NINTH

EDITION

ORGANIZATIONAL BEHAVIOUR

UNDERSTANDING AND MANAGING LIFE AT WORK

GARY JOHNS
Concordia University

ALAN M. SAKS
University of Toronto

PEARSON

Toronto

Vice-President, Editorial Director: Gary Bennett
Editor-in-Chief: Nicole Lukach
Acquisitions Editor: Nick Durie
Sponsoring Editor: Jennifer Parks
Marketing Manager: Leigh-Anne Graham
Developmental Editor: Joanne Sutherland
Project Manager: Deborah Starks
Manufacturing Manager/Coordinator: Jane Schell
Production Editor: Sapna Rastogi (Cenveo® Publisher Services)
Copy Editor: Cat Haggert
Proofreader: Linda Jenkins
Compositor: Cenveo® Publisher Services
Photo Researcher: Julie Pratt
Permissions Researcher: Rachel Irwin
Art Director: Julia Hall
Cover and Interior Designer: Miriam Blier
Cover Image: Top left: Getty Images/Digital Vision
              Top right: Getty Images/Digital Vision
              Bottom left: Getty Images/Digital Vision
              Bottom right: Getty Images/Studio Blond

Credits and acknowledgments of material borrowed from other sources and reproduced, with permission, in this textbook appear on the appropriate page within the text and on p. 687.

If you purchased this book outside the United States or Canada, you should be aware that it has been imported without the approval of the publisher or author.

10 9 8 [CKV]

Library and Archives Canada Cataloguing in Publication

Johns, Gary, 1946–
    Organizational behaviour : understanding and managing life at work / Gary Johns, Alan M. Saks. — 9th ed.

Includes bibliographical references and index.
ISBN 978-0-13-216112-1

    1. Organizational behavior—Textbooks. 2. Management—Textbooks. I. Saks, Alan M. (Alan Michael), 1960– II. Title.

HD58.7.J64 2013   302.3′5   C2012-908229-5

PEARSON

BRIEF CONTENTS

PART ONE   AN INTRODUCTION   1

Chapter 1   Organizational Behaviour and Management   2

PART TWO   INDIVIDUAL BEHAVIOUR   41

Chapter 2   Personality and Learning   42
Chapter 3   Perception, Attribution, and Diversity   78
Chapter 4   Values, Attitudes, and Work Behaviour   118
Chapter 5   Theories of Work Motivation   152
Chapter 6   Motivation in Practice   188

PART THREE   SOCIAL BEHAVIOUR AND ORGANIZATIONAL PROCESSES   227

Chapter 7   Groups and Teamwork   228
Chapter 8   Social Influence, Socialization, and Organizational Culture   262
Chapter 9   Leadership   304
Chapter 10   Communication   352
Chapter 11   Decision Making   384
Chapter 12   Power, Politics, and Ethics   418
Chapter 13   Conflict and Stress   452

PART FOUR   THE TOTAL ORGANIZATION   491

Chapter 14   Organizational Structure   492
Chapter 15   Environment, Strategy, and Technology   530
Chapter 16   Organizational Change, Development, and Innovation   566

Appendix   Research in Organizational Behaviour   603
References   619
Index   660
Photo Credits   687

CONTENTS

Preface xix

About the Authors xxviii

PART ONE **AN INTRODUCTION** 1

Chapter 1 **Organizational Behaviour and Management** 2

VIGNETTE **Sodexo Canada** 2

What Are Organizations? 4
Social Inventions 4 Goal Accomplishment 5 Group Effort 5

What Is Organizational Behaviour? 5

Why Study Organizational Behaviour? 6
Organizational Behaviour Is Interesting 7 Organizational Behaviour
Is Important 7 Organizational Behaviour Makes a Difference 7

How Much Do You Know About Organizational Behaviour? 8

● **RESEARCH FOCUS**
ARE THE BEST COMPANIES TO WORK FOR THE BEST COMPANIES? 9

Goals of Organizational Behaviour 10
Predicting Organizational Behaviour 10 Explaining Organizational
Behaviour 10 Managing Organizational Behaviour 11

Early Prescriptions Concerning Management 11
The Classical View and Bureaucracy 11

● **YOU BE THE MANAGER**
TORONTO'S TROUBLED TRANSIT SYSTEM 12
The Human Relations Movement and a Critique of Bureaucracy 13

Contemporary Management—The Contingency Approach 14

What Do Managers Do? 15
Managerial Roles 15 Managerial Activities 16 Managerial
Agendas 17 Managerial Minds 18 International Managers 18

Some Contemporary Management Concerns 19
Diversity—Local and Global 19 A Positive Work Environment
and Employee Well-Being 20 Talent Management and Employee
Engagement 22 Corporate Social Responsibility 23

● **APPLIED FOCUS**
GREEN MANAGEMENT AT THE DELTA CHELSEA HOTEL 24

● **THE MANAGER'S NOTEBOOK**
TORONTO'S TROUBLED TRANSIT SYSTEM 25

Learning Objectives Checklist 26
Discussion Questions 26
On-the-Job Challenge Question
The Ultimate Perk 27
Experiential Exercise
Good Job, Bad Job 28
Experiential Exercise

OB on TV   28
Experiential Exercise
OB in the News   29
Case Incident
My Mother's Visit   29
Case Study   30
Integrative Case   34

PART TWO   INDIVIDUAL BEHAVIOUR   41

Chapter 2   **Personality and Learning**   42

VIGNETTE **Economical Insurance**   42

What Is Personality?   44

Personality and Organizational Behaviour   45
The Five-Factor Model of Personality *46* Locus of Control *48*

● **RESEARCH FOCUS**
CEO PERSONALITY AND FIRM PERFORMANCE 49
Self-Monitoring *49* Self-Esteem *50*

New Developments in Personality and Organizational Behaviour   51
Positive and Negative Affectivity *51* Proactive Personality *52*
General Self-Efficacy *52* Core Self-Evaluations *52*

What Is Learning?   53
What Do Employees Learn? *53* Operant Learning Theory *54*

Increasing the Probability of Behaviour   54
Positive Reinforcement *54* Negative Reinforcement *55*
Organizational Errors Involving Reinforcement *55*

Reinforcement Strategies   57

Reducing the Probability of Behaviour   58
Extinction *58* Punishment *58* Using Punishment Effectively *59*

Social Cognitive Theory   60
Observational Learning *61*

● **RESEARCH FOCUS**
THE TRICKLE-DOWN EFFECTS OF ABUSIVE MANAGEMENT 62
Self-Efficacy Beliefs *62* Self-Regulation *63*

Organizational Learning Practices   65
Organizational Behaviour Modification *65* Employee Recognition
Programs *66* Training and Development Programs *67*

● **YOU BE THE MANAGER**
CALGARY INTERNATIONAL AIRPORT'S YYC MILES RECOGNITION PROGRAM 68
Career Development *69*

● **THE MANAGER'S NOTEBOOK**
CALGARY INTERNATIONAL AIRPORT'S YYC MILES RECOGNITION
PROGRAM 69

Learning Objectives Checklist   70
Discussion Questions   71
Integrative Discussion Questions   72
On-the-Job Challenge Question
Playing Hooky   72
Experiential Exercise
Proactive Personality Scale   73

Case Incident
Courier Cats   75
Case Study
Howe 2 Ski Stores   75

Chapter 3   Perception, Attribution, and Diversity   78

VIGNETTE   **KPMG**   78

What Is Perception?   80

Components of Perception   80
The Perceiver *81* The Target *81* The Situation *82*

Social Identity Theory   82

A Model of the Perceptual Process   83

Basic Biases in Person Perception   84
Primacy and Recency Effects *84* Reliance on Central Traits *85*
Implicit Personality Theories *85* Projection *85* Stereotyping *86*

● **RESEARCH FOCUS**
WEIGHT-BASED BIAS IN THE WORKPLACE 86

Attribution: Perceiving Causes and Motives   87
Consistency Cues *88* Consensus Cues *88* Distinctiveness Cues *88*
Attribution in Action *89* Biases in Attribution *89*

Person Perception and Workforce Diversity   91
The Changing Workplace *91* Valuing Diversity *91*
Stereotypes and Workforce Diversity *92*

● **ETHICAL FOCUS**
WHAT'S IN A NAME? YOU'RE HIRED . . . OR NOT! 94
Managing Workforce Diversity *98*

● **YOU BE THE MANAGER**
AMERICAN EXPRESS CANADA'S SKILLED IMMIGRANT
STRATEGY 100

Perceptions of Trust   101

Perceived Organizational Support   101

Person Perception in Human Resources   103
Perceptions of Recruitment and Selection *103* Perceptions in the
Employment Interview *104* Perceptions and the Performance
Appraisal *105*

● **THE MANAGER'S NOTEBOOK**
AMERICAN EXPRESS CANADA'S SKILLED IMMIGRANT
STRATEGY 108

Learning Objectives Checklist   109
Discussion Questions   110
Integrative Discussion Questions   110
On-the-Job Challenge Question 1
Australia's Jobs Bonus Initiative   111
On-the-Job Challenge Question 2
Citizens Medical Centre's New Hiring Policy   111
Experiential Exercise
Beliefs about Older Workers   112
Case Incident
The New CEO   113
Case Study
CTV Newsnet   114

Chapter 4   Values, Attitudes, and Work Behaviour   118

VIGNETTE **L'Oréal Canada**   118

What Are Values?   120
Generational Differences in Values *120* Cultural Differences in Values *121* Implications of Cultural Variation *124*

● **GLOBAL FOCUS**
CANADIANS HAVE CULTURAL INTELLIGENCE *126*

What Are Attitudes?   126

What Is Job Satisfaction?   127

What Determines Job Satisfaction?   128
Discrepancy *128* Fairness *128*

● **GLOBAL FOCUS**
IS THE IMPORTANCE OF FAIRNESS UNIVERSAL ACROSS CULTURES? *131*
Disposition *131* Mood and Emotion *132* Some Key Contributors to Job Satisfaction *134*

● **YOU BE THE MANAGER**
THE FUTURE OF WORK @ CAPITAL ONE *136*

Consequences of Job Satisfaction   136
Absence from Work *136* Turnover *137* Performance *138* Organizational Citizenship Behaviour *139* Customer Satisfaction and Profit *140*

What Is Organizational Commitment?   141
Key Contributors to Organizational Commitment *142* Consequences of Organizational Commitment *142* Changes in the Workplace and Employee Commitment *143*

● **THE MANAGER'S NOTEBOOK**
CAPITAL ONE *144*

Learning Objectives Checklist   145
Discussion Questions   145
Integrative Discussion Questions   146
On-the-Job Challenge Question
Mr. Winston   146
Experiential Exercise
Attitudes Toward Absenteeism from Work   146
Case Incident
How Much Do You Get Paid?   147
Case Study
Gen Y in the Workforce   147

Chapter 5   Theories of Work Motivation   152

VIGNETTE **Great Little Box Company Ltd.**   152

Why Study Motivation?   154

What Is Motivation?   154
Basic Characteristics of Motivation *154* Extrinsic and Intrinsic Motivation and Self-Determination Theory *155* Motivation and Performance *156*

● **RESEARCH FOCUS**
DOES EDUCATION PREDICT JOB PERFORMANCE? *157*
The Motivation–Performance Relationship *159*

Need Theories of Work Motivation   159

Maslow's Hierarchy of Needs *159* Alderfer's ERG Theory *161*
McClelland's Theory of Needs *162* Research Support for Need
Theories *163* Managerial Implications of Need Theories *163*

Process Theories of Work Motivation   164

Expectancy Theory *164* Research Support for Expectancy
Theory *167* Managerial Implications of Expectancy Theory *167*
Equity Theory *168* Research Support for Equity Theory *169*
Managerial Implications of Equity Theory *170* Goal Setting
Theory *170* What Kinds of Goals Are Motivational? *170* Enhancing
Goal Commitment *171* Goal Orientation and Proximity *173*
Research Support for Goal Setting Theory *173* Managerial
Implications of Goal Setting Theory *174*

● **RESEARCH FOCUS**
EFFECTS OF SUBCONSCIOUS GOALS ON PERFORMANCE 175

Do Motivation Theories Translate Across Cultures?   175

● **YOU BE THE MANAGER**
YOUR TIPS OR YOUR JOB 176

Putting It All Together: Integrating Theories of Work Motivation   178

● **THE MANAGER'S NOTEBOOK**
YOUR TIPS OR YOUR JOB 179

Learning Objectives Checklist   180
Discussion Questions   181
Integrative Discussion Questions   182
On-the-Job Challenge Question
Employee Time Theft   182
Experiential Exercise
What Is Your Goal Orientation?   183
Case Incident
Mayfield Department Stores   184
Case Study
Datatronic   184

Chapter 6   **Motivation in Practice**   188

VIGNETTE **Ellisdon Corporation**   188

Money as a Motivator   190

Linking Pay to Performance on Production Jobs *190* Potential
Problems with Wage Incentives *191* Linking Pay to Performance
on White-Collar Jobs *193*

● **YOU BE THE MANAGER**
THE "MONEY FOR NOTHING" MERIT PAY SYSTEM 194
Potential Problems with Merit Pay Plans *195*

● **ETHICAL FOCUS**
INCENTIVE COMPENSATION AND UNETHICAL BEHAVIOUR 196
Using Pay to Motivate Teamwork *197*

Job Design as a Motivator   200

Traditional Views of Job Design *201* Job Scope and
Motivation *201* The Job Characteristics Model *203*
Job Enrichment *206* Potential Problems with Job
Enrichment *207* New Developments in Job Design *208*

● **GLOBAL FOCUS**
NATIONAL CULTURE AND JOB DESIGN 210

Management by Objectives   210

Alternative Working Schedules as Motivators for a Diverse Workforce   212
Flex-Time *212* Compressed Workweek *213* Job and Work
Sharing *214* Telecommuting *215*

Motivation Practices in Perspective   216

• THE MANAGER'S NOTEBOOK
THE "MONEY FOR NOTHING" MERIT PAY SYSTEM 217

Learning Objectives Checklist   218
Discussion Questions   219
Integrative Discussion Questions   220
On-the-Job Challenge Question
Profit Sharing or Hourly Wages?   220
Experiential Exercise
Task Characteristics Scale   220
Case Incident
The Junior Accountant   222
Case Study
Chang Koh Metal Ptd. Ltd. in China   223
Integrative Case
Deloitte & Touche: Integrating Arthur Andersen   225

PART THREE SOCIAL BEHAVIOUR
AND ORGANIZATIONAL
PROCESSES   227

Chapter 7 **Groups and Teamwork**   228

VIGNETTE **IDEO**   228

What Is a Group?   230

Group Development   230
Typical Stages of Group Development *231* Punctuated
Equilibrium *232*

Group Structure and Its Consequences   233
Group Size *233* Diversity of Group Membership *235*
Group Norms *235* Roles *236*

• RESEARCH FOCUS
ABSENCE CULTURES—NORMS IN ACTION 237
Status *239*

Group Cohesiveness   240
Factors Influencing Cohesiveness *240* Consequences of
Cohesiveness *242*

Social Loafing   243

What Is a Team?   244

Designing Effective Work Teams   245
Self-Managed Work Teams *245* Cross-Functional Teams *248*

• GLOBAL FOCUS
A DIVERSE GLOBAL TEAM CREATES THE CAMARO 249
Virtual Teams *250*

• APPLIED FOCUS
BLOG SUPPORTS VIRTUAL CHANGE TEAM 251

● **YOU BE THE MANAGER**
CREATING TRUST IN VIRTUAL TEAMS AT ORANGE 252

A Word of Caution: Teams as a Panacea   254

● **THE MANAGER'S NOTEBOOK**
CREATING TRUST IN VIRTUAL TEAMS AT ORANGE 254

Learning Objectives Checklist   255
Discussion Questions   256
Integrative Discussion Questions   256
On-the-Job Challenge Question
Self-Managed Teams at ISE Communications   257
Experiential Exercise
NASA   257
Case Incident
The Group Assignment   258
Case Study
The Creativity Development Committee   259

Chapter 8   **Social Influence, Socialization, and Organizational Culture**   262

VIGNETTE **Google Canada**   262

Social Influence in Organizations   264
Information Dependence and Effect Dependence *264* The Social
Influence Process and Conformity *265*

Organizational Socialization   265
Stages of Socialization *266*

Unrealistic Expectations and the Psychological Contract   267
Unrealistic Expectations *268* Psychological Contract *268*

Methods of Organizational Socialization   269
Realistic Job Previews *269* Employee Orientation Programs *271*

● **GLOBAL FOCUS**
ROPES AND CULTURAL SOCIALIZATION 271
Socialization Tactics *272*

● **ETHICAL FOCUS**
SOCIALIZATION TACTICS AND ETHICAL CONFLICT 275
Mentoring *275* Proactive Socialization *279*

Organizational Culture   280
What Is Organizational Culture? *280* The "Strong Culture"
Concept *281* Assets of Strong Cultures *282*

● **APPLIED FOCUS**
CULTURE AND CUSTOMER SERVICE AT PRINT AUDIT 283
Liabilities of Strong Cultures *284* Contributors to the
Culture *285* Diagnosing a Culture *287*

● **YOU BE THE MANAGER**
CHANGING THE CULTURE AT KINAXIS 288

● **THE MANAGER'S NOTEBOOK**
CHANGING THE CULTURE AT KINAXIS 290

Learning Objectives Checklist   290
Discussion Questions   291
Integrative Discussion Questions   292
On-the-Job Challenge Question
CN Rail   292

Experiential Exercise
Socialization Preferences and Experience   293
Case Incident
The Reality Shock   295
Case Study   295

Chapter 9   **Leadership**   304

VIGNETTE   **Bonnie Brooks of Hudson's Bay Company**   304

What Is Leadership?   306

Are Leaders Born? The Trait Theory of Leadership   308
Research on Leadership Traits *308* Limitations of the Trait
Approach *309*

The Behaviour of Leaders   309

● **RESEARCH FOCUS**
LEADER CATEGORIZATION THEORY AND RACIAL BIAS 310
Consideration and Initiating Structure *310*

● **YOU BE THE MANAGER**
LEADERSHIP DEVELOPMENT AT BUSINESS DEVELOPMENT BANK
OF CANADA (BDC) 311
The Consequences of Consideration and Structure *312* Leader Reward
and Punishment Behaviours *312*

Situational Theories of Leadership   313
Fiedler's Contingency Theory and Cognitive Resource Theory *313*
House's Path–Goal Theory *315*

Participative Leadership: Involving Employees in Decisions   317
What Is Participation? *317* Potential Advantages of Participative Leadership *318* Potential Problems of Participative Leadership *319* Vroom
and Jago's Situational Model of Participation *319*

Leader–Member Exchange (LMX) Theory   321

Transactional and Transformational Leadership Theory   322
Intellectual Stimulation *323* Individualized Consideration *323*
Inspirational Motivation *323* Charisma *323*

Global Leadership   325

New and Emerging Theories of Leadership   326
Empowering Leadership *326* Ethical Leadership *327* Authentic
Leadership *328* Servant Leadership *330*

Culture and Leadership   331

Gender and Leadership   332

● **APPLIED FOCUS**
THE ADVANCEMENT OF WOMEN INITIATIVE AT SCOTIABANK 336

● **THE MANAGER'S NOTEBOOK**
LEADERSHIP DEVELOPMENT AT BUSINESS DEVELOPMENT
BANK OF CANADA (BDC) 337

Learning Objectives Checklist   338
Discussion Questions   339
Integrative Discussion Questions   340
On-the-Job Challenge Question
The RCMP's New Boss   340
Experiential Exercise
Ethical Leadership Scale (ELS)   341
Scoring and Interpretation   341

Experiential Exercise
Leadership Empowerment Behaviour   342
Scoring and Interpretation   342
Experiential Exercise
Leadership Jazz   343
Procedure   343
Discussion   344
Case Incident
Fran-Tech   344
Case Study
Transforming ICRISAT: The Leadership of Dr. William Dar   345

Chapter 10   **Communication**   352

VIGNETTE **The University of Guelph Rumour Mill**   352

What Is Communication?   354

Basics of Organizational Communication   355
Communication by Strict Chain of Command *355* Deficiencies in the
Chain of Command *355*

Voice, Silence, and the Mum Effect   356

The Grapevine   357
Characteristics of the Grapevine *357* Who Participates in the
Grapevine? *357* Pros and Cons of the Grapevine *358*

● **ETHICAL FOCUS**
BLOGS: EFFECTIVE COMMUNICATION TOOL OR CYBERSPACE MENACE? 359

The Verbal Language of Work   359

The Non-Verbal Language of Work   360
Body Language *360* Props, Artifacts, and Costumes *361*

Gender Differences in Communication   363

Cross-Cultural Communication   365
Language Differences *365* Non-Verbal Communication across
Cultures *365* Etiquette and Politeness across Cultures *366*

● **GLOBAL FOCUS**
SELF-PRESENTATION BIAS: WHO'S MOST AND LEAST MODEST IN JOB
APPLICATIONS? 367
Social Conventions across Cultures *367* Cultural Context *368*

● **YOU BE THE MANAGER**
FOUR SEASONS GOES TO PARIS 370

Computer-Mediated Communication   371

Personal Approaches to Improving Communication   373
Basic Principles of Effective Communication *373* When in
Rome... *375*

Organizational Approaches to Improving Communication   375
Provision of Explanations *375* 360-Degree Feedback *376* Employee
Surveys and Survey Feedback *376* Suggestion Systems and Query
Systems *376* Telephone Hotlines, Intranets, and Webcasts *377*
Management Training *377*

● **THE MANAGER'S NOTEBOOK**
FOUR SEASONS GOES TO PARIS 378

Learning Objectives Checklist   379
Discussion Questions   379
Integrative Discussion Questions   380

On-the-Job Challenge Question
Carol Bartz and Yahoo!   380
Experiential Exercise
Communication Technology and Media Dilemmas   380
Case Incident
Email Madness   382
Case Study
Facebook (A)   382
Facebook (B)   383

Chapter 11   Decision Making   384

VIGNETTE **JPMorgan Chase Loses $2 Billion**   384

What Is Decision Making?   386
Well-Structured Problems *386* Ill-Structured Problems *387*

The Compleat Decision Maker—A Rational Decision-Making Model   387
Perfect versus Bounded Rationality *387* Problem Identification and
Framing *389* Information Search *390* Alternative Development,
Evaluation, and Choice *391* Risky Business *393* Solution
Implementation *394* Solution Evaluation *394*

● **ETHICAL FOCUS**
ROGUE TRADERS GET TRAPPED IN ESCALATION *396*
How Emotion and Mood Affect Decision Making *396* Rational
Decision Making—A Summary *398*

● **YOU BE THE MANAGER**
PREVENTING SURGICAL DECISION ERRORS AT TORONTO
GENERAL HOSPITAL *399*

Group Decision Making   400
Why Use Groups? *401* Do Groups Actually Make Higher-Quality
Decisions than Individuals? *402* Disadvantages of Group Decision
Making *402*

● **APPLIED FOCUS**
DECISION MAKING AT RIM *404*
How Do Groups Handle Risk? *405*

Improving Decision Making in Organizations   406
Training Discussion Leaders *406* Stimulating and Managing
Controversy *407* Traditional and Electronic Brainstorming *407*
Nominal Group Technique *408* The Delphi Technique *409*

● **THE MANAGER'S NOTEBOOK**
PREVENTING SURGICAL DECISION ERRORS AT TORONTO
GENERAL HOSPITAL *410*

Learning Objectives Checklist   411
Discussion Questions   412
Integrative Discussion Questions   412
On-the-Job Challenge Question
Toronto Ritz-Carlton Nixes Poppies   412
Experiential Exercise
The New Truck Dilemma   413
Preparation for Role-Playing   413
The Role-Playing Process   413
Collection of Results   413
Discussion of Results   413

General Instructions   413
Case Incident
The Restaurant Review   414
Case Study
Standard Media Plan   415

Chapter 12   Power, Politics, and Ethics   418

VIGNETTE **Sexual Harassment at the Royal Canadian
Mounted Police**   418

What Is Power?   420

The Bases of Individual Power   420
Legitimate Power *420* Reward Power *421* Coercive Power *421*
Referent Power *421* Expert Power *422*

How Do People Obtain Power?   423
Doing the Right Things *423* Cultivating the Right People *423*

Empowerment—Putting Power Where It Is Needed   424

• **APPLIED FOCUS**
TIM HORTONS FRANCHISE LACKS EMPOWERMENT 426

Influence Tactics—Putting Power to Work   427

Who Wants Power?   428

Controlling Strategic Contingencies—How Subunits Obtain Power   429
Scarcity *429* Uncertainty *430* Centrality *430*
Substitutability *430*

Organizational Politics—Using and Abusing Power   431
The Basics of Organizational Politics *431*

• **ETHICAL FOCUS**
KNOWLEDGE HIDING IN ORGANIZATIONS 432
The Facets of Political Skill *433* Machiavellianism—
The Harder Side of Politics *435* Defensiveness—Reactive
Politics *436*

Ethics in Organizations   437
The Nature of Ethical Dilemmas *437*

• **YOU BE THE MANAGER**
YAHOO'S RESUME SCANDAL 439
Causes of Unethical Behaviour *440* Whistle-Blowing *442*
Sexual Harassment—When Power and Ethics Collide *442*
Employing Ethical Guidelines *444*

• **THE MANAGER'S NOTEBOOK**
YAHOO'S RESUME SCANDAL 445

Learning Objectives Checklist   445
Discussion Questions   446
Integrative Discussion Questions   447
On-the-Job Challenge Question
CBC's Steven Smart   447
Experiential Exercise
Political Skill Inventory   447
Scoring and Interpretation   447
Case Incident
Doubling Up   448
Case Study
OrangeWerks: A Question of Ethics   448

Chapter 13   Conflict and Stress   452

VIGNETTE **The Toronto Hair War: Glo versus Gliss**   452

What Is Conflict?   454

Causes of Organizational Conflict   454
Group Identification and Intergroup Bias *454* Interdepen-
dence *455* Differences in Power, Status, and Culture *455*
Ambiguity *456* Scarce Resources *456*

Types of Conflict   456

Conflict Dynamics   457

Modes of Managing Conflict   457
Avoiding *458* Accommodating *458* Competing *458*
Compromise *458* Collaborating *459*

Managing Conflict with Negotiation   459
Distributive Negotiation Tactics *460* Integrative Negotiation
Tactics *462* Third Party Involvement *463*

Is All Conflict Bad?   464

A Model of Stress in Organizations   465
Stressors *465* Stress *465* Stress Reactions *465* Personality
and Stress *466*

Stressors in Organizational Life   467
Executive and Managerial Stressors *467* Operative-Level
Stressors *468* Boundary Role Stressors, Burnout, and Emotional
Labour *468* The Job Demands–Resources Model and Work
Engagement *470* Some General Stressors *470*

● **YOU BE THE MANAGER**
BULLYING AT VETERANS AFFAIRS 473

Reactions to Organizational Stress   475
Behavioural Reactions to Stress *475*

● **RESEARCH FOCUS**
PRESENTEEISM IN THE WORKPLACE 477
Psychological Reactions to Stress *477* Physiological Reactions to
Stress *478*

Organizational Strategies for Managing Stress   478
Job Redesign *479* "Family-Friendly" Human
Resource Policies *479*

● **APPLIED FOCUS**
QUEBEC CERTIFIES WORK–LIFE BALANCE 480
Stress Management Programs *481* Work–Life Balance, Fitness, and
Wellness Programs *481*

● **THE MANAGER'S NOTEBOOK**
BULLYING AT VETERANS AFFAIRS 482

Learning Objectives Checklist   482
Discussion Questions   483
Integrative Discussion Questions   484
On-the-Job Challenge Question
   Why Don't People Take Their Vacations?   484
Experiential Exercise
   Strategies for Managing Conflict   484
Case Incident
   Bringing Baby to Work   485

Case Study   486
Integrative Case
  Deloitte & Touche: Integrating Arthur Andersen   489

PART FOUR   THE TOTAL ORGANIZATION   491

Chapter 14   Organizational Structure   492

VIGNETTE   **Flight Centre: Family, Village, Tribe**   492

What Is Organizational Structure?   494

The Division and Coordination of Labour   494
Vertical Division of Labour *494* Horizontal Division of
Labour *495* Departmentation *497* Basic Methods of Coordinating
Divided Labour *501* Other Methods of Coordination *503*

Traditional Structural Characteristics   504
Span of Control *504* Flat versus Tall *505* Formalization *505*
Centralization *506*

• APPLIED FOCUS
DID BP'S ORGANIZATIONAL STRUCTURE CONTRIBUTE TO THE GULF OIL
SPILL? 507
Complexity *508*

Summarizing Structure—Organic versus Mechanistic   508

Contemporary Organic Structures   509
The Ambidextrous Organization *510* Network and Virtual
Organizations *511* The Modular Organization *513* The
Boundaryless Organization *514*

• APPLIED FOCUS
NETWORK-CENTRIC INNOVATION: BOEING'S 787 DREAMLINER 515

The Impact of Size   516
Size and Structure *516* Downsizing *517*

• YOU BE THE MANAGER
THE TOYOTA RECALL PROBLEM 518

A Footnote: Symptoms of Structural Problems   520

• THE MANAGER'S NOTEBOOK
THE TOYOTA RECALL PROBLEM 521

Learning Objectives Checklist   521
Discussion Questions   522
Integrative Discussion Questions   522
On-the-Job Challenge Question
  Span of Control at Google   523
Experiential Exercise
  Organizational Structure Preference Scale   523
  Scoring and Interpretation   524
Case Incident   524
Case Study   524

Chapter 15   Environment, Strategy, and Technology   530

VIGNETTE   **Ford Motor Company**   530

The External Environment of Organizations   532
Organizations as Open Systems *533* Components of the External
Environment *534* Environmental Uncertainty *536* Resource
Dependence *538*

Strategic Responses to Uncertainty and Resource Dependence   539

● **RESEARCH FOCUS**
CEO NARCISSISM AND FIRM STRATEGY 540
Organizational Structure as a Strategic Response *541* Other Forms of
Strategic Response *542*

● **YOU BE THE MANAGER**
LOBLAW COMPANIES LIMITED BUYS T&T SUPERMARKET 545

The Technologies of Organizations   547
Basic Dimensions of Technology *548* Structuring to Cope with
Technology *550*

Implications of Advanced Information Technology   552

● **RESEARCH FOCUS**
THE ADOPTION AND USE OF TECHNOLOGY: WHAT'S
THE DIFFERENCE? 552
The Two Faces of Advanced Technology *553* Advanced Manufacturing
Technology *553* Advanced Office Technology *555*

● **THE MANAGER'S NOTEBOOK**
LOBLAW COMPANIES LIMITED BUYS T&T SUPERMARKET 557

Learning Objectives Checklist   558
Discussion Questions   559
Integrative Discussion Questions   559
On-the-Job Challenge Question
   The Learjet 60XRs   560
Experiential Exercise
   Diagnosing an Organization   560
Experiential Exercise
   Effects of Advanced Information Technology   561
Case Incident   561
Case Study   562

Chapter 16   **Organizational Change, Development, and Innovation**   566

VIGNETTE **Best Buy**   566

The Concept of Organizational Change   568
Why Organizations Must Change *568* What Organizations
Can Change *569* The Change Process *570* The Learning
Organization *571*

● **RESEARCH FOCUS**
DO ORGANIZATIONS LEARN MORE FROM SUCCESS OR FAILURE? 573

Issues in the Change Process   574
Diagnosis *574* Resistance *575* Evaluation and
Institutionalization *577*

Organizational Development: Planned Organizational Change   578

● **YOU BE THE MANAGER**
CHANGING THE FACE OF THE VICTORIA POLICE FORCE 579

Some Specific Organizational Development Strategies   580
Team Building *580* Survey Feedback *581* Total Quality
Management *582* Reengineering *585*

Does Organizational Development Work?   587

The Innovation Process   588
What Is Innovation? *588* Generating and Implementing Innovative
Ideas *589*

● **APPLIED FOCUS**
WHY AREN'T HIGH-QUALITY HEALTH CARE INNOVATIONS IMPLEMENTED? 590
Diffusing Innovative Ideas *594*

A Footnote: The Knowing–Doing Gap   595

● **THE MANAGER'S NOTEBOOK**
CHANGING THE FACE OF THE VICTORIA POLICE FORCE 596

Learning Objectives Checklist   597
Discussion Questions   598
Integrative Discussion Questions   598
On-the-Job Challenge Question
The Hacker Way at Facebook   599
Experiential Exercise
Measuring Tolerance for Ambiguity   599
Scoring and Interpretation   599
Case Incident
Dandy Toys   600
Case Study
First Canadian Club   600
First Canadian Club   600
Integrative Case
Deloitte & Touche: Integrating Arthur Andersen   602

Appendix   **Research in Organizational Behaviour**   603

The Basics of Organizational Behaviour Research   604
Types of Variables *604* Measurement of Variables *605*

Observational Techniques   605
Participant Observation *606* Direct Observation *607* Correlational
Techniques *608* Correlation and Causation *609*

Experimental Techniques   610

A Continuum of Research Techniques   613

Combining Research Techniques   613

Issues and Concerns in Organizational Behaviour Research   614
Sampling *614* Hawthorne Effect *615* Ethics *616*

Learning Objectives Checklist   616

References   619

Index   660

Photo Credits   687

PREFACE

Welcome to the ninth edition of *Organizational Behaviour: Understanding and Managing Life at Work*! This edition marks the 30th anniversary of the text, which has been rigorously updated over the years to present students with the latest knowledge and research on both the science and practice of organizational behaviour. First published in 1983, *Organizational Behaviour* is the longest-running, continuously published, and regularly revised organizational behaviour textbook authored in Canada.

In writing the ninth edition of this book, we have been guided by three goals. First, we wish to convey the genuine excitement inherent in the subject of organizational behaviour by sharing our enthusiasm about the subject with students who are reading and learning about it for the first time.

Second, we want the presentation of the material to have both academic and practical integrity, acknowledging the debt of the field to both behavioural science research and organizational practice. To put it another way, we want this book to be useful and enjoyable to read without oversimplifying key subjects on the premise that this somehow makes them easier to understand. This requires striking a balance between research and theory on the one hand, and practice and application on the other hand. The ninth edition of *Organizational Behaviour* includes the most recent research and theory in the field (e.g., psychological capital, Chapter 1; generational differences in values, Chapter 4; relational job design, Chapter 6; servant leadership, Chapter 9; work engagement, Chapter 13; ambidextrous organizations, Chapter 14; and the "Research Focus" features) as well as many examples of the application and practice of organizational behaviour that are throughout the text and showcased in the chapter-opening vignettes, the "Applied Focus" features, and the "You Be the Manager" features.

Third, we want students to not only learn about organizational behaviour but also to understand the connections and linkages across topics and how to integrate theory, principles, and concepts across chapters rather than see them as separate or isolated topics. Special features designed to enhance this skill include an integrative case that runs through each section of the text and integrative discussion questions at the end of every chapter. We sincerely hope these goals have resulted in a textbook that is interesting and enjoyable to read and that conveys the importance of organizational behaviour.

NEW TO THE NINTH EDITION

The ninth edition of *Organizational Behaviour* adds substantial new content, features, and pedagogy while remaining faithful to the general format and structure of the eighth edition.

While the major topics of the eighth edition remain in this edition, we have added new content to reflect recent research as well as new and emerging themes in the organizational behaviour literature in every chapter of the text. Examples of new topics, sections, and definitions that can be found in the ninth edition include

- Chapter 1: a positive work environment and employee well-being; workplace spirituality; psychological capital
- Chapter 2: trait activation theory; peer recognition programs
- Chapter 3: frame-of-reference training
- Chapter 4: progression of withdrawal from the organization
- Chapter 5: more coverage of self-determination theory
- Chapter 6: relational job design and prosocial motivation

- Chapter 7: information sharing in virtual teams
- Chapter 8: social information processing theory; developmental networks
- Chapter 9: social exchange theory; empowering and servant leadership
- Chapter 10: employee voice and silence
- Chapter 12: effects of strong organizational identification on ethical lapses
- Chapter 14: the merits and demerits of centralization; more coverage of network and virtual organizations
- Chapter 15: the adoption and use of technology
- Chapter 16: the Mayflower Group employee survey consortium; creative deviance

We have updated many other areas throughout the text with the most current and recent research from the practising management literature, academic literature, and the popular and business press. We have also replaced the content of many of the features and added new ones. In total, the ninth edition contains 9 new chapter-opening vignettes, 15 new "Focus" boxes, and 7 new "You Be the Manager" features. These features have been carefully chosen to represent current and exciting examples of organizational behaviour. Of those examples that we have retained from the eighth edition, many have been substantially updated.

In addition to new and updated content, the ninth edition includes several new exhibits. For example, Chapter 4 includes a new depiction of cultural values across nations (Exhibit 4.4), new data on what contributes to employee job satisfaction (Exhibit 4.7), and a graphical portrayal of the progression of withdrawal from an organization (Exhibit 4.10).

Finally, in the end-of-chapter material, there are six new case studies, three new case incidents, and four new experiential exercises. You will also find many new discussion questions.

ABOUT THE COVER

The cover of the ninth edition of *Organizational Behaviour: Understanding and Managing Life at Work*, along with the pictures throughout the text, features musicians from a performing jazz band. What does a jazz band have to do with organizational behaviour? A great deal! Jazz has been used as a metaphor for organizations and organizational behaviour for many years.

In 1998, the journal *Organizational Science* published a special issue on jazz improvisation as a metaphor for organizations (vol. 9, no. 5), a result of a symposium called "Jazz as a Metaphor for Organizing in the Twenty-First Century" that was held at the 1995 Academy of Management Conference in Vancouver, British Columbia. The idea was to think about the twenty-first-century organization in the context of the jazz metaphor for organizing. The jazz metaphor has also been adopted by some organizations. In its 1996 annual report, the LEGO Corporation featured its top-management team as a jazz ensemble with the CEO playing the saxophone—the CEO wanted to highlight the importance of improvisation at all levels of management.

Organizations and organizational behaviour are like jazz in many ways. Jazz involves improvisation, innovation, and flexibility, all of which are important attributes of individuals and groups in organizations as well as organizations themselves. Organizations and the people in them must be flexible and capable of innovation and improvisation to survive and adapt to change. Innovation and flexibility are especially important for contemporary organizations.

In his book *Leadership Jazz*, Max De Pree argues that leadership in organizations is like a jazz band: "Jazz-band leaders must choose the music, find the right musicians, and perform—in public. But the effect of the performance depends on so many things—the environment, the volunteers playing in the band, the need for everybody to perform as individuals and as a group, the absolute dependence of the leader on the members of the band, the need of the leader for the followers to play well. What a summary of an organization!"

Finally, as noted by Mary Jo Hatch, one of the chairs of the jazz symposium, the characteristics that are associated with the twenty-first-century organization are very similar to those of a jazz band: It is flexible, adaptable, and responsive to the environment, and it has loose boundaries and minimal hierarchy. Organizational behaviour is very much like a jazz band—individuals working together in the spirit of innovation, improvisation, and inspiration.

GENERAL CONTENT AND WRITING STYLE

Organizational Behaviour, Ninth Edition, is comprehensive—the material is authoritative and up to date, and reflects current research and practical concerns. Both traditional subjects (such as expectancy theory) and newer topics (like workplace spirituality, psychological capital, bullying, whistle-blowing, servant leadership, virtual teams, collective efficacy, emotional intelligence, creative deviance, and organizational learning) are addressed. Balanced treatment is provided to micro topics (covered in the earlier chapters) and macro topics (covered in the later chapters).

Although *Organizational Behaviour* is comprehensive, we have avoided the temptation to include too many concepts, theories, and ideas. Rather than composing a long laundry list of marginally related concepts, each chapter is organized in interlocked topics. The topics are actively interrelated and are treated in enough detail to ensure understanding. Special attention has been devoted to the flow and sequencing of the topics.

The writing style is personal and conversational. Excessive use of jargon is avoided and important ideas are well defined and illustrated. Special attention has been paid to consistency of terminology throughout the book. We have tried to foster critical thinking about the concepts under discussion by using devices like asking the reader questions in the body of the text.

Believing that a well-tailored example can illuminate the most complex concept, we have used examples liberally throughout the text to clarify the points under consideration. The reader is not left wondering how a key idea applies to the world of organizations. The book is illustrated with exhibits, cartoons, and excerpts from the business press, such as *Report on Business*, *Canadian Business*, *Fortune*, and *Canadian HR Reporter*, to enhance the flow of the material and reinforce the relevance of the examples for students.

We have treated the subject matter generically, recognizing that organizational behaviour occurs in all organizations. The reader will find vignettes, cases, "Focus" selections, "You Be the Manager" features, and examples drawn from a variety of settings, including large and small businesses, high-tech firms, manufacturing firms, hospitals, schools, and the military. In addition, care has been taken to demonstrate that the material covered is relevant to various levels and jobs within these organizations.

ORGANIZATION

Organizational Behaviour is organized in a simple but effective building-block manner. Part One: An Introduction defines organizational behaviour, discusses the nature of organizations, introduces the concept of management, and reviews contemporary management concerns. Part Two: Individual Behaviour covers the topics of personality, learning, perception, attribution, diversity, attitudes, job satisfaction, organizational commitment, and motivation. Part Three: Social Behaviour and Organizational Processes discusses groups, teamwork, socialization, culture, leadership, communication, decision making, power, politics, ethics, conflict, negotiation, and stress. Part Four: The Total Organization considers organizational structure, environment, strategy, technology, change, and innovation.

Some instructors may prefer to revise the order in which students read particular chapters, and they can accomplish this easily. However, Chapter 5, Theories of Work Motivation, should be read before Chapter 6, Motivation in Practice. Also, Chapter 14, Organizational Structure, should be read before Chapter 15, Environment, Strategy, and Technology. The book has been designed to be used in either a quarter or semester course.

MAJOR THEMES AND CONTENT

In preparing the ninth edition of *Organizational Behaviour*, we concentrated on developing several themes that are current in contemporary organizational life. This development included adding new content, expanding previous coverage, and addressing the themes throughout the text to enhance integration.

The **global aspects of organizational life** continue to receive strong treatment in this edition to enable students to become more comfortable and competent in dealing with people from other cultures. Major sections on this theme appear in Chapters 4, 5, 9, and 10, which deal respectively with values, motivation, leadership, and communication. Pedagogical support for the global theme includes "Global Focus" features (Chapters 4, 6, 7, 8, and 10), two "You Be the Manager" features (Chapters 10 and 14), and two case studies (Chapters 6 and 9).

The changing nature of workplace demographics and a need to provide a welcoming work environment for all organizational members has led to explicit coverage of **workforce diversity**. The major treatment of this topic occurs in Chapter 3 in the context of perception and attribution. Additional treatment occurs in the context of motivation (Chapter 5), teams (Chapter 7), and communication (Chapter 10). Pedagogical support for the diversity theme can be found in the "You Be the Manager" feature in Chapters 3, 10, and 16. We also see it in an "Applied Focus" feature (Chapter 9), a "Research Focus" feature (Chapter 9), a "Global Focus" feature (Chapter 7), three chapter-opening vignettes (Chapters 3, 4, and 12), a case incident (Chapter 3), two case studies (Chapters 3 and 4), and an experiential exercise (Chapter 3).

Contemporary organizations are focusing more and more on **teamwork**. This has led to expanded coverage of teams (such as virtual teams), and the most recent research findings on team characteristics and group effectiveness can be found in Chapter 7. Coverage of group decision making is included in Chapter 11. Pedagogical backup for the teamwork theme includes a chapter-opening vignette, "You Be the Manager" feature, "Global Focus" feature, "Applied Focus" feature, a case study, a case incident, and an experiential exercise (all in Chapter 7).

Many organizations continue to undergo major *change and transformation*. Interrelated topics involving organizational change such as **reengineering**, **downsizing**, and **advanced technology** continue to receive detailed coverage and are the focus of another theme highlighted in this edition. Coverage of reengineering can be found in Chapter 16, and related coverage on downsizing can be found in Chapter 14. Although principal coverage of advanced technology is discussed in Chapter 15, the role of technology in communication and decision making can also be found in Chapters 10 and 11, where computer-mediated communication, company intranets, and electronic brainstorming are covered. Other relevant topics include telecommuting (Chapter 6) as well as sections on virtual, modular, ambidextrous, and boundaryless organizational structures (Chapter 14). Several features also portray the use and abuse of advanced technology, such as the "Ethical Focus" feature in Chapter 10. Pedagogical backup for the change theme includes two chapter-opening vignettes (Chapters 15 and 16), two "You Be the Manager" features (Chapters 8 and 16), an experiential exercise (Chapter 10), a case incident (Chapter 16), two case studies (Chapters 8 and 16), and the Integrative Case.

Finally, the ninth edition of *Organizational Behaviour* reflects the continuing issue of **ethics** in organizations. The major formal coverage of ethics is included in Chapter 12 along with a discussion of power and politics. In addition, coverage of ethical leadership can be found in Chapter 9. Pedagogical support for the ethics theme can be found in a chapter-opening vignette and the "You Be the Manager" feature in Chapter 12, and several "Ethical Focus" features (Chapters 3, 6, 8, 10, 11, and 12). Case studies are particularly good vehicles for examining the complexity surrounding ethical issues, and the case incidents in Chapters 9 and 12 and the case studies in Chapters 10 and 12 deal with explicit ethical dilemmas. One of the experiential exercises in Chapter 9 deals with ethical leadership.

PEDAGOGICAL FEATURES

The ninth edition's pedagogical features are designed to complement, supplement, and reinforce the textual material. More specifically, they are designed to promote self-awareness, critical thinking, and an appreciation of how the subject matter applies in actual organizations. The ninth edition of *Organizational Behaviour* includes all of the features found in the previous edition, including three different kinds of cases (case studies, case incidents, and an integrative case), four types of "Focus" boxes ("Applied Focus," "Research Focus," "Ethical Focus," and "Global Focus"), "You Be the Manager" features, experiential exercises, and "On-the-Job Challenge" questions, which can be found at the end of each chapter, along with discussion questions for each chapter and integrative discussion questions.

- All chapters begin with an **Opening Vignette** chosen to stimulate interest in the chapter's subject matter. All of these vignettes concern real people in real organizations. Each vignette is carefully analyzed at several points in the chapter to illustrate the ideas under consideration. For example, Chapter 3 begins with a discussion of diversity at KPMG, and Chapter 12 describes sexual harassment at the RCMP. The ninth edition of *Organizational Behaviour* includes nine new and three updated opening vignettes.

- Each chapter opens with **Learning Objectives** to help focus the student's attention on the chapter's subject matter. The Learning Objectives also appear within the chapter, in the margin, beside content relevant to each objective.

- In each chapter, students encounter a "**You Be the Manager**" feature that invites them to stop and reflect on the relevance of the material they are studying to a real problem in a real organization. Venues range from the Toronto Transit Commission (Chapter 1), the Calgary International Airport (Chapter 2), to Loblaw's acquisition of T&T Supermarket (Chapter 15). Problems range from improving customer service (Chapter 1), managing diversity (Chapter 3), and changing an organization's culture (Chapter 8), to bullying at work (Chapter 13). At the end of each chapter, "**The Manager's Notebook**" offers some observations about the problem and reveals what the organization actually did. The ninth edition of *Organizational Behaviour* includes seven new "You Be the Manager" features.

- All chapters contain some combination of the following "Focus" features: "**Research Focus**," "**Applied Focus**," "**Global Focus**," or "**Ethical Focus**." These features illustrate or supplement the textual material with material from the practising management literature (e.g., *Canadian HR Reporter*), the research literature (e.g., *Academy of Management Journal*), and the popular press (e.g., *Toronto Star*, *National Post*). They are chosen to exemplify real-world problems and practices as they relate to organizational behaviour. The "Research Focus" feature provides examples of organizational behaviour research, such as the effects of subconscious goals on performance (Chapter 5) and presenteeism in the workplace (Chapter 13). The "Applied Focus" features provide practical examples of the application of the text material in organizations. For example, the "Applied Focus" box in Chapter 1 describes green management at the Delta Chelsea Hotel, and the box in Chapter 12 describes employee empowerment at Tim Hortons. These two features help to reinforce the importance of both the research and practice of organizational behaviour. The "Ethical Focus" feature provides examples of ethics in organizational behaviour research, such as incentive compensation and unethical behaviour (Chapter 6) and knowledge hiding in the workplace (Chapter 12). This feature reinforces the importance of ethics in management and organizational behaviour. The "Global Focus" feature provides examples of organizational behaviour around the globe, such as illustrating who has high cultural intelligence (Chapter 4) and the role of national culture in job design (Chapter 6). This feature reinforces the importance of cross-cultural issues in management and organizational behaviour. The ninth edition of *Organizational Behaviour* includes 15 new Focus features.

- **Key terms** in each chapter are set in boldface type when they are discussed in the body of the text and are defined in the margin in a **running glossary**. To help students find the definitions they need, key terms are highlighted in the index, with page references for definitions, also in boldface.

- Each chapter concludes with a **Learning Objectives Checklist** (keyed to the chapter **Learning Objectives**) and **Discussion Questions**. In addition, each chapter includes two or three **Integrative Discussion Questions**. While the traditional discussion questions deal with issues within each chapter, the integrative discussion questions require students to relate and integrate the material in a current chapter with concepts and theories from previous chapters. For example, one of the questions in Chapter 12 ("Power, Politics, and Ethics") requires students to use the material on organizational learning practices (Chapter 2) and contributors to organizational culture (Chapter 8) to understand how an organization can create an ethical workplace. This feature is designed to facilitate student integration of various concepts and theories throughout the text.

- **On-the-Job Challenge Questions** appear after the Integrative Discussion Questions in each chapter. These questions differ from the other discussion questions in several respects. First, they are based on real issues and problems facing organizations. Second, they are more complex and challenging in that they require students to use their knowledge of all the material in the chapter. Third, these questions are very practical and require students to apply the text material to an actual situation or event facing an organization. For example, the question in Chapter 8 asks students to consider how the culture of CN Rail might have contributed to collisions and derailments and how the culture might be changed to improve safety. The answers to these questions are not simple or straightforward and require the student to apply the text material to a real issue or problem facing an organization. We hope that these questions provide students with an interesting and engaging opportunity to use their knowledge of organizational behaviour to address real problems facing organizations today. The ninth edition of *Organizational Behaviour* includes ten new on-the-job challenge questions.

- Each chapter includes at least one **Experiential Exercise**. These exercises span individual self-assessment, role-playing, and group activities. In addition, to enhance student understanding and encourage discussion and interaction, most of the exercises include a group component in which groups of students work together on an exercise or discuss the results of a self-assessment and answer a series of questions. To ensure confidence in the feedback students receive, the self-assessments generally have a research base. The ninth edition of *Organizational Behaviour* includes four new experiential exercises.

- **Case Incidents** are included in every chapter. Case incidents are shorter than the case studies and are designed to focus on a particular topic within a chapter. Because they are short (one or two paragraphs) and deal with realistic scenarios of organizational life, they enable an instructor to quickly generate class discussion on a key theme within each chapter. They can be used at the beginning of a class to introduce a topic and to stimulate student thinking and interest, during the class when a particular topic is being discussed, or at the end of a class when the focus turns to applying the text material. The ninth edition of *Organizational Behaviour* includes three new case incidents.

- A **Case Study** is found in each chapter. The cases are of medium length, allowing great flexibility in tailoring their use to an instructor's personal style. We have selected cases that require active analysis and decision making, not simply passive description. Cases span important topics in contemporary organizations, such as diversity (Chapter 3), introducing teams (Chapter 7), and changing corporate culture (Chapter 8). The ninth edition of *Organizational Behaviour* includes six new case studies.

- The **Integrative Case** is presented at the end of Part One of the text. Unlike the case studies, which focus only on the material in each chapter, the integrative case requires students to use the material throughout the text to understand the case material. Integrative case questions can be found at the end of each of the four parts of the text. The questions deal with the main issues and themes of the chapters within each part. This enables students to gain an increasing awareness and understanding of the case material upon completion of each part of the text. Answering the case questions requires the integration of material from the chapters within each part as well as preceding parts of the text. Therefore, upon completion of the text and the integrative case questions, the student will have acquired a comprehensive understanding of the case through the integration of issues pertaining to individual behaviour, social behaviour and organizational processes, and the total organization.

RESOURCES FOR STUDENTS

A successful OB course requires more than a well-written book. A total package of resources extends this edition's emphasis on creating value for you. The following aids support *Organizational Behaviour*.

MyManagementLab...where learning comes to life!

An access code to MyManagementLab at www.mymanagementlab.com is included with this textbook. MyManagementLab is a state-of-the-art interactive and instructive solution designed to help you master organizational behaviour. MyManagementLab provides access to a wealth of resources all geared to meet your learning needs.

Features include

- Personalized study plans—Pre- and post-tests with remediation activities directed to help you understand and apply the concepts you need the most help with.

- OB Mini-Cases, Decision-Making Mini-Sims, and Talking OB quizzes allow you to test your knowledge.

- Interactive elements such as audio chapter summaries, glossary flashcards, and annotated figures let you experience and learn firsthand.

- Your eText gives you access to your textbook online. eText pages look exactly like your printed text but offer powerful functionality such as quick navigation, full-text search, and the ability to create notes and highlight text in different colours. With your eText you can also create bookmarks, zoom, and link to media files such as videos, simulations, and other activities that may be associated with the book.

Study on the Go

Featured at the end of each chapter, you will find a unique barcode providing access to Study on the Go, an unprecedented mobile integration between text and online content. Link to Pearson's unique Study on the Go content directly from your smartphone, allowing you to study whenever and wherever you wish! Go to one of the sites below to see how you can download an app to your smartphone for free. Once the app is installed, your phone will scan the code and link to a website containing Pearson's Study on the Go content, including popular study tools such as Glossary Flashcards, Audio Summaries, and Quizzes, which can be accessed anytime.

ScanLife http://www.scanlife.com/en/gl-apps

NeoReader http://get.neoreader.com/

QuickMark http://www.quickmark.com.tw/

CourseSmart for Students

CourseSmart goes beyond traditional expectations—providing instant, online access to the textbooks and course materials you need at an average savings of 60 percent. With instant access from any computer and the ability to search your text, you'll find the content you need quickly, no matter where you are. And with online tools like highlighting and note-taking, you can save time and study efficiently. See all the benefits at www.coursesmart.com/students.

RESOURCES FOR INSTRUCTORS

Instructor resources are password protected and available for download via **www.pearsoned.ca.**

- **Instructor's Resource Manual.** Written by the text authors to ensure close coordination with the book, this extensive manual includes chapter objectives, a chapter outline, answers to all of the text questions and cases, supplemental lecture material, video case teaching notes, and teaching notes for each chapter. Available for download from the Pearson online catalogue.

- **MyTest**: Our testbank is available in MyTest in MyManagementLab. MyTest is a powerful assessment-generation program that helps instructors easily create and print quizzes, tests, exams, as well as homework or practice handouts. The testbank consists of about 1700 questions, including a mix of factual and application questions. Multiple-choice, true/false, and short-answer formats are provided. The testbank is also available in a Word version for download from the Pearson online catalogue.

- **PowerPoint® Presentations.** Each chapter of the text is outlined in a series of PowerPoint slides prepared by the text authors, which include key points, exhibits, and tables. Available for download from the Pearson online catalogue.

CourseSmart for Instructors

CourseSmart goes beyond traditional expectations—providing instant, online access to the textbooks and course materials you need at a lower cost for students. And even as students save money, you can save time and hassle with a digital eTextbook that allows you to search for the most relevant content at the very moment you need it. Whether it's evaluating textbooks or creating lecture notes to help students with difficult concepts, CourseSmart can make life a little easier. See how when you visit http://www.coursesmart.com/instructors.

Pearson Custom Library

For enrolments of at least 25 students you can create your own textbook by choosing the chapters that best suit your own course needs. To begin building your custom text, visit www.pearsoncustomlibrary.com. You may also work with a dedicated Pearson Custom editor to create your ideal text—publishing your own original content or mixing and matching Pearson content. Contact your local Pearson Representative to get started.

peerScholar

Firmly grounded in published research, peerScholar is a powerful online pedagogical tool that helps develop your students' critical and creative thinking skills. peerScholar facilitates this through the process of creation, evaluation, and reflection. Working in stages, students begin by submitting a written assignment. peerScholar then circulates their work for others to review, a process that can be anonymous or not depending on your preference. Students receive peer feedback and evaluations immediately, reinforcing their learning and driving the development of higher-order thinking skills. Students can then re-submit revised work, again depending on your preference. Contact your Pearson Representative to learn more about peerScholar and the research behind it.

Technology Specialists

Pearson's Technology Specialists work with faculty and campus course designers to ensure that Pearson technology products, assessment tools, and online course materials are tailored to meet your specific needs. This highly qualified team is dedicated to helping schools take full advantage of a wide range of educational resources, by assisting in the integration of a variety of instructional materials and media formats. Your local Pearson Education sales representative can provide you with more details on this service program.

ACKNOWLEDGMENTS

Books are not written in a vacuum. In writing *Organizational Behaviour*, Ninth Edition, we have profited from the advice and support of a number of individuals. This is our chance to say thank you.

First, we would like to thank our reviewers for this edition, who provided us with a wealth of insights about how to improve the text:

Vishwanath Baba, McMaster University

Ingrid Brand, Durham College

Ann Brosseau, McGill University

Sinan Caykoylu, Simon Fraser University

Debby Cleveland, BCIT

Aaron Dresner, Concordia University

Claude Dupuis, Athabasca University

Kelly Dye, Acadia University

Joanne Leck, University of Ottawa

Jane Mullen, Mount Allison University

Don Miskiman, University of the Fraser Valley

Second, we wish to thank our many colleagues who have provided us with helpful feedback, insights, and general support for the book: Blake Ashforth, Jennifer Berdahl, Stéphane Côté, Marylene Gagné, Jamie Gruman, Geoffrey Leonardelli, Julie McCarthy, Samantha Montes, Robert Oppenheimer, Lyman Porter, Phani Radhakrishnan, Simon Taggar, Soo Min Toh, John Trougakos, V.V. Baba, and David Zweig.

Third, we want to thank John Vongas and Raghid Al Hajj, whose excellent research and organizational skills contributed greatly to the timeliness and relevance of the revision.

Fourth, we want to thank the team at Pearson Education Canada. We wish to extend our genuine appreciation to a group of extremely competent professionals who were wonderful to work with and who have greatly contributed to the quality of this text: Nick Durie (Acquisitions Editor), Jennifer Parks (Sponsoring Editor), Jenna Wulff (Marketing Manager), Joanne Sutherland (Developmental Editor), Deborah Starks (Project Manager), Cat Haggert (Copy Editor); the permissions team of Amanda Campbell and Joanne Tang; and Miriam Blier (Designer). We did our best to make this book interesting, informative, and enjoyable to read; making it look as good as it does is icing on the cake. Thanks to everyone at Pearson who contributed to this book. They represent a great example of what this textbook is all about: *individuals working together to accomplish goals through group effort.*

Finally, each of us wishes to give thanks to those in our lives who have contributed to our work and the writing of this text:

I (Gary Johns) am grateful to my Concordia University Management Department colleagues for their interest, support, and ideas. Additionally, I would like to thank my students over the years. In one way or another, many of their questions, comments, challenges, and suggestions are reflected in the book. Also, thanks to all my colleagues who have taken time to suggest ideas for the book when we have met at professional conferences. Finally, thanks to Monika Jörg for her continuing enthusiasm, caring, humour, support, and advice.

I (Alan Saks) am grateful to my colleagues at the University of Toronto who have all been very supportive of this textbook. I would like to express my appreciation to my parents who have provided me with love and support throughout my career and continue to celebrate every step along the way. I also wish to thank my family, Kelly, Justin, and Brooke, who have had to endure my long hours of work for the past year. Although they did not write a single word in this book, in many ways their contribution is as significant as mine. Thanks for understanding, making me laugh, and for waiting so long for it to end!

Gary Johns   Alan M. Saks

ABOUT THE AUTHORS

Gary Johns (PhD, Wayne State University) is Professor of Management and the Concordia University Research Chair in Management in the John Molson School of Business, Concordia University, Montreal. He has research interests in absenteeism from work, presenteeism, personality, job design, research methodology, and the impact of context on organizational behaviour. He has published in *Journal of Applied Psychology, Academy of Management Journal, Academy of Management Review, Organizational Behavior and Human Decision Processes, Personnel Psychology, Journal of Management, Research in Organizational Behavior, Research in Personnel and Human Resources Management, Journal of Organizational Behavior,* Journal of Occupational and Organizational Psychology, International Review of Industrial and Organizational Psychology, Journal of Occupational Health Psychology, Canadian Psychology, Human Resource Management Review, Human Relations, Applied Psychology: An International Review, Canadian Journal of Administrative Sciences,* and *Psychology Today.* Co-author of *Organizational Behaviour: Understanding and Managing Life at Work* (9th Edition, Pearson Prentice Hall). Recipient of Academy of Management Organizational Behavior Division's New Concept Award, Society for Industrial and Organizational Psychology's Edwin E. Ghiselli Research Design Award, the Canadian Society for Industrial and Organizational Psychology's Award for Distinguished Contributions to Industrial and Organizational Psychology, the Concordia University Research Award, and the award for the best article published in *Human Relations* in 2007. Elected Fellow of SIOP, American Psychological Association, Canadian Psychological Association, and Academy of Management. Former Chair of the Canadian Society for Industrial and Organizational Psychology. Associate Editor, *Journal of Organizational Behavior,* 1998–2006. Currently on editorial boards of *Journal of Applied Psychology, Human Relations, International Journal of Selection and Assessment,* and *Applied Psychology: An International Review.* Formerly on editorial boards of *Academy of Management Journal, Journal of Management, Personnel Psychology, Organizational Behavior and Human Decision Processes, Journal of Occupational Health Psychology, Canadian Journal of Administrative Sciences,* and *Journal of Occupational and Organizational Psychology.* Held visiting positions at University of Sheffield, University of Oregon, Queensland University of Technology, Australian Graduate School of Management and Australian School of Business (University of New South Wales), Hong Kong University of Science and Technology, and Singapore Management University.

Alan M. Saks (PhD, University of Toronto) is a Professor of Organizational Behaviour and Human Resources Management at the University of Toronto, where he holds a joint appointment in the Department of Management—UTSC, the Centre for Industrial Relations and Human Resources, and the Joseph L. Rotman School of Management. Prior to joining the University of Toronto, Professor Saks was a member of the Department of Management at Concordia University and the School of Administrative Studies at York University. Professor Saks earned an HBA in Psychology from the University of Western Ontario, an MASc in Industrial–Organizational Psychology from the University of Waterloo, and a PhD in Organizational Behaviour and Human Resources from the University of Toronto. His research interests include recruitment, job search, training, employee engagement, and the socialization and on-boarding of new employees. Professor

Saks has published his research in refereed journals such as the *Journal of Applied Psychology, Personnel Psychology, Academy of Management Journal, Journal of Organizational Behavior, Journal of Vocational Behavior, Journal of Business and Psychology, Human Resource Management, The International Journal of Human Resource Management, International Journal of Training and Development,* and *Human Resource Management Review,* as well as in professional journals such as *HR Professional Magazine, The Learning Journal,* and *Canadian HR Reporter.* In addition to *Organizational Behaviour: Understanding and Managing Life at Work,* he is also the author of *Research, Measurement, and Evaluation of Human Resources* and co-author of *Managing Performance through Training and Development.* Professor Saks is currently on the editorial boards of the *Journal of Vocational Behavior, Human Resource Development Review, Journal of Leadership and Organizational Studies,* and *International Journal of Training and Development* and is an Associate Editor of the *Journal of Business and Psychology.*

For Bill and Jean Johns and for Monika Jörg
Gary Johns

For Kelly, Justin, Brooke, and my parents
Simon and Renee Saks
Alan M. Saks

This edition is dedicated to the memory of our friend and colleague, Robert (Bob) J. House.

PART

AN INTRODUCTION

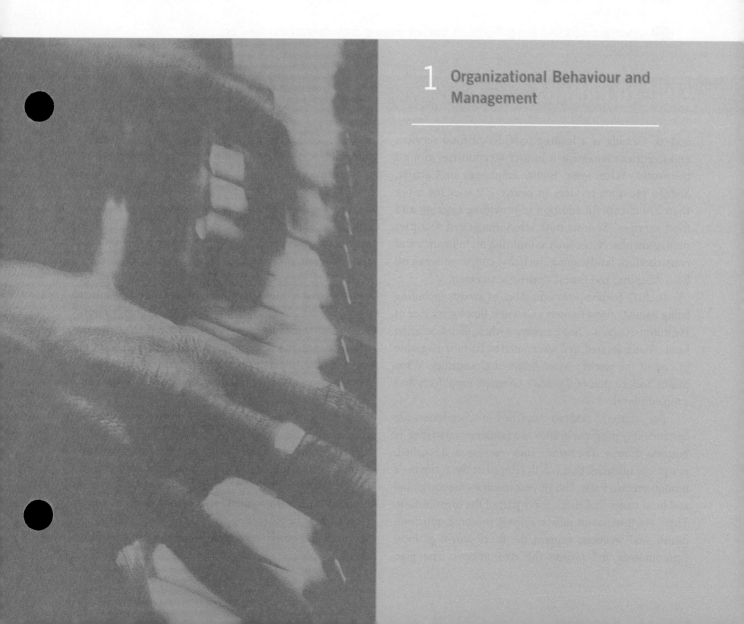

1 Organizational Behaviour and Management

ORGANIZATIONAL BEHAVIOUR AND MANAGEMENT

LEARNING OBJECTIVES

After reading Chapter 1, you should be able to:

1.1 Define *organizations* and describe their basic characteristics.

1.2 Explain the concept of *organizational behaviour* and describe the goals of the field.

1.3 Define *management* and describe what managers do to accomplish goals.

1.4 Contrast the *classical viewpoint* of management with that which the *human relations movement* advocated.

1.5 Describe the *contemporary contingency approach* to management.

1.6 Explain what managers do—their roles, activities, agendas for action, and thought processes.

1.7 Describe the societal and global trends that are shaping contemporary management concerns.

SODEXO CANADA

Sodexo Canada is a leading provider of food services and facilities management in over 80 countries around the world. With some 10,000 employees in Canada, Sodexo provides services to nearly 750 sites for more than 230 clients. In addition to providing catering and food services, Sodexo now offers integrated facilities management services such as building maintenance and construction, landscaping, security, concierge services, housekeeping, and fitness centre management.

In 2012 Sodexo won a number of awards including being named one of Canada's Greenest Employers, one of Hamilton-Niagara's Top Employers where their Canadian head office is located, and was named by *Fortune* magazine as one of the world's Most Admired Companies. What makes Sodexo one of Canada's Greenest Employers and a top employer?

For starters, Sodexo launched a corporate-wide sustainability program in 2009 as a fundamental part of its business strategy. The *Better Tomorrow Plan*, as it is called, is a global initiative that was developed at the company's headquarters in Paris. The 10-year vision focuses on global and local issues that touch every part of the organization. There are three main pillars: actively promote nutrition, health, and wellness; support the development of local communities; and protect the environment. The plan includes companywide commitments to reduce its carbon footprint, water consumption, and waste diversion and composting.

In Canada, the initiative rolled out in a number of ways. An online toolkit was created to communicate to and engage employees. It featured posters, presentations for employees and clients, and elearning links. An employee-run committee called the Green Team also works to educate and engage employees and inspire them to adopt practices that reduce waste and preserve the environment. This includes bimonthly initiatives around energy awareness, charitable events, and Earth Day activities. Quarterly newsletters go out to employees along with weekly ebulletins and news briefs that incorporate a sustainability piece. There's also an annual progress report on corporate citizenship initiatives.

According to Chris Roberts, Director of Corporate Citizenship, "Having a decentralized employee population and accounts right across the country is tough so we need to rely on the support of cross-functional teams within the company to help with these initiatives." The team members come from different divisions, such as supply management or marketing and sales. "They help support my goals and objectives of implementing and communicating the plan across Canada."

As part of the plan, the company worked with the World Wildlife Fund (WWF) to implement a national sustainable seafood policy, which committed Sodexo to eliminating at-risk species from its menus by the end of 2011 and sourcing 100 percent of its seafood from sustainable sources by 2015.

What makes Sodexo one of Hamilton-Niagara's Top Employers? Sodexo supports ongoing employee education, which includes tuition subsidies and offers a variety of in-house training programs as well as mentoring and formal leadership programs. Employees have a range of career opportunities at locations across Canada and around the world. Sodexo provides several financial benefits such as a new employee referral bonus, a share purchase plan, a defined contribution pension plan, and matching RSP contributions. New employees receive three weeks paid vacation and the longest-serving employees receive six weeks.

Sodexo also has a culture of diversity and inclusion that includes a number of initiatives including a Diversity Business and Leadership Summit (DBLS) that involves a day of professional development focused on building skills, knowledge, and awareness around different dimensions of diversity. The company recently launched a Virtual Diversity Business and Leadership Summit to provide easy access to diversity and inclusion training. Sodexo also celebrates diversity and inclusion by having a Federal Heritage Month education and awareness program.

In recognition of its diversity initiatives, Sodexo received the 2012 Catalyst Award in North America, which honours exceptional business initiatives that advance women in the workplace. The award was in recognition of Sodexo's initiative, *Making Every Day Count: Driving Business Success Through the Employee Experience*, which is a systematic strategy to provide the tools, resources, and support necessary to ensure the success of all employees. From 2003 to 2010, the number of women in leadership at Sodexo increased by 74 percent and the number of women on the executive committee increased from three to five. Sodexo also received the Innovations in Diversity Award by *Profiles in Diversity Journal* in recognition of its Virtual Diversity and Business Leadership Summit.

How do employees at Sodexo feel about their organization? According to Susan Black, Senior Vice-President of Human Resources at Sodexo Canada, "People feel good about being part of this organization because we do some great work in the communities and to support the environment."[1]

There are a variety of different organizations in which individuals work together to accomplish goals through group effort. Though the motivation of a television news station might differ from other organizations, all organizations strive for goal accomplishment and survival.

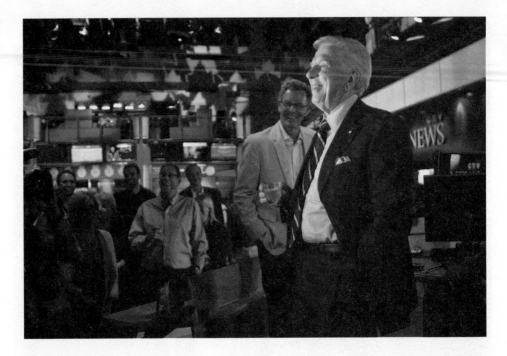

What we have here is an example of worklife and management—just what this book is about. The example also highlights many important aspects of organizational behaviour, such as learning, diversity, teams, communication, and corporate citizenship and social responsibility. It raises some very interesting questions: Why does Sodexo have a corporate sustainability program? Why does Sodexo have programs that promote diversity and inclusion? Why do they provide employees with financial benefits and what effect does this have on employee attitudes and behaviour? Why is Sodexo so concerned about the community and the environment? This book will help you uncover the answers to these kinds of questions.

In this chapter, we will define *organizations* and *organizational behaviour* and examine their relationship to management. We will explore historical and contemporary approaches to management and consider what managers do and how they think. The chapter concludes with some issues of concern to contemporary managers.

LO 1.1

Define *organizations* and describe their basic characteristics.

Organizations.
Social inventions for accomplishing common goals through group effort.

WHAT ARE ORGANIZATIONS?

This book is about what happens in organizations. Most of us will earn our livelihood working in organizations and our well-being as well as that of our communities depends on organizations. We are often identified, in part, by what we do and where we do it. We live in an organizational society.[2] But what exactly is an organization?

Organizations are social inventions for accomplishing common goals through group effort. Sodexo Canada is obviously an organization, but so are the Toronto Blue Jays, the CTV, and a college sorority or fraternity.

Social Inventions

When we say that organizations are social inventions, we mean that their essential characteristic is the coordinated presence of *people*, not necessarily things. Sodexo Canada owns a lot of things, such as equipment and offices. However, you are probably aware that, through advanced information technology and contracting out work, some contemporary organizations make and sell products, such as computers or clothes, without owning much of anything. Also, many service organizations, such as consulting firms, have little physical capital. Still, these organizations have people—people who present both opportunities and challenges. *The field of organizational behaviour is about understanding people and managing them to work effectively.*

Goal Accomplishment

Individuals are assembled into organizations for a reason. The organizations mentioned above have the very basic goals of providing food and facilities management services, winning baseball games, and delivering news. Non-profit organizations have goals such as saving souls, promoting the arts, helping the needy, or educating people. Virtually all organizations have survival as a goal. Despite this, consider the list of organizations that have failed to survive—Canadian Airlines, Eaton's, the Montreal Expos, and Columbia House, just to name a few. *The field of organizational behaviour is concerned with how organizations can survive and adapt to change.* Certain behaviours are necessary for survival and adaptation. People have to

- be motivated to join and remain in the organization;
- carry out their basic work reliably, in terms of productivity, quality, and service;
- be willing to continuously learn and upgrade their knowledge and skills; and
- be flexible and innovative.[3]

The field of organizational behaviour is concerned with all these basic activities. Innovation and flexibility, which provide for adaptation to change, are especially important for contemporary organizations. Management guru Tom Peters has gone so far as to advise firms to "Get Innovative or Get Dead."[4]

Group Effort

The final component of our definition of organizations is that they are based on group effort. At its most general level, this means that organizations depend on interaction and coordination among people to accomplish their goals. Much of the intellectual and physical work done in organizations is quite literally performed by groups, whether they are permanent work teams or short-term project teams. Also, informal grouping occurs in all organizations because friendships develop and individuals form informal alliances to accomplish work. The quality of this informal contact in terms of communication and morale can have a strong impact on goal achievement. For all these reasons, *the field of organizational behaviour is concerned with how to get people to practise effective teamwork.*

Now that we have reviewed the basic characteristics of organizations, let's look more directly at the meaning and scope of organizational behaviour.

WHAT IS ORGANIZATIONAL BEHAVIOUR?

Organizational behaviour refers to the attitudes and behaviours of individuals and groups in organizations. The discipline of organizational behaviour systematically studies these attitudes and behaviours and provides insight about effectively managing and changing them. It also studies how organizations can be structured more effectively and how events in their external environments affect organizations. Those who study organizational behaviour are interested in attitudes—how satisfied people are with their jobs, how committed they feel to the goals of the organization, or how supportive they are of promoting women or minorities into management positions. Behaviours like cooperation, conflict, innovation, resignation, or ethical lapses are important areas of study in the field of organizational behaviour.

HERMAN MILLER: MANAGERS AS LEADERS Go to MyManagementLab to watch a video about managers as leaders.

Explain the concept of *organizational behaviour* and describe the goals of the field.

Organizational behaviour. The attitudes and behaviours of individuals and groups in organizations.

Human resources management. Programs, practices, and systems to acquire, develop, and retain employees in organizations.

A closely related but distinct discipline is human resources management. **Human resources management** refers to programs, practices, and systems to acquire, develop, and retain employees in organizations. You are probably familiar with many human resource practices such as recruitment and selection, compensation, and training and development. As you will see throughout this text, knowledge of organizational behaviour will help you understand the use and effectiveness of human resource practices. For example, in Chapter 3 you will learn about the role that perceptions play in human resources management. In Chapter 4, you will learn about employee absenteeism and turnover (which is necessary for developing effective human resource practices to lower absenteeism and retain employees). In Chapters 5 and 6 you will learn how theories of motivation help us understand the effects of different pay plans on employee motivation and performance. In Chapter 8 you will learn how human resource practices such as realistic job previews and employee orientation programs contribute to the socialization process in organizations. Thus, learning about organizational behaviour will improve your understanding of human resources management.

Using an organizational behaviour perspective, reconsider the Sodexo Canada vignette that opened the chapter. The immediate question is: *What are the factors that make an organization competitive and a great place to work?* Although we will not answer this question directly, we can pose some subsidiary questions highlighting some of the topics that the field of organizational behaviour covers, which we will explore in later chapters.

- How do employees learn, and what is the role of training and development and career planning? At Sodexo Canada, employees have access to tuition subsidies, a variety of training programs, and career opportunities to help them advance in their careers. Learning is important for employee behaviour and performance. It is discussed in Chapter 2.

- What should organizations do to manage a diverse workforce? Sodexo offers a Diversity Business and Leadership Summit (DBLS) to build skills, knowledge, and awareness around different dimensions of diversity and celebrates diversity and inclusion by having a Federal Heritage Month education and awareness program. Workforce diversity and how to manage it is discussed in Chapter 3.

- How can organizations motivate employees, and how important is compensation? Sodexo Canada offers employees a share purchase plan, a defined contribution pension plan, and matching RSP contributions. Chapter 5 describes different theories of motivation, and the role of money as a motivator is discussed in Chapter 6.

- What is a cross-functional team and how do you design effective teams? Sodexo Canada uses cross-functional teams to help implement and communicate the Better Tomorrow Plan. You will learn about teams in Chapter 7.

- What is an organizational culture and what role does it play in an organization's success? The culture at Sodexo Canada emphasizes corporate social responsibility, diversity and inclusion, sustainability, and concern for the environment. How cultures are built and maintained is covered in Chapter 8.

These questions provide a good overview of some issues that those in the field of organizational behaviour study. Accurate answers to these questions would go a long way toward understanding why Sodexo Canada is a successful organization and how other organizations can make changes to become more effective. Analysis followed by action is what organizational behaviour is all about.

WHY STUDY ORGANIZATIONAL BEHAVIOUR?

Why should you attempt to read and understand the material in *Organizational Behaviour*?

Organizational Behaviour Is Interesting

At its core, organizational behaviour is interesting because it is about people and human nature. Why does Sodexo Canada focus so much on diversity, and what effect does this have on employee attitudes and behaviour? These questions are interesting because they help us understand why employees become committed to an organization and what motivates them to work hard.

Organizational Behaviour includes interesting examples of success as well as failure. Later in the text, we will study a company that has a wellness program that rewards employees for making changes in their health-related behaviours and lifestyle (Economical Insurance, Chapter 2); a company that has won awards for integrating skilled immigrants into the workplace (KPMG, Chapter 3); a company that successfully integrates generations in the workplace (L'Oreal Canada, Chapter 4); a company that excels at staffing project teams (IDEO, Chapter 7); and a company organized into families, villages, and tribes (Flight Centre, Chapter 14). All of these companies are extremely successful, and organizational behaviour helps explain why.

Organizational behaviour does not have to be exotic to be interesting. Anyone who has negotiated with a recalcitrant bureaucrat or had a really excellent boss has probably wondered what made them behave the way they did. Organizational behaviour provides the tools to find out why.

Organizational Behaviour Is Important

Looking through the lens of other disciplines, it would be possible to frame Sodexo Canada's success in terms of marketing and sales. Notice, however, that underlying these perspectives, it is *still* about organizational behaviour. What happens in organizations often has a profound impact on people. It is clear that the impact of organizational behaviour does not stop at the walls of the organization. The consumers of an organization's products and services are also affected, such as the customers who rely on Sodexo Canada's services. Thus, organizational behaviour is important to managers, employees, and consumers, and understanding it can make us more effective managers, employees, or consumers.

We sometimes fail to appreciate that there is tremendous variation in organizational behaviour. For example, skilled salespeople in insurance or real estate make many, many more sales than some of their peers. Similarly, for every Greenpeace or Sierra Club, there are dozens of failed organizations that were dedicated to saving the environment. The field of organizational behaviour is concerned with explaining these differences and using the explanations to improve organizational effectiveness and efficiency.

Organizational Behaviour Makes a Difference

In his book *Competitive Advantage Through People*, Jeffrey Pfeffer argues that organizations can no longer achieve a competitive advantage through the traditional sources of success, such as technology, regulated markets, access to financial resources, and economies of scale.[5] Today, the main factor that differentiates organizations is their workforce and human capital. The results of a recent study that reviewed research on human capital are unequivocal: human capital is strongly related to and a key determinant of firm performance.[6] Thus, sustained competitive advantage and organizational effectiveness are increasingly related to the management of human capital and organizational behaviour.

On the basis of a review of the popular and academic literature, Pfeffer identified 16 practices of companies that are effective through their management of people. Many of these practices, such as incentive pay, participation and empowerment, teams, job redesign, and training and skill development, are important topics in organizational behaviour and are discussed in this book. Pfeffer's research helps to point out that organizational behaviour is not just interesting and important but that it also makes a big difference for the effectiveness and competitiveness of organizations.

Many of the best companies to work for and organizations like Sodexo that have been named top employers are living examples of the importance of organizational behaviour. As shown in Exhibit 1.1, the best companies to work for in Canada have implemented management practices that have their basis in organizational behaviour such as flexible work schedules, diversity programs, and employee recognition and reward programs. This raises an interesting question: Are the best companies to work for also the most profitable? Some might argue that just because an organization is a great place to work does not necessarily mean that it is a great organization when it comes to competitiveness and performance. What do you think? To find out more, see the Research Focus: *Are the Best Companies to Work for the Best Companies?*

HOW MUCH DO YOU KNOW ABOUT ORGANIZATIONAL BEHAVIOUR?

Although this is probably your first formal course in organizational behaviour, you already have a number of opinions about the subject. To illustrate this, consider whether the following statements are true or false. Please jot down a one-sentence rationale for your answer. There are no tricks involved!

1. Effective organizational leaders tend to possess identical personality traits.

2. Nearly all workers prefer stimulating, challenging jobs.

3. Managers have a very accurate idea about how much their peers and superiors are paid.

4. Workers have a very accurate idea about how often they are absent from work.

5. Pay is the best way to motivate most employees and improve job performance.

Now that you have your answers, do one more thing. Assume that the correct answer is opposite to the one you have given; that is, if your answer is "true" for a statement, assume that it is actually false, and vice versa. Now, give a one-sentence rationale why this opposite answer could also be correct.

Each of these statements concerns the behaviour of people in organizations. Furthermore, each statement has important implications for the functioning of organizations. If effective leaders possess identical personality traits, then organizations might sensibly hire

Explore

Go to MyManagementLab to see an annotated version of this figure.

EXHIBIT 1.1 Management practices of the best companies to work for in Canada.
Sources: Brearton, S., & Daly, J. (2003, January). The 50 best companies to work for in Canada. *Report on Business Magazine, 19*(2), 53–66; Hannon, G. (2002, January). The 50 best companies to work for. *Report on Business Magazine, 18*(7), 41–52.

- Flexible work schedules (flex-time, telecommuting, job sharing, and compressed workweek)
- Stock options, profit sharing plans, and performance bonuses
- Extensive training and development programs
- Family assistance programs
- On-site fitness facilities, daycare, and wellness programs
- Career days and formal career plans
- Flexible or cafeteria-style benefit plans
- Monthly staff socials, family Christmas parties, and picnics
- Stress reduction programs
- Monthly all-employee meetings
- Formal workplace diversity programs to encourage women and minorities
- Employee recognition and reward programs

RESEARCH FOCUS

ARE THE BEST COMPANIES TO WORK FOR THE BEST COMPANIES?

In recent years, surveys of the best companies to work for have become very popular. While there is no doubt that being a great place to work is important, some have wondered whether the best places to work are also the best companies. For example, are the additional costs associated with being a great place to work (e.g., employee-friendly practices, outstanding pay and benefits) justified by higher firm performance? Do good employee relations and positive job attitudes contribute to the bottom line?

To find out, Ingrid Fulmer, Barry Gerhart, and Kimberly Scott conducted a study in which they compared 50 of the companies from *Fortune* magazine's 100 best list to a matched set of firms that have never been on the 100 best list but are comparable in terms of industry, size, and operating performance. Comparisons between the two samples indicated that the 100 best companies outperformed the matched group of companies on financial performance and stock returns. Financial performance as measured by return on assets (ROA) and market-to-book value of equity was generally better among the 100 best than among the matched group of organizations over a six-year period. Further, the six-year cumulative stock returns of the companies on the 100 best list outperformed a composite market index by 183 percentage points, or 95 percent!

To confirm this, they compared the sample from the 100 best companies to another sample of organizations from Hewitt Associates and The Gallup Organization on a measure of employee attitudes. The results indicated that the companies on the 100 best list had more positive employee relations and attitudes compared to the other companies. Further, to assess the stability of job attitudes, the authors examined the relationship between the employee attitude measure over two years. The results indicated that the relationship was positive and significant and that there was little change from one year to the next. In other words, employee attitudes at the 100 best firms were highly positive and stable over time, providing support for the belief that positive employee relations are a source of sustainable competitive advantage.

These findings provide the strongest evidence to date of a direct positive link between employee relations and attitudes and financial performance. They suggest that companies can create attractive workplaces without hurting the bottom line, and in many cases the 100 best exhibit superior performance.

Source: Based on Fulmer, I.S., Gerhart, B., & Scott, K.S. (2003). Are the 100 best better? An empirical investigation of the relationship between being a "great place to work" and firm performance. *Personnel Psychology, 56,* 965–993; Romero, E.J. (2004). Are the great places to work also great performers? *Academy of Management Executive, 18,* 150–152.

leaders who have such traits. Similarly, if most employees prefer stimulating jobs, there are many jobs that could benefit from upgrading. In this book, we will investigate the extent to which statements such as these are true or false and why they are true or false.

The answers to this quiz may surprise you. Substantial research indicates that each of the statements in the quiz is essentially false. Of course, there are exceptions, but in general, researchers have found that the personalities of effective leaders vary a fair amount, many people prefer routine jobs, managers are not well informed about the pay of their peers and superiors, workers underestimate their own absenteeism, and pay is not always the most effective way to motivate workers and improve job performance. However, you should not jump to unwarranted conclusions based on the inaccuracy of these statements until we determine *why* they tend to be incorrect. There are good reasons for an organization to tie pay to job performance to motivate employees and to improve their performance. Also, we can predict who might prefer challenging jobs and who will be motivated by pay. We will discuss these issues in more detail in later chapters.

Experience indicates that people are amazingly good at giving sensible reasons why the same statement is either true or false. Thus, pay will always motivate workers because most people want to make more money and will work harder to get more pay. Conversely, workers will only work as hard as they have to, regardless of how much money they are paid. The ease with which people can generate such contradictory responses suggests that "common sense" develops through unsystematic and incomplete experiences with organizational behaviour.

However, because common sense and opinions about organizational behaviour do affect management practice, practice should be based on informed opinion and systematic study. To learn more about how to study organizational behaviour, see the Appendix. Now, let's consider the goals of organizational behaviour.

GOALS OF ORGANIZATIONAL BEHAVIOUR

Like any discipline, the field of organizational behaviour has a number of commonly agreed-upon goals. Chief among these are effectively predicting, explaining, and managing behaviour that occurs in organizations. For example, in Chapter 6 we will discuss the factors that predict which pay plans are most effective in motivating individuals and groups. Then we will explain the reasons for this effectiveness and describe how managers can implement effective pay plans.

Predicting Organizational Behaviour

Predicting the behaviour of others is an essential requirement for everyday life, both inside and outside of organizations. Our lives are made considerably easier by our ability to anticipate when our friends will get angry, when our professors will respond favourably to a completed assignment, and when salespeople and politicians are telling us the truth about a new product or the state of the nation. In organizations, there is considerable interest in predicting when people will make ethical decisions, create innovative products, or engage in sexual harassment.

The very regularity of behaviour in organizations permits the prediction of its future occurrence. However, untutored predictions of organizational behaviour are not always as accurate. Through systematic study, the field of organizational behaviour provides a scientific foundation that helps improve predictions of organizational events. Of course, being able to predict organizational behaviour does not guarantee that we can explain the reason for the behaviour and develop an effective strategy to manage it. This brings us to the second goal of the field.

Explaining Organizational Behaviour

Another goal of organizational behaviour is to explain events in organizations—why do they occur? Prediction and explanation are not synonymous. Ancient societies were capable of predicting the regular setting of the sun but were unable to explain where it went or why it went there. In general, accurate prediction precedes explanation. Thus, the very regularity of the sun's disappearance gave some clues about why it was disappearing.

Organizational behaviour is especially interested in determining why people are more or less motivated, satisfied, or prone to resign. Explaining events is more complicated than predicting them. For one thing, a particular behaviour could have multiple causes. People may resign from their jobs because they are dissatisfied with their pay, because they are discriminated against, or because they have failed to respond appropriately to an organizational crisis. An organization that finds itself with a "turnover problem" is going to have to find out why this is happening before it can put an effective correction into place. This behaviour could have many different causes, each of which would require a specific solution. Furthermore, explanation is also complicated by the fact that the underlying causes of some event or behaviour can change over time. For example, the reasons people quit may vary greatly depending on the overall economy and whether there is high or low unemployment in the field in question. Throughout the book, we will consider material that should improve your grasp of organizational behaviour. The ability to understand behaviour is a necessary prerequisite for effectively managing it.

Managing Organizational Behaviour

Management is defined as the art of getting things accomplished in organizations through others. Managers acquire, allocate, and utilize physical and human resources to accomplish goals.[7] This definition does not include a prescription about how to get things accomplished. As we proceed through the text, you will learn that a variety of management styles might be effective depending on the situation at hand.

If behaviour can be predicted and explained, it can often be managed. That is, if we truly understand the reasons for high-quality service, ethical behaviour, or anything else, we can often take sensible action to manage it effectively. If prediction and explanation constitute analysis, then management constitutes action. Unfortunately, we see all too many cases in which managers act without analysis, looking for a quick fix to problems. The result is often disaster. The point is not to overanalyze a problem. Rather, it is to approach a problem with a systematic understanding of behavioural science and organizational behaviour and to use that understanding to make decisions; this is known as evidence-based management.

Evidence-based management involves translating principles based on the best scientific evidence into organizational practices. By using evidence-based management, managers can make decisions based on the best available scientific evidence from social science and organizational research, rather than personal preference and unsystematic experience. Evidence-based management derives principles from research evidence and translates them into practices that solve organizational problems. The use of evidence-based management is more likely to result in the attainment of organizational goals, including those affecting employees, stockholders, and the public in general.[8]

Now that you are familiar with the goals of organizational behaviour, read You Be the Manager: *Toronto's Troubled Transit System* and answer the questions. At the end of the chapter, find out what the TTC is doing in The Manager's Notebook. This is not a test but rather an exercise to improve critical thinking, analytical skills, and management skills. Pause and reflect on these application features as you encounter them in each chapter.

EARLY PRESCRIPTIONS CONCERNING MANAGEMENT

For many years, experts interested in organizations were concerned with prescribing the "correct" way to manage an organization to achieve its goals. There were two basic phases to this prescription, which experts often call the classical view and the human relations view. A summary of these viewpoints will illustrate how the history of management thought and organizational behaviour has developed.

The Classical View and Bureaucracy

Most of the major advocates of the classical viewpoint were experienced managers or consultants who took the time to write down their thoughts on organizing. For the most part, this activity occurred in the early 1900s. The classical writers acquired their experience in military settings, mining operations, and factories that produced everything from cars to candy. Prominent names include Henri Fayol, General Motors executive James D. Mooney, and consultant Lyndall Urwick.[9] Although exceptions existed, the **classical viewpoint** tended to advocate a very high degree of specialization of labour and a very high degree of coordination. Each department was to tend to its own affairs, with centralized decision making from upper management providing coordination. To maintain control, the classical view suggested that managers have fairly few workers, except for lower-level jobs where machine pacing might substitute for close supervision.

LO 1.3

Define *management* and describe what managers do to accomplish goals.

Management. The art of getting things accomplished in organizations through others.

Evidence-based management. Translating principles based on the best scientific evidence into organizational practices.

LO 1.4

Contrast the *classical viewpoint* of management with that which the *human relations movement* advocated.

Classical viewpoint. An early prescription on management that advocated high specialization of labour, intensive coordination, and centralized decision making.

YOU BE THE MANAGER

Toronto's Troubled Transit System

The Toronto Transit Commission (TTC) is the third-largest public transit system in North America, after New York and Mexico City. With 12 500 employees, the TTC moves 1.5 million riders every weekday.

In January of 2010, on the heels of a TTC fare hike and token shortages, a TTC rider took a photo of a subway ticket collector sprawled back in his chair, his mouth agape, and apparently snoozing while on the job. The photo was posted in the web and went viral.

At first people were amused, but then it grew rapidly into anger and the sleeping ticket collector who became known as "TTC Sleeper" became a lightning rod for transit riders frustrated with the TTC.

Soon more photos of sleeping TTC employees began to surface and riders complained about everything from TTC employees sleeping, reading, or watching DVDs, to more serious allegations of dangerous driving, verbal rudeness, and even assault. And then in February the TTC was once again under fire for a video taken of an employee who left a bus idling while he took a lengthy, unscheduled break in a doughnut shop.

Reports of customer complaints indicate that they increased by nearly 20 percent, from about 26 000 in the first 11 months of 2008 to about 31 000 in the same period the following year. While many riders complained about the fare increase, the top two complaints for the year were bus and streetcar delays and "discourtesy" from TTC workers. There were 3851 complaints about discourteous employees.

Former TTC chief general manager Gary Webster issued a scolding memo to all employees declaring, "The culture of complacency and malaise that has seeped into our organization will end" and he warned that workers would be "held accountable for their poor performance."

Then TTC chairman Adam Giambrone announced the creation of a blue-ribbon customer service advisory panel of private-sector experts to review the TTC's customer service practices and make recommendations of how the TTC could improve customer service. The Amalgamated Transit Union Local 113 announced that it would hold a series of town hall meetings to address the strained relationship between passengers and workers.

In April 2010, the TTC released hundreds of customer complaints to the *Toronto Star* through a freedom of information request. The complaints painted a picture of a transit system troubled by a culture of indifference and disdain toward customers. Riders say they are verbally abused and harassed by TTC staff daily. Poor people skills, not delays or fare disputes, appeared to be the main concern for transit customers.

Customer complaints paint a picture of a transit system troubled by a culture of indifference and disdain toward customers.

Questions

1. What issues are particularly relevant from an organizational behaviour perspective? What can the TTC learn about the customer service problem from organizational behaviour?

2. How can the goals of organizational behaviour help solve the problems at the TTC and improve customer service?

To find out what the TTC is doing to improve customer service, see The Manager's Notebook at the end of the chapter.

Sources: Kalinowski, T. (2010, January 20). TTC seeks outside aid to fix customer beefs. *Toronto Star*, GT5; Kalinowski, T. (2010, January 28). 'We owe our riders an apology,' TTC boss concedes; Giambrone's news conference was classic damage control. But will it work? *Toronto Star*, A1; Kalinowski, T. (2010, January 28). Customer service checklist. *Toronto Star*, A19; Ferenc, L. (2010, February 3). Can much-maligned TTC pass our test? After all the promises on improvements, Star reporter boards for 2 hours of scrutiny. *Toronto Star*, GT3; Kalinowski, T. (2010, February 4). TTC driver takes coffee break as fuming riders wait and wait. *Toronto Star*, A2; Anonymous (2010, February 9). TTC's culture of complacency. *Toronto Star*, A18; Kennedy, B. (2010, April 1). Unhappy TTC riders get chance to sound off to employees. *Toronto Star*, 1; Doolittle, R. (2010, April 20). Crude, rude TTC staff top list of complaints; Dreadful lack of people skills, not delays or fare disputes, main concern for commuters. *Toronto Star*, 1; Yang, J. (2010, January 22). TTC catnaps ignite rider fury amid higher fares. *Toronto Star*, www.thestar.com/printarticle/754753; Anonymous (2010, August 23). TTC Customer Service Advisory Panel Report.

Frederick Taylor (1856–1915), the father of **scientific management**, was also a contributor to the classical school, although he was mainly concerned with job design and the structure of work on the shop floor.[10] Rather than informal "rules of thumb" for job design, Taylor's scientific management advocated the use of careful research to determine the optimum degree of specialization and standardization. He also supported the development of written instructions that clearly defined work procedures, and he encouraged supervisors to standardize workers' movements and breaks for maximum efficiency. Taylor even extended scientific management to the supervisor's job, advocating "functional foremanship" whereby supervisors would specialize in particular functions. For example, one might become a specialist in training workers, while another might fulfill the role of a disciplinarian.

The practising managers and consultants had an academically in Max Weber (1864–1920), the distinguished German social theorist. Weber made the term "bureaucracy" famous by advocating it as a means of rationally managing complex organizations. During Weber's lifetime, managers were certainly in need of advice. In this time of industrial growth and development, most management was done by intuition, and nepotism and favouritism were rampant. According to Weber, a **bureaucracy** has the following qualities:

- A strict chain of command in which each member reports to only a single superior.
- Criteria for selection and promotion based on impersonal technical skills rather than nepotism or favouritism.
- A set of detailed rules, regulations, and procedures ensuring that the job gets done regardless of who the specific worker is.
- The use of strict specialization to match duties with technical competence.
- The centralization of power at the top of the organization.[11]

Weber saw bureaucracy as an "ideal type" or theoretical model that would standardize behaviour in organizations and provide workers with security and a sense of purpose. Jobs would be performed as intended rather than following the whims of the specific role occupant. In exchange for this conformity, workers would have a fair chance of being promoted and rising in the power structure. Rules, regulations, and a clear-cut chain of command that further clarified required behaviour provided the workers with a sense of security.

Even during this period, some observers, such as the "business philosopher" Mary Parker Follett (1868–1933), noted that the classical view of management seemed to take for granted an essential conflict of interest between managers and employees.[12] This sentiment found expression in the human relations movement.

The Human Relations Movement and a Critique of Bureaucracy

The human relations movement generally began with the famous **Hawthorne studies** of the 1920s and 1930s.[13] These studies, conducted at the Hawthorne plant of Western Electric near Chicago, began in the strict tradition of industrial engineering. They were concerned with the impact of fatigue, rest pauses, and lighting on productivity. However, during the course of the studies, the researchers (among others, Harvard University's Elton Mayo and Fritz Roethlisberger, and Hawthorne's William J. Dickson) began to notice the effects of psychological and social processes on productivity and work adjustment. This impact suggested that there could be dysfunctional aspects to how work was organized. One obvious sign was resistance to management through strong informal group mechanisms, such as norms that limited productivity to less than what management wanted.

After the Second World War, a number of theorists and researchers, who were mostly academics, took up the theme begun at Hawthorne. Prominent names included Chris Argyris, Alvin Gouldner, and Rensis Likert. The **human relations movement** called attention to certain dysfunctional aspects of classical management and bureaucracy and advocated

Scientific management. Frederick Taylor's system for using research to determine the optimum degree of specialization and standardization of work tasks.

Bureaucracy. Max Weber's ideal type of organization that included a strict chain of command, detailed rules, high specialization, centralized power, and selection and promotion based on technical competence.

Hawthorne studies. Research conducted at the Hawthorne plant of Western Electric near Chicago in the 1920s and 1930s that illustrated how psychological and social processes affect productivity and work adjustment.

Human relations movement. A critique of classical management and bureaucracy that advocated management styles that were more participative and oriented toward employee needs.

more people-oriented styles of management that catered more to the social and psychological needs of employees. This critique of bureaucracy addressed several specific problems:

- Strict specialization is incompatible with human needs for growth and achievement.[14] This can lead to employee alienation from the organization and its clients.

- Strong centralization and reliance on formal authority often fail to take advantage of the creative ideas and knowledge of lower-level members, who are often closer to the customer.[15] As a result, the organization will fail to learn from its mistakes, which threatens innovation and adaptation. Resistance to change will occur as a matter of course.

- Strict, impersonal rules lead members to adopt the minimum acceptable level of performance that the rules specify.[16] If a rule states that employees must process at least eight claims a day, eight claims will become the norm, even though higher performance levels are possible.

- Strong specialization causes employees to lose sight of the overall goals of the organization.[17] Forms, procedures, and required signatures become ends in themselves, divorced from the true needs of customers, clients, and other departments in the organization. This is the "red-tape mentality" that we sometimes observe in bureaucracies.

Obviously, not all bureaucratic organizations have these problems. However, they were common enough that human relations advocates and others began to call for the adoption of more flexible systems of management and the design of more interesting jobs. They also advocated open communication, more employee participation in decision making, and less rigid, more decentralized forms of control.

Simulate

WHAT IS MANAGEMENT? Go to MyManagementLab to complete a simulation about management.

LO **1.5**

Describe the *contemporary contingency approach* to management.

CONTEMPORARY MANAGEMENT— THE CONTINGENCY APPROACH

How has the apparent tension between the classical approach and the human relations approach been resolved? First, contemporary scholars and managers recognize the merits of both approaches. The classical advocates pointed out the critical role of control and coordination in getting organizations to achieve their goals. The human relationists pointed out the dangers of certain forms of control and coordination and addressed the need for flexibility and adaptability. Second, as we will study in later chapters, contemporary scholars have learned that management approaches need to be tailored to fit the situation. For example, we would generally manage a payroll department more bureaucratically than a research and development department. Getting out a payroll every week is a routine task with no margin for error. Research requires creativity that is fostered by a more flexible work environment.

Reconsider the five questions we posed earlier about the factors that make an organization competitive and a great place to work. Answering these questions is not an easy task, partly because human nature is so complex. This complexity means that an organizational behaviour text cannot be a "cookbook." In what follows, you will not find recipes to improve job satisfaction or service quality, with one cup of leadership style and two cups of group dynamics. We have not discovered a simple set of laws of organizational behaviour that you can memorize and then retrieve when necessary to solve any organizational problem. It is this "quick fix" mentality that produces simplistic and costly management fads and fashions.[18]

There is a growing body of research and management experience to help sort out the complexities of what happens in organizations. However, the general answer to many of the questions we will pose in the following chapters is *It depends*. Which leadership style is most effective? This depends on the characteristics of the leader, those of the people being led, and what the leader is trying to achieve. Will an increase in pay lead to an increase in performance? This depends on who is getting the increase and the exact reason for the increase.

These dependencies are called contingencies. The **contingency approach** to management recognizes that there is no one best way to manage; rather, an appropriate style depends on the demands of the situation. Thus, the effectiveness of a leadership style is contingent on the abilities of the followers, and the consequence of a pay increase is partly contingent on the need for money. Contingencies illustrate the complexity of organizational behaviour and show why we should study it systematically. Throughout the text we will discuss organizational behaviour with the contingency approach in mind.

WHAT DO MANAGERS DO?

Organizational behaviour is not just for managers or aspiring managers. As we noted earlier, a good understanding of the field can be useful for consumers or anyone else who has to interact with organizations or get things done through them. Nevertheless, many readers of this text have an interest in management as a potential career. Managers can have a strong impact on what happens in and to organizations. They both influence and are influenced by organizational behaviour, and the net result can have important consequences for organizational effectiveness.

There is no shortage of texts and popular press books oriented toward what managers *should* do. However, the field of organizational behaviour is also concerned with what really happens in organizations. Let's look at several research studies that explore what managers *do* do. This provides a context for appreciating the usefulness of understanding organizational behaviour.

Managerial Roles

Canadian management theorist Henry Mintzberg conducted an in-depth study of the behaviour of several managers.[19] The study earned him a PhD from the Massachusetts Institute of Technology (MIT) in 1968. In the Appendix we discuss how he conducted the study and some of its more basic findings. Here, however, we are concerned with Mintzberg's discovery of a rather complex set of roles played by the managers: figurehead, leader, liaison person, monitor, disseminator, spokesperson, entrepreneur, disturbance handler, resource allocator, and negotiator. These roles are summarized in Exhibit 1.2.

INTERPERSONAL ROLES
Interpersonal roles are expected behaviours that have to do with establishing and maintaining interpersonal relations. In the *figurehead role*, managers serve as symbols of their organization rather than active decision makers. Examples of the figurehead role are making a speech to a trade group, entertaining clients, or signing legal documents. In the *leadership role*, managers select, mentor, reward, and discipline employees. In the *liaison role*, managers maintain horizontal contacts inside and outside the organization. This might include discussing a project with a colleague in another department or touching base with an embassy delegate of a country where the company hopes to do future business.

Contingency approach. An approach to management that recognizes that there is no one best way to manage, and that an appropriate management style depends on the demands of the situation.

LO 1.6

Explain what managers do—their roles, activities, agendas for action, and thought processes.

Informational Roles	Interpersonal Roles	Decisional Roles
Monitor Disseminator Spokesperson	Figurehead Leader Liaison	Entrepreneur Disturbance handler Resource allocator Negotiator

EXHIBIT 1.2 Mintzberg's managerial roles.
Source: ODONNELL & KELLY, PORTALES: COMUNIDAD & CULTURA & WORKBK PKG, 1st Edition, © 2003. Reprinted by permission of Pearson Education, Inc. Upper Saddle River, NJ. Reprinted by permission.

INFORMATIONAL ROLES These roles are concerned with the various ways managers receive and transmit information. In the *monitor role*, managers scan the internal and external environments of the firm to follow current performance and to keep themselves informed of new ideas and trends. For example, the head of research and development might attend a professional engineering conference. In the *disseminator role*, managers send information on both facts and preferences to others. For example, the R&D head might summarize what he or she learned at the conference in an email to employees. The *spokesperson role* concerns mainly sending messages into the organization's external environment—for example, drafting an annual report to stockholders or giving an interview to the press.

DECISIONAL ROLES The final set of managerial roles Mintzberg discussed deals with decision making. In the *entrepreneur role*, managers turn problems and opportunities into plans for improved changes. This might include suggesting a new product or service that will please customers. In the *disturbance handler role*, managers deal with problems stemming from employee conflicts and address threats to resources and turf. In their *resource allocation role*, managers decide how to deploy time, money, personnel, and other critical resources. Finally, in their *negotiator role*, managers conduct major negotiations with other organizations or individuals.

Of course, the relative importance of these roles will vary with management level and organizational technology.[20] First-level supervisors do more disturbance handling and less figureheading. Still, Mintzberg's major contribution to organizational behaviour is to highlight the *complexity* of the roles managers are required to play and the variety of skills they must have to be effective, including leadership, communication, and negotiation. His work also illustrates the complex balancing act managers face when they must play different roles for different audiences. A good grasp of organizational behaviour is at the heart of acquiring these skills and performing this balancing act.

Managerial Activities

Fred Luthans, Richard Hodgetts, and Stuart Rosenkrantz studied the behaviour of a large number of managers in a variety of different kinds of organizations.[21] They determined that the managers engage in four basic types of activities:

- *Routine communication.* This includes the formal sending and receiving of information (as in meetings) and the handling of paperwork.
- *Traditional management.* Planning, decision making, and controlling are the primary types of traditional management.
- *Networking.* Networking consists of interacting with people outside of the organization and informal socializing and politicking with insiders.
- *Human resource management.* This includes motivating and reinforcing, disciplining and punishing, managing conflict, staffing, and training and developing employees.

Exhibit 1.3 summarizes these managerial activities and shows how a sample of 248 managers divided their time and effort, as determined by research observers (discipline and punishment were done in private and were not open to observation). Perhaps the most striking observation about this figure is how all these managerial activities involve dealing with people.

One of Luthans and colleagues' most fascinating findings is how emphasis on these various activities correlated with managerial success. If we define success as moving up the ranks of the organization quickly, networking proved to be critical. The people who were promoted quickly tended to do more networking (politicking, socializing, and making contacts) and less human resource management than the averages in Exhibit 1.3. If we define success in terms of unit effectiveness and employee satisfaction and commitment, the

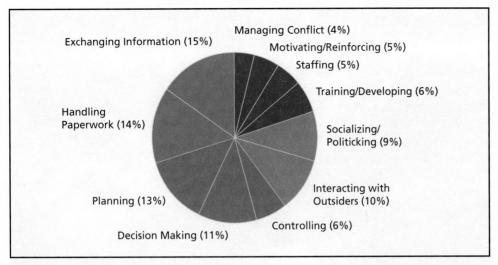

EXHIBIT 1.3 Summary of managerial activities.
Source: Adapted from Luthans, F., Hodgetts, R.M., & Rosenkrantz, S.A. (1988). *Real managers.* Cambridge, MA: Ballinger. Reprinted by permission of Dr. F. Luthans on behalf of the authors.

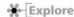 Explore

Go to MyManagementLab to see an annotated version of this figure.

more successful managers were those who devoted more time and effort to human resource management and less to networking than the averages in the exhibit. A good understanding of organizational behaviour should help you manage this trade-off more effectively, reconciling the realities of organizational politics with the demands of accomplishing things through others.

Managerial Agendas

John Kotter studied the behaviour patterns of a number of successful general managers.[22] Although he found some differences among them, he also found a strong pattern of similarities that he grouped into the categories of agenda setting, networking, and agenda implementation.

AGENDA SETTING Kotter's managers, given their positions, all gradually developed agendas of what they wanted to accomplish for the organization. Many began these agendas even before they assumed their positions. These agendas were almost always informal and unwritten, and they were much more concerned with "people issues" and were less numerical than most formal strategic plans. The managers based their agendas on wide-ranging informal discussions with a wide variety of people.

NETWORKING Kotter's managers established a wide formal and informal network of key people both inside and outside of their organizations. Insiders included peers, employees, and bosses, but they also extended to these people's employees and bosses. Outsiders included customers, suppliers, competitors, government officials, and the press. This network provided managers with information and established cooperative relationships relevant to their agendas. Formal hiring, firing, and reassigning shaped the network, but so did informal liaisons in which managers created dependencies by doing favours for others.

AGENDA IMPLEMENTATION The managers used networks to implement the agendas. They would go *anywhere* in the network for help—up or down, in or out of the organization. In addition, they employed a wide range of influence tactics, from direct orders to subtle language and stories that conveyed their message indirectly.

The theme that runs through Kotter's findings is the high degree of informal interaction and concern with people issues that were necessary for the managers to achieve their agendas. To be sure, the managers used their formal organizational power, but they often found themselves dependent on people over whom they wielded no power. An understanding of organizational behaviour helps to recognize and manage these realities.

John Kotter's research of successful business managers showed that exemplary managers practise agenda setting, networking, and agenda implementation. Michael Dell, of Dell Computers, is an example of such a manager.

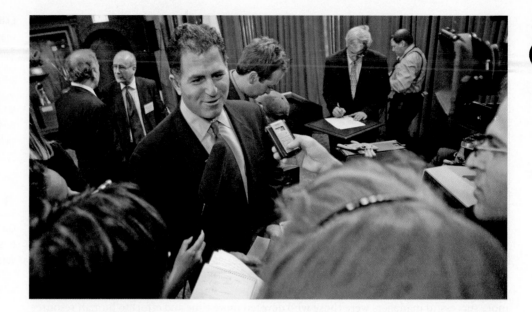

Managerial Minds

In contrast to exploring how managers act, which is the focus of the previous section, Herbert Simon and Daniel Isenberg have both explored how managers think.[23] Although they offer a wealth of observations, we will concentrate here on a specific issue that each examined in independent research—managerial intuition.

Some people think that organizational behaviour and its implications for management are just common sense. However, careful observers of successful managers have often noted that intuition seems to guide many of their actions. Isenberg's research suggests that experienced managers use intuition in several ways:

- to sense that a problem exists;
- to perform well-learned mental tasks rapidly (e.g., sizing up a written contract);
- to synthesize isolated pieces of information and data; and
- to double-check more formal or mechanical analyses ("Do these projections look correct?").

Does the use of intuition mean that managerial thinking is random, irrational, or undisciplined? Both Simon and Isenberg say no. In fact, both strongly dispute the idea that intuition is the opposite of rationality or that intuitive means unanalytical. Rather, good intuition is problem identification and problem solving based on a long history of systematic and extensive education and experience that enables the manager to locate problems within a network of previously acquired information. The theories, research, and management practices that we cover in *Organizational Behaviour* will contribute to your own information network and give you better managerial intuition about decisions that involve how to make an organization a great place to work and a financial success.

International Managers

The research we discussed above describes how managers act and think in North America. Would managers in other global locations act and think the same way? Up to a point, the answer is probably yes. After all, we are dealing here with some very basic behaviours and thought processes. However, the style in which managers do what they do and the emphasis they give to various activities will vary greatly across cultures because of cross-cultural variations in values that affect both managers' and employees' expectations about interpersonal interaction. Thus, in

International managers must adapt to cross-cultural differences to successfully interact with potential clients and overseas affiliates.

Chapter 5 we study cross-cultural differences in motivation. In Chapter 9 we study cultural differences in leadership, and in Chapter 10 we explore how communication varies across cultures.

Geert Hofstede has done pioneering work on cross-cultural differences in values that we will study in Chapter 4. Hofstede provides some interesting observations about how these value differences promote contrasts in the general role that managers play across cultures.[24] He asserts that managers are cultural heroes and are even a distinct social class in North America, where individualism is treasured. In contrast, Germany tends to worship engineers and have fewer managerial types. In Japan, managers are required to pay obsessive attention to group solidarity rather than to star employees. In the Netherlands, managers are supposed to exhibit modesty and strive for consensus. In the family-run businesses of Taiwan and Singapore, "professional" management, North American style, is greatly downplayed. The contrasts that Hofstede raises are fascinating because the technical requirements for accomplishing goals are actually the same across cultures. It is only the *behavioural* requirements that differ. Thus, national culture is one of the most important contingency variables in organizational behaviour. The appropriateness of various leadership styles, motivation techniques, and communication methods depends on where one is in the world.

 Watch

PTC: EMPLOYEE ENGAGEMENT Go to MyManagementLab to watch a video about employee engagement.

SOME CONTEMPORARY MANAGEMENT CONCERNS

 LO **1.7**

To conclude the chapter, we will briefly examine four issues with which organizations and managers are currently concerned. As with previous sections, our goal is to illustrate how the field of organizational behaviour can help you understand and manage these issues.

Describe the societal and global trends that are shaping contemporary management concerns.

Diversity—Local and Global

The demographics of the North American population and workforce are changing and, as a result, both the labour force and customers are becoming increasingly culturally diverse. Contributing to this is the increased movement of women into paid employment as well as immigration patterns. In Canada, visible minorities are the fastest growing segment of the population.[25] Employment and Immigration Canada has projected that two-thirds of today's new entrants to the Canadian labour force will be women, visible minorities, Aboriginal people, and persons with disabilities.[26] A report by Statistics Canada predicted that the number of visible minorities in Canada is expected to double by 2017 and will form more than half the population in greater Toronto and Vancouver, and immigrants will account for 22 percent of the population.[27] Native-born Caucasian North Americans frequently find themselves working with people whose ethnic backgrounds are very different from their own.

Diversity of age is also having an impact in organizations. In less than a decade, the workforce will be dominated by people over the age of 40. By the year 2015, 48 percent of Canada's working-age population will be between the ages of 45 and 64, compared to 29 percent in 1991.[28] With the elimination of mandatory retirement at age 65, along with the recent global recession in which many people saw their life savings diminish, a growing number of Canadians over 65 will remain in the workforce. A recent survey found that older Canadians are redefining the concept of retirement and that 75 percent of the participants who had not yet retired expected to continue working past the age of 65.[29] Perhaps you have observed people of various ages working in fast-food restaurants that were at one time staffed solely by young people. Both the re-entry of retired people into the workforce and the trend to remove vertical layers in organizations have contributed to much more intergenerational contact in the workplace than was common in the past. Organizations are beginning to adopt new programs in response to this demographic shift, such as flexible benefit plans, compressed workdays, and part-time jobs, to attract and retain older workers. For example, Orkin/PCO Services Corp. of Mississauga, a pest-control service, dealt with a shortage of pest-control specialists by introducing a more flexible part-time schedule with benefits to attract and retain employees who would otherwise have retired or left the industry.[30]

Diversity is also coming to the fore as many organizations realize that they have not treated certain segments of the population, such as women, homosexuals, and the disabled, fairly in many aspects of employment. Organizations have to be able to get the best from *everyone* to be truly competitive. Although legal pressures (such as the *Employment Equity Act*) have contributed to this awareness, general social pressure, especially from customers and clients, has also done so.

Finally, diversity issues are having an increasing impact as organizations "go global." Foreign sales by multinational corporations have exceeded $7 trillion and are growing 20 to 30 percent faster than their sales of exports.[31] Multinational expansion, strategic alliances, and joint ventures increasingly require employees and managers to come into contact with their counterparts from other cultures. Although many of these people have an interest in North American consumer goods and entertainment, it is naïve to assume that business values are rapidly converging on a North American model. As a result, North American organizations that operate in other countries need to understand how the workforce and customers in those countries are diverse and culturally different.

What does diversity have to do with organizational behaviour? The field has long been concerned with stereotypes, conflict, cooperation, and teamwork. These are just some of the factors that managers must manage effectively for organizations to benefit from the considerable opportunities that a diverse workforce affords. We will have more to say about workforce diversity in Chapter 3 and cultural differences in values in Chapter 4.

A Positive Work Environment and Employee Well-Being

During the past decade, employees have faced increasing concerns over job security, increasing job demands, and work-related stress that have contributed to a deterioration of their physical and psychological health and well-being. At the same time, organizations are faced with employees who are disengaged, disillusioned, and suffering from physical and mental sicknesses.

Absenteeism and employee turnover in Canadian organizations are also on the rise. According to Statistics Canada, there has been an alarming and unprecedented increase in absenteeism rates since the mid-1990s. The increase in absenteeism has been found across all age groups and sectors and translates into millions of dollars in lost productivity. It has been estimated that the total cost of reported absenteeism in Canada is $15 billion annually. Although there is no one definitive cause, increasing stress levels and poorly designed jobs are major contributors. In fact, all types of employees are experiencing more workplace stress today than a decade ago, and the incidence of work-related illness is also on the rise.[32]

A study of Canadian employees estimated that the direct cost of absenteeism due to high work–life conflict—a major stressor in the workplace—is approximately $3 to $5 billion per year, and when both direct and indirect costs are included in the calculation, work–life conflict costs Canadians approximately $6 to $10 billion per year.[33] Exhibit 1.4 presents some of the major findings from this study.

In response to these concerns, employees are searching for meaning and purpose in their work lives and organizations have begun to focus on employee physical and mental health by creating more positive work environments. What does a positive work environment and employee well-being have to do with organizational behaviour?

For one thing, organizational behaviour is concerned with creating positive work environments that contribute to employee health and wellness. A good example of this is a spiritual workplace or workplace spirituality. **Workplace spirituality** refers to workplaces that provide employees with meaning, purpose, a sense of community, and a connection to others. It is important to realize that workplace spirituality is not about religion in the workplace, but rather providing employees with a meaningful worklife that is aligned with their values. In a spiritual workplace, employees have interesting work that provides meaning and a feeling of purpose, a sense that they belong to and are part of a caring and supportive community, and a sense of connection to their work and others. Employees in a spiritual workplace have opportunities for personal growth and development and they feel valued and supported.[34]

An increasing number of organizations are showing interest in spiritual workplaces. For example, TELUS provides quiet rooms where employees can decompress, meditate, or pray; they offer seminars on topics such as nutrition, parenting, and work–life balance, and

Workplace spirituality.
A workplace that provides employees with meaning, purpose, a sense of community, and a connection to others.

These findings are based on a sample of 31 571 Canadian employees who work for 100 medium to large organizations in the public, private, and nonprofit sections of the economy. The authors of the report concluded that the majority of Canada's largest employers cannot be considered to be best-practice employers.	
What Workers Experience	**Percentage of Employees**
Employees reporting high levels of role overload	58%
Work responsibilities interfere with the ability to fulfill responsibilities at home	28%
Negative spillover from work to family	44%
Employees reporting high levels of stress	33%
Employees reporting high levels of burnout	32%
Employees reporting highly depressed mood	36%
Employees reporting high levels of job satisfaction	46%
Employees reporting high levels of organizational commitment	53%
Employees who think of leaving their current organization once a week or more	28%
Employees indicating high levels of absenteeism	46%
Employees reporting high levels of life satisfaction	41%

EXHIBIT 1.4 Work–life conflict in Canadian organizations.
Source: Higgins, C., & Duxbury, L. (2003). *2001 national work–life conflict study* (Ottawa: Health Canada). Reproduced with permission of the authors.

Explore

Go to MyManagementLab to see an annotated version of this figure.

employees have access to books and CDs on spirituality; on-site fitness classes like yoga and tai chi are also available. Employees at TELUS get three personal days off a year to use at their discretion and can work from home. These spirituality initiatives help to create a positive work environment that promotes health and wellness and reduced absenteeism.[35]

Organizational behaviour is also concerned with developing employees and providing them with the resources they need to achieve their goals and for their well-being. An important contributor to employee success and well-being is psychological capital (PsyCap). **Psychological capital** refers to an individual's positive psychological state of development that is characterized by self-efficacy, optimism, hope, and resilience. Self-efficacy refers to one's confidence to take on and put in the necessary effort to succeed at challenging tasks (see Chapter 2 for a more detailed discussion of self-efficacy); optimism involves making internal attributions about positive events in the present and future and external attributions about negative events (see Chapter 3 for a more detailed discussion on attributions); hope refers to persevering toward one's goals, and when necessary making changes and using multiple pathways to achieve one's goals (see Chapter 5 for a more detailed discussion of goals and goal setting); and resilience refers to one's ability to bounce back or rebound from adversity and setbacks to attain success.[36]

It is important to note that each of the components of PsyCap are considered to be states or positive work-related psychological resources that can be changed, modified, and developed. In other words, they are not fixed, stable, or static personality traits.[37]

Research on PsyCap has found that it is positively related to employee psychological well-being as well as more positive job attitudes, behaviours, and job performance, and negatively related to undesirable attitudes and behaviours such as employee anxiety, stress, and turnover intentions.[38] There is also evidence that PsyCap interventions (PCI) that focus on enhancing each of the components of PsyCap are effective for developing employees' PsyCap. Thus, one way for organizations to improve employee health and well-being is to develop their PsyCap.[39]

In summary, creating a positive and spiritual work environment where employees can experience meaning and purpose and the development of employees' PsyCap are important factors that contribute to employee health and well-being as well as positive job attitudes and behaviours. The field of organizational behaviour is deeply concerned with such issues.

Talent Management and Employee Engagement

During the last decade, organizations have become increasingly concerned about talent and employee engagement. Consider this: A survey of senior executives from all over the world found that talent was ranked as the second most critical challenge just behind business growth.[40] **Talent management** refers to an organization's processes for attracting, developing, retaining, and utilizing people with the required skills to meet current and future business needs.[41]

The ability of organizations to attract and retain talent has always been important; however, today it has become especially critical for many organizations that are struggling to find the employees they need to compete and survive. As a result, the management of talent has become a major organizational concern that involves a concerted effort and the involvement of all levels of management.

An increasing number of organizations are having trouble finding qualified people, a problem stemming in part from changing demographics that will result in a dramatic shortage of skilled workers over the next 10 years. The baby boomers will begin to retire in the next few years, which will create a large skills gap. It is predicted that there will be a 30 percent shortfall of workers between the ages of 25 and 44. This, combined with the increasing willingness of knowledge workers to relocate anywhere in the world and fewer Canadians entering the skilled trades, means that Canadian organizations will increasingly face severe shortages of labour. There are already shortages in scientific, technical, and high-tech industries and in senior management, communications, and marketing positions. A

Psychological capital (PsyCap). An individual's positive psychological state of development that is characterized by self-efficacy, optimism, hope, and resilience.

Talent management. An organization's processes for attracting, developing, retaining, and utilizing people with the required skills to meet current and future business needs.

recent poll found that more than 60 percent of Canadian employers say that labour shortages are limiting their productivity and efficiency. Most of Canada's top CEOs believe that retaining employees has become their number-one priority, and attracting new employees is their fourth priority, just behind financial performance and profitability. Three-quarters of CEOs say they cannot find enough competent employees.[42]

Organizations have also become increasingly concerned about employee engagement. As you will learn in Chapter 13, **work engagement** is a positive work-related state of mind that is characterized by vigour, dedication, and absorption.[43] It has been reported that only one-third of workers are engaged and yet engaged workers have more positive work attitudes and higher job performance. Employee engagement is considered to be key to an organization's success and competitiveness and it can have a significant impact on productivity, customer satisfaction, profitability, innovation, and quality. One study found that in a sample of 65 firms from different industries, the top 25 percent on an engagement index had greater return on assets (ROA), greater profitability, and more than double the shareholder value compared to the bottom 25 percent.[44]

What does organizational behaviour have to do with talent management and employee engagement? Organizational behaviour provides the means for organizations to be designed and managed in ways that optimize the attraction, development, retention, engagement, and performance of talent.[45] For example, providing opportunities for learning and designing jobs that are challenging, meaningful, and rewarding; providing recognition and monetary rewards for performance; managing a diverse workforce; offering flexible work arrangements; and providing effective leadership are just some of the factors that are important for the effective management of talent and employee engagement. These are, of course, some of the practices of the best companies to work for in Canada (see Exhibit 1.1), and their annual rate of turnover is lower than the national average and half that of some other companies.[46]

Corporate Social Responsibility

Organizations like Sodexo have become increasingly concerned about corporate social responsibility (CSR) and the need to be a good corporate citizen. **Corporate social responsibility** refers to an organization taking responsibility for the impact of its decisions and actions on its stakeholders. It has to do with an organization's overall impact on society at large and extends beyond the interests of shareholders to the interests and needs of employees and the community in which it operates. CSR involves a variety of issues that range from community involvement, environmental protection, safe products, ethical marketing, employee diversity, and local and global labour practices. Ultimately, CSR has to do with how an organization performs its core functions of producing goods and providing services and that it does so in a socially responsible way.[47] Sodexo's Better Tomorrow Plan is a good example of this.

What does a focus on social responsibility have to do with organizational behaviour? For starters, many CSR issues have to do with organizational behaviour, such as an organization's treatment of employees, management practices such as managing diversity, work–family balance, and employment equity. Organizations that rank high on CSR are good employers because of the way they treat their employees and because of their management practices that promote employee well-being. As indicated earlier, these are the kinds of practices employed by the best companies to work for in Canada.

CSR also involves environmental, social, and governance (ESG) issues. Sodexo Canada's Better Tomorrow Plan is a good example of an organization that has made a commitment to social issues and the environment. Organizations' social and environmental actions are increasingly being scrutinized, and shareholders and consumers are holding firms to higher CSR standards on the environment, employment, and other social issues. Governance issues such as executive compensation have also begun to receive greater attention. CSR is so important that a number of research firms now rank and rate organizations on CSR.[48]

Work engagement.
A positive work-related state of mind that is characterized by vigour, dedication, and absorption.

Corporate social responsibility (CSR).
An organization taking responsibility for the impact of its decisions and actions on its stakeholders.

 Watch

HONEST TEA: CORPORATE SOCIAL RESPONSIBILITY Go to MyManagementLab to watch a video about corporate social responsibility.

In 2009, *Maclean's* published its inaugural list of the 50 Most Socially Responsible Corporations in Canada, corporations that are raising the standard of what it means to be a good corporate citizen.[49] These rankings, along with the belief that CSR has implications for an organization's reputation and financial performance, have led to an increasing number of organizations placing greater emphasis on CSR initiatives.

For example, many organizations make donations to charitable organizations and have implemented programs to help their communities. Sodexo Canada created the Sodexo Foundation, which is an independent charitable organization that donates meals to at-risk youth.[50] Cameo Corp. of Saskatoon, one of the world's largest producers of uranium, has a community investment program that focuses on improving the quality of life for people in the communities in which it operates. The company has contributed $3 million to the University of Saskatchewan to promote greater access for Aboriginal peoples, women, and northerners to studies in engineering and science. Unilever Canada has a community vitality fund and donates 1 percent of pre-tax profits to initiatives in children's health and water resources, which are both linked to its products. The company also encourages volunteerism and gives employees four afternoons off each year for community activities.[51]

A concern for the environment and green initiatives is also an example of CSR. Recall that Sodexo Canada is one of Canada's greenest employers. What does going green have to do with organizational behaviour? Green programs require changes in employees' attitudes and behaviours. For example, at Fairmont Hotels and Resorts, employees volunteer to be on green teams that meet monthly to brainstorm environmental initiatives. The company also recognizes and rewards employees for their efforts. The program has had a positive effect on employee engagement and motivation, and employees are proud to be working for an environmentally responsible organization.[52] For another example, see the Applied Focus: *Green Management at the Delta Chelsea Hotel.*

APPLIED FOCUS

Green Management at the Delta Chelsea Hotel

In 2008, several hundred employees of the Delta Chelsea Hotel in Toronto took a tour at Turtle Island Recycling. The visit helped get employees more engaged in green initiatives by providing a big picture of what happens to the waste from the hotel and its impact on the environment.

"Those tours made a huge difference because our [recycling] results drastically improved after those visits," says Tracy Ford, public relations manager at the Delta Chelsea. "It's made such a difference in what our goals are with the hotel."

In 2008, 76 percent of all waste from the hotel was recycled, and by February 2009, that figure had risen to 81 percent. Much of that success is attributed to a green team made up of representatives from various departments—such as stewarding, catering, and housekeeping—that sets up a strategic plan and updates the hotel's environmental policy.

To spread the word, employee orientation includes a presentation on the hotel's green initiatives and policies, an internal newsletter dedicates a page to the environment, posters in elevators and message boards on employee floors tout the cause, and a health and wellness day profiling the green team challenges employees to take a quiz for prizes.

The Delta Chelsea has also set a goal to be carbon-neutral. To help, the hotel recently launched a LivClean Eco-Stay Program, whereby guests can voluntarily pay $1 per stay to support emission-reduction projects. This will enable environmental initiatives within the hotel, facilitate assessment and reporting of its environmental impact, and assist in the development and expansion of the Hotel Association of Canada's Green Key Program, an "ECOmmodation" rating program. The hotel has been given a Green Key rating of four out of five.

The hotel's efforts have been recognized with an energy and environmental award from the Hotel Association of Canada. Going forward, the Delta plans to get a better understanding of the impact of its green initiatives on employee engagement by including questions on the green program in its annual employee survey.

Source: Based on Dobson, S. (2009, April 20). It pays to be green. *Canadian HR Reporter, 22*(8), 15.

In summary, CSR is becoming a major concern for organizations today, and some organizations even issue CSR reports along with their annual reports. Hudson's Bay Company (HBC) publishes a Corporate Social Responsibility Report every year that is available on its website. An organization's CSR activities and policies are associated with a firm's financial performance as well as positive employee attitudes, engagement, and performance.[53] CSR also has implications for the recruitment and retention of employees as an increasing number of workers want to work for organizations that are environmentally friendly and rank high on CSR. For example, job candidates are attracted to HBC because of its corporate social responsibility program. At Husky Injection Molding Systems Ltd. in Bolton, Ontario, job candidates and employees choose to work at the company because of its environmental responsibility program.[54] Organizational behaviour has much to offer organizations in their quest to become more socially responsible.

We hope this brief discussion of some of the issues that are of concern to organizations and managers has reinforced your awareness of using organizational behaviour to better understand and manage life at work. These concerns permeate today's workplace, and we will cover them in more detail throughout the text.

THE MANAGER'S NOTEBOOK

Toronto's Troubled Transit System

1. Organizational behaviour refers to the attitudes and behaviours of individuals and groups in organizations, and the discipline of organizational behaviour provides insight about effectively managing and changing attitudes and behaviours. The complaints made by TTC riders indicate employee indifference and disdain toward customers and discourteous and rude behaviour. Organizational behaviour can help to address the TTC's customer service problems by creating positive attitudes toward customer service and changing employee behaviours when interacting with customers. This might involve motivating employees to be more courteous and it will probably involve a change in the culture of the TTC toward a greater emphasis on customer service. Organizational behaviour topics that are particularly relevant include learning (Chapter 2), attitudes (Chapter 4), motivation (Chapters 5 and 6), socialization and organizational culture (Chapter 8), leadership (Chapter 9), communication (Chapter 10), and organizational change (Chapter 16).

2. The goals of organizational behaviour are predicting, explaining, and managing organizational behaviour. Based on customer complaints, it is possible to predict the things that customers will complain about and that many of the complaints will be about poor customer service and discourteous employee behaviour. However, what is not so clear is the explanation or reason for the discourteous and rude behaviours.

Explaining these behaviours is important because it will make it possible to manage them. There are many possible reasons for the discourteous behaviours and poor customer service, such as learning—perhaps employees have not be trained to provide good customer service or maybe they are not rewarded for it. Or perhaps the importance of customer service has not been clearly communicated to employees and they are not given feedback about their customer service performance. Each of these explanations will require a different and specific solution. So if we understand the reasons for poor customer service, we can take action to manage and improve it. Along these lines, the TTC announced a series of customer service improvements that they promise will make the TTC "the better way" in Toronto. The TTC promised better communication and courtesy including screening new hires for "customer service aptitude" and evaluating all 12 000 employees on their customer service performance. A comprehensive review of customer service training for new employees and recertification for older staff is also planned. The report by the Customer Service Advisory Panel made a number of recommendations that involve a renewed focus on customer service. Many of the recommendations involve organizational behaviour such as the creation of a culture of customer service, improving internal communications, customer service training courses, and a review of recognition programs.

LEARNING OBJECTIVES CHECKLIST

1.1 *Organizations* are social inventions for accomplishing common goals through group effort. The basic characteristic of organizations is that they involve the coordinated efforts of people working together to accomplish common goals.

1.2 *Organizational behaviour* refers to the attitudes and behaviours of individuals and groups in an organizational context. The field of organizational behaviour systematically studies these attitudes and behaviours and provides advice about how organizations can manage them effectively. The goals of the field include the prediction, explanation, and management of organizational behaviour.

1.3 *Management* is the art of getting things accomplished in organizations through others. It consists of acquiring, allocating, and utilizing physical and human resources to accomplish goals.

1.4 The *classical view* of management advocated a high degree of employee specialization and a high degree of coordination of labour from the top of the organization. Taylor's scientific management and Weber's views on bureaucracy are in line with the classical position. The *human relations*

movement pointed out the "people problems" that the classical management style sometimes provoked and advocated more interesting job design, more employee participation in decisions, and less centralized control.

1.5 The *contemporary contingency approach* to management suggests that the most effective management styles and organizational designs are dependent on the demands of the situation.

1.6 Research on what managers do shows that they fulfill interpersonal, informational, and decisional roles. Important activities include routine communication, traditional management, networking, and human resource management. Managers pursue agendas through networking and use intuition to guide decision making. The demands on managers vary across cultures. A good grasp of organizational behaviour is essential for effective management.

1.7 A number of societal and global trends are shaping contemporary management concerns, including local and global diversity; positive work environments and employee well-being; talent management and employee engagement; and a focus on corporate social responsibility.

DISCUSSION QUESTIONS

1. What are your goals in studying organizational behaviour? What practical advantages might this study have for you?

2. Consider absence from work as an example of organizational behaviour. What are some of the factors that might predict who is likely to be absent from work? How might you explain absence from work? What are some techniques that organizations use to manage absence? Now do the same for turnover as an example of organizational behaviour.

3. Describe the assumptions about organizational behaviour that are reflected in television shows

such as situation comedies and police dramas. How accurate are these portrayals? Do they influence our thinking about what occurs in organizations?

4. To demonstrate that you grasp the idea of contingencies in organizational behaviour, consider how closely managers should supervise the work of their employees. What are some factors on which closeness of supervision might be contingent?

5. Management is the art of getting things accomplished in organizations through others. Given this definition, what are some factors that make

management a difficult, or at least a challenging, occupation?

6. Use the contingency approach to describe a task or an organizational department where a more classical management style might be effective. Then do the same for a task or department where the human relations style would be effective.

7. What is corporate social responsibility (CSR) and what does it have to do with organizational behaviour? Explain how an understanding of organizational behaviour can help organizations become more socially responsible.

8. Why do studies of managerial behaviour reveal the importance of networking? What about the importance of human resource management? Explain the differences between these two behaviours and their importance for success.

9. What are some of the demands that increased workforce diversity and increased global operations make on managers? What are some of the opportunities that these trends offer to managers?

10. Describe how management practices and organizational behaviour can help organizations deal with the contemporary management concerns discussed in the chapter. In other words, what are some of the things that organizations can do to (a) manage local and global diversity, (b) create a positive work environment and improve employee well-being, (c) improve and facilitate the management of talent and employee engagement, and (e) promote corporate social responsibility?

11. What is the meaning of workplace spirituality and how is it different from religion in the workplace? What does an organization have to do to become a spiritual workplace? Would you want to work in a spiritual workplace? Explain your answer.

12. What is the meaning of psychological capital and what does it have to do with organizational behaviour? Describe each of the components of psychological capital and how they can help you in your studies.

ON-THE-JOB CHALLENGE QUESTION

The Ultimate Perk

Social Media Group helps organizations develop strategies for the effective use of social media. The company's clients include Fortune 500 organizations such as 3M, Ford Motor Company, CNN, and Thomson Reuters.

The company's CEO, Maggie Fox, recently stopped tracking vacation days and introduced an unlimited paid vacation policy. "We're playing with the big boys and our incredible team has to deliver their A plus game. Every. Single. Day," said Fox. "Why shouldn't an employee be able to take an afternoon off to play with her kids?"

According to Leona Hobbs, vice-president of at Social Media Group, "We really want to recognize the contributions of our people and how much effort they put into the work."

Each employee is responsible for his own mental health, his colleagues, and his clients. Time off has to be cleared with supervisors, but it's an informal process. The company does not keep formal statistics, but Fox believes people are taking more time off overall, and says that's a good thing.

Netflix introduced open-ended vacations in 2004 and IBM Canada has eliminated tracking of vacation days except in its Quebec manufacturing plant. IBM guidelines say employees get a three-week vacation to start, but there is no policing and employees are empowered to take vacation whenever they want.

Do people at the Social Media Group abuse the program? Not at all, says Fox. "We work hard and play hard. I hire people who do great work. If I hire someone who takes advantage of the program, it's my problem, because I've made a bad decision."

What do you think about Social Media Group's unlimited vacation policy? Using an organizational behaviour perspective, what effect do you think the unlimited vacation policy will have on employees' attitudes and behaviour? Discuss the implications of the unlimited vacation policy for each of the contemporary management concerns discussed in the chapter. Do you think it is a good idea for organizations to have an unlimited vacation policy? Explain your answer.

Source: Based on Smolkin, S. (2011, August 9). And now the ultimate perk—unlimited vacation time. *Toronto Star*, A1, A2; Klie, S. (2010, November 15). Unlimited paid vacation? Some firms trying it. *Canadian HR Reporter, 23*(20), 1, 10.

EXPERIENTIAL EXERCISE

Good Job, Bad Job

The purpose of this exercise is to help you get acquainted with some of your classmates by learning something about their experiences with work and organizations. To do this, we will focus on an important and traditional topic in organizational behaviour—what makes people satisfied or dissatisfied with their jobs (a topic that we will cover in detail in Chapter 4).

1. Students should break into groups of four to six people. Each group should choose a recording secretary.

2. In each group, members should take turns introducing themselves and then describing to the others either the best job or the worst job that they have ever had. Take particular care to explain why this particular job was either satisfying or dissatisfying. For example, did factors such as pay, co-workers, your boss, or the work itself affect your level of satisfaction? The recording secretary should make a list of the jobs group members held, noting which were "good" and which were "bad." (15 minutes)

3. Using the information from Step 2, each group should develop a profile of four or five characteristics that seem to contribute to dissatisfaction in a job and four or five characteristics that contribute to satisfaction. In other words, are there some common experiences among the group members? (10 minutes)

4. Each group should write its "good job" and "bad job" characteristics on the board. (3 minutes)

5. The class should reconvene, and each group's recording secretary should report on the specific jobs the group considered good or bad. The instructor will discuss the profiles on the board, noting similarities and differences. Other issues worth probing are behavioural consequences of job attitudes (e.g., quitting) and differences of opinion within the groups (e.g., one person's bad job may have seemed attractive to someone else). (15 minutes)

6. Why do you think that a good job for some people might be a bad job for others and vice versa? What are the implications of this for management and organizational behaviour?

EXPERIENTIAL EXERCISE

OB on TV

The purpose of this exercise is to explore the portrayal of organizational behaviour on television. Most experts on the function of TV as a communication medium agree on two points. First, although TV may present an inaccurate or distorted view of many specific events, the overall content of TV programming does accurately reflect the general values and concerns of society. Second, TV has the power to shape the attitudes and expectations of viewers. If this is so, we should pay some attention to the portrayal of work and organizational behaviour on TV.

Prepare this exercise before its assigned class:

1. Choose a prime-time TV show that interests you. (This means a show that airs between 8 p.m. and 10 p.m. in your viewing area. If your schedule prohibits this, choose another time.) The show in question could be a comedy, a drama, or a documentary, for example, *Mr. D*, *Republic of Doyle*, *CSI*, or *Marketplace*. Your instructor may give you more specific instructions about what to watch.

2. On a piece of paper, list the name of the program and its date and time of broadcast. Write the answers to the following questions during or immediately following the broadcast:

   a. What industry is the primary focus of the program? Use the following list to categorize your answer: agriculture; mining; construction; manufacturing; transportation; communication; wholesale trade; retail trade; finance; service; public administration. (Examples of service industries include hotel, health, law, education, newspaper, entertainment, and private investigation. Examples of public administration include justice, police work, and national security.)

   b. What industries or occupations are of secondary focus in the program?

   c. What exact job categories or occupational roles do the main characters in the program play? Use this list to categorize your answers: managerial; clerical; professional; sales; service; craftsperson; machine operator; labourer; law enforcement, military personnel; customer/patient/client; homemaker.

   d. Write several paragraphs describing how organizational life is portrayed in the program. For example, is it fun or boring? Does it involve conflict or cooperation? Are people treated fairly? Do they seem motivated? Is worklife stressful?

e. What aspects of the TV portrayal of organizational behaviour do you think were realistic? Which were unrealistic?

3. Be prepared to discuss your findings in class. Your instructor will have some research information about

how organizational life has actually been portrayed on TV over the years.

Source: Inspired by the research of Leah Vande Berg and Nick Trujillo, as reported in Vande Berg, L., & Trujillo, N. (1989). *Organizational life on television.* Copyright © 1989. Ablex Publishing. Reproduced with permission of ABC-CLIO, LLC.

EXPERIENTIAL EXERCISE

OB in the News

Every day there are stories in the news about organizations, the workplace, careers, and jobs. Now that you are learning about organizational behaviour, you can begin to interpret and understand these stories in a more informed manner. So let's get started. Look for an article in your local newspaper that has something to do with work or organizations. Pay particular attention to articles in the business or careers section of the paper. Read the article as you normally would and then write a short summary of the article and what you have learned from it. Then read the article again, but this time answer the following questions:

1. What does the article tell you about organizational behaviour? Refer to the sections *What Are Organizations?* and *What Is Organizational Behaviour?* in this chapter to answer this question.

2. Use the events described in the article to explain why organizational behaviour is important and makes a difference.

3. How can the goals of organizational behaviour be used to better understand the events in the article or solve a problem or concern that is noted in the article? Be sure to relate each of the goals of organizational behaviour to the article (i.e., predicting, explaining, and managing behaviour in organizational behaviour).

4. Does the article address any of the contemporary management concerns described in the chapter? Try to interpret the article in terms of one or more of the contemporary management concerns.

5. Compare your first reading and interpretation of the article to your second reading and interpretation. What did you learn about the events in the article when interpreting it through your new organizational behaviour "lens"?

6. How can learning about organizational behaviour improve your understanding and interpretation of stories and events like the one described in your article?

CASE INCIDENT

My Mother's Visit

Last year, George was preparing for his mother's first visit to Canada. George had immigrated to Canada from Haiti six years ago. His dream was for his mother to come to Canada to meet his new family and live with them. He had been working hard and saving money for many years to pay for his mother's airfare. Finally, everything was coming together. His mother's flight was booked and a big celebration was planned to mark her arrival. George had arranged to leave work at lunchtime to pick his mother up at the airport and take her to his house, where the guests would be waiting. He spent months planning the celebration and making the arrangements.

However, when the big day arrived, George's boss handed him an assignment and told him he was not to leave until it was completed. When George described his plans, his boss cut him off and reminded him that the organization depends on employees to do whatever it takes to get the job done: "No excuses, George. You are not to leave until the job is done!" George had to arrange for a taxi to pick up his mother, and her welcome celebration took place without him. George did not get home until late in the evening. The guests had left and his mother had gone to bed. George wondered why the assignment could not have waited until the next day, or why one of his co-workers couldn't have done it.

1. What does this incident tell you about management and organizational behaviour at George's organization?

2. How can organizational behaviour help to predict and explain the behaviour of George and his boss? What advice would you give to George and his boss in terms of managing organizational behaviour in the future?

3. What does this incident tell you about management and organizational behaviour in general?

CASE STUDY

A Zero Wage Increase Again?

The owner of a large hardware, furniture, and building centre faced a dilemma regarding how to manage the upcoming wage review process. After two consecutive years of frozen wages, employees were impatient for financial progress, but there was no spare money in the budget. It was possible to pump savings from upcoming process-improvement initiatives to a wage increase; however, the owner had limited motivation to channel hard-won funds to underperforming employees. On the other hand, he was eager to reward the people who added value. A plan that rewarded only some employees could result in an angry backlash. He had to decide if he wanted to divert the savings into compensation and if so, he needed an effective distribution plan.

As store owner Mark Coglin walked up to the service desk, he heard Simon, the floor manager, finishing a phone conversation. Mark paused at the counter as he listened to the tail end of the interchange. Simon said, "Are you sure you can't make it in? This is kind of leaving me in a bind, Dougie. Yeah, I get it. Okay. Hopefully we'll see you tomorrow." Replacing the receiver into the cradle, Simon glanced up, shrugged in response to Mark's raised eyebrow, and said, "That was Dougie Suzor calling in again. He thinks he has the flu." Mark rolled his eyes and the two men started walking towards the front of the large home hardware and building centre.

Once they were out of earshot of any customers or other staff members, Mark commented under his breath, "It's funny how that flu bug always seems to hit Dougie the Monday following a long weekend."

Simon nodded, and said, "He's not the only one. Four other employees called in before him, and I have a feeling there will be a couple more calls from people whose shifts start in the afternoon."

Mark sighed loudly in exasperation. "What is it about us that makes people think we are dumb, Simon?" He pointed to his freshly-pressed button-up shirt with the company logo embroidered on the left side, and said, "This says the name of the store is 'House, Hearth & Home', not 'House of the-ones-who-will-believe-anything,' right?" Simon chuckled, but didn't comment or break stride. This wasn't the first time he had heard this line of joke. Mark continued, "Do they think we're not going to notice that they miss every Monday after a long weekend? Especially when they come in on the Tuesday talking about the great road trip they had. Is it really that likely that they will catch the flu for *one day only* every time? Sheesh."

Simon laughed as he reached for the buzzing cell clipped to his belt. After a quick glance at the text display, he paused and shoved several pieces of paper into Mark's hand. Changing direction, he asked over his shoulder, "Would you mind giving these to Donna at the front for me? They're about to send out that order for the Avondale project, and I want to check a few things with Wesley in the yard before it goes." Not waiting for an answer, Simon took off towards the warehouse.

Watching Simon's retreating back, Mark was impressed once again by the dedication he had to doing things right, even though it had unfortunately interrupted his venting. As the floor manager, Simon never had a shortage of issues clamoring for his attention. Somehow he managed to juggle a lot of balls at the same time, very rarely dropping any of them. As one of the owners of House, Hearth & Home, it was very reassuring for Mark to have Simon on the job. He was a key employee.

Mark knew a business as big as his needed employees like Simon. As he made his way to the front of the store, he was able to glimpse only part of the 39 000 square feet devoted to hardware and building supplies. An additional 12 000 square feet were filled with home furnishings, leaving 8000 square feet as warehouse space. No one person could manage the one hundred staff members, the truckloads of inventory, and the annual sales of more than Cdn$20 million. Although every employee could make a difference in the success of the establishment, there were certain employees who would be very hard to replace and Simon was one of them.

After delivering the papers to Donna and chatting with her for a few minutes, Mark walked towards the kitchen department to check out how the new displays looked. Customers really seemed enthusiastic about the kitchen displays, but they took up a lot of valuable floor space. Mark wanted to reassure himself that the new ones were as nice as or even better than the old ones. As he came around the end of an aisle, he noticed Marie and Anne, two employees from the flooring department, talking and laughing as they stocked a shelf. He could hear they were talking about a television show that had been on the night before. Part way down the aisle, a customer was looking perplexed as she scanned the upper shelves. Annoyed, but trying not to show it, Mark smiled as he paused beside Marie and Anne, and said, "I think you have a customer, ladies." Looking around, they acted as though they hadn't noticed her before. Marie mumbled an apology and jumped up to ask her if she needed assistance.

Mark shook his head as he walked away. He thought, "We have trained our employees to make customer service a priority, yet those two acted like that customer was invisible. Why will certain employees not do the right thing unless someone is standing over them? And why do they think I would be so gullible as to believe they hadn't seen her?"

Before he could find an answer to this question, Mark was distracted by the sight of the new kitchen displays. They looked very impressive and he stopped to congratulate the kitchen designer for her good work. Glancing at his watch, Mark realized it was almost time for his meeting with Aaron, the company controller. As he excused himself and started heading towards Aaron's back office, Mark thought about the reason for this meeting and felt a little nervousness in his stomach. He had asked Aaron to figure out if there was any money for wage increases this year. Mark knew enough about the balance sheet to suspect the news would not be good.

Like many other businesses, the global downturn had negatively affected House, Hearth & Home. Sales had shrunk by almost Cdn$4 million a year.

Profit margins had tightened or disappeared in several areas.

Employees had seemed to understand why there had been no raises in 2009 and in 2010. However, Mark felt it would be hard to sell a zero percent increase for the third year in a row.

As usual, Aaron was behind his desk with a spreadsheet open on his computer and a cup of coffee half-forgotten among the many papers on his desk. With the company for over six years, Aaron adeptly handled many of the accounting and human resource issues, freeing up Mark to spend more time out on the floor troubleshooting. He smiled as Mark came in and said, "Hey, you're right on time. Grab a seat. I'm just printing out a little report for our meeting." The printer behind him started to whirr, and Aaron rolled over in his chair to pull two sheets as they emerged.

Rubbing his eyes as he handed one to Mark, he said, "You asked me if I could find any money for raises this year. Well, I've gone over the latest numbers and the quick answer, I'm afraid, is no." Aaron waited a moment to let Mark scan the sheet before he continued. "As you know, sales have been down, we've written off some old inventory this year, and there have been a few unexpected expenses that have really cut into profits. I've laid it out in broad brush strokes in this table. I don't think any of it will be surprising to you."

Mark exhaled loudly as he began to go through each line with Aaron. He was surprised by how disappointed he was feeling. Listening to Aaron as he walked him through the numbers, Mark let a part of his brain consider why he felt such disquiet at the idea of another year with no increases. What was he afraid would happen? A mutiny? A mass exodus? Sabotage?

The sound of the printer running again made Mark realize that he had not been giving the conversation enough attention. He said, "I'm sorry, Aaron I didn't catch all of that. What was the last part?"

As he handed Mark another sheet, Aaron replied, "I was saying that the first sheet is a fair accounting of the business. There aren't more than a few thousand spare dollars to go towards raises. However, there may be some ways we can 'find' some money in there."

Mark cleared his throat, and asked, "Legally?"

Aaron rolled his eyes, and said:

Of course. I wouldn't recommend anything the auditors would pull apart. I'm just saying that if we change what we're spending money on, we might be able to divert some towards a wage increase. For example, I've heard you say that we're not getting much of a return from our advertising spending. We could "save" some money there. Or there may be room to reduce our inventory even further. Of course, you may decide that savings made by process improvements should go to things other than wages. The downturn isn't over yet. If we do find some money, there are many other places in this company where you could invest it. For example, we could use a better security system. Or we could pay down some of our debt. Or we could do some overdue building maintenance to ensure we look good for the customers. It's a tough decision. You think about it.

Mark looked at the second sheet with interest. Aaron had listed a number of different areas where they could cut expenses or save some money. Some of them had been raised, but they had never been presented in such a detailed fashion. Beside each he had given an estimate of the dollar amounts that could be saved. If they were able to implement all of these ideas, there would be enough money to give all employees maybe a 2.5 to 3.0 per cent increase. This was a little higher than the annual inflation rate.

This type of increase would not make up for the two years of zero increases, but it would be a movement in the right direction.

Mark waited for a sense of relief to wash over him, but for some reason, he did not feel as excited about this news as he had expected. This didn't make sense. He had been disappointed the moment before when he thought there was no change. Aaron had given him an opening to make this raise happen.

Knowing that Aaron had put a lot of work into this idea, Mark made an effort to show some enthusiasm and to thank Aaron for his creative thinking. However, he ended the meeting shortly afterwards with an assurance that he would think about everything Aaron had presented. Mark needed to let his thoughts settle down before he could sort them out.

Walking back onto the floor, Mark decided that some fresh air might do him some good. He headed outside to the side yard where the lumber, drywall, and other large materials were transferred directly to customers or to the delivery trucks. He scanned the yard for Wesley, the yard foreman. An eight year employee,

Wes had the responsibility to keep the yard organized and safe. When things got sloppy in the yard, accidents increased, people were more likely to get hurt, and inventory was likely to be lost or damaged. Like Simon the floor manager inside, Wes was always ready to step up and make sure things were done correctly.

Wesley was in the far end of the yard speaking to a young man on a forklift. As Mark walked closer, he could hear them discussing the best way to prep large customer orders. Instead of interrupting, Mark paused to straighten out a pile of lumber that a customer had just finished picking through. At the sound of forklift moving off, Mark looked up to see Wes watching him work while leaning against a skit of siding.

What a smirk, Mark asked, "You enjoying yourself there?"

Wes nodded but stepped over to pick up a few boards that had fallen to the ground. Placing them back with the others, Wes said, "Hey, it's not every day that I get to see you actually working."

Looking at the neat pile with satisfaction, Mark straightened out his back and replied, "From what I can see, that young kid is doing most of the work out here."

Wes laughed out loud, and said, "Ouch! But good catch, Mark. Kyle is doing a lot out here. I wish I had 10 more just like him. He just brought me another great idea for doing things better. He has only been here for two months, and he already seems to understand how everything should flow together. There are guys who have been here for five years who can't do that." As Wes talked, they watched Kyle expertly maneuver the forklift as he picked an order of drywall for a contractor.

Looking back at Mark, Wes said, "Hey, I don't think you came out here to pick up boards or talk about Kyle. Did you need me to do something?"

Mark shook his head and replied, "Nah. Just hanging out. Maybe I'm wondering if I could leave my problems inside, and get a job with you cleaning up the yard. Seems like it would be a lot less stressful, and I could get lots of fresh air. What do you say?"

Wes laughed again, and replied as he looked down at his cell phone, "Sorry, no openings. You don't really want to work here anyway. Kyle would just make you look bad! Gotta go." Wes turned away to sort out a delivery problem that was holding up a job on the other side of town, and Mark found himself on his own again.

Realizing the answers he sought were not in the yard, Mark wandered back to his office. Shutting the door, he turned off his phone and sat back in his leather office chair so he could try again to straighten out his thinking like he had straightened up the pile of lumber.

Pulling out a blank notepad, Mark wrote down the thoughts that were rolling around his head. He knew it was probably unreasonable to ask his employees to accept a wage freeze for the third year in a row. A subgroup of the employees already seemed to dislike their jobs and it was scary to imagine how hard they would be to deal with if their morale level sunk even lower. There were already issues with "lost" inventory—perhaps the employee theft problem would skyrocket if there was no wage increase. Employees who felt cheated might feel entitled to help themselves to a different sort of raise. The store was full of items that most people would want—it would be easy for a disgruntled employee to smuggle some of the smaller items out of the store in lieu of a raise.

The ideas for cost savings given by Aaron could probably be accomplished, but it would be a lot of work. Thinking about the time and effort that would be necessary to make it happen, Mark wasn't sure if he wanted it bad enough. He already worked long hours, six days a week. If he was honest with himself, he had to admit that he was not particularly motivated to find a way to give raises to some of his employees. There were certain employees who didn't even seem to earn the money they were already making. It was hard to justify giving them even more money.

Mark realized that at least 15 per cent of his employees would probably save the company money if they left. These were the people like Dougie who were unreliable, dishonest, incompetent, or always in the middle of the latest workplace drama. It was hard to get motivated to work extra hours for months on end to reward this behaviour.

Of course, there were twice as many really good employees like Kyle. These were the employees that cared about their work, and went that extra mile, even when no one was watching. They were the lifeblood of the business. They should be recognized. At the very top of this pile sat Aaron the controller, Simon the floor manager, and Wesley the yard foreman. Mark jotted down a note that it was imperative to show at least these three that they were really appreciated. He also knew that giving a raise to only some people and not others could create new problems.

Mark thought hard about the options scrawled across the page. Should he give an increase to everyone, to no one, or to the deserving minor-

ity? Should he do something else entirely? He knew there would be big consequences to any decision he made.

Source: Karen MacMillan wrote this case solely to provide material for class discussion. The author does not intend to illustrate either effective or ineffective handling of a managerial situation. The author may have disguised certain names and other identifying information to protect confidentiality.

QUESTIONS

1. Explain the relevance and importance of organizational behaviour for the issues described in the case and the wage review dilemma. What are the main issues and what do they have to do with organizational behaviour?

2. Use the goals of organizational behaviour to address the wage review dilemma. In other words, what needs to be predicted, explained, and managed? What do you think will happen if there is not a wage increase? What will happen if there is a wage increase? What will happen if only some employees receive a wage increase? How can the goals of organizational behaviour help Mark make a decision about the wage dilemma?

3. Consider the relevance of each of the managerial roles and activities for Mark Coglin. What roles and activities are most important for dealing with the wage dilemma? What does Mark need to do and how should he proceed?

4. Do you think Mark should give all or none of the employees a wage increase? Should Mark give only some of the employees a wage increase? What are the implications of each decision and how can organizational behaviour help Mark make this decision and understand the implications?

5. What do you think Mark should do and why? Is there something else he could do besides a wage increase? Will Mark's decision have an effect on the attitudes and behaviours of the employees? Explain your answers.

IVEY

Richard Ivey School of Business
The University of Western Ontario

INTEGRATIVE CASE

Deloitte & Touche: Integrating Arthur Andersen

Written by Ken Mark and Gerard Seijts

Introduction

It was a rainy September morning. Terry Noble, the Toronto Group Managing Partner for Deloitte & Touche (Deloitte), stretched his back and contemplated the results of the most recent "Pulse Survey" that were just presented to him.

Noble co-chaired the national integration team that was faced with a huge challenge: to develop a company-wide plan to create support materials to aid the Deloitte people in integrating more than 1000 Arthur Andersen (Andersen) people into their 5600 person strong organization. Noble's team monitored the integration process through a monthly Pulse Survey, which would allow the team to benchmark unit to unit over time, and to take remedial action if, at specific stages, the integration goals were not attained.

The data that Noble just had seen did not come as a total surprise. In fact, he and the Deloitte senior management team were feeling a certain degree of backlash from a number of people in their own organization. Some Deloitte employees, it seemed, feared that Deloitte management, in its haste to consummate this new deal and welcome Andersen, was forgetting about its own employees. There was an attitude among some employees within Deloitte, the larger organization, that people coming from Andersen were "damaged goods" and that these people should be grateful that they had found a good home. Comments such as "Damn the torpedoes and let's get on with business," and "It's our way or the highway . . . after all, we acquired the Andersen business" began to surface. The cultural issues were showing up in day-to-day behaviour. Noble mulled over how he might best address this issue. Should he address it at all? For example, he did not yet know whether the opinions voiced came from a few vocal employees, or if others in the Deloitte organization shared their sentiment. The integration issues were rather complicated because, at the outset, the integration message was interpreted by some as "a merger of two equals."

The Integration

On June 3, 2002, across Canada, approximately 1000 Andersen people (700 professional staff, 200 support staff, and 70 partners) would join Deloitte, effectively creating the country's largest professional services organization. The large majority of these people would be located in Toronto. Noble estimated that the value of Andersen annual billings brought to Deloitte was between Cdn$100 million and Cdn$180 million. If the integration were somehow mismanaged, annual billings would be around Cdn$90 million or even less. However, if the integration were successful, the number would be closer to the Cdn$180 million mark. The combined entity would employ 6600 people in total, representing annual billings of approximately Cdn$1.1 billion.

A welcome breakfast involving 1300 people was planned to kick off the integration at the Metro Toronto Convention Centre, followed by a series of introductory speeches. Colin Taylor, Deloitte's chief executive and managing partner stated:

Now we're integrating the Andersen people and clients into Deloitte with the same energy, enthusiasm, and speed that we brought to closing the transaction. We have a lot of work ahead of us and our goal is to make this transition absolutely seamless for our clients and as smooth as possible for our people.

At Deloitte, "Making a Difference Together" was the vision for the integrated organization that expressed the combined company's commitment to its clients and each other. It also expressed the belief that the integration with Andersen would strengthen existing capabilities. Deloitte included these words in a new logo created to highlight all integration communications. The logo symbolized Deloitte's conviction that, as the number one professional services firm in Canada, it will be even stronger and more successful in the marketplace (see Exhibit 1).

Deloitte & Touche

Deloitte in Canada was part of a worldwide group named Deloitte Touche Tohmatsu. Deloitte Touche Tohmatsu was a Swiss Verein, an association, and each of its national practices was a separate and independent legal entity.

In Canada, Deloitte had 2001 revenues of Cdn$895 million and 5600 people (including 515 partners). Its main services were fourfold. Assurance and Advisory services provided attest services (financial audits of organizations, rendering an independent opinion). Financial Advisory services included investigative

EXHIBIT 1 Deloitte's new logo for the integrated organization.
Source: Company files.

services directed at solving business crime and reorganization services to allow managers to regain control amid organizational crisis—essentially crisis management services. In addition, this group facilitated public offerings of stock or debt, mergers and acquisitions, and performed due diligence work for clients. Consulting-type services were offered to help clients develop and enhance their business strategies. Tax services supported personal and corporate filings as well as advised clients on how to achieve tax savings. Deloitte had offices in all major cities across Canada. The four services listed above were offered in each of these offices.

Andersen

Andersen Worldwide SC, a Swiss Societe Cooperative, was a coordinating entity for its autonomous member firms that had agreed to cooperate in the market with a common brand, philosophy, and technologies and practice methods. Thus, each Andersen Worldwide member firm, including Andersen in the United States and Andersen in Canada, had its own governance and capital structure. There were Andersen consultants serving clients in 390 locations around the world.

In 1960, Andersen established its Canadian practice with 26 people. Prior to 2002, it was considered the smallest of the five largest accounting firms in Canada with 1300 people. At the time of the integration in 2002, Andersen had sized itself down to approximately 970 employees. The firm serviced clients across the country from seven offices located in Vancouver, Calgary, Winnipeg, Mississauga, Toronto, Ottawa, and Montreal. It offered services that were very similar to those offered by Deloitte.

Noble was impressed with the Andersen organization in Canada, stating:

We knew that Andersen had the best litigation record of any professional services firm in Canada. We admired and envied Andersen. At Deloitte, we would often hold Andersen practices up as the industry benchmark, including their tools, skills, marketing, and knowledge management capabilities. Their link to a global network of consultants with expertise in a multitude of areas, and which could be accessed at any given time, was unparalleled.

The Events That Led up to the Integration

In 1999, Enron had been the seventh largest U.S. company (based on reported revenues). For the last 10 years, it had evolved from a regional natural gas provider to, among other things, a trader of natural gas, electricity, and other commodities, with retail operations in energy and other products. In 1998, Enron was number 73 on Fortune's annual list of "100 Best Companies to Work For."

Andersen U.S. provided Enron with internal audit services as well as serving as Enron's external auditor. Although Andersen's international branches were legally separate from Andersen U.S., the Andersen name became a huge liability as a result of the Enron scandal. Andersen U.S. faced a felony charge of obstruction of justice, accused of trying to block a Securities and Exchange Commission (SEC) investigation into Enron's financial disclosures by destroying documents related to the accounting firm's audits.

In statements released to the media, Andersen stated that the action taken against its firm by the U.S. Department of Justice was "both factually and legally baseless." Nevertheless, the damage had been done and the company faced a crisis from which it would not recover.

Enron's collapse and allegations of illegal activity by Andersen created debate around auditor independence and scope of services. Criminal indictment of Andersen U.S. created a negative impact on the accounting profession. One of the questions that persisted in the public arena was whether an accounting firm could objectively perform an audit when it also made millions of dollars providing other services to the same client. Audit firms refuted that an audit could be enhanced by the extra knowledge the firm gained through its consulting arm.

The collapse of Enron and the court of public opinion effectively destroyed the Andersen brand in a few months. In accepting Andersen professionals, some Deloitte managers were concerned that the Enron fallout might carry over to the Deloitte brand.

The Integration Talks

Although it was thought that rival accounting firms—either KPMG or Ernst & Young—already had a deal to acquire Andersen, Deloitte's senior management team was pleasantly surprised when it found out that Andersen's U.S. tax practice had urged Andersen Canada to talk to Deloitte. In the United States, Andersen's tax practice had aligned with its Deloitte counterpart. In the first week of April 2002, Andersen Canada contacted Deloitte to begin integration talks.

On Friday, April 12, 2002, Deloitte completed a memorandum of agreement with Andersen Canada to integrate its practice with Deloitte. This transaction was subject to a due diligence review, partner approvals by both firms, and regulatory approval. Because of its size, the transaction was subject to regulatory review by the Competition Bureau under Canada's *Competition Act*. Noble stated:

> The run-up to the integration has been a disaster for Andersen. Despite their Canadian client base and staff remaining loyal, their phones were not ringing. Even when they were the frontrunner for new business, potential clients would almost always shy away from them. The day-to-day press surrounding Andersen was very negative.

Andersen had been negotiating with KPMG and the media was speculating that a deal was imminent. Deloitte took a less public profile, avoiding speculation. Because both sides moved rapidly, the transaction was completed in six weeks. Closing the

transaction quickly was critical because a lengthy process increased the risk that a major client and a significant number of talented professionals would be lost.

Alan Booth, director of National Human Resources with Deloitte, explained that the detailed negotiations on people and other critical integration issues proved very challenging due to various reasons, including:

1. Strict limitations on contact between Deloitte and Andersen to permit regulatory review;

2. Imminent systems loss at Andersen set to occur when it would withdraw from Andersen Worldwide;

3. Numerous rumours that fed anxiety among people in both organizations; and

4. Coordination of messages to people from Deloitte and Andersen was greatly affected by the necessary contact limitations.

On Friday, May 31, 2002, at 5:00 p.m. Pacific Daylight Time, Andersen Canada "went dark." All its systems including phones, e-mail, and personal computers (PCs) were disconnected from the worldwide Andersen network. This signalled the beginning of the actual integration of the former Andersen people into the Deloitte organization.

The National Integration Team

A national integration team consisting of 12 individuals was formed to lead the integration. The team was co-chaired by Terry Noble, who had trained as a chartered accountant with Andersen in Canada, and Russ Robertson, Andersen's managing partner. Colin Taylor, Deloitte's chief executive, knew that both men had been classmates at the Western Business School undergraduate program at the University of Western Ontario, London, Canada, in the 1960s, and thus knew each other. Equal numbers of Deloitte and Andersen personnel were represented on the team. An effort was made to ensure that key people from both sides were involved to guide the integration challenge. For example, heads of functions, integrating officers from the five Deloitte offices, and several "thought leaders" were part of the team.

The main goals of the integration team were to put together a companywide plan for integration and to create support materials (e.g., "A Primer on Organizational Grieving") to aid the Deloitte people in integrating their new colleagues into their organization. Geographic and functional leaders were to execute

EXHIBIT 2 Pulse Survey questions.

No.	Questions
1.	Overall, the integration is going well.
2.	The firm is committed to making the integration as smooth as possible for our people.
3.	I am being kept informed about how the integration will affect me.
4.	I am being treated fairly during the integration.
5.	My ability to do my job effectively has been maintained or improved as a result of the integration.
6.	I am confident dealing with client questions about the integration.
7.	Client service levels have been maintained or improved as a result of the integration.
8.	My clients are feeling positive about the integration.
9.	I intend to be with D&T one year from now.
	Overall score.

the plan with support from national functions such as human resources (HR), information technology (IT) and finance. For example, HR was, to a large extent, responsible for communicating the Deloitte policies, as well as explaining administrative items, such as compensation, the incentive plan, pensions and benefits, and promotion policies. The IT department was responsible for issues such as a seamless transition of e-mail, telephone systems, and computer applications. There were significant differences in the IT systems between the two companies. However, by the end of Monday, June 3, 2002, almost all new Deloitte people had their PCs reconfigured to the Deloitte systems, a new phone number, a connection to the network, and new business cards to give to their clients.

The national integration team would monitor the integration process through an Internet-based Pulse Survey, which would allow the team to benchmark unit to unit over time, and to take immediate remedial action if in the various stages the integration goals were not attained. The Pulse Survey was conducted every month with a random sample of people from both organizations. For example, among other things, people were asked:

1. How they felt the integration was proceeding overall;

2. If they were kept informed about the personal impact integration would have on them;

3. Whether they perceived fair treatment;

4. Whether their ability to do their jobs was maintained or increased;

5. If they felt that client service levels were being maintained or improved; and

6. If they intended to remain with Deloitte one year into the future.

Participants in the survey were also given the opportunity to provide open comments on how they felt the integration was progressing, or any other message they wanted to communicate in confidence. All offices received detailed feedback on all of the questions that were incorporated in the survey. The questions that were part of the Pulse Survey are listed in Exhibit 2.

Once every two weeks, the managing partners of each of the five Deloitte offices would convene for a conference call to share updates and ideas, some of which resulted from the Pulse Survey. Best practices were identified, and integrating officers were encouraged to implement these practices across offices. Last, the integration team would present status updates to Deloitte's executive committee and board of directors.

Commenting on the Deloitte and Andersen integration, in November of 2002, Noble stated:

Integration is easier said than done. It takes at least three to five years. There is often a strong tendency on the part of those leading the change efforts to declare victory too soon. Early on we need to outline the present and future state of our organization. Cultures do not change that quickly. We do not want a situation where the integration unravels and turns into a bad business deal because we did not manage the process, people, systems, and business fundamentals in a proper fashion.

One thousand Andersen professionals are joining us and not one of them had chosen to be part of our organization. The integration is like an arranged marriage and we have to find common ground. The Andersen people probably have a fear that they will be taken over and their identity and sense of value will be lost. I'm sure that they are not prepared to let that happen.

There are workplace productivity issues that we will have to manage. At first, the Andersen people will be busy getting used to their new titles, new surroundings, and new colleagues. Many people will be concerned with "me" issues: my office, my promotion, my salary, my computer, my role and responsibilities, and so forth. While they have all that to sort through, our job is to figure out how to mitigate the productivity drop. A significant drop in our productivity could tie up the organization for years.

Of course, we want to be able to retain all of our clients—particularly those that are brought in by Andersen. We want our new clients to be proud of their association with Deloitte and confident in the ability of the combined entity to deliver quality and excellent service. Our combined client base needs to be convinced that Deloitte will not be affected by the aftershocks of the Andersen events in the U.S. We cannot afford to slip on our client service delivery. Otherwise there would not be enough work for our people.

Risks Identified by the Integration Team

As Noble saw it, the real challenge for the Deloitte and Andersen organizations was to move beyond the integrated HR and IT systems toward a unified,

market-leading organization. The actual successes achieved in the marketplace would hold the combined entities together. For example, financial success served as glue and, as Noble observed, would all but ensure that partners felt they had shared in the success of the transaction. Essential to the long-term success of the integration, therefore, was that individuals would see (or feel in their pocket) that investing significant resources in the transaction, time and money, was indeed worth it. Noble believed that the Andersen people would be blamed if the combined organization missed the financial targets that it intended to achieve. Such scapegoating would detract from the integration efforts.

Noble identified the top three risk factors that threatened to derail the success of the integration: cultural misalignment and subsequent conflict, insufficient integration, and lack of organizational synergies. Exhibits 3 and 4 describe the method and results of the cultural assessment that was conducted in July 2002 to determine the differences between the Deloitte and Andersen cultures.

The results of the assessment revealed how each organization viewed itself, the "other" organization and the challenges of the integration. The cultural gaps between members of the two organizations identified critical organizational issues that required special attention from the national integration team. It was quite clear that people from Deloitte and

EXHIBIT 3
Methodology used to test cultural alignment between Deloitte and Andersen.
Source: Company files.

Deloitte & Touche

Overall Assessment

CULTURAL SYNERGIES		CULTURAL GAPS	
Dimension	**Degree of Alignment**	**Dimension**	**Degree of Alignment**
Commitment to Quality	●	Bureaucracy	⊕
Client Orientation	●	Market Orientation	◑
Teamwork	◖	Diversity	⊕
Communication	◖	Action Orientation and Accountability	◑
Openness	◖	Learning and Development	◑
Integrity	◖	Reward and Recognition	◑
External Competitiveness	◖	Organizational Values	◑
Results Orientation	◖	Work Lifestyle Balance	◑
Risk Propensity	◖	Management Support	◑
Vision and Mission	◕	Goal Definition and Alignment	◑

Legend: Degree of Cultural Alignment

⊕ ◑ ◖ ◗ ●

Ten areas were identified as having either a moderate or low degree of cultural alignment. The remaining ten areas revealed a relatively high degree of cultural alignment.

EXHIBIT 4 Results of cultural assessment.
Source: Company files.

Andersen were different from an organizational culture point of view.

Noble elaborated:

The Andersen organization is being told that they will join a new organization. They would not have volunteered to integrate with us if not for the crisis that occurred in the U.S. Will they be enthusiastic about the integration? Some of them may be. However, others may not completely understand why we do things in a certain way here at Deloitte. Addressing the differences between the two cultures was essential to successfully guiding the integration.

The great payoff will be, that if we do this right, and utilize the talent of Andersen employees, we will not only become the best professional services firm, but also the largest in the country.

Ultimately, this is a talent play for us. We've got the best 1000 people coming into our organization fully trained. We have to figure out how we can get their commitment to us and to serve our clients. We want the Andersen people to be proud of their new organization.

We will lose people, but we want to lose them for the right reasons. People may have goals or values that are different from the ones espoused at Deloitte. However, we don't want to lose people because of poor interpersonal treatment.

The September Meeting

The data from the Pulse Survey (the third since June of 2002) that Noble had received earlier in the morning confirmed, at least to some extent, what he had been hearing through the grapevine. The data suggested that a number of Deloitte employees feared that Deloitte management, in its haste to consummate the deal with Andersen and welcome the new employees, was forgetting about its own people. Some elements within the Deloitte organization did not understand the amount of attention given to the Andersen people, whom they viewed as "damaged goods." Comments indicating that it was time for all people involved in the integration to "get on with business and focus on the market" began to surface.

However, Noble was not certain of the number of individuals that shared such views. Were these the concerns of a few vocal people? Or did these individuals voice what many others in the Deloitte organization were thinking? Clearly, this was not the kind of feedback he was hoping for. The results from the Pulse Survey led Noble to contemplate how he and his colleagues from the integration team could best deal with the cultural differences in the short term. In his words:

There is the naïve view that a new culture will be formed with relative ease. I doubt it. Cultures involve deep-seated beliefs. For example, at Andersen, there had always been a strong drive to focus on the clients' needs above everything else. In contrast, at Deloitte, while acknowledging the importance of commitment to quality and the client's needs, there was also a focus on employee issues.

A Frenchman and an Englishman will always retain their culture. But they can learn to work together to achieve a common goal. Or can they really?

It takes a lot of effort and patience to help new behaviours and practices grow deep roots.

In Noble's mind, this was a complex issue to manage. Furthermore, there were a number of situational constraints on actions that could be undertaken to address the issue. For example, Noble and his integration team had to contend with the fact that people were constantly on-site at the client's business. How then should managers work to resolve tensions that might arise between the two cultures? Moreover, taking the people from the two organizations to an off-site location to deal with the issue of cultural differences would certainly affect billable hours. Were we prepared to do that? On the other hand, addressing these and other issues in a timely and proper fashion could make the difference between being a good organization versus being great organization. True integration would be hard to achieve without the knowledge, skill, and, above all, the commitment of the Deloitte people. It was 10:29 a.m., and Noble got up to go to the meeting with the integration team.

Source: Ken Mark prepared this case under the supervision of Professor Gerard Seijts solely to provide material for class

discussion. The authors do not intend to illustrate either effective or ineffective handling of a managerial situation. The authors may have disguised certain names and other identifying information to protect confidentiality.

QUESTIONS

1. Discuss the relevance of organizational behaviour for the issues that Deloitte & Touche are facing. How can organizational behaviour be used to help the integration team ensure that the integration is successful?

2. Explain how the goals of organizational behaviour can be used by the integration team to ensure that the integration is successful. Describe some of the things that the integration team might want to predict, explain, and manage.

3. Consider Terry Noble's role as co-chair of the national integration team in terms of Mintzberg's managerial roles. What roles does he exhibit and how effective is he in performing each role? What roles are most important and why?

4. To what extent are some of the contemporary management concerns described in Chapter 1 relevant for the integration team? What does the integration team need to be most concerned about and what should they do to be successful in managing the contemporary management concerns?

PART **2**

INDIVIDUAL BEHAVIOUR

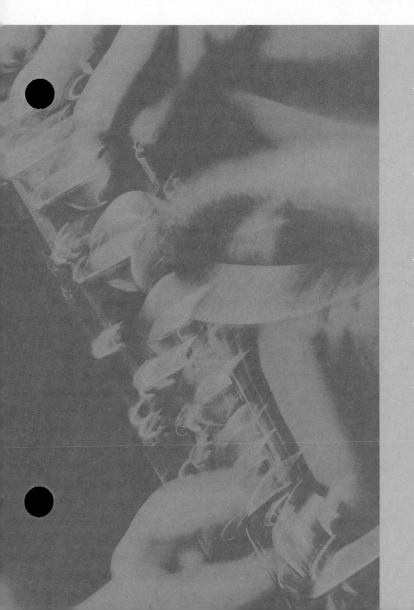

2 Personality and Learning

3 Perception, Attribution, and Diversity

4 Values, Attitudes, and Work Behaviour

5 Theories of Work Motivation

6 Motivation in Practice

CHAPTER 2

PERSONALITY AND LEARNING

LEARNING OBJECTIVES

After reading Chapter 2, you should be able to:

2.1 Define *personality* and discuss its general role in influencing organizational behaviour.

2.2 Describe the *dispositional*, *situational*, and *interactionist* approaches to organizational behaviour and *trait activation theory*.

2.3 Discuss the Five-Factor Model of personality.

2.4 Describe and discuss the consequences of *locus of control*, *self-monitoring*, and *self-esteem*.

2.5 Discuss *positive* and *negative affectivity*, *proactive personality*, *general self-efficacy*, and *core self-evaluations* and their consequences.

2.6 Define *learning* and describe what is learned in organizations.

2.7 Explain *operant learning theory* and differentiate between *positive* and *negative reinforcements*.

2.8 Explain when to use immediate versus delayed reinforcement and when to use continuous versus partial reinforcement.

2.9 Distinguish between *extinction* and *punishment* and explain how to use punishment effectively.

2.10 Explain *social cognitive theory* and discuss *observational learning*, *self-efficacy beliefs*, and *self-regulation*.

2.11 Describe the following organizational learning practices: *organizational behaviour modification*, *employee recognition programs*, *training and development programs*, and *career development*.

ECONOMICAL INSURANCE

Economical Insurance is a property and casualty insurance company that was founded in 1871. Its first insurance policy was written on a barn in Berlin, Ontario. Today, Economical has nearly 2500 employees and it is one of the largest property and casualty insurance companies in Canada. From its head office in Waterloo, Ontario, and an additional 17 branches and member companies across Canada, Economical offers a wide range of personal, commercial, farm, and surety products.

A few years ago, the company's medical plan costs had been increasing at an annual rate of 8 to 12 percent. So in the summer of 2008, members of the human resources department began to think seriously about a wellness strategy. Economical needed a program that would meet the following goals: build employee awareness of individual health; enhance employee engagement; reward employees for a broad range of wellness behaviours; enhance organiza-

tional health; have the flexibility to evolve as needs change; and produce measureable results in group benefits experience, absenteeism, and other key areas in three to five years.

In the first year of the program, the company focused on enhancing the awareness of individual employees and overall organizational health, as this would set the baseline for future strategies and initiatives. A wellness campaign was designed, including biometric clinics and wellness assessments, and a new personal wellness account was introduced.

The biometric screening clinics involved voluntary, confidential 15-minute appointments with a registered nurse to look for six heart disease risk factors. Employees were provided with wallet cards documenting their measures so they could monitor changes, speak with their physicians, and enter the information into their wellness assessments.

The confidential wellness assessment was housed on the benefit carrier's website and contained 32 questions

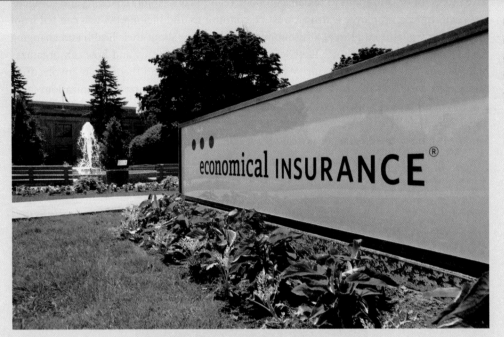

assessing 10 health risks (such as health habits, readiness to change, culture, and productivity). Each employee received an individualized report summarizing their results, along with tips to improve areas needing attention. Employees who completed the assessment within the promoted time frame were provided with $300 in wellness credits deposited into a personal wellness account through their flexible benefit plan. The credits can be used for things such as fitness/sports equipment, lessons, and weight management programs. More than one-half (54 percent) of employees participated.

In the second year of the program, Economical added a team wellness challenge to the program to create action and behaviour changes. This required employees to take action by focusing on particular risk areas. Teams worked toward common health goals and logged activities using an online journal.

The main challenge included a minimum amount of physical activity. For each minute of exercise, participants got a point. In addition, teams received bonus points for participation in focus areas (e.g., eating five fruits and veggies a day, drinking water, and taking time for oneself). Individual scores were combined to make team scores and the team with the most points won.

Employees who did the team challenge were rewarded with $150 for their personal wellness accounts while those who completed a wellness assessment received a further $150. The change in the incentive strategy from the first year to the second year is a purposeful, multi-year approach that progressively requires employees to adjust behaviours.

To create a year-round focus on physical activity, Economical also launched a four-week spring walking challenge (Stride into Summer) that involved more than 70 percent of employees walking more than 112 000 kilometres. Senior executives acted as role models by sharing their personal wellness-related stories.

Reviewing the results against the objectives indicates that employees are learning more about their individual health. Ninety-two percent of biometric screening participants said it helped them learn more about cardiovascular health and 71 percent said they will be making changes to their lifestyle. Testimonials from employees who have begun to change their lifestyles and see real health gains also indicate that the program has been effective.

Employees will now be challenged to sustain the changes they have made in their behaviour. Economical expects that within another two years, the program should see measureable improvements in the group benefits experience and absenteeism. It is also hoped that the program will enhance employee engagement and productivity, and help contain rising health-care costs.[1]

Learning is a critical requirement for effective organizational behaviour, and as you probably have heard, for organizations to remain competitive in today's rapidly changing and competitive environment, employee learning must be continuous and lifelong. As you can tell from the opening vignette, employees at Economical are learning about their health and changing their behaviour to live healthier lifestyles. But how do people learn and how can organizations change employees' behaviour? What learning principles and theories are involved? In this chapter we will focus on the learning process and see how learning in organizations takes place. While learning is necessary for people to change their behaviours, studies in organizational behaviour have shown that behaviour is also a function of people's personalities. Therefore, we begin this chapter by considering personality and organizational behaviour.

Kirmac Collision Services focuses on personality when recruiting and hiring employees.

WHAT IS PERSONALITY?

LO 2.1

Define *personality* and discuss its general role in influencing organizational behaviour.

The notion of personality permeates thought and discussion in our culture. We are bombarded with information about "personalities" in the print and broadcast media. We are sometimes promised exciting introductions to people with "nice" personalities. We occasionally meet people who seem to have "no personality."

Personality is so important that some companies focus on personality when hiring employees. For example, Kirmac Collision Services, an automotive collision repair company based in Coquitlam, British Columbia, has taken a new approach to recruiting and hiring employees that focuses less on industry-specific experience and skills and more on personality.[2] But what exactly *is* personality?

Personality. The relatively stable set of psychological characteristics that influences the way an individual interacts with his or her environment.

Personality is the relatively stable set of psychological characteristics that influences the way an individual interacts with his or her environment and how he or she feels, thinks, and behaves. An individual's personality summarizes his or her personal style of dealing with the world. You have certainly noticed differences in personal style among your parents, friends, professors, bosses, and employees. They are reflected in the distinctive way that they react to people, situations, and problems.

Where does personality come from? Personality consists of a number of dimensions and traits that are determined in a complex way by genetic predisposition and by one's long-term learning history. Although personality is relatively stable, it is certainly susceptible to change through adult learning experiences. And while we often use labels such as "high self-esteem" to describe people, we should always remember that people have a *variety* of personality characteristics. Excessive typing of people does not help us to appreciate their unique potential to contribute to an organization.

PERSONALITY AND ORGANIZATIONAL BEHAVIOUR

Personality has a rather long and rocky history in organizational behaviour. Initially, it was believed that personality was an important factor in many areas of organizational behaviour, including motivation, attitudes, performance, and leadership. In fact, after the Second World War, the use of personality tests for the selection of military personnel became widespread, and, in the 1950s and 1960s it became popular in business organizations.

This approach to organizational behaviour is known as the **dispositional approach** because it focuses on individual dispositions and personality. According to the dispositional approach, individuals possess stable traits or characteristics that influence their attitudes and behaviours. In other words, individuals are predisposed to behave in certain ways. However, decades of research produced mixed and inconsistent findings that failed to support the usefulness of personality as a predictor of organizational behaviour and job performance. As a result, there was a dramatic decrease in personality research and a decline in the use of personality tests for selection.

Researchers began to shift their attention to factors in the work environment that might predict and explain organizational behaviour. This approach became known as the **situational approach**. According to the situational approach, characteristics of the organizational setting, such as rewards and punishment, influence people's feelings, attitudes, and behaviour. For example, many studies have shown that job satisfaction and other work-related attitudes are largely determined by situational factors such as the characteristics of work tasks.[3]

Over the years, proponents of both approaches have argued about the importance of dispositions versus the situation in what is known as the "person–situation debate." Although researchers argued over which approach was the right one, it is now believed that both approaches are important for predicting and understanding organizational behaviour. This led to a third approach to organizational behaviour, known as the "interactionist approach," or "interactionism." According to the **interactionist approach**, organizational behaviour is a function of both dispositions and the situation. In other words, to predict and understand organizational behaviour, one must know something about an individual's personality and the setting in which he or she works. This approach is now the most widely accepted perspective within organizational behaviour.[4]

To give you an example of the interactionist perspective, consider the role of personality in different situations. To keep it simple, we will describe situations as being either "weak" or "strong." In weak situations it is not always clear how a person should behave, while in strong situations there are clear expectations for appropriate behaviour. As a result, personality has the most impact in weak situations. This is because in these situations (e.g., a newly formed volunteer community organization) there are loosely defined roles, few rules, and weak reward and punishment contingencies. However, in strong situations, which have more defined roles, rules, and contingencies (e.g., routine military operations), personality tends to have less impact.[5] Thus, as you can see, the extent to which personality influences people's attitudes and behaviour depends on the situation. Later in the text you will learn that the extent to which people perceive stressors as stressful and the way they react to stress is also influenced by their personality. This is another example of the interactionist approach to organizational behaviour.

One of the most important implications of the interactionist perspective is that some personality characteristics are useful in certain organizational situations. According to

 Simulate

INDIVIDUAL BEHAVIOUR Go to MyManagementLab to complete a simulation about individual behaviour.

LO

Describe the *dispositional*, *situational*, and *interactionist* approaches to organizational behaviour and *trait activation theory*.

Dispositional approach. Individuals possess stable traits or characteristics that influence their attitudes and behaviours.

Situational approach. Characteristics of the organizational setting influence people's attitudes and behaviour.

Interactionist approach. Individuals' attitudes and behaviour are a function of both dispositions and the situation.

Trait activation theory.
Traits lead to certain
behaviours only when the
situation makes the need
for the trait salient.

trait activation theory, traits lead to certain behaviours only when the situation makes the need for that trait salient. In other words, personality characteristics influence people's behaviour when the situation calls for a particular personality characteristic.[6] Thus, there is no one best personality and managers need to appreciate the advantages of employee diversity. A key concept here is *fit*: putting the right person in the right job, group, or organization and exposing different employees to different management styles.

In recent years, there has been a resurgence of interest in personality research in organizational behaviour. One of the main problems with the early research on personality was the use of inadequate measures of personality characteristics. However, advances in measurement and trends in organizations have prompted renewed interest. For example, increased emphasis on service jobs with customer contact, concern about ethics and integrity, and contemporary interest in teamwork and cooperation all point to the potential contribution of personality.[7]

Another reason for the renewed interest in personality has been the development of a framework of personality characteristics known as the Five-Factor Model, or the "Big Five," which provides a framework for classifying personality characteristics into five general dimensions. This framework makes it much easier to understand and study the role of personality in organizational behaviour.[8]

In what follows, we first discuss the five general personality dimensions of the Five-Factor Model. Then we cover three well-known personality characteristics with special relevance to organizational behaviour. We then discuss recent developments in personality research. Later in the text, we will explore the impact of personality characteristics on job satisfaction, motivation, leadership, ethics, organizational politics, and stress.

LO **2.3**

Discuss the Five-Factor
Model of personality.

The Five-Factor Model of Personality

People are unique, people are complex, and there are literally hundreds of adjectives that we can use to reflect this unique complexity. Yet, over the years, psychologists have discovered that there are about five basic but general dimensions that describe personality. These Big Five dimensions are known as the Five-Factor Model (FFM) of personality and are summarized in Exhibit 2.1 along with some illustrative traits.[9] The dimensions are:

- **Extraversion.** This is the extent to which a person is outgoing versus shy. Persons who score high on extraversion tend to be sociable, outgoing, energetic, joyful, and assertive. High extraverts enjoy social situations, while those low on this dimension (introverts) avoid them. Extraversion is especially important for jobs that require a lot of interpersonal interaction, such as sales and management, where being sociable, assertive, energetic, and ambitious is important for success.

- **Emotional stability/Neuroticism.** This is degree to which a person has appropriate emotional control. People with high emotional stability (low neuroticism) are self-confident and have high self-esteem. Those with lower emotional stability (high neuroticism) tend toward self-doubt and depression. They tend to be anxious, hostile, impulsive, depressed, insecure, and more prone to stress. As a result, for almost any job the performance of persons with low emotional stability is likely to suffer. Persons

  Explore

Go to MyManagementLab
to see an annotated
version of this figure.

EXHIBIT 2.1
**The Five-Factor Model
of personality.**

Extraversion	Emotional Stability	Agreeableness	Conscientiousness	Openness to Experience
Sociable, Talkative vs. Withdrawn, Shy	Stable, Confident vs. Depressed, Anxious	Tolerant, Cooperative vs. Cold, Rude	Dependable, Responsible vs. Careless, Impulsive	Curious, Original vs. Dull, Unimaginative

who score high on emotional stability are likely to have more effective interactions with co-workers and customers because they tend to be more calm and secure.

- **Agreeableness.** This is the extent to which a person is friendly and approachable. More agreeable people are warm, considerate, altruistic, friendly, sympathetic, cooperative, and eager to help others. Less agreeable people tend to be cold and aloof. They tend to be more argumentative, inflexible, uncooperative, uncaring, intolerant, and disagreeable. Agreeableness is most likely to contribute to job performance in jobs that require interaction and involve helping, cooperating, and nurturing others, as well as in jobs that involve teamwork and cooperation.

- **Conscientiousness.** This is the degree to which a person is responsible and achievement-oriented. More conscientious people are dependable and positively motivated. They are orderly, self-disciplined, hard-working, and achievement-striving, while less conscientious people are irresponsible, lazy, and impulsive. Persons who are high on conscientiousness are likely to perform well on most jobs given their tendency toward hard work and achievement.

- **Openness to experience.** This is the extent to which a person thinks flexibly and is receptive to new ideas. More open people tend toward creativity and innovation. Less open people favour the status quo. People who are high on openness to experience are likely to do well in jobs that involve learning and creativity given that they tend to be intellectual, curious, and imaginative, and to have broad interests.

The Big Five dimensions are relatively independent. That is, you could be higher or lower in any combination of dimensions. Also, they tend to hold up well cross-culturally. Thus, people in different cultures use these same dimensions when describing the personalities of friends and acquaintances. There is also evidence that the Big Five traits have a genetic basis.[10]

RESEARCH EVIDENCE Research has linked the Big Five personality dimensions to organizational behaviour. First, there is evidence that each of the Big Five dimensions is related to job performance and organizational citizenship behaviours (voluntary behaviour that contributes to organizational effectiveness such as helping co-workers; see Chapter 4 for a detailed discussion of organizational citizenship behaviour).[11] Generally, traits like those in the top half of Exhibit 2.1 lead to better job performance and more citizenship behaviours. Further, the Big Five dimensions that best predict job performance depend on the occupation. For example, high extraversion is important for managers and salespeople. However, high conscientiousness predicts performance in all jobs across occupations and is also the strongest predictor of all the Big Five dimensions of overall job performance.[12]

Second, research has also found that the Big Five are related to other work behaviours. For example, one study showed that conscientiousness is related to retention and attendance at work and is also an important antidote for counterproductive behaviours such as theft, absenteeism, and disciplinary problems.[13] Extraversion has also been found to be related to absenteeism; extraverts tend to be absent more often than introverts.[14]

The Big Five are also related to work motivation and job satisfaction. In a study that investigated the relationship between the Big Five and different indicators of work motivation, the Big Five were found to be significantly related to motivation. Among the five dimensions, neuroticism and conscientiousness were the strongest predictors of motivation, with the former being negatively related and the latter being positively related.[15] In another study, the Big Five were shown to be significantly related to job satisfaction. The strongest predictor was neuroticism (i.e., emotional stability) followed by conscientiousness, extraversion, and, to a lesser extent, agreeableness. Openness to experience was not related to job satisfaction. Higher neuroticism was associated with lower job satisfaction, while higher extraversion, conscientiousness, and agreeableness were associated with higher job satisfaction. Similar results have been found for life satisfaction. In addition, individuals with higher conscientiousness, extraversion, agreeableness, and emotional stability perform better on a team in terms of their performance of important team-relevant behaviours such as cooperation, concern, and courtesy to team members.[16]

The Big Five are also related to job search and career success. Extraversion, conscientiousness, openness to experience, and agreeableness have been found to relate positively to the intensity of a job seeker's job search, while neuroticism was negatively related. As well, conscientiousness was found to be positively related to the probability of obtaining employment.[17] In addition, high conscientiousness and extraversion and low neuroticism have been found to be associated with a higher income and occupational status. Perhaps most interesting is the fact that these personality traits were related to career success even when the influence of general mental ability was taken into account. Furthermore, both childhood and adult measures of personality predicted career success during adulthood over a period of 50 years. These results suggest that the effects of personality on career success are relatively enduring.[18]

The above findings all indicate that one's personality can influence one's attitudes and behaviours. But can the personality of a CEO influence the performance of an organization? To find out, see the Research Focus: *CEO Personality and Firm Performance.*

As noted earlier, the Big Five personality dimensions are basic and general. However, years of research have also identified a number of more specific personality characteristics that influence organizational behaviour, including locus of control, self-monitoring, and self-esteem. Let's now consider each of these.

Locus of Control

Consider the following comparison. Laurie and Stan are both management trainees in large banks. However, they have rather different expectations regarding their futures. Laurie has just enrolled in an evening Master of Business Administration (MBA) program in a nearby university. Although some of her MBA courses are not immediately applicable to her job, Laurie feels that she must be prepared for greater responsibility as she moves up in the bank hierarchy. Laurie is convinced that she will achieve promotions because she studies hard, works hard, and does her job properly. She feels that an individual makes her own way in the world and that she can control her own destiny. She is certain that she can someday be the president of the bank if she really wants to be. Her personal motto is "I can do it."

Stan, on the other hand, sees no use in pursuing additional education beyond his bachelor's degree. According to him, such activities just do not pay off. People who get promoted are just plain lucky or have special connections, and further academic preparation or hard work has nothing to do with it. Stan feels that it is impossible to predict his own future, but he knows that the world is pretty unfair.

Laurie and Stan differ on a personality dimension called **locus of control**. This variable refers to individuals' beliefs about the *location* of the factors that control their behaviour. At one end of the continuum are high internals (like Laurie), who believe that the opportunity to control their own behaviour resides within themselves. At the other end of the continuum are high externals (like Stan), who believe that external forces determine their behaviour. Not surprisingly, compared with internals, externals see the world as an unpredictable, chancy place in which luck, fate, or powerful people control their destinies (see Exhibit 2.2).[19]

Internals tend to see stronger links between the effort they put into their jobs and the performance level that they achieve. In addition, they perceive to a greater degree than externals that the organization will notice high performance and reward it.[20] Since internals believe that their work behaviour will influence the rewards they achieve, they are more likely to be aware of and to take advantage of information that will enable them to perform effectively.[21]

LO 2.4

Describe and discuss the consequences of *locus of control, self-monitoring,* and *self-esteem.*

✳ Explore

Go to MyManagementLab to see an annotated version of this figure.

EXHIBIT 2.2
The internal/external locus of control continuum.

Locus of control.
A set of beliefs about whether one's behaviour is controlled mainly by internal or external forces.

RESEARCH FOCUS

CEO PERSONALITY AND FIRM PERFORMANCE

As organizations struggle to remain competitive in today's increasingly global environment, a key success factor is the ability to adapt quickly to environmental changes or what is known as *strategic flexibility*. Strategic flexibility has been shown to drive firm performance.

The CEO of an organization plays a key role in driving strategic change and can have a profound effect on an organization's strategic direction and performance. But can the CEO's personality influence strategic flexibility and firm performance?

To find out, Sucheta Nadkarni and Pol Herrmann conducted a study of CEOs of 195 small and medium-sized enterprises (SMEs) from the Indian business process outsourcing industry. Offshore business process outsourcing is the transfer of the operational ownership of one or more of a firm's processes to an external provider from another country that then manages the processes according to predetermined metrics. India is the leader in business process outsourcing services, an industry where strategic flexibility is central to success and survival.

The researchers predicted that a CEO's personality can influence firm performance by either enhancing or inhibiting strategic flexibility. This is because the CEO's personality will influence how he/she searches for and interprets information that is central to developing strategic flexibility.

Nadkarni and Herrmann focused on the five dimensions of the Five-Factor Model and predicted that each dimension will be positively or negatively related to strategic flexibility. The CEOs completed a personality and demographic survey, and at least two top managers that report directly to the CEO completed a strategic flexibility survey. Financial performance records were obtained from each firm.

The results indicated that emotional stability, extraversion, and openness to experience were positively related to strategic flexibility while conscientiousness was negatively related. Medium levels of agreeableness were related to the most strategic flexibility. In addition, strategic flexibility was positively related to firm performance.

These results indicate that CEO extraversion, emotional stability, and openness to experience enhanced firm performance by fostering strategic flexibility, whereas CEO conscientiousness undermined firm performance by inhibiting flexibility. Medium levels of agreeableness maximized strategic flexibility and firm performance.

This study highlights the importance of CEO personality in fostering strategic flexibility and firm performance.

Source: Based on Nadkarni, S., & Herrmann, P. (2010). CEO personality, strategic flexibility, and firm performance: The case of the Indian business process outsourcing industry. *Academy of Management Journal, 53*, 1050–1073.

Research shows that locus of control influences organizational behaviour in a variety of occupational settings. Evidently, because they perceive themselves as being able to control what happens to them, people who are high on internal control are more satisfied with their jobs, more committed to their organizations, earn more money, and achieve higher organizational positions.[22] In addition, they seem to perceive less stress, to cope with stress better and experience less burnout, and to engage in more careful career planning. They are also less likely to be absent from work and to be more satisfied with their lives.[23]

Self-Monitoring

We are sure that you have known people who tend to "wear their heart on their sleeve." These are people who act the way they feel and say what they think in spite of their social surroundings. We are also sure that you have known people who are a lot more sensitive to their social surroundings, a lot more likely to fit what they say and do to the nature of those surroundings regardless of how they think or feel. What we have here is a contrast in **self-monitoring**, which is the extent to which people observe and regulate how they appear and behave in social settings and relationships.[24] The people who "wear their heart on their sleeve" are low self-monitors. They are not so concerned with scoping out and fitting in with those around them. Their opposites are high self-monitors, who take great care to observe the thoughts, actions, and feelings of those around them and control the images that they project. In this sense, high

Self-monitoring. The extent to which people observe and regulate how they appear and behave in social settings and relationships.

self-monitors behave somewhat like actors. In particular, high self-monitors tend to show concern for socially appropriate emotions and behaviours, to tune in to social and interpersonal cues, and to regulate their behaviour and self-presentation according to these cues.

How does self-monitoring affect organizational behaviour?[25] For one thing, high self-monitors tend to gravitate toward jobs that require, by their nature, a degree of role-playing and the exercise of their self-presentation skills. Sales, law, public relations, and politics are examples. In such jobs, the ability to adapt to one's clients and contacts is critical; so are communication skills and persuasive abilities, characteristics that high self-monitors frequently exhibit. High self-monitors perform particularly well in occupations that call for flexibility and adaptiveness in dealings with diverse constituencies. As well, a number of studies show that managers are inclined to be higher self-monitors than non-managers in the same organization. Self-monitoring is also significantly related to a number of work-related outcomes. High self-monitors tend to be more involved in their jobs, to perform at a higher level, and to be more likely to emerge as leaders. However, high self-monitors are also likely to experience more role stress and show less commitment to their organization.[26]

Promotion in the management ranks is often a function of subjective performance appraisals, and the ability to read and conform to the boss's expectations can be critical for advancement. Thus, the ability to regulate and adapt one's behaviour in social situations and to manage the impressions others form of them might be a career advantage for high self-monitors. In fact, in a study that tracked the careers of a sample of MBA graduates, high self-monitors were more likely to change employers and locations and to receive more promotions than low self-monitors.[27]

Are high self-monitors always at an organizational advantage? Not likely. They are unlikely to feel comfortable in ambiguous social settings in which it is hard to determine exactly what behaviours are socially appropriate. Dealing with unfamiliar cultures (national or corporate) might provoke stress. Also, some roles require people to go against the grain or really stand up for what they truly believe in. Thus, high self-monitoring types would seem to be weak innovators and would have difficulty resisting social pressure.

Self-Esteem

How well do you like yourself? This is the essence of the personality characteristic called self-esteem. More formally, **self-esteem** is the degree to which a person has a positive self-evaluation. People with high self-esteem have favourable self-images. People with low self-esteem have unfavourable self-images. They also tend to be uncertain about the correctness of their opinions, attitudes, and behaviours. In general, people tend to be highly motivated to protect themselves from threats to their self-esteem.

One of the most interesting differences between people with high and low self-esteem has to do with the *plasticity* of their thoughts, attitudes, and behaviour, or what is known as "behavioural plasticity." According to **behavioural plasticity theory**, people with low self-esteem tend to be more susceptible to external and social influences than those who have high self-esteem—that is, they are more pliable. Thus, events and people in the organizational environment have more impact on the beliefs and actions of employees with low self-esteem. This occurs because, being unsure of their own views and behaviour, they are more likely to look to others for information and confirmation. In addition, people who have low self-esteem seek social approval from others, approval that they might gain from adopting others' views, and they do not react well to ambiguous and stressful situations. This is another example of the interactionist approach, in that the effect of the work environment on people's beliefs and actions is partly a function of their self-esteem.[28]

Employees with low self-esteem also tend to react badly to negative feedback—it lowers their subsequent performance.[29] This means that managers should be especially cautious when using negative reinforcement and punishment, as discussed later in this chapter,

Self-esteem. The degree to which a person has a positive self-evaluation.

Behavioural plasticity theory. People with low self-esteem tend to be more susceptible to external and social influences than those who have high self-esteem.

with employees with low self-esteem. If external causes are thought to be responsible for a performance problem, this should be made very clear. Also, managers should direct criticism at the performance difficulty and not at the person. As we will explain shortly, modelling the correct behaviour should be especially effective with employees with low self-esteem, who are quite willing to imitate credible models and who also respond well to mentoring. Finally, organizations should try to avoid assigning those with low self-esteem to jobs (such as life insurance sales) that inherently provide a lot of negative feedback.

Organizations will generally benefit from a workforce with high self-esteem. Such people tend to make more fulfilling career decisions, they exhibit higher job satisfaction and job performance, and they are generally more resilient to the strains of everyday worklife.[30] What can organizations do to bolster self-esteem? Opportunity for participation in decision making, autonomy, and interesting work have been fairly consistently found to be positively related to self-esteem.[31] Also, organizations should avoid creating a culture with excessive and petty work rules that signal to employees that they are incompetent or untrustworthy.[32]

NEW DEVELOPMENTS IN PERSONALITY AND ORGANIZATIONAL BEHAVIOUR

In recent years, there have been a number of exciting developments in personality research in organizational behaviour. In this section, we describe five recent personality variables that have been found to be important for organizational behaviour: positive and negative affectivity, proactive personality, general self-efficacy, and core self-evaluations.

LO 2.5

Discuss *positive* and *negative affectivity*, *proactive personality*, *general self-efficacy*, and *core self-evaluations* and their consequences.

Positive and Negative Affectivity

Have you ever known somebody who is always happy, cheerful, and in a good mood? Or perhaps you know someone who is always unhappy and in a bad mood. Chances are you have noticed these differences in people. Some people are happy most of the time, while others are almost always unhappy. These differences reflect two affective dispositions known as positive affectivity (PA) and negative affectivity (NA). Research has found that they are enduring personality characteristics and that there might be a genetic and biological bases to them.

People who are high on **positive affectivity** experience positive emotions and moods like joy and excitement and view the world in a positive light, including themselves and other people. They tend to be cheerful, enthusiastic, lively, sociable, and energetic. People who are high on **negative affectivity** experience negative emotions and moods like fear and anxiety and view the world in a negative light. They have an overall negative view of themselves and the world around them, and they tend to be distressed, depressed, and unhappy.[33] It is important to understand that PA and NA are not opposite ends of a continuum but are relatively independent dimensions.[34]

Unlike the other personality traits discussed in this chapter, positive and negative affectivity are emotional dispositions that predict people's general emotional tendencies. Thus, they can influence people's emotions and mood states at work and influence job attitudes and work behaviours. Research has found that people who are high on PA have higher job satisfaction, job performance, and engage in more organizational citizenship behaviours. High PA employees have also been found to be more creative at work. Individuals who are high on NA report lower job satisfaction and have poorer job performance. High NA employees tend to experience more stressful work conditions and report higher levels of workplace stress and strain. NA has also been found to be associated with counterproductive work behaviours (e.g., harassment and physical aggression), withdrawal behaviours (e.g., absenteeism and turnover), and occupational injury. Finally, there is some evidence that PA is a key factor that links happiness to success in life and at work.[35]

Positive affectivity. Propensity to view the world, including oneself and other people, in a positive light.

Negative affectivity. Propensity to view the world, including oneself and other people, in a negative light.

Proactive Personality

How effective are you at taking initiative and changing your circumstances? Taking initiative to improve one's current circumstances or creating new ones is known as **proactive behaviour.** It involves challenging the status quo rather than passively adapting to present conditions. Some people are actually better at this than others because they have a stable disposition toward proactive behaviour, known as a "proactive personality." Individuals who have a **proactive personality** are relatively unconstrained by situational forces and act to change and influence their environment. Proactive personality is a stable personal disposition that reflects a tendency to take personal initiative across a range of activities and situations and to effect positive change in one's environment.[36]

Proactive individuals search for and identify opportunities, show initiative, take action, and persevere until they bring about meaningful change. People who do not have a proactive personality are more likely to be passive and to react and adapt to their environment. As a result, they tend to endure and to be shaped by the environment instead of trying to change it.[37]

Proactive personality has been found to be related to a number of work outcomes, including job satisfaction, job performance, organizational citizenship behaviours, tolerance for stress in demanding jobs, leadership effectiveness, participation in organizational initiatives, work team performance, and entrepreneurship. One study found that proactive personality is associated with higher performance evaluations because individuals with a proactive personality develop strong supportive networks and perform initiative-taking behaviours such as implementing solutions to organization or departmental problems or spearheading new programs. Individuals with a proactive personality have also been found to have high-quality relationships with their supervisors. There is also evidence that persons with a proactive personality are more successful in searching for employment and career success. They are more likely to find a job, to receive higher salaries and more frequent promotions, and to have more satisfying careers.[38]

General Self-Efficacy

General self-efficacy (GSE) is a general trait that refers to an individual's belief in his or her ability to perform successfully in a variety of challenging situations.[39] GSE is considered to be a *motivational* trait rather than an *affective* trait because it reflects an individual's belief that he or she can succeed at a variety of tasks rather than how an individual feels about him or herself. An individual's GSE is believed to develop over the lifespan as repeated successes and failures are experienced across a variety of tasks and situations. Thus, if you have experienced many successes in your life, you probably have high GSE, whereas somebody who has experienced many failures probably has low GSE. Individuals who are high on GSE are better able to adapt to novel, uncertain, and adverse situations. In addition, employees with higher GSE have higher job satisfaction and job performance.[40]

Core Self-Evaluations

Unlike the other personality characteristics described in this chapter, which are specific in themselves, **core self-evaluations** refers to a broad personality concept that consists of more specific traits. The idea behind the theory of core self-evaluations is that individuals hold evaluations about themselves and their self-worth or worthiness, competence, and capability.[41] In a review of the personality literature, Timothy Judge, Edwin Locke, and Cathy Durham identified four traits that make up a person's core self-evaluation. The four traits have already been described in this chapter; they include self-esteem, general self-efficacy, locus of control, and neuroticism (emotional stability).

Research on core self-evaluations has found that these traits are among the best dispositional predictors of job satisfaction and job performance. People with more positive core self-evaluations have higher job satisfaction, organizational commitment, and job performance. Furthermore, research has shown that core self-evaluations measured in childhood and in early adulthood are related to job satisfaction in middle adulthood. This suggests that core self-evaluations are related to job satisfaction over time. Core self-evaluations have also been found to be positively related to life and career satisfaction, and individuals with higher CSE perceive fewer stressors and experience less stress and conflict at work. One of the reasons for the relationship between core self-evaluations and work outcomes is that individuals with a positive self-regard are more likely to perceive and pay attention to the positive aspects of their environments. They experience their job as more intrinsically satisfying and have higher perceptions of fairness and support.[42]

WHAT IS LEARNING?

LO 2.6

Define *learning* and describe what is learned in organizations.

So far in this chapter we have described how people's personalities can influence their work attitudes and behaviours. However, recall our earlier discussion that the organizational setting can also can have a strong effect on an individual's attitudes and behaviour. As you will learn in this section, the environment can change people's behaviour and even shape personalities. As described at the start of the chapter, employees at Economical changed their lifestyle behaviours. But how does this happen? How and why do people change their behaviour? To try and answer this question, let's examine the concept of learning.

Learning occurs when practice or experience leads to a relatively permanent change in behaviour potential. The words *practice* or *experience* rule out viewing behavioural changes caused by factors like drug intake or biological maturation as learning. One does not learn to be relaxed after taking a tranquilizer, and a boy does not suddenly learn to be a bass singer at the age of 14. The practice or experience that prompts learning stems from an environment that gives feedback concerning the consequences of behaviour. But what do employees learn in organizations?

Learning. A relatively permanent change in behaviour potential that occurs due to practice or experience.

What Do Employees Learn?

Learning in organizations can be understood in terms of taxonomies that indicate what employees learn, how they learn, and different types of learning experiences. The "what" aspect of learning can be described as learning content, of which there are four primary categories: practical skills, intrapersonal skills, interpersonal skills, and cultural awareness.[43]

Practical skills include job-specific skills, knowledge, and technical competence. Employees frequently learn new skills and technologies to continually improve performance and to keep organizations competitive. Constant improvement has become a major goal in many organizations today, and learning can give an organization a competitive advantage.[44] *Intrapersonal skills* are skills such as problem solving, critical thinking, learning about alternative work processes, and risk taking. *Interpersonal skills* include interactive skills such as communicating, teamwork, and conflict resolution. Later in this book, we will discuss the ways in which teams are becoming the major building blocks of organizations, as well as the importance of effective communication for organizational success.

Finally, *cultural awareness* involves learning the social norms of organizations and understanding company goals, business operations, and company expectations and priorities. All employees need to learn the cultural norms and expectations of their organizations to function as effective organizational members. We discuss the learning of social norms and organizational culture in more detail in Chapter 8.

Now that we have considered what people learn in organizations, let's turn to two theories that describe how people in organizations like Economical learn.

LO 2.7

Explain *operant learning theory* and differentiate between *positive* and *negative reinforcements*.

Operant learning. Learning by which the subject learns to operate on the environment to achieve certain consequences.

Operant Learning Theory

In the 1930s, psychologist B.F. Skinner investigated the behaviour of rats confined in a box containing a lever that delivered food pellets when pulled. Initially, the rats ignored the lever, but at some point they would accidentally pull it and a pellet would appear. Over time, the rats gradually acquired the lever-pulling response as a means of obtaining food. In other words, they *learned* to pull the lever. The kind of learning Skinner studied is called **operant learning** because the subject learns to operate on the environment to achieve certain consequences. The rats learned to operate the lever to achieve food. Notice that operantly learned behaviour is controlled by the consequences that follow it. These consequences usually depend on the behaviour, and this connection is what is learned. For example, salespeople learn effective sales techniques to achieve commissions and avoid criticism from their managers. The consequences of commissions and criticism depend on which sales behaviours salespeople exhibit.

Operant learning can be used to increase the probability of desired behaviours and to reduce or eliminate the probability of undesirable behaviours. Let's now consider how this is done.

INCREASING THE PROBABILITY OF BEHAVIOUR

Reinforcement. The process by which stimuli strengthen behaviours.

One of the most important consequences that influences behaviour is reinforcement. **Reinforcement** is the process by which stimuli strengthen behaviours. Thus, a *reinforcer* is a stimulus that follows some behaviour and increases or maintains the probability of that behaviour. The sales commissions and criticism mentioned earlier are reinforcers for salespeople. In each case, reinforcement serves to strengthen behaviours, such as proper sales techniques, that fulfill organizational goals. In general, organizations are interested in maintaining or increasing the probability of behaviours such as correct performance, prompt attendance, and accurate decision making. As described at the beginning of the chapter, Economical is interested in maintaining and increasing the probability of various employee wellness behaviours, such as physical activity and healthy eating. As we shall see, positive reinforcers work by their application to a situation, while negative reinforcers work by their removal from a situation.

Positive Reinforcement

Positive reinforcement. The application or addition of a stimulus that increases or maintains the probability of some behaviour.

Positive reinforcement increases or maintains the probability of some behaviour by the *application* or *addition* of a stimulus to the situation in question. Such a stimulus is a positive reinforcer. In the basic Skinnerian learning situation described earlier, we can assume that reinforcement occurred because the probability of the lever operation increased over time. We can further assume that the food pellets were positive reinforcers because they were introduced after the lever was pulled.

Consider the experienced securities analyst who tends to read a particular set of financial newspapers regularly. If we had been able to observe the development of this reading habit, we might have found that it occurred as the result of a series of successful business decisions. That is, the analyst learns to scan those papers because his or her reading is positively reinforced by subsequent successful decisions. In this example, something is added to the situation (favourable decisions) that increases the probability of certain behaviour (selective reading). Also, the appearance of the reinforcer is dependent or contingent on the occurrence of that behaviour.

In general, positive reinforcers tend to be pleasant things, such as food, praise, money, or business success. However, the intrinsic character of stimuli does not determine whether they are positive reinforcers, and pleasant stimuli are not positive reinforcers when considered in the abstract. Whether or not something is a positive reinforcer depends only on whether it increases or maintains the occurrence of some behaviour by its application. Thus, it is improbable that the holiday turkey that employers give to all the employees of a manufacturing plant positively reinforces anything. The only behaviour that the receipt of the turkey is contingent on is being employed by the company during the third week of December. It is unlikely that the turkey increases the probability that employees will remain for another year or work harder.

Negative Reinforcement

Negative reinforcement increases or maintains the probability of some behaviour by the *removal* of a stimulus from the situation in question. Also, negative reinforcement occurs when a response *prevents* some event or stimulus from occurring. In each case, the removed or prevented stimulus is a *negative reinforcer.* Negative reinforcers are usually aversive or unpleasant stimuli, and it stands to reason that we will learn to repeat behaviours that remove or prevent these stimuli.

Let's repeat this point, because it frequently confuses students of organizational behaviour: Negative reinforcers *increase* the probability of behaviour. Suppose we rig a cage with an electrified floor so that it provides a mild shock to its inhabitant. In addition, we install a lever that will turn off the electricity. On the first few trials, a rat put in the cage will become very upset when shocked. Sooner or later, however, it will accidentally operate the lever and turn off the current. Gradually, the rat will learn to operate the lever as soon as it feels the shock. The shock serves as a negative reinforcer for the lever pulling, increasing the probability of the behaviour by its removal.

Managers who continually nag their employees unless the employees work hard are attempting to use negative reinforcement. The only way employees can stop the aversive nagging is to work hard and be diligent. The nagging maintains the probability of productive responses by its removal. In this situation, employees often get pretty good at anticipating the onset of nagging by the look on their boss's face. This look serves as a signal that they can avoid the nagging altogether if they work harder.

Negative reinforcers generally tend to be unpleasant things, such as shock, nagging, or threat of fines. Again, however, negative reinforcers are defined only by what they do and how they work, not by their unpleasantness. Above, we indicated that nagging could serve as a negative reinforcer to increase the probability of productive responses. However, nagging could also serve as a positive reinforcer to increase the probability of unproductive responses if an employee has a need for attention and nagging is the only attention the manager provides. In the first case, nagging is a negative reinforcer—it is terminated following productive responses. In the second case, nagging is a positive reinforcer—it is applied following unproductive responses. In both cases, the responses increase in probability.

Organizational Errors Involving Reinforcement

Experience indicates that managers sometimes make errors in trying to use reinforcement. The most common errors are confusing rewards with reinforcers, neglecting diversity in preferences for reinforcers, and neglecting important sources of reinforcement.

CONFUSING REWARDS WITH REINFORCERS   Organizations and individual managers frequently "reward" workers with things such as pay, promotions, fringe benefits, paid vacations, overtime work, and the opportunity to perform challenging tasks. Such rewards can fail to serve as reinforcers, however, because organizations do not make them contingent on specific behaviours that are of interest to the organization, such as attendance, innovation, or productivity. For example, many organizations assign overtime work on the basis of seniority, rather than performance or good attendance, even when the union contract does not require it. Although the opportunity to earn extra money might have strong potential as a reinforcer, it is seldom made contingent on some desired behaviour. Notice how the incentives and points awarded as part of Economical's wellness program were all contingent on specific behaviours.

Negative reinforcement. The removal of a stimulus that in turn increases or maintains the probability of some behaviour.

NEGLECTING DIVERSITY IN PREFERENCES FOR REINFORCERS Organizations often fail to appreciate individual differences in preferences for reinforcers. In this case, even if managers administer rewards after a desired behaviour, they may fail to have a reinforcing effect. Intuitively, it seems questionable to reinforce a workaholic's extra effort with time off from work, yet such a strategy is fairly common. A more appropriate reinforcer might be the assignment of some challenging task, such as work on a very demanding key project. Some labour contracts include clauses that dictate that supervisors assign overtime to the workers who have the greatest seniority. Not surprisingly, high-seniority workers are often the best paid and the least in need of the extra pay available through overtime. Even if it is administered so that the best-performing high-seniority workers get the overtime, such a strategy might not prove reinforcing—the usual time off might be preferred over extra money.

Managers should carefully explore the possible range of stimuli under their control (such as task assignment and time off from work) for their applicability as reinforcers for particular employees. For example, there is some evidence that employee preferences vary as a function of generational differences with younger workers in their 20s and 30s preferring cash rewards and older workers preferring more experiential rewards, like a vacation.[45] Furthermore, organizations should attempt to administer their formal rewards (such as pay and promotions) to capitalize on their reinforcing effects for various individuals.

NEGLECTING IMPORTANT SOURCES OF REINFORCEMENT There are many reinforcers of organizational behaviour that are not especially obvious. While concentrating on potential reinforcers of a formal nature, such as pay or promotions, organizations and their managers often neglect those that are administered by co-workers or are intrinsic to the jobs being performed. Many managers cannot understand why a worker would persist in potentially dangerous horseplay despite threats of a pay penalty or dismissal. Frequently, such activity is positively reinforced by the attention provided by the joker's co-workers. In fact, on a particularly boring job, such threats might act as positive reinforcers for horseplay by relieving the boredom, especially if the threats are never carried out. Two important sources of reinforcement that managers often ignore are performance feedback and social recognition.

Performance feedback. Providing quantitative or qualitative information on past performance for the purpose of changing or maintaining performance in specific ways.

- *Performance feedback.* **Performance feedback** involves providing quantitative or qualitative information on past performance for the purpose of changing or maintaining performance in specific ways. This reinforcement is available for jobs that provide feedback concerning the adequacy of performance. For example, in some jobs, feedback contingent on performance is readily available. Doctors can observe the success of their treatment by observing the progress of their patients' health, and mechanics can take the cars they repair for a test drive. In other jobs, organizations must build some special feedback mechanism into the job. Performance feedback is most effective when it is (a) conveyed in a positive manner, (b) delivered immediately after the performance is observed, (c) represented visually, such as in graph or chart form, and (d) specific to the behaviour that is being targeted for feedback.[46]

Social recognition. Informal acknowledgement, attention, praise, approval, or genuine appreciation for work well done from one individual or group to another.

- *Social recognition.* **Social recognition** involves informal acknowledgement, attention, praise, approval, or genuine appreciation for work well done from one individual or group to another. Research has shown that when social recognition is made contingent on employee behaviour it can be an effective means for performance improvement.[47]

In summary, managers should understand that positive feedback and a "pat on the back" for a job well done are positive reinforcers that are easy to administer and likely to reinforce desirable behaviours.

REINFORCEMENT STRATEGIES

LO 2.8

What is the best way to administer reinforcers? Should we apply a reinforcer immediately after the behaviour of interest occurs, or should we wait for some period of time? Should we reinforce every correct behaviour, or should we reinforce only a portion of correct responses?

To obtain the *fast acquisition* of some response, continuous and immediate reinforcement should be used—that is, the reinforcer should be applied every time the behaviour of interest occurs, and it should be applied without delay after each occurrence. Many conditions exist in which the fast acquisition of responses is desirable. These include correcting the behaviour of "problem" employees, training employees for emergency operations, and dealing with unsafe work behaviours. Consider the otherwise excellent performer who tends to be late for work. Under pressure to demote or fire this good worker, the boss might sensibly attempt to positively reinforce instances of prompt attendance with compliments and encouragement. To modify the employee's behaviour as quickly as possible, the supervisor might station herself near the office door each morning to supply these reinforcers regularly and immediately.

You might wonder when one would not want to use a continuous, immediate reinforcement strategy to mould organizational behaviour. Put simply, behaviour that individuals learn under such conditions tends not to persist when reinforced less frequently or stopped. Intuitively, this should not be surprising. For example, under normal conditions, operating the power switch on your iPod is continuously and immediately reinforced by music. If the system develops a short circuit and fails to produce music, your switch-operating behaviour will cease very quickly. In the example in the preceding paragraph, the need for fast learning justified the use of continuous, immediate reinforcement. Under more typical circumstances, we would hope that prompt attendance could occur without such close attention.

Behaviour tends to be *persistent* when it is learned under conditions of partial and delayed reinforcement. That is, it will tend to persist under reduced or terminated reinforcement when not every instance of the behaviour is reinforced during learning or when some time period elapses between its enactment and reinforcement. In most cases, the supervisor who wishes to reinforce prompt attendance knows that he or she will not be able to stand by the shop door every morning to compliment the crew's timely entry. Given this constraint, the supervisor should compliment prompt attendance occasionally, perhaps later in the day. This should increase the persistence of promptness and reduce the employees' reliance on the boss's monitoring.

Let's recap. Continuous, immediate reinforcement facilitates fast learning, and delayed, partial reinforcement facilitates persistent learning (see Exhibit 2.3). Notice that it is impossible to maximize both speed and persistence with a single reinforcement strategy. Also, many responses in our everyday lives cannot be continuously and immediately reinforced, so in

Explain when to use immediate versus delayed reinforcement and when to use continuous versus partial reinforcement.

EXHIBIT 2.3 Summary of reinforcement strategies and their effects.

[Explore

Go to MyManagementLab to see an annotated version of this figure.

many cases it pays to sacrifice some speed in learning to prepare the learner for this fact of life. All this suggests that managers have to tailor reinforcement strategies to the needs of the situation. Often, managers must alter the strategies over time to achieve effective learning and maintenance of behaviour. For example, the manager training a new employee should probably use a reinforcement strategy that is fairly continuous and immediate (whatever the reinforcer). Looking over the employee's shoulder to obtain the fast acquisition of behaviour is appropriate. Gradually, however, the supervisor should probably reduce the frequency of reinforcement and perhaps build some delay into its presentation to reduce the employee's dependency on his or her attention.

LO 2.9

Distinguish between *extinction* and *punishment* and explain how to use punishment effectively.

REDUCING THE PROBABILITY OF BEHAVIOUR

Thus far in our discussion of learning, we have been interested in *increasing* the probability of various work behaviours, such as attendance or good performance. Both positive and negative reinforcement can accomplish this goal. However, in many cases, we encounter learned behaviours that we wish to *stop* from occurring. Such behaviours are detrimental to the operation of the organization and could be detrimental to the health or safety of an individual employee.

There are two strategies that can reduce the probability of learned behaviour: extinction and punishment.

Extinction

Extinction. The gradual dissipation of behaviour following the termination of reinforcement.

Extinction simply involves terminating the reinforcement that is maintaining some unwanted behaviour. If the behaviour is not reinforced, it will gradually dissipate or be extinguished.

Consider the case of a bright, young marketing expert who was headed for the "fast track" in his organization. Although his boss, the vice-president of marketing, was considering him for promotion, the young expert had developed a very disruptive habit—the tendency to play comedian during department meetings. The vice-president observed that this wisecracking was reinforced by the appreciative laughs of two other department members. He proceeded to enlist their aid to extinguish the joking. After the vice-president explained the problem to them, they agreed to ignore the disruptive one-liners and puns. At the same time, the vice-president took special pains to positively reinforce constructive comments by the young marketer. Very quickly, joking was extinguished, and the young man's future with the company improved.[48]

This example illustrates that extinction works best when coupled with the reinforcement of some desired substitute behaviour. Remember that behaviours that have been learned under delayed or partial reinforcement schedules are more difficult to extinguish than those learned under continuous, immediate reinforcement. Ironically, it would be harder to extinguish the joke-telling behaviour of a committee member who was only partially successful at getting a laugh than of one who was always successful at getting a laugh.

Punishment

Punishment. The application of an aversive stimulus following some behaviour designed to decrease the probability of that behaviour.

Punishment involves following an unwanted behaviour with some unpleasant, aversive stimulus. In theory, when the actor learns that the behaviour leads to unwanted consequences, this should reduce the probability of the response. Notice the difference between punishment and

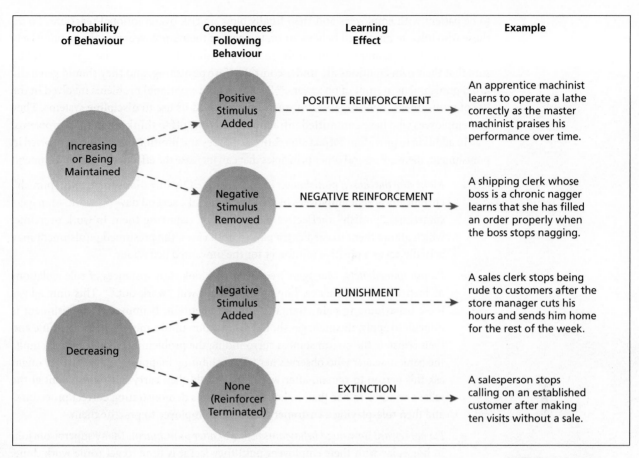

Probability of Behaviour	Consequences Following Behaviour	Learning Effect	Example
Increasing or Being Maintained	Positive Stimulus Added	POSITIVE REINFORCEMENT	An apprentice machinist learns to operate a lathe correctly as the master machinist praises his performance over time.
	Negative Stimulus Removed	NEGATIVE REINFORCEMENT	A shipping clerk whose boss is a chronic nagger learns that she has filled an order properly when the boss stops nagging.
Decreasing	Negative Stimulus Added	PUNISHMENT	A sales clerk stops being rude to customers after the store manager cuts his hours and sends him home for the rest of the week.
	None (Reinforcer Terminated)	EXTINCTION	A salesperson stops calling on an established customer after making ten visits without a sale.

EXHIBIT 2.4 Summary of learning effects.

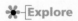 Explore

Go to MyManagementLab to see an annotated version of this figure.

negative reinforcement. In negative reinforcement a nasty stimulus is *removed* following some behaviour, increasing the probability of that behaviour. With punishment, a nasty stimulus is *applied* after some behaviour, *decreasing* the probability of that behaviour. If a boss criticizes her assistant after seeing her use the office phone for personal calls, we expect to see less of this activity in the future. Exhibit 2.4 compares punishment with reinforcement and extinction.

Using Punishment Effectively

In theory, punishment should be useful in eliminating unwanted behaviour. After all, it seems unreasonable to repeat actions that cause us trouble. Unfortunately, punishment has some unique characteristics that often limit its effectiveness in stopping unwanted activity. First, while punishment provides a clear signal as to which activities are inappropriate, it does not by itself demonstrate which activities should *replace* the punished response. Reconsider the executive who chastises her assistant for making personal calls at the office. If the assistant makes personal calls only when she has caught up on her work, she might legitimately wonder what she is supposed to be doing during her occasional free time. If the boss fails to provide substitute activities, the message contained in the punishment may be lost.

Both positive and negative reinforcers specify which behaviours are appropriate. Punishment indicates only what is not appropriate. Since no reinforced substitute behaviour is provided, punishment only temporarily suppresses the unwanted response. When surveillance is removed, the response will tend to recur. Constant monitoring is very time consuming, and individuals become amazingly adept at learning when they can get away with the forbidden activity. The assistant will soon learn when she can make personal calls without detection. The moral here is clear: *Provide an acceptable alternative for the punished response.*

A second difficulty with punishment is that it has a tendency to provoke a strong emotional reaction on the part of the punished individual.[49] This is especially likely when the punishment is delivered in anger or perceived to be unfair. Managers who try overly hard to be patient with employees and then finally blow up risk overemotional reactions. So do those who tolerate unwanted behaviour on the part of their employees and then impulsively decide to make an example of one individual by punishing him or her. Managers should be sure that their own emotions are under control before punishing, and they should generally avoid punishment in front of observers.[50] Because of the emotional problems involved in the use of punishment, some organizations have downplayed its use in discipline systems. They give employees who have committed infractions *paid* time off to think about their problems.

In addition to providing correct alternative responses and limiting the emotions involved in punishment, there are several other principles that can increase the effectiveness of punishment.

- *Make sure the chosen punishment is truly aversive.* Organizations frequently "punish" chronically absent employees by making them take several days off work. Managers sometimes "punish" ineffective performers by requiring them to work overtime, which allows them to earn extra pay. In both cases, the presumed punishment may actually act as a positive reinforcer for the unwanted behaviour.

- *Punish immediately.* Managers frequently overlook early instances of rule violations or ineffective performance, hoping that things will "work out."[51] This only allows these behaviours to gain strength through repetition. If immediate punishment is difficult to apply, the manager should delay action until a more appropriate time and then reinstate the circumstances surrounding the problem behaviour. For example, the bank manager who observes her teller exhibiting inappropriate behaviour might ask this person to remain after work. She should then carry out punishment at the teller's window rather than in her office, perhaps demonstrating correct procedures and then role-playing a customer to allow the employee to practise them.

- *Do not reward unwanted behaviours before or after punishment.* Many supervisors join in horseplay with their employees until they feel it is time to get some work done. Then, unexpectedly, they do an about-face and punish those who are still "goofing around." Sometimes, managers feel guilty about punishing their employees for some rule infraction and then quickly attempt to make up with displays of good-natured sympathy or affection. For example, the boss who criticizes her assistant for personal calls might show up an hour later with a gift. Such actions present employees with extremely confusing signals about how they should behave, since the manager could be unwittingly reinforcing the very response that he or she wants to terminate.

- *Do not inadvertently punish desirable behaviour.* This happens commonly in organizations. The manager who does not use all his capital budget for a given fiscal year might have the department's budget for the next year reduced, punishing the prudence of his employees. Government employees who "blow the whistle" on wasteful or inefficient practices might find themselves demoted.[52] University professors who are considered excellent teachers might be assigned to onerous, time-consuming duty on a curriculum committee, cutting into their class preparation time.

In summary, punishment can be an effective means of stopping undesirable behaviour. However, managers must apply it very carefully and deliberately to achieve this effectiveness. In general, reinforcing correct behaviours and extinguishing unwanted responses are safer strategies for managers than the frequent use of punishment.

SOCIAL COGNITIVE THEORY

LO 2.10

Explain *social cognitive theory* and discuss *observational learning*, *self-efficacy beliefs*, and *self-regulation*.

It has perhaps occurred to you that learning and behaviour sometimes takes place in organizations without the conscious control of positive and negative reinforcers by managers. People often learn and behave through their own volition and self-influence. Thus, human behaviour is not simply due to environmental influences. Rather, people have the cognitive capacity to regulate and control their own thoughts, feelings, motivation, and actions. Unlike operant learning theory, **social cognitive theory (SCT)** emphasizes the role of *cognitive processes* in regulating people's behaviour.

According to SCT, people learn by observing the behaviour of others. Individuals also manage their own behaviour by thinking about the consequences of their actions (forethought), setting performance goals, monitoring their performance and comparing it to their goals, and rewarding themselves for goal accomplishment. People also develop beliefs about their abilities through their interaction with the environment, and these beliefs influence their thoughts and behaviour.[53]

Social cognitive theory suggests that human behaviour can best be explained through a system of *triadic reciprocal causation*, in which personal factors and environmental factors work together and interact to influence people's behaviour. In addition, people's behaviour can also influence personal factors and the environment. Thus, SCT complements operant learning in explaining how people learn and organizational behaviour.[54]

According to Albert Bandura, who is responsible for the development of social cognitive theory, SCT involves three key components: observational learning, self-efficacy beliefs, and self-regulation.[55]

Observational Learning

Besides directly experiencing consequences, people also learn by observing the behaviour of others. For instance, after experiencing just a couple of executive committee meetings, a newly promoted vice-president might look like an "old pro," bringing appropriate materials to the meeting, asking questions in an approved style, and so on. How can we account for such learning?

Observational learning is the process of observing and imitating the behaviour of others. With observational learning, learning occurs by observing or imagining the behaviour of others (models), rather than through direct personal experience.[56] Generally, observational learning involves examining the behaviour of others, seeing what consequences they experience, and thinking about what might happen if we act the same way. If we expect favourable consequences, we might imitate the behaviour. Thus, the new vice-president doubtless modelled his behaviour on that of the more experienced peers on the executive committee. But has reinforcement occurred here? It is *self-reinforcement* that occurs in the observational learning process. For one thing, it is reinforcing to acquire an understanding of others who are viewed positively. In addition, we are able to imagine that the reinforcers that the model experiences will come our way when we imitate his or her behaviour. Surely, this is why we imitate the behaviour of sports heroes and entertainers, a fact that advertisers capitalize on when they choose them to endorse products.

What kinds of models are likely to provoke the greatest degree of imitation? In general, attractive, credible, competent, high-status people stand a good chance of being imitated. In addition, it is important that the model's behaviour provoke consequences that are seen as positive and successful by the observer. You might recall that in the chapter-opening vignette senior executives at Economical acted as role models by sharing their personal wellness-related stories.

Finally, it helps if the model's behaviour is vivid and memorable—bores do not make good models.[57] In business schools, it is not unusual to find students who have developed philosophies or approaches that are modelled on credible, successful, high-profile business leaders. Popular examples include Microsoft's Bill Gates and former General Electric CEO Jack Welch, both of whom have been the object of extensive coverage in the business and popular press.

The extent of observational learning as a means of learning in organizations suggests that managers should pay more attention to the process. For one thing, managers who operate on a principle of "do as I say, not as I do" will find that what they do is more likely to be imitated, including undesirable behaviours such as expense account abuse. Also, in the

Social cognitive theory (SCT). Emphasizes the role of cognitive processes in learning and in the regulation of people's behaviour.

Observational learning. The process of observing and imitating the behaviour of others.

RESEARCH FOCUS

THE TRICKLE-DOWN EFFECTS OF ABUSIVE MANAGEMENT

There is strong evidence that abusive supervisors (e.g., telling a subordinate that his or her thoughts or feelings are stupid or putting the subordinate down in front of others) result in negative employee attitudes, behaviours, and psychological health. But why are supervisors abusive and does their abusive behaviour make their employees more likely to be abusive?

To find out, Mary Bardes Mawritz and colleagues tested a model of the trickle-down effects of abusive manager behaviour that suggests that abusive behaviour in organizations can flow downward from higher levels of management to lower level employees. The model predicts that employees will be negatively impacted by abusive manager behaviour through their direct supervisor's abusive behaviour.

The model and predictions are based on social cognitive theory and observational learning such that abusive behaviour at higher levels in an organization is role modelled by those at lower levels (i.e., supervisors and employees). In other words, supervisors role model the abusive behaviour of their managers and engage in similar abusive behaviour with their own employees. Employees then model their supervisor's abusive behaviour which leads to workgroup interpersonal deviance (i.e., employees' abusive behaviours directed at other organizational members).

The researchers also predicted that the effect of abusive supervisor behaviour on workgroup interpersonal deviance will be especially strong when the workgroup climate is hostile (a climate that is characterized by consistent acrimonious, antagonistic, and suspicious feelings within the work group). In a hostile climate, workgroup members feel envious, less trusting, and aggressive toward others.

Employees in different organizations completed a survey and asked four of their co-workers and their immediate supervisor to also complete the survey. As expected, abusive manager behaviour was positively related to abusive supervisor behaviour, and abusive supervisor behaviour was positively related to workgroup interpersonal deviance. In other words, supervisors who have managers who are abusive toward them are abusive toward their employees, who in turn treat each other in an abusive manner.

The results also indicated that employees were more likely to model their supervisor's abusive behaviour when the climate of their workgroup was hostile. When the workgroup climate was non-hostile it actually reversed the negative effects of abusive supervisor behaviour on workgroup interpersonal deviance. Thus, employees in a non-hostile work climate did not model their supervisor's abusive behaviour.

These results indicate that employees observe and imitate their supervisor's negative and abusive behaviours. Thus, managers and supervisors should act as positive role models because their behaviours, both positive and negative, will trickle down and be observed and imitated by their employees.

Source: Based on Bardes Mawritz, M., Mayer, D.M., Hoobler, J.M., Wayne, S.J., & Marinova, S.V. (2012). A trickle-down model of abusive supervision. *Personnel Psychology, 65,* 325–357.

absence of credible management models, workers might imitate dysfunctional peer behaviour if peers meet the criteria for strong models. For example, one study found that the antisocial behaviour of a work group was a significant predictor of an individual's antisocial workplace behaviour. Thus, individual's antisocial workplace behaviour can be shaped, in part, through the process of observation.[58] Furthermore, as described in the Research Focus: *The Trickle-Down Effects of Abusive Management,* abusive behaviour on the part of managers and supervisors can lead to abusive behaviour among employees. On a more positive note, well-designed performance appraisal and reward systems permit organizations to publicize the kind of organizational behaviour that should be learned and imitated.

Self-Efficacy Beliefs

Self-efficacy beliefs.
Beliefs people have about their ability to successfully perform a specific task.

While observational learning may have helped the vice-president learn how to behave in an executive committee meeting, you may have wondered what made him so confident. Was he not full of self-doubt and worried that he would fail? This belief is known as self-efficacy. **Self-efficacy beliefs** refer to beliefs people have about their ability to successfully perform

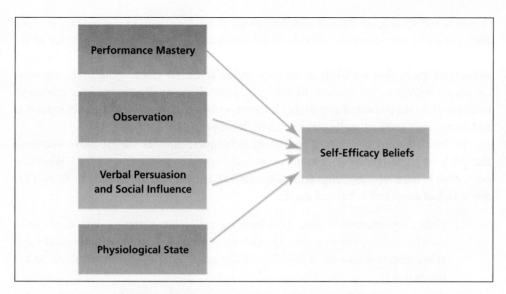

EXHIBIT 2.5
**Determinants of
self-efficacy beliefs.**

Explore

Go to MyManagementLab
to see an annotated
version of this figure.

a specific task. At this point, it is important to note the difference between task-specific self-efficacy and some of the general personality traits discussed earlier in the chapter. In particular, unlike self-esteem and general self-efficacy, which are general personality traits, self-efficacy is a task-specific cognitive appraisal of one's ability to perform a specific task. Thus, it is not a generalized personality trait. Furthermore, people can have different self-efficacy beliefs for different tasks. For example, the vice-president might have strong self-efficacy for conducting an executive committee meeting, but low self-efficacy for doing well in a course on organizational behaviour![59]

Because self-efficacy is a cognitive belief rather than a stable personality trait, it can be changed and modified in response to different sources of information. As shown in Exhibit 2.5, self-efficacy beliefs are influenced by one's experiences and success performing the task in question (performance mastery), observation of others performing the task, verbal persuasion and social influence, and one's physiological or emotional state. Thus, the self-efficacy of the vice-president could have been strengthened by observing the behaviour of others during meetings, by encouragement from peers that he would do a great job, and perhaps by his own sense of comfort and relaxation rather than feelings of anxiety and stress while attending meetings. Finally, his mastery displayed during the meeting is also likely to further strengthen his self-efficacy beliefs.

Self-efficacy beliefs are important because they influence the activities people choose to perform, the amount of effort and persistence they devote to a task, affective and stress reactions, and job performance.[60] In the case of the vice-president, his strong sense of self-efficacy beliefs obviously contributed to his ability to perform like an "old pro" at the meeting.

Self-Regulation

In much of this chapter we have been concerned with how organizations and individual managers can use learning principles to manage the behaviour of organizational members. However, according to social cognitive theory, employees can use learning principles to manage their *own* behaviour, making external control less necessary. This process is called **self-regulation**.[61]

How does self-regulation occur? You will recall that observational learning involved factors such as observation of models, imagination, imitation, and self-reinforcement. Individuals can use these and similar techniques in an intentional way to control their own behaviour. The basic process involves observing one's own behaviour (i.e., self-observation), comparing the behaviour with a standard (i.e., self-evaluation), and rewarding oneself if the behaviour meets the standard (i.e., self-reinforcement). A key part of the process is people's

Self-regulation.
The use of learning principles to regulate one's own behaviour.

pursuit of self-set goals that guide their behaviour. When there exists a discrepancy between one's goals and performance, individuals are motivated to modify their behaviour in the pursuit of goal attainment, a process known as *discrepancy reduction*. When individuals attain their goals, they are likely to set even higher and more challenging goals, a process known as *discrepancy production*. In this way, people continually engage in a process of setting goals in the pursuit of ever higher levels of performance. Thus, discrepancy reduction and discrepancy production lie at the heart of the self-regulatory process.[62]

To illustrate some specific self-regulation techniques, consider the executive who finds that she is taking too much work home to do in the evenings and over weekends. While her peers seem to have most evenings and weekends free, her own family is ready to disown her due to lack of attention! What can she do?[63]

- *Collect self-observation data.* This involves collecting objective data about one's own behaviour. For example, the executive might keep a log of phone calls and other interruptions for a few days if she suspects that these contribute to her inefficiency.
- *Observe models.* The executive might examine the time-management skills of her peers to find someone successful to imitate.
- *Set goals.* The executive might set specific short-term goals to reduce telephone interruptions and unscheduled personal visits, enlisting the aid of her assistant, and using self-observation data to monitor her progress. Longer-term goals might involve four free nights a week and no more than four hours of work on weekends.
- *Rehearse.* The executive might anticipate that she will have to educate her co-workers about her reduced availability. So as not to offend them, she might practise explaining the reason for her revised accessibility.
- *Reinforce oneself.* The executive might promise herself a weekend at the beach with her family the first time she gets her take-home workload down to her target level.

Research has found that self-regulation can improve learning and result in a change in behaviour. For example, one study showed how a self-regulation program was used to improve work attendance among unionized maintenance employees. Those who had used over half their sick leave were invited by the human resources department to participate in an eight-week program with the following features:

- Discussion of general reasons for use of sick leave. High on the list were transportation problems, family difficulties, and problems with supervisors and co-workers.
- Self-assessment of personal reasons for absence and development of personal coping strategies.
- Goal setting to engage in behaviours that should improve attendance (short-term goals) and to improve attendance by a specific amount (long-term goal).
- Self-observation using charts and diaries. Employees recorded their own attendance, reasons for missing work, and steps they took to get to work.
- Identification of specific reinforcers and punishers to be self-administered for reaching or not reaching goals.

Compared with a group of employees who did not attend the program, the employees who were exposed to the program achieved a significant improvement in attendance, and they also felt more confident (i.e., higher self-efficacy) that they would be able to come to work when confronted with various obstacles to attendance.[64] In another study, training in self-regulation was found to significantly improve the sales performance of a sample of insurance salespeople.[65] Self-regulation programs have been successful in changing a variety of work behaviours and are an effective method of training and learning.[66]

ORGANIZATIONAL LEARNING PRACTICES

We began our discussion of learning by defining learning and describing learning content, and then we focused on theories of how people learn. In this final section, we review a number of organizational learning practices (including an application of operant learning called organizational behaviour modification), employee recognition programs, training and development programs, and career development.

Organizational Behaviour Modification

Most reinforcement occurs naturally, rather than as the result of a conscious attempt to manage behaviour. However, if you recall the wellness program at Economical described at the beginning of the chapter, you will notice that reinforcers (i.e., points and money) were used for specific health-related behaviours such as exercise and healthy eating. In other words, the reinforcers were made contingent on specific behaviours. This is an example of organizational behaviour modification.

Organizational behaviour modification (O.B. Mod) involves the systematic use of learning principles to influence organizational behaviour. For example, consider how one company used organizational behaviour modification through the reinforcement of safe working behaviour in a food-manufacturing plant. At first glance, accidents appeared to be chance events or wholly under the control of factors such as equipment failures. However, the researchers felt that accidents could be reduced if specific safe working practices could be identified and reinforced. These practices were identified with the help of past accident reports and advice from supervisors. Systematic observation of working behaviour indicated that employees followed safe practices only about 74 percent of the time. A brief slide show was prepared to illustrate safe versus unsafe job behaviours. Then, two reinforcers of safe practices were introduced into the workplace. The first consisted of a feedback chart that was conspicuously posted in the workplace to indicate the percentage of safe behaviours observers noted. This chart included the percentages achieved in observational sessions before the slide show, as well as those achieved every three days after the slide show. A second source of reinforcement was supervisors, who were encouraged to praise instances of safe performance that they observed. These interventions were successful in raising the percentage of safe working practices to around 97 percent almost immediately. The plant moved from last to first place in the company standings and received a safety plaque from the company "in recognition of successfully working 280 000 hours without a disabling injury" over a period of 10 months. (See Exhibit 2.6.)[67]

LO 2.11

Describe the following organizational learning practices: *organizational behaviour modification, employee recognition programs, training and development programs,* and *career development.*

Organizational behaviour modification (O.B. Mod). The systematic use of learning principles to influence organizational behaviour.

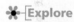
Explore

Go to MyManagementLab to see an annotated version of this figure.

EXHIBIT 2.6 Percentage of safe working practices achieved with and without reinforcement.
Source: Adapted from Komaki, J., et al. (1978, August). A behavioral approach to occupational safety: Pinpointing and reinforcing safe performance in a food manufacturing plant. *Journal of Applied Psychology, 63* (4), 439. Copyright © 1978 by American Psychological Association. Adapted by permission.

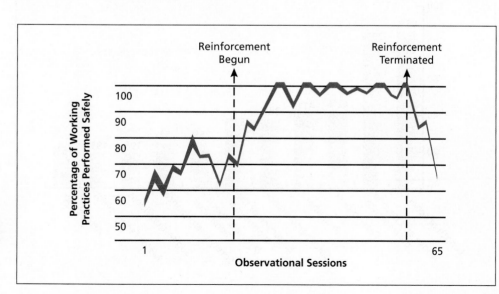

In general, research supports the effectiveness of organizational behaviour modification programs. In addition to improvements in safety, O.B. Mod has also been found to have a positive effect on improving work attendance and task performance. The effects on task performance, however, tend to be stronger in manufacturing than in service organizations. As well, money, feedback, and social recognition have all been found to be effective forms of positive reinforcement. Although money has been found to have stronger effects on performance than social recognition and performance feedback, the use of all three together has the strongest effect on task performance. Research has also found that the effect of money on performance is greater when it is provided systematically through O.B. Mod compared to a routine pay-for-performance program.[68]

Employee Recognition Programs

A popular example of an organizational learning practice that uses positive reinforcement is employee recognition programs. **Employee recognition programs** are formal organizational programs that publicly recognize and reward employees for specific behaviours. Exhibit 2.7 shows some of the most popular types of employee recognition programs.

Many companies in Canada have some form of employee recognition program, and employees in the best companies to work for in Canada believe that they receive adequate recognition beyond compensation for their contributions and accomplishments. To be effective, however, a formal employee recognition program must specify (a) how a person will be recognized, (b) the type of behaviour being encouraged, (c) the manner of the public acknowledgement, and (d) a token or icon of the event for the recipient. A key part of an employee recognition program is public acknowledgement. Thus, a financial reward for good performance would not qualify as an employee recognition program if it was not accompanied by some form of public praise and recognition.[69]

An increasing number of organizations have begun to implement a new kind of recognition program called peer recognition. **Peer recognition programs** are formal programs in which employees can publicly acknowledge, recognize, and reward their co-workers for exceptional work and performance. For example, at Ceridian Canada Ltd. employees can nominate co-workers for monthly prizes, quarterly cash awards, and the chance to win the annual President's Club Award, which includes a paid vacation to a holiday destination. Ceridian recognizes 28 "star" employees each quarter and gives each a $100 gift certificate. At year end, 15 are selected to go on an overseas trip with spouses and senior executives. IT/NET Ottawa Inc. has

Employee recognition programs. Formal organizational programs that publicly recognize and reward employees for specific behaviours.

Peer recognition programs. Formal programs in which employees can publicly acknowledge, recognize, and reward their co-workers for exceptional work and performance.

EXHIBIT 2.7 Types of recognition programs.
Source: Trends in Employee Recognition/WorldatWork. (2008, August 11). Service awards most popular. *Canadian HR Reporter, 21* (14), 4.

 Explore

Go to MyManagementLab to see an annotated version of this figure.

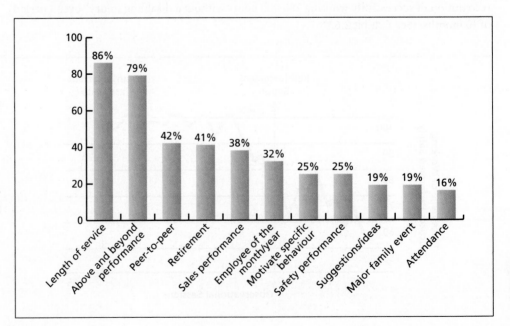

a peer-to-peer recognition program called "My Thanks," in which employees are encouraged to acknowledge co-workers' exceptional work by sending them a cash-valued gift certificate. The value of the certificate is determined by who is awarding it and it can be done any time and as often as employees choose to recognize a co-worker.[70] Before continuing, consider You Be the Manager: *Calgary International Airport's YYC Miles Recognition Program.*

Employee recognition programs have been found to result in a number of individual and organizational outcomes, including job satisfaction, performance and productivity, and lower turnover.[71] One study compared a public recognition program for improving work attendance with several other interventions. Employees with perfect attendance for an entire month had their names posted with a gold star for that month. At the end of each quarter, employees with no more than two absences received a personal card notifying and congratulating them. In addition, at the end of the year there was a plant-wide meeting to recognize good attendance, and small engraved mementos were awarded to employees who had perfect attendance during the entire year. The results indicated that employees had favourable perceptions of the program and that the program resulted in a decrease in absenteeism.[72] A survey of 26 000 employees in 31 organizations in the United States found that companies that invest the most in recognition programs have more than triple the profits of those that invest the least.[73]

Training and Development Programs

Training and development is one of the most common types of formal learning in organizations. Training refers to planned organizational activities that are designed to facilitate knowledge and skill acquisition to change behaviour and improve performance on one's current job; development focuses on future job responsibilities.[74] Employees learn a variety of skills by attending formal training and development programs. In addition to teaching employees technical skills required to perform their jobs, training and development programs also teach employees non-technical skills such as how to work in teams, how to provide excellent customer service, and ways to understand and appreciate cultural diversity.

Effective training and development programs include many of the principles of learning described earlier in the chapter, such as positive reinforcement, feedback, observational

Training and development. Training is planned organizational activities that are designed to facilitate knowledge and skill acquisition to change behaviour and improve performance on one's current job; development focuses on future job responsibilities.

YOU BE THE MANAGER

Calgary International Airport's YYC Miles Recognition Program

The Calgary Airport Authority is a not-for-profit corporation that is responsible for the management, maintenance, operation, and development of Calgary International Airport and Springbank Airport.

Several years ago, a volunteer employee committee developed a recognition program in response to a low score to a question on an employee engagement survey. The low score was for the statement, "I feel my contributions are recognized and valued."

According to Cynthia Tremblay, Senior Director of Human Resources at the Calgary Airport Authority, "We did some employee focus groups (asking), 'What can we do to help address this issue?' and a recognition program was the idea that came out of that. It is very much employee-driven," she says.

The program, called the YYC Miles recognition program—based on the Calgary airport locator code—allows employees to recognize their co-workers for going above and beyond their role, such as helping a confused passenger find his/her way around the airport.

When the program was launched, the employee committee made a promotional video based on the TV show *The Office* and showed it to all employees at a company retreat. To make sure they are continually promoting the program, the committee writes regular articles about it for the company newsletter and mentions it in meetings.

What do you think of the Calgary Airport's YYC Miles recognition program? You be the manager.

Employees at the Calgary International Airport can recognize their co-workers for going above and beyond their role.

Questions

1. How would you design the YYC Miles peer recognition program if you were using the principles of operant learning theory?

2. How should peer recognition programs be designed to be most effective?

To find learn more about the YYC miles recognition program, see The Manager's Notebook.

Sources: Based on Silliker, A. (2011, October 10). Calgary airport's recognition program—YYC Miles—takes flight. *Canadian HR Reporter, 24* (17), 19; information on Calgary International Airport (www.calgaryairport.com).

Behaviour modelling training (BMT). One of the most widely used and effective methods of training, involving five steps based on the observational learning component of social cognitive theory.

learning, strengthening employees' self-efficacy beliefs, and self-regulation. One of the most widely used and effective methods of training is **behaviour modelling training** (BMT), which is based on the observational learning component of social cognitive theory and involves the following steps:[75]

- Describe to trainees a set of well-defined behaviours (skills) to be learned.
- Provide a model or models displaying the effective use of those behaviours.
- Provide opportunities for trainees to practise using those behaviours.
- Provide feedback and social reinforcement to trainees following practice.
- Take steps to maximize the transfer of those behaviours to the job.

Many organizations have used behavioural modelling training to develop supervisory, communications, sales, and customer service skills. A review of BMT research concluded that it has a positive effect on learning, skills, and job behaviour. The effects on behaviour were greatest when trainees were instructed to set goals and when rewards and sanctions were used in the trainees' work environment.[76] Training has been found to increase trainees' self-efficacy in addition to having a positive effect on learning and job behaviour.[77]

Career Development

Career development is an ongoing process in which individuals progress through a series of stages that consist of a unique set of issues, themes, and tasks. This usually involves a career planning and career management component. Career planning involves the assessment of an individual's interests, skills, and abilities in order to develop goals and career plans. Career management involves taking the necessary steps to achieve an individual's goals and career plans. This often involves special assignments and activities that are designed to assist employees in their career development.[78]

Given the increasing emphasis on and importance of continuous and lifelong learning, many organizations now have career development programs. For example, Dun & Bradstreet Canada, a business information services company, has a career development program for all of its employees. Employees have a file called a Leadership Action Plan that lists their strengths and career aspirations as well as a plan on how they will achieve their goals. The file is reviewed by a supervisor four times a year. In addition, an intranet site is available to help employees perform career assessments and access information about job opportunities within the company.[79]

When TD Bank Financial Group surveyed its employees, it found that skills development and career development were very important factors for them. As a result, the company decided to invest more in employee career management and created a website to help employees with all aspects of managing their careers. The Career Advisor site is a comprehensive tool that enables employees to determine how best to develop themselves and overcome career challenges. Employees have access to a combination of interactive diagnostic instruments, personal reports, advice, tools, and action planning exercises.[80]

> **Career development.**
> An ongoing process in which individuals progress through a series of stages that consist of a unique set of issues, themes, and tasks.

THE MANAGER'S NOTEBOOK

Calgary International Airport's YYC Miles Recognition Program

1. According to operant learning theory, rewards should be contingent on specific behaviours that are of interest to the organization, such as attendance, innovation, or productivity. This is especially important in a peer recognition program because employees are responsible for choosing co-workers for recognition, and such choices should not simply be based on who is most liked or who has the most friends in the company. The program also has to consider individual preferences for reinforcers. Rewards will not have a reinforcing effect if they are not desired by employees. Therefore, it is important that a variety of rewards be available to suit individual preferences. With respect to the YYC Miles program, each employee is given 1000 points per month to recognize co-workers. When an employee sees a co-worker go above and beyond his role, she fills out a form online saying why she's recognizing him and how many points he is receiving—which is completely at the discretion of the employee. One point is equivalent to one cent and points can be accumulated for a wide range of gifts from the YYC Miles online catalogue, starting at 1250 points for a movie ticket all the way up to 450 000 points for an LCD TV.

2. Peer recognition programs should be designed in the same manner as formal employee recognition programs. To be effective, they should specify (a) how a person will be recognized, (b) the type of behaviour being encouraged, (c) the manner of the public acknowledgement, and (d) a token or icon of the event for the recipient. Because the employee's peers are responsible for deciding who will be recognized, careful attention should be given to how this is done to ensure that the process is fair and that the expected behaviour has been demonstrated. With respect to the YYC Miles program, the committee monitors the program to make sure people are nominating each other for appropriate things. When filling out a recognition form, employees need to specify which of five pillars of excellence the co-worker displayed—dedicated people, responsible investing, great partnerships, operational efficiency, or Western hospitality.

MyManagementLab   Visit MyManagementLab at **www.mymanagementlab** **.com** for access to online tutorials, interactive exercises, videos, and much more.

LEARNING OBJECTIVES CHECKLIST

2.1 *Personality* is the relatively stable set of psychological characteristics that influences the way we interact with our environment. It has more impact on behaviour in weak situations than in strong situations.

2.2 According to the *dispositional approach*, stable individual characteristics influence people's attitudes and behaviours. The *situational approach* argues that characteristics in the work environment influence people's attitudes and behaviour. The *interactionist approach* posits that organizational behaviour is a function of both dispositions and the situation. According to *trait activation theory*, traits lead to certain behaviours only when the situation makes the need for that trait salient.

2.3 The Five-Factor Model consists of five basic dimensions of personality: *extraversion*, *emotional stability/neuroticism*, *agreeableness*, *conscientiousness*, and *openness to experience*. Research has found that the Big Five are related to job performance, motivation, job satisfaction, and career outcomes.

2.4 *Locus of control* refers to individuals' beliefs about the location of the factors that control their behaviour. High internals believe that the opportunity to control their own behaviour resides within themselves, while high externals believe that external forces determine their behaviour. People who have an internal locus of control are more satisfied with their jobs, earn more money, and achieve higher organizational positions. *Self-monitoring* is the extent to which people observe and regulate how they appear and behave in social settings and relationships. High self-monitors have good communication skills and persuasive abilities and are more likely to change employers and locations and to receive more promotions than individuals who are low self-monitors. *Self-esteem* is the degree

to which a person has a positive self-evaluation. People with high self-esteem tend to make more fulfilling career decisions, to exhibit higher job satisfaction and job performance, and to be generally more resilient to the strains of everyday worklife.

2.5 People who are high on *positive affectivity* experience positive emotions and moods and tend to view the world in a positive light, including themselves and other people. People who are high on *negative affectivity* experience negative emotions and moods and tend to view the world in a negative light. *Proactive personality* is a stable personal disposition that reflects a tendency to take personal initiative across a range of activities and situations and to effect positive change in one's environment. *General self-efficacy* (GSE) is a general trait that refers to an individual's belief in his or her ability to perform successfully in a variety of challenging situations. *Core self-evaluations* refer to a broad personality concept that consists of more specific traits.

2.6 *Learning* occurs when practice or experience leads to a relatively permanent change in behaviour potential. The content of learning in organizations consists of practical, intrapersonal and interpersonal skills, and cultural awareness.

2.7 *Operant learning* occurs as a function of the consequences of behaviour. If some behaviour is occurring regularly or increasing in probability, you can assume that it is being reinforced. If the reinforcer is added to the situation following the behaviour, it is a *positive reinforcer*. If the reinforcer is removed from the situation following the behaviour, it is a *negative reinforcer*.

2.8 Behaviour is learned quickly when it is reinforced immediately and continuously. Behaviour tends to be persistent under reduced or terminated reinforcement when it is learned under conditions of delayed or partial reinforcement.

2.9 If some behaviour decreases in probability, you can assume that it is being either extinguished or punished. If the behaviour is followed by no observable consequence, it is being extinguished; that is, some reinforcer that was maintaining the behaviour has been terminated. If the behaviour is followed by the application of some unpleasant consequence, it is being punished.

2.10 According to social cognitive theory, people have the cognitive capacity to regulate and control their own thoughts, feelings, motivation, and actions. The main components of social cognitive theory are observational learning, self-efficacy beliefs, and self-regulation. *Observational learning* is the process of imitating others. Models are most likely to be imitated when they are high in status, attractive, competent, credible, successful, and vivid. *Self-efficacy beliefs* refer to the belief that one can successfully perform a specific task and is influenced by performance mastery, observation of others performing the task, verbal persuasion and social influence, and physiological arousal. *Self-regulation* occurs when people use learning principles to manage their own behaviour, thus reducing the need for external control. Aspects of self-regulation include collecting self-observation data, observing models, goal setting, rehearsing, and using self-reinforcement.

2.11 Organizational learning practices include organizational behaviour modification, employee recognition programs, training and development programs, and career development. *Organizational behaviour modification* is the systematic use of learning principles to influence organizational behaviour. Companies have successfully used it to improve employees' attendance, task performance, and workplace safety. *Employee recognition programs* are formal organizational programs that publicly recognize and reward employees for specific behaviours. *Training programs* involve planned organizational activities that are designed to facilitate knowledge and skill acquisition and to change behaviour and improve performance on one's current job, while *development* focuses on future job responsibilities. *Career development* is an ongoing process in which individuals progress through a series of stages that consist of a unique set of issues, themes, and tasks. It involves a career planning and career management component.

DISCUSSION QUESTIONS

1. Consider the relevance of the dispositional, situational, and interactionist approaches to your own behaviour. Describe examples of your behaviour in a school or work situation that demonstrate each perspective of organizational behaviour.

2. Suppose that you are the manager of two employees, one who has an internal locus of control and another who has an external locus of control. Describe the leadership tactics that you would use with each employee. Contrast the management styles that you would employ for employees with high versus low self-esteem.

3. Consider some examples of behaviour that you repeat fairly regularly (such as studying or going to work every morning). What are the positive and negative reinforcers that maintain this behaviour?

4. We pointed out that managers frequently resort to punishing ineffective behaviour. What are some of the practical demands of the typical manager's job that lead to this state of affairs?

5. Discuss a situation that you have observed in which the use of punishment was ineffective in terminating some unwanted behaviour. Why was punishment ineffective in this case? What would have made it more effective?

6. Describe a situation in which you think an employer could use organizational behaviour modification and an employee recognition program to improve or correct employee behaviour. Can you anticipate any dangers in using these approaches?

7. A supervisor in a textile factory observes that one of her employees is violating a safety rule

that could result in severe injury. What combination of reinforcement, punishment, and extinction could she use to correct this behaviour? What does social cognitive theory suggest that she do to correct the behaviour?

8. Describe a job in which you think an employee recognition program might be an effective means for changing and improving employee behaviour. Explain how you would design the program and how you would use principles from operant learning theory and social cognitive theory.

9. Do you think that organizations should base their hiring decisions on applicants' personality? What are the advantages and disadvantages of doing this? If an organization were to do this, what personality characteristics do you think they should focus on when assessing and choosing applicants?

10. Refer to the Research Focus: *CEO Personality and Firm Performance* and consider the relationship between the Big Five personality characteristics and strategic flexibility. Why do you think conscientiousness was the only trait negatively related to strategic flexibility given that it has been found to be the best predictor of job performance among the Big Five? Why are openness to experience, extraversion, and emotional stability positively related, and why is medium agreeableness better for strategic flexibility than high or low agreeableness?

11. Employee of the month (EOM) programs are one of the most popular forms of recognition in organizations. However, there is some evidence that such programs are not effective and can even have detrimental effects such as sabotage and unhealthy competition. Based on the material presented in this chapter, why do you think that the typical EOM program is not effective, and how should EOM programs be designed to make them more effective?

INTEGRATIVE DISCUSSION QUESTIONS

1. Refer to the material in Chapter 1 on Mintzberg's managerial roles and consider how personality might be a factor in how effectively a manager performs each role. Discuss the relationships among the Big Five personality dimensions, locus of control, self-monitoring, self-esteem, proactive personality, and general self-efficacy with each of the managerial roles.

2. Discuss how each of the organizational learning practices described in the chapter can be used by organizations to deal effectively with the contemporary management concerns discussed in Chapter 1.

ON-THE-JOB CHALLENGE QUESTION

Playing Hooky

In the summer of 2012, a *Toronto Star* investigation reported that construction and maintenance workers who were supposed to be working at Toronto public schools were spending their mornings at Tim Hortons, drinking in bars, and even kissing in cars. One worker was spotted delivering pamphlets to houses and offering to perform odd jobs for pay on school board time. The workers submitted time sheets and were paid their wages as if they had put in a full day's work.

In some cases, workers have signed in to work at a school and then announced they had to go get "parts" and were later discovered by Toronto District School Board officials drinking in a bar. In another case, a male worker was found in a board vehicle with a female "fooling around," according to a board source. In the case of the pamphlets, board sources say a worker was using board time to distribute flyers advertising his services for odd jobs, apparently using board equipment.

How can we explain these behaviours? Based on what you know about learning theory, explain why workers engaged in these inappropriate behaviours during work hours and why they were not doing what they were supposed to be doing. What do you think needs to be done to stop these behaviours and increase the probability that workers will do what they are supposed to be doing?

Source: Based on Donovan, K., & Welsh, M. (2012, June 22). School workers playing hooky. *Toronto Star*, A1, A4.

EXPERIENTIAL EXERCISE

Proactive Personality Scale

Do you have a proactive personality? To find out, answer the 17 questions below as frankly and honestly as possible using the following response scale:

1–Disagree very much

2–Disagree moderately

3–Disagree slightly

4–Neither agree or disagree

5–Agree slightly

6–Agree moderately

7–Agree very much

____ 1. I am constantly on the lookout for new ways to improve my life.

____ 2. I feel driven to make a difference in my community, and maybe the world.

____ 3. I tend to let others take the initiative to start new projects.

____ 4. Wherever I have been, I have been a powerful force for constructive change.

____ 5. I enjoy facing and overcoming obstacles to my ideas.

____ 6. Nothing is more exciting than seeing my ideas turn into reality.

____ 7. If I see something I don't like, I fix it.

____ 8. No matter what the odds, if I believe in something I will make it happen.

____ 9. I love being a champion for my ideas, even against others' opposition.

____ 10. I excel at identifying opportunities.

____ 11. I am always looking for better ways to do things.

____ 12. If I believe in an idea, no obstacle will prevent me from making it happen.

____ 13. I love to challenge the status quo.

____ 14. When I have a problem, I tackle it head-on.

____ 15. I am great at turning problems into opportunities.

____ 16. I can spot a good opportunity long before others can.

____ 17. If I see someone in trouble, I help out in any way I can.

Source: Bateman, T.S., & Crant, J.M. (1993). The proactive component of organizational behavior: A measure and correlates. *Journal of Organizational Behavior, 14*, 103–118. © 1993 John Wiley & Sons Limited. Reprinted with permission.

Scoring and Interpretation

You have just completed the Proactive Personality Scale developed by Thomas Bateman and J. Michael Crant.

To obtain your score, first subtract your response to question 3 from 8. For example, if you gave a response of 7 to question 3, give yourself a 1 (8 minus 7). Then add up your scores to all 17 items. Your total should be somewhere between 17 and 119. The higher you scored, the more proactive your personality is—you feel that you can change things in your environment.

The average score of 134 first-year MBA students with full-time work experience was 90.7. Thus, these people tended to see themselves as very proactive. In this research, people with a proactive personality tended to report more extracurricular and service activities and major personal achievements that involve making constructive changes to the world around them.

General Self-Efficacy

Want to learn about your general self-efficacy? Answer the eight questions below as frankly and honestly as possible using the following response scale:

1–Strongly disagree

2–Disagree

3–Neither agree nor disagree

4–Agree

5–Strongly agree

6–Agree moderately

____ 1. I will be able to achieve most of the goals that I have set for myself.

____ 2. When facing difficult tasks, I am certain that I will accomplish them.

____ 3. In general, I think that I can obtain outcomes that are important to me.

____ 4. I believe I can succeed at most any endeavour to which I set my mind.

____ 5. I will be able to successfully overcome many challenges.

____ 6. I am confident that I can perform effectively on many different tasks.

____ 7. Compared to other people, I can do most tasks very well.

____ 8. Even when things are tough, I can perform quite well.

Source: Chen, G., Gully, S.M., & Eden, D. (2001). Validation of a new general self-efficacy scale. *Organizational Research Methods, 4*, 62–83.

Scoring and Interpretation

You have just completed the New General Self-Efficacy Scale developed by Gilad Chen, Stanley M. Gully, and Dov Eden. To obtain your general self-efficacy (GSE) score, add up your scores to all 8 items and divide by 8. Your score should be somewhere between 1 and 5. The higher your score, the greater your general self-efficacy.

GSE enables individuals to effectively adapt to novel and adverse environments and can help to explain motivation and performance in a variety of work contexts. The average score of 323 undergraduate students enrolled in several upper-level psychology courses was 3.87.

The Core Self-Evaluations Scale (CSES)

To find out about your core self-evaluations, answer the 12 questions below as frankly and honestly as possible using the following response scale:

1–Strongly disagree

2–Disagree

3–Neither agree nor disagree

4–Agree

5–Strongly agree

____ 1. I am confident I get the success I deserve in life.

____ 2. Sometimes I feel depressed.

____ 3. When I try, I generally succeed.

____ 4. Sometimes when I fail I feel worthless.

____ 5. I complete tasks successfully.

____ 6. Sometimes, I do not feel in control of my work.

____ 7. Overall, I am satisfied with myself.

____ 8. I am filled with doubts about my competence.

____ 9. I determine what will happen in my life.

____ 10. I do not feel in control of my success in my career.

____ 11. I am capable of coping with most of my problems.

____ 12. There are times when things look pretty bleak and hopeless to me.

Source: Judge, T.A., Erez, A., Bono, J.E., & Thoresen, C.J. (2003). The core self-evaluations scale: Development of a measure. *Personnel Psychology, 56*, 303–313.

Scoring and Interpretation

You have just completed the Core Self-Evaluations Scale (CSES) developed by Timothy Judge, Amir Erez, Joyce Bono, and Carl Thoresen. To obtain your score, first subtract your response to questions 2, 4, 6, 8, 10, and 12 from 6. For example, if you gave a response of 1 to question 2, give yourself a 5 (6 minus 1). Then add up your scores to all 12 items and divide by 12. Your score should be somewhere between 1 and 5. The higher your score, the higher your core self-evaluations.

Core self-evaluations (CSE) are a broad personality concept that reflect evaluations people hold about themselves and their self-worth. Core self-evaluations consist of self-esteem, general self-efficacy, locus of control, and neuroticism. The average score of undergraduate students in two studies was 3.83 and 3.78. Scores on the CSES have been found to be positively related to job satisfaction, job performance, and life satisfaction.

Questions

To facilitate class discussion and your understanding of proactive personality, GSE, and CSE, form a small group with several other members of the class and consider the following questions:

1. Each group member should present their proactive personality, GSE, and CSE scores. Next, consider the extent to which each member has been involved in extracurricular and service activities and in personal accomplishments that involved making changes to their circumstances and how they have adapted to novel and difficult situations. Each member should also consider how satisfied they are with a current or previous job and how satisfied they are with their life (1 = not satisfied at all to 5 = very satisfied). Have students with higher proactive personality scores been more involved in extracurricular and service activities? What about personal accomplishments and constructive change? Have students with higher GSE scores been more effective in adapting to novel and difficult situations? And are students with higher CSE scores more satisfied with their current or a previous job and are they more satisfied with their life? (Alternatively, members of the class may write their proactive personality, GSE, and CSE scores, extracurricular and service activities, personal accomplishments, experiences adapting to novel and difficult situations, and job and life satisfaction on a piece of paper and hand it in to the instructor. The instructor can then write the responses on the board for class discussion.)

2. When are a proactive personality, GSE, and CSE most likely to be beneficial? When are they least likely to be beneficial?

3. Do you think organizations should hire people based on whether they have a proactive personality and on their GSE and CSE scores? What are the implications of this?

4. Based on your proactive personality, GSE, and CSE scores, what have you learned about yourself and your behaviour in different situations?

5. How can your knowledge of your proactive personality, GSE, and CSE scores help you at school and at work? What can you do to become more proactive? What can you do to strengthen your GSE and CSE?

CASE INCIDENT

Courier Cats

To stay competitive, many organizations regularly upgrade their computer technology. This was the case for Courier Cats, a small but profitable courier firm. To improve the delivery and tracking of parcels, the company decided to invest in new software. It was expected that the new software would not only allow the company to expand its business but also improve the quality of service. Because the new software was much more complex and sophisticated than what the company had been using, employees had to attend a one-day training program to learn how to use the new system. However, six months after the system was implemented, many employees were still using the old system. Some employees refused to use the new software, while others did not think they would ever be able to learn how to use it.

1. Why do you think that the employees did not use the new software?

2. Can personality explain why some employees refused to use the new software? What personality characteristics are most relevant for explaining why some employees refused to use the new software while others had no trouble learning and using it?

3. What are some of the implications that stem from operant learning theory and social cognitive theory for increasing the probability that the employees will use the new software? What do you recommend for improving the use of the new software?

CASE STUDY

Howe 2 Ski Stores

The Howe 2 Ski Stores are a chain of three ski and windsurfing shops located in the suburbs of a large western coastal city. Maria Howe, a ski enthusiast and business major, opened the first store 10 years ago after her university graduation with financial backing from her family and several friends. From its inception, the Howe 2 store was intended to provide state-of-the-art equipment and clothing for skiers at all ski levels, from beginner to champion. It was to be staffed by employees who were themselves advanced skiers and could provide expert advice on the choice of clothing and equipment, and it was intended to have a quick response time that would permit the last-minute purchase of equipment and clothing to a ski trip.

Howe originally drew from a pool of skiing friends and fellow students to staff the stores and still prefers to hire part-time employees with skiing expertise who might leave in a year over more stable, full-time employees with less expertise and interest in the sport. Whether administrative staff, cashiers, clerks, or moulders (employees who fit bindings to skis), employees were encouraged to keep up to date on the latest skiing equipment and trends, attend ski vendor shows, try out demo equipment, and give feedback on the store's inventory to help provide the highest quality equipment and advice for the customer. Suggestion boxes were placed in the store, and Howe herself regularly collected, read, and acted upon the suggestions made by the clerks and customers. She developed special advertising campaigns to build an image for the nearby slopes to increase the market. As the business grew, Howe even added a line of rental equipment to lower the costs and encourage people to try the sport.

Although profits grew irregularly due to weather effects and the faddish nature of the sport, Howe's efforts paid off in the long term, and within four years business had grown sufficiently to permit the opening of a second Howe 2 Ski Store in another suburb about 16 kilometres from the location of the first store. To even out sales across the year, about six years ago Howe took a chance on the growing windsurfing market and the coastal location and added a line of equipment for this sport. This expanded market has enabled her to smooth out the number of sales occurring throughout the year.

Three years ago, Howe was able to open a third store, located within a 25-kilometre radius of the other two locations. Although managers have been hired to run each of the stores and the total number of employees has grown to 65, Howe's basic strategy has remained the same—high quality, state-of-the-art products, a knowledgeable staff, and quick response time. Profits from the stores have continued to grow, although at a slower rate. Competition from other ski stores has also increased noticeably within the last two years.

The threat of increased competition has been exacerbated by signs that employee productivity has begun to slide. Last year, there were eight occasions where expensive ski orders were not delivered in time for the customer's ski vacation. Although Howe used a variety of manoeuvres to retain the customers' patronage (e.g., paying for the customer to rent equipment of equivalent quality, arranging express delivery of the equipment to the customer as soon as it was received at the store, and lowering the price of the equipment), the costs of these late orders were high. She realized that word of mouth about these kinds of incidents could significantly damage the store's reputation. Furthermore, at least 15 percent of all ski orders were delivered more than two days late, even though customers did not miss a trip or vacation as a result.

In an attempt to respond to these difficulties, Howe instituted a merit performance system for the moulders (employees who fit the binding to skis). Although productivity seemed to increase for a while, waves of discontent popped up all over the stores. The moulders felt that their merit ratings were inaccurate because the store managers could not observe them working much of the time. Further, they argued that their performance levels would have been much higher had not other employees interrupted them with questions about appropriate bindings or failed to clearly identify the appropriate equipment on the sales orders. Other employees also complained

because they were not given the opportunity for merit pay. The buyers, who visit ski shows, examine catalogues, and talk with sales representatives to decide on the inventory, argued that their work was essential for high sales figures and quality equipment. Sales clerks claimed that their in-depth familiarity with an extensive inventory and their sales skills were essential to increasing sales. They also noted their important role in negotiating a delivery date that the moulders could meet. Similar arguments were made by the people in the credit office who arranged for short-term financing if necessary and the cashiers who verified costs and checked credit card approvals. Even the stockers noted that the store would be in a bad way if they did not locate the correct equipment in a warehouse full of inventory and deliver it in a timely manner to the moulders.

Howe had to concede that the employees were correct on many of these points, so she suspended the merit plan at the end of the ski season and promised to re-evaluate its fairness. Even more convincing were several indications that productivity problems were not limited to moulder employees. Complaints about customer service increased 20 percent during the year. Several customers noted that they were allowed to stand, merchandise in hand, waiting for a clerk to help them, while clerks engaged in deep conversations among themselves. Although Howe mentioned this to employees in the stores when she visited and asked the store managers to discuss it in staff meetings, the complaints continued. A record number of "as is" skis were sold at the end of the season sale because they were damaged in the warehouse or the store or by the moulders. The closing inventory revealed that 20 percent of the rental equipment had been lost or seriously damaged without resulting charges to the renters because records were poorly maintained. Regular checks of the suggestion boxes in the store revealed fewer and fewer comments. Although less extreme, similar problems occurred in windsurfing season. Employees just didn't seem to notice these problems or, worse, didn't seem to care.

Howe was very bothered by all these factors and felt they could not be attributed to the growth of the business alone. She knew it would be impossible to maintain her competitive position with these events occurring.

Source: From NKOMO/MCAFEE/QUARRIE. Applications in Human Resource Management, 1E. © 2007 Nelson Education Ltd. Reproduced by permission. www.cengage.com/permissions

QUESTIONS

1. What are the main problems occurring in the Howe 2 Ski Stores? To what extent are the problems due to personality and characteristics of the work environment?

2. What behaviours need to be maintained or increased, and what behaviours should be reduced or eliminated?

3. What do you think of Maria Howe's attempt to respond to the difficulties in the stores? Use operant learning theory and social cognitive theory to explain the effects of her merit performance system. Why wasn't it more effective?

4. What do you think Maria Howe should do to respond to the difficulties in the stores? Refer to operant learning theory and social cognitive theory in answering this question.

5. What organizational learning practices might be effective for changing employee behaviours? Consider the potential of organizational behaviour modification, employee recognition programs, and training and development programs. Explain how you would implement each of these and their potential effectiveness.

6. What advice would you give Maria Howe on how to address the problems in her stores? Should she pay more attention to the personalities of the people she hires and/or should she make changes to the work environment? What employees and what behaviours should she focus on? Explain your answer.

PERCEPTION, ATTRIBUTION, AND DIVERSITY

LEARNING OBJECTIVES

After reading Chapter 3, you should be able to:

3.1 Define *perception* and discuss some of the general factors that influence perception.

3.2 Explain *social identity theory* and *Bruner's model* of the perceptual process.

3.3 Describe the main biases in person perception.

3.4 Describe how people form *attributions* about the causes of behaviour.

3.5 Discuss various biases in attribution.

3.6 Discuss the concepts of *workforce diversity* and valuing diversity.

3.7 Discuss how racial, ethnic, religious, gender, and age *stereotypes* affect organizational behaviour and what organizations can do to manage diversity.

3.8 Define *trust* perceptions and *perceived organizational support*, and describe *organizational support theory*.

3.9 Discuss person perception and perceptual biases in human resources.

KPMG

KPMG is a leading accounting and professional services firm that provides audit, tax, and financial advisory services to businesses across Canada. KPMG is one of Canada's oldest accounting firms with offices in 33 locations across the country and more than 675 partners and 5000 employees.

Several years ago, Michael Bach, a manager in the professional services IT consulting practice at KPMG in Toronto, approached the human resources director about creating a full-time position responsible for diversity and promoting diversity at the company. He was told to write a business case. So he did.

His business case was about bringing the company's diversity practices under one umbrella and making them a companywide priority. A month later, he presented it to the board of directors and got a new job, a team, and a budget of just over $500 000. "I was told to go rock the boat," said Bach, who is now KPMG's national director of diversity, equity, and inclusion and reports directly to the chief HR officer and CEO.

In four years, Bach launched initiatives and programs to recruit and retain employees from diverse backgrounds

as well as a mandatory online-training program for employees on diversity issues. KPMG now has diversity councils at many of its 33 offices in Canada. The company also has a number of social clubs, including an international club, where members meet regularly to offer support to employees who are new to the country. Bach has also introduced networks and clubs such as Women's Interchange Network, Parents of Children with Special Needs, religious groups, and pride@kpmg, a network for LGBT employees.

Bach also created an open recruiting process for skilled immigrants and introduced diversity training for all new hires and cultural competence training for managers. "There was a lot of education, making sure that people got that being educated and working outside of Canada is not a bad thing," said Bach. A targeted recruitment strategy to increase the number of women and visible minority employees by 10 percent over five years was also implemented.

Other initiatives Bach has spearheaded include reaching out to immigrant communities through career fairs to identify professional candidates and participating in the

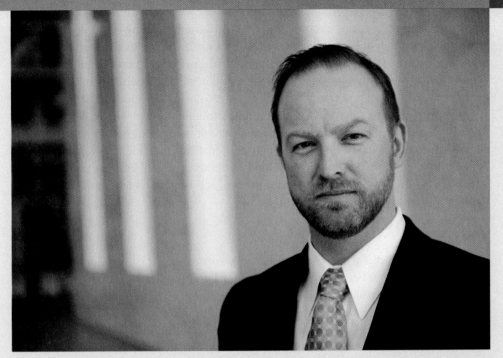

Michael Bach of KPMG has initiated many diversity programs at KPMG, and the firm is now recognized as one of Canada's Best Diversity Employers and one of the Best Employers for New Canadians.

Internationally Educated Professionals conference. But Bach is most proud of the fact that KPMG helps immigrants with foreign accounting accreditation attain their Canadian designation, be it a Certified Accountant (CA) or Certified Public Accountant (CPA) designation.

When KPMG looked at women's advancement into its equity partnership they saw that they had only moved about 3 percent and were only at about 10 percent to begin with. "Quite frankly, they were at a glacier pace," said Bach. So they set targets for women to become partners at the firm and became the first accounting firm in Canada to do so.

Multipurpose reflection rooms have also been created in most KPMG offices. They are a dedicated space for quiet observation, prayers, meditation, or breast-feeding. The idea came from a Muslim employee who wondered aloud if there was some quiet place at work where he could pray for a few minutes. "I realized it was a reasonable request, and we need a place for not only prayers, but others things, too," said Bach.

The biggest roadblock was lack of understanding and awareness, said Bach. "There was some skepticism as people thought they would lose out in some way when we talked about being more diverse. The message that we had was: It's not about losing anything, but offering everyone equal opportunities and that can benefit the company."

Today, almost 15 percent of the firm's workforce in the Toronto area is foreign-trained and nearly 40 percent were born outside Canada. The number of women partners has now reached 18 percent and the proportion of women and visible minorities in new partner classes at KPMG has gone from 40 percent in 2009 to 51 percent in 2010.

For his work, Bach received the *Canadian HR Reporter* Individual Achievement award as part of the Toronto Region Immigrant Employment Council's (TRIEC's) fourth annual Immigrant Success (IS) Awards, which recognize innovation and leadership in integrating skilled immigrants into the workplace. Catalyst Canada also recognized Bach in 2011 for his work to improve diversity within KPMG.

In 2012, KPMG was chosen as one of Canada's Best Diversity Employers and one of the Best Employers for New Canadians for the fifth year in a row, in addition to being selected as one of Canada's Top 100 Employers.[1]

Why has KPMG made workplace diversity a top priority? What effect do diversity programs have on employee attitudes and behaviour? And why do organizations often harbour false assumptions and myths about women, visible minority employees, and immigrants? These are the kinds of questions that we will attempt to answer in this chapter. First, we will define *perception* and examine how various aspects of the perceiver, the object or person being perceived, and the situation influence perception. Following this we will present a theory and model of the perceptual process and we will consider some of the perceptual tendencies that we employ in forming impressions of people and attributing causes to their behaviour. We will then examine the role of perception in achieving a diverse workforce and how to manage diversity, perceptions of trust, perceived organizational support, and person perception in human resources. In general, you will learn that perception and attribution influence who gets into organizations, how they are treated as members, and how they interpret this treatment.

WHAT IS PERCEPTION?

LO 3.1

Define *perception* and discuss some of the general factors that influence perception.

Perception. The process of interpreting the messages of our senses to provide order and meaning to the environment.

Perception is the process of interpreting the messages of our senses to provide order and meaning to the environment. Perception helps sort out and organize the complex and varied input received by our senses of sight, smell, touch, taste, and hearing. The key word in this definition is *interpreting*. People frequently base their actions on the interpretation of reality that their perceptual system provides, rather than on reality itself. If you perceive your pay to be very low, you might seek employment in another firm. The reality—that you are the best-paid person in your department—will not matter if you are unaware of the fact. However, to go a step further, you might be aware that you are the best-paid person and *still* perceive your pay as low in comparison with that of the CEO of your organization or your ostentatious next-door neighbour.

Some of the most important perceptions that influence organizational behaviour are the perceptions that organizational members have of each other. Because of this, we will concentrate on person perception in this chapter.

COMPONENTS OF PERCEPTION

Perception has three components—a perceiver, a target that is being perceived, and some situational context in which the perception is occurring. Each of these components influences the perceiver's impression or interpretation of the target (Exhibit 3.1).

"I'm only firing you to impress the people that I'm not firing."

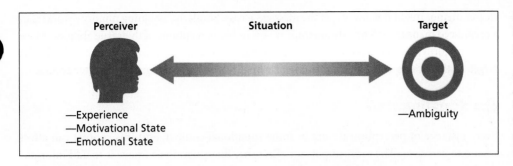

EXHIBIT 3.1
Factors that influence perception.

✖ Explore

Go to MyManagementLab to see an annotated version of this figure.

The Perceiver

The perceiver's experience, needs, and emotions can affect his or her perceptions of a target.

One of the most important characteristics of the perceiver that influences his or her impressions of a target is experience. Past experiences lead the perceiver to develop expectations, and these expectations affect current perceptions. An interesting example of the influence of experience on perception is shown in Exhibit 3.2. It illustrates the perceptions of 268 managerial personnel in a Fortune 500 company concerning the influence of race and gender on promotion opportunities. As you can see, Caucasian men were much less likely to perceive race or gender barriers to promotion than were Caucasian women, non-Caucasian men, and non-Caucasian women.[2] Remember, these people were ostensibly viewing the same "objective" promotion system.

Frequently, our needs unconsciously influence our perceptions by causing us to perceive what we wish to perceive. Research has demonstrated that perceivers who have been deprived of food will tend to "see" more edible things in ambiguous pictures than will well-fed observers. Similarly, lonely university students might misperceive the most innocent actions of members of the opposite sex as indicating interest in them.

Emotions, such as anger, happiness, or fear, can influence our perceptions. We have all had the experience of misperceiving the innocent comment of a friend or acquaintance when we were angry. For example, a worker who is upset about not getting a promotion might perceive the consolation provided by a co-worker as gloating condescension. On the other hand, consider the worker who does get a promotion. She is so happy that she fails to notice how upset her co-worker is because he was not the one promoted.

In some cases, our perceptual system serves to defend us against unpleasant emotions. This phenomenon is known as **perceptual defence**. We have all experienced cases in which we "see what we want to see" or "hear what we want to hear." In many of these instances, our perceptual system is working to ensure that we do not see or hear things that are threatening.

Perceptual defence. The tendency for the perceptual system to defend the perceiver against unpleasant emotions.

✖ Explore

Go to MyManagementLab to see an annotated version of this figure.

The Target

Perception involves interpretation and the addition of meaning to the target, and ambiguous targets are especially susceptible to interpretation and addition. Perceivers have a need to resolve such ambiguities. You might be tempted to believe that providing more information about the target will improve perceptual accuracy. Unfortunately, this is not always the case. Writing

EXHIBIT 3.2
Ratings of the perceived importance of race and gender for promotion opportunity in executive jobs.

Note: Table values are the percentages saying that race or gender was important or very important. N = number of cases.

Source: Reprinted with permission of the publisher from *Cultural diversity in organizations: Theory, research, & practice.* © 1993 by T. Cox Jr. Berrett-Koehler Publishers, Inc., San Francisco, CA. All rights reserved. www.bkconnection.com.

	Caucasian Men (N = 123)	Caucasian Women (N = 76)	Non-Caucasian Men (N = 52)	Non-Caucasian Women (N = 17)
Race	26	62	75	76
Gender	31	87	71	82

clearer memos might not always get the message across. Similarly, assigning minority workers to a prejudiced manager will not always improve his or her perceptions of their true abilities. As we shall see shortly, the perceiver does not or cannot always use all the information provided by the target. In these cases, a reduction in ambiguity might not be accompanied by greater accuracy.

The Situation

Every instance of perception occurs in some situational context, and this context can affect what one perceives. The most important effect that the situation can have is to add information about the target. Imagine a casual critical comment about your performance from your boss the week before she is to decide whether or not you will be promoted. You will likely perceive this comment very differently from how you would if you were not up for promotion. Also, a worker might perceive a racial joke overheard on the job very differently before and after racial strife has occurred in the plant. In both of these examples, the perceiver and the target are the same, but the perception of the target changes with the situation.

LO **3.2**

Explain *social identity theory* and *Bruner's model* of the perceptual process.

Social identity theory. A theory that states that people form perceptions of themselves based on their personal characteristics and memberships in social categories.

SOCIAL IDENTITY THEORY

In the previous section, we described how characteristics of the perceiver, the target, and the situation influence the perceiver's interpretation of the target. In this section, we discuss social identity theory to help us understand how this happens. Let's begin with a simple question: "Who are you?" Chances are when you answer this question you say things like "student," "Canadian," "accountant," and so on. In other words, you respond in terms of various social categories to which you believe you belong. This is what social identity theory is all about.

According to **social identity theory**, people form perceptions of themselves based on their personal characteristics and memberships in social categories. As a result, our sense of self is composed of a personal identity and a social identity. Our *personal identity* is based on our unique personal characteristics, such as our interests, abilities, and traits. *Social identity* is based on our perception that we belong to various social groups, such as our gender, nationality, religion, occupation, and so on. Personal and social identities help us answer the question "Who am I?"

But why and how do we do this? As individuals, we categorize ourselves and others to make sense of and understand the social environment. The choice of specific categories depends on what is most salient and appropriate to the situation. For example, we might define people in a meeting according to their job title. Once a category is chosen, we tend to see members of that category as embodying the most typical attributes of that category, or what are called "prototypes." Similarly, once we locate ourselves in a social category we tend to perceive ourselves as embodying the prototypical characteristics of the category. In this way, we develop a sense of who and what we are, as well as our values, beliefs, and ways of thinking, acting, and feeling.[3]

In addition to forming self-perceptions based on our social memberships, we also form perceptions of others based on their memberships in social categories. This is because social identities are relational and comparative. In other words, we define members of a category relative to members of other categories. For example, the category of professor is meaningful in relation to the category of student. As the comparison category changes, so will certain aspects of the focal social identity. So when the authors of this text are in the classroom, they are perceived as professors by their students and as having whatever attributes the students attribute to professors. However, one of the authors of this text lives next door to a university student who perceives him not as a professor, but as a "baby boomer." Notice how her social categorization differs from those of the students in the classroom. As a result, her perception of the author will also differ because the attributes and characteristics associated with the generation category of a "baby boomer" differ from those of the occupational category of "professor."

Social identity theory helps us understand how the components of the perceptual system operate in the formation of perceptions. We perceive people in terms of the attributes and characteristics that we associate with their social category relative to other categories. Thus, your perception of others is a function of how you categorize yourself (e.g., student) and your target (e.g., professor). If the situation changes, so might the categorization and the relation between the perceiver and the target. For example, in a hospital, medical students might be perceived as doctors by nurses and patients, but in the classroom they are perceived as medical students by their professors.[4]

Because people tend to perceive members of their own social categories in more positive and favourable ways than those who are different and belong to other categories, social identity theory is useful for understanding stereotyping and discrimination, topics we discuss later in this chapter. Now let's turn to a more detailed understanding and model of the perceptual process.

A MODEL OF THE PERCEPTUAL PROCESS

In the previous section, we described how we form perceptions of ourselves and others based on social categories. But exactly how does the perceiver go about putting together the information contained in the target and the situation to form a picture of the target? Respected psychologist Jerome Bruner has developed a model of the perceptual process that can provide a useful framework for this discussion.[5] According to Bruner, when the perceiver encounters an unfamiliar target, the perceiver is very open to the informational cues contained in the target and the situation surrounding it. In this unfamiliar state, the perceiver really needs information on which to base perceptions of the target and will actively seek out cues to resolve this ambiguity. Gradually, the perceiver encounters some familiar cues (note the role of the perceiver's experience here) that enable her or him to make a crude categorization of the target, which follows from social identity theory. At this point, the cue search becomes less open and more selective. The perceiver begins to search out cues that confirm the categorization of the target. As this categorization becomes stronger, the perceiver actively ignores or even distorts cues that violate initial perceptions (see the left side of Exhibit 3.3). This does not mean that an early categorization cannot be changed. It does mean, however, that it will take a good many contradictory cues before one re-categorizes the target, and that these cues will have to overcome the expectations that have been developed.

Model	Example
Unfamiliar target encountered	New co-worker
Openness to target cues	Observation; search for information
Familiar cues encountered	Co-worker is Stanford graduate with good grades
Target categorized	Co-worker is "good man" with "great potential"
Cue selectivity	Co-worker's poor performance ignored or distorted
Categorization strengthened	Co-worker is still "good man" with "great potential"

EXHIBIT 3.3
Bruner's model of the perceptual process and an example.

 Explore

Go to MyManagementLab to see an annotated version of this figure.

Let's clarify your understanding of Bruner's perceptual model with an example, shown on the right side of Exhibit 3.3. Imagine that a woman who works as an engineer for a large aircraft company is trying to size up a newly hired co-worker. Since he is an unfamiliar target, she will be especially open to any cues that might provide information about him. In the course of her cue search, she discovers that he has a master's degree in aeronautical engineering from Stanford University and that he graduated with top grades. These are familiar cues because she knows that Stanford is a top school in the field, and she has worked with many excellent Stanford graduates. She then proceeds to categorize her new co-worker as a "good man" with "great potential." With these perceptions, she takes a special interest in observing his performance, which is good for several months. This increases the strength of her initial categorization. Gradually, however, the engineer's performance deteriorates for some reason, and his work becomes less and less satisfactory. This is clear to everyone except the other engineer, who continues to see him as adequate and excuses his most obvious errors as stemming from external factors beyond his control.

Bruner's model demonstrates three important characteristics of the perceptual process. First, perception is *selective*. Perceivers do not use all the available cues, and those they do use are thus given special emphasis. This means that our perception is efficient, and this efficiency can both aid and hinder our perceptual accuracy. Second, Bruner's model illustrates that our perceptual system works to paint a constant picture of the target. Perceptual *constancy* refers to the tendency for the target to be perceived in the same way over time or across situations. We have all had the experience of "getting off on the wrong foot" with a teacher or a boss and finding it difficult to change his or her constant perception of us. Third, the perceptual system also creates a consistent picture of the target. Perceptual *consistency* refers to the tendency to select, ignore, and distort cues in such a manner that they fit together to form a homogeneous picture of the target. We strive for consistency in our perception of people. We do not tend to see the same person as both good and bad or dependable and untrustworthy. Often, we distort cues that are discrepant with our general image of a person to make the cues consistent with this image. In the next section, we consider some specific perceptual biases that contribute to selectivity, constancy, and consistency in our perception of people.

LO 3.3

Describe the main biases in person perception.

BASIC BIASES IN PERSON PERCEPTION

For accuracy's sake, it would be convenient if we could encounter others under laboratory conditions, in a vacuum or a test tube, as it were. Because the real world lacks such ideal conditions, the impressions that we form of others are susceptible to a number of perceptual biases.

Primacy and Recency Effects

Primacy effect. The tendency for a perceiver to rely on early cues or first impressions.

Given the examples of person perception that we have discussed thus far, you might gather that we form our impressions of others fairly quickly. One reason for this fast impression formation is our tendency to rely on the cues that we encounter early in a relationship. This reliance on early cues or first impressions is known as the **primacy effect**. Primacy often has a lasting impact. Thus, the worker who can favourably impress his or her boss in the first few days on the job is in an advantageous position due to primacy. Similarly, the labour negotiator who comes across as "tough" on the first day of contract talks might find this image difficult to shake as the talks continue. Primacy is a form of selectivity, and its lasting effects illustrate the operation of constancy.

Recency effect. The tendency for a perceiver to rely on recent cues or last impressions.

Sometimes, a **recency effect** occurs, in which people give undue weight to the cues they encountered most recently. In other words, last impressions count most. Landing a big contract today might be perceived as excusing a whole year's bad sales performance.

Reliance on Central Traits

Even though perceivers tend to rely on early information when developing their perceptions, these early cues do not receive equal weight. People tend to organize their perceptions around **central traits**, personal characteristics of the target that are of special interest to them. In developing her perceptions of her new co-worker, the experienced engineer seemed to organize her impressions around the trait of intellectual capacity. The centrality of traits depends on the perceiver's interests and the situation. Thus, not all engineers would organize their perceptions of the new worker around his intellectual abilities, and the established engineer might not use this trait as a central factor in forming impressions of the people she meets at a party.

Central traits. Personal characteristics of a target person that are of particular interest to a perceiver.

Central traits often have a very powerful influence on our perceptions of others. Physical appearance is a common central trait in work settings that is related to a variety of job-related outcomes. Research shows an overwhelming tendency for those who are "attractive" to also be perceived as "good," especially when it comes to judgments about their social competence, qualifications, and potential job success.[6]

In general, research shows that conventionally attractive people are more likely to fare better than unattractive people in terms of a variety of job-related outcomes, including employment potential, getting hired, being chosen as a business partner, receiving good performance evaluations, or being promoted.[7] Physical height, which is one of the most obvious aspects of appearance, has also been found to be related to job performance, promotions, and career success.[8] Taller and more attractive people are also more likely to be paid more. However, as discussed in the Research Focus: *Weight-Based Bias in the Workplace,* individuals who are overweight tend to be evaluated negatively on a number of workplace outcomes. This bias is particularly troublesome given that the rate of obesity among adults in North America has been increasing over the last 20 years.

Implicit Personality Theories

Each of us has a "theory" about which personality characteristics go together. These are called **implicit personality theories**. Perhaps you expect hardworking people to also be honest. Perhaps you feel that people of average intelligence tend to be most friendly. To the extent that such implicit theories are inaccurate, they provide a basis for misunderstanding.[9] The employee who assumes that her very formal boss is also insensitive might be reluctant to discuss a work-related problem with him that could be solved fairly easily.

Implicit personality theories. Personal theories that people have about which personality characteristics go together.

Projection

In the absence of information to the contrary, and sometimes in spite of it, people often assume that others are like themselves. This tendency to attribute one's own thoughts and feelings to others is called **projection**. In some cases, projection is an efficient and sensible perceptual strategy. After all, people with similar backgrounds or interests often *do* think and feel similarly. Thus, it is not unreasonable for a capitalistic business person to assume that other business people favour the free enterprise system and disapprove of government intervention in this system. However, projection can also lead to perceptual difficulties. The chairperson who feels that an issue has been resolved and perceives committee members to feel the same way might be very surprised when a vote is taken. The honest warehouse manager who perceives others as honest might find inventory disappearing. In the case of threatening or undesirable characteristics, projection can serve as a form of perceptual defence. The dishonest worker might say, "Sure I steal from the company, but so does everyone else." Such perceptions can be used to justify the perceiver's thievery.

Projection. The tendency for perceivers to attribute their own thoughts and feelings to others.

Stereotyping

One way to form a consistent impression of other people is simply to assume that they have certain characteristics by virtue of some category that they fall into as suggested by social identity theory. This perceptual tendency is known as **stereotyping**, or the tendency to generalize about people in a social category and ignore variations among them. Categories on which people might base a stereotype include race, age, gender, ethnic background, religion, social class, and occupation.[10] There are three specific aspects to stereotyping.[11]

Stereotyping. The tendency to generalize about people in a certain social category and ignore variations among them.

- We distinguish some category of people (university professors).

- We assume that the individuals in this category have certain traits (absent-minded, disorganized, ivory-tower mentality).

- We perceive that everyone in this category possesses these traits ("All my professors this year will be absent-minded, disorganized, and have an ivory-tower mentality").

People can evoke stereotypes with incredibly little information. In a "first impressions" study, the mere fact that a woman preferred to be addressed as "Ms." led to her being perceived as more masculine, more achievement-oriented, and less likeable than those who preferred the traditional titles "Miss" or "Mrs."[12]

Not all stereotypes are unfavourable. You probably hold favourable stereotypes of the social categories of which you are a member, such as student. However, these stereotypes

RESEARCH FOCUS

WEIGHT-BASED BIAS IN THE WORKPLACE

Researchers have been investigating how body weight affects workplace outcomes such as hiring decisions and performance appraisals for nearly 30 years. Many studies have found evidence of a bias against overweight individuals in the workplace and have concluded that overweight individuals are systematically denigrated in comparison to their non-overweight co-workers. In fact, the evidence for discrimination against overweight individuals can be found at virtually every stage of the employment process, including hiring, placement, compensation, promotion, discipline, and termination.

Research on negative attitudes toward overweight people in the workplace has found that overweight individuals are perceived by their co-workers and supervisors as lacking self-discipline and self-control, being lazy and not trying as hard as others at work, possessing poor work habits, and having less conscientiousness, competency, skills, and ability than individuals of "average" weight. Overweight individuals are also viewed as being more likely to be absent from work and less likely to get along with and be accepted by their co-workers and subordinates.

In an effort to better understand the extent of the bias against overweight individuals in the workplace, Cort Rudolph and colleagues examined the results of

previous research on body weight and workplace outcomes. Based on the results of 25 studies that have investigated weight-based bias in the workplace, the authors found that there is a significant negative relationship between body weight across all relevant evaluative workplace outcomes, including hiring decisions, promotion, and performance evaluation.

They also found that the negative effect of weight bias on hiring outcomes was significantly stronger than the effect on performance outcomes. Why might this be? The authors suggest that it is because the effects of bias are stronger when decision makers lack performance-relevant information about a target, such as when making hiring decisions. On the other hand, when decision makers have performance-relevant information about a target, such as when making performance evaluations or promotion decisions, the effects of bias are much lower. Without relevant information about a target, a decision maker is more likely to resort to body weight stereotypes and to make biased decisions.

Source: Reprinted from *Journal of Vocational Behaviour*, 74, Rudolph, C.W., Wells, C.L., Weller, M.D., & Baltes, B.B. A meta-analysis of empirical studies of weight-based bias in the workplace, 1–10, Copyright © 2009, with permission from Elsevier.

are often less well developed and less rigid than others you hold. Stereotypes help us develop impressions of ambiguous targets, and we are usually pretty familiar with the people in our own groups. In addition, this contact helps us appreciate individual differences among group members, and such differences work against the development of stereotypes.

Language can be easily twisted to turn neutral or even favourable information into a basis for unfavourable stereotypes. For example, if British people do tend to be reserved, it is fairly easy to interpret this reserve as snobbishness. Similarly, if women who achieve executive positions have had to be assertive, it is easy to interpret this assertiveness as pushiness.

Knowing a person's occupation or field of study, we often make assumptions about his or her behaviour and personality. Accountants might be stereotyped as compulsive, precise, and one-dimensional, while engineers might be perceived as cold and calculating. Reflect on your own stereotypes of psychology or business students.

Not all stereotypes are inaccurate. You probably hold fairly correct stereotypes about the educational level of the typical university professor and the on-the-job demeanour of the typical telephone operator. These accurate stereotypes ease the task of developing perceptions of others. However, it is probably safe to say that most stereotypes are inaccurate, especially when we use them to develop perceptions of specific individuals. This follows from the fact that stereotypes are most likely to develop when we do not have good information about a particular group.

This raises an interesting question: If many stereotypes are inaccurate, why do they persist?[13] After all, reliance on inaccurate information to develop our perceptions would seem to be punishing in the long run. In reality, a couple of factors work to *reinforce* inaccurate stereotypes. For one thing, even incorrect stereotypes help us process information about others quickly and efficiently. Sometimes, it is easier for the perceiver to rely on an inaccurate stereotype than it is to discover the true nature of the target. The male manager who is required to recommend one of his 20 employees for a promotion might find it easier to automatically rule out promoting a woman than to carefully evaluate all his employees, regardless of gender. Second, inaccurate stereotypes are often reinforced by selective perception and the selective application of language that was discussed above. The Hispanic worker who stereotypes all non-Hispanic managers as unfair might be on the lookout for behaviours to confirm these stereotypes and fail to notice examples of fair and friendly treatment. If such treatment *is* noticed, it might be perceived as patronizing rather than helpful.

ATTRIBUTION: PERCEIVING CAUSES AND MOTIVES

LO 3.4

Describe how people form *attributions* about the causes of behaviour.

Thus far, we have considered the components of perception, social identity theory, and Bruner's model of the perceptual process, and we have discussed some specific perceptual tendencies that operate as we form impressions of others. We will now consider a further aspect of impression formation—how we perceive people's motives. **Attribution** is the process by which we assign causes or motives to explain people's behaviour. The attribution process is important because many rewards and punishments in organizations are based on judgments about what really caused a target person to behave in a certain way.

In making attributions about behaviour, an important goal is to determine whether the behaviour is caused by dispositional or situational factors. **Dispositional attributions** suggest that some personality or intellectual characteristic unique to the person is responsible for the behaviour and that the behaviour thus reflects the "true person." If we explain a behaviour as a function of intelligence, greed, friendliness, or laziness, we are making dispositional attributions.

Situational attributions suggest that the external situation or environment in which the target person exists was responsible for the behaviour and that the person might have had little control over the behaviour. If we explain behaviour as a function of bad weather, good luck, proper tools, or poor advice, we are making situational attributions.

Attribution. The process by which causes or motives are assigned to explain people's behaviour.

Dispositional attributions. Explanations for behaviour based on an actor's personality or intellect.

Situational attributions. Explanations for behaviour based on an actor's external situation or environment.

Obviously, it would be nice to be able to read minds to understand people's motives. Since we cannot do this, we are forced to rely on external cues and make inferences from these cues. Research indicates that as we gain experience with the behaviour of a target person, three implicit questions guide our decisions as to whether we should attribute the behaviour to dispositional or situational causes.[14]

- Does the person engage in the behaviour regularly and consistently? (Consistency cues)
- Do most people engage in the behaviour, or is it unique to this person? (Consensus cues)
- Does the person engage in the behaviour in many situations, or is it distinctive to one situation? (Distinctiveness cues)

Let's examine consistency, consensus, and distinctiveness cues in more detail.

Consistency Cues

Consistency cues.
Attribution cues that reflect how consistently a person engages in a behaviour over time.

Consistency cues reflect how consistently a person engages in a behaviour over time. For example, unless we see clear evidence of external constraints that force a behaviour to occur, we tend to perceive behaviour that a person performs regularly as indicative of his or her true motives. In other words, high consistency leads to dispositional attributions. Thus, one might assume that the professor who has generous office hours and is always there for consultation really cares about his or her students. Similarly, we are likely to make dispositional attributions about workers who are consistently good or poor performers, perhaps perceiving the former as "dedicated" and the latter as "lazy." When behaviour occurs inconsistently, we begin to consider situational attributions. For example, if a person's performance cycles between mediocre and excellent, we might look to variations in workload to explain the cycles.

Consensus Cues

Consensus cues.
Attribution cues that reflect how a person's behaviour compares with that of others.

Consensus cues reflect how a person's behaviour compares with that of others. In general, acts that deviate from social expectations provide us with more information about the actor's motives than conforming behaviours do. Thus, unusual, low-consensus behaviour leads to more dispositional attributions than typical, high-consensus behaviour. The person who acts differently from the majority is seen as revealing more of his or her true motives. The informational effects of low-consensus behaviour are magnified when the actor is expected to suffer negative consequences because of the deviance. Consider the job applicant who makes favourable statements about the role of big business in society while being interviewed for a job at General Electric. Such statements are so predictable in this situation that the interviewer can place little confidence in what they really indicate about the candidate's true feelings and motives. On the other hand, imagine an applicant who makes critical comments about big business in the same situation. Such comments are hardly expected and could clearly lead to rejection. In this case, the interviewer would be more confident about the applicant's true disposition regarding big business.

Distinctiveness Cues

Distinctiveness cues.
Attribution cues that reflect the extent to which a person engages in some behaviour across a variety of situations.

Distinctiveness cues reflect the extent to which a person engages in some behaviour across a variety of situations. When a behaviour occurs across a variety of situations, it lacks distinctiveness, and the observer is prone to provide a dispositional attribution about its cause. We reason that the behaviour reflects a person's true motives if it "stands up" in a variety of environments. Thus, the professor who has generous office hours, stays after class to talk to students, and attends student functions is seen as truly student-oriented. The worker whose performance was good in his first job as well as several subsequent jobs is perceived as having real ability. When a behaviour is highly distinctive, in that it occurs in only one situation, we are likely to assume that some aspect of the situation caused the behaviour. If the only student-oriented behaviour that we observe is generous office hours, we assume that they are dictated by department policy. If a worker performed well on only one job, back in 1995, we suspect that his uncle owned the company!

Attribution in Action

Frequently, observers of real-life behaviour have information at hand about consistency, consensus, and distinctiveness. Let's take an example that shows how the observer puts such information together in forming attributions. At the same time, the example will serve to review the previous discussion. Imagine that Roshani, Mika, and Sam are employees who work in separate firms. Each is absent from work today, and a manager must develop an attribution about the cause to decide which action is warranted.

- *Roshani*—Roshani is absent a lot, her co-workers are seldom absent, and she was absent a lot in her previous job.
- *Mika*—Mika is absent a lot, her co-workers are also absent a lot, but she was almost never absent in her previous job.
- *Sam*—Sam is seldom absent, her co-workers are seldom absent, and she was seldom absent in her previous job.

Just what kind of attributions are managers likely to make regarding the absences of Roshani, Mika, and Sam? Roshani's absence is highly consistent, it is a low-consensus behaviour, and it is not distinctive, since she was absent in her previous job. As shown in Exhibit 3.4, this combination of cues is very likely to prompt a dispositional attribution, perhaps that Roshani is lazy or irresponsible. Mika is also absent consistently, but it is high-consensus behaviour in that her peers also exhibit absence. In addition, the behaviour is highly distinctive—she is absent only on this job. As indicated, this combination of cues will usually result in a situational attribution, perhaps that working conditions are terrible, or that the boss is nasty. Finally, Sam's absence is inconsistent. In addition, it is similar to that of co-workers and not distinctive, in that she was inconsistently absent on her previous job as well. As shown, this combination of cues suggests that some temporary, short-term situational factor is causing her absence. It is possible that a sick child occasionally requires her to stay home.

Biases in Attribution

As the preceding section indicates, observers often operate in a rational, logical manner in forming attributions about behaviour. The various cue combinations and the resulting attributions have a sensible appearance. This does not mean that such attributions are always correct, but they do represent good bets about why some behaviour occurred. Having made this observation, it would be naïve to assume that attributions are always free from bias or error. Earlier, we discussed a number of very basic perceptual biases, and it stands to reason that the complex task of attribution would also be open to bias. Let's consider three biases in attribution: the fundamental attribution error, actor–observer effect, and self-serving bias.[15]

LO 3.5

Discuss various biases in attribution.

**EXHIBIT 3.4
Cue combinations and resulting attributions.**

 Explore

Go to MyManagementLab to see an annotated version of this figure.

	Consistency	Consensus	Distinctiveness	Likely Attribution
Roshani	High	Low	Low	Disposition
Mika	High	High	High	Situation
Sam	Low	High	Low	Temporary Situation

FUNDAMENTAL ATTRIBUTION ERROR Suppose you make a mistake in attributing a cause to someone else's behaviour. Would you be likely to err on the side of a dispositional cause or a situational cause? Substantial evidence indicates that when we make judgments about the behaviour of people other than ourselves, we tend to overemphasize dispositional explanations at the expense of situational explanations. This is called the **fundamental attribution error**.[16]

Why does the fundamental attribution error occur? For one thing, we often discount the strong effects that social roles can have on behaviour. We might see bankers as truly conservative people because we ignore the fact that their occupational role and their employer dictate that they act conservatively. Second, many people whom we observe are seen in rather constrained, constant situations (at work or at school) that reduce our appreciation of how their behaviour may vary in other situations. Thus, we fail to realize that the observed behaviour is distinctive to a particular situation. That conservative banker might actually be a weekend skydiver!

The fundamental attribution error can lead to problems for managers of poorly performing employees. It suggests that dispositional explanations for the poor performance will sometimes be made even when situational factors are the true cause. Laziness or low aptitude might be cited, while poor training or a bad sales territory is ignored. However, this is less likely when the manager has had actual experience in performing the employee's job and is thus aware of situational roadblocks to good performance.[17]

ACTOR–OBSERVER EFFECT It is not surprising that actors and observers often view the causes for the actor's behaviour very differently. This difference in attributional perspectives is called the **actor–observer effect**.[18] Specifically, while the observer might be busy committing the fundamental attribution error, the actor might be emphasizing the role of the situation in explaining his or her own behaviour. Thus, as actors, we are often particularly sensitive to those environmental events that led us to be late or absent. As observers of the same behaviour in others, we are more likely to invoke dispositional causes.

We see some of the most striking examples of this effect in cases of illegal behaviour, such as price fixing and the bribery of government officials. The perpetrators and those close to them often cite stiff competition or management pressure as causes of their ethical lapses. Observers see the perpetrators as immoral or unintelligent.[19]

Why are actors prone to attribute much of their own behaviour to situational causes? First, they might be more aware than observers of the constraints and advantages that the environment offered. At the same time, they are aware of their private thoughts, feelings, and intentions regarding the behaviour, all of which might be unknown to the observer. Thus, I might know that I sincerely wanted to get to the meeting on time, that I left home extra early, and that the accident that delayed me was truly unusual. My boss might be unaware of all of this information and figure that I am just unreliable.

Research on the actor–observer effect has recently found that the effect is not as pervasive as once believed. For example, it appears to be more likely under particular conditions such as when explaining negative events. The opposite effect seems to occur for positive events (i.e., the actor makes a dispositional attribution while the observer makes a situational attribution).[20]

SELF-SERVING BIAS It has probably already occurred to you that certain forms of attributions have the capacity to make us feel good or bad about ourselves. In fact, people have a tendency to take credit and responsibility for successful outcomes of their behaviour and to deny credit and responsibility for failures.[21] This tendency is called **self-serving bias**, and it is interesting because it suggests that people will explain the very same behaviour differently on the basis of events that happened *after* the behaviour occurred. If the vice-president of marketing champions a product that turns out to be a sales success, she might attribute this to her retailing savvy. If the very same marketing process leads to failure, she might attribute this to the poor performance of the marketing research firm that she used. Notice that the self-serving

Fundamental attribution error. The tendency to overemphasize dispositional explanations for behaviour at the expense of situational explanations.

Actor–observer effect. The propensity for actors and observers to view the causes of the actor's behaviour differently.

Self-serving bias. The tendency to take credit for successful outcomes and to deny responsibility for failures.

bias can overcome the tendency for actors to attribute their behaviour to situational factors. In this example, the vice-president invokes a dispositional explanation ("I'm an intelligent, competent person") when the behaviour is successful.

Self-serving bias can reflect intentional self-promotion or excuse making. However, again, it is possible that it reflects unique information on the part of the actor. Especially when behaviour has negative consequences, the actor might scan the environment and find situational causes for the failure.[22] To be sure, when a student does very well on an exam, she is very likely to make a dispositional attribution. However, upon receiving a failing grade, the same student is much more likely to find situational causes to explain her grade!

PERSON PERCEPTION AND WORKFORCE DIVERSITY

The realities of workforce diversity have become an important factor for many organizations in recent years. **Workforce diversity** refers to differences among employees or potential recruits in characteristics such as gender, race, age, religion, cultural background, physical ability, or sexual orientation. The interest in diversity stems from at least two broad facts. First, the workforce is becoming more diverse. Second, there is growing recognition that many organizations have not successfully managed workforce diversity.

The Changing Workplace

As we mentioned in Chapter 1, the composition of the Canadian labour force is changing.[23] Fifty years ago, it was mainly Caucasian and male. Now, changing immigration patterns, the aging of baby boomers, and the increasing movement of women into paid employment result in a lot more variety. Immigrants to Canada from all parts of the world are making the Canadian population and labour force increasingly multicultural and multiethnic. The diversity of Canada's population is expected to continue to grow during the next 20 years. According to Statistics Canada, the number of visible minorities in Canada is expected to double by 2017 and visible minorities will form more than half the population in greater Toronto and Vancouver. If current trends continue, one in every five persons in Canada will be non-white when Canada celebrates its 150th birthday in 2017.[24] According to projections, between 25 and 28 percent of the Canadian population will be foreign-born by 2031, and in less than a decade 48 percent of Canada's working-age population will be between the ages of 45 and 64.[25]

The labour pool is changing, and at the same time many organizations are seeking to recruit more representatively from this pool so that they employ people who reflect their customer base—an effort to better mirror their markets. This is especially true in the growing service sector, where contact between organizational members and customers is very direct. As discussed in the chapter-opening vignette, KPMG has been very active in developing programs to hire, develop, and promote visible minorities, women, and immigrants, as have many other companies, including the YMCA in Toronto, Shell Canada Ltd., Federal Express Canada Ltd., and the Royal Bank of Canada (RBC).[26]

The changing employment pool is not the only factor that has prompted interest in diversity issues. Globalization, mergers, and strategic alliances mean that many employees are required to interact with people from substantially different national or corporate cultures. Compounding all this is an increased emphasis on teamwork as a means of job design and quality enhancement.

Valuing Diversity

In the past, organizations were thought to be doing the right thing if they merely tolerated diversity—that is, if they engaged in fair hiring and employment practices with respect to women and minorities. Firms were considered to be doing especially well if they assisted these

LO **3.6**

Discuss the concepts of *workforce diversity* and valuing diversity.

Workforce diversity.
Differences among recruits and employees in characteristics such as gender, race, age, religion, cultural background, physical ability, or sexual orientation.

VERIZON: DIVERSITY
Go to MyManagementLab to watch a video about diversity.

GLOBAL CULTURE AND DIVERSITY Go to MyManagementLab to complete a simulation about global culture and diversity.

EXHIBIT 3.5
Competitive advantages to valuing and managing a diverse workforce.
Source: Cox, T.H., & Blake, S. (1991, August). Managing cultural diversity: Implications for organizational competitive-ness. *Academy of Management Executive, 47,* 45–56.

1. Cost Argument	As organizations become more diverse, the cost of a poor job in integrating workers will increase. Those who handle this well will thus create cost advantages over those who don't.
2. Resource-Acquisition Argument	Companies develop reputations on favourability as prospective employers for women and ethnic minorities. Those with the best reputations for managing diversity will win the competition for the best personnel. As the labour pool shrinks and changes composition, this edge will become increasingly important.
3. Marketing Argument	For multinational organizations, the insight and cultural sensitivity that members with roots in other countries bring to the marketing effort should improve these efforts in important ways. The same rationale applies to marketing to subpopulations within domestic operations.
4. Creativity Argument	Diversity of perspectives and less emphasis on conformity to norms of the past (which characterize the modern approach to management of diversity) should improve the level of creativity.
5. Problem-Solving Argument	Heterogeneity in decision and problem solving groups potentially produces better decisions through a wider range of perspectives and more thorough critical analysis of issues.
6. System Flexibility Argument	An implication of the multicultural model for managing diversity is that the system will become less determinant, less standardized, and therefore more fluid. The increased fluidity should create greater flexibility to react to environmental changes (i.e., reactions should be faster and at less cost).

people to "fit in" with the mainstream corporate culture by "fixing" what was different about them.[27] For example, women managers were sometimes given assertiveness training to enable them to be as hard-nosed and aggressive as their male counterparts!

Recently, some have argued that organizations should *value* diversity, not just tolerate it or try to blend everyone into a narrow mainstream. To be sure, a critical motive is the basic fairness of valuing diversity. However, there is increasing awareness that diversity and its proper management can yield strategic and competitive advantages. These advantages include the potential for improved problem solving and creativity when diverse perspectives are brought to bear on an organizational problem such as product or service quality. They also include improved recruiting and marketing when the firm's human resources profile matches that of the labour pool and customer base (see Exhibit 3.5). The results of a recent study indicate that more organizations are adopting diversity as part of their corporate strategy to improve their competitiveness in global markets. Furthermore, a diversity climate (the extent to which an organization promotes equal employment opportunity and inclusion) has been found to be associated with business-unit performance. Another study found that organizations with more gender-diverse management teams have superior financial performance.[28]

However, if there is a single concept that serves as a barrier to valuing diversity, it is the stereotype. Let's now examine several workplace stereotypes and their consequences.

 LO **3.7**

Discuss how racial, ethnic, religious, gender, and age *stereotypes* affect organizational behaviour and what organizations can do to manage diversity.

Stereotypes and Workforce Diversity

As described earlier, a stereotype is the tendency to generalize about people in a certain social category and ignore variations among them. Common workplace stereotypes are based on gender, age, race, religion, and ethnicity. In the following section, we describe how stereotypes can have negative effects on how individuals are treated in organizations. It is also worth noting that in some situations in which a negative stereotype is salient, just the perception that one might be judged on the basis of a stereotype can have a negative effect on their behaviour and performance, something that is known as stereotype threat.

Stereotype threat occurs when members of a social group (e.g., visible minorities or women) feel they might be judged or treated according to a stereotype and that their behaviour and/or performance will confirm the stereotype. Thus, the existence of a stereotype threat can undermine a person's performance. Research has found evidence for stereotype threat effects for ethnicity/race stereotypes and gender-based stereotypes. The activation of a salient negative stereotype threat in a testing situation (e.g., asking test takers to report demographics prior to taking a test) has been found to result in lower cognitive ability and math test performance scores of minorities and women compared to non-threatening situations.[29] Let's now consider the nature of these stereotypes and their consequences in the workplace.

Stereotype threat. Members of a social group feel they might be judged or treated according to a stereotype and that their behaviour and/or performance will confirm the stereotype.

RACIAL, ETHNIC, AND RELIGIOUS STEREOTYPES

Racial, ethnic, and religious stereotypes are pervasive, persistent, frequently negative, and often self-contradictory. Most of us hold at least some stereotypical views of other races, religions, or cultures. Over the years, such stereotypes exhibit remarkable stability unless some major event, such as a war, intervenes to change them. Then, former allies can acquire negative attributes in short order.

Personal experience is unnecessary for such stereotype formation. In one study, people were asked to describe the traits of a number of ethnic groups, including several fictional ones. Although they had never met a Danerian, a Pirenian, or a Wallonian, this did not inhibit them from assigning traits, and those they assigned were usually unfavourable![30] Such stereotypes often contain contradictory elements. A common reaction is to describe a particular group as being too lazy, while at the same time criticizing it for taking one's job opportunities away.

There is a remarkable shortage of serious research into racial, ethnic, and religious matters in organizations.[31] However, what evidence there is shows that just getting in the door can be a problem. For example, whites have been found to advance further in the hiring process than blacks even when the applicants are the same age and physical size, have identical education and work experience, and share similar personalities.[32] A study on religious discrimination found that female job applicants who appeared to be Muslim experienced more negative interpersonal behaviour and discrimination (e.g., rudeness or hostility) than non-Muslim female applicants.[33] Discrimination in hiring has also been found to occur when job applicants have an ethnic-sounding name. To learn more, see the Ethical Focus: *What's in a Name? You're Hired...or Not!*

Even after visible minorities get in the door, career advancement based on racial or ethnic stereotypes are common. A study on the career satisfaction and advancement of visible minorities in Canada found that visible minorities perceive more barriers in their career advancement, including a lack of fairness in the process, and report less career satisfaction than white colleagues. In addition, 47 percent of visible minority managers and professionals reported feeling they were held to a higher standard of performance and 69 percent of visible minority respondents reported that in their career, "who you know" is more important than "what you know."[34] In the United States, almost one-quarter of workers from diverse backgrounds reported being discriminated against or treated unfairly at work. The most common example was not receiving credit for their work.[35]

Attributions can play an important role in determining how job performance is interpreted. For example, one study found that good performance on the part of African-American managers was seen to be due to help from others (a situational attribution), while good performance by Caucasian managers was seen to be due to their effort and abilities (a dispositional attribution).[36]

Racial and ethnic stereotypes are also important in the context of the increasing globalization of business. In one study, researchers asked American business students to describe Japanese and American managers along a number of dimensions. The students viewed Japanese managers as having more productive employees and being better overall managers. However, the students preferred to work for an American manager.[37] One can wonder how such students will respond to international assignments. Of course, all groups have stereotypes of each other. Japanese stereotypes of Americans probably contribute to Americans not being promoted above a certain level in Japanese firms.

ETHICAL FOCUS

WHAT'S IN A NAME? YOU'RE HIRED . . . OR NOT!

Have you ever thought about how your name might influence your chances of being invited for a job interview or receiving a job offer? Chances are you probably have not thought about this.

However, there is evidence that name discrimination is a problem when it comes to screening resumes and that having an ethnic-sounding name might put a job applicant at a disadvantage. Furthermore, this might explain in part why the unemployment rate of recent immigrants to Canada is almost twice as high as similarly aged non-immigrants even though Canada's immigration policy focuses on skilled immigrants with high levels of education and experience.

To find out if the name of a job applicant influences recruiter decisions, a study was conducted by Metropolis British Columbia and authors Philip Oreopoulos and Diane Dechief of the University of Toronto. The study involved sending out over 7000 resumes by email in response to job postings across multiple occupations in Toronto, Montreal, and Vancouver. The jobs required at least a bachelor's degree, fluency in English, and four to six years of work experience. All of the resumes indicated that the applicant had Canadian work experience, Canadian education, and solid credentials. However, they differed in terms of the name of the applicant. Some of the resumes had common Anglophone sounding names such as John Smith, while others had popular Greek, Indian, or Chinese names.

The main outcome variable of the study was whether or not a resume generates a callback from an employer indicating interest in meeting or further discussing the applicant's credentials. A callback is the most important step for obtaining a job offer.

The results indicated that resumes with English-sounding names were 35 percent more likely to receive a callback for a job interview than resumes with Indian or Chinese names across the three cities. Resumes with English-sounding names also received more callbacks than resumes with Greek-sounding names. These results remained even when taking into account many other factors on the resumes such as a degree from a top-ranking university, active social extracurricular activities, or job experience from a large, multinational firm.

These results indicate the existence of employer discrimination against job applicants with ethnic-sounding names. According to the authors of the study, subconscious or implicit discrimination may be one reason why recruiters are less likely to call back applicants with ethnic-sounding names. An applicant's name or country of origin may trigger stereotypes that cause employers to focus on the stereotype and overemphasize potential concerns such as social and language skills and to ignore other important factors on the resume such as education and experience.

These results provide one explanation for a common complaint from immigrants to Canada that they never hear back from prospective employers, even when they apply for jobs that precisely match their expertise. What's more, the results also indicate that even Canadian-raised and educated job applicants might be discriminated against if they have an ethnic-sounding name.

Sources: Oreopoulos, P., & Dechief, D. (2011). *Why do some employers prefer to interview Matthew, but not Samir? New evidence from Toronto, Montreal, and Vancouver.* Metropolis British Columbia Centre of Excellence for Research on Immigration and Diversity, Working Paper Series, No.11-13; Dobson, S. (2011, November 21). "Matthew, you're hired. Good luck next time, Samir." *Canadian HR Reporter, 24*(20), 1, 20; Immen, W. (2011, November 18). How an ethnic-sounding name may affect the job hunt; Hiring managers tend to bypass resumes with foreign-sounding names even if education, experience meet the grade, study finds. *The Globe and Mail,* B21.

Finally, recent evidence suggests that organizations are simply reflections of the environments of which they are a part. Thus, if prejudice, negative stereotyping, ethnocentrism, and discrimination exist within the environment that an organization inhabits, it is very likely that these problems will surface within the organization itself.[38]

GENDER STEREOTYPES One of the most problematic stereotypes for organizations is the gender stereotype. Considering their numbers in the workforce, women are severely underrepresented in managerial and administrative jobs. Although women now occupy a significant and growing proportion of entry- and mid-level management positions, this is not the case for top-level positions, where they remain significantly underrepresented. According to a study of 500 of Canada's top companies by Catalyst Canada, women hold only 14.4 percent of corporate officer positions, including presidents, executive vice-presidents, and chief operating officers. As a result, it's predicted that women's overall representation in corporate Canada will not reach 25 percent until 2025.[39]

There is evidence that gender stereotypes are partially responsible for discouraging women from business careers and blocking their ascent to managerial positions. This under-representation of women managers and administrators happens because stereotypes of women do not correspond especially well with stereotypes of business people or managers.

What is the nature of gender stereotypes? A series of studies have had managers describe men in general, women in general, and typical "successful middle managers." These studies have determined that successful middle managers are perceived as having traits and atti-tudes that are similar to those generally ascribed to men. That is, successful managers are seen as more similar to men in qualities such as leadership ability, competitiveness, self-confidence, ambitiousness, and objectivity.[40] Thus, stereotypes of successful middle manag-ers do not correspond to stereotypes of women. The trend over time in the results of these studies contains some bad news and some good news. The bad news is that *male* managers today hold the same dysfunctional stereotypes about women and management that they held in the early 1970s when researchers conducted the first of these studies. At that time, women managers held the same stereotypes as the men. The good news is that the recent research shows a shift by the women—they now see successful middle managers as possessing atti-tudes and characteristics that describe *both* men and women in general. However, although good managers are described today as possessing fewer masculine characteristics than in past decades, the recent research indicates that both men and women of varying age, educa-tion, and work experience still describe a good manager as possessing predominantly mascu-line characteristics. In other words, the stereotype of a leader is culturally masculine. People perceive leaders as similar to men but not very similar to women.[41]

Granting that gender stereotypes exist, do they lead to biased human resources deci-sions? The answer would appear to be yes. In a typical study, researchers asked male bank supervisors to make hypothetical decisions about workers who were described equivalently except for gender.[42] Women were discriminated against for promotion to a branch manager's position. They were also discriminated against when they requested to attend a professional development conference. In addition, female supervisors were less likely than their male counterparts to receive support for their request that a problem employee be fired. In one case, bias worked to *favour* women. The bank supervisors were more likely to approve a request for a leave of absence to care for one's children when it came from a female. This finding is similar to others that show that gender stereotypes tend to favour women when they are being considered for "women's" jobs (such as secretary) or for "women's" tasks (such as supervising other women), but not for traditional male jobs.[43] One recent study found that when women are successful in traditional male jobs, they are less liked, and being disliked had a negative effect on their evaluations and recommendations for rewards, including salary and special job opportunities.[44]

In general, research suggests that the above findings are fairly typical. Women suffer from a stereotype that is detrimental to their hiring, development, promotion, and salaries. Female managers are also more likely than male managers to have to make off-the-job sacri-fices and compromises in family life to maintain their careers.[45] However, there is growing evidence that the detrimental effects of such stereotypes are reduced or removed when deci-sion makers have good information about the qualifications and performance of particular women and an accurate picture of the job that they are applying for or seeking promotion into.[46] In particular, several studies reveal convincingly that women do not generally suffer from gender stereotypes in *performance evaluations* that their supervisors provide.[47] This is not altogether surprising. As we noted earlier, stereotypes help us process information in ambiguous situations. To the extent that we have good information on which to base our perceptions of people, reliance on stereotypes is less necessary. Day-to-day performance is often fairly easy to observe, and gender stereotypes do not intrude on evaluations. Along these lines, a recent review of research on gender differences in job performance ratings found that females scored slightly higher than males; however, males received higher ratings of promotion potential.[48]

1.	L.V. Lomes Limited
2.	Admiral Insurance
3.	DEL Property Management Inc.
4.	Nycomed, a Takeda Company
5.	Royal Lepage Performance Realty
6.	SaskCentral (Credit Union Central of Saskatchewan)
7.	Ariad Communications
8.	T4G Limited
9.	Lutherwood
10.	Achievers (Formerly I Love Rewards)

Fortunately, as shown in Exhibit 3.6, many Canadian organizations have made efforts to ensure that women are represented in senior positions and have been recognized for their endeavours. For example, at Shell Canada Ltd. of Calgary there are more women than men on the list of potential senior managers.[49] Women have made the most significant progress moving into senior management and executive positions in the financial services industry. On the other hand, industries that tend to be stereotypically male, such as paper and forest products, steel production, motor vehicles and parts, oil and gas, and general manufacturing and construction, continue to have the lowest representation of women in senior positions.[50]

AGE STEREOTYPES Another kind of stereotype that presents problems for organizations is the age stereotype. Knowing that a person falls into a certain age range or belongs to a particular age generation, we have a tendency to make certain assumptions about the person's physical, psychological, and intellectual capabilities. We will have more to say about generation differences and values in Chapter 4.

What is the nature of work-related age stereotypes? Older workers are seen as having less *capacity for performance*. They tend to be viewed as less productive, creative, logical, and capable of performing under pressure than younger workers. In addition, older workers are seen as having less *potential for development*. Compared with younger workers, they are considered more rigid and dogmatic and less adaptable to new corporate cultures. Not all stereotypes of older workers are negative, however. They tend to be perceived as more honest, dependable, and trustworthy (in short, more *stable*). In general, these stereotypes are held by both younger and older individuals.[51]

It is worth noting that these stereotypes are essentially inaccurate. For example, age seldom limits the capacity for development until post-employment years.[52] Furthermore, the most comprehensive study on age and job performance found that age is not related to task performance or creativity but it is related to other forms of job performance. For example, older workers were found to exhibit more citizenship behaviours and greater safety-related behaviour, and fewer counterproductive work behaviours. Older workers were also found to exhibit less workplace aggression, on-the-job substance use, tardiness, and absenteeism. Thus, by all accounts older workers perform as well or better than younger workers across numerous dimensions of job performance.[53]

However, the relevant question remains: Do age stereotypes affect human resources decisions? It would appear that such stereotypes can affect decisions regarding hiring, promotion, and skills development. In one study, researchers had university students make hypothetical recommendations regarding younger and older male workers. An older man was less likely to be hired for a finance job that required rapid, high-risk decisions. An older man was considered less promotable for a marketing position that required creative solutions to difficult problems. Finally, an older worker was less likely to be permitted to attend

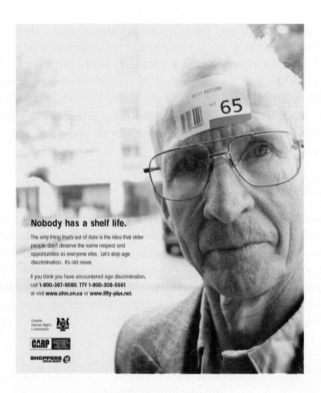

A public awareness campaign to combat age stereotypes and discrimination sponsored by Canada's Association for the Fifty-Plus and the Ontario Human Rights Commission featured this poster with the tag line "Nobody has a shelf life."

a conference on advanced production systems.[54] These decisions reflect the stereotypes of the older worker depicted above, and they are doubtless indicative of the tendency for older employees to be laid off during corporate restructuring.

Unfortunately, the reality for older workers is consistent with the research. According to the Ontario Human Rights Commission, discrimination on the basis of age is experienced by people as young as 40 to 45, who are often passed over for merit pay and promotions or pressured to take early retirement. In a blatant example of such discrimination, a job fair held in Toronto several years ago stated that the target audience was 18- to 54-year-olds. Many older workers were offended, and a complaint was made to the Ontario Human Rights Commission.[55] Again, however, we should recognize that age stereotypes may have less impact on human resources decisions when managers have good information about the capacities of the particular employee in question.

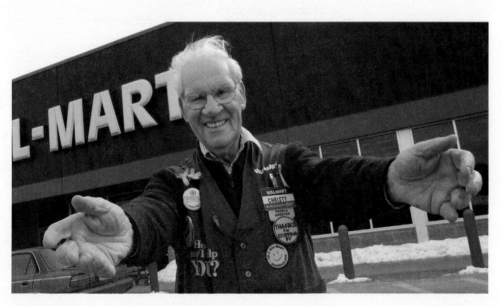

Walmart Canada is a repeat winner of the Best Employer Awards for 50-plus Canadians for its efforts in attracting and hiring older workers.

To combat age stereotypes and discrimination, Canada's Association for the Fifty-Plus (CARP) has worked with the Ontario Human Rights Commission on a public awareness campaign that included a poster featuring photographs of older people with the tag line "Nobody has a shelf life. Stop age discrimination now."[56] Some organizations have implemented programs and practices to promote the hiring and retention of older workers. A good example is Walmart Canada, which has been recognized for its efforts in attracting and hiring older workers. The company is a repeat winner of the Best Employer Awards for 50-plus Canadians.[57]

Managing Workforce Diversity

←●┤Simulate

HUMAN RESOURCES AND DIVERSITY Go to MyManagementLab to complete a simulation about human resources and diversity.

Given the prevalence of the stereotypes noted above, valuing diversity is not something that occurs automatically. Rather, diversity needs to be *managed* to have a positive impact on work behaviour and an organization. What can organizations do to achieve and manage a diverse workforce? Before continuing, try to answer this question by taking another look at the chapter-opening vignette on KPMG to see what they do to manage a diverse workforce.

Exhibit 3.7 lists some of the common activities that are often included in diversity programs. Some additional examples are listed below.[58]

EXHIBIT 3.7
Common activities included in diversity programs.
Source: Jayne, M.E.A., & Dipboye, R.L. (2004, Winter). Leveraging diversity to improve business performance: Research findings and recommendations for organizations. *Human Resource Management*, *43(4)*, 409–424. © 2004 John Wiley & Sons, Inc. Used by permission.

Strategic Initiative	Sample Interventions
Recruiting	• Employee referral programs • Diverse recruiting teams • Internship programs and sponsored scholarships • Job posting and advertising initiatives targeting specific groups • Minority conference and job fair attendance • Recruiting efforts targeting universities and community colleges with diverse student bodies
Retention	• Corporate-sponsored employee resource or affinity groups • Employee benefits (e.g., adoption, domestic partner, elder care, flexible health, and dependent spending accounts) • Work–life programs and incentives (e.g., on-site child care, flexible work schedules, and on-site lactation facilities)
Development	• Leadership development training programs • Mentoring programs
External Partnership	• Minority supplier programs • Community service outreach
Communication	• Award programs providing public recognition of managers and employees for diversity achievement • Newsletters, internal websites on diversity • Senior leadership addresses, town hall meetings, business updates
Training	• Awareness training on the organization's diversity initiative • Issue-based/prevention training (e.g., sexual harassment and men and women as colleagues) • Team-building and group-process training
Staffing and Infrastructure	• Dedicated diversity staff • Executive and local diversity councils

- Select enough minority members to get them beyond token status. When this happens, the majority starts to look at individual accomplishments rather than group membership because they can see variation in the behaviours of the minority. In recent years, an increasing number of Canadian organizations have become more interested in diversity recruiting and, as indicted in the chapter-opening vignette, KPMG actively recruits immigrants and has set targets for promoting women.[59]

- Encourage teamwork that brings minority and majority members together.

- Ensure that those making career decisions about employees have accurate information about them rather than having to rely on hearsay and second-hand opinion.

- Train people to be aware of stereotypes and to value diversity. As indicated in the chapter-opening vignette, KPMG made diversity training mandatory for all employees and new hires.

A good example of a company that manages workforce diversity is Boeing Canada, which has been recognized as one of Canada's Best Diversity Employers. The company actively promotes diversity, which helps to create a positive and respectful workplace and contributes to the overall success of the organization. In addition to employing deaf people and providing them with BlackBerrys to communicate with co-workers and their supervisors, the company also employs the following diversity strategies:[60]

- Diversity days that feature a lunch from a particular culture accompanied by presentations that include dancers and singers to help employees learn about the diverse backgrounds of their co-workers.

- Diversity training that includes formal educational classes on respecting and honouring co-worker's origins, leanings, and affiliations.

- Language training for recent immigrants and others who want to improve their English, as well as training in American Sign Language (ASL).

- Monthly awareness campaigns that profile events in the calendar such as Ramadan.

- Aboriginal recruitment in partnership with the Centre for Aboriginal Human Resource Development in Winnipeg.

- A women's committee to assist female employees with personal and professional development.

- Partnering with the Society for Manitobans with Disabilities (SMD) to provide employment opportunities to disabled job seekers.

- Job shadowing in cooperation with Red River College's deaf students program in Winnipeg so that students can see and communicate with deaf employees at work.

- A volunteer employment equity and diversity team that meets biweekly to identify and discuss diversity initiatives and plan awareness programs.

Although diversity training programs are one of the most common approaches for managing diversity, there is little hard research on the success of these programs. However, there is some anecdotal evidence that these programs can actually cause disruption and bad feelings when all they do is get people to open up and voice their stereotypes and then send them back to work.[61] Awareness training should be accompanied by skills training that is relevant to the particular needs of the organization. This might include training in resolving intercultural conflict, team building, handling a charge of sexual harassment, or learning a second language. Basic awareness and skills training are not the only components of managing diversity. Organizations must use a number of other tactics. What is perhaps most important is that organizations integrate diversity into all of its policies and practices rather than treat diversity as a stand-alone practice. Organizations that have been successful in managing diversity have an inclusive culture that values individual differences.[62]

In future chapters, we will consider the following diversity practices:

- The implications of generational differences in values and work attitudes (Chapter 4).
- Recognizing diversity in employee needs and motives (Chapter 5).
- Using alternative working schedules to offer employees flexibility (Chapter 6).
- Using employee surveys to foster better communication (Chapters 10 and 16).

YOU BE THE MANAGER

American Express Canada's Skilled Immigrant Strategy

American Express in Canada operates as AMEX Canada Inc. and AMEX Bank of Canada. AMEX Canada Inc. and AMEX Band of Canada employ over 3000 Canadians in 13 cities coast to coast.

AMEX Canada has had a diverse workforce for many years. However, with the expected growth in the coming years, the company realized that it needed to do more to attract, retain, and develop skilled immigrants.

Nancy Steele, Director of AMEX technologies (AET), was puzzled that the company's policy of hiring skilled immigrant workers seemed to be failing. "Quite often, you would on-board them, then find they weren't successful and have to remove them and have them leave the organization" she said.

As a solution, Steele initiated a skilled immigrant strategy. "The broader strategy was to look at talent in general across the organization," she said. "As we're going to grow, take on new people and invest a lot in Canada, we looked at what we're going to do to keep up the pace of growth and diversity a little bit."

In looking at ways to hire new employees, she realized there needed to be more work done to hire immigrants. "There were a lot of gaps in the process of how we hire and recruit, where we hire and recruit, and the type of talent we're getting," she said. "There were many opportunities we didn't see."

Furthermore, managers sometimes struggled to understand other cultures and help staff to succeed.

To retain skilled immigrants, Steele implemented initiatives to encourage these employees to grow within the company. "We looked at strategies to improve the process to help individuals not only get better jobs or jobs that are more suited to their skills, but develop them when they're on-site and help them progress in their career," she said.

What should AMEX Canada do to improve the hiring and retention of skilled immigrants? You be the manager.

Fernanda Silva (left) is a Brazillian immigrant who was hired by AMEX technologies as a quality assurance analyst through a skilled immigrant hiring program that was initiated by company director, Nancy Steele.

Questions

1. What should AMEX Canada do to attract and hire skilled immigrants?

2. What strategies are needed to develop and retain skilled immigrants?

To find out what AMEX Canada did, consult The Manager's Notebook at the end of the chapter.

Sources: Based on Silliker, A. (2011, March 28). Firms honoured for work with skilled immigrants. *Canadian HR Reporter, 24*(6), 1, 20; Dalby, P. (2011, March 9). New hiring approach improves success rate for immigrants. *Toronto Star,* www.thestar.com/printarticle/950769; Anonymous (2011, October 6). Nancy Steele spearheads skilled immigrant strategy at American Express Canada. *TRIEC,* www.triec.ca/2011/nancy-steele-spearheads-skilled-immigrant-strategy; www.americanexpress.com/ca.

Finally, one area of diversity that is of particular concern to governments and organizations is the hiring and integration of skilled immigrants, something that KPMG has been doing very well. To find out how another organization is doing this, read You Be the Manager: *American Express Canada's Skilled Immigrant Strategy*.

PERCEPTIONS OF TRUST

LO 3.8

Define *trust* perceptions and *perceived organizational support*, and describe organizational support theory.

Do you trust your boss and organization? What about your co-workers? These are questions that more and more people are asking themselves today, and research has found that employee trust toward management is on the decline.[63] One survey found that 47 percent of those who responded agreed that a lack of trust is a problem in their organization. In another survey, 40 percent indicated that they do not believe what management says.[64] A decline in trust can be a serious problem because trust perceptions influence organizational processes and outcomes, such as sales levels, net profits, and employee turnover.[65]

Trust has been defined as a willingness to be vulnerable and to take risks with respect to the actions of another party.[66] More specifically, "trust is a psychological state comprising the intention to accept vulnerability based upon positive expectations of the intentions or behaviour of another."[67] Trust perceptions toward management are based on three distinct perceptions: ability, benevolence, and integrity.[68] *Ability* refers to employee perceptions regarding management's competence and skills. *Benevolence* refers to the extent that employees perceive management as caring and concerned for their interests and willing to do good for them. *Integrity* refers to employee perceptions that management adheres to and behaves according to a set of values and principles that the employee finds acceptable. The combination of these three factors influences trust perceptions.

Trust. A psychological state in which one has a willingness to be vulnerable and to take risks with respect to the actions of another party.

Not surprisingly, higher perceptions of management ability, benevolence, and integrity are associated with greater perceptions of trust. There is also some evidence that perceptions of fairness (see Chapter 4 for a discussion of fairness) are associated with trust perceptions. Employees who perceived their supervisor as more fair report higher levels of trust.[69] Furthermore, perceptions of trust in management are positively related to job satisfaction, organizational commitment, job performance, and organizational citizenship behaviour, and negatively related to turnover intentions.[70]

Trust is also considered to be the most critical factor when judging best workplaces in Canada. According to the Great Place to Work Institute Canada, trust is the foundation for quality jobs and performance excellence. When the institute evaluates organizations for the best workplaces, they use a "Trust Index" to assess employees' perspective on what it is like to work in their organization. As shown in Exhibit 3.8, the trust model consists of five dimensions. To create a great workplace, managers need to build trust, which is achieved by practising credibility, respect, and fairness, and by encouraging pride and camaraderie among employees.[71]

Finally, it should also be noted that trust among co-workers is also important. A study of firefighters found that higher levels of trust toward one's co-workers was related to fewer physical symptoms (e.g., trouble sleeping) and less withdrawal (e.g., thoughts of being absent).[72]

PERCEIVED ORGANIZATIONAL SUPPORT

Whether or not you trust your boss and organization probably has a lot to do with how much they support you or, rather, your perceptions of support. **Perceived organizational support** (POS) refers to employees' general belief that their organization values their contribution and cares about their well-being. When employees have positive perceptions of organizational support, they believe their organization will provide assistance when they need it to perform their job effectively and to deal with stressful situations.[73]

Perceived organizational support (POS). Employees' general belief that their organization values their contribution and cares about their well-being.

EXHIBIT 3.8
Trust model.
Source: © 2005 Great Place to Work® Institute, Inc. All Rights Reserved.

Explore

Go to MyManagementLab to see an annotated version of this figure.

CREDIBILITY
- ▶ Being approachable and easy to talk with, answering hard questions, and making expectations clear
- ▶ Trusting people without looking over their shoulders
- ▶ Being reliable, delivering on promises, and "walking the talk"
- ▶ Articulating a clear vision for the company or department

RESPECT
- ▶ Showing appreciation for employees' efforts and contributions
- ▶ Ensuring that people have the equipment they need to do their jobs
- ▶ Seeking employees' opinions and involving them in important decisions
- ▶ Caring for employees as people with lives outside of work

FAIRNESS
- ▶ Ensuring all employees have opportunities for rewards and recognition
- ▶ Avoiding playing favourites, especially when promoting people
- ▶ Treating all employees fairly, regardless of age, race, or sex
- ▶ Ensuring employees are paid fairly

TRUST

PRIDE
- ▶ Helping employees feel they personally make a difference in their work
- ▶ Inspiring employees to feel pride in team accomplishments
- ▶ Helping employees feel proud of the whole company and its contributions to the community

CAMARADERIE
- ▶ Creating a workplace atmosphere where employees can be themselves and care about each other
- ▶ Welcoming new employees to a friendly environment and celebrating special events
- ▶ Creating a cooperative work environment and demonstrating that people are "all in this together"

Organizational support theory. A theory that states that employees who have strong perceptions of organizational support feel an obligation to care about the organization's welfare and to help the organization achieve its objectives.

According to **organizational support theory**, employees who have strong perceptions of organizational support feel an obligation to care about the organization's welfare and to help the organization achieve its objectives. They feel a greater sense of purpose and meaning, and a strong sense of belonging to the organization. As a result, employees incorporate their membership and role within the organization into their social identity. In addition, when POS is strong, employees feel obligated to reciprocate the organization's care and support. As a result, POS has a number of positive consequences.

Research has found that employees who have greater POS have higher job performance and are more satisfied with their jobs, more committed to the organization, and less likely to be absent from work and to quit. They are also more likely to have a positive mood at work and to be more involved in their job, and they are less likely to experience strain symptoms such as fatigue, burnout, anxiety, and headaches.[74]

As shown in Exhibit 3.9, there are a number of factors that contribute to employees' POS. First, because supervisors function as representatives of the organization through their actions and decisions, they represent the organization to employees. As a result, favourable treatment and support from supervisors, or *perceived supervisor support*, contributes strongly to POS. Interestingly, supervisors with more positive perceptions of POS are themselves perceived by employees as being more supportive. In addition, fair organizational procedures as well as favourable rewards and job conditions are also strongly related to POS.[75]

What can organizations do to improve employee perceptions of organizational support? One study found that supportive human resources practices that demonstrate an investment

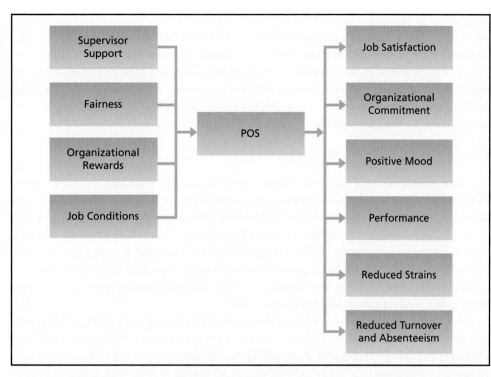

EXHIBIT 3.9
**Predictors and conse-
quences of perceived
organizational support.**
Source: Based on Rhoades, L.,
& Eisenberger, R. (2002).
Perceived organizational sup-
port: A review of the literature.
Journal of Applied Psychology,
87, 698–714.

Go to MyManagementLab
to see an annotated
version of this figure.

in employees and recognition of employee contributions are most likely to lead to the development of greater POS. Such practices signal to employees that the organization values and
cares about them. Some examples of supportive human resources practices include participation in decision making, opportunities for growth and development, and a fair reward and
recognition system.[76] Of course, equality and diversity programs such as those at KPMG also
help to increase POS.

PERSON PERCEPTION IN HUMAN RESOURCES

LO **3.9**

Perceptions play an important role in human resources and can influence who gets hired and
how employees are evaluated once they are hired. Job applicants also form perceptions during
the recruitment and selection process, and their perceptions influence their attraction to an
organization and whether or not they decide to accept a job offer.

Discuss person
perception and
perceptual biases in
human resources.

In this section, we consider the role of perceptions in three important areas of human
resources: recruitment and selection, the employment interview, and the performance appraisal.

Perceptions of Recruitment and Selection

When you meet recruiters and complete employment tests, chances are you form perceptions
of the organization. In fact, research indicates that how job applicants are treated during the
recruitment and selection process influences their perceptions toward the organization and
their likelihood of accepting a job offer. According to **signalling theory**, job applicants have
incomplete information about jobs and organizations so they interpret their recruitment experiences as cues or signals about unknown characteristics of an organization and what it would
be like to work there. For example, questions that are invasive and discriminatory might send
a signal that the organization discriminates and does not value diversity; poor treatment during the hiring process might signal a lack of professionalism and respect of employees. These
perceptions are important because they influence a job applicant's likelihood of remaining in
the selection process and accepting a job offer.[77]

Signalling theory. Job
applicants interpret their
recruitment experiences
as cues or signals about
unknown characteristics of
an organization and what
it will be like to work in an
organization.

Applicants also form perceptions toward organizations based on the selection tests used
for hiring. This research has its basis in *organizational justice theory*, which is described in

more detail in Chapter 4. Essentially, job applicants form more positive perceptions of the selection process when selection procedures are perceived to be fair. Furthermore, applicants who have more positive perceptions of selection fairness are more likely to view the organization favourably and to have stronger intentions to accept a job offer and recommend the organization to others. Among various selection procedures, employment interviews and work samples are perceived more favourably than cognitive ability tests, which are perceived more favourably than personality tests and honesty tests.[78]

Perceptions in the Employment Interview

You have probably had the pleasure (or displeasure!) of sitting through one or more job interviews in your life. After all, the interview is one of the most common organizational selection devices, applied with equal opportunity to applicants for everything from the janitorial staff to the executive suite. With our futures on the line, we would like to think that the interview is a fair and accurate selection device, but is it? Research shows that the interview is a valid selection device, although it is far from perfectly accurate, especially when the interviewer conducts it in an unstructured, free-form format. The validity of the interview improves when interviewers conduct a more structured interview.[79]

What factors threaten the validity of the interview? To consider the most obvious problem first, applicants are usually motivated to present an especially favourable impression of themselves. As our discussion of the perception of people implies, it is difficult enough to gain a clear picture of another individual without having to cope with active deception! A couple of the perceptual tendencies that we already discussed in this chapter can also operate in the interview. For one thing, there is evidence that interviewers compare applicants to a stereotype of the ideal applicant.[80] In and of itself, this is not a bad thing. However, this ideal stereotype must be accurate, and this requires a clear understanding of the nature of the job in question and the kind of person who can do well in this job. This is a tall order, especially for the interviewer who is hiring applicants for a wide variety of jobs. Second, interviewers have a tendency to exhibit primacy reactions.[81] Minimally, this means that information the interviewer acquired early in the interview will have an undue impact on the final decision. However, it also means that information the interviewer obtained *before* the interview (for instance, by scanning the application form or resume) can have an exaggerated influence on the interview outcome.

The interview is a difficult setting in which to form accurate impressions about a candidate. Interview validity increases when interviews are more structured.

A couple of perceptual tendencies that we have not discussed are also at work in interviews. First, interviewers have a tendency to give less importance to positive information about the applicant.[82] This tendency means that negative information has undue impact on the decision.[83] It might occur because interviewers get more feedback about unsuccessful hiring than successful hiring ("Why did you send me that idiot?"). It might also happen because positive information is not perceived as telling the interviewer much, since the candidate is motivated to put up a good front. In addition, **contrast effects** sometimes occur in the interview.[84] This means that the applicants who have been interviewed earlier affect the interviewer's perception of a current applicant, leading to an exaggeration of differences between applicants. For example, if the interviewer has seen two excellent candidates and then encounters an average candidate, she might rate this person lower than if he had been preceded by two average applicants (see Exhibit 3.10). This is an example of the impact of the situation on perception.

Contrast effects.
Previously interviewed job applicants affect an interviewer's perception of a current applicant, leading to an exaggeration of differences between applicants.

It is clear that the interview constitutes a fairly difficult setting in which to form accurate impressions about others. It is of short duration, a lot of information is generated, and the applicant is motivated to present a favourable image. Thus, interviewers often adopt "perceptual crutches" that hinder accurate perception. At KPMG, employees involved in the recruitment process receive bias-free interview training.[85]

Earlier, we noted that the validity of the interview improves when it is structured. But what exactly is a structured interview? According to a study by Derek Chapman of the

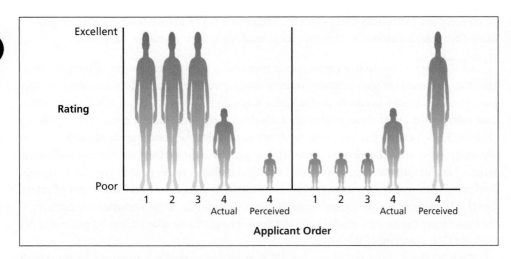

EXHIBIT 3.10
Two examples of contrast effects.

Explore

Go to MyManagementLab to see an annotated version of this figure.

University of Calgary and David Zweig of the University of Toronto, interview structure involves four dimensions: *evaluation standardization* (the extent to which the interviewer uses standardized and numeric scoring procedures); *question sophistication* (the extent to which the interviewer uses job-related behavioural questions and situational questions); *question consistency* (the extent to which the interviewer asks the same questions in the same order of every candidate); and *rapport building* (the extent to which the interviewer does *not* ask personal questions that are unrelated to the job). They also found that interviews were more likely to be structured when the interviewer had formal interview training and focused on selection rather than recruitment during the interview.[86] Structured interviews probably reduce information overload and ensure that applicants can be more easily compared, since they have all responded to an identical sequence of questions.[87]

Perceptions and the Performance Appraisal

Once a person is hired, however imperfectly, further perceptual tasks confront organization members. Specifically, the organization will want some index of the person's job performance for decisions regarding pay raises, promotions, transfers, and training needs.

OBJECTIVE AND SUBJECTIVE MEASURES   It is possible to find objective measures of performance for certain aspects of some jobs. These are measures that do not involve a substantial degree of human judgment. The number of publications that a professor has in top journals is a good example. In general, though, as we move up the organizational hierarchy, it becomes more difficult to find objective indicators of performance. Thus, it is often hard to find quantifiable evidence of a manager's success or failure. When objective indicators of performance do exist, they are often contaminated by situational factors. For example, it might be very difficult to compare the dollar sales of a snowmobile salesperson whose territory covers British Columbia with one whose territory is Nova Scotia. Also, while dollar sales might be a good indicator of current sales performance, it says little about a person's capacity for promotion to district sales manager.

Because of the difficulties that objective performance indicators present, organizations must often rely on subjective measures of effectiveness, usually provided by managers. However, the manager is confronted by a number of perceptual roadblocks. He or she might not be in a position to observe many instances of effective and ineffective performance. This is especially likely when the employee's job activities cannot be monitored directly. For example, a police sergeant cannot ride around in six squad cars at the same time, and a telephone company supervisor cannot visit customers' homes or climb telephone poles with all of his or her installers. Such situations mean that the target (the employee's performance) is frequently ambiguous, and we have seen that the perceptual system resolves ambiguities in an efficient but often inaccurate manner. Even when performance is observable, employees often alter their behaviour so that they look good when their manager is around.

RATER ERRORS Subjective performance appraisal is susceptible to some of the perceptual biases we discussed earlier—primacy, recency, and stereotypes. In addition, a number of other perceptual tendencies occur in performance evaluation. They are often called rater errors. One interrelated set of these tendencies includes leniency, harshness, and central tendency (Exhibit 3.11). **Leniency** refers to the tendency to perceive the performance of one's ratees as especially good, while **harshness** is the tendency to see their performance as especially ineffective. Lenient raters tend to give "good" ratings, and harsh raters tend to give "bad" ratings. Professors with reputations as easy graders or tough graders exemplify these types of raters. **Central tendency** involves assigning most ratees to a middle-range performance category— the extremes of the rating categories are not used. The professor who assigns 80 percent of her students *C*s is committing this error.

Each of these three rating tendencies is probably partially a function of the rater's personal experiences. For example, the manager who has had an especially good group of employees might respond with special harshness when management transfers him to supervise a group of slightly less able workers. It is worth noting that not all instances of leniency, harshness, and central tendency necessarily represent perceptual errors. In some cases, raters intentionally commit these errors, even though they have accurate perceptions of workers' performance. For example, a manager might use leniency or central tendency in performance reviews so that his employees do not react negatively to his evaluation.

Another perceptual error that is frequently committed by performance raters is called the **halo effect**.[88] The halo effect occurs when the observer allows the rating of an individual on one trait or characteristic to colour the ratings on other traits or characteristics. For example, in a teacher evaluation system, a student might perceive his instructor as a nice person, and this might favourably influence his perception of the instructor's knowledge of the material and speed in returning exams and papers. Similarly, a manager might rate an employee as frequently late for work, and this might in turn lead her to devalue the employee's productivity and quality of work. As these examples illustrate, halo can work either for or against the ratee. In both cases, the rater fails to perceive differences *within* ratees. The halo effect tends to be organized around central traits that the rater considers important. The student feels that being nice is an especially important quality, while the manager places special emphasis on promptness. Ratings on these characteristics then affect the rater's perceptions of other characteristics.

The **similar-to-me effect** is an additional rater error that may, in part, reflect perceptual bias. The rater tends to give more favourable evaluations to people who are similar to the rater in terms of background or attitudes. For example, the manager with an MBA degree

Leniency. The tendency to perceive the job performance of ratees as especially good.

Harshness. The tendency to perceive the job performance of ratees as especially ineffective.

Central tendency. The tendency to assign most ratees to middle-range job performance categories.

Halo effect. The rating of an individual on one trait or characteristic tends to colour ratings on other traits or characteristics.

Similar-to-me effect. A rater gives more favourable evaluations to people who are similar to the rater in terms of background or attitudes.

EXHIBIT 3.11
Leniency, harshness, and central tendency rater errors.

Explore

Go to MyManagementLab to see an annotated version of this figure.

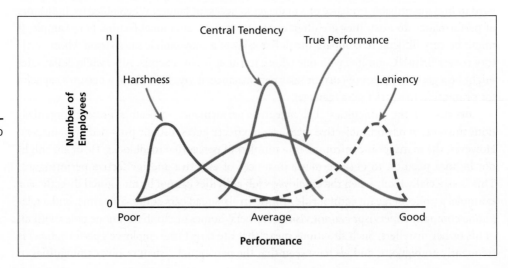

who comes from an upper-middle-class family might perceive a similar employee as a good performer even though the person is only average. Similarly, a rater might overestimate the performance of an individual who holds similar religious and political views. Such reactions probably stem from a tendency to view our own performance, attitudes, and background as "good." We then tend to generalize this evaluation to others who are, to some degree, similar to us. Raters with diverse employees should be especially wary of this error.

Given all these problems, it should be clear that it is difficult to obtain good subjective evaluations of employee performance. Because of this, human resources specialists have explored various techniques for reducing perceptual errors and biases. There has been a tendency to attempt to reduce rater errors by using rating scales with more specific behavioural labels. The assumption here is that giving specific examples of effective and ineffective performance will facilitate the rater's perceptual processes and recall.

Exhibit 3.12 shows a **behaviourally anchored rating scale (BARS)** that gives very specific behavioural examples (from top to bottom) of good, average, and poor customer service. It was developed for the J.C. Penney Company. With such an aid, the rater may be less susceptible to perceptual errors when completing the rating task, although the evidence for this is mixed.[89]

Another approach for reducing perceptual errors and biases and improving the accuracy of performance appraisals is rater training. One of the best known approaches is

Behaviourally anchored rating scale (BARS). A rating scale with specific behavioural examples of good, average, and poor performance.

EXHIBIT 3.12
Behaviourally anchored rating scale (BARS) for rating customer service.
Source: Campbell, J.P., Dunnette, M.D., Lawler, E.E., III, & Weick, K.E., Jr. (1970). *Managerial behavior, performance, and effectiveness.* New York: McGraw-Hill. © The McGraw-Hill Companies, Inc. Used by permission.

✳ Explore

Go to MyManagementLab to see an annotated version of this figure.

Could be expected to exchange a blouse purchased in a distant town and to impress the customer so much that she would buy three dresses and three pairs of shoes.

Could be expected to smooth things over beautifully with an irate customer who returned a sweater with a hole in it and turn her into a satisfied customer.

Could be expected to be friendly and tactful and to agree to reline a coat for a customer who wants a new coat because the lining had worn out in "only" two years.

Could be expected to courteously exchange a pair of gloves that are too small.

Could be expected to handle the after-Christmas rush of refunds and exchanges in a reasonable manner.

Could be expected to make a refund for a sweater only if the customer insists.

Could be expected to be quite abrupt with customers who want to exchange merchandise for a different colour or style.

Could be expected to tell a customer that a "six-week-old" order could not be changed even though the merchandise had actually been ordered only two weeks previously.

Could be expected to tell a customer who tried to return a shirt bought in Hawaii that a store in the States had no use for a Hawaiian shirt.

Frame-of-reference (FOR) training. A training method to improve rating accuracy that involves providing raters with a common frame of reference to use when rating individuals.

called **frame-of-reference (FOR) training**. FOR training involves providing raters with a common frame of reference to use when rating individuals. Raters learn about each performance dimension and are provided with examples of good, average, and poor performance. They then practise making performance ratings and receive feedback on their accuracy. As a result, raters learn what behaviours reflect different levels of performance on each performance dimension and to use the same frame of reference when rating all individuals. Research on FOR training has shown that it is a very effective method for improving rating accuracy.[90]

THE MANAGER'S NOTEBOOK

American Express Canada's Skilled Immigrant Strategy

AMEX Canada's skilled immigrant strategy was implemented in 2009 and earned Nancy Steele the *Canadian HR Reporter* Individual Achievement Award in 2011 at the Immigrant Success Awards presented by the Toronto Region Immigrant Employment Council (TRIEC). This is a good example of how a strategy for managing diversity includes skilled immigrants and that this requires special initiatives for hiring, developing, and retaining them. In 2012, AMEX Canada was named one of Canada's Best Diversity Employers.

1. To recruit skilled immigrants, Nancy Steele worked with TRIEC and organized a mass recruitment day. TRIEC, which pre-screens applicants, brought in 200 immigrants and 10 managers and went through the interview process with the recruits. There have been two sessions like this to date, with more scheduled. So far 11 skilled immigrants have been hired through the program, or 10 percent of hires in the AET division. They have filled key positions such as quality assurance analysts, business analysts, project managers, and programming.

2. To develop and retain skilled immigrants, a number of initiatives were implemented. Language training is available for those skilled immigrants whose language skills many not be "quite as robust" as what is needed, said Steele. English language training enhances integration and promotion. Managers undergo cross-cultural training to learn how to understand the challenges immigrants might be facing and evaluate any potential gaps in their training or performance, so they can coach them appropriately, said Steele. The success of the program is demonstrated in improved retention rates. "What makes me most proud is the feedback I get directly from our new skilled immigrant hires. They thank me for the opportunity to work here and grow their career with the company," says Steele.

Sources: Based on Silliker, A. (2011, March 28). Firms honoured for work with skilled immigrants. *Canadian HR Reporter, 24*(6), 1, 20; Dalby, P. (2011, March 9). New hiring approach improves success rate for immigrants. *Toronto Star*, www.thestar.com/printarticle/950769; Anonymous (2011, October 6). Nancy Steele spearheads skilled immigrant strategy at American Express Canada. *TRIEC*, www.triec.ca/2011/nancy-steele-spearheads-skilled-immigrant-strategy; www.americanexpress.com/ca.

MyManagementLab   Visit MyManagementLab at **www.mymanagementlab .com** for access to online tutorials, interactive exercises, videos, and much more.

LEARNING OBJECTIVES CHECKLIST

3.1 *Perception* involves interpreting the input from our senses to provide meaning to our environment. Any instance of perception involves a perceiver, a target, and a situational context. The experience, needs, and emotions of the perceiver affect perception, as does the ambiguity of the target.

3.2 According to *social identity theory*, people form perceptions of themselves and others based on their characteristics and memberships in social categories. Bruner's model of the perceptual process suggests that we are very receptive to cues provided by the target and the situation when we encounter an unfamiliar target. However, as we discover familiar cues, we quickly categorize the target and process other cues in a selective manner to maintain a consistent and constant picture of the target.

3.3 The main biases in person perception include *primacy*, *recency*, *implicit personality theory*, *reliance on central traits*, *projection*, and *stereotyping*. Stereotypes of gender, age, race, ethnicity, and religion are especially problematic for organizations.

3.4 *Attribution* is the process of assigning causes or motives to people's behaviour. The observer is often interested in determining whether the behaviour is due to *dispositional* (internal) or *situational* (external) causes. Behaviour is likely to be attributed to the disposition of the actor when the behaviour (1) is performed consistently, (2) differs from that exhibited by other people, and (3) occurs in a variety of situations or environments. An opposite set of cues will prompt a situational attribution.

3.5 The tendency of observers to overemphasize dispositional attributions is known as the *fundamental attribution error*. In contrast, actors are more likely to explain their own behaviour in situational terms, and this actor–observer difference in attributions is known as the *actor–observer effect*. Our tendency to take credit for success and to deny responsibility for failure is known as the *self-serving bias*.

3.6 The changing nature of the workplace and increasing diversity have highlighted the importance of valuing and managing employee diversity, which can yield strategic, competitive, and performance advantages for the organization.

3.7 Racial, ethnic, religious, gender, and age stereotypes can result in discriminatory human resources decisions and are a major barrier to valuing diversity. Organizations can use a number of tactics, including training, to manage diversity. However, to be most effective, diversity should be integrated into all organization policies and practices and part of an inclusive culture that values individual differences.

3.8 Perceptions of *trust* involve a willingness to be vulnerable and to take risks with respect to the actions of another party. Trust perceptions toward management are based on perceptions of ability, benevolence, and integrity. *Perceived organizational support* (POS) refers to perceptions about how much an organization values an individual's contribution and cares about one's well-being. According to *organizational support theory*, employees who have strong perceptions of organizational support feel an obligation to care about the organization's welfare and to help the organization achieve its objectives.

3.9 According to *signalling theory*, job applicants have incomplete information about jobs and organizations so they interpret their recruitment and selection experiences as cues or signals about unknown characteristics of an organization. Job applicants form more positive perceptions of the selection process when the selection procedures are perceived to be fair. Judging the suitability of job applicants in an interview and appraising job performance are especially difficult perceptual tasks, in part because the target is motivated to convey a good impression. In addition, interviewers and performance raters exhibit a number of perceptual tendencies that are reflected in inaccurate judgments, including *leniency*, *harshness*, *central tendency*, and *contrast*, *halo*, and *similar-to-me effects*. Structured interviews can improve the accuracy of perceptions in the employment interview, and *behaviourally anchored rating scales (BARS)* and *frame-of-reference (FOR)* training can improve the accuracy of performance appraisals.

DISCUSSION QUESTIONS

1. Discuss how differences in the experiences of students and professors might affect their perceptions of students' written work and class comments.

2. Using implicit personality theory, explain how physical attractiveness influences job-related outcomes in employment interviews and performance appraisals.

3. Discuss the occupational stereotypes that you hold about computer programmers, the clergy, truck drivers, bartenders, and bankers. How do you think these stereotypes have developed? Has an occupational stereotype ever caused you to commit a socially embarrassing error when meeting someone for the first time?

4. Use Bruner's perceptual model (Exhibit 3.3) and social identity theory to explain why performance appraisals and interviewers' judgments are frequently inaccurate.

5. Discuss how perceptions of organizational support can influence employees' attitudes and behaviour. What can organizations do to develop positive perceptions of organizational support?

6. Suppose an employee does a particularly poor job on an assigned project. Discuss the attribution process that this person's manager will use to form judgments about this poor performance. Be sure to discuss how the manager will use consistency, consensus, and distinctiveness cues.

7. A study of small business failures found that owners generally cited factors such as economic depression or strong competition as causes.

However, creditors of these failed businesses were much more likely to cite ineffective management. What attribution bias is indicated by these findings? Why do you think the difference in attribution occurs?

8. Discuss the factors that make it difficult for employment interviewers to form accurate perceptions of interviewees. Explain why a gender or racial stereotype might be more likely to affect a hiring decision than a performance appraisal decision. How can interviews and performance appraisals be designed to improve the accuracy of perceptions?

9. What are the implications of social identity theory for diversity in organizations? Describe some of the things that an organization can do to remove the barriers to workplace diversity. List some of the advantages gained by organizations that effectively manage a diverse workforce.

10. Explain stereotype threat effects and provide some examples of how they might occur in organizations and the consequences. What can organizations do to prevent stereotype threat effects?

11. Review the Ethical Focus feature, *What's in a Name? You're Hired . . . or Not!*, and use Bruner's model of the perceptual process to explain why job applicants with ethnic-sounding names are less likely to receive callbacks. What perceptual biases might explain the lower callbacks received for resumes with ethnic-sounding names? What should organizations do to avoid name discrimination? What should job applicants do?

INTEGRATIVE DISCUSSION QUESTIONS

1. Describe how the principles of operant learning theory and social cognitive theory can be used to manage workplace diversity and reduce the effects of workplace stereotypes. How can the organizational learning practices described in Chapter 2 be used for managing diversity?

2. Consider how the four basic types of managerial activities described in Chapter 1 (i.e.,

routine communication, traditional management, networking, and human resource management) can influence employees' perceptions of trust and perceived organizational support (POS). How should managers perform each of these activities to improve employees' perceptions of trust and POS?

ON-THE-JOB CHALLENGE QUESTION 1

Australia's Jobs Bonus Initiative

In 2012, the Australian government launched a new initiative that will pay employers to hire older workers. Employers will receive $1000 for every worker aged 50 or older that they hire and retain for at least three months. The government has committed $10 million over four years to the Jobs Bonus initiative in response to a report which highlights the value of older workers.

According to Mark Butler, the Minister for Ageing, "We still need to deal with a cultural issue in the Australian business community that sometimes looks past the value of older workers. We know that older workers have lower absenteeism, they have higher retention rates, and they bring with them extraordinary wisdom and experience. We just need to push through this barrier that some Australian employers still have."

However, according to Susan Eng, vice-president of advocacy at CARP, a Toronto-based advocacy group for people over 50, this may not be the right course of action. "I understand the motivation but I'm not particularly thrilled with the method. It suggests that an older worker is somehow flawed and you, therefore, have to pay somebody to hire them," she said. "If you're trying to resolve and overcome age discrimination in hiring, why reinforce this stereotype by offering a sweetener?"

What do you think about the Australian government's Jobs Bonus initiative? Do perceptions have anything to do with this initiative? Do you think this will help or hurt older workers and the perception and stereotype of them? Is this something that Canadian governments should consider doing? What are the implications for employees and organizations?

Source: Silliker, A. (2012, May 21). Australia offers $1000 for hiring of older workers. *Canadian HR Reporter, 25*(10), 1, 10.

ON-THE-JOB CHALLENGE QUESTION 2

Citizens Medical Centre's New Hiring Policy

Citizens Medical Centre, a hospital in Victoria, Texas, recently instituted a new hiring policy that bans job applicants from employment for being overweight. The new policy states that the hospital will not hire anyone with a body mass index (BMI which is a formula used to determine fat) of 35 or higher. This is the equivalent of someone who is five feet five inches tall and weighs 210 pounds or someone who is 5 feet 10 inches tall and weighs 245 pounds.

According to the policy, an employee's physique "should fit with a representational image or specific mental projection of the job of a health-care professional." David Brown, the hospital's CEO, stated, "The majority of our patients are over 65 and they have expectations that cannot be ignored in terms of personal appearance." He further stated that, "We have the ability as an employer to characterize our process and to have a policy that says what's best for our business and our patients."

As part of the hiring process, job applicants are screened by a physician who assesses their fitness for work, which includes their body mass index. Existing workers who become obese during employment are not terminated; however, job applicants have been turned away as a result of the policy.

Although the laws in Texas do not prohibit weight discrimination in hiring, they do prohibit discrimination based on race, age, or religion.

However, according to Peggy Howell, public relations director for the National Association to Advance Fat Acceptance, "This is discrimination plain and simple. So the field of medicine is no longer an option for people of larger body size? What a waste of talent." She said that a hospital should know that lots of medical conditions lead to obesity or weight gain.

According to CEO David Brown, excessive weight has "all kinds of encumbrances" for the hospital and its health plan, and there's evidence that extremely obese employees are absent from work more often.

What do you think about Citizens Medical Centre's new hiring policy? Do perceptions, attributions, and stereotypes have anything to do with the hiring policy? What do you think is the reason for such a policy and do you believe it is in the best interests of the hospital and its patients? Is this something that other organizations should consider doing? What are the implications?

Sources: Silliker, A. (2012, May 21). U.S. hospital balks a hiring obese workers. *Canadian HR Reporter, 25*(10), 1, 3; Ramshaw, E. (March 26, 2012). Victoria hospital won't hire very obese workers. *The Texas Tribune*, www.texastribune.org; (2012, April 5). Hospital in weight row after hiring policy BANS obese job applicants. *Daily Mail Reporter*, www.dailymail.co.uk/news/article-2125385.

EXPERIENTIAL EXERCISE

Beliefs about Older Workers

Answer the 27 questions listed here. The questions are an attempt to assess the attitudes people have about older workers. The statements cover many different points of view; you may find yourself agreeing strongly with some of the statements, disagreeing just as strongly with others, and perhaps feeling uncertain about others. After you have answered all 27 questions, follow the instructions below to obtain your score.

Read each statement carefully. Using the numbers from 1 to 5 on the rating scale, mark your personal opinion about each statement in the blank space next to each statement. Remember, give your personal opinion according to how much you agree or disagree with each item. In all cases, older refers to people who are 50 years of age or older.

—1—	—2—	—3—	—4—	—5—
Strongly agree	Agree	Neither agree nor disagree	Disagree	Strongly disagree

____ 1. Older employees have fewer accidents on the job.

____ 2. Most companies are unfair to older employees.

____ 3. Older employees are harder to train for jobs.

____ 4. Older employees are absent more often than younger employees.

____ 5. Younger employees have more serious accidents than older workers.

____ 6. If two workers had similar skills, I'd pick the older worker to work with me.

____ 7. Occupational diseases are more likely to occur among younger employees.

____ 8. Older employees usually turn out work of higher quality.

____ 9. Older employees are grouchier on the job.

____ 10. Younger workers are more cooperative on the job.

____ 11. Older workers are more dependable.

____ 12. Most older workers cannot keep up with the speed of modern industry.

____ 13. Older employees are most loyal to the company.

____ 14. Older workers resist change and are too set in their ways.

____ 15. Younger workers are more interested than older workers in challenging jobs.

____ 16. Older workers can learn new skills as easily as other employees.

____ 17. Older employees are better employees.

____ 18. Older employees do not want jobs with increased responsibilities.

____ 19. Older workers are not interested in learning new skills.

____ 20. Older employees should "step aside" (take a less demanding job) to give younger employees advancement opportunities.

____ 21. The majority of older employees would quit work if they could afford it.

____ 22. Older workers are usually outgoing and friendly at work.

____ 23. Older workers prefer less challenging jobs than those they held when they were younger.

____ 24. It is a better investment to train younger workers rather than older workers.

____ 25. Older employees in our department work just as hard as anyone else.

____ 26. Given a choice, I would not work with an older worker on a daily basis.

____ 27. A person's performance declines significantly with age.

Scoring and Interpretation

The scale you have just completed measures your attitudes toward older workers. To score your beliefs about older workers, subtract your responses to each of the following items from 6: 1, 2, 5, 6, 7, 8, 11, 13, 16, 17, 22, and 25. For example, if you put 2 for item 1, give yourself a 4 (6 minus 2). Then simply add up your resulting responses to all 27 items. Your score should fall somewhere between 27 and 135. Low scores indicate an overall negative belief about older workers, while high scores indicate positive beliefs. The higher your score, the more favourable your attitudes are toward older workers.

Research on older workers has generally found that a negative stereotype of older workers exists in organizations. The danger of this is that it can lead to negative attitudes and discriminatory behaviour toward older workers.

A study of 179 employees from three organizations obtained scores that ranged from 54 to 118. The average score was 90, which indicated somewhat positive beliefs about older workers. As reported in other studies, older workers had more positive beliefs about older workers than younger workers. However, younger workers who had more interactions with older workers were found to have more positive beliefs about older workers.

To facilitate class discussion and your understanding of age stereotypes, form a small group with several other members of the class and consider the following questions. (Note that the instructor can also do this as a class exercise. Students should write their score, age, and interactions with older workers on a piece of paper and hand it in to the instructor, who can then determine the relationship between age, interactions with older workers, and beliefs about older workers.)

1. Students should first compare their scores to each other's and to the average score indicated above (90). Do group members have positive or negative beliefs about older workers? Do some group members have more positive or negative beliefs than others in the group?

2. Each member of the group should indicate his or her age. Determine the average age of the group and categorize those members above the average as being "older" and those below the average as being "younger." Then calculate the average score of the two age groups. Is there a difference in beliefs about older workers between older and younger group members?

3. Each group member should indicate how often they interact with older workers (daily, several times a week, once a week, or monthly). Based on group members' responses, create two categories that correspond to high and low interactions with older workers. Calculate the average score of these two groups. Is there a difference in beliefs about older workers between those who have more and those you have less interaction with older workers?

4. Why do some students have positive or negative beliefs about older workers? What are the implications of these beliefs at work and outside of work?

5. What can you do to develop more positive beliefs about older workers? What are the implications of doing so?

Source: Hassell, B.L., & Perrewe, P.L. (1995). An examination of beliefs about older workers: Do stereotypes still exist? *Journal of Organizational Behavior, 16,* 457–468.

CASE INCIDENT

The New CEO

In March 2009, the Canadian National Institute for the Blind (CNIB) announced the appointment of John M. Rafferty as the organization's new president and CEO. CNIB is a nationwide charity that provides services and support to Canadians who are blind or visually impaired. Rafferty left a lucrative private-sector job to join CNIB. According to Al Jameson, chair of CNIB's national board of directors, Rafferty is an exceptional business leader whose skills and experience make him an excellent fit for CNIB. In fact, Rafferty has 13 years of national and international experience as a senior executive who has served in numerous leadership positions.

However, Rafferty's appointment upset many people in the community and prompted criticism of CNIB. Some even referred to his hiring as despicable and a step backward. Unlike all his predecessors and every top executive in the 91-year history of

CNIB, Rafferty can see. He is CNIB's first "sighted" president and CEO. His hiring resulted in a complicated debate about identity and employment equity within Canada's diverse blind and visually impaired community.

According to John Rae, vice-president of the Alliance for Equality of Blind Canadians (AEBC), the hiring of a sighted person as CEO is yet another example of CNIB "turning its back on the people it was set up to serve." By selecting Rafferty, CNIB has implied that blind Canadians qualified to lead a major organization do not exist. How can CNIB lobby corporations to hire the blind when it will not do so itself?

Sources: Dale, D. (2009, May 3). Debate stirs over hiring of sighted CNIB head: Board defends choice as critics ask how it can lobby firms to hire blind when it will not do so itself. *Toronto Star,* A1; Meet the President: John M. Rafferty. www.cnib.ca/en/about/who/president/default.aspx.

1. Discuss the role of perceptions in people's reactions to the hiring of John Rafferty. Use Bruner's model of the perceptual process and social identity theory to explain people's perceptions and reactions.

2. Do you think CNIB should have hired John Rafferty as the organization's new president and

CEO, or should they have hired an individual who is blind or visually impaired? Explain your answer.

3. Does this incident have anything to do with equity and diversity? Explain your answer.

CASE STUDY

CTV Newsnet

On January 15, 2000, Henry Kowalski, senior vice-president, news, had to move quickly to save the reputation of CTV (Canadian Television) Newsnet. Because of a technical error, a tape of its anchor-person, Avery Haines, making degrading remarks about various minorities, had been aired during a newscast. He had no doubt whatsoever about the integrity of Haines and that the apparent slurs were part of a private self-deprecating joke made, she believed, off-air. Still, none of these facts made his dilemma easier. It was up to him to address the situation, without delay.

CTV's Position in the Canadian Broadcasting Industry

CTV Inc. was one of Canada's pre-eminent communications companies, with conventional television operations across Canada. Its broadcasting signals reached 99 percent of English-speaking Canadians and offered a wide range of quality news, sports, information, and entertainment programming. CTV Inc. had been in preliminary discussions with BCE (Bell Canada Enterprises), which announced a formal offer to purchase in March 2000.

During the previous four years, the company saw significant growth from its roots in family-run regional broadcasting, such as CFTO in Toronto. In February 1999, CTV Inc. was hoping to complete strategic negotiations that would expand the scale of its online operations. It was planning to launch an interactive site in the fall of 2000. At the CTV Inc. annual general meeting, Ivan Fecan, the chief executive officer, announced: "We expect to move into entertainment content production in a meaningful way, in fiscal 2000." While Fecan was clearly excited and optimistic about the direction the company was taking, he also, however, drew attention to the extra interest costs that would be incurred by acquisitions.

CTV's main competitor was Global Television, and at the beginning of the year both companies were claiming to have won the 1999 fall ratings war, each interpreting differently the statistics compiled by Nielsen Research. Each of the competing broadcasters would have liked to be able to demonstrate definitively its edge in viewer numbers over the other, knowing the weight that advertisers would give to such ratings.

CTV's Goals and Corporate Philosophy

Fiscal 1999 was the first year of operation for the newly formed CTV Inc., although the brand known as CTV Network had been very well-known to Canadian audiences and advertisers for the past two decades. The consolidation of CTV and its owned affiliates, along with recent restructuring and innovations, had resulted in the creation of a truly integrated Canadian broadcasting and communications company.

Scope of operations included 25 television stations in Ontario, Saskatchewan, Alberta, British Columbia, Nova Scotia, and New Brunswick. Of these stations, 18 were affiliates of CTV, six were CBC affiliate television stations and one, CIVT, Vancouver, was an independent television station. CTV also owned ASN, a satellite-to-cable program undertaking and had ownership interests in four speciality cable television services: The Comedy Network; Outdoor Life Network; a headline news channel, CTV Newsnet; and CTV Sportsnet.

CTV Inc. had a 12 percent interest in History Television Inc. and held a licence for an additional speciality service, TalkTV, which was scheduled to launch in September 2000. CTV Inc. also had a controlling interest in Sports Specials/Pay-Per-View for digital and DTH.

On March 5, 1999, CTV acquired a 68.46 percent interest in NetStar Communications Inc. The acquisition of NetStar was held in trust pending regulatory approvals. NetStar owned the Sports Network Inc. (TSN); Le Reseau des Sports (RDS) Inc.; Dome Productions Inc. (one of the largest mobile production facilities in Canada); and, through its 80 percent owned subsidiary, operated the Discovery Channel. NetStar also had a 24.95 percent interest in Viewer's Choice Canada Inc. CTV Inc. also had a 50 percent interest in Landscape Entertainment Corp., a production venture that would produce worldwide content for film, television, and the Internet.

At fiscal year-end 1999, CTV Inc.'s. balance sheet showed total assets of $1.1 billion compared with $760 million at end of the previous year. Revenues for the first quarter of 2000 showed a slight decline over the same period the previous year, due mostly to softness in conventional television, which was down four percent compared with the previous year. Consequently, speciality channels such as CTV Newsnet and the Comedy Network were making significant revenue contributions and it was in this area that CTV Inc. would continue to focus.

Ivan Fecan further remarked that "CTV Inc. is still in the process of becoming the powerful, integrated broadcasting and communications organization it can and will be. We are leveraging the strengths of every part of the company to create a strong whole." He emphasized the company goal of helping clients to "extend their brands along the entire value chain, from the internet to local retail," and the need to maintain strong personal relationships and community roots across Canada.

CTV Inc. was clearly moving forward and enthusiastic about further expansion in the future, but it was also determined to continue to demonstrate that social commitment was still a priority. Fecan commended the involvement of individual employees in various fundraising and charitable activities. He also pointed to the contribution of CTV's programming, especially the Signature Series, which "had a significant impact on national awareness of injustice and sexual harassment of children," and stated the intention do many more projects like that.

The 24-hour news channel, CTV Newsnet, had always observed the company philosophy in its reporting, giving generous broadcast time to social issues, local, national, and global. In January 2000, Canadian farmers were voicing their desperation about the crisis in Canadian agriculture, and the impossibility of family-owned farms remaining viable without increased government support. On January 16, a massive benefit concert was planned in Toronto solely to create awareness among urban dwellers on the problems faced by Canadian farmers.

One organizer, Liberal MP (Broadview-Greenwood) Dennis Mills, was quoted in *The Toronto Star* (January 13) as saying: "if we can get people to make legislators who live in cities—and 80 percent of Canada's parliamentarians do—more accountable in dealing with farming and agricultural issues, we'll have succeeded."

Canada's public station, CBC (Canadian Broadcasting Corporation), was planning to air a farm crisis program from 10:00 am Sunday, January 16 until 2:00 AM Monday, January 17. On the morning of Saturday, January 15, CTV Newsnet, in keeping with its social awareness and community interest policies, was about to air the first of a series of its reports on the situation.

Henry Kowalski

Kowalski was a 25-year veteran of television news and had been with the CTV family since 1984. In the first six years of his career, he worked as head of assignment, specials producer, Toronto bureau chief, and Vancouver bureau chief. In 1992, he was promoted to chief news editor, where he retooled the newscast and added several innovative features and segments.

His responsibilities included CTV's flagship *CTV News* with Lloyd Robertson and Sandie Rinaldo, all local newscasts on CTV's owned and operated stations across Canada, *Canada AM*, and the highly acclaimed *W5*. Under his leadership, *CTV News* became Canada's most-watched newscast, consistently ranking in the Nielsen top twenty.

In January 1997, Kowalski was promoted to senior vice-president and general manager, CTV News. He was responsible for guiding a team towards the successful launch of CTV Newsnet in October 1997 and for the remake of CFTO News, where he increased the audience and cemented it in first place in the competitive Toronto/Hamilton market.

CTV Newsnet's mandate was to become a significant force in Canadian journalism. In the highly competitive and over-serviced Canadian television market, Kowalski knew that a significant effort would be required to build a new service that would take a leadership position. He was no stranger to this type of challenge.

A New Anchorperson

Early in December 1999, Kowalski signed 33-year-old Haines on a probationary contract to anchor the station's 24-hour cable news channel. Haines had been with the Toronto radio station CFRB for 11 years, having been hired straight from college by Bill Carroll, its news director.

Haines was eager to make the move from radio to television, and Kowalski was impressed with her qualifications; not only had she won several awards in newscasting, but she was well liked and respected by her peers and superiors and was already a popular radio personality with an enthusiastic following. He felt that she would be a good fit in the fast-paced and demanding milieu of television news and had the ability, ambition, and charisma that CTV Newsnet was looking to acquire. He had enjoyed the interview and found Haines relaxed, animated, composed, and personable. In all, he was very confident that Haines would quickly adapt and grow into this challenging position.

An Excellent Fit

Nearly two months had passed, and Kowalski was very pleased with Haines's progress. She had adjusted adeptly to the new medium, and her charisma translated well from voice to visual; she had impressive screen presence. Besides the implicit public approval, Haines seemed already to have gained the support and even affection of all her co-workers. She appeared inherently interested in everyone and everything and exuded a natural enthusiasm and charm.

It was not only personality, however, that distinguished the new employee but also her work ethic. Haines gave full commitment to her job; always willing to accept criticism and advice, to apply herself completely to every task, she was also creative and innovative where appropriate. Kowalski felt he had made a good decision and had acquired an employee who would be a great asset to CTV Newsnet.

Flubbed Lines

On Saturday, January 15, Haines was in the studio taping an introduction to a report on aid for Canadian farmers. For some reason, whether through lack of concentration, or simply because of a slip of the tongue, Haines stammered her way through the opening lines and completely garbled the message. Fortunately this was not a live broadcast, but as a relative newcomer in a very responsible position, Haines felt vulnerable and awkward.

Partly to cover her own embarrassment, but also to ease the tension for the other people in the studio, Haines started to make fun of her own ineptness. "I kind of like the stuttering thing," she laughed, "It's like equal opportunity, right? We've got a stuttering newscaster. We've got the black; we've got the Asian; we've got the woman. I could be a lesbian-folk-dancing-black-woman-stutterer." Someone joined in the banter, adding a few other possibilities, and Haines, responded in kind: "In a wheelchair…with a gimping rubber leg. Yeah, really. I'd have a successful career, let me tell you." Everyone in the studio knew the statements were very politically incorrect, but the repartee was harmless among those who understood its self-deprecating context and so typical of the gallows humour among journalists. No one was in the least offended, since Haines herself was a woman of African-Asian heritage. They knew she was poking fun at herself.

Meanwhile, everyone had relaxed, the technicians were ready to roll with a new tape, the original with the flubbed lines having been set aside. Haines went flawlessly through her farm-and-aid report, and the segment was ready to be aired later in the day.

A Technical Error

It had been a busy Saturday for the technical crew, but despite the re-take, everything was ready to go for the latest broadcast. The control room technician hit play and Haines, composed and pleasant, was on screen—stumbling through her intro to the farm-aid report. "Oh—! Oh—! Wrong tape! Wrong tape!" The cries went up in the studio control room. But things got worse. They realized that not only was the audience seeing Haines, CTV's Newsnet anchor, talking gibberish, they were watching and listening to the appallingly inappropriate exchange that had followed the flawed intro. The tape was rolling and the technical crews were so stunned that before they could react, the short tape had been played in its entirety.

Public Reaction

The phone lines at CTV's Agincourt studios were flashing instantly with messages from horrified and angry viewers, viewers who had come to trust the integrity and professionalism of CTV. Haines was doing another taped interview when her line-up editor rushed in to tell her about the awful error. Everyone scrambled, as they knew that Haines's comments would be aired by every competitive media source in the Greater Toronto area and could potentially spread beyond. It was essential to apologize on air as soon as possible. Haines was shaken and devastated, more for those she must have horribly offended than for her own sake. She was deeply disturbed that the public would inevitably, and quite understandably, assume that her remarks represented her real views. She also knew that her position on CTV Newsnet was in jeopardy.

Henry Kowalski's Dilemma

Even before Haines's apologies were aired, Kowalski was in the CTV Newsnet studio, quickly trying to get a take on public reaction and to establish just how this major breach of process could have happened. Regardless of the details or of who was to blame, he was ultimately responsible for managing the brand created by CTV News and now he was faced with the unthinkable—damage control in the wake of a serious error.

Avery Haines had already demonstrated her talent and potential and clearly was a victim in the fiasco. Nevertheless, Kowalski had to consider the effects of the incident not so much on individuals as on the growing reputation of CTV Newsnet and its ultimate backlash on the parent company, CTV Inc. They could lose major advertisers if the right actions weren't taken. Clearly, this was not going to be a good weekend.

Source: Professors Carol Tattersall and Christina A. Cavanagh prepared this case solely to provide material for class discussion. The authors do not intend to illustrate either effective or ineffective handling of a managerial situation. The authors may have disguised certain names and other identifying information to protect confidentiality.

QUESTIONS

1. What are people's perceptions of Avery Haines? Be sure to refer to the perceptions of Henry Kowalski, her co-workers, and CTV Newsnet viewers.

2. Why do viewers have different perceptions of Avery Haines than her co-workers? Use Bruner's model of the perceptual process to explain people's perceptions of Avery Haines.

3. Use attribution theory to explain how co-workers and viewers responded to Haines's inappropriate comments. Why did her co-workers and the public react so differently?

4. Do you think the public's reaction to Haines's comments was reasonable? Discuss the possibility that the public response may be due to biases in person perception and attribution.

5. Haines was deeply disturbed that the public would assume that the bigotry inherent in her remarks represented her real views. Use the material in the chapter on perceptions and attributions to explain why the public believed that her remarks represented her real views. What does this case tell us about perceptions and attributions?

6. What do you think Avery Haines should do? What should Henry Kowalski do? Should Avery Haines be fired? Explain your answers.

VALUES, ATTITUDES, AND WORK BEHAVIOUR

LEARNING OBJECTIVES

After reading Chapter 4, you should be able to:

4.1 Define *values* and discuss the implications of cross-cultural variation in values for organizational behaviour.

4.2 Define *attitudes* and explain how people develop attitudes.

4.3 Explain the concept of *job satisfaction* and discuss some of its key contributors, including discrepancy, fairness, disposition, mood, and emotion.

4.4 Explain the relationship between job satisfaction and absenteeism, turnover, performance, organizational citizenship behaviour, and customer satisfaction.

4.5 Differentiate *affective*, *continuance*, and *normative commitment* and explain how organizations can foster *organizational commitment*.

L'ORÉAL CANADA

Montreal's L'Oréal Canada is a subsidiary of the French L'Oréal Group, a prominent producer of cosmetics and personal care products. Their lines include L'Oréal Paris, Giorgio Armani, Ralph Lauren, Redken, Garnier, Biotherm, and The Body Shop. Journalist Donna Nebenzahl describes three generations of L'Oréal employees.

It's not a new phenomenon, three generations in a single workplace, but the latest generation on the scene is causing a flurry of concern. That message came loud and clear to Marjolaine Rompré, director of learning development at L'Oréal Canada, a company that hires a large number of the Gen Y population, the most recent generation in the workplace.

By the late 1990s, the company realized that a work population that is one-third boomer (1947–1966), one-third Generation X (1967–1979), and one-third Generation Y (1980–1995) was going to have to figure out how to cope with the winds of change blown in by this younger generation. So it was up to Rompré, a young boomer (born in 1961), to do something to alleviate the stress. Earlier generations, when they started at work, would go into meetings and observe and hardly speak, not wanting to ruffle feathers. Not so for the Gen Y population. "This new generation is so candid about participating and a lot freer," she said. "When we saw that, we realized we could

be faced with an interesting problem. We called it Generation Shock."

So they decided to create a program for L'Oréal workers that would "valorize generational differences," which became the title, because they felt that Gen Y already received a lot of attention and the goal was to ensure that every group understood the other. In the end, she says, "the Ys told us they were so happy to learn why the baby boomers were so conservative and why Gen X didn't want to share information with them." They have brought in 500 employees so far, in an effort to reveal the values of each generation—and the common truth that each generation is more rebellious than the one before and always wants to change the world.

For instance, when they talk about security, the groups learn that for the post-war generation, the smallest, oldest group now known as Traditionalists, security meant their savings. "They bought with cash and they had money in the bank," she said. For baby boomers, "their security was in the pension plan, because that was really created with their generation. You just had job security and pension plan." For the X generation, who came into a saturated market and had to fight for their jobs, security meant having a strong resume. On the other hand, Rompré says, "for Gen Y, *security* is not a word in their

L'Oréal employees Jean Cardinal, Rosalie Nolin, and Dominic Savaria span the baby boom–Gen X–Gen Y gap.

vocabulary because they have such a safety net; their parents are there for them. They don't have the same outlook."

There's a certain self importance in this group, she says, mixed with extreme loyalty toward their colleagues, with whom many form lasting friendships. "There's a greater sense of community than among the Gen X. Baby boomers are about the team, while Gen X were very career-oriented, all about themselves." This, of course, is a response to Gen X's entrée into a very competitive and tight workplace, compared with Gen Y, who see work as a continuum from university. "For them, it's just another way of learning. They're really focused on their development," Rompré said. "They want to continue to grow and learn." At the same time, she points out, "they have an amazing sense of community and friendship. Families are smaller, with fewer siblings, so friends are important when growing up. Plus, mom and daddy are working." So when they get into the workplace, their colleagues become their friends and their social life takes place partly at work.

On the other hand, the previous generations were a lot more career and results focused. It was clear that when you started in a company, you would start at the bottom and work hard in order to earn your place. Not so for Gen Y. "This generation is the most schooled generation ever, and they want to have responsibility very early on," she said. They really want to be autonomous, yet they also want validation. They want to be independent, but like to work in teams. They want rapid success within the company, yet have a very strong desire to maintain work–life balance. They practise extensive freedom of speech and are very candid, but they lack political savvy. They want to be everywhere at the same time, but have real difficulty managing priorities. They have great tolerance about religion, race, and nationality, but are very quick to pass judgment on the competency of their bosses. "They won't respect you because you're their boss. They'll respect you because you're competent and approachable," Rompré said.

At L'Oréal, the course has been a huge success, generating so much buzz that the company had to add to the half-day sessions. Another sidenote within the company, where there are actually a number of Gen Ys who are now managing boomers and Gen Xs: Most of the Ys are children of baby boomers so there is an interesting relationship between the two groups. "The Xs had to fight much more, waiting for boomers to get out, but the baby boomers aren't threatened by Gen Y," she said. "In fact, they love to share and to show them the ropes."[1]

The L'Oréal Canada story illustrates how generational differences in values and work attitudes affect workplace behaviour. In this chapter we will discuss such values and attitudes. Our discussion of values will be particularly oriented toward cross-cultural variations in values and their implications for organizational behaviour. Our discussion of attitudes will explain attitude formation. Two critical attitudes are job satisfaction and organizational commitment. We will consider the causes and consequences of both.

WHAT ARE VALUES?

LO 4.1

Define *values* and discuss the implications of cross-cultural variation in values for organizational behaviour.

Values. A broad tendency to prefer certain states of affairs over others.

We might define **values** as "a broad tendency to prefer certain states of affairs over others."[2] The *preference* aspect of this definition means that values have to do with what we consider good and bad. Values are motivational, since they signal the attractive aspects of our environment that we seek and the unattractive aspects that we try to avoid or change. They also signal how we believe we *should* and *should not* behave.[3] The words *broad tendency* mean that values are very general and that they do not predict behaviour in specific situations very well. Knowing that a person generally embraces the values that support capitalism does not tell us much about how he or she will respond to a homeless person on the street this afternoon.

People tend to hold values structured around such factors as achievement, power, autonomy, conformity, tradition, and social welfare.[4] Not everyone holds the same values. Managers might value high productivity (an achievement value), while union officials might be more concerned with enlightened supervision and full employment (social values). We learn values through the reinforcement processes we discussed in Chapter 2. Most are socially reinforced by parents, teachers, and representatives of religions.

To solidify your understanding of values and their impact on organizational behaviour, let's examine some generational differences in values and see how work values differ across cultures.

Generational Differences in Values

Like L'Oréal Canada, many contemporary organizations are attempting to understand the implications of having four rather distinctive generations in the workplace who are often required to work with one another. As shown in Exhibit 4.1, these generations comprise what are often called the Traditionalists, the baby boomers, Generation X, and the Millennials (or Generation Y). These generations are of course demarcated by being of different ages, but they are also distinguished by having grown up under rather different socialization experiences. For example, many Traditionalists grew up in the shadow of two wars, baby boomers faced a vibrant economy (not to mention the sexual revolution and the advent of rock 'n' roll!), and Gen X and Y experienced more dual-career families and more divorce when growing up. It has been argued that these contrasting experiences, in turn, have led to notable value differences between the generations. For example, "latchkey kids" and those who know divorce might come to value the advice of authority figures less and the advice of friends more, compared to earlier generations. Such value differences might then underlie the differential workplace assets and preferences for leadership style highlighted in Exhibit 4.1.

The popular press contains many stereotypes (Chapter 3) concerning the generations, some of which are apparent in the exhibit.[5] Thus, the Traditionalists are portrayed as being respectful of authority and having a high work ethic; boomers are viewed as optimistic workaholics; Gen X is seen as cynical, confident, and pragmatic; and Gen Y is said to be confident, social, demanding of feedback, and somewhat unfocused. In general, the latter two generations are seen as more accepting of diversity and striving for good work–life balance, and their comfort with technology is notable.

Are these stereotypes accurate? It has to be said that the study of inter-generational values and of related attitudes and behaviour is in its infancy. And it is inherently hard to tease

Generation	Percentage of Workforce	Assets in the Workplace	Leadership Style Preferences
Traditionalists Born 1922–1945	8%	Hard working, stable, loyal, thorough, detail-oriented, focused, emotional maturity	Fair, consistent, clear, direct, respectful
Baby Boomers Born 1946–1964	44%	Team perspective, delicated, experienced, knowledgeable, service-oriented	Treat as equals, warm and caring, mission-defined, democratic approach
Generation X Born 1965–1980	34%	Independent, adaptable, creative, techno-literate, willing to challenge the status quo	Direct, competent, genuine, informal, flexible, results-oriented, supportive of learning opportunities
Millennials Born 1981–2000	14% and increasing rapidly	Optimistic, able to multitask, tenacious, technologically savvy, driven to learn and grow, team-oriented, socially responsible	Motivational, collaborative, positive, educational, organized, achievement-oriented, able to coach

EXHIBIT 4.1
Four generations in today's workplace.
Source: Society for Human Resource Management (2009). The multigenerational workforce: Opportunity for competitive success. *SHRM Research Quarterly*, First Quarter, 1–9. Compiled from AARP (2007). *Leading a multigenerational workforce*. Washington, DC: AARP; Sabatini Fraone, J., Hartmann, D., & McNally, K. (2008). *The multigenerational workforce: Management implications and strategies for collaboration*. Boston: Boston College Center for Work & Family; Zemke, R., Raines, C., & Filipezak, B. (2000). *Generations at work*. New York: American Management Association.

out generational effects from those that simply reflect age or work experience. Most recent research points to more similarities than differences in values across generations.[6] However, there is some indication that Gen X and Y are more inclined to value money, status, and rapid career growth than are boomers.[7] This may reflect valuing what one does not yet have, but it could also reflect the positive self-esteem movement to which later generations have been exposed. Indeed, there is evidence that the self-esteem of university students has increased over the years, along with narcissism.[8] There is also evidence that Gen Ys and Xs, compared to boomers, see work as less central, value leisure more, and are more inclined toward work–life balance.[9] Research conducted by the Center for Creative Leadership concluded that all work generations share the same values but express them differently. For instance, most people value respect, but for older employees this means being deferred to, while for Gen X and Y this means being listened to.[10]

Explore

Go to MyManagementLab to see an annotated version of this figure.

Any generational differences in work values or in the way values are expressed is important because there is much evidence that good "fit" between a person's values and those of the organization (person–organization fit) leads to positive work attitudes and behaviours, including reduced chances of quitting.[11] This means that organizations may have to tailor job designs, leadership styles, and benefits to the generational mix of their workforces.

Cultural Differences in Values

It is by now a cliché to observe that business has become global in its scope—Korean cars dot North American roads, your Dell helpdesk service provider resides in India, and entire lines of "Italian" cookware are made in China. All this activity obscures just how difficult it can be to forge business links across cultures. For example, research shows that anywhere from 16 to 40 percent of managers who receive foreign assignments terminate them early because they perform poorly or do not adjust to the culture.[12] Similarly, a lengthy history of failed business negotiations is attributable to a lack of understanding of cross-cultural differences. At the root of many of these problems is a lack of appreciation of basic differences in work-related values across cultures.

WORK CENTRALITY   Work itself is valued differently across cultures. One large-scale survey of over 8000 individuals in several nations found marked cross-national differences in the extent to which people perceived work as a central life interest.[13] Japan topped the list, with very high work centrality. Belgians and Americans exhibited average work centrality, and the British scored low. One question in the survey asked respondents whether they would continue working if they won a large amount of money in a lottery. Those with more central interest in work were more likely to report that they would continue working despite the new-found wealth.

Customer-friendly service is a high work priority in Japan. Tokyo Disneyland is considered the safest, cleanest, and most orderly Disney park in the world.

The survey also found that people for whom work was a central life interest tended to work more hours. A reflection of this can be seen in Exhibit 4.2, which shows great variation in vacation time across cultures. This illustrates how cross-cultural differences in work centrality can lead to adjustment problems for foreign employees and managers. Imagine the unprepared British executive who is posted to Japan only to find that Japanese managers commonly work late and then socialize with co-workers or customers long into the night. In Japan, this is all part of the job, often to the chagrin of the lonely spouse. On the other hand, consider the Japanese executive posted to Britain who finds out that an evening at the pub is *not* viewed as an extension of the day at the office and is therefore not a time to continue talking business.

HOFSTEDE'S STUDY Dutch social scientist Geert Hofstede questioned over 116 000 IBM employees located in 40 countries about their work-related values. In subsequent work he added another 36 countries and regions to his database.[14] When Hofstede analyzed the results, he discovered four basic dimensions along which work-related values differed across cultures: power distance, uncertainty avoidance, masculinity/femininity, and individualism/

EXHIBIT 4.2
Vacation time across cultures.
Source: World Tourism Organization (WTO) as cited in Travel Industry Association of America (2002). World Tourism Overview. Retrieved July 18, 2003, from http://www.tia.org/ivis/worldtourism.asp#vacation. Reprinted by permission. © UNWTO, 9284403309.

 Explore

Go to MyManagementLab to see an annotated version of this figure.

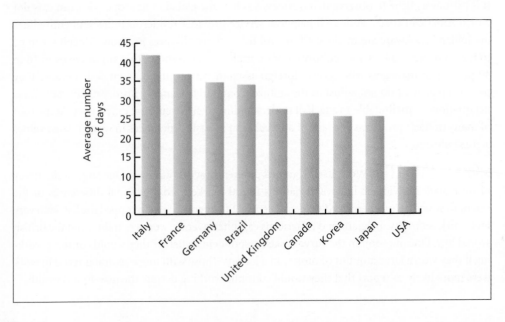

collectivism. Subsequent work with Canadian Michael Bond that catered more to Eastern cultures resulted in a fifth dimension, the long-term/short-term orientation.[15] More recently, the dimensions were verified and supplemented by the GLOBE project, headed by Professor Robert House.[16] You will learn more about this research, which involved more than 17 000 managers in 62 societies, when we cover leadership in Chapter 9.

- *Power distance.* **Power distance** refers to the extent to which society members accept an unequal distribution of power, including those who hold more power and those who hold less. In small power distance cultures, inequality is minimized, superiors are accessible, and power differences are downplayed. In large power distance societies, inequality is accepted as natural, superiors are inaccessible, and power differences are highlighted. Small power distance societies include Denmark, New Zealand, Israel, and Austria. Large power distance societies include the Philippines, Russia, and Mexico. Out of 76 countries and regions, Canada and the United States rank 15 and 16, respectively, falling on the low power distance side of the average, which would be 38.

- *Uncertainty avoidance.* **Uncertainty avoidance** refers to the extent to which people are uncomfortable with uncertain and ambiguous situations. Strong uncertainty avoidance cultures stress rules and regulations, hard work, conformity, and security. Cultures with weak uncertainty avoidance are less concerned with rules, conformity, and security, and hard work is not seen as a virtue. However, risk taking is valued. Strong uncertainty avoidance cultures include Japan, Greece, and Portugal. Weak uncertainty avoidance cultures include Singapore, Denmark, and Sweden. On uncertainty avoidance, the United States and Canada are well below average (i.e., exhibiting weak uncertainty avoidance), ranking 13 and 15, respectively, out of 76.

- *Masculinity/femininity.* More masculine cultures clearly differentiate gender roles, support the dominance of men, and stress economic performance. More feminine cultures accept fluid gender roles, stress sexual equality, and stress quality of life. In Hofstede's research, Slovakia and Japan are the most masculine societies, followed by Austria, Venezuela, and Mexico. The Scandinavian countries are the most feminine. Canada ranks about mid-pack, and the United States is fairly masculine, falling about halfway between Canada and Japan. The GLOBE research identified two aspects to this dimension—how assertive people are and how much they value gender equality.

- *Individualism/collectivism.* More **individualistic** societies tend to stress independence, individual initiative, and privacy. More **collective** cultures favour interdependence and loyalty to one's family or clan. The United States, Australia, Great Britain, and Canada are among the most individualistic societies. Venezuela, Columbia, and Pakistan are among the most collective, with Japan falling about mid-pack. The GLOBE research uncovered two aspects to this dimension—how much the collective distribution of resources is stressed and how much one's group or organization elicits loyalty.

- *Long-term/short-term orientation.* Cultures with a long-term orientation tend to stress persistence, perseverance, thrift, and close attention to status differences. Cultures with a short-term orientation stress personal steadiness and stability, face-saving, and social niceties. China, Hong Kong, Taiwan, Japan, and South Korea tend to be characterized by a long-term orientation. The United States, Canada, Great Britain, Zimbabwe, and Nigeria characterized by a more short-term orientation. Hofstede and Bond argue that the long-term orientation, in part, explains prolific East Asian entrepreneurship.

Exhibit 4.3 compares the United States, Canada, Mexico, Japan, and West Africa on Hofstede's value dimensions. Note that the profiles for Canada and the United States are very similar, but they differ considerably from that of Mexico.

Hofstede has produced a number of interesting "cultural maps" that show how countries and regions cluster together on pairs of cultural dimensions. The map in Exhibit 4.4 shows

Power distance. The extent to which an unequal distribution of power is accepted by society members.

Uncertainty avoidance. The extent to which people are uncomfortable with uncertain and ambiguous situations.

Individualism vs. collectivism. Individualistic societies stress independence, individual initiative, and privacy. Collective cultures favour interdependence and loyalty to family or clan.

EXHIBIT 4.3
Cross-cultural value comparisons.

Note: Time orientation data for Mexico unavailable.

Source: Graph by Gary Johns and Alan Saks. Based on data from Hofstede, G. (2005). Cultures and organizations: Software of the mind.

[Explore

Go to MyManagementLab to see an annotated version of this figure.

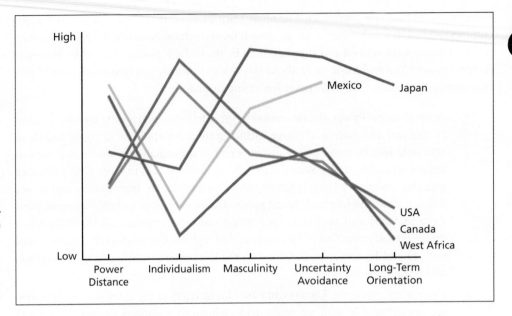

the relationship between power distance and degree of individualism. As you can see, these two values tend to be related. Cultures that are more individualistic tend to downplay power differences, while those that are more collectivistic tend to accentuate power differences.[17]

Implications of Cultural Variation

EXPORTING OB THEORIES An important message from the cross-cultural study of values is that organizational behaviour theories, research, and practices from North America might not translate well to other societies, even the one located just south of Texas.[18] The basic questions (How should I lead? How should we make this decision?) remain the same. It is just the *answers* that differ. For example, North American managers tend to encourage participation in work decisions by employees. This corresponds to the fairly low degree of power distance valued here. Trying to translate this leadership style to cultures that value high power distance might prove unwise. In these cultures, people might be more comfortable deferring to the boss's decision. Similarly, in individualistic North America, calling attention to one's accomplishments is expected and often rewarded in organizations. In more collective Asian or South American cultures, individual success might be devalued, and it might make sense to reward groups rather than individuals. Finally, in extremely masculine cultures, integrating women into management positions might require special sensitivity.

IMPORTING OB THEORIES Not all theories and practices that concern organizational behaviour are designed in North America or even in the West. The most obvious examples are "Japanese management" techniques, such as quality circles, total quality management, and just-in-time production. Although there are success stories of importing these techniques from Japan to North America, there are also examples of difficulties and failure. Many of the problems stem from basic value differences between Japan and North America. For example, the quest for continuous improvement and the heavy reliance on employee suggestions for improvement has had a mixed reaction.[19] In Japan, cultural values have traditionally dictated a fairly high degree of employment security. Thus, working at a fast pace and providing suggestions for improvement will not put one out of a job. North American workers are uncertain about this.

Many of the Japanese-inspired means of organizing work are team-oriented. Since Japan has fairly collective cultural values, submerging one's own interests in those of the team is natural. Although employers have successfully used teams in North America, as you will see in Chapter 7, our more individualistic culture dictates that careful selection of team members is necessary.

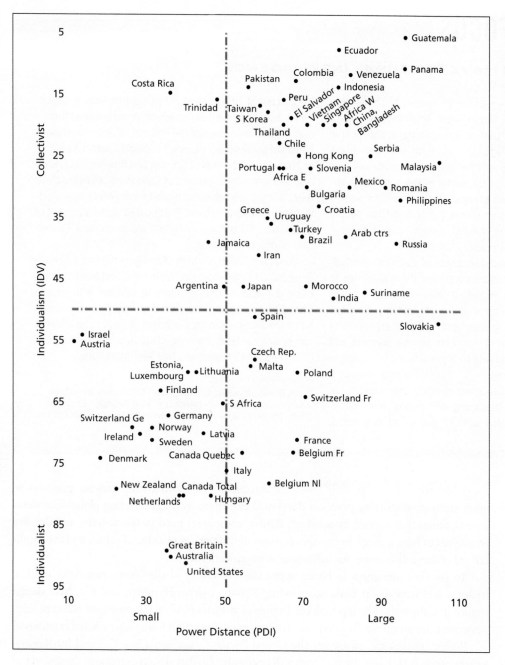

EXHIBIT 4.4
Power distance and individualism values for various countries and regions.
Source: Adapted from Hofstede, G., Hofstede, G.J., & Minkov, M. (2010). *Cultures and organizations: Software of the mind* (3rd ed.). New York: McGraw-Hill, p. 103.

Understanding cultural value differences can enable organizations to successfully import management practices by tailoring the practice to the home culture's concerns.

APPRECIATING GLOBAL CUSTOMERS
An appreciation of cross-cultural differences in values is essential to understanding the needs and tastes of customers or clients around the world. Once relegated to the status of a marketing problem, it is now clear that such understanding fundamentally has to do with organizational behaviour. Errors occur with regularity. For instance, the initial French response to the Disneyland Paris theme park was less enthusiastic than Disney management had expected, probably due in part to Disney's failure to truly appreciate French tastes in food, lifestyle, and entertainment. South Korea's Samsung recalled a calendar featuring models displaying its products that was destined for overseas customers. Some North Americans were offended by Miss July's see-through blouse.

Appreciating the values of global customers is also important when the customers enter your own culture. Many firms have profited from an understanding of the increasing ethnic diversity in the United States, Canada, and Australia.

■ GLOBAL FOCUS

CANADIANS HAVE CULTURAL INTELLIGENCE

First there was IQ—intelligence quotient. Then there was EQ—emotional intelligence. Now there's a new kind of intelligence that is increasingly indispensable in today's global village. CQ—cultural intelligence—is a must-have skill, not just for foreign diplomats but also for business people, public sector workers, military personnel, and just about everyone in multicultural societies. And Canadians score more highly in it than people in the United States, United Kingdom, and France, according to a recent study.

CQ is a heightened awareness of cultures—including one's own—that makes a person more sensitive to people from diverse origins. It implies having a broad knowledge of customs and beliefs among different nationalities, ethnic groups, and faiths. It also reflects a person's motivation to overcome cultural barriers and confidence in one's ability to communicate with people from different cultures.

Four out of ten Canadians strongly agreed with the statement: "I enjoy interacting with people from different cultures," compared with 37 percent of Americans, 24 percent of Britons, and 30 percent of French respondents. Sixteen percent of Canadians strongly agreed that: "I have a good knowledge of the cultural values and religious beliefs of some other cultures," compared with 13 percent of Americans, 9 percent of Britons, and 5 percent of French respondents. Fifteen percent of Canadians strongly agreed that: "I adjust my behaviour when I meet people from a culture that is unfamiliar to me," compared with 13 percent of Americans, 10 percent of British residents, and 12 percent of people in France.

Canadians' relatively high CQ reflects the fact that multicultural cities like Toronto, Vancouver, and Montreal give citizens plenty of opportunities to interact with people from diverse origins, said Jack Jedwab, executive director of the Association for Canadian Studies. The internet survey was carried out among 3000 international respondents and 2345 Canadians by Léger Marketing.

Source: Excerpted from Scott, M. (2012, January 5). Canadians are leaders in cultural intelligence. *The Gazette* (Montreal), p. A4. © Copyright The Montreal Gazette. For more about the scientific underpinnings of CI see www.culturalq.com.

DEVELOPING GLOBAL EMPLOYEES Success in translating management practices to other cultures, importing practices developed elsewhere, and appreciating global customers are not things that happen by accident. Rather, companies need to select, train, and develop employees to have a much better appreciation of differences in cultural values and the implications of these differences for behaviour in organizations.

To get their designers to better appreciate the values of the North American market, Japanese and Korean car makers, including Nissan, Toyota, Hyundai, and Kia, have design studios in California. The top ranks of Detroit's automakers, once the protected realm of midwesterners, are now liberally filled with Europeans or those with European or Asian experience.

Before continuing, please see the Global Focus: *Canadians Have Cultural Intelligence*. As you proceed through the text, you will encounter further discussion about the impact of cultural values on organizational behaviour. Now, let's examine attitudes and see how they are related to values.

LO 4.2

Define *attitudes* and explain how people develop attitudes.

Attitude. A fairly stable evaluative tendency to respond consistently to some specific object, situation, person, or category of people.

WHAT ARE ATTITUDES?

An **attitude** is a fairly stable evaluative tendency to respond consistently to some specific object, situation, person, or category of people. First, notice that attitudes involve *evaluations* directed toward *specific* targets. If I inquire about your attitude toward your boss, you will probably tell me something about how well you *like* him or her. This illustrates the evaluative aspect of attitudes. Attitudes are also much more specific than values, which dictate only broad preferences. For example, you could value working quite highly but still dislike your specific job.

Our definition indicates that attitudes are *tendencies to respond* to the target of the attitude. Thus, attitudes often influence our behaviour toward some object, situation, person, or group.

Attitude ⟶ Behaviour

Of course, not everyone who likes the boss goes around praising him or her in public for fear of being seen as too political. Similarly, people who dislike the boss do not always engage in public criticism for fear of retaliation. These examples indicate that attitudes are not always consistent with behaviour, and that attitudes provide useful information over and above the actions that we can observe. Behaviour is most likely to correspond to attitudes when people have direct experience with the target of the attitude and when the attitude is held confidently.[20]

Where do attitudes come from? Put simply, attitudes are a function of what we think and what we feel. That is, attitudes are the product of a related belief and value.[21] Given this point of view, we can now expand the attitude model presented above to include the thinking and feeling aspects of attitudes represented by beliefs and values.

$$BELIEF + VALUE \Rightarrow Attitude \longrightarrow Behaviour$$

Thus, we can imagine the following sequence of ideas in the case of a person experiencing work–family conflict:

"My job is interfering with my family life." (Belief)
"I dislike anything that hurts my family." (Value)
"I dislike my job." (Attitude)
"I'll search for another job." (Behaviour)

This simple example shows how attitudes (in this case, job satisfaction) develop from basic beliefs and values, and how they affect organizational behaviour (in this case, turnover from the organization). The specific attitudes we are now going to cover, job satisfaction and organizational commitment, have a strong impact on people's positive contributions to their work.[22]

WHAT IS JOB SATISFACTION?

Job satisfaction refers to a collection of attitudes that people have about their jobs. We can differentiate two aspects of satisfaction. The first of these is facet satisfaction, the tendency for an employee to be more or less satisfied with various facets of the job. The notion of facet satisfaction is obvious when we hear someone say, "I love my work but hate my boss" or "This place pays lousy, but the people I work with are great." Both these statements represent different attitudes toward separate facets of the speaker's job. The most relevant attitudes toward jobs are contained in a rather small group of facets: the work itself, compensation, career opportunities, recognition, benefits, working conditions, supervision, co-workers, and organizational policy.[23]

In addition to facet satisfaction, we can also conceive of overall satisfaction, an overall or summary indicator of a person's attitude toward his or her job that cuts across the various facets.[24] The statement "On the whole, I really like my job, although a couple of aspects could stand some improvement" is indicative of the nature of overall satisfaction. Overall satisfaction is an average or total of the attitudes individuals hold toward various facets of the job. Thus, two employees might express the same level of overall satisfaction for different reasons.

A popular measure of job satisfaction is the *Job Descriptive Index* (JDI).[25] This questionnaire is designed to evaluate five facets of satisfaction: people, pay, supervision, promotions, and the work itself. Employees are asked to respond "yes," "no," or "?" (cannot decide) in describing whether a particular word or phrase is descriptive of these facets. For example, for the pay facet, they are asked whether they are "well paid." A scoring system is available to provide an index of satisfaction for each facet. In addition, there is a scale that provides an overall measure of satisfaction.

Another carefully constructed measure of satisfaction, using a somewhat different set of facets, is the *Minnesota Satisfaction Questionnaire* (MSQ).[26] On this measure, respondents indicate how happy they are with various aspects of their job on a scale ranging from "very satisfied" to "very dissatisfied." Sample items from the short form of the MSQ include

- the competence of my supervisor in making decisions;
- the way my job provides for steady employment; and
- my pay and the amount of work I do.

Watch

JOIE DE VIVRE HOSPITALITY: EMPLOYEE MOTIVATION Go to MyManagementLab to watch a video about employee motivation.

Watch

PTC: EMPLOYEE ENGAGEMENT Go to MyManagementLab to watch a video about employee engagement.

LO 4.3

Explain the concept of *job satisfaction* and discuss some of its key contributors, including discrepancy, fairness, disposition, mood, and emotion.

Job satisfaction. A collection of attitudes that workers have about their jobs.

Scoring the responses to these items provides an index of overall satisfaction as well as satisfaction on the facets on which the MSQ is based.

Firms such as Best Buy, Marriott, Scotiabank, The Keg, and Microsoft make extensive use of employee attitude surveys. We will cover the details of such surveys in Chapter 10 when we explore communication and in Chapter 16 when we cover organizational change and development.

WHAT DETERMINES JOB SATISFACTION?

When employees on a variety of jobs complete the JDI or the MSQ, we often find differences in the average scores across jobs. Of course, we could almost expect such differences. The various jobs might differ objectively in the facets that contribute to satisfaction. Thus, you would not be astonished to learn that a corporate vice-president was more satisfied with her job than a janitor in the same company. Of greater interest is the fact that we frequently find decided differences in job satisfaction expressed by individuals performing the same job in a given organization. For example, two nurses who work side by side might indicate radically different satisfaction in response to the MSQ item "The chance to do things for other people." How does this happen?

Discrepancy

You will recall that attitudes, such as job satisfaction, are the product of associated beliefs and values. These two factors cause differences in job satisfaction even when jobs are identical. First, people might differ in their beliefs about the job in question. That is, they might differ in their *perceptions* concerning the actual nature of the job. For example, one of the nurses might perceive that most of her working time is devoted to direct patient care, while the other might perceive that most of her time is spent on administrative functions. To the extent that they both value patient care, the former nurse should be more satisfied with this aspect of the job than the latter nurse. Second, even if individuals perceive their jobs as equivalent, they might differ in what they *want* from the jobs. Such desires are preferences that are dictated, in part, by the workers' value systems. Thus, if the two nurses perceive their opportunities to engage in direct patient care as high, the one who values this activity more will be more satisfied with the patient care aspect of work. The **discrepancy theory** of job satisfaction asserts that satisfaction is a function of the discrepancy between the job outcomes people want and the outcomes that they perceive they obtain.[27] For instance, there is strong evidence that satisfaction with one's pay is high when there is a small gap between the pay received and the perception of how much pay *should* be received.[28] For example, at L'Oréal generational differences in values could have an impact on job satisfaction levels.

Discrepancy theory.
A theory that job satisfaction stems from the discrepancy between the job outcomes wanted and the outcomes that are perceived to be obtained.

Fairness

In addition to the discrepancy between the outcomes people receive and those they desire, another factor that determines job satisfaction is fairness. Issues of fairness affect both what people want from their jobs and how they react to the inevitable discrepancies of organizational life. As you will see, there are three basic kinds of fairness. Distributive fairness has to do with the outcomes we receive, procedural fairness concerns the process that led to those outcomes, and interactional fairness concerns how these matters were communicated to us.[29]

Distributive fairness.
Fairness that occurs when people receive the outcomes they think they deserve from their jobs

DISTRIBUTIVE FAIRNESS   **Distributive fairness** (often called *distributive justice*) occurs when people receive the outcomes they think they deserve from their jobs; that is, it involves the ultimate *distribution* of work rewards and resources. Above, we indicated that what people want from their jobs is a partial function of their value systems. In fact, however, there are

practical limitations to this notion. You might value money and the luxurious lifestyle that it can buy very highly, but this does not suggest that you expect to receive a salary of $200 000 a year. In the case of many job facets, individuals want "what's fair." And how do we develop our conception of what is fair? **Equity theory** states that the inputs that people perceive themselves as investing in a job and the outcomes that the job provides are compared against the inputs and outcomes of some other relevant person or group.[30] Equity will be perceived when the following distribution ratios exist:

$$\frac{\text{My outcomes}}{\text{My inputs}} = \frac{\text{Other's outcomes}}{\text{Other's inputs}}$$

In these ratios, **inputs** consist of anything that individuals consider relevant to their exchange with the organization, anything that they give up, offer, or trade to their organization. These might include factors such as education, training, seniority, hard work, and high-quality work. **Outcomes** are those factors that the organization distributes to employees in return for their inputs. The most relevant outcomes are represented by the job facets we discussed earlier—pay, career opportunities, supervision, the nature of the work, and so on. The "other" in the ratio above might be a co-worker performing the same job, a number of co-workers, or even one's conception of all the individuals in one's occupation.[31] For example, the CEO of Microsoft probably compares his outcome/input ratio with those that he assumes exist for the CEOs of Google and Intel. You probably compare your outcome/input ratio in your organizational behaviour class with that of one or more fellow students.

Equity theory has important implications for job satisfaction. First, inequity itself is a dissatisfying state, especially when we are on the "short end of the stick." For example, suppose you see the hours spent studying as your main input to your organizational behaviour class and the final grade as an important outcome. Imagine that a friend in the class is your comparison person. Under these conditions, the following situations appear equitable and should not provoke dissatisfaction on your part:

You	Friend		You	Friend
C grade	A grade	Or	A grade	C grade
50 hours	100 hours		60 hours	30 hours

In each of these cases, a fair relationship seems to exist between study time and grades distributed. Now consider the following relationships:

You	Friend		You	Friend
C grade	A grade	Or	A grade	C grade
100 hours	50 hours		30 hours	60 hours

In each of these situations, an unfair connection appears to exist between study time and grades received, and you should perceive inequity. However, the situation on the left, in which you put in more work for a lower grade, should be most likely to prompt dissatisfaction. This is a "short end of the stick" situation. For example, the employee who frequently remains on the job after regular hours (input) and receives no special praise or extra pay (outcome) might perceive inequity and feel dissatisfied. Equity considerations also have an indirect effect on job satisfaction by influencing what people want from their jobs. If you study for 100 hours while the rest of the class averages 50 hours, you will expect a higher grade than the class average.

Consider a practical example of equity in action. During a business recession, the Canadian-based luxury hotel company Four Seasons did not lay off employees and thus threaten customer service like many of its competitors. Rather, executives accepted a pay freeze and workers were asked to vote on a temporary move to a four-day work week rather than five.

Equity theory. A theory that job satisfaction stems from a comparison of the inputs one invests in a job and the outcomes one receives in comparison with the inputs and outcomes of another person or group.

Inputs. Anything that people give up, offer, or trade to their organization in exchange for outcomes.

Outcomes. Factors that an organization distributes to employees in exchange for their inputs.

The offer was accepted enthusiastically because it was seen as fair given extensive industry layoffs and the sacrifices made by company executives.[32]

The equity concept suggests that outcomes should be tied to individual contributions or inputs. This corresponds well with the individualistic North American culture. In more collective cultures, *equality* of outcomes might produce more feelings of distributive fairness. In more feminine cultures, allocating outcomes according to *need* (rather than performance) might provide for distributive fairness.

PROCEDURAL FAIRNESS   **Procedural fairness** (often called *procedural justice*) occurs when individuals see the process used to determine outcomes as reasonable; that is, rather than involving the actual distribution of resources or rewards, it is concerned with how these outcomes are decided and allocated. An example will illustrate the difference between distributive and procedural fairness. Out of the blue, Greg's boss tells him that she has completed his performance evaluation and that he will receive a healthy pay raise starting next month. Greg has been working very hard, and he is pleased with the pay raise (distributive fairness). However, he is vaguely unhappy about the fact that all this occurred without his participation. Where he to work, the employee and the boss would complete independent performance evaluation forms and then sit down and discuss any differences. This provided good feedback for the employee. Greg wonders how his peers who got less generous raises are reacting to the boss's style.

Procedural fairness is particularly relevant to outcomes such as performance evaluations, pay raises, promotions, layoffs, and work assignments. In allocating such outcomes, the following factors contribute to perceptions of procedural fairness.[33] The allocator

- follows consistent procedures over time and across people;
- uses accurate information and appears unbiased;
- allows two-way communication during the allocation process; and
- welcomes appeals of the procedure or allocation.

Procedural fairness is especially likely to provoke dissatisfaction when people also see distributive fairness as being low.[34] One view notes that dissatisfaction will be "maximized when people believe that they *would* have obtained better outcomes if the decision maker had used other procedures that *should* have been implemented."[35] (Students who receive lower grades than their friends will recognize the wisdom of this observation!) Thus, Greg, mentioned above, will probably not react too badly to the lack of consultation while his peers who did not receive large raises might strongly resent the process that the boss used.

INTERACTIONAL FAIRNESS   **Interactional fairness** (often called *interactional justice*) occurs when people feel that they have received respectful and informative communication about some outcome.[36] In other words, it extends beyond the actual procedures used to the interpersonal treatment received when learning about the outcome. Respectful communication is sincere and polite and treats the individual with dignity; informative communication is candid, timely, and thorough. Interactional fairness is important because it is possible for absolutely fair outcomes or procedures to be perceived as unfair when they are inadequately or uncaringly explained.

Sometimes, lower-level managers have little control over procedures that are used to allocate resources. However, they almost always have the opportunity to explain these procedures in a thorough, truthful, and caring manner. Frequently, people who experience procedural unfairness are dissatisfied with the "system." On the other hand, people who experience interactional unfairness are more likely to be dissatisfied with the boss.

Both procedural and interactional fairness can to some extent offset the negative effects of distributive unfairness. In one interesting study, nurses who received a pay cut due to hospital policy changes exhibited less insomnia when their supervisors were trained in the principles of interactional fairness compared to nurses with untrained supervisors.[37]

Procedural fairness. Fairness that occurs when the process used to determine work outcomes is seen as reasonable.

Interactional fairness. Fairness that occurs when people feel they have received respectful and informative communication about an outcome.

GLOBAL FOCUS

IS THE IMPORTANCE OF FAIRNESS UNIVERSAL ACROSS CULTURES?

Most research concerning fairness at work has been done in North America. In general, this research shows that fairness is an important determinant of job satisfaction, commitment to the organization, and trust in the organization and managers. But are these findings universal across cultures, or is fairness a particular preoccupation of North Americans?

Andrew Li and Russell Cropanzano compared the research on fairness at work that has been done in North America with that conducted in East Asia (mainland China, Japan, Hong Kong, South Korea, Taiwan, and Singapore). On one hand, we might guess that individualistic, low-power–distance North Americans would be more sensitive to incidents of unfairness. On the other hand, most such incidents are interpersonal (e.g., a boss gives a biased performance evaluation), and the more collective, social features of East Asian cultures might point to greater fairness sensitivity.

Li and Cropanzano found that distributive and procedural fairness predicted satisfaction, commitment, and trust in both regions. However, the associations were somewhat weaker in East Asia, suggesting a greater tolerance for unfairness there. The authors suggested that a need for interpersonal harmony, prevalent in the more collective East Asian cultures, might have led to this result.

The authors concluded that fairness seems important for people with a range of cultural backgrounds. However, they also noted that managers should be extra alert for feelings of unfairness among East Asians because they might not signal it in their attitudes and behaviour, hoping to maintain social harmony.

Source: Li, A., & Cropanzano, R. (2009). Do East Asians respond more/less strongly to organizational justice than North Americans? *Journal of Management Studies, 46*, 787–805.

Before continuing, see the Global Focus: *Is the Importance of Fairness Universal across Cultures?*

Disposition

Could your personality contribute to your feelings of job satisfaction? This is the essential question guiding research on the relationship between disposition and job satisfaction. Underlying the dispositional view is the idea that some people are *predisposed* by virtue of their personalities to be more or less satisfied despite changes in discrepancy or fairness. Some of the research that suggests that disposition contributes to job satisfaction is fascinating:[38]

- Identical twins raised apart from early childhood tend to have similar levels of job satisfaction.

- Job satisfaction tends to be fairly stable over time, even when changes in employer occur.

- Disposition measured early in adolescence is correlated with one's job satisfaction as a mature adult.

Taken together, these findings suggest that some personality characteristics originating in genetics or early learning contribute to adult job satisfaction. In fact, recent research has linked dopamine and serotonin genes to satisfaction.[39]

Research on disposition and job satisfaction has centred around the Big Five personality traits (Chapter 2). People who are extraverted and conscientious tend to be more satisfied with their jobs, while those high in neuroticism are less satisfied.[40] Also, people who are high in self-esteem and internal locus of control are more satisfied.[41] Thus, in general, people who are more optimistic and proactive report higher job satisfaction. Mood and emotion may contribute to this connection, so we will now examine these topics.

Watch

EAST HAVEN FIRE DEPARTMENT: EMOTIONS AND MOODS Go to MyManagementLab to watch a video about emotions and moods.

Emotions. Intense, often short-lived feelings caused by a particular event.

Moods. Less intense, longer-lived, and more diffuse feelings.

Emotional contagion. Tendency for moods and emotions to spread between people or throughout a group.

Emotional regulation. Requirement for people to conform to certain "display rules" in their job behaviour in spite of their true mood or emotions.

Mood and Emotion

The picture we have painted so far of the determinants of job satisfaction has been mostly one of calculation and rationality: people calculate discrepancies, compare job inputs to outcomes, and so on. But what about the intense feelings that are sometimes seen in work settings—the joy of a closed business deal or the despair that leads to workplace homicides? Or what about that vague feeling of a lack of accomplishment that blunts the pleasure of a dream job? We are speaking here about the role of affect as a determinant of job satisfaction. Affect is simply a broad label for feelings. These feelings include **emotions**, which are intense, often short-lived, and caused by a particular event such as a bad performance appraisal. Common emotions include joy, pride, anger, fear, and sadness. Affect also refers to **moods**, which are less intense, longer-lived, and more diffuse feelings.

How do emotions and moods affect job satisfaction? Affective events theory, proposed by Howard Weiss and Russell Cropanzano, addresses this question.[42] Basically, the theory reminds us that jobs actually consist of a series of events and happenings that have the potential to provoke emotions or to influence moods, depending on how we appraise these events and happenings. Thus, seeing a co-worker being berated by a manager might provoke emotional disgust and lower one's job satisfaction, especially if it is a frequent occurrence. This illustrates that perceived unfairness, as discussed earlier, can affect job satisfaction via emotion.[43] Also, a person's disposition can interact with job events to influence satisfaction. For instance, those who are neurotic and pessimistic may react to a minor series of job setbacks with a negative mood that depresses their job satisfaction.

An interesting way in which mood and emotion can influence job satisfaction is through **emotional contagion**. This is the tendency for moods and emotions to spread between people or throughout a group. Thus, people's moods and emotions tend to converge with interaction. Generally, teams experiencing more positive affect tend to be more cooperative, helpful, and successful, all of which are conditions that contribute to job satisfaction.[44] Emotional contagion can also occur in dealing with customers such that pleasant service encounters contribute to the service provider's satisfaction as well as to that of the customer.

Another interesting way in which mood and emotion can influence job satisfaction is through the need for **emotional regulation**. This is the requirement for people to conform to certain "display rules" in their job behaviour, in spite of their true mood or emotions. Often, this is referred to informally as "emotional labour." In one version, employees are expected to be perky and upbeat whether they feel that way or not, thus exaggerating positive emotions. In the other version, employees are supposed to remain calm and civil even when hassled or insulted, thus suppressing negative emotions. One study found that call centre employees averaged 10 incidents of customer aggression a day.[45] All jobs have their implicit display rules, such as not acting angry in front of the boss. However, service roles such as waiter, bank teller, and flight attendant are especially laden with display rules, some of which may be made explicit in training and via cues from managers.

What are the consequences of the requirement for emotional regulation? There is solid evidence that the frequent need to suppress negative emotions and fake emotions that you do not really feel take a toll on job satisfaction and increase stress.[46] Flight attendants can humour only so many drunk or angry air passengers before the experience wears thin! On the other hand, the jury is still out on the requirement to express positive emotions, especially when you really are feeling positive. Some research suggests that this display rule boosts job satisfaction.[47] If so, positive contagion from happy customers may be responsible. Of course, disposition may again enter the picture, as extraverts may be energized by requirements for positive display.

Do organizations pay a premium for emotional labour? The answer is sometimes. Theresa Glomb, John Kammeyer-Mueller, and Maria Rotundo studied the emotional labour and cognitive demands (thinking, decision making) required in various occupations (see Exhibit 4.5).[48]

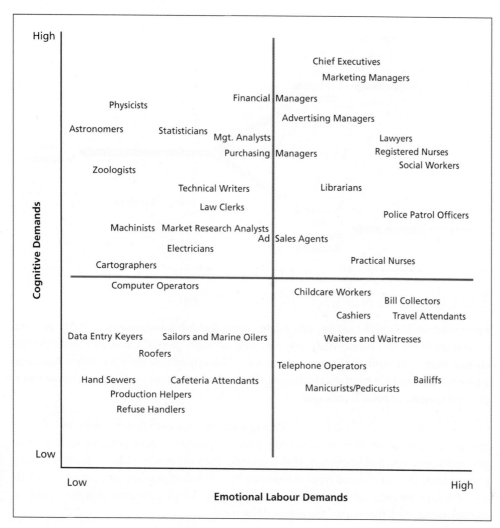

EXHIBIT 4.5
Occupations plotted by emotional labour and cognitive demands.
Source: Adapted from Glomb, T.M., Kammeyer-Mueller, J.D., & Rotundo, M. (2004). Emotional labor demands and compensating wage differentials. *Journal of Applied Psychology,* 89, 700–714.

✳ Explore

Go to MyManagementLab to see an annotated version of this figure.

They found that those in occupations with high cognitive demands (the upper portion of the exhibit) tend to be paid more when the jobs are also high in emotional labour. Thus, lawyers tend to earn more than zoologists. On the other hand, occupations with low cognitive demands entail a wage penalty when emotional labour is higher. Thus, the "people jobs" in the lower right quadrant of the exhibit tend to be less well paid than the jobs in the lower left quadrant. As we will see shortly, pay is an important determinant of job satisfaction.

Consideration of mood and emotion helps explain a curious but commonplace phenomenon: how people with similar beliefs and values doing the same job for the same compensation can still exhibit very different satisfaction levels. This difference is probably a result of emotional events and subtle differences in mood that add up over time. We will revisit emotion when we study emotional intelligence (Chapter 5), decision making (Chapter 11), stress (Chapter 13), and organizational change (Chapter 16).

Exhibit 4.6 summarizes what research has to say about the determinants of job satisfaction. To recapitulate, satisfaction is a function of certain dispositional factors, the discrepancy between the job outcomes a person wants and the outcomes received, and mood and emotion. More specifically, people experience greater satisfaction when they meet or exceed the job outcomes they want, perceive the job outcomes they receive as equitable compared with those others receive, and believe that fair procedures determine job outcomes. The outcomes that people want from a job are a function of their personal value systems, moderated by equity considerations. The outcomes that people perceive themselves as receiving from the job represent their beliefs about the nature of that job.

EXHIBIT 4.6
How discrepancy,
fairness, disposition,
mood, and emotion
affect job satisfaction.

 Explore

Go to MyManagementLab
to see an annotated
version of this figure.

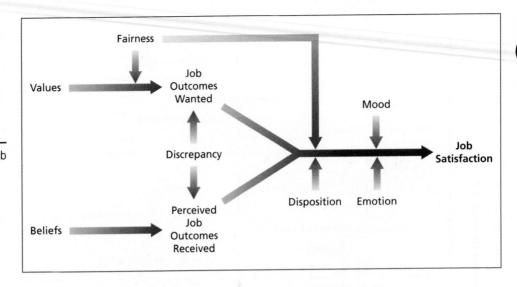

Some Key Contributors to Job Satisfaction

From what we have said thus far, you might expect that job satisfaction is a highly personal experience. While this is essentially true, we can make some general statements about the facets that seem to contribute the most to feelings of job satisfaction for most North American workers. These include mentally challenging work, adequate compensation, career opportunities, and friendly or helpful colleagues.[49]

MENTALLY CHALLENGING WORK This is work that tests employees' skills and abilities and allows them to set their own working pace. Employees usually perceive such work as personally involving and important. It also provides the worker with clear feedback regarding performance. Of course, some types of work can be too challenging, and this can result in feelings of failure and reduced satisfaction. In addition, some employees seem to prefer repetitive, unchallenging work that makes few demands on them.

ADEQUATE COMPENSATION It should not surprise you that pay and satisfaction are positively related. However, not everyone is equally desirous of money, and some people are certainly willing to accept less responsibility or fewer working hours for lower pay. In most companies, one finds a group of employees who are especially anxious to earn extra money through overtime and another group that actively avoids overtime work.

CAREER OPPORTUNITIES The availability of career opportunities contributes to job satisfaction. Opportunity for promotion is an important contributor to job satisfaction because promotions contain a number of valued signals about a person's self-worth. Some of these signals may be material (such as an accompanying raise), while others are of a social nature (recognition within the organization and increased prestige in the community). Of course, there are cultural and individual differences in what people see as constituting a fair promotion system. Some employees might prefer a strict seniority system, while others might wish for a system based strictly on job performance. Many of today's flatter organizations no longer offer the promotion opportunities of the past. Well-run firms have offset this by designing lateral moves that provide for challenging work. Also, as discussed in Chapter 2, career development helps prepare employees to assume challenging assignments.

PEOPLE It should not surprise you that friendly, considerate, good-natured superiors and co-workers contribute to job satisfaction, especially via positive moods and emotions. There is, however, another aspect to interpersonal relationships on the job that contributes to job satisfaction. Specifically, we tend to be satisfied in the presence of people who help us attain job outcomes that we value. Such outcomes might include doing our work better or more easily, obtaining a raise or promotion, or even staying alive. For example, a company of soldiers in battle might be less concerned with how friendly their commanding officer is than with how competently he is able to act to keep them from being overrun by the enemy. Similarly, an aggressive young executive might like a considerate boss but prefer even more a boss who can clarify her work objectives and reward her for attaining them. The friendliness aspect of interpersonal relationships seems most important in lower-level jobs with clear duties and in various dead-end jobs. If pay is tied to performance or as jobs become more complex or promotion opportunities increase, the ability of others to help us do our work well contributes more to job satisfaction.

Context can certainly affect what contributes most to job satisfaction. Exhibit 4.7 shows the results of a survey conducted by the Society for Human Resource Management in 2011. As you can see, job security and the organization's financial stability were high on the list.

In the high-tech and creative domains, organizational success depends on attracting and retaining the very best talent and creating an atmosphere free from distractions and inconveniences so that the creative juices can flow. The stress of project deadlines is commonplace. Because of these factors, firms such as Google, Microsoft, Pixar, and Research In Motion (RIM) go to extraordinary lengths to foster employee job satisfaction. Perks range from the provision of "fun" campus-like environments to free meals to the availability of services such as transportation, dry cleaning, and car washes. To see how Capital One enhances job satisfaction, check out You Be the Manager.

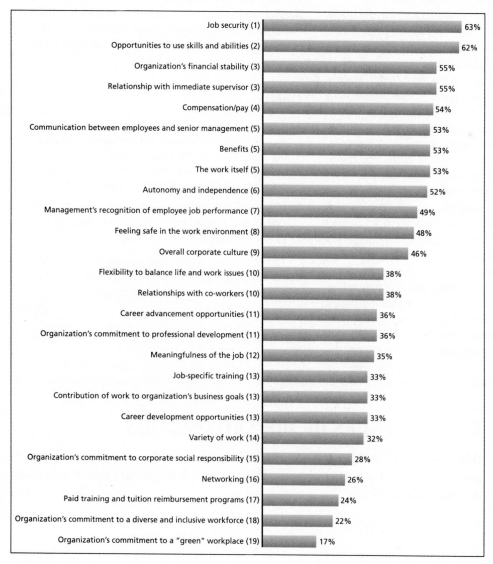

EXHIBIT 4.7
"Very important" aspects of employee job satisfaction.
Note: Percentages reflect respondents who answered "very important" on a scale where 1 = "very unimportant" and 4 = "very important."
Source: Society for Human Resource Management. (2011). *2011 Employee job satisfaction and engagement.* Alexandria, VA: SHRM, p.7. © Society for Human Resource Management. Used by permission.

Job security (1) — 63%
Opportunities to use skills and abilities (2) — 62%
Organization's financial stability (3) — 55%
Relationship with immediate supervisor (3) — 55%
Compensation/pay (4) — 54%
Communication between employees and senior management (5) — 53%
Benefits (5) — 53%
The work itself (5) — 53%
Autonomy and independence (6) — 52%
Management's recognition of employee job performance (7) — 49%
Feeling safe in the work environment (8) — 48%
Overall corporate culture (9) — 46%
Flexibility to balance life and work issues (10) — 38%
Relationships with co-workers (10) — 38%
Career advancement opportunities (11) — 36%
Organization's commitment to professional development (11) — 36%
Meaningfulness of the job (12) — 35%
Job-specific training (13) — 33%
Contribution of work to organization's business goals (13) — 33%
Career development opportunities (13) — 33%
Variety of work (14) — 32%
Organization's commitment to corporate social responsibility (15) — 28%
Networking (16) — 26%
Paid training and tuition reimbursement programs (17) — 24%
Organization's commitment to a diverse and inclusive workforce (18) — 22%
Organization's commitment to a "green" workplace (19) — 17%

YOU BE THE MANAGER

The Future of Work @ Capital One

The nature of the work to which people are drawn reflects the values that individuals espouse. Over the past century, work has moved from primarily blue collar, assembly-line jobs toward white collar, knowledge-based jobs. With the transition, employee values have also changed. Knowledge workers, who make up approximately one-third of the workforce in North America, seek a work environment that supports not only teamwork and collaboration but also privacy and flexibility. When the work environment cannot support these needs, employees can become dissatisfied because inability to concentrate and accomplish tasks can create frustration and anxiety, as can the challenges of trying to balance worklife with personal life. When employees are not able to work when they want, how they want, and with whom they want, satisfaction can decline, resulting in absenteeism, turnover, and lower productivity.

At Capital One, one of the top 15 banks in the United States, caring for their knowledge workers has always been a top priority. Considered one of the best places to work by *Fortune* magazine, Capital One's key values include "Excellence" and "Do the Right Thing." Employees are encouraged to achieve corporate objectives by thinking independently and taking ownership of their ideas. The "test and learn" culture is played out through teamwork, collaboration, and innovative work practices. At the core of Capital One's culture is the importance of making data-driven decisions, which has positioned the IT function, and technology itself, in a strategic role.

To satisfy their knowledge workers, Capital One has invested in creating workspaces that support employee values. In the late 1990s, they embarked on a program with the aim of creating state-of-the-art facilities that encourage teamwork and collaboration. Drawing on theories of building and furniture utilization, Capital One implemented a standardized design of offices, cubicles, and conference rooms. But Capital One soon discovered a significant underutilization of office resources. They found that, on a daily basis,

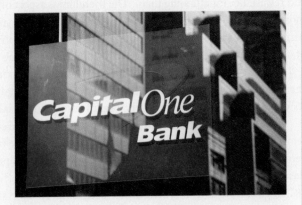

40 percent of cubicles were left vacant, while another 30 percent were unoccupied for certain hours of the day. It appeared that employees were not using their workspace as originally intended. Capital One took this problem seriously. Even though the company had been recognized for its state-of-the-art facilities, changing workplace values were signalling that standard office designs were a thing of the past.

Questions

1. Although Capital One had implemented a state-of-the-art facility, employees did not appear to be taking advantage of the office resources in the way management intended. How could the work environment be affecting employees' job satisfaction?

2. How could the office space be redesigned to meet employees' needs? What role could technology play in the redesign of the office space?

To find out how Capital One increased job satisfaction by redesigning their office space, see The Manager's Notebook at the end of the chapter.

Source: Adapted from Khana, S., & New, J.R. (2008). Revolutionizing the workplace: A case study of the future of work program at Capital One. *Human Resource Management, 47*, 795–808.

Explain the relationship between job satisfaction and absenteeism, turnover, performance, organizational citizenship behaviour, and customer satisfaction.

CONSEQUENCES OF JOB SATISFACTION

Dell, Sears, and L'Oréal Canada are firms that have maintained a competitive advantage by paying particular attention to employee satisfaction. Why is this so? Let's look at some consequences of job satisfaction.

Absence from Work

Absenteeism is an expensive behaviour in North America, costing billions of dollars each year. Such costs are attributable to "sick pay," lost productivity, and chronic overstaffing to compensate for absentees. Many more days are lost to absenteeism than to strikes and other industrial disputes. Research shows that less-satisfied employees are more likely to be absent and that satisfaction with the content of the work is the best predictor of absenteeism.[50] However, the absence–satisfaction connection is not very strong. Several factors constrain the ability of many people to convert their like or dislike of work into corresponding attendance patterns:

- Some absence is simply unavoidable because of illness, weather conditions, or child care problems. Thus, some very happy employees will occasionally be absent owing to circumstances beyond their control.

- Some organizations have attendance control policies that influence absence more than satisfaction does. In a company that does not pay workers for missed days (typical of many workplaces with hourly pay), absence may be more related to economic needs than to dissatisfaction. The unhappy worker who absolutely needs money will probably show up for work. By the same token, dissatisfied and satisfied workers might be equally responsive to threats of dismissal for absenteeism.

- In many jobs it may be unclear to employees how much absenteeism is reasonable or sensible. With a lack of company guidelines, workers may look to the behaviour of their peers for a norm to guide their behaviour. This norm and its corresponding "absence culture" (see Chapter 7) might have a stronger effect than the individual employee's satisfaction with his or her job.[51]

Turnover

Turnover refers to resignation from an organization, and it can be incredibly expensive. For example, it costs several thousand dollars to replace a nurse or a bank teller who resigns. As we move up the organizational hierarchy, or into technologically complex jobs, such costs escalate dramatically. For example, it costs millions of dollars to hire and train a single military fighter pilot. Estimates of turnover costs usually include the price of hiring, training, and developing to proficiency a replacement employee. Such figures probably underestimate the true costs of turnover, however, because they do not include intangible costs, such as work group disruption or the loss of employees who informally acquire special skills and knowledge over time on a job. All this would not be so bad if turnover were concentrated among poorer performers. Unfortunately, this is not always the case. In one study, 23 percent of scientists and engineers who left an organization were among the top 10 percent of performers.[52]

What is the relationship between job satisfaction and turnover? Research indicates a moderately strong connection, with less-satisfied workers being more likely to quit.[53] However, the relationship between the attitude (job satisfaction) and the behaviour in question (turnover) is far from perfect. Exhibit 4.8 presents a model of turnover that can help explain this.[54] In the model, circles represent attitudes, ovals represent elements of the turnover process, and squares denote situational factors. The model shows that job satisfaction as well as commitment to the organization and various "shocks" (both discussed below) can contribute to intentions to leave. Research shows that such intentions are very good predictors of turnover.[55] As shown, such intentions sometimes prompt turnover directly, even impulsively. On the other hand, reduced satisfaction or commitment can also stimulate a more deliberate evaluation of the utility of quitting and a careful job search and evaluation of job alternatives. The following are some reasons why satisfied people sometimes quit their jobs or dissatisfied people stay:

- Certain "shocks," such as a marital breakup, the birth of a child, or an unsolicited job offer in an attractive location, might stimulate turnover despite satisfaction with the current job.

- An employee's dissatisfaction with his or her specific job might be offset by a strong commitment to the overall values and mission of the organization.

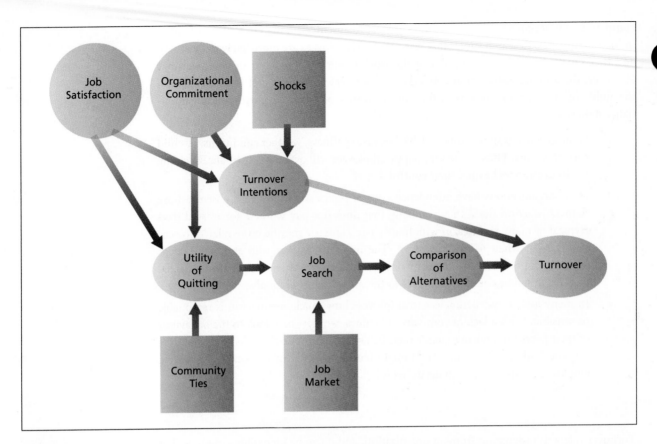

EXHIBIT 4.8
A model of employee turnover.

Explore

Go to MyManagementLab to see an annotated version of this figure.

- An employee might be so embedded in the community (due to involvement with churches, schools, or sports) that he or she is willing to endure a dissatisfying job rather than move.

- A weak job market might result in limited employment alternatives. Dissatisfaction is most likely to result in turnover when jobs are plentiful.[56]

Despite these exceptions, a decrease in job satisfaction often precedes turnover, and those who quit experience a boost in satisfaction on their new job. However, some of this boost might be due to a "honeymoon effect," in which the bad facets of the old job are gone, the good facets of the new job are apparent, and the bad facets of the new job are not yet known. Over time, as these bad facets are recognized, a "hangover effect" can occur, in which overall satisfaction with the new job decreases.[57] This pattern is shown in Exhibit 4.9, which traces job satisfaction at five points in time as a person moves between jobs A and B.

Performance

It seems sensible that job satisfaction contributes to less absenteeism and turnover, but does it also lead to improved job performance? After all, employees might be so "satisfied" that no work is accomplished! In fact, research has confirmed what folk wisdom and business magazines have advocated for many years—job satisfaction is associated with enhanced performance.[58] However, the connection between satisfaction and performance is complicated, because many factors influence motivation and performance besides job satisfaction (as we'll see in Chapter 5). Thus, research has led to some qualifications to the idea that "a happy worker is a productive worker."

All satisfaction facets are not equal in terms of stimulating performance. The most important facet has to do with the content of the work itself.[59] Thus, interesting, challenging jobs are most likely to stimulate high performance (we will see how to design such jobs in Chapter 6). One consequence of this is the fact that the connection between job satisfaction and performance is stronger for complex, high-tech jobs in science, engineering, and

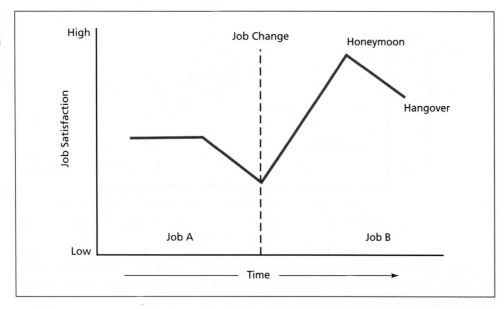

EXHIBIT 4.9
**The honeymoon–
hangover effect.**
Source: Drawing by the
authors, based on Boswell,
W.R., Boudreau, J.W., & Tichy,
J. (2005). The relationship
between employee job change
and job satisfaction: The
honeymoon–hangover effect.
Journal of Applied Psychology,
90, 882–892.

 Explore

Go to MyManagementLab
to see an annotated
version of this figure.

computers and less strong for more routine labour jobs. In part, this is because people doing complex jobs have more control over their level of performance.

Another issue in the connection between job satisfaction and performance has to do with which of these is the cause and which the effect. Although job satisfaction contributes to performance, performance could also contribute to job satisfaction.[60] When good performance is *followed by rewards*, employees are more likely to be satisfied. However, many organizations do not reward good performance sufficiently. Thus, contemporary research indicates that satisfaction is more likely to affect performance, rather than the reverse.[61]

In addition to boosting formal job performance, satisfaction can also contribute to employees' informal, everyday behaviour and actions that help their organizations and their co-workers. Let's turn now to a discussion of this.

Organizational Citizenship Behaviour

Organizational citizenship behaviour (OCB) is voluntary, informal behaviour that contributes to organizational effectiveness.[62] In many cases, the formal performance evaluation system does not detect and reward it. Job satisfaction contributes greatly to the occurrence of OCB, more than it does to regular task performance, in fact.[63]

An example of OCB should clarify the concept. You are struggling to master a particularly difficult piece of software. A colleague at the next desk, busy on her own rush job, comes over and offers assistance. Irritated with the software, you are not even very grateful at first, but within 10 minutes you have solved the problem with her help. Notice the defining characteristics of this example of OCB:

- The behaviour is voluntary. It is not included in her job description.
- The behaviour is spontaneous. Someone did not order or suggest it.
- The behaviour contributes to organizational effectiveness. It extends beyond simply doing you a personal favour.
- The behaviour is unlikely to be explicitly picked up and rewarded by the performance evaluation system, especially since it is not part of the job description.

What forms might OCB take? As the software example indicates, one prominent form is *helping* behaviour, offering assistance to others. Another might be *conscientiousness* to the details of work, including getting in on the snowiest day of the year and not wasting organizational resources. A third involves being a *good sport* when the inevitable frustrations of organizational life crop up—not everyone can have the best office or the best parking spot.

**Organizational
citizenship behaviour
(OCB).** Voluntary, informal
behaviour that contributes
to organizational
effectiveness.

**EXHIBIT 4.10
Progression of
withdrawal**

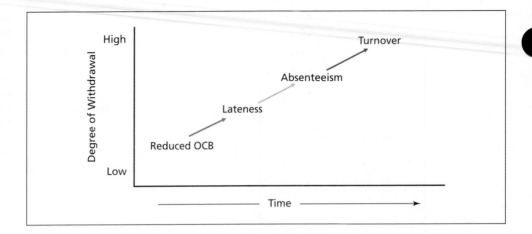

A final form of OCB is *courtesy and cooperation*.[64] Examples might include warning the photocopy unit about a big job that is on the way or delaying one's own work to assist a colleague on a rush job.

Just how does job satisfaction contribute to OCB? Fairness is the key. Although distributive fairness (especially in terms of pay) is important, procedural and interactional fairness from a supportive manager seem especially critical.[65] If the manager strays from the prescriptions for procedural fairness we gave earlier, OCB can suffer. If one feels unfairly treated, it might be difficult to lower formal performance for fear of dire consequences. It might be much easier to withdraw the less visible, informal activities that make up OCB. On the other hand, fair treatment and its resulting satisfaction might be reciprocated with OCB, a truly personalized input. OCB is also influenced by employees' mood at work. People in a pleasant, relaxed, optimistic mood are more likely to provide special assistance to others.[66]

OCB contributes to organizational productivity and efficiency and to reduced turnover.[67] Because of this, some firms do try to formally recognize OCBs. Xilinx, the highly innovative leader in programmable logic components, fosters and publicizes nominations of people who go "above and beyond duty" to help peers, selecting some for special recognition and a token cash award.[68]

Research shows that there is sometimes a progression of withdrawal in response to job dissatisfaction (and to reduced commitment, discussed below).[69] That is, people withdraw their attention or work effort in an attempt to compensate for dissatisfaction, beginning with more subtle behaviours and progressing to more extreme, until some equilibrium is struck. As shown in Exhibit 4.10, reduction of OCB is often the first withdrawal response, as these are voluntary behaviours. This may be followed, in turn, by coming to work late, then absenteeism, and ultimately turnover. Managers should be alert to increases in the lower forms of withdrawal, because they may signal bigger problems in the future.

Customer Satisfaction and Profit

So far, we have established that job satisfaction can reduce employee absenteeism and turnover and increase employee performance and citizenship behaviour. But is it possible that employee satisfaction could actually affect *customer* satisfaction? That is, do happy employees translate into happy customers? And do happy employees actually contribute to the bottom line of the organization by increasing organizational profits? After all, we have warned that the translation of positive attitudes into positive employee behaviours is less than perfect and that such attitudes therefore might not affect the bottom line.

A growing body of evidence has established that employee job satisfaction is indeed translated into customer or client satisfaction and organizational profitability.[70] Thus, organizations with higher average levels of employee satisfaction are more effective. The same

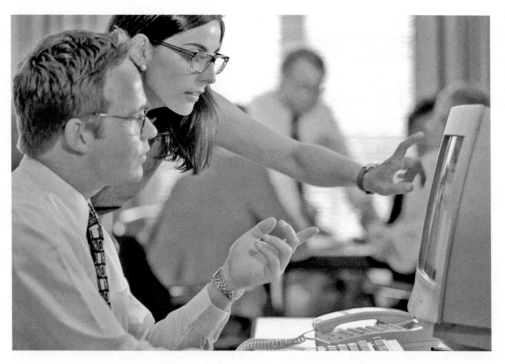

When one worker voluntarily helps out another, it is an example of organizational citizenship, which positively affects organizational effectiveness.

applies to units within larger organizations. Hence, local bank branches or insurance claims offices with more satisfied employees should tend to have more satisfied clients and generate more profits for the larger firm. Thus, it makes good sense to use employee satisfaction as one criterion in judging the effectiveness of local unit managers.

How does employee satisfaction translate into customer satisfaction? Reduced absenteeism and turnover contribute to the seamless delivery of service, as do the OCBs that stimulate good teamwork. Also, the mood mechanism, mentioned earlier, should not be discounted, as good mood among employees can be contagious for customers.

The Ford Motor Company (see Chapter 16) and Sears have been particularly attentive to the links among employee satisfaction, customer satisfaction, and profit. In an 800-store study, Sears found a clear positive relationship between employee satisfaction and store profitability. In addition, improvements in employee satisfaction were mirrored in customer satisfaction, resulting in an estimated $200 million in added annual revenue.[71]

Let's turn now to another important work attitude—organizational commitment.

WHAT IS ORGANIZATIONAL COMMITMENT?

Organizational commitment is an attitude that reflects the strength of the linkage between an employee and an organization. This linkage has implications for whether someone tends to remain in an organization. Researchers John Meyer and Natalie Allen have identified three very different types of organizational commitment:[72]

- **Affective commitment** is commitment based on a person's identification and involvement with an organization. People with high affective commitment stay with an organization because they *want* to.

- **Continuance commitment** is commitment based on the costs that would be incurred in leaving an organization. People with high continuance commitment stay with an organization because they *have* to.

- **Normative commitment** is commitment based on ideology or a feeling of obligation to an organization. People with high normative commitment stay with an organization because they think that they *should* do so.

LO 4.5

Differentiate *affective*, *continuance*, and *normative commitment* and explain how organizations can foster *organizational commitment*.

Organizational commitment. An attitude that reflects the strength of the linkage between an employee and an organization.

Affective commitment. Commitment based on identification and involvement with an organization.

Continuance commitment. Commitment based on the costs that would be incurred in leaving an organization.

Normative commitment. Commitment based on ideology or a feeling of obligation to an organization.

Employees can be committed not only to their organization but also to various constituencies within and outside the organization. Thus, each type of commitment could also apply to one's work team, union, or profession.[73]

Key Contributors to Organizational Commitment

The causes of the three forms of commitment tend to differ. By far the best predictor of affective commitment is interesting, satisfying work of the type found in enriched jobs (see Chapter 6).[74] One mistake that organizations sometimes make is starting employees out in unchallenging jobs so they do not make any serious errors. This can have a negative impact on affective commitment. Role clarity and having one's expectations met after being hired also contribute to affective commitment.[75]

Continuance commitment occurs when people feel that leaving the organization will result in personal sacrifice, or they perceive that good alternative employment is lacking. Building up "side bets" in pension funds, obtaining rapid promotion, or being well integrated into the community where the firm is located can lock employees into organizations even though they would rather go elsewhere. Not surprisingly, continuance commitment increases with the time a person is employed by an organization.

Normative commitment ("I *should* stay here") can be fostered by benefits that build a sense of obligation to the organization. These might include tuition reimbursements or special training that enhances one's skills. Strong identification with an organization's product or service ("I should stay here because the Sierra Club is doing important work") can also foster normative commitment. Finally, certain socialization practices (see Chapter 8) that emphasize loyalty to the organization can stimulate normative commitment. For example, sports coaches often haze players who miss practice to stress the importance of loyalty to the team.

Consequences of Organizational Commitment

There is good evidence that all forms of commitment reduce turnover intentions and actual turnover.[76] Organizations plagued with turnover problems among key employees should look carefully at tactics that foster commitment. This is especially called for when turnover gets so bad that it threatens customer service. Many service organizations (e.g., restaurants and hotels), however, have traditionally accepted high turnover rates.

Organizations should take care, though, in their targeting of the kind of commitment to boost. Affective commitment is positively related to performance because it focuses attention on goals and thus enhances motivation (see Chapter 5).[77] However, continuance commitment is *negatively* related to performance, something you might have observed in dealing with burned-out bureaucrats.[78] An especially bad combination for both the employee and the organization is high continuance commitment coupled with low affective commitment—people locked into organizations that they detest. This happens very frequently during recessions.

Is there a downside to organizational commitment? Very high levels of commitment can cause conflicts between family life and worklife. Also, very high levels of commitment have often been implicated in unethical and illegal behaviour, including a General Electric price-fixing conspiracy. Finally, high levels of commitment to a particular *form* or *style* of organization can cause a lack of innovation and lead to resistance when a change in the culture is necessary.[79]

Changes in the Workplace and Employee Commitment

Organizations are experiencing unprecedented change as a result of shifts in workforce demographics, technological innovations, and global competition.[80] In an era of layoffs, downsizing, outsourcing, restructuring, and reengineering, there is evidence that employees are losing commitment to their organizations.[81] People often view their careers as a series of jobs with a variety of potential employers, or they even see themselves as freelancers rather than having a series of jobs in one organization.

John Meyer, Natalie Allen, and Laryssa Topolnytsky have studied commitment in a changing world of work, and they note that the impact of changes in the workplace on employee commitment can be seen in three main areas:[82]

- *Changes in the nature of employees' commitment to the organization.* Depending on the nature of workplace changes and how they are managed, employees' levels of affective, continuance, and normative commitment can increase or decrease. Thus, the commitment profiles of employees following a change will be different from what they were prior to the change, and maintaining high levels of affective commitment will be particularly challenging. Changes that are made in the organization's best interest but that are detrimental to employees' well-being are most likely to damage affective commitment.

- *Changes in the focus of employees' commitment.* Employees generally have multiple commitments. In particular, employee commitment can be directed to others within the organization, such as subunits or divisions, teams, the "new" organization, as well as entities outside the organization, such as one's occupation, career, or union. Therefore, changes in the workplace might alter the focus of employees' commitments both within and outside of the organization. As organizations increase in size following mergers and acquisitions, for example, employees are likely to shift their commitment to smaller organizational units, such as their particular division, branch, or team. As well, changes that threaten employees' future in the organization might result in a shift in commitment to entities outside the organization, such as one's profession, occupation, or personal career.

- *The multiplicity of employer–employee relationships within organizations.* As organizations attempt to cope and adapt to rapid change, they need to be flexible enough to shrink or expand their workforce. At the same time, they need a workforce that is flexible enough to get any job done. This creates a potential conflict as employees who do not have guaranteed job security may be unwilling to be as flexible as the organization would like or to have a strong affective commitment toward the organization. A potential solution to this problem is for organizations to have different relationships with employee groups. For example, an organization might have a group of core employees who perform the key operations required for organizational success. It would be important for this group of employees to have a high level of affective organizational commitment. Other employee groups would consist of those with contractual arrangements or individuals hired on a temporary basis who do not perform the core tasks and whose commitment to the organization is not as important.

In summary, changes in the workplace are having an impact on the nature of employee commitment and employee–employer relationships. It is therefore important that organizations understand how changes in the workplace can change the profile and focus of employees' commitment and the impact this can have on employee behaviour and organizational success.

THE MANAGER'S NOTEBOOK

Capital One

1. Capital One's original workspace design was based on a "one size fits all" approach. Using conventional theories of building and furniture utilization, they standardized the size of offices and cubicles and assigned office space based on hierarchy. Conference rooms were established as iconic representations of the corporate culture, taking up ample space in prime areas of the building. Although employees were provided with the tools to do their work, such as high-powered desktop computers and feature-rich phones, the design was based on the assumption that employees would either be in their cubicles working or in conference rooms for meetings. Capital One did not consider that their knowledge workers sought a diversity of workspace solutions that allowed them to work anywhere (within or outside the building), whenever and however they wanted. In lieu of working the way they were expected, they sought out workspaces that supported their need to collaborate, work independently, and work away from the office when required. Upon realizing the underutilization of resources, Capital One established a new program, called "The Future of Work." With the intent to increase job satisfaction, and ultimately business productivity, Capital One focused the program on the employee. With their employees they aimed to discover what their knowledge workers needed to be most productive and most happy. Capital One realized that, with the many generations of workers in their company and with the diversity of cultures, employee needs varied considerably throughout the workday and the workweek. Their Future of Work program sought to provide a rich variety of work environments that allowed employees the flexibility they craved.

2. Capital One's Future of Work program was primarily concerned with the satisfaction of employees. Although reducing facility costs and boosting productivity were also considered important, Capital One believed that things start with the employee. The Future of Work program therefore redirected the facility savings into technology programs in order to "untether" employees from their desks. Mobility tools such as laptops, mobile phones, BlackBerries, and voice-over-Internet Protocol (VOIP) telephone solutions were made available to ensure that employees could work from anywhere, whenever they chose, as long as WiFi or hard-wired internet connections were available. Workers were classified by the type of work they did and their mobility preferences. Each type of worker was then assigned a certain amount of office space and a set of mobility tools to support their work habits. For example, executives and directors were provided with both office space and BlackBerries or laptops, since they are often in the office during the day but also continue working when they leave. Teleworkers and mobile workers, on the other hand, were provided with plenty of mobility tools, but with shared rather than dedicated office space, in consideration of the fact that they were in the office less. In addition to the technology, the workspace itself was redesigned to include a variety of spaces, ranging from small enclaves to large project rooms, along with lounges and café-style settings, supported by power and data connections. Did all this work? Employees reported a 41 percent increase in overall workplace satisfaction, while facilities costs per employee dropped by almost half. Although overall productivity increases are difficult to measure, employees did report a greater facility in getting their work done, on their own and with their teams.

LEARNING OBJECTIVES CHECKLIST

4.1 *Values* are broad preferences for particular states of affairs. Values tend to differ across generations and across cultures. Critical cross-cultural dimensions of values include power distance, uncertainty avoidance, masculinity/femininity, individualism/collectivism, and time orientation. Differences in values across cultures set constraints on the export and import of organizational behaviour theories and management practices. They also have implications for satisfying global customers and developing globally aware employees.

4.2 *Attitudes* are a function of what we think about the world (our beliefs) and how we feel about the world (our values). Attitudes are important because they influence how we behave, although we have discussed several factors that reduce the correspondence between our attitudes and behaviours.

4.3 *Job satisfaction* is an especially important attitude for organizations. Satisfaction is a function of the discrepancy between what individuals want from their jobs and what they perceive that they obtain, taking into account fairness. Dispositional factors, moods, and emotions also influence job satisfaction. Factors such as challenging work, adequate compensation, career opportunities, and friendly, helpful co-workers contribute to job satisfaction.

4.4 Job satisfaction is important because it promotes several positive outcomes for organizations. Satisfied employees tend to be less likely to be absent or leave their jobs. While links between satisfaction and performance are not always strong, satisfaction with the work itself has been linked to better performance. Satisfaction linked to perceptions of fairness can also lead to citizenship behaviours on the part of employees. Satisfied workers may also enhance customer satisfaction.

4.5 *Organizational commitment* is an attitude that reflects the strength of the linkage between an employee and an organization. *Affective commitment* is based on a person's identification with an organization. *Continuance commitment* is based on the costs of leaving an organization. *Normative commitment* is based on ideology or feelings of obligation. Changes in the workplace can change the nature and focus of employee commitment as well as employer–employee relationships. To foster commitment, organizations need to be sensitive to the expectations of employees and consider the impact of policy decisions beyond economic issues.

DISCUSSION QUESTIONS

1. What are some of the conditions under which a person's attitudes might not predict his or her work behaviour?

2. What is the difference between procedural and interactional fairness? Give an example of each.

3. Explain how these people might have to regulate their emotions when doing their jobs: hair salon owner, bill collector, police officer, teacher. How will this regulation of emotion affect job satisfaction?

4. Using the model of the turnover process in Exhibit 4.8, explain why a very dissatisfied employee might not quit his or her job.

5. Explain why employees who are very satisfied with their jobs might not be better performers than those who are less satisfied.

6. Use equity theory to explain why a dentist who earns $100 000 a year might be more dissatisfied with her job than a factory worker who earns $40 000.

7. Mexico has a fairly high power distance culture, while the United States and Canada have lower power distance cultures. Discuss how effective management techniques might vary between Mexico and its neighbours to the north.

8. Describe some job aspects that might contribute to job satisfaction for a person in a more collective culture. Do the same for a person in a more individualistic culture.

9. Give an example of an employee who is experiencing distributive fairness but not procedural fairness. Give an example of an employee who is experiencing procedural fairness but not distributive fairness.

INTEGRATIVE DISCUSSION QUESTIONS

1. What role do perceptions play in the determination of job satisfaction? Refer to the components of perception in Chapter 3 and describe how perception plays a role in the determination of job satisfaction according to discrepancy theory, equity theory, and dispositions. How can perceptions be changed to increase job satisfaction?

2. Does personality influence values and job attitudes? Discuss how the Big Five personality dimensions—locus of control, self-monitoring, self-esteem, and positive and negative affectivity—might influence occupational choice, job satisfaction, and organizational commitment (affective, continuance, and normative). If personality influences job satisfaction and organizational commitment, how can organizations foster high levels of these attitudes?

ON-THE-JOB CHALLENGE QUESTION

Mr. Winston

In 2006, Arthur Winston died at age 100. He had worked for 76 years for the Los Angeles Metropolitan Transportation Authority cleaning trains and buses. Although this is remarkable enough, it is even more remarkable that he missed only one day of work in his last 72 years, the day of his wife's funeral in 1988. At the time of his retirement on the eve of becoming 100, he headed a crew of 11 workers. Although he had aspired to become a mechanic when younger, the racial biases of the 1930s and 1940s prevented this career advancement. In 1996, Mr. Winston received a congressional citation from the U.S. president as "Employee of the Century." Mr. Winston's incredible record was the object of extensive media coverage, both at home and abroad.

Use the material in the chapter to speculate on various reasons for Mr. Winston's awesome attendance record. What accounts for the great media interest in Mr. Winston?

Sources: (2006, April 14). MTA employee who retired at 100 has died in his sleep. http://cbs2.com/local/Arthur.Winston. MTA.2.515610.html; Marquez, M. (2006, March 22). Los Angeles man retires at 100. abcnews.go.com/US/WNT/story?id=1756219.

EXPERIENTIAL EXERCISE

Attitudes Toward Absenteeism from Work

In this exercise we will examine your attitudes toward absenteeism from work. Although you learned in the chapter that absence can stem from job dissatisfaction, the scenarios below show that a number of other factors can also come into play.

1. Working alone, please indicate the extent to which you think that the employee's absence in each of the following scenarios is legitimate or illegitimate by using one of the six answer categories that appear below. A legitimate absence might be considered acceptable, while an illegitimate absence might be considered unacceptable. This is a measure of your personal attitudes; there are no right or wrong answers. Add up your scores and divide by 7 to obtain an average. Lower scores represent less favourable attitudes toward absenteeism.

2. Working in groups of 3 to 5 people, discuss the ratings that each of you gave to each scenario. What are the major reasons that contributed to each of your ratings? Compare your average scores.

3. As a group, decide which scenario is *most* legitimate, and explain why. Then decide which scenario is *least* legitimate, and explain why. Compare with the norms provided below.

4. As managers, how would you react to the least legitimate situation? What would you do?

6	5	4	3	2	1
Extremely legitimate	Moderately legitimate	Slightly legitimate	Slightly illegitimate	Moderately illegitimate	Extremely illegitimate

1. Susan is a highly productive employee, but she is absent more often than her co-workers. She has decided to be absent from work to engage in some recreational activities because she believes that her absence would not affect her overall productivity. _____

2. John is an active member of his community social club. Occasionally, the club organizes community activities with the aim of improving the quality of community life. A few days before a planned community activity, much of the work has not been done and the club members are concerned that the activities will be unsuccessful. John has therefore decided to be absent from work to help the club organize its forthcoming activities. ____

3. Peter is a member of a project team that was charged with the responsibility of converting the company's information systems. The work entailed long hours, but the team was able to finish the project on time. Now that the project is completed, the long working hours have taken a toll and Peter feels quite stressed, so he has decided to stay away from work to recuperate. ____

4. Jane works in a low-paying job for which she is overqualified. She has been searching for a more suitable job through advertisements in the newspapers. She has been called for a job interview and has decided to call in sick to attend the interview. ____

5. Frank has a few months before his retirement and has lost the enthusiasm he used to have for his work. He believes he has contributed to making the company the success it is today. He recently joined a retired persons association where he feels his services are needed more. The association is organizing a safety awareness program for senior citizens, so he has decided to stay away from work to help. ____

6. Joan's co-workers normally use up all their sick leave. She is moving into a new house, and since she has not used up all her permitted sick leave, she has decided to call in sick so that she can finish packing for the move. ____

7. Anne does not feel challenged by her job and believes that she is not making any meaningful contribution to her organization. Her mother is going to the doctor for a routine medical checkup and because Anne believes the company will not miss her, she decided to stay away from work to accompany her mother. ____

Source: Scenarios developed by Helena M. Addae. Used with permission.

Scoring and Interpretation

As noted, lower scores represent less favourable attitudes toward absenteeism. Helena Addae, who developed the scenarios, administered them to over 1500 employees in nine countries. The average rating across the 7 scenarios was 3.09. Respectively, the average ratings for each scenario were: S1 = 2.39; S2 = 2.88; S3 = 3.96; S4 = 3.52; S5 = 3.12; S6 = 3.03; S7 = 2.70. Higher numbers indicate more legitimacy.

CASE INCIDENT

How Much Do You Get Paid?

Joan had been working as a reporter for a large television network for seven years. She was an experienced and hardworking reporter who had won many awards over the years for her outstanding work. The work was exciting and challenging, and at $75 000 a year plus benefits she felt well paid and satisfied. Then she found out that two recent graduates from one of the best schools of journalism in the United States had just been hired by her network at a starting salary of $80 000. Further, two other reporters who worked with Joan and had similar track records had just received job offers from American networks and were being offered $150 000 plus $10 000 for every award won for their reporting.

1. According to equity theory, how will these incidents influence Joan's job satisfaction and behaviour?

2. What should Joan do in response to her situation? What should her organization do?

CASE STUDY

Gen Y in the Workforce
"RU BRD?"[1]

The text message from Ashok stood out in bold block letters on the small screen of Josh Lewis's iPhone. Am I ever, Josh thought, stuffing the device back into his pocket and emphatically rolling his chair away from his PC and the backlit spreadsheets and formulas that had made his eyes bloodshot and his mood sour. He stood up, stretched, and took a minute to consider his plight: For the past three days, he'd been crunching U.S. and international

---

1 Are you bored?

film sales, attendance, and merchandising figures nonstop for his boss, Sarah Bennett, the marketing chief of the movie division of Rising Entertainment. Bennett and her team were in the midst of prepping the promotions, advertising, and branding plan for the next *Fire Force Five* film; her presentation to the company's CEO, its head of distribution, and other unit leaders was planned for Friday.

Two more days—many more hours, many more stats to go over before I sleep, the 23-year-old marketing associate estimated. He plunked himself back down in his chair.

A recent graduate of the University of Southern California, Josh had had visions of making films that offered strong social commentary—like Al Gore's *An Inconvenient Truth* or Morgan Spurlock's *Super Size Me*—and distributing them on open platforms so that his message could reach the greatest number of people. With some championing from his uncle—a well-regarded TV producer who knew people who knew people—Josh joined Rising Entertainment, one of the top three multimedia production and distribution houses in the world. The company boasted large film, television, home video, music, and licensed merchandise units, with a catalogue of thousands of properties. Josh expected that the studio, with its location in the heart of Los Angeles and satellite offices in six countries, would offer plenty of excitement and opportunity—ever-present TV and film shoots on the lots, hobnobbing with industry power brokers, the inevitable offers from competing studios, and, of course, the terrific LA nightlife. But now, with 10 months on job, and most of that time relegated to mundane ancillary projects that informed the bigger initiatives his boss was spearheading, Josh was feeling numb. Who would have thought that life in a big movie studio could be so routine? He thought to himself.

Suddenly there was that familiar vibration from his iPhone and another text message from Ashok: "WRUD? TAB?"[2] A break sounded great. He replied immediately—"BRT"[3]—and set off for their favourite meeting spot. As he was heading out, it occurred to Josh that he should let Sarah know where he was. He fired off another quick text message.

---

2 What are you doing? Take a break?

3 Be right there

Sounding Bored

By the time Josh got to the high-backed purple booth in the corner of the commissary, Ashok and Jessica were already there. Ashok Devi worked in Rising Entertainment's TV division as a promotions associate. Jessica Sadler had started out in the film division but, for now at least, was working as an assistant in the company's legal group—ostensibly to help out a team in transition but really to figure out if law school was in her future. The three had been at USC together, studying a broad mix of business, communications, and film, but they had become particularly good friends since joining the company around the same time, braving orientation together, and now commiserating with one another about the flaws in their respective work groups—in which each was among the youngest on staff.

"Aw, what's wrong, Josh?" Jessica said, noticing Josh's serious expression as he shuffled over to the table. "Did your mom call HR again?" Ashok, who was sitting next to Jessica, just grinned and shook his head.

Josh shot them both a look. "Whatever. I've been buried all week with ridiculous busy-work. Sarah's all amped about this distribution and marketing plan for the Triple-F series. But I'm just not feeling it," he vented.

"Have you tried explaining that to Sarah?" Jessica asked.

Josh had. A few weeks earlier, during a small team meeting in which Sarah was outlining her marketing premise for *Fire Force Five: Resignation*—the details of which centered primarily on TV ads and an aggressive print campaign—Josh had causally joked about how 1990s the whole plan was. It was as though DVRs, film-related websites and blogs, virtual worlds, and YouTube didn't exist, he thought. As though the question of how to capitalize on the free-content movement was still something plaguing the guys in the record business and not anyone else.

No one watches network TV anymore—or network TV ads, Josh had pointed out during the meeting. Instead of relying chiefly on traditional marketing channels, he said, why not try new media? Make the movie theme song available for download for Guitar Hero. Or, even better, make one or more of the *Fire Force Five* movies available online and embed teasers for the latest sequel within them.

Sarah had immediately balked, noting the creaky Rising Entertainment website, which boasted very little traffic and even less functionality. A "successful" online campaign for the third Triple-F movie in 2005 had nearly taken down the studio's entire network—including critical sales force connections.

"So how about striking deals with, like, Hulu or There or Gaia? They're well suited to handle the traffic—much better than we are," Josh replied. These days it was just so much easier to download music, movies, and TV shows how and when you wanted them. To have, as Jessica joked, old *90210* and new *90210* existing peacefully on your laptop. "We'd be leveraging one of Rising Entertainment's biggest strengths, its library, in a way that gets the company out in front of the movement to free content."

"All great points," Sarah had responded. "But our budget is soft right now—everything is soft right now. I'm not sure we have the time and resources to throw at these channels." Josh opened his mouth to respond, but the marketing chief cut off the discussion there and went on to her other notes.

That was the end of that, Josh explained to his friends. "I guess I just expected that I would get to act on more of my ideas," he complained, as they finished crunching through a large order of lime-cilantro chips and salsa. "And that the higher-ups here would have figured out by now that the model's changing." By the time Ashok, Jessica, and Josh had gotten down to salty crumbs, the three were in firm agreement: Sarah just didn't get it.

The View from Above

Should all the bullet points be flame balls? Sarah Bennett wondered, only half joking with herself. She was in the midst of building her PowerPoint slides for Friday's meeting with CEO Sam Smith stone and, as always, fighting the urge to add crazy animation and special effects to her presentation. After 10 years at Rising Entertainment, the 37-year-old marketing chief still saw herself as a budding creative rather than an established suit. But she understood her role in the hierarchy: manage the people and the details.

Still, it was a far cry from where she started. A native of Long Island, Sarah had gotten her MBA from New York University's Stern School of Business and held an undergraduate degree in film studies from NYU's prestigious Tisch School. She moved to Los Angeles and worked her way up in Rising Entertainment, from an entry-level copywriter, to

marketing associate, to head of the 22-person film-marketing unit. Sarah had a lot riding on the latest *Fire Force Five* release. A big opening weekend would go a long way toward helping her lobby for one of the positions she was really interested in: EVP in either international business development or family films.

The *Fire Force Five* series was one of the company's strongest and best-known properties: The three Triple-F movies released over the past 10 years had generated more than $2.4 billion in box-office receipts and almost as much in merchandise sales. The buzz was building for the upcoming fourth release. Already, Sarah had leveraged the decade-long relationships she'd cultivated with reporters at *Entertainment Weekly*, *Variety*, and other magazines to place behind-the-scenes and making-of feature articles—each of which stoked the chatter and anticipation among Triple-F fans. She'd overseen the production of a high-impact trailer that would be reviewed in Friday's meeting, and she'd also been coordinating with Rising Entertainment's publicity department to get most of the *Fire Force* quintet booked on the usual morning and late-night talk shows.

Now, Sarah was staring anxiously at the envelope icon in the bottom-right corner of her screen: Where were the numbers she'd asked Josh to generate? Sarah just couldn't afford to stay at the office tonight; every minute she was late to pick up four-month-old Rosie from day care was costing her (financially and psychically), and she had already logged plenty of overtime this week. Sarah was ready to alert her husband that he'd have to handle the pickup, when the Outlook message popped up: "You have new unopened items." It was close to 5:30 PM when Josh's report arrived, and the last couple of case studies looked pretty sketchy, as if he'd thrown them together quickly. But there wasn't enough time to send them back for revision, Sarah decided. She'd work on them further in the morning.

Sarah quickly dropped the numbers into her slide deck and was about to log off when she spotted the bright pink "coaching" sticky note slapped on the side of her monitor. A few months ago she and the other frontline managers at Rising Entertainment had gone through a special HR-facilitated training session about integrating the newer, younger hires into the company. "Invest the time," the managers were told. But what many of them heard was "Sugarcoat."

Sarah quickly dashed off an e-mail to Josh. "Great job! You're the best." Who was she kidding? He'd done a half-assed job, and he knew it. Like so many of the young people hired by the studio recently, Sarah thought, Josh was far more concerned with *getting* praise than with *earning* praise. How else to explain that "look at me" move in the team meeting a few weeks back? Not that Josh's ideas were bad, Sarah recalled. They just weren't very well informed; he hadn't bothered to think about things like, well, money and infrastructure and talent. If I had tried something like that when I was an associate, I would have been back at square one in a heartbeat, she thought.

No one had even bothered to show her the ropes until she'd been on board awhile, Sarah recalled. But, following HR's directives, she promised herself she'd take time to explain to Josh exactly how his analysis had been received, how it fit into the overall presentation, and how she'd structured the pitch—after the meeting. The clock was ticking.

Bypassing the Boss

Sam Smithstone was already late for a dinner meeting with a couple of potential clients at the Ivy. The freeway would be murder. So he didn't take too kindly to Josh Lewis's overly solicitous greeting in the hallway late on Thursday and his attempts to conduct a drive-by pitch. "Stop by my office at 8:15 a.m. tomorrow," he told the marketing associate. "Or walk with me, if you want. But keep up."

The break-time discussion with his friends the day before had emboldened Josh. As soon as he'd returned to his cubicle, he sent Jessica and Ashok an urgent e-mail: "Who would know details of our current distribution and intellectual property agreements for the Triple-F films?" Jessica shared the name of a veteran IP lawyer in her department. Ashok had no contacts to share but responded nonetheless with a morale-boosting "XLNT!"[4] Rather than devote even more time to Sarah's assignment, Josh opted to turn in a "good enough" version near day's end. Then he had raced off to legal to find Jessica's colleague. He'd spent most of Thursday morning and afternoon fleshing out his plan.

Now, walking alongside the studio head, Josh took a moment to establish his pedigree, telling the executive where he went to school and why he chose Rising Entertainment. As Josh chatted up the CEO

with ease, Sam was instantly reminded of his daughter—who was around the same age, now living back at home, and would similarly corral him to talk gadgets, politics, and pop culture.

"I'm glad you're enjoying it here—so what did you want to run by me?" Sam said, trying to get Josh to cut to the chase before they reached the lobby.

Josh carefully but quickly laid out his ideas for putting the Triple-F series online as a marketing ploy for the new instalment and employing nontraditional distribution and promotion channels. Even before Josh was done, Sam stopped and smiled. "That's some fresh thinking—I like it," he said. "Can you talk through these ideas during tomorrow's meeting? Maybe provide some P&L projections or a point-by-point comparison of your plan against the plans we've used to market and distribute Triple-F in the past?"

"I can," Josh replied, neglecting to tell the senior leader that he hadn't actually been invited to the meeting and wasn't even sure where it was being held. "I will. Thanks, Mr. Smithstone." Sam was only seconds out the door when Josh grabbed for his phone and typed an urgent message to Ashok and Jessica: "AYT?[5] SOS!"

"Oops!" Sarah literally bumped into her boss as they were both getting coffee in the commissary early on Friday morning. She had been so fixated on the slight stain on her blouse—spit-up? orange juice?—that she hadn't even seen Sam Smithstone approaching, Styrofoam cup in hand. Good thing there's a cover on that, Sarah thought.

"Great work cultivating the new guys, Sarah. I'm looking forward to hearing more from Josh," the CEO said in passing. "I love his approach, and even better, I love the wiki he sent around last night explaining his idea. See you in a bit."

Sarah stared after Sam. What? Wikis? She was amazed on every level, starting with the fact that the CEO even knew who Josh was. I wasn't even sure he knew who *I* was, she thought. Her astonishment slowly abated—replaced with a burning desire to talk things over with her young marketing colleague, particularly before the Triple-F meeting in a few hours.

Sarah pulled out her BlackBerry and punched out a message: "Josh, in my office please, in 10."

Source: Case prepared by Tamara J. Erikson.

---

4 Excellent!

5 Are you there?

QUESTIONS

1. What are the sources of generational conflict between Josh Lewis and Sarah Bennett? How do their values differ?

2. What are the sources of job dissatisfaction for Josh? What are the sources of job dissatisfaction for Sarah? In both cases, consider discrepancy between wanted and received job outcomes and issues of fairness.

3. Was Josh correct to bypass Sarah and intervene directly with studio head Sam Smithstone?

4. In this series of events, could Josh have acted more effectively? Could Sarah have acted more effectively? In each case, explain your reasoning.

5. What should Sarah do right now? Should she punish Josh, or commend his diligence, or invite him to the meeting, or commandeer his ideas, or something else?

6. What should Sarah do in the longer term?

THEORIES OF WORK MOTIVATION

LEARNING OBJECTIVES

After reading Chapter 5, you should be able to:

5.1 Define *motivation*, discuss its basic properties, and distinguish it from *performance*.

5.2 Compare and contrast *intrinsic* and *extrinsic motivation* and describe *self-determination theory*, *autonomous motivation*, and *controlled motivation*.

5.3 Explain and discuss the different factors that predict *performance* and define *general cognitive ability* and *emotional intelligence*.

5.4 Explain and discuss *need theories* of motivation.

5.5 Explain and discuss *expectancy theory*.

5.6 Explain and discuss *equity theory*.

5.7 Explain and discuss *goal setting theory*, *goal orientation*, and *proximal* and *distal goals*.

5.8 Discuss the cross-cultural limitations of theories of motivation.

5.9 Summarize the relationships among the various theories of motivation, performance, and job satisfaction.

GREAT LITTLE BOX COMPANY LTD.

Great Little Box Company Ltd. (GLBC) is a leading designer and manufacturer of custom and stock corrugated boxes, point-of-purchase displays, folding cartons, labels, and protective packaging. It began operations in 1982 in Burnaby, British Columbia, with just three employees. Today, the company has grown to more than 200 full- and part-time employees. It has locations in Kelowna, Victoria, and Everett, Washington, in addition to its head office in Vancouver.

The company has had remarkable success since it began, with annual sales today of $35 million. Much of its success is attributed to the hard work and dedication of its employees, who receive ongoing skills training and career and personal development, as well as above-average compensation and benefits. To ensure that salaries are competitive, the company participates in salary surveys and reviews individual salaries every 12 months.

Incentive compensation is linked to the company's overall business goals and to objectives that are part of employees' goals. At the beginning of each year, employees meet with their immediate supervisor to set individual performance goals. Performance reviews are held every three months, and employees meet with their supervisor to review how well they met their goals and to establish goals for the next quarter. Performance feedback is also obtained from co-workers and managers who are familiar with each employee's work.

Exceptional performance is recognized with special dinners, cash awards, and preferred parking spots. A suggestion program rewards employees for cost-saving ideas. Employees whose suggestions are implemented receive a share of the financial savings to the company. Employees can also receive a $10 reward any day of the week for catching a mistake, improving a work process, or providing better ideas for manufacturing in what is known as the $10'ers program. Incentives have also been established for each department and are paid out weekly, monthly, and quarterly.

GLBC also has a profit-sharing plan and encourages employees to save for their retirement through matching RSP contributions. Employees are kept up to date on the company's profits through monthly meetings that include frank discussions about all financial matters relating to the business. The company opens its books to employees and provides details on the company's financial status. The meetings ensure that employees know how the company is doing and what can be done to improve things. The meetings are also a forum for employee input and for recog-

Motivated employees are the key to the success of the Great Little Box Company, which has been named one of Canada's Top 100 Employers and one of British Columbia's Top Employers.

nizing and rewarding employees for their efforts. Every month, 15 percent of the previous month's profits are shared equally among all employees regardless of an employee's position, seniority, and wage.

Employees also share the benefits of the company's success when it reaches its annual profitability goal. The annual profitability goal is known as the Big Outrageous Xtravaganza goal (or BOX goal), and when it is reached, the company treats all of its employees to an all-expenses-paid vacation to a sunny destination. Over the past 13 years, GLBC employees have enjoyed vacations to places such as Cabo San Lucas, Puerto Vallarta, and Las Vegas.

GLBC has consistently been recognized as one of Canada's Best Managed Companies and a great employer. In 2012 it was chosen as one of Canada's Top 100 Employers, one of the *Financial Post*'s Ten Best Companies to Work For, and one of British Columbia's Top Employers. According to GLBC president and CEO Robert Meggy, "It is clear that happy and motivated employees are the key to success and longevity."[1]

Would you be motivated if you worked for Great Little Box Company? What kind of person would respond well to the company's motivational techniques? What underlying philosophy of motivation is GLBC using and what effect does it have on employees' motivation and performance? These are some of the questions that this chapter will explore.

First we will define motivation and distinguish it from performance. After that we will describe several popular theories of work motivation and contrast them. Then we will explore whether these theories translate across cultures. Finally we will present a model that links motivation, performance, and job satisfaction.

WHY STUDY MOTIVATION?

Motivation is one of the most traditional topics in organizational behaviour, and it has interested managers, researchers, teachers, and sports coaches for years. However, a good case can be made that motivation has become even more important in contemporary organizations. Much of this is a result of the need for increased productivity to be globally competitive. It is also a result of the rapid changes that contemporary organizations are undergoing. Stable systems of rules, regulations, and procedures that once guided behaviour are being replaced by requirements for flexibility and attention to customers that necessitate higher levels of initiative. This initiative depends on motivation. According to GLBC president and CEO Robert Meggy, "Everything we do has to be by people who are well-motivated. I see it in the bottom line for us."[2]

What would a good motivation theory look like? In fact, as we shall see, there is no single all-purpose motivation theory. Rather, we will consider several theories that serve somewhat different purposes. In combination, though, a good set of theories should recognize human diversity and consider that the same conditions will not motivate everyone. Also, a good set of theories should be able to explain how it is that some people seem to be self-motivated, while others seem to require external motivation. Finally, a good set of theories should recognize the social aspect of human beings—people's motivation is often affected by how they see others being treated. Before getting to our theories, let's first define motivation more precisely.

WHAT IS MOTIVATION?

LO 5.1

Define *motivation*, discuss its basic properties, and distinguish it from *performance*.

Motivation. The extent to which persistent effort is directed toward a goal.

  Watch

JOIE DE VIVRE HOSPITALITY: EMPLOYEE MOTIVATION Go to MyManagementLab to watch a video about employee motivation.

The term *motivation* is not easy to define. However, from an organization's perspective, when we speak of a person as being motivated, we usually mean that the person works "hard," "keeps at" his or her work, and directs his or her behaviour toward appropriate outcomes.

Basic Characteristics of Motivation

We can formally define **motivation** as the extent to which persistent effort is directed toward a goal.[3]

EFFORT The first aspect of motivation is the strength of the person's work-related behaviour, or the amount of *effort* the person exhibits on the job. Clearly, this involves different kinds of activities on different kinds of jobs. A loading-dock worker might exhibit greater effort by carrying heavier crates, while a researcher might reveal greater effort by searching out an article in some obscure foreign technical journal. Both are exerting effort in a manner appropriate to their jobs.

PERSISTENCE The second characteristic of motivation is the *persistence* that individuals exhibit in applying effort to their work tasks. The organization would not be likely to think of the loading-dock worker who stacks the heaviest crates for two hours and then goofs off for six hours as especially highly motivated. Similarly, the researcher who makes an important discovery early in her career and then rests on her laurels for five years would not be considered especially highly motivated. In each case, workers have not been persistent in the application of their effort.

DIRECTION Effort and persistence refer mainly to the quantity of work an individual produces. Of equal importance is the quality of a person's work. Thus, the third characteristic of motivation is the *direction* of the person's work-related behaviour. In other words, do workers channel persistent effort in a direction that benefits the organization? Employers expect motivated stockbrokers to advise their clients of good investment opportunities and motivated software designers to design software, not play computer games. These correct decisions increase the probability that persistent effort is actually translated into accepted organizational outcomes. Thus, motivation means working smart as well as working hard.

GOALS Ultimately, all motivated behaviour has some goal or objective toward which it is directed. We have presented the preceding discussion from an organizational perspective—that is, we assume that motivated people act to enhance organizational objectives. In this case, employee goals might include high productivity, good attendance, or creative decisions. Of course, employees can also be motivated by goals that are contrary to the objectives of the organization, including absenteeism, sabotage, and embezzlement. In these cases, they are channelling their persistent efforts in directions that are dysfunctional for the organization.

Extrinsic and Intrinsic Motivation and Self-Determination Theory

Some hold the view that people are motivated by factors in the external environment (such as supervision or pay), while others believe that people can, in some sense, be self-motivated without the application of these external factors. You might have experienced this distinction. As a worker, you might recall tasks that you enthusiastically performed simply for the sake of doing them and others that you performed only to keep your job or placate your boss.

Experts in organizational behaviour distinguish between intrinsic and extrinsic motivation. At the outset, we should emphasize that there is only weak consensus concerning the exact definitions of these concepts and even weaker agreement about whether we should label specific motivators as intrinsic or extrinsic.[4] However, the following definitions and examples seem to capture the distinction fairly well.

Intrinsic motivation stems from the direct relationship between the worker and the task and is usually self-applied. Feelings of achievement, accomplishment, challenge, and competence derived from performing one's job are examples of intrinsic motivators, as is sheer interest in the job itself. Off the job, avid participation in sports and hobbies is often intrinsically motivated.

Extrinsic motivation stems from the work environment external to the task and is usually applied by someone other than the person being motivated. Pay, fringe benefits, company policies, and various forms of supervision are examples of extrinsic motivators. At GLBC, profit sharing and cash awards for exceptional performance are examples of extrinsic motivators.

Obviously, employers cannot package all conceivable motivators as neatly as these definitions suggest. For example, a promotion or a compliment might be applied by the boss but might also be a clear signal of achievement and competence. Thus, some motivators have both extrinsic and intrinsic qualities.

The relationship between intrinsic and extrinsic motivators has been the subject of a great deal of debate.[5] Some research studies have reached the conclusion that the availability of extrinsic motivators can reduce the intrinsic motivation stemming from the task itself.[6] The notion is that when extrinsic rewards depend on performance, then the motivating potential of intrinsic rewards decreases. Proponents of this view have suggested that making extrinsic rewards contingent on performance makes individuals feel less competent and less in control of their own behaviour. That is, they come to believe that their performance is controlled by the environment and that they perform well only because of the money.[7] As a result, their intrinsic motivation suffers.

However, a review of research in this area reached the conclusion that the negative effect of extrinsic rewards on intrinsic motivation occurs only under very limited conditions, and

---

LO **5.2**

Compare and contrast *intrinsic* and *extrinsic motivation* and describe *self-determination theory, autonomous motivation,* and *controlled motivation.*

Intrinsic motivation. Motivation that stems from the direct relationship between the worker and the task; it is usually self-applied.

Extrinsic motivation. Motivation that stems from the work environment external to the task; it is usually applied by others.

they are easily avoidable.[8] As well, in organizational settings in which individuals see extrinsic rewards as symbols of success and as signals of what to do to achieve future rewards, they increase their task performance.[9] Thus, it is safe to assume that both kinds of rewards are important and compatible in enhancing work motivation.

Despite the fact that the distinction between intrinsic and extrinsic motivation can be fuzzy, many theories of motivation make the distinction. For example, intrinsic and extrinsic factors are used in **self-determination theory** (SDT) to explain what motivates people and whether motivation is autonomous or controlled. When people are motivated by intrinsic factors, they are in control of their motivation or what is known as **autonomous motivation**. When motivation is autonomous, individuals are engaged in a task because they choose to be and their actions are internally regulated. This is often the case when people perform a task because they find it interesting or fun to do.

When people are motivated to obtain a desired consequence or extrinsic reward, their motivation is controlled externally or what is known as **controlled motivation**. When motivation is controlled, individuals feel they have no choice and they have to engage in a task. Thus, their behaviour is externally regulated. This is the case when people do something to obtain a desired consequence, avoid punishment, or because the boss is watching them.

The distinction between autonomous and controlled motivation is important because autonomous motivation has been shown to facilitate effective performance, especially on complex tasks. Autonomous motivation is also associated with other work outcomes such as positive work attitudes and psychological well-being.[10] Later in the chapter you will see how other theories of motivation treat intrinsic and extrinsic motivation. Let's now consider the relationship between motivation and performance.

Motivation and Performance

At this point, you may well be saying, "Wait a minute, I know many people who are 'highly motivated' but just don't seem to perform well. They work long and hard, but they just don't measure up." This is certainly a sensible observation, and it points to the important distinction between motivation and performance. **Performance** can be defined as the extent to which an organizational member contributes to achieving the objectives of the organization.

Some of the factors that contribute to individual performance in organizations are shown in Exhibit 5.1.[11] While motivation clearly contributes to performance, the relationship is not one-to-one because a number of other factors also influence performance. For example, recall from Chapter 2 that personality traits such as the Big Five and core self-evaluations also predict job performance. You might also be wondering about the role of intelligence—doesn't it influence performance? The answer, of course, is yes—intelligence, or what is also known as mental ability, does predict performance. Two forms of intelligence that are particularly important for performance are general cognitive ability and emotional intelligence. Let's consider each before we discuss motivation.

GENERAL COGNITIVE ABILITY The term *cognitive ability* is often used to refer to what most people call intelligence or mental ability. Although there are many different types of specific cognitive abilities, in organizational behaviour we are often concerned with what is known as *general cognitive ability*. **General cognitive ability** is a term used to refer to a

---

Self-determination theory. A theory of motivation that considers whether people's motivation is autonomous or controlled.

Autonomous motivation. When people are self-motivated by intrinsic factors.

Controlled motivation. When people are motivated to obtain a desired consequence or extrinsic reward.

LO **5.3**

Explain and discuss the different factors that predict *performance* and define *general cognitive ability* and *emotional intelligence*.

Performance. The extent to which an organizational member contributes to achieving the objectives of the organization.

General cognitive ability. A person's basic information-processing capacities and cognitive resources.

EXHIBIT 5.1
Factors contributing to individual job performance.

Go to MyManagementLab to see an annotated version of this figure.

person's basic information-processing capacities and cognitive resources. It reflects an individual's overall capacity and efficiency for processing information, and it includes a number of cognitive abilities, such as verbal, numerical, spatial, and reasoning abilities, that are required to perform mental tasks. Cognitive ability is usually measured by a number of specific aptitude tests that measure these abilities.[12]

Research has found that general cognitive ability predicts learning, training, and career success as well as job performance in all kinds of jobs and occupations, including those that involve both manual and mental tasks. This should not come as a surprise because many cognitive skills are required to perform most kinds of jobs. General cognitive ability is an even better predictor of performance for more complex and higher-level jobs that require the use of more cognitive skills and involve more information processing.[13] Thus, both general cognitive ability and motivation are necessary for performance.

Given that cognitive ability is a strong predictor of performance, you might also wonder about the role of education in job performance. As you probably know, education is an important indicator of one's intelligence and it is important for obtaining employment. But how important is education for job performance? To find out, see the Research Focus: *Does Education Predict Job Performance?*

EMOTIONAL INTELLIGENCE Although the importance of general cognitive ability for job performance has been known for many years, researchers have only recently begun to study emotional intelligence. **Emotional intelligence** (EI) has to do with an individual's ability to understand and manage his or her own and others' feelings and emotions. It involves the ability to perceive and express emotion, assimilate emotion in thought, understand and reason about

Emotional intelligence.
The ability to understand and manage one's own and other's feelings and emotions.

RESEARCH FOCUS

DOES EDUCATION PREDICT JOB PERFORMANCE?

Most organizations use education as an indicator of a job applicant's skill levels and ability and use education as a prerequisite in hiring decisions. There is substantial evidence that individuals' educational attainments are associated with positive career outcomes, including salary level, number of promotions, development opportunities, and job mobility. But does educational level predict job performance?

To find out, Thomas W.H. Ng and Daniel C. Feldman examined the results of 293 studies on education and job performance. They looked at three kinds of job performance. Core task performance refers to the basic required duties of a particular job. Citizenship performance refers to those extra behaviours engaged in by employees, over and above their core task requirements, that actively promote and strengthen an organization's effectiveness (e.g., creativity). Counterproductive performance refers to voluntary behaviours that harm the well-being of the organization (e.g., theft, absenteeism). Education level refers to the academic credentials or degrees an individual has obtained.

The authors predicted that education would be positively related to core task performance and citizenship performance and negatively related to counterproductive performance as a result of the acquisition of

task-relevant knowledge and work values that promote organizational effectiveness.

The results indicated that education was related to all three types of performance. More highly educated workers have higher core task performance, display greater creativity, and demonstrate more citizenship behaviours than less educated workers. Highly educated workers also engage in less counterproductive behaviours (i.e., workplace aggression, substance use, and absenteeism). The authors also found that the relationships between education and performance were stronger for men than for women and stronger for Caucasian employees than for racial minorities. In addition, the relationship between education and core task performance was stronger for more complex jobs.

Overall, the results of this study confirm the long-held belief that education predicts job performance and provides some validity for the use of education level as a factor in the hiring process and for the benefits of an educated workforce.

Source: Excerpted from Ng, T.W.H., & Feldman, D.C. (2009). How broadly does education contribute to job performance? *Personnel Psychology, 62,* 89–134. Reprinted with permission of Wiley-Blackwell Publishing.

emotions, and manage emotions in oneself and others. Individuals high in EI are able to iden-tify and understand the meanings of emotions and to manage and regulate their emotions as a basis for problem solving, reasoning, thinking, and action.[14]

Peter Salovey and John Mayer, who are credited with first coining the term *emotional intelligence*, have developed an EI model that consists of four interrelated sets of skills, or branches. The four skills represent sequential steps that form a hierarchy. The perception of emotion is at the bottom of the hierarchy, followed by (in ascending order) using emotions to facilitate thinking, understanding emotions, and managing and regulating emotions. The four-branch model of EI is shown in Exhibit 5.2 and described below.[15]

1. *Perceiving emotions accurately in oneself and others:* This involves the ability to perceive emotions and to accurately identify one's own emotions and the emotions of others. An example of this is the ability to accurately identify emotions in people's faces and in non-verbal behaviour. People differ in the extent to which they can accurately identify emotions in others, particularly from facial expressions.[16] This step is the most basic level of EI and is necessary to be able to perform the other steps in the model.

2. *Using emotions to facilitate thinking:* This refers to the ability to use and assimilate emo-tions and emotional experiences to guide and facilitate one's thinking and reasoning. This means that one is able to use emotions in functional ways, such as making decisions and other cognitive processes (e.g., creativity, integrative thinking, and inductive reasoning). This stage also involves being able to shift one's emotions and generate new emotions that can help one to see things in different ways and from different perspectives. This is an important skill because, as will be described in Chapter 11, emotions and moods affect what and how people think when making decisions.[17]

3. *Understanding emotions, emotional language, and the signals conveyed by emotions:* This stage involves being able to understand emotional information, the determinants and consequences of emotions, and how emotions evolve and change over time. At this stage, people understand how different situations and events generate emotions as well as how they and others are influenced by various emotions.[18] Individuals who are good at this know not to ask somebody who is in a bad mood for a favour, but rather to wait until the person is in a better mood or to just ask somebody else!

4. *Managing emotions so as to attain specific goals:* This involves the ability to manage one's own and others' feelings and emotions as well as emotional relationships. This is the highest level of EI because it requires one to have mastered the previous stages. At this stage, an individual is able to regulate, adjust, and change his or her own emotions as well as others' emotions to suit the situation. Examples of this include being able to stay calm when feel-ing angry or upset; being able to excite and enthuse others; or being able to lower another person's anger. To be effective at managing emotions one must be able to perceive emotions, integrate and assimilate emotions, and be knowledgeable of and understand emotions.

Research on EI has found that it predicts performance in a number of areas, includ-ing job performance and academic performance.[19] One study found that college students' EI measured at the start of the academic year predicted their grade point averages at the end of the year. A review of research on emotional intelligence and job performance found that EI is not only positively related to job performance, but that it predicts job performance above and beyond cognitive ability and the Big Five personality variables.[20] There is also some evidence that EI is most strongly related to job performance in jobs that require high levels of emotional labour, such as police officers and customer service representatives.[21] Accord-ing to the results of one study, the importance of emotional intelligence for job performance depends on one's cognitive ability. Emotional intelligence was found to be most important for the job performance of employees with lower levels of cognitive ability and of less impor-tance for the job performance of employees with high levels of cognitive ability.[22]

Explore

Go to MyManagementLab to see an annotated version of this figure.

EXHIBIT 5.2
Four-branch model of emotional intelligence.
Source: Based on Mayer, J.D., Caruso, D.R., & Salovey, P. (2000). Emotional Intelligence meets traditional standards for an intelligence. *Intelligence, 27*, 267–298; Salovey, P., & Mayer, J.D. (1990). Emotional Intelligence. *Imagination, Cognition & Personality, 9*, 185–211. Used by permission of Baywood Publishing.

The Motivation–Performance Relationship

As shown in Exhibit 5.1, it is certainly possible for performance to be low even when a person is highly motivated. In addition to personality, general cognitive ability, and emotional intelligence, poor performance could also be due to a poor understanding of the task or luck and chance factors that can damage the performance of the most highly motivated individuals. Of course, an opposite effect is also possible. An individual with rather marginal motivation might have high general cognitive ability or emotional intelligence or might understand the task so well that some compensation occurs—what little effort the individual makes is expended very efficiently in terms of goal accomplishment. Also, a person with weak motivation might perform well because of some luck or chance factor that boosts performance. Thus, it is no wonder that workers sometimes complain that they receive lower performance ratings than colleagues who "don't work as hard."

In this chapter, we will concentrate on the motivational components of performance rather than on the other determinants in Exhibit 5.1. However, the message here should be clear: We cannot consider motivation in isolation. High motivation will not result in high performance if employees have low general cognitive ability and emotional intelligence, do not understand their jobs, or encounter unavoidable obstacles over which they have no control. Motivational interventions, such as linking pay to performance, simply *will not work* if employees are deficient in important skills and abilities.[23] Let's now turn to theories of motivation to better understand what motivates people and the process of motivation.

NEED THEORIES OF WORK MOTIVATION

The first three theories of motivation that we will consider are **need theories**. These theories attempt to specify the kinds of needs people have and the conditions under which they will be motivated to satisfy these needs in a way that contributes to performance. Needs are physiological and psychological wants or desires that individuals can satisfy by acquiring certain incentives or achieving particular goals. It is the behaviour stimulated by this acquisition process that reveals the motivational character of needs:

NEEDS ⟶ BEHAVIOUR ⟶ INCENTIVES AND GOALS

Notice that need theories are concerned with *what* motivates workers (needs and their associated incentives or goals). They can be contrasted with *process theories*, which are concerned with exactly *how* various factors motivate people. Need and process theories are complementary rather than contradictory. Thus, a need theory might contend that money can be an important motivator (what), and a process theory might explain the actual mechanics by which money motivates (how).[24] In this section, we will examine three prominent need theories of motivation.

Maslow's Hierarchy of Needs

Abraham Maslow was a psychologist who developed and refined a general theory of human motivation.[25] According to Maslow, humans have five sets of needs that are arranged in a hierarchy, beginning with the most basic and compelling needs (see the left side of Exhibit 5.3). These needs include

1. *Physiological needs.* These include the needs that must be satisfied for the person to survive, such as food, water, oxygen, and shelter. Organizational factors that might satisfy these needs include the minimum pay necessary for survival and working conditions that promote existence.

2. *Safety needs.* These include needs for security, stability, freedom from anxiety, and a structured and ordered environment. Organizational conditions that might meet these needs

Watch

MOTIVATION Go to MyManagementLab to watch a video about motivation.

LO 5.4

Explain and discuss *need theories* of motivation.

Need theories. Motivation theories that specify the kinds of needs people have and the conditions under which they will be motivated to satisfy these needs in a way that contributes to performance.

EXHIBIT 5.3
Relationship between Maslow's and Alderfer's need theories.

Explore

Go to MyManagementLab to see an annotated version of this figure.

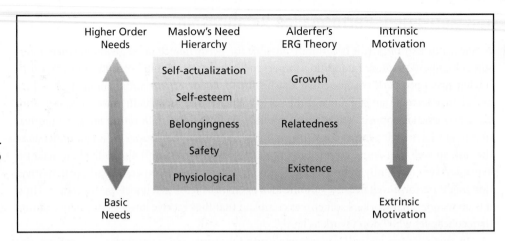

include safe working conditions, fair and sensible rules and regulations, job security, a comfortable work environment, pension and insurance plans, and pay above the minimum needed for survival.

3. *Belongingness needs.* These include needs for social interaction, affection, love, companionship, and friendship. Organizational factors that might meet these needs include the opportunity to interact with others on the job, friendly and supportive supervision, opportunity for teamwork, and opportunity to develop new social relationships.

4. *Esteem needs.* These include needs for feelings of adequacy, competence, independence, strength, and confidence, and the appreciation and recognition of these characteristics by others. Organizational factors that might satisfy these needs include the opportunity to master tasks leading to feelings of achievement and responsibility. Also, awards, promotions, prestigious job titles, professional recognition, and the like might satisfy these needs when they are felt to be truly deserved.

5. *Self-actualization needs.* These needs are the most difficult to define. They involve the desire to develop one's true potential as an individual to the fullest extent and to express one's skills, talents, and emotions in a manner that is most personally fulfilling. Maslow suggests that self-actualizing people have clear perceptions of reality, accept themselves and others, and are independent, creative, and appreciative of the world around them. Organizational conditions that might provide self-actualization include absorbing jobs with the potential for creativity and growth as well as a relaxation of structure to permit self-development and personal progression.

Given the fact that individuals may have these needs, in what sense do they form the basis of a theory of motivation? That is, what exactly is the motivational premise of **Maslow's hierarchy of needs**? Put simply, the lowest-level unsatisfied need category has the greatest motivating potential. Thus, none of the needs is a "best" motivator; motivation depends on the person's position in the need hierarchy. According to Maslow, individuals are motivated to satisfy their physiological needs before they reveal an interest in safety needs, and safety must be satisfied before social needs become motivational, and so on. When a need is unsatisfied, it exerts a powerful effect on the individual's thinking and behaviour, and this is the sense in which needs are motivational. However, when needs at a particular level of the hierarchy are satisfied, the individual turns his or her attention to the next higher level. Notice the clear implication here that a *satisfied need is no longer an effective motivator*. Once one has adequate physiological resources and feels safe and secure, one does not seek more of the factors that met these needs but looks elsewhere for gratification. According to Maslow, the single exception to this rule involves self-actualization needs. He felt that these were "growth" needs that become stronger as they are gratified.

Maslow's hierarchy of needs. A five-level hierarchical need theory of motivation that specifies that the lowest-level unsatisfied need has the greatest motivating potential.

Alderfer's ERG Theory

Clayton Alderfer developed another need-based theory, called **ERG theory.**[26] It streamlines Maslow's need classifications and makes some different assumptions about the relationship between needs and motivation. The name ERG stems from Alderfer's compression of Maslow's five-category need system into three categories—existence, relatedness, and growth needs.

ERG theory. A three-level hierarchical need theory of motivation (existence, relatedness, growth) that allows for movement up and down the hierarchy.

1. *Existence needs.* These are needs that are satisfied by some material substance or condition. As such, they correspond closely to Maslow's physiological needs and to those safety needs that are satisfied by material conditions rather than interpersonal relations. These include the need for food, shelter, pay, and safe working conditions.

2. *Relatedness needs.* These are needs that are satisfied by open communication and the exchange of thoughts and feelings with other organizational members. They correspond fairly closely to Maslow's belongingness needs and to those esteem needs that involve feedback from others. However, Alderfer stresses that relatedness needs are satisfied by open, accurate, honest interaction rather than by uncritical pleasantness.

3. *Growth needs.* These are needs that are fulfilled by strong personal involvement in the work setting. They involve the full utilization of one's skills and abilities and the creative development of new skills and abilities. Growth needs correspond to Maslow's need for self-actualization and the aspects of his esteem needs that concern achievement and responsibility.

As you can see in Exhibit 5.3, Alderfer's need classification system does not represent a radical departure from that of Maslow. In addition, Alderfer agrees with Maslow that as lower-level needs are satisfied, the desire to have higher-level needs satisfied will increase. Thus, as existence needs are fulfilled, relatedness needs gain motivational power. Alderfer explains this by arguing that as more "concrete" needs are satisfied, energy can be directed toward satisfying less concrete needs. Finally, Alderfer agrees with Maslow that the least concrete needs—growth needs—become *more* compelling and *more* desired as they are fulfilled.

It is, of course, the differences between ERG theory and the need hierarchy that represent Alderfer's contribution to the understanding of motivation. First, unlike the need hierarchy, ERG theory does not assume that a lower-level need *must* be gratified before a less concrete need becomes operative. Thus, ERG theory does not propose a rigid hierarchy of needs. Some individuals, owing to background and experience, might seek relatedness or growth even though their existence needs are ungratified. Hence, ERG theory seems to account for a wide variety of individual differences in motive structure. Second, ERG theory assumes that if the higher-level needs are ungratified, individuals will increase their desire for the gratification of lower-level needs. Notice that this represents a *radical* departure from Maslow. According to Maslow, if esteem needs are strong but ungratified, a person will not revert to an interest in belongingness needs because these have necessarily already been gratified. (Remember, he argues that satisfied needs are not motivational.) According to Alderfer, however, the frustration of higher-order needs will lead workers to regress to a more concrete need category. For example, the software designer who is unable to establish rewarding social relationships with superiors or co-workers might increase his interest in fulfilling existence needs, perhaps by seeking a pay increase. Thus, according to Alderfer, an apparently satisfied need can act as a motivator by substituting for an unsatisfied need.

Given the preceding description of ERG theory, we can identify its two major motivational premises as follows:

1. The more lower-level needs are gratified, the more higher-level need satisfaction is desired.

2. The less higher-level needs are gratified, the more lower-level need satisfaction is desired.

McClelland's Theory of Needs

McClelland's theory of needs. A nonhierarchical need theory of motivation that outlines the conditions under which certain needs result in particular patterns of motivation.

Psychologist David McClelland has spent several decades studying the human need structure and its implications for motivation. According to **McClelland's theory of needs**, needs reflect relatively stable personality characteristics that one acquires through early life experiences and exposure to selected aspects of one's society. Unlike Maslow and Alderfer, McClelland has not been interested in specifying a hierarchical relationship among needs. Rather, he has been more concerned with the specific behavioural consequences of needs. In other words, under what conditions are certain needs likely to result in particular patterns of motivation? The three needs that McClelland studied most have special relevance for organizational behaviour—needs for achievement, affiliation, and power.[27]

Need for achievement. A strong desire to perform challenging tasks well.

Individuals who are high in **need for achievement** (*n* Ach) have a strong desire to perform challenging tasks well. More specifically, they exhibit the following characteristics:

- *A preference for situations in which personal responsibility can be taken for outcomes.* Those high in *n* Ach do not prefer situations in which outcomes are determined by chance because success in such situations does not provide an experience of achievement.

- *A tendency to set moderately difficult goals that provide for calculated risks.* Success with easy goals will provide little sense of achievement, while extremely difficult goals might never be reached. The calculation of successful risks is stimulating to the high–*n* Ach person.

- *A desire for performance feedback.* Such feedback permits individuals with high *n* Ach to modify their goal attainment strategies to ensure success and signals them when success has been reached.[28]

People who are high in *n* Ach are concerned with bettering their own performance or that of others. They are often concerned with innovation and long-term goal involvement. However, these things are not done to please others or to damage the interests of others. Rather, they are done because they are *intrinsically* satisfying. Thus, *n* Ach would appear to be an example of a growth or self-actualization need.

Need for affiliation. A strong desire to establish and maintain friendly, compatible interpersonal relationships.

People who are high in **need for affiliation** (*n* Aff) have a strong desire to establish and maintain friendly, compatible interpersonal relationships. In other words, they like to like others, and they want others to like them! More specifically, they have an ability to learn social networking quickly and a tendency to communicate frequently with others, either face to face, by telephone, or in writing. Also, they prefer to avoid conflict and competition with others, and they sometimes exhibit strong conformity to the wishes of their friends. The *n* Aff motive is obviously an example of a belongingness or relatedness need.

Need for power. A strong desire to influence others, making a significant impact or impression.

People who are high in **need for power** (*n* Pow) strongly desire to have influence over others. In other words, they wish to make a significant impact or impression on them. People who are high in *n* Pow seek out social settings in which they can be influential. When in small groups, they act in a "high-profile," attention-getting manner. There is some tendency for those who are high in *n* Pow to advocate risky positions. Also, some people who are high in *n* Pow show a strong concern for personal prestige. The need for power is a complex need because power can be used in a variety of ways, some of which serve the power seeker and some of which serve other people or the organization. However, *n* Pow seems to correspond most closely to Maslow's self-esteem need.

McClelland predicts that people will be motivated to seek out and perform well in jobs that match their needs. Thus, people with high *n* Ach should be strongly motivated by sales jobs or entrepreneurial positions, such as running a small business. Such jobs offer the feedback, personal responsibility, and opportunity to set goals, as noted above. People who are high in *n* Aff will be motivated by jobs such as social work or customer relations because these jobs have as a primary task establishing good relations with others.

Finally, high *n* Pow will result in high motivation in jobs that enable one to have a strong impact on others—jobs such as journalism and management. In fact, McClelland has found that the most effective managers have a low need for affiliation, a high need for power, and the ability to direct power toward organizational goals.[29] (We will study this further in Chapter 12.)

Research Support for Need Theories

Maslow's need hierarchy suggests two main hypotheses. First, specific needs should cluster into the five main need categories that Maslow proposes. Second, as the needs in a given category are satisfied, they should become less important, while the needs in the adjacent higher-need category should become more important. This second hypothesis captures the progressive, hierarchical aspect of the theory. In general, research support for both these hypotheses is weak or negative. This is probably a function of the rigidity of the theory, which suggests that most people experience the same needs in the same hierarchical order. However, there is fair support for a simpler, two-level need hierarchy comprising the needs toward the top and the bottom of Maslow's hierarchy.[30]

This latter finding provides some indirect encouragement for the compressed need hierarchy found in Alderfer's ERG theory. Several tests indicate fairly good support for many of the predictions generated by the theory, including expected changes in need strength. Particularly interesting is the confirmation that the frustration of relatedness needs increases the strength of existence needs.[31] The simplicity and flexibility of ERG theory seem to capture the human need structure better than the greater complexity and rigidity of Maslow's theory.

McClelland's need theory has generated a wealth of predictions about many aspects of human motivation. Researchers have tested more and more of these predictions in organizational settings, and the results are generally supportive of the idea that particular needs are motivational when the work setting permits the satisfaction of these needs.[32]

Managerial Implications of Need Theories

The need theories have some important things to say about managerial attempts to motivate employees.

APPRECIATE DIVERSITY The lack of support for the fairly rigid need hierarchy suggests that managers must be adept at evaluating the needs of individual employees and offering incentives or goals that correspond to their needs. Unfounded stereotypes about the needs of the "typical" employee and naïve assumptions about the universality of need satisfaction are bound to reduce the effectiveness of chosen motivational strategies. The best salesperson might not make the best sales manager! The needs of a young recent college graduate probably differ from those of an older employee preparing for retirement. Thus, it is important to survey employees to find out what their needs are and then offer programs that meet their needs. For example, GLBC conducts an annual employee satisfaction survey to find out what employees want most and what they think of their salary.[33]

APPRECIATE INTRINSIC MOTIVATION The need theories also serve the valuable function of alerting managers to the existence of higher-order needs (whatever specific label we apply to them). The recognition of these needs in many employees is important for two key reasons. One of the basic conditions for organizational survival is the expression of some creative and innovative behaviour on the part of members. Such behaviour seems most likely to occur during the pursuit of higher-order need fulfillment, and ignorance of this factor can cause the demotivation of the people who have the most to offer the organization. Second, observation and research evidence support Alderfer's idea that the frustration of higher-order needs prompts demands for greater satisfaction of lower-order needs. This can lead to a vicious motivational cycle—that is, because the factors that gratify lower-level needs are fairly easy to administer (e.g., pay and fringe benefits), management has grown to rely on them to motivate employees. In turn, some employees, deprived of higher-order need gratification, come to expect more and more of these extrinsic factors in exchange for their services. Thus, a cycle of deprivation, regression, and temporary gratification continues, at great cost to the organization.[34]

How can organizations benefit from the intrinsic motivation that is inherent in strong higher-order needs? First, such needs will fail to develop for most employees unless lower-level needs are reasonably well gratified.[35] Thus, very poor pay, job insecurity, and unsafe working conditions will preoccupy most workers at the expense of higher-order outcomes. Second, if basic needs are met, jobs can be "enriched" to be more stimulating and challenging and to provide feelings of responsibility and achievement (we will have more to say about this in Chapter 6). Finally, organizations could pay more attention to designing career paths that enable interested workers to progress through a series of jobs that continue to challenge their higher-order needs. Individual managers could also assign tasks to employees with this goal in mind.

PROCESS THEORIES OF WORK MOTIVATION

Process theories. Motivation theories that specify the details of how motivation occurs.

In contrast to need theories of motivation, which concentrate on *what* motivates people, **process theories** concentrate on *how* motivation occurs. In this section, we will examine three important process theories—expectancy theory, equity theory, and goal setting theory.

LO 5.5

Explain and discuss *expectancy theory.*

Expectancy Theory

Expectancy theory. A process theory that states that motivation is determined by the outcomes that people expect to occur as a result of their actions on the job.

The basic idea underlying **expectancy theory** is the belief that motivation is determined by the outcomes that people expect to occur as a result of their actions on the job. Psychologist Victor Vroom is usually credited with developing the first complete version of expectancy theory and applying it to the work setting.[36] The basic components of Vroom's theory are shown in Exhibit 5.4 and are described in more detail below.

Outcomes. Consequences that follow work behaviour.

- **Outcomes** are the consequences that may follow certain work behaviours. First-level outcomes are of particular interest to the organization, such as high productivity versus average productivity, illustrated in Exhibit 5.4, or good attendance versus poor attendance. Expectancy theory is concerned with specifying how an employee might attempt to choose one first-level outcome instead of another. Second-level outcomes are consequences that follow the attainment of a particular first-level outcome. Contrasted with first-level outcomes, second-level outcomes are most personally relevant to the individual worker and might involve amount of pay, sense of accomplishment, acceptance by peers, fatigue, and so on.

Instrumentality. The probability that a particular first-level outcome will be followed by a particular second-level outcome.

- **Instrumentality** is the probability that a particular first-level outcome (such as high productivity) will be followed by a particular second-level outcome (such as pay) (this is also known as the *performance* ⟶ *outcome* link). For example, a bank teller might figure that the odds are 50/50 (instrumentality = .5) that a good performance rating will result in a pay raise.

Valence. The expected value of work outcomes; the extent to which they are attractive or unattractive.

- **Valence** is the expected value of outcomes, the extent to which they are attractive or unattractive to the individual. Thus, good pay, peer acceptance, the chance of being fired, or any other second-level outcome might be more or less attractive to particular workers. According to Vroom, the valence of first-level outcomes is the sum of products of the associated second-level outcomes and their instrumentalities—that is,

$$\text{the valence of a particualr first-level outcome} = \sum \text{instrumentalities} \times \text{second-level valences}$$

EXHIBIT 5.4
A hypothetical expectancy model (E = Expectancy, I = Instrumentality, V = Valence).

✳️—Explore

Go to MyManagementLab to see an annotated version of this figure.

In other words, the valence of a first-level outcome depends on the extent to which it leads to favourable second-level outcomes.

- **Expectancy** is the probability that the worker can actually achieve a particular first-level outcome (this is also known as the *effort ⟶ performance* link). For example, a machinist might be absolutely certain (expectancy = 1.0) that she can perform at an average level (producing 15 units a day), but less certain (expectancy = .6) that she can perform at a high level (producing 20 units a day).

- **Force** is the end product of the other components of the theory. It represents the relative degree of effort that will be directed toward various first-level outcomes.

According to Vroom, the force directed toward a first-level outcome is a product of the valence of that outcome and the expectancy that it can be achieved. Thus,

$$force = first\text{-}level\ valence \times expectancy$$

We can expect an individual's effort to be directed toward the first-level outcome that has the largest force product. Notice that no matter the valence of a particular first-level

Expectancy. The probability that a particular first-level outcome can be achieved.

Force. The effort directed toward a first-level outcome.

outcome a person will not be motivated to achieve it if the expectancy of accomplishment approaches zero.

Believe it or not, the mechanics of expectancy theory can be distilled into a couple of simple sentences! In fact, these sentences nicely capture the premises of the theory:

- People will be motivated to perform in those work activities that they find attractive and that they feel they can accomplish.

- The attractiveness of various work activities depends on the extent to which they lead to favourable personal consequences.

It is extremely important to understand that expectancy theory is based on the perceptions of the individual worker. Thus, expectancies, valences, instrumentalities, and relevant second-level outcomes depend on the perceptual system of the person whose motivation we are analyzing. For example, two employees performing the same job might attach different valences to money, differ in their perceptions of the instrumentality of performance for obtaining high pay, and differ in their expectations of being able to perform at a high level. Therefore, they would likely exhibit different patterns of motivation.

Although expectancy theory does not concern itself directly with the distinction between extrinsic and intrinsic motivators, it can handle any form of second-level outcome that has relevance for the person in question. Thus, some people might find second-level outcomes of an intrinsic nature, such as feeling good about performing a task well, positively valent. Others might find extrinsic outcomes, such as high pay, positively valent.

To firm up your understanding of expectancy theory, consider Tony Angelas, a middle manager in a firm that operates a chain of retail stores (Exhibit 5.5). Second-level outcomes

EXHIBIT 5.5
Expectancy model for Tony Angelas (E = Expectancy, I = Instrumentality, V = Valence).

Explore

Go to MyManagementLab to see an annotated version of this figure.

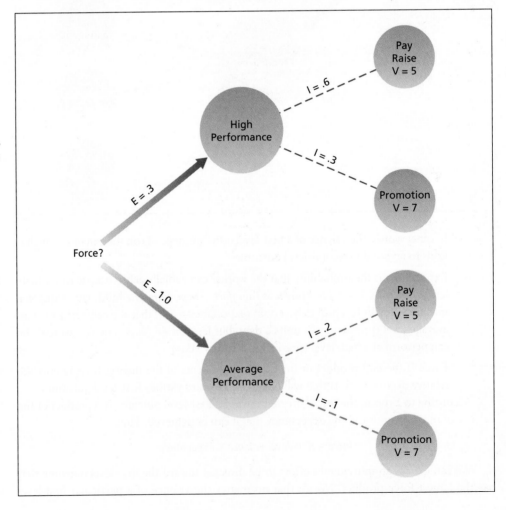

that are relevant to him include the opportunity to obtain a raise and the chance to receive a promotion. The promotion is more highly valent to Tony than the raise (7 versus 5 on a scale of 10) because the promotion means more money *and* increased prestige. Tony figures that if he can perform at a very high level in the next few months, the odds are 6 in 10 that he will receive a raise. Thus, the instrumentality of high performance for obtaining a raise is .6. Promotions are harder to come by, and Tony figures the odds at .3 if he performs well. The instrumentality of average performance for achieving these favourable second-level outcomes is a good bit lower (.2 for the raise and only .1 for the promotion). Recall that the valence of a first-level outcome is the sum of the products of second-level outcomes and their instrumentalities. Thus, the valence of high performance for Tony is $(5 \times .6) + (7 \times .3) = 5.1$. Similarly, the valence of average performance is $(5 \times .2) + (7 \times .1) = 1.7$. We can conclude that high performance is more valent for Tony than average performance.

Does this mean that Tony will necessarily try to perform at a high level in the next few months? To determine this, we must take into account his expectancy that he can actually achieve the competing first-level outcomes. As shown in Exhibit 5.5, Tony is absolutely certain that he can perform at an average level (expectancy = 1.0) but much less certain (.3) that he can sustain high performance. Force is a product of these expectancies and the valence of their respective first-level outcomes. Thus, the force associated with high performance is .3 $\times$ 5.1 = 1.53, while that associated with average performance is 1.0 $\times$ 1.7 = 1.70. As a result, although high performance is attractive to Tony, he will probably perform at an average level.

With all this complicated figuring, you might be thinking, "Look, would Tony really do all this calculation to decide his motivational strategy? Do people actually think this way?" The answer to these questions is probably no. Rather, the argument is that people *implicitly* take expectancy, valence, and instrumentality into account as they go about their daily business of being motivated. If you reflect for a moment on your behaviour at work or school, you will realize that you have certain expectancies about what you can accomplish, the chances that these accomplishments will lead to certain other outcomes, and the value of these outcomes for you.

Research Support for Expectancy Theory

Tests have provided moderately favourable support for expectancy theory.[37] In particular, there is especially good evidence that the valence of first-level outcomes depends on the extent to which they lead to favourable second-level consequences. We must recognize, however, that the sheer complexity of expectancy theory makes it difficult to test. We have already suggested that people are not used to *thinking* in expectancy terminology. Thus, some research studies show that individuals have a difficult time discriminating between instrumentalities and second-level valences. Despite this and other technical problems, experts in motivation generally accept expectancy theory.

Managerial Implications of Expectancy Theory

The motivational practices suggested by expectancy theory involve "juggling the numbers" that individuals attach to expectancies, instrumentalities, and valences.

BOOST EXPECTANCIES One of the most basic things managers can do is ensure that their employees *expect* to be able to achieve first-level outcomes that are of interest to the organization. No matter how positively valent high productivity or good attendance might be, the force equation suggests that workers will not pursue these goals if expectancy is low. Low expectancies can take many forms, but a few examples will suffice to make the point.

- Employees might feel that poor equipment, poor tools, or lazy co-workers impede their work progress.

- Employees might not understand what the organization considers to be good performance or see how they can achieve it.
- If performance is evaluated by a subjective supervisory rating, employees might see the process as capricious and arbitrary, not understanding how to obtain a good rating.

Although the specific solutions to these problems vary, expectancies can usually be enhanced by providing proper equipment and training, demonstrating correct work procedures, carefully explaining how performance is evaluated, and listening to employee performance problems. The point of all this is to clarify the path to beneficial first-level outcomes.

CLARIFY REWARD CONTINGENCIES Managers should also attempt to ensure that the paths between first- and second-level outcomes are clear. Employees should be convinced that first-level outcomes desired by the organization are clearly *instrumental* in obtaining positive second-level outcomes and avoiding negative outcomes. If a manager has a policy of recommending good performers for promotion, she should spell out this policy. Similarly, if managers desire regular attendance, they should clarify the consequences of good and poor attendance. To ensure that instrumentalities are strongly established, they should be clearly stated and then acted on by the manager. Managers should also attempt to provide stimulating, challenging tasks for workers who appear to be interested in such work. On such tasks, the instrumentality of good performance for feelings of achievement, accomplishment, and competence is almost necessarily high. The ready availability of intrinsic motivation reduces the need for the manager to constantly monitor and clarify instrumentalities.[38]

APPRECIATE DIVERSE NEEDS Obviously, it might be difficult for managers to change the valences that employees attach to second-level outcomes. Individual preferences for high pay, promotion, interesting work, and so on are the product of a long history of development and are unlikely to change rapidly. However, managers would do well to analyze the diverse preferences of particular employees and attempt to design individualized "motivational packages" to meet their needs. Recall that at GLBC exceptional performance is recognized by a variety of rewards such as cash, special dinners, and preferred parking spots. Of course, all concerned must perceive such rewards to be fair. Let's examine another process theory that is concerned specifically with the motivational consequences of fairness.

Equity Theory

LO **5.6**

Explain and discuss *equity theory.*

Equity theory. A process theory that states that motivation stems from a comparison of the inputs one invests in a job and the outcomes one receives in comparison with the inputs and outcomes of another person or group.

In Chapter 4, we discussed the role of **equity theory** in explaining job satisfaction. To review, the theory asserts that workers compare the inputs that they invest in their jobs and the outcomes that they receive against the inputs and outcomes of some other relevant person or group. When these ratios are equal, the worker should feel that a fair and equitable exchange exists with the employing organization. Such fair exchange contributes to job satisfaction. When the ratios are unequal, workers perceive inequity, and they should experience job dissatisfaction, at least if the exchange puts the worker at a disadvantage vis-à-vis others.

But in what sense is equity theory a theory of motivation? Put simply, *individuals are motivated to maintain an equitable exchange relationship.* Inequity is unpleasant and tension-producing, and people will devote considerable energy to reducing inequity and achieving equity. What tactics can do this? Psychologist J. Stacey Adams has suggested the following possibilities:[39]

- Perceptually distort one's own inputs or outcomes.
- Perceptually distort the inputs or outcomes of the comparison person or group.
- Choose another comparison person or group.
- Alter one's inputs or alter one's outcomes.
- Leave the exchange relationship.

Notice that the first three tactics for reducing inequity are essentially psychological, while the last two involve overt behaviour.

To clarify the motivational implications of equity theory, consider Terry, a middle manager in a consumer products company. He has five years' work experience and an MBA degree and considers himself a good performer. His salary is $75 000 a year. Terry finds out that Maxine, a co-worker with whom he identifies closely, makes the same salary he does. However, she has only a Bachelor's degree and one year of experience, and he sees her performance as average rather than good. Thus, from Terry's perspective, the following outcome/input ratios exist:

$$\frac{\text{TERRY \$75 000}}{\text{Good performance MBA, 5 years}} \neq \frac{\text{MAXINE \$75 000}}{\text{Average performance Bachelor's, 1 year}}$$

In Terry's view, he is underpaid and should be experiencing inequity. What might he do to resolve this inequity? Psychologically, he might distort the outcomes that he is receiving, rationalizing that he is due for a certain promotion that will bring his pay into line with his inputs. Behaviourally, he might try to increase his outcomes (by seeking an immediate raise) or reduce his inputs. Input reduction could include a decrease in work effort or perhaps excessive absenteeism. Finally, Terry might resign from the organization to take what he perceives to be a more equitable job somewhere else.

Let's reverse the coin and assume that Maxine views the exchange relationship identically to Terry—same inputs, same outcomes. Notice that she too should be experiencing inequity, this time from relative overpayment. It does not take a genius to understand that Maxine would be unlikely to seek equity by marching into the boss's office and demanding a pay cut. However, she might well attempt to increase her inputs by working harder or enrolling in an MBA program. Alternatively, she might distort her view of Terry's performance to make it seem closer to her own. As this example implies, equity theory is somewhat vague about just when individuals will employ various inequity reduction strategies.

GENDER AND EQUITY As an addendum to the previous example, it is extremely interesting to learn that both women and men have some tendency to choose same-sex comparison persons—that is, when judging the fairness of the outcomes that they receive, men tend to compare themselves with other men, and women tend to compare themselves with other women. This might provide a partial explanation for why women are paid less than men, even for the same job. If women restrict their equity comparisons to (lesser paid) women, they are less likely to be motivated to correct what we observers see as wage inequities.[40]

Research Support for Equity Theory

Most research on equity theory has been restricted to economic outcomes and has concentrated on the alteration of inputs and outcomes as a means of reducing inequity. In general, this research is very supportive of the theory when inequity occurs because of *underpayment*.[41] For example, when workers are underpaid on an hourly basis, they tend to lower their inputs by producing less work. This brings inputs in line with (low) outcomes. Also, when workers are underpaid on a piece-rate basis (e.g., paid $1 for each market research interview conducted), they tend to produce a high volume of low-quality work. This enables them to raise their outcomes to achieve equity. Finally, there is also evidence that underpayment inequity leads to resignation. Presumably, some underpaid workers thus seek equity in another organizational setting.

The theory's predictions regarding *overpayment* inequity have received less support.[42] The theory suggests that such inequity can be reduced behaviourally by increasing inputs or by reducing one's outcomes. The weak support for these strategies suggests either that people tolerate overpayment more than underpayment, or that they use perceptual distortion to reduce overpayment inequity.

Managerial Implications of Equity Theory

The most straightforward implication of equity theory is that perceived underpayment will have a variety of negative motivational consequences for the organization, including low productivity, low quality, theft, or turnover. On the other hand, attempting to solve organizational problems through overpayment (disguised bribery) might not have the intended motivational effect. The trick here is to strike an equitable balance.

But how can such a balance be struck? Managers must understand that feelings about equity stem from a *perceptual* social comparison process in which the worker "controls the equation"—that is, employees decide what are considered relevant inputs, outcomes, and comparison persons, and management must be sensitive to these decisions. For example, offering the outcome of more interesting work might not redress inequity if better pay is considered a more relevant outcome. Similarly, basing pay only on performance might not be perceived as equitable if employees consider seniority an important job input.

Understanding the role of comparison people is especially crucial.[43] Even if the best engineer in the design department earns $2000 more than anyone else in the department, she might still have feelings of inequity if she compares her salary with that of more prosperous colleagues in *other* companies. Awareness of the comparison people chosen by workers might suggest strategies for reducing felt inequity. Perhaps the company will have to pay even more to retain its star engineer.

Notice how equity is achieved at GLBC. Salary surveys are conducted and individual salaries are reviewed every 12 months to make sure that salaries are competitive. In addition, all employees share equally in profit sharing. President and CEO Robert Meggy says, "I certainly believe in fair pay. You don't have to be the best paying but you have to be fair."[44]

LO **5.7**

Explain and discuss *goal setting theory*, *goal orientation*, and *proximal* and *distal goals*.

Goal. The object or aim of an action.

Goal Setting Theory

At the beginning of the chapter, motivation was defined as persistent effort directed toward a goal. But what is a goal? A **goal** is the object or aim of an action.[45] One of the basic characteristics of all organizations is that they have goals. As indicated in the chapter-opening vignette, GLBC sets business goals and objectives for the organization as well as departments. In addition, employees meet with their immediate supervisor to set individual performance goals and to review how well they have met their goals. Thus, if employees are to achieve acceptable performance, some method of translating organizational goals into individual goals must be implemented.

Unfortunately, there is ample reason to believe that personal performance goals are vague or nonexistent for many organizational members. Employees frequently report that their role in the organization is unclear, or that they do not really know what their boss expects of them. Even in cases in which performance goals would seem to be obvious because of the nature of the task (e.g., filling packing crates to the maximum to avoid excessive freight charges), employees might be ignorant of their current performance. This suggests that the implicit performance goals simply are not making an impression.

The notion of goal setting as a motivator has been around for a long time. However, theoretical developments and some very practical research have demonstrated when and how goal setting can be effective.[46]

Goal setting theory. A process theory that states that goals are motivational when they are specific, challenging, when organizational members are committed to them, and when feedback about progress toward goal attainment is provided.

What Kinds of Goals Are Motivational?

According to **goal setting theory**, goals are most motivational when they are *specific* and *challenging* and when organizational members are *committed* to them. In addition, *feedback* about progress toward goal attainment should be provided.[47] The positive effects of goals are due to four mechanisms: they *direct* attention toward goal-relevant activities, they lead to greater *effort*, they increase and prolong *persistence*, and they lead to the discovery and use of task-relevant

EXHIBIT 5.6
The mechanisms of goal setting.
Source: Locke, E.A., & Latham, G.P. (2002). Building a practically useful theory of goal setting and task motivation. *American Psychologist, 57,* 705–717.

Explore

Go to MyManagementLab to see an annotated version of this figure.

strategies for goal attainment.[48] Exhibit 5.6 shows the characteristics of goals that are motivational and the mechanisms that explain the effects of goals on performance.

GOAL SPECIFICITY Specific goals are goals that specify an exact level of achievement for people to accomplish in a particular time frame. For example, "I will enrol in five courses next semester and achieve a B or better in each course" is a specific goal. Similarly, "I will increase my net sales by 20 percent in the coming business quarter" is a specific goal. On the other hand, "I will do my best" is not a specific goal, since level of achievement and time frame are both vague.

GOAL CHALLENGE Obviously, specific goals that are especially easy to achieve will not motivate effective performance. But goal challenge is a much more personal matter than goal specificity, since it depends on the experience and basic skills of the organizational member. One thing is certain, however—when goals become so difficult that they are perceived as *impossible* to achieve, they will lose their potential to motivate. Thus, goal challenge is best when it is pegged to the competence of individual workers and increased as the particular task is mastered. One practical way to do this is to base initial goals on past performance. For example, an academic counsellor might encourage a D student to set a goal of achieving Cs in the coming semester and encourage a C student to set a goal of achieving Bs. Similarly, a sales manager might ask a new salesperson to try to increase his sales by 5 percent in the next quarter and ask an experienced salesperson to try to increase her sales by 10 percent.

GOAL COMMITMENT Individuals must be committed to specific, challenging goals if the goals are to have effective motivational properties. The effect of goals on performance is strongest when individuals have high goal commitment. In a sense, goals really are not goals and cannot improve performance unless an individual accepts them and is committed to working toward them. This is especially important when goals are challenging and difficult to achieve. In a following section, we will discuss some factors that affect goal commitment.

GOAL FEEDBACK Specific and challenging goals have the most beneficial effect when they are accompanied by ongoing feedback that enables the person to compare current performance with the goal. This is why a schedule of tasks to be completed often motivates goal accomplishment. Progress against the schedule provides feedback. To be most effective, feedback should be accurate, specific, credible, and timely. Recall that at GLBC performance reviews are held every three months at which time employees meet with their supervisor to review how well they met their goals and to establish goals for the next quarter. Performance feedback is also obtained from co-workers and managers who are familiar with each employee's work and informal progress reviews are also held throughout the year.

Enhancing Goal Commitment

It has probably not escaped you that the requirements for goal challenge and goal commitment seem potentially incompatible. After all, you might be quite amenable to accepting an easy goal but balk at accepting a tough one. Therefore, it is important to consider some of the factors that might affect commitment to challenging, specific goals, including participation, rewards, and management support.

PARTICIPATION It seems reasonable that organizational members should be more committed to goals that are set with their participation than to those simply handed down by their superior. Sensible as this sounds, the research evidence on the effects of participation is very mixed—sometimes participation in goal setting increases performance, and sometimes it does not.[49] If goal commitment is a potential *problem*, participation might prove beneficial.[50] When a climate of distrust between superiors and employees exists, or when participation provides information that assists in the establishment of fair, realistic goals, then it should facilitate performance. On the other hand, when employees trust their boss and when the boss has a good understanding of the capability of the employees, participation might be quite unnecessary for goal commitment.[51] Interestingly, research shows that participation can improve performance by increasing the *difficulty* of the goals that employees adopt.[52] This might occur because participation induces competition or a feeling of team spirit among members of the work unit, which leads them to exceed the goal expectations of the supervisor.

REWARDS Will the promise of extrinsic rewards (such as money) for goal accomplishment increase goal commitment? Probably, but there is plenty of evidence that goal setting has led to performance increases *without* the introduction of monetary incentives for goal accomplishment. One reason for this might be that many ambitious goals involve no more than doing the job as it was designed to be done in the first place. For example, encouraging employees to pack crates or load trucks to within 5 percent of their maximum capacity does not really involve a greater expenditure of effort or more work. It simply requires more attention to detail. Goal setting should, however, be compatible with any system to tie pay to performance that already exists for the job in question.

SUPPORTIVENESS There is considerable agreement about one factor that will *reduce* commitment to specific, challenging performance goals. When supervisors behave in a coercive manner to encourage goal accomplishment, they can badly damage employee goal commitment. For goal setting to work properly, supervisors must demonstrate a desire to assist employees in goal accomplishment and behave supportively if failure occurs, even adjusting the goal downward if it proves to be unrealistically high. Threat and punishment in response to failure will be extremely counterproductive.[53]

"Nobody came back from the Goal Setting Workshop. They all left to find better jobs."

Goal Orientation and Proximity

A recent development in goal setting theory is research on people's preferences for different kinds of goals, or what is known as *goal orientation*. **Goal orientation** refers to an individual's goal preferences in achievement situations. It is a stable individual difference that affects performance. Some individuals have a preference for learning goals while others have a preference for performance goals (performance-prove or performance-avoid goals). Individuals with a **learning goal orientation** are most concerned about learning something new and developing their competence in an activity by acquiring new skills and mastering new situations; they focus on acquiring new knowledge and skills and developing their competence. Individuals with a **performance-prove goal orientation** are concerned about demonstrating their competence in performing a task by seeking favourable judgments about the outcome of their performance. Individuals with a **performance-avoid goal orientation** are concerned about avoiding negative judgments about the outcome of their performance.[54]

In the last several years, research has found that goal orientation is important for learning and performance. For example, a learning goal orientation has been found to be positively related to learning as well as academic, task, and job performance, while a performance-avoid orientation is negatively related to learning and lower task and job performance. A performance-prove orientation is not related to learning or performance outcomes. Thus, a learning goal orientation is most effective for learning and performance outcomes, while a performance-avoid goal orientation is detrimental for learning and performance.[55]

Goals can also be distinguished in terms of whether they are distal or proximal goals. A **distal goal** is a long-term or end goal, such as achieving a certain level of sales performance. A **proximal goal** is a short-term goal or sub-goal that is instrumental for achieving a distal goal. Proximal goals involve breaking down a distal goal into smaller, more attainable sub-goals. Proximal goals provide clear markers of progress toward a distal goal because they result in more frequent feedback. As a result, individuals can evaluate their ongoing performance and identify appropriate strategies for the attainment of a distal goal. Distal goals are too far removed to provide markers of one's progress, making it difficult for individuals to know how they are doing and to adjust their strategies.[56]

Research Support for Goal Setting Theory

Goal setting theory is considered to be one of the most valid and practical theories of employee motivation. Several decades of research have demonstrated that specific, difficult goals lead to improved performance and productivity on a wide variety of tasks and occupations, including servicing drink machines, entering data, selling, teaching, and typing text. Further, the effect of group goal setting on group performance is similar to the effect of individual goal setting. Group goals result in superior group performance, especially when groups set specific goals and when the group members participate in setting the goals.[57] Studies also reveal that the positive effects of goal setting are not short lived—they persist over a long enough time to have practical value.[58]

For example, in a now classic study conducted at Weyerhaeuser Company, a large forest products firm headquartered in Tacoma, Washington, truck drivers were assigned a specific, challenging performance goal of loading their trucks to 94 percent of legal weight capacity. Before setting this goal, management had simply asked the drivers to do their best to maximize their weight. Over the first several weeks, load capacity gradually increased to more than 90 percent and remained at this high level for seven years! In the first nine months alone, the company accountants conservatively estimated the savings at $250 000. These results were achieved without driver participation in setting the goal and without monetary incentives for goal accomplishment. Drivers evidently found the 94 percent goal motivating in and of itself; they frequently recorded their weights in informal competition with other drivers.[59]

In recent years, research has found that the effects of goal setting on performance depend on a number of factors. For example, when individuals lack the knowledge or skill to

Goal orientation. An individual's goal preferences in achievement situations.

Learning goal orientation. A preference to learn new things and develop competence in an activity by acquiring new skills and mastering new situations.

Performance-prove goal orientation. A preference to obtain favourable judgments about the outcome of one's performance.

Performance-avoid goal orientation. A preference to avoid negative judgments about the outcome of one's performance.

Distal goal. Long-term or end goal.

Proximal goal. Short-term goal or sub-goal.

Drivers at Weyerhaeuser Company were assigned a specific, challenging performance goal of loading their trucks to 94 percent of legal weight capacity.

perform a novel or complex task, a specific and challenging performance goal can decrease rather than increase performance relative to a do-your-best goal. On the other hand, when a task is straightforward, a specific, high-performance goal results in higher performance than a do-your-best goal. Thus, a high-performance goal is most effective when individuals already have the ability to perform a task. However, when individuals are learning to perform a novel or complex task, setting a specific, high-learning goal that focuses on knowledge and skill acquisition will be more effective than a specific, high-performance goal or a do-your-best goal. This is because effective performance of complex tasks requires the acquisition of knowledge and skills, and a specific learning goal focuses one's attention on learning.[60]

In addition, proximal goals have been found to be especially important for novel and complex tasks and distal goals can have a negative effect. However, when distal goals are accompanied with proximal goals they have a significant positive effect on the discovery and use of task-relevant strategies, self-efficacy, and performance.[61]

Research on goal setting theory has recently begun to consider the potential effects of subconscious goals. To learn more, see the Research Focus: *Effects of Subconscious Goals on Performance.*

Managerial Implications of Goal Setting Theory

The managerial implications of goal setting theory seem straightforward: set specific and challenging goals and provide ongoing feedback so that individuals can compare their performance with the goal. While goals can be motivational in certain circumstances, they obviously have some limitations. For example, as indicated earlier, the performance impact of specific, challenging goals is stronger for simpler jobs than for more complex jobs, such as scientific and engineering work. Thus, when a task is novel or complex and individuals need to acquire new knowledge and skills for good performance, setting a specific learning goal will be more effective than setting a high-performance goal. Setting a high-performance goal will be most effective when individuals already have the ability to perform a task effectively. In addition, proximal goals should be set in conjunction with distal goals when employees are learning a new task or performing a complex one.[62] In the next chapter, we will discuss a more elaborate application of goal setting theory, called *Management by Objectives.*

Now that you are familiar with the motivation theories, please consult You Be the Manager: *Your Tips or Your Job.*

RESEARCH FOCUS

EFFECTS OF SUBCONSCIOUS GOALS ON PERFORMANCE

When we think of goals and goal setting, we naturally assume that it is a conscious process, and in fact goal setting theory is focused entirely on conscious motivation. But there is some evidence that subconscious goals can have the same effect on behaviour and performance as conscious goals. But how can people have subconscious goals?

The answer is priming. Participants are exposed to stimuli such as a word or a picture of something relevant to the goal that one wants to prime them for. The stimulus triggers automatic goal activation that affects goal-directed cognition and behaviour without the person being aware of the process. Thus, subconscious goal motivation operates automatically, without intention, awareness, or conscious guidance.

A number of laboratory experiments have found that priming results in subconscious goals that influence behaviour and performance. But can priming result in subconscious goals in the workplace? To find out, Amanda Shantz and Gary Latham conducted an experiment in which they tested the effect of a primed goal alone and a specific, difficult, consciously set goal on the performance of call centre employees who were fundraising for a university. Employees were randomly assigned to one of four conditions: a primed goal only, a conscious goal only, a primed goal and conscious goal, and a "do-your-best" goal condition.

At the start of their three-hour shift, the employees received an information packet that contained information about the university for whom they would be soliciting donations and recent awards to faculty and the university. To prime a subconscious goal, an achievement-related photograph of a woman winning a race was shown in the backdrop of the paper that the information was printed on. The photograph was of Sonia O'Sullivan, an Irish athlete who won a silver medal in the 2000 Olympics. Participants in the conscious goal condition were given a specific high goal of $1200 to attain on their shift. The employees were told that management wanted to determine the usefulness of the information in the packet on their ability to raise money. They did not know that they were in an experiment.

To test the effects of the goal conditions, the employees in the four groups were compared on the amount of dollars they raised at the end of their shift. The results indicated that employees who were primed raised significantly more money than employees who were not primed and that employees who were assigned a conscious, difficult goal raised more money than employees who were told to do their best. Thus, both the primed and conscious goals increased performance. However, employees in the conscious goal condition raised more money than employees in the primed-subconscious goal condition.

The results of this study suggest that organizations can motivate employees to achieve higher levels of performance by priming them with a subconscious achievement-related goal through the use of an image that depicts achievement. This study also shows that motivation is not always conscious and that subconscious goals can be activated through priming.

Sources: Reprinted from *Organizational Behavior and Human Decision Processes, 109,* Shantz, A., & Latham, G. P., An exploratory field experiment of the effect of subconscious and conscious goals on employee performance, 9–17, Copyright © 2009 Elsevier Inc. All rights reserved; Stajkovic, A.D., Locke, E.A., & Blair, E.S. (2006). A first examination of the relationships between primed subconscious goals, assigned conscious goals, and task performance, *Journal of Applied Psychology, 91,* 1172–1180. Copyright © 2006 by American Psychological Association. Reprinted by permission.

DO MOTIVATION THEORIES TRANSLATE ACROSS CULTURES?

LO 5.8

Discuss the cross-cultural limitations of theories of motivation.

Are the motivation theories that we have described in this chapter culture-bound? That is, do they apply only to North America, where they were developed? The answer to this question is important for North American organizations that must understand motivational patterns in their international operations. It is also important to foreign managers, who are often exposed to North American theory and practice as part of their training and development.

It is safe to assume that most theories that revolve around human needs will come up against cultural limitations to their generality. For example, both Maslow and Alderfer suggest that people pass through a social stage (belongingness, relatedness) on their way to a

YOU BE THE MANAGER

Your Tips or Your Job

During the summer of 2012, a Marriott beach resort hotel in Ontario, The Rousseau Muskoka, issued an ultimatum to its spa employees. The ultimatum came in the form of a three-page letter to employees that made the front page of the *Toronto Star*.

In the letter, the employees were informed that spa customers will be charged a new higher gratuity fee (20 percent) on manicures, body wraps, massages, and other treatments and spa employees will receive 50 percent of the gratuity.

The gratuity was previously 18 percent with 2 percent going to the spa's administrative staff and the rest to the spa employee who performed the service. Under the new gratuity policy, the spa staff will receive 10 percent, 8.75 percent will go to the hotel, and 1.25 will go to administrative staff. If customers wish to tip more than the 20 percent gratuity, the extra portion would go to the employee.

The letter indicated that the new policy is necessary to efficiently manage costs and to remain competitive within the industry. Employees were told that if the new policy was not acceptable to them, their employment would be terminated.

Under the *Employment Standards Act*, there is nothing to stop organizations and managers from taking tips from their employees. However, at the time of the letter, New Democrat MPP Michael Prue introduced a private member's bill at Queen's Park that would outlaw owners and managers from taking a cut of worker's tips. Prue's proposal would amend the law to specify "an employer shall not take any portion of an employee's tips or other gratuities."

In the *Toronto Star* article, it was reported that sources at the hotel said most spa employees had reluctantly consented to the new policy because they

Employees at the Rousseau Muskoka were told to accept a reduction in gratuities or have their employment terminated.

need their jobs. But what about their motivation and job performance? You be the manager.

Questions

1. What do you think of the resort's new policy? Use the theories of motivation to explain the effects it might have on employees' motivation and performance.

2. Do you think the resort should proceed with its new policy? Explain your answer.

To find out what happened, see The Manager's Notebook at the end of the chapter.

Sources: Based on Ferguson, R. (June 27, 2012). Your tips or your jobs, posh hotel warns staff. *Toronto Star*, A1, A6; Ferguson, R. (June 29, 2012). Staff can keep tips—and their jobs. *Toronto Star*, A1, A14; Silliker, A. (2012). Hotel nixes plan to skim employee tips. *Canadian HR Reporter, 25*(14), 3, 6.

---

higher-level personal growth or self-actualization stage. However, as we discussed in Chapter 4, it is well established that there are differences in the extent to which societies value a more collective or a more individualistic approach to life.[63] In individualistic societies (e.g., Canada, the United States, Great Britain, and Australia), people tend to value individual initiative, privacy, and taking care of oneself. In more collective societies (e.g., Mexico, Singapore, and Pakistan), more closely knit social bonds are observed, in which members of one's in-group (family, clan, or organization) are expected to take care of each other in exchange for strong loyalty to the in-group.[64] This suggests that there might be no superiority to self-actualization as a motive in more collective cultures. In some cases, for example, appealing to employee loyalty might prove more motivational than the opportunity for self-expression because it relates to strong belongingness needs that stem from cultural values. Also, cultures differ in

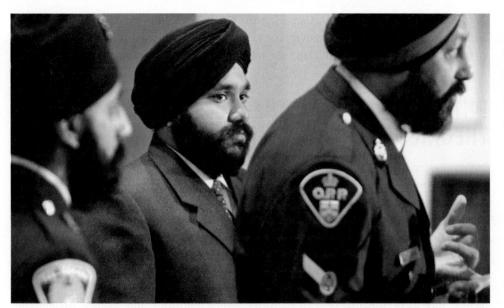

Cultures differ in how they define achievement. In collective societies where group solidarity is dominant, achievement may be more group-oriented than in individualistic societies.

the extent to which they value achievement as it is defined in North America, and conceptions of achievement might be more group-oriented in collective cultures than in individualistic North America. Similarly, the whole concept of intrinsic motivation might be more relevant to wealthy societies than to developing societies.

With respect to equity theory, we noted earlier that people should be appropriately motivated when outcomes received "match" job inputs. Thus, higher producers are likely to expect superior outcomes compared with lower producers. This is only one way to allocate rewards, however, and it is one that is most likely to be endorsed in individualistic cultures. In collective cultures, there is a tendency to favour reward allocation based on equality rather than equity.[65] In other words, everyone should receive the same outcomes despite individual differences in productivity, and group solidarity is a dominant motive. Trying to motivate employees with a "fair" reward system might backfire if your definition of fairness is equity and theirs is equality.

Because of its flexibility, expectancy theory is very effective when applied cross-culturally. The theory allows for the possibility that there may be cross-cultural differences in the expectancy that effort will result in high performance. It also allows for the fact that work outcomes (such as social acceptance versus individual recognition) may have different valences across cultures.[66]

Finally, setting specific and challenging goals should also be motivational when applied cross-culturally, and, in fact, goal setting has been found to predict, influence, and explain behaviour in numerous countries around the world.[67] However, for goal setting to be effective, careful attention will be required to adjust the goal setting process in different cultures. For example, individual goals are not likely to be accepted or motivational in collectivist cultures, where group rather than individual goals should be used. Power distance is also likely to be important in the goal setting process. In cultures where power distance is large, it would be expected that goals be assigned by superiors. However, in some small power distance cultures in which power differences are downplayed, participative goal setting would be more appropriate. One limitation to the positive effect of goal setting might occur in those (mainly Far Eastern) cultures in which saving face is important. That is, a specific and challenging goal may not be very motivating if it suggests that failure could occur and if it results in a negative reaction. This would seem to be especially bad if it were in the context of the less-than-preferred individual goal setting. Failure in the achievement of a very specific goal could lead to loss of face. As well, in the so-called being-oriented cultures where people work only as much as needed to live and avoid continuous work, there tends to be some resistance to goal setting.[68]

International management expert Nancy Adler has shown how cultural blinders often lead to motivational errors.[69] A primary theme running through this discussion is that appreciating cultural diversity is critical in maximizing motivation.

PUTTING IT ALL TOGETHER: INTEGRATING THEORIES OF WORK MOTIVATION

In this chapter, we have presented several theories of work motivation and attempted to distinguish between motivation and performance. In Chapter 4, we discussed the relationship between job performance and job satisfaction. At this point, it seems appropriate to review just how all these concepts fit together. Exhibit 5.7 presents a model that integrates these relationships.

Each of the theories helps us to understand the motivational process. First, for individuals to obtain rewards they must achieve designated levels of performance. We know from earlier in this chapter that performance is a function of motivation as well as other factors, such as personality, general cognitive ability, emotional intelligence, understanding of the task, and chance. In terms of motivation, we are concerned with the amount, persistence, and direction of effort. Therefore, Boxes 1 through 5 in Exhibit 5.7 explain these relationships.

Perceptions of expectancy and instrumentality (expectancy theory) relate to all three components of motivation (*Box 1*). In other words, individuals direct their effort toward a particular first-level outcome (expectancy) and increase the amount and persistence of effort to the extent that they believe it will result in second-level outcomes (instrumentality). Goal setting theory (*Box 2*) indicates that specific and challenging goals that people are committed to, as well as feedback about progress toward goal attainment, will have a positive effect on amount, persistence, and direction of effort. Goal specificity should also strengthen both expectancy and instrumentality connections. The individual will have a clear picture of a first-level outcome to which her effort should be directed and greater certainty about the consequences of achieving this outcome.

Boxes 3 through 5 illustrate that motivation (*Box 3*) will be translated into good performance (*Box 5*) if the worker has the levels of general cognitive ability and emotional intelligence relevant to the job, and if the worker understands the task (*Box 4*). Chance can also help to translate motivation into good performance. If these conditions are not met, high motivation will not result in good performance.

LO **5.9**

Summarize the relationships among the various theories of motivation, performance, and job satisfaction.

✳ Explore

Go to MyManagementLab to see an annotated version of this figure.

EXHIBIT 5.7
Integrative model of motivation theories.

Second, a particular level of performance (*Box 5*) will be followed by certain outcomes. To the extent that performance is followed by outcomes that fulfill individual needs (need theory) and are positively valent second-level outcomes (expectancy theory), they can be considered rewards for good performance (*Box 6*). In general, the connection between performance and the occurrence of intrinsic rewards should be strong and reliable because such rewards are self-administered. For example, the nurse who assists several very sick patients back to health is almost certain to feel a sense of competence and achievement because such feelings stem directly from the job. On the other hand, the connection between performance and extrinsic rewards might be much less reliable because the occurrence of such rewards depends on the actions of management. Thus, the head nurse may or may not recommend attendance at a nursing conference (an extrinsic fringe benefit) for the nurse's good performance.

THE MANAGER'S NOTEBOOK

Your Tips or Your Job

1. According to one employee at the spa, "Everyone feels disgusted. Morale is low." The theories of motivation suggest that the new policy is also going to hurt employee motivation. The employees are probably motivated to fulfill their physiological or existence needs and are thus motivated to earn the extra money they receive from tips. The reduction in tips will lower their motivation given that they will be receiving lower tips for the same work. Their lower motivation is most clearly evident from an equity theory perspective. According to equity theory, workers compare the inputs that they invest in their jobs and the outcomes that they receive against the inputs and outcomes of some other relevant person or group. When these ratios are equal, the worker should feel that a fair and equitable exchange exists with the employing organization. When the ratios are unequal, workers perceive inequity. The employees at the resort will perceive their situation as inequitable because they will be obtaining lower outcomes (i.e., tips) for the same amount of work (i.e., inputs). Given that individuals are motivated to maintain an equitable exchange relationship, we would expect the employees to lower their inputs to bring them in line with the lower tips they will be receiving. This could include a decrease in work effort or quality, or perhaps excessive absenteeism. Employees might also try to increase their outcomes through theft. Expectancy theory also suggests that employees will lower their motivation because performing at the same level will no longer result in the same outcome. As a result, employees might be motivated to work at a lower level given that a high level of performance is not going to result in the same outcome as previously. In expectancy theory terms, the valence of the tip (second-level outcome) might be reduced thereby lowering the valence of the first-level outcome (e.g., high performance). Ultimately, what might happen is that the employees will work faster so that they can service more clients, which will result in more tips. This will probably result in poorer customer service (e.g., less time to chat with customers), lower quality work, and a greater potential for mistakes.

2. It didn't take long for the resort to change its mind about the new policy. An angry public and media backlash forced them to scrap the new policy just two days after the story appeared on the front page of the *Toronto Star*. In a statement to the *Star*, the general manager said, "In response to feedback from staff and clientele about our company's recent decision to change our current gratuity structure at Spa Rousseau, we believe it prudent to reverse this decision and to maintain the gratuity structure as it is." He also told the *Star* that other steps will be taken to ensure the financial viability of the spa.

Sources: Based on Ferguson, R. (June 27, 2012). Your tips or your jobs, posh hotel warns staff. *Toronto Star*, A1, A6; Ferguson, R. (June 29, 2012). Staff can keep tips—and their jobs. *Toronto Star*, A1, A14.

Third, to the extent that the rewards fulfill individual needs (need theory), then they will be motivational, as depicted by the path from rewards (*Box 6*) to motivation (*Box 3*). In addition, the rewards that individuals receive are also the outcomes of the equity theory equation and will be used by individuals to form perceptions of equity (*Box 7*). Perceptions of equity also influence motivation (*Box 3*) and job satisfaction (*Box 8*). You will recall that this relationship between job outcomes, equity, and job satisfaction was discussed in Chapter 4. According to equity theory, individuals in a state of equity have high job satisfaction. Individuals who are in a state of inequity experience job dissatisfaction. Also, recall from Chapter 4 that good performance leads to job satisfaction if that performance is rewarded, and job satisfaction in turn leads to good performance.

In summary, each theory of motivation helps us to understand a different part of the motivational process. Understanding how the different theories of motivation can be integrated brings us to the topic of the next chapter—practical methods of motivation that apply the theories we have been studying in this chapter.

MyManagementLab

Visit MyManagementLab at **www.mymanagementlab .com** for access to online tutorials, interactive exercises, videos, and much more.

LEARNING OBJECTIVES CHECKLIST

5.1 *Motivation* is the extent to which persistent effort is directed toward a goal. *Performance* is the extent to which an organizational member contributes to achieving the objectives of the organization.

5.2 *Intrinsic motivation* stems from the direct relationship between the worker and the task and is usually self-applied. *Extrinsic motivation* stems from the environment surrounding the task and is applied by others. *Self-determination theory* focuses on whether motivation is autonomous or controlled. Motivation is *autonomous* when people are motivated by intrinsic factors and they are in control of their motivation. Motivation is *controlled* when people are motivated to obtain a desired consequence or extrinsic reward.

5.3 *Performance* is influenced by motivation as well as personality, general cognitive ability, emotional intelligence, task understanding, and chance factors. *General cognitive ability* refers to a person's basic information-processing capacities and cognitive resources. *Emotional intelligence* refers to the ability to manage one's own and other's feelings and emotions. Motivation will be translated into good performance if an individual has the general cognitive ability and

emotional intelligence relevant to the job, and if he or she understands the task.

5.4 *Need theories* propose that motivation will occur when employee behaviour can be directed toward goals or incentives that satisfy personal wants or desires. The three need theories discussed are *Maslow's need hierarchy, Alderfer's ERG theory*, and *McClelland's theory of needs* for achievement, affiliation, and power. Maslow and Alderfer have concentrated on the hierarchical arrangement of needs and the distinction between intrinsic and extrinsic motivation. McClelland has focused on the conditions under which particular need patterns stimulate high motivation.

5.5 *Process theories* attempt to explain how motivation occurs rather than what specific factors are motivational. *Expectancy theory* argues that people will be motivated to engage in work activities that they find attractive and that they feel they can accomplish. The attractiveness of these activities depends on the extent to which they lead to favourable personal consequences.

5.6 *Equity theory* states that workers compare the inputs that they apply to their jobs and the outcomes that they get from their jobs with the inputs and outcomes of others. When these outcome/input ratios are unequal, inequity exists, and workers will be motivated to restore equity.

5.7 *Goal setting theory* states that goals are motivational when they are specific and challenging and when workers are committed to them and receive feedback about progress toward goal attainment. In some cases, companies can facilitate goal commitment through employee participation in goal setting and by financial incentives for goal attainment, but freedom from coercion and punishment seems to be the key factor in achieving goal commitment. *Goal orientation* refers to an individual's goal preferences in achievement situations. A *learning* goal orientation is a preference to learn new things and develop competence in an activity by acquiring new skills and mastering new situations. A *performance-prove goal orientation* is a preference to obtain favourable judgments about the outcome of one's performance, and a *performance-avoid goal orientation* is a preference to avoid negative judgments about the outcome of one's performance. A *distal goal* is a long-term or end goal, and a *proximal goal* is a short-term goal or sub-goal.

5.8 There are some cross-cultural limitations of the theories of motivation. For example, most theories that revolve around human needs will come up against cultural limitations to their generality as a result of differences in values across cultures. As for equity theory, trying to motivate employees with a "fair" reward system might backfire if the definition of fairness is other than

equity (e.g., equality). Because of its flexibility, expectancy theory is very effective when applied cross-culturally and allows for the possibility that there may be cross-cultural differences in the expectancy that effort will result in high performance. It also allows for the fact that work outcomes (such as social acceptance versus individual recognition) may have different valences across cultures. Setting specific and challenging goals should also be motivational when applied cross-culturally. However, for goal setting to be effective, careful attention will be required to adjust the goal setting process in different cultures.

5.9 Performance is a function of motivation as well as other factors, such as personality, general cognitive ability, emotional intelligence, understanding of the task, and chance. Perceptions of expectancy and instrumentality influence motivation, as do specific and challenging goals that people are committed to and that are accompanied with feedback. Motivation will be translated into good performance if the worker has the levels of general cognitive ability and emotional intelligence relevant to the job and if the worker understands the task. Chance can also help to translate motivation into good performance. To the extent that performance leads to rewards that fulfill individual needs and are positively valent, they will be motivational. When the rewards are perceived as equitable, they will have a positive effect on motivation and job satisfaction. Furthermore, good performance leads to job satisfaction if that performance is rewarded, and job satisfaction in turn leads to good performance.

DISCUSSION QUESTIONS

1. Many millionaires continue to work long, hard hours, sometimes even beyond the usual age of retirement. Use the ideas developed in the chapter to speculate about the reasons for this motivational pattern. Is the acquisition of wealth still a motivator for these individuals?

2. Discuss a time when you were highly motivated to perform well (at work, at school, in a sports contest) but performed poorly in spite of your high motivation. How do you know that your

motivation was really high? What factors interfered with good performance? What did you learn from this experience?

3. Use Maslow's hierarchy of needs and Alderfer's ERG theory to explain why assembly line workers and executive vice-presidents might be susceptible to different forms of motivation.

4. Colleen is high in need for achievement, Eugene is high in need for power, and Max is high in need for affiliation. They are thinking about

starting a business partnership. To maximize the motivation of each, what business should they go into, and who should assume which roles or jobs?

5. Reconsider the case of Tony Angelas, which was used to illustrate expectancy theory. Imagine that you are Tony's boss and you think that he can be motivated to perform at a high level. Suppose you cannot modify second-level outcomes or their valences, but you can affect expectancies and instrumentalities. What would you do to motivate Tony? Prove that you have succeeded by recalculating the force equations to demonstrate that Tony will now perform at a high level.

6. Debate the following statements: Of all the motivational theories we discussed in this chapter, goal setting theory is the simplest to implement. Goal setting is no more than doing what a good manager should be doing anyway.

7. What are the implications of goal orientation for motivating a group of employees? When would it be best to set a learning goal versus a performance goal? When it would be best to set a proxi-

mal versus a distal goal? Describe a situation in which it would be best to set a learning goal and a situation in which it would be best to set a performance goal. Describe a situation in which it would be best to set a proximal goal and a situation in which it would be best to set a distal goal.

8. Critique the following assertion: People are basically the same. Thus, the motivation theories discussed in the chapter apply equally around the globe.

9. Describe self-determination theory and provide an example of when your motivation was controlled and when it was autonomous. What factors contributed to your autonomous and controlled motivation and what effect did your motivation have on your performance?

10. What is the relationship between cognitive ability and emotional intelligence with job performance? When would emotional intelligence be most important for a person's job performance? When is cognitive ability especially important for job performance?

INTEGRATIVE DISCUSSION QUESTIONS

1. Refer to the cross-cultural dimensions of values described in Chapter 4 (i.e., work centrality, power distance, uncertainty avoidance, masculinity/femininity, individualism/collectivism, and long-term/short-term orientation) and discuss the implications of each value for exporting the work motivation theories discussed in this chapter across cultures. Based on your analysis, how useful are the theories described in this chapter for understanding and

managing motivation across cultures? What are the implications?

2. Consider the basic characteristics of motivation in relation to operant learning theory and social cognitive theory. What are the implications of operant learning theory and social cognitive theory for motivation, and how do they compare to the theories of work motivation described in this chapter?

ON-THE-JOB CHALLENGE QUESTION

Employee Time Theft

Employee theft is a major problem for organizations in Canada and the United States. According to one study, employee theft costs Canadian organizations more than $120 billion a year and is the cause of 30 percent of business failures. The study also found that 79 percent of employees admit to stealing or considering it. Another study found that as many as one out of every 28 employees was apprehended for theft in 2007 in the United States. Although employee

theft has usually involved things like inflated expense accounts, cooking the books, stealing merchandise, or pocketing money from cash sales, organizations are increasingly finding themselves the victims of time theft.

Time theft occurs when employees steal their employer's time by engaging in unauthorized personal activities during working hours, such as visiting social networking sites and chat lines or spending time out of the office fulfilling one's personal agenda (e.g., playing golf) rather than meeting with clients or making sales calls. Time theft also occurs when employees take longer breaks for coffee or meals, make personal phone calls at work, send or receive email not related to work, and surf the Web for personal reasons.

Why are employees motivated to steal from their organization? Use the theories of motivation discussed in the chapter to answer this question. What can organizations do to prevent employee time theft? Consider the implications of each theory of motivation for preventing all forms of employee theft.

Sources: Sherr, I. (2009, July 11). U.S. retailers struggle with theft by employees; Outpaces shoplifting, fraud. Tech solutions yield surprises. *Gazette* (Montreal), C6; Levitt, H. (2009, May 20). Employers must beware of the time wasters: Ways to make staff accountable for time away from the office. *Edmonton Journal*, F4; Levitt, H. (2008, August 20). Hands off the cookie jar or pay the price. *Ottawa Citizen*, F3; Buckingham, R. (2008, April 1). Time theft growing in the workplace. *Telegraph-Journal* (Saint John), B1.

EXPERIENTIAL EXERCISE

What Is Your Goal Orientation?

The following scale is a measure of goal orientation. Answer each of the statements as accurately and honestly as possible using the following response scale:

1–Strongly disagree

2–Moderately disagree

3–Slightly disagree

4–Neither disagree nor agree

5–Slightly agree

6–Moderately agree

7–Strongly agree

____ **1.** It's important for me to impress others by doing a good job.

____ **2.** If I don't succeed at a difficult task, I plan to try harder the next time.

____ **3.** I worry that I won't always be able to meet the standards set by others.

____ **4.** I avoid tasks that I may not be able to complete.

____ **5.** It's better to stick with what works than risk failing at a task.

____ **6.** The opportunity to extend my range of abilities is important to me.

____ **7.** I avoid circumstances where my performance will be compared to that of others.

____ **8.** I like to meet others' expectations of me.

____ **9.** The opportunity to learn new things is important to me.

____ **10.** I'm not interested in impressing others with my performance.

____ **11.** I am always challenging myself to learn new concepts.

____ **12.** I get upset when other people do better than I do.

____ **13.** Most of the time, I stay away from tasks that I know I won't be able to complete.

____ **14.** I don't care what others think of my performance.

____ **15.** I don't enjoy taking on tasks if I am unsure whether I will complete them successfully.

____ **16.** The opportunity to do challenging work is important to me.

____ **17.** Typically, I like to be sure that I can successfully perform a task before I attempt it.

____ **18.** I value what others think of my performance.

____ **19.** I prefer to work on tasks that force me to learn new things.

____ **20.** In learning situations, I tend to set fairly challenging goals for myself.

____ **21.** I don't like having my performance compared negatively to that of others.

Scoring and Interpretation

To obtain your score, first subtract your response to questions 10 and 14 from 8. For example, if you gave a response of 1 to question 10, give yourself a 7 (8 minus 1). To obtain your score on each type of goal orientation, add your scores as follows:

Learning goal orientation: Add items 2, 6, 9, 11, 16, 19, and 20.

Performance-prove goal orientation: Add items 1, 5, 8, 12, 18, and 10.

Performance-avoid goal orientation: Add items 3, 4, 7, 13, 15, 17, and 21.

Your total for each of the three goal orientations should be somewhere between 7 and 49. The higher your score, the higher your goal orientation. Rank your scores from highest to lowest to identify your primary goal orientation. To facilitate class discussion and your understanding of goal orientation, form a small group with several other members of the class and consider the following questions:

1. Each group member should present their goal orientation scores. Rank your three scores from highest to lowest. What is your primary goal orientation? What is the primary goal orientation of most members of your group?

2. Given your primary goal orientation, how might it affect your academic performance? How might it affect your performance at work?

3. Given your primary goal orientation, what type of goal should you set for yourself in the future? When should you set a learning goal versus a performance goal?

4. How can knowledge of your primary goal orientation help you in your future studies and grades? How can it help you at work and in your career?

5. Based on the results of this exercise, what have you learned about yourself? What kind of goals should you focus on at school and at work? Explain your answers.

Source: Zweig, D., and Webster, J. (2004). Validation of a multidimensional measure of goal orientation. *Canadian Journal of Behavioural Science, 36*(3), 232–243. Copyright 2004, Canadian Psychological Association. Used with permission.

CASE INCIDENT

Mayfield Department Stores

As competition in the retail market began to heat up, it became necessary to find ways to motivate the sales staff of Mayfield Department Stores to increase sales. Therefore, a motivational program was developed with the help of a consulting firm. Each month, employees in the department with the highest sales would have a chance to win a trip to Mexico. At the end of the year, the names of all employees in those departments that had the highest sales for at least one month would have their name entered into a draw and three names would be chosen to win a one-week trip to Mexico paid for by Mayfield.

1. According to need theories of motivation and goal setting theory, will this program be motivational? Explain your answer.

2. Discuss the motivational potential of the program according to expectancy theory and equity theory. Will the program motivate the sales staff and improve sales?

3. How would you change the program to make it more effective for motivating employees? Use expectancy theory, equity theory, and goal setting theory to support your plan to make the program more effective.

CASE STUDY

DATATRONIC

DATATRONIC is a company started by George Pandry and Rolin Martin, two friends who had just graduated with degrees in business administration and saw an opportunity to start their own business. With an increasing number of organizations conducting employee attitude surveys, they saw a need for data input and analyses as well as for the design of Web-based surveys. With a loan from their parents, they rented space, purchased 20 used computers, and set up shop. They hired some students they knew at the university and began advertising their services. Employees were paid minimum wage and usually worked three-hour shifts in the mornings and afternoons several days a week.

The assignment of projects to employees was fairly straightforward. Whenever a new project was accepted by DATATRONIC, Rolin would review the job and then set a deadline for completion based on the nature of the project and the customer's needs. While some employees only worked on Web-based surveys, all employees were able to input data and conduct some basic data analyses. If a project required more advanced data analysis, it was assigned to one of a handful of employees who were able to do it. It was George's responsibility to check on the progress of projects and make sure they were completed by the deadline. Once a project was completed, Rolin would review it and check for mistakes and errors. If a project was found to have errors, Rolin would send it back to the employee who worked on it, with instructions on what needed to be corrected and the new deadline. If the corrections were minor, then the employee would be asked to do them immediately and put aside what he or she was currently working on. If the corrections were more substantial, then the employee's current project would be given to another employee so that the employee could work on the project that required corrections.

Within a relatively short period of time, DATATRONIC was having trouble keeping up with demand. In fact, business was so good they had to hire more employees and purchase more computers. After about six months, however, they began to notice some problems. An increasing number of projects were not being completed on time, and customers were beginning to complain. In some cases, George and Rolin had to give big discounts to customers who threatened to take their business elsewhere.

In order to try to deal with the increasing missed deadlines, George decided to keep a close eye on employees during their shifts. He soon came to the conclusion that many of them were friends and spent too much time chatting and socializing while they were supposed to be working.

After discussing the problem with Rolin, it was decided that the best thing to do was to keep a closer eye on employees while they worked. So the next day, George began watching employees and even standing over them while they worked. Whenever some of the employees began to talk with each other, George rushed over to remind them that they were there to work and not to talk. Some of the employees were surprised at this sudden change and didn't understand what the problem was. George told them that too many projects were not being completed on time

and that talking would no longer be tolerated while employees are working. "You get paid for working here, not socializing and talking to your friends," George was often heard saying. "Stop talking and get back to work."

By the end of the month, however, things still had not improved. While the employees were no longer talking to each other when George was watching over them, many projects were still not being completed on time. George and Rolin decided that they should focus on those employees who were the main source of the problem. After reviewing the records of all employees, they made a list showing the number of projects each employee had completed on time as well as the number that were late. They then posted the list on a large board at the front of the room. Employees were told that from now on, George and Rolin would be keeping track of how many employees' projects were completed on time and that they would fire people who were late completing more than one project a month.

This did not sit well with the employees. Many of them complained that it was unfair to blame them for being late because some projects were much more demanding than others and the deadlines were often unreasonable. However, George and Rolin insisted that the deadlines were based on the size and difficulty of the projects.

Many of the students relied on the extra money they made from DATATRONIC to pay for their books, supplies, and the occasional dinner or night out, so being fired was a concern to them. Within a few weeks, almost all projects were being completed on time. George and Rolin concluded that their latest strategy was working, and the list of employees at the front of the room was showing a marked increase in projects completed on time for all employees.

However, by the end of the month a new problem became apparent. Many of the completed data files were full of mistakes, the data analysis was often incomplete and incorrect, and the Web-based surveys were often missing questions and contained all sorts of errors. As a result, almost 50 percent (15 jobs per month) of all jobs had to be completely redone. This turned out to be a rather costly problem. Each job took between 10 and 50 hours and cost DATATRONIC hundreds of dollars to fix. This also meant that projects were not being completed on time because they had to be redone and checked after the deadline. More and more customers began to complain and to demand a reduction in the cost of their projects.

To make matters worse, some of the best employees decided to quit. Over a period of three months, DATATRONIC lost an average of three employees a month. Every time an employee quit, they had to replace him or her, and the cost of replacement was beginning to be a problem. The cost of advertising, interviewing, and hiring a new employee was estimated to be about $5000.

While employees were at one time bringing their friends to work DATATRONIC, this was no longer enough to fill all the jobs. As a result, it became increasingly difficult to find and hire new workers. In desperation, George and Rolin decided to increase the pay to new hires to above minimum wage. This, however, did not sit well with current employees, some of whom had been with DATATRONIC since it first began. Some of DATATRONIC's experienced employees threatened to quit if they did not receive a pay increase. George and Rolin did not see how they could increase the pay of all their current employees. However, they realized that something had to be done—and fast.

They came up with a three-pronged approach. First, they decided to give those employees who were threatening to quit a pay increase equal to what new hires were receiving. Second, they decided to offer a $100 bonus at the end of every month to the employee who performed best on completion time and quality. The employee with the most projects completed with the fewest errors would receive the bonus. And third, they decided that employees who turned in projects with substantial errors would be required to correct them on their own time, without pay.

When the employees heard about these changes they became less cooperative with each other and less willing to offer help and assistance. Before the announcement, although employees engaged in less socializing during working hours, they maintained a friendly and collegial atmosphere, with workers frequently asking each other for help and providing assistance to new hires. However, with the new bonus program and the possibility of having to correct errors without pay, this was no longer the case. Employees not only stopped talking to each other, they also stopped helping each other.

This was especially hard on the new hires who often needed help and advice from the more experienced employees.

At the end of the first month under the new bonus program, George and Rolin called a meeting and told the employees that Mika Salomn had completed three projects and had made only one error. She happily accepted her bonus of $100 and was congratulated for her excellent performance. Some of the other employees clapped and congratulated her, but others seemed less enthused. Nonetheless, the number of mistakes and projects that had to be returned to workers for corrections began to decline.

George and Rolin felt that they had finally found the solution to solving the problems at DATATRONIC. However, by the end of the week, three other employees began demanding a pay increase and several others complained that they should have received the bonus because their performance was just as good as Mika's. To make matters worse, three new hires and two of DATATRONIC's most experienced employees decided to quit.

George and Rolin couldn't understand how something so good had become so bad. They wondered whether they should give all employees a pay increase equal to the new hires or perhaps they need to do something about the bonus program. They were at a loss as to what to do next and wondered if maybe they needed to hire a consultant to provide some advice and direction.

QUESTIONS

1. What factors do you think contribute to the performance of the employees at DATATRONIC? Refer to Exhibit 5.1 to explain your answer.
2. Consider the needs of the employees at DATATRONIC. What is most likely to motivate them? How important are intrinsic and extrinsic motivators? Is their motivation autonomous or controlled?
3. Discuss the motivational strategies being used at DATATRONIC. What are employees motivated to do? How do the theories of motivation help us understand employees' motivation and performance and the effectiveness of the motivational strategies?

4. Using the theories of motivation, what advice would you give George and Rolin on how to motivate employees at DATATRONIC? Be sure to refer to the need theories and the process theories of motivation.

5. What would you do to motivate DATATRONIC employees? Be specific in terms of how to motivate them to complete projects on time, to complete projects without errors, and to continue to work at DATATRONIC. Justify your answers using the theories of motivation.

MOTIVATION IN PRACTICE

LEARNING OBJECTIVES

After reading Chapter 6, you should be able to:

6.1 Discuss how to tie pay to performance on production jobs and the difficulties of *wage incentive plans*.

6.2 Explain how to tie pay to performance on white-collar jobs and the difficulties of *merit pay plans*.

6.3 Understand how to use pay to motivate teamwork.

6.4 Describe the details of the *Job Characteristics Model*.

6.5 Describe the motivational properties of *job enrichment*.

6.6 Discuss *work design characteristics* and the *relational architecture of jobs*.

6.7 Understand the connection between goal setting and *Management by Objectives*.

6.8 Explain how alternative work schedules respect employee diversity.

6.9 Describe the factors that organizations should consider when choosing motivational practices.

ELLISDON CORPORATION

EllisDon Corporation is a privately and employee-held company and one of the largest general contracting, construction, and project management organizations in Canada. The company has been involved in construction projects across the country and around the world. Some of its most exciting projects in Canada include the Rogers Centre in Toronto, the Centre for the Built Environment at the Nova Scotia Community College, and the Sioux Lookout Meno Ya Win Health Centre.

What is it like to work at EllisDon? Just ask Lee Pearsons. He worked as the assistant project manager for the George Brown College Centre for Health Sciences building in Toronto. His job was to make sure the structure was closed in with sealed glass units before winter in 2011. The deadline was Christmas.

Working at EllisDon means that how Lee Pearsons gets from here to there is his business. "We have freedom to do things our own way," he says. "We still have to meet the goals, but how you go about it is up to you."

According to Neil Crawford, leader of Aon Hewitt's Best Employer surveys, EllisDon fosters "an entre-

preneurial culture where people have a lot of freedom in how they're going to get things done.... They give people new challenges and support them. They create opportunities for individuals to make what they want of their employment."

When working at the George Brown job site, Pearsons and his team made decisions every day about scheduling, making the tower crane available as needed, working overtime when necessary, all to reach the goal of a closed-in building by Christmas. "We have the freedom to govern ourselves on site as required," he says. "It's almost like it's our own little mini-business." According to Janine Szczepanowski, Vice-President of Leadership and Entrepreneurial Development, "We put the accountability and decision making with the people who are closest to the opportunity, the problem, the client, the issue." The result is a company full of people "who are running their own thing."

Human Resources Manager Monica Darroch says, "When EllisDon hires somebody, it hires the best of the best and then leaves you alone to do a great job, entrusting all the employees to take ownership." Finding the right employees who fit with EllisDon isn't just a matter of filling a job vacancy. "It's about getting the right people on the bus and then finding a seat for them after," says Darroch. "And determining whether they want to go in a direction that's aligned with where we're going as a company."

In addition to fostering an entrepreneurial culture and a feeling of ownership, EllisDon shares its success with all of its employees. It provides employees with generous compensation, a profit-sharing plan, and a stock-purchase plan. Employees are allowed to buy an equity stake in the company on an annual basis. Every 12 months the company participates in salary surveys to keep salaries competitive and it reviews individual salaries. Other perks include early closing time on Friday afternoons in the summer, sports ticket giveaways, and use of box seats at the Rogers Centre.

Benefits include a defined contribution pension plan with employer contributions (up to 5% of salary), retirement planning assistance, and subsidized home and auto insurance. Some employees, depending on their position, can work flexible hours, telecommute, and participate in a reduced summer hours program.

In 2012, EllisDon was ranked the best large employer in the Greater Toronto Area as well as one of Canada's Top 100 Employers and a Top Employer for Canadians Over 40.[1]

Notice the motivational strategies that EllisDon employs: generous compensation, a profit-sharing plan, employee stock ownership, flexible working hours, telecommuting, and lots of freedom and autonomy in how to perform one's job. In this chapter, we will discuss four motivational techniques: money, job design, Management by Objectives, and alternative working schedules. In each case, we will consider the practical problems that are involved in implementing these techniques. The chapter will conclude with a discussion of the factors that an organization needs to consider when choosing a motivational strategy.

◄●▪ Simulate

MOTIVATION Go to MyManagementLab to complete a simulation about motivation.

MONEY AS A MOTIVATOR

The money that employees receive in exchange for organizational membership is in reality a package made up of pay and various fringe benefits that have dollar values, such as insurance plans, sick leave, and vacation time. Here, we will be concerned with the motivational characteristics of pay itself.

So just how effective is pay as a motivator? How important is pay for you? Chances are you do not think pay is as important as it really is for you. In fact, employees and managers seriously underestimate the importance of pay as a motivator.[2] Yet the motivation theories described in Chapter 5 suggest that pay is, in fact, a very important motivator.

According to Maslow and Alderfer, pay should prove especially motivational to people who have strong lower-level needs. For these people, pay can be exchanged for food, shelter, and other necessities of life. However, suppose you receive a healthy pay raise. Doubtless, this raise will enable you to purchase food and shelter, but it might also give you prestige among friends and family, signal your competence as a worker, and demonstrate that your boss cares about you. Thus, using need hierarchy terminology, pay can also function to satisfy social, self-esteem, and self-actualization needs. If pay has this capacity to fulfill a variety of needs, then it should have especially good potential as a motivator. How can this potential be realized? Expectancy theory provides the clearest answer to this question. According to expectancy theory, if pay can satisfy a variety of needs, it should be highly valent, and it should be a good motivator to the extent that *it is clearly tied to performance.*

Research on pay and financial incentives is consistent with the predictions of need theory and expectancy theory. Financial incentives and pay-for-performance plans have been found to increase performance and lower turnover. Research not only supports the motivational effects of pay but also suggests that pay may well be the most important and effective motivator of performance. In general, the ability to earn money for outstanding performance is a competitive advantage for attracting, motivating, and retaining employees, and recent reports indicate that an increasing number of Canadian organizations are using financial incentives.[3] Let's now consider how to link pay to performance on production jobs.

LO 6.1

Discuss how to tie pay to performance on production jobs and the difficulties of *wage incentive plans.*

Piece-rate. A pay system in which individual workers are paid a certain sum of money for each unit of production completed.

Wage incentive plans. Various systems that link pay to performance on production jobs.

Linking Pay to Performance on Production Jobs

The prototype of all schemes to link pay to performance on production jobs is piece-rate. In its pure form, **piece-rate** is set up so that individual workers are paid a certain sum of money for each unit of production they complete. For example, sewing machine operators might be paid 2 dollars for each dress stitched, or punch press operators might be paid a few cents for each piece of metal fabricated. More common than pure piece-rate is a system whereby workers are paid a basic hourly wage and paid a piece-rate differential on top of this hourly wage. For example, a forge operator might be paid 8 dollars an hour plus 30 cents for each unit he produces. In some cases, of course, it is very difficult to measure the productivity of an individual worker because of the nature of the production process. Under these circumstances, group incentives are sometimes employed. For example, workers in a steel mill might be paid an hourly wage and a monthly bonus for each tonne of steel produced over some minimum quota. These various schemes to link pay to performance on production jobs are called **wage incentive plans**.

Compared with straight hourly pay, the introduction of wage incentives usually leads to substantial increases in productivity.[4] One review reports a median productivity improvement of 30 percent following the installation of piece-rate pay, an increase not matched by goal setting or job enrichment.[5] Also, a study of 400 manufacturing companies found that those with wage incentive plans achieved 43 to 64 percent greater productivity than those without such plans.[6]

One of the best examples of the successful use of a wage incentive plan is the Lincoln Electric Company. Lincoln Electric is the world's largest producer of arc welding equipment, and it also makes electric motors. The company offers what some say are the best-paid factory jobs in the world. They use an intricate piece-rate pay plan that rewards workers for what they produce. The firm has turned a handsome profit every quarter for more than 50 years and has not laid off anyone for more than 40 years. Employee turnover is extremely low, and Lincoln workers are estimated to be roughly twice as productive as other manufacturing workers.[7] Other companies that use wage incentive plans include Steelcase, the Michigan manufacturer of office furniture, and Nucor, a steel producer. However, not as many organizations use wage incentives as we might expect. What accounts for this relatively low utilization of a motivational system that has proven results?[8]

Potential Problems with Wage Incentives

Despite their theoretical and practical attractiveness, wage incentives have some potential problems when they are not managed with care.

LOWERED QUALITY It is sometimes argued that wage incentives can increase productivity at the expense of quality. While this may be true in some cases, it does not require particular ingenuity to devise a system to monitor and maintain quality in manufacturing. However, the quality issue can be a problem when employers use incentives to motivate faster "people processing," such as conducting consumer interviews on the street or in stores. Here, quality control is more difficult.

DIFFERENTIAL OPPORTUNITY A threat to the establishment of wage incentives exists when workers have different opportunities to produce at a high level. If the supply of raw

Wage incentive programs that link pay to performance on production jobs have been shown to improve employee productivity.

materials or the quality of production equipment varies from workplace to workplace, some workers will be at an unfair disadvantage under an incentive system. In expectancy theory terminology, workers will differ in the expectancy that they can produce at a high level.

REDUCED COOPERATION Wage incentives that reward individual productivity might decrease cooperation among workers. For example, to maintain a high wage rate, machinists might hoard raw materials or refuse to engage in peripheral tasks, such as keeping the shop clean or unloading supplies.

Consider what happened when Solar Press, an Illinois printing and packaging company, installed a team wage incentive. It was not long before both managers and employees began to spot problems. Because of the pressure to produce, teams did not perform regular maintenance on the equipment, so machines broke down more often than before. When people found better or faster ways to do things, some hoarded them from fellow employees for fear of reducing the amount of their own payments. Others grumbled that work assignments were not fairly distributed, that some jobs demanded more work than others. They did, but the system did not take this into account.[9]

INCOMPATIBLE JOB DESIGN In some cases, the way jobs are designed can make it very difficult to implement wage incentives. On an assembly line it is almost impossible to identify and reward individual contributions to productivity. As pointed out above, wage incentive systems can be designed to reward team productivity in such a circumstance. However, as the size of the team *increases*, the relationship between any individual's productivity and his or her pay *decreases*. For example, the impact of your productivity in a team of two is much greater than the impact of your productivity in a team of ten. As team size increases, the linkage between your performance and your pay is erased, removing the intended incentive effect.

RESTRICTION OF PRODUCTIVITY A chief psychological impediment to the use of wage incentives is the tendency for workers to restrict productivity. This restriction is illustrated graphically in Exhibit 6.1. Under normal circumstances, without wage incentives, we can often expect productivity to be distributed in a "bell-shaped" manner—a few workers are especially low producers, a few are especially high producers, and most produce in the middle range. When wage incentives are introduced, however, workers sometimes come to an informal agreement about what constitutes a fair day's work and artificially limit their output accordingly. In many cases, this **restriction of productivity** can decrease the expected benefits of the incentive system, as in Exhibit 6.1.

Restriction of productivity. The artificial limitation of work output that can occur under wage incentive plans.

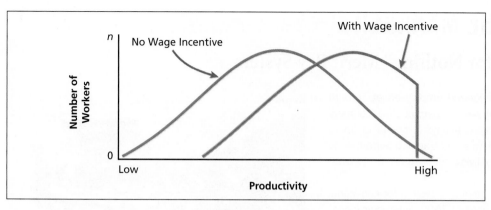

EXHIBIT 6.1
Hypothetical productivity distributions, with and without wage incentives, when incentives promote restriction.

✳-[Explore

Go to MyManagementLab to see an annotated version of this figure.

Why does restriction often occur under wage incentive systems? Sometimes it happens because workers feel that increased productivity due to the incentive will lead to reductions in the workforce. More frequently, however, employees fear that if they produce at an especially high level, an employer will reduce the rate of payment to cut labour costs. In the early days of industrialization, when unions were non-existent or weak, this often happened. Engineers studied workers under normal circumstances, and management would set a payment rate for each unit of productivity. When management introduced the incentive system, workers employed legitimate shortcuts that they had learned on the job to produce at a higher rate than expected. In response to this, management simply changed the rate to require more output for a given amount of pay! Stories of such rate-cutting are often passed down from one generation of workers to another in support of restricting output under incentive systems. As you might expect, restriction seems less likely when a climate of trust and a history of good relations exist between employees and management.

Linking Pay to Performance on White-Collar Jobs

LO 6.2

Explain how to tie pay to performance on white-collar jobs and the difficulties of *merit pay plans*.

Merit pay plans.
Systems that attempt to link pay to performance on white-collar jobs.

Compared to production jobs, white-collar jobs (including clerical, professional, and managerial) frequently offer fewer objective performance criteria to which pay can be tied. To be sure, company presidents are often paid annual bonuses that are tied to the profitability of the firm, and salespeople are frequently paid commissions on sales. However, trustworthy objective indicators of individual performance for the majority of white-collar jobs are often difficult to find. Thus, performance in many such jobs is evaluated by the subjective judgment of the performer's manager.

Attempts to link pay to performance on white-collar jobs are often called **merit pay plans**. Just as straight piece-rate is the prototype for most wage incentive plans, there is also a prototype for most merit pay plans: Periodically (usually yearly), managers are required to evaluate the performance of employees on some form of rating scale or by means of a written description of performance. Using these evaluations, the managers then recommend that some amount of merit pay be awarded to individuals over and above their basic salaries. This pay is usually incorporated into the subsequent year's salary. Since the indicators of good performance on some white-collar jobs (especially managerial jobs) can be unclear or highly subjective, merit pay can provide an especially tangible signal that the organization considers an employee's performance "on track." Individuals who see a strong link between rewards and performance tend to perform better.[10] In addition, white-collar workers (especially managers) particularly support the notion that performance should be an important determinant of pay.[11]

Merit pay plans are employed with a much greater frequency than wage incentive plans and have become one of the most common forms of motivation in Canadian organizations.[12] In a tight labour market, merit pay is often used by organizations to attract and retain employees and as an alternative to wage increases.[13] Furthermore, there is some evidence that pay-for-performance merit pay plans can be effective for improving the performance of professionals.[14]

However, despite the fact that merit pay can stimulate effective performance, that substantial support exists for the idea of merit pay, and that most organizations claim to

YOU BE THE MANAGER

The "Money for Nothing" Merit Pay System

Managerial and non-unionized employees at Toronto City Hall receive merit pay as part of their compensation package. The system pays a bonus of up to 3 percent to managers who meet agreed performance goals, on top of cost-of-living increases of up to 3.25 percent.

However, the city's merit pay system for non-unionized staff became an issue in 2009, when politicians, led by Councillor Peter Milczyn, urged the budget committee to cut the $8.5 million set aside for it.

The city's merit pay system has long been controversial. Critics have argued that a major flaw in the system is that most non-union city hall staff are eligible for it and most get it. Managers get the 3 percent for "satisfactory or better performance."

In all, some 1684 employees are eligible, and city finance officials say about 90 percent of them get the maximum merit pay, which amounts to 3 percent of their salaries, while another 5 percent receive a 1 percent increase on top of the cost-of-living increases and raises for moving up the salary scale. The cost of all these hikes is $133 million, of which about $8.5 million is pure bonus.

Councillor Peter Milczyn has stated that the performance merit pay system is exorbitant. "It does not achieve the goals of truly rewarding those who perform exceptionally." He has argued that "unless you're doing something extraordinary for the city, you're already being paid a good wage with excellent benefits and a fabulous pension and job security. Why should we give you a bonus as well?" He told reporters that an automatic performance bonus is wrong and it does not provide value for the money being spent. He called for a review of the system which lumps together employees who are rated as exceptional with those deemed satisfactory.

Many of the city councillors want to overhaul the system because it does not distinguish between "satisfactory" work and really good work. However, the city's last attempt to cap merit pay resulted in a lawsuit. In 2004, the city tried to reduce the merit pay bonus from 3 percent to 1 percent but lost the case in arbitration.

What do you think about the City of Toronto's merit pay and bonus system? You be the manager.

Managerial and non-unionized employees at Toronto City Hall receive a bonus of up to 3 percent on top of cost-of-living increases.

Questions

1. What do you think is wrong with the city's merit pay and bonus system? Why has it been described as being broken?

2. If you were to change the city's merit pay system, what would you do to make it more effective?

To find out what the city is doing, see The Manager's Notebook at the end of the chapter.

Sources: Peat, D. (2012, July 13). Mayor votes with left in curbing non-union raises, bonuses. *Toronto Sun.com*, www.torontosun.com; Peat, D. (2012, June 5). City committee approves non-union pay hikes, *Sun.com*, www.torontosun.com; Moloney, P. (2012, June 5). City of Toronto managers in line for big pay hike. *Thestar.com*, www.thestar.com; Peat, D. (2011, February 1). City to overhaul 'money for nothing' bonuses. *Toronto Sun.com*, www.torontosun.com; Moloney, P. (2011, February 1). Pay hike yes, bonus no, for city managers. *Thestar. com*, www.thestar.com; Vincent, D. *Sun.com*, www.torontosun.com (2009, February 20). Merit pay on mayor's chopping block: City's generous system long been controversial. *Toronto Star*, A3; Hanes, A. (2009, February 20). Miller reviews bonus system of senior staff: Acknowledges criticism of cash beyond salaries. *National Post*, A8; Vincent, D., Moloney, P., & Spears, J. (2009, April 8). Councillors freeze pay for others: City politicians under fire for eliminating staffers' cost-of-living while keeping their own. *Toronto Star*, GT2; Levy, S. (2008, December 23). Merit pay blues at City Hall. *Toronto Sun* (online), www.torontosun. com; Lewington, J. (2008, July 12). City wants tighter merit purse strings. *Globe and Mail*, A9; Lewington, J. (2009, March 24). Miller wants to freeze non-union salaries. *Globe and Mail*, A11.

provide merit pay, it appears that many of these systems now in use are *ineffective*. In reality, a survey found that 83 percent of organizations with a pay-for-performance system said it was only somewhat successful or not working at all.[15]

Many individuals who work under such plans do not perceive a link between their job performance and their pay. There is also evidence that pay is, in fact, *not* related to performance under some merit plans.[16] Adding more evidence of ineffectiveness are studies that track pay increases over time. For example, one study of managers showed that pay increases in a given year were often uncorrelated with pay increases in adjacent years.[17] From what we know about the consistency of human performance, such a result seems unlikely if organizations are truly tying pay to performance. In most organizations, seniority, the number of employees, and job level account for more variation in pay than performance does.

Potential Problems with Merit Pay Plans

As with wage incentive plans, merit pay plans have several potential problems if employers do not manage them carefully. Before continuing, read You Be the Manager: *The "Money for Nothing" Merit Pay System.*

LOW DISCRIMINATION One reason that many merit pay plans fail to achieve their intended effect is that managers might be unable or unwilling to discriminate between good performers and poor performers. In Chapter 3, we pointed out that subjective evaluations of performance can be difficult to make and are often distorted by a number of perceptual errors. In the absence of performance rating systems designed to control these problems, managers might feel that the only fair response is to rate most employees as equal performers. Effective rating systems are rarely employed. Surveys show consistent dissatisfaction with both giving and receiving performance evaluations.[18] Even when managers feel capable of clearly discriminating between good and poor performers, they might be reluctant to do so. If the performance evaluation system does not assist the manager in giving feedback about his or her decisions to employees, the equalization strategy might be employed to prevent conflicts with them or among them. If there are true performance differences among employees, equalization over-rewards poorer performers and under-rewards better performers.[19]

SMALL INCREASES A second threat to the effectiveness of merit pay plans exists when merit increases are simply too small to be effective motivators. In this case, even if rewards are carefully tied to performance and managers do a good job of discriminating between more and less effective performers, the intended motivational effects of pay increases may not be realized. Ironically, some firms all but abandon merit when inflation soars or when they encounter economic difficulties. Just when high motivation is needed, the motivational impact of merit pay is removed. Sometimes a reasonable amount of merit pay is provided, but its motivational impact is reduced because it is spread out over a year or because the organization fails to communicate how much of a raise is for merit and how much is for cost of living.

To overcome this visibility problem, some firms have replaced conventional merit pay with a **lump sum bonus** that is paid out all at one time and not built into base pay. Such bonuses have become a common method to motivate and retain employees at all levels of an organization. They get people's attention! In 2011, the Ontario Lottery and Gaming Corporation (OLG) paid out $11.6 million in one-time pay-for-performance bonuses to about 6000 employees.[20]

When merit pay makes up a substantial portion of the compensation package, management has to take extreme care to ensure that it ties the merit pay to performance criteria that truly benefit the organization. Otherwise, employees could be motivated to earn their yearly bonus at the expense of long-term organizational goals. To learn more about how this can happen, see the Ethical Focus: *Incentive Compensation and Unethical Behaviour.*

Lump sum bonus. Merit pay that is awarded in a single payment and not built into base pay.

ETHICAL FOCUS

INCENTIVE COMPENSATION AND UNETHICAL BEHAVIOUR

In the United States, executive compensation is believed to be one of the reasons why many companies engaged in the kind of risky and unethical behaviour that helped trigger the financial crisis and a global recession. It is believed that the lure of financial incentives contributed to an increase in accounting fraud and risky and unethical behaviours. But how and why does this happen?

One explanation is the use of target-based incentive systems. With a target-based incentive, an employee has to achieve a certain level of performance to obtain a bonus. As a result, employees might be tempted to lie about their performance (e.g., billable hours), take short cuts, and engage in risky and unethical behaviours to reach the target and receive the bonus.

To find out if target-based bonuses encourage unethical behaviour, C. Bram Cadsby, Fei Song, and Francis Tapon conducted an experiment in which university students performed an anagram task that required them to make as many words as possible out of seven letters.

The experiment involved seven 1-minute rounds and consisted of three different compensation schemes: 1. *Linear piece-rate*: participants were paid 40 or 10 cents for each word they created; 2. *Target-based bonus*: participants were paid $3.60 for each of the seven rounds in which they created nine words or more; and 3. *Tournament-based bonus*: participants were paid $3.60 for each of the seven rounds in which their performance was at or above the 85th percentile relative to other participants in the same session.

At the end of the seven sessions, the participants had to check the words of another participant while one of the participants checked their words. Participants then had their work returned to them and were told to check their work to make sure that all the correct words had been marked "correct" and the incorrect words had been marked "incorrect." They were given permission to correct any mistakes that had been made and were told to accurately report the number of correct words they had created. Participants were then asked to record the number of correct words they had created on a performance record sheet and to hand it in to get paid.

The results indicated that the number of correct words that a participant created during the seven rounds did not differ across the three compensation schemes. In other words, all three compensation schemes resulted in the same performance.

However, the results for over reporting of performance (i.e., cheating) indicated that the number of words reported by participants in the target-based bonus condition that were incorrect was two and half times higher than the other conditions. In other words, participants in the target-based bonus condition lied about the number of correct words they created.

The results of this study indicate that incentive compensation programs that link pay to numerical targets result in more cheating than other compensation systems. Thus, incentive compensation systems need to be carefully designed to encourage appropriate behaviours and to discourage inappropriate and unethical behaviours.

Source: Cadsby, C.B., Song, F., & Tapon, F. (2010). Are you paying your employees to cheat? An experimental investigation. *The B.E. Journal of Economic Analysis and Policy, 10*(1), 1–30.

PAY SECRECY A final threat to the effectiveness of merit pay plans is the extreme secrecy that surrounds salaries in most organizations. It has long been a principle of human resource management that salaries are confidential information, and management frequently implores employees who receive merit increases not to discuss these increases with their co-workers. Notice the implication of such secrecy for merit pay plans: even if merit pay is administered fairly, is contingent on performance, and is generous, employees might remain ignorant of these facts because they have no way of comparing their own merit treatment with that of others. As a consequence, such secrecy might severely damage the motivational impact of a well-designed merit plan. Rather incredibly, many organizations fail to inform employees about the average raise received by those doing similar work.

Given this extreme secrecy, you might expect that employees would profess profound ignorance about the salaries of other organizational members. In fact, this is not true—in the absence of better information, employees are inclined to "invent" salaries for other members. Unfortunately, this invention seems to reduce both satisfaction and motivation. Specifically, several studies have shown that managers have a tendency to overestimate the pay of their

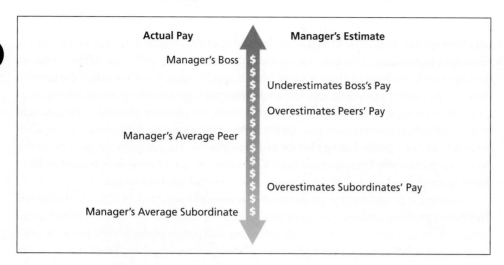

EXHIBIT 6.2
A manager's estimates of pay earned by boss, peers, and subordinates.

Explore

Go to MyManagementLab to see an annotated version of this figure.

employees and their peers and to underestimate the pay of their superiors (see Exhibit 6.2).[21] In general, these tendencies will reduce satisfaction with pay, damage perceptions of the linkage between performance and rewards, and reduce the valence of promotion to a higher level of management.

An interesting experiment examined the effects of pay disclosure on the performance and satisfaction of pharmaceutical salespeople who operated under a merit pay system. At the time of a regularly scheduled district sales meeting, each of the 14 managers in the experimental group presented to his or her employees the new open salary administration program. The sales staff were given the individual low, overall average, and individual high merit raise amounts for the previous year. The raises ranged from no raise to $75 a month, with a company average of $43. Raises were classified according to district, region, and company increases in pay. Likewise, salary levels (low, average, and high) were given for sales staff on the basis of their years with the company (1 to 5; 5 to 10; 10 to 20; and more than 20 years). Specific individual names and base salaries were not disclosed to the sales staff. However, this information could be obtained from the supervisor. Each person's performance evaluation was also made available by the district manager for review by his or her other sales staff.[22]

After the pay disclosure was implemented, the sales staff in the experimental group revealed significant increases in performance and satisfaction with pay. However, since performance consisted of supervisory ratings, it is possible that supervisors felt pressured to give better ratings under the open pay system, in which their actions were open to scrutiny. This, of course, raises an important point. If performance evaluation systems are inadequate and poorly implemented, a more open pay policy will simply expose the inadequacy of the merit system and lead managers to evaluate performance in a manner that reduces conflict. Unfortunately, this might be why most organizations maintain relative secrecy concerning pay. One exception was the now defunct NeXT Computers, founded by the late Steve Jobs, which had a completely open salary system. Although many public and civil service jobs have open pay systems, most make little pretence of paying for performance.

Using Pay to Motivate Teamwork

Some of the dysfunctional aspects of wage incentives and merit pay stem from their highly individual orientations. People sometimes end up pursuing their own agendas (and pay) at the expense of the goals of their work group, department, or organization. As a result, some firms have either replaced or supplemented individual incentive pay with plans designed to foster more cooperation and teamwork.[23] Notice that each of the plans we discuss below has a somewhat different motivational focus. Organizations have to choose pay plans that support their strategic needs.

LO **6.3**

Understand how to use pay to motivate teamwork

Profit sharing. The return of some company profit to employees in the form of a cash bonus or a retirement supplement.

PROFIT SHARING

Profit sharing is one of the most commonly used group-oriented incentive systems and, as described at the beginning of the chapter, it is a key component of EllisDon's motivational system. In years in which the firm makes a profit, some of this is returned to employees in the form of a bonus, sometimes in cash and sometimes in a deferred retirement fund. Such money is surely welcome, and it may reinforce some identification with the organization. For example, at Apex Public Relations in Toronto, the company allocates 15 percent of its profit to all of its employees every year. Larsen & Shaw Ltd., a hinge-making company in Walkerton, Ontario, has a profit-sharing plan for its 100 employees. The company shares 11 percent of its pre-tax profits every December and June. The amount an employee receives is based on his or her years of service, base pay, and performance, which is evaluated twice a year.[24]

However, it is unlikely that profit sharing, as normally practised, is highly motivational. Its greatest problem is that too many factors beyond the control of the workforce (such as the general economy) can affect profits no matter how well people perform their jobs. Also, in a large firm, it is difficult to see the impact of one's own actions on profits. Profit sharing seems to work best in smaller firms that regularly turn a handsome profit, like WestJet Airlines. The company is small and has consistently been profitable.

Employee stock ownership plans (ESOPs). Incentive plans that allow employees to own a set amount of a company's shares and provide employees with a stake in the company's future earnings and success.

EMPLOYEE STOCK OWNERSHIP PLANS (ESOPS)

In recent years, **employee stock ownership plans (ESOPs)** have become a popular group-oriented incentive. These plans allow employees to own a set amount of the company's shares that they are allowed to purchase at a fixed price. For example, employees at EllisDon are allowed to buy an equity stake in the company on an annual basis. Some organizations like WestJet match employee contributions.

ESOPs provide employees with a stake in a company's future earnings and success and help to create a sense of ownership. They also serve a number of other purposes, including attracting and retaining talent; motivating employee performance; focusing employee attention on organizational performance; creating a culture of ownership; educating employees about the business; and conserving cash by substituting options for cash.[25]

In Canada, many of the best companies to work for, including EllisDon, offer stock options to a majority of their employees. For example, at the Royal Bank of Canada, 85 percent of employees are enrolled in a share ownership plan that matches 50 cents for every dollar an employee invests, up to 6 percent of his or her salary. At PCL Constructors in Edmonton, only employees are permitted to own company stock. The company has realized a profit every year since 1977, when it became 100 percent employee owned.[26] Husky Injection Molding Systems Ltd. has a share-purchasing plan in which approximately 25 percent of the company's shares are held by employees. Employees at Husky can earn company shares by doing things that help the environment and community. At Hudson's Bay Company, employees receive $1 worth of company shares for every $6 they invest, an immediate return of 17 percent.[27]

Employee stock options are believed to increase employees' loyalty and motivation because they align employees' goals and interests with those of the organization and create a sense of legal and psychological ownership. There is some evidence that ESOPs can improve employee retention and profitability.[28] A study conducted by the Toronto Stock Exchange found that companies with employee stock ownership plans outperformed those that do not on a number of performance indicators, including profit growth, net profit margin, productivity, return on average total equity, and return on capital.[29]

However, like profit sharing, ESOPs work best in small organizations that regularly turn a profit. In larger organizations it is more difficult for employees to see the connection between their efforts and company profits because many factors can influence the value of a company's stock besides employee effort and performance. In addition, ESOPs lose their motivational potential in a weak economy when a company's share price goes down.

Gainsharing. A group pay incentive plan based on productivity or performance improvements over which the workforce has some control.

GAINSHARING

Gainsharing plans are group incentive plans that are based on improved productivity or performance over which the workforce has some control.[30] Such plans often include reductions in the cost of labour, material, or supplies. When measured costs decrease, the company pays a monthly bonus according to a predetermined formula that shares this "gain" between employees and the firm. For example, a plan installed by Canadian pulp and paper producer Fraser Papers rewards employees for low scrap and low steam usage during production. The plan sidesteps the cost of steam generation and the international price for paper, things over which the workforce lacks control.[31]

Gainsharing plans have usually been installed using committees that include extensive workforce participation. This builds trust and commitment to the formulas that are used to convert gains into bonuses. Also, most plans include all members of the work unit, including production people, managers, and support staff.

The most common gainsharing plan is the Scanlon Plan, developed by union leader Joe Scanlon in the 1930s.[32] The plan stresses participatory management and joint problem solving between employees and managers, but it also stresses using the pay system to reward employees for this cooperative behaviour. Thus, pay is used to align company and employee goals. The Scanlon Plan has been used successfully by many small, family-owned manufacturing firms. Also, in recent years, many large corporations (such as General Electric, Motorola, Carrier, and Dana) have installed Scanlon-like plans in some manufacturing plants.[33] The turnaround of the motorcycle producer Harley-Davidson is, in part, attributed to the institution of gainsharing.

In a study in a unionized auto parts manufacturing plant, a Scanlon gainsharing program was negotiated as part of a joint union–management effort to respond to economic downturns and competitive challenges in the auto industry. Management and the union were extensively involved in the development and implementation of the plan, which consisted of a formal employee suggestion program and a formula for determining the amount of total cost savings that was to be divided equally among plant employees. The plan had a positive effect on the number of suggestions provided by employees, and the cumulative number of suggestions implemented was associated with lower production costs.[34] In general, productivity improvements following the introduction of Scanlon-type plans support the motivational impact of this group wage incentive.[35] However, perception that the plan is fair is critical.[36]

SKILL-BASED PAY

SKILL-BASED PAY The idea behind **skill-based pay** (also called *pay for knowledge*) is to motivate employees to learn a wide variety of work tasks, irrespective of the job that they might be doing at any given time. The more skills that are acquired, the higher the person's pay.[37] Companies use skill-based pay to encourage employee flexibility in task assignments and to give them a broader picture of the work process. It is especially useful on self-managed teams (Chapter 7), in which employees divide up the work as they see fit. It is also useful in flexible

Skill-based pay. A system in which people are paid according to the number of job skills they have acquired.

At Quebec's Bell Helicopter Textron plant, skill-based pay encourages flexibility in the aircraft assemblers' work assignments and provides them with an overall picture of the work process.

PAY PLAN	DESCRIPTION	ADVANTAGES	DISADVANTAGES
Profit sharing	Employees receive a cash bonus based on organization profits	• Employees have a sense of ownership. • Aligns employee goals with organization goals. • Only pays when the organization makes a profit.	• Many factors beyond the control of employees can affect profits. • It is difficult for employees to see the impact of their actions on organization profits.
Employee stock ownership	Employees can own a set amount of the organization's shares.	• Creates a sense of legal and psychological ownership for employees. • Aligns employees' goals and interests with those of the organization.	• Many factors can influence the value of an organization's shares, regardless of employees' effort and performance. • It is difficult for employees to see the connection between their efforts and the value of their organization's stocks. • They lose their motivational potential in a weak economy when the value of an organization's stocks decline.
Gainsharing	When measured costs decrease, employees receive a bonus based on a predetermined formula.	• Aligns organization and employee goals. • Encourages teamwork and cooperative behaviour.	• Bonuses might be paid even when the organization does not make a profit. • Employees might neglect objectives that are not included in the formula.
Skill-based pay	Employees are paid according to the number of job skills they acquire.	• Encourages employees to learn new skills. • Greater flexibility in task assignments. • Provides employees with a broader picture of the work process.	• Increases the cost of training. • Labour costs can increase as employees acquire more skills.

EXHIBIT 6.3
Teamwork pay plans.

Go to MyManagementLab to see an annotated version of this figure.

HERMAN MILLER: MOTIVATION, LEADERSHIP & TEAMWORK Go to MyManagementLab to watch a video about leadership and teamwork.

Job design. The structure, content, and configuration of a person's work tasks and roles.

manufacturing (Chapter 15), in which rapid changes in job demands can occur. Quebec's Bell Helicopter Textron plant uses skill-based pay for its aircraft assemblers to enhance their flexibility.

Training costs can be high with a skill-based pay system. Also, when the system is in place, it has to be used. Sometimes managers want to keep employees on a task they are good at rather than letting them acquire new skills. However, skill-based programs can have positive consequences. A study on the effects of a skill-based pay system in a large organization that manufactures vehicle safety systems reported an increase in productivity, lower labour costs per part, and a reduction in scrap following implementation of a skill-based pay program.[38]

Exhibit 6.3 compares the various pay plans that organizations use to motivate teamwork. Research has found that group-based financial incentives can have a positive effect on the collective efforts of employees and business-unit outcomes.[39]

JOB DESIGN AS A MOTIVATOR

If the use of money as a motivator is primarily an attempt to capitalize on extrinsic motivation, current approaches to using job design as a motivator represent an attempt to capitalize on intrinsic motivation. **Job design** refers to the structure, content, and configuration of a person's work tasks and roles.[40] In essence, the goal of job design is to identify the characteristics that make some tasks more motivating than others and to capture these characteristics in the design of jobs. Although it is often believed that money is the primary work motivator, many workers are actually motivated more by stimulating, challenging, and meaningful work.[41] But how do you design jobs to make them more motivating? Let's begin with a review of traditional views of job design.

Traditional Views of Job Design

From the beginning of the Industrial Revolution until the 1960s, the prevailing philosophy regarding the design of most non-managerial jobs was job simplification. The historical roots of job simplification are found in social, economic, and technological forces that existed even before the Industrial Revolution. This preindustrial period was characterized by increasing urbanization and the growth of a free market economy, which prompted a demand for manufactured goods. Thus, a division of labour within society occurred, and specialized industrial concerns using newly developed machinery emerged to meet this demand. With complex machinery and an uneducated, untrained workforce, these organizations recognized that *specialization* was the key to efficient productivity. If the production of an object could be broken down into very basic, simple steps, even an uneducated and minimally trained worker could contribute his or her share by mastering one of these steps.

The zenith of job simplification occurred in the early 1900s, when industrial engineer Frederick Winslow Taylor presented the industrial community with his principles of scientific management.[42] From Chapter 1, you will recall that Taylor advocated extreme division of labour and specialization, even extending to the specialization of supervisors in roles such as trainer, disciplinarian, and so on. Also, he advocated careful standardization and regulation of work activities and rest pauses. Intuitively, jobs designed according to the principles of scientific management do not seem intrinsically motivating. The motivational strategies that management used during this period consisted of close supervision and the use of piece-rate pay. But it would do a disservice to history to conclude that job simplification was unwelcomed by workers, who were mostly non-unionized, uneducated, and fighting to fulfill their basic needs. Such simplification helped them to achieve a reasonable standard of living. However, with a better-educated workforce whose basic needs are fairly well met, behavioural scientists have begun to question the impact of job simplification on performance, customer satisfaction, and the quality of working life.

Job Scope and Motivation

Job scope can be defined as the breadth and depth of a job.[43] **Breadth** refers to the number of different activities performed on the job, while **depth** refers to the degree of discretion or control the worker has over how these tasks are performed. "Broad" jobs require workers to *do* a number of different tasks, while "deep" jobs emphasize freedom in *planning* how to do the work.

As shown in Exhibit 6.4, jobs that have great breadth and depth are called high-scope jobs. A professor's job is a good example of a high-scope job. It is broad because it involves the

Job scope. The breadth and depth of a job.

Breadth. The number of different activities performed on a job.

Depth. The degree of discretion or control a worker has over how work tasks are performed.

EXHIBIT 6.4
Job scope as a function of job depth and job breadth.

Go to MyManagementLab to see an annotated version of this figure.

Job Depth (vertical axis: Low to High)

Job Breadth (horizontal axis: Low to High)

- Quality Control / Equipment Monitoring (high depth, low breadth)
- **High-Scope** — Manager, Professor (high depth, high breadth)
- **Low-Scope** — Traditional Assembly Line Job (low depth, low breadth)
- Assembly Line Utility Worker (low depth, high breadth)

performance of a number of different tasks, such as teaching, grading, doing research, writing, and participating in committees. It is also deep because there is considerable discretion in how academics perform these tasks. In general, professors have a fair amount of freedom to choose a particular teaching style, grading format, and research area. Similarly, management jobs are high-scope jobs. Managers perform a wide variety of activities (supervision, training, performance evaluation, report writing) and have some discretion over how they accomplish these activities.

The classic example of a low-scope job is the traditional assembly line job. This job is both "shallow" and "narrow" in the sense that a single task (such as bolting on car wheels) is performed repetitively and ritually, with no discretion as to method. Traditional views of job design were attempts to construct low-scope jobs in which workers specialized in a single task.

Occasionally, we encounter jobs that have high breadth but little depth, or vice versa. For motivational purposes, we can also consider these jobs to be relatively low in scope. For example, a utility worker on an assembly line fills in for absent workers on various parts of the line. While this job involves the performance of a number of tasks, it involves little discretion as to when or how the worker performs the tasks. On the other hand, some jobs involve a fair amount of discretion over a single, narrowly defined task. For example, quality control inspectors perform a single, repetitive task, but they might be required to exercise a fair degree of judgment in performing this task. Similarly, workers who monitor the performance of equipment (such as in a nuclear power plant) might perform a single task but again be required to exercise considerable discretion when a problem arises.

The motivational theories we discussed in the previous chapter suggest that high-scope jobs (*both* broad and deep) should provide more intrinsic motivation than low-scope jobs. Maslow's need hierarchy and ERG theory both seem to indicate that people can fulfill higher-order needs by the opportunity to perform high-scope jobs. Expectancy theory suggests that high-scope jobs can provide intrinsic motivation if the outcomes derived from such jobs are attractive.

One way to increase the scope of a job is to assign employees *stretch assignments*, something that many organizations have begun to do. Stretch assignments offer employees challenging opportunities to broaden their skills by working on a variety of tasks with new responsibilities. Oakville, Ontario–based Javelin Technologies Inc., which develops design and engineering software for the manufacturing industry, uses stretch assignments as a way to keep employees interested and challenged in their positions.[44]

Another approach for increasing the scope of an individual's job is **job rotation**, which involves rotating employees to different tasks and jobs in an organization. This often

Job rotation. Rotating employees to different tasks and jobs in an organization.

In his classic film *Modern Times*, Charlie Chaplin performed a typical low-scope job working on an assembly line.

involves working in different functional areas and departments. Job rotation is used by many companies, such as Bell Canada, Telus Corp., and Pitney Bowes, and it has been increasing in popularity. Each year, Pitney Bowes Canada assigns five or six new recruits two years in job rotation. In addition to providing employees with a variety of challenging assignments, job rotation is also effective for developing new skills and expertise that can prepare employees for future roles.[45] In the next section, we discuss a model of how to design high-scope jobs.

The Job Characteristics Model

The concept of job scope provides an easy-to-understand introduction to why some jobs seem more intrinsically motivating than others. However, we can find a more rigorous delineation of the motivational properties of jobs in the Job Characteristics Model that J. Richard Hackman and Greg Oldham developed (Exhibit 6.5).[46] As you can observe, the Job Characteristics Model proposes that there are several "core" job characteristics that have a certain psychological impact on workers. In turn, the psychological states induced by the nature of the job lead to certain outcomes that are relevant to the worker and the organization. Finally, several other factors (moderators) influence the extent to which these relationships hold true.

CORE JOB CHARACTERISTICS The Job Characteristics Model shows that there are five core job characteristics that have particularly strong potential to affect worker motivation: skill variety, task identity, task significance, autonomy, and job feedback. In general, higher levels of these characteristics should lead to the favourable outcomes shown in Exhibit 6.5. Notice that **skill variety**, the opportunity to do a variety of job activities using various skills and talents, corresponds fairly closely to the notion of job breadth we discussed earlier. **Autonomy**, the freedom to schedule one's own work activities and decide work procedures, corresponds to job depth. However, Hackman and

LO 6.4

Describe the details of the *Job Characteristics Model*.

Skill variety. The opportunity to do a variety of job activities using various skills and talents.

Autonomy. The freedom to schedule one's own work activities and decide work procedures.

✱—[Explore

Go to MyManagementLab to see an annotated version of this figure.

EXHIBIT 6.5
The Job Characteristics Model.
Source: Hackman, J.R., & Oldham, G.R. *Work redesign* (Prentice Hall Organizational Development Series), 1st Ed. © 1980. Reproduced by Pearson Education, Inc., Upper Saddle River, NJ. Electronically reproduced by permission of Pearson Education, Inc., Upper Saddle River, NJ.

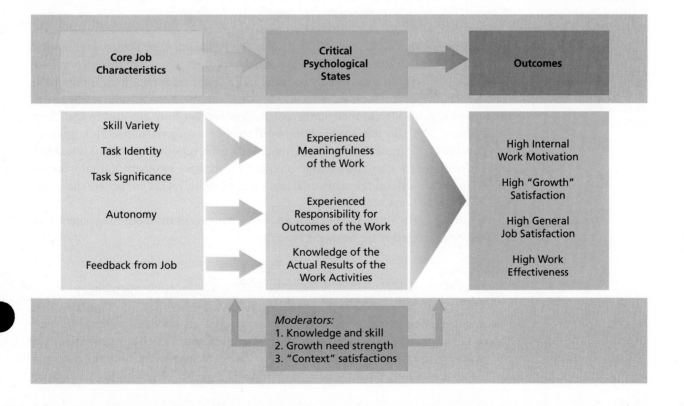

EXHIBIT 6.6
Core job characteristics examples.

Go to MyManagementLab to see an annotated version of this figure.

1. Skill variety
High variety: The owner-operator of a garage who does electrical repair, rebuilds engines, does body work, and interacts with customers.
Low variety: A body shop worker who sprays paint eight hours a day.

2. Task identity
High identity: A cabinet maker who designs a piece of furniture, selects the wood, builds the object, and finishes it to perfection.
Low identity: A worker in a furniture factory who operates a lathe solely to make table legs.

3. Task significance
High significance: Nursing the sick in a hospital intensive care unit.
Low significance: Sweeping hospital floors.

4. Autonomy
High autonomy: A telephone installer who schedules his or her own work for the day, makes visits without supervision, and decides on the most effective techniques for a particular installation.
Low autonomy: A telephone operator who must handle calls as they come according to a routine, highly specified procedure.

5. Job feedback
High feedback: An electronics factory worker who assembles a radio and then tests it to determine if it operates properly.
Low feedback: An electronics factory worker who assembles a radio and then routes it to a quality control inspector who tests it for proper operation and makes needed adjustments.

Task significance. The impact that a job has on other people.

Task identity. The extent to which a job involves doing a complete piece of work, from beginning to end.

Feedback. Information about the effectiveness of one's work performance.

Oldham recognized that one could have a high degree of control over a variety of skills that were perceived as meaningless or fragmented. Thus, the concepts of task significance and task identity were introduced. **Task significance** is the impact that a job has on others. **Task identity** is the extent to which a job involves doing a complete piece of work, from beginning to end. In addition, they recognized that **feedback**, information about one's performance effectiveness, is also essential for high intrinsic motivation. People are not motivated for long if they do not know how well they are doing. High and low levels of each of the core job characteristics are described in Exhibit 6.6.

Hackman and Oldham developed a questionnaire called the Job Diagnostic Survey (JDS) to measure the core characteristics of jobs. The JDS requires job holders to report the amount of the various core characteristics contained in their jobs. From these reports, we can construct profiles to compare the motivational properties of various jobs. For example, consider the JDS profiles for lower-level managers in a utility company (collected by one of the authors of this text) and those for keypunchers in another firm (reported by Hackman and Oldham). While the managers perform a full range of managerial duties, the keypunchers perform a highly regulated job—anonymous work from various departments is assigned to them by a supervisor, and their output is verified for accuracy by others. Not surprisingly, the JDS profiles reveal that the managerial jobs are consistently higher on the core characteristics than are the keypunching jobs.

According to Hackman and Oldham, an overall measure of the motivating potential of a job can be calculated by the following formula:

$$\text{Motivating potential score} = \frac{\text{Skill variety} + \text{Task identity} + \text{Task significance}}{3} \times \text{Autonomy} \times \text{Job feedback}$$

Since the JDS measures the job characteristics on seven-point scales, a motivating potential score could theoretically range from 1 to 343. For example, the motivating potential score for the keypunchers' jobs is 20, while that for the managers' jobs is 159. Thus, the managers are more likely than the keypunchers to be motivated by the job itself. The average motivating potential score for 6930 employees on 876 jobs has been calculated at 128.[47]

CRITICAL PSYCHOLOGICAL STATES Why are jobs that are higher on the core characteristics more intrinsically motivating? What is their psychological impact? Hackman and Oldham argue that work will be intrinsically motivating when it is perceived as meaningful, when the worker feels responsible for the outcomes of the work, and when the worker has knowledge about his or her work progress. As shown in Exhibit 6.5, the Job Characteristics Model proposes that the core job characteristics affect meaningfulness, responsibility, and knowledge of results in a systematic manner. When an individual uses a variety of skills to do a "whole" job that is perceived as significant to others, he or she perceives the work as meaningful. When a person has autonomy to organize and perform the job as he or she sees fit, the person feels personally responsible for the outcome of the work. Finally, when the job provides feedback about performance, the worker will have knowledge of the results of this opportunity to exercise responsibility.

OUTCOMES The presence of the critical psychological states leads to a number of outcomes that are relevant to both the individual and the organization. Chief among these is high intrinsic motivation. When the worker is truly in control of a challenging job that provides good feedback about performance, the key prerequisites for intrinsic motivation are present. The relationship between the work and the worker is emphasized, and the worker is able to draw motivation from the job itself. This will result in high-quality productivity. By the same token, workers will report satisfaction with higher-order needs (growth needs) and general satisfaction with the job itself. This should lead to reduced absenteeism and turnover.

MODERATORS Hackman and Oldham recognize that jobs that are high in motivating potential do not always lead to favourable outcomes. Thus, as shown in Exhibit 6.5, they propose certain moderator or contingency variables (Chapter 1) that intervene between job characteristics and outcomes. One of these is the job-relevant knowledge and skill of the worker. Put simply, workers with weak knowledge and skills should not respond favourably to jobs that are high in motivating potential, since such jobs will prove too demanding. Another proposed moderator is **growth need strength**, which refers to the extent to which people desire to achieve higher-order need satisfaction by performing their jobs. Hackman and Oldham argue that those with high growth needs should be most responsive to challenging work. Finally, they argue that workers who are dissatisfied with the context factors surrounding the job (such as pay, supervision, and company policy) will be less responsive to challenging work than those who are reasonably satisfied with context factors.

Growth need strength. The extent to which people desire to achieve higher-order need satisfaction by performing their jobs.

RESEARCH EVIDENCE In tests of the Job Characteristics Model, researchers usually require workers to describe their jobs by means of the JDS and then measure their reactions to these jobs. Although there is some discrepancy regarding the relative importance of the various core characteristics, these tests have generally been very supportive of the basic prediction of the model— workers tend to respond more favourably to jobs that are higher in motivating potential.[48]

A review of research on the Job Characteristics Model found that all five core job characteristics were positively related to the outcomes in the model (i.e., job satisfaction, growth satisfaction, and internal work motivation) as well as other outcomes, including supervisor satisfaction, co-worker satisfaction, compensation satisfaction, promotion satisfaction, organizational commitment, and job involvement. In addition, some of the core job characteristics (e.g., autonomy and feedback from the job) were also related to behavioural (e.g., absenteeism and performance) and well-being (e.g., anxiety and stress) outcomes. With respect to the critical psychological states, there was strong support for the role of experienced meaningfulness of the work but less support for experienced responsibility and no support for the role of knowledge of results. These results suggest that experienced meaningfulness is the most critical psychological state.[49] Where the model seems to falter is in its predictions about growth needs and context satisfaction. Evidence that these factors influence reactions to job design is weak or contradictory.[50]

LO 6.5

Describe the motivational properties of *job enrichment*.

Job enrichment. The design of jobs to enhance intrinsic motivation, quality of working life, and job involvement.

Job involvement. A cognitive state of psychological identification with one's job and the importance of work to one's total self-image.

Job Enrichment

Job enrichment is the design of jobs to enhance intrinsic motivation, the quality of working life, and job involvement. **Job involvement** refers to a cognitive state of psychological identification with one's job and the importance of work to one's total self-image. Employees who have challenging and enriched jobs tend to have higher levels of job involvement. In fact, all of the core job characteristics have been found to be positively related to job involvement. Employees who are more involved in their job have higher job satisfaction and organizational commitment and are less likely to consider leaving their organization.[51]

EllisDon is a good example of an organization that has designed jobs according to the principles of job enrichment. As indicated in the chapter-opening vignette, employees at Ellis-Don have a great deal of autonomy in how they perform their jobs and the freedom to make important decisions. In general, job enrichment involves increasing the motivating potential of jobs via the arrangement of their core characteristics. There are no hard and fast rules for the enrichment of jobs. Specific enrichment procedures depend on a careful diagnosis of the work to be accomplished, the available technology, and the organizational context in which enrichment is to take place. However, many job enrichment schemes combine tasks, establish client relationships, reduce supervision, form teams, or make feedback more direct.[52]

- *Combining tasks.* This involves assigning tasks that might be performed by different workers to a single individual. For example, in a furniture factory a lathe operator, an assembler, a sander, and a stainer might become four "chair makers"; each worker would then do all four tasks. Such a strategy should increase the variety of skills employed and might contribute to task identity as each worker approaches doing a unified job from start to finish.

- *Establishing external client relationships.* This involves putting employees in touch with people outside the organization who depend on their products or services. An example of this might be to give line workers letters from customers who have problems with service or a product.[53] Such a strategy might involve the use of new (interpersonal) skills, increase the identity and significance of the job, and increase feedback about one's performance.

- *Establishing internal client relationships.* This involves putting employees in touch with people who depend on their products or services within the organization. For example, billers and expediters in a manufacturing firm might be assigned permanently to certain salespeople, rather than working on any salesperson's order as it comes in. The advantages are similar to those mentioned for establishing external client relationships.

- *Reducing supervision or reliance on others.* The goal here is to increase autonomy and control over one's own work. For example, management might permit clerical employees to check their own work for errors instead of having someone else do it. Similarly, firms might allow workers to order needed supplies or contract for outside services up to some dollar amount without obtaining permission.

- *Forming work teams.* Management can use this format as an alternative to a sequence of "small" jobs that individual workers perform when a product or service is too large or complex for one person to complete alone. For example, social workers who have particular skills might operate as a true team to assist a particular client, rather than passing the client from person to person. Similarly, stable teams can form to construct an entire product, such as a car or boat, in lieu of an assembly line approach.

Such approaches should lead to the formal and informal development of a variety of skills and increase the identity of the job.

- *Making feedback more direct.* This technique is usually used in conjunction with other job design aspects that permit workers to be identified with their "own" product or service. For example, an electronics firm might have assemblers "sign" their output on a tag that includes an address and toll-free phone number. If a customer encounters problems, he or she contacts the assembler directly. In Sweden, workers who build trucks by team assembly are responsible for service and warranty work on "their" trucks that are sold locally.

Potential Problems with Job Enrichment

Despite the theoretical attractiveness of job enrichment as a motivational strategy, and despite the fact that many organizations have experimented with such programs, enrichment can encounter a number of challenging problems.

POOR DIAGNOSIS Problems with job enrichment can occur when it is instituted without a careful diagnosis of the needs of the organization and the particular jobs in question. Some enrichment attempts might be half-hearted tactical exercises that really do not increase the motivating potential of the job adequately. An especially likely error here is increasing job breadth by giving employees more tasks to perform at the same level while leaving the other crucial core characteristics unchanged—a practice known as **job enlargement**. Thus, workers are simply given *more* boring, fragmented, routine tasks to do, such as bolting intake manifolds and water pumps onto engines. On the other side of the coin, in their zeal to use enrichment as a cure-all, organizations might attempt to enrich jobs that are already perceived as too rich by their incumbents (some refer to this as *job engorgement*!).[54] This has happened in some "downsized" firms in which the remaining employees have been assigned too many extra responsibilities. Rather than increasing motivation, this can lead to role overload and work stress.

Job enlargement. Increasing job breadth by giving employees more tasks at the same level to perform but leaving other core characteristics unchanged.

LACK OF DESIRE OR SKILL Put simply, some workers do not *desire* enriched jobs. Almost by definition, enrichment places greater demands on workers, and some might not relish this extra responsibility. Even when people have no basic objections to enrichment in theory, they might lack the skills and competence necessary to perform enriched jobs effectively. Thus, for some poorly educated or trained workforces, enrichment might entail substantial training costs. In addition, it might be difficult to train some workers in certain skills required by enriched jobs, such as social skills.

DEMAND FOR REWARDS Occasionally, workers who experience job enrichment ask that greater extrinsic rewards, such as pay, accompany their redesigned jobs. Most frequently, this desire is probably prompted by the fact that such jobs require the development of new skills and entail greater responsibility. Sometimes such requests are motivated by the wish to share in the financial benefits of a successful enrichment exercise. In one documented case, workers with radically enriched jobs in a General Foods dog food plant in Topeka, Kansas, sought a financial bonus based on the system's success.[55] Equity in action!

UNION RESISTANCE Traditionally, North American unions have not been enthusiastic about job enrichment. In part, this is due to a historical focus on negotiating with management about easily quantified extrinsic motivators, such as money, rather than the soft stuff of job design. Also, unions have tended to equate the narrow division of labour with preserving jobs for their members. Faced with global competition, the need for flexibility, and the need for employee initiative to foster quality, companies and unions have begun to dismantle restrictive contract provisions regarding job design. Fewer job classifications mean more opportunities for flexibility by combining tasks and using team approaches.

SUPERVISORY RESISTANCE Even when enrichment schemes are carefully implemented to truly enhance the motivating potential of deserving jobs, they might fail because of their unanticipated impact on other jobs or other parts of the organizational system. A key problem here concerns the supervisors of the workers whose jobs have been enriched. By definition, enrichment increases the autonomy of employees. Unfortunately, such a change might "dis-enrich" the boss's job, a consequence that will hardly facilitate the smooth implementation of the job redesign. Some organizations have responded to this problem by effectively doing away with direct supervision of workers performing enriched jobs. Others use the supervisor as a trainer and developer of individuals in enriched jobs. Enrichment can increase the need for this supervisory function.

New Developments in Job Design

LO **6.6**

Discuss *work design characteristics* and the *relational architecture of jobs*.

Although the Job Characteristics Model and job enrichment have received the most attention and are considered to be the most dominant theoretical models of job design, they have been criticized for being too narrow in that they focus on a limited number of motivational job characteristics. In recent years, more comprehensive models of job design have been developed that go beyond the core job characteristics and include other important aspects of job design, such as social and contextual characteristics. Two areas of particular note are work design and relational job design.

WORK DESIGN Based on a review of the literature, Frederick Morgeson and Stephen Humphrey developed a work design model (they use the term *work design* as opposed to *job design* because it acknowledges both the job and the broader work environment) that consists of a wider variety of work design characteristics.

Work design characteristics.
Attributes of the task, job, and social and organizational environment.

Work design characteristics refer to the attributes of the task, job, and social and organizational environment and consist of three categories: motivational characteristics, social characteristics, and work context characteristics. The motivational characteristics category includes *task characteristics*, which are similar to the core job characteristics of the Job Characteristics Model (autonomy, task variety, task significance, task identity, and feedback from the job), as well as *knowledge characteristics* that refer to the kinds of knowledge, skill, and ability demands required to perform a job. Note that they make a distinction between task variety and skill variety in that task variety involves the degree to which a job requires employees to perform a wide range of tasks on the job, while skill variety reflects the extent to which a job requires an individual to use a variety of different skills to perform a job.

Social characteristics have to do with the interpersonal and social aspects of work and include social support, interdependence, interaction outside of the organization, and feedback from others. *Work context characteristics* refer to the context within which work is performed and consist of ergonomics, physical demands, work conditions, and equipment use. See Exhibit 6.7 for more detail on the work design characteristics.

Morgeson and Humphrey developed a scale called the Work Design Questionnaire (WDQ) to measure the work design characteristics, and it is currently the most comprehensive measure of work design available. The scale can be used for research purposes and as a diagnostic tool to assess the motivational properties of jobs prior to work redesign.

Although much less research has been conducted on the knowledge and social and work context characteristics than the task characteristics, research has found that they are also related to job attitudes and behaviours. In fact, the social characteristics are even more strongly related to some outcomes (i.e., turnover intentions and organizational commitment) than the motivational characteristics (i.e., task characteristics and knowledge characteristics). Overall, the work design characteristics were found to have a large and significant effect on employee attitudes and behaviours.[56]

RELATIONAL JOB DESIGN Employees are often motivated to make a difference in other people's lives but they are often disconnected from those who benefit from their work. Adam

Task Characteristics. How the work itself is accomplished and the range and nature of tasks associated with a particular job.
   a. *Autonomy*. The extent to which a job allows freedom, independence, and discretion to schedule work, make decisions, and choose the methods used to perform tasks.
   b. *Task variety*. The degree to which a job requires employees to perform a wide range of tasks on the job.
   c. *Task significance*. The degree to which a job infuences the lives of others, whether inside or outside the organization.
   d. *Task identity*. The degree to which a job involves a whole piece of work, the results of which can be easily identified.
   e. *Feedback from job*. The degree to which the job provides direct and clear information about the effectiveness of task performance.

Knowledge Characteristics. The kinds of knowledge, skill, and ability demands that are placed on an individual as a function of what is done on the job.
   a. *Job complexity*. The extent to which the tasks on a job are complex and difficult to perform.
   b. *Information processing*. The degree to which a job requires attending to and processing data or other information.
   c. *Problem solving*. The degree to which a job requires unique ideas or solutions and reflects the more active cognitive processing requirements of a job.
   d. *Skill variety*. The extent to which a job requires an individual to use a variety of different skills to complete the work.
   e. *Specialization*. The extent to which a job involves performing specialized tasks or possessing specialized knowledge and skill.

Social Characteristics. The interpersonal and social aspects of work.
   a. *Social support*. The degree to which a job provides opportunities for advice and assistance from others.
   b. *Interdependence*. The degree to which the job depends on others and others depend on it to complete the work.
   c. *Interaction outside the organization*. The extent to which the job requires employees to interact and communicate with individuals external to the organization.
   d. *Feedback from others*. The extent to which others (e.g., co-workers and supervisors) in the organization provide information about performance.

Contextual Characteristics. The context within which work is performed including the physical and environmental contexts.
   a. *Ergonomics*. The degree to which a job allows correct or appropriate posture and movement.
   b. *Physical demands*. The amount of physical activity or effort required on the job.
   c. *Work conditions*. The environment within which a job is performed (e.g., the presence of health hazards, noise, temperature, and cleanliness of the working environment).
   d. *Equipment use*. The variety and complexity of the technology and equipment used in a job.

EXHIBIT 6.7
Work design characteristics.
Source: Morgeson, F.P., & Humphrey, S.E. (2006). The work design questionnaire (WDQ): Developing and validating a comprehensive measure for assessing job design and the nature of work, *Journal of Applied Psychology*, *91*, 1321–1339; Humphrey, S.E. Nahrgang, J.D., & Morgeson, F.P. (2007). Integrating motivational, social, and contextual work design features: A meta-analytic summary and theoretical extension of the work design literature. *Journal of Applied Psychology*, *92*, 1332–1356. Copyright © 2006, 2007 by the American Psychological Association. Reproduced with permission.

✳ Explore

Go to MyManagementLab to see an annotated version of this figure.

Grant, however, has recently developed a model to explain how jobs can be designed to motivate employees to make a difference in other's lives. This is known as **prosocial motivation** and it refers to the desire to expend effort to benefit other people.[57]

Grant calls this approach to job design the **relational architecture of jobs**, which refers to the structural properties of work that shape employees' opportunities to connect and interact with other people. The basic idea is that jobs can be designed so that employees can see the impact of their actions on others. Clearly, jobs vary in terms of their potential to have an impact on the lives of others. For example, firefighters and surgeons have frequent opportunities to make a lasting difference in the lives of others, while janitorial jobs and cashiers have few such opportunities. However, jobs can be relationally designed to provide employees with opportunities to interact and communicate with the people affected by their work, thereby allowing them to see the benefits and significance of their work for others.[58]

For example, in a study of call centre employees who raise funds for a university, callers who had a brief exposure to a scholarship recipient who benefited from their work showed a significant increase in persistence (i.e., time spent on the phone) and performance (i.e., money raised). In a related study, callers who read stories about how former callers helped to

Prosocial motivation. The desire to expend effort to benefit other people.

Relational architecture of jobs. The structural properties of work that shape employees' opportunities to connect and interact with other people.

GLOBAL FOCUS

NATIONAL CULTURE AND JOB DESIGN

The emergence of new approaches to job design was in response to Taylor's approach to job design, which focused on efficiency and productivity. Taylor failed to consider the importance of job design to a person's sense of self-worth and well-being, which is crucial for motivating employees. However, the type of job design that will maximize a person's sense of self-worth and well-being depends on national culture. In fact, different approaches to job design have emerged in different cultures.

The effect of culture on job design can be seen in three major job design models that emerged in three different cultures—the United States, northern Europe, and Japan—all at about the same time and all aimed at enhancing employees' self-worth and well-being.

First, Hackman and Oldham's Job Characteristics Model emerged in the United States, where there is a high level of individualism and a relatively low level of power distance. The job characteristics of autonomy and personal feedback satisfy the motives of self-worth and well-being of individuals. whose cultural values prize high individualism and low power distance.

Second, an approach to job design emerged in northern Europe known as socio-technical systems. Unlike the Job Characteristics Model, this approach to job design focused on the integration of the social and technical aspects of work and on the group rather than individual employees. This led to the emergence of autonomous work groups, the most famous example being at the Volvo plant in Sweden. Employees in autonomous work groups are trained to have multiple roles so that they can switch roles when necessary. This approach to job design reflects a culture that prizes the value of collectivism and the importance of the group rather than the individual.

Third, in Japan an approach to job design known as Quality Control (QC) Circles began in the 1960s. A QC Circle is a small group, consisting of first-line employees who operate autonomously to continually control and improve the quality of their network, products, and services. Their objective is to generate ideas for quality improvement, to identify problems, and to implement solutions.

Two cultural values support the emergence of QC Circles in Japan—collectivism and power distance. The high level of collectivism in Japan supports a work design model at the group rather than the individual level. Japan also has a high level of power distance compared to the United States and northern Europe, and so the QC Circles are part of a hierarchical organizational system. Thus, employees in QC Circles meet in teams to generate ideas for quality improvement that must then be presented to and approved by their managers.

In summary, all three job design models are approaches to job enrichment that aim to increase a person's self-worth and well-being. Each approach defines job meaningfulness in different terms that are congruent with the respective cultural values. Thus, cultural values shape the preferred model of job design.

Source: Based on Erez, M. (2010). Culture and job design. *Journal of Organizational Behavior, 31,* 389–400.

finance student scholarships more than doubled the number of weekly pledges they earned and the amount of weekly donations they raised. These studies demonstrate that by redesigning and emphasizing the relational aspects of jobs and their social impact and value it is possible to improve employee motivation and performance. One way to do this is by designing jobs so that employees have contact with those who benefit from their work.[59]

Now that you are familiar with the design of jobs, do you think that culture can influence job design? To learn more, see the Global Focus: *National Culture and Job Design.*

LO 6.7

Understand the connection between goal setting and *Management by Objectives.*

MANAGEMENT BY OBJECTIVES

In Chapter 5, we discussed goal setting theory, which states that goals are most motivational when they are specific, when they are challenging, when organizational members are committed to them, and when feedback about progress toward goal attainment is provided.

Management by Objectives (MBO) is an elaborate, systematic, ongoing management program designed to facilitate goal establishment, goal accomplishment, and employee development.[60]

The concept was developed by management theorist Peter Drucker. The objectives in MBO are simply another label for goals. In a well-designed MBO program, objectives for the organization as a whole are developed by top management and diffused down through the organization through the MBO process. In this manner, organizational objectives are translated into specific behavioural objectives for individual members. Our primary focus here is with the nature of the interaction between managers and individual workers in an MBO program.

Although there are many variations on the MBO theme, most manager–employee interactions share the following similarities:

1. The manager meets with individual workers to develop and agree on employee objectives for the coming months. These objectives usually involve both current job performance and personal development that may prepare the worker to perform other tasks or seek promotion. The objectives are made as specific as possible and quantified, if feasible, to assist in subsequent evaluation of accomplishment. Time frames for accomplishment are specified, and the objectives may be given priority according to their agreed importance. The methods to achieve the objectives may or may not be topics of discussion. Objectives, time frames, and priorities are put in writing.

2. There are periodic meetings to monitor employee progress in achieving objectives. During these meetings, people can modify objectives if new needs or problems are encountered.

3. An appraisal meeting is held to evaluate the extent to which the agreed upon objectives have been achieved. Special emphasis is placed on diagnosing the reasons for success or failure so that the meeting serves as a learning experience for both parties.

4. The MBO cycle is repeated.

Over the years, a wide variety of organizations have implemented MBO programs. At Hewlett-Packard, MBO and metrics to measure progress were the cornerstone of the company's management philosophy for nearly six decades.[61] At Toronto-based pharmaceutical firm Janssen-Ortho Inc., each employee's goals are tied to a list of corporate objectives. Employees can earn a yearly bonus of up to 20 percent if they and the company meet their goals.[62]

RESEARCH EVIDENCE   The research evidence shows that MBO programs result in clear productivity gains.[63] However, a number of factors are associated with the failure of MBO programs. For one thing, MBO is an elaborate, difficult, time-consuming process, and its implementation must have the full commitment of top management. One careful review showed a 56 percent average gain in productivity for programs with high top management commitment, and a 6 percent gain for those with low commitment.[64] If such commitment is absent, managers at lower levels simply go through the motions of practising MBO. At the very least, this reaction will lead to the haphazard specification of objectives and thus subvert the very core of MBO—goal setting. A frequent symptom of this degeneration is the complaint that MBO is "just a bunch of paperwork."[65] Indeed, at this stage, it is!

Even with the best of intentions, setting specific, quantifiable objectives can be a difficult process. This might lead to an overemphasis on measurable objectives at the expense of more qualitative objectives. For example, it might be much easier to agree on production goals than on goals that involve employee development, although both might be equally important. Also, excessive short-term orientation can be a problem with MBO. Finally,

Management by Objectives (MBO). An elaborate, systematic, ongoing program designed to facilitate goal establishment, goal accomplishment, and employee development.

even if reasonable objectives are established, MBO can still be subverted if the performance review becomes an exercise in browbeating or punishing employees for failure to achieve objectives.[66]

LO **6.8**

Explain how alternative work schedules respect employee diversity.

ALTERNATIVE WORKING SCHEDULES AS MOTIVATORS FOR A DIVERSE WORKFORCE

Most Canadians work a five-day week of approximately 40 hours—the "nine-to-five grind." However, many organizations have modified these traditional working schedules. For example, some employees at EllisDon can work flexible hours, telecommute, and participate in a reduced summer hours program. In fact, nearly half of Canadian workers say their workplaces offer some form of alternative working arrangement.[67] The purpose of these modifications is not to motivate people to work harder and thus produce direct performance benefits. Rather, the purpose is to meet diverse workforce needs and promote job satisfaction. In turn, this should facilitate recruiting the best talent and reduce costly absenteeism and turnover. Let's now take a closer look at some of the most common alternative working schedules.

Flex-Time

Flex-time. An alternative work schedule in which arrival and departure times are flexible.

One alternative to traditional working schedules is **flex-time**, which was first introduced on a large scale in Europe. In its most simple and common form, management requires employees to report for work on each working day and work a given number of hours. However, the times at which they arrive and leave are flexible, as long as they are present during certain core times. For example, companies might permit employees to begin their day anytime after 7 a.m. and work until 6 p.m., as long as they put in eight hours and are present during the core times of 9:15 a.m. until noon and 2:00 p.m. until 4:15 p.m. (Exhibit 6.8). Other systems permit employees to tally hours on a weekly or monthly basis, although they are still usually required to be present during the core time of each working day.[68]

Flex-time is obviously well suited to meeting the needs of a diverse workforce, since it allows employees to tailor arrival and departure times to their own transportation and child

EXHIBIT 6.8
An example of a flex-time schedule.
Source: Adapted from Ronen, S. (1981). *Flexible working hours: An innovation in the quality of work life.* New York: McGraw-Hill, p. 42. Reprinted by permission of the author.

 Explore

Go to MyManagementLab to see an annotated version of this figure.

"... AM I INTERESTED IN AN ALTERNATIVE WORK
ARRANGEMENT?,... YES,... I'D LIKE TO TELECOMMUTE
FROM A COMPUTER EQUIPPED HOT TUB ON FLEX TIME..."

care situations. It should reduce absenteeism, since employees can handle personal matters during conventional business hours.[69] Also, flexible working hours signal a degree of prestige and trust that is usually reserved for executives and professionals.

When jobs are highly interdependent, such as on an assembly line, flex-time becomes an unlikely strategy. To cite an even more extreme example, we simply cannot have members of a hospital operating room team showing up for work whenever it suits them! In addition, flex-time might lead to problems in achieving adequate supervisory coverage. For these reasons, not surprisingly, flex-time is most frequently implemented in office environments. For instance, in a bank, the core hours might be when the bank is open to the public.

Although flex-time has generally been limited to white-collar workers, it has been applied in a variety of organizations, including insurance companies (ING Insurance), financial institutions (RBC), and government offices (many Canadian and American public service positions). According to one survey, 66 percent of organizations offer flexible work schedules.[70]

RESEARCH EVIDENCE   We can draw a number of conclusions from the research on flex-time.[71] First, employees who work under flex-time almost always prefer the system to fixed hours. In addition, work attitudes generally become more positive, and employers report minimal abuse of the arrangement. When measured, absenteeism and tardiness have often shown decreases following the introduction of flex-time, and first-line supervisors and managers are usually positively inclined toward the system. Interestingly, slight productivity gains are often reported under flex-time, probably due to better use of scarce resources or equipment rather than to increased motivation. A review of research on flex-time concluded that it has a positive effect on productivity, job satisfaction, and satisfaction with work schedule, and that it lowers employee absenteeism.[72]

Compressed Workweek

A second alternative to traditional working schedules is the **compressed workweek**. This system compresses the hours worked each week into fewer days. The most common compressed workweek is the 4–40 system, in which employees work four 10-hour days each week rather than the traditional five 8-hour days. Thus, the organization or department might operate Monday through Thursday or Tuesday through Friday, although rotation schemes that keep the organization open five days a week are also employed.[73]

Compressed workweek. An alternative work schedule in which employees work fewer than the normal five days a week but still put in a normal number of hours per week.

Like flex-time, the shorter workweek might be expected to reduce absenteeism because employees can pursue personal business or family matters in what had been working time. In addition, the 4–40 schedule reduces commuting costs and time by 20 percent and provides an extra day a week for leisure or family pursuits. Although the longer workday could pose a problem for single parents, a working couple with staggered off-days could actually provide their own child care on two of five "working" days.

Technical roadblocks to the implementation of the 4–40 workweek include the possibility of reduced customer service and the negative effects of fatigue that can accompany longer working days. The latter problem is likely to be especially acute when the work is strenuous.

RESEARCH EVIDENCE   Although research on the effects of the four-day week is less extensive than that for flex-time, a couple of conclusions do stand out.[74] First, people who have experienced the four-day system seem to *like* it. Sometimes this liking is accompanied by increased job satisfaction, but the effect might be short-lived.[75] In many cases, the impact of the compressed workweek might be better for family life than for worklife. Second, workers have often reported an increase in fatigue following the introduction of the compressed week. This might be responsible for the uneven impact of the system on absenteeism, sometimes decreasing it and sometimes not. Potential gains in attendance might be nullified as workers take an occasional day off to recuperate from fatigue.[76] Finally, the more sophisticated research studies do not report lasting changes in productivity due to the shortened workweek.[77] According to a review of research on the compressed workweek, there is a positive effect on job satisfaction and satisfaction with work schedule, but no effect on absenteeism or productivity.[78]

Job and Work Sharing

Job sharing occurs when two part-time employees divide the work (and perhaps the benefits) of a full-time job.[79] The two can share all aspects of the job equally, or some kind of complementary arrangement can occur in which one party does some tasks and the co-holder does other tasks.

Job sharing is obviously attractive to people who want to spend more time with small children or sick elders than a conventional five-day-a-week routine permits. By the same token, it can enable organizations to attract or retain highly capable employees who might otherwise decide against full-time employment.

Work sharing involves reducing the number of hours employees work to avoid layoffs when there is a reduction in normal business activity. The Government of Canada has a work-sharing program that is designed to help employers and workers avoid temporary layoffs. For example, NORDX/CDT, a Montreal-based firm that makes cables used in fibre-optic networks, introduced a work-sharing program to cut costs while keeping workers employed. The program reduces the workweek by one to three days for some employees over a short-term period; 272 employees work one day less per week. Employees receive employment-insurance benefits for the days they are not working, up to 55 percent of their salary.[80]

Many companies all across Canada implemented work sharing programs to save jobs and avoid layoffs during the recession. For example, Rogers Communications gave full-time staff the opportunity to reduce their workweek and accept a 20 percent pay cut to avoid layoffs to 20 percent of its staff. Buhler Industries Inc. of Winnipeg implemented a three-day workweek for its 200 employees instead of letting 90 workers go and shutting down its tractor-manufacturing plant for four months. In British Columbia, Photon Control Inc. saved 10 jobs by implementing a four-day workweek when its revenues declined, saving the company about $17 000 a month without having to downsize. Work sharing not only cuts costs, saves jobs, and avoids layoffs, but it allows organizations to retain highly skilled workers so they can quickly rebound when the economy and business improves.[81]

Job sharing. An alternative work schedule in which two part-time employees divide the work of a full-time job.

Work sharing. Reducing the number of hours employees work to avoid layoffs when there is a reduction in normal business activity.

RESEARCH EVIDENCE There is virtually no hard research on job and work sharing. However, anecdotal reports suggest that the job sharers must make a concerted effort to communicate well with each other and with superiors, co-workers, and clients. Such communication is greatly facilitated by contemporary computer technology and voice mail. However, job sharing can result in coordination problems if communication is not adequate. Also, problems with performance appraisal can occur when two individuals share one job.

Telecommuting

In recent years, an increasing number of organizations have begun to offer employees telecommuting, or what is also known as telework or teleworking. By **telecommuting**, employees are able to work at home but stay in touch with their offices through the use of communications technology, such as a computer network, voice mail, and electronic messages.[82] Like the other types of alternative working arrangements, telecommuting provides workers with greater flexibility in their work schedules.

Many companies first began implementing telecommuting in response to employee requests for more flexible work arrangements.[83] With the growth in communication technologies, however, other factors have also influenced the spread of telecommuting. For example, telecommuting is changing the way that organizations recruit and hire people. When telecommuting is an option, companies can hire the best person for a job, regardless of where they live in the world, through *distant staffing*.[84] Distant staffing enables employees to work for a company without ever having to come into the office or even be in the same country!

Telecommuting has grown considerably over the last few years, and demand is expected to continue to grow in the coming years. It is estimated that approximately 11 million North Americans are telecommuting and that 51 percent of North American companies offer some form of telecommuting, including one in four Fortune 1000 companies. In Canada, it has been estimated that more than 1.5 million Canadians are telecommuting and more organizations plan to offer it to their employees over the next few years.[85]

Telecommuting.
A system by which employees are able to work at home but stay in touch with their offices through the use of communications technology, such as a computer network, voice mail, and electronic messages.

An interesting trend in telecommuting is telework centres that provide workers all of the amenities of a home office in a location close to their home. Related to this is the emergence of *distributed work programs*, which involve a combination of remote work arrangements that allow employees to work at their business office, a satellite office, and a home office. At Bell Canada, all employees are eligible to participate in the company's distributed work program. Employees can choose to work from home all of the time, or they can work a few days a week at one of Bell's satellite offices. More than 2000 of its 42 000 workers in Canada telecommute, either from home or from one of 13 satellite offices.[86]

RESEARCH EVIDENCE Telecommuting has often been touted as having benefits to organizations and individuals. For example, organizations stand to benefit from lower costs as a result of a reduction in turnover and need for office space and equipment, and they can attract employees who see it as a desirable benefit. For individuals, it has been suggested that telecommuting can improve work–life balance and increase productivity.[87] But does telecommuting deliver on these benefits?

A review of research on telecommuting found that telecommuting has small but positive effects on perceived autonomy and lower work–family conflict. It also has a positive effect on job satisfaction and job performance and results in lower stress and turnover intentions. Telecommuting was found to have no detrimental effect on the quality of workplace relationships or one's career prospects. In addition, a greater frequency of telecommuting (more than 2.5 days a week) was associated with a greater reduction in work–family conflict and stress. The authors found that the positive effects of telecommuting were mostly due to an increase in perceived autonomy. In other words, one of the reasons that telecommuting has positive effects on attitudes and behaviours is because it increases employees' sense of autonomy.[88]

Negative aspects of telecommuting can result from damage to informal communication. These include decreased visibility when promotions are considered, problems in handling rush projects, and workload spillover for non-telecommuters. More frequent telecommuting also has a negative effect on relationships with co-workers.[89] Other potential problems include distractions in the home environment, feelings of isolation, and overwork. In addition, telecommuting may not be appropriate in organizations where customers are frequently at the office or where co-workers need to constantly collaborate on rush projects. Nor is telecommuting appropriate for all employees.[90]

Despite the benefits and the growing popularity of telecommuting, many companies are hesitant to implement telecommuting programs because of concerns about trust and control and worries that employees will not be as productive. Many managers are uncomfortable with the prospect of not being able to keep an eye on their employees while they work.[91] Therefore, a strong perception of trust between employees and management must exist before an organization implements a telecommuting program and the program must be preceded by careful planning and accompanied by clear guidelines to govern the arrangement.

LO **6.9**

Describe the factors that organizations should consider when choosing motivational practices.

MOTIVATION PRACTICES IN PERSPECTIVE

As we have illustrated in this chapter, organizations have a lot of options when it comes to motivating their employees. Confused about what they should do?

As we indicated in Chapter 1, there are no simple formulas to improve employee attitudes and performance, nor is there a set of laws of organizational behaviour that can be used to solve organizational problems. Like all of organizational behaviour, when it comes to employee motivation, there is no "cookbook" to follow. Thus, while many of the best companies to work for in Canada use the motivational practices described in this chapter, this does not mean that these practices will always be effective or that other organizations should follow suit. Clearly, the motivational practices used by the best companies are effective because they *fit* in to and are part of a larger organizational culture and system of management practices. For example, the motivational practices of EllisDon described at the beginning of the chapter are part of an organizational culture that fosters entrepreneurship and employee ownership.

The choice of motivational practices requires a thorough diagnosis of the organization and the needs and desires of employees. The most effective approach will depend on a combination of factors, including employee needs (e.g., money and challenging work), the nature of the job (e.g., individual or group work), characteristics of the organization (e.g., strategy and culture), and the outcome that an organization wants to achieve (e.g., diversity and learning). Ultimately, motivational systems that make use of a variety of motivators—such as performance-based pay and job enrichment—used in conjunction with one another are likely to be most effective.[92]

■ THE MANAGER'S NOTEBOOK ■

The "Money for Nothing" Merit Pay System

1. There are a number of problems with the merit pay and bonus system at Toronto City Hall. For starters, almost everybody eligible for merit not only receives it but they receive the maximum permitted. This of course means that merit pay is not tied to performance. A related issue is that the performance review process is not discriminating levels of performance. Managers are either unable or unwilling to discriminate between good performers and poor performers. As a result, most employees are rated as equal performers. Thus, the system over-rewards poor performers and under-rewards the best performers. All this suggests that the merit pay system is not having the intended motivational effects and, like most merit pay systems, is ineffective. The system has been described as broken because almost everyone at the top pay rate receives the 3 percent bonus so there is no motivation to work harder. As a result, the system does not reward high-performing employees any differently than average or satisfactory performers.

2. For the City of Toronto's merit pay program to be effective it must be tied to performance. There must be a performance evaluation system that requires managers to discriminate between good and poor performers. The system must clearly indicate the criteria for merit pay, and it should be given only to those employees who meet or exceed the criteria. As stated by Deputy Mayor Doug Holyday, the system should be revamped for everyone, not just senior management, and merit pay should go only to exceptional employees. Giving it to everybody makes a mockery of the concept, according to Holyday. Councillor Peter Milczyn said that merit pay should be awarded only for "extraordinary achievement," such as a project that saves the city money. The bonus was suspended in 2009 to cut costs and in 2012 the employee and labour relations committee proposed a merit pay system that will hand out bonuses ranging from 0 percent to 5 percent depending on employees' annual performance. It was recommended that senior managers who exceed expectations receive a 5 percent bonus. According to Human Resources staff, up to 20 percent of managers will make the 5 percent bonus; 70 percent who meet expectations will get a 2.5 percent bonus; and those who meet most expectations will receive a 1 percent bonus. The city's employee and labour relations committee was told that the bonuses should be reinstated to give managers a performance incentive. According to Holyday, the bonuses must be re-earned each year by meeting or exceeding job expectations. However, in July of 2012 city council lowered the proposed merit pay from 5 percent for those exceeding expectations to 3 percent and to 2 percent for those meeting expectations.

MyManagementLab　Visit MyManagementLab at **www.mymanagementlab .com** for access to online tutorials, interactive exercises, videos, and much more.

LEARNING OBJECTIVES CHECKLIST

6.1 Money should be most effective as a motivator when it is made contingent on performance. Schemes to link pay to performance on production jobs are called *wage incentive plans*. *Piece-rate*, in which workers are paid a certain amount of money for each item produced, is the prototype of all wage incentive plans. In general, wage incentives increase productivity, but their introduction can be accompanied by a number of problems, one of which is the restriction of production.

6.2 Attempts to link pay to performance on white-collar jobs are called *merit pay plans*. Evidence suggests that many merit pay plans are less effective than they could be because merit pay is inadequate, performance ratings are mistrusted, or extreme secrecy about pay levels prevails.

6.3 Compensation plans to enhance teamwork include *profit sharing, employee stock ownership plans, gainsharing,* and *skill-based pay*. Each of these plans has a different motivational focus, so organizations must choose a plan that supports their strategic needs.

6.4 Recent views advocate increasing the scope (breadth and depth) of jobs to capitalize on their inherent motivational properties, as opposed to the job simplification of the past. The *Job Characteristics Model*, developed by Hackman and Oldham, suggests that jobs have five core characteristics that affect their motivating potential: *skill variety, task identity, task significance, autonomy,* and *feedback*. When jobs are high in these characteristics, favourable motivational and attitudinal consequences should result.

6.5 Job enrichment involves designing jobs to enhance intrinsic motivation, job involvement, and the quality of working life. Some specific enrichment techniques include combining tasks, establishing client relationships, reducing supervision and reliance on others, forming work teams, and making feedback more direct.

6.6 In recent years, more comprehensive models of job design have been developed that go beyond the core job characteristics and include other important work design characteristics. *Work design characteristics* refer to the attributes of the task, job, and social and organizational environment. The *relational architecture of jobs* refers to the structural properties of work that shape employees' opportunities to connect and interact with other people. The basic idea is that jobs can be designed to connect employees to those who benefit from their work, so that employees can see the impact of their actions on others.

6.7 *Management by Objectives (MBO)* is an elaborate goal-setting and evaluation process that organizations typically use for management jobs. Objectives for the organization as a whole are developed by top management and diffused down through the organization and translated into specific behavioural objectives for individual members.

6.8 Some organizations have adopted alternative working schedules, such as *flex-time, compressed workweeks, job and work sharing,* or *telecommuting,* with expectations of motivational benefits. These schemes have the potential to reduce absenteeism and turnover and to enhance the quality of working life for a diverse workforce.

6.9 Organizations need to conduct a diagnostic evaluation to determine the motivational practices that will be most effective. This requires a consideration of employee needs, the nature of the job, organizational characteristics, and the outcome that is of most concern to the organization.

DISCUSSION QUESTIONS

1. Describe some jobs for which you think it would be difficult to link pay to performance. What is it about these jobs that provokes this difficulty?

2. Why do you think employees and managers seriously underestimate the importance of pay as a motivator? What are the implications of this for organizations' use of pay to motivate employees? What are the consequences?

3. Imagine two insurance companies that have merit pay plans for salaried, white-collar employees. In one organization, the plan truly rewards good performers, while in the other it does not. Both companies decide to make salaries completely public. What will be the consequences of such a change for each company? (Be specific, using concepts such as expectancy, instrumentality, job satisfaction, and turnover.)

4. You are, of course, familiar with the annual lists of the world's 10 worst-dressed people or 10 worst movies. Here's a new one: A job enrichment consultant has developed a list of the 10 worst jobs, which includes a highway toll collector, roofer, bank guard, garbage collector, and elevator operator. Use the five core job characteristics to describe each of these jobs. Could you enrich any of these jobs? How? Which should be completely automated? Can you add some jobs to the list?

5. What are the essential distinctions between gainsharing, profit sharing, and employee stock ownership plans? How effective is each pay plan, and what are the advantages and disadvantages?

6. Some observers have argued that the jobs of the prime minister of Canada and the president of the United States are "too big" for one person to perform adequately. This probably means that the jobs are perceived as having too much scope or being too enriched. Use the Job Characteristics Model to explore the accuracy of this observation.

7. Imagine an office setting in which a change to a four-day workweek, flex-time, or telecommuting would appear to be equally feasible to introduce. What would be the pros and cons of each system? How would factors such as the nature of the business, the age of the workforce, and the average commuting distance affect the choice of systems?

8. How is the concept of workforce diversity related to the motivational techniques discussed in the chapter?

9. Although an increasing number of organizations are offering their employees the opportunity to telecommute, many employees who have tried it don't like it and prefer to be in the workplace. Why do you think some employees do not want to telecommute and some have even returned to the workplace after trying it? What can organizations do to ensure that employees' telecommuting experiences are successful?

10. Refer to the work design characteristics in Exhibit 6.7. What work design characteristics are most important for you and why? If you were to redesign the job you currently hold or a job you have previously held, what work design characteristics would you change?

11. Incentive compensation plans are believed to have a number of advantages for organizations. However, they can also have negative consequences for employees and organizations. Discuss how the design of compensation programs can lead to inappropriate and unethical behaviours. How should incentive compensation programs be designed to encourage positive behaviours and discourage negative ones?

12. What is the relational architecture of jobs and why is this important for job design? Discuss your current or most recent job in terms of its relational architecture. How can the relational architecture of your job be improved and what effect would this have on your motivation?

INTEGRATIVE DISCUSSION QUESTIONS

1. Merit pay plans often require managers to conduct performance evaluations of their employees to determine the amount of merit pay to be awarded. Discuss some of the perceptual problems and biases described in Chapter 3 that could create problems for a merit pay plan. What can be done to improve performance evaluations and the success of merit pay plans?

2. Using each of the motivation theories described in Chapter 5, explain how job design and job enrichment can be motivational. According to each theory, when is job design and job enrichment most likely to be effective for motivating workers?

3. In Chapter 2, employee recognition programs were discussed as an organizational learning practice. Using the material presented in this chapter, describe the potential for employee recognition programs to be used as a motivational practice. What aspects of employee recognition programs might be especially important for a motivational program?

ON-THE-JOB CHALLENGE QUESTION

Profit Sharing or Hourly Wages?

Ken Lewenza, president of the Canadian Auto Workers union (CAW) says the union is under pressure from Chrysler, Ford, and General Motors to accept performance pay and bonuses rather than across-the-board salary increases. He said the automakers want the recent deal made with auto workers in the United Sates to be the model to follow in Canada.

In the United States, the United Auto Workers union accepted a deal that links pay to company performance in its last two contracts in lieu of higher hourly wages. However, Lewenza says his union remains firmly opposed to the concept of profit sharing. "We have managed to resist what we call gimmick pay…I want us to stick to the traditional way of compensating workers, with no gimmicks attached," he said. "At the end of the day our position is pretty entrenched. The best way to improve compensation for our members is through hourly increases in wages."

Do you agree that profit sharing is "gimmick" pay and the best way to improve compensation for autoworkers is through hourly wage increases? What are the implications of these two pay strategies for employee motivation? What are the implications of each strategy for employees, the union, and the automakers? What are the advantages and disadvantages for all concerned? What do you think is the best pay strategy? Explain your answer.

Sources: Van Alphen, T. (2010, December 9). CAW cool to sharing in profits. *Toronto Star*, B1, B2; (2012, March 7). CAW continues to reject profit-sharing but says it faces intense pressure from Detroit Three to accept deal like UAW's. *The Windsor Star*, blogs.windsorstar.com/2012/03/07/caw-continues-to-reject-profit-sharing-but-says-…

EXPERIENTIAL EXERCISE

Task Characteristics Scale

How would you describe your job? The questions below are from the Work Design Questionnaire (WDQ). They provide you the opportunity to evaluate the task characteristics of the job you currently hold or one you have held in the past. For each question, indicate the extent to which you agree or disagree. Alternatively, you can use this scale to assess your task characteristics preferences by replacing the beginning of each question with "I would like a job that allows me to…"

Use the following response scale when answering each question.

1–Strongly disagree

2–Disagree

3–Neither disagree nor agree

4–Agree

5–Strongly agree

____ 1. The job allows me to make my own decisions about how to schedule my work.

____ 2. The job allows me to decide on the order in which things are done on the job.

____ 3. The job allows me to plan how I do my work.

____ 4. The job gives me a chance to use my personal initiative or judgment in carrying out the work.

____ 5. The job allows me to make a lot of decisions on my own.

____ 6. The job provides me with significant autonomy in making decisions.

____ 7. The job allows me to make decisions about what methods I use to complete my work.

____ 8. The job gives me considerable opportunity for independence and freedom in how I do the work.

____ 9. The job allows me to decide on my own how to go about doing my work.

____ 10. The job involves a great deal of task variety.

____ 11. The job involves doing a number of different things.

____ 12. The job requires the performance of a wide range of tasks.

____ 13. The job involves performing a variety of tasks.

____ 14. The results of my work are likely to significantly affect the lives of other people.

____ 15. The job itself is very significant and important in the broader scheme of things.

____ 16. The job has a large impact on people outside the organization.

____ 17. The work performed on the job has a significant impact on people outside the organization.

____ 18. The job involves completing a piece of work that has an obvious beginning and end.

____ 19. The job is arranged so that I can do an entire piece of work from beginning to end.

____ 20. The job provides me the chance to completely finish the pieces of work I begin.

____ 21. The job allows me to complete work I start.

____ 22. The work activities themselves provide direct and clear information about the effectiveness (e.g., quality and quantity) of my job performance.

____ 23. The job itself provides feedback on my performance.

____ 24. The job itself provides me with information about my performance.

Scoring and Interpretation

You have just completed the task characteristics scales of the Work Design Questionnaire (WDQ). A study of a sample of 540 individuals who had at least 10 years of full-time work experience resulted in the following mean scores for each task characteristic (scores range from 1 to 5; note that there are three different scales for autonomy: work scheduling autonomy, decision-making autonomy, and work methods autonomy):

Work scheduling autonomy:	3.93
Decision-making autonomy:	4.12
Work methods autonomy:	3.99
Task variety:	4.13
Task significance:	3.95
Task identity:	3.61
Feedback from the job:	3.91

To obtain your score on each task characteristic, calculate your scores as shown below. Note that your scores can range from 1 to 5, with higher scores indicating a greater amount of the task characteristic in your job (or in the case of preferences, a greater preference for the task characteristic).

Work scheduling autonomy: Add items 1, 2, and 3 and divide by three.

Decision-making autonomy: Add items 4, 5, and 6 and divide by three.

Work methods autonomy: Add items 7, 8, and 9 and divide by three.

(Note that you can obtain an overall score of autonomy by adding your score for questions 1 to 9 and dividing by nine).

Task variety: Add items 10, 11, 12, and 13 and divide by four.

Task significance: Add items 14, 15, 16, and 17 and divide by four.

Task identity: Add items 18, 19, 20, and 21 and divide by four.

Feedback from job: Add items 22, 23, and 24 and divide by three.

Source: Morgeson, F.P., & Humphrey, S.E. (2006). The work design questionnaire (WDQ): Developing and validating a comprehensive measure for assessing job design and the nature of work. *Journal of Applied Psychology, 91*, 1321–1339. Copyright © 2006 by the American Psychological Association. Reproduced with permission.

To facilitate class discussion and your understanding of the task characteristics and job design, form a small group with several other members of the class and consider the following questions:

1. Each group member should present his or her score on each task characteristic. What task characteristics do group members score high and low on? Is there any consistency among group members in terms of the highest and lowest task characteristics? (Note: If you answered the question in terms of task characteristics preferences, discuss your highest and lowest preferences).

2. Each group member should describe his or her job and provide specific examples of what contributes to their task characteristics scores. What is it about the job that contributes to a high or low score on each task characteristic? (Note: If you answered the question in terms of task characteristics preferences, discuss your ideal job based on your task characteristics scores. Be specific in terms of how you would like your job to be designed).

3. Consider your job attitudes (e.g., job satisfaction and organizational commitment) and behaviours (e.g., job performance, absenteeism, and intention to quit) in terms of your task characteristics scores. To what extent do the task characteristics contribute to your job attitudes and behaviours? (Note: If you answered the question in terms of task characteristics preferences, describe how the task characteristics might influence your job attitudes and behaviours. What task characteristics do you think would be most important for you and why?)

4. If you could redesign your job, what task characteristics would you focus on? What exactly would you do to redesign your job? Be specific in terms of how your job would change. What effect do you think these changes would have on your job attitudes and behaviours? (Note: If you answered the question in terms of task characteristics preferences, discuss how knowledge of your task characteristics scores can assist you in your job search, questions you will ask interviewers, and your job choice decision. How will knowledge of your task characteristics preferences assist in you in the future?)

5. What have you learned about job design and task characteristics? How can you use this information as an employee and as a manager?

CASE INCIDENT

The Junior Accountant

After graduating from business school, Sabrita received a job offer from a large accounting firm to work as a junior accountant. She was ranked in the top 10 of her class and could not have been happier.

During the first six months, however, Sabrita began to reconsider her decision to join a large firm. This is how she described her job: Every day her supervisor brought several files for her to audit. He told her exactly in what order to do them and how to plan her day and work. At the end of the day, the supervisor would return to pick up the completed files. The supervisor collected the files from several other junior accountants and put them all together and completed the audit himself. The supervisor would then meet the client to review and discuss the audit. Sabrita did not ever meet the clients, and her supervisor never talked about his meeting with them or the final report.

Sabrita felt very discouraged and wanted to quit. She was even beginning to reconsider her choice of accounting as a career.

1. Describe the job characteristics and critical psychological states of Sabrita's job. According to the Job Characteristics Model, how motivated is Sabrita and what is the effect on her job attitudes and behaviours?

2. Evaluate Sabrita's job on each of the work design characteristics described in Exhibit 6.7. What work design characteristics are particularly low? Based on your evaluation, what factors do you

think are contributing to Sabrita's attitudes and intention to quit?

3. How would you redesign Sabrita's job to increase its motivating potential? Be sure to describe changes you would make to the work design characteristics as well as job enrichment schemes that you might use to redesign her job.

CASE STUDY

Chang Koh Metal Ptd. Ltd. in China

Chang Koh Metal Ptd. Ltd. was founded in Singapore in 1982 by Teo Kai San, a first generation Straits-born Chinese. The company's operations were in the production of metal-stamping precision parts. In 1993, the company expanded its operations by establishing a plant in Putian, China, the area of China from which Teo Kai San's parents had emigrated. The founder's son, Andrew Teo, was appointed as general manager.

Andrew was 29 years old and had an engineering degree from the National University of Singapore. Prior to joining his father's company, Andrew had worked for an American multinational company in Singapore and had progressed to the rank of line manager, a position with substantial authority and responsibility. Andrew joined his father's company because he felt that his success in the multinational was a sign of his skills, indicating that he deserved a senior position in his father's company on the basis of merit rather than family connections. He also felt that the systems and practices he had learned at the multinational would enable him to bring more updated management practices to Chang Koh Metal.

Since Andrew's father believed it was important to have in a position of authority a person who was knowledgeable about the local area, he appointed a relative from Putian, Jian Wei, as the plant manager to assist Andrew in the plant's operations. A primary reason for choosing China as the site for a plant was the belief that Singaporean Chinese should find it easy to work with the Chinese in China. After all, the two groups shared a common cultural heritage. The other advantages were the readily available supply of labour—Singapore was experiencing full employment, and the company found it difficult to recruit qualified production workers—and the lower operating costs.

After a year in China, however, Andrew was not sure the plan to venture there had been wise. Although the labour costs were much lower than in Singapore, productivity was disappointing, and a number of management and labour problems had arisen, which he felt were frustrating his efforts to control the plant efficiently.

Staffing Procedure

Andrew had learned from his previous work experience that it was important to hire the right people with the appropriate qualifications and place them in the positions to which they were best suited in order to ensure smooth operations. But his efforts were hindered by Jian Wei's peculiar hiring practices.

To fill open positions, Jian Wei would contact city officials and friends and relatives and ask them for recommendations on whom to hire. Most of the time the people hired did not have the skills needed to perform the tasks for which they were hired. Andrew vigorously protested against Jian Wei's practices and instituted formalized procedures to follow in recruitment and selection that called for systematic advertising of positions, evaluation of candidates, and hiring based on qualifications. Jian Wei became upset because he argued that his practices were necessary as a way to keep the channels of communication and mutual exchange open with important officials because the company might need their help in future business dealings. This disagreement created tension between the two men.

Productivity and Quality Issues

The plant in China employed about 150 workers. Andrew adopted the same salary system as he had seen used by his former employer and paid these workers a fixed salary based on the number of hours worked. However, their productivity rates were very low, and the workers demonstrated very little commitment to meeting the company's goals.

After three months, Andrew scrapped the salary system and instead instituted a piece-rate system in which the workers were paid a minimum base salary supplemented by an incremental rate for each unit produced above a certain number. In other words, if the workers produced at or below the minimum production standard for the day, they received the minimum wage. If they produced above that rate, they received additional money for each extra piece produced.

For the following two months, Andrew was proud of his innovative management because the results were impressive. Company productivity targets were met, the workers were exerting themselves energetically, and they were even willing to work overtime at the same rate as the usual work day in order to make extra money. However, within a short period of time, he began to receive several complaints from customers about the low quality of the goods they were receiving from the company. Parts that should have been rejected were instead shipped to customers.

In response, Andrew had the quality control and manufacturing specifications printed on large posters and posted around the plant for all to see. He set up a quality control department and implemented 100 percent quality checks. However, all these efforts failed to stop poor-quality products from reaching the customers.

As he investigated, he discovered that those in the quality control department were inspecting the parts but were passing almost everything that they inspected. He held a training session for the quality control inspectors, pointed out defective parts to them, and had them demonstrate to him that they could distinguish poor quality from good quality. Since it was clear that they could do so, he sent them back to the production floor, convinced that they would now begin to perform as a true quality control unit. Yet within a short period of time it became apparent that the unit was not doing the job any better than it had before the training session.

Andrew expressed his frustration to Jian Wei and demanded that he take action to improve the situation. Jian Wei protested that the quality control members' actions were completely understandable—they knew that rejected parts would not be added to the total that would count toward the incentive rate compensation and would therefore reduce the wages production workers would receive. They would not take money out of the pockets of the production workers.

Andrew felt that the quality control workers should be shown that failure to act would take money out of their own pockets, so he suggested that a system of demerit points be set up for the quality control employees that would lead to deductions from their wages. However, Jian Wei strongly disagreed with the idea, arguing that it was unfair to penalize these employees for doing what they believed was right.

Finally, a compromise was reached in which more supervisors were hired for the quality control department to provide closer supervision of the workers. In addition, Andrew arranged to have all final products shipped to Singapore for final inspection before they were sent out to customers.

Rules and Regulations

About 15 technicians were responsible for the maintenance of machinery. At any one time, one machine would be set aside for maintenance work. Ninety percent of the time, a machine that was designated as "in maintenance" actually sat unused.

To Andrew's dismay, he found that the technicians regularly used the "in maintenance" machine to do moonlighting work to make extra income. To Andrew, this practice was a clear violation of company rules and regulations, a fact that warranted dismissal of the supervisor of the technicians, who had not only condoned the activity but had actually participated in it.

Jian Wei supported the employees. He argued that the machine would have been left idle anyway, so what was the harm? All activities were conducted outside normal working hours, and the technicians' jobs were not being neglected. No additional costs were incurred by the factory, except in the operation of the machine. Jian Wei thought that, as boss, Andrew needed to show much more understanding and sensitivity to the issue than he had. It was unfair to single out one person for punishment, especially when the company had not suffered any losses. In addition, Jian Wei was dismayed to hear Andrew talk about dismissing an employee. He said that such practice just was not done in China—no true Chinese person would think about removing a person's "iron rice bowl." Reluctantly, Andrew agreed to Jian Wei's recommendation to resolve the issue by transferring the technicians' supervisor to another department.

Problems like these made Andrew very doubtful that the operation in China could ever be turned into a profitable venture. His father had been willing to grant Andrew some time to get the plant up and running before he expected results, but now he was starting to ask questions about why the plant was still losing money and why no trend in the direction of profitability was evident in the financial performance figures. He had recently asked Andrew to come up with a concrete plan to turn the situation around. Andrew was wondering what he could do.

Source: Begley, T. (1998). Chang Koh Metal Ptd. Ltd. In China. In G. Oddou and M. Mendenhall (Eds.), *Cases in International Organizational Behaviour*. Reprinted by permission of John Wiley & Sons, Inc.

QUESTIONS

1. Comment on the fixed salary system that Andrew adopted from his former employer. Why was this system not effective for motivating the plant workers?

2. Do you think that scrapping the fixed salary system and replacing it with the piece-rate system was a good idea? What are some of the strengths and weaknesses of the piece-rate system?

3. Why was Andrew unsuccessful in his efforts to improve product quality? Do you think that a system of demerit points and wage deductions for the quality control workers would have been effective? Would having more supervisors in the quality control department and shipping products to Singapore for final inspection solve the problem? What do you think would be an effective way to improve product quality?

4. Were cross-cultural differences a factor in the effectiveness of the salary systems? How effective do you think each system would have been if the plant was located in North America?

5. Discuss the potential effects of implementing an MBO program in the plant. Do you think it would improve productivity and solve some of the problems?

6. Are there any conditions under which the piece-rate system might have been more effective?

7. What are some alternative ways to use pay to motivate the workers at the plant? Are there alternatives to the piece-rate system? How effective are they likely to be? What does this case say about using money as a motivator?

8. What should Andrew do now? What would you do?

INTEGRATIVE CASE

Deloitte & Touche: Integrating Arthur Andersen

At the end of Chapter 1 you were introduced to the Deloitte & Touche: Integrating Arthur Andersen Integrative Case. The case questions focused on issues pertaining to the relevance and goals of organizational behaviour, managerial roles, and contemporary management concerns. Now that you have completed Part 2 of the text and the chapters on Individual Behaviour, you can return to the Integrative Case and focus on issues related to learning, perceptions, fairness and job attitudes, motivation, and pay plans by answering the following questions.

QUESTIONS

1. How important is learning for the successful integration of the two firms? What do employees need to learn and what organizational learning practices should be used? Be sure to consider the use and application of each of the organizational learning practices described in Chapter 2.

2. Consider the perceptions held by employees of both firms. To what extent are person perception biases affecting these perceptions? What are the implications of these perceptions for the integration of the two firms and what does the integration team need to do?

3. Use social identity theory to explain the perceptions that employees at each firm have of themselves and those at the other firm. According to social identity theory, what does the integration team need to understand and what should they do?

4. Consider the role of trust and perceived organizational support (POS) in the case. How

important are they for the successful integration of the two firms and to what extent do employees at each firm have positive perceptions of trust and organizational support? What should the integration team and management do to create positive perceptions of trust and organizational support?

5. Discuss in detail how issues of fairness are relevant to this case. Do you expect that distributive, procedural, or interactional fairness is most important here? Please be sure to consider both the current Deloitte personnel and the incoming Andersen personnel.

6. Speculate about how mood and emotion might have figured in the case events. Was there a need for emotional regulation?

7. Consider the job satisfaction and organizational commitment of the Andersen employees.

What should the integration team focus on if they want the Andersen employees to be satisfied with their new jobs, committed to their new organization, and willing to stay rather than quit? What about the Deloitte & Touche employees?

8. Discuss the relevance of motivation in the case. How important is motivation and describe what employees need to be motivated to do and how to motivate them to do it. Explain how each of the theories of motivation can be used to motivate employees.

9. Do you think the integration team should consider using money to motivate employees? What kind of pay plan would you recommend and why? What other motivational practices would you recommend for the successful integration of the two firms? Explain your answer.

PART 3

SOCIAL BEHAVIOUR AND ORGANIZATIONAL PROCESSES

7 **Groups and Teamwork**

8 **Social Influence, Socialization, and Organizational Culture**

9 **Leadership**

10 **Communication**

11 **Decision Making**

12 **Power, Politics, and Ethics**

13 **Conflict and Stress**

GROUPS AND TEAMWORK

LEARNING OBJECTIVES

After reading Chapter 7, you should be able to:

7.1 Define *groups* and distinguish between *formal* and *informal* groups.

7.2 Discuss group development.

7.3 Explain how group size and member diversity influence what occurs in groups.

7.4 Review how *norms*, *roles*, and *status* affect social interaction.

7.5 Discuss the causes and consequences of *group cohesiveness*.

7.6 Explain the dynamics of *social loafing*.

7.7 Discuss how to design and support *self-managed teams*.

7.8 Explain the logic behind *cross-functional teams* and describe how they can operate effectively.

7.9 Understand *virtual teams* and what makes them effective.

IDEO

IDEO is considered to be one of the most innovative and influential global design and innovation consultancy firms in the world. IDEO has received numerous domestic and international awards for design excellence, including 38 Red Dot awards and 28 iF Hanover awards. Signature products have included the first Apple computer mouse, Nike sunglasses, and the Steelcase Node chair.

With offices in major cities in the U.S., Europe, and Asia, IDEO employs people working on projects for clients ranging from startups to premier organizations in food and beverage (Nestlé), retail (Target), philanthropy (Oxfam), telecommunications (Nokia), computing (Microsoft), medicine (Mayo Clinic), banking (Bank of America), and manufacturing (Ford Motor Company).

As a design firm, IDEO uses an approach that relies heavily on interdisciplinary project teams. For example, for a Kentucky-based project headed by The Community Builders, the largest nonprofit developer of public housing in the U.S., an IDEO team was assembled consisting of anthropologists, architects, psychologists, and industrial designers. To accomplish their mandate, team members interviewed builders, urban planners, municipal authorities, and service providers. The real insights, however, occurred when the team broke into groups to stay overnight with three families from Park DuValle, a mixed-income community in Louisville. By doing so, the team was able to uncover the latent needs of home dwellers whose income levels and life trajectories were vastly different from one another.

Since the challenges facing IDEO are complex, assembling the right teams is critical to ensuring its success. In his book *Change by Design*, CEO Tim Brown suggests that a popular saying throughout the company – "All of us are smarter than any of us" – is purportedly what drives the company's insistence on a collective ownership of ideas. Staffing a project with teammates from a multiplicity of disciplines takes patience, however. To become part of an IDEO team, an individual must possess not only depth in the skill required to make a tangible contribution, but also

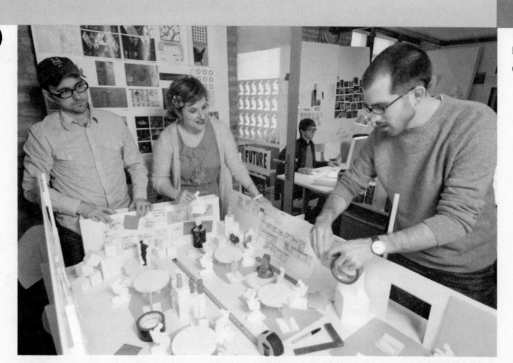

IDEO design team. Image courtesy of IDEO.

a capacity for handling role ambiguity and a disposition for collaborating with others across fields. Several best practices are therefore instilled to provide the firm with guidance in designing effective teams.

First, since new teams are marshaled for every project, team members must be passionate about the project they are assigned to. Without passion, IDEO believes that the motivation needed to generate creative solutions will be absent.

Second, status differences between team members are eliminated because IDEO considers hierarchy as stifling to innovation. As such, formal position titles on business cards and segregated corner offices are rejected because they impose mental and physical barriers between teams and individuals. Another element minimizing employee status differences and facilitating virtual communication is the company's intranet, known widely as "The Tube." Considered to be the centerpiece of how IDEO interacts as a global organization, The Tube encourages teams to collaborate and share their passions and expertise through social-networking tools such as blogs, wikis, and real-time screen sharing.

An innovation project with a dedicated beginning, middle, and end is more likely to keep the team motivated and focused on moving forward. Since clients may unnecessarily delay their engagement after the presentation of a consultant's report, IDEO encourages its client to participate in all aspects of the team's research, analysis, and development process. Unlike many traditional design consulting firms, IDEO's teams help shorten the time between conception and sale, thereby reinforcing its competitive advantage.[1]

This vignette shows how critical groups or teams are in determining organizational success. In this chapter, we will define the term *group* and discuss the nature of formal groups and informal groups in organizations. After this, we will present the details of group development. Then, we will consider how groups differ from one another structurally and explore the consequences of these differences. We will also cover the problem of social loafing. Finally, we will examine how to design effective work teams.

WHAT IS A GROUP?

LO 7.1

Define *groups* and distinguish between *formal* and *informal* groups.

Group. Two or more people interacting interdependently to achieve a common goal.

We use the word "group" rather casually in everyday discourse—for example, special-interest group or ethnic group. However, for behavioural scientists, a **group** consists of two or more people interacting interdependently to achieve a common goal.

Interaction is the most basic aspect of a group—it suggests who is in the group and who is not. The interaction of group members need not be face to face, and it need not be verbal. For example, employees who telecommute can be part of their work group at the office even though they live kilometres away and communicate via email. Interdependence simply means that group members rely to some degree on each other to accomplish goals. All groups have one or more goals that their members seek to achieve. These goals can range from having fun to marketing a new product to achieving world peace.

Group memberships are very important for two reasons. First, groups exert a tremendous influence on us. They are the social mechanisms by which we acquire many beliefs, values, attitudes, and behaviours. Group membership is also important because groups provide a context in which *we* are able to exert influence on *others*.

Formal work groups. Groups that are established by organizations to facilitate the achievement of organizational goals.

Formal work groups are groups that organizations establish to facilitate the achievement of organizational goals. They are intentionally designed to channel individual effort in an appropriate direction. The most common formal group consists of a manager and the employees who report to that manager. In a manufacturing company, one such group might consist of a production manager and the six shift supervisors who report to him or her. In turn, the shift supervisors head work groups composed of themselves and their respective subordinates. Thus, the hierarchy of most organizations is a series of formal, interlocked work groups.

Other types of formal work groups include task forces, project teams, and committees. *Task forces* and *project teams* are temporary groups that meet to achieve particular goals or to solve particular problems, such as suggesting productivity improvements. At IDEO, the design of products and services is accomplished via formal but temporary interdisciplinary project teams. *Committees* are usually permanent groups that handle recurrent assignments outside the usual work group structures. For example, a firm might have a standing committee on work–family balance.

Informal groups. Groups that emerge naturally in response to the common interests of organizational members.

In addition to formal groups sanctioned by management to achieve organizational goals, informal grouping occurs in all organizations. **Informal groups** are groups that emerge naturally in response to the common interests of organizational members. They are seldom sanctioned by the organization, and their membership often cuts across formal groups. Informal groups can either help or hurt an organization, depending on their norms for behaviour. We will consider this in detail later.

GROUP DEVELOPMENT

LO 7.2

Discuss group development.

Even relatively simple groups are actually complex social devices that require a fair amount of negotiation and trial and error before individual members begin to function as a true group. While employees often know each other before new teams are formed, simple familiarity does not replace the necessity for team development.

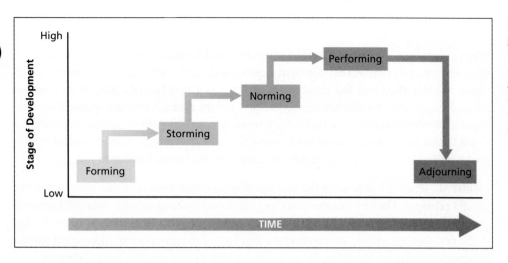

EXHIBIT 7.1 Stages of group development.

Go to MyManagementLab to see an annotated version of this figure.

Typical Stages of Group Development

Leaders and trainers have observed that many groups develop through a series of stages over time.[2] Each stage presents the members with a series of challenges they must master to achieve the next stage. These stages (forming, storming, norming, performing, and adjourning) are presented in Exhibit 7.1.

FORMING At this early stage, group members try to orient themselves by "testing the waters." What are we doing here? What are the others like? What is our purpose? The situation is often ambiguous, and members are aware of their dependency on each other.

STORMING At this second stage, conflict often emerges. Confrontation and criticism occur as members determine whether they will go along with the way the group is developing. Sorting out roles and responsibilities is often at issue here. Problems are more likely to happen earlier, rather than later, in group development.

NORMING At this stage, members resolve the issues that provoked the storming, and they develop social consensus. Compromise is often necessary. Interdependence is recognized, norms are agreed to, and the group becomes more cohesive (we will study these processes later). Information and opinions flow freely.

PERFORMING With its social structure sorted out, the group devotes its energies toward task accomplishment. Achievement, creativity, and mutual assistance are prominent themes of this stage.

ADJOURNING Some groups, such as task forces and design project teams, have a definite lifespan and disperse after achieving their goals. Also, some groups disperse when corporate layoffs and downsizing occur. At this adjourning stage, rites and rituals that affirm the group's previous successful development are common (such as ceremonies and parties). Members often exhibit emotional support for each other.[3]

The stages model is a good tool for monitoring and troubleshooting how groups are developing. However, not all groups go through these stages of development. The process applies mainly to new groups that have never met before. Well-acquainted task forces and committees can short-circuit these stages when they have a new problem to work out.[4] Also, some organizational settings are so structured that storming and norming are unnecessary for even strangers to coalesce into a team. For example, most commercial airline cockpit crews perform effectively even though they can be made up of virtual strangers who meet just before takeoff.[5]

Punctuated Equilibrium

Punctuated equilibrium model. A model of group development that describes how groups with deadlines are affected by their first meetings and crucial midpoint transitions.

When groups have a specific deadline by which to complete some problem-solving task, we can often observe a very different development sequence from that described above. Connie Gersick, whose research uncovered this sequence, describes it as a **punctuated equilibrium model** of group development.[6] *Equilibrium* means stability, and the research revealed apparent stretches of group stability punctuated by a critical first meeting, a midpoint change in group activity, and a rush to task completion. In addition to many business work groups, Gersick studied student groups doing class projects, so see if this sequence of events sounds familiar to you.

PHASE 1 Phase 1 begins with the first meeting and continues until the midpoint in the group's existence. The very first meeting is critical in setting the agenda for what will happen in the remainder of this phase. Assumptions, approaches, and precedents that members develop in the first meeting end up dominating the first half of the group's life. Although it gathers information and holds meetings, the group makes little visible progress toward the goal.

MIDPOINT TRANSITION The midpoint transition occurs at almost exactly the halfway point in time toward the group's deadline. For instance, if the group has a two-month deadline, the transition will occur at about one month. The transition marks a change in the group's approach, and how the group manages the change is critical for the group to show progress. The need to move forward is apparent, and the group may seek outside advice. This transition may consolidate previously acquired information or even mark a completely new approach, but it crystallizes the group's activities for Phase 2 just as the first meeting did for Phase 1.

PHASE 2 For better or for worse, decisions and approaches adopted at the midpoint get played out in Phase 2. It concludes with a final meeting that reveals a burst of activity and a concern for how outsiders will evaluate the product.

Exhibit 7.2 shows how the punctuated equilibrium model works for groups that successfully or unsuccessfully manage the midpoint transition.

What advice does the punctuated equilibrium model offer for managing product development teams, advertising groups, or class project groups?[7]

- Prepare carefully for the first meeting. What is decided here will strongly determine what happens in the rest of Phase 1. If you are the coach or adviser of the group, stress *motivation and excitement* about the project.
- As long as people are working, do not look for radical progress during Phase 1.
- Manage the midpoint transition carefully. Evaluate the strengths and weaknesses of the ideas that people generated in Phase 1. Clarify any questions with whoever is

EXHIBIT 7.2
The punctuated equilibrium model of group development for two groups.

Explore

Go to MyManagementLab to see an annotated version of this figure.

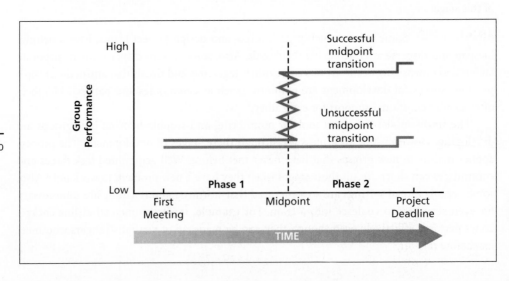

commissioning your work. Recognize that a fundamental change in approach must occur here for progress to occur. Essential issues are not likely to "work themselves out" during Phase 2. At this point, a group coach should focus on the *strategy* to be used in Phase 2.

- Be sure that adequate resources are available to actually execute the Phase 2 plan.
- Resist deadline changes. These could damage the midpoint transition.

As noted, the concept of punctuated equilibrium applies to groups with deadlines. Such groups might also exhibit some of the stages of development noted earlier, with a new cycle of storming and norming following the midpoint transition.

GROUP STRUCTURE AND ITS CONSEQUENCES

Group structure refers to the characteristics of the stable social organization of a group—the way a group is "put together." The most basic structural characteristics along which groups vary are size and member diversity. Other structural characteristics are the expectations that members have about each other's behaviour (norms), agreements about "who does what" in the group (roles), the rewards and prestige allocated to various group members (status), and how attractive the group is to its members (cohesiveness).

Group Size

LO 7.3

Explain how group size and member diversity influence what occurs in groups.

Of one thing we can be certain—the smallest possible group consists of two people, such as a manager and a particular employee. It is possible to engage in much theoretical nitpicking about just what constitutes an upper limit on group size. However, given the definition of group that we presented earlier, it would seem that congressional or parliamentary size (300 to 400 members) is somewhere close to this limit. In practice, most work groups, including task forces and committees, usually have between 3 and 20 members.

SIZE AND SATISFACTION
The more the merrier? In theory, yes. In fact, however, members of larger groups rather consistently report less satisfaction with group membership than those who find themselves in smaller groups.[8] What accounts for this apparent contradiction?

For one thing, as opportunities for friendship increase, the chance to work on and develop these opportunities might decrease owing to the sheer time and energy required. In addition, in incorporating more members with different viewpoints, larger groups might prompt conflict and dissension, which work against member satisfaction. As group size increases, the time available for verbal participation by each member decreases. Also, many people are inhibited about participating in larger groups.[9] Finally, in larger groups, individual members identify less easily with the success and accomplishments of the group. For example, a particular member of a 4-person cancer research team should be able to identify his or her personal contributions to a research breakthrough more easily than a member of a 20-person team can.

SIZE AND PERFORMANCE
Satisfaction aside, do large groups perform tasks better than small groups? This question has great relevance to practical organizational decisions: How many people should a bank assign to evaluate loan applications? How many carpenters should a construction company assign to build a garage? If a school system decides to implement team teaching, how big should the teams be? The answers to these and similar questions depend on the exact task that the group needs to accomplish and on how we define good performance.[10]

Some tasks are **additive tasks**. This means that we can predict potential performance by adding the performances of individual group members together. Building a house is an additive task, and we can estimate potential speed of construction by adding the efforts of individual carpenters. Thus, for additive tasks, the potential performance of the group increases with group size.

Additive tasks. Tasks in which group performance is dependent on the sum of the performance of individual group members.

Disjunctive tasks.
Tasks in which group performance is dependent on the performance of the best group member.

Process losses. Group performance difficulties stemming from the problems of motivating and coordinating larger groups.

Conjunctive tasks.
Tasks in which group performance is limited by the performance of the poorest group member.

Some tasks are **disjunctive tasks**. This means that the potential performance of the group depends on the performance of its *best member*. For example, suppose that a research team is looking for a single error in a complicated computer program. In this case, the performance of the team might hinge on its containing at least one bright, attentive, logical-minded individual. Obviously, the potential performance of groups doing disjunctive tasks also increases with group size because the probability that the group includes a superior performer is greater.

We use the term "potential performance" consistently in the preceding two paragraphs for the following reason: As groups performing tasks get bigger, they tend to suffer from process losses.[11] **Process losses** are performance difficulties that stem from the problems of motivating and coordinating larger groups. Even with good intentions, problems of communication and decision making increase with size—imagine 50 carpenters trying to build a house. Thus, actual performance = potential performance − process losses.

These points are summarized in Exhibit 7.3. As you can see in part (a), both potential performance and process losses increase with group size for additive and disjunctive tasks. The net effect is shown in part (b), which demonstrates that actual performance increases with size up to a point and then falls off. Part (c) shows that the *average* performance of group members decreases as size gets bigger. Thus, up to a point, larger groups might perform better as groups, but their individual members tend to be less efficient.

We should note one other kind of task. **Conjunctive tasks** are those in which the performance of the group is limited by its *poorest performer*. For example, an assembly-line operation is limited by its weakest link. Also, if team teaching is the technique used to train employees how to perform a complicated, sequential job, one poor teacher in the sequence will severely damage the effectiveness of the team. Both the potential and actual performance of conjunctive tasks would decrease as group size increases because the probability of including a weak link in the group goes up.

EXHIBIT 7.3
Relationships among group size, productivity, and process losses.
Source: From Steiner, I.D. (1972). *Group process and productivity.* New York: Academic Press, p. 96. Copyright © 1972.

✳─Explore

Go to MyManagementLab to see an annotated version of this figure.

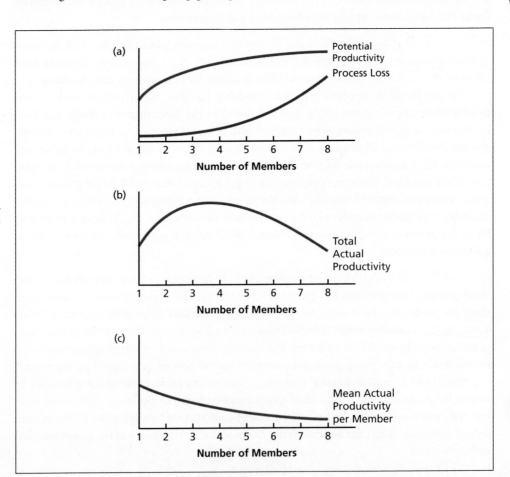

In summary, for additive and disjunctive tasks, larger groups might perform better up to a point but at increasing costs to the efficiency of individual members. By any standard, performance on purely conjunctive tasks should decrease as group size increases.

Diversity of Group Membership

Imagine an eight-member product development task force composed exclusively of 30-something white males of Western European heritage. Then imagine another task force with 50 percent men and 50 percent women from eight different ethnic or racial backgrounds and an age range from 25 to 55. The first group is obviously homogeneous in its membership, while the latter is heterogeneous or diverse. Which task force do you think would develop more quickly as a group? Which would be most creative?

Group diversity has a strong impact on interaction patterns—more diverse groups have a more difficult time communicating effectively and becoming cohesive (we will study cohesiveness in more detail shortly).[12] This means that diverse groups might tend to take longer to do their forming, storming, and norming.[13] Once they do develop, more and less diverse groups can be equally cohesive and productive.[14] However, diverse groups sometimes perform better on certain tasks. For example, diversity in educational background and functional specialty (e.g., marketing versus product design) enhances team creativity and innovation because a wider variety of ideas are considered.[15] In general, any negative effects of "surface diversity" in age, gender, or race are small or wear off over time. For instance, age diversity is unrelated to group performance, while racial and gender diversity have small negative effects.[16] However, "deep diversity" in attitudes toward work or how to accomplish a goal can badly damage cohesiveness.[17]

All this speaks well for the concepts of valuing and managing diversity, which we discussed in Chapter 3. When management values and manages diversity, it offsets some of the initial process loss costs of diversity and capitalizes on its benefits for group performance.

Group Norms

Social **norms** are collective expectations that members of social units have regarding the behaviour of each other. As such, they are codes of conduct that specify what individuals ought and ought not to do and standards against which we evaluate the appropriateness of behaviour.

Much normative influence is unconscious, and we are often aware of such influence only in special circumstances, such as when we see children struggling to master adult norms or international visitors sparring with the norms of our culture. We also become conscious of norms when we encounter ones that seem to conflict with each other ("Get ahead" but "Don't step on others") or when we enter new social situations. For instance, the first day on a new job, workers frequently search for cues about what is considered proper office etiquette: Should I call the boss "mister"? Can I personalize my workspace?

NORM DEVELOPMENT *Why* do norms develop? The most important function that norms serve is to provide regularity and predictability to behaviour. This consistency provides important psychological security and permits us to carry out our daily business with minimal disruption.

What do norms develop *about?* Norms develop to regulate behaviours that are considered at least marginally important to their supporters. For example, managers are more likely to adopt norms regarding the performance and attendance of employees than norms concerning how employees personalize and decorate their offices. In general, less deviation is accepted from norms that concern more important behaviours.

How do norms develop? As we discussed in Chapter 4, individuals develop attitudes as a function of a related belief and value. In many cases, their attitudes affect their behaviour. When the members of a group *share* related beliefs and values, we can expect them to share consequent attitudes. These shared attitudes then form the basis for norms.[18] Notice that it

LO 7.4

Review how *norms*, *roles*, and *status* affect social interaction.

Norms. Collective expectations that members of social units have regarding the behaviour of each other.

really does not make sense to talk about "my personal norm." Norms are *collectively* held expectations, depending on two or more people for their existence.

Why do individuals tend to comply with norms? Much compliance occurs simply because the norm corresponds to privately held attitudes. In addition, even when norms support trivial social niceties (such as when to shake hands or when to look serious), they often save time and prevent social confusion. Most interesting, however, is the case in which individuals comply with norms that *go against* their privately held attitudes and opinions. For example, couples without religious convictions frequently get married in religious services, and people who hate neckties often wear them to work. In short, groups have an extraordinary range of rewards and punishments available to induce conformity to norms.

SOME TYPICAL NORMS   There are some classes of norms that seem to crop up in most organizations and affect the behaviour of members. They include the following:

- *Dress norms.* Social norms frequently dictate the kind of clothing people wear to work.[19] Military and quasi-military organizations tend to invoke formal norms that support polished buttons and razor-sharp creases. Even in organizations that have adopted casual dress policies, employees often express considerable concern about what they wear at work. Such is the power of social norms.

- *Reward allocation norms.* There are at least four norms that might dictate how rewards, such as pay, promotions, and informal favours could be allocated in organizations:

  a. Equity—reward according to inputs, such as effort, performance, or seniority.

  b. Equality—reward everyone equally.

  c. Reciprocity—reward people the way they reward you.

  d. Social responsibility—reward those who truly need the reward.[20]

  Most Western organizations tend to stress allocation according to some combination of equity and equality—give employees what they deserve, and no favouritism.

- *Performance norms.* The performance of organizational members might be as much a function of social expectations as it is of inherent ability, personal motivation, or technology.[21] Work groups provide their members with potent cues about what an appropriate level of performance is. New group members are alert for these cues: Is it all right to take a break now? Under what circumstances can I be absent from work without being punished? (See the Research Focus: *Absence Cultures—Norms in Action.*) The official organizational norms that managers send to employees usually favour high performance. However, work groups often establish their own informal performance norms, such as those that restrict productivity under a piece-rate pay system. In accordance with the discussion in Chapter 5, groups that set specific, challenging goals will perform at a high level.[22]

Roles

Roles. Positions in a group that have a set of expected behaviours attached to them.

Roles are positions in a group that have a set of expected behaviours attached to them. Thus, roles represent "packages" of norms that apply to particular group members. As we implied in the previous section, many norms apply to all group members to be sure that they engage in *similar* behaviours (such as restricting productivity or dressing a certain way). However, the development of roles is indicative of the fact that group members might also be required to act *differently* from one another.

In organizations, we find two basic kinds of roles. Designated or *assigned roles* are formally prescribed by an organization as a means of dividing labour and responsibility to facilitate task achievement. In general, assigned roles indicate "who does what" and "who can tell others what to do." In a software firm, labels that we might apply to formal roles include president, software engineer, analyst, programmer, and sales manager. In addition to assigned

RESEARCH FOCUS

ABSENCE CULTURES—NORMS IN ACTION

On first thought, you might assume that absenteeism from work is a very individualized behaviour, a product of random sickness or of personal job dissatisfaction. Although these factors contribute to absenteeism, there is growing evidence that group norms also have a strong impact on how much work people miss.

We can see cross-national differences in absenteeism. Traditionally, absence has been rather high in Scandinavia, lower in the United States and Canada, and lower yet in Japan and Switzerland. Clearly, these differences are not due to sickness but rather to differences in cultural values about the legitimacy of taking time off work. These differences get reflected in work group norms.

Within the same country and company we can still see group differences in absenteeism. A company that Gary Johns studied had four plants that made the same products and had identical human resources policies. Despite this, one plant had a 12 percent absence rate while another had an absence rate of 5 percent. Within one plant, some departments had virtually no absence while others approached a rate of 25 percent!

Moving to the small group level, Johns also studied small customer service groups in a utility company. Despite the fact that all employees were doing the same

work in the same firm, there were again striking cross-group differences in absenteeism, ranging from 1 to 13 percent.

These normative differences in absenteeism across groups are called absence cultures. How do they develop? People tend to adjust their own absence behaviour to what they see as typical of their group. Then, other factors come into play. In the utility company study, the groups that monitored each other's behaviour more closely had lower absence. A Canadian study found that air traffic controllers traded off calling in sick so that their colleagues could replace them at double overtime. A U.K. study found that industrial workers actually posted "absence schedules" so that they could take time off without things getting out of hand! All these are examples of norms in action.

The norms underlying absence cultures can dictate presence as well as absence. Recent studies show that "presenteeism," coming to work when feeling unwell, is prevalent in many human services occupations.

Source: Some of the research bearing on absence cultures is described in Johns, G. (2008). Absenteeism and presenteeism: Not at work or not working well. In J. Barling & C.L. Cooper (Eds.), Sage Handbook of Organizational Behavior (Vol. 1). London: Sage.

---

roles, we invariably see the development of *emergent roles*. These are roles that develop naturally to meet the social–emotional needs of group members or to assist in formal job accomplishment. The class clown and the office gossip fulfill emergent social–emotional roles, while an "old pro" might emerge to assist new group members learn their jobs. Other emergent roles might be assumed by informal leaders or by scapegoats who are the targets of group hostility.

ROLE AMBIGUITY   **Role ambiguity** exists when the goals of one's job or the methods of performing it are unclear. Ambiguity might be characterized by confusion about how performance is evaluated, how good performance can be achieved, or what the limits of one's authority and responsibility are.

Exhibit 7.4 shows a model of the process that is involved in assuming an organizational role. As you can see, certain organizational factors lead role senders (such as managers) to

Role ambiguity. Lack of clarity of job goals or methods.

 Explore

Go to MyManagementLab to see an annotated version of this figure.

EXHIBIT 7.4
A model of the role assumption process.
Source: Adapted from Katz, D. et al. (1966, 1978). *The Social Psychology of Organizations*, 2nd edition, p.196. © 1966, 1978 John Wiley & Sons Inc. New York. Reprinted by permission of John Wiley & Sons, Inc.

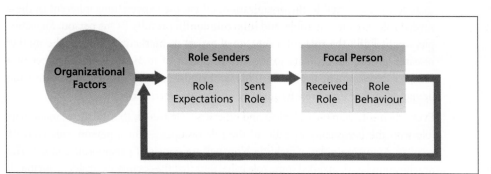

develop role expectations and "send" roles to focal people (such as employees). The focal person "receives" the role and then tries to engage in behaviour to fulfill the role. This model reveals a variety of elements that can lead to ambiguity.

- *Organizational factors.* Some roles seem inherently ambiguous because of their function in the organization. For example, middle management roles might fail to provide the "big picture" that upper management roles do. Also, middle management roles do not require the attention to supervision necessary in lower management roles.
- *The role sender.* Role senders might have unclear expectations of a focal person. Even when the sender has specific role expectations, they might be ineffectively sent to the focal person. A weak orientation session, vague performance reviews, or inconsistent feedback and discipline may send ambiguous role messages to employees.
- *The focal person.* Even role expectations that are clearly developed and sent might not be fully digested by the focal person. This is especially true when he or she is new to the role. Ambiguity tends to decrease as length of time in the job role increases.[23]

What are the practical consequences of role ambiguity? The most frequent outcomes appear to be job stress, dissatisfaction, reduced organizational commitment, lowered performance, and intentions to quit.[24] Managers can do much to reduce unnecessary role ambiguity by providing clear performance expectations and performance feedback, especially for new employees and for those in more intrinsically ambiguous jobs.

ROLE CONFLICT

Role conflict exists when an individual is faced with incompatible role expectations. Conflict can be distinguished from ambiguity in that role expectations might be crystal clear but incompatible in the sense that they are mutually exclusive, cannot be fulfilled simultaneously, or do not suit the role occupant.

- **Intrasender role conflict** occurs when a single role sender provides incompatible role expectations to the role occupant. For example, a manager might tell an employee to take it easy and not work so hard, while delivering yet another batch of reports that require immediate attention. This form of role conflict seems especially likely to also provoke ambiguity.
- If two or more role senders differ in their expectations for a role occupant, **intersender role conflict** can develop. Employees who straddle the boundary between the organization and its clients or customers are especially likely to encounter this form of conflict. Intersender conflict can also stem exclusively from within the organization. The classic example here is the first-level manager, who serves as the interface between "management" and "the workers." From above, the manager might be pressured to get the work out and keep the troops in line. From below, he or she might be encouraged to behave in a considerate and friendly manner.
- Organizational members necessarily play several roles at one time, especially if we include roles external to the organization. Often, the expectations inherent in these several roles are incompatible, and **interrole conflict** results.[25] One person, for example, might fulfill the roles of a functional expert in marketing, head of the market research group, subordinate to the vice-president of marketing, and member of a product development task force. This is obviously a busy person, and competing demands for her time are a frequent symptom of interrole conflict.
- Even when role demands are clear and otherwise congruent, they might be incompatible with the personality or skills of the role occupant—thus, **person–role conflict** results.[26] Many examples of "whistle-blowing" are signals of person–role conflict. The organization has demanded some role behaviour that the occupant considers unethical.

Role conflict. A condition of being faced with incompatible role expectations.

Intrasender role conflict. A single role sender provides incompatible role expectations to a role occupant.

Intersender role conflict. Two or more role senders provide a role occupant with incompatible expectations.

Interrole conflict. Several roles held by a role occupant involve incompatible expectations.

Person–role conflict. Role demands call for behaviour that is incompatible with the personality or skills of a role occupant.

As with role ambiguity, the most consistent consequences of role conflict are job dissatisfaction, stress reactions, lowered organizational commitment, and turnover intentions.[27] Managers can help prevent employee role conflict by avoiding self-contradictory messages, conferring with other role senders, being sensitive to multiple role demands, and fitting the right person to the right role.

Status

Status is the rank, social position, or prestige accorded to group members. Put another way, it represents the group's *evaluation* of a member. Just *what* is evaluated depends on the status system in question. However, when a status system works smoothly, the group will exhibit clear norms about who should be accorded higher or lower status.

Status. The rank, social position, or prestige accorded to group members.

FORMAL STATUS SYSTEMS All organizations have both formal and informal status systems. Since formal systems are most obvious to observers, let's begin there. The formal status system represents management's attempt to publicly identify those people who have higher status than others. It is so obvious because this identification is implemented by the application of *status symbols* that are tangible indicators of status. Status symbols might include titles, particular working relationships, pay packages, work schedules, and the physical working environment. Just what are the criteria for achieving formal organizational status? One criterion is often seniority in one's work group. Employees who have been with the group longer might acquire the privilege of choosing day shift work or a more favourable office location. Even more important than seniority, however, is one's assigned role in the organization—one's job. Because they perform different jobs, secretaries, labourers, managers, and executives acquire different statuses. Organizations often go to great pains to tie status symbols to assigned roles.

Why do organizations go to all this trouble to differentiate status? For one thing, status and the symbols connected to it serve as powerful magnets to induce members to aspire to higher organizational positions (recall Maslow's need for self-esteem). Second, status differentiation reinforces the authority hierarchy in work groups and in the organization as a whole, since people *pay attention* to high-status individuals.

INFORMAL STATUS SYSTEMS In addition to formal status systems, one can detect informal status systems in organizations. Such systems are not well advertised, and they might lack the conspicuous symbols and systematic support that people usually accord the formal system. Nevertheless, they can operate just as effectively. Sometimes, job performance is a basis for the acquisition of informal status. The "power hitters" on a baseball team or the "cool heads" in a hospital emergency unit might be highly evaluated by co-workers for their ability to assist in task accomplishment. Some managers who perform well early in their careers are identified as "fast trackers" and given special job assignments that correspond to their elevated status. Just as frequently, though, informal status is linked to factors other than job performance, such as gender or race. For example, the man who takes a day off work to care for a sick child may be praised as a model father. The woman who does the same may be questioned about her work commitment.

CONSEQUENCES OF STATUS DIFFERENCES Status differences have a paradoxical effect on communication patterns. Most people like to communicate with others at their own status or higher rather than with people who are below them.[28] The result should be a tendency for communication to move up the status hierarchy. However, if status differences are large, people can be inhibited from communicating upward. These opposing effects mean that much communication gets stalled.

People pay attention to and respect status.[29] Thus, status also affects the amount of various group members' communication and their influence in group affairs. As you might guess, higher-status members do more talking and have more influence.[30] Some of the most convincing evidence comes from studies of jury deliberations, in which jurors with higher social status (such as managers and professionals) participate more and have more effect on the verdict.[31] Unfortunately, there is no guarantee that the highest-status person is the most knowledgeable about the problem at hand!

REDUCING STATUS BARRIERS Although status differences can be powerful motivators, their tendency to inhibit the free flow of communication has led many organizations to downplay status differentiation by doing away with questionable status symbols. The goal is to foster a culture of teamwork and cooperation across the ranks, as seen in the IDEO vignette that opened the chapter. The high-tech culture of Silicon Valley is egalitarian and lacking in conspicuous status symbols, but even old-line industries are getting on the bandwagon, doing away with reserved parking and fancy offices for executives.

Some organizations employ phoney or misguided attempts to bridge the status barrier. Some examples of "casual Friday" policies (which permit the wearing of casual clothes on Fridays) only underline status differences the rest of the week if no other cultural changes are made.

Many observers note that email has levelled status barriers.[32] High-speed transmission, direct access, and the opportunity to avoid live confrontation often encourage lower-status parties to communicate directly with organizational VIPs. This has even been seen in the rank-conscious military.

LO 7.5

Discuss the causes and consequences of *group cohesiveness*.

Group cohesiveness. The degree to which a group is attractive to its members.

GROUP COHESIVENESS

Group cohesiveness is a critical property of groups. Cohesive groups are those that are especially attractive to their members. Because of this attractiveness, members are especially desirous of staying in the group and tend to describe the group in favourable terms.[33]

The arch-stereotype of a cohesive group is the major league baseball team that begins September looking like a good bet to win its division and make it to the World Series. On the field we see well-oiled, precision teamwork. In the clubhouse, all is sweetness and joviality, and interviewed players tell the world how fine it is to be playing with "a great bunch of guys."

Cohesiveness is a relative, rather than absolute, property of groups. While some groups are more cohesive than others, there is no objective line between cohesive and non-cohesive groups. Thus, we will use the adjective *cohesive* to refer to groups that are more attractive than average for their members.

Factors Influencing Cohesiveness

What makes some groups more cohesive than others? Important factors include threat, competition, success, member diversity, group size, and toughness of initiation.

THREAT AND COMPETITION External threat to the survival of the group increases cohesiveness in a wide variety of situations.[34] As an example, consider the wrangling, uncoordinated corporate board of directors that quickly forms a united front in the face of a takeover bid. Honest competition with another group can also promote cohesiveness.[35] This is the case with the World Series contenders.

Why do groups often become more cohesive in response to threat or competition? They probably feel a need to improve communication and coordination so that they can better cope with the situation at hand. Members now perceive the group as more attractive because it is seen as capable of doing what has to be done to ward off threat or to win. However, under *extreme* threat or very *unbalanced* competition, increased cohesiveness will serve little purpose. For example, the partners in a firm faced with certain financial disaster would be unlikely to exhibit cohesiveness because it would do nothing to combat the severe threat.

SUCCESS It should come as no surprise that a group becomes more attractive to its members when it has successfully accomplished some important goal, such as defending itself

Cohesive groups lead to effective goal accomplishment.

against threat or winning a prize.[36] By the same token, cohesiveness will decrease after failure, although there may be "misery loves company" exceptions. The situation for competition is shown graphically in Exhibit 7.5. Fit-Rite Jeans owns two small clothing stores (A and B) in a large city. To boost sales, it holds a contest between the two stores, offering $150 worth of merchandise to each employee of the store that achieves the highest sales during the next business quarter. Before the competition begins, the staff of each store is equally cohesive. As we suggested above, when competition begins, both groups become more cohesive. The members become more cooperative with each other, and in each store there is much talk about "us" versus "them." At the end of the quarter, store A wins the prize and becomes yet more cohesive. The group is especially attractive to its members because it has succeeded in the attainment of a desired goal. On the other hand, cohesiveness plummets in the losing store B—the group has become less attractive to its members.

MEMBER DIVERSITY Earlier, we pointed out that groups that are diverse in terms of gender, age, and race can have a harder time becoming cohesive than more homogeneous groups. However, if the group is in agreement about how to accomplish some particular task,

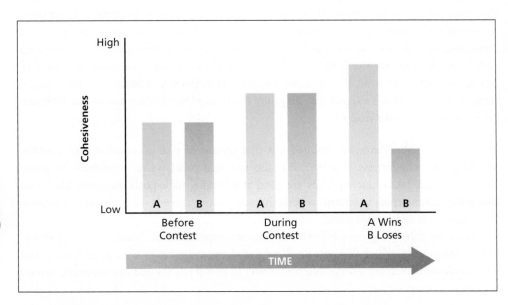

EXHIBIT 7.5
Competition, success, and cohesiveness.

✳ Explore

Go to MyManagementLab to see an annotated version of this figure.

its success in performing the task will often outweigh surface dissimilarity in determining cohesiveness.[37]

SIZE Other things being equal, bigger groups should have a more difficult time becoming and staying cohesive. In general, such groups should have a more difficult time agreeing on goals and more problems communicating and coordinating efforts to achieve those goals. Earlier, we pointed out that large groups frequently divide into subgroups. Clearly, such subgrouping is contrary to the cohesiveness of the larger group.

TOUGHNESS OF INITIATION Despite its rigorous admissions policies, the Harvard Business School does not lack applicants. Similarly, exclusive yacht and golf clubs might have waiting lists for membership extending several years into the future. All this suggests that groups that are tough to get into should be more attractive than those that are easy to join.[38] This is well known in the armed forces, where rigorous physical training and stressful "survival schools" precede entry into elite units such as the Canadian Special Operations Forces Command or the U.S. Army Rangers.

Consequences of Cohesiveness

From the previous section, it should be clear that managers or group members might be able to influence the level of cohesiveness of work groups by using competition or threat, varying group size or composition, or manipulating membership requirements. The question remains, however, as to whether *more* or *less* cohesiveness is a desirable group property. This, of course, depends on the consequences of group cohesiveness and who is doing the judging.

MORE PARTICIPATION IN GROUP ACTIVITIES Because members wish to remain in the group, voluntary turnover from cohesive groups should be low. Also, members like being with each other; therefore, absence should be lower than in less cohesive groups. In addition, participation should be reflected in a high degree of communication within the group as members strive to cooperate with and assist each other. This communication might well be of a more friendly and supportive nature, depending on the key goals of the group.[39]

MORE CONFORMITY Because they are so attractive and coordinated, cohesive groups are well equipped to supply information, rewards, and punishment to individual members. These factors take on special significance when they are administered by those who hold a special interest for us. Thus, highly cohesive groups are in a superb position to induce conformity to group norms.

Members of cohesive groups are especially motivated to engage in activities that will *keep* the group cohesive. Chief among these activities is applying pressure to deviants to get them to comply with group norms. Cohesive groups react to deviants by increasing the amount of communication directed at these individuals.[40] Such communication contains information to help the deviant "see the light," as well as veiled threats about what might happen if he or she does not. Over time, if such communication is ineffective in inducing conformity, it tends to decrease. This is a signal that the group has isolated the deviant member to maintain cohesiveness among the majority.

MORE SUCCESS Above, we pointed out that successful goal accomplishment contributes to group cohesiveness. However, it is also true that cohesiveness contributes to group success—in general, cohesive groups are good at achieving their goals. Research has found that group cohesiveness is related to performance.[41] Thus, there is a reciprocal relationship between success and cohesiveness.

Why are cohesive groups effective at goal accomplishment? Probably because of the other consequences of cohesiveness we discussed above. A high degree of participation and communication, coupled with active conformity to group norms and commitment, should

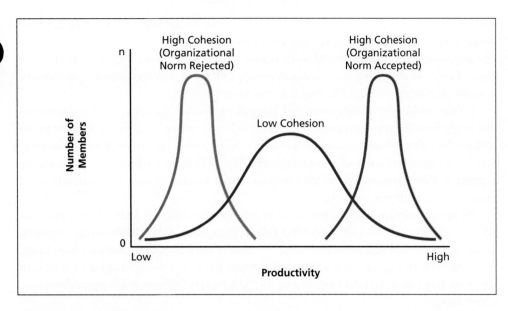

EXHIBIT 7.6
**Hypothetical
productivity curves
for groups varying in
cohesiveness.**

✳-[Explore

Go to MyManagementLab
to see an annotated
version of this figure.

ensure a high degree of agreement about the goals the group is pursuing and the methods it is using to achieve those goals. Thus, coordinated effort pays dividends to the group.

Since cohesiveness contributes to goal accomplishment, should managers attempt to increase the cohesiveness of work groups by juggling the factors that influence cohesiveness? To answer this question, we must emphasize that cohesive groups are especially effective at accomplishing *their own* goals. If these goals happen to correspond with those of the organization, increased cohesiveness should have substantial benefits for group performance. If not, organizational effectiveness might be threatened.[42] One large-scale study of work groups reached the following conclusions:

- In highly cohesive groups, the productivity of individual group members tends to be fairly similar to that of other members. In less cohesive groups there is more variation in productivity.

- Highly cohesive groups tend to be *more* or *less* productive than less cohesive groups, depending on a number of variables.[43]

These two facts are shown graphically in Exhibit 7.6. The lower variability of productivity in more cohesive groups stems from the power of such groups to induce conformity. To the extent that work groups have productivity norms, more cohesive groups should be better able to enforce them. Furthermore, if cohesive groups accept organizational norms regarding productivity, they should be highly productive. If cohesive groups reject such norms, they are especially effective in limiting productivity.

One other factor that influences the impact of cohesiveness on productivity is the extent to which the task really requires interdependence and cooperation among group members (e.g., a football team versus a golf team). Cohesiveness is more likely to pay off when the task requires more interdependence.[44]

In summary, cohesive groups tend to be successful in accomplishing what they wish to accomplish. In a good labour relations climate, group cohesiveness on interdependent tasks should contribute to high productivity. If the climate is marked by tension and disagreement, cohesive groups may pursue goals that result in low productivity.

SOCIAL LOAFING

Have you ever participated in a group project at work or school in which you did not contribute as much as you could have because other people were there to take up the slack? Or have you ever reduced your effort in a group project because you felt that others were not pulling

Explain the dynamics of
social loafing.

Social loafing. The tendency to withhold physical or intellectual effort when performing a group task.

their weight? If so, you have been guilty of social loafing. **Social loafing** is the tendency that people have to withhold physical or intellectual effort when they are performing a group task.[45] The implication is that they would work harder if they were alone rather than part of the group. Earlier we said that process losses in groups could be due to coordination problems or to motivation problems. Social loafing is a motivation problem.

People working in groups often feel trapped in a social dilemma, in that something that might benefit them individually—slacking off in the group—will result in poor group performance if everybody behaves the same way. Social loafers resolve the dilemma in a way that hurts organizational goal accomplishment. Notice that the tendency for social loafing is probably more pronounced in individualistic North America than in more collective and group-oriented cultures.

As the questions above suggest, social loafing has two different forms. In the *free rider effect*, people lower their effort to get a free ride at the expense of their fellow group members. In the *sucker effect*, people lower their effort because of the feeling that others are free riding, that is, they are trying to restore equity in the group. You can probably imagine a scenario in which the free riders start slacking off and then the suckers follow suit. Group performance suffers badly.

What are some ways to counteract social loafing?[46]

- *Make individual performance more visible.* Where appropriate, the simplest way to do this is to keep the group small in size. Then, individual contributions are less likely to be hidden. Posting performance levels and making presentations of one's accomplishments can also facilitate visibility.

- *Make sure that the work is interesting.* If the work is involving, intrinsic motivation should counteract social loafing.

- *Increase feelings of indispensability.* Group members might slack off because they feel that their inputs are unnecessary for group success. This can be counteracted by using training and the status system to provide group members with unique inputs (e.g., having one person master computer graphics programs).

- *Increase performance feedback.* Some social loafing happens because groups or individual members simply are not aware of their performance. Increased feedback, as appropriate, from the boss, peers, and customers (internal or external) should encourage self-correction.

- *Reward group performance.* Members are more likely to monitor and maximize their own performance (and attend to that of their colleagues) when the *group* receives rewards for effectiveness.[47]

WHAT IS A TEAM?

HERMAN MILLER: ORGANIZATIONAL BEHAVIOUR Go to MyManagementLab to watch a video about organizational behaviour.

TEAMS Go to MyManagementLab to complete a simulation about teams.

Collective efficacy. Shared beliefs that a team can successfully perform a given task.

Some have suggested that a team is something more than a group. They suggest that a group becomes a team when there exists a strong sense of shared commitment and when a synergy develops such that the group's efforts are greater than the sum of its parts.[48] While such differences might be evident in some instances, our definition of a group is sufficient to describe most teams that can be found in organizations. The term *team* is generally used to describe "groups" in organizational settings. Therefore, for our purposes in this chapter, we use the terms interchangeably. Teams have become a major building block of organizations and are now quite common in North America.[49] Research has shown improvements in organizational performance in terms of both efficiency and quality as a result of team-based work arrangements.[50]

You will recall that in Chapter 2 we defined self-efficacy as beliefs individuals have about their ability to successfully perform a task. When it comes to teams, collective efficacy is also important to ensure high performance.[51] **Collective efficacy** consists of *shared* beliefs that a team can successfully perform a given task. Notice that self-efficacy does not necessarily translate into collective efficacy—five skilled musicians do not necessarily result in a good band. In the following sections we cover the factors that contribute to collective efficacy in a team.

DESIGNING EFFECTIVE WORK TEAMS

The double-edged nature of group cohesiveness suggests that a delicate balance of factors dictates whether a work group is effective or ineffective. In turn, this suggests that organizations should pay considerable attention to how work groups are designed and managed.

A good model for thinking about the design of effective work groups is to consider a successful sports team. In most cases, such teams are small groups made up of highly skilled individuals who are able to meld these skills into a cohesive effort. The task they are performing is intrinsically motivating and provides very direct feedback. If there are status differences on the team, the basis for these differences is contribution to the team, not some extraneous factor. The team shows an obsessive concern with obtaining the right personnel, relying on tryouts or player drafts, and the team is coached, not supervised. With this informal model in mind, let's examine the concept of group effectiveness more closely.

J. Richard Hackman of Harvard University (co-developer of the Job Characteristics Model, Chapter 6) has written extensively about work group effectiveness.[52] According to Hackman, a work group is effective when (1) its physical or intellectual output is acceptable to management and to the other parts of the organization that use this output, (2) group members' needs are satisfied rather than frustrated by the group, and (3) the group experience enables members to *continue* to work together.

What leads to group effectiveness? In colloquial language, "sweat, smarts, and style." Put more formally, as Hackman notes, group effectiveness occurs when high effort is directed toward the group's task, when great knowledge and skill are directed toward the task, and when the group adopts sensible strategies for accomplishing its goals. And just how does an organization achieve this? There is growing awareness in many organizations that the answer is self-managed work teams.

Self-Managed Work Teams

Self-managed work teams generally provide their members with the opportunity to do challenging work under reduced supervision. Other labels that we often apply to such groups are autonomous, semi-autonomous, and self-directed. The general idea, which is more important than the label, is that the groups regulate much of their own members' behaviour. Much interest in such teams was spurred by the success of teams in Japanese industry. Critical to the success of self-managed teams are the nature of the task, the composition of the group, and the various support mechanisms in place.[53]

TASKS FOR SELF-MANAGED TEAMS Experts agree that tasks assigned to self-managed work teams should be complex and challenging, requiring high interdependence among team members for accomplishment. In general, these tasks should have the qualities of enriched jobs (Chapter 6). Thus, teams should see the task as significant, they should perform the task from beginning to end, and they should use a variety of skills. Self-managed teams have to have something useful to self-manage, and it is fairly complex tasks that capitalize on the diverse knowledge and skills of a group. Taking a number of olive stuffers on a food-processing assembly line, putting them in distinctive jumpsuits, calling them the Olive Squad, and telling them to self-manage will be unlikely to yield dividends in terms of effort expended or brainpower employed. The basic task will still be boring, a prime recipe for social loafing!

LO **7.7**

Discuss how to design and support *self-managed teams*.

Self-managed work teams. Work groups that have the opportunity to do challenging work under reduced supervision.

Outside the complexity requirement, the actual range of tasks for which organizations have used self-managed teams is wide, spanning both blue- and white-collar jobs. In the white-collar domain, complex service and design jobs seem especially conducive to self-management. In the blue-collar domain, General Mills and Chaparral Steel of Midlothian, Texas, make extensive use of self-managed work groups. In general, these groups are responsible for dividing labour among various subtasks as they see fit and making a variety of decisions about matters that impinge on the group. When a work site is formed from scratch and lacks an existing culture, the range of these activities can be very broad. Consider the self-managed teams formed in a new U.K. confectionery plant.

> *Production employees worked in groups of 8 to 12 people, all of whom were expected to carry out each of eight types of jobs involved in the production process. Group members were collectively responsible for allocating jobs among themselves, reaching production targets and meeting quality and hygiene standards, solving local production problems, recording production data for information systems, organizing breaks, ordering and collecting raw materials and delivering finished goods to stores, calling for engineering support, and training new recruits. They also participated in selecting new employees. Within each group, individuals had considerable control over the amount of variety they experienced by rotating their tasks, and each production group was responsible for one product line. Group members interacted informally throughout the working day but made the most important decisions—for example, regarding job allocation—at formal weekly group meetings where performance was also discussed.*[54]

If a theme runs through this discussion of tasks for self-managed teams, it is the breakdown of traditional, conventional, specialized *roles* in the group. Group members adopt roles that will make the group effective, not ones that are simply related to a narrow specialty.

COMPOSITION OF SELF-MANAGED TEAMS How should organizations assemble self-managed teams to ensure effectiveness? "Stable, small, and smart" might be a fast answer.[55]

- *Stability.* Self-managed teams require considerable interaction and high cohesiveness among their members. This, in turn, requires understanding and trust. To achieve this, group membership must be fairly stable. Rotating members into and out of the group will cause it to fail to develop a true group identity.[56]

- *Size.* In keeping with the demands of the task, self-managed teams should be as small as is feasible. The goal here is to keep coordination problems and social loafing to a minimum. These negative factors can be a problem for all groups, but they can be especially difficult for self-managed groups. This is because reduced supervision means that there is no boss to coordinate the group's activities and search out social loafers who do not do their share of the work.

- *Expertise.* Group members should have a high level of expertise about the task at hand. Everybody does not have to know everything, but the group as a *whole* should be very knowledgeable about the task. Again, reduced supervision discourages "running to the boss" when problems arise, but the group must have the resources to successfully solve these problems. One set of skills that all members should probably possess to some degree is social skills. Understanding how to talk things out, communicate effectively, and resolve conflict is especially important.

- *Diversity.* Put simply, a team should have members who are similar enough to work well together and diverse enough to bring a variety of perspectives and skills to the task at hand. A product planning group consisting exclusively of new male MBAs might work well together but lack the different perspectives that are necessary for creativity.

One way of maintaining appropriate group composition might be to let the group choose its own members, as occurred at the confectionery plant we described above. A potential problem with this is that the group might use some irrelevant criterion (such as race or gender) to unfairly exclude others. Thus, human resources department oversight is necessary, as are very clear selection criteria (in terms of behaviours, skills, and credentials). The selection stage is critical, since some studies (including the one conducted in the confectionary plant) have shown elevated turnover in self-managed teams.[57] Such turnover can damage team effectiveness because it reduces the capacity for the team to learn and adapt.[58] Thus, "fit" is important, and it is well worth expending the extra effort to find the right people. At Britain's Pret A Manger sandwich and coffee shops, job seekers work in a shop for a day and then the staff votes on whether they can join the team.[59]

The theme running through this discussion of team composition favours *high cohesiveness* and the development of group *norms* that stress group effectiveness.

SUPPORTING SELF-MANAGED TEAMS A number of support factors can assist self-managed teams in becoming and staying effective. Reports of problems with teams can usually be traced back to inadequate support.

- *Training.* In almost every conceivable instance, members of self-managed teams require extensive training. The kind of training depends on the exact job design and on the needs of the workforce. However, some common areas include:
  - *Technical training.* This might include math, computer use, or any tasks that a supervisor formerly handled. Cross-training in the specialties of other teammates is common.
  - *Social skills.* Assertiveness, problem solving, and routine dispute resolution are skills that help the team operate smoothly.
  - *Language skills.* This can be important for ethnically diverse teams. Good communication is critical on self-managed teams.
  - *Business training.* Some firms provide training in the basic elements of finance, accounting, and production so that employees can better grasp how their team's work fits into the larger picture.

- *Rewards.* The general rule here is to mostly tie rewards to team accomplishment rather than to individual accomplishment while still providing team members with some individual performance feedback to counteract social loafing. Microsoft's European product support group went from individual rewards to team-based rewards when it found that the former discouraged engineers from taking on difficult cases.[60] Gain sharing, profit sharing, and skill-based pay (Chapter 6) are compatible reward systems for a team environment. Skill-based pay is especially attractive because it rewards the acquisition of multiple skills that can support the team.

- *Management.* Self-management will not receive the best support when managers feel threatened and see it as reducing their own power or promotion opportunities. Some schooled in the traditional role of manager may simply not adapt. Those who do can serve important functions by mediating relations *between* teams and by dealing with union concerns, since unions are often worried about the cross-functional job sharing in self-management. One study found that the most effective managers in a self-management environment encouraged groups to observe, evaluate, and reinforce their own task behaviour.[61] This suggests that coaching teams to be independent enhances their effectiveness.[62]

Exhibit 7.7 summarizes the factors that determine work group effectiveness. Michael Campion and colleagues studied these factors in teams of professional and non-professional workers.[63] Their results provide strong support for many of the relationships shown in the exhibit. Overall, research has shown improvements in team productivity, quality, customer satisfaction, and safety following the implementation of self-managed work teams.[64]

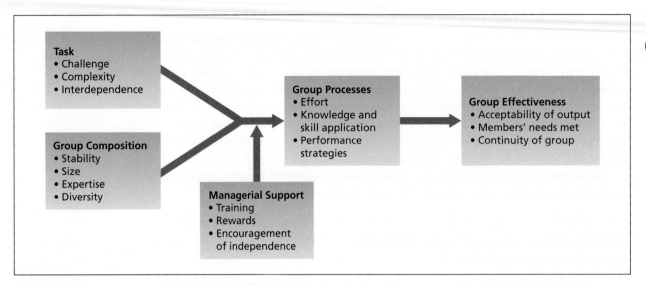

EXHIBIT 7.7
Factors influencing work group effectiveness.

Source: Based in part on Hackman, J.R. (1987). "The Design of Work Teams" in J.W. Lorsch (Ed.), *Handbook of organizational behaviour*. Englewood Cliffs, NJ: Pearson Education. Used by permission of J.W. Lorsch.

 Explore

Go to MyManagementLab to see an annotated version of this figure.

LO **7.8**

Explain the logic behind *cross-functional teams* and describe how they can operate effectively.

Cross-functional teams. Work groups that bring people with different functional specialties together to better invent, design, or deliver a product or service.

Cross-Functional Teams

Let's look at another kind of team that contemporary organizations are using with increasing frequency. **Cross-functional teams** bring people with different functional specialties together to better invent, design, or deliver a product or service. For example, recall that the IDEO Kentucky public housing project brought together experts in architecture, design, anthropology, and psychology.

A cross-functional team might be self-managed and permanent if it is doing a recurrent task that is not too complex. If the task is complex and unique (such as designing a car), cross-functional teams require formal leadership, and their lives will generally be limited to the life of the specific project. In both cases, the "cross-functional" label means that such diverse specialties are necessary that cross-training is not feasible. People have to be experts in their own area but able to cooperate with others.

Cross-functional teams, which have been used in service industries such as banking and hospitals, are probably best known for their successes in product development.[65] Thus, Rubbermaid uses teams to invent and design a remarkable variety of innovative household products. Pharmaceutical development teams at Novartis and Wyeth include toxicologists, biologists, clinicians, chemists, and marketers.

The general goals of using cross-functional teams include some combination of innovation, speed, and quality that comes from early coordination among the various specialties. We can see their value by looking at the traditional way auto manufacturers used to design cars in North America.[66] First, stylists determined what the car would look like and then passed their design on to engineering, which developed mechanical specifications and blueprints. In turn, manufacturing considered how to construct what the stylists and engineers designed. Somewhere down the line, marketing and accounting got their say. This process invariably leads to problems. One link in the chain might have a difficult time understanding what the previous link meant. Worse, one department might resist the ideas of another simply because they "were not invented here." The result of all this is slow, expensive development and early quality problems. In contrast, the cross-functional approach gets all the specialties working together from day one. A complex project, such as a car design, might have over 30 cross-functional teams working at the same time. Global Focus: *A Diverse Global Team Creates the Camaro* describes a small part of the cross-functional teamwork that produced the sporty Chevy, which is built in Oshawa, Ontario.

The speed factor can be dramatic. Manufacturers have reduced the development of a new car model by several years. Boeing used a cross-functional team to reduce certain design analyses from two weeks to only a few minutes.

GLOBAL FOCUS

A DIVERSE GLOBAL TEAM CREATES THE CAMARO

The handful of designers who gave birth to the reborn Camaro were a diverse group. That theme continued as it was developed all around the globe. When Design Director Tom Peters got a hush-hush assignment from Ed Welburn, VP of Global Design, to come up with a new Camaro to be shown at an upcoming auto show, he was beyond excited. The chance to redefine an American icon is every car designer's dream. Trying to keep his project top secret, he assembled a small team of his most talented young designers. They were SangYup Lee and Steve Kim from Korea and Vlad Kapitonov from Russia. Tom wanted a diverse group who didn't grow up with the Camaro in their backyard—who would bring a fresh perspective to the design. He asked his team to design "the meanest street-fighting dog they've ever seen" and to look at modern aircraft for influence. He did this right before a holiday break.

SangYup took that directive literally, feverishly sketching at the airport on his way to visit family in Korea. Vlad and Steve sketched over the break too, and when everybody regrouped at the design lair known as Studio X, Tom knew he had picked the right guys. Sketches were chosen—SangYup's for the front, and Vlad's for the rear. Designer Micah Jones nailed the interior, fusing high design with high technology. Using these sketches as a guide, the car was fast-tracked to a full-size clay and then fitted with an engine and drivetrain so that it could swagger onto the world's stage at the 2006 North American International Auto Show. And that's where the story really began. Tom and his team now had to build a production car that would lose none of the jaw-dropping style of the concept—a job that would require a flawless blend of engineering and technology.

The team crisscrossed the world in this effort, beginning in Australia. There, the engineering group at Holden were chosen because of their rear-wheel-drive prowess.

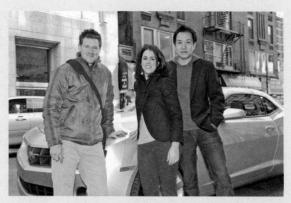

Three GM designers who worked on the Camaro: Micah Jones, Rebecca Waldmeir, and SangYup Lee.

Working closely with Tom's team, they created a platform that delivered the pure power any car bearing the name Camaro would need. The Camaro took plenty of other side trips on its journey from concept to production car. It was cold-weather tested in Sweden. Warm-weather tested in Death Valley. And the mighty SS was track tested at Nürburgring, where it clocked a world-class 8:19.

The result of all this combined passion is nothing short of spectacular. You might see a beautifully modern American car when you look at the new Camaro. But Tom Peters sees a car drawn by a Korean, engineered in Australia, tested in Germany, and built in North America. Because he knows firsthand that the only way to build a world-class car is to have the best people in the world build it!

Sources: Excerpted from Chevrolet advertising copy. (2009, May). *Road & Track*, 30. General Motors Corp. Used with permission, GM Media Archives.

PRINCIPLES FOR EFFECTIVENESS A number of factors contribute to the effectiveness of cross-functional teams. We will illustrate several with examples from a past redesign of the Ford Mustang.[67]

- *Composition.* All relevant specialties are necessary, and effective teams are sure not to overlook anyone. Auto companies put labour representatives on car design teams to warn of assembly problems. On the Mustang project, outside suppliers were represented. At IDEO, clients are represented on design teams.

- *Superordinate goals.* **Superordinate goals** are attractive outcomes that can only be achieved by collaboration. They override detailed functional objectives that might be in conflict (e.g., finance versus design). On the Mustang project, the superordinate goal was to keep the legendary name alive in the face of corporate cost cutting.

Superordinate goals. Attractive outcomes that can only be achieved by collaboration.

- *Physical proximity.* Team members have to be located (sometimes relocated) close to each other to facilitate informal contact. Mustang used a former furniture warehouse in Allen Park, Michigan, to house its teams.

- *Autonomy.* Cross-functional teams need some autonomy from the larger organization, and functional specialists need some authority to commit their function to project decisions. This prevents meddling or "micromanaging" by upper-level or functional managers.

- *Rules and procedures.* Although petty rules and procedures are to be avoided, some basic decision procedures must be laid down to prevent anarchy. On the Mustang project, it was agreed that a single manufacturing person would have a veto over radical body changes.

- *Leadership.* Because of the potential for conflict, cross-functional team leaders need especially strong people skills in addition to task expertise. The "tough engineer" who headed the Mustang project succeeded in developing his people skills for that task.

Several of these principles ensure that team members share mental models. **Shared mental models** mean that team members share identical information about how they should interact and what their task is. Shared mental models enhance coordination and contribute greatly to effective team performance, at least when the shared knowledge reflects reality.[68] Although shared mental models are important for all teams, they are a particular challenge to instill in cross-functional teams due to the divergent backgrounds of the team members. Consider this product development team:

> *The team is given the mandate to make a "tough truck." The designer, thinking in terms of styling, conceptualizes "tough" as "powerful looking." The designer then sketches a vehicle with a large grille and large tires, creating a very powerful stance. When seeing this mock-up, an engineer, thinking in terms of functionality and conceptualizing tough as implying durability, is unhappy with the design because it compromises the vehicle's power. Maintaining hauling capacity with large tires implies the need for greater torque output from the engine, adding expense and difficulty to the engineer's part of the problem. When the engineer suggests 16- rather than 20-inch wheels, the designer balks, claiming it makes the vehicle look cartoonish rather than tough.[69]*

Clearly, the designer and the engineer don't share mental models of what "tough" means, and this problem can be greatly magnified with the participation of other functions and disciplines. It can also be magnified in virtual teams, a subject we will now turn to.

Virtual Teams

With the increasing trends toward globalization and the rapid development of high-tech communication tools, a new type of team has emerged that will surely be critical to organizations' success for years to come: virtual teams. **Virtual teams** are work groups that use technology to communicate and collaborate across space, time, and organizational boundaries.[70] Along with their reliance on computer and electronic technology, the primary feature of these teams is the lack of face-to-face contact between team members due to geographic dispersion. This separation often entails linkages across countries and cultures. Furthermore, virtual teams are often cross-functional. Technologies used by virtual teams can be either asynchronous (email, fax, voice mail), allowing team members to reflect before responding, or synchronous (chat, groupware), allowing team members to communicate dynamically in real time. Although not so long ago they were only a dream, virtual teams are now spreading across the business landscape and are used by numerous companies, such as CAE, Sabre, IBM, and Texas Instruments. For an example of a virtual team supported by a blog, see the Applied Focus: *Blog Supports Virtual Change Team.*

Shared mental models. Team members share identical information about how they should interact and what their task is.

Simulate

VIRTUAL TEAMS Go to MyManagementLab to complete a simulation about virtual teams.

LO **7.9**

Understand *virtual teams* and what makes them effective.

Virtual teams. Work groups that use technology to communicate and collaborate across time, space, and organizational boundaries.

■ APPLIED FOCUS

BLOG SUPPORTS VIRTUAL CHANGE TEAM

An office services firm was implementing major benefits changes for its U.S. employees. Part of the benefits strategy change was a shift away from a paternalistic approach to more employee responsibility. The company knew this represented a major change-management opportunity. It wanted to have its best change-management team lead efforts to announce, engage and manage change efforts but without letting advance word leak out. The change-management team was scattered across the United States, but had to work closely together for several months to effect the desired change results. To work as a virtual team, a secure blog was created for the change-management team members. Only team members had access to ongoing discussions and draft change documents. The blog was a convenient way to provide real-time collaboration as well as a record of discussions and decisions for team members who could not make the live conversations. Team members learned to use the blog as the central repository for all planning and implementation tools. It was the most accessed site on a daily basis, even if no synchronous communication was required between members. The change team's success using the blog for virtual team collaboration was noted as a key element of the change process. The blog tool has since been used by other virtual teams throughout the organization.

Source: Excerpted from Society for Human Resource Management. (2010, First Quarter). Successfully transitioning to a virtual organization: Challenges, impact and technology. *SHRM Research Quarterly*, p. 6.

ADVANTAGES OF VIRTUAL TEAMS Why are these teams becoming so popular? Because linking minds through technology has some definite advantages:

- *Around-the-clock work.* Globally, a virtual team is a 24-hour team that never sleeps. In these "follow the sun" teams, a team member can begin a process in London and pass it on to another team member in New York for more input. From New York, the work can be forwarded to a colleague in San Francisco who, after more work, can send it along to Hong Kong for completion.[71] In today's non-stop economy, the benefits of such continuous workflows are huge.

- *Reduced travel time and cost.* Virtual teaming reduces travel costs associated with face-to-face meetings. In the past, important meetings, key negotiation sessions, and critical junctures in projects required team members to board planes and travel long distances. In the virtual environment, expensive and time-consuming travel can be mostly eliminated. Virtual teams can therefore lead to significant savings of time and money, and concerns over air travel also make virtual teams an attractive alternative.

- *Larger talent pool.* Virtual teams allow companies to expand their potential labour markets and to go after the best people, even if these people have no interest in relocating. The nature of virtual teams can also give employees added flexibility, allowing for a better work–life balance, which is an effective recruiting feature.[72]

CHALLENGES OF VIRTUAL TEAMS While the advantages highlighted above are appealing, virtual teams can also involve some disadvantages.[73] Managers must recognize that these teams present unique challenges and should not be treated as regular teams that just happen to use technology.

- *Trust.* Commentators have noted that trust is difficult to develop between virtual team members. People typically establish trust through physical contact and socialization, which are simply not available to virtual team members. For more on this challenge, see You Be the Manager: *Creating Trust in Virtual Teams at Orange.*

YOU BE THE MANAGER

Creating Trust in Virtual Teams at Orange

Multinational companies have a dual challenge of globalizing operations for purposes of efficiencies and localizing delivery of products and services to support national differences. At Orange, this challenge became all the more obvious when it expanded operations in the late 1990s to become a large, pan-European company. Orange is the mobile operator of France Telecom, providing services to 57 million customers across 17 countries. With presence in Europe, the Middle East, and Africa, Orange realized that to protect and strengthen the Orange brand, product development previously performed within host countries needed to become a global initiative. Although it is tempting to centralize a team that has a global mandate, Orange pursued virtual-team collaboration, which allows firms to increase diversity in their teams and potentially achieve greater productivity and creativity. At Orange, virtual teams were becoming a way of life, as with many high-tech, global corporations, but there were clearly challenges, rooted in the fact that there were less interpersonal similarities (e.g., common backgrounds and experience) among team members.

Within the product development organization at Orange, virtual teams were usually led by a product manager. Members of the team not only had primary responsibilities to the virtual team but also did work for local teams and various functions. As with other virtual teams, those at Orange were required to work across time zones, cultures, and reporting lines. Virtuality meant that team members were unable to interact informally, in face-to-face meetings. Communicating through electronic media (e.g., email, phone, and video conferencing) greatly reduced the ability to interact through non-verbal cues. The lack of informal communication was considered to be a large barrier in team productivity. As one team leader expressed, "Work really only starts after that first face-to-face meeting."

Cultural distance also affected the virtual teams at Orange. In one virtual team, conference calls between the U.K. and Paris offices became particularly strained. The British employees, in an effort to enhance meeting productivity, used humour to encourage participation, but this approach backfired. Without the benefit of seeing facial expressions, paired with the difficulty

At Orange, the creation and leadership of virtual teams is based on the fundamental need to create trust quickly and embed this trust throughout the life of the team.

of relating to the jokes themselves, Parisian employees felt increasingly isolated from their British counterparts and, as with other virtual teams at Orange, had low trust in their colleagues' ability to perform.

Because virtual teams at Orange were vital to the company's overall global strategy, management was keen to find ways to enhance team performance, productivity, and innovation. It was clear that work had to be done to overcome the trust barrier that existed between many of the virtual team members.

Questions

1. Why is trust important in virtual teams, and what influences the degree of trust among team members?

2. How can trust be developed and maintained in virtual teams?

To find out how Orange increased trust between virtual team members, see The Manager's Notebook at the end of this chapter.

Source: Adapted from Lawley, D. (2006, May/June). Creating trust in virtual teams at Orange. *Knowledge Management Review, 9* (2), 12–17.

- *Miscommunication.* The loss of face-to-face communication presents certain risks for virtual teams. Humans use many non-verbal cues to communicate meaning and feeling in a message. Using technology, the richness of face-to-face communication is lost and miscommunication can result (see Chapter 10). These risks can be particularly high on global virtual teams, as attempts at humour or the use of unfamiliar terms can lead to messages being misconstrued. Some organizations, such as Chevron, encourage global team members to avoid humour or metaphors when communicating online.[74]

- *Isolation.* People have needs for companionship. In self-contained offices, co-workers can meet for lunch, share stories, talk about their kids, and socialize outside of work. Unfortunately, these more casual interactions are not usually possible for virtual teams, a lack that can lead to team members having feelings of isolation and detachment.

- *High costs.* Savings in areas such as travel must be weighed against the costs of cutting-edge technology. Initial set-up costs can be substantial. Budgets must also be devoted to maintenance since, in the virtual environment, the firm's technology must run flawlessly, 24 hours a day, 7 days a week.

- *Management issues.* For managers, virtual teams can create new challenges in terms of dealing with subordinates who are no longer in view. How can you assess individual performance, monitor diligence, and ensure fairness in treatment when your team is dispersed around the globe?

Jessica Mesmer-Magnus and colleagues conducted an informative review of the research on information sharing in virtual teams versus face-to-face teams.[75] They found that virtual teams engaged in a lower volume of information sharing but were in fact more likely to share unique information that was not known by other team members. They suggested that the uniqueness advantage is because virtuality encourages more reflection compared to direct interaction. Paradoxically, however, the performance of virtual teams was especially dependent on them also having a high volume of open communication to complement the unique ideas. This is because openness facilitates the development of cooperation, cohesion, and trust, all of which are challenges for virtuality. The authors also found support for the idea that hybrid teams that combine face-to-face interaction with virtual interaction are especially likely to share information, a point reinforced in the following section.

LESSONS CONCERNING VIRTUAL TEAMS Overall, a number of lessons are beginning to emerge about what managers must do or keep watch for when developing virtual teams.[76]

- *Recruitment.* Choose team members carefully in terms of attitude and personality so that they are excited about these types of teams and can handle the independence and isolation that often define them. Find people with good interpersonal skills, not just technical expertise.

- *Training.* Invest in training for both technical and interpersonal skills. In many cases, virtual teams falter not due to weak technical skills but due to poor communication and cooperation.

- *Personalization.* Encourage team members to get to know one another, either by encouraging informal communication using technology or by arranging face-to-face meetings whenever possible. Reduce feelings of isolation by setting aside time for chit-chat, acknowledging birthdays, and so on.

- *Goals and ground rules.* On the management side, virtual team leaders should define goals clearly, set rules for communication standards and responses, and provide feedback to keep team members informed of progress and the big picture.

The key appears to be recognizing the ways in which these teams are different from those based in a single office environment but not falling into the trap of focusing solely on technology. Many of the general recommendations that apply to any work team also apply to virtual teams. These teams are made up of individuals who have the same feelings and needs as workers in more traditional environments. Virtual teams must be real teams, if not by location, then in mind and spirit.

A WORD OF CAUTION: TEAMS AS A PANACEA

Teams can be a powerful resource for organizations, and this chapter has identified some of the important lessons leading to team success. However, switching from a traditional structure to a team-based configuration is not a cure-all for an organization's problems, even though some managers fall prey to the "romance of teams."[77] It is likely that the research to date on teams has focused almost exclusively on viable, ongoing teams, with little attention being paid to unsuccessful teams. Some observers suggest that the team approach puts unwanted pressure and responsibilities on workers. Others have noted that many organizations have rushed to deploy teams with little planning, often resulting in confusion and contradictory signals to employees. Good planning and continuing support are necessary for the effective use of teams.[78]

THE MANAGER'S NOTEBOOK

Creating Trust in Virtual Teams at Orange

1. Trust is an important ingredient in all teams, regardless of the proximity of members. Trust is considered to enhance overall team performance because it reduces the need for formal checks and balances and increases team members' ability to work through interpersonal challenges. When trust is low, teams require a higher degree of control and leadership, which reduces overall productivity and increases costs. In virtual teams, trust is harder to achieve due to the perceived distances (e.g., geographical and cultural) between team members. To overcome this challenge, members of virtual teams need to be aligned in their thoughts and actions about the work they have been assigned. In virtual teams, trust is built on the perceived ability of team members, benevolence between team members, positive feelings about each other, and the overall integrity of the group. At Orange, experience confirmed that three principles are necessary for building trust in teams: small team size, strong leadership, and a common working framework. At first, Orange attempted to run large, lengthy, cross-functional initiatives through the use of virtual teams. But the company found that the number of relationships and the complexity of the work created significant trust barriers. Over time, Orange moved to smaller virtual teams (under 10 members) to achieve more focused mandates over a shorter period. In addition, Orange recognized that more effective leaders were those who could recognize cultural differences and bridge those differences between members through the use of a common framework. For example, one way to ensure "equality" in a team is to have everyone join a conference call by phone, regardless of the fact that some members are located in the same place and could talk face to face.

2. At Orange, experience indicated that leaders of virtual teams are better off focusing on outputs rather than on team processes. Since it is impossible to know what each team member is doing at any particular time, measuring outputs allows each team member to work when and how he or she chooses, respecting local customs and norms. Orange and their consultants also realized that the start-up of a team is a crucial period when leaders need to develop clear team objectives. To encourage a culture of trust within the team, leaders must therefore be good communicators and coaches, be able to foster an atmosphere of trust, and be independent workers. From the start, the leader must demonstrate trust in team members and encourage trust among team members by identifying their track records and nature of expertise. This effort must be complemented by seeking trust from stakeholders of the project, which, in turn, will generate further trust within the team. At Orange, the creation and leadership of virtual teams is now based on the fundamental need to create trust quickly and to embed this trust throughout the life of the team. Trust has become a planned activity to be achieved through the building of knowledge (understanding objectives and the contribution of others) and team formation.

LEARNING OBJECTIVES CHECKLIST

7.1 A *group* consists of two or more people interacting interdependently to achieve a common goal. *Formal work groups* are groups that organizations establish to facilitate the achievement of organizational goals. *Informal groups* are groups that emerge naturally in response to the common interests of organizational members.

7.2 Some groups go through a series of developmental stages: forming, storming, norming, performing, and adjourning. However, the *punctuated equilibrium* model stresses a first meeting, a period of little apparent progress, a critical midpoint transition, and a phase of goal-directed activity.

7.3 As groups get bigger, they provide less opportunity for member satisfaction. When tasks are *additive* (performance depends on the addition of individual effort) or *disjunctive* (performance depends on that of the best member), larger groups should perform better than smaller groups if the group can avoid *process losses* due to poor communication and motivation. When tasks are *conjunctive* (performance is limited by the weakest member), performance decreases as the group gets bigger, because the chance of adding a weak member increases. Diverse groups generally develop at a slower pace and be less cohesive than homogeneous groups. While the effects of surface-level demographic diversity can wear off over time, deep diversity differences regarding attitudes are more difficult to overcome.

7.4 *Norms* are expectations that group members have about one another's behaviour. They provide consistency to behaviour and develop as a function of shared attitudes. In organizations, both formal and informal norms often develop to control dress, reward allocation, and performance. *Roles* are positions in a group that have a set of expected behaviours associated with

them. *Role ambiguity* refers to a lack of clarity of job goals or methods. *Role conflict* exists when an individual is faced with incompatible role expectations, and it can take four forms: *intra-sender, intersender, interrole,* and *person–role*. Both ambiguity and conflict have been shown to provoke job dissatisfaction, stress, and lowered commitment. *Status* is the rank or prestige that a group accords its members. Formal status systems use status symbols to reinforce the authority hierarchy and reward progression. Informal status systems also operate in organizations. Although status differences are motivational, they also lead to communication barriers.

7.5 *Cohesive groups* are especially attractive to their members. Threat, competition, success, and small size contribute to cohesiveness, as does a tough initiation into the group. The consequences of cohesiveness include increased participation in group affairs, improved communication, and increased conformity. Cohesive groups are especially effective in accomplishing their own goals, which may or may not be those of the organization.

7.6 *Social loafing* occurs when people withhold effort when performing a group task. This is less likely when individual performance is visible, the task is interesting, there is good performance feedback, and the organization rewards group achievement.

7.7 Members of *self-managed work teams* do challenging work under reduced supervision. For greatest effectiveness, such teams should be stable, small, well trained, and moderately diverse in membership. Group-oriented rewards are most appropriate. Teams perform best when they have high *collective efficacy*, a shared belief that they can perform a given task. Sharing identical information (*shared mental models*) contributes to such efficacy.

7.8 *Cross-functional teams* bring people with different functional specialties together to better invent, design, or deliver a product or service. They should have diverse membership, a *superordinate* goal, some basic decision rules, and reasonable autonomy. Members should work in the same physical location, and team leaders require people skills as well as task skills.

7.9 *Virtual teams* use technology to communicate and collaborate across time, space, and organizational boundaries. These teams offer many advantages, such as reduced travel costs, greater potential talent, and continuous workflows, but pose dangers in terms of miscommunication, trust, and feelings of isolation.

DISCUSSION QUESTIONS

1. Describe the kind of skills that you would look for in members of self-managed teams. Explain your choices. Do the same for virtual teams.

2. Debate: *Effective teamwork is more difficult for individualistic Americans, Canadians, and Australians than for more collectivist Japanese.*

3. When would an organization create self-managed teams? When would it use cross-functional teams? When would it employ virtual teams?

4. Suppose that a group of United Nations representatives from various countries forms to draft a resolution regarding world hunger. Is this an additive, disjunctive, or conjunctive task? What kinds of process losses would such a group be likely to suffer? Can you offer a prediction about the size of this group and its performance?

5. Explain how a cross-functional team could contribute to product or service quality. Explain how a cross-functional team could contribute to speeding up product design.

6. Mark Allen, a representative for an international engineering company, is a very religious person who is active in his church. Mark's direct superior has instructed him to use "any legal means" to sell a large construction project to a foreign government. The vice-president of international operations had informed Mark that he could offer a generous "kickback" to government officials to clinch the deal, although such practices are illegal. Discuss the three kinds of role conflict that Mark is experiencing.

7. Some organizations have made concerted efforts to do away with many of the status symbols associated with differences in organizational rank. All employees now park in the same lot, eat in the same dining room, and have similar offices and privileges. Discuss the pros and cons of such a strategy. How might such a change affect organizational communications?

8. You are an executive in a consumer products corporation. The president assigns you to form a task force to develop new marketing strategies for the organization. You are permitted to choose its members. What things would you do to make this group as cohesive as possible? What are the dangers of group cohesiveness for the group itself and for the organization of which the group is a part?

INTEGRATIVE DISCUSSION QUESTIONS

1. What role do perceptions play in group development? Refer to the discussion of perceptual process and biases in Chapter 3 and discuss the implications for each stage of group development. What are the implications for improving the development of groups?

2. How can groups be motivated? Consider the implications of each of the work motivation theories described in Chapter 5. What do the theories tell us about how to motivate groups?

ON-THE-JOB CHALLENGE QUESTION

Self-Managed Teams at ISE Communications

ISE Communications was one of the pioneers in using self-managed work teams. The teams were put in place to improve manufacturing flexibility and customer service, both factors being crucial in the highly competitive circuit board industry. Its conversion from an assembly-line style of circuit board manufacturing to teams who identified with "their own" products and customers was deemed a great success by industry observers. One interesting result was that the teams became extremely obsessed with monitoring the promptness and attendance of their members, more so than managers had been before the conversion to teams. They even posted attendance charts and created punishments for slack team members.

Use your understanding of both group dynamics and teams to explain why the employees became so concerned about attendance when they were organized into teams. What had changed?

Source: Barker, J.R. (1993). Tightening the iron cage: Concertive control in self-managing teams. *Administrative Science Quarterly, 38*, 408–437.

EXPERIENTIAL EXERCISE

NASA

The purpose of this exercise is to compare individual and group problem solving and to explore the group dynamics that occur in a problem-solving session. It can also be used in conjunction with Chapter 11. The instructor will begin by forming groups of four to seven members.

The situation described in this problem is based on actual cases in which men and women lived or died, depending on the survival decisions they made. Your "life" or "death" will depend on how well your group can share its present knowledge of a relatively unfamiliar problem, so that the group can make decisions that will lead to your survival.

The Problem

You are a member of a space crew originally scheduled to rendezvous with a mother ship on the lighted surface of the moon. Due to mechanical difficulties, however, your ship was forced to land at a spot some 200 miles from the rendezvous point. During landing, much of the equipment aboard was damaged, and, because survival depends on reaching the mother ship, the most critical items available must be chosen for the 200-mile trip. On the next page are listed the 15 items left intact and undamaged after the landing. Your task is to rank them in terms of their importance to your crew in reaching the rendezvous point. In the first column (step 1) place the number 1 by the first most important, and so on, through number 15, the least important. You have 15 minutes to complete this phase of the exercise.

After the individual rankings are complete, participants should be formed into groups having from four to seven members. Each group should then rank the 15 items as a team. This group ranking should be a general consensus after a discussion of the issues, not just the average of each individual ranking. While it is unlikely that everyone will agree exactly on the group ranking, an effort should be made to reach at least a decision that everyone can live with. It is important to treat differences of opinion as a means of gathering more information and clarifying issues and as an incentive to force the group to seek better alternatives. The group ranking should be listed in the second column (step 2).

The third phase of the exercise consists of the instructor providing the expert's rankings, which should be entered in the third column (step 3). Each participant should compute the difference between the individual ranking (step 1) and the expert's ranking (step 3), and between the group ranking (step 2) and the expert's ranking (step 3). Then add the two "difference" columns—the smaller the score, the closer the ranking is to the view of the experts.

Source: From Ritchie, *Organization and people*, 3rd edition. © 1984 South-Western, a part of Cenage Learning, Inc. Reproduced by permission. www.cengage.com/permissions.

Discussion

The instructor will summarize the results on the board for each group, including (a) the average individual accuracy score, (b) the group accuracy score, (c) the gain or loss between the average individual score and the group score, and (d) the lowest individual score (i.e., the best score) in each group.

The following questions will help guide the discussion:

1. As a group task, is the NASA exercise an additive, disjunctive, or conjunctive task?

2. What would be the impact of group size on performance in this task?

3. Did any norms develop in your group that guided how information was exchanged or how the decision was reached?

4. Did any special roles emerge in your group? These could include a leader, a secretary, an "expert," a critic, or a humourist. How did these roles contribute to or hinder group performance?

5. Consider the factors that contribute to effective self-managed teams. How do they pertain to a group's performance on this exercise?

6. How would group diversity help or hinder performance on the exercise?

NASA tally sheet

Items	Step 1 Your individual ranking	Step 2 The team's ranking	Step 3 Survival expert's ranking	Step 4 Difference between Step 1 & 3	Step 5 Difference between Step 2 & 3
Box of matches					
Food concentrate					
50 feet of nylon rope					
Parachute silk					
Portable heating unit					
Two .45 calibre pistols					
One case dehydrated milk					
Two 100-lb. tanks of oxygen					
Stellar map (of the moon's constellation)					
Life raft					
Magnetic compass					
5 gallons of water					
Signal flares					
First aid kit containing injection needles					
Solar-powered FM receiver-transmitter					
			Total		
		(The lower the score the better)		Your score	Team score

CASE INCIDENT

The Group Assignment

Janet, a student, never liked working on group assignments; however, this time she thought it would be different because she knew most of the people in her group. But it was not long before things started going badly. After the first meeting, the group could not agree when to meet again. When they finally did meet, nobody had done anything, and the assignment was due in two weeks. The group then agreed to meet again the next day to figure out what to do. However, two of the group members did not show up. The following week Janet tried in vain to arrange for another meeting, but the other group members said they were too busy and that it would be best to divide the assignment up and have each member work on a section. The night before the assignment was due the group members met to give Janet their work. Finally, Janet thought, we are making progress. However, when she got home and read what the other members had written she was shocked at how bad it was. Janet spent the rest of the night and early morning doing the whole assignment herself. Once the course ended, Janet never spoke to any of the group members again.

1. Refer to the typical stages of group development and explain the development of Janet's group.

2. To what extent was group cohesiveness a problem in Janet's work group? What might have made the group more cohesive?

CASE STUDY

The Creativity Development Committee

Tom was the manager of three research and development laboratories for a large chemical and materials corporation. He supervised general operations, budgeting, personnel, and proposal development for the labs. Each lab had several projects, and each project team was headed by a project director, who was usually a scientist or an engineer. Tom had been project director for 10 years in another of the corporation's labs and had been promoted to lab manager four years ago. Although he had to transfer across the country to take this job, he felt he had earned the respect of his subordinates. He had been regarded as an outsider at first, but he worked hard to be accepted, and the lab's productivity had gone up over the last two years. Tom's major worry was keeping track of everything. His busy schedule kept him from close supervision over projects.

As in most labs, each project generally went its own way. As long as it produced results, a project enjoyed a high degree of autonomy. Morale was usually high among research staff. They knew they were on the leading edge of the corporation's success and they enjoyed it. The visibility and importance of innovative research were shown by the fact that project directors were regularly promoted upward.

It was in this milieu that Tom decided that productivity might be further increased if research creativity were heightened. Research teams often met to discuss ideas and to decide on future directions. In these meetings ideas were often improved upon, but they could also be killed or cut off. Tom had studied research on decision making, which indicated that groups often suppress good ideas without a hearing; the research suggested ways of preventing this suppression and enhancing group creativity. Tom hoped to harness these findings by developing standard procedures through which idea development would be enhanced rather than hindered in these meetings. Tom asked four project directors if they were willing to work with him to review the research and meet regularly over the summer to help formulate appropriate procedures. The four agreed to take on the task and the group began its work enthusiastically.

During the first six weeks of the summer the group met weekly to discuss relevant articles and books and to hear consultants. The group was able to narrow down a set of about 15 procedures and programs to 4 prime possibilities. Eventually, 2 programs emerged as possibilities. However, as the list was narrowed from 4 to 2, there was a clear split in how the group felt.

One procedure was strongly favoured by three of the project directors. The fourth project director liked the procedure better than the other option but was less vocal in showing her support for it. In general, the project directors felt the procedure they favoured was far more consistent with what project teams were currently doing and with the problems faced by the corporation. They believed the second program, which involved a lot of writing and the use of special voting procedures, was too abstract for working research scientists to accept. It would be difficult, they said, to use this procedure because everyone would have to fill out forms and explain ideas in writing before a meeting could be held. Because of already heavy workloads, their people would not go along with the program. Researchers would ridicule the program and be prejudiced against future attempts to stimulate creativity.

Tom argued that the second program was more comprehensive, had a broader conception of problems, and would help develop more creative ideas than the first, which was a fairly conservative "brainstorming" process. Although discussion focused on the substantive nature of each program and its reaction to the objective of creativity, the project directors knew that the program Tom favoured was one he had been trained in at his former lab. Tom was a good friend of the consultant who had developed it. The project directors talked outside meetings about this friendship and questioned whether it was shaping Tom's attitudes. The climate of the group, which had initially been positive and enthusiastic, grew tense as issues connected to the power relations between the manager and project directors surfaced.

Although the project directors knew Tom could choose the program he wanted, how the final choice would be made was never clarified at the beginning of the summer. The time that the project directors spent reading and evaluating the programs created an implicit expectation that they would have an equal say in the final choice. At the same time, the project directors had all worked at the lab for at least four years and had experienced first-hand the relative power of managers and project directors. They heard horror stories of project directors who had got on the manager's "wrong side" and been denied promotion or fired. When push came to shove, they expected the manager to have greater power and to be willing to use it.

At its final meeting the group discussed the two programs for quite some time, but there seemed to be little movement. Somewhat hesitantly, Tom turned to each project director individually and asked, "How upset would you be if I choose the program I prefer?" One project director said he was uncomfortable answering. Two indicated that they felt they would have difficulty using the creativity program as it was currently designed. The fourth said that she thought she could live with it. After these answers were given, Tom told the project directors he would leave a memo in their mailboxes informing them of the final decision.

Two weeks after this discussion, the project directors were told that the second program, the one the manager preferred, would be ordered. The memo also said that the other program would be used, on an experimental basis, by one of the 18 projects. The decision caused considerable resentment. The project directors felt "used." They saw little reason in having spent too much time discussing programs if Tom was just going to choose the program he wanted, regardless of their preferences. When the program began in the fall, one of the project directors told his team that the program would be recommended rather than required, and he explained that it might have to be adapted extensively to fit the unit's style. He made this decision without telling the manager. While the move was in clear violation of Tom's authority, he knew Tom could not visit the teams often and was therefore unlikely to find out about it. Another project director instituted the program but commented afterward that he felt he had not integrated it into his unit well. He questioned how much effort he had actually invested in making the program "work."

The incident had a significant impact on the way Tom was seen by the project directors. Several commented that they had lost their respect for Tom, that they saw Tom as someone who was willing to manipulate people for his own purposes. This opinion filtered to other project directors and scientists through the "grapevine" and caused Tom considerable difficulties in a labour grievance during the following year. In this dispute several researchers banded together and defied the manager because they believed he would eventually back down. In addition, the project director who made the program optional for these workers served as a model for similar defiance by others. Once the directors saw that "optional" use of the program would be go unpunished, they felt free to do it themselves, and Tom's control was further reduced. Tom eventually transferred to another division of the corporation.

Source: FOLGER, JOSEPH P.; POOLE, MARSHALL SCOTT; STUTMAN, RANDALL K., WORKING THROUGH CONFLICT: STRATEGIES FOR RELATIONSHIPS, GROUPS, AND ORGANIZATIONS, 3rd Ed, © 1997, pp. 107–109. Reprinted and Electronically reproduced by permission of Pearson Education, Inc., Upper Saddle River, New Jersey.

QUESTIONS

1. Discuss how the stages of group development and the punctuated equilibrium model apply to the Creativity Development Committee. Did the

group progress through any of the stages of these models? Did the group fail to resolve any issues implied by these models?

2. Is the choice of the best creativity development program an additive, disjunctive, or conjunctive task? Explain your reasoning. Discuss the implications of the task type for what happened on the committee.

3. Did role ambiguity surface in the case? If so, how so?
4. Did role conflict surface in the case? If so, which type or types occurred?
5. How did status issues emerge in the committee?
6. Did the committee share a mental model about its goals and procedures?

CHAPTER 8

SOCIAL INFLUENCE, SOCIALIZATION, AND ORGANIZATIONAL CULTURE

LEARNING OBJECTIVES

After reading Chapter 8, you should be able to:

8.1 Understand the difference between *information dependence* and *effect dependence*.

8.2 Differentiate *compliance*, *identification*, and *internalization* as motives for social conformity.

8.3 Describe the *socialization* process and the stages of organizational socialization.

8.4 Describe the implications of *unrealistic expectations* and the *psychological contract* for socialization.

8.5 Describe the main *methods of socialization* and how newcomers can be *proactive* in their socialization.

8.6 Define *organizational culture* and discuss the contributors to a culture.

8.7 Discuss the assets and liabilities of *strong cultures*.

8.8 Describe how to diagnose an organizational culture.

GOOGLE CANADA

Google was co-founded by Larry Page and Sergey Brin in 1998 while they were students at Stanford University. Today, Google is one of the world's largest internet search engines and the most popular website. Google's world headquarters building, known as the Googleplex, is located in Mountain View, California.

Google has more than 30 000 employees in offices around the world, and its employees speak dozens of languages. However, it has managed to maintain a small-company feel thanks to a culture of collaboration, a flat structure with very little hierarchy, small focused teams of employees, kitchens that serve healthy food and encourage employees to eat together and socialize, and perks such as in-house massages. The company even has a chief culture officer to ensure that it maintains its core values and culture. To encourage a sense of ownership, Google employees receive stock grants or options.

Google Canada has about 300 employees working in offices in Toronto, Waterloo, Ottawa, and Montreal. In 2008, Google Canada opened its first official Canadian headquarters in downtown Toronto. Given the company's commitment to being environmentally responsible,

the Toronto headquarters was built with the environment in mind. For example, they kept the existing concrete floor rather than using new floor material. The cafeteria floor is made of recycled Canadian bicycle tires from landfills. And rather than using new chairs in the lobby waiting area, the company purchased stadium seats from the old Montreal Forum. Many of the green ideas came from employees and involved using existing materials of the building or reusing or recycling other materials.

As part of the company's green initiative, employees are encouraged to use public transportation or their own green solution to get to work; those that do so receive a monthly subsidy that is added to their pay. A bike room with showers is provided to encourage a healthy lifestyle. The company also believes in taking good care of its people. The cafeteria offers free breakfasts, lunch, and snacks, and a dietary expert is responsible for the selection of food along with a menu that details how healthy each item is. Google recently launched a program called "Are You Fiscally Fit," to provide employees with resources such as seminars, free books, and one-on-one consultations to

Google Canada has been ranked as the best place to work in Canada thanks to a culture that emphasizes collaboration, innovation, transparency, and a commitment to environmental responsibility.

help them increase their financial knowledge. The company also encourages employees to be more involved in the community through initiatives such as Google's donation-matching program.

Google's culture also emphasizes innovation and entrepreneurialism through its "20 percent time" program, which enables employees to work together or separately one day out of five on something other than their job that they are passionate about. This allows employees to work on new ideas and collaborate with each other. Some of Google's most innovative products, such as Gmail and Google Outreach, came out of the 20 percent time program. The entrepreneurial culture is also fostered through flexible hours and a focus on results and productive time rather than face time.

Another important part of the Google culture is transparency and open communication. The company holds weekly TGIF meetings, where company executives and founders Sergey Brin and Larry Page address employees and answer any questions they have about Google. The Google culture of open communication also influences the hiring process, which involves several rounds of interviews in which employees and managers participate. As a result, employees have some input into the direction of the company and who they will be working with.

Google has won many awards for its work environment. *Fortune* magazine has ranked Google as one of America's most admired companies and the best place to work in the United States. In 2012, Google Canada was ranked as the best place to work in Canada for the second year in a row.[1]

This description of Google Canada raises a number of interesting questions. What exactly is an organizational culture and what effect does it have on employees? What does it mean to have a strong culture and what are the assets and liabilities of strong cultures? How are cultures built and maintained and how do new employees learn about an organization's culture? These are the kinds of questions that we will probe in this chapter.

First we will examine the general issue of social influence in organizations—how members have an impact on each other's behaviour and attitudes. Social norms hold an organization together, and conformity to such norms is a product of the social influence process. Following this we consider the elaborate process of organizational socialization, the learning of attitudes, knowledge, and behaviours that are necessary to function in an organization. Socialization both contributes to and results from the organizational culture, the final topic that we will explore.

SOCIAL INFLUENCE IN ORGANIZATIONS

In the previous chapter we pointed out that groups exert influence over the attitudes and behaviour of their individual members. As a result of social influence, people often feel or act differently from how they would as independent operators. What accounts for such influence? In short, in many social settings, and especially in groups, people are highly *dependent* on others. This dependence sets the stage for influence to occur.

Information Dependence and Effect Dependence

LO 8.1

Understand the difference between *information dependence* and *effect dependence*.

Information dependence. Reliance on others for information about how to think, feel, and act.

Social information processing theory. Information from others is used to interpret events and develop expectations about appropriate and acceptable attitudes and behaviours.

Effect dependence. Reliance on others due to their capacity to provide rewards and punishment.

We are frequently dependent on others for information about the adequacy and appropriateness of our behaviour, thoughts, and feelings. How satisfying is this job of mine? How nice is our boss? How much work should I take home to do over the weekend? Should we protest the bad design at the meeting? Objective, concrete answers to such questions might be hard to come by. Thus, we must often rely on information that others provide.[2] In turn, this **information dependence** gives others the opportunity to influence our thoughts, feelings, and actions via the signals they send to us.[3]

The process through which this occurs is explained by social information processing theory. According to **social information processing theory**, organizational members use information from others to interpret events and develop expectations about appropriate and acceptable attitudes and behaviours. Thus, organizational members look to others for information and cues about how they should behave.[4] Individuals are often motivated to compare their own thoughts, feelings, and actions with those of others as a means of acquiring information about their adequacy. The effects of social information can be very strong, often exerting as much or more influence over others as objective reality. As a result, individual behaviour is influenced and shaped by others.[5]

As if group members were not busy enough tuning in to information provided by the group, they must also be sensitive to the rewards and punishments the group has at its disposal. Thus, individuals are dependent on the *effects* of their behaviour as determined by the rewards and punishments provided by others. **Effect dependence** actually involves two complementary processes. First, the group frequently has a vested interest in how individual members think and act because such matters can affect the goal attainment of the group. Second, the members frequently desire the approval of the group. In combination, these circumstances promote effect dependence.

In organizations, plenty of effects are available to keep individual members "under the influence." Managers typically have a fair array of rewards and punishments available, including promotions, raises, and the assignment of more or less favourable tasks. At the informal level, the variety of such effects available to co-workers is staggering. They might reward cooperative behaviour with praise, friendship, and a helping hand on the job. Lack of cooperation might result in nagging, harassment, name calling, or social isolation.

The Social Influence Process and Conformity

One of the most obvious consequences of information and effect dependence is the tendency for group members to conform to the social norms that have been established by the group. In the last chapter, we discussed the development and function of such norms, but we have postponed until now the discussion of why norms are supported. Put simply, much of the information and many of the effects on which group members are dependent are oriented toward enforcing group norms. As described below, there are three different motives for social conformity.[6]

To understand the motives for social conformity, consider Mark, an idealistic graduate of a university social work program who acquires a job with a social services agency. Mark loves helping people but hates the bureaucratic red tape and reams of paperwork that are necessary to accomplish this goal. However, to acquire the approval of his boss and co-workers and to avoid trouble, he follows the rules to the letter of the law. This is pure compliance. **Compliance** is the simplest, most direct motive for conformity to group norms. It occurs because a member wishes to acquire rewards from the group and avoid punishment. As such, it primarily involves effect dependence. Although the complying individual adjusts his or her behaviour to the norm, he or she does not really subscribe to the beliefs, values, and attitudes that underlie the norm.

Over time, however, Mark begins to *identify* with his boss and more experienced co-workers because they are in the enviable position of controlling those very rewards and punishments that are so important to him. Obviously, if he is to *be* one of them, he must begin to think and feel like them. **Identification** as a motive for conformity is often revealed by an imitation process in which established members serve as models for the behaviour of others. Although there are elements of effect dependence here, information dependence is especially important—if someone is basically similar to you, then you will be motivated to rely on that person for information about how to think and act.

Finally, Mark is promoted to a supervisory position, partly because he is so cooperative. Breaking in a new social worker, Mark is heard to say, "Our rules and forms are very important. You don't understand now, but you will." The metamorphosis is complete—Mark has *internalized* the beliefs and values that support the bureaucratic norms of his agency. **Internalization** occurs when individuals have truly and wholly accepted the beliefs, values, and attitudes that underlie the norm. Conformity occurs because it is seen as *right*, not because it achieves rewards, avoids punishment, or pleases others. That is, conformity is due to internal, rather than external, forces.

Although this story is slightly dramatized, the point that it makes is accurate—simple compliance can set the stage for more complete identification and involvement with organizational norms and roles. The process through which this occurs in organizations is known as *organizational socialization* and it is the focus of the next section.

ORGANIZATIONAL SOCIALIZATION

The story of Mark, the social worker, in the previous section describes how one individual was socialized into a particular organization. **Socialization** is the process by which people learn the attitudes, knowledge, and behaviours that are necessary to function in a group or organization. It is a learning process in which new members must acquire knowledge, change their attitudes, and perform new behaviours. Socialization is also the primary means by which organizations communicate their culture and values to new members.[7]

Exhibit 8.1 depicts the socialization process. In particular, it shows how different socialization methods (e.g., employee orientation programs) influence a number of immediate or proximal socialization outcomes, such as learning, which lead to more distal or longer-term outcomes, such as attitudes (e.g., job satisfaction) and behaviours (e.g., turnover).

Learning during socialization has often been described in terms of content areas or domains of learning, such as the task, role, group, and organization domain. Newcomers need to acquire the knowledge and skills necessary to perform their job duties and *tasks*;

LO

Differentiate *compliance*, *identification*, and *internalization* as motives for social conformity.

Compliance. Conformity to a social norm prompted by the desire to acquire rewards or avoid punishment.

Identification. Conformity to a social norm prompted by perceptions that those who promote the norm are attractive or similar to oneself.

Internalization. Conformity to a social norm prompted by true acceptance of the beliefs, values, and attitudes that underlie the norm.

LO **8.3**

Describe the *socialization* process and the stages of organizational socialization.

Socialization. The process by which people learn the attitudes, knowledge, and behaviours that are necessary to function in a group or organization.

Socialization Methods		Proximal Socialization Outcomes	Distal Socialization Outcomes
Realistic job previews		Learning	Job satisfaction
Employee orientation programs		Task mastery	Organizational commitment
Socialization tactics		Social integration	Organizational identification
Mentoring		Role conflict	Organizational citizenship behaviour
Proactive tactics		Role ambiguity	Job performance
		Person–job fit	Stress
		Person–organization fit	Turnover

EXHIBIT 8.1
The socialization process.

 Explore

Go to MyManagementLab to see an annotated version of this figure.

Person–job fit. The match between an employee's knowledge, skills, and abilities and the requirements of a job.

Person–organization fit. The match between an employee's personal values and the values of an organization.

Organizational identification. The extent to which individuals define themselves in terms of the organization and what it is perceived to represent.

they need to learn the appropriate behaviours and expectations of their *role*; they need to learn the norms and values of their *work group*; and they need to learn about the *organization*, such as its history, traditions, language, politics, mission, and culture. As newcomers learn about each of these areas, they should begin to master their tasks and integrate with others in their workgroup and the organization. This should also help to reduce their role ambiguity and role conflict. In Chapter 7, we described how different factors can lead to role ambiguity and role conflict. One of the goals of socialization is to provide new hires with information and knowledge about their role to avoid problems of role conflict and role ambiguity.

An important objective of organizational socialization is for newcomers to achieve a good fit. There are generally two kinds of fit that are important for socialization. First, newcomers must acquire the knowledge and skills necessary to perform their work tasks and roles. This is known as person–job fit, or PJ fit. **Person–job fit** refers to the match between an employee's knowledge, skills, and abilities and the requirements of a job. Second, newcomers must also learn the values and beliefs that are important to the group and organization. This is known as **person–organization fit**, or PO fit, and it refers to the match between an employee's personal values and the values of an organization.[8] Research has found that both PJ and PO fit are strongly influenced by the socialization process and are related to job attitudes and behaviours.[9]

One of the primary goals of organizational socialization is to ensure that new employees learn and understand the key beliefs, values, and assumptions of an organization's culture, and for individuals to define themselves in terms of the organization and what it is perceived to represent. This is known as **organizational identification**, and as shown in Exhibit 8.1, it is also a distal outcome of socialization. Organizational identification reflects an individual's learning and acceptance of an organization's culture.[10]

In summary, socialization is important because it has a direct effect on proximal socialization outcomes (e.g., learning, PJ fit, and PO fit), which lead to more positive distal outcomes (e.g., organizational identification). As we shall see, some of this process might occur before organization membership formally begins, while some of it occurs once the new member enters the organization. Furthermore, socialization is an ongoing process by virtue of continuous interaction with others in the organization. However, socialization is most potent during certain periods of membership transition, such as when one is promoted or assigned to a new work group or department, and especially when one joins a new organization.[11]

Stages of Socialization

Since organizational socialization is an ongoing process, it is useful to divide this process into three stages.[12] One of these stages occurs before entry, another immediately follows entry, and the last occurs after one has been a member for some period of time. In a sense, the first two stages represent hurdles for achieving passage into the third stage (see Exhibit 8.2).

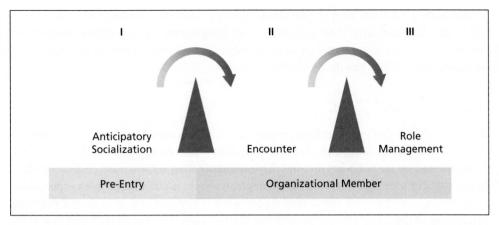

EXHIBIT 8.2
Stages of organizational socialization.
Source: Based on Feldman, D.C. (1976). A contingency theory of socialization. *Administrative Science Quarterly, 21,* 433–452; Feldman, D.C. (1981). The multiple socialization of organization members. *Academy of Management Review, 6,* 309–318.

Explore

Go to MyManagementLab to see an annotated version of this figure.

ANTICIPATORY SOCIALIZATION A considerable amount of socialization occurs even before a person becomes a member of a particular organization. This process is called anticipatory socialization. Some anticipatory socialization includes a formal process of skill and attitude acquisition, such as that which might occur by attending college or university. Other anticipatory socialization might be informal, such as that acquired through a series of summer jobs or even by watching the portrayal of organizational life in television shows and movies. Some organizations begin to socialize job candidates even before they are hired at recruitment events, where organizational representatives discuss the organization with potential hires. As we shall see shortly, organizations vary in the extent to which they encourage anticipatory socialization in advance of entry. As well, not all anticipatory socialization is accurate and useful for the new member.

ENCOUNTER In the encounter stage, the new recruit, armed with some expectations about organizational life, encounters the day-to-day reality of this life. Formal aspects of this stage might include orientation programs and rotation through various parts of the organization. Informal aspects include getting to know and understand the style and personality of one's boss and co-workers. At this stage, the organization and its experienced members are looking for an acceptable degree of conformity to organizational norms and the gradual acquisition of appropriate role behaviour. Recruits, on the other hand, are interested in having their personal needs and expectations fulfilled. If successful, the recruit will have complied with critical organizational norms and should begin to identify with experienced organizational members.

ROLE MANAGEMENT Having survived the encounter stage and acquired basic role behaviours, the new member's attention shifts to fine tuning and actively managing his or her role in the organization. Following some conformity to group norms, the new recruit might now be in a position to modify the role to better serve the organization. This might require forming connections outside the immediate workgroup. The organizational member must also confront balancing the now-familiar organizational role with non-work roles and family demands. Each of these experiences provides additional socialization to the role occupant, who might begin to internalize the norms and values that are prominent in the organization.

Now that we have seen a basic sketch of how socialization proceeds, let's take a closer look at some of the key issues in the process.

UNREALISTIC EXPECTATIONS AND THE PSYCHOLOGICAL CONTRACT

LO **8.4**

Describe the implications of *unrealistic expectations* and the *psychological contract* for socialization.

People seldom join organizations without expectations about what membership will be like and what they expect to receive in return for their efforts. In fact, it is just such expectations that lead them to choose one career, job, or organization over another. Management majors have some expectations about what they will be doing when they become management trainees at IBM. Similarly, even 18-year-old army recruits have notions about what military life will be like. Unfortunately, these expectations are often unrealistic, and agreements between new members and organizations are often breached. Let's now consider the implications of unrealistic expectations and the psychological contract.

UNREALISTIC EXPECTATIONS

Research indicates that people entering organizations hold many expectations that are inaccurate and often unrealistically high. As a result, once they enter an organization they realize that their expectations are not being met and they experience what is known as a "reality shock."[13] In one study of telephone operators, for example, researchers obtained people's expectations about the nature of the job *before* they started work. They also looked at these employees' perceptions of the actual job shortly *after* they started work. The results indicated that many perceptions were less favourable than expectations. A similar result occurred for students entering an MBA program. The extent to which newcomers' expectations are met (or unmet) has important implications for their socialization. Research has found that newcomers who have higher met expectations have higher job satisfaction, organizational commitment, job performance, and job survival and lower intentions to leave.[14]

Why do new members often have unrealistic expectations about the organizations they join?[15] To some extent, occupational stereotypes, such as those we discussed in Chapter 3, could be responsible. The media often communicate such stereotypes. For example, a person entering nursing training might have gained some expectations about hospital life from watching the television show *Grey's Anatomy*. Those of us who teach might also be guilty of communicating stereotypes. After four years of study, the new management trainee at IBM might be dismayed to find that the emphasis is on *trainee* rather than *management*! Finally, unrealistic expectations may also stem from overzealous recruiters who paint rosy pictures to attract job candidates to the organization. Taken together, these factors demonstrate the need for socialization and for helping recruits acquire more realistic expectations.

PSYCHOLOGICAL CONTRACT

Psychological contract.
Beliefs held by employees regarding the reciprocal obligations and promises between them and their organization.

When people join organizations, they have beliefs and expectations about what they will receive from the organization in return for what they will give the organization. Such beliefs form what is known as the psychological contract. A **psychological contract** refers to beliefs held by employees regarding the reciprocal obligations and promises between them and their organization.[16] For example, an employee might expect to receive bonuses and promotions in return for hard work and loyalty.

Psychological contract breach. Employee perceptions that his or her organization has failed to fulfill one or more of its promises or obligations in the psychological contract.

Unfortunately, psychological contract breach appears to be a common occurrence. Perceptions of **psychological contract breach** occur when an employee perceives that his or her organization has failed to fulfill one or more of its promises or obligations in the psychological contract. One study found that 55 percent of recent MBA graduates reported that some aspect of their psychological contract had been broken by their employer.[17] This often results in feelings of anger and betrayal and can have a negative effect on employees' work attitudes and behaviour.

A review of research on the impact of psychological contract breach found that breach is related to affective reactions (higher feelings of contract violation and mistrust toward management), work attitudes (lower job satisfaction and organizational commitment, and higher turnover intentions), and work behaviours (lower organizational citizenship behaviour and job performance). These effects are due to the formation of negative emotions that stem from feelings of violation and mistrust toward management.[18] Employee perceptions of psychological contract breach have also been found to be associated with a decrease in innovation-related behaviours (e.g., coming up with new ideas) and lower customer satisfaction, both of which can have negative consequences for organizations.[19]

Why does psychological contract breach occur? As is the case with unrealistic expectations, recruiters are often tempted to promise more than their organization can provide to attract the best job applicants. In addition, newcomers often lack sufficient information to form accurate perceptions concerning their psychological contract. As a result, there will be some incongruence or differences in understanding between an employee and the organization about promised obligations. In addition, organizational changes, such as downsizing and restructuring, can cause organizations to knowingly break promises made to an employee that they are either unable or unwilling to keep.[20]

It is therefore important that newcomers develop accurate perceptions in the formation of a psychological contract. Many of the terms of the psychological contract are established during anticipatory socialization. Therefore, organizations need to ensure that truthful and accurate information about promises and obligations is communicated to new members before and after they join an organization. Incongruence and psychological contract breach are less likely in organizations where socialization is intense.[21] Furthermore, there is some evidence that what organizations actually give employees is itself especially important.[22] This further demonstrates the importance and need for organizational socialization. Let's now take a closer look at how organizations socialize new members.

HUMAN RESOURCES Go to MyManagementLab to complete a simulation about human resources.

LO **8.5**

Describe the main *methods of socialization* and how newcomers can be *proactive* in their socialization.

METHODS OF ORGANIZATIONAL SOCIALIZATION

Organizations differ in the extent to which they socialize their new hires. This is in part owing to the fact that some organizations make use of other organizations to help socialize their members. For example, hospitals do not develop experienced cardiologists from scratch. Rather, they depend on medical schools to socialize potential doctors in the basic role requirements of being a physician. Similarly, business firms rely on business schools to send them recruits who think and act in a business-like manner. In this way, a fair degree of anticipatory socialization may exist before a person joins an organization. On the other hand, organizations such as police forces, the military, and religious institutions are less likely to rely on external socialization. Police academies, boot camps, and seminaries are set up as extensions of these organizations to aid in socialization.

Organizations that handle their own socialization are especially interested in maintaining the continuity and stability of job behaviours over a period of time. Conversely, those that rely on external agencies to perform anticipatory socialization are oriented toward maintaining the potential for creative, innovative behaviour on the part of members—there is less "inbreeding." Of course, reliance on external agents might present problems. The engineer who is socialized in university courses to respect design elegance might find it difficult to accept cost restrictions when he or she is employed by an engineering firm. For this reason, organizations that rely heavily on external socialization always supplement it with formal training and orientation or informal on-the-job training.

The point is that organizations differ in terms of *who* does the socializing, *how* it is done, and *how much* is done. Most organizations, however, make use of a number of methods of socialization, including realistic job previews, employee orientation programs, socialization tactics, and mentoring. Let's now take a closer look at each of these methods of organizational socialization.

Realistic Job Previews

We noted earlier that new organizational members often have unrealistic, inflated expectations about what their jobs will be like. When the job actually begins and it fails to live up to these expectations, individuals experience a "reality shock," and job dissatisfaction results. As a consequence, costly turnover is most likely to occur among newer employees who are unable to survive the discrepancy between expectations and reality. For the organization, this sequence of events represents a failure of socialization.

EXHIBIT 8.3 Traditional and realistic job previews compared.

Source: Wanous, J.P. (1975). Tell it like it is at realistic job previews. *Personnel, 52*(4), 50–60 © 1975 American Management Association, New York. All rights reserved.

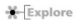[Explore

Go to MyManagementLab to see an annotated version of this figure.

Traditional Procedures	Realistic Procedures
Set initial job expectations too high	Set job expectations realistically
Job is typically viewed as attractive	Job may or may not be attractive, depending on individual's needs
High rate of job offer acceptance	Some accept, some reject job offer
Work experience disconfirms expectations	Work experience confirms expectations
Dissatisfaction and realization that job not matched to needs	Satisfaction; needs matched to job
Low job survival, dissatisfaction, frequent thoughts of quitting	High job survival, satisfaction, infrequent thoughts of quitting

Realistic job previews. The provision of a balanced, realistic picture of the positive and negative aspects of a job to applicants.

Obviously, organizations cannot control all sources of unrealistic job expectations, such as those provided by television shows and glorified occupational stereotypes. However, they *can* control those generated during the recruitment process by providing job applicants with realistic job previews. **Realistic job previews** provide a balanced, realistic picture of the positive and negative aspects of the job to applicants.[23] Thus, they provide "corrective action" to expectations at the anticipatory socialization stage. Exhibit 8.3 compares the realistic job preview process with the traditional preview process that often sets expectations too high by ignoring the negative aspects of the job.

How do organizations design and conduct realistic job previews? Generally, they obtain the views of experienced employees and human resources staff about the positive and negative aspects of the job. Then, they incorporate these views into booklets or video presentations for applicants.[24] A video might involve interviews with job incumbents discussing the pros and cons of their jobs. Some companies have managers and employees communicate realistic information to job candidates in person. For example, Scotiabank has managers from various business lines explain the day-to-day job realities to prospective job candidates.[25] Realistic previews have been designed for jobs as diverse as telephone operators, life insurance salespeople, U.S. Marine Corps recruits, and supermarket workers.

Sometimes realistic previews use simulations to permit applicants to actually sample the work. For example, in an effort to recruit more women, the Ontario Provincial Police (OPP) have staged recruiting camps in which the women experience typical OPP policing activities, including shooting a handgun, completing 6 a.m. fitness drills, and responding to mock crimes.[26]

RESEARCH EVIDENCE Evidence shows that realistic job previews are effective in reducing inflated expectations and turnover and improving job performance.[27] What is less clear is exactly why turnover reduction occurs. Reduced expectations and increased job satisfaction are part of the answer. It also appears that realistic previews cause those not cut out for the job or who have low PJ and PO fit perceptions to withdraw from the application process, a process known as *self-selection*.[28] As a result, applicants who perceive a good PJ and PO fit are more likely to accept a job offer and remain on the job. There is also some evidence that organizations that provide realistic job previews are perceived by job applicants as more honest and trustworthy and this encourages employees to remain with the organization once they are hired.[29] Although the turnover reductions generated by realistic previews are small, they can result in substantial financial savings for organizations.[30] Thus, providing realistic job previews is a low-investment strategy that can reduce turnover and also help prevent perceptions of psychological contract breach.[31]

Employee Orientation Programs

Once newcomers enter an organization, socialization during the encounter stage usually begins with an orientation program. **Employee orientation programs** are designed to introduce new employees to their job, the people they will be working with, and the organization. The main content of most orientation programs consists of health and safety issues, terms and conditions of employment, and information about the organization, such as its history and traditions. Another purpose of employee orientation programs is to begin conveying and forming the psychological contract and to teach newcomers how to cope with stressful work situations.[32]

Orientation programs that are designed to help newcomers cope with stress are called **Realistic Orientation Program for Entry Stress (ROPES)**. Like a realistic job preview, ROPES provides newcomers with realistic information; however, it also teaches newcomers how to use cognitive and behavioural coping techniques to manage workplace stressors. For an example of a ROPES program, see the Global Focus: *ROPES and Cultural Socialization.*

Employee orientation programs. Programs designed to introduce new employees to their job, the people they will be working with, and the organization.

Realistic Orientation Program for Entry Stress (ROPES). An orientation program that is designed to teach newcomers coping techniques to manage workplace stressors.

■ GLOBAL FOCUS ■

ROPES AND CULTURAL SOCIALIZATION

As business becomes increasingly global, more workers are relocating to different countries. This means that socialization needs to focus on preparing new hires and current employees not only for the organization where they will be working (organizational socialization) but also for the culture (cultural socialization). But how do you socialize people for different countries and prepare them for the enormous amount of stress they will experience working and living in a different culture?

The answer is a new kind of orientation program called ROPES, which stands for Realistic Orientation Program for Entry Stress. ROPES provides realistic information about tasks and the environment, and also teaches cognitive and behavioural coping techniques to manage stressors and lower stress. But how effective is ROPES for cultural socialization?

To find out, Jinyan Fan and John P. Wanous conducted a study among new Asian international graduate students at a large university in the United States in which they compared ROPES to a more traditional orientation program. Based on interviews with international students, ROPES was designed to teach international students how to cope with three major stressors: (1) the fast pace of the academic quarter system (the university has three quarters versus the more common two semester system), (2) language difficulties, and (3) social interaction difficulties.

The 72 participants were randomly assigned to receive ROPES or a more traditional orientation session that focused mostly on students' immediate concerns, such as how to keep legal status in the United States, how to ensure personal safety, how to connect a home phone, and so forth.

To test the effectiveness of ROPES, participants completed questionnaires to measure their expectations, anxiety, stress, and adjustment. The results indicated that the ROPES participants reported lower expectations at the end of the orientation program, lower stress and higher academic and interaction adjustment six and nine months after the program, and higher retention two years later. Further, the positive effects of ROPES became stronger over time. The results also indicated that the better academic and interaction adjustment of the ROPES participants was partly due to a reduction in stress. In other words, ROPES was more effective for cultural socialization than the traditional orientation program because it lowered stress.

Source: Based on Fan, J., & Wanous, J.P. (2008). Organizational and cultural entry: A new type of orientation program for multiple boundary crossings. *Journal of Applied Psychology 93*, 1390–1400. Copyright © 2008 by the American Psychological Association. Reproduced with permission.

Most orientation programs take place during the first week of entry and last one day to one week. Some organizations realize the importance of orientation and invest a considerable amount of time and resources in it. For example, Capital Power, an independent power producer in Edmonton, recently designed and implemented a new orientation program called "Strong Start." The program combines elearning modules with classroom instruction that provides information about the organization (e.g., vision, values, and policies) and its business. The modules are interactive and include video clips, online coaching, an intranet scavenger hunt, and knowledge checks. After completing the elearning modules, new hires participate in a day-and-a-half classroom session that includes a talk from the CEO or another senior executive. New hires are also required to create a 100-day initial development plan with their manager. Capital Power has seen a 30 percent increase in organizational knowledge among participants since the program was launched.[33]

RESEARCH EVIDENCE Orientation programs are an important method of socialization because they can have an immediate effect on learning and a lasting effect on the job attitudes and behaviours of new hires. One study found that newly hired employees who attended an orientation program were more socialized in terms of their knowledge and understanding of the organization's goals and values, history, and involvement with people, and also reported higher organizational commitment compared to employees who did not attend the orientation program.[34] A study conducted at Corning Inc. concluded that employees who completed a full orientation program were 69 percent more likely to remain with the company after three years. Other companies have also seen substantial decreases in their rate of turnover as a result of employee orientation programs.[35]

Socialization Tactics

Although realistic job previews and orientation programs play an important role in the socialization of new employees, the socialization process does not end at the conclusion of an orientation program. In fact, it often continues for months after an individual has entered the organization, and in some organizations it continues throughout the entire first year. So what happens to new hires once the orientation program has ended?

John Van Maanen and Edgar Schein developed a theory of socialization that helps us understand and explain the socialization process. They suggested that there are six **socialization tactics** that organizations can use to structure the early work experiences of new hires and individuals who are in transition from one role to another. As shown in Exhibit 8.4, each of the six tactics consists of a bipolar continuum that can be grouped into two separate patterns of socialization that are called institutionalized and individualized socialization (see Exhibit 8.5 for descriptions of each of the tactics).[36]

Socialization tactics. The manner in which organizations structure the early work experiences of newcomers and individuals who are in transition from one role to another.

EXHIBIT 8.4
Socialization tactics.

Explore

Go to MyManagementLab to see an annotated version of this figure.

INSTITUTIONALIZED SOCIALIZATION		INDIVIDUALIZED SOCIALIZATION
Collective Formal	CONTEXT TACTICS	Individual Informal
Sequential Fixed	CONTENT TACTICS	Random Variable
Serial Investiture	SOCIAL TACTICS	Disjunctive Divestiture

Collective versus Individual Tactics When using the collective tactic, a number of new members are socialized as a group, going through the same experiences and facing the same challenges. Army boot camps, fraternity pledge classes, and training classes for salespeople and flight attendants are common examples. In contrast, the individual tactic consists of socialization experiences that are tailor-made for each new member. Simple on-the-job training and apprenticeship to develop skilled craftspeople constitute individual socialization.

Formal versus Informal Tactics Formal tactics involve segregating newcomers from regular organizational members and providing them with formal learning experiences during the period of socialization. Informal tactics, however, do not distinguish a newcomer from more experienced members and rely more on informal and on-the-job learning.

Sequential versus Random Tactics Sequential versus random tactics have to do with whether there is a clear sequence of steps or stages during the socialization process. With a sequential tactic, there is a fixed sequence of steps leading to the assumption of the role, whereas with the random tactic, there is an ambiguous or changing sequence.

Fixed versus Variable Tactics If socialization is fixed, there is a timetable for the newcomer's assumption of the role. If the tactic is variable, then there is no time frame to indicate when the socialization process ends and the newcomer assumes his or her new role.

Serial versus Disjunctive Tactics The serial tactic refers to a process in which newcomers are socialized by experienced members of the organization. The disjunctive tactic refers to a socialization process where role models and experienced organization members do not groom new members or "show them the ropes."

Investiture versus Divestiture Tactics Divestiture tactics refer to what is also known as debasement and hazing. This occurs when organizations put new members through a series of experiences that are designed to humble them and strip away some of their initial self-confidence and change their attitudes and beliefs. Debasement is a way of testing the commitment of new members and correcting for faulty anticipatory socialization. Having been humbled and stripped of preconceptions, members are then ready to learn the norms of the organization. An extreme example is the rough treatment and shaved heads of U.S. Marine Corps recruits. Sometimes organizations prefer not to use debasement or hazing as part of the socialization of newcomers. Rather, they employ the investiture socialization tactic, which affirms the incoming identity and attributes of new hires rather than denying them and stripping them away. Organizations that carefully select new members for certain attributes and characteristics would be more likely to use this tactic.

EXHIBIT 8.5
Descriptions of the socialization tactics.
Source: Van Maanen, J., & Schein, E.H. (1979). Toward a theory of organizational socialization. In B.M. Staw (Ed.), *Research in organizational behavior*, Vol. 1. Greenwich, CT: JAI Press, 209–264.

Institutionalized socialization consists of collective, formal, sequential, fixed, serial, and investiture tactics. *Individualized socialization* consists of individual, informal, random, variable, disjunctive, and divestiture tactics. The main difference between these two approaches to socialization is that institutionalized socialization involves a more formalized and structured program of socialization that reduces uncertainty and encourages new hires to accept organizational norms and maintain the status quo. On the other hand, individualized socialization reflects a relative absence of structure that creates ambiguity and encourages new hires to question the status quo and develop their own approach to their role.

In addition, the tactics have also been distinguished in terms of the *context* in which information is presented to new hires, the *content* provided to new hires, and the *social* aspects of socialization.[37] As shown in Exhibit 8.4, the collective–individual and formal–informal tactics represent the context of socialization; the sequential–random and fixed–variable tactics represent the content of socialization; and the serial–disjunctive and investiture–divestiture tactics represent the social aspects of socialization.

Some socialization tactics, such as debasement and hazing, are designed to strip new members of their old beliefs, values, and attitudes and get them to internalize new ones.

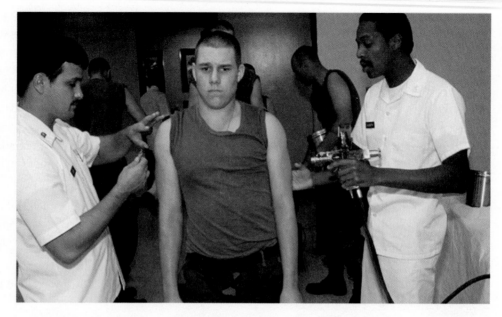

Why would an organization choose institutionalized over individualized socialization? Institutionalized socialization tactics are effective in promoting organizational loyalty and uniformity of behaviour among those being socialized. This last characteristic is often very important. No matter where they are in the world, soldiers know whom to salute and how to do it. Similarly, air passengers need not expect any surprises from cabin crew, thanks to the flight attendants' institutionalized socialization.

When socialization is individualized, new members are more likely to take on the particular characteristics and style of those who are socializing them. Thus, two newly hired real estate agents who receive on-the-job training from their bosses might soon think and act more like their bosses than like each other. As you can see, uniformity is less likely under individualized socialization.

Institutionalized socialization is always followed up by some individualized socialization as the member joins his or her regular work unit. For example, rookie police officers are routinely partnered with more experienced officers. At this point, they will begin to develop some individuality in the style with which they perform their jobs.

RESEARCH EVIDENCE Research on socialization tactics supports the basic predictions regarding the effects of institutionalized and individualized socialization on newcomers' roles, attitudes, and behaviour. Institutionalized socialization tactics have been found to be related to proximal outcomes, such as lower role ambiguity and conflict and more positive perceptions of PJ and PO fit, as well as distal outcomes, such as more positive job satisfaction and organizational commitment and lower stress and turnover. In addition, the institutionalized socialization tactics result in a more custodial role orientation, in which new hires accept the status quo and the requirements of their tasks and roles. On the other hand, the individualized socialization tactics result in a more innovative role orientation, in which new recruits might change or modify the way they perform their tasks and roles.

It is also worth noting that among the different socialization tactics, the social tactics (serial–disjunctive and investiture–divestiture) have been found to be the most strongly related to socialization outcomes. This is consistent with research that has found that organizations that are more successful at socializing newcomers help them to establish a broad network of relationships with co-workers.[38] Furthermore, as described in the Ethical Focus: *Socialization Tactics and Ethical Conflict*, divestiture socialization tactics can also result in ethical conflict at work.

ETHICAL FOCUS

SOCIALIZATION TACTICS AND ETHICAL CONFLICT

Professionals in fields such as law, medicine, psychology, and teaching receive extensive training in ethics and resolving ethical conflicts that can arise in their fields. Thus, one might think that ethical misconduct would be rare among professionals. However, even trained professionals experience a significant amount of ethical conflict in their work and these ethical conflicts can cause employees to feel frustrated and emotionally exhausted.

Ethical conflict is a subjective sense that expectations for one's behaviour are inconsistent with one's beliefs regarding what is right and wrong. Thus, ethical conflict arises when there is a perceived discrepancy between the ethical climate of the organization and the ethics of the individual and the individual must choose between two competing principles. This is especially problematic when the organization has lower ethical standards than the individual.

But what can cause an individual to experience ethical conflict at work and what are the consequences of it?

According to John D. Kammeyer-Mueller, Lauren S. Simon, and Bruce L. Rich, ethical conflicts can occur when an organization's socialization practices encourage new employees to behave counter to their own sense of right and wrong. In particular, they predicted that divestiture socialization tactics are most likely to result in ethical conflict because they discourage employees from using their own belief systems and replace them with the organization's attitudes and beliefs, whereas investiture socialization tactics encourage employees to rely on their own sense of what is right. The authors also predicted that divestiture tactics and ethical conflict will result in more emotional exhaustion and ethical conflict will lead to lower career fulfillment.

To test these predictions, the authors conducted a study of 371 early-career lawyers. The lawyers completed a survey that asked them about their socialization, the extent to which they have experienced various conflicts during their first years on the job as a practising lawyer (e.g., conflict between your personal values and the directives of your supervisors), and their experience of emotional exhaustion (e.g., feeling rundown) and career fulfillment (e.g., pay level and promotion).

As predicted, the authors found that divestiture socialization was positively related to ethical conflict and emotional exhaustion. In addition, ethical conflict was positively related to emotional exhaustion and emotional exhaustion was negatively related to career fulfillment.

The results of this study indicate that early-career lawyers who experience higher levels of divestiture socialization experience more ethical conflict at work, which in turn results in more emotional exhaustion and lower career fulfillment.

These results do not mean that divestiture socialization should always be avoided. In fact, there are some occupations such police, military, and emergency medical teams where uniformity of behaviour is extremely important and divestiture socialization is required. The point that the authors are making is that divestiture socialization tactics should be designed to clarify and support newcomers' beliefs about ethical behaviour and teach them that following the organization's rules for behaviour is consistent with achieving their desired ethical ends.

Source: Based on Kammeyer-Mueller, J.D., Simon, L.S., & Rich, B.L. (2012). The psychic cost of doing wrong: Ethical conflict, divestiture socialization, and emotional exhaustion. *Journal of Management, 38*, 784–808.

Mentoring

It should be apparent from our discussion of socialization tactics that supervisors and peers play an important role in the socialization process. While effective relationships between supervisors and their employees do influence the socialization and career success of individuals within an organization, one particularly important relationship is between a newcomer or apprentice and a mentor.

A **mentor** is an experienced or more senior person in the organization who gives a junior person (the apprentice or protégé) guidance and special attention, such as giving advice and creating opportunities to assist him or her during the early stages of his or her career. While someone other than the junior person's boss can serve as a mentor, often the supervisor is in a unique position to provide mentoring.

Mentor. An experienced or more senior person in the organization who gives a junior person guidance and special attention, such as giving advice and creating opportunities to assist him or her during the early stages of his or her career.

Mentoring is a type of developmental relationship that produces benefits for a protégé's work and/or career.[39] However, for mentors to be effective they must perform two types of developmental functions: career and psychosocial functions.

CAREER FUNCTIONS OF MENTORING

A mentor provides many career-enhancing benefits to an apprentice.[40] These benefits are made possible by the senior person's experience, status, knowledge of how the organization works, and influence with powerful people in the organization. The career functions of mentoring include

- *Sponsorship.* The mentor might nominate the apprentice for advantageous transfers and promotions.
- *Exposure and visibility.* The mentor might provide opportunities to work with key people and see other parts of the organization.
- *Coaching and feedback.* The mentor might suggest work strategies and identify strengths and weaknesses in the apprentice's performance.
- *Developmental assignments.* The mentor can provide challenging work assignments that will help develop key skills and knowledge that are crucial to career progress.

PSYCHOSOCIAL FUNCTIONS OF MENTORING

Besides helping directly with career progress, mentors can provide certain psychosocial functions that are helpful in developing the apprentice's self-confidence, sense of identity, and ability to cope with emotional traumas that can damage a person's effectiveness. These include

- *Role modelling.* This provides a set of attitudes, values, and behaviours for the junior person to imitate.
- *Providing acceptance and confirmation.* This provides encouragement and support and helps the apprentice gain self-confidence.
- *Counselling.* This provides an opportunity to discuss personal concerns and anxieties concerning career prospects, work–family conflicts, and so on.

Formal mentoring programs.
Organizationally sponsored programs in which seasoned employees are recruited as mentors and matched with protégés.

Mentoring relationships have often been of an informal nature, in that the individuals involved chose to enter into a mentoring relationship with each other without the direct involvement of their organization. However, **formal mentoring programs**, in which seasoned employees are recruited as mentors and matched with protégés as part of an organizationally sponsored program, have become increasingly popular in recent years and are now provided by many organizations.[41] For example, Telvent Canada Ltd., a Calgary-based company that develops information management systems, started a formal mentoring program a number of years ago. Although it was originally offered to new hires to help get them up to speed, it is now available to all of the company's employees. Bell Canada launched a companywide online mentor program several years ago called Mentor Match, which is open to all of its employees. The program is available on the company's intranet, and employees must apply to be either a mentor or a protégé.[42]

WOMEN AND MENTORING

One factor that inhibits women's career development compared with that of their male counterparts is the difficulty women have historically faced in establishing an apprentice–mentor relationship with a senior person in the organization.[43] The lack of mentors and role models is a major barrier for the career advancement of many women.[44] The problem goes well beyond the traditional gender stereotyping we discussed in Chapter 3. It stems from the fact that the senior people who are in the best position to be mentors are frequently men, and men are also more likely to serve as mentors than are women.[45] Further, a young woman attempting to establish a productive relationship with a senior male associate faces complexities that the male apprentice does not. Often, a woman's concerns are different from those her male mentor experienced at that stage in his career. As a result, the strategies

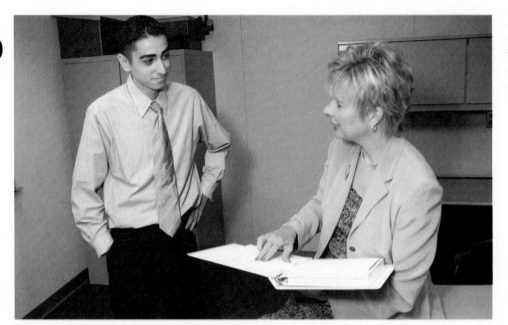

Many research efforts have documented the importance of having a mentor when starting one's career and how it can influence career success.

that he models might have limited relevance to the female apprentice. Perhaps the greatest difficulty is associated with fears that their relationship will be perceived as involving intimacy. Concerns about appearances and what others will say can make both people uncomfortable and get in the way of a productive relationship.

Because of these concerns, the prospective female apprentice faces more constraints than her male counterpart. Research has confirmed that cross-gender mentor–apprentice dyads are less likely to get involved in informal after-work social activities. These activities can help apprentices establish relationships with other influential people in a relaxed setting. Research also confirms that apprentices in a cross-gender dyad are less likely to see their mentor as a role model and, therefore, are less likely to realize the developmental benefits of an effective model.[46]

However, with many organizations now providing formal mentoring programs, the barriers facing women in finding a mentor have been removed. In fact, a recent review of gender differences in mentoring found that males and females are equally likely to have been a protégé. And while male and female protégés report receiving equal amounts of career development mentoring, female protégés reported receiving more psychosocial support.[47] Similarly, a recent study on formal mentoring programs found that the negative effects associated with cross-gender dyads dissipates as the mentoring relationship develops over time. Thus, protégés in cross-gender dyads receive just as much career and psychosocial mentoring as those in same-gender relationships.[48]

How critical is mentoring to a woman's career? The research evidence suggests that mentoring is even more critical to women's career success than it is to men's. Women who make it to executive positions invariably had a mentor along the way. This is true for one-half to two-thirds of male executives.[49] Recent studies also indicate that a majority of women (61 percent) have had a mentor, and almost all (99 percent) say that their mentor has had an impact on the advancement of their career.[50] There is also some evidence that female managers and professionals benefit the most from a senior male mentor in male-dominated industries.[51]

Thus, for women with career aspirations, finding a mentor appears to be a difficult but crucial task. The good news is that an increasing number of organizations are developing mentoring and networking programs. For example, Deloitte has a program called Developing Leaders, in which experienced partners mentor and coach male and female partners who demonstrate leadership potential. Mentors are carefully chosen, and their skills and experience are matched to the new partner's goals and aspirations. In addition, women at Deloitte have developed networking and mentoring opportunities for themselves through a program called Women's Business Development Groups. The group organizes networking events and meets with other women's business groups and organizes an annual Spring Breakfast during which prominent women are invited to speak.[52] These kinds of networking opportunities are extremely important because research has found that exclusion from informal networks is one of the major roadblocks to the advancement of women.[53]

RACE, ETHNICITY, AND MENTORING   Limited racial and ethnic diversity at higher levels of organizations constrain the mentoring opportunities available to younger minority group employees. Research shows that mentors tend to select apprentices who are similar to them in terms of race and nationality as well as gender.[54] While there are exceptions, research confirms that minority apprentices in cross-ethnic group mentoring relationships tend to report less assistance than those with same-race mentors.[55]

Cross-race mentoring relationships seem to focus on instrumental or career functions of mentoring (e.g., sponsorship, coaching, and feedback) and provide less psychosocial support functions (e.g., role modelling and counselling) than is generally seen in same-race dyads.[56] Although the increasing diversity of organizations makes this tendency less problematic, it suggests that minority group members should put extra efforts into developing a supportive network of peers who can provide emotional support and role modelling as well as the career functions. It also means that organizations must do more to provide mentoring opportunities for minority employees, just as some have done for women. One organization that is doing this is IBM, where an Asian Task Force identifies and develops talented Asian employees across North America who might benefit from mentoring.[57]

RESEARCH EVIDENCE   Many research studies have documented the importance of having a mentor when starting one's career and how it can influence career success.[58] A review of this research found that mentored individuals had higher objective career outcomes, such as compensation and number of promotions, and higher subjective outcomes, including greater satisfaction with one's job and career and greater career commitment. They were also more likely to believe that they would advance in their career. However, mentoring tends to be more strongly related to the subjective than to the objective career outcomes. Furthermore, in comparisons of the effects of the two mentoring functions, the psychosocial function was found to be more strongly related to satisfaction with the mentoring relationship, while the career function was more strongly related to compensation and advancement. Both functions were found to be just as important in generating positive attitudes toward one's job and career.[59]

Research on formal mentoring programs has found that they are just as beneficial as informal mentoring relationships and are certainly more beneficial than not having mentors at all. In addition, formal mentoring programs have been found to be most effective when the mentor and protégé have input into the matching process and when they receive training prior to the mentoring relationship, especially training that is perceived to be of a high quality.[60]

In recent years, it has become apparent that many newcomers have more than a single mentor and that mentoring support can come from several people inside and outside of the organization, or what is known as a developmental network. **Developmental networks** refer to groups of people who take an active interest in and actions toward advancing a protégé's career by providing developmental assistance. Thus, unlike a traditional mentoring relationship that involves one protégé and one mentor, in a developmental network a protégé can have multiple developers from inside and outside (e.g., family and community) of the organization and include people from different hierarchical levels of the organization (e.g., peers, superiors, subordinates, and senior managers). With a developmental network, a newcomer is more likely to obtain different types of support (e.g., career and psychosocial) and a broader range of career outcomes.[61]

Developmental networks. Groups of people who take an active interest in and actions toward advancing a protégé's career by providing developmental assistance.

PROACTIVE SOCIALIZATION

You may recall from Chapter 2 that individuals learn by observing and imitating the behaviour of others and that proactive behaviours involve taking initiative to improve current circumstances or create new ones. Thus, it should not surprise you that these forms of learning are also important for socialization. That is, newcomers can be proactive in their socialization and in the management of their careers through the use of proactive behaviours.

Proactive socialization refers to the process in which newcomers play an active role in their socialization through the use of a number of proactive behaviours. Exhibit 8.6 describes the major types of proactive socialization behaviours. Two of the most important proactive behaviours are to request feedback about one's work and job performance (feedback seeking) and to seek information about one's work tasks, roles, work group, and organization (information seeking). Recall that organizational socialization is about learning the attitudes, knowledge, and behaviours that are necessary to function as an effective member of a group and organization. One way for new employees to learn is to seek information from others in the organization.[62]

Newcomers can acquire information by requesting it, by asking questions, and by observing the behaviour of others. In addition, there are different sources that can be used to acquire information, such as supervisors, co-workers, mentors, and written documents. However, research has found that newcomers rely primarily on observation, followed by interpersonal sources (i.e., supervisors and co-workers). Furthermore, they tend to seek out task-related information the most, especially during the early period of socialization, followed by role, group, and organization information.[63]

In addition to feedback seeking and information seeking, newcomers can also be proactive by participating in social events (general socializing), developing friendships and relationships with co-workers (relationship building), developing a friendship and relationship with one's boss (boss-relationship building), getting to know people outside of one's department or work area (networking), and attempting to change or modify one's tasks to improve PJ fit (job change negotiation).[64]

RESEARCH EVIDENCE   Research has found that newcomers who engage in proactive behaviours more frequently are more likely to obtain the corresponding proactive outcomes. For example, newcomers who frequently seek feedback are more likely to obtain it and those who engage in relationship building are more likely to have developed friendships with co-workers. As a result, newcomers who are more proactive obtain more feedback and information, and develop more friendships and relationships, which results in more positive proximal and distal socialization outcomes. Thus, it pays to be proactive![65]

Proactive socialization. The process through which newcomers play an active role in their own socialization through the use of a number of proactive socialization behaviours.

EXHIBIT 8.6
Proactive socialization behaviours.
Source: Ashford, S.J., & Black, J.S. (1996). Proactivity during organizational entry: The role of desire for control. *Journal of Applied Psychology, 81,* 199–214.

Feedback seeking Requesting information about how one is performing one's tasks and role.

Information seeking Requesting information about one's job, role, group, and organization.

General socializing Participating in social office events and attending social gatherings (e.g., parties, outings, clubs, and lunches).

Relationship building Initiating social interactions and building relationships with others in one's area or department.

Boss-relationship building Initiating social interactions to get to know and form a relationship with one's boss.

Networking Socializing with and getting to know members of the organization from various departments and functions.

Job change negotiation Attempts to change one's job duties or the manner and means by which one performs one's job in order to increase the fit between oneself and the job.

**BLACKBIRD
GUITARS** Go to
MyManagementLab to
watch a video about
organizational culture.

**ZAPPOS: MOTIVATING
EMPLOYEES
THROUGH COMPANY
CULTURE** Go to
MyManagementLab to
watch a video about
motivating employees
through company
culture.

**ORGANIZATIONAL
CULTURE** Go to
MyManagementLab to
complete a simulation
about organizational
culture.

LO **8.6**

Define *organizational
culture* and discuss the
contributors to a culture.

Organizational culture.
The shared beliefs, values,
and assumptions that exist
in an organization.

ORGANIZATIONAL CULTURE

The last several pages have been concerned with socialization into an organization. To a large degree, the course of that socialization both depends on and shapes the culture of the organization. As indicated in the chapter-opening vignette, Google Canada has a unique culture that has been described as entrepreneurial, innovative, open, and transparent. But what exactly is an organizational culture? Let's now examine culture, a concept that has gained the attention of both researchers and practising managers.

What Is Organizational Culture?

At the outset, we can say that organizational culture is not the easiest concept to define. But to get you thinking about what a culture is like, consider this example. The day before game 7 of the 2011 Stanley Cup finals between the Vancouver Canucks and the Boston Bruins, Tracy Redies, CEO of Coast Capital Savings Credit Union, received an email from a customer service representative asking her to consider closing branches with extended hours early so that employees would be able to watch game 7 with their families. Many businesses would not have considered such a request. However, an important part of Coast Capital's culture is caring and this was a great opportunity to show employees that the organization cares about them. So within a few hours, Redies sent out an email announcing that the branches would be closing early and customers would be directed to the call centre. Employees working at the call centre would get large screen TVs and pizza so they too could watch the game. Within 30 seconds of the announcement, Redies received hundreds of emails from thrilled employees including many who did not even work at the extended hour branches but were happy for their co-workers. One customer service representative sent her an email in bold that read: "I love you CEO."[66]

Informally, culture might be thought of as an organization's style, atmosphere, or personality. This style, atmosphere, or personality is most obvious when we contrast what it must be like to work in various organizations, such as Suncor Energy Inc., the Royal Bank of Canada, WestJet, or Google Canada. Even from their mention in the popular press, we can imagine that these organizations provide very different work environments. Thus, culture provides uniqueness and social identity to organizations.

More formally, **organizational culture** consists of the shared beliefs, values, and assumptions that exist in an organization.[67] In turn, these shared beliefs, values, and assumptions determine the norms that develop and the patterns of behaviour that emerge from these norms. The term *shared* does not necessarily mean that members are in close agreement on these matters, although they may well be. Rather, it means that they have had uniform exposure to them and have some minimum common understanding of them. Several other characteristics of culture are important.

- Culture represents a true "way of life" for organizational members, who often take its influence for granted. Frequently, an organization's culture becomes obvious only when it is contrasted with that of other organizations or when it undergoes changes.

- Because culture involves basic assumptions, values, and beliefs, it tends to be fairly stable over time. In addition, once a culture is well established, it can persist despite turnover among organizational members, providing social continuity.

- The content of a culture can involve matters that are internal to the organization or external. Internally, a culture might support innovation, risk taking, or secrecy of information. Externally, a culture might support "putting the customer first" or behaving unethically toward competitors.

- Culture can have a strong impact on both organizational performance and member satisfaction.

Culture is truly a social variable, reflecting yet another aspect of the kind of social influence that we have been discussing in this chapter. Thus, culture is not simply an automatic consequence of an organization's technology, products, or size. For example, there is some tendency for organizations to become more bureaucratic as they get larger. However, the culture of a particular large organization might support an informal, non-bureaucratic atmosphere as is the case at Google, which has maintained a small-company, informal work environment.

Can an organization have several cultures? The answer is yes. Often, unique **subcultures** develop that reflect departmental differences or differences in occupation or training.[68] A researcher who studied Silicon Valley computer companies found that technical and professional employees were divided into "hardware types" and "software types." In turn, hardware types subdivided into engineers and technicians, and software types subdivided into software engineers and computer scientists. Each group had its own values, beliefs, and assumptions about how to design computer systems.[69] Effective organizations will develop an overarching culture that manages such divisions. For instance, a widely shared norm might exist that in effect says, "We fight like hell until a final design is chosen, and then we all pull together."

Subcultures. Smaller cultures that develop within a larger organizational culture that are based on differences in training, occupation, or departmental goals.

The "Strong Culture" Concept

Some cultures have more impact on the behaviour of organizational members than others. In a **strong culture**, the beliefs, values, and assumptions that make up the culture are both intense and pervasive across the organization.[70] In other words, they are strongly supported by the majority of members, even cutting across any subcultures that might exist. Thus, the strong culture provides great consensus concerning "what the organization is about" or what it stands for. In weak cultures, on the other hand, beliefs, values, and assumptions are less strongly ingrained or less widely shared across the organization. Weak cultures are thus fragmented and have less impact on organizational members. All organizations have a culture, although it may be hard to detect the details of weak cultures.

To firm up your understanding of strong cultures, let's consider thumbnail sketches of some organizations that are generally agreed to have strong cultures.

LO 8.7

Discuss the assets and liabilities of *strong cultures.*

Strong culture. An organizational culture with intense and pervasive beliefs, values, and assumptions.

- *Hilti (Canada) Corp.* The construction-equipment manufacturer in Mississauga, Ontario, developed a can-do attitude using "Gung Ho!" as its mantra and a culture that emphasizes the importance of worthwhile work, being in control of achieving your goals, and celebrating others' successes. The company takes its culture so seriously that "Gung Ho!" was transformed into a program called "Our Culture Journey" to ensure that all employees know what Hilti stands for and expects. Most of the company's employees have gone through the mandatory two-day Culture Journey, which reintroduces them to the company's culture. In addition, all new recruits get two days of "culture training" before they begin four weeks of product and sales training, and that is after four weeks of pre-training! Hilti has been ranked as one of the best workplaces in Canada.[71]

- *Boston Pizza.* Based in Richmond, British Columbia, Boston Pizza is the number-one casual dining chain in Canada, with more than 340 restaurants across the country. It has a culture of teamwork and fun that emphasizes PO fit over skills when hiring. The company hires people who fit the culture, or what they call the Boston Pizza fit. A three-pillar success strategy involves a commitment to franchisee profitability, building the brand, and continually improving the guest experience. Incentive programs reward franchisees and their staff for delivering above-standard quality. Boston Pizza has been recognized as having one of Canada's most admired corporate cultures.[72]

- *WestJet Airlines.* WestJet is known for its relaxed, fun, and youthful culture and for fostering a family atmosphere and a desire to maximize profits that has inspired

Agrium Inc.
CIBC
Coast Capital Savings Credit Union
ING Direct Canada
Kinross Gold Corporation
Ledcor Group of Companies
Loblaw Companies Limited
RBC
Shoppers Drug Mart
WestJet Airlines

extremely high employee motivation and commitment. WestJet has consistently been ranked as having one of the 10 most admired corporate cultures in Canada and even has a culture department to ensure that employees remain happy and engaged. Interestingly, the airline and its culture are modelled after the successful Dallas-based airline Southwest Airlines.[73]

To find out about some of the other companies with the most admired corporate cultures in Canada, see Exhibit 8.7.

Three points are worth emphasizing about strong cultures. First, an organization need not be big to have a strong culture. If its members agree strongly about certain beliefs, values, and assumptions, a small business, school, or social service agency can have a strong culture. Second, strong cultures do not necessarily result in blind conformity. For example, a strong culture at 3M supports and rewards *non*-conformity in the form of innovation and creativity. Finally, Hilti, Boston Pizza, and WestJet are obviously successful organizations. Thus, strong cultures are associated with greater success and effectiveness. Let's now consider the assets and liabilities of strong cultures. For a good example of the assets, see the Applied Focus: *Culture and Customer Service at Print Audit.*

Assets of Strong Cultures

Organizations with strong cultures have several potential advantages over those lacking a strong culture.

COORDINATION In effective organizations, the right hand (e.g., finance) knows what the left hand (e.g., production) is doing. The overarching values and assumptions of strong cultures can facilitate such communication. In turn, different parts of the organization can learn from each other and can coordinate their efforts. This is especially important in decentralized, team-oriented organizations. Notice that coordination and collaboration are facilitated at Google Canada by providing places for employees to communicate and socialize with each other, its "20 percent time" program, and weekly TGIF meetings.

CONFLICT RESOLUTION You might be tempted to think that a strong culture would produce strong conflicts within an organization—that is, you might expect the intensity associated with strongly held assumptions and values to lead to friction among organizational members. There may be some truth to this. Nevertheless, sharing core values can be a powerful mechanism that helps to ultimately resolve conflicts—a light in a storm, as it were. For example, in a firm with a core value of excellent customer service, it is still possible for managers to differ about how to handle a particular customer problem. However, the core value will often suggest an appropriate dispute resolution mechanism—"Let's have the person who is closest to the customer make the final decision."

■ APPLIED FOCUS ■

CULTURE AND CUSTOMER SERVICE AT PRINT AUDIT

Print Audit is a fast-growing print management software company based in Calgary, Alberta. It develops print tracking and auditing software that enables organizations to analyze, reduce, and recover their printing volumes and costs. According to President and Chief Executive Officer John MacInnes, the company enables its 5000 customers around the world to lower the cost and environmental impact of printing and photocopying.

In addition to its environmental achievements, Print Audit has also been winning awards for its customer service and technical support. In 2004 the company received the National Quality Institute's (NQI) Canada Award of Excellence for Quality, and in 2005 and 2008 it received the Gold Customer Service Award for Small Business. The NQI bases its award in part on a company's culture, and it was impressed with Print Audit's vision statement: "To have fun, build great products and 'wow' the customer."

Key to Print Audit's success is its high-quality customer service and close relationships with its customers. Unlike other companies, which emphasize how fast you get somebody off the phone, Print Audit is concerned with whether they solved an issue to the caller's 100 percent satisfaction. They even call customers back to make sure they are satisfied. Callers are greeted by a live person and not an automated message, and the company contacts customers 15 and 45 days after they purchase any product or service to ensure they are fully satisfied.

What makes Print Audit's approach different? The company's five corporate values: family first, fun, growth, integrity, and respect. "Nowhere in our values does it say, 'Get them off the phone,'" says MacInnes. "It comes down to respect. These people have paid us money that they've worked hard for and it is our job to make sure they are satisfied with what they've bought from us." Employees are encouraged to send thank-you cards as well as flowers and gifts to customers. The company's annual flower bill is $10 000.

According to MacInnes, "The biggest hurdle is making sure that the people working here share the same values." So when hiring, Print Audit conducts multiple interviews, including one that thoroughly assesses a job candidate's fit with its service-oriented culture. This is one reason why the company has a retention rate close to 100 percent. In fact, only two people have left Print Audit during its nine years in business.

In the last eight years, Print Audit has achieved an average of 362 percent annual growth. As for the awards the company has won, MacInnes says, "The most meaningful awards we receive are the ones which recognize the values and priorities that we hold most dear."

Sources: Dunsdon, N. (2008, October 14). The customer is all right. *Globe and Mail*, E6; Anonymous (2008, September 9). Print Audit wins National Customer Service Award. Targeted News Service; Atchison, C. (2009, May). Masters of one (Guaranteeing 'wow' service every time.) *Profit*, 28(2), 18; www.printaudit.com.

FINANCIAL SUCCESS Does a strong culture pay off in terms of dollars and cents—that is, do the assets we discussed above get translated into bottom-line financial success? The answer seems to be yes, as long as the liabilities discussed below can be avoided.

One study of insurance companies found that firms whose managers responded more consistently to a culture survey (thus indicating agreement about the firm's culture) had greater asset and premium growth than those indicating disagreement.[74] Another study had members of six international accounting firms complete an organizational culture values survey. Because all firms were in the same business, there is some similarity to their value profiles (e.g., attention to detail is valued over innovation). However, close inspection shows that the six firms actually differ a good deal in their value profiles. Two of the firms tended to emphasize the work task values of detail and stability and to deemphasize a team orientation and respect for people. Comparatively, three other firms tended to emphasize these interpersonal relationship values. The author determined that the two firms that emphasized work task values had much higher employee turnover rates compared to the three firms that emphasized interpersonal relationship values, a fact that was estimated to cost them between $6 and $9 million a year.[75]

There is growing consensus that strong cultures contribute to financial success and other indicators of organizational effectiveness *when the culture supports the mission, strategy, and goals of the organization.*[76] A good example is WestJet Airlines. A key aspect of West-Jet's corporate culture is a universal desire to maximize profits. The company has not only become one of the most profitable airlines in North America, but it is also the most successful low-cost carrier in Canadian history. According to former company CEO Clive Beddoe, WestJet's corporate culture is the primary reason for its extraordinary performance. "The entire environment is conducive to bringing out the best in people," he says. "It's the culture that creates the passion to succeed."[77]

Perhaps it is no wonder, then, that executives across Canada have consistently ranked WestJet as having one of the most admired corporate cultures in Canada. Most of the executive respondents also believe that there is a direct correlation between culture and an organization's health and financial performance and that corporate culture has a tangible impact on their long-term success and an organization's ability to recruit, manage, and retain the best people. In fact, the most admired corporate cultures have been found to have a three-year average revenue growth that was 37 percent higher than that of the S&P/TSX 60, and a three-year average asset growth that was 147 percent higher than the S&P/TSX 60.[78]

Liabilities of Strong Cultures

On the other side of the coin, strong cultures can be a liability under some circumstances.

RESISTANCE TO CHANGE The mission, strategy, or specific goals of an organization can change in response to external pressures, and a strong culture that was appropriate for past success might not support the new order. That is, the strong consensus about common values and appropriate behaviour that makes for a strong culture can prove to be very resistant to change. This means that a strong culture can damage a firm's ability to innovate.

An excellent example is the case of IBM. A strong culture dedicated to selling and providing excellent service for mainframe computers contributed to the firm's remarkable success. However, this strong culture also bred strong complacency that damaged the company's ability to compete effectively with smaller, more innovative firms. IBM's strong mainframe culture limited its competitiveness in desktop computing, software development, and systems compatibility.

Another good example is the sales culture of software giant Oracle Corporation, which has been described as hyperaggressive and tough as nails—the toughest ever seen in the industry. Oracle salespeople were accused of using brute-force tactics, heavy-handed sales pitches, and even routinely running roughshod over customers. Although the culture was once the envy of the industry and the major reason Oracle became the world's second-largest software company, when the industry changed the culture was described as its own worst enemy. CEO Larry Ellison set out to change the company's aggressive sales culture, and one of the first things he did was eliminate a long-established incentive system that encouraged furious sales pushes, over-promising, and steep discounts.[79]

CULTURE CLASH Strong cultures can mix as badly as oil and water when a merger or acquisition pushes two of them together under the same corporate banner.[80] Both General Electric and Xerox, large organizations with strong cultures of their own, had less-than-perfect experiences when they acquired small high-tech Silicon Valley companies with unique cultures. In both cases, the typical scenario concerns a freewheeling smaller unit confronting a more bureaucratic larger unit.

The merger of Hewlett-Packard and Compaq also raised concerns about a culture clash given the different work habits, attitudes, and strategies of the two companies. For example, Hewlett-Packard was known for careful, methodical decision making while Compaq had a reputation for moving fast and correcting mistakes later. Hewlett-Packard was engineering-oriented and Compaq was sales-oriented. The merger involved a vicious battle inside Hewlett-Packard that was described as a corporate civil war. When the companies merged, employees who were once rivals had to work together and learn new systems. They had to resolve culture clashes and overcome the fact that more often than not, high-tech mergers fail. This, however, was nothing new to Compaq. The company experienced a culture clash when it merged with Digital Equipment Corp. in 1998. Many of the promised benefits did not materialize, product decisions were not made quickly or were changed, and confused customers took their business elsewhere.[81]

PATHOLOGY Some strong cultures can threaten organizational effectiveness simply because the cultures are, in some sense, pathological.[82] Such cultures may be based on beliefs, values, and assumptions that support infighting, secrecy, and paranoia, pursuits that hardly leave time for doing business. The collapse of Enron has been blamed in part on a culture that valued lies and deception rather than honesty and truth, and the collapse of WorldCom has been attributed to a culture of secrecy and blind obedience in which executives were encouraged to hide information from directors and auditors and told to simply follow orders. The use of unethical and fraudulent accounting practices was part and parcel of both cultures. Similarly, when Garth Drabinsky and Myron Gottlieb, co-founders of the theatre company Livent Inc., were sentenced for fraud and forgery, Superior Court Justice Mary Lou Benotto stated that the two men presided over a corporation whose culture was one of dishonesty and what she called a "cheating culture."[83]

Another example of a pathological culture is NASA's culture of risk taking. Although the cause of the fatal crash of the *Columbia* space shuttle in February 2003 was a chunk of foam about the size of a briefcase, the root cause was NASA's culture that downplayed space-flight risks and suppressed dissent. A report by the Columbia Accident Investigation Board concluded that "NASA's organizational culture had as much to do with this accident as foam did." The report indicated that the culture of NASA has sacrificed safety in the pursuit of budget efficiency and tight schedules. One of the board's recommendations was that the "self-deceptive" and "overconfident" culture be changed.[84]

The RCMP has also been singled out as having a pathological culture. Recent allegations and law suits of sexual harassment by former Mounties have been attributed to a culture of silence in which employees are afraid to speak up and sexual harassment was so pervasive that many victims felt that they had no choice but to tolerate it because their complaints went unanswered.[85]

Contributors to the Culture

How are cultures built and maintained? In this section, we consider two key factors that contribute to the foundation and continuation of organizational cultures: the founder's role and socialization.

THE FOUNDER'S ROLE It is certainly possible for cultures to emerge over time without the guidance of a key individual. However, it is remarkable how many cultures, especially strong cultures, reflect the values of an organization's founder.[86] The imprint of Walt Disney on the Disney Company, Sam Walton on Walmart, Ray Kroc on McDonald's, Thomas Watson on IBM, Frank Stronach on Magna International, Mary Kay Ash on Mary Kay Cosmetics, and Bill Gates on Microsoft is obvious. As we shall see shortly, such an imprint is often kept alive through a series of stories about the founder passed on to successive generations of new employees. This provides continuing reinforcement of the firm's core values.

In a similar vein, most experts agree that top management strongly shapes the organization's culture. The culture will usually begin to emulate what top management "pays

Honorary Chairman Frank Stronach of Magna International is a classic example of a founder whose values have shaped the organization's culture.

attention to." For example, the culture of IBM today is much different than it was under the leadership of Thomas Watson, who created a culture that reflected his own personality. Louis Gerstner, Jr., who took over as CEO in 1993 until his retirement in 2002, made diversity a top priority. As a result, the culture of IBM became a more people-friendly one in which individuals are valued for their unique traits, skills, and contributions—a sharp contrast to the culture of conformity under the leadership of Thomas Watson. Today, IBM is regarded as a leader in workplace diversity.[87]

Sometimes the culture begun by the founder can cause conflict when top management wishes to see an organization change direction. At Apple Computer, the late Steven Jobs nurtured a culture based on new technology and new products—innovation was everything. When top management perceived this strategy to be damaging profits, it introduced a series of controls and changes that led to Jobs' resignation as board chair.[88]

SOCIALIZATION The precise nature of the socialization process is a key to the culture that emerges in an organization because socialization is one of the primary means by which individuals can learn the culture's beliefs, values, and assumptions. Weak or fragmented cultures often feature haphazard selection and a nearly random series of job assignments that fail to present the new hire with a coherent set of experiences. On the other hand, Richard Pascale, of the University of Oxford, notes that organizations with strong cultures go to great pains to expose employees to a careful, step-by-step socialization process (Exhibit 8.8).[89]

- *Step 1—Selecting Employees.* New employees are carefully selected to obtain those who will be able to adapt to the existing culture, and realistic job previews are provided to allow candidates to deselect themselves (i.e., self-selection). As an example, Pascale cites Procter & Gamble's series of individual interviews, group interviews, and tests for brand management positions. Another good example is the interview process conducted by Google, in which employees participate in the selection of new hires who fit the Google culture. An increasing number of organizations now emphasize recruiting and selecting employees for their fit to the company's values and culture (PO fit).[90]

EXHIBIT 8.8
Socialization steps in strong cultures.
Source: The Regents of the University of California. (1985). Reprinted from the *California Management Review,* *27*(2) by permission of The Regents.

✦ Explore

Go to MyManagementLab to see an annotated version of this figure.

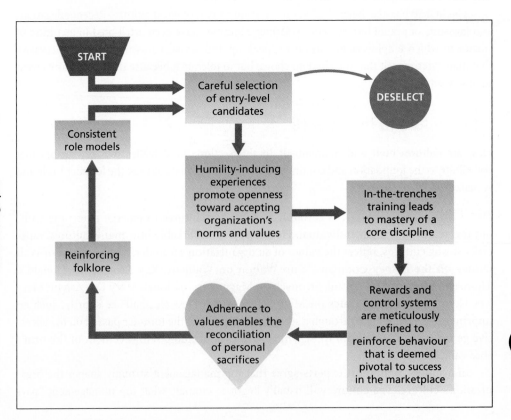

- *Step 2—Debasement and Hazing.* Debasement and hazing provoke humility in new hires so that they are open to the norms of the organization.

- *Step 3—Training "in the Trenches."* Training begins "in the trenches" so that employees begin to master one of the core areas of the organization. For example, even experienced MBAs will start at the bottom of the professional ladder to ensure that they understand how *this* organization works. At Lincoln Electric, an extremely successful producer of industrial products, new MBAs literally spend eight weeks on the welding line so that they truly come to understand and appreciate Lincoln's unique shop floor culture.

- *Step 4—Reward and Promotion.* The reward and promotion system is carefully used to reinforce those employees who perform well in areas that support the values and goals of the organization. For example, at Agrium Inc., a supplier of agricultural products and services, rewards and recognition programs are closely aligned with behaviours that exemplify the corporate values.[91]

- *Step 5—Exposure to Core Culture.* Again and again, the culture's core beliefs, values, and assumptions are asserted to provide guidance for member behaviour. This is done to emphasize that the personal sacrifices required by the socialization process have a true purpose.

- *Step 6—Organizational Folklore.* Members are exposed to folklore about the organization, stories that reinforce the nature of the culture. We examine this in more detail below.

- *Step 7—Role Models.* Identifying people as "fast-trackers" provides new members with role models whose actions and views are consistent with the culture. These role models serve as tangible examples for new members to imitate.

Pascale is careful to note that it is the *consistency* among these steps and their mutually reinforcing properties that make for a strong culture. For example, it is remarkable how many of these tactics the Disney company uses. Selection is rigorous, and grooming standards serve as mild debasement. Everyone begins at the bottom of the hierarchy. Pay is low, but promotion is tied to performance. Folklore stresses core values ("Walt's in the park"). And better performers serve as role models at Disney University or in paired training.

At Four Seasons Hotels and Resorts, where the company wants new employees to buy in to the team philosophy and a "service mindset," all new hires—from hotel managers to dishwashers—go through four interviews during the selection process; once hired, they enter a three-month socialization program.[92]

Although we have been discussing how cultures are built and maintained, very often organizations have to change their culture, especially when there are changes in an organization's business strategy. We will have more to say about organizational change in Chapter 16, but for now please consult You Be the Manager: *Changing the Culture at Kinaxis.*

Diagnosing a Culture

Earlier we noted that culture represents a "way of life" for organizational members. Even when the culture is strong, this way of life might be difficult for uninitiated outsiders to read and understand. One way to grasp a culture is to examine the symbols, rituals, and stories that characterize the organization's way of life. For insiders, these symbols, rituals, and stories are mechanisms that teach, communicate, and reinforce the company's culture.

SYMBOLS At the innovative Chaparral Steel Company in Texas, employees have to walk through the human resources department to get to their lockers. Although this facilitates communication, it also serves as a powerful symbol of the importance that the company places on its human resources. For years, IBM's "respect for the individual" held strong symbolic value, which was somewhat shaken with its first-ever layoffs. Such symbolism is a strong indicator of corporate culture.[93]

LO 8.8

Describe how to diagnose an organizational culture.

YOU BE THE MANAGER

Changing the Culture at Kinaxis

Kinaxis is a provider of software for supply chain management (SCM) and sales and operations planning (S&OP). Founded in Ottawa in 1984, Kinaxis now has offices around the world.

However, after being in business for 20 years, Kinaxis underwent a major transformation. With the goal of growing faster and gaining more value, the software company completely changed what it sold, how it sold it, and who it sold it to.

According to company COO John Sicard, "We had to differentiate ourselves. We were competing with some pretty large competitors and we found ourselves competing under their terms, not our own."

While Kinaxis was seeing some surprising gains in its professional services, its software sales were sliding and software maintenance was only growing marginally—not a healthy trend, said Sicard. "We realized for us to actually win more and grow, we had to change our approach."

The company decided to make several business changes including shifting the software to subscription from perpetual, on-demand from on-premise, and configured from custom. In 2008, Kinaxis attempted a similar change that was unsuccessful. After the executive team explained that the company was shifting to subscription software from perpetual, they went back on their word and approved a perpetual software sale for one employee which quickly snowballed to many other employees.

Fundamentally changing the business—and implementing all the changes at the same time—required support from all employees because it affected every single department in the organization, said Sicard.

Kinaxis made several business changes that required a change in the company's culture

Since people are often uncomfortable with change, the executive team had to be prepared for resistance and figure out a way to gain employee support.

But what other changes are required to successfully transform the business? Does it require a change in culture? You be the manager.

Questions

1. Do you think that Kinaxis needs to change its culture? If so, how should they proceed? Explain your reasoning.

2. What can Kinaxis do to gain employee support, and how will the changes affect the selection of new employees?

To find out what Kinaxis did, see The Manager's Notebook at the end of the chapter.

Some executives are particularly skilled at using symbols consciously to reinforce cultural values. Retired chairman and CEO Carl Reichardt of Wells Fargo was known as a fanatical cost cutter. According to one story, Reichardt received managers requesting capital budget increases while sitting in a tatty chair. As managers made their cases, Reichardt picked at the chair's exposed stuffing, sending a strong symbolic message of fiscal austerity. This was in case they had missed the message conveyed by having to pay for their own coffee and their own office Christmas decorations![94]

RITUALS Observers have noted how rites, rituals, and ceremonies can convey the essence of a culture.[95] For example, at Coast Capital Savings Credit Union, Canada's second-largest credit union, the company's executives dress up in costumes during the employee recognition awards event. During the 2011 Stanley Cup playoffs, staff held noon-hour street hockey games in the parking lot to support the Vancouver Canucks. These events are indicative of a culture of fun and light-heartedness.[96] The Disney picnics, beach parties, and employee nights are indicative of a peer-oriented, youth-oriented culture. At Flight Centre, the monthly parties called "buzz nights," at which employees are recognized for their accomplishments, are indicative of a youthful, energetic, and fun culture. At Mary Kay Cosmetics, elaborate "seminars" with the flavour of a Hollywood premiere combined with a revival meeting are used to make the sales force feel good about themselves and the company. Pink Cadillacs and other extravagant sales awards reinforce the cultural imperative that any Mary Kay woman can be successful. Rituals need not be so exotic to send a cultural message. In some companies, the annual performance review is an act of feedback and development. In others, it might be viewed as an exercise in punishment and debasement.

STORIES   As we noted earlier, the folklore of organizations—stories about past organizational events—is a common aspect of culture. These stories, told repeatedly to successive generations of new employees, are evidently meant to communicate "how things work," whether they are true, false, or a bit of both. Anyone who has spent much time in a particular organization is familiar with such stories, and they often appear to reflect the uniqueness of organizational cultures. However, research indicates that a few common themes underlie many organizational stories:

- Is the big boss human?
- Can the little person rise to the top?
- Will I get fired?
- Will the organization help me when I have to move?
- How will the boss react to mistakes?
- How will the organization deal with obstacles?[97]

Issues of equality, security, and control underlie the stories that pursue these themes. Also, such stories often have a "good" version, in which things turn out well, and a "bad" version, in which things go sour. For example, there is a story that Ray Kroc, McDonald's founder, cancelled a franchise after finding a single fly in the restaurant.[98] This is an example of a sour ending to a "How will the boss react to mistakes?" story. Whether the story is true, its retelling is indicative of one of the core values of the McDonald's culture—a fanatical dedication to clean premises.

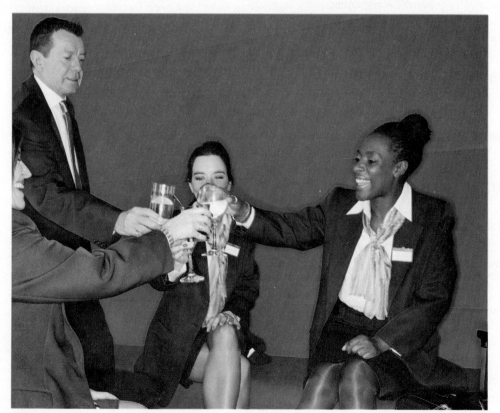

Fun is an essential part of the culture of Flight Centre, where employees attend monthly parties called "buzz nights."

THE MANAGER'S NOTEBOOK

Changing the Culture at Kinaxis

The Kinaxis story is an excellent example of how changes in an organization's business strategy often require changes in the company's culture. In 2011, Kinaxis was named Company of the Year by the Ottawa Centre for Research and Innovation (OCRI) and was named one of the top 100 employers by the National Capital Region's Top Employer in 2010, which recognizes Ottawa-area employers that offer an exceptional place to work.

1. The change in business strategy required a new culture that would support the business initiatives. To get employees behind the new plan, Kinaxis involved them in the new vision for the company. It created an online community shaped by four key pillars—learn, laugh, share, and connect—that became anchors to the new company culture. The website was also revamped to reflect the new culture, which included changing the title of a video from "Stuff Happens" to "Sh*t happens." "Everyone went, 'We can't have that on our website,' and we said, 'Yes, we can because that's what people think—it's edgy and it's OK,' said Sicard. "We modernized the website, changed our voice. Rather than sounding like a big tech library, we really started to speak in a more conversational manner." Kinaxis also hired a community manager to help transform employees and get them used to being social. "That was a big part of our cultural shift. (We were) very enterprise-focused, closed doors, everything is very, very serious—and developers never came out," said Sicard. "But we had to change the way people thought about this."

2. To gain employee support, Kinaxis offered financial incentives for any employee who would contribute to the website. They were encouraged to be provocative, but respectful, bold, and edgy in their comments—because that's how you get people talking, said Sicard. In keeping with this new, edgy brand, Kinaxis developed its own TV show called the *Late Late Supply Chain Show* starring Kinaxis employees as well as a video comedy series called *New Kinexions*. Ongoing communication with employees was also a key aspect in how Kinaxis survived the transformation. The company's CEO "errs on telling everything"—through newsletters, one-on-one sessions, and town-hall meetings—so employees can really understand what's going on at the organization. The HR department was also affected by the change and the biggest shift was in how it screened candidates and determined fit, said Sicard. "In the past, we might have been hyper-focused on a potential employee's fit from a technical know-how/skill side of the equation and, of course, we're still looking for 'Will they work well in a team?' but now (we look at) "Will they thrive under this culture?"

MyManagementLab

Visit MyManagementLab at **www.mymanagementlab .com** for access to online tutorials, interactive exercises, videos, and much more.

LEARNING OBJECTIVES CHECKLIST

8.1 There are two basic forms of social dependence. *Information dependence* means that we rely on others for information about how we should think, feel, and act. *Effect dependence* means that we rely on rewards and punishments provided by others. Both contribute to conformity to norms.

8.2 There are several motives for conformity to social norms. One is *compliance*, in which conformity occurs mainly to achieve rewards and avoid punishment. It is mostly indicative of effect dependence. Another motive for conformity is *identification* with other group members. Here, the person sees himself or herself as similar to other organizational members and relies on them for information. Finally, conformity may be motivated by the *internalization* of norms, and the person is no longer conforming simply because of social dependence.

8.3 *Socialization* is the process by which people learn the attitudes, knowledge, and behaviours that are necessary to function in a group or organization. It is a process that affects proximal socialization outcomes (e.g., learning about one's tasks, roles, group, and organization) as well as distal socialization outcomes (e.g., job satisfaction and turnover). Organizational members learn norm and role requirements through three stages of socialization: anticipatory, encounter, and role management.

8.4 People entering organizations tend to have expectations that are inaccurate and unrealistically high and that can cause them to experience reality shock. The *psychological contract* refers to beliefs held by employees regarding the reciprocal obligations and promises between them and their organization. *Psychological contract breach* is common and can have a negative effect on employees' work attitudes and behaviours. Socialization programs can help new hires form realistic expectations and accurate perceptions of the psychological contract.

8.5 *Realistic job previews* can help new members cope with initial unrealistic expectations. *Employee orientation programs* introduce new employees to their job, the people they will be working with, and the organization. *Socialization tactics* refer to the manner in which organizations structure the early work experiences of newcomers and individuals who are in transition from one role to another. Institutionalized socialization reflects a formalized and structured program of socialization, while individualized socialization reflects a relative absence of structure. *Mentors* can assist new members during socialization and influence their career success by performing career and psychosocial functions. *Formal mentoring programs* are organizationally sponsored programs in which seasoned employees are recruited as mentors and matched with protégés. *Developmental networks* refer to groups of people who take an active interest in and actions toward advancing a protégé's career by providing developmental assistance. New members can play an active role in their socialization through the use of *proactive socialization* behaviours, such as feedback seeking and information seeking.

8.6 *Organizational culture* consists of the shared beliefs, values, and assumptions that exist in an organization. *Subcultures* can develop that reflect departmental or occupational differences. In *strong cultures*, beliefs, values, and assumptions are intense, pervasive, and supported by consensus. An organization's founder and its socialization practices can strongly shape a culture.

8.7 The assets of a strong culture include good coordination, appropriate conflict resolution, and financial success. Liabilities of a strong culture include inherent pathology, resistance to change, and culture clash when mergers or acquisitions occur.

8.8 Symbols, rituals, and stories are often useful for diagnosing a culture.

DISCUSSION QUESTIONS

1. Compare and contrast information dependence with effect dependence. Under which conditions should people be especially information-dependent? Under which conditions should people be especially effect-dependent?

2. Describe an instance of social conformity that you have observed in an organizational setting. Did compliance, identification, or internalization motivate this incident? Were the results beneficial for the organization? Were they beneficial to the individual involved?

3. Consider how you were socialized into the college or university where you are taking your organizational behaviour course. Did you have some unrealistic expectations? Where did your expectations come from? What outside experiences prepared you for college or university? Did you experience institutionalized or individualized socialization? What proactive socialization behaviours did you employ to facilitate your socialization?

4. What are the pros and cons of providing realistic job previews for a job that is objectively pretty bad? What about for a job that is pretty good?

5. Imagine that you are starting a new business in the retail trade. You are strongly oriented toward providing excellent customer service. What could you do to nurture a strong organizational culture that would support such a mission?

6. Discuss the advantages and disadvantages of developing a strong organizational culture and some socialization practices that you would recommend for building a strong organizational culture.

7. Describe how you would design a new-employee orientation program. Be sure to indicate the content of your program and what knowledge and information employees will acquire from attending the program. What are some of the outcomes that you would expect from your orientation program?

8. What does it mean to be proactive during the socialization process and what are the different ways that newcomers can be proactive? To what extent have you used each of the proactive behaviours described in the chapter (see Exhibit 8.6) in a current or previous job, and what effect did it have on your socialization?

9. What are the main functions performed by mentors, and what effect do they have on protégés? Do you think organizations should implement formal mentoring programs or should they remain informal? What are the advantages and disadvantages of each approach?

10. What is the difference between a traditional orientation program and a Realistic Orientation Program for Entry Stress (ROPES)? What is the difference between a realistic job preview and ROPES? Why and when would you use each of these (traditional orientation program, ROPES, and realistic job preview) during the socialization process?

INTEGRATIVE DISCUSSION QUESTIONS

1. What are the implications of social cognitive theory for social influence and socialization? Discuss the practical implications of each component of social cognitive theory (i.e., observational learning, self-efficacy, and self-regulation) for the socialization of new organization members. Describe how you would design an orientation program for new employees based on social cognitive theory. Consider the implications of social cognitive theory for mentoring. What does social cognitive theory say about why mentoring is important and how to make it effective?

2. Refer to the work-related values that differ across cultures presented in Chapter 4 (i.e., work centrality, power distance, uncertainty avoidance, masculinity/femininity, individualism/collectivism, and long-term/short-term orientation) and consider how the culture of an organization in Canada might lead to conflicts in a country with different work-related values. Give some examples of the kind of organizational culture that might conflict with the various work-related values in other countries. What are the implications of this for Canadian companies that wish to expand abroad?

ON-THE-JOB CHALLENGE QUESTION

CN Rail

CN Rail is the largest freight railway in Canada, with 22 696 employees. It operates the largest rail network in Canada and the only transcontinental network in North America—in eight provinces in Canada and 16 states in the United States. In 1995, CN went public after decades of government ownership. The company underwent a transformation that involved acquiring the Illinois Central Railroad in 1998. As a result, it is now considered to be "North America's Railroad."

In 2007, Canada's Transport minister ordered a review of the railway after a five-year period in which there was a steep increase in collisions and derailments. One of the conclusions of the resulting report was the following: "CN's strict adherence to a rules-based approach, focused largely on disciplinary actions when mistakes are made, has instilled a 'culture of fear and discipline' and is counter to an effective safety management system. CN needs to acknowledge this openly and take concrete steps to improve."

CN's goal is to be the best transportation company in North America. Does it need to change the culture to obtain its goal?

Explain how the culture at CN Rail can contribute to collisions and derailments. How can safety be influenced by an organization's culture? How important is it for CN to change its culture? What do they need to do to change the culture and improve safety?

Sources: Vu, U. (2008, July 14). Culture of fear rules safety at CN. *Canadian HR Reporter, 21*(13), 1, 20; Johnson, J., Dakens, L., Edwards, P., & Morse, N. (2008). *Switchpoints*. Hoboken, NJ: John Wiley & Sons, Inc.; www.cn.ca.

EXPERIENTIAL EXERCISE

Socialization Preferences and Experience

The purpose of this exercise is for you to learn about how you would like to be socialized when you join an organization and how you have been socialized in a current or previous organization. By comparing your preferences to your most recent socialization experience, you can better understand how socialization can influence your job attitudes and behaviour.

Part 1: Your Socialization Preferences

Indicate your preference for each of the socialization experiences listed below using the following response scale:

1–Dislike very much

2–Dislike

3–Neither like nor dislike

4–Like

5–Like very much

To what extent would you like or dislike

_____ 1. To be extensively involved with other new hires in common, job-related training activities.

_____ 2. To go through a set of training experiences that are specifically designed to give newcomers a thorough knowledge of job-related skills.

_____ 3. The organization to change your values and beliefs.

_____ 4. To see a clear pattern in the way one role leads to another or one job assignment leads to another.

_____ 5. To have experienced organizational members see advising or training newcomers as one of their main job responsibilities.

_____ 6. To be able to predict your future career path in the organization by observing other people's experiences.

_____ 7. To have other newcomers be instrumental in helping you to understand your job requirements.

_____ 8. To be physically apart from regular organizational members during your training.

_____ 9. To have to "pay your dues" before you are fully accepted.

_____ 10. For each stage of the training process to expand and build upon the job knowledge gained during the preceding stages of the process.

_____ 11. To gain a clear understanding of your role in the organization by observing your senior colleagues.

_____ 12. To have good knowledge of the time it will take you to go through the various stages of the training process in the organization.

_____ 13. For the organization to put all newcomers through the same set of learning experiences.

_____ 14. To avoid performing any of your normal job responsibilities until you are thoroughly familiar with departmental procedures and work methods.

_____ 15. To be transformed or changed into a different kind of person.

_____ 16. For the movement from role to role and function to function to build up experience and a track record to be very apparent in the organization.

_____ 17. To receive little guidance from experienced organizational members about how you should perform your job.

_____ 18. To have your progress through the organization follow a fixed timetable of events.

_____ 19. For most of your training to be carried out apart from other newcomers.

_____ 20. For much of your job knowledge to be acquired informally on a trial and error basis.

_____ 21. To be accepted by the organization for who you are as a person.

_____ 22. For the organization to put newcomers through an identifiable sequence of learning experiences.

_____ 23. To have a lot of access to people who have previously performed your role in the organization.

____ 24. To have a clear idea of when to expect a new job assignment or training exercise in the organization.

____ 25. To experience a sense of "being in the same boat" among newcomers in the organization.

____ 26. To be very aware that you are seen as "learning the ropes" in the organization.

____ 27. To feel that experienced organizational members hold you at a distance until you conform to their expectations.

____ 28. To have the steps in the career ladder clearly specified in the organization.

____ 29. To generally be left alone to discover what your role should be in the organization.

____ 30. For most of your knowledge of what may happen to you in the future to come informally, through the grapevine, rather than through regular organizational channels.

Part 2: Your Socialization Experience

Answer each of the questions above again but this time in terms how you were socialized in your current organization if you are employed or the most recent organization where you were last employed. For each statement, use the following scale to indicate how accurately it describes your socialization experiences when you joined the organization:

1 = Strongly disagree
2 = Disagree
3 = Neither agree nor disagree
4 = Agree
5 = Strong agree

Scoring and Interpretation

This scale measures the six socialization tactics. To calculate your scores on each tactic, you first must subtract your response to questions 3, 9, 15, 17, 19, 20, 27, 29, and 39 from 6. For example, if you gave a response of 5 to question 3, give yourself a 1 (6 minus 5). Then calculate your score for each socialization tactic by adding up your answers as follows:

Collective versus individual tactic: Add your answers to questions 1, 7, 13, 19, and 25.

Formal versus informal tactic: Add your answers to questions 2, 8, 14, 20, and 26.

Investiture versus divestiture tactic: Add your answers to questions 3, 9, 15, 21, and 27.

Sequential versus random tactic: Add your answers to questions 4, 10, 16, 22, and 28.

Serial versus disjunctive tactic: Add your answers to questions 5, 11, 17, 23, and 29.

Fixed versus variable tactic: Add your answers to questions 6, 12, 18, 24, and 30.

For each scale your total score should be somewhere between 5 and 25. Higher scores reflect the institutionalized end of the scale (collective, formal, investiture, sequential, serial, and fixed). You can calculate a total score for all tactics by adding your responses to all 30 questions. Your total scale should fall between 30 and 150. Higher scores reflect a preference for institutionalized socialization. To calculate your socialization experience scores, follow the same procedures but this time use your answers from Part 2.

To compare your socialization preferences to your socialization experience, calculate a socialization preference difference score by subtracting your socialization experience score from your socialization preference score for each tactic. For example, if your collective–individual socialization preference score was 25 and your socialization experience score was 10, the difference would be 15. A small difference indicates greater congruence between your socialization preference and experience. Large differences indicate a discrepancy between how you prefer to be socialized and the way you were socialized.

To facilitate class discussion and your understanding of socialization tactics, form a small group with several other members of the class and consider the following questions:

1. Each group member should present their preference score of each socialization tactic. What is the average of the group for each tactic? For each of the six tactics, do most group members prefer the institutionalized or individualized tactic? Each group member should explain their preference for each tactic.

2. Each group member should present their experience score of each socialization tactic. What is the average of the group for each tactic? For each of the six tactics, did most group members experience institutionalized or individualized socialization? Each group member should explain how they were socialized and what effect it had on them.

3. Each group member should present their socialization preference–experience difference score for each tactic. What are largest and smallest differences and for which tactics? Do some members have larger differences than others? Compare and contrast the experiences of those who have large difference scores to those

who have smaller difference scores. Be sure to consider the effect of your socialization on your learning, job attitudes, and behaviour.

4. How can an understanding of your socialization preferences assist in your future jobs? How can organizations improve their socialization process by understanding the socialization preferences of new hires?

5. What are the implications for organizations that do not consider the socialization preferences of

new hires? What are the implications for new hires whose socialization experience is inconsistent with their preferences?

Source: Based on Jones, G.R. (1986). Socialization tactics, self-efficacy, and newcomers' adjustments to organizations. *Academy of Management Journal, 29,* 262–279; Ashforth, B.E., Sluss, D.M., & Saks, A.M. (2007). Socialization tactics, proactive behavior, and newcomer learning: Integrating socialization models. *Journal of Vocational Behavior, 70,* 447–462.

CASE INCIDENT

The Reality Shock

Soon after starting his new job, Jason began to wonder about the challenging work he was supposed to be doing, the great co-workers he had been told about, and the ability to attend training and development programs. None of these things seemed to be happening as promised and as he had expected. To make matters worse, he had spent most of the first month working on his own and reading about the organization's mission, history, policies, and so on. Jason began to wonder whether he had chosen the right job and organization. He was feeling very dissatisfied and seriously thinking about quitting.

1. Explain how Jason's anticipatory socialization might be contributing to his disappointment and

job attitudes. How might this situation have been prevented?

2. Explain how unrealistic expectations and the psychological contract can help us understand Jason's situation.

3. Comment on the use of socialization tactics in Jason's socialization. What tactics do you think were used and what effect did they have on Jason?

4. Given Jason's current situation, is there anything the organization can do to prevent him from quitting? What should Jason do? Is there anything the organization should do so other new hires don't have the same experience as Jason?

CASE STUDY

Employee Engagement at Modern Appliances Inc.

Written by Jeffrey Gandz.

James Bradshaw, chief executive officer (CEO) of Modern Appliances (Modern), had never expected such a radical proposal for improving customer satisfaction as the one that has just been presented at the first ModernIzation workshop. But the one that was on the table promised to be challenging. Bradshaw could see some real advantages to approving it, but there were also some risks. The biggest among these was the potential for publicly overriding the vice-president of finance, who Bradshaw believed would be firmly against the proposal. On the other hand, it was clear that the recommendation represented a

breakthrough of sorts, and turning it down could set back the efforts being made to increase employee engagement at Modern.

Modern Appliances

Modern Appliances had been in business for almost 75 years and manufactured a wide range of refrigerators, freezers, washing machines, dryers, dishwashers, and other large appliances. With sales in excess of $2 billion, Modern was considered a quality manufacturer and a good marketer. However, in recent years, the company had come under severe competitive pressure from a number of sources; North American companies had outsourced manufacture to China and Vietnam, but domestic Chinese manufacturers were learning to compete effectively outside their home markets and were importing into Modern's traditionally strong North American markets. European companies were focusing on styling to tempt people away from traditional North American suppliers, and they were luring away segments of the market to whom innovative design was appealing.

One way that Modern had managed to stay competitive was through its control systems. There were very strict and comprehensive cost controls in place within the company and even the most modest expenditures required two or three levels of approval. Supplies were all ordered centrally and a very professional and aggressive purchasing department negotiated very good prices and central supply contracts.

For a long time, Bradshaw had believed that Modern could defend against these newer entrants to the North American market only if the workforce was fully engaged in the challenge of creating a truly superior value proposition for its customers and then sustaining that value proposition through everything they did to manufacture the product and market it through their trade channels. After all, these were bulky items and not that easy or inexpensive to ship from Asia. Surely, sitting on top of the North American market, Modern ought to be able to come up with designs that were appealing to the North American family that did not have to cope with tiny houses or apartments that needed all the space-saving design elements built into the European sourced products. Modern knew its customers and that was the key to everything.

Well, not quite everything. Bradshaw was aware that, over the years, Modern had become more than a little complacent with its position as the market leader in quality appliances. Design was a little old fashioned but, more than that, there were issues with both costs and quality. Modern was unionized but, while unionization certainly posed some challenges for costs and labour-force flexibility, Bradshaw did not blame the unions. He felt that it was management, many generations of management, that was to blame. Modern employees had simply not been sufficiently engaged in understanding the business, in analyzing how Modern could do better, or in participating in the development changes to the way that business was done. Costs were higher than they should be because there were too many low-value-added processes in the company, people

did not do the right things in the right way the first time. Also, the re-work of poor quality production—from incorrect invoicing to parts missing from appliances—drove up costs. Modern caught most of the quality problems before they left its plants, but after-sales service and warranty costs were unacceptably high.

True, over the years there had been a large number of employee involvement initiatives, such as quality circles, total quality management (TQM), ISO certification, even Kanbans and other interventions. Many of these had met with some success but had not fundamentally resulted in a changed culture. After the events, people went back to doing things the way they had always done them until the next corporate initiative was launched.

Changing The Culture

Bradshaw had always been impressed with what he had read about the way that Jack Welch had operated at General Electric (GE). Despite having inherited a very successful company, Welch had proceeded to change the fundamental culture of GE from a vast bureaucracy to an agile, fast-paced company that was remarkably innovative for its size. Central to the changes that Welch had implemented at GE was the idea of "Work-out!" which meant, quite literally, driving low-value-added bureaucratic work out of the organization, thereby speeding up the way things were done and creating a culture of change, innovation, self-confidence and engagement among GE employees.

As Welch had described it, it was a multi-year initiative rather than a quick fix. It had required a huge commitment of time and money, over many years, as he sought a permanent culture change rather than just a series of "improvement events." Work-Out! had laid the basis for the subsequent introduction of Six Sigma at GE. By getting rid of the low-value-added processes, GE was able to focus on improving the processes that were important, which laid the groundwork for productivity improvements that continued long after Welch had retired from GE. Speeding up processes had also reduced working capital, money that had subsequently been used as part of GE's acquisition strategy through the 1980s and 1990s.

One of Welch's pieces of advice to other business leaders was to "Plagiarize with Pride"—copy other successful initiatives. And that was just what

Bradshaw had done. Just over a year ago, he had raised the issue of doing something quite dramatic with his executive team. His proposal was that the company would start a series of workshops modelled on the GE Work-Out! Process, and they commit to continue to run these, following up on the recommendations, for at least three years. Every single employee in the company would be given the opportunity to participate in one or more of these events. The entire overhauling process would be accompanied by a fundamental redefinition of the roles of managers, different measurement systems would be put into place that were aligned with a changed culture, and it would be made clear to all managers that establishing and maintaining an engaged workforce would be considered as important as achieving financial goals. Most importantly, these changes would be made by the people who would be affected by them. Individual employees would be involved in identifying the need for change as well as recommending the specific actions to be taken, and these same people would be involved in driving the proposed changes through to completion.

Bradshaw's views about the roles of managers and employees were simple; he believed that the vast majority of employees wanted to do a good job, wanted to add value of the company, wanted to please customers . . . and so on. The role of managers was to enable this to happen. They should act as trainers, coaches, problem solvers, process enablers, and resource acquirers rather than as overseers or bosses in the traditional sense.

The reaction from Bradshaw's managements team had been mixed His vice-president of human resources, Anne Armstrong, had been enthusiastic; she was, however, skeptical that the unions representing employees would be supportive, especially if the recommended changes affected terms or conditions of employment. "On the other hand, something like this might be just the type of thing that we need to break the hostility cycle in which we've been embedded for the last 25 years," she said.

The head of production had sat quietly throughout the early parts of the discussion and then raised the question: "Why do you think this process will be any better than the things that we have tried in the past?" The vice-president of finance pointed out, quite correctly, that Modern was well known for the very tight controls that it maintained and that any loosening of those controls would likely be viewed poorly by suppliers, customers, analysts, and others that dealt with the firm. Bradshaw knew that his head of finance was progressive in pursuit of business improvement but was also convinced that those types of initiatives should be led by the Business Improvement Group (BIG) attached to Finance and should not lead to any lessening of controls.

Others at the meeting—the vice-presidents of sales, marketing, research, legal, and government affairs—had all seemed supportive if not openly enthusiastic. They were skeptical about whether such events would actually create culture change, whether employees who lacked expertise in certain critical areas would be the right ones to do the analysis and propose change or whether these should be tackled by managers and consultants, whether the changes would be profound or just cosmetic, and so on. They were a little alarmed at the idea that discussion of the proposals would take place publicly. "Frankly," said the vice-president of marketing, "I can see that some of these proposals may have issues that we don't want to air in public. Besides which, we may not agree among ourselves, and we may need some time to talk them through and reach consensus."

All of these concerns seemed reasonable to James Bradshaw:

Frankly, if you're not skeptical about some of these things, then I'm not sure I really want you as an executive.... It suggests that you're not that bright! But surely it's worth taking a chance or two to see what can materialize from this kind of initiative. Sure, we'll make mistakes, but nothing that will be fatal.

Despite the lack of overwhelming support, Bradshaw had decided to go ahead and launch the new initiative, ModernIzation...i.e., Modern's drive to change its culture from a traditional, top-down, management-driven company to one in which every employee felt engaged in finding ways to achieve organizational goals.

I believe, fundamentally, that employees want what management wants, at least most of the time. They want to use their initiative, their ideas about how to do things better. They want to make products that please the customer, give good service, be appreciated. They hate useless bureaucracy and excessive controls just as managements dislike the expense associated with those and the ways in which they slow down business processes. They want a clear sense of direction, a goal toward which they can strive. But they also want some input into deciding what these goals should be. True, they also want more pay—but we in management don't have a problem with paying more if we are getting more in return! Our challenge in management is to liberate these "wants" and turn them into outcomes that benefit both employees and shareholders. That way it will be sustainable.

The September Workshop

In September 60 employees gathered at a hotel on the airport strip for the first employee workshop in the ModernIzation process. They were drawn from various functions in the company, none were managers, some were unionized, some had university degrees or college diplomas, others had only a couple of years of high school. They had been informed of the reason for the meeting a couple of weeks previously: to identify obstacles to Modern being among the very best companies for customer service as viewed by their customers. But they had very little idea about what would actually happen at the session. That was soon changed when James Bradshaw entered the hotel ballroom in which they were gathered.

The choice of "customer service" as the theme for the first workshop had been a deliberate one on the part of James Bradshaw.

Customer service is something that both non-management and management employees can agree is needed if we are to be successful. Moreover, everyone wants us to be good at customer service. We may disagree about how to do it best, but that's a disagreement over means rather than ends. And that we should be able to work out.

The 60 employees were drawn at random from different parts of the company. There were clerks from accounting, salespeople, mechanics from the maintenance department, IT analysts, service technicians who drove maintenance trucks, a couple of administrative assistants, production line workers and others. None were managers or supervisors. The session was kicked off by James Bradshaw with his whole executive team present. He used about 20 minutes to present some market research data that indicated how important after-sales service was to the customer's buying decision process and where Modern ranked in the customer's perceptions about service. He then threw out this challenge to the assembled people:

I need you to identify what it's going to take to make us the best customer-service oriented company in this country, one that people talk about when you ask them for examples of great customer service companies. What's getting in the way of our being No. 1, and what do we need to change to make it happen? We—the management team—are going to leave you to work this out for us over the next couple of days. Then we'll rejoin you on Wednesday morning to listen to what you have to say. And I promise you this—every recommendation you make will be either approved and implemented or, if it's not, we'll give the reason why not. Only if we're not sure whether it's legal or it costs a lot of money for questionable returns will we say "maybe," and then we'll commit to give you a firm "yes" or "no" within 30 days. One more thing—your recommendations will stand a better chance of being accepted if there is a "champion" from the group prepared to stay involved in seeing the recommendation through to implementation.

With those comments, Bradshaw and his team left the meeting in the hands of Jeff Meredith, an outside consultant, and his team of six facilitators.

Over the next two days, the 60 Modern employees, guided by Meredith and his team of facilitators, went through a simple process of identification, analysis, solution-seeking, consensus building, and recommendation (see Exhibit 1).

The Modernization Workshop Process

In randomly assigned groups of 10, the Modern employees spent 90 minutes brainstorming a single question: "What gets in the way of Modern Appliances being considered the best customer service company in the world?" Each team generated more than a dozen reasons and, using a "round robin" debriefing in which Team 1 presented one of its reasons, then Team 2 presented a different reason, Team 3 a different one, and so on back to Team 1, they collected 28 different reasons why the company was not truly excellent in the area of customer service.

These reasons were posted on flip charts and, by allocating up to 10 points (sticky dots) per reason, all 60 people effectively "voted" on the reasons, which resulted in a prioritized list. The group members were then asked to break into teams in order to analyze each of the reasons and to propose a recommendation. The teams were allowed to call other people in the company if they needed additional information, but they found little need to do this. Since all the activity was taking place in one large hotel ballroom, the teams found enough expertise among the 60 people present to be able to answer most of their questions. People sometime left their "home" teams to give some help to other teams that needed their input. The facilitators—all of whom were well-trained process-mappers—gave process help to the teams but did not attempt to influence their conclusions or recommendations.

At different points during the process, teams were asked to present their analyses and conclusions to the full, 60-person group. People made observations, added their views, challenged conclusions, and recommendations were modified. Gradually recommendations emerged and people were asked to consider how these would be implemented. At this stage, the consultant and his facilitation team took on the role of challenging the analyses and recommendations for consistency, comprehensiveness, and practicality; under these challenges the recommendations were refined.

By the end of this process—which took two days—14 recommendations were left standing. On the evening of the second day, the teams worked feverishly to get these recommendations into a format that could be presented to James Bradshaw and the management team the following morning. In this effort, they were helped by the facilitators, using pre-prepared templates for presenting their analyses and recommendations in a form that would be conducive to easy decision making and follow-up.

The Warranty Process

One of the very first problems identified by the randomly assigned team on the first morning was the Modern Appliances warranty program. This problem was adopted as an important issue that was worth addressing by a "solutions" team, ranking third overall in priority.

Modern had a great warranty on its refrigerators. Simply put, if the appliance broke down within 12 months of purchase, the company would repair or replace it free of charge and, moreover, it would also pay for any food spoiled as a consequence of the breakdown. This warranty was an industry standard, but it was also a major source of customer dissatisfaction, not because it happened often, but because when it did happen, the warranty claims process was time-consuming and seemed to give the impression that Modern did not care about the customer experience. Recently, there had been a very negative comment in one of the largest-circulation consumer products review magazines that had been picked up by one of the popular television shows. The negative publicity had been damaging.

The issue of the warranty process emerged from the very first problem-identification session in three different teams and was eventually ranked as No. 4 in the issues to be dealt with in the analysis and recommendations session. The rough process map, which was determined by a team consisting of a couple of customer service technicians, a customer service clerk, a sales associate, an IT analyst, two plant workers, and an accounts payable clerk, is shown in Exhibit 2. The key features of the process were described by one of the group whose sister had bought a FoodCenter freezer unit from Modern, and the rest of group shared their understanding of the process. As presented to the other groups following their initial problem-identification stage, the process map looked like this:

1. The customer first noticed that something was wrong when she came into the kitchen on a Wednesday morning and saw a puddle of water in front of the appliance. Checking it over, she thought that the appliance did not seem very cold.

2. She went to the telephone book to find the warranty service. It was not in the phone book because Modern did not identify its individual brands—in this case, FoodCenter—separately.

3. She then called the dealer from which she had bought the appliance. Recognizing this as a warranty repair, for which Modern paid its dealers very little, the dealer referred her to Modern, giving the customer the telephone number.

4. When the customer called Modern, she reached a customer service representative (CSR) who took her name, address, particulars of the model, the details of the problem and promised to dispatch a service representative "quickly."

5. The customer service representative (CSR) filled out a screen on her computer form and sent it to

the customer service manager. Actually, it went to his incoming mail queue since the customer service manager was away on the two-day course on improving customer service!

6. When he returned, the following Monday, it took the CSM a couple of days to clear his mail backlog, but on Wednesday he dispatched a customer service technician (CST) who was fully equipped to fix the problem. The CST called on the householder, diagnosed the problem (a 79-cent O-ring that had failed) and repaired it in 30 minutes.

7. However, because it had taken a week to make the fix, a good deal of food had spoiled. The householder gave a verbal list to the CST...two pounds of bacon, three roasts, a leg of lamb, a dozen frozen TV dinners and some other items. All told, she estimated that she had lost about $200 worth of food because of the breakdown.

8. The CST noted all of this down on a form and, at the end of the day, this form was handed into the customer service manager.

9. The next day, this form was keyed into the computer system (M-Track) and a copy sent to the CSR. She called the customer to check on the customer's claim for ruined food. By then, over a week had passed. The customer had not kept a detailed record of the food lost, and she was irritated by the delay; she also was very busy that day, looking after her own children as well as a neighbour's. The list of spoiled food she gave to the CSR was considerably larger than the one that she had given to the customer service technician. The group was not surprised to hear this: "This list increases in direct proportion to the time it takes to fix the problem," said one of the customer service technicians. The reason for CSR checking back with the customer was the subject of much discussion among the group: some thought it was control system, other saw it as a sign that the customer service technicians, all of whom were unionized employees, were not trusted to do the job properly, others put it down to "past practice."

10. Faced with this discrepancy, the CSR called a meeting with the customer service manager and the customer service technician. This meeting took a week to arrange. They agreed that they had little option except to agree to the new fig-

ure. "After all, the CST said, "she hardly had time to investigate what she had lost when I visited her.... The new figure is probably more accurate."

11. The next day, the customer service representative (CSR) called back to the customer, acknowledged her claim, and said that she would be compensated.

12. The CSR then sent another electronic form to the accounts payable department at Modern. There it sat for 30 days since the company's policy was to pay on a "net-30" basis. After 30 days, the accounts payable clerk sent a cheque requisition to the accounts payable manager; he was actually away on a course, and the requisition sat on *his* desk for three days. When he came back, the accounts payable manager signed the requisition, which was processed two days later and a cheque was sent by mail to the customer. "By the way," asked one of the group members, "what value did the accounts payable manager add to this process? He knew none the circumstances surrounding the case. What was he really approving?"

13. It took seven days for the cheque to reach the customer. At last, she was compensated. It had taken 60 days from the time that the problem had occurred. During that time she had complained to all her friends and, indeed, to complete strangers about Modern's terrible customer service. "I'd never buy another appliance from them! They just don't stand by their warranty promise."

Other employees who were at the session were not all that surprised by what they heard. When questioned about this by the workshop leader, one of the participants said:

Modern has lots of processes like these. Slow, slow, slow! Checks, controls, approvals … too many people involved in issues. And it's usually the customer who pays the price. By the way, we—the employees—hate these processes too. They don't let us do our jobs well.

After each of the groups had presented its specific problem areas, all of the issues were posted on the wall of the meeting room, people re-voted on the importance of the issues, and people also volunteered to work on up to two of them. Modern's warranty process ranked third in order of importance in the minds of the participants, and six people volunteered to work on it by writing their names on sticky notes and attaching them to a flipchart sheet identifying the warranty process as an issue. During the next two hours they went away and tried to figure out how to improve the warranty process.

Discussion in the group went backwards and forwards—computerizing the process more, creating a shortcut for warranty claims that would eliminate the 30-day waiting period on accounts payable, empowering the service representatives to dispatch a service technician without waiting for a manager's approval, and so on. About two-thirds of the way through the discussion, one of the service technicians asked a question:

"Does anyone know the average value of one of these claims? And what are the highs and low"? A quick call to the accounting department produced this data: the average claim in the last 12 months had been $193.27, and 90 percent of the claims had been under $280. "In which case," said the service technician, "I have a simple solution to this issue." He proceeded to describe his solution to the group. There was a lot of discussion and some modifications before the group reached consensus—this was worth proposing to the plenary session and, if they agreed, to the management team at the end of the session.

The Presentation

On the morning of the third day, the whole management team of Modern showed up at the hotel and found the 60 people split into seven different teams. Each team had two issues they had worked through, had presented each issue to their colleagues, refined the details, and were now ready to present to the management team.

John Antozyk, the chair of Modern's local union branch and also a service representative who had never made a presentation before in his life except at union meetings, walked to the front of the meeting room. He briefly described the warranty issue, which they had analyzed using a couple of transparencies to illustrate the current process. He gave the team's recommendation:

We propose that: (a) we list the brand names of our appliances in the telephone books and Internet listings together with the warranty numbers; (b) we empower the customer

service representatives to dispatch the service technicians; (c) we issue chequebooks to service technicians, and if the amount of the claim is under $300, they are empowered to settle the claim on the spot. That way we can settle a claim in six hours instead of 60 days and, since there will be minimal time between the customer having the problem and our settling the claim, the claim amount will be less, there will be no badmouthing of Modern, and we will generate a lot of goodwill. I'm prepared to work with the management team to make this happen.

This recommendation was not a surprise to Bradshaw. Jeff Meredith, the workshop leader, had called him the previous evening to give him a general briefing about all of the recommendations that were emerging from the various team discussions. They were not in finished form since the teams were still working on them, but Bradshaw had a pretty good idea of what they were likely to be. As the team made its recommendation on the warranty process, Bradshaw could not resist looking for the response of his vice-president of finance. Roger Allenby was white as a sheet. His hands were gripping the edge of the table where he sat, and Bradshaw swore that he saw beads of perspiration dripping down Allenby's forehead.

When John Antozyk finished his presentation, sitting down to applause from the assembled group, James Bradshaw turned to his management team and said, "So what do you think? Should we approve this or not? We have about 15 minutes to discuss each recommendation, and all discussion will take place here, in front of the people making the recommendations."

Source: Richard Ivey School of Business. Case 9B07C035 by Jeffrey Gandz, 2007. Professor Jeffrey Gandz wrote this case solely to provide material for class discussion. The author does not intend to illustrate either effective or ineffective handling of a managerial situation. The author may have disguised certain names and other identifying information to protect confidentiality.

EXHIBIT 1
The Workshop Process

The Workshop Process

Explain Concept → Charge by Business Leader → Management Team Leaves → Obstacle Identification → Prioritization

Election-In → Analysis → Recommendation(s) → Presentation for Inputs → Action Planning

Presentation for Approval → Follow-Through → Follow-Up

EXHIBIT 2
The Warranty System

Modern CSC

① ② ③ ST SPVR
⑧
⑨ ⑦ ④
⑥ ⑩ MTG CSC S/T SPVR
⑤ S/T
7–9 Weeks
List of spoiled food
⑪ ⑫
Accept payable → Check
⑭ ⑬
Accept payable SPVR
⑮
Canada post

QUESTIONS

1. Describe the culture at Modern Appliances. What values, norms, and behaviours are associated with the culture? How has the culture contributed to Modern's success?

2. What are some of the concerns that James Bradshaw has about Modern Appliances? To address these concerns, he believes that a change in culture is needed. Do you agree that the culture should be changed? Explain your answer.

3. What kind of culture does Bradshaw want to create and how does it differ from the existing culture? Do you think this new culture will improve customer service? Explain your answer.

4. Describe the ModernIzation workshop process. Do you think that this is an effective way to change the culture of an organization? Refer to the material in the chapter on contributors to culture and Exhibit 8.8 and describe what else might be required to change the culture of Modern Appliances.

5. Compare and contrast the current warranty process at Modern Appliances to the team's recommendation for how to change the process. Describe how these two processes differ in terms of organizational values, norms, and employee behaviours. Do you think the new warranty process will contribute to a change in culture and improve customer service? Explain your answer.

6. What are some of the assets and liabilities of Modern Appliances existing culture and the proposed culture?

CHAPTER 9

LEADERSHIP

LEARNING OBJECTIVES

After reading Chapter 9, you should be able to:

9.1 Define *leadership* and discuss the role of formal leadership in organizations.

9.2 Explain and critically evaluate the *trait theory of leadership*.

9.3 Describe the following leadership behaviours and their consequences: *consideration*, *initiating structure*, *leader reward*, and *leader punishment*.

9.4 Describe and evaluate the following situational theories of leadership: *Fiedler's contingency theory*, *cognitive resource theory*, and *House's path–goal theory*.

9.5 Discuss participative leadership and how and when to use *participative leadership* using the Vroom and Jago model.

9.6 Describe and evaluate *leader–member exchange (LMX) theory*.

9.7 Describe *transactional* and *transformational* leadership and their consequences.

9.8 Discuss *global leadership* and describe the characteristics of global leaders.

9.9 Discuss the new and emerging theories of leadership including *empowering leadership*, *ethical leadership*, *authentic leadership*, and *servant leadership*.

9.10 Discuss the GLOBE project and explain the role that culture plays in leadership effectiveness.

9.11 Describe gender differences in leadership and explain why women are underrepresented in leadership roles in organizations.

BONNIE BROOKS OF HUDSON'S BAY COMPANY

Bonnie Brooks is a Canadian with prominent international retail and leadership experience. In 2008, she was appointed president and CEO of The Bay, the company's first female CEO. Her mandate was to boost sales and breathe new life into the tired but storied department store and to lead The Bay's ambitious revival strategy.

The Bay is Canada's oldest department store, with 94 stores across the country. However, like many other department stores in North America, store productivity had been slipping for years, and The Bay was losing market share to big-box specialty chains and global discounters. The Bay had to make dramatic changes to survive. The vision was to make it the dominant Canadian department store by improving the quality of its brands, its stores, its service, and the customer experience.

However, The Bay has been subject to numerous failed makeovers over the past decade. While there are many skeptics, according to industry experts Brooks is one of the few executives with the savvy to change The Bay.

They said she will bring a sense of fashion, style, and glamour to the job.

Brooks has more than 35 years of experience in the retail fashion industry. Before taking the job at The Bay, she was president of Lane Crawford Joyce Group, a Hong Kong retail conglomerate that runs more than 500 stores in nine Asian countries. In this role she oversaw all aspects of the company including Lane Crawford department stores, Joyce Boutiques, Pedder Group, and the LCJG Distribution Company, and spearheaded the company's turnaround. Brooks is credited with transforming Lane Crawford into a luxury retailer. In 2008, Lane Crawford won the 2008 International Retailer of the Year award.

Brooks began her career at Fairweather, where she worked her way up from stylist and copywriter to head of marketing. She was also editor-in-chief of *Flare*, Canada's largest fashion and lifestyle magazine, and senior vice-president of marketing and executive vice-president and

Bonnie Brooks is credited with The Bay's exceptional turnaround and was named president of Hudson's Bay Company in 2012.

general merchandise manager at Holt Renfrew. At Holt Renfrew she played a part in the company's reinvigoration in the late 1980s.

So why did she decide to return to Canada to lead The Bay? According to Brooks, "The role to transform The Bay from its existing format to world class was too compelling to pass up. Building exceptional retail destinations is not only my profession, it's my passion." Her goal was to make The Bay the best department store in Canada. However, after six months her ambitions grew to make The Bay an international company and one of the best department stores in the world.

While many believed that consumers had lost interest in department stores, Brooks rebuilt The Bay brand in her own image and introduced The Bay to a new audience. She brought a personal touch to everything she did. Brooks was the voice of The Bay on radio spots and she refreshed all aspects of the business including its restaurants and hair salons. She discontinued unpopular brands in favour of edgy new ones and obtained exclusive fashion deals with brands such as Ralph Lauren.

According to David Riddiford, chief executive of Links of London, who worked with Brooks at Lane Crawford, "Bonnie's whole essence is about communication. She is a fabulous networker and fabulous negotiator, and she believes in bringing people onside." When asked about her leadership style, Brooks said that she tries to motivate people to exceed their own expectations. A favourite saying of hers is "A man's reach must always exceed his grasp."

Today, Bonnie Brooks is credited with The Bay's exceptional turnaround and for making The Bay relevant again. Under her leadership, The Bay celebrated its most profitable year ever. In the first half of 2011, sales were up 4% at stores open for more than a year and rose to 9% in the second half of 2011. In the fall quarter of 2011, it had its highest sales in history.

In 2012, Bonnie Brooks was named president of Hudson's Bay Company as part of its purchase of its U.S. sister company, Lord & Taylor Holdings LLC. As president, she is now responsible for merchandising, marketing, and store operations at The Bay and Lord & Taylor. In commenting on her new position, Brooks said "It's a chance to do something innovative. Lord & Taylor is just a terrific company and they have been doing really, really well for the last three years. I hope we can keep up that momentum."

Lord & Taylor is one of the oldest upscale chains in the United States. With 47 stores in nine northeastern states, it too is in need of a makeover and Brooks is being counted on to do it again. According to Richard Baker, Governor and CEO of the Hudson's Bay Company, "Bonnie's extraordinary leadership at The Bay and previous global retailing expertise from Lane Crawford are a natural fit to lead this new integrated organization as we move to our next phase of growth and evolution. The turnaround and speed of growth at The Bay under Bonnie's leadership is unprecedented in modern times." As for Lord & Taylor, Baker says, "I believe Bonnie and the team will continue to make progress and continue to innovate. Bonnie is always an agent of change."

Bonnie Brooks' leadership has not gone unnoticed. She is recognized as one the most innovative international retail experts. In 2010, *Fast Company* magazine named her one of the 100 most creative people in business, and *Monocle Magazine* named her one of the top 25 Top Retailers in the world. She has also been recognized as one of Canada's Most Powerful Women.[1]

Watch

LEADERSHIP Go to MyManagementLab to watch a video about leadership.

Simulate

LEADERSHIP Go to MyManagementLab to complete a simulation about leadership.

LO 9.1

Define *leadership* and discuss the role of formal leadership in organizations.

Leadership. The influence that particular individuals exert on the goal achievement of others in an organizational context.

Bonnie Brooks is a case study in leadership. But what exactly is leadership, and what makes a leader successful? Would Bonnie Brooks be successful in other organizations and in other leadership situations? These are the kinds of issues that this chapter tackles.

First we will define leadership and find out if we can identify special leadership traits associated with successful leaders. After this we will examine the consequences of various leadership behaviours and examine theories contending that effective leadership depends on the nature of the work situation. Following this are discussions of participative leadership, leader–member exchange theory, transactional and transformational leadership theory, and global leadership. Next we discuss several new and emerging leadership theories including empowering leadership, ethical leadership, authentic leadership, and servant leadership. We conclude the chapter with a discussion of cultural issues and gender differences in leadership.

WHAT IS LEADERSHIP?

Several years ago, an article in *Report on Business Magazine* highlighted the perceived importance of leadership in business and public affairs. The cover story, "The Toughest SOBs in Business," profiled Canada's toughest bosses and suggested that effective leaders have a rare combination of vision, skills, expertise, and toughness. In another cover story on the 25 most powerful executives in Canada, it is suggested that powerful leaders have influence and the ability to get their way with governments, the public, partners, and peers. Perhaps it is not surprising that organizations in North America spend billions of dollars each year to make their leaders more effective.[2] But what exactly is leadership and what makes a leader effective?

Leadership occurs when particular individuals exert influence on the goal achievement of others in an organizational context. Effective leadership exerts influence in a way that achieves organizational goals by enhancing the productivity, innovation, satisfaction, and commitment of the workforce. Leadership is about motivating people and gaining their commitment. Effective leaders can change the way people think, feel, and behave, and they can have a positive effect on individuals, groups, units, and even entire organizations.[3]

As demonstrated in the chapter-opening vignette, leadership has a strong effect on an organization's strategy, success, and very survival. Just consider Bonnie Brooks' role in transforming The Bay and making it a more profitable and viable organization. Her role and actions demonstrate the important role that leaders play in changing the direction and strategy of an organization or what is known as strategic leadership.

Strategic leadership refers to a leader's "ability to anticipate, envision, maintain flexibility, think strategically, and work with others to initiate changes that will create a viable future for the organization." Strategic leaders can provide an organization with a sustainable competitive advantage by helping their organizations compete in turbulent and unpredictable environments and by exploiting growth opportunities. Strategic leaders are open and honest in their interactions with the organization's stakeholders, and they focus on the future.[4]

In theory, *any* organizational member can exert influence on other members, thus engaging in leadership. In practice, though, some members are in a better position to be leaders than others. Individuals with titles such as *manager, executive, supervisor,* and *department head* occupy formal or assigned leadership roles. As part of these roles they are *expected* to influence others, and they are given specific authority to direct employees. Of course, the presence of a formal leadership role is no guarantee that there is leadership. Some managers and supervisors fail to exert any influence on others. These people will usually be judged to be ineffective leaders. Thus, leadership involves going beyond formal role requirements to influence others.

Individuals might also emerge to occupy informal leadership roles. Since informal leaders do not have formal authority, they must rely on being well liked or being perceived as highly skilled to exert influence. In this chapter we will concentrate on formal leadership. In the next section, we discuss one of the earliest theories of leadership. Before continuing, try to answer this question: *Do you think people are born to be leaders?*

Strategic leadership. Leadership that involves the ability to anticipate, envision, maintain flexibility, think strategically, and work with others to initiate changes that will create a viable future for the organization.

" Some men are born great, some achieve greatness, and some are allowed to work for great men like me. "

LO 9.2

Explain and critically evaluate the *trait theory of leadership*.

Trait theory of leadership. Leadership depends on the personal qualities or traits of the leader.

Traits. Individual characteristics such as physical attributes, intellectual ability, and personality.

Intelligence
Energy and drive
Self-confidence
Dominance
Motivation to lead
Emotional stability
Honesty and integrity
Need for achievement
Sociability

EXHIBIT 9.1
Traits associated with leadership effectiveness.

ARE LEADERS BORN? THE TRAIT THEORY OF LEADERSHIP

Given Bonnie Brooks' track record as an effective leader, you might be tempted to conclude that she is a born leader. But then again, given her years of experience you might just as easily conclude that she has, in fact, learned how to become a good leader.

Throughout history, social observers have been fascinated by obvious examples of successful interpersonal influence, whether the consequences of this influence were good, bad, or mixed. Individuals such as Henry Ford, Martin Luther King, Jr., Barbara Jordan, Ralph Nader, and Jack Welch have been analyzed and reanalyzed to discover what made them leaders and what set them apart from less successful leaders. The implicit assumption here is that those who become leaders and do a good job of it possess a special set of traits that distinguish them from the masses of followers. This approach to leadership is known as the trait theory of leadership. According to the **trait theory of leadership**, leadership depends on the personal qualities or traits of the leader.[5] While philosophers and the popular media have advocated such a position for centuries, trait theories of leadership did not receive serious scientific attention until the 1900s. Let's take a closer look at the research on leadership traits.

Research on Leadership Traits

During the First World War the U.S. military recognized that it had a leadership problem. Never before had the country mounted such a massive war effort, and able officers were in short supply. Thus, the search for leadership traits that might be useful in identifying potential officers began. Following the war, and continuing through the Second World War, this interest expanded to include searching for leadership traits in populations as diverse as school children and business executives. Some studies tried to differentiate traits of leaders and followers, while others were a search for traits that predicted leader effectiveness or distinguished lower-level leaders from higher-level leaders.[6]

Just what is a trait, anyway? **Traits** are personal characteristics of individuals such as physical characteristics, intellectual ability, and personality. Research on leadership has mostly focused on traits associated with demographics (e.g., gender, age, and education), task competence (e.g., intelligence), and interpersonal attributes (e.g., extraversion).[7] Research has shown that many, many traits are not associated with whether people become leaders or how effective they are as leaders. Research also shows that some traits are associated with leadership. Exhibit 9.1 provides a list of the traits that have often been found to be related to leadership.[8] As you might expect, leaders (or more successful leaders) tend to be higher than average on these dimensions, although the connections are not very strong. Notice that the list portrays a high-energy person who really wants to have an impact on others but at the same time is smart and stable enough not to abuse his or her power. Interestingly, this is a very accurate summary description of Bonnie Brooks.

In recent years, there has been a renewed interest in the study of leadership traits, and a number of studies have shown that certain traits are more closely linked to leadership emergence and effectiveness. For example, all five of the Big Five dimensions of personality have been found to be related to leadership emergence and success, with extraversion and conscientiousness being the most consistent predictors of leadership effectiveness.[9] A review of research on intelligence and leadership found that although there is a significant relationship between intelligence and leadership effectiveness, it is considerably lower than previously thought.[10] It is also worth noting that the relationship between traits and leadership effectiveness is stronger for affective and relational measures of effectiveness (e.g., satisfaction with the leader) than for performance-related measures. Perhaps not surprisingly, many contemporary organizations use a wide variety of trait-based assessments to measure leadership traits when making hiring and promotion decisions.[11] However, there are some aspects to the trait approach that limit its ultimate usefulness.

Limitations of the Trait Approach

Even though some traits appear to be related to leadership and leader effectiveness, there are several reasons why the trait approach is not the best means of understanding and improving leadership.

In many cases, it is difficult to determine whether traits make the leader or whether the opportunity for leadership produces the traits. For example, do dominant individuals tend to become leaders, or do employees become more dominant *after* they successfully occupy leadership roles? This distinction is important. If the former is true, we might wish to seek out dominant people and appoint them to leadership roles. If the latter is true, this strategy will not work.

Even if we know that dominance, intelligence, or tallness is associated with effective leadership, we have few clues about what dominant or intelligent or tall people *do* to influence others successfully. As a result, we have little information about how to train and develop leaders and no way to diagnose failures of leadership.

The most crucial problem of the trait approach to leadership is its failure to take into account the *situation* in which leadership occurs. Intuitively, it seems reasonable that top executives and first-level supervisors might require different traits to be successful. Similarly, physical prowess might be useful in directing a logging crew but irrelevant to managing a team of scientists.

Finally, because the trait approach leads us to believe that people are more likely to become a leader or to be a more effective leader simply because they possess certain traits, this can lead to bias and discrimination when it comes to evaluating a leader's effectiveness and decisions about promoting people to leadership positions. To learn more, see the Research Focus: *Leader Categorization Theory and Racial Bias.*

In summary, although there are some traits that are associated with leadership success, traits alone are not sufficient for successful leadership. Traits are only a precondition for certain actions that a leader must take to be successful. In other words, possessing the appropriate traits for leadership makes it possible—and even more likely—that certain actions will be taken and will be successful.[12] In fact, there is some evidence that one of the reasons that traits are related to leadership effectiveness is because of their association with leadership behaviours that are important for effective leadership. This research also indicates that leader behaviours have a greater impact on leadership effectiveness than leader traits and, unlike traits, behaviours can be learned and developed.[13] Before continuing, see You Be the Manager: *Leadership Development at Business Development Bank of Canada (BDC).*

THE BEHAVIOUR OF LEADERS

The trait approach is mainly concerned with what leaders *bring* to a group setting. The limitations of this approach gradually promoted an interest in what leaders *do* in group settings. Of particular interest were the behaviours of certain group members that caused them to *become* leaders and the behaviour of assigned or appointed leaders. What are the crucial behaviours such leaders engage in, and how do these behaviours influence employee performance and satisfaction? In other words, is there a particular *leadership style* that is more effective than other possible styles?

LO 9.3

Describe the following leadership behaviours and their consequences: *consideration, initiating structure, leader reward,* and *leader punishment.*

■ RESEARCH FOCUS

LEADER CATEGORIZATION THEORY AND RACIAL BIAS

Are you more likely to think that somebody is a leader just because of their race? According to research by Ashleigh Rosette, Geoffrey Leonardelli, and Katherine Phillips, there is a good chance that you are more likely to view somebody who is white as a leader than somebody who is a racial minority. The authors based their predictions on a theory called leadership categorization theory. According to *leadership categorization theory*, people are more likely to view somebody as a leader and to evaluate them as a more effective leader when they possess prototypical characteristics of leadership.

A leadership prototype is a standard example or typical leader category that individuals develop over time based on a set of beliefs about the behaviours and characteristics of leaders. Persons who possess the characteristics that are consistent with an observer's leadership prototype are more likely to be viewed as leaders and to be evaluated more favourably.

The authors predicted that this might explain racial bias in who occupies top leadership positions. That is, race, and specifically being white, might be a central characteristic of the business leader prototype.

To find out, the authors conducted four studies in which student participants read a newspaper article about a fictitious company and then answered questions about the race of the leader and the effectiveness of the leader described in the article.

As predicted by leader categorization theory, leaders, but not employees, were more often assumed to be white by white and non-white participants regardless of whether the organization portrayed in the article was in the financial services or social services industry and regardless of the percentage of white individuals in the organization and in leadership positions.

White and non-white participants also evaluated white leaders as more effective and as having more leadership potential than non-white leaders when the leader was credited with their organization's success. This is the very situation in which racial bias can undermine non-white leaders' career potential.

These results demonstrate that being white is a characteristic of the business leader prototype. In other words, whites are perceived to be prototypical business leaders and receive more favourable evaluations compared to non-white leaders.

Thus, race can result in biased evaluations of leadership through the process of leader categorization, and this has implications for the likelihood that an individual will be promoted to leadership positions and a leader's likelihood of career advancement.

Source: Based on Rosette, A.S., Leonardelli, G.J., & Phillips, K.W. (2008). The White standard: Racial bias in leader categorization. *Journal of Applied Psychology, 93*, 758–777. Used with permission. Copyright © 2008 by the American Psychological Association. Adapted with permission.

Co-operators president and CEO Kathy Bardswick is a good example of a leader who exhibits leader consideration behaviour.

Consideration. The extent to which a leader is approachable and shows personal concern and respect for employees.

The most involved, systematic study of leadership took place at Ohio State University in the 1940s. The Ohio State researchers began by having employees describe their superiors along a number of behavioural dimensions. Statistical analyses of these descriptions revealed that they boiled down to two basic kinds of behaviour—consideration and initiating structure.

Consideration and Initiating Structure

Consideration is the extent to which a leader is approachable and shows personal concern and respect for employees. The considerate leader is seen as friendly and egalitarian, expresses appreciation and support, and is protective of group welfare. Co-operators Group president and CEO Kathy Bardswick is a good example of someone who exhibits leader consideration behaviour. After she became CEO in 2001, she participated in 90 town hall meetings across the country to learn about employee concerns and answer their questions. Upon learning that employees were stressed and feeling the heat of public outrage at the high cost of auto insurance, she introduced a number of initiatives to assist employees, including a wellness program, recognition programs, and flexible work hours. In 2004, for the first time, the Co-operators were named one of the 50 Best Employers in Canada.[14]

YOU BE THE MANAGER

Leadership Development at Business Development Bank of Canada (BDC)

Many organizations report a gap between their current leadership talent and future leadership needs. To address leadership gaps, companies such as Business Development Bank of Canada (BDC) identify employees who have the potential to move into leadership roles.

BDC is a Crown corporation based in Montreal that provides financing and consulting services for small and medium-sized businesses. It focuses primarily on the technology and export sectors of the economy and provides entrepreneurs with financing and a range of business consulting services. It serves its clients through a network of 92 branches across Canada.

To ensure it has future leaders, BDC selects employees for promotion based on their skills and achievements. However, very often the employees selected do not have experience leading, managing, and inspiring others and may face various challenges when they are promoted into management positions.

At one point, BDC realized that a significant number of employees (one in five) who were promoted were having difficulties achieving the expected results and required remedial training and coaching.

Other companies have had similar problems with high-potential employees who are not prepared for leadership roles. One study found that 27 percent of 109 employees who were rated as having high potential for senior management were rated as high risks for failure once they were promoted.

To address this problem, BDC implemented a leadership transition program to better prepare and develop employees with leadership potential. But how do you prepare employees to be leaders? You be the manager.

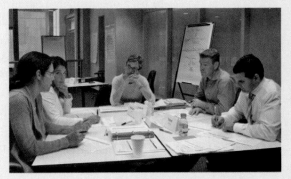

Business Development Bank of Canada (BDC) has implemented a program to evaluate and develop employees with leadership potential.

Questions

1. What kinds of experiences should the leadership transition program provide employees with leadership potential?

2. How effective will the program be in increasing the success of new leaders? Can you "make" effective leaders?

To find out more about BDC's leadership transition program, see The Manager's Notebook at the end of the chapter.

Sources: Immen, W. (2007, November 23). Primed to sail, not to fail. *Globe and Mail*, C1; Carlson, D. (2007, March 3). Potential managers play high-stakes game. *Vancouver Sun*, D4; Klie, S. (2008, October 20). Holistic approach to developing leaders best. *Canadian HR Reporter, 21*(18), 14; Yerema, R., & Caballero, R. (2009, January 12). Employer Review: Business Development Bank of Canada/BDC, www.eluta.ca/top-employer-bdc; www.bdc.ca.

Initiating structure is the degree to which a leader concentrates on group goal attainment. The structuring leader clearly defines and organizes his or her role and the roles of followers, stresses standard procedures, schedules the work to be done, and assigns employees to particular tasks.

It is important to note that consideration and initiating structure are not incompatible; a leader could be high, low, or average on one or both dimensions.

Initiating structure. The degree to which a leader concentrates on group goal attainment.

The Consequences of Consideration and Structure

The association between leader consideration, leader initiating structure, and employee responses has been the subject of hundreds of research studies. In general, this research shows that consideration and initiating structure both contribute positively to employees' motivation, job satisfaction, and leader effectiveness. However, consideration tends to be more strongly related to follower satisfaction (leader satisfaction and job satisfaction), motivation, and leader effectiveness, while initiating structure is slightly more strongly related to leader job performance and group performance.[15] In addition, there is some evidence that the relative importance of consideration and initiating structure varies according to the nature of the leadership situation. To verify this, consider the following:

- When employees are under a high degree of pressure due to deadlines, unclear tasks, or external threat, initiating structure increases satisfaction and performance. (Soldiers stranded behind enemy lines should perform better under directive leadership.)

- When the task itself is intrinsically satisfying, the need for high consideration and high structure is generally reduced. (The teacher who really enjoys teaching should be able to function with less social–emotional support and less direction from the principal.)

- When the goals and methods of performing the job are very clear and certain, consideration should promote employee satisfaction, while structure might promote dissatisfaction. (The job of refuse collection is clear in goals and methods. Here, employees should appreciate social support but view excessive structure as redundant and unnecessary.)

- When employees lack knowledge as to how to perform a job, or the job itself has vague goals or methods, consideration becomes less important, while initiating structure takes on additional importance. (The new astronaut recruit should appreciate direction in learning a complex, unfamiliar job.)[16]

As you can see, the effects of consideration and initiating structure often depend on characteristics of the task, the employee, and the setting in which work is performed. We will have more to say about this when we discuss the situational theories of leadership. But first, let's consider two more examples of leader behaviours.

Leader Reward and Punishment Behaviours

Two additional leader behaviours that have been the focus of research are leader reward behaviour and leader punishment behaviour. **Leader reward behaviour** provides employees with compliments, tangible benefits, and deserved special treatment. When such rewards are made *contingent on performance*, employees should perform at a high level and experience job satisfaction. Under such leadership, employees have a clear picture of what is expected of them, and they understand that positive outcomes will occur if they achieve these expectations.

Leader punishment behaviour involves the use of reprimands or unfavourable task assignments and the active withholding of raises, promotions, and other rewards. You will recall from Chapter 2 that punishment is extremely difficult to use effectively and, when it is perceived as random and not contingent on employee behaviour, employees react negatively, with great dissatisfaction.

Research on leader reward and punishment behaviour has found these behaviours to be very effective. Contingent leader reward behaviour is positively related to employees'

Leader reward behaviour. The leader's use of compliments, tangible benefits, and deserved special treatment.

Leader punishment behaviour. The leader's use of reprimands or unfavourable task assignments and the active withholding of rewards.

perceptions (e.g., trust in supervisor), attitudes (e.g., job satisfaction and organizational commitment), and behaviour (e.g., effort, performance, and organizational citizenship behaviour). And while contingent leader punishment behaviour is related to more favourable employee perceptions, attitudes, and behaviour, *non-contingent* punishment behaviour is related to unfavourable outcomes. Furthermore, the relationships are much stronger when rewards and punishment are made contingent on employee behaviour, which means the manner in which leaders administer rewards and punishment is a critical determinant of their effectiveness. The reason leader reward and punishment behaviours are related to employee attitudes and behaviours is because they lead to more positive perceptions of justice and lower role ambiguity.[17]

SITUATIONAL THEORIES OF LEADERSHIP

We have referred to the potential impact of the situation on leadership effectiveness several times. Specifically, *situation* refers to the *setting* in which influence attempts occur. The basic premise of situational theories of leadership is that the effectiveness of a leadership style is contingent on the setting. The setting includes the characteristics of the employees, the nature of the task they are performing, and characteristics of the organization.

A good example of the importance of the situation for leadership effectiveness comes from WestJet Airlines. A number of years ago, the airline hired Steve Smith to take over as CEO. At the time, Smith was running Air Canada's regional airline in Ontario. West-Jet liked his amiable, energetic personality. However, once he was on the job it became apparent that Smith's top-down leadership style and lack of openness with employees did not fit with WestJet's more open, bottom-up, collaborative style of leadership. WestJet's employee association resented his approach and Smith eventually resigned. This is a good example of how the effectiveness of a leader's style is contingent on the situation. Thus, a leader who is effective in one situation might not be as effective in another situation.[18]

The situational leadership theories described below are among the best known and most studied. They consider situational variables that seem especially likely to influence leadership effectiveness.

Fiedler's Contingency Theory and Cognitive Resource Theory

Fred Fiedler of the University of Washington has spent decades developing and refining a situational theory of leadership called **contingency theory**.[19] This name stems from the notion that the association between *leadership orientation* and *group effectiveness* is contingent on (depends on) the extent to which the *situation is favourable* for the exertion of influence. In other words, some situations are more favourable for leadership than others, and these situations require different orientations on the part of the leader.

Leadership orientation is measured by having leaders describe their **least preferred co-worker** (LPC). This person may be a current or past co-worker. In either case, it is someone with whom the leader has had a difficult time getting the job done. The leader who describes the LPC relatively favourably (a high LPC score) can be considered *relationship* oriented—that is, despite the fact that the LPC is or was difficult to work with, the leader can still find positive qualities in him or her. On the other hand, the leader who describes the LPC unfavourably (a low LPC score) can be considered *task* oriented. This person allows the low task competence of the LPC to colour his or her views of the personal qualities of the LPC ("If he's no good at the job, then he's not good, period").

LO 9.4

Describe and evaluate the following situational theories of leadership: *Fiedler's contingency theory, cognitive resource theory,* and *House's path–goal theory.*

Contingency theory. Fred Fiedler's theory that states that the association between leadership orientation and group effectiveness is contingent on how favourable the situation is for exerting influence.

Least preferred co-worker. A current or past co-worker with whom a leader has had a difficult time accomplishing a task.

Situational theories of leadership explain how leadership style must be tailored to the demands of the task and the qualities of employees.

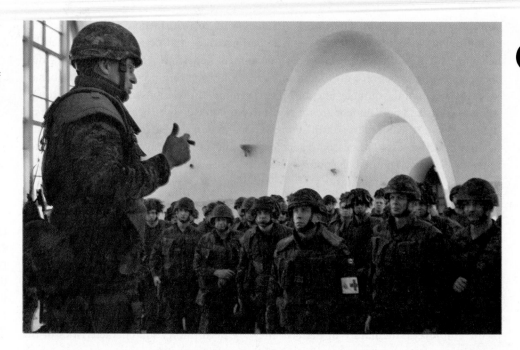

Fiedler has argued that the LPC score reveals a personality trait that reflects the leader's motivational structure. High LPC leaders are motivated to maintain interpersonal relations, while low LPC leaders are motivated to accomplish the task. Despite the apparent similarity, the LPC score is *not* a measure of consideration or initiating structure. These are observed *behaviours*, while the LPC score is evidently an *attitude* of the leader toward work relationships.

Situational favourableness is the "contingency" part of contingency theory—that is, it specifies when a particular LPC orientation should contribute most to group effectiveness. A situation is considered to be most favourable when the relationship between the leader and the group members is good (leader–member relations), the task at hand is highly structured (task structure), and when the leader has been granted formal authority by the organization to tell others what to do (position power). The situation is least favourable when leader–member relations are poor, the task is unstructured, and the leader has weak position power.

As shown in Exhibit 9.2, we can arrange the possible combinations of situational factors into eight octants that form a continuum of favourability. The model indicates that a task orientation (low LPC) is most effective when the leadership situation is very favourable

EXHIBIT 9.2
Predictions of leader effectiveness from Fiedler's contingency theory of leadership.

 Explore

Go to MyManagementLab to see an annotated version of this figure.

Favourableness	High							Low
Leader-Member Relations	Good				Poor			
Task Structure	Structured		Unstructured		Structured		Unstructured	
Position Power	Strong	Weak	Strong	Weak	Strong	Weak	Strong	Weak
	I	II	III	IV	V	VI	VII	VIII
Most Effective Leader Orientation	Task				Relationship			Task

(octants I, II, and III) *or* when it is very unfavourable (octant VIII). On the other hand, a relationship orientation (high LPC) is most effective in conditions of medium favourability (octants IV, V, VI, and VII). Why is this so? In essence, Fiedler argues that leaders can "get away" with a task orientation when the situation is favourable—employees are "ready" to be influenced. Conversely, when the situation is very unfavourable for leadership, task orientation is necessary to get anything accomplished. In conditions of medium favourability, the boss is faced with some combination of an unclear task or a poor relationship with employees. Here, a relationship orientation will help to make the best of a situation that is stress-provoking but not impossibly bad.

In recent years, Fiedler has revised contingency theory and developed a new leadership theory called **cognitive resource theory** (CRT). The focus of CRT is the conditions in which a leader's cognitive resources (intelligence, expertise, and experience) contribute to effective leadership. The essence of CRT is that the importance of intelligence for leadership effectiveness depends on the directiveness of the leader, group support for the leader, and the stressfulness of the situation. Leader intelligence is predicted to be most important when the leader is directive, the group supports the leader, and the situation is low-stress, because the leader is able to think clearly and use his or her intelligence. In high-stress situations a leader's cognitive resources are impaired, so his or her work experience will be most important.[20]

> **Cognitive resource theory.** A leadership theory that focuses on the conditions in which a leader's cognitive resources (intelligence, expertise, and experience) contribute to effective leadership.

RESEARCH EVIDENCE The conclusions about leadership effectiveness in Exhibit 9.2 are derived from many studies that Fiedler summarizes.[21] However, contingency theory has been the subject of as much debate as any theory in organizational behaviour.[22] Fiedler's explanation for the superior performance of high LPC leaders in the middle octants is not especially convincing, and the exact meaning of the LPC score is one of the great mysteries of organizational behaviour. It does not seem to be correlated with other personality measures or predictive of specific leader behaviour. It now appears that a major source of the many inconsistent findings regarding contingency theory is the small sample sizes that researchers used in many of the studies. Advances in correcting for this problem statistically have led recent reviewers to conclude that there is reasonable support for the theory.[23] However, Fiedler's prescription for task leadership in octant II (good relations, structured task, weak position power) seems contradicted by the evidence, suggesting that his theory needs some refinement.

Research on CRT has found some support for the prediction that experience predicts performance in high-stress situations, while intelligence predicts performance in low-stress situations.[24] Leader intelligence has also been found to be more strongly related to group performance when the leader is directive and has the support of the group.[25] Thus, CRT indicates that traits (e.g., intelligence) are important for leadership effectiveness in certain situations.

House's Path–Goal Theory

Robert House, building on the work of Martin Evans, proposed a situational theory of leadership called path–goal theory.[26] Unlike Fiedler's contingency theory, which relies on the somewhat ambiguous LPC trait, **path–goal theory** is concerned with the situations under which various leader *behaviours* are most effective.

> **Path–goal theory.** Robert House's theory concerned with the situations under which various leader behaviours (directive, supportive, participative, achievement oriented) are most effective.

THE THEORY Why did House choose the name "path–goal" for his theory? According to House, the most important activities of leaders are those that clarify the paths to various goals of interest to employees. Such goals might include a promotion, a sense of accomplishment, or a pleasant work climate. In turn, the opportunity to achieve such goals should promote job satisfaction, leader acceptance, and high effort. Thus, *the effective leader forms a connection between employee goals and organizational goals.*

House argues that to provide *job satisfaction* and *leader acceptance*, leader behaviour must be perceived as immediately satisfying or as leading to future satisfaction. Leader behaviour that employees see as unnecessary or unhelpful will be resented. House contends that to promote employee *effort*, leaders must make rewards dependent on performance and ensure that employees have a clear picture of how they can achieve these rewards. To do this, the leader might have to provide support through direction, guidance, and coaching. For example, the bank teller who wishes to be promoted to supervisor should exhibit superior effort when his boss promises a recommendation contingent on good work and explains carefully how the teller can do better on his current job.

LEADER BEHAVIOUR Path–goal theory is concerned with the following four specific kinds of leader behaviour:

- *Directive behaviour.* Directive leaders schedule work, maintain performance standards, and let employees know what is expected of them. This behaviour is essentially identical to initiating structure.

- *Supportive behaviour.* Supportive leaders are friendly, approachable, and concerned with pleasant interpersonal relationships. This behaviour is essentially identical to consideration.

- *Participative behaviour.* Participative leaders consult with employees about work-related matters and consider their opinions.

- *Achievement-oriented behaviour.* Achievement-oriented leaders encourage employees to exert high effort and strive for a high level of goal accomplishment. They express confidence that employees can reach these goals.

According to path–goal theory, the effectiveness of each set of behaviours depends on the situation that the leader encounters.

SITUATIONAL FACTORS Path–goal theory concerns itself with two primary classes of situational factors—employee characteristics and environmental factors. Exhibit 9.3 illustrates the role of these situational factors in the theory. Put simply, the impact of leader behaviour on employee satisfaction, effort, and acceptance of the leader depends on the nature of the employees and the work environment. Let's consider these two situational factors in turn, along with some of the theory's predictions.

According to the theory, different types of employees need or prefer different forms of leadership. For example,

- Employees who are high need achievers (Chapter 5) should work well under achievement-oriented leadership.

- Employees who prefer being told what to do should respond best to a directive leadership style.

Explore

Go to MyManagementLab to see an annotated version of this figure.

EXHIBIT 9.3
The path–goal theory of leadership.
Source: From *Journal of Contemporary Business, 3*(4), 89. Reprinted by permission.

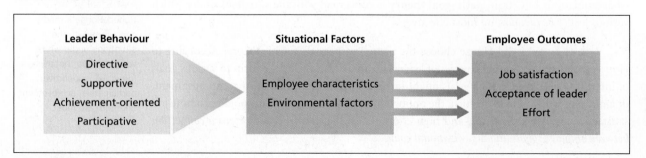

Leader Behaviour	Situational Factors	Employee Outcomes
Directive		Job satisfaction
Supportive	Employee characteristics	Acceptance of leader
Achievement-oriented	Environmental factors	Effort
Participative		

- When employees feel that they have rather low task abilities, they should appreciate directive leadership and coaching behaviour. When they feel quite capable of performing the task, they will view such behaviours as unnecessary and irritating.

As you can observe from these examples, leaders might have to tailor their behaviour to the needs, abilities, and personalities of individual employees.

Also, according to the theory, the effectiveness of leadership behaviour depends on the particular work environment. For example,

- When tasks are clear and routine, employees should perceive directive leadership as a redundant and unnecessary imposition. This should reduce satisfaction and acceptance of the leader. Similarly, participative leadership would not seem to be useful when tasks are clear, since there is little in which to participate. Obviously, such tasks are most common at lower organizational levels.

- When tasks are challenging but ambiguous, employees should appreciate both directive and participative leadership. Such styles should clarify the path to good performance and demonstrate that the leader is concerned with helping employees to do a good job. Obviously, such tasks are most common at higher organizational levels.

- Frustrating, dissatisfying jobs should increase employee appreciation of supportive behaviour. To some degree, such support should compensate for a disliked job, although it should probably do little to increase effort.

As you can see from these examples of environmental factors, effective leadership should *take advantage of* the motivating and satisfying aspects of jobs while *offsetting* or *compensating for* those job aspects that demotivate or dissatisfy.

RESEARCH EVIDENCE In general, there is some research support for most of the situational propositions discussed above. In particular, there is substantial evidence that supportive or considerate leader behaviour is most beneficial in supervising routine, frustrating, or dissatisfying jobs and some evidence that directive or structuring leader behaviour is most effective on ambiguous, less-structured jobs.[27] The theory appears to work better in predicting employees' job satisfaction and acceptance of the leader than in predicting job performance.[28]

PARTICIPATIVE LEADERSHIP: INVOLVING EMPLOYEES IN DECISIONS

In the discussion of path–goal theory, we raised the issue of participative leadership. Because this is such an important leadership style, we will devote further attention to participation.

What Is Participation?

At a very general level, **participative leadership** means involving employees in making work-related decisions. The term *involving* is intentionally broad. Participation is not a fixed or absolute property but a relative concept. This is illustrated in Exhibit 9.4. Here, we see that leaders can vary in the extent to which they involve employees in decision making. Minimally, participation involves obtaining employee opinions before making a decision. Maximally, it allows employees to make their own decisions within agreed-on limits. As the "area of freedom" on the part of employees increases, the leader is behaving in a more participative manner. There is, however, an upper limit to the area of employee freedom available under participation. Participative leadership should not be confused with the *abdication* of leadership, which is almost always ineffective.

Participation can involve individual employees or the entire group of employees that reports to the leader. For example, participation on an individual basis might work best

LO 9.5

Discuss participative leadership and how and when to use *participative leadership* using the Vroom and Jago model.

Participative leadership. Involving employees in making work-related decisions.

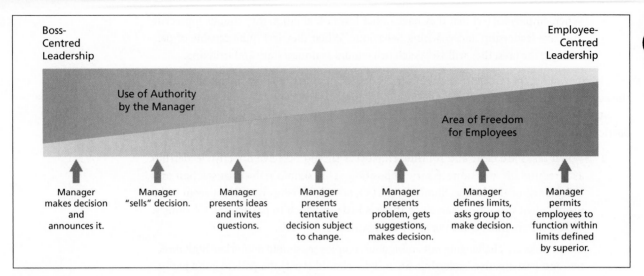

EXHIBIT 9.4

Employee participation in decision making can vary.

Source: An exhibit from Tannenbaum, R., & Schmidt, W.H. (1958, March/April). "How to choose a leadership pattern." Printed by permission of the *Harvard Business Review.* Copyright © 1958 by the President and Fellows of Harvard College; all rights reserved.

 Explore

Go to MyManagementLab to see an annotated version of this figure.

when setting performance goals for particular employees, planning employee development, or dealing with problem employees. On the other hand, the leader might involve the entire work group in decision making when determining vacation schedules, arranging for telephone coverage during lunch hour, or deciding how to allocate scarce resources such as travel money or secretarial help. As these examples suggest, the choice of an individual or group participation strategy should be tailored to specific situations.

Potential Advantages of Participative Leadership

Just why might participation be a useful leadership technique? What are its potential advantages?

MOTIVATION Participation can increase the motivation of employees.[29] In some cases participation permits them to contribute to the establishment of work goals and to decide how they can accomplish these goals. It might also occur to you that participation can increase intrinsic motivation by enriching employees' jobs. In Chapter 6, you learned that enriched jobs include high task variety and increased employee autonomy. Participation adds some variety to the job and promotes autonomy by increasing the "area of freedom" (see Exhibit 9.4).

QUALITY Participation can enhance quality in at least two ways. First, an old saying argues that "two heads are better than one." While this is not always true, there do seem to be many cases in which "two heads" (participation) lead to higher-quality decisions than the leader could make alone.[30] In particular, this is most likely when employees have special knowledge to contribute to the decision. In many research and engineering departments it is common for the professional employees to have technical knowledge that is superior to that of their boss. This occurs either because the boss is not a professional or because the boss's knowledge has become outdated. Under these conditions, employee participation in technical matters should enhance the quality of decisions.

Participation can also enhance quality because high levels of participation often empower employees to take direct action to solve problems without checking every detail with the boss. Empowerment gives employees the authority, opportunity, and motivation to take initiative and solve problems.

ACCEPTANCE Even when participation does not promote motivation or increase the quality of decisions, it can increase the employees' acceptance of decisions. This is especially likely when issues of *fairness* are involved.[31] For example, consider the problems of scheduling vacations or telephone coverage during lunch hours. Here, the leader could probably make high-quality decisions without involving employees. However, the decisions might be totally unacceptable to the employees because they perceive them as unfair. Involving employees in decision making could result in solutions of equal quality that do not provoke dissatisfaction. Public commitment and ego involvement probably contribute to the acceptance of such decisions.

Potential Problems of Participative Leadership

You have no doubt learned that every issue in organizational behaviour has two sides. Consider the potential difficulties of participation.

TIME AND ENERGY Participation is not a state of mind. It involves specific behaviours on the part of the leader (soliciting ideas, calling meetings), and these behaviours use time and energy. When a quick decision is needed, participation is not an appropriate leadership strategy. The hospital emergency room is not the place to implement participation on a continuous basis!

LOSS OF POWER Some leaders feel that a participative style will reduce their power and influence. Sometimes they respond by asking employees to make trivial decisions of the "what colour shall we paint the lounge" type. Clearly, the consequences of such decisions (for motivation, quality, and acceptance) are near zero. A lack of trust in employees and a fear that they will make mistakes is often the hallmark of an insecure manager. On the other hand, the contemporary call for flatter hierarchies and increased teamwork make such sharing of power inevitable.

LACK OF RECEPTIVITY OR KNOWLEDGE Employees might not be receptive to participation. When the leader is distrusted, or when a poor labour climate exists, they might resent "having to do management's work." Even when receptive, employees might lack the knowledge to contribute effectively to decisions. Usually, this occurs because they are unaware of *external constraints* on their decisions.

Vroom and Jago's Situational Model of Participation

How can leaders capitalize on the potential advantages of participation while avoiding its pitfalls? Victor Vroom and Arthur Jago developed a model that attempts to specify in a practical manner when leaders should use participation and to what extent they should use it. (The model was originally developed by Vroom and Philip Yetton).[32]

Vroom and Jago begin with the recognition that there are various degrees of participation that a leader can exhibit. For issues involving the entire work group, the following range of behaviours is plausible (*A* stands for autocratic, *C* for consultative, and *G* for group; I indicates an individual, and II indicates that a group is involved):

AI. You solve the problem or make the decision yourself, using information available to you at the time.

AII. You obtain the necessary information from your employees, then decide the solution to the problem yourself. You may or may not tell your employees what the problem is when getting the information from them. The role played by your employees in making the decision is clearly one of providing the necessary information to you, rather than generating or evaluating alternative solutions.

CI. You share the problem with the relevant employees individually, getting their ideas and suggestions without bringing them together as a group. Then you make the decision, which may or may not reflect your employees' influence.

CII. You share the problem with your employees as a group, obtaining their collective ideas and suggestions. Then you make the decision, which may or may not reflect your employees' influence.

✱ Explore

Go to MyManagementLab
to see an annotated
version of this figure.

EXHIBIT 9.5
**The Vroom and Jago
decision tree for
participative leadership.**
Source: Reprinted from Vroom,
V.H., & Jago, A.G. (1988). *The
new leadership: Managing participation in organizations*, "The
Vroom and Jago Decision Tree
for Participative Leadership,"
© 1988 Pearson Education,
Inc. Reproduced by permission
of Pearson Education, Inc.

GII. You share the problem with your employees as a group. Together you generate and
evaluate alternatives and attempt to reach agreement (consensus) on a solution. Your
role is much like that of chairperson. You do not try to influence the group to adopt
"your" solution, and you are willing to accept and implement any solution that has the
support of the entire group.[33]

Which of these strategies is most effective? According to Vroom and Jago, this depends
on the situation or problem at hand. In general, the leader's goal should be to make high-
quality decisions to which employees will be adequately committed without undue delay.
To do this, he or she must consider the questions in Exhibit 9.5. The quality requirement
(QR) for a problem might be low if it is very unlikely that a technically bad decision could be
made or if all feasible alternatives are equal in quality. Otherwise, QR is probably high. The
commitment requirement (CR) is likely to be high if employees are very concerned about
which alternative is chosen or if they will have to actually implement the decision. The problem is structured (ST) when the leader understands the current situation, the desired situation, and how to get from one to the other. Unfamiliarity, uncertainty, or novelty in any of

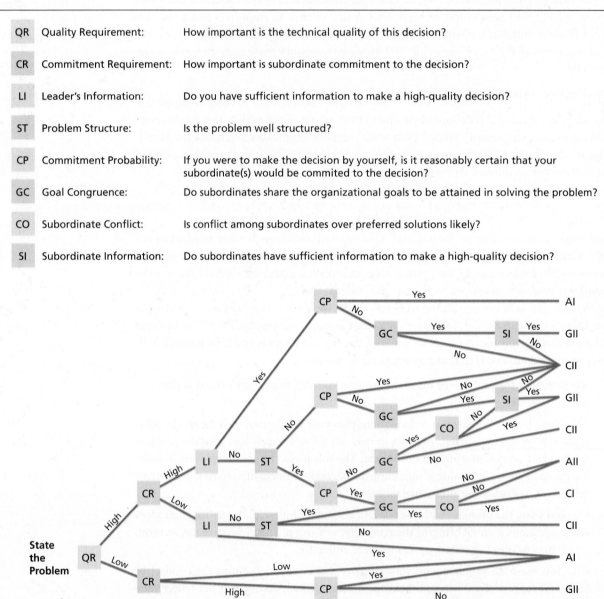

QR	Quality Requirement:	How important is the technical quality of this decision?
CR	Commitment Requirement:	How important is subordinate commitment to the decision?
LI	Leader's Information:	Do you have sufficient information to make a high-quality decision?
ST	Problem Structure:	Is the problem well structured?
CP	Commitment Probability:	If you were to make the decision by yourself, is it reasonably certain that your subordinate(s) would be commited to the decision?
GC	Goal Congruence:	Do subordinates share the organizational goals to be attained in solving the problem?
CO	Subordinate Conflict:	Is conflict among subordinates over preferred solutions likely?
SI	Subordinate Information:	Do subordinates have sufficient information to make a high-quality decision?

these matters reduces problem structure. The other questions in Exhibit 9.5 are fairly self-explanatory. Notice, however, that all are oriented toward preserving either decision quality or commitment to the decision.

By tracing a problem through the decision tree, the leader encounters the prescribed degree of participation for that problem. In every case, the tree shows the fastest approach possible (i.e., the most autocratic) that still maintains decision quality and commitment. In many cases, if the leader is willing to sacrifice some speed, a more participative approach could stimulate employee development (as long as quality or commitment is not threatened).

RESEARCH EVIDENCE The original decision model developed by Vroom and Yetton, on which the Vroom and Jago model is based, has substantial research support.[34] Following the model's prescriptions is more likely to lead to successful managerial decisions than unsuccessful decisions. The model has been used frequently in management development seminars.

But does participative leadership result in beneficial outcomes? There is substantial evidence that employees who have the opportunity to participate in work-related decisions report more job satisfaction and higher task performance and organizational citizenship behaviour toward the organization than those who do not. These results are due in part to a positive effect on employee empowerment and trust in one's supervisor. Thus, most workers seem to *prefer* a participative work environment. However, for participation to be translated into higher productivity, it would appear that certain facilitating conditions must exist. Specifically, participation should work best when employees feel favourably toward it, when they are intelligent and knowledgeable about the issue at hand, and when the task is complex enough to make participation useful.[35] In general, these conditions are incorporated into the Vroom and Jago model. Like any other leadership strategy, the usefulness of participation depends on the constraints of the situation.

LEADER–MEMBER EXCHANGE (LMX) THEORY

LO

Do you like your boss and do you have a good relationship with him or her? People often talk about their leaders in terms of how well they get along with them and if they like them or not. Thus, it should not surprise you that an important component of leadership is the nature of the relationship that develops between leaders and employees. One theory of leadership that explains leader–employee relationships is **leader–member exchange** or **LMX theory**. Unlike other theories of leadership that focus on leader traits and behaviours, LMX theory focuses on the relationship that develops between a leader and an employee. Thus, it is a social exchange relationship-based approach to leadership.

The basic idea behind LMX theory is that over time and through the course of their interactions, different types of relationships develop between leaders and employees. As a result, each relationship that a leader develops with an employee will be different and unique and these relationships will differ in terms of the *quality* of the relationship. Effective leadership processes result when leaders and employees develop and maintain high-quality social exchange relationships.[36]

The basis for the effects of LMX is **social exchange theory** and the norm of reciprocity, which posits that individuals who are treated favourably by others will feel a sense of obligation to reciprocate by responding positively and returning that favourable treatment in some manner. Thus, employees who are in a high-quality relationship with their supervisor will reciprocate with extra effort and higher commitment and performance.[37]

High-quality relationships, or high LMX, involve a high degree of mutual influence and obligation as well as trust, loyalty, open communication, and respect between a leader and an employee. High LMX leaders provide employees with challenging tasks and opportunities, greater latitude and discretion, task-related resources, and recognition. In high-quality relationships, employees perform tasks beyond their job descriptions, as suggested by social

Describe and evaluate *leader–member exchange (LMX) theory*.

Leader–member exchange (LMX) theory. A theory of leadership that focuses on the quality of the relationship that develops between a leader and an employee.

Social exchange theory. Individuals who are treated favourably by others feel obliged to reciprocate by responding positively and returning that favourable treatment in some manner.

exchange theory. At the other extreme are low-quality relationships, or low LMX. Low LMX is characterized by low levels of trust, respect, obligation, and mutual support. In low-quality relationships, the leader provides less attention and latitude to employees, and so employees do only what their job descriptions and formal role requirements demand.[38]

RESEARCH EVIDENCE Research on LMX theory has found that the relationships between leaders and employees do in fact differ in terms of the quality of the relationship and this has implications for work outcomes. Employees with higher quality LMX have higher self-efficacy, overall satisfaction, satisfaction with supervision, organizational commitment, organizational citizenship behaviour, role clarity, job performance, and creativity, and lower role conflict and turnover intentions. In general, research on LMX theory has found that higher quality LMX relationships is associated with positive outcomes for leaders, employees, work units, and organizations.[39]

LO 9.7

Describe *transactional* and *transformational* leadership and their consequences.

Transactional leadership. Leadership that is based on a straightforward exchange relationship between the leader and the followers.

Management by exception. Leadership that involves the leader taking corrective action on the basis of the results of leader–follower transactions.

Transformational leadership. Leadership that provides followers with a new vision that instills true commitment.

TRANSACTIONAL AND TRANSFORMATIONAL LEADERSHIP THEORY

Thus far in the chapter we have been describing traditional theories of leadership involving an approach to leadership that is known as transactional leadership. **Transactional leadership** is leadership that is based on a straightforward exchange relationship between the leader and the followers—leaders set goals and provide direction and support, employees perform well, and the leader rewards them; the leader uses a participatory style, and the employees come up with good ideas.

Transactional leadership behaviour involves *contingent reward behaviour*, as discussed earlier in the chapter, and management by exception. Similar to path–goal theory, the leader clarifies expectations and establishes the rewards for meeting them. **Management by exception** is the degree to which leaders take corrective action on the basis of results of leader–follower transactions. Thus, they monitor follower behaviour, anticipate problems, and take corrective actions before the behaviour creates serious problems.[40] Although it might be difficult to do well, such leadership is routine, in the sense that it is directed mainly toward bringing employee behaviour in line with organizational goals.

However, you might be aware of some more dramatic examples of leadership in which leaders have had a more profound effect on followers by giving them a new vision that instilled true commitment to a project, a department, or an organization. Such leadership is called **transformational leadership** because the leader decisively changes the beliefs and attitudes of followers to correspond to this new vision and motivates them to achieve performance beyond expectations.[41]

Popular examples of transformational leadership are easy to find—consider Herb Kelleher's founding of Southwest Airlines, former Disney CEO Michael Eisner's role in improving Disney's performance, the late Steven Jobs' vision in bringing the Apple Macintosh to fruition, or former Hewlett-Packard CEO Carly Fiorina's orchestration of the merger with Compaq Computer and her transformation of Hewlett-Packard's structure and culture. Each of these leaders went beyond a mere institutional figurehead role and even beyond a transactional leadership role to truly transform employees' thinking about the nature of their businesses. However, these prominent examples should not obscure the fact that transformational leadership can occur in less visible settings. For example, a new coach might revitalize a sorry peewee soccer team, or an energetic new director might turn around a moribund community association using the same types of skills.

But what *are* the behaviours of these transformational leaders who encourage considerable effort and dedication on the part of followers? Bernard Bass of the State University of New York at Binghamton has conducted extensive research on transformational leaders.[42] Bass notes that transformational leaders are usually good at the transactional aspects of clarifying paths to goals and rewarding good performance. But he also notes other qualities that set transformational leaders apart from their transactional colleagues. In particular, there are four key dimensions of transformational leader behaviour: intellectual stimulation, individualized consideration, inspirational motivation, and charisma.[43] Let's now take a closer look at each of these behaviours.

Intellectual Stimulation

Intellectual stimulation contributes, in part, to the "new vision" aspect of transformational leadership. People are stimulated to think about problems, issues, and strategies in new ways. The leader challenges assumptions, takes risks, and solicits followers' ideas. Often, creativity and novelty are at work here. For example, the late Steve Jobs was convinced that the Apple Macintosh had to be extremely user friendly. As you might imagine, many of the technical types who wanted to sign on to the Mac project needed to be convinced of the importance of this quality, and Jobs was just the person to do it, raising their consciousness about what it felt like to be a new computer user.

Individualized Consideration

Individualized consideration involves treating employees as distinct individuals, indicating concern for their needs and personal development, and serving as a mentor or coach when appropriate. The emphasis is a one-on-one attempt to meet the concerns and needs of the individual in question in the context of the overall goal or mission. Bass implies that individualized consideration is particularly striking when military leaders exhibit it because the military culture generally stresses impersonality and "equal" treatment. The late General "Stormin'" Norman Schwarzkopf, commander of American troops during the Gulf War, is a good example of this.

Inspirational Motivation

Inspirational motivation involves the communication of visions that are appealing and inspiring to followers. Leaders with inspirational motivation have a strong vision for the future based on values and ideals. They stimulate enthusiasm, challenge followers with high standards, communicate optimism about future goal attainment, and provide meaning for the task at hand. They inspire followers using symbolic actions and persuasion.[44]

Charisma

Charisma (also known as *idealized influence*) is the fourth and by far the most important aspect of transformational leadership. In fact, many authors simply talk about charismatic leadership, although a good case can be made that a person could have charisma without being a leader. **Charisma** is a term stemming from a Greek word meaning *favoured* or *gifted*.

Charismatic individuals have been portrayed throughout history as having personal qualities that give them the potential to have extraordinary influence over others. They tend to command strong loyalty and devotion, and this, in turn, inspires enthusiastic dedication and effort directed toward the leader's chosen mission. In terms of the concepts we developed in Chapter 8, followers come to trust and *identify* with charismatic leaders and to *internalize* the values and goals they hold. Charisma provides the *emotional* aspect of transformational leadership.

It appears that the emergence of charisma is a complex function of traits, behaviours, and being in the right place at the right time.[45] Prominent traits include self-confidence, dominance, and a strong conviction in one's beliefs. Charismatic leaders often act to create an impression of personal success and accomplishment. They hold high expectations for follower performance while at the same time expressing confidence in followers' capabilities.

Charisma. The ability to command strong loyalty and devotion from followers and thus have the potential for strong influence among them.

Richard Branson of Virgin Group is a charismatic leader who commands strong loyalty and devotion from his employees.

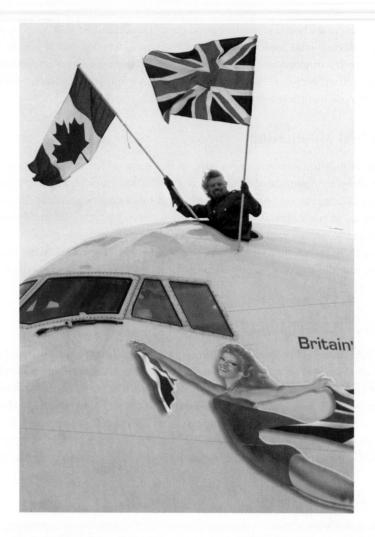

This enhances the self-esteem of the followers. The goals set by charismatic leaders often have a moral or ideological flavour to them. In addition, charismatic leaders often emerge to articulate the feelings of followers in times of stress or discord. If these feelings go against an existing power structure, the leader might be perceived as especially courageous.

Although charisma is considered to be an important aspect of transformational leadership, it has also been treated as a distinct theory of leadership in its own right and often studied independent of the other dimensions of transformational leadership. Charismatic leadership has been found to be strongly related to follower satisfaction and leadership effectiveness.[46]

Several studies have investigated the charisma of CEOs and its relationship to organizational performance. The results of these studies, however, are mixed. Although CEOs who are perceived to be charismatic are perceived as more effective, only one study has provided evidence that charismatic leadership is directly related to firm performance. This appears to be especially the case when the environment was perceived to be uncertain.[47]

RESEARCH EVIDENCE In the last two decades there have been more published studies on transformational leadership than all other popular theories of leadership. A review of all these studies found transformational leadership to be strongly related to follower motivation and satisfaction (satisfaction with leader and job satisfaction), leader performance, leader effectiveness, and individual, group, and organizational performance.[48]

Comparisons between transformational leadership and contingent reward behaviours indicate that transformational leadership is more strongly related to follower satisfaction with the leader and leader effectiveness, while contingent reward is more strongly related to follower job satisfaction and leader job performance. However, compared to other forms of leader behaviour (initiating structure, consideration, contingent reward behaviour), transformational leadership has been found to be the most consistent predictor of effective leadership.[49] In addition, several studies have also found that CEO transformational leadership is positively related to organizational performance.[50] Transformational leadership seems to be especially effective during times of change and for obtaining employees' commitment to a change. Employees with transformational leaders have been found to be more committed to and less likely to resist a large-scale organizational change.[51]

Why are transformational leaders so effective? According to several studies, transformational leaders are instrumental in developing high-quality LMX relationships, identification with one's work unit, self-efficacy, person–organization value congruence, and for enhancing employees' perceptions of the five core job characteristics of the job characteristics model (see Chapter 6). Overall, research indicates that the best leaders are both transformational and transactional.[52]

GLOBAL LEADERSHIP

For multinational organizations, global leadership is a critical success factor. But what is global leadership? **Global leadership** involves having leadership capabilities to function effectively in different cultures and being able to cross language, social, economic, and political borders.[53] The essence of global leadership is the ability to influence people who are not like the leader and come from different cultural backgrounds. This means that to succeed, global leaders need to have a global mindset, tolerate high levels of ambiguity, and exhibit cultural adaptability and flexibility.[54]

As indicated in the chapter-opening vignette, Bonnie Brooks is a good example of a global leader. She has more than 35 years of international retail experience, including 11 years in Hong Kong, where she was president of Lane Crawford Joyce Group. But what else makes one a good global leader?

According to Hal Gregersen, Allen Morrison, and Stewart Black, global leaders have the following four characteristics:[55]

- *Unbridled inquisitiveness.* Global leaders must be able to function effectively in different cultures in which they are required to cross language, social, economic, and political borders. A key characteristic of global leaders is that they relish the opportunity to see and experience new things.

- *Personal character.* Personal character consists of two components: an emotional connection to people from different cultures and uncompromising integrity. The ability to connect with others involves a sincere interest and concern for them and a willingness to listen to and understand others' viewpoints. Global leaders also demonstrate an uncompromising integrity by maintaining high ethical standards and loyalty to their organization's values. This demonstration of integrity results in a high level of trust throughout the organization.

- *Duality.* For global leaders, duality means that they must be able to manage uncertainty and balance global and local tensions. Global leaders are able to balance the tensions and dualities of global integration and local demands.

- *Savvy.* Because of the greater challenges and opportunities of global business, global leaders need to have business and organizational savvy. Global business savvy means that global leaders understand the conditions they face in different countries and are able to recognize new market opportunities for their organization's goods and services. Organizational savvy means that global leaders are well informed of their organization's capabilities and international ventures. You might recall from the chapter-opening vignette that Bonnie Brooks was believed to be one of the few executives with the savvy to lead a turnaround of The Bay.

LO **9.8**

Discuss *global leadership* and describe the characteristics of global leaders.

Global leadership. A set of leadership capabilities required to function effectively in different cultures and the ability to cross language, social, economic, and political borders.

Individuals with the potential to become global leaders have experience working or living in different cultures, they speak more than one language, and have an aptitude for global business. However, becoming an effective global leader requires extensive training that consists of travel to foreign countries, teamwork with members of diverse backgrounds, and formal training programs that provide instruction on topics such as international and global strategy, business and ethics, cross-cultural communication, and multicultural team leadership. The most powerful strategy for developing global leaders is work experience, transfers, and international assignments. Long-term international assignments are considered to be especially effective.[56] Many companies, such as GE, Citigroup, Shell, Siemens, and Nokia, use international assignments to develop global leaders.[57]

Developing global leaders is becoming increasingly important for organizations around the world. To be successful in the global economy, it is critical for an organization to identify and develop leaders who have the capability to become global leaders. For many organizations, however, this will not be easy, as many report that they do not have enough global leaders now or for the future, and they do not have a system in place for developing them.[58]

However, there is some evidence that certain countries produce more global leaders than others. Karl Moore and Henry Mintzberg of McGill University found that those countries that are considered to be the most global in terms of their involvement in world trade and investment, such as Canada, the Netherlands, Switzerland, Belgium, Ireland, Sweden, Denmark, Singapore, Australia, and Finland, tend to have more than their share of good global leaders given their size. Why is this? They are all middle-economy countries that are dependent on foreign trade. As a result, they must be able to understand and empathize with persons in other cultures. For Canadians, this comes naturally. According to Moore and Mintzberg, it is a strength of Canadians that they learn from the cradle to take into account other perspectives, a key requirement of global managers working for global companies. Living in a multicultural environment like Canada is excellent preparation for being a global manager. As a result, Canadian companies like Bombardier are way ahead of most organizations in big countries like the United States when it comes to global leadership.[59]

LO 9.9

Discuss the new and emerging theories of leadership including *empowering leadership*, *ethical leadership*, *authentic leadership*, and *servant leadership*.

NEW AND EMERGING THEORIES OF LEADERSHIP

Over the last decade, leadership research has begun to focus on more than just the leader but also the broader context of the leadership process. This has involved a greater focus on followers and it has led to the emergence of new forms of leadership behaviours and theories.[60] In this section we describe four new and emerging theories of leadership: empowering leadership, ethical leadership, authentic leadership, and servant leadership. Pay particular attention to how each of these new forms of leadership differ from the more traditional styles and theories of leadership described earlier in the chapter.

Empowering Leadership

Traditional theories of leadership focus on how leaders influence and motivate employees to work toward organizational goals largely through initiating structure and directive behaviours. These theories were developed at a time when organizations were more hierarchical and bureaucratic. Many organizations today, however, are flatter, more flexible, and less bureaucratic and employees in these organizations have more autonomy and responsibility in how they perform their jobs. This calls for a style of leadership that enables employees to make decisions and take actions on their own without direct supervision, or what is known as empowering leadership.

Empowering leadership involves implementing conditions that enable power to be shared with employees. Empowering leaders highlight the significance of employees' work, provide participation and autonomy in decision making, express confidence in employees'

Empowering leadership. Implementing conditions that enable power to be shared with employees.

capabilities, and remove bureaucratic constraints or hindrances to performance. As a result, employees experience a state of psychological empowerment that consists of a feeling that their work is personally important (meaning), a belief in their ability to successfully perform work tasks (competence), freedom to choose how to initiate and carry out one's tasks (self-determination), and a belief that one's behaviour is making a difference (impact). Thus, empowering leadership provides employees with a greater feeling of control over their work and a sense that they can make a difference in their organization's effectiveness.[61]

To date, only a few studies have studied empowering leadership. One study found that empowering leadership was associated with higher self-efficacy and adaptability of sales-people in a pharmaceutical company, which was related to higher job performance and customer-service satisfaction. Interestingly, employees with less product/industry knowl-edge and experience benefited the most from empowering leadership.[62] In another study, the authors argued that empowering leadership is especially important for employees who do creative work because employees must be given autonomy and latitude in the creative process. The authors found that professional employees in a major information technology company in the People's Republic of China (PRC) who had empowering leaders experienced a greater degree of psychological empowerment, which was associated with more creativity-relevant behaviours.[63] Thus, the effectiveness of empowering leadership is likely to depend on situational factors such as the task at hand and employee characteristics.

Ethical Leadership

Most theories of leadership focus on how leaders can improve the performance and effective-ness of individuals and groups. This should not be surprising, as most organizations want competent leaders who can make the company profitable. However, given the profound impact that leaders can have on the lives of so many people inside and outside of an organiza-tion, ethics is also is a fundamental part of effective leadership. It is now generally understood that ethical leadership is a critical component of leadership effectiveness and long-term busi-ness success.

Ethical leadership involves the demonstration of normatively appropriate conduct (e.g., openness, fairness, and honesty) through personal actions and interpersonal relationships, and the promotion of such conduct to followers through two-way communication, rein-forcement, and decision making. Ethical leaders model what is deemed to be normatively appropriate behaviour, such as honesty, trustworthiness, fairness, and care. They make ethics salient in the workplace and draw attention to it by engaging in explicit ethics-related communications and by setting ethical standards. They reward ethical behaviour and disci-pline those who do not follow ethical standards and punish unethical behaviour (notice the use of contingent leader reward and punishment behaviour). Ethical leaders also consider the ethical consequences of their decisions and make principled and fair decisions that can be observed and emulated by others. Ethical leaders care about people and the broader society and seek to do the right thing personally and professionally.[64]

What should leaders do to develop an ethical culture and workplace? According to Terry Thomas, John Schermerhorn, and John Dienhart, leaders must have a strong commitment to ethics and be willing to do even small, everyday things that help to raise awareness and reinforce the importance of ethics, including[65]

- *Communicate a clear and consistent positive ethics message from the top.* Commit-ment to ethics must be stated often and clearly; ethics messages must be supported by positive examples of senior executives making tough choices that are driven by company values.
- *Create and embrace opportunities for everyone in the organization to communicate posi-tive ethics, values, and practices.* Employees must experience a "voice" in the ethics culture and be encouraged to express concerns and preferences; they must have easy

Ethical leadership. The demonstration of normatively appropriate conduct through personal actions and interpersonal relationships.

and secure access to mechanisms for doing so, including advice lines and tip lines for reporting violations; all questions and concerns must be followed to closure; all systematic sources of recurring problems must be traced and rectified.

- *Ensure consequences for ethical and unethical conduct.* Ethical performance should be recognized and rewarded, visibly and regularly; unethical behaviour should be met with sanctions up to and including termination, with no exclusions for senior executives.

Boeing's CEO Jim McNerney is a good example of an ethical leader who has taken these kinds of initiatives in an effort to build an ethical culture. For example, he has linked pay and bonuses to how well executives embrace "Boeing values," such as promoting integrity and avoiding abusive behaviour. He has also established financial incentives for managers based not solely on a rising stock price but on improved performance.[66]

Research on ethical leadership has found that it is positively associated with employee perceptions of honesty, fairness, and effectiveness, and with fewer counterproductive behaviours. Employees of ethical leaders are more satisfied with their supervisor, more willing to devote extra effort to their job, more likely to engage in citizenship behaviours, and more willing to report problems to management. One study found that the extent to which ethics was an important part of an organization's culture was influenced by the ethics and moral development of the leader. In other words, the ethical behaviour of leaders had a significant influence on the ethical culture of the organization. This is because ethical leaders set ethical standards, they model ethical behaviours, and they use rewards and punishment to ensure ethical behaviour on the part of employees. Along these lines, a recent study found that ethical leadership was related to less unethical behaviour in work units and less relationship conflict among employees.[67]

Ethical leaders have also been found to have a positive effect on employees' job performance in part because they improve employee perceptions of leader–member exchange (LMX) quality, self-efficacy, organizational identification, task significance, and effort.[68] Although ethical leadership is important at all levels of an organization, ethical leadership on the part of the immediate supervisor is likely to have the greatest effect on employees.[69]

Authentic Leadership

Have you ever questioned the real feelings and beliefs of a leader? Have you ever wondered if perhaps a leader was hiding his or her real thoughts and beliefs? We like to believe that our leaders always act in a manner that is consistent with their true personal values and beliefs and in the best interests of employees and the organization. However, as it turns out, some leaders are more authentic than others when it comes to what they say and what they do.

Authentic leadership.
A positive form of leadership that involves being true to oneself.

Authentic leadership is a positive form of leadership that involves being true to oneself. Authentic leaders know and act upon their true values, beliefs, and strengths, and they help others do the same. Their conduct and behaviour is guided by their internal values. In other words, there is a consistency between their true values, beliefs, and actions. As a result, authentic leaders earn the respect and trust of their followers. Authentic leaders are perceived by their followers as being high in moral perspective and as open and fair in decision making.[70]

A good example of an authentic leader is Maple Leafs Foods CEO Michael McCain. At the time of the listeriosis outbreak in 2008, he apologized and expressed sympathy for the victims and accepted full responsibility and accountability. He said that he was doing what was right, and doing what was right came directly from the company's ingrained values. According to McCain, "The core principle here was to first do what's in the interest of public health, and second to be open and transparent in taking accountability. For the team, this was almost not a decision—it was obvious. It's just what we are."[71] McCain's words and actions are an excellent example of authentic leadership.

Authentic leadership involves four distinct but related behaviours:[72]

- *Self-awareness.* An accurate understanding of one's strengths and weaknesses and an awareness of one's impact on others. Authentic leaders gain insight into themselves through interactions with others and possess accurate self-knowledge.

- *Relational transparency.* The presenting of one's true or authentic self to others and the open sharing of information and expressions of one's true thoughts and feelings.

- *Balanced processing.* The objective analysis of all relevant information before making a decision and consideration of views that challenge one's own position.

- *Internalized moral perspective.* They have internal moral standards and values that guide their behaviour and decision making. Authentic leaders exhibit behaviour that is consistent with their internal values and standards and they resist social pressures.

Over the last several years an increasing number of studies have found that authentic leadership has positive effects on a number of work-related outcomes. For example, followers of authentic leaders have been found to have higher organizational commitment, job satisfaction, and satisfaction with their supervisor and to exhibit higher organizational citizenship behaviour, work engagement, ethical, and pro-social behaviours.[73]

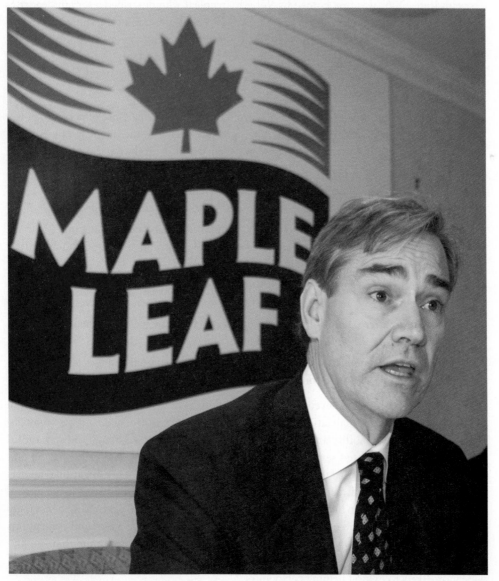

Maple Leaf Foods CEO Michael McCain's words and actions in response to the listeriosis outbreak is an example of authentic leadership.

Authentic leadership has also been found to have a positive effect on work groups. For example, in a study on work groups in a large bank, authentic leadership was positively related to the psychological capital of the group (self-efficacy, hope, optimism, and resilience; see Chapter 1 for definitions) and trust among group members, which led to a higher level of group citizenship behaviours and performance.[74] A study on military teams found that team leader authenticity was related to team members' authenticity. In other words, team members were more likely to be authentic when their leader was authentic. The study also found that team member authenticity was related to higher-quality teamwork behaviour and team productivity.[75]

Servant Leadership

If you think about the focus of most theories of leadership, what you find is a leader exerting influence on others for his or her own self-interest and that of the organization and its objectives. But what about the interests and needs of the leader's followers? Unlike other theories of leadership, the focus of servant leadership is a concern for the needs of followers and their well-being.

Servant leadership is a form of leadership that involves going beyond one's own self-interests and having a genuine concern to serve others and a motivation to lead. Servant leadership emphasizes the needs of followers and their growth and development. The phrase "servant leadership" was first coined by Robert Greenleaf who described a servant leader as somebody who wants to serve first and lead second rather than somebody who wants to lead first. Thus, servant leaders have a need to serve combined with a motivation to lead.[76]

But what exactly distinguishes a servant leader from other leaders? A recent review and synthesis of the research on servant leadership identified the following six key characteristics of servant leader behaviour:[77]

> **Servant leadership.** A form of leadership that involves going beyond one's own self-interests and having a genuine concern to serve others and a motivation to lead.

- *Empowering and developing people.* Providing others with a sense of personal power and encouraging their personal development. A belief in the intrinsic value of each individual and the realization of each person's abilities and what the person can still learn.

- *Humility.* Actively seeking the contributions of others and placing their interests first. Facilitating the performance of others and providing them with support.

- *Authenticity.* Similar to authentic leadership, this involves expressing one's true self in ways that are consistent with one's inner feelings and thoughts, and accurately representing internal states, intentions, and commitments.

- *Interpersonal acceptance.* The ability to understand and experience the feelings of others and to create an atmosphere of trust in which others will feel accepted.

- *Providing direction.* Ensuring that people know what is expected of them and considering followers' abilities, needs, and input when providing direction.

- *Stewardship.* Focusing on service rather than control and self-interest, and encouraging others to act in the common interest.

Servant leadership is believed to encourage followers to become the very best they can be and to lead to self-actualization, positive job attitudes, performance, and an organizational focus on sustainability and corporate social responsibility. Although only a handful of studies have investigated servant leadership, the research to date indicates that servant leadership is positively related to trust in management, perceptions of organizational justice, need satisfaction, job satisfaction, organizational commitment, and creative behaviours.[78] Servant leadership has also been found to be related to organizational citizenship behaviours because it increases employees' self-efficacy, commitment to the supervisor, and perceptions of procedural justice. A study of departments in a chain of grocery stores found that employees in departments that had servant leaders had higher perceptions of being treated fairly and were more likely to exhibit helping behaviours.[79]

CULTURE AND LEADERSHIP

LO 9.10

Discuss the GLOBE project and explain the role that culture plays in leadership effectiveness.

If you consider the cultural differences in values described in Chapter 4, you might be wondering if the leadership styles we have been discussing in this chapter are equally effective across cultures. This is a question that researchers have been asking for decades. Fortunately, we have learned a great deal about this over the last 25 years, thanks to the most extensive and ambitious study ever undertaken on global leadership.

The Global Leadership and Organizational Behaviour Effectiveness (GLOBE) research project involved 170 researchers who worked together for 10 years collecting and analyzing data on cultural values and practices and leadership attributes from over 17 000 managers in 62 societal cultures. The results provide a rich and detailed account of cultural attributes and global leadership dimensions around the world.[80]

The project team first identified nine cultural dimensions that distinguish one society from another and have important managerial implications. Some of these dimensions are similar to Hofstede's, which were described in Chapter 4, but many of them were developed by GLOBE. Exhibit 9.6 lists and defines the nine cultural dimensions. Using these nine dimensions, GLOBE identified 10 culture clusters from the 62 culture samples. The culture clusters differ with respect to how they score on the nine culture dimensions.

GLOBE wanted to know whether the same attributes that lead to successful leadership in one country lead to success in other countries. What they found was that citizens in each nation have implicit assumptions regarding requisite leadership qualities, something known as implicit leadership theory. According to **implicit leadership theory**, individuals hold a set of beliefs about the kinds of attributes, personality characteristics,

Implicit leadership theory. A theory that states that individuals hold a set of beliefs about the kinds of attributes, personality characteristics, skills, and behaviours that contribute to or impede outstanding leadership.

EXHIBIT 9.6
Cultural dimensions from the GLOBE project
Source: Javidan, M., Dorfman, P.W., de Luque, M.S., & House, R.J. In the eye of the beholder: Cross-cultural lessons in leadership from Project GLOBE. *Academy of Management Perspectives, 20,* Table 4, p. 75.

The GLOBE project conceptualized and developed measures of nine cultural dimensions. These are aspects of a country's culture that distinguish one society from another and have important managerial implications. The nine cultural dimensions are as follows:

Performance Orientation: The degree to which a collective encourages and rewards (and should encourage and reward) its members for improvement and excellence in their performance.

Assertiveness: The degree to which individuals are (and should be) assertive, confrontational, and aggressive in their interactions with others.

Future Orientation: The extent to which individuals prepare (and should prepare) for the future, for example, by delaying gratification, planning ahead, and investing in the future.

Humane Orientation: The degree to which a collective encourages and rewards (and should encourage and reward) individuals for their fairness, altruism, generosity, caring, and kindness to others.

Institutional Collectivism: The degree to which the institutional practices of organizations and society encourage and reward (and should encourage and reward) collective distribution of resources and collective action.

In-Group Collectivism: The degree to which individuals express (and should express) pride, loyalty, and cohesiveness in their families or organizations.

Gender Egalitarianism: The degree to which a collective minimizes (and should minimize) gender inequality.

Power Distance: The degree to which members of a collective expect (and should expect) power to be distributed evenly.

Uncertainty Avoidance: The extent to which a society, organization, or group relies (and should rely) on social norms, rules, and procedures to lessen the unpredictability of future events.

skills, and behaviours that contribute to or impede outstanding leadership. These belief systems are assumed to affect the extent to which an individual accepts and responds to others as leaders. GLOBE found that these belief systems are shared among individuals in common cultures, something they call *culturally endorsed implicit leadership theory (CLT)*. Further, they identified 21 primary and 6 global leadership dimensions that are contributors to or inhibitors of outstanding leadership. The six global leadership dimensions are as follows:[81]

- *Charismatic/Value-Based.* A broadly defined leadership dimension that reflects the ability to inspire, to motivate, and to expect high performance outcomes from others on the basis of firmly held core beliefs.

- *Team-Oriented.* Emphasizes effective team building and implementation of a common purpose or goal among team members.

- *Participative.* The degree to which managers involve others in making and implementing decisions.

- *Humane-Oriented.* Reflects supportive and considerate leadership, but also includes compassion and generosity.

- *Autonomous.* Refers to independent and individualistic leadership.

- *Self-Protective.* Focuses on ensuring the safety and security of the individual.

GLOBE then created leadership profiles for each national culture and cluster of cultures based on their scores on the six global leadership dimensions. They compared the ten culture clusters on the leadership profiles and found that cultures and clusters differ significantly on all six of the global leadership dimensions. For example, compared to other culture clusters, Canada and the United States score high on the charismatic/value-based, participative, and humane-oriented dimensions, low on the self-protective dimension, and medium on the team-oriented and the autonomous dimensions.

Finally, to determine what is considered important for leadership effectiveness across cultures, GLOBE examined a large number of leader attributes. They found that while the cultures do differ on many aspects of leadership effectiveness, they also have many similarities. In fact, they found many attributes, such as being honest, decisive, motivational, and dynamic, to be universally desirable; these are believed to facilitate outstanding leadership in all GLOBE countries. They also found leadership attributes such as being loners, irritable, egocentric, and ruthless to be deemed ineffective in all GLOBE countries. And as you might expect, they also found that some attributes are *culturally contingent*. In other words, some attributes are effective in some cultures but are either ineffective or even dysfunctional in others. Exhibit 9.7 provides some examples of universally desirable, universally undesirable, and culturally contingent leadership attributes.[82]

The results of the GLOBE project are important because they show that while there are similarities across cultures in terms of what are considered to be desirable and undesirable leadership attributes, there are also important differences. This means that managers need to understand the similarities and differences in what makes someone an effective leader across cultures if they are to be effective global leaders.

LO 9.11

Describe gender differences in leadership and explain why women are underrepresented in leadership roles in organizations.

GENDER AND LEADERSHIP

Do men and women adopt different leadership styles? A number of popular books have argued that women leaders tend to be more intuitive, less hierarchically oriented, and more collaborative than their male counterparts. Is this true? Notice that two opposing logics could be at work here. On the one hand, different socialization experiences could lead men and women

The following is a partial list of leadership attributes that are universal facilitators, universal inhibitors, or culturally contingent.

Universal Facilitators of Leadership Effectiveness

- Demonstrating trustworthiness, a sense of justice, and honesty
- Having foresight and planning ahead
- Encouraging, motivating, and building confidence; being positive and dynamic
- Being communicative, informed, a coordinator, and team integrator (team builder)

Universal Impediments to Leadership Effectiveness

- Being a loner and asocial
- Being irritable and uncooperative
- Imposing your views on others

Culturally Contingent Endorsement of Leader Attributes

- Being individualistic
- Being constantly conscious of status
- Taking risks

EXHIBIT 9.7 Cultural views of leadership effectiveness from the GLOBE project.
Source: Javidan, M., Dorfman, P.W., de Luque, M.S., & House, R.J. In the eye of the beholder: Cross-cultural lessons in leadership from Project GLOBE. *Academy of Management Perspectives, 20,* 69–70.

to learn different ways of exerting influence on others. On the other hand, men and women should be equally capable of gravitating toward the style that is most appropriate in a given setting. This would result in no general difference in style.

However, a number of reviews have found that there are some differences in leadership style between men and women in organizational settings. For example, researchers Alice Eagly and Blair Johnson concluded that women have a tendency to be more participative or democratic than men, and as a result, they are changing the business world.[83] How is this so? One theory holds that women have better social skills, which enable them to successfully manage the give-and-take that participation requires. Another theory holds that women avoid more autocratic styles because they violate gender stereotypes and lead to negative reactions. This might explain why a study on gender and leadership found that women are perceived by themselves and their co-workers as performing significantly better as managers than do men.[84]

In a review of the leadership styles of men and women based on 45 studies, women leaders were found to be more transformational than men leaders, and they also engaged in more of the contingent reward behaviours associated with transactional leadership. Men leaders engaged in more of the other components of transactional leadership, such as management by exception and **laissez-faire leadership**, which is a passive form of leadership that involves the avoidance or absence of leadership and is negatively related to leader effectiveness.[85]

What is most interesting about these findings is that those aspects of leadership style in which women exceed men are all positively related to leadership effectiveness, while those leadership aspects in which men exceed women have weak, negative, or null relations to leadership effectiveness. The authors concluded that these findings attest to the ability of women to be highly effective leaders in contemporary organizations.[86]

While the evidence clearly indicates that women can be highly effective leaders, the reality is that women hold very few top leadership positions in Canadian organizations. Bonnie

Laissez-faire leadership. A style of leadership that involves the avoidance or absence of leadership.

Brooks of Hudson's Bay Company is an exception, as is Elyse Allan, President and CEO of General Electric Canada. She has been recognized as one of the 25 Most Powerful People in Canada and one of Canada's Top Women of Influence.[87]

The most recent census of women corporate officers and top earners of the FP500 indicates that women hold only 16.9 percent of corporate officer roles. This is particularly low when you consider that women make up 47 percent of the total workforce and 37.2 percent of management positions. Further, only 37 women occupy top executive offices (vice-presidents, chief operating officers, chief financial officers) of Canada's 100 largest publicly traded companies and only 2 percent of CEOs at Canada's 1000 largest public companies are women. According to Statistics Canada, the proportion of women in senior management positions has not changed in the past two decades. Since 1987, men have been two to three times more likely to hold a senior management position and one-and-a-half times more likely to hold a middle management position. Women also hold a minority of senior leadership positions in the United States and Europe.[88] How can we explain this obvious gender bias in leadership?

Glass ceiling. An invisible barrier that prevents women from advancing to senior leadership positions in organizations.

For decades the explanation has been the **glass ceiling** metaphor—the invisible barrier that prevents women from advancing to senior leadership positions in organizations. However, Alice Eagly and Linda Carli have suggested that a more accurate metaphor is a *labyrinth*, because of the many twists, turns, detours, and dead ends that women encounter along their way up the organizational hierarchy. In other words, the lack of women leaders is the sum of all of the barriers women face rather than one particular barrier (i.e., the glass ceiling) at the top of the organization.[89]

So what are the barriers that women encounter in organizations? According to Eagly and Carli, they include[90]

- *Vestiges of prejudice.* Men continue to receive higher wages and faster promotions than women with equal qualifications at all organizational levels.
- *Resistance to women's leadership.* As indicated in Chapter 3, the stereotypes of leaders are very much masculine. Leaders are perceived as similar to men and not very

Elyse Allan is President and CEO of General Electric Canada and one of the few women to hold a senior leadership position in Canada.

Agentic Traits

Dedicated: Logs long hours to meet deadlines.
Charismatic: Motivates employees when speaking.
Intelligent: Displays talent and ability in all aspects of the job.
Determined: Does not give up easily when issues arise.
Aggressive: Fights to get necessary resources for one's team.

Communal Traits

Caring: Shows concern for the well being of one's team.
Sensitive: Sympathetic and responsive to the feelings of employees.
Honest: Does not take credit for employees' good ideas.
Understanding: Listens when subordinates are having a personal conflict.
Compassionate: Extends deadlines when employees have family commitments.

EXHIBIT 9.8 Agentic and communal leadership traits
Source: Reprinted from *Organizational Behavior and Human Decision Processes 101*, Scott, K. A., & Brown, D. J. (2006). Female first, leader second? Gender bias in the encoding of leadership behavior, 230–242. Copyright © 2006 Elsevier Inc. All Rights Reserved. Reprinted with permission from Elsevier.

Explore

Go to MyManagementLab to see an annotated version of this figure.

similar to women, as more "agentic" than communal, and as more masculine than feminine.[91] Men are perceived as having *agentic* traits, which convey assertion and control and are generally associated with effective leadership. Women are perceived as having *communal* traits, which convey a concern for the compassionate treatment of others. Agentic leadership traits tend to be associated with male leaders to a greater extent than with female leaders. In other words, males are perceived as having traits that are associated with leadership. Exhibit 9.8 shows some common agentic and communal leadership traits.

- *Issues of leadership style.* Women leaders often struggle to find an appropriate leadership style that reconciles the communal traits associated with females and the agentic traits associated with leaders. This results in a double bind. When women exhibit an agentic style they are criticized for lacking communal traits, and when they exhibit a communal style they are criticized for not being agentic enough to be a leader. However, as shown in Exhibit 9.9, many of the qualities of successful women executives are in fact agentic.

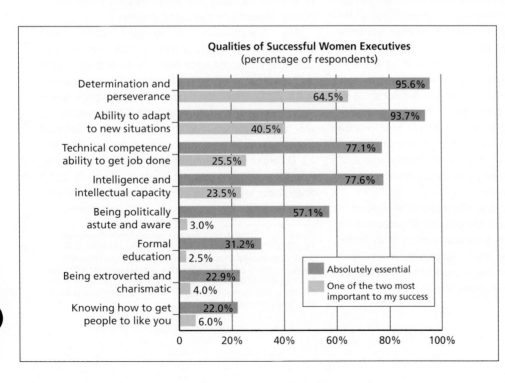

Qualities of Successful Women Executives
(percentage of respondents)

Quality	Absolutely essential	One of the two most important to my success
Determination and perseverance	95.6%	64.5%
Ability to adapt to new situations	93.7%	40.5%
Technical competence/ability to get job done	77.1%	25.5%
Intelligence and intellectual capacity	77.6%	23.5%
Being politically astute and aware	57.1%	3.0%
Formal education	31.2%	2.5%
Being extroverted and charismatic	22.9%	4.0%
Knowing how to get people to like you	22.0%	6.0%

EXHIBIT 9.9 Qualities of successful women executives.
Source: Women in Management, Richard Ivey School of Business, The University of Western Ontario.

Explore

Go to MyManagementLab to see an annotated version of this figure.

- *Demands of family life.* Women remain more responsible for domestic work and child rearing, and as a result they have fewer years of work experience and fewer hours of employment. This slows their career progress and results in lower pay.
- *Underinvestment in social capital.* Women have less time for socializing with colleagues and developing social networks and often have difficulty breaking in to social networks because these are predominantly male. As a result, women have less social capital.

Given the many obstacles that women face, what can organizations do to increase the number of women in senior leadership positions? As shown in Exhibit 9.10, a combination of programs and interventions is required such as reducing the subjectivity of performance evaluation, changing the norm of long work hours, and establishing family-friendly human resources practices. To find out how one organization has increased the number of women in senior leadership positions, see the Applied Focus: *The Advancement of Women Initiative at Scotiabank.*

APPLIED FOCUS

THE ADVANCEMENT OF WOMEN INITIATIVE AT SCOTIABANK

In 1993, Scotiabank established a task force on the advancement of women in an effort to recruit, develop, and advance more women into senior leadership positions. However, the program did not set targets for fear of a negative backlash within the bank, and there were no measures of progress. As a result, 10 years later women still held less than 20 percent of senior management positions.

In 2003, the bank re-launched the Advancement of Women (AoW) Initiative with some important changes. For example, ScotiaWomen's Connection provides an online resources guide with information and tools to support networking and mentoring. Quarterly networking sessions are held for women at all levels of the organization that feature speakers, professional development, and career information sessions.

In addition, the bank now measures women's progress toward targets in senior-level positions on an ongoing basis. Managers and all executive vice-presidents are accountable for the advancement of women. It is part of their performance review, which, in turn, is tied to compensation.

Today, women comprise 70 percent of Scotiabank's total Canadian workforce and just over 50 percent of its management staff. The number of women at all senior levels in the bank has nearly doubled between 2003 and 2006. Scotiabank has increased the percentage of women at the senior management level from 18.9

percent in 2003 to 31.0 percent in 2006. In the most senior roles, the percentage of women has increased from 26.7 percent in 2003 to 36.8 percent in 2006.

In 2007, three of Scotiabank's female vice-presidents were on the 100 most powerful Canadian women list, and three other of its leaders were listed on the 100 most powerful Canadian women alumnae. In the same year, Scotiabank received the prestigious Catalyst Award in recognition of its Advancement of Women Initiative and its innovative programs to recruit, develop, and advance women.

The Advancement of Women Initiative was expanded in 2007 and can now be found in many countries where the bank operates. It is considered to be a model of how to develop and promote female leaders.

In 2010, Sylvia Chrominska, Scotiabank's Group Head, Global Human Resources & Communications, was named an inaugural recipient of the Catalyst Canada Honours in the category of Human Resources/Diversity Leader for her contribution in advancing women within and beyond the workplace. In 2012 Scotiabank was ranked as one of the best employers in Canada and one of Canada's best workplaces.

Sources: Klie, S. (2009, April 6). Women make small gains. *Canadian HR Reporter, 22*(7), 2, 3; Galt, V. (2007, April 5). How to hammer the glass ceiling. *Globe and Mail,* B1; Diversity Is strength: Advancement of women. www.scotiabank.com; Scotiabank—Unlocking potential, delivering results: The Advancement of Women (AoW) Initiative. 2007 Catalyst Award Winner; www.catalyst.org; Breaking the barriers (Women in banking: A case study of Scotiabank. www.scotiabank.com.

According to Alice Eagly and Linda Carli, legislation that requires organizations to eliminate inequitable practices is not effective for the advancement of women when inequality in an organization is embedded in the organization's culture and structure. If organizations want to remove the barriers that prevent women from advancing to leadership roles, they should do the following:

- Increase people's awareness of the psychological drivers of prejudice toward female leaders, and work to dispel those perceptions.
- Change the long-hours norm.
- Reduce the subjectivity of performance evaluation.
- Use open-recruitment tools, such as advertising and employment agencies, rather than relying on informal social networks and referrals to fill positions.
- Ensure a critical mass of women in executive positions—not just one or two women—to head off the problems that come with tokenism.
- Avoid having a sole female member of any team.
- Help shore up social capital.
- Prepare women for line management with appropriately demanding assignments.
- Establish family-friendly human resources practices.
- Allow employees who have significant parental responsibility more time to prove themselves worthy of promotion.
- Welcome women back.
- Encourage male participation in family-friendly benefits.

EXHIBIT 9.10 The advancement of women in organizations
Source: A.H. Eagly and L.L. Carli. (2007). Exhibit from "Women and the Labyrinth of Leadership," 101. Reprinted by permission of the *Harvard Business Review*. Copyright © 2007 by the Harvard Business School Publishing Corporation; all rights reserved.

 Explore

Go to MyManagementLab to see an annotated version of this figure.

THE MANAGER'S NOTEBOOK

Leadership Development at Business Development Bank of Canada (BDC)

BDC has been recognized for its leadership practices. In 2007, it was the first and only Canadian organization listed on Fortune's list of Top Companies for Leaders. BDC has also been recognized for its excellence in leadership development. In 2011 it received the Gold prize of the Canadian Awards for Training Excellence in recognition of its leadership development program. BDC has also been selected as one of Canada's Top 100 Employers every year from 2007 to 2012.

1. The leadership transition program includes classroom learning, job shadowing, and coaching. High potentials are also given projects that stretch their experiences. Participants attend an Executive Assessment Centre, where they participate in a simulation in which they role-play a manager. The simulation involves juggling a variety of tasks, making vital business decisions, and staying in character while role-playing a day in the life of a specifically titled executive.

Performances are recorded on video and reviewed. BDC is one of an increasing number of organizations using the assessment centre to identify potential leaders and prepare them to move up the corporate ladder. According to BDC's senior director of learning strategies, "Basically, we're preparing people who would be put into first level of managerial roles within 18 to 24 months."

2. The program has improved the transition to leadership and increased the number of newly promoted managers that meet expectations. High-potential employees are now better prepared for leadership roles, and their transition is smoother and more successful. Further, those who realize that management is not for them drop out of the program before moving into a leadership role. Thus, employees who have the potential to become leaders need to be developed to become effective leaders.

MyManagementLab   Visit MyManagementLab at **www.mymanagementlab** **.com** for access to online tutorials, interactive exercises, videos, and much more.

LEARNING OBJECTIVES CHECKLIST

9.1 *Leadership* occurs when an individual exerts influence on others' goal achievement in an organizational context. Individuals with titles such as manager, executive, supervisor, and department head occupy formal or assigned leadership roles. As part of these roles, they are expected to influence others, and they are given specific authority to direct employees. Individuals may also emerge to occupy informal leadership roles. Since informal leaders do not have formal authority, they must rely on being well liked or being perceived as highly skilled to exert influence.

9.2 The *trait theory of leadership* was concerned with identifying physical, psychological, and intellectual *traits* that might predict leader effectiveness. While some traits appear to be related to leadership capacity, there are no traits that guarantee leadership across various situations. However, of the Big Five dimensions of personality, extraversion and conscientiousness have been found to be the most consistent predictors of leadership effectiveness.

9.3 Studies of the behaviour of leaders have concentrated on *initiating structure* and *consideration* as well as *leader reward* and *punishment behaviours*. Both consideration and initiating structure contribute positively to employees' motivation, job satisfaction, and leader effectiveness. Consideration tends to be more strongly related to follower satisfaction, motivation, and leader effectiveness, while initiating structure is slightly more strongly related to leader job performance and group performance. Leader contingent reward and punishment behaviour is positively related to employees' perceptions, attitudes, and behaviour.

9.4 *Fiedler's contingency theory* is a situational theory of leadership that suggests that different leadership orientations are necessary depending on the favourableness of the situation for the leader. Favourableness depends on the structure of the task, the position power of the leader, and the relationship between the leader and the group. Fiedler argues that *task-oriented* leaders perform best in situations that are either very favourable or very unfavourable. *Relationship-oriented* leaders are said to perform best in situations of medium favourability. *Cognitive resource theory* (CRT) is a refinement of contingency theory that focuses on the conditions in which a leader's cognitive resources contribute to effective leadership. *House's path–goal theory* is a situational theory of leadership that suggests that leaders will be most effective when they are able to clarify the paths to various subordinate goals that are also of interest to the organization. According to House, the effectiveness of directive, supportive, participative, and achievement-oriented behaviour depends on the nature of the subordinates and the characteristics of the work environment.

9.5 *Participative leadership* involves employees in making work-related decisions. Participation can increase employee motivation and lead to higher quality and more acceptable decisions. The *Vroom and Jago model* specifies how much participation is best for various kinds of decisions. Participation works best when employees are desirous of participation, when they are intelligent and knowledgeable, and when the task is reasonably complex.

9.6 *Leader–member exchange (LMX) theory* is concerned with the quality of the relationship that develops between a leader and an employee. High-quality relationships, or high LMX, involve a high degree of mutual influence and obligation as well as trust, loyalty, and respect between a leader and an employee. Higher quality LMX relationships result in positive outcomes for leaders, employees, work units, and organizations.

9.7 *Transactional leadership* is leadership that is based on a straightforward exchange relationship between the leader and followers and involves *contingent reward behaviour* and *management by exception*. *Transformational leadership* refers to leaders that provide followers with a new vision that instills true commitment. They provide intellectual stimulation, individualized consideration, and inspirational motivation. They also have *charisma*, the ability to command extraordinary loyalty, dedication, and effort from followers.

9.8 *Global leadership* involves having a set of leadership capabilities required to function effectively in different cultures and the ability to cross language, social, economic, and political borders. Global leaders are characterized by their inquisitiveness, personal character, global business and organizational savvy, and their ability to manage the dualities of global integration and local demands.

9.9 *Empowering leadership* involves implementing conditions that enable the sharing of power with employees. *Ethical leadership* involves the demonstration of normatively appropriate conduct through personal actions and interpersonal relationships and the promotion of such conduct to followers through two-way communication, reinforcement, and decision making. *Authentic leadership* is a positive form of leadership that involves being true to oneself. Authentic leaders know and act upon their true values, beliefs, and strengths and they help others do the same. *Servant leadership* is a form of leadership that involves going beyond one's own self-interests and having a genuine concern to serve others.

9.10 The GLOBE project found that there are many leadership attributes that are universally desirable or universally undesirable in all cultures, as well as some attributes that are culturally contingent, that is, they will be effective in some cultures but ineffective or dysfunctional in others.

9.11 There are some differences in leadership style between men and women in organizational settings. Female leaders tend to be more transformational than male leaders, and they also engage in more contingent reward behaviours. Male leaders engage in more management by exception and laissez-faire leadership. Women remain underrepresented in senior leadership positions as a result of many barriers and obstacles that have been described as a labyrinth of leadership.

DISCUSSION QUESTIONS

1. Are leaders born or made? Consider each perspective (leaders born versus made) and the implications of each for organizations. What does each perspective suggest that organizations should do to ensure that they have effective leaders? Based on the information in this chapter, do you think that leaders can be developed?

2. Contrast the relative merits of consideration and initiating structure as well as leader reward and punishment behaviour in the following leadership situations: running the daily operations of a bank branch; commanding an army unit under enemy fire; and supervising a group of college students who are performing a hot, dirty, boring summer job. Use House's path–goal theory to support your arguments.

3. What is the main premise behind cognitive resource theory (CRT) and how does it extend Fiedler's contingency theory? What does CRT say about research on leadership traits? What does it tell us about the role of traits for leadership effectiveness?

4. Describe a situation that would be ideal for having employees participate in a work-related decision. Discuss the employees, the problem, and the setting. Describe a situation in which participative decision making would be an especially unwise leadership strategy. Why is this so?

5. What are transformational leaders skilled at doing that gives them extraordinary influence over others? Why do you think women are more likely to be transformational leaders than men? Describe a leadership situation in which a transformational leader would probably not be the right person for the job.

6. What are the main findings from the GLOBE project and what are the implications for leadership across cultures? If a leader from Canada

takes on an assignment in another culture, will he or she be successful? What is most likely to improve the chances of success?

7. Identify a leader who you think is a global leader and describe the characteristics and behaviours that make that person a global leader. What advice would you give an organization that needs more global leaders?

8. Leadership traits are considered to be important for leadership because they can lead to certain actions that are required for effective leadership. Review each of the traits in Exhibit 9.1 and discuss how they might be related to different leadership styles and behaviours (e.g., consideration, initiating structure, directive, supportive, participative, achievement oriented, transformational, LMX, global, empowering, ethical, authentic, and servant). What traits do you think are most important for each leadership style? What traits are most important for being an effective leader?

9. What does it mean to be an ethical leader, and how can ethical or unethical leadership affect an organization? What about an authentic leader? A servant leader?

10. Describe leadership categorization theory and how it explains racial and gender bias in leadership. What can organizations do to remove the barriers that restrict the movement of non-whites and women into leadership positions?

11. If your task was to design a leadership development program, what would you include and what would you emphasize? What would be the focus of your leadership development program? Explain and justify your answer.

12. Discuss the four new and emerging theories of leadership (empowering, ethical, authentic, and servant). How is each type of leadership different from traditional theories of leadership? Do you think these theories extend our knowledge and understanding of effective leadership? Explain your answer.

INTEGRATIVE DISCUSSION QUESTIONS

1. Consider the relationship between leadership and organizational culture. Using the approaches to leadership discussed in this chapter (e.g., leadership traits, behaviours, situational theories, participative leadership, LMX theory, transformational leadership, and empowering, ethical, authentic, and servant leadership), describe how a leader can influence the culture of an organization. Based on your analysis, do you think that leaders have a strong influence on an organization's culture?

2. What effect does leadership have on employee motivation? Using each of the theories of motivation described in Chapter 5, discuss the implications for leadership. In other words, according to each theory, what should a leader do to motivate employees?

3. Refer to the material in Chapter 3 on perceptions and gender stereotypes and compare and contrast it with the material presented in this chapter on women and leadership. What does the material in Chapter 3 tell us about women and leadership? Why do you think women are more likely to be transformational leaders than men? Can women be more effective leaders than men? What have you learned about perceptions, stereotypes, and reality when it comes to women and leadership?

4. Refer to the material in Chapter 2 on learning and discuss the implications of learning theories for ethical leadership. In other words, what should ethical leaders do to create an ethical workplace? Similarly, refer to the material in Chapter 8 on culture and explain what a leader might do to create an ethical organizational culture.

ON-THE-JOB CHALLENGE QUESTION

The RCMP's New Boss

In November of 2011, Bob Paulson was appointed as the new Commissioner of the Royal Canadian Mounted Police (RCMP), becoming the 23rd Commissioner.

However, Paulson's appointment came at a critical time for the RCMP amid a string of scandals including numerous allegations of sexual harassment. Several former members of the RCMP stated that they endured years of sexual harassment from senior officers. According to a staff relations representative, morale within the force has withered to an "all-time low."

During a press conference at the House of Commons, Paulson promised to reform the RCMP, stating, "First on my plate will be addressing the issue of harassment and sexual harassment" and "I will sort this out in a way that Canadians can have faith and trust in the RCMP." He said that "accountability and leadership" will be at the top of his long list of priorities.

Canadians have been questioning the RCMP's ability to safeguard the public as complaints of botched investigations, excessive use of force, and institutional dysfunction have become routine.

The Minister of Public Safety, Vic Toews, stated, "The RCMP has been pursuing an ambitious course of change over recent years, and navigating that change has been the challenge of successive commissioners over the years, and it will be no different for the new commissioner…he recognizes that change is necessary."

Paulson replaces former Commissioner William Elliott, who stepped down after being accused by some senior members of the management team for having an abrasive leadership style.

Refer to the theories and approaches to leadership discussed in the chapter and describe the kind of leader that Bob Paulson should be and the type of leadership that is required to change the RCMP. What do the theories of leadership suggest he needs to do to be an effective leader? What advice would you give him? What leadership style and behaviours do you recommend and why?

Sources: Freeze, C., LeBlanc, D., & Sher, J. (2011, November 16). New RCMP Commissioner sets out to rebuild trust. *The Globe and Mail*; Kennedy, M., & Quan, D. (2011, November 16). Bob Paulson to be named new RCMP commissioner. *National Post*; Kennedy, M. (2011, November 16). New RCMP boss named as sexual harassment claims are referred to police watchdog. *National Post*.

EXPERIENTIAL EXERCISE

Ethical Leadership Scale (ELS)

How ethical is your leader? To find out, answer the 10 questions below as frankly and honestly as possible about your current supervisor if you are employed or the most recent supervisor you had in your last job. Use the following response scale:

1–Strongly disagree

2–Disagree

3–Neither agree or disagree

4–Agree

5–Strongly agree

My supervisor…

____ 1. Listens to what employees have to say.

____ 2. Disciplines employees who violate ethical standards.

____ 3. Conducts his/her personal life in an ethical manner.

____ 4. Has the best interests of employees in mind.

____ 5. Makes fair and balanced decisions.

____ 6. Can be trusted.

____ 7. Discusses business ethics or values with employees.

____ 8. Sets an example of how to do things the right way in terms of ethics.

____ 9. Defines success not just by results but also by the way that they are obtained.

____ 10. When making decisions, asks, "What is the right thing to do?"

Scoring and Interpretation

You have just completed the Ethical Leadership Scale (ELS) developed by Michael E. Brown, Linda K. Trevino, and David A. Harrison. To obtain your score, add up your responses to the 10 questions and divide by 10. Your total should be somewhere between 1 and 5. Higher scores indicate a more ethical leader. The average score of 87 MBA students in a large public university in the United States was 3.37. In a sample of 123 undergraduate seniors in business, the average ELS score was 3.46.

Source: Brown, M.E., Trevino, L.K. & Harrison, D.A. (2005). Ethical leadership: A social learning perspective for construct development and testing *Organizational Behavior and Human Decision Processes 97*, 117–134. Copyright © 2005 Elsevier Inc. All Rights Reserved. Reprinted with permission from Elsevier.

To facilitate class discussion and your understanding of ethical leadership, form a small group with several members of the class and consider the following questions:

1. Each group member should present their ELS score. What is the range of scores (highest and lowest) and the average score in your group? Overall, how ethical are group members' supervisors?

2. Each group member should provide examples of what makes their supervisor an ethical or unethical leader. Be specific in describing supervisor behaviours that are ethical or unethical. Based on group members' answers, what are some of the main differences between ethical and unethical leaders?

3. Each group member should consider the impact that their supervisor has had on them, their co-workers, and the organization. Be specific in describing the effects that their ethical or unethical behaviour has had on people's attitudes and behaviours as well as on the organization (e.g., reputation, sales, or productivity).

4. What does your supervisor need to do differently to be a more ethical leader?

5. If you are now or have been in a leadership position in the past, how ethical have you been? Take the ELS again but this time thinking about yourself in a current or previous leadership role. How ethical are you (or were you)? What do you have to do to become a more ethical leader?

EXPERIENTIAL EXERCISE

Leadership Empowerment Behaviour

Have you ever had a leader who was empowering? To find out, answer the 12 questions below as frankly and honestly as possible about your current supervisor if you are employed or the most recent supervisor you had in your last job. Use the following response scale:

1–Strongly disagree

2–Disagree

3–Neither agree or disagree

4–Agree

5–Strongly agree

My supervisor…

____ 1. helps me understand how my objectives and goals relate to those of the company.

____ 2. helps me understand the importance of my work to the overall effectiveness of the company.

____ 3. helps me understand how my job fits into the bigger picture.

____ 4. makes many decisions together with me.

____ 5. often consults me on strategic decisions.

____ 6. solicits my opinion on decisions that may affect me.

____ 7. believes that I can handle demanding tasks.

____ 8. believes in my ability to improve even when I make mistakes.

____ 9. expresses confidence in my ability to perform at a high level.

____ 10. allows me to do my job my way.

____ 11. makes it more efficient for me to do my job by keeping the rules and regulations simple.

____ 12. allows me to make important decisions quickly to satisfy customer needs.

Scoring and Interpretation

You have just completed the Leadership Empowerment Behaviour (LEB) scale developed by Michael Ahearne, John Mathieu, and Adam Rapp. The scale measures four dimensions of empowering leadership: 1. Enhancing the meaningfulness of work (questions 1, 2, and 3); 2. Fostering participation in decision making (questions 4, 5, and 6); 3. Expressing confidence in high performance (questions 7, 8, and 9); and 4. Providing autonomy from bureaucratic constraints (questions 10, 11, and 12). To obtain your overall score, add up your responses to the 12 questions and divide by 12. Your total should be somewhere between 1 and 5. Higher scores indicate a more empowering leader. The average score of 367 professional-level employees in a major information technology (IT) company in China was 3.67. You can also determine the score on each dimension by adding the three items for each dimension and then dividing by 3.

Sources: Zhang, X., & Bartol, K. (2010). Linking empowering leadership and employee creativity: The influence of psychological empowerment, intrinsic motivation, and creative process engagement. *Academy of Management Journal, 53,* 107–128; Ahearne, M.,

Mathieu, J., & Rapp, A. (2005). To empower or not to empower your sales force? An empirical examination of the influence of leadership empowerment behavior on customer satisfaction and performance. *Journal of Applied Psychology, 90*, 945–955.

To facilitate class discussion and your understanding of empowering leadership, form a small group with several members of the class and consider the following questions:

1. Each group member should present their LEB score. What is the range of scores (highest and lowest) and the average score in your group? Overall, how empowering are group members' supervisors?

2. Each group member should provide examples of what makes their supervisor an empowering leader. Be specific in describing how your supervisor scored on each of the four dimensions. Based on group members' answers, what are some of the main reasons why a supervisor is or is not empowering?

3. Each group member should consider the impact that their supervisor has had on them, their co-workers, and the organization. Be specific in describing the effects that an empowering leader has had on people's attitudes, behaviours, and creativity.

4. What does your supervisor need to do differently to be a more empowering leader?

5. Do you think that all leaders should be empowering leaders? Explain your answer. If you had a choice, would you want to have an empowering leader? Explain your answer.

EXPERIENTIAL EXERCISE

Leadership Jazz

The purpose of this exercise is to learn about the effect of leadership on individual and group creativity. It can also be used in conjunction with Chapter 16 (i.e., creativity). For this exercise, students will work in small groups (no more than five people). The instructor will assign a leader to each group and will also decide what kind of leader he or she will be. Each group will be required to create musical instruments using only the resources they have with them, which they will use to play a tune/song in front of the class. The class will evaluate each group's performance.

Procedure

Students should form small groups with no more than five people. The instructor will then assign a leader in each group and instruct that person on what kind of leader to be (e.g., transactional, transformational, considerate, task oriented, participative, empowering, servant, etc.). This will enable comparisons across groups. Alternatively, the instructor can let the leaders of each group choose their leadership style. Whatever the case, the leader should not reveal to the group his/her leadership style until after the exercise. The leader of each group is responsible for his or her group's performance in creating musical instruments and for their performance of a tune or song. Once the groups have been formed and the leaders assigned, the exercise should proceed as follows:

Step 1: Each group will have 10–15 minutes to create musical instruments using any materials they have with them. They must not leave the room or their workspace to search for materials. Groups should try to create as many musical instruments as they can, creating a variety of instruments that can be used in a band or orchestra. Thus, the goal is both quantitative (number of instruments) and qualitative (variety of instruments).

Step 2: Each group will have 10–15 minutes to decide on several tunes/songs to play and to rehearse them in preparation for their performance in front of the class. The group should decide on what tune to play for the class and focus on the quality of their performance. Each group should have a backup tune/song in case another group plays the same one they have chosen. This will help to ensure that each group plays a different tune/song. Keep in mind that the quality of the performance is important.

Step 3: Each group will perform a tune/song (two to three minutes maximum) in front of the class that no other group has performed (each group should be prepared to perform more than one song in case their first choice is played by another group).

Step 4: The class will rate the performance of each group using the following criteria:

- quantity of instruments used;
- variety of instruments used;
- recognizability of tune/song;
- uniqueness of tune/song; and
- quality of performance.

After all the groups have performed their tune/song, the class votes for the best group for each of the criteria listed above and for the overall best group.

Discussion

The discussion should focus on how the group members responded to the leader and the effect of the leader on the group's creativity and performance. To facilitate class discussion, consider the following questions:

1. How did group members respond to their leader and what effect did the leader have on individual group member's behaviour, creativity, and performance?

2. What effect did the leader have on the creativity and performance of each group? Group members should comment on what their leader did that was helpful and encouraged creativity and what their leader did that was not helpful and did not encourage creativity. What else could the leader have done to improve the group's creativity and performance? How important is leadership for individual and group creativity? What can leaders do to encourage creativity?

3. What style of leadership was most effective? At this point, the leaders can disclose their leadership style. What type of leader was associated with the group that received the highest score on the performance criteria? What type of leader was associated with the group that received the lowest score on the performance criteria? What type of leadership was most effective for overall group creativity and performance?

4. Consider the role of situational theories of leadership. Does the task of creating and playing musical instruments require a certain style of leadership? Did some members of each group respond better to their leader than others?

5. If you were to do this task over again, what type of leader would you prefer and why? What type of leader would be most effective? Discuss the theories of leadership to support your answers.

Source: Lengnick-Hall, M.L., & Lengnick-Hall, C.A. (1999). Leadership jazz: An exercise in creativity. *Journal of Management Education, 23,* 65–70. Copyright © 1999, OBTS Teaching Society for Management Educators. Reprinted by Permission of SAGE Publications.

CASE INCIDENT

Fran-Tech

A mid-level manager at Fran-Tech, a Seattle software company, received a CD-ROM set containing the source code for a competitor's software product. The competitor is the market leader in the software niche in which both companies compete; it is crushing Fran-Tech in the marketplace. An anonymous note accompanying the package stated that the package was sent by a disgruntled employee of the competitor and urged the recipient to use the data "as you see fit." The manager receiving the data was considered to be a "star" performer by her boss and her peers.

1. What do you think the manager is likely to do in this situation? What should she do and why?

2. Explain the relevance of ethical leadership in this situation. What will an ethical leader do and why? What will an unethical leader do?

3. Consider how the manager's response to this situation can impact the ethical behaviour of her employees in the organization. What are some of the potential implications of her actions for employees and the organization?

Source: Thomas, T., Schermerhorn, J.R., Jr., & Dienhart, J.W. (2004). Strategic leadership of ethical behavior in business. *Academy of Management Executive, 18,* 56–66.

CASE STUDY

Transforming ICRISAT: The Leadership of Dr. William Dar

As he walked in the Hyderabad, India campus of the International Crops Research Institute for the Semi-Arid Tropics (ICRISAT), Dr. William Dar, ICRISAT's recently appointed director general (DG), saw several things that bothered him. From overgrown shrubs to uninspired employees and a generally uncongenial work environment, a number of points required improvement at ICRISAT. As a result, the sprawling 3000-acre campus appeared to be desolate. Dar had observed this less-than-satisfactory state of affairs from an early point in his involvement with the institute and had politely conveyed his concerns to the chief of general services; however, even after a month, there was no visible improvement to the campus.

Sitting in his office, Dar asked himself whether he had made the right decision in leaving a secure and highly influential position in the Philippines and relocating to India. Prior to joining ICRISAT as the DG only two weeks ago, Dar had served as the presidential advisor for rural development and as the secretary of agriculture. Now he was considering giving up on his new assignment and returning to the Philippines where his previous job awaited him, rather than sticking with the riskier option of attempting to revive the ailing institute as DG. Unstable leadership over the past three years had resulted in stunted growth and had negatively impacted research at ICRISAT. Dar had tried to remain confident that he had everything to gain and nothing to lose by staying with the institute—but now he was not so sure that was true.

A Succession of Challenges

The past few years had been particularly difficult for ICRISAT. Leadership had failed at all levels, staff morale was low, and research output was abysmal. Employee turnover rates were unusually high—particularly at senior management levels—and the leadership at ICRISAT had been unable to decrease them. Prior to Dar's appointment, the institute had been through four director generals and four deputy director generals (DDGs) in quick succession. The contrasting personalities and divergent views of these leaders had added further uncertainty to the already volatile atmosphere at ICRISAT.

In addition to withstanding unstable leadership, the institute had also faced financial problems. Until the late 1990s, ICRISAT had had the luxury of virtually unlimited funding and unrestricted spending due to generous support from donors; however, by the time Dar joined the institute, the donors had started questioning ICRISAT's funding due to its poor performance and research output in recent years, initiating a marked reduction in financial resources. When Dar was appointed DG, he found that in the past five years the institute's funding had been reduced by 50 percent, which was making it difficult to sustain minimal research even at existing levels. The governing body, which consisted of independent members,[1] had recently decided to reduce funding further and had asked ICRISAT to achieve self-sustainability if it wanted to continue to exist as a research institute.

Compounding difficulties was the fact that ICRISAT was due for a major external review form the Consultative Group for International Agricultural Research (CGIAR) in the coming year. CGIAR was a global partnership and a nodal body coordinating the research being carried out by various organizations for sustainable development. Its vision was "to reduce poverty and hunger, improve human health and nutrition and enhance ecosystem resilience thought high-quality international agricultural research, partnership and leadership."[2] Since CGIAR had a controlling stake in the organization's existence, the institute had good cause to worry. Due to ICRISAT's unsatisfactory research output, CGIAR had already asked the ICRISAT management and governing board to assess the viability of the organization for the future (taking further financial reductions into account) and to propose a plan for its contribution to agricultural development. This was a direct indication of the loss of trust that ICRISAT faced from its donors and CGIAR, and the increasingly difficult circumstances that were expected in the future. In order to survive, the institute was going to have to perform admirably despite huge cuts in finances. All of these problems had significantly affected the atmosphere at ICRISAT and the grim state of affairs was reflected openly in the "strategic drift" the organization was currently experiencing.

The shifting of ICRISAT headquarters to Africa was another challenge threatening the future of the organization. An external review panel had recently indicated that there was a need to shift the institute's major centres of administration and research to Sub-Saharan Africa (SSA). CGIAR, which had carried out an external program review (EPR), reported that ICRISAT was losing its competitive advantage in Asia. It felt that the institute did not have a strong base in Africa where there was an urgent need for agricultural research and development, and that many activities that could prove significant for development in Africa needed to be phased out in Asia and moved to Africa. To this effect, the panel had strongly recommended the transfer of ICRISAT's headquarters and all of its programs to Africa—with the exception of the genetic resources management and enhancement program, which was the only branch of ICRISAT that would be retained at the Hyderabad campus.[3] From the time Dar became DG, there was tremendous pressure on him to facilitate the process of shifting ICRISAT's programs and headquarters from India to Africa.

Another major issue that plagued ICRISAT was that of low staff morale. Just prior to Dar's appointment as DG, many staff members had been coerced into accepting a kind of "golden handshake" scheme that provided certain employees with security in the event of loss of employment. Ironically, this actually suggested serious insecurity in the minds of many staff members, and a number of senior scientists and employees opted for voluntary retirement schemes and joined other more stable research organizations instead. Those who remained at ICRISAT were overburdened with work thrust upon them due to the exodus of employees. This added and unjustifiable workload further demoralized any staff that had stayed. The egress of talent and high turnover among staff resulted in inconsistencies in research and development, further reducing the institute's research output. In addition, after the financial cuts of the past few years, obtaining sufficient funding for new staff positions had become extremely challenging and serious concerns regarding ICRISAT's insufficient research output were being registered by monitoring agencies.

About the Institute: ICRISAT

The genesis of ICRISAT lay in the widespread awareness that developed in the 1960s and early 1970s about famine and hunger in certain underdeveloped countries of Asia and Africa. The suffering seen in these regions mobilized more than 50 countries and other development agencies and banks into action. After extensive consultations and research it was observed that, of all the difficulties that plagued these regions, lack of food was the most critical. Thus, the need for research in agriculture was felt to be a major factor in the alleviation of poverty. Once the need for agricultural research was acknowledged, an informal network was established and this body came to be known as CGIAR.

CGIAR began with one centre in the South Indian city of Hyderabad in 1972 and eventually grew to 16 centres, mainly located in developing nations (see Exhibit 1). In addition to the main centre in India, two regional hubs were established in Kenya and Mali and four other centres were established in Niger, Zimbabwe, Malawi and Mozambique. The organization felt that these centres represented areas in the greatest need of efforts to eradicate poverty.

Established on July 5, 1972, ICRISAT originated as an international research centre for improving crop yield and drought-resistant growth (see Exhibit 2). The institute observed that agricultural development of the semi-arid tropics (SAT) in Asia and Africa was in a state of neglect. The main crops of these regions were certain cereals and legumes that were crucial resources for the people that lived in these areas. As these crops were not a staple of the average diet in the developed world, research of these crops had been ignored; however, unless this research was addressed, it was unlikely that the SAT region would emerge from the food security problems it faced. Based on the needs of SAT populations, ICRISAT's prime areas of agricultural research included crops such as sorghum, pearl millet, chickpeas, pigeon peas and groundnuts, which were staples among the diets of these populations.

The SAT region included major portions of the South Asian Peninsula, certain parts of Southeast Asia and Latin America, and the entire continent of Africa—with some exceptions in the central and southern parts of the continent. Nearly 20 per cent of the world's population lived in this region, which suffered from harsh weather conditions, marginal soil, erratic rainfall, overexploitation of land, land degradation and overpopulation. All these factors posted tremendous challenges to agricultural production and the less advantaged (i.e., the majority of the population in the SAT region) inevitably bore the brunt of these difficulties.

Vision and Mission of Icrisat

While ICRISAT's goal was "to harness the power of technology for agricultural development, food security, poverty alleviation and environmental protection,"[4] its overall objective was to improve the quality of crops in order to provide better nourishment to subsistence farmers while simultaneously providing them with an opportunity to increase their household incomes through higher productivity of land. Based on these goals, ICRISAT's mission was to improve the well-being of the marginal farmers in the SAT region by increasing agricultural productivity, providing food security and reducing poverty through agricultural research.

In accordance with this objective, the primary role of ICRISAT was to carry out research in developing robust crops capable of withstanding the extreme climate of SAT region. Such crops would lead to enhancement and sustainable production and improvement in conservation of the limited natural resources of the area. Once such crops were developed, ICRISAT was required to disseminate the information through available platforms, including workshops, networks, training, library services and publishing. Within India, these new developments reached ICRISAT's target group (local farmers) with the help of central government departments like the India Council of Agricultural Research (ICAR), state government departments like the Department of Agriculture and agricultural universities. ICRISAT was responsible for liaising between all four agencies—researchers, government agencies, state government agencies and the farmers.

The onset of the new millennium brought significantly increased donor expectations for ICRISAT. The United Nations' proposed Millennium Development Goals included poverty/hunger reduction and environmental sustainability as a part of its agenda, and noted that agricultural research was one of the primary factors that could help in eradicating poverty and hunger.[5] It was therefore expected that ICRISAT would take a major role in achieving these convergent goals.

In pursuing the vision and mission of ICRISAT, the DG was responsible for fostering, sustaining and enabling a collaborative environment that would encourage excellence in research output and solidarity in the workplace. It was imperative that the DG have tact and excellent public relations skills in order to maintain good international relations as well as alliances and partnerships that would cultivate donors for resource mobilization and assist in disseminating research output to the end users (i.e., farmers). To facilitate the achievement of the institute's objectives, the DG was assisted by the four DDGs, who were responsible for guiding the DG in steering ICRISAT at an operational and strategic level—including managing the day-to-day functioning of ICRISAT, giving scientific direction and optimizing strategic and operational efficiency of the institute.

Background of William Dar

William Dar was born in Danumán West, a village in the province of Santa Maria, Philippines. Being from a farming background, he first learned about farming from his father. Dar graduate from Benguet State University (BSU—then the Mountain State Agricultural Collage) in 1973 with bachelor of science degree in agricultural education, followed by a master of science in agronomy. He later entered a doctoral program in Horticulture at the University of the Philippines Los Baños and received his doctorate in 1980.[6]

Prior to joining ICRISAT, Dar had served as a professor and vice-president at BSU.[7] He had been instrumental in expanding the university's research capabilities and funding, and in the commencement of applicable agricultural training programs. His professional competence and leadership qualities resulted in his appointment as the first director of the Bureau of Agricultural Research (BAR), where he managed the organization, formulated strategies for improving the quality of research output and took significant actions in implementing various projects of the Department of Agriculture.

Dar's leadership qualities and commitment to his work brought him recognition and he became the executive director of the Philippine Council for Agriculture, Forestry and Natural Resources Research and Development (PCARRD), "a powerful national commission for administering knowledge-based agriculture and related sciences in the country."[8] At PCARRD, he was active in implementing a number of programs to benefit farmers and led the council to new successes through empowerment, knowledge dissemination and resource mobilization. Dar believed that neither the government nor the farmers could sustain agricultural development in isolation; he therefore advocated the novel concept of public-private partnership, in which both parties worked together for mutual benefit.

Dar's Leadership Style

During his work at BSU and BAR, Dar's distinctive leadership style had drawn a lot of attention; he frequently challenged the status quo and believed in continuously raising the bar in achievement of organizational objectives.

His personal involvement in research activities motivated and guided employees by ensuring that they were well supported in terms of their research development and their well-being. Dar's decisive leadership methods encouraged proactive governance and decentralized management of research. Under his direction, free seeds and seedlings were distributed among the farmers in and around Hyderabad. Dar involved the DDGs in decisions and made sure that all the decision makers acted as a team. It became his mantra to "take the team along" and foster the active involvement of his subordinates in all initiatives.

Although Dar understood the common resistance to change, he was determined to turn that resistance to commitment through involvement. He influenced people to go beyond their own interests for the betterment of the organization; for example, he encouraged all ICRISAT employees in contributing to the institute's larger vision of attaining self-sustainability, and discouraged them from restricting themselves to their limited domains.

Furthermore, Dar believed that a free-flowing channel of communication at all levels facilitated faster adaptation to change. His main strength was the ability to clearly articulate a vision for the future, as was evident in his previous endeavours at Philippine Council for Agricultural Research and Rural Development (PCARRD). He believed that he had the ability to engineer a collaborative community of talented individuals who were willing to go beyond the normal standards of performance and align their own goals with the goals of the organization.

Eradication of poverty was an issue close to Dar's heart. While growing up in Philippines, he had observed that unless extreme poverty was alleviated in underdeveloped and developing countries, there would be no respite from hunger and malnourishment. This core objective became imprinted in Dar's style of leadership as he rose to positions of influence. Upon his appointment at ICRISAT, Dar created a shared vision for eradicating poverty and malnourishment in the SAT region through research in the field of agriculture, which was in alignment with CGIAR's aim of breaking the stubborn grip of poverty, hunger, malnutrition and environmental degradation through agricultural development in the same areas.

This helped Dar in convincing the board to support his ideas and goals for the future course of the institute. He argued that the research and development of agricultural science at ICRISAT would help reduce poverty by making farmers self-sustainable and that various projects undertaken by ICRISAT (such as watershed programs) would also reduce effects leading to environmental degradation.

The Road Ahead

When he joined ICRISAT, Dar brought with him a history of experience in turning adversity into opportunity. He knew that poverty was one of the main problems in developing countries—in fact, he knew what it was like to live in poverty—and he wanted to help make the world free from this malady. It was therefore his vision to improve the well-being of SAT populations through agricultural research undertaken by ICRISAT. Furthermore, in doing so, Dar felt that these disadvantaged populations needed to be treated in a humane manager—an approach he referred to as "science with a human face," which he incorporated into the ICRISAT logo.[9]

Recognizing the urgent need for transformational change at ICRISAT, Dar started by mapping out a new vision, mission and research strategy for the organization. Within a week of becoming DG, he had realized that ICRISAT had spawned substantial research output in the last 28 years; however, what was lacking now was the ability to turn that technology into practical assistance for small and marginal farmers. This would help in revolutionizing agricultural productivity and, consequently, help in the reduction of poverty. While these efforts had been undertaken in the past on a trial basis at a few locations in India and Africa, Dar's intent was to succeed at the global level. He wanted to capitalize on the transfer of technology to the farm sector by instituting positive public-private-farmer relationships.

Since Dar was well versed in agricultural issues, he had quickly realized that it was in the institute's best interests for the ICRISAT headquarters to remain at the current location for two main reasons. Firstly, from a strategic perspective aimed at assisting developing countries, Southeast Asia represented an area in dire need of research, due to low yield in terms of acreage. Shifting the institute's headquarters to Africa may be unnecessary since many other aspects of ICRISAT had already been transferred to Africa, and such a move could result in Southeast Asia being ignored. Secondary, the current location at Hyderabad had the advantage of access to red, black and intermediate soil types, thus providing a variety of soils for research, unlike the African locations. For these reasons, Dar was sure he could convince the board that ICRISAT could generate sufficient funds to increase focus and investment for Africa without transferring headquarters.

As far as the institute's survival was concerned, Dar was able to buy some time for ICRISAT from CGIAR and the board by convincing them of the importance of the institute's existence to the future of the SAT region and its farming communities. Since CGIAR was guided by a similar vision of reducing poverty, hunger and malnutrition, the concerted efforts towards poverty reduction through agricultural research advocated by Dar were viewed positively by the group. As part of his argument, Dar cited the agricultural prosperity seen in the vicinity of the Hyderabad campus and in central and southern India—primarily due to intervention from ICRISAT scientists in the past, which demonstrated ICRISAT's ability to influence the farmers in the SAT region.

Next Dar tracked the issue of general untidiness and negative atmosphere on campus. He displayed his exemplary leadership skills when he summoned the chief security officer and established a plan to clean up the Hyderabad campus and to show Team ICRISAT that he meant business. By setting a personal example, he ensured that the campus was rid of all litter, and soon the departments started noticing that the new DG had very clear and firm views on the importance of the organization's image. Gradually, the employees began to help out willingly and started looking up.

However, several questions still remained unanswered regarding the future of ICRISAT: How should Dar address the other issues that were still pushing ICRISAT towards failure? How should he ensure proper projection of the institute so that the board would notice and appreciate its research focus? Most importantly, how should he convince the board and the donors about the need to provide fresh impetus to the institute?

Source: Richard Ivey School of Business. Case 8B12C016 by Sunita Mehta and Surya Kant Sharma 2012. Sunita Mehta and Surya Kant Sharma wrote this case solely to provide material for class discussion. The authors do not intend to illustrate either effective of ineffective handling of a managerial situation. The authors may have disguised certain names and other identifying information of protect confidentiality.

Adjudged second best case at the ISB-Ivey Case Competition 2011, held in partnership with Richard Ivey School of Business and the Association of Indian Management Schools and sponsored by the Certified Management Accountants.

QUESTIONS

1. Discuss the problems facing ICRISAT. To what extent are these problems the result of its leadership over the past several years?

2. Describe Dr. Dar's leadership experience. What kind of leadership behaviour and style has he exhibited and what effect has his leadership had on others? Has he been an effective leader? Explain your answer.

3. Use Fiedler's contingency theory and House's path–goal theory to analyze the leadership situation facing Dr. Dar at ICRISAT. What leadership style does each theory suggest?

4. Discuss the merits of LMX theory and transactional and transformational leadership for the leadership situation facing Dr. Dar and in light of the role of the Director General. What type of leadership would be most effective and why?

5. Given the many challenges facing ICRISAT and Dr. Dar (e.g., low staff morale, poor performance and research output, reduced funding), what type of leadership do you think is required? Consider each of the following types of leadership with respect to its potential effectiveness for dealing with each of the challenges: (a) strategic leadership, (b) initiating structure, (c) consideration, (d) participative leadership, (e) transactional leadership, (f) transformational leadership, (g) empowering leadership, (h) ethical leader-

ship, (i) authentic leadership, and (j) servant leadership. Overall, what style of leadership would you recommend for Dr. Dar to be an effective leader? Explain your answer.

6. What does this case tell us about the role of leadership and its effects on people and organizations? What does it tell us about leadership behaviours, the situation, and leadership effectiveness? Explain your answer.

EXHIBIT 1
Dispersion of CGIAR Centres
Source: Company files.

Dispersion of CGIAR Centres

EXHIBIT 2
ICRISAT Locations in the Semi-Arid Tropics
Source: Company files.

ICRISAT Locations in the Semi-ARID Tropics

1 "Report of Sixth External Program and Management Review (EPMR) of the International Crops Research Institute for the Semi-Arid Tropics (ICRISAT): February 2009," p. 86, www.cgiar.org/exco/exco16/exco16_icrisat_epmr.pdf.

2 CGIAR. "Who We Are," www.cgiar.org/who/index.html.

3 CGIAR. (2003, September). Report of the Fifth External Programme Review of the International Crops Research Institute for the Semi-Arid Tropics (ICRISAT), p. xi, www.cgiar.org/pdf/agm03/agm03bus_icrisat_epr.pdf.

4 ICRISAT. (2011, May). Ireland and ICRISAT: Reducing Hunger and Poverty in the Drylands of Africa, www.icrisat.org/who-we-are/investors-partners/donor-flyers/Ireland%20and%20ICRISAT.pdf.

5 United Nations Millennium Declaration. Resolution adopted by the General Assembly 55/2, pp. 4–6, www.un.org/millennium/declaration/areas552e.pdf, accessed March 22, 2012.

6 Hilario, F.A. (2009, October 10). Servant-Leader William Dar. Can't follow, can't lead. *ICRISAT Watch*, www.icrisat-watch.blogspot.com/2009/10/servant-leader-william-dar-cant-follow.html.

7 ICRISAT. (n.d.). Director General's Biography, www.icrisat.org/icrisat-dg-biography.htm.

8 Hilario, F.A. (2009, October 10). Servant-Leader William Dar. Can't follow, can't lead. *ICRISAT Watch,* www.icrisatwatch.blogspot.com/2009/10/servant-leader-william-dar-cant-follow.html.

9 *www.icrisat.org/icrisat-logo.htm, www.icrisat.org/Icrisat-aboutus.htm.*

COMMUNICATION

LEARNING OBJECTIVES

After reading Chapter 10, you should be able to:

10.1 Define *communication* and explain why communication by the strict chain of command is often ineffective.

10.2 Explain the factors that contribute to *voice* versus *silence*.

10.3 Explain the organizational *grapevine* and discuss its main features.

10.4 Review the role of verbal and *non-verbal communication* at work.

10.5 Discuss gender differences in communication and identify how a failure to recognize these differences can cause communication problems.

10.6 Discuss challenges relating to *cross-cultural communication* and identify useful strategies to deter miscommunication.

10.7 Define *computer-mediated communication* and highlight its strengths and weaknesses.

10.8 Review personal strategies and organizational initiatives aimed at enhancing communication.

THE UNIVERSITY OF GUELPH RUMOUR MILL

When the University of Guelph launched the Rumour Mill two years ago, a series of informal question-and-answer sessions with President Alastair Summerlee and Provost Maureen Mancuso, the bottom hadn't yet fallen out of world financial markets. University endowment and pension funds were still healthy, and there was no sign of pending budget cuts. The sessions were meant to give members of the university community a chance to ask Dr. Summerlee and Dr. Mancuso about rumours circulating on campus and to discuss whatever else was on their minds. It was, Dr. Summerlee says, part of his longstanding plan to make senior administration more accountable.

Then the economy took a nosedive, and universities were suddenly faced with the prospect of budget cuts, tuition increases, hiring freezes, and possible layoffs. By the end of last year, Dr. Summerlee was facing some sharp criticisms about the university's investment decisions and pointed questions about his own proposed salary increase.

"It's almost like my own reality TV show," quips Dr. Summerlee with a laugh. It isn't easy, he admits, facing such public accusations and criticism. But the Rumour Mill will continue as planned.

"In my view this is an important piece of the role of a leader of a public institution," Dr. Summerlee says. "You need to be accountable to the people who are here, and sometimes those people have a very different perception of you, of what's going on, and your role and relevance to the place. And it's pretty difficult sometimes, but you owe it to them to listen and to take it." And besides, he adds, it helps boost listenership of the Rumour Mill podcasts: "It's quite good real-life drama."

The Rumour Mill is just one medium U of Guelph's leaders are using to communicate with faculty, staff, and students in these uncertain economic times. Faced with what seems to be a never-ending litany of bad news, university chiefs across Canada are trying to find ways to reach out to the university community.

U of Guelph, for example, has posted on its website letters, memos, and a webcast of a statement by President Summerlee, laying out the full scope of Guelph's financial

The Rumour Mill, informal question-and-answer sessions with President Alastair Summerlee, is just one medium University of Guelph's leaders are using to communicate with faculty, staff, and students.

difficulties—its endowment losses, pension fund deficit, and budget shortfall—and the proposed measures for dealing with them. The site includes a suggestion box inviting visitors to email ideas they have to help the university pare its costs.

Several other university leaders have held town hall meetings and other public forums recently, and have set up task forces to consult with the university community. And though the news they are delivering is usually sobering, "I think overall people appreciate being kept in the loop," Dr. Summerlee says.

That's the goal of any successful communications strategy, says Peter Eckel, director of programs and initiatives at the American Council on Education's Center for Effective Leadership, based in Washington, D.C. The best method of getting a message across will depend on a number of factors, such as the size and culture of the campus. What works well for one won't necessarily work for another. Town hall meetings may be better suited to smaller institutions, for example. Both large and small institutions, however, present their own particular communications challenges. Smaller universities tend to have a tight-knit group of scholars, students, and alumni, and that can make rumours difficult to control. A good communication plan should focus on keeping those rumours in check. At larger institutions, the goal should be to deliver a single clear and consistent message. This can be difficult when the university community is spread out over several campuses, often miles apart, Dr. Eckel says.[1]

Simulate

COMMUNICATION Go
to MyManagementLab
to complete a simulation
about communication.

LO

Define *communication*
and explain why
communication by the
strict chain of command
is often ineffective.

Communication. The
process by which information
is exchanged between a
sender and a receiver.

Explore

Go to MyManagementLab
to see an annotated
version of this figure.

**EXHIBIT 10.1 A model
of the communication
process and an example.**
Source: Glueck, W.F. (1980).
Management, 2nd Ed. Hinsdale,
Ill: Dryden Press. South-West-
ern, a part of Cengage Learning,
Inc. Reproduced by permission,
www.cengage.com/permissions.
Example by authors.

The University of Guelph story exemplifies the importance of good electronic and face-to-face communication. In this chapter, we will explore these and other aspects of communication in organizations. First, we will define *communication* and present a model of the communication process. We will investigate voice, silence, the "grapevine," the verbal and non-verbal language of work, gender differences, cross-cultural communication, and computer-mediated communication. Finally, we will discuss personal and organizational means of improving communication.

WHAT IS COMMUNICATION?

Communication is the process by which information is exchanged between a sender and a receiver. The kind of communication we are concerned with in this chapter is *interpersonal* communication—the exchange of information between people. The simplest prototype for interpersonal communication is a one-on-one exchange between two individuals. Exhibit 10.1 presents a model of the interpersonal communication process and an example of a communication episode between a purchasing manager and her assistant. As you can see, the sender must *encode* his or her thoughts into some form that can be *transmitted* to the receiver. In this case, the manager has chosen to encode her thoughts in writing and transmit them via email. Alternatively, the manager could have encoded her thoughts in speech and transmitted them via voice mail or face to face. The assistant, as a receiver, must *perceive* the message and accurately decode it to achieve accurate understanding. In this case, the assistant uses an online parts catalogue to decode the meaning of an "A-40." To provide *feedback*, the assistant might send the manager a copy of the order for the flange bolts. Such feedback involves yet another communication episode that tells the original sender that her assistant received and understood the message.

This simple communication model is valuable because it points out the complexity of the communication process and demonstrates a number of points at which errors can occur. Such errors lead to a lack of correspondence between the sender's initial thoughts and the receiver's understanding of the intended message. A slip of the finger on the keyboard can lead to improper encoding. A poor email system can lead to ineffective transmission. An outdated parts catalogue can result in inaccurate decoding. Encoding and decoding may be prone to even more error when the message is inherently ambiguous or emotional. This is because the two parties may have very different perceptions of the "facts" at hand.

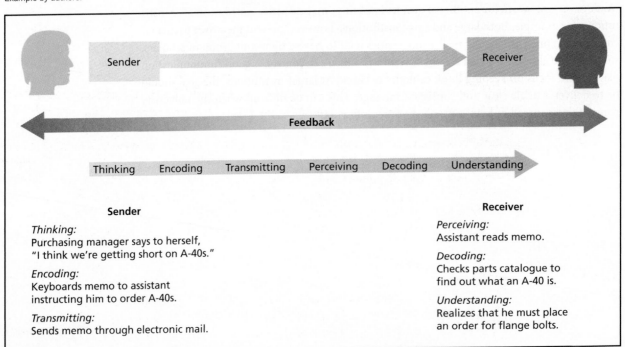

Effective communication occurs when the right people receive the right information in a timely manner. Violating any of these three conditions results in a communication episode that is ineffective.

BASICS OF ORGANIZATIONAL COMMUNICATION

Let's consider a few basic issues about organizational communication.

Communication by Strict Chain of Command

The lines on an organizational chart represent lines of authority and reporting relationships. For example, a vice-president has authority over the plant manager, who has authority over the production supervisors. Conversely, production workers report to their supervisors, who report to the plant manager, and so on. In theory, organizational communication could stick to this strict **chain of command**. Under this system, three necessary forms of communication can be accomplished.

Downward communication flows from the top of the organization toward the bottom. For example, a vice-president of production might instruct a plant manager to gear up for manufacturing a new product. In turn, the plant manager would provide specifics to supervisors, who would instruct the production workers accordingly.

Upward communication flows from the bottom of the organization toward the top. For instance, a chemical engineer might conceive a new plastic formula with unique properties. She might then pass this on to the research and development manager, who would then inform the relevant vice-president.

Horizontal communication occurs between departments or functional units, usually as a means of coordinating effort. Within a strict chain of command, such communication would flow up to and then down from a *common manager*. For example, suppose a salesperson gets an idea for a new product from a customer. To get this idea to the research staff, it would have to be transmitted up to and down from the vice-presidents of marketing and research, the common managers for these departments.

Clearly, a lot of organizational communication does follow the formal lines of authority shown on organizational charts. This is especially true for the examples of upward and downward communication given above—directives and instructions usually pass downward through the chain of command, and ideas and suggestions pass upward. However, the reality of organizational communication shows that the formal chain of command is an incomplete and sometimes ineffective path of communication.

Deficiencies in the Chain of Command

Managers recognize that sticking strictly to the chain of command is often ineffective.

INFORMAL COMMUNICATION The chain of command obviously fails to consider *informal* communication between members. In previous chapters, we discussed how informal interaction helps people accomplish their jobs more effectively. Of course, not all informal communication benefits the organization. An informal grapevine might spread unsavoury, inaccurate rumours across the organization.

FILTERING Getting the right information to the right people is often inhibited by filtering. **Filtering** is the tendency for a message to be watered down or stopped altogether at some point during transmission, and it is something of a double-edged sword. On the one hand, employees are *supposed* to filter information. For example, CEOs are not expected to communicate every detail of the management of the company right down to the shop floor. However, overzealous filtering will preclude the right people from getting the right information, and the organization will suffer accordingly. Upward filtering often occurs because employees are

Effective communication. Communication whereby the right people receive the right information in a timely manner.

Chain of command. Lines of authority and formal reporting relationships.

Downward communication. Information that flows from the top of the organization toward the bottom.

Upward communication. Information that flows from the bottom of the organization toward the top.

Horizontal communication. Information that flows between departments or functional units, usually as a means of coordinating effort.

Filtering. The tendency for a message to be watered down or stopped during transmission.

afraid that their boss will use the information against them. Downward filtering is often due to time pressures or simple lack of attention to detail, but more sinister motives may be at work. As the old saying goes, "information is power," and some managers filter downward communications to maintain an edge on their subordinates. For example, a manager who feels that an up-and-coming employee could be promoted over him might filter crucial information to make the subordinate look bad at a staff meeting.

SLOWNESS   Even when the chain of command transmits information faithfully, it can be painfully slow. The chain of command can be even slower for horizontal communication between departments, and it is not a good mechanism for reacting quickly to customer problems. Cross-functional teams and employee empowerment, concepts we introduced earlier in the text, have been used to improve communication in these areas by short-circuiting the chain of command.

In summary, informal communication and the recognition of filtering and time constraints guarantee that organizations will develop channels of communication beyond the strict chain of command.

VOICE, SILENCE, AND THE MUM EFFECT

LO 10.2

Explain the factors that contribute to *voice* versus *silence*.

Voice. The constructive expression of disagreement or concern about work unit or organizational practices.

Speaking generally, the free flow of information contributes to effective communication. One aspect of this free flow is employee **voice**, the constructive expression of disagreement or concern about work unit or organizational practices.[2] Voice refers to "speaking up" and can be contrasted with silence, which in this context means withholding relevant information. Voice might be directed horizontally, to teammates, or vertically, to the boss or to management in general. When it is not morally or legally required, voice can be considered a form of organizational citizenship behaviour (Chapter 4) that enables organizations to learn and change. Hence, it is in their interest to encourage voice. However, speaking up can be perceived as risky due to inherent power differentials in organizations.

Who is inclined to exercise voice, and when? Interestingly, more satisfied employees who identify more strongly with their work unit or organization are most likely to speak up, as are those who are conscientious and extraverted.[3] Also, direct supervisors and higher level managers play an absolutely critical role in creating a climate in which constructive dissent can emerge.[4] Both direct support (or lack thereof) for dissent as well as symbolic stories about what has happened to those who exercise voice are strong determinants of such a climate. Also, meeting employees informally on their own turf and not unfairly punishing honest mistakes can foster a positive climate for voice. All of these factors can contribute to an atmosphere of **psychological safety**, a shared belief that it is safe to take social risks.[5] Indeed, high "voicers" report less work stress than those who remain silent.[6]

Psychological safety. A shared belief that it is safe to take social risks.

On the other hand, self-censorship will result in a climate of silence. One study found that the following implicit notions contributed to silence: I can't attack the boss's pet idea; I don't have solid data to speak up; I can't bypass the boss; I can't publically embarrass the boss; I can't look like I'm not a team player.[7]

Mum effect. The tendency to avoid communicating unfavourable news to others.

A more general factor that contributes to silence and works against voice is the **mum effect**, the tendency to avoid communicating unfavourable news to others.[8] Often, people would rather "keep mum" than convey bad news that might provoke negative reactions. The sender need not actually be responsible for the bad news for the mum effect to occur, but the tendency is even more likely when the sender *is* responsible for the bad news. For example, the nurse who mistakenly administers an incorrect drug dose might be very reluctant to inform the head nurse of his or her error. Employees with strong aspirations for upward mobility are especially likely to encounter communication difficulties with their bosses.[9] This might be due, in part, to the mum effect—employees who desire to impress their bosses to achieve a promotion have strong motives to withhold bad news.[10]

The mum effect does not apply only to subordinates. A boss might be reluctant to transmit bad news downward. One of your authors found that employees who had good performance ratings were more likely to know those ratings than employees who had bad ratings. Managers evidently avoided communicating bad news for which they were partly responsible, since they themselves had done the ratings. Given this, it is not surprising that managers and their employees often differ in their perceptions of employee performance.[11]

At the University of Guelph, the Rumour Mill was implemented to counter the tendency toward the mum effect and provide a mechanism for voice. Issues of voice and silence are especially relevant to power dynamics, organizational politics, and ethics, topics we will cover in Chapter 12.

THE GRAPEVINE

LO 10.3

Explain the organizational *grapevine* and discuss its main features.

Just inside the gates of the steel mill where one of your authors used to work there was a large sign that read "*X* days without a major accident." The sign was revised each day to impress on the workforce the importance of safe working practices. A zero posted on the sign caught one's attention immediately, since this meant that a serious accident or fatality had just occurred. Seeing a zero on entering the mill, workers seldom took more than five minutes to find someone who knew the details. While the victim's name might be unknown, the location and nature of the accident were always accurate, even though the mill was very large and the accident had often occurred on the previous shift. How did this information get around so quickly? It travelled through the "grapevine."

Characteristics of the Grapevine

The **grapevine** is the informal communication network that exists in any organization. As such, the grapevine often cuts across formal lines of communication that are recognized by management. Observation suggests several distinguishing features of grapevine systems:

Grapevine. An organization's informal communication network.

- We generally think of the grapevine as communicating information by word of mouth. However, written notes, emails, and fax messages can contribute to the transmission of information. For example, a fax operator in the New York office might tell the Zurich office that the chairman's wife just had a baby.

- Organizations often have several grapevine systems, some of which may be loosely coordinated. For instance, a secretary who is part of the "office grapevine" might communicate information to a mail carrier, who passes it on to the "warehouse grapevine."

- The grapevine can transmit information relevant to the performance of the organization as well as personal gossip.[12] Many times, it is difficult to distinguish between the two: "You won't *believe* who just got fired!"

How accurate is the grapevine? One expert concludes that at least 75 percent of the non-controversial organization-related information carried by the grapevine is correct.[13] Personal information and emotionally charged information are most likely to be distorted.

Who Participates in the Grapevine?

Just who is likely to tell—that is, who is likely to be a transmitter of grapevine information? Personality characteristics may play a role. For instance, extraverts might be more likely to pass on information than introverts. Similarly, those who lack self-esteem might pass on information that gives them a personal advantage.

The nature of the information might also influence who chooses to pass it on. In a hospital, the news that a doctor has obtained a substantial cancer research grant might follow a very different path from news involving his affair with a nurse!

Finally, it is obvious that the *physical* location of organizational members is related to their opportunity to both receive and transmit news via the "vine." Occupants of work stations that receive a lot of traffic are good candidates to be grapevine transmitters. A warm control room in a cold plant or an air-conditioned computer room in a sweltering factory might provide their occupants with a steady stream of potential receivers for juicy information. On the other side of the coin, jobs that require movement throughout the organization also give their holders much opportunity to serve as grapevine transmitters. Mail carriers and IT troubleshooters are good examples.

Pros and Cons of the Grapevine

Is the grapevine desirable from the organization's point of view? For one thing, it can keep employees informed about important organizational matters, such as job security. In some organizations, management is so notoriously lax at this that the grapevine is a regular substitute for formal communication. The grapevine can also provide a test of employee reactions to proposed changes without making formal commitments. Managers have been known to "leak" ideas to the grapevine to probe their potential acceptance. Anita Roddick, the late founder of The Body Shop, was known for planting ideas with the office gossips to tap in to the organization's informal networks.[14] Finally, when grapevine information extends outside the organization, it can serve as a potent informal recruiting source.[15]

The grapevine can become a real problem for the organization when it becomes a constant pipeline for rumours, such as those at the University of Guelph described in the chapter-opening vignette. A **rumour** is an unverified belief that is in general circulation.[16] The key word here is "unverified"—although it is possible for a rumour to be true, it is not likely to *remain* true as it runs through the grapevine. Because people cannot verify the information as accurate, rumours are susceptible to severe distortion as they are passed from person to person.

Rumours seem to spread fastest and farthest when the information is especially ambiguous, when the content of the rumour is important to those involved, when the rumour seems credible, and when the recipient is anxious.[17]

Increasingly difficult global competition, staff reductions, and restructuring have placed a premium on rumour control. At the same time, organizations should avoid the tendency to be mum about giving bad news. For a concrete example of the pros and cons of the grapevine, see the Ethical Focus: *Blogs: Effective Communication Tool or Cyberspace Menace?*

Rumour. An unverified belief that is in general circulation.

ETHICAL FOCUS

BLOGS: EFFECTIVE COMMUNICATION TOOL OR CYBERSPACE MENACE?

Weblogs, popularly known as blogs, are online journals in which an individual can share his or her personal thoughts and views on almost any topic. Blogs are becoming one of the most popular forms of communication in cyberspace and allow their authors to publish opinions on movies, politics, fashion, and so on, and give their readers a peek into their daily lives. Increasingly, employees are using blogs to communicate information and views concerning their employers. This can represent both an opportunity and a threat for companies. On the one hand, some companies have embraced blogs as a way of assessing the internal climate of the workforce and gaining access to the employee grapevine. Microsoft has more than 2000 in-house bloggers and views them in a positive light, because many blogs actually promote company products. Other companies arrange blogs themselves or set up internal blogs as an extension of their intranet. The ultimate employee blog is the chief executive's, who can use the internet to connect with employees and disseminate information. Companies who manage their company-related blogs well can reap the benefits of improved communication.

Blogs, however, also have a dark side. They can be a breeding ground for personal attacks against managers and unfounded rumours and gossip, and they can also disseminate confidential company information. To make matters worse, the more vicious bloggers usually use their computer expertise to remain anonymous. "A blogger can go out and make any statement about anybody, and you can't control it," says Steven Down, general manager of bike lock maker Kryptonite, a company that was under attack from bloggers over flaws in their products—with many of the claims proving to be untrue. To defend against potential brand damage caused by smear campaigns, employers can engage and respond to the bloggers directly, which could open them to further ridicule, or pursue legal action, which may be difficult if the blogger's identity cannot be easily determined.

The risks can also be high for the bloggers themselves. While blogging during work hours can lead to disciplinary action and disclosing confidential company information or slandering managers is grounds for dismissal and legal action, some bloggers have found out the hard way that their tongue-in-cheek musings about work can be a fast track to the unemployment line. Companies such as Google, Delta Airlines, and the Wells Fargo bank have fired employees for their blogging activities. Mark Jen, formally of Google, and Joe Gordon, formally of the U.K. bookstore chain Waterstone's, were both fired due to blog posts that management viewed as damaging to the company. The bloggers indicated that their weblogs were similar to chatting about work with family and friends, and both offered to stop blogging about work if the company desired it; but they were fired anyway.

Experts recommend that companies create policies on blogging for their employees, outlining what is and is not acceptable in blogs. For instance, IBM has developed guidelines concerning blogging. Overall, it seems clear that weblogs are here to stay and that what goes on in the workplace will always be a favourite topic for bloggers. Whether blogs represent a positive tool for employee communication, however, remains to be seen.

Sources: Brody, R.G., & Wheelin, B.J. (2005). Blogging: The new computer "virus" for employers. *HR. Human Resource Planning, 28,* 12; Lyons, D. (2005, November 14). Attack of the blogs. *Forbes,* 128–138 (Down quote); Murphy, C. (2006, March 21). Blogging. *Personnel Today,* 26–27; Weinman, J.J. (2005). What the dooce! Blogging about work. *Journal of Internet Law, 9,* 3–6.

THE VERBAL LANGUAGE OF WORK

 LO 10.4

Review the role of verbal and *non-verbal communication* at work.

A friend of one of your authors just moved into a new neighbourhood. In casual conversation with a neighbour, he mentioned that he was "writing a book on OB." She replied with some enthusiasm, "Oh, that's great. My husband's in obstetrics too!" The author's friend, of course, is a management professor who was writing a book on organizational behaviour. The neighbour's husband was a physician who specialized in delivering babies.

Every student knows what it means to do a little "cramming in the caf" before an exam. Although this phrase might sound strange to the uninitiated listener, it reveals how circumstances shape our language and how we often take this shaping for granted. In many jobs, occupations, and organizations we see the development of a specialized language, or **jargon**,

Jargon. Specialized language used by job holders or members of particular occupations or organizations.

that members use to communicate with one another. Thus, *OB* means *organizational behaviour* to management professors and *obstetrics* to physicians.

Rosabeth Moss Kanter, in studying a large corporation, discovered its attempt to foster COMVOC, or "common vocabulary," among its managers.[18] Here, the goal was to facilitate communication among employees who were often geographically separated, unknown to each other, and "meeting" impersonally through memos.

COMVOC provided a common basis for interaction among virtual strangers. In addition, managers developed their own informal supplements to COMVOC. Upward mobility, an especially important topic in the corporation, was reflected in multiple labels for the same concept:

Fast trackers	One performers
High fliers	Boy (girl) wonders
Superstars	Water walkers

While jargon is an efficient means of communicating with peers and provides a touch of status to those who have mastered it, it can also serve as a *barrier* to communicating with others. For example, local jargon might serve as a barrier to clear communication between departments such as sales and engineering. New organizational members often find the use of jargon especially intimidating and confusing.

A second serious problem with the use of jargon is the communication barrier that it presents to those *outside* of the organization or profession. Consider the language of the corporate takeover, with its greenmail, poison pills, and white knights!

THE NON-VERBAL LANGUAGE OF WORK

Have you ever come away from a conversation having heard one thing yet believing the opposite of what was said? Professors frequently hear students say that they understand a concept but somehow know that they do not. Students often hear professors say, "Come up to my office any time" but somehow know that they do not mean it. How can we account for these messages that we receive in spite of the words we hear? The answer is often non-verbal communication.

Non-verbal communication refers to the transmission of messages by some medium other than speech or writing. As indicated above, non-verbal messages can be very powerful in that they often convey "the real stuff," while words serve as a smoke screen. Raised eyebrows, an emphatic shrug, or an abrupt departure convey a lot of information with great economy. The minutes of dramatic meetings (or even verbatim transcripts) can make for extremely boring reading because they are stripped of non-verbal cues. These examples involve the transmission of information by body language. Below, we consider body language and the manipulation of objects as major forms of non-verbal COMMUNICATION.

Non-verbal communication. The transmission of messages by some medium other than speech or writing.

Body Language

Body language is non-verbal communication that occurs by means of the sender's bodily motions and facial expressions or the sender's physical location in relation to the receiver.[19] Although we can communicate a variety of information via body language, two important messages are the extent to which the sender likes and is interested in the receiver and the sender's views concerning the relative status of the sender and the receiver.

In general, senders communicate liking and interest in the receiver when they

Body language. Non-verbal communication by means of a sender's bodily motions, facial expressions, or physical location.

- position themselves physically close to the receiver;
- touch the receiver during the interaction;

- maintain eye contact with the receiver;
- lean forward during the interaction; and
- direct their torso toward the receiver.[20]

Each of these behaviours demonstrates that the sender has genuine consideration for the receiver's point of view.

Senders who feel themselves to be of higher status than the receiver act more *relaxed* than those who perceive themselves to be of lower status. Relaxation is demonstrated by

- the casual, asymmetrical placement of arms and legs;
- a reclining, non-erect seating position; and
- a lack of fidgeting and nervous activity.[21]

In other words, the greater the difference in relaxation between two parties, the more they communicate a status differential to each other.

People often attempt to use non-verbal behaviour to communicate with others, just like they use verbal behaviour. This use could include showing our true feelings, "editing" our feelings, or trying to actively deceive others. It is difficult to regulate non-verbal behaviour when we are feeling very strong emotions. However, people are otherwise pretty good at non-verbal "posing," such as looking relaxed when they are not. On the other hand, observers also show some capacity to detect such posing.[22]

One area in which research shows that body language has an impact is on the outcome of employment interview decisions. Employment interviewers are usually faced with applicants who are motivated to make a good verbal impression. Thus, in accordance with the idea that "the body doesn't lie," interviewers might consciously or unconsciously turn their attention to non-verbal cues on the assumption that they are less likely to be censored than verbal cues. Non-verbal behaviours, such as smiling, gesturing, and maintaining eye contact, have a favourable impact on interviewers when they are not overdone.[23] However, it is unlikely that such body language can overcome bad credentials or poor verbal performance.[24] Rather, positive body language might give the edge to applicants who are otherwise equally well qualified. Remember, in an employment interview, it is not just what you say, but also what you do!

Props, Artifacts, and Costumes

In addition to the use of body language, non-verbal communication can also occur through the use of various objects such as props, artifacts, and costumes.

OFFICE DECOR AND ARRANGEMENT Consider the manner in which people decorate and arrange their offices. Does this tell visitors anything about the occupant? Does it communicate any useful information? The answer is yes. One study found that students would feel more welcome and comfortable in professors' offices when the office was (1) tidy, (2) decorated with posters and plants, and (3) the desk was against the wall instead of between the student and the professor.[25] A neat office evidently signalled that the professor was well organized and had time to talk to them. Perhaps personal decoration signalled "I'm human." When the desk was against the wall, there was no tangible barrier between the parties. Inferences of this type appear to have some validity. Another study found that strangers were able to accurately infer certain Big Five personality traits (Chapter 2) of the occupants of business offices. In particular, they could assess how conscientious and how open to experience the person was simply by seeing his or her office. Neatness was a typical cue for conscientiousness and distinctive decor for openness.[26]

Researcher Kimberly Elsbach found that middle managers working in the California information technology sector (mostly at Intel and Hewlett-Packard) used office decor to

The decor and arrangement of furniture in a person's office conveys non-verbal information to visitors.

"profile" the identity and status of office occupants.[27] Exhibit 10.2 shows some of the inferences they made about their fellow employees, both flattering and unflattering.

DOES CLOTHING COMMUNICATE? "Wardrobe engineer" John T. Molloy is convinced that the clothing organizational members wear sends clear signals about their competence, seriousness, and promotability—that is, receivers unconsciously attach certain stereotyped meanings to various clothing and then treat the wearer accordingly. For example, Molloy

EXHIBIT 10.2 Inferences from office decor.

Source: Adapted from Elsbach, K.D. (2004). Interpreting workplace identities: The role of office décor. *Journal of Organizational Behavior, 25*(1), 99–128. © 2004 John Wiley & Sons Limited. Reproduced with permission of John Wiley & Sons Ltd.

Office Decor	Distinctiveness Categorizations	Status Categorizations
Family photos	Family oriented, balanced, not work focused	Not a 'player'
Hobby photos, calendar, poster, artifacts	Ambitious, outgoing, well-rounded	Unprofessional
Funny, unusual artifacts and conversation pieces	Fun person, joker, off-beat, approachable, lazy, needs attention	Not serious, unprofessional
Formal decor, artifacts	Professional, successful, vain, distant, snobbish	High status, authority figure
Informal, messy office	Easy-going, busy, true engineer, disorganized, unskilled	Unprofessional
Awards, diplomas	Show-off, hard-working, successful, pretentious, vain	Accomplished, intimidating
Professional products	Functional expert, "company person," geek	Accomplished
Ideological artifacts	Patriotic, says "I have a social conscience," extreme, radical	Insecure, unprofessional
Salient, flashy artifacts	Needs to get attention, flashy	Insecure
High conformity artifacts	Predictable, reliable, conservative, not innovative	Insecure

insists that a black raincoat is the kiss of death for an aspiring male executive. He claims that black raincoats signal "lower-middle class," while beige raincoats lead to "executive" treatment. For the same reason, Molloy strongly vetoes sweaters for women executives. Molloy stresses that proper clothing will not make up for a lack of ambition, intelligence, and savvy. Rather, he argues that the wrong clothing will prevent others from detecting these qualities. To this end, he prescribes detailed "business uniforms," the men's built around a conservative suit and the women's around a skirted suit and blouse.[28]

Research reveals that clothing does indeed communicate.[29] Even at the ages of 10 to 12 years, children associate various brand names of jeans with different personality characteristics of the wearer! Such effects persist into adulthood. Research simulations have shown that more masculinely dressed and groomed women are more likely to be selected for executive jobs. However, one study shows that there might be a point at which women's dress becomes "too masculine" and thus damages their prospects.[30] The non-profit organization Dress for Success provides disadvantaged women with professional apparel appropriate for job interviews in various industries and additional apparel when they are hired.[31]

Proper clothing may enhance self-esteem and self-confidence to a noticeable degree. One study contrived to have some student job applicants appear for an interview in street clothes, while others had time to dress in more appropriate formal interview gear. Those who wore more formal clothes felt that they had made a better impression on the interviewer. They also asked for a starting salary that was $4000 higher than the job seekers who wore street clothes![32]

GENDER DIFFERENCES IN COMMUNICATION

LO 10.5

Discuss gender differences in communication and identify how a failure to recognize these differences can cause communication problems.

According to Deborah Tannen, there are gender differences in communication styles, and these differences influence the way that men and women are perceived and treated in the workplace. Gender differences in communication have their origin in childhood. Girls see conversations as a way to develop relationships and networks of connection and intimacy. Boys view conversations as a way for them to achieve status within groups and to maintain independence. These childhood differences persist in the workplace, where they influence who gets recognized and who is valued.[33]

A typical example of how these differences are played out is in a business meeting in which a woman comes up with a great idea and by the end of the meeting one of her male peers receives the credit for it.[34] In these instances, what often happens is that a man picks up the idea of a female co-worker and spends more time talking about it. As a result, he gets the credit.[35]

Gender differences in communication revolve around what Tannen refers to as the "One Up, One Down" position. Men tend to be more sensitive to power dynamics and will use communication as a way to position themselves in a one-up situation. Women are more concerned with rapport building, and they communicate in ways that avoid putting others down. As a result, women often find themselves in a one-down position, which can have a negative effect on the rewards they receive and their careers.[36]

On the basis of her research, Tannen has found that there are a number of key differences in male and female communication styles and rituals that often place women in a one-down position:

- *Getting credit.* Men are more likely than women to blow their own horn about something good they have done.

- *Confidence and boasting.* Men tend to be more boastful about themselves and their capabilities and to minimize their doubts compared with women, who downplay their certainty. As a result, men tend to be perceived as more confident.

- *Asking questions.* Most people know that men do not like to ask for directions when they are lost. This is because they realize that asking questions can put them in a one-down position and reflect negatively on them. Therefore, men are less likely than women to ask questions.

- *Apologies.* Women will often say "I'm sorry" as a way of expressing concern, such as when a friend has had a bad day. For women, apologies are part of a ritual that is used to establish rapport. Men, however, see ritual apologies as weakness.

- *Feedback.* Women will often buffer criticism by beginning with praise as a way to save face for the person receiving the criticism and avoid putting them in a one-down position. Men, however, tend to be much more blunt and straightforward. These differences can lead to misunderstandings, as when a man interprets a woman's praise, rather than the criticism, as the main message.

- *Compliments.* If a friend of yours has just completed a class presentation and asks for your thoughts about it, what would you say? Women are more likely to provide a compliment such as "Great presentation" or "Good job." Men, however, are more likely to interpret the question literally and provide a critique.

- *Ritual opposition.* Men often use ritual opposition as a form of communication and to exchange ideas. This takes the form of attacking others' points of view, challenging them in public, and being argumentative. For women, ritual opposition is seen as a personal attack and something to be avoided.

- *Managing up and down.* Many women believe that, to be recognized and rewarded, what matters most is doing a good job. Unfortunately, this is not always the case. What also matters is who you communicate with and what you discuss. Men spend much more time communicating with their superiors and talking about their achievements. This type of communication influences who gets recognized and promoted. When in positions of power, women tend to downplay their superiority, leading others to believe that they cannot project their authority.

- *Indirectness.* What would be your response if your supervisor asked you a relatively simple question such as "How would you feel about helping the human resources department hire a new person for our department?" Would you then think about how you "feel" about helping or would you interpret this as a request to actually do it? In North America, persons in positions of authority are expected to give direct orders when asking subordinates to do something. Women in positions of authority, however, tend to be indirect when giving orders. For instance, in the above example, what is really being said is, "Help the human resource department hire a person for our department." Such indirectness can lead to misunderstandings and be perceived as a lack of appropriate demeanour and confidence.[37]

The differences in communication styles between men and women almost always reflect negatively on women and place them in a one-down position. Does this mean that women should change the way they communicate? The communication styles that women are accustomed to are most appropriate when communicating with other women, and the same goes for men. Problems arise when those communicating do not understand each other's rituals and styles. The key, according to Deborah Tannen, is to recognize that people have different linguistic styles and to be flexible so that you can adjust your style when necessary. For example, men should learn to admit when they make a mistake and women could learn to be more direct when asking subordinates to do something. Being able to use different communication styles allows people to adjust their style to any given situation.[38] This is also important for effective cross-cultural communication, which is our next topic.

CROSS-CULTURAL COMMUNICATION

LO 10.6

Consider a commonplace exchange in the world of international business:

> A Japanese businessman wants to tell his Norwegian client that he is uninterested in a particular sale. To be polite, the Japanese says, "That will be very difficult." The Norwegian interprets the statement to mean that there are still unresolved problems, not that the deal is off. He responds by asking how his company can help solve the problems. The Japanese, believing he has sent the message that there will be no sale, is mystified by the response.[39]

Discuss challenges relating to *cross-cultural communication* and identify useful strategies to deter miscommunication.

Obviously, ineffective communication has occurred between our international business people, since the Norwegian has not received the right information about the (non) sale. From the Norwegian's point of view, the Japanese has not encoded his message in a clear manner. The Japanese, on the other hand, might criticize the weak decoding skills of his Scandinavian client. Let's examine some important dimensions of cross-cultural communication.

Language Differences

Communication is generally better between individuals or groups who share similar cultural values. This is even more true when they share a common language. Thus, despite acknowledged differences in terminology ("lift" versus "elevator," "petrol" versus "gasoline"), language should not be a communication barrier for the North American executive who is posted to a British subsidiary. Despite this generality, the role of language in communication involves some subtle ironies. For example, a common language can sometimes cause visitors to misunderstand or be surprised by legitimate cultural differences because they get lulled into complacency. Boarding a Qantas Airlines flight in Australia, one of your authors was attempting to pick up a magazine from a rack when he was admonished by a flight attendant with the sharp words "First class, mate." Grinning sheepishly, he headed back to his economy class seat without the magazine. Wise to the ways of Australia, he was not offended by this display of brash informality. However, a less familiar North American, assuming that "they speak English, they're just like us," might have been less forgiving, attributing the flight attendant's behaviour to a rude personality rather than national style. By the same token, the flight attendant would be surprised to learn that someone might be offended by his words.

As the Qantas example indicates, speaking the same language is no guarantee of perfect communication. In fact, the Norwegian and Japanese business people described above may have negotiated in a common language, such as English. Even then, the Norwegian did not get the message. Speaking generally, however, learning a second language should facilitate cross-cultural communication. This is especially true when the second-language facility provides extra insight into the communication style of the other culture. Thus, the Norwegian would profit from understanding that the Japanese have sixteen subtle ways to say no, even if he could not understand the language perfectly.[40]

Non-Verbal Communication across Cultures

From our earlier discussion of non-verbal communication, you might be tempted to assume that it would hold up better than verbal communication across cultures. While there are some similarities across cultures in non-verbal communication, there are also many differences. Here are a few examples.

- *Facial expressions.* People are very good at decoding basic, simple emotions in facial expressions, even across cultures. Americans, Japanese, and members of New Guinea tribes can accurately detect anger, surprise, fear, and sadness in the same set of facial photographs.[41] Thus, paying particular attention to the face in cross-cultural encounters will often yield communication dividends. However, this does not always work because some cultures (such as that of Japan) frown on the display of negative facial expressions, no doubt prompting the "inscrutable" label.

- *Gestures.* Except for literal mimicry ("I need food," "Sign here"), gestures do not translate well across cultures. This is because they involve symbolism that is not shared. Most amusing are those cases in which the same gesture has different meanings across cultures:

  In the United States, a raised thumb is used as a signal of approval or approbation, the thumbs-up signal, but in Greece, it is employed as an insult, often being associated with the expression *katsa pano*, or "sit on this." Another example is the ring sign, performed by bringing the tips of the thumb and finger together so that they form a circle. For most English-speaking people it means okay and is, in fact, known as the "okay gesture." But in some sections of France, the ring means zero or worthless. In English-speaking countries, disagreement is signalled by shaking the head, but in Greece and southern Italy the head-toss is employed to signify disagreement.[42]

- *Gaze.* There are considerable cross-cultural differences in the extent to which it is considered suitable to look others directly in the eye. Latin Americans and Arabs favour an extended gaze, while Europeans do not. In many parts of East Asia, avoiding eye contact is a means of showing respect. In North America, it often connotes disrespect.

- *Touch.* In some cultures, people tend to stand close to one another when meeting and often touch each other as an adjunct to conversation. This is common in Arab, Latin American, and Southern European countries. On the other hand, Northern Europeans and North Americans prefer to "keep their distance."[43]

In an interesting experiment on non-verbal cross-cultural communication, English people received training in social skills that were appropriate to the Arab world. These included standing or sitting close to others and looking into their eyes, coupled with extensive touching, smiling, and handshaking. Experimenters then introduced Arabs to a trained subject and to a control subject who had only been exposed to general information about the Middle East. When asked whom they liked better, the Arabs preferred the people who had received training in their own non-verbal communication style.[44] We can well imagine a business meeting between English and Saudi bankers, both true to their cultures. The Saudis, gazing and touching, finish the meeting wondering why the English are so inattentive and aloof. The English, avoiding eye contact and shrinking from touch, wonder why the Saudis are so aggressive and threatening!

Etiquette and Politeness across Cultures

Cultures differ considerably in how etiquette and politeness are expressed.[45] Very often, this involves saying things that one does not literally mean. The problem is that the exact form that this takes varies across cultures, and careful decoding is necessary to avoid confusion and embarrassment. Literal decoding will almost always lead to trouble. Consider the North American manager who says to an employee, "Would you like to calculate those figures for me?" This is really a mild order, not an opportunity to say no to the boss's "invitation." However, put yourself in the place of a foreign employee who has learned that Americans generally speak directly and expect directness in return. Should she say no to the boss?

In some cultures, politeness is expressed with modesty that seems excessive to North Americans. Consider, for example, the Chinese visitor's response to a Canadian who told him that his wife was very attractive. The Chinese modestly responded, "No, no, my wife is ugly." Needless to say, what was said was not what the Chinese visitor really meant. For an example of national variations in modesty, see the Global Focus: *Self-Presentation Bias: Who's Most and Least Modest in Job Applications?*

GLOBAL FOCUS

SELF-PRESENTATION BIAS: WHO'S MOST AND LEAST MODEST IN JOB APPLICATIONS?

Cornelius König and colleagues studied an aspect of communication that is important to both job seekers and potential employers—self-presentation in the job application process. Self-presentation refers to a range of communication behaviours that might be subsumed under the label of faking. This could include exaggerating one's positive qualities and downplaying one's negative qualities as well as more blatant examples, such as fabricating experience that one does not really have. The overall goal of self-presentation is to create a favourable impression of the candidate in the eyes of HR personnel and managers. Using an elaborate technique designed to ensure anonymity encourage honest responding, the researchers questioned Swiss and Icelandic respondents about what they communicated during a recent job application. The goal was to compare the results with previous research done in the United States. Given that modesty is a particularly valued trait in both Iceland and Switzerland (e.g., tourist guidebooks often extol Swiss modesty),

but less so in the United States, it was expected that the Icelanders and Swiss would report having employed less self-presentation in job applications. For the most part, the Europeans reported much less self-presentation bias than the Americans on a wide range of items. For example, while no Swiss or Icelandic respondents reported outright fabrication of information about themselves, 17% of U.S. respondents did so. Also, 5% of the Swiss, 17% of the Icelanders, and 56% of the Americans admitted to exaggerating their positive attributes such as efficiency and industriousness. Such communication tendencies might favour U.S. applicants in international recruiting situations and lead to overlooking the positive qualities of more modest European applicants.

Source: König, C.J., Hafsteinson, L.G., Jansen, A., & Stadelmann, E.H. (2011). Applicants' self-presentational behaviors across cultures: Less self-presentation in Switzerland and Iceland than in the United States. *International Journal of Selection and Assessment, 19*, 331–339.

In social situations, the Japanese are particularly interested in maintaining feelings of interdependence and harmony. To do this, they use a large number of set phrases or "lubricant expressions" to express sympathy and understanding, soften rejection, say no indirectly, or facilitate apology.[46] When the Japanese told the Norwegian "that will be very difficult" rather than "no," he was using such an expression. To Northern Europeans and North Americans, who do not understand the purpose of these ritual expressions, they may seem at best to be small talk and at worst to be insincere.

Social Conventions across Cultures

Over and above the issue of politeness and etiquette, there are a number of social conventions that vary across cultures and can lead to communication problems.[47] We have already alluded to the issue of directness. Especially in business dealings, North Americans tend to favour "getting down to brass tacks" and being specific about the issue at hand. Thus, the uninitiated business person might be quite surprised at the rather long period of informal chat that will begin business meetings in the Arab world or the indirectness and vagueness of many Japanese negotiators.

Greetings and how people say hello also vary across cultures, and these differences can lead to misunderstandings. For example, in North America people often greet one another by asking, "How are you?" and yet seem uninterested in the response. While this is an acceptable way of saying hello to North Americans, visitors from other cultures find this to be hypocritical. In other cultures, people greet each other by asking, "Where are you going?" Such a question is considered intrusive to North Americans who do not realize that this too is just a way of greeting somebody.[48]

What individuals consider a proper degree of loudness for speech also varies across cultures, and people from "quieter" societies (such as the United Kingdom) might unfairly view those from "louder" societies (such as the Middle East) as pushy or intimidating.

EXHIBIT 10.3 Pace of life in six countries.
Source: Levine, R., & Wolff, E. (1985, March). Social time: The heartbeat of culture. *Psychology Today*, 26–35. Reprinted with permission from *Psychology Today Maga-zine*, copyright © 1985 Sussex Publishers, LLC.

✳-Explore

Go to MyManagementLab to see an annotated version of this figure.

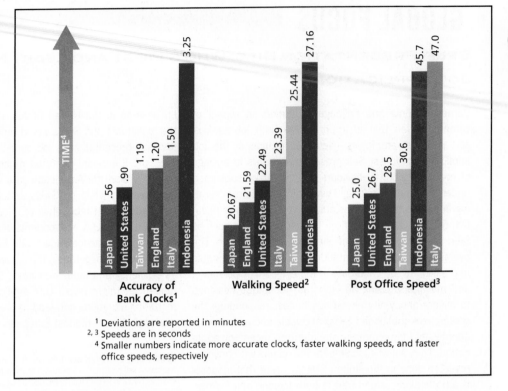

What people consider proper punctuality also varies greatly around the world. In North America and Japan, punctuality at meetings and social engagements is expected and esteemed. In the Arab world and Latin America, being late for a meeting is not viewed nega-tively. In fact, one study found that being on time for an appointment connoted success in the United States and being *late* connoted success in Brazil.[49] Notice how an American business person might decode a Brazilian's lateness as disrespect, while the Brazilian was just trying to make a proper impression.

Exhibit 10.3 shows the results of a study of differences in the pace of life across cultures. It illustrates the accuracy of clocks, the time to walk 100 feet, and the time to get served in a post office. As you can see, Japan is the most time conscious, while Indonesia is quite leisurely. Such differences are especially likely to provoke communication problems when we attribute them to a *person* and ignore the overall influence of the culture.

Finally, nepotism, favouring one's relatives in spite of their qualifications, is generally frowned on in more individualistic societies, such as North America and Northern Europe. However, in more collective cultures, such as those found in Africa and Latin America, people are expected to help their relatives. Hence, an American manager might view his Nigerian colleague's hiring his own son as irresponsible. The Nigerian might see it as irresponsible *not* to hire his own flesh and blood.

Cultural Context

Cultural context. The cultural information that surrounds a communication episode.

In the previous sections, we provided many examples of communication differences across cul-tures. Is there some organizing principle underlying these differences, something that helps to summarize them? The concept of *cultural context* provides a partial answer. **Cultural context** is the cultural information that surrounds a communication episode. It is safe to say that context is always important in accurately decoding a message. Still, as Exhibit 10.4 shows, cultures tend to differ in the importance to which context influences the meaning to be put on communications.[50]

Some cultures, including many East Asian, Latin American, African, and Arab cultures, are high-context cultures. This means that the message contained in communication is

EXHIBIT 10.4 High- versus low-context cultures.
Source: Klopf & McCroskey, *Intercultural Communication Encounters*, Figure 10.1 "Where Different Cultures Fall on the Context Scale," p. 187, © 2007 Pearson Education, Inc. Reproduced by permission of Pearson Education, Inc.

Go to MyManagementLab to see an annotated version of this figure.

strongly influenced by the context in which the message is sent. In high-context cultures, literal interpretations are often incorrect. Examples include those mentioned earlier—the Japanese really meant that the business deal was dead, and the Chinese did not really mean that his wife was unattractive.

Low-context cultures include North America, Australia, Northern Europe (excluding France), and Scandinavia. Here, messages can be interpreted more literally because more meaning resides in the message than in the context in which the communication occurs. The "straight talk" that Americans favour is such an example. However, such straight talk is not any straighter in meaning than that heard in high-context cultures if one also learns to attend to the context when decoding messages.

Differences in the importance of context across cultures have some interesting implications for organizational communication, especially when we consider what might occur during business negotiations. Consider the following:[51]

- People from high-context cultures want to know about you and the company that you represent in great detail. This personal and organizational information provides a context for understanding your messages to them.

- Getting to the point quickly is not a style of communication that people in high-context cultures favour. Longer presentations and meetings allow people to get to know one another and to consider a proposal in a series of stages.

- When communicating with people from a high-context culture, give careful consideration to the age and rank of the communicator. Age and seniority tend to be valued in high-context cultures, and the status of the communicator is an important contextual factor that gives credibility to a message. Younger fast-trackers will do fine in low-context cultures where "it's the message that counts."

■ YOU BE THE MANAGER ■

Four Seasons Goes to Paris

Four Seasons Hotels and Resorts manages 86 properties in 35 countries and is widely regarded as the world's leading operator of luxury hotels. For 15 years in a row, the Canadian company has made Fortune's list of the Top 100 Best Companies to Work for in North America (since the list began) and has experienced impressive financial results during that same period.

Four Seasons is known for its strong organizational culture, which is based on the Golden Rule of "treating others as you wish they would treat you." The culture is supported by a philosophy focusing on modesty, individual accountability, a strong allegiance to the firm, global service standards, and intelligent, anticipatory, and enthusiastic customer service. When Four Seasons decided to expand internationally, many wondered if its corporate culture—undoubtedly a major factor in its North American success—would be easy to transfer to employees in other countries. This question was particularly important when Four Seasons signed a deal to manage the famous George V hotel in Paris in 1996.

The French have a distinct national culture and a particular philosophy of customer service. They believe it is degrading to be "in the service" of someone else, but honourable to "give service" if it is deserved. This view is quite the opposite of what Four Seasons' North American employees believe. The French have also had management–employee relationships that traditionally tended to be adversarial, not cooperative, and they are not known for taking initiative without checking with a higher-up first. At the Four Seasons, however, the culture focuses on individual initiative with accountability, and strong cooperation between managers and employees.

A further problem for the Four Seasons was France's strong labour laws. The company was forced to keep all existing employees who wished to stay with the hotel. The George V is one of six grand, historic, and luxurious hotels in Paris classified as "Palaces," but in the 1980s and 1990s service had lapsed to the point where many wondered if it was worthy of the "Palace" name. Having to keep some of the employees who worked during these down years meant that communicating and implementing a new, customer-focused culture would be difficult, to say the least. The Four Seasons also had to contend with France's past experiences with other North American firms that had showed little cultural sensitivity when they came to

The George V balances Four Seasons corporate culture with French national culture.

Europe and earned the resentment and ridicule of the French (e.g., Disneyland Paris).

To contend with all these daunting hurdles, Four Seasons played up its Canadian identity to emphasize its open-mindedness to different cultures. Further, Didier Le Calvez, a native of France who had spent the last 25 years working outside the country, was appointed as general manager of the George V. Le Calvez and his team knew that "Four Seasonizing" the hotel would be no easy task.

Questions

1. Given Four Seasons' operations in 35 countries, what important factors must the firm's managers be aware of to properly communicate with staff at their hotels? Should all policies and procedures be communicated and implemented universally?

2. Considering France's national culture and the fact that the George V had been acquired and is now being operated by foreign interests, what specific tactics could Le Calvez use to communicate Four Seasons' culture and approach to employees and to the French public?

To find out what Four Seasons did, see The Manager's Notebook at the end of the chapter.

Source: Adapted (with updates) from Hallowell, R., Bowen, D.E., & Knoop, C.I. (2002, November). Four Seasons goes to Paris. *Academy of Management Executive*, 7–24; Updates from http://money.cnn.com/magazines/fortune/best-companies/2012/snapshots/85.html.

- Because they tend to devalue cultural context, people from low-context cultures tend to favour very detailed business contracts. For them, the meaning is in the message itself. High-context cultures place less emphasis on lengthy contracts because the context in which the deal is sealed is critical.

Some more general advice for good cross-cultural communication will be presented shortly, but for now, consider the You Be the Manager: *Four Seasons Goes to Paris* feature about cross-cultural communication when a company expands to a new country, as was the case when Four Seasons took over one of Paris's most renowned hotels.

COMPUTER-MEDIATED COMMUNICATION

Does communicating electronically differ from communicating face to face? This is clearly an important topic given the pervasive use of routine email, "chat"-type decision support software, teleconferencing, videoconferencing, and other electronic communication media. A good way to begin thinking about this issue is to consider **information richness**, the potential information-carrying capacity of a communication medium.[52] Various media can be ranked in terms of their information richness. A face-to-face transmission of information is very high in richness because the sender is personally present, audio and visual channels are used, body language and verbal language are occurring, and feedback to the sender is immediate and ongoing. A telephone conversation is also fairly rich, but it is limited to the audio channel, and it does not permit the observation of body language. At the other extreme, communicating via numeric computer output lacks richness because it is impersonal and uses only numeric language. Feedback on such communication might also be very slow.

Exhibit 10.5 shows two important dimensions of information richness: the degree to which information is synchronous between senders and receivers, and the extent to which both parties can receive non-verbal and para-verbal cues. Highly synchronous communication, such as face-to-face speech, is two-way, in real time. On the low side of synchronization, memos, letters, and even emails are essentially a series of one-way messages, although email has the clear potential for speedy response. Face-to-face interaction and videoconferencing are high in non-verbal (e.g., body language) and para-verbal (e.g., tone of voice) cues, while these are essentially absent in the text-based media. In general, the media in the upper right sector of Exhibit 10.5 (highly synchronous, high in non-verbal and para-verbal cues) exemplify the most information richness and those in the lower left sector exhibit the least richness.

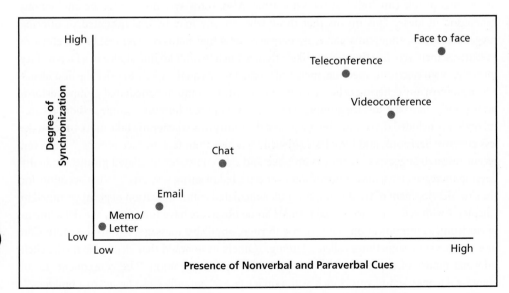

EXHIBIT 10.5 **Communication media arranged according to synchronization and cue availability.**

Source: Reprinted from Baltes, B., Dickson, M.W., Sherman, M.P., Bauer, C.C., & LaGanke, J.S. (2002). Computer-mediated communication and group decision making: A meta-analysis, *Organizational Behavior and Human Decision Processes 87*, 156–179. Copyright © 2001 Elsevier Science (USA). All rights reserved. Reprinted with permission from Elsevier.

LO 10.7

Define *computer-mediated communication* and highlight its strengths and weaknesses.

Information richness. The potential information-carrying capacity of a communication medium.

 Watch

COMMUNICATION Go to MyManagementLab to watch a video about communication.

Watch

GAWKER MEDIA: MANAGERS & COMMUNICATIONS Go to MyManagementLab to watch a video about managers and communication.

Explore

Go to MyManagementLab to see an annotated version of this figure.

Computer-mediated
communication includes
videoconferencing.

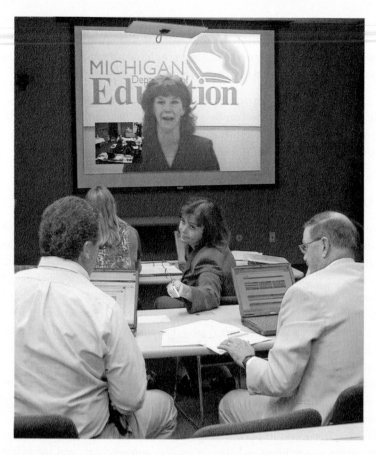

**Computer-mediated
communication (CMC).**
Forms of communication
that rely on computer
technology to facilitate
information exchange.

As shown in Exhibit 10.5, email, chat systems, teleconferencing, and videoconferencing are commonly classified as **computer-mediated communication** (CMC) in that they rely on computer technology to facilitate information exchange. All of these media permit discussion and decision making without employees having to be in the same location, potentially saving time, money, and travel hassles. But does such potential efficiency result in effective communication as we defined it earlier?

Most research to date has focused on "chat"-type group-decision support systems that rely on text-based computer conferencing to generate ideas and make decisions. Such systems have been shown to enhance the sheer number of ideas generated when brainstorming a problem (Chapter 11).[53] Several factors contribute to this. In electronic groups, computer memory means that people can "talk" at the same time. Also, some systems permit the anonymous generation of ideas. This means that those who are shy may be less inhibited in offering suggestions. Also, anonymity can erase perceived or actual status differences. In one study of executives, men were five times more likely than women to offer an initial idea in a face-to-face meeting. In an electronic meeting, men and women were equally likely to offer the first idea.[54]

By almost any criterion other than generating ideas, computer-mediated groups perform more poorly than face-to-face groups, at least when they meet for only a single session. A careful review concluded that computer-mediated decision groups generally take more time, make less effective decisions, and have less-satisfied members than face-to-face groups.[55] However, recent research suggests that time is an issue and that computer-mediated groups gradually develop increased trust and cooperation over repeated meeting sessions.[56] What accounts for the slow development of trust using computer-mediated communication (a point we noted in Chapter 7 with reference to virtual teams)? Some observers have found that the detachment of electronic communication can give rise to rude, impulsive messages and to the expression of extreme views, sometimes called "flaming." Others have noted that electronic media elicit informal modes of expression that are prone to misinterpretation. The consequent use of emotional icons ("emoticons") such as the smiley face ☺ can only go so far as trust builders.[57]

In addition, the lack of non-verbal cues may make it difficult to recognize subtle trends toward consensus. Finally, although computer mediation can reduce status differences and promote equality, people can still detect some differences in text-based messages. For instance, people exhibit some degree of accuracy in deducing whether a message was sent by a man or a woman![58]

As suggested by Exhibit 10.5, email may be even more prone to miscommunication than chat formats. Jason Kruger and colleagues conducted five experiments that showed that people strongly overestimated their skill in both communicating and interpreting sarcasm, humour, and emotions via email. They concluded that people tend to be egocentric and exaggerate the extent to which others share their own perspective.[59] Other research suggests that people may interpret some emails as more emotionally negative than they really are.[60]

People readily make negative inferences about the intelligence and trustworthiness of those who send emails with spelling and grammar errors, unless they are known to hail from foreign cultures. However, cultural background of the sender is not excused in the case of etiquette errors such as terse messages.[61]

Some people have argued that telecommuting can lead to professional isolation from bosses and co-workers, presumably due to less face-to-face interaction and reliance on less rich communication media (e.g., email). However, a review of research suggests that this is not a problem.[62] Another study showed that professional isolation was less likely when richer media were available (e.g., audio and video conferencing, whiteboard collaborative software).[63]

To summarize, a good rule to follow is that less routine communication requires richer communication media.[64] Memos, reports, emails, and web portals are fine for recurrent, non-controversial, impersonal communication in which information is merely being disseminated. Important decisions, intended changes, controversial messages, and emotional issues generally call for richer (i.e., face-to-face or video) media. At the University of Guelph, the town hall meetings, the webcasts, and the Rumour Mill podcasts are rich media suited to the serious news being delivered.

PERSONAL APPROACHES TO IMPROVING COMMUNICATION

LO 10.8

Review personal strategies and organizational initiatives aimed at enhancing communication.

More and more people are learning that developing their communication skills is just as sensible as developing their accounting skills, their computer skills, or anything else that will give them an edge in the job market. Improvements in communication skills are very reinforcing. When you communicate well, people generally respond to you in a positive way, even if they are not totally happy with your message. Poor communication can provoke a negative response that is self-perpetuating, in that it leads to even *poorer* communication. This happens when the other party becomes resistant, defensive, deceptive, or hostile.

Basic Principles of Effective Communication

Let's consider some basic principles of effective face-to-face communication.[65] These principles are basic, in that they apply to upward, downward, horizontal, and outside communication. They generally apply to cross-cultural encounters, too, as long as they are applied in conjunction with the advice in the following section, "When in Rome…"

TAKE THE TIME   Good communication takes time. Managers in particular have to devote extra effort to developing good rapport with employees. Not taking adequate time often leads to the selection of the wrong communication medium. One of your authors has seen a "don't do this" memo sent to 130 employees because two of them committed some offence. Of course, the memo irritated 128 people, and the two offenders really did not grasp the problem. The boss should have taken the time to meet face to face with the two people in question.

BE ACCEPTING OF THE OTHER PERSON

Try to be accepting of the other person as an individual who has the right to have feelings and perceptions that may differ from your own. You can accept the person even if you are unhappy with something that he or she has done. Having empathy with others (trying to put yourself in their place and see things from their perspective) will increase your acceptance of them. Acting superior or arrogant works against acceptance.

DO NOT CONFUSE THE PERSON WITH THE PROBLEM

Although you should be accepting of others, it is generally useful to be problem-oriented rather than person-oriented. For example, suppose an employee does something that you think might have offended a client. It is probably better to focus on this view of the problem than to impute motives to the employee ("Don't you care about the client's needs?"). The focus should be on what the person did, not who the person is. Along these same lines, try to be more descriptive rather than evaluative. Again, focus on what exactly the employee did to the client, not how bad the consequences are.

Congruence. A condition in which a person's words, thoughts, feelings, and actions all contain the same message.

SAY WHAT YOU FEEL

More specifically, be sure that your words, thoughts, feelings, and actions exhibit **congruence**—that they all contain the same message. A common problem is soft-pedalling bad news, such as saying that someone's job is probably secure when you feel that it probably is not. However, congruence can also be a problem with positive messages. Some managers find it notoriously difficult to praise excellent work or even to reinforce routine good performance. Congruence can be thought of as honesty or authenticity, but you should not confuse it with brutal frankness or cruelty. Also, remember that in some high-context cultures, "saying what you feel" is done very indirectly. Still, the words and feelings are congruent in their own context.

Active listening. A technique for improving the accuracy of information reception by paying close attention to the sender.

LISTEN ACTIVELY

Effective communication requires good listening. People who are preoccupied with themselves or who simply hear what they expect to hear are not good listeners. Good listening improves the accuracy of your reception, but it also shows acceptance of the speaker and encourages self-reflection on his or her part. Good listening is not a passive process. Rather, good communicators employ active listening to get the most out of an interaction. Techniques of **active listening** include the following:

- *Watch your body language.* Sit up, lean forward, and maintain eye contact with the speaker. This shows that you are paying attention and are interested in what the speaker is saying (this is another aspect of congruence).

- *Paraphrase what the speaker means.* Reflecting back what the speaker has said shows interest and ensures that you have received the correct message.

- *Show empathy.* When appropriate, show that you understand the feelings that the speaker is trying to convey. A phrase such as "Yes, that client has irritated me, too" might fill the bill.

- *Ask questions.* Have people repeat, clarify, or elaborate what they are saying. Avoid asking leading questions that are designed to pursue some agenda that *you* have.

- *Wait out pauses.* Do not feel pressured to talk when the speaker goes silent. This discourages him or her from elaborating.

The San Francisco Police Department has trained several hundred officers in active listening as part of its peer support program to deal with work stress.[66]

GIVE TIMELY AND SPECIFIC FEEDBACK

When you initiate communication to provide others with feedback about their behaviour, do it soon and be explicit. Speed maximizes the reinforcement potential of the message, and explicitness maximizes its usefulness to the recipient. Say *what* was good about the person's presentation to the client, and say it soon.

When in Rome...

Frankly, you are off to a pretty good start in cross-cultural communication if you can do a careful job of applying the basic communication principles we discussed above. However, people's basic skills sometimes actually *deteriorate* when they get nervous about a cross-cultural encounter. Let's cover a few more principles for those situations.

ASSUME DIFFERENCES UNTIL YOU KNOW OTHERWISE The material we presented earlier on cross-cultural communication and that in Chapter 3 on workforce diversity should sensitize you to the general tendency for cross-cultural differences to exist. In a cross-cultural situation, caution dictates we should assume that such differences exist until we are proven wrong. Remember, we have a tendency to project our own feelings and beliefs onto ambiguous targets (Chapter 3), leading us to ignore differences. Be particularly alert when dealing with proficient English speakers from cultures that emphasize harmony and avoidance of conflict (e.g., Japan). Their good English will tempt you to think that they think like you do, and their good manners will inhibit them from telling you otherwise.

RECOGNIZE DIFFERENCES WITHIN CULTURES Appreciating differences between cultures can sometimes blind us to the differences among people within a culture. This, of course, is what stereotypes do (Chapter 3). Remember, your German employees will have as many different personalities, skills, and problems as your North American employees. Remember, too, that there are occupational and social class differences in other countries just like there are at home, although they can be harder to decipher (this is why one of your authors once shook hands with the chef at a French business school, mistaking him for the dean!).

WATCH YOUR LANGUAGE (AND THEIRS) Unless the person with whom you are communicating is very fluent in English, speak particularly clearly, slowly, and simply. Avoid clichés, jargon, and slang. Consider how mystifying phrases such as "I'm all ears," "Let's get rolling," and "So long" must be.[67] By the same token, do not assume that those who can speak your language well are smarter, more skilled, or more honest than those who cannot.

ORGANIZATIONAL APPROACHES TO IMPROVING COMMUNICATION

In this section, we discuss some organizational techniques that can improve communication. We consider other techniques in Chapter 13 (concerning conflict reduction) and Chapter 16 (with regard to organizational development).

Provision of Explanations

Organizations sometimes have to enact controversial policies that have the potential to spark much employee resistance. Examples might involve restructuring, layoffs, pay rollbacks, smoking bans, or affirmative action programs. Often, there are good reasons for the introduction of such policies. However, in line with the mum effect, many organizations simply announce such policies with little or no explanation, evidently fearing to dwell on negative news or provoke lawsuits. This is a bad idea, and there are communication approaches that can greatly improve the perceived fairness of controversial policies. Notions of procedural and interactional fairness (Chapter 4) underlie such effective communication.

Two factors are critical to the perceived fairness of controversial policies: the adequacy of the explanation and the style with which it is delivered.[68] Adequate explanations are specific and detailed, highlighting the reasons for the policy, how the decision was made, and the benefits that will accrue from it. Equally important, the delivery of the message should be truthful, sincere, respectful, and sensitive. When appropriate, the communicator should express sincere remorse for having to implement the policy (e.g., a pay rollback) and acknowledge any suffering that the policy might cause. All of this requires the use of a rich communication medium, such as a personal appearance by the CEO or other high organizational representative. A research review concluded that an adequate explanation for a policy decision reduced employees' tendencies to retaliate by 43 percent. It also concluded that an inadequate explanation is seen as less fair than no explanation at all.[69]

360-Degree Feedback

Traditionally, employee performance appraisal has been viewed as an exercise in downward communication in which the boss tells the employee how he or she is doing. More recently, performance appraisal has become a two-way communication process in which employees are also able to have upward impact concerning their appraisal. Most recently, some firms have expanded the communication channels in performance appraisal to include not only superior and self-ratings but also ratings by subordinates, peers, and clients or customers. This is called *multisource* or **360-degree feedback**. Firms that use it include Air Canada and Bell Canada.

The 360-degree system usually focuses on required behavioural competencies rather than bottom-line performance. It is usually used for employee development rather than salary determination. It is possible that the various sources of feedback could contradict each other, and ratees may need some assistance in putting all this input together. However, in a well-designed 360-degree system, the various information sources ideally should provide unique data about a person's performance. Research shows that 360-degree feedback leads to subsequent performance improvements.[70]

360-degree feedback. Performance appraisal that uses the input of supervisors, employees, peers, and clients or customers of the appraised individual.

Employee Surveys and Survey Feedback

Surveys of the attitudes and opinions of current employees can provide a useful means of upward communication. Since surveys are usually conducted with questionnaires that provide for anonymous responses, employees should feel free to voice their genuine views. A good **employee survey** contains questions that reliably tap employee concerns and also provide information that is useful for practical purposes. Survey specialists must summarize (encode) results in a manner that is easily decoded by management. Surveys are especially useful when they are administered periodically. In this case, managers can detect changes in employee feelings that may deserve attention.

When survey results are fed back to employees, along with management responses and any plans for changes, this feedback should enhance downward communication. Survey feedback shows employees that management has heard and considered their comments. Plans for changes in response to survey concerns indicate a commitment to two-way communication.[71] In Chapter 16 you will learn more about employee surveys.

Employee survey. An anonymous questionnaire that enables employees to state their candid opinions and attitudes about an organization and its practices.

Suggestion Systems and Query Systems

Suggestion systems are designed to enhance upward communication by soliciting ideas for improved work operations from employees. They represent a formal attempt to encourage useful ideas and prevent their filtering through the chain of command. The simplest example of a suggestion system involves the use of a suggestion box into which employees put written ideas for improvements (usually anonymously). This simple system is usually not very effective, since there is no tangible incentive for making a submission and no clear mechanism to show that management considered a submission.

Much better are programs that *reward* employees for suggestions that are actually adopted and provide feedback as to how management evaluated each suggestion. For simple suggestions a flat fee is usually paid (perhaps $500). For complex suggestions of a technical nature that might result in substantial savings to the firm, a percentage of the anticipated savings is often awarded (perhaps several thousand dollars). An example of such a suggestion might be how to reduce paper use and promote environmental sustainability. When strong

Suggestion systems. Programs designed to enhance upward communication by soliciting ideas for improved work operations from employees.

publicity follows the adopted suggestions (such as explaining them in the organization's employee newsletter), downward communication is also enhanced, since employees receive information about the kind of innovations desired. At RBC Financial Group, employees can receive up to $25 000 for a suggestion, and around 550 a month are submitted.[72]

Related to suggestion systems are *query systems*, which provide a formal means of answering questions that employees may have about the organization. These systems foster two-way communication and are most effective when questions and answers are widely disseminated. Many organizations have a column of questions and answers in their employee newsletters, the content ranging from questions about benefits to the firm's stock performance.

Telephone Hotlines, Intranets, and Webcasts

Many organizations have adopted *telephone hotlines* to further communication. Some hotlines use a news format to present company information. News may be presented live at prearranged times or recorded for 24-hour availability. Such hotlines prove especially valuable at times of crisis, such as during storms or strikes.[73] Other hotlines serve as query systems, in that employees can call in for answers to their questions, either by using an automated attendant or by talking live to support personnel (e.g., Human Resources). In some instances, companies use hotlines for ethics reporting, so that employees can call in to report unethical behaviour they have either experienced or witnessed. These hotlines can support anonymous reporting. McMaster University uses such a system, which is operated by the firm EthicsPoint.[74]

Many companies use their corporate intranet portals as a means of communicating important announcements or engaging employees in electronic discussions (e.g., corporate blogs). Intranet portals represent an important information source on various topics of interest to employees and can also allow employees to communicate information to the organization, such as changes of address or benefits enrolment.[75]

One excellent technique for fostering communication is a company-managed webcasting solution. Corporate webcasting constitutes a rich communication medium that allows for the broadcasting of both audio and video and can reach employees located anywhere in the world. Multipoint webcasting allows for a number of presenters who can be located in multiple cities. Such communication mediums are especially good for general information sessions, training, and new product introduction. The synchronous, interactive nature of webcasts supports audience engagement either through written questions, audio questions, or, where possible, video interaction.

The attraction of webcasting is that it not only can reach many employees in an effective manner but can also be made available after the fact. Employees who either missed the original webcast or want to review what they learned can watch the webcast at their leisure, in whole or in part.

To reduce costs and enhance communication, some organizations use podcasts. The benefit of podcasts is that there is no need for camera equipment. A simple recording of the audio presentation will suffice. Although podcasts lack the richness of video, they still capture the emotion of the speaker and, when used live, allow for audio question-and-answer periods. As with webcasts, recorded podcasts can be placed on an organizational intranet so employees can listen at a later date. Although each University of Guelph Rumour Mill session is hosted live on campus, it is also recorded and posted on the university's website for anyone to listen to. In a university setting, where students and faculty are never all available all at once, recorded podcasts are an effective means of reaching all constituents in a given period of time.

Management Training

Managers face a fundamental challenge in balancing social-emotional and task demands in their communication with employees, and proper training can improve the communication skills of managers. Notice the specific use of the word "skills" here. Vague lectures about the importance of good communication simply do not tell managers how to communicate better. However, isolating specific communication skills and giving the boss an opportunity to practise these skills should have positive effects. The manager who has confidence in how to handle delicate matters should be better able to handle the balance between social-emotional and task demands.

Effective training programs often present videotaped models correctly handling a typical communication problem. Managers then role-play the problem and are reinforced by the trainers when they exhibit effective skills. At General Electric, for example, typical communication problems that this kind of training addresses have included discussing undesirable work habits, reviewing work performance, discussing salary changes, and dealing with employee-initiated discussions.[76] North Carolina's Center for Creative Leadership incorporates 360-degree feedback data from peers, superiors, and subordinates into its training.

It might seem that training of this nature is essentially focused on downward communication. However, the disclosure of one's attitudes and feelings promotes reciprocity on the part of the receiver.[77] Thus, the manager who can communicate effectively downward can expect increased upward communication in return.

THE MANAGER'S NOTEBOOK

Four Seasons Goes to Paris

1. While Four Seasons encourages strict adherence to its core values, it allows the management and employees of each hotel to be true to their national culture. As such, Four Seasons takes a "when in Rome..." approach to the hotel business. Not every country has the same social conventions, or the same idea of what is considered polite and proper etiquette. Four Seasons goes out of its way to ensure that its hotels communicate fundamental values to staff and guests but in a way that allows employees to have discretion at the local level. To underline this point, Four Seasons trimmed its written operating standards from 800 to 270 to allow greater discretion at the local level when dealing with different social conventions across cultures. As such, an Italian employee in Italy or an Egyptian employee in Egypt would be free to behave in a manner and provide service in a way that is congruent with his or her national identity. Four Seasons' cultural sensitivity extends to human resource practices, such as performance evaluations, that are not common in Europe and the Middle East. Managers are free to modify human resource forms and procedures to respect local customs and traditions.

2. Four Seasons' managers noted that, in France, words were not enough to communicate values and that French employees take a wait-and-see approach before jumping on board. Therefore, how the values were presented to employees and enacted by managers were key parts of the communication process. In addition to the presentation style, some concrete communication tactics were also used. A 35-person task force was assembled to help people understand how the company does things, to listen for problems, and to control the rumour mill. In an attempt to defuse the traditional labour tensions in France, Le Calvez took the representatives of the various unions to lunch so that important conversations could take place face to face in an inclusive manner. The company also carefully explained the use of procedures, such as employee evaluations, and framed them as opportunities for open and constructive dialogue. Furthermore, to promote communication and problem solving, Four Seasons implemented a "direct line" process in which, once a month, the general manager would meet with employees, supervisors, and managers in groups of 30. Finally, Le Calvez and his team carefully cultivated culturally sensitive external communications with the press. So what was the outcome? Responses from employee surveys have been extremely positive, clearly showing that employees have bought in to the culture. Furthermore, the hotel received several industry awards since Four Seasons took control. Overall, through intelligent communication tactics and cultural sensitivity, Four Seasons was able to maintain the standards of excellence at the George V and to make believers of employees and the public alike.

MyManagementLab Visit MyManagementLab at **www.mymanagementlab .com** for access to online tutorials, interactive exercises, videos, and much more.

LEARNING OBJECTIVES CHECKLIST

10.1 *Communication* is the process by which information is exchanged between a sender and a receiver. Effective communication involves getting the right information to the right people in a timely manner. Although much routine communication can occur via the chain of command, the chain tends to be slow and prone to filtering. It also ignores informal communication.

10.2 *Voice* is expressing constructive disagreement with organizational practices. It is most likely in an atmosphere of *psychological safety* that encourages social risk taking. The *mum effect* (the reluctance to transmit bad news) discourages voice.

10.3 The *grapevine* is an organization's informal communication network. Key physical locations or jobs that require movement around the organization encourage certain members to pass on information. The grapevine can be useful to the organization, and it often transmits information accurately. However, it becomes problematic when rumours (unverified beliefs) circulate.

10.4 Verbal language that is tailored to the needs of a particular occupation or organization is known as *jargon*. While jargon aids communication between experienced co-workers, it can often prove confusing for new organizational members and people outside the organization. *Non-verbal communication* is the transmission of messages by a medium other than speech or writing. One major form is *body language*, which involves body movement or the placement of the body in relation to the receiver. Much body language is subtle and automatic, communicating factors such as liking, interest, and status differences. Other forms of non-verbal communication involve office decoration, office arrangement, and the clothing worn at work.

10.5 Communication styles between men and women differ. Speaking generally, women are more inclined to ask questions, make apologies, and give compliments; men are more likely to take credit, act confident, and express opposition.

10.6 Communication across cultures can be difficult owing to obvious language differences, but also to less obvious differences in non-verbal style, social conventions, and matters of etiquette. In low-context cultures, individuals tend to interpret messages more literally than in high-context cultures, where issues surrounding a message are more critical to understanding it. When communicating cross-culturally, assume cultural differences until you know otherwise, recognize differences within cultures, and use simple language.

10.7 *Computer-mediated communication* is communication that relies on computer technology to facilitate information exchange. Examples include email, chat systems, teleconferencing, and video-conferencing. Computer-mediated communication is useful for disseminating routine messages and soliciting ideas, but richer (e.g., face to face) communication media are superior for non-routine decision tasks and messages.

10.8 Personal approaches to improving communication include taking time, being accepting of others, concentrating on the problem, saying what you feel, listening actively, and giving timely and specific feedback. Organizational approaches to improving communication include 360-degree feedback, employee surveys, suggestion and query systems, telephone hotlines, corporate intranets, webcasts, podcasts, and management training.

DISCUSSION QUESTIONS

1. Using Exhibit 10.1 as a guide, describe a communication episode that you have observed in an organization. Who were the sender and receiver? Was the episode effective? Why or why not?

2. Debate: Since more and more global business is being conducted in English, North Americans will not have cross-cultural communication problems in the future.

3. Why is computer-mediated communication attractive? What are its problems?

4. List six reasons why employees might respond with silence rather than voice to an organizational problem. Then, for each reason, explain how the organization could act to encourage voice.

5. Discuss the pros and cons of the existence of the grapevine in organizations. Suppose an organization wanted to "kill" the grapevine. How easy do you think this would be?

6. Discuss a case in which you heard one message communicated verbally and "saw" another transmitted non-verbally. What was the content of each message? Which one did you believe?

7. Under what conditions might body language or clothing have a strong communicative effect? When might the effect be weaker?

8. Debate: As more women move into management positions in organizations, the gender differences in communication between men and women will eventually disappear, and so will communication problems.

INTEGRATIVE DISCUSSION QUESTIONS

1. What role do perceptions play in gender differences in communication? Refer to the perceptual system in Chapter 3 and use its components to explain how differences in communication styles between men and women can result in misunderstandings and inaccurate perceptions. What effect might these misunderstandings and inaccurate perceptions have on gender stereotypes?

2. How does a manager's leadership style affect manager–employee communication? Refer to the theories of leadership described in Chapter 9 (e.g., ethical and authentic leadership, leadership traits, behaviours, situational theories, participative leadership, and LMX theory) and explain their implications for effective manager–employee communication.

ON-THE-JOB CHALLENGE QUESTION

Carol Bartz and Yahoo!

Carol Bartz, Yahoo's hard-driving CEO, was fired "over the telephone" in a conversation with Chairman of the Board Roy Bostock. The firing came with more than a year left on her contract, as Yahoo continued to lose ground to Google and failed to recognize the competitive threat posed by Facebook. Bartz was well known for her abrasive, confrontational communication style, and she was especially known for her extreme use of profanity. A number of observers wondered whether Bartz's salty language was an issue because she is a woman.

Was it appropriate to fire Carol Bartz via a telephone call? Why or why not? Would a profane communication style be more likely to damage the reputation of a male or female CEO, and why? Do expectations play a role?

Sources: Grinberg, E. (2011, September 12). Carol Bartz, swearing and a ------- in the workplace CNN.com.; Efrati, A. & Lublin, J.S. (2011, September 7). Yahoo ousts Bartz as CEO. wsj.com.

EXPERIENTIAL EXERCISE

Communication Technology and Media Dilemmas

The advent of various forms of advanced communication technology and associated media have benefited organizations and their employees in many ways, but they have also led to an assortment of problems and conflicts. Several themes are apparent in the scenarios presented below. For one thing, contemporary communication media have blurred the distinction between the work and nonwork domains. Second, the scenarios suggest communication contradictions—Facebook postings could be grounds for firing, but the medium can also facilitate work-related communication. Third, much contemporary communication occurs in a context in which one is not sure just who the receiver might be.

The exercise can be conducted in several ways: Students can independently prepare their reflections on the scenarios for class discussion. Alternatively, learning teams can discuss one or more scenarios and report their reflections to the class. Finally, the instructor might organize a debate around each scenario. In any case, use your imagination when reflecting on the scenarios. How would you feel if you were an employee in the scenario? How would you feel if you were a manager?

1. The American Lifeguard Association has recorded a notable increase in complaints concerning lifeguards texting on the job, and some drowning tragedies have reportedly occurred at pools where such texting occurred. Many lifeguards are students who evidently feel the need to "stay connected" when at work, even though lifeguard training specifies vigilant 10-second scanning cycles of the water. Incidents of lifeguards concealing forbidden cellphones have been reported. Of course, it can be pretty boring sitting up there in a lifeguard's chair all day! What do you think about this issue?

2. A survey of Canadian companies found that 57 percent block access to online sites for shopping. Others reported keeping tabs on the frequency of use of such sites by their employees. On one hand, it seems reasonable to insist that workers do their personal shopping on their own time. On the other hand, many people are so overwhelmed by dual career juggling, child care logistics, and taking assignments home that a few spare minutes at work might be their only opportunity to shop. What's wrong with hitting e-Bay or Amazon during your break?

3. Would you hire BlazinWeedClown@mail.com? In a study of 15 000 online job applications for distribution centre positions, 3 percent of email addresses were judged antisocial (referencing insanity, sex, drugs, or meanness; e.g., insanekid33) and 22 percent were judged otherwise unprofessional (referencing hobbies, immaturity, popular culture, nerdiness; e.g., cyborg22). The study also found that observers readily made attributions about the intelligence, professionalism, and conscientiousness of these email applicants. Such judgments could, of course, affect an applicant's chances of being hired. But should they?

4. Two employees were fired by British Columbia's West Coast Mazda for making postings on their personal Facebook pages that were critical of the company and its management. Although the general public did not have access to the postings, nearly 500 Facebook friends, including former and current West Coast employees, did so. The comments, some lewd and others hinting at workplace violence, were deemed "offensive, insulting, and disrespectful" by an arbitration board, which upheld the dismissals as indicative of insubordination. Was this just natural, private grumbling about the workplace, or was it grounds to be fired?

5. PhoneDog, a web-based company that provides news, reviews, and advice concerning mobile phones and service providers, sued a former employee for taking his 17 000 Twitter followers with him when he changed jobs. The company contended that the followers comprised a customer database and that they had invested substantial resources to leverage social media to enhance awareness of their brand. Hence, the list was their "property." Is this list of followers some proprietary trade secret, or is it list of people with too much time on their hands? And who "owns" it?

6. Atos, a European IT services firm with 74 000 employees in 42 countries, announced that it would put in place a "zero email policy" for internal communications, claiming that email contains too much (90 percent) time-wasting trivia. Instead, its CEO touted the advantages of communicating in person, by phone, by text, or via various real-time social media such as Facebook or business collaboration software. Supporters of the plan noted that younger people had already deserted email for more social media and texting. Critiques asserted that people will "waste" time communicating no matter what media or technology are used, as it's just human nature. What do you say? And is email passé for internal business communications?

7. Do U txt @ wrk? Some members of the police SWAT team in Ontario, California, did, and it got them into hot water. The officers were given department-issued pagers and were permitted to use them for personal texting if they reimbursed the department. Fed up with doing the accounting to get reimbursement, and surprised by the volume of personal texts (in a month, only 57 out of one officer's 456 texts were work-related), the department accessed the texts via the mobile carrier. They contained a good bit of sexually explicit content. The department had a formal policy to monitor emails but had not explicitly mentioned pagers. The officers and a lower level court claimed that this was a violation of privacy rights. Under appeal, the U.S. Supreme Court was unanimous that the employer was within its rights to access the texts. Many employees are issued pagers, mobile phones, and so on for the convenience of the employer. Should employees expect some privacy if they use them occasionally for personal purposes?

8. A Quebec IBM employee on long-term disability leave for major depression was surprised when the company's insurance company terminated her benefits and declared her fit to work. It appeared that their decision was partly influenced by photos on her Facebook page showing her cavorting on a beach, enjoying a birthday celebration, and visiting a male strip bar. Is it fair game to use this social media source as evidence concerning a medical claim? Did the poster use good judgment?

9. Writer Bob Green puts it succinctly: In the days before cellphones, would an employer permit an employee to install a personal phone line in the office to make personal calls at will? Certainly not, but the advent of cellphones has effectively led to an analogous situation. Green recounts a series of complaints from store managers, restaurant proprietors, and factory bosses, some of whom have instituted no-cell policies. Especially worrisome are reports of extensive cell use by hospital

staff, even in the operating room. Of course, as Green notes, some of these same employers see nothing unusual about texting or calling employees after work hours or on the weekend, expecting 24/7 responses. How big of an issue is this? Should personal cell phone use at work be prohibited or restricted in any way?

Sources: Exercise prepared by Gary Johns. (1) Tedeschi, B. (2010, September 10). Texts from lifeguard chair are raising concerns over safety. *The New York Times*, A21; (2) Simons, P. (2011, December 11). Personal browsing a workplace issue. *The Gazette* (Montreal), D20; (3) Blackhurst, E., Congemi, P., Meyer, J., & Sachau, D. (2011). Should you hire BlazinWeed-Clown@Mail.Com? *The Industrial-Organizational Psychologist, 49*(2), 27–37; (4) Ringseis, E. (2011). Careful what you write when you LOL. *The Canadian Industrial-Organizational Psychologist, 27*(2), 6–7; (5) Booth, R. (2011, December 28). Company sues ex-worker for Twitter followers. *The Globe and Mail*, B10; (6) Staff. (2011, December 16). Work: Life without email. *THE WEEK*; (7) Groscup, J. (2010, May). RU txting at wrk? *Monitor on Psychology*, 22; (8) Vicini, J. (2010, June 17). Court allows search of text messages on pager. Reuters, www.reuters.com; (9) Staff. (2009, November 21). Depressed woman loses benefits over Facebook photos. CBC News, www.cbc.ca/news; (10) Green, B. (2012, January 7). Is 2012 the year to hang up the phone? CNN opinion. CNN.com.

CASE INCIDENT

Email Madness

The email just said "Cancel it." Carol Graves couldn't believe her eyes. Carol was a marketing coordinator for Monkland Pharmaceuticals. One of her duties was to organize a professional development visiting speaker series for her marketing colleagues, mostly featuring prominent univer professors or health care professionals. Given how busy people were, it was very hard to get a commitment from speakers and to schedule the talks at times that were suitable for all. Even getting a proper room for the speakers' presentations was difficult due to competition for meeting space. The "cancel it" email had come from Carol's boss Anastasia Bulos when Carol had informed her (by email) that the monthly coordination meeting that Anastasia had just announced conflicted with one of Carol's hard-gotten scheduled speakers.

In response to the "cancel it" message, Carol had composed a heated message that accused Anastasia of undermining her, exhibiting professional disinterest, and ignoring the unit events calendar. Just before Carol was about to hit the send icon, a ping alerted her to another email from Anastasia. The sole message consisted of "☺". The "cancel it" message had been a joke! Shortly thereafter, Anastasia announced a new date for the monthly meeting that did not conflict with the planned speaker.

1. Communication problems can occur in any medium, but what particular problems with email are apparent in this incident?

2. What are some informal "rules" about using email that might avoid the problems illustrated in incidents of this nature?

CASE STUDY

Facebook (A)

Miranda Shaw was stymied. She had been on the verge of hiring a highly talented recent business school graduate, Rick Parsons, as a senior analyst for her project team. It had been a choice between Parsons and Deborah Jones, another very promising hire. Both Parsons and Jones had graduated from the same highly ranked business school that Shaw had attended, had the appropriate work backgrounds, and had performed well in their multiple rounds of interviews. From their conversations, Shaw believed either one would be a good choice for the company. While she had had a hard time deciding, she was leaning toward hiring Parsons because of his leadership skills and his reputation for tireless

energy and great communication skills. Before making her final decision, Shaw—almost in desperation, because she needed to submit her recommendation to human resources immediately—had "Googled" both of the candidates. What she had discovered about Parsons both on-line and at Facebook.com,[1] while not necessarily a deal-breaker, was disturbing enough that she had to rethink her opinion.[2]

Shaw was a manager at a leading consulting firm. She had worked her way up from intern after four years and was on the fast track to making partner. Her company was a special place and, as she had seen over the last few years, it took a special type of consultant to work there. She remembered plenty of cases where new hires had left the company in the first few months because they did not fit in with the high-energy and high-commitment work environment. She had seen several projects delayed or worse because of personnel issues. This high turnover was not good for the company because it invested significant time, energy, and funds to train and mentor new hires. Shaw believed in the adage that "you are only as good as the people who work for you," and she knew that making the right hiring decisions was critical to her success at the firm. Shaw had to take these factors into consideration as she decided between two equally qualified candidates for the position.

In her web search, Shaw was initially impressed with Parsons. He was obviously very involved in non-profit work and had won a number of community service awards. But she then discovered his Facebook page and found herself quite dismayed. There were several pictures of Parsons with his fraternity brothers; in most, they were drinking, smoking cigarettes, and—in his own words—"smokin' blunts." This term, Shaw learned after a little research, meant smoking cigars hollowed out and stuffed with marijuana.

She then turned her Google efforts to Jones. She did not discover any personal information about Jones, nor did she find Jones on Facebook. There were only work-related sites that listed Jones as an effective project member.

Shaw sighed in dismay. She had been poised, only an hour earlier, to submit her recommendation to hire Parsons. Now she was not sure what to do.

---

[1]Facebook is a social networking website; see www.facebook.com.

[2]Facebook's default privacy settings allowed users belonging to the same network to see each other's profiles, which is how Shaw had been able to access Parson's profile.

QUESTIONS

1. Discuss how the web and new media such as Facebook have (a) aided, and (b) complicated organizational communication. Be sure to consider the implications of sending a message when you do not know who the receiver might be.

2. Suppose that Miranda had just heard a rumour about Rick's activities as opposed to seeing them on Facebook. Would her reaction have been the same? Incorporate the concept of media richness in framing your answer.

3. Do the prominence of Rick on the web and the relative absence of Deborah reflect gender differences in communication?

4. What should Miranda do?

Facebook (B)

Based on her Google search and the Facebook.com photographs, Miranda Shaw concluded that Rick Parsons would not fit in with the professional work environment at the company and of the team in particular. She knew how much time and money could be wasted on hiring the wrong person. She concluded that she should offer the position to Deborah Jones.

While she was mostly proud of her resourcefulness, Shaw was a little uneasy about her decision. Although information on the internet was public and people controlled what they posted online, Shaw was not certain that it was fair to use web information in her hiring decision. After all, the candidate had not offered it willingly, and Shaw had not told Parsons or Jones that she would be researching them online. She did not, however, have either the time or resources to waste on hiring another bad fit. She was sure that most employers used Google and other internet sources in hiring, though few admitted it. Nonetheless, she was not comfortable with her research methods and wondered how long this discomfort would last.

Source: This case was prepared by Bidhan Parmar (MBA '07), Jenny Mead, Senior Ethics Research Associate, and R. Edward Freeman, Elis & Signe Olsson Professor of Business Ethics. It was written as a basis for class discussion rather than to illustrate effective or ineffective handling of an administrative situation. Copyright © 2008 by the University of Virginia Darden School Foundation, Charlottesville, VA. All rights reserved.

QUESTIONS

5. Was it ethical for Miranda to avail herself of these indirect, web-based sources of communication to find out about the job applicants?

6. If Miranda hires Deborah, should she explain to Rick the issue that damaged his chances? Why or why not?

7. If Miranda does tell Rick, how should she do so? In answering, consider the chapter sections Basic Principles of Effective Communication and Provision of Explanations.

DECISION MAKING

JPMORGAN CHASE LOSES $2 BILLION

In the years leading up to JPMorgan Chase's $2 billion trading loss [in May 2012], risk managers and some senior investment bankers raised concerns that the bank was making increasingly large investments involving complex trades that were hard to understand. But even as the size of the bets climbed steadily, these former employees say, their concerns about the dangers were ignored or dismissed. An increased appetite for such trades had the approval of the upper echelons of the bank, including Jamie Dimon, the chief executive, current and former employees said. Initially, this led to sharply higher investing profits, but they said it also contributed to the bank's lowering its guard. "There was a lopsided situation, between really risky positions and relatively weaker risk managers," said a former trader with the chief investment office, the JPMorgan unit that suffered the recent loss. Instead, the bank maintains that the losses were largely the fault of the chief investment office. Overall tolerance for risky trading did not increase, current executives said, just the scale of the office's activities because of the bank's acquisition of Washington Mutual in 2008 and its more risky credit portfolio.

Top investment bank executives raised concerns about the growing size and complexity of the bets held by the bank's chief investment office as early as 2007, according to interviews with half a dozen current and former bank officials. Within the investment office, led by Ina Drew, who resigned on Monday [May 14, 2012], the bets were directed by the head of the Europe trading desk in London, Achilles Macris.

Under Mr. Dimon's stewardship, JPMorgan Chase has long had a reputation for its strong risk-management abilities—indeed, it came through the 2008 financial crisis largely unscathed, unlike many big banks. For their part, senior bank officials on Monday disputed the assertions that the company weakened risk management in recent years while seeking higher trading profits. Risk managers were largely sidelined by Mr. Macris, who had wide latitude and also had Ms. Drew's support, with only modest interference from her. At one point, after concerns were raised about positions assembled by Bruno Iksil, now known as the London Whale, Mr. Macris brought in a risk officer with whom he had worked closely in the past. Risk officers are empowered to halt trades deemed too dangerous, so the coziness of the arrangement generated talk in New York as well, according to the former trader within the chief investment office.

Part of the breakdown in supervision, current executives said, was a fundamental disconnect between the chief investment office in London and the rest of the bank. Even within the chief investment office there were heightening concerns that the bets being made in London were

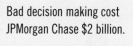

Bad decision making cost JPMorgan Chase $2 billion.

incredibly complex and not fully understood by management in New York. What is more, said another senior former executive, Mr. Dimon had other fires to put out, and the chief investment office wasn't a "problem child" for either top managers or the board of directors, despite its rapid expansion. Gigantic losses were piling up from bad mortgages, and new regulations were threatening the profitability of traditional banking, among other pressing matters. All of these factors may explain why Mr. Dimon, an executive known for his ability to sense risk who also was familiar with the minutiae of his business, failed to heed the first alarm bells that were sounded in early April [2012].

Sirens had gone off after a series of erratic trading sessions in late March resulted in big gains one day, followed by even bigger losses the next on the London trading desk of the bank's chief investment office. Mr. Dimon was convinced by Ms. Drew and her team that the turbulence was "manageable," executives said. Nor did anyone on the operating committee, of which Ms. Drew is a member, question her conclusion—in fact the full operating committee wasn't told of the scope of the problem till early last week [the week of May 7, 2012], just days before Mr. Dimon went public. The alarm bells were silenced in early April, but days after first-quarter earnings were reported on April 13, the erratic trading pattern continued, except this time there were few gains to offset the losses, and the red ink was flowing faster by the day. Mr. Dimon convened a second round of checks, which soon concluded there was a ticking time bomb, but by then it was too late, a situation made worse as traders actually increased their bets instead of shrinking them, resulting in a loss that now totals more than $2 billion and threatens a management team that until now could seemingly do no wrong.[1]

At JPMorgan Chase, how could so many people misjudge the risks and make such a series of apparently bad decisions? We will find out in this chapter. First we will define decision making and present a model of a rational decision-making process. As we work through this model, we will be especially concerned with the practical limitations of rationality. After this we will investigate the use of groups to make decisions. Finally, the chapter closes with a description of some techniques to improve decision making.

WHAT IS DECISION MAKING?

Consider the following questions that might arise in a variety of organizational settings:

- How much inventory should our store carry?
- Where should we locate the proposed community mental health centre?
- Should I remain at this job or accept another?
- How many classes of Philosophy 200 should our department offer next semester?
- Should our diplomats attend the summit conference?

Common sense tells us that someone is going to have to do some decision making to answer such questions. **Decision making** is the process of developing a commitment to some course of action.[2] Three things are noteworthy about this definition. First, decision making involves making a *choice* among several action alternatives—the store can carry more or less inventory, and the mental health centre can be located at the north or south end of town. Second, decision making is a *process* that involves more than simply the final choice among alternatives—if you decide to accept the offer of a new job, we want to know *how* this decision was reached. Finally, the "commitment" mentioned in the definition usually involves some commitment of *resources*, such as time, money, or personnel—if the store carries a large inventory, it will tie up cash.

In addition to conceiving of decision making as the commitment of resources, we can describe it as a process of problem solving.[3] A **problem** exists when a gap is perceived between some existing state and some desired state. For example, the chairperson of the Philosophy department might observe that there is a projected increase in university enrolment for the upcoming year and that his course schedule is not completed (existing state). In addition, he might wish to adequately service the new students with Philosophy 200 classes and at the same time satisfy his dean with a timely, sensible schedule (desired state). In this case, the decision-making process involves the perception of the existing state, the conception of the desired state, and the steps that the chairperson takes to move from one state to the other.

Well-Structured Problems

For a **well-structured problem**, the existing state is clear, the desired state is clear, and how to get from one state to the other is fairly obvious. Intuitively, these problems are simple, and their solutions arouse little controversy. This is because such problems are repetitive and familiar.

- Assistant bank manager—which of these 10 car loan applications should I approve?
- Welfare officer—how much assistance should this client receive?
- Courier—which delivery route should I use?

Because decision making takes time and is prone to error, organizations (and individuals) attempt to program the decision making for well-structured problems. A **program** is simply a standardized way of solving a problem. As such, programs short-circuit the decision-making process by enabling the decision maker to go directly from problem identification to solution.

Programs usually go under labels such as *rules*, *routines*, *standard operating procedures*, or *rules of thumb*. Some programs come from experience and exist only "in the head." Other programs are more formal. At UPS, drivers' routes are programmed to avoid left-hand

LO

Define *decision making* and differentiate well-structured and ill-structured problems.

 Watch

DECISION MAKING Go to MyManagementLab to watch a video about decision making.

Decision making. The process of developing a commitment to some course of action.

 Simulate

DECISION MAKING Go to MyManagementLab to complete a simulation about decision making.

Problem. A perceived gap between an existing state and a desired state.

Well-structured problem. A problem for which the existing state is clear, the desired state is clear, and how to get from one state to the other is fairly obvious.

Program. A standardized way of solving a problem.

turns so that they do not idle waiting for oncoming traffic to clear. In one year, this saved three million gallons of fuel and reduced emissions by 32 000 tonnes.[4] You are probably aware that routine loan applications are "scored" by banks according to a fixed formula that takes into account income, debt, previous credit, and so on.

Many of the problems encountered in organizations are well structured, and programmed decision making provides a useful means of solving these problems. However, programs are only as good as the decision-making process that led to the adoption of the program in the first place. In computer terminology, "garbage in" will result in "garbage out." For example, Nebraska enacted a "safe haven" law by which unwanted infants could be left at hospitals rather than abandoned. However, the law used the word "child," which resulted in a number of unruly teenagers (some from other states) being deposited at Nebraska hospitals![5]

Ill-Structured Problems

The extreme example of an **ill-structured problem** is one in which the existing and desired states are unclear and the method of getting to the desired state (even if clarified) is unknown. For example, a vice-president of marketing might have a vague feeling that the sales of a particular product are too low. However, she might lack precise information about the product's market share (existing state) and the market share of its most successful competitor (ideal state). In addition, she might be unaware of exactly how to increase the sales of this particular product.

Ill-structured problems are generally unique; that is, they are unusual and have not been encountered before. In addition, they tend to be complex and involve a high degree of uncertainty. As a result, they frequently arouse controversy and conflict among the people who are interested in the decision. For example, consider the following:

- Should we vaccinate the population against a new flu strain when the vaccination may have some bad side effects?
- Should we implement a risky attempt to rescue political hostages?
- In which part of the country should we build a new plant?

It should be obvious that ill-structured problems such as these cannot be solved with programmed decisions. Rather, the decision makers must resort to non-programmed decision making. This simply means that they are likely to try to gather more information and be more self-consciously analytical in their approach. Ill-structured problems can entail high risk and stimulate strong political considerations. There was some evidence of this in the JPMorgan Chase trading loss fiasco. We will concentrate on such ill-structured problems in this chapter.

Exhibit 11.1 presents a model of the decision process that a rational decision maker might use. When a problem is identified, a search for information is begun. This information clarifies the nature of the problem and suggests alternative solutions. These are carefully evaluated, and the best is chosen for implementation. The implemented solution is then monitored over time to ensure its immediate and continued effectiveness. If difficulties occur at any point in the process, repetition or recycling may be affected.

It might occur to you that we have not yet determined exactly what a "rational" decision maker is. Before we discuss the specific steps of the model in detail, let's contrast two forms of rationality.

THE COMPLEAT DECISION MAKER— A RATIONAL DECISION-MAKING MODEL

Perfect versus Bounded Rationality

The prototype for **perfect rationality** is the familiar Economic Person (formerly Economic Man), whom we meet in the first chapter of most introductory textbooks in economics. Economic Person is the perfect, cool, calculating decision maker. More specifically, he or she

Ill-structured problem. A problem for which the existing and desired states are unclear and the method of getting to the desired state is unknown.

LO 11.2

Compare and contrast perfectly *rational decision making* with decision making *under bounded rationality.*

Perfect rationality. A decision strategy that is completely informed, perfectly logical, and oriented toward economic gain.

EXHIBIT 11.1 The rational decision-making process.

Explore

Go to MyManagementLab to see an annotated version of this figure.

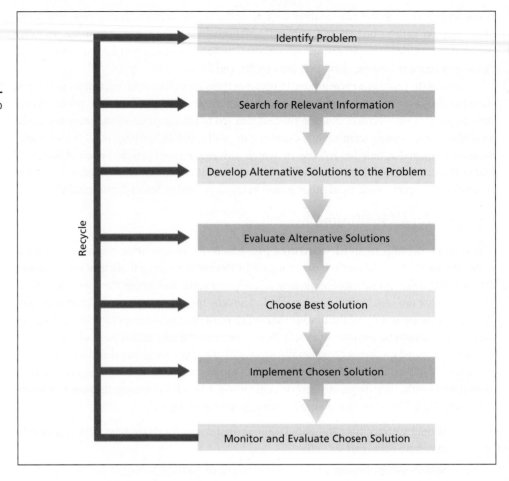

- can gather information about problems and solutions without cost and is thus completely informed;

- is perfectly logical—if solution A is preferred over solution B, and B is preferred over C, then A is necessarily preferable to C; and

- has only one criterion for decision making—economic gain.

While Economic Person is useful for theoretical purposes, the perfectly rational characteristics embodied in Economic Person do not exist in real decision makers. Nobel Prize winner Herbert Simon recognized this and suggested that managers use **bounded rationality** rather than perfect rationality.[6] That is, while they try to act rationally, they are limited in their capacity to acquire and process information. In addition, time constraints and political considerations (such as the need to please others in the organization) act as bounds to rationality.

Framing and cognitive biases both illustrate the operation of bounded rationality, as does the impact of emotions and mood on decisions. **Framing** refers to the (sometimes subtle) aspects of the presentation of information about a problem that are assumed by decision makers.[7] A frame could include assumptions about the boundaries of a problem, the possible outcomes of a decision, or the reference points used to decide if a decision is successful.[8] As we shall see, how problems and decision alternatives are framed can have a powerful impact on resulting decisions.

Cognitive biases are tendencies to acquire and process information in a particular way that is prone to error. These biases constitute assumptions and shortcuts that can improve decision-making efficiency, but they frequently lead to serious errors in judgment. We will see how they work in the following pages.

Bounded rationality.
A decision strategy that relies on limited information and that reflects time constraints and political considerations.

Framing. Aspects of the presentation of information about a problem that are assumed by decision makers.

Cognitive biases. Tendencies to acquire and process information in an error-prone way.

After we work through the rational decision-making model, we will consider how emotions and mood affect decisions.

Problem Identification and Framing

Discuss the impact of *framing* and *cognitive biases* on the decision process.

You will recall that a problem exists when a gap occurs between existing and desired conditions. Such gaps might be signalled by dissatisfied customers or vigilant employees. Similarly, the press might contain articles about legislation or ads for competing products that signal difficulties for the organization. The perfectly rational decision maker, infinitely sensitive and completely informed, should be a great problem identifier. Bounded rationality, however, can lead to the following difficulties in problem identification:[9]

- *Perceptual defence.* In Chapter 3, we pointed out that the perceptual system may act to defend the perceiver against unpleasant perceptions. For example, at JPMorgan Chase, executives might have been unconsciously motivated not to "see" signals of the trading problem.

- *Problem defined in terms of functional specialty.* Selective perception can cause decision makers to view a problem as being in the domain of their own specialty even when some other perspective might be warranted. For example, employees with a marketing background might fixate on a marketing solution to poor sales even though the problem resides in bad design.

- *Problem defined in terms of solution.* This form of jumping to conclusions effectively short-circuits the rational decision-making process. When Coca-Cola changed its time-honoured formula in 1985 to produce a "new" Coke, it appears that it prematurely defined its market share problem in terms of a particular solution—we need to change our existing product.

- *Problem diagnosed in terms of symptoms.* "What we have here is a morale problem." While this might be true, a concentration on surface symptoms will provide the decision maker with few clues about an adequate solution. The real problem here involves the cause of the morale problem. Low morale due to poor pay suggests different solutions than does low morale due to boring work.

When a problem is identified, it is necessarily framed in some way. Consider how different it is to frame a $10 000 expenditure as a cost (something to be avoided) versus an investment (something to be pursued). Or, consider how different it is to frame a new product

"IT'S BEGINNING TO SHOW SOME HUMAN CHARACTERISTICS—FAULTY REASONING, FORGETFULNESS AND REPETITION."

introduction as a military campaign against competitors versus a crusade to help customers. In each case, the facts of the matter might be the same, but the different decision frames might lead to very different decisions.

Rational decision makers should try to be very self-conscious about how they have framed problems ("We have assumed that this is a product innovation problem."). Also, they should try out alternative frames ("Let's imagine that we don't need a new product here."). Finally, decision makers should avoid overarching, universal frames (corporate culture gone wild). While it is a good idea to "put customers first," we do not want to frame every problem as a customer service problem.[10]

Information Search

As you can see in Exhibit 11.1, once a problem is identified, a search for information is instigated. This information search may clarify the nature or extent of the problem and begin to suggest alternative solutions. Again, our perfectly rational Economic Person is in good shape at this second stage of the decision-making process. He or she has free and instantaneous access to all information necessary to clarify the problem and develop alternative solutions. Bounded rationality, however, presents a different picture. The information search might be slow and costly.

TOO LITTLE INFORMATION Sometimes decision makers do not acquire enough information to make a good decision. Several cognitive biases contribute to this. For one thing, people tend to be mentally lazy and use whatever information is most readily available to them. Often, this resides in the memory, and we tend to remember *vivid recent* events.[11] Although such events might prove irrelevant in the context of the current problem, we curtail our information search and rely on familiar experience. The manager who remembers that "the last time we went to an outside supplier for parts, we got burned" may be ignoring the wisdom of contracting out a current order.

Confirmation bias. The tendency to seek out information that conforms to one's own definition of or solution to a problem.

Another cognitive bias that contributes to an incomplete information search is the well-documented tendency for people to be overconfident in their decision making.[12] This difficulty is exacerbated by **confirmation bias**, the tendency to seek out information that conforms to one's own definition of or solution to a problem. According to one expert, this ceremonial information search leads to "decision-based evidence making" rather than evidence-based decision making![13]

Critics of the U.S. invasion of Iraq cited both overconfidence and confirmation bias. Similarly, in the fatal 1986 *Challenger* space launch, only a limited range of data about the impact of temperature on mechanical failure were examined, leading to a disastrous cold weather launch choice. Another sort of inadequate information was apparent in the JPMorgan Chase loss of $2 billion. Many of the bank's derivative financial products were so mathematically complicated that executives simply did not understand how risky they were.

Information overload. The reception of more information than is necessary to make effective decisions.

TOO MUCH INFORMATION While the bounds of rationality often force us to make decisions with incomplete or imperfect information, *too much* information can also damage the quality of decisions. **Information overload** is the reception of more information than is necessary to make effective decisions. As you might guess, information overload can lead to errors, omissions, delays, and cutting corners.[14] In addition, decision makers facing overload often attempt to use all the information at hand, then get confused and permit low-quality information or irrelevant information to influence their decisions.[15] Perhaps you have experienced this when writing a term paper—trying to incorporate too many references and too many viewpoints into a short paper can lead to a confusing, low-quality end product. More is not necessarily better. The chapter-opening vignette suggests that information overload might have distracted chief executive Jaime Dimon at JPMorgan Chase from attending to the evolving trading irregularities.

Information overload can lead to errors, omissions, delays, and stress.

However, decision makers seem to *think* that more is better. Why is this so? For one thing, even if decisions do not improve with additional information, confidence in the decisions will increase.[16] Second, decision makers may fear being "kept in the dark" and associate the possession of information with power. One research review concludes that managers

- gather much information that has little decision relevance;
- use information that they collected and gathered after a decision to justify that decision;
- request information that they do not use;
- request more information, regardless of what is already available; and
- complain that there is not enough information to make a decision even though they ignore available information.[17]

Finally, information search often involves seeking advice from various parties, including trade associations, government agencies, and consultants. Research reveals that people have a cognitive bias to value advice for which they have paid over free advice of equal quality. No wonder there are so many consulting firms![18]

Alternative Development, Evaluation, and Choice

Perfectly informed or not, the decision maker can now list alternative solutions to the problem, examine the solutions, and choose the best one. For the perfectly rational, totally informed, ideal decision maker, this is easy. He or she conceives of all alternatives, knows the ultimate value of each alternative, and knows the probability that each alternative will work. In this case, the decision maker can exhibit **maximization**—that is, he or she can choose the alternative with the greatest expected value. Consider a simple example:

Maximization. The choice of the decision alternative with the greatest expected value.

	Ultimate Value	Probability	Expected Value
Alternative 1	$100 000 Profit	.4	$40 000 Profit
Alternative 2	$ 60 000 Profit	.8	$48 000 Profit

Here, the expected value of each alternative is calculated by multiplying its ultimate value by its probability. In this case, the perfectly rational decision maker would choose to implement the second alternative.

Unfortunately, things do not go so smoothly for the decision maker working under bounded rationality. He may not know all alternative solutions, and he may be ignorant of the ultimate values and probabilities of success of those solutions that he knows. Again, cognitive biases come into play. In particular, people are especially weak intuitive statisticians, and they frequently violate standard statistical principles. For example,[19]

- People avoid incorporating known existing data about the likelihood of events ("base rates") into their decisions. For instance, firms continue to launch novelty food products (e.g., foods squeezed from tubes or foods developed by celebrities) even though they have a very high failure rate in the market.

- Large samples warrant more confidence than small samples. Despite this, data from a couple of (vivid) focus groups might be given more weight than data from a large (but anonymous) national survey.

- Decision makers often overestimate the odds of complex chains of events occurring—the scenario sounds sensible despite being less likely with every added link in the chain. During the 2008–2009 economic meltdown, it was implicitly assumed that the economy would remain healthy *and* real estate prices would continue to rise *and* people would find a way to pay their escalating mortgages.

- People are poor at revising estimates of probabilities and values as they acquire additional information. A good example is the **anchoring effect**, which illustrates that decision makers do not adjust their estimates enough from some initial estimate that serves as an anchor. For example, in one study, real estate agents allowed the *asking price* of a house to unduly influence their *professional evaluation* of the house.[20]

Anchoring effect. The inadequate adjustment of subsequent estimates from an initial estimate that serves as an anchor.

It is possible to reduce some of these basic cognitive biases by making people more accountable for their decisions. This might include requiring reasoned reports, formal presentations of how the decision was reached, and so on. However, it is critical that this accountability be in place *before* a decision is reached. After-the-fact accountability often increases the probability of biases, as people try to protect their identity as good decision makers.[21] It is now clear that deregulation of the banking industry reduced accountability and contributed to the 2008–2009 economic meltdown.

The perfectly rational decision maker can evaluate alternative solutions against a single criterion—economic gain. The decision maker who is bounded by reality might have to factor in other criteria as well, such as the political acceptability of the solution to other organizational members—will the boss like it? Since these additional criteria have their own values and probabilities, the decision-making task increases in complexity.

Satisficing. Establishing an adequate level of acceptability for a solution to a problem and then screening solutions until one that exceeds this level is found.

The bottom line here is that the decision maker working under bounded rationality frequently "satisfices" rather than maximizes.[22] **Satisficing** means that the decision maker establishes an adequate level of acceptability for a solution and then screens solutions until he or she finds one that exceeds this level. When this occurs, evaluation of alternatives ceases, and the solution is chosen for implementation. For instance, the human resources manager who feels that absenteeism has become too high might choose a somewhat arbitrary acceptable level (e.g., the rate one year earlier), and then accept the first solution that seems likely to achieve this level. Few organizations seek to *maximize* attendance.

Decision expert Paul Nutt found that the search for alternatives is often very limited in strategic decision making and that firms invest very little money in exploring alternatives.[23] What this leads to is a kind of tunnel vision in which some hastily chosen option is viewed much too favourably.[24] Thus, the provision of information concerning alternatives is crucial to good decision making.[25] Successful consulting firms often fulfill this role.

Risky Business

Choosing between decision alternatives often involves an element of risk, and the research evidence on how people handle such risks is fascinating. Consider this scenario that decision researcher Max Bazerman developed. Which alternative would you choose?

> *Robert Davis, head of the legal staff of a Fortune 500 company, has delayed making one of the most critical recommendations in the organization's history. The company is faced with a class action suit from a hostile group of consumers. While the organization believes that it is innocent, it realizes that a court may not have the same perspective. The organization is expected to lose $50 million if the suit is lost in court. Davis predicts a 50 percent chance of losing the case. The organization has the option of settling out of court by paying $25 million to the "injured" parties. Davis' senior staff has been collecting information and organizing the case for over six months. It is time for action. What should Davis recommend?*

Alternative A	Settle out of court and accept a sure *loss* of $25 million,
	or
Alternative B	Go to court expecting a 50 percent probability of a $50 million loss.[26]

Notice that these two solutions are functionally equivalent in terms of dollars and cents (50 percent of $50 million = $25 million). Nonetheless, you probably tended to choose alternative B—about 80 percent of students do. Notice also that alternative B is the riskier of the two alternatives in that it exposes the firm to a *potential* for greater loss.

Now, consider two further descriptions of the alternatives. Which solution would you choose?

Alternative C	Settle out of court and *save* $25 million that could be lost in court,
	or
Alternative D	Go to court expecting a 50 percent probability of *saving* $50 million.

Again, these two solutions are functionally equivalent in monetary terms (and equivalent to options A and B). Yet, you probably chose solution C—80 percent of students do. Notice that this is the *less* risky alternative, in that the firm is not exposed to a potential $50 million loss.

This is a graphic example of the power of framing. Alternatives A and B frame the problem as a choice between losses, while C and D frame it as a choice between gains or savings. Research by Daniel Kahneman and Amos Tversky shows that when people view a problem as a choice between losses, they tend to make risky decisions, rolling the dice in the face of a sure loss. When people frame the alternatives as a choice between gains they tend to make conservative decisions, protecting the sure win.[27] It is very important to be aware of what reference point you are using when you frame decision alternatives. It is not necessarily wrong to frame a problem as a choice between losses, but this can contribute to a foolish level of risk taking.

We should emphasize that learning history can modify these general preferences for or against risk.[28] For example, suppose that a firm has become very successful by virtue of a series of risky decisions and is now faced with sitting on a handsome market share or investing in a product that could boost its share even higher. This win-win scenario would normally provoke conservatism, but the firm's historical success may tempt managers to choose the risky course of action and invest in the new product.

Solution Implementation

When a decision is made to choose a particular solution to a problem, the solution must be implemented. The perfectly rational decision maker will have factored any possible implementation problems in to his or her choice of solutions. Of course, the bounded decision maker will attempt to do the same when estimating probabilities of success. However, in organizations, decision makers are often dependent on others to implement their decisions, and it might be difficult to anticipate their ability or motivation to do so.

A good example of implementation problems occurs when products such as cars are designed, engineered, and produced in a lengthy series of stages. For example, engineering might have to implement decisions made by designers, and production planning might have to implement decisions made by engineering. As we noted in Chapter 7, this sequential process frequently leads to confusion, conflict, and delay unless cross-functional teams are used during the decision-making process. When they work well, such teams are sensitive to implementation problems.

LO 11.4

Explain the process of *escalation of commitment* to an apparently failing course of action.

Solution Evaluation

When the time comes to evaluate the implemented solution, the decision maker is effectively examining the possibility that a new problem has occurred: Does the (new) existing state match the desired state? Has the decision been effective? For all the reasons we stated previously, the perfectly rational decision maker should be able to evaluate the effectiveness of the decision with calm, objective detachment. Again, however, the bounded decision maker might encounter problems at this stage of the process.

JUSTIFICATION   As we said earlier, people tend to be overconfident about the adequacy of their decisions. Thus, substantial dissonance can be aroused when a decision turns out to be faulty. One way to prevent such dissonance is to avoid careful tests of the adequacy of the decision. As a result, many organizations are notoriously lax when it comes to evaluating the effectiveness of expensive training programs or advertising campaigns. If the bad news cannot be avoided, the erring decision maker may devote his or her energy to trying to justify the faulty decision.

Sunk costs. Permanent losses of resources incurred as the result of a decision.

Escalation of commitment. The tendency to invest additional resources in an apparently failing course of action.

The justification of faulty decisions is best seen in the irrational treatment of sunk costs. **Sunk costs** are permanent losses of resources incurred as the result of a decision.[29] The key word here is *permanent*. Since these resources have been lost (sunk) due to a past decision, they should not enter into future decisions. Psychologist Barry Staw has studied how, despite this, people often "throw good resources after bad," acting as if they can recoup sunk costs. This process is **escalation of commitment** to an apparently failing course of action, in which the escalation involves devoting more and more resources to actions implied by the decision.[30] For example, suppose an executive authorizes the purchase of several new machines to improve plant productivity. The machines turn out to be very unreliable, and they are frequently out of commission for repairs. Perfect rationality suggests admitting to a mistake here. However, the executive might authorize an order for more machines from the same manufacturer to "prove" that he was right all along, hoping to recoup sunk costs with improved productivity from an even greater number of machines. As indicated in the final paragraph of the chapter-opening vignette, escalation seems to have contributed to the JPMorgan Chase trading loss.

Dissonance reduction is not the only reason that escalation of commitment to a faulty decision may occur. A social norm that favours *consistent* behaviour by managers may also be at work.[31] Changing one's mind and reversing previous decisions might be perceived as a sign of weakness, a fate to be avoided at all costs.

Escalation of commitment sometimes happens even when the current decision maker is not responsible for previous sunk costs. For example, politicians might continue an expensive, unnecessary public works project that was begun by a previous political administration. Here, dissonance reduction and the appearance of consistency are irrelevant, suggesting some other causes of escalation. For one thing, decision makers might be motivated to not appear wasteful.[32] ("Even though the airport construction is way over budget and flight traffic doesn't justify a new airport, let's finish the thing. Otherwise, the taxpayers will think we've squandered their money.") Also, escalation of commitment might be due to the way in which decision makers frame the problem once some resources have been sunk. Rather than seeing the savings involved in reversing the decision, they may frame the problem as a decision between a sure loss of x dollars (which have been sunk) and an uncertain loss of $x + y$ dollars (maybe the additional investment will succeed). As we noted earlier, when problems are framed this way, people tend to avoid the certain loss and go with the riskier choice, which in this case is escalation.[33] In addition to these situational causes, personality, moods, and emotions can affect escalation. For instance, people high on neuroticism and negative affectivity (Chapter 2) are *less* likely to escalate since they try to avoid stressful predicaments.[34]

Escalation can occur in both competitive and non-competitive situations. A non-competitive example can be seen in the overvaluation of stocks by Wall Street analysts in advance of a market crash. Competitive, auction-like situations seem especially likely to prompt escalation because they often involve time pressure, rivalry, interested audiences, and the desire to be the first mover. These factors contribute to emotional arousal (see below) and stimulate escalation.[35] The Vietnam and Iraq wars have been cited as prime examples of competitive escalation.

Are there any ways to prevent the tendency to escalate commitment to a failing course of action? Logic and research suggest the following:[36]

- Encourage continuous experimentation with reframing the problem to avoid the decision trap of feeling that more resources *have* to be invested. Shift the frame to saving rather than spending.

- Set specific goals for the project in advance that must be met if more resources are to be invested. This prevents escalation when early results are "unclear."

- Place more emphasis when evaluating managers on *how* they made decisions and less on decision outcomes. This kind of accountability is the sensible way to teach managers not to fear or hide failure.

- Separate initial and subsequent decision making so that individuals who make the initial decision to embark on a course of action are assisted or replaced by others who decide if a course of action should be continued. Banks often do this when trying to decide what to do about problem loans. However, at JPMorgan Chase, risk managers failed to flag problematic trading.

It may be tempting to think that using groups to make decisions will reduce the tendency toward escalation. However, groups are *more* prone than individuals to escalate commitment.[37]

For a particularly dark example of non-competitive escalation, see the Ethical Focus: *Rogue Traders Get Trapped in Escalation*. It illustrates how more and more resources are dedicated to trying to turn around a flawed investment strategy.

HINDSIGHT The careful evaluation of decisions is also inhibited by faulty hindsight. **Hindsight** refers to the tendency to review the decision-making process that was used to find out what was done right (in the case of success) or wrong (in the case of failure). While hindsight can prove useful, it often reflects a cognitive bias.

Hindsight. The tendency to review the decision-making process to find what was done right or wrong.

ETHICAL FOCUS

ROGUE TRADERS GET TRAPPED IN ESCALATION

Backed by the wealth of large investment companies, traders deal in financial instruments on their employers' behalf. Over the years, a number of traders have gone "rogue," losing tonnes of money and repeatedly covering up the fact, trying to recoup their losses and refusing to accept sunk costs.

One of the most notorious rogue traders is Jérôme Kerviel, who was charged in 2008 for losing five billion euros trading on behalf of France's Société Générale. Kerviel was accused of fraudulent activity because he knowingly broke company policies in an effort to create an exorbitant amount of wealth.

Not all rogue traders, however, appear to be motivated by personal gain. Take, for example, John Rusnak, who lost US$691 million at Allfirst Bank. Unlike some rogue traders, Rusnak was considered to be an introverted family man. According to court documents, he received a modest salary of $108 000 and a bonus of $78 000 in 2001. When Rusnak was arrested in 2002, he appeared to be less of an intentional fraud and more of a cover-up artist, a term used by consultant Hugo Pound for traders who make risky, high-return investments in an effort to recoup earlier losses. Apparently Rusnak's trouble began in 1997, when he lost a large amount of money in a questionable trading strategy. Instead of admitting failure to the bank, because he had positioned himself as a savvy trader, Rusnak sold

fictitious options, which generated fictitious returns. He then invested heavily in real options, hoping to recover his losses. Over a four-year period, Rusnak repeatedly threw good company money after his bad investments, digging himself deeper and deeper into a hole.

Rusnak's behaviour, as with other cover-up artists, is a clear example of escalation of commitment. In this case, Rusnak could not accept his original losses and write them off as sunk costs. Although he likely knew that the facade would one day come undone, he continued along the destructive path in order to please his employer and save face. As explained by Nick Leeson, another infamous cover-up artist, "For the trader, it feels like being carried away by a hot-air balloon; if you don't jump off immediately, you can't jump off at all." In 2009, John Rusnak was released on parole before the end of his seven-and-a-half-year jail term. Although he legally owes $691 million, it is not clear how much he will actually be able to pay back.

Sources: Anonymous. (2009, January 29). Rogue trader Rusnak released from prison. *Toronto Star*, B2; DiBiagio, T.M. (2002). *Indictment of United States of America versus John M. Rusnak*. The United States District Court for the District of Maryland, www.usdoj.gov/; Leith, W. (2002, October 26). How to lose a billion. *Guardian* (online), www.guardian.co.uk (quote); Lichfield, J. (2009, January 23). Jérôme Kerviel: Secrets of the rogue trader. *The Independent* (online), www.independent.co.uk; McNee, A. (2002). Allied Irish banks case study. *eRisk*, www.erisk.com; Pignal, S. (2009, January 24). They bet the bank. *Financial Times*, 24; Barry Staw, personal communication (2009, July 31).

The classic example of hindsight involves the armchair quarterback who "knew" that a chancy intercepted pass in the first quarter was unnecessary because the team won the game anyway! The armchair critic is exhibiting the knew-it-all-along effect. This is the tendency to assume, after the fact, that we knew all along what the outcome of a decision would be. In effect, our faulty memory adjusts the probabilities that we estimated before making the decision to correspond to what actually happened.[38] This can prove quite dangerous. The money manager who consciously makes a very risky investment that turns out to be successful might revise her memory to assume that the decision was a sure thing. The next time, the now-confident investor might not be so lucky!

Another form of faulty hindsight is the tendency to take personal responsibility for successful decision outcomes while denying responsibility for unsuccessful outcomes.[39] Thus, when things work out well, it is because *we* made a careful, logical decision. When things go poorly, some unexpected *external* factor messed up our sensible decision!

LO **11.5**

Consider how emotions and mood affect decision making.

How Emotion and Mood Affect Decision Making

Thus far we have discussed decision making from a mainly cognitive perspective, focusing on the rational decision-making model and illustrating the limits to rationality. However, our coverage of decision justification and hindsight suggests a considerable emotional component to many organizational decisions—people do not like to be wrong, and they often become emotionally attached to the failing course of action that signals escalation of commitment.

Decision makers in a good mood can overestimate the likelihood of good events and use shortcut decision strategies.

At the outset, it should be emphasized that emotionless decision making would be poor decision making, and the rational model is not meant to suggest otherwise. Some of the most graphic evidence for this comes from unfortunate cases in which people suffer brain injuries that blunt their emotions while leaving their intellectual functions intact. Such individuals often proceed to make a series of poor life decisions because they are unable to properly evaluate the impact of these decisions on themselves and others; they have no feeling.[40] One can imagine the negative consequences if NASA's manned spacecraft were designed by emotionless rather than caring engineers. In fact, during the 2005 *Discovery* mission, it was suggested that some of the caution-focused decisions, such as the delay in landing and decision to set down in California, were made by mission control personnel still suffering emotional effects of the 2003 *Columbia* tragedy. Strong emotions frequently figure in the decision-making process that corrects ethical errors (Chapter 12), and so-called whistle-blowers often report that they were motivated by emotion to protest decision errors. Strong (positive) emotion has also been implicated in creative decision making and the proper use of intuition to solve problems. Such intuition (Chapter 1) can lead to the successful short-circuiting of the steps in the rational model when speed is of the essence.

Despite these examples of how emotion can help decision making, there are many cases in which strong emotions are a hindrance. The folk saying "blinded by emotion" has some truth to it, as people experiencing strong emotions are often self-focused and distracted from the actual demands of the problem at hand. Most of our information about the impact of emotions on decisions is anecdotal, because people are often reluctant to participate in field research about emotional issues and because it is not ethical to invoke strong emotions in lab research. One clever field study did document how excessive pride led highly paid CEOs to pay too much for firms they were acquiring.[41] Other business-press evidence implicates angry CEOs losing their heads in competitive bidding for acquisitions (escalation of commitment). A common theme over the years has been how excessive emotional conflict between business partners or family business members provokes questionable business decisions.

In contrast to the case for strong emotions, there is much research on the impact of mood on decision making. You will recall from Chapter 4 that moods are relatively mild, unfocused states of positive or negative feeling. The research on mood and decision making reveals some very interesting paradoxes. For one thing, mood is a pretty low-key state, and you might be inclined to think it would not have much impact on decisions. In fact, there is plenty of evidence that mood affects *what* and *how* people think when making decisions. Also, you might imagine that the impact of mood would be restricted to mundane, structured decision problems. In fact, mood has its greatest impact on uncertain, ambiguous decisions of the type that are especially crucial for organizations. Here is what the research reveals:[42]

- People in a positive mood tend to remember positive information. Those in a negative mood remember negative information.

- People in a positive mood tend to evaluate objects, people, and events more positively. Those in a negative mood provide more negative evaluations.

- People in a good mood tend to overestimate the likelihood that good events will occur and underestimate the occurrence of bad events. People in a bad mood do the opposite.

- People in a good mood adopt simplified, shortcut decision-making strategies, more likely violating the rational model. People in a negative mood are prone to approach decisions in a more deliberate, systematic, detailed way.

- Positive mood promotes more creative, intuitive decision making.

As you can see, it makes perfect sense to hope for your job interview to be conducted by a person in a good mood or to try to create a good mood on the part of your clients! Notice that the impact of mood on decision making is not necessarily dysfunctional. If the excesses of optimism can be controlled, those in a good mood can make creative decisions. If the excesses of pessimism can be controlled, those in a negative mood can actually process information more carefully and effectively. In a very interesting simulation of foreign currency trading, it was found that traders in a good mood performed more poorly (by losing money) than those in bad or neutral moods. Those in a bad mood performed better, but were rather conservative. Traders in a neutral mood did best, tolerating risk but not being overconfident.[43] Thus, the investment practitioners' advice to remain calm during turbulent markets has some validity.

A fine example of how mood and emotion can lead to faulty decision making can be seen in the "dot.com meltdown" that began in the late 1990s. In this era, hundreds of firms were formed to exploit the potential wealth of e-commerce. An economic boom, ready capital, advancing technology, and the model of a few overnight "internet millionaires" created a positive mood that led to overly intuitive decisions, false creativity, and exaggerated optimism. Mood is contagious, and many start-up firms, fearing to be left behind, were founded with vague goals and vaguer business plans. Many consisted of little more than a website, and "hits" were confused with cash flow. The ensuing crash left the firms founded on careful business decision–making principles to enjoy the spoils of the technology revolution. It was exactly this kind of giddy emotion, fuelled by big bonuses, that led Wall Street executives to ignore the subprime mortgage meltdown that occurred in 2008–2009.

Before continuing, check out You Be the Manager: *Preventing Surgical Decision Errors at Toronto General Hospital.*

Rational Decision Making—A Summary

The rational decision-making model in Exhibit 11.1 provides a good guide for how many decisions *should* be made but offers only a partially accurate view of how they *are* made. For complex, unfamiliar decisions, such as choosing an occupation, the rational model provides a pretty good picture of how people actually make decisions.[44] Also, organizational decision makers often follow the rational model when they agree about the goals they are pursuing.[45] On the other hand, there is plenty of case study evidence of short-circuiting the rational model

YOU BE THE MANAGER

Preventing Surgical Decision Errors at Toronto General Hospital

Every year, between 9000 and 23 000 people die in Canadian hospitals due to surgical errors. Although many preventable deaths occur during an operation, some of them also stem from pre-op or post-op errors. Surgical operations are done by some of the most highly trained professionals, yet still mistakes are made in this emotion-laden environment.

Toronto General Hospital and its two sister hospitals, Toronto Western and Princess Margaret, form the University Health Network (UHN). These hospitals, like all other hospitals in the country, sometimes fall victim to human error. Considering that the complication rate in higher-income area hospitals is approximately 10.3 percent, more than 2000 of the UHN's 23 000 annual surgical patients may suffer from preventable complications.

"[Surgery] is one of the areas where we have tremendous skills and resources," says Dr. Ross Baker, a health policy professor at the University of Toronto. "And then we go in and somebody forgets to do something they should do as a matter of course, and the outcome is an infection or complication of some sort."

For years, medical researchers have sought ways to reduce errors that occur in the operating room, not only to save lives but also to save money. Prevention requires an understanding of possible negative events and their associated causes. Once the scenarios have been identified, a set of procedures can be created to help prevent them from occurring. Also at issue is establishing means to manage any negative events that do occur to avoid adverse complications. Both approaches come with challenges. First, it may be difficult to predict potential problems because hospital staff and procedures are constantly changing. Second, errors may not always be identified in real time.

One might wonder why a highly professional team of doctors and nurses would fail to identify or respond to a potentially deadly error, especially when they have the collective technical knowledge to identify such errors. The problem, it seems, is not so much related to knowledge; rather, it often stems from the complex professional relationships that exist between doctors and nurses, and between the surgical leader and the rest of the team. Like a pilot in command of a plane, the lead surgeon carries significant responsibility and authority. Team members often feel threatened about speaking up, even if they believe that a problem exists.

In surgical teams, members often find it difficult to speak up, even if they believe that a problem exists.

Eliminating preventable complications, therefore, requires both systemic and behavioural changes.

Dr. Bryce Taylor, UHN's surgeon in chief, takes the problem very seriously: "With approximately 234 million surgeries performed each year worldwide, we owe it to our patients to look at every opportunity to prevent complications during and after surgery."

Questions

1. Is there a programmed decision-making process that would support the prevention and correction of surgical errors?

2. What role may emotions play in the decision behaviour of operating room personnel?

To find out what happened at Toronto General, see The Manager's Notebook at the end of the chapter.

Sources: Blackwell, T. (2009, January 15). Checklists cut surgical mistakes by a third. *National Post*, A1, A5 (Baker quote); Blatt, R., Christianson, M.K., & Sutcliffe, K.M. (2006). A sensemaking lens on reliability. *Journal of Organizational Behavior, 27*, 491–515; Haynes, A.B., Weiser, T.G., Berry, W.R., Lipsitz, S.R., Breizat, A-H.S., Dellinger, et al. (2009). A surgical safety checklist to reduce morbidity and mortality in a global population. *New England Journal of Medicine, 360*, 491–499; Nembhardi, I.M., & Edmondson, A.C. (2006). Making it safe: The effects of leader inclusiveness and professional status on psychological safety and improvement efforts in health care teams. *Journal of Organizational Behavior, 27*, 941–966; Priest, L. (2009, January 15). Simple checklist saves lives in the operating room, study finds. *Globe and Mail*, A4; Anonymous (2009, January 14). Results show surgical safety checklist drops deaths and complications by more than one third, University Health Network, www.uhn.com (Taylor quote).

EXHIBIT 11.2
Perfectly rational decision making contrasted with bounded rationality.

Explore

Go to MyManagementLab to see an annotated version of this figure.

Stage	Perfect Rationality	Bounded Rationality
Problem Identification	Easy, accurate perception of gaps that constitute problems	Perceptual defence; jump to solutions; attention to symptoms rather than problems; mood affects memory
Information Search	Free; fast; right amount obtained	Slow; costly; reliance on flawed memory; obtain too little or too much
Development of Alternative Solutions	Can conceive of all	Not all known
Evaluation of Alternative Solutions	Ultimate value of each known; probability of each known; only criterion is economic gain	Potential ignorance of or miscalculation of values and probabilities; criteria include political factors; affected by mood
Solution Choice	Maximizes	Satisfices
Solution Implementation	Considered in evaluation of alternatives	May be difficult owing to reliance on others
Solution Evaluation	Objective, according to previous steps	May involve justification, escalation to recover sunk costs, faulty hindsight

in organizational decisions, in part because of the biases we discussed above.[46] A study of 356 decisions in medium to large organizations found that half of them failed. These failures were found to be primarily due to the use of poor tactics on the part of managers who impose solutions, limit the search for alternatives, and use power to implement their plans.[47] However, true experts in a field will often short-circuit the rational model, using their intuitive knowledge base stored in memory to skip steps logically.[48] Exhibit 11.2 summarizes the operation of perfect and bounded rationality at each stage of the decision process. Exhibit 11.3 summarizes the various cognitive biases that we have covered.

LO 11.6

Summarize the pros and cons of using groups to make decisions, with attention to the *groupthink* phenomenon and risk assessment.

GROUP DECISION MAKING

Many, many organizational decisions are made by groups rather than individuals, especially when problems are ill structured. In this section, we consider the advantages and problems of group decision making.

EXHIBIT 11.3
Summary of cognitive biases in decision making.

Explore

Go to MyManagementLab to see an annotated version of this figure.

- Decision makers tend to be overconfident about the decisions that they make.
- Decision makers tend to seek out information that confirms their own problem definitions and solutions. (Confirmation bias)
- Decision makers tend to remember and incorporate vivid, recent events into their decisions.
- Decision makers fail to incorporate known existing data about the likelihood of events into their decisions.
- Decision makers ignore sample sizes when evaluating samples of information.
- Decision makers overestimate the odds of complex chains of events occurring.
- Decision makers do not adjust estimates enough from some initial estimate that serves as an anchor as they acquire more information. (Anchoring effect)
- Decision makers have difficulty ignoring sunk costs when making subsequent decisions.
- Decision makers overestimate their ability to have predicted events after-the-fact, take responsibility for successful decision outcomes, and deny responsibility for unsuccessful outcomes. (Hindsight)

Why Use Groups?

There are a number of reasons for employing groups to make organizational decisions.

DECISION QUALITY Experts often argue that groups or teams can make higher-quality decisions than individuals. This argument is based on the following three assumptions:

- Groups are *more vigilant* than individuals are—more people are scanning the environment.
- Groups can *generate more ideas* than individuals can.
- Groups can *evaluate ideas better* than individuals can.

At the problem identification and information search stages, vigilance is especially advantageous. For example, a member of the board of directors might notice a short article in an obscure business publication that has great relevance for the firm. In searching for information to clarify the problem suggested in the article, other members of the board might possess unique information that proves useful.

When it comes to developing alternative solutions, more people should literally have more ideas, if only because someone remembers something that others have forgotten. In addition, members with different backgrounds and experiences may bring different perspectives to the problem. This is why undergraduate students, graduate students, faculty, and administrators are often included on university task forces to improve the library or course evaluation system.

When it comes to evaluating solutions and choosing the best one, groups have the advantage of checks and balances—that is, an extreme position or incorrect notion held by one member should be offset by the pooled judgments of the rest of the group.

These characteristics suggest that groups *should* make higher-quality decisions than individuals can. Shortly, we will find out whether they actually do.

DECISION ACCEPTANCE AND COMMITMENT As we pointed out in our discussion of participative leadership in Chapter 9, groups are often used to make decisions on the premise that a decision made in this way will be more acceptable to those involved. Again, there are several assumptions underlying this premise:

- People wish to be involved in decisions that will affect them.
- People will better understand a decision in which they participated.
- People will be more committed to a decision in which they invested personal time and energy.

The acceptability of group decisions is especially useful in dealing with a problem described earlier—getting the decision implemented. If decision makers truly understand the decision and feel committed to it, they should be willing to follow through and see that it is carried out.

DIFFUSION OF RESPONSIBILITY High quality and acceptance are sensible reasons for using groups to make decisions. A less admirable reason to employ groups is to allow for **diffusion of responsibility** across the members in case the decision turns out poorly. In this case, each member of the group will share part of the burden of the negative consequences, and no one person will be singled out for punishment. Of course, when this happens, individual group members often "abandon ship" and exhibit biased hindsight—"I knew all along that the bid was too high to be accepted, but they made me go along with them."

Diffusion of responsibility. The ability of group members to share the burden of the negative consequences of a poor decision.

Do Groups Actually Make Higher-Quality Decisions than Individuals?

Is the frequent use of groups to make decisions warranted by evidence? The answer is yes. One review concludes that "groups usually produce more and better solutions to problems than do individuals working alone."[49] Another concludes that group performance is superior to that of the average individual in the group.[50] More specifically, groups should perform better than individuals when

- the group members differ in relevant skills and abilities, as long as they do not differ so much that conflict occurs;
- some division of labour can occur;
- memory for facts is an important issue; and
- individual judgments can be combined by weighting them to reflect the expertise of the various members.[51]

To consolidate your understanding of these conditions, consider a situation that should favour group decision making: A small construction company wishes to bid on a contract to build an apartment complex. The president, the controller, a construction boss, and an engineer work together to formulate the bid. Since they have diverse backgrounds and skills, they divide the task initially. The president reviews recent bids on similar projects in the community; the controller gets estimates on materials costs; the engineer and construction boss review the blueprints. During this process, each racks his or her brain to recall lessons learned from making previous bids. Finally, they put their information together, and each member voices an opinion about what the bid should be. The president decides to average these opinions to arrive at the actual bid, since each person is equally expert in his or her own area.

Equal weighting of opinions and averaging is inappropriate when some group members have more expertise concerning a particular problem, and it is critical for decision success that such expertise is recognized by the group. However, if several group members share the same view about a problem, this shared view can prevail in spite of the knowledge held by a single expert.[52] Extensive discussion of the problem is one way that accurate but minority viewpoints can positively influence decisions.[53]

Disadvantages of Group Decision Making

Although groups have the ability to develop high-quality, acceptable decisions, there are a number of potential disadvantages to group decision making.

TIME   Groups seldom work quickly or efficiently compared with individuals. This is because of the process losses (Chapter 7) involved in discussion, debate, and coordination. The time problem increases with group size. When the speed of arriving at a solution to a problem is a prime factor, organizations should avoid using groups.

CONFLICT   Participants in group decisions may have their own personal axes to grind or their own resources to protect. When this occurs, decision quality may take a back seat to political wrangling and infighting. In the example about the construction company we presented earlier, the construction boss might see it to his advantage to overestimate the size of the crew required to build the apartments. On the other hand, the controller might make it her personal crusade to pare labour costs. A simple compromise between these two extreme points of view might not result in the highest quality or most creative decision. In general, groups will make better decisions when their members feel psychologically safe.

DOMINATION The advantages of group decision making will seldom be realized if meetings are dominated by a single individual or a small coalition. Even if a dominant person has good information, this style is not likely to lead to group acceptance and commitment. If the dominant person is particularly misinformed, the group decision is very likely to be ineffective.

GROUPTHINK Have you ever been involved in a group decision that you knew was a "loser" but that you felt unable to protest? Perhaps you thought you were the only one who had doubts about the chosen course of action. Perhaps you tried to speak up, but others criticized you for not being on the team. Maybe you found yourself searching for information to confirm that the decision was correct and ignoring evidence that the decision was bad. What was happening? Were you suffering from some strange form of possession? Mind control?

In Chapter 8, we discussed the process of conformity, which can have a strong influence on the decisions that groups make. The most extreme influence is seen when **groupthink** occurs. This happens when group pressures lead to reduced mental efficiency, poor testing of reality, and lax moral judgment.[54] In effect, unanimous acceptance of decisions is stressed over quality of decisions.

Psychologist Irving Janis, who developed the groupthink concept, felt that high group cohesiveness was at its root. It now appears that other factors are more important.[55] These include strong identification with the group, concern for their approval, and the isolation of the group from other sources of information. However, the promotion of a particular decision by the group leader appears to be the strongest cause.[56] Janis provides a detailed list of groupthink symptoms:

Groupthink. The capacity for group pressure to damage the mental efficiency, reality testing, and moral judgment of decision-making groups.

- *Illusion of invulnerability.* Members are overconfident and willing to assume great risks. They ignore obvious danger signals.

- *Rationalization.* Problems and counter-arguments that members cannot ignore are "rationalized away." That is, seemingly logical but improbable excuses are given.

- *Illusion of morality.* The decisions the group adopts are not only perceived as sensible, they are also perceived as *morally* correct.

- *Stereotypes of outsiders.* The group constructs unfavourable stereotypes of those outside the group who are the targets of their decisions.

- *Pressure for conformity.* Members pressure each other to fall in line and conform with the group's views.

- *Self-censorship.* Members convince themselves to avoid voicing opinions contrary to the group.

- *Illusion of unanimity.* Members perceive that unanimous support exists for their chosen course of action.

- *Mindguards.* Some group members may adopt the role of "protecting" the group from information that goes against its decisions.[57]

Obviously, victims of groupthink are operating in an atmosphere of unreality that should lead to low-quality decisions. We can see this in the decision-making process concerning NASA's Hubble Space Telescope in the 1990s, where an aberration in the telescope's primary mirror was the source of astronomical repair costs.[58] To begin with, a dominant leader in charge of the internal mirror tests appears to have isolated the mirror project team from outside sources of information. Symptoms of groupthink followed: At least three sets of danger signals that the mirror was flawed were ignored or explained away (illusion of invulnerability and rationalization); an outside firm, Kodak, was dismissed as too incompetent to test the mirror (stereotype of outsiders); the consultant who suggested that Kodak test the mirror received bitter criticism but still felt he did not protest enough in the end (mind-guarding and self-censorship); and the defence of the isolated working methods was viewed as more "theological" than technical (illusion of morality).

APPLIED FOCUS

Decision Making at RIM

On January 22, 2012, Research in Motion (RIM) announced that its co-CEOs and co-chairmen of the board, Mike Lazaridis and Jim Balsillie, were stepping down. The two, who created a company that revolutionized mobile communication by practically inventing mobile email and thus defining the smartphone as we know it, left behind a different RIM from the one that dominated the smartphone industry only a few years earlier. In a relatively short time, RIM witnessed the loss of much of its share value, dwindling subscriber growth, and major layoffs.

In an open letter written after RIM issued a profit warning, industry analyst Sameet Kanade questioned RIM's decision making, blaming the dual CEO structure for the company's poor performance. In fact, RIM grew so fast that management structures well suited to the early start-up firm now slowed decision making in a fast evolving, innovation-based industry. Although Lazaridis and Balsillie always dominated the decisions made by RIM's board, they also had a preference for securing board consensus. This approach, which took time, diluted accountability and motivated senior executives to go along with whatever the pair decided, or else nothing would move along. The effect was failure to recognize imminent competitive threats and a lag in response time, as seen in RIM's failure to capitalize on the expressed need of its corporate customers for upscaling the Black-Berry years before Apple introduced its iPad. In 2007, Lazaridis commented to the *Guardian* on the release of Apple's iPhone, saying "How much presence does Apple have in business? It's vanishingly small." An engineer, he only seemed to focus on the short battery life of the iPhone and BlackBerry's superior security protocols. This narrow view prevented RIM from identifying the shift in the market toward general consumer products that provide a superior media consumption experience. Smartphones were becoming less and less about secure business communication, and RIM was trailing in the application race.

The sense of invulnerability nurtured by early successes led RIM to announce unrealistic deadlines that either resulted in delays, as in the case of the BlackBerry 10, or the release of products noted for deficiencies (e.g., no email), as in the case of the PlayBook. The latter lacked many features until proper software updates became available. Another problem was including the Bridge application in PlayBook, allowing BlackBerry users to access the internet without buying a separate data plan. The potential loss of revenue was not well received by the carriers, which had been the firm's faithful allies, and three major carriers did not support the PlayBook on its launch. Despite negative market feedback, RIM remained committed to it, and both CEOs expressed confidence in the product. However, the numbers were less optimistic with PlayBook making up just 1.1 percent of the tablet market at the beginning of 2012, even after sharp price discounts.

An impediment to effective decision making at RIM was the strongly held custom of promoting from within rather than seeking outside talent. Although internal recruiting has some advantages, it also limited RIM's access to crucial information about what was going on in the industry and bred insular thinking. Attracting new blood from Google or Apple would have given RIM valuable insight into the industry and provided a new cache of ideas.

A few years ago, calls for the sale or break up of RIM would have been considered absurd. Whether RIM turns the tide is yet to be seen, but what is certain is that the best decision the company can make at this stage is to change the way it makes its decisions.

Sources: Castaldo, J. (2011, June 17). Does RIM need a new CEO? *Canadian-Business*, www.canadianbusiness.com/blog/business_briefings/30381-does-rim-need-a-new-ceo; Castaldo, J. (2012, January 19). How management has failed at RIM. *CanadianBusiness*, www.canadianbusiness.com/article/66599-how-management-has-failed-at-rim; Castaldo, J. (2012, March 30). New CEO charts different course for RIM. *CanadianBusiness*, www.canadianbusiness.com/article/77636-new-ceo-charts-different-course-for-rim; Martinson, J. (2007, March 2). Mr BlackBerry—$2bn geek who started with Lego. *The Guardian*, www.guardian.co.uk/business/2007/mar/02/12.

What can prevent groupthink? Leaders must be careful to avoid exerting undue pressure for a particular decision outcome and concentrate on good decision processes. Also, leaders should establish norms that encourage and even reward responsible dissent, and outside experts should be brought in from time to time to challenge the group's views.[59] Some of the decision-making techniques we discuss later in the chapter should help prevent the tendency as well.

Before continuing, consider the Applied Focus: *Decision Making at RIM.*

How Do Groups Handle Risk?

Almost by definition, problems that are suitable for group decision making involve some degree of risk and uncertainty. This raises a very important question: Do groups make decisions that are more or less risky than those of individuals? Or will the degree of risk assumed by the group simply equal the average risk preferred by its individual members? Consider the following scenario:

> *An accident has just occurred at a nuclear power plant. Several corrections exist, ranging from expensive and safe to low-cost but risky. On the way to an emergency meeting, each nuclear engineer formulates an opinion about what should be done. But what will the group decide?*

Conventional wisdom provides few clear predictions about what the group of engineers will decide to do. It is sometimes argued that groups will make riskier decisions than individuals because there is security in numbers—that is, diffusion of responsibility for a bad decision encourages the group to take greater chances. On the other hand, it is often argued that groups are cautious, with the members checking and balancing each other so much that a conservative outcome is sure to occur. Just contrast the committee-laden civil service with the swashbuckling style of independent operators such as Ted Turner and Donald Trump!

Given this contradiction of common sense, the history of research into group decision making and risk is instructive. A Massachusetts Institute of Technology student, J.A.F. Stoner, reported in a master's thesis that he had discovered clear evidence of a **risky shift** in decision making.[60] Participants in the research reviewed hypothetical cases involving risk, such as those involving career choices or investment decisions. As individuals, they recommended a course of action. Then they were formed into groups, and the groups discussed each case and came to a joint decision. In general, the groups tended to advise riskier courses of action than the average risk initially advocated by their members. This is the risky shift. As studies were conducted by others to explore the reasons for its causes, things got more complicated. For some groups and some decisions, **conservative shifts** were observed. In other words, groups came to decisions that were *less* risky than those of the individual members before interaction.

It is now clear that both risky and conservative shifts are possible, and that they occur in a wide variety of real settings, including investment and purchasing decisions. But what determines which kind of shift occurs? A key factor appears to be the initial positions of the group members before they discuss the problem. This is illustrated in Exhibit 11.4. As you can see, when group members are somewhat conservative before interaction (the Xs), they tend to exhibit a conservative shift when they discuss the problem. When group members are somewhat risky initially (the dots), they exhibit a risky shift after discussion. In other words, *group discussion seems to polarize or exaggerate the initial position of the group.*[61] Returning to the nuclear accident, if the engineers initially prefer a somewhat conservative solution, they would likely adopt an even more conservative strategy during the meeting.

Risky shift. The tendency for groups to make riskier decisions than the average risk initially advocated by their individual members.

Conservative shift. The tendency for groups to make less risky decisions than the average risk initially advocated by their individual members.

EXHIBIT 11.4
The dynamics of risky and conservative shifts for two groups.

 Explore

Go to MyManagementLab to see an annotated version of this figure.

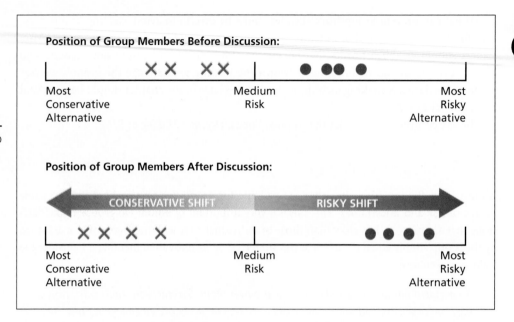

Why do risky and conservative shifts occur when groups make decisions? Evidence indicates two main factors:[62]

● Group discussion generates ideas and arguments that individual members have not considered before. This information naturally favours the members' initial tendency toward risk or toward conservatism. Since discussion provides "more" and "better" reasons for the initial tendency, the tendency ends up being exaggerated.

● Group members try to present themselves as basically similar to other members but "even better." Thus, they try to one-up others in discussion by adopting a slightly more extreme version of the group's initial stance.

A somewhat worrisome research finding is that groups that communicate via computer (Chapter 10) are inclined to polarize even more than face-to-face groups.[63]

In summary, managers should be aware of the tendency for group interaction to polarize initial risk levels. If this polarization results from the sensible exchange of information, it might actually improve the group's decision. However, if it results from one-upmanship, it might lead to low-quality decisions.

LO 11.7

Discuss techniques for improving organizational decision making.

IMPROVING DECISION MAKING IN ORGANIZATIONS

Managers can improve the success of their decisions by using various tactics, such as making the need for action clear at the outset, setting objectives, carrying out an unrestricted search for solutions, and getting key people to participate.[64] It stands to reason that organizational decision making can improve if decision makers receive encouragement to follow more closely the rational decision-making model shown in Exhibit 11.1. This should help to preclude the various biases and errors that we have alluded to throughout the chapter. Each of the following techniques has this goal.

Training Discussion Leaders

When organizations use group decision making, an appointed leader often convenes the group and guides the discussion. The actions of this leader can "make or break" the decision. On the one hand, if the leader behaves autocratically, trying to "sell" a preconceived decision, the advantages of using a group are obliterated, and decision acceptance can suffer. If the leader fails to exert *any* influence, however, the group might develop a low-quality solution that does not meet the needs of the organization. The use of role-playing training to develop these leadership skills has increased the quality and acceptance of group decisions. The following are examples of the skills that people learn in discussion-leader training:[65]

- State the problem in a non-defensive, objective manner. Do not suggest solutions or preferences.

- Supply essential facts and clarify any constraints on solutions (e.g., "We can't spend more than $25 000.").

- Draw out all group members. Prevent domination by one person, and protect members from being attacked or severely criticized.

- Wait out pauses. Do not make suggestions or ask leading questions.

- Ask stimulating questions that move the discussion forward.

- Summarize and clarify at several points to mark progress.

Stimulating and Managing Controversy

Full-blown conflict among organizational members is hardly conducive to good decision making. Individuals will withhold information, and personal or group goals will take precedence over developing a decision that solves organizational problems. On the other hand, a complete lack of controversy can be equally damaging, since alternative points of view that may be very relevant to the issue at hand will never surface. Such a lack of controversy is partially responsible for the groupthink effect, and it also contributes to many cases of escalation of commitment.

Research shows a variety of ways to stimulate controversy in decision-making groups: incorporating members with diverse ideas and backgrounds, forming subgroups to "tear the problem apart," and establishing norms that favour the open sharing of information.[66] However, these tactics must be managed carefully to ensure that open conflict does not result.

One interesting method of controversy stimulation is the appointment of a **devil's advocate** to challenge existing plans and strategies. The advocate's role is to challenge the weaknesses of the plan or strategy and state why it should not be adopted. For example, a bank might be considering offering an innovative kind of account. Details to be decided include interest rate, required minimum balance, and so on. A committee might be assigned to develop a position paper. Before a decision is made, someone would be assigned to read the paper and "tear it apart," noting potential weaknesses. Thus, a decision is made in full recognition of the pros and cons of the plan. The controversy promoted by the devil's advocate improves decision quality.[67] However, to be effective, the advocate must present his or her views in an objective, unemotional manner.

Devil's advocate. A person appointed to identify and challenge the weaknesses of a proposed plan or strategy.

Traditional and Electronic Brainstorming

Brainstorming is the brainchild of a Madison Avenue advertising executive.[68] Its major purpose is to increase the number of creative solution alternatives to problems. Thus, **brainstorming** focuses on the *generation* of ideas rather than the *evaluation* of ideas. If a group generates a large number of ideas, the chance of obtaining a truly creative solution is increased.

Brainstorming was originally conceived as a group technique. It was assumed that, in generating ideas, group members could feed off each other's suggestions and be stimulated

Brainstorming. An attempt to increase the number of creative solution alternatives to problems by focusing on idea generation rather than evaluation.

to offer more creative solutions. To ensure this, the group is encouraged to operate in a free-wheeling, off-the-wall manner. No ideas should be considered too extreme or unusual to be voiced. In addition, no criticism of ideas should be offered, since this can inhibit useful lines of thinking. For instance, an advertising agency might convene a group to generate names for a new toothpaste or soft drink. Similarly, a government agency might convene a group to generate possible solutions for welfare fraud.

Traditional brainstorming has not fulfilled its full creative promise. Research has shown conclusively that individuals working alone tend to generate more ideas than those in groups.[69] In other words, four people working independently (and encouraged to be creative and non-evaluative) will usually generate more ideas than the same people working as a team. Why is this? Likely explanations include inhibition, domination of the group by an ineffective member, or the sheer physical limitations of people trying to talk simultaneously.

However, brainstorming can provide advantages that extend beyond the mere number of ideas generated. Researchers Robert Sutton and Andrew Hargadon studied IDEO, the incredibly successful product and services design firm based in Palo Alto, California. One of the most innovative companies in the world, IDEO makes extensive use of brainstorming. They found that the procedure results in a number of important creative and business advantages. In terms of the organizational culture, they found that it helps organizational memory and supports a culture of wisdom—that is, ideas from one session can be used on subsequent, unrelated projects, and participants learn to appreciate the good ideas of others. At the individual level, the sessions motivate and stimulate the engineers and allow them to show off their good ideas to their colleagues. Finally, IDEO uses the brainstorming sessions to impress their clients, who really get to see how the design process unfolds. Thus, brainstorming shapes the organizational culture, helps retain good talent, and contributes to client confidence.[70]

Electronic brainstorming. The use of computer-mediated technology to improve traditional brainstorming practices.

An alternative to traditional brainstorming is electronic brainstorming. **Electronic brainstorming** uses computer-mediated communication to accomplish the same goal as traditional brainstorming: the generation of novel ideas without evaluation. As we noted, face-to-face interaction actually reduces individual brainstorming performance. But what happens if people brainstorm as an electronic group?

Once over the size of two members, electronic brainstorming groups perform better than face-to-face groups in terms of both quantity and quality of ideas.[71] Also, as electronic groups get larger, they tend to produce more ideas, but the ideas-per-person measure remains stable. In contrast, as face-to-face groups get bigger, fewer and fewer ideas per person are generated (recall social loafing from Chapter 7). What accounts for the success of electronic brainstorming? Reduced inhibition about participating and the ability for people to enter ideas simultaneously without waiting for others seem to be the main reasons. Notice that these factors become especially critical as the group gets bigger. Some organizations have done electronic brainstorming with groups of up to 30 members.

Nominal group technique. A structured group decision-making technique in which ideas are generated without group interaction and then systematically evaluated by the group.

Nominal Group Technique

The fact that nominal (in name only) brainstorming groups generate more ideas than interacting brainstorming groups gave rise to the **nominal group technique** (NGT) of decision making. Unlike brainstorming, NGT is concerned with both the generation of ideas and the evaluation of these ideas.

Imagine a meeting room in which 7 to 10 individuals are sitting around a table in full view of each other; however, at the beginning of the meeting they do not speak to each other. Instead, each individual is writing ideas on a pad of paper in front of him or her. At the end of 5 to 10 minutes, a structured sharing of ideas takes place. Each individual, in round-robin fashion, presents one idea from his or her private list. A recorder writes that idea on a flip chart in full view of other members. There is still no discussion at this point of the meeting—only the recording of privately narrated ideas. Round-robin listing continues until all members indicate they have no further ideas to share. Discussion follows during the next phase of the meeting; however, it is structured so that each idea receives attention before independent voting. This is accomplished by asking for clarification, or stating support or nonsupport of each idea listed on the flip chart. Independent voting then takes place. Each member privately, in writing, selects priorities by rank-ordering (or rating). The group decision is the mathematically pooled outcome of the individual votes.[72]

As you can see, NGT carefully separates the generation of ideas from their evaluation. Ideas are generated nominally (without interaction) to prevent inhibition and conformity. Evaluation permits interaction and discussion, but it occurs in a fairly structured manner to be sure that each idea gets adequate attention. NGT's chief disadvantage would seem to be the time and resources required to assemble the group for face-to-face interaction. The Delphi technique was developed, in part, to overcome this problem.

The Delphi Technique

The **Delphi technique** of decision making was developed at the Rand Corporation to forecast changes in technology. Its name derives from the future-telling ability of the famous Greek Delphic Oracle.[73] Unlike NGT, the Delphi process relies solely on a nominal group—participants do not engage in face-to-face interaction. Thus, it is possible to poll a large number of experts without assembling them in the same place at the same time. We should emphasize that these experts do not actually make a final decision; rather, they provide information for organizational decision makers.

The heart of Delphi is a series of questionnaires sent to respondents. Minimally, there are two waves of questionnaires, but more is not unusual. The first questionnaire is usually general in nature and permits free responses to the problem. For example, suppose the CEO of a large corporation wishes to evaluate and improve the firm's customer service. A random sample of employees who have worked closely with customers would receive an initial questionnaire asking them to list the strengths and weaknesses of the existing approach to customers. The staff would collate the responses and develop a second questionnaire that might share these responses and ask for suggested improvements. A final questionnaire might then be sent asking respondents to rate or rank each improvement. The staff would then merge the ratings or rankings mathematically and present them to the president for consideration.

A chief disadvantage of Delphi is the rather lengthy time frame involved in the questionnaire phases, although email and other web-based solutions can speed up sending and receiving. In addition, its effectiveness depends on the writing skills of the respondents and their interest in the problem, since they must work on their own rather than as part of an actual group. Despite these problems, Delphi is an efficient method of pooling a large number of expert judgments while avoiding the problems of conformity and domination that can occur in interacting groups.

Delphi technique. A method of pooling a large number of expert judgments by using a series of increasingly refined questionnaires.

THE MANAGER'S NOTEBOOK

Preventing Surgical Decision Errors at Toronto General Hospital

1. To help cut surgical errors, medical researchers drew upon the experience of airline pilots, who use a safety checklist before takeoff. In 2008, the World Health Organization issued a set of guidelines for safe surgery. Harvard professor Dr. Atul Gawande and a team of physicians from eight city hospitals worldwide (including Toronto General) transformed the WHO guidelines into a 19-item Surgical Safety Checklist. Such checklists are especially effective for preventing procedural errors. The checklist is applied at three critical stages of the surgical process: before anaesthesia, before skin incision, and before the patient leaves the operating room. As part of their research, Dr. Gawande and his team, including UHN Chief Surgeon Dr. Bryce Taylor, tested the checklist in each of the eight hospitals, with impressive results. Although there was a greater decrease in preventable deaths in lower-income versus higher-income hospitals, all eight institutions experienced significant drops in complication rates. Dr. Taylor was so impressed with the results that the checklist is now being used by all three UHN hospitals under his watch. Should the checklist be fully implemented across Canada, it is possible that more than 60 000 complications could be avoided each year. Dr. Gawande's own experience convinced him that the checklist should be used worldwide; he argues that its use could prevent millions of complications and deaths each year and save billions of dollars in health-care costs.

2. Studies have indicated that nurses do not always speak up in the operating room out of fear of reprisal. Although both nurses and doctors ultimately serve the needs of the patient, their respective training serves different purposes. Physicians have in-depth knowledge on surgical procedures, positioning them as leaders in the operating room. Consequently, because nurses are on the lower end of the status hierarchy, they may refrain from challenging physicians out of fear of being punished. The traditional operating room structure, in which the lead surgeon is considered to be the ultimate boss, may also intimidate residents and anaesthesiologists. So when problems do arise, they may be overlooked by a submissive surgical team. The essential problem is one in which the emotions of discomfort or outright fear lead to decisions being made with inadequate information. Thus, the person on the team who is most knowledgeable about a problem may not offer decision input. Toronto General Hospital understood that changing the surgical team culture from one of command-and-control to one of collaborative learning could encourage effective group decision making through the elimination of fear. The introduction of the Surgical Safety Checklist encouraged all team members to speak up either prior to, during, or after the operation. The researchers from Toronto General Hospital were so convinced that the procedures borrowed from aviation could save lives that they even invited a senior Air Canada training pilot to talk with the surgical teams.

MyManagementLab

Visit MyManagementLab at **www.mymanagementlab .com** for access to online tutorials, interactive exercises, videos, and much more.

LEARNING OBJECTIVES CHECKLIST

11.1 *Decision making* is the process of developing a commitment to some course of action. Alternatively, it is a problem-solving process. A problem exists when a gap is perceived between some existing state and some desired state. Some problems are well structured. This means that existing and desired states are clear, as is the means of getting from one state to the other. Well-structured problems are often solved with programs that simply standardize solutions. Programmed decision making is effective as long as the program is developed rationally and as long as conditions do not change. Ill-structured problems contain some combination of an unclear existing state, an unclear desired state, or unclear methods of getting from one state to the other. They tend to be unique and non-recurrent, and they require non-programmed decision making, in which the rational model comes into play.

11.2 *Rational decision making* includes (1) problem identification, (2) information search, (3) development of alternative solutions, (4) evaluation of alternatives, (5) choice of the best alternative, (6) implementation, and (7) ongoing evaluation of the implemented alternative. The imaginary, perfectly rational decision maker has free and easy access to all relevant information, can process it accurately, and has a single ultimate goal—economic maximization. Real decision makers must suffer from *bounded rationality*. They do not have free and easy access to information, and the human mind has limited information processing capacity and is susceptible to a variety of cognitive biases. In addition, time constraints and political considerations can outweigh anticipated economic gain. As a result, bounded decision makers usually *satisfice* (choose a solution that is "good enough") rather than maximize.

11.3 *Framing* refers to the aspects of the presentation of information about a problem that are assumed by decision makers. A frame could include assumptions about the boundaries of a problem, the possible outcomes of a decision, or the reference points used to decide if a decision is successful. Problems that are framed as an investment versus a cost, or as a potential gain versus a potential loss, can affect decision-making processes. *Cognitive biases* are tendencies to acquire and process information in a particular way that is prone to error. These biases constitute assumptions and shortcuts that can improve decision-making efficiency, but they frequently lead to serious errors in judgment. Examples include overemphasizing recent information, overconfidence based on past success, perceptual defence, and faulty hindsight.

11.4 *Escalation of commitment* is the tendency to invest additional resources in an apparently failing course of action. This tendency emerges from people's desires to justify past decisions and attempts to recoup sunk costs incurred as the result of a past decision.

11.5 Although emotions can enhance the decision-making process in relation to correcting ethical errors or when dealing with creative problems, they can also distract and unsettle decision makers and lead to poor choices. Research has shown that mood can also have an important impact on the decision-making process, especially for uncertain or ambiguous problems. Mood can affect information recall, evaluation, creativity, time reference, and projected outcomes.

11.6 Groups can often make higher-quality decisions than individuals because of their vigilance and their potential capacity to generate and evaluate more ideas. Also, group members might accept more readily a decision that they have been involved in making. Given the appropriate problem, groups will frequently make higher-quality decisions than individuals. However, using groups takes a lot of time and may provoke conflict. In addition, groups may fall prey to *groupthink*, in which social pressures to conform to a particular decision outweigh rationality. Groups may also make decisions that are more risky or conservative than those of individuals.

11.7 Attempts to improve organizational decision making have involved training discussion leaders, stimulating controversy, *brainstorming*, *the nominal group technique*, and the *Delphi technique*.

DISCUSSION QUESTIONS

1. The director of an urban hospital feels that there is a turnover problem among the hospital's nurses. About 25 percent of the staff resigns each year, leading to high replacement costs and disruption of services. Use the decision model in Exhibit 11.1 to explore how the director might proceed to solve this problem. Discuss probable bounds to the rationality of the director's decision.

2. Describe a decision-making episode (in school, work, or your personal life) in which you experienced information overload. How did you respond to this overload? Did it affect the quality of your decision?

3. Many universities must register thousands of students for courses each semester. Is this a well-structured problem or an ill-structured problem? Does it require programmed decisions or non-programmed decisions? Elaborate.

4. An auditing team fails to detect a case of embezzlement that has gone on for several months at a bank. How might the team members use hindsight to justify their faulty decisions?

5. A very cohesive planning group for a major oil company is about to develop a long-range strategic plan. The head of the unit is aware of the groupthink problem and wishes to prevent it. What steps should she take?

6. Discuss the implications of diffusion of responsibility, risky shift, and conservative shift for the members of a parole board. Also, consider the role of emotion and mood.

7. Discuss how the concepts of groupthink and escalation of commitment might be related to some cases of unethical decision making (and its cover-up) in business.

8. What are the similarities and differences of the nominal group technique and the Delphi technique? What are the comparative advantages and disadvantages?

INTEGRATIVE DISCUSSION QUESTIONS

1. Consider the role of communication in decision making. Explain how various communication problems can affect decision making in organizations. How can personal and organizational approaches for improving communication improve decision making?

2. Does group structure influence group decision making? Explain how each of the following structural characteristics might influence group decision quality, acceptance and commitment, and diffusion of responsibility: group size, diversity, norms, roles, status, and cohesiveness.

ON-THE-JOB CHALLENGE QUESTION

Toronto Ritz-Carlton Nixes Poppies

It happens every year: A prominent organization bans a practice the public holds dear; an uproar ensues; the organization backs down in the face of bad publicity. So it happened at Toronto's posh new Ritz-Carlton hotel. The hotel had issued a memo to employees forbidding the wearing of poppies as a reminder of Remembrance Day, November 11, which marks the end of World War I and serves to honour all military veterans. In general, Ritz policy forbids the wearing of any ribbons, pins, or badges that make a statement or support a cause. After complaints and media attention, the poppy ban was withdrawn. About the same time, the international soccer association FIFA initially banned the English team from wearing poppies in a match against Spain and then backed down after a public uproar and an intervention by Prince William.

Imagine the decision process that underpins the Ritz-Carlton policy against wearing ribbons, pins, or badges on one's uniform. What are some pros and some cons of such a policy? What does this story say about the role of rationality versus emotion in decision making? How do you account for the regularity with which managers reverse themselves on decisions like this?

Sources: Staff. (2011, November 10). Hotel rescinds poppy ban. *National Post*, A5; Burtt, J. (November 9, 2011). FIFA backs down and allows England players to wear poppies on black armband against Spain. *The Telegraph*.

EXPERIENTIAL EXERCISE

The New Truck Dilemma

Preparation for Role-Playing

The instructor will

1. Read the general instructions to the class as a whole.

2. Place data regarding name, length of service, and make and age of truck on the board for ready reference by all.

3. Divide the class into groups of six. Ask any remaining members will to join one of the groups and serve as observers.

4. Assign roles to each group by handing out slips with the names Chris Marshall, Terry, Sal, Jan, Sam, and Charlie. Ask each person to read his or her own role only. Instructions should not be consulted once role-playing has begun.

5. Ask the Chris Marshalls to stand up when they have completed reading their instructions.

6. When all Chris Marshalls are standing, ask that each crew member display conspicuously the slip of paper with his or her role name so that Chris can tell who is who.

The Role-Playing Process

1. The instructor will start the role-playing with a statement such as the following: "Chris Marshall has asked the crew to wait in the office. Apparently Chris wants to discuss something with the crew. When Chris sits down that will mean he or she has returned. What you say to each other is entirely up to you. Are you ready? All Chris Marshalls please sit down."

2. Role-playing proceeds for 25 to 30 minutes. Most groups reach agreement during this interval.

Collection of Results

1. Each supervisor in turn reports his or her crew's solution. The instructor summarizes these on the board by listing the initials of each repair person and indicating with arrows which truck goes to whom.

2. A tabulation should be made of the number of people getting a different truck, the crew members considering the solution unfair, and the supervisor's evaluation of the solution.

Discussion of Results

1. A comparison of solutions will reveal differences in the number of people getting a different truck, who gets the new one, the number dissatisfied, and so on. Discuss why the same facts yield different outcomes.

2. The quality of the solution can be measured by the trucks retained. Highest quality would require the poorest truck to be discarded. Evaluate the quality of the solutions achieved.

3. Acceptance is indicated by the low number of dissatisfied repair people. Evaluate solutions achieved on this dimension.

4. List problems that are similar to the new truck problem. See how widely the group will generalize.

General Instructions

This is a role-playing exercise. Do not read the roles given below until assigned to do so by your instructor!

Assume that you are a repair person for a large utility company. Each day you drive to various locations in the city to do repair work. Each repair person drives a small truck, and you take pride in keeping yours looking good. You have a possessive feeling about your truck and like to keep it in good running order. Naturally, you would like to have a new truck too, because a new truck gives you a feeling of pride.

Here are some facts about the trucks and the crew that reports to Chris Marshall, the supervisor of repairs:

> Terry—17 years with the company, has a 2-year-old Ford
>
> Sal—11 years with the company, has a 5-year-old Dodge
>
> Jan—10 years with the company, has a 4-year-old Ford
>
> Sam—5 years with the company, has a 3-year-old Ford
>
> Charlie—3 years with the company, has a 5-year-old Chevrolet

PART THREE SOCIAL BEHAVIOUR AND ORGANIZATIONAL PROCESSESES

Most of you do all your driving in the city, but Jan and Sam cover the jobs in the suburbs.

You will be one of the people mentioned above and will be given some further individual instructions. In acting your part in role-playing, accept the facts as well as assume the attitude supplied in your specific role. From this point on, let your feelings develop in accordance with the events that transpire in the role-playing process. When facts or events arise that are not covered by the roles, make up things that are consistent with the way it might be in a real-life situation.

When the role-playing begins, assume that Chris Marshall called the crew into the repair office.

Role for Chris Marshall, Supervisor. You are the supervisor of a repair crew, each of whom drives a small service truck to and from various jobs. Every so often you get a new truck to exchange for an old one, and you have the problem of deciding which one of your crew gets the new truck. Often there are hard feelings because each person seems to feel entitled to the new truck, so you have a tough time being fair. As a matter of fact, it usually turns out that whatever you decide, most of the crew consider it wrong. You now have to face the issue again because a new truck has just been allocated to you for assignment. The new truck is a Chevrolet.

To handle this problem, you have decided to put the decision up to the crew themselves. You will tell them about the new truck and will put the problem in terms of what would be the fairest way to assign the truck. Do not take a position yourself because you want to do what the crew thinks is most fair. However, be sure that the group reaches a decision.

Role for Terry. When a new Chevrolet truck becomes available, you think you should get it because you have most seniority and do not like your present truck.

Your own car is a Chevrolet, and you prefer a Chevrolet truck such as you drove before you got the Ford.

Role for Sal. You feel you deserve a new truck. Your present truck is old, and since the more senior crew member has a fairly new truck, you should get the next one. You have taken excellent care of your present Dodge and have kept it looking like new. People deserve to be rewarded if they treat a company truck like their own.

Role for Jan. You have to do more driving than most of the other crew because you work in the suburbs. You have a fairly old truck and feel you should have a new one because you do so much driving.

Role for Sam. The heater in your present truck is inadequate. Since Charlie backed into the door of your truck, it has never been repaired to fit right. The door lets in too much cold air, and you attribute your frequent colds to this. You want a warm truck since you have a good deal of driving to do. As long as it has good tires, brakes, and is comfortable, you do not care about its make.

Role for Charlie. You have the poorest truck in the crew. It is five years old, and before you got it, it had been in a bad wreck. It has never been good, and you have put up with it for three years. It is about time you got a good truck to drive, and you feel the next one should be yours. You have a good accident record. The only accident you had was when you sprung the door of Sam's truck when he opened it as you backed out of the garage. You hope the new truck is a Ford, since you prefer to drive one.

Source: Adapted from Maier, N.R.F., & Verser, G.C. (1982). *Psychology in industrial organizations* (5th ed.). Copyright 1982 Wadsworth, a part of Cengage Learning, Inc. Adapted by permission, www.cengage.com/permissions.

CASE INCIDENT

The Restaurant Review

After emigrating from New Orleans to his adopted city of Vancouver, Christophe Touché had worked as head chef at a neighbourhood pub for five years while saving money and planning to open his own restaurant. At the pub, he perfected several Cajun specialties that would form the core of the menu of his new restaurant, Cajun Sensation. After his restaurant had been open for two months, Christophe was delighted

to receive a phone call from the local newspaper food critic who had dined anonymously at the restaurant the previous evening and was calling to verify some of the ingredients and techniques he used in his cooking. Two days later, delight turned to dismay as Christophe read the restaurant review. Although the critic praised the inventiveness of some dishes, others were described as "heavy handed." The staff was described as "charming but amateurish." And the wine list was described as "well chosen but overpriced." The review concluded, "In sum, this very new restaurant has both problems and promise." It was local custom to post restaurant reviews prominently at the restaurant entrance to capture walk-by trade. At a staff meeting, opinions varied about what to do. One member suggested posting the review, as it noted that the new establishment had been open only two months. Another suggested posting only favourable excerpts from the review. A third offered to write an angry letter to the paper's editor. Christophe wasn't sure what to do.

1. What are some of the factors that might lead Christophe to make a poor decision about the review?

2. What would you do in this situation, and why?

CASE STUDY

Standard Media Plan

It was a late Saturday afternoon in mid-December, and Bob Smith, a research analyst for L&H Marketing Research, was working furiously to complete the media plan portion of the Standard Grooming Products report. Standard was considering introducing a men's hairspray and needed demographic characteristics and media habits of male hairspray users, as well as attitudinal information about such product attributes as oiliness, stickiness, masculinity, and fragrance.

The findings were to be presented Monday afternoon, and a long series of problems and delays had forced Bob to come in on Saturday to finish the report. Complicating matters, Bob felt that his boss, Barry Michaels, expected the statistical analysis to be consistent with L&H's initial recommendations to Standard. Bob, Barry and Marjorie Glass, from Standard's advertising agency, were to meet Monday morning to finalize L&H's presentation to Standard.

Back in September, Bob had recommended surveying 250 users of men's hairspray from each of 15 metropolitan areas. Charles Chastain from Standard's marketing department had argued that conclusions about local usage in each city would not be accurate unless each city's sample size was proportional to its population. That is, the sample sizes for larger cities should be larger than for smaller cities. Furthermore, Charles feared that males in metropolitan areas differed from rural males on usage or other important characteristics. Bob finally convinced Charles that sample sizes proportional to population would mean only 5 to 10 interviews in some smaller cities—too few to draw statistically valid conclusions. Furthermore, expanding the survey to include rural users would have required committing more money to the project—money Standard didn't want to spend. Since Standard was a new account with big potential, a long-term relationship with them would be valuable. (Business at L&H had been slow this past year.) Feeling "under the gun," Bob met with Barry and Charles, who agreed to reduce the sample to 200 men in each of only 11 metropolitan areas.

In October, a Des Moines, Iowa, pretest revealed that the questionnaire's length was driving the cost per completed interview to about $18. Total expenses would be well over budget if that cost held for the 15 metro areas. If the survey costs exceeded $65 000 (counting the pilot study), precious little money would be left for the focus groups, advertising, and packaging pretesting in L&H's contract with Standard (see Table 11.1).

Table 11.1 Proposed Budget

Type of Expense	Amount (US$)
Phone survey	58 000
Focus group study	8 000
Advertising pretesting	25 000
Package pretesting	14 000
Miscellaneous expenses	5 000
Proposal total expenses	110 000

In early November, a new problem arose. After surveying eight metro areas, Bob discovered that his assistant, with whom he had a good long-term relationship, had accidentally deleted all questions on media habits from the questionnaire given to L&H's vendor for the phone interviews. When telling Barry and Charles of the missing questions problem, Bob omitted indicating the source of the problem. Barry and Charles became visibly angry at the vendor, but after much discussion, they decided there was too little time to hire a new vendor and resample the eight areas. Therefore, they agreed to reinsert the media questions for the remaining three cities and just finish the survey.

Bob's task now was to make the most of the data he had. Because responses from each of the three cities were reasonably similar, and each city came from a different region (East, West, and Midwest), Bob felt confident that the three-city data were representative. Therefore, he decided to base the media plan on the large differences between his results and the national averages for adult men—making sports magazines and newspapers the primary vehicles for Standard's advertising (see Table 11.2).

Table 11.2   Comparison of Media Habits, Three-City Sample of Male Hairspray Users versus U.S. Adult Males

Male Media-Use	Male Hairspray Users in Three Cities	National Male Hairspray Users
Magazines, % of users (at least one subscription)		
News	28	19
Entertainment	4	3
Sports	39	20
Other	9	6
Newspaper subscription, % of users (at least one daily)	35	14
Favourite radio format, % of users		
Pop/rock	51	48
Country	26	37
EZ listening	7	6
News/talk	5	4
Other	11	5
Hours watching television per week, per user		
Total	17.5	23.5
Dramas	6.3	8.4
Comedies	7.8	7.3
News	1.1	3.9
Other	2.3	3.9

Bob's confidence in the media plan based on sports magazines and newspapers was bolstered by a phone conversation with Marjorie Glass. Until a short time ago, her agency had handled the advertising for American Toiletries, so she had valuable information about this competitor's possible responses to Standard's new product. Marjorie liked Bob's recommendations, had no misgivings about using information about a former client, and agreed to support the media plan in Monday's meeting. Indeed, Bob thought, Marjorie had been a big help.

The Standard project had put a great deal of stress on Bob, who hated spending weekends away from his family—especially near Christmas! If the presentation went well and more business was forthcoming, Bob suspected he would be spending even more weekends here. But if the presentation went poorly or the data collection errors became an issue, then Standard might look elsewhere for market research, thus jeopardizing Bob's future with L&H. Either way, he felt apprehensive. He wondered how he should present his results and how much information he should share with the client. Should he reveal to Standard any or all of the problems L&H experienced in conducting the project? Or should he simply present his results and recommendation as credible bases to proceed with Standard's media plan and not mention technical issues? The question really was about the level of understanding that his client would want about the basis of the recommendations. He also thought that his boss, Barry Michaels, would be much more concerned about how well the proposals fit with L&H's initial recommendations and would certainly be upset if he lost the account. The choices weren't easy. Bob wished he could turn to somebody outside the organization to share his dilemma and seek a fresh, independent perspective.

Source: Excerpted from Boland, R.J., Jr., Singh, J., Salipante, P., Aram, J.D., Fay, S.Y., & Kanawattanachai, P. (2001). Knowledge representations and knowledge transfer. *Academy of Management Journal, 44*, 393–417, Appendix B.

QUESTIONS

1. Given the formal definition of the word "problem" presented in the chapter, what is the problem faced by Bob Smith? Is the problem well-structured or ill-structured?

2. What are some of the bounds or limits on rationality that affect attempts to solve the problem Bob faces? What would a satisficing solution be?

3. Is Bob suffering from too little information or too much? Defend your answer.

4. How has Bob framed his problem? What would be an alternative frame?

5. Does the case contain any elements of groupthink or escalation of commitment? Explain.

6. Discuss how confirmation bias and the anchoring effect (Exhibit 11.3) pertain to Bob's concern about Barry Michaels' interest that the marketing proposal fit the initial recommendation to the client.

7. Are there ethical issues in this case?

8. What should Bob do?

POWER, POLITICS, AND ETHICS

LEARNING OBJECTIVES

After reading Chapter 12, you should be able to:

12.1 Define *power* and review the bases of individual power.

12.2 Explain how people obtain power in organizations.

12.3 Discuss the concept of *empowerment*.

12.4 Review various *influence tactics*.

12.5 Provide a profile of power seekers.

12.6 Explain *strategic contingencies* and discuss how subunits obtain power.

12.7 Define *organizational politics* and discuss its various forms.

12.8 Define *ethics* and review the ethical dilemmas that managers and employees face.

12.9 Define *sexual harassment* and discuss what organizations can do to prevent it and how they should respond to allegations.

SEXUAL HARASSMENT AT THE ROYAL CANADIAN MOUNTED POLICE

The Royal Canadian Mounted Police (RCMP) recruited its first female officers in May 1974, some 101 years after its founding. Occasionally making headlines, sexual harassment has been an issue in the force for years. In 2004 the RCMP reached a settlement on a lawsuit filed by four female officers claiming to had been sexually harassed. More recently, in 2011, Corporal Catherine Galliford, the spokesperson for the RCMP on several high-profile investigations, made public her allegations of sexual harassment against several superior officers and colleagues. Galliford, in a 115-page complaint, described how for almost two decades she was the target of harassment and bullying due to her gender. Galliford's courage emboldened several other female officers to come forward with similar stories of abuse. The allegations spanned years and snowballed into one of the biggest scandals to hit the force since its creation. Recently, more than 100 victims have started organizing for a possible class action lawsuit against the RCMP. Their allegations include indecent exposure, sexual remarks and advances, coerced sexual activities, double standards, and threats to benefits. Harassment has had serious effects on the victims. Most who went public have taken sick leave after being diagnosed with post-traumatic stress disorder, depression, anxiety, and insomnia, and some even attempted suicide. Some substance abuse has occurred, but the more common story is one of failed careers, damaged family relations, and low quality of life.

As allegations have been brought to light, it becomes clear that power, politics, and a strict hierarchal organizational structure play a role in fuelling the unethical behaviour. On one hand, the RCMP provides not so easily replaceable service in many of the provinces, which causes provincial and federal authorities to be more forgiving about some of the transgressions that have been attributed to the force. On the other hand, the RCMP has all the ingredients needed for a perfect storm when it comes to harassment issues. Similar to other paramilitary organizations, it has a rigid male-dominated hierarchy with strict power differentials under which Mounties are expected to follow commands or risk being punished. Within such organizations, criticizing and whistle-blowing are often not tolerated and can have serious consequences for complainants. Female officers have reported observing or

The RCMP has been plagued by repeated charges of sexual harassment and power abuse.

experiencing how voicing one's opinions about such issues have led to poor performance evaluations, transfer to less desirable assignments, being labelled as a whiner, and eventually being "stressed" out of the force. Even those who dare to object have had their complaints fall onto deaf ears. Constable Janet Merlo, whose lawsuit could evolve into a class action, wrote to former RCMP commissioner William Elliott concerning an unfair transfer only to get a standard reply more than two years later. Former commissioner Elliott was himself on the receiving end of intimidation accusations by his deputies. A senior officer charged with fixing the harassment mess was accused of brokering a deal that got a Staff Sergeant accused of harassing two female Mounties off the hook with a deduction of a day's pay and an order to get counselling after pleading guilty to charges well below what the two women were accusing him of. The same transgressor was soon after promoted.

Yet another problem is inadequate policies and procedures to investigate and manage such incidents. The Division Staff Relations Representative Program, the body responsible for handling formal complaints within the RCMP, rarely acted when it came to harassment issues. Victims can go on indefinite paid sick leave, which basically avoids having to fix the problem. A 2007 task force on RCMP governance and culture heavily criticized its management structure and suggested that complaints against Mounties be handled by a civilian body rather than an internal division. The suggestion has yet to be implemented.

Following Catherine Galliford's public accusations and the storm that followed, steps have been taken to initiate change. The RCMP Public Complaints Commission was assigned to inspect whether regulations were impartially respected when investigating complaints of harassment and whether existing RCMP guidelines in that respect needed updating. An informal review based on focus group meetings with some 400 female Mounties found that there is a general distrust in the current reporting system. As such, recommendations were made for a new, more confidential system for reporting incidents and better harassment awareness programs. Building on these findings, a gender-based nation-wide audit is being conducted by the RCMP to tackle those subjects in addition to areas such as women's engagement and advancement in the workplace. The supervision of harassment complaints has been centralized in Ottawa, and British Columbia has trained 100 RCMP officers in harassment investigation.[1]

This vignette illustrates the main themes of this chapter—power, politics, and ethics. First we will define power and discuss the bases of individual power. Then we will examine how people get and use power and who seeks it. After this we will explore how organizational subunits, such as particular departments, obtain power, define organizational politics, and explore the relationship of politics to power. Finally, we will look at ethics in organizations and sexual harassment.

At one time, power and politics were not considered polite topics for coverage in organizational behaviour textbooks. At best, they were seen as irrational and at worst, as evil. Now, though, organizational scholars recognize what managers have known all along—that power and politics are *natural* expressions of life in organizations. They often develop as a rational response to a complex set of needs and goals, and their expression can be beneficial. However, they can also turn bad and put a strain on ethical standards, as at the RCMP.

LO 12.1

Define *power* and review the bases of individual power.

Power. The capacity to influence others who are in a state of dependence.

WHAT IS POWER?

Power is the capacity to influence others who are in a state of dependence. First, notice that power is the *capacity* to influence the behaviour of others. Power is not always perceived or exercised.[2] For example, most professors hold a great degree of potential power over students in terms of grades, assignment load, and the ability to embarrass students in class. Under normal circumstances, professors use only a small amount of this power.

Second, the fact that the target of power is dependent on the power holder does not imply that a poor relationship exists between the two. For instance, your best friend has power to influence your behaviour and attitudes because you are dependent on him or her for friendly reactions and social support. Presumably, you can exert reciprocal influence for similar reasons.

Third, power can flow in any direction in an organization. Often members at higher organizational levels have more power than those at lower levels. However, in specific cases, reversals can occur. For example, the janitor who finds the president in a compromising position with a subordinate might find himself in a powerful position if the president wishes to maintain his reputation in the organization!

Finally, power is a broad concept that applies to both individuals and groups. On the one hand, an individual marketing manager might exert considerable influence over the staff who report to her. On the other, the marketing department at XYZ Foods might be the most powerful department in the company, able to get its way more often than other departments. But from where do the marketing manager and the marketing department obtain their power? We explore this issue in the following sections. First, we consider individual bases of power. Then we examine how organizational subunits, such as the marketing department, obtain power.

THE BASES OF INDIVIDUAL POWER

If you wanted to marshal some power to influence others in your organization, where would you get it? As psychologists John French and Bertram Raven explained, power can be found in the *position* that you occupy in the organization or the *resources* that you are able to command.[3] The first base of power—legitimate power—is dependent on one's position or job. The other bases (reward, coercive, referent, and expert power) involve the control of important resources.

Legitimate power. Power derived from a person's position or job in an organization.

Legitimate Power

Legitimate power derives from a person's position or job in the organization. It constitutes the organization's judgment about who is formally permitted to influence whom, and it is often called authority. As we move up the organization's hierarchy, we find that members possess more and more legitimate power. In theory, organizational equals (e.g., all vice-presidents) have equal legitimate power. Of course, some people are more likely than others to *invoke* their legitimate power—"Look, *I'm* the boss around here." In the RCMP, one's legitimate power corresponds to one's rank in the organization's hierarchy.

Organizations differ greatly in the extent to which they emphasize and reinforce legitimate power. At one extreme is the military, which has many levels of command, differentiating uniforms, and rituals (e.g., salutes), all designed to emphasize legitimate power. On the other hand, the academic hierarchy of universities tends to downplay differences in the legitimate power of lecturers, professors, chairpeople, and deans.

When legitimate power works, it often does so because people have been socialized to accept its influence. Experiences with parents, teachers, and law enforcement officials cause members to enter organizations with a degree of readiness to submit to (and exercise) legitimate power. In fact, employees consistently cite legitimate power as a major reason for following their boss's directives, even across various cultures.[4] This is one reason why juries often fail to believe that top executives are "out of the loop" in ethical scandals.

Reward Power

Reward power means that the power holder can exert influence by providing positive outcomes and preventing negative outcomes. In general, it corresponds to the concept of positive reinforcement discussed in Chapter 2. Reward power often backs up legitimate power. That is, managers are given the chance to recommend raises, do performance evaluations, and assign preferred tasks to employees. Of course, *any* organizational member can attempt to exert influence over others with praise, compliments, and flattery, which also constitute rewards.

Reward power. Power derived from the ability to provide positive outcomes and prevent negative outcomes.

Coercive Power

Coercive power is available when the power holder can exert influence using punishment and threat. Like reward power, it is often a support for legitimate power. Managers might be permitted to dock pay, assign unfavourable tasks, or block promotions. Despite a strong civil service system, even U.S. government agencies provide their executives with plenty of coercive power. In the RCMP, some more senior male officers have abused their legitimate power and engaged in sexual coercion.

Coercive power. Power derived from the use of punishment and threat.

Of course, coercive power is not perfectly correlated with legitimate power. Lower-level organizational members can also apply their share of coercion. For example, consider work-to-rule campaigns that slow productivity by strictly adhering to organizational procedures. Cohesive work groups are especially skilful at enforcing such campaigns.

In Chapter 2, we pointed out that the use of punishment to control behaviour is very problematic because of emotional side effects. Thus, it is not surprising that when managers use coercive power, it is generally ineffective and can provoke considerable employee resistance.[5]

Referent Power

Referent power exists when the power holder is *well liked* by others. It is not surprising that people we like readily influence us. We are prone to consider their points of view, ignore their failures, seek their approval, and use them as role models. In fact, it is often highly dissonant to hold a point of view that is discrepant from that held by someone we like.[6]

Referent power. Power derived from being well liked by others.

Referent power is especially potent for two reasons. First, it stems from *identification* with the power holder. Thus, it represents a truer or deeper base of power than reward or coercion, which may stimulate mere compliance to achieve rewards or avoid punishment. In this sense, charismatic leaders (Chapter 9) have referent power. Second, *anyone* in the organization may be well liked, irrespective of his or her other bases of power. Thus, referent power is available to everyone from the janitor to the president.

Friendly interpersonal relations often permit influence to extend across the organization, outside the usual channels of legitimate authority, reward, and coercion. For example, a production manager who becomes friendly with the design engineer through participation in a task force might later use this contact to ask for a favour in solving a production problem.

Expert Power

Expert power. Power derived from having special information or expertise that is valued by an organization.

A person has **expert power** when he or she has special information or expertise that the organization values. In any circumstance, we tend to be influenced by experts or by those who perform their jobs well. However, the more crucial and unusual this expertise, the greater is the expert power available. Thus, expert power corresponds to difficulty of replacement. Consider the business school that has one highly published professor who is an internationally known scholar and past federal cabinet minister. Such a person would obviously be difficult to replace and should have much greater expert power than an unpublished lecturer.

One of the most fascinating aspects of expert power occurs when lower-level organizational members accrue it. Many secretaries have acquired expert power through long experience in dealing with clients, keeping records, or sparring with the bureaucracy. Frequently they have been around longer than those they serve. In this case it is not unusual for bosses to create special titles and develop new job classifications to reward their expertise and prevent their resignation.

Of all the bases of managerial power, expertise is most consistently associated with employee effectiveness.[7] Also, research shows that employees perceive women managers as more likely than male managers to be high in expert power.[8] Women often lack easy access to more organizationally based forms of power, and expertise is free for self-development. Thus, being "better" than their male counterparts is one strategy that women managers have used to gain influence.

Exhibit 12.1 summarizes likely employee responses to various bases of managerial power. As you can see, coercion is likely to produce resistance and lack of cooperation. Legitimate power and reward power are likely to produce compliance with the boss's wishes. Referent and expert power are most likely to generate true commitment and enthusiasm for the manager's agenda.

EXHIBIT 12.1
Employee responses to bases of power.
Source: Steers, R.M., & Black, J.S. (1994). *Organizational behavior,* 4th ed. © 1991. Reproduced by permission of Pearson Education, Inc., Upper Saddle River, NJ.

 Explore

Go to MyManagementLab to see an annotated version of this figure.

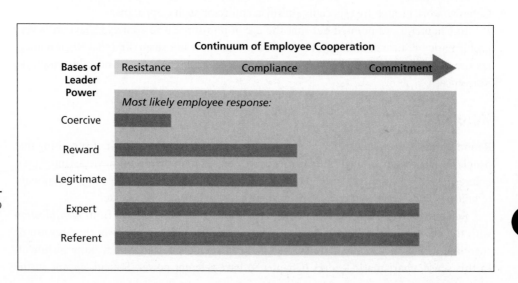

HOW DO PEOPLE OBTAIN POWER?

LO 12.2

Now that we have discussed the individual bases of power, we can turn to the issue of how people *get* power. Rosabeth Moss Kanter has provided a succinct recipe: Do the right things, and cultivate the right people.[9]

Explain how people obtain power in organizations.

Doing the Right Things

According to Kanter, some activities are "righter" than others for obtaining power. She argues that activities lead to power when they are extraordinary, highly visible, and especially relevant to the solution of organizational problems.

EXTRAORDINARY ACTIVITIES Excellent performance of a routine job might not be enough to obtain power. What one needs is excellent performance in *unusual* or *non-routine* activities. In the large company that Kanter studied, these activities included occupying new positions, managing substantial changes, and taking great risks. For example, consider the manager who establishes and directs a new customer service program. This is a risky, major change that involves the occupancy of a new position. If successful, the manager should acquire substantial power.

VISIBLE ACTIVITIES Extraordinary activities will fail to generate power if no one knows about them. People who have an interest in power are especially good at identifying visible activities and publicizing them. The successful marketing executive whose philosophy is profiled in *Fortune* will reap the benefits of power. Similarly, the innovative surgeon whose techniques are reported in the *New England Journal of Medicine* will enhance his influence in the hospital.

RELEVANT ACTIVITIES Extraordinary, visible work may fail to generate power if no one cares. If nobody sees the work as relevant to the solution of important organizational problems, it will not add to one's influence. The English professor who wins two Pulitzer Prizes will probably not accrue much power if his small college is financially strapped and hurting for students. He would not be seen as contributing to the solution of pressing organizational problems. In another college, these extraordinary, visible activities might generate considerable influence.

Cultivating the Right People

An old saying advises, "It's not what you know, it's *who* you know." In reference to power in organizations, there is probably more than a grain of truth to the latter part of this statement. Kanter explains that developing informal relationships with the right people can prove a useful means of acquiring power.

OUTSIDERS Establishing good relationships with key people outside one's organization can lead to increased power within the organization. Sometimes this power is merely a reflection of the status of the outsider, but, all the same, it may add to one's internal influence. The assistant director of a hospital who is friendly with the president of the American Medical Association might find herself holding power by association. Cultivating outsiders may also contribute to more tangible sources of power. Organizational members who are on the boards of directors of other companies might acquire critical information about business conditions that they can use in their own firms.

SUBORDINATES At first blush, it might seem unlikely that power can be enhanced by cultivating relationships with subordinates. However, as Kanter notes, an individual can gain influence if she is closely identified with certain up-and-coming subordinates—"I taught her everything she knows." In academics, some professors are better known for the brilliant PhD students they have supervised than for their own published work. Of course, there is also the possibility that an outstanding subordinate will one day become one's boss! Having cultivated the relationship earlier, one might then be rewarded with special influence.

Cultivating subordinate interests can also provide power when a manager can demonstrate that he or she is backed by a cohesive team. The research director who can oppose a policy change by honestly insisting that "My people won't stand for this" knows that there is strength in numbers.

PEERS Cultivating good relationships with peers is mainly a means of ensuring that nothing gets in the way of one's *future* acquisition of power. As one moves up through the ranks, favours can be asked of former associates, and fears of being "stabbed in the back" for a past misdeed are precluded. Organizations often reward good "team players" with promotions on the assumption that they have demonstrated good interpersonal skills. On the other side of the coin, people often avoid contact with peers whose reputation is seen as questionable.

SUPERIORS Liaisons with key superiors probably represent the best way of obtaining power through cultivating others. As we discussed in Chapter 8, such superiors are often called *mentors* or *sponsors* because of the special interest they show in a promising subordinate. Mentors can provide power in several ways. Obviously, it is useful to be identified as a protégé of someone higher in the organization. More concretely, mentors can provide special information and useful introductions to other "right people."

Although cultivating others can add to one's power base, associates of people who have power sometimes develop an exaggerated and illusory sense of their own power, status, and influence. This phenomenon seems much more prevalent among men than women.[10] Celebrity hangers-on and political staff personnel (e.g., aides to prime ministers and senators) can be classic examples of this illusory power by association.

LO 12.3

Discuss the concept of *empowerment*.

Empowerment. Giving people the authority, opportunity, and motivation to take initiative and solve organizational problems.

EMPOWERMENT—PUTTING POWER WHERE IT IS NEEDED

Early organizational scholars treated power as something of a fixed quantity: An organization had so much, the people on the top had a lot, and lower-level employees had a little. Our earlier analysis of the more informal sources of power (such as being liked and being an expert) hints at the weakness of this idea. Thus, contemporary views of power treat it less as a fixed-sum phenomenon. This is best seen in the concept of **empowerment**, which means giving people the authority, opportunity, and motivation to take initiative to solve organizational problems.[11]

In practice, having the authority to solve an organizational problem means having legitimate power. This might be included in a job description, or a boss might delegate it to a subordinate.

Having opportunity usually means freedom from bureaucratic barriers and other system problems that block initiative. In a service encounter, if you have ever heard "Sorry, the computer won't let me do that" or "That's not my job," you have been the victim of limited opportunity. Opportunity also includes any relevant training and information about the impact of one's actions on other parts of the organization.

The motivation part of the empowerment equation suggests hiring people who will be intrinsically motivated by power and opportunity and aligning extrinsic rewards with successful performance. Also, leaders who express confidence in subordinates' abilities and foster conditions that facilitate the sharing of power (see transformational and empowering leadership, Chapter 9) can contribute to empowerment.[12] A good example occurred when a nay-saying union shop steward, doubting General Electric's commitment to changing its corporate culture, explained a recurrent problem with a supplier's component. His manager, sensing he was correct, chartered a plane, and the subordinate left that same night to visit the supplier and solve the problem.[13] It goes without saying that managers have to be tolerant of occasional mistakes from empowered employees.

People who are empowered have a strong sense of self-efficacy (Chapter 2), the feeling that they are capable of doing their jobs well and "making things happen." Empowering lower-level employees can be critical in service organizations, where providing customers with a good initial encounter or correcting any problems that develop can be essential for repeat business. The Nordstrom chain of stores is one firm that is known for empowering sales personnel to make on-the-spot adjustments or search out merchandise at other stores. Customers have even had enthusiastic store personnel change flat tires.

Under its Power to Please program, staff at Canada's Delta Hotels have the authority to handle special guest requests without seeking manager approval, deal with customer complaints on the spot, and have input on how they fulfill their tasks. For example, staff can handle requests for extra towels or more coffee directly, housekeepers have input on the type of cleaning products the hotel uses, and front desk staffers can take it upon themselves to send up a platter from room service following a guest complaint.[14]

There is growing evidence that empowerment fosters job satisfaction, organizational commitment, organizational citizenship behaviours, and high performance.[15] However, empowerment does not mean providing employees with a maximum amount of unfettered power. Rather, used properly, empowerment puts power where it is *needed* to make the organization effective. This depends on organizational strategy and customer expectations. The average Taco Bell customer does not expect highly empowered counter personnel who offer to make adjustments to the posted menu—a friendly, fast, efficient encounter will do. On the other hand, the unempowered waiter in a fancy restaurant who is fearful of accommodating reasonable adjustments and substitutions can really irritate customers. Speaking generally, service encounters predicated on high volume and low cost need careful engineering. Those predicated on customized, personalized service need more empowered personnel.[16] For an instructive exception, see the Applied Focus: *Tim Hortons Franchise Lacks Empowerment.*

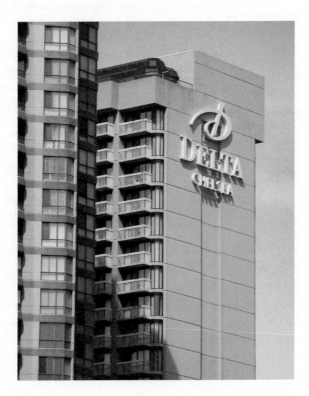

Delta Hotels focuses on empowerment.

■ APPLIED FOCUS

TIM HORTONS FRANCHISE LACKS EMPOWERMENT

Tim Hortons Inc. has squelched what could have become a PR disaster over the Timbit Affair. At the same time, the company has been served a stinging lesson on how following franchise rules too zealously can stifle the ability of front-line workers to keep the customer satisfied. The coffee and doughnut chain, one of the most valued brands in the country, rehired a London, Ontario, employee just hours after she was fired for giving away one 16-cent Timbit to the restless child of a regular customer.

"When the dust settles, Tim Hortons did absolutely the right thing, which is to reconsider and say, 'if we had to do it over again, we wouldn't do it quite this way,'" said Hugh Christie, a lawyer who heads the labour and employment national group at Gowlings.

Media outlets jumped on the tale of the 27-year-old single mother of four shunted aside by a Canadian corporate icon. Head office didn't take long to respond. Rather than go on the offensive, Tims ate humble pie. Hours after her firing, Nicole Lilliman was reinstated. But she doesn't want to go back to the same store. Ms. Lilliman will now work at a nearby location, said spokeswoman Rachel Douglas. She will be paid for the missed days. "When something comes out of London and gets this amount of press coverage, it's a learning [experience] for the entire chain," Ms. Douglas said. "The lesson is appropriate ways to treat your staff. Using proper processes...and making sure everyone's aware." She stressed that the whole sorry saga was a "mistake that shouldn't have happened," and that franchises set their own policies on freebies.

Events unfolded Monday, when a long-time customer came in with a fussy toddler. Ms. Lilliman, who's worked at the store for three years, spontaneously gave the child a doughnut hole to quiet her. She thought nothing of it, according to the *London Free Press*, until Wednesday, when she was hauled into the office and told she'd been caught on video giving away free food. The experience "was hell," she told the newspaper. "When I told my daughter I lost my job she started crying. She's only six, and she doesn't know. She said 'We won't have any food any more.'"

The fate of her manager is still being decided. It certainly hit a nerve with the public. *Globe* readers posted more than 800 comments on the story yesterday, making it one of the most-talked about stories in the history of globeandmail.com.

The Timbit Affair offers insights into how much discretion individual employees should have, and how front-line workers are the real faces of the corporate brand. "The best customer service happens when people on the front lines have decision-making power and it's assumed that they can problem-solve on the spot," said Kadi Kaljuste, senior vice-president at consultant firm Hill & Knowlton, who praised Ms. Lilliman for using common sense. Giving employees leeway to figure out solutions isn't a new idea. U.S. fashion retailer Nordstrom Inc. and airline WestJet Airlines Ltd. have both won plaudits for their customer service—and handing that trust to employees is partly why, Ms. Kaljuste says. It's an important reminder of how "the brand values cascade right down to the front line," said Paul Cubbon, marketing instructor at UBC's Sauder School of Business.

So what are policies like at Tims competitors? Dunkin Donuts lets stores set policies on giveaways. Starbucks lets customers try food and drinks.

You might wonder whether organizational members could have *too much* power. Exhibit 12.2 nicely illustrates the answer. People are empowered, and should exhibit effective performance, when they have sufficient power to carry out their jobs. Above, we mainly contrasted empowerment with situations in which people had inadequate power for effective performance. However, as the exhibit shows, excessive power can lead to

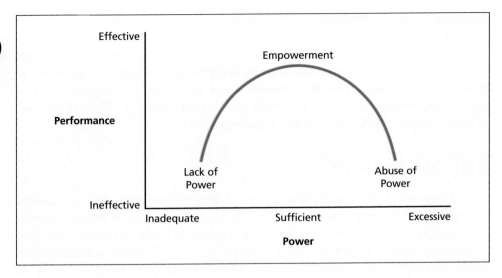

EXHIBIT 12.2
Relationship between power and performance.
Source: Whetten, D.A., Cameron, K.S. (1995). *Developing Management Skills*, 3rd ed. Reproduced by permission of Pearson Education, Inc., Upper Saddle River, NJ.

Go to MyManagementLab to see an annotated version of this figure.

abuse and ineffective performance. One is reminded of the recurrent and inappropriate use of government aircraft by political bigwigs as an example. As we will see in the following sections, the fact that people can have too much power does not always inhibit them from seeking it anyway!

INFLUENCE TACTICS—PUTTING POWER TO WORK

As we discussed earlier, power is the potential to influence others. But exactly how does power result in influence? Research has shown that various **influence tactics** convert power into actual influence. These are specific behaviours that people use to affect others and manage other's impressions of themselves.[17] These tactics include the following:

- Assertiveness—ordering, nagging, setting deadlines, and verbally confronting others;
- Ingratiation—using flattery and acting friendly, polite, or humble;
- Rationality—using logic, reason, planning, and compromise;
- Exchange—doing favours or offering to trade favours;
- Upward appeal—making formal or informal appeals to organizational superiors for intervention; and
- Coalition formation—seeking united support from other organizational members.

What determines which influence tactics you might use? For one thing, your bases of power.[18] Other things being equal, someone with coercive power might gravitate toward assertiveness, someone with referent power might gravitate toward ingratiation, and someone with expert power might try rationality. Of course, rationality or its appearance is a highly prized quality in organizations, and its use is viewed positively by others. Thus, surveys show that people report trying to use rationality very frequently.

As you can guess, the use of influence tactics is also dependent on just whom you are trying to influence—subordinates, peers, or superiors. Subordinates are more likely to be the recipients of assertiveness than peers or superiors. Despite the general popularity of rationality, it is most likely to be directed toward superiors. Exchange, ingratiation, and upward appeal are favoured tactics for influencing both peers and subordinates.[19]

Which influence tactics are most effective? Some of the most interesting research has concerned upward influence attempts directed toward superiors. It shows that, at least for men, using rationality as an influence tactic was associated with receiving better performance

LO 12.4

Review various *influence tactics.*

Influence tactics. Tactics that are used to convert power into actual influence over others.

evaluations, earning more money, and experiencing less work stress. A particularly ineffective influence style is a "shotgun" style that is high on all tactics with particular emphasis on assertiveness and exchange. In this series of studies, women who used ingratiation as an influence tactic received the highest performance evaluations (from male managers).[20] Another study showed that top managers who used ingratiation with their CEOs were inclined to receive appointments to corporate boards with whom the CEO was connected.[21] Thus, flattery and opinion conformity work even at the very top of organizations!

WHO WANTS POWER?

LO 12.5

Provide a profile of power seekers.

Who wants power? At first glance, the answer would seem to be everybody. After all, it is both convenient and rewarding to be able to exert influence over others. Power whisks celebrities to the front of movie lines, gets rock stars the best restaurant tables, and enables executives to shape organizations in their own image. Actually, there are considerable individual differences in the extent to which individuals pursue and enjoy power. On television talk shows, we occasionally see celebrities recount considerable embarrassment over the unwarranted power that public recognition brings.

Earlier we indicated that some people consider power a manifestation of evil. This is due, in no small part, to the historic image of power seekers that some psychologists and political scientists have portrayed. This is that power seekers are neurotics who are covering up feelings of inferiority, striving to compensate for childhood deprivation, or substituting power for lack of affection.[22]

There can be little doubt that these characteristics do apply to some power seekers. Underlying this negative image of power seeking is the idea that some power seekers feel weak and resort primarily to coercive power to cover up, compensate for, or substitute for this weakness. Power is sought for its own sake and is used irresponsibly to hurt others. Adolf Hitler comes to mind as an extreme example.

But can one use power responsibly to influence others? Psychologist David McClelland says yes. In Chapter 5, we discussed McClelland's research on need for power (n Pow). You will recall that n Pow is the need to have strong influence over others. This need is a reliable personality characteristic—some people have more n Pow than others.[23] Also, just as many women have high n Pow as men.[24] People who are high in n Pow in its "pure" form conform to the negative stereotype depicted above—they are rude, sexually exploitative, abuse alcohol, and show a great concern with status symbols. However, when n Pow is responsible and controlled, these negative properties are not observed. Specifically, McClelland argues that the most effective managers

- have high n Pow;
- use their power to achieve organizational goals;
- adopt a participative or "coaching" leadership style; and
- are relatively unconcerned with how much others like them.

McClelland calls such managers *institutional managers* because they use their power for the good of the institution rather than for self-aggrandizement. They refrain from coercive leadership and do not play favourites, since they are not worried about being well liked. His research reveals that institutional managers are more effective than *personal power managers* (who use their power for personal gain) and *affiliative managers* (who are more concerned with being liked than with exercising power). Exhibit 12.3 shows that institutional managers are generally superior in giving subordinates a sense of responsibility, clarifying organizational priorities, and instilling team spirit.[25] We can conclude that the need for power can be a useful asset, as long as it is not a neurotic expression of perceived weakness.

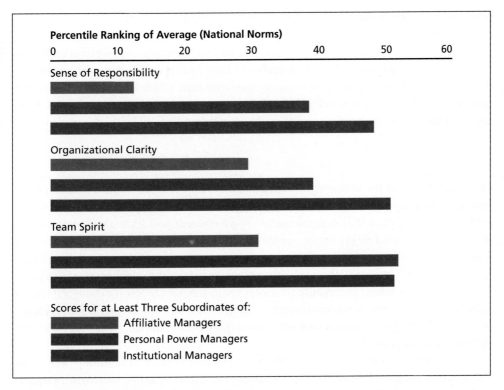

Percentile Ranking of Average (National Norms)

Sense of Responsibility

Organizational Clarity

Team Spirit

Scores for at Least Three Subordinates of:
Affiliative Managers
Personal Power Managers
Institutional Managers

EXHIBIT 12.3 Responses of subordinates of managers with different motive profiles.
Source: McClelland, D.C., & Burnham, D.H. (1976, March/April). Power is the great motivator. *Harvard Business Review.* Copyright © 1976 by the President and Fellows of Harvard College; all rights reserved.

 Explore

Go to MyManagementLab to see an annotated version of this figure.

Research has shown that CEOs who are very powerful relative to their top management team tend to pursue extreme strategies, with big successes or failures. However, a powerful board of directors can temper these extremes and promote successful strategic outcomes.[26]

CONTROLLING STRATEGIC CONTINGENCIES—HOW SUBUNITS OBTAIN POWER

Thus far, we have been concerned with the bases of *individual* power and how individual organizational members obtain influence. In this section, we shift our concern to **subunit power**. Most straightforwardly, the term *subunit* applies to organizational departments. In some cases, subunits could also refer to particular jobs, such as those held by software engineers or environmental lawyers.

How do organizational subunits acquire power—that is, how do they achieve influence that enables them to grow in size, get a bigger share of the budget, obtain better facilities, and have greater impact on decisions? In short, they control **strategic contingencies**, which are critical factors affecting organizational effectiveness. This means that the work *other* subunits perform is contingent on the activities and performance of a key subunit. Again, we see the critical role of *dependence* in power relationships. If some subunits are dependent on others for smooth operations (or their very existence), they are susceptible to influence. We turn now to the conditions under which subunits can control strategic contingencies.

Scarcity

Differences in subunit power are likely to be magnified when resources become scarce.[27] When there is plenty of budget money or office space or support staff for all subunits, they will seldom waste their energies jockeying for power. If cutbacks occur, however, differences in power will become apparent. For example, well-funded quality-of-worklife programs or organizational

 LO **12.6**

Explain *strategic contingencies* and discuss how subunits obtain power.

Subunit power. The degree of power held by various organizational subunits, such as departments.

Strategic contingencies. Critical factors affecting organizational effectiveness that are controlled by a key subunit.

development efforts might disappear when economic setbacks occur because the subunits that control them are not essential to the firm's existence.

Subunits tend to acquire power when they are able to *secure* scarce resources that are important to the organization as a whole. One study of a large American state university found that the power of academic departments was associated with their ability to obtain funds through consulting contracts and research grants. This mastery over economic resources was more crucial to their power than was the number of undergraduates taught by the department.[28]

Uncertainty

Organizations detest the unknown. Unanticipated events wreak havoc with financial commitments, long-range plans, and tomorrow's operations. The basic sources of uncertainty exist mainly in the organization's environment—government policies might change, sources of supply and demand might dry up, or the economy might take an unanticipated turn. It stands to reason that the subunits that are most capable of coping with uncertainty will tend to acquire power.[29] In a sense, these subunits are able to protect the others from serious problems. By the same token, uncertainty promotes confusion, which permits *changes* in power priorities as the organizational environment changes. Those functions that can provide the organization with greater control over what it finds problematic and can create more certainty will acquire more power.[30]

Changes in the sources of uncertainty frequently lead to shifts in subunit power. Thus, HR departments gained power when government legislation regarding employment opportunity was first passed, and departments concerned with environmental impact have gained power with the current interest in "green" organizations. Units dealing with business ethics or environmental concerns gain or lose power in response to the latest scandal or the newest piece of legislation involving clean air or water.

Centrality

Other things being equal, subunits whose activities are most central to the mission or work flow of the organization should acquire more power than those whose activities are more peripheral.[31] A subunit's activities can be central in at least three senses. First, it may influence the work of most other subunits. The finance or accounting department is a good example here—its authority to approve expenses and make payments affects every other department in the firm.

Centrality also exists when a subunit has an especially crucial impact on the quantity or quality of the organization's key product or service. This is one reason for the former low power of human resources departments—their activities were then seen as fairly remote from the primary goals of the organization.

Finally, a subunit's activities are more central when their impact is more immediate. As an example, consider a large city government with a fire department, a police department, and a public works department. The impact of a lapse in fire or police services will be felt more immediately than a lapse in street repairs. This gives the former departments more potential for power acquisition.

One of the reasons that organizations such as the RCMP have trouble instituting effective anti-harassment units is that the role of such units is not seen as central to the organization's primary mission of crime fighting.

Substitutability

A subunit will have relatively little power if others inside or outside the organization can perform its activities. If the subunit's staff is non-substitutable, however, it can acquire substantial power.[32] One crucial factor here is the labour market for the specialty performed by the subunit. A change in the labour market can result in a change in the subunit's influence. For example, the market for scientists and engineers is notoriously cyclical. When jobs are plentiful, these professionals command high salaries and high influence in organizations. When jobs are scarce, this power wanes. In the 1990s, there was a shortage of engineers and scientists, with a consequent increase in their bargaining power. Precisely in line with the strategic contingencies idea, this shortage provided real opportunities for properly trained women and members of minorities to move into positions of power from which they were excluded when there were plenty of white male engineers and scientists to go around.[33]

If work can be contracted out, the power of the subunit that usually performs these activities is reduced. Typical examples include temporary office help, off-premises data entry, and contracted maintenance, laboratory, and security services. The subunits that control these activities often lack power because the threat of "going outside" can counter their influence attempts.

ORGANIZATIONAL POLITICS—USING AND ABUSING POWER

Define *organizational politics* and discuss its various forms.

In the previous pages, we have avoided using the terms "politics" or "political" in describing the acquisition and use of power. This is because not all uses of power constitute politics.

The Basics of Organizational Politics

Organizational politics is the pursuit of self-interest within an organization, whether or not this self-interest corresponds to organizational goals.[34] Frequently, politics involves using means of influence that the organization does not sanction or pursuing ends or goals that it does not sanction.[35]

Political activity is self-conscious and intentional. This separates politics from ignorance or lack of experience with approved means and ends. Also, we can conceive of politics as either individual activity or subunit activity. Either a person or a whole department could act politically. Finally, it is possible for political activity to have beneficial outcomes for the organization, even though these outcomes are achieved by questionable tactics.

We can explore organizational politics using the means/ends matrix in Exhibit 12.4. It is the association between influence means and influence ends that determines whether activities are political and whether these activities benefit the organization.

> • *I. Sanctioned means/sanctioned ends.* Here, power is used routinely to pursue agreed-on goals. Familiar, accepted means of influence are employed to achieve sanctioned outcomes. For example, a manager agrees to recommend a raise for an employee if she increases her net sales by 30 percent in the next six months. There is nothing political about this.

Organizational politics. The pursuit of self-interest in an organization, whether or not this self-interest corresponds to organizational goals.

Go to MyManagementLab to see an annotated version of this figure.

EXHIBIT 12.4 The dimensions of organizational politics. *Source:* From Mayes, B.T., & Allen, R.T. (1977). Toward a definition of organizational politics, *Academy of Management Review, 2,* 672–678. Reprinted by permission.

Influence Means	Influence Ends	
	Organizationally Sanctioned	Not Sanctioned by Organization
Organizationally Sanctioned	Nonpolitical job behaviour **I**	**II** Organizationally dysfunctional political behaviour
Not Sanctioned by Organization	Political behaviour potentially functional to the organization **III**	**IV** Organizationally dysfunctional political behaviour

- *II. Sanctioned means/not-sanctioned ends.* In this case, acceptable means of influence are abused to pursue goals that the organization does not approve of. For instance, a head nurse agrees to assign a subordinate nurse to a more favourable job if the nurse agrees not to report the superior for stealing medical supplies. While job assignment is often a sanctioned means of influence, covering up theft is not a sanctioned end. This is dysfunctional political behaviour.

- *III. Not-sanctioned means/sanctioned ends.* Here, ends that are useful for the organization are pursued through questionable means. For example, although officials of the Salt Lake City Olympic Committee were pursuing a sanctioned end—the 2002 Winter Olympics—the use of bribery and vote-buying as a means of influence was not sanctioned by the committee.

- *IV. Not-sanctioned means/not-sanctioned ends.* This quadrant may exemplify the most flagrant abuse of power, since disapproved tactics are used to pursue disapproved outcomes. For example, to increase his personal power, the head of an already overstaffed legal department wishes to increase its size. He intends to hire several of his friends in the process. To do this, he falsifies workload documents and promises special service to the accounting department in exchange for the support of its manager.

We have all seen cases in which politics have been played out publicly to "teach someone a lesson." More frequently, though, politicians conceal their activities with a "cover story" or "smoke screen" to make them appear legitimate.[36] Such a tactic will increase the odds of success and avoid punishment from superiors. A common strategy is to cover non-sanctioned means and ends with a cloak of rationality. For an example, see the Ethical Focus: *Knowledge Hiding in Organizations*.

Do political activities occur under particular conditions or in particular locations in organizations? Research suggests the following:[37]

- Managers report that most political manoeuvring occurs at middle and upper management levels rather than at lower levels.

- Some subunits are more prone to politicking than others. Clear goals and routine tasks (e.g., production) might provoke less political activity than vague goals and complex tasks (e.g., research and development).

ETHICAL FOCUS

KNOWLEDGE HIDING IN ORGANIZATIONS

Canadian researchers Catherine Connelly, David Zweig, Jane Webster, and John Trougakos studied knowledge hiding in organizations. Knowledge hiding is a form of political behaviour that entails intentionally concealing or withholding information that has been requested by or is relevant to another organizational member. Although the sharing of knowledge is essential for organizational success and has been extensively studied, little is known about the active hiding of organizational-relevant knowledge from co-workers. A preliminary study determined that about 10 percent of knowledge transfer events consisted of knowledge hiding rather than sharing, and that people were quite open about the process: "There are always ways to answer questions without answering questions...." A second study established three forms of hiding: *Playing dumb* (pretending to be ignorant about requested knowledge); *evasive hiding* (providing misinformation or falsely promising knowledge in the future); *rationalized hiding* (justifying the failure to share by claiming extenuating circumstances or blaming others). What factors promote knowledge hiding? Interpersonal mistrust of the other party is a critical motivator of all three types of hiding. In addition, evasive hiding is more likely when knowledge is complex and more task-related. The researchers also expect that knowledge hiding is elevated when there is great competition among employees for individual recognition.

Source: Connelly, C., Zweig, D., Webster, J. & Trougakos, J. (2012). Knowledge hiding in organizations. *Journal of Organizational Behavior, 33*, 64–88.

- Some issues are more likely than others to stimulate political activity. Budget allocation, reorganization, and personnel changes are likely to be the subjects of politicking. Setting performance standards and purchasing equipment are not.

- In general, scarce resources, uncertainty, and important issues provoke political behaviour.

Highly political climates result in lowered job satisfaction, commitment, and organizational citizenship, and increased stress and turnover intentions.[38] When it comes to performance, politics take a toll on older workers but not on younger workers, perhaps due to stress factors.[39]

The Facets of Political Skill

It is one thing to engage in organizational politics, but it is another thing to do it skilfully, because pursuing self-interest can encounter resistance. Gerald Ferris and colleagues define **political skill** as "the ability to understand others at work and to use that knowledge to influence others to act in ways that enhance one's personal or organizational objectives."[40] Notice that this definition includes two aspects—comprehending others and translating this comprehension into influence. Research by Ferris and colleagues indicates that there are four facets to political skill:

- *Social astuteness.* Good politicians are careful observers who are tuned in to others' needs and motives. They can "read" people and thus possess emotional intelligence, as discussed in Chapter 5. They are active self-monitors (Chapter 2) who know how to present themselves to others.

- *Interpersonal influence.* The politically skilled have a convincing and persuasive interpersonal style but employ it flexibly to meet the needs of the situation. They put others at ease.

- *Apparent sincerity.* Influence attempts will be seen as manipulative unless they are accompanied by sincerity. A good politician comes across as genuine and exhibits high integrity.

- *Networking ability.* **Networking** involves establishing good relations with key organizational members or outsiders to accomplish one's goals. Networks provide a channel for favours to be asked for and given. An effective network enhances one's organizational reputation, thus aiding influence attempts.

Political skill, as measured by these four facets, is positively related to rated job performance. Also, more skilled politicians are less inclined to feel stressed in response to role conflict, evidently due to better coping.[41] If you would like to assess your own political skill, complete the Experiential Exercise *Political Skill Inventory* at the end of the chapter.

Because networking is such a critical aspect of power acquisition and political success, let's examine it in more detail. In essence, networking involves developing informal social contacts to enlist the cooperation of others when their support is necessary. Upper-level managers often establish very large political networks both inside and outside the organization (Exhibit 12.5). Lower-level organizational members might have a more restricted network, but the principle remains the same. One study of general managers found that they used face-to-face encounters and informal small talk to bolster their political networks. They also did favours for others and stressed the obligations of others to them. Personnel were hired, fired, and transferred to bolster a workable network, and the managers forged connections among network members to create a climate conducive to goal accomplishment.[42]

Monica Forret and Thomas Dougherty determined that there are several aspects to networking:[43]

Political skill. The ability to understand others at work and to use that knowledge to influence others to act in ways that enhance one's personal or organizational objectives.

Networking. Establishing good relations with key organizational members and outsiders to accomplish one's goals.

EXHIBIT 12.5
A typical upper-level manager's external network.

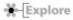Explore

Go to MyManagementLab to see an annotated version of this figure.

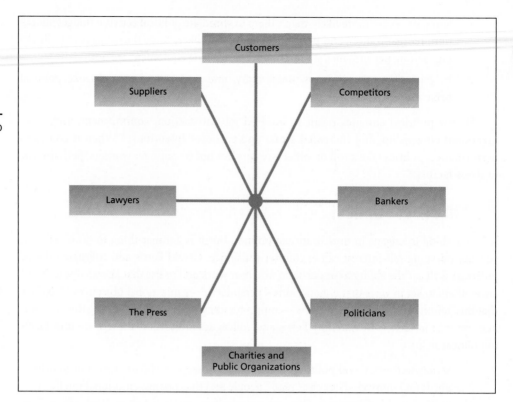

- Maintaining contacts—giving out business cards, sending gifts and thank you notes;
- Socializing—playing golf, participating in company sports leagues, having drinks after work;
- Engaging in professional activities—giving a workshop, accepting a speaking engagement, teaching, publishing, appearing in the media;
- Participating in community activities—being active in civic groups, clubs, church events; and
- Increasing internal visibility—accepting high-profile work projects, sitting on important committees and task forces.

The authors found that those high in self-esteem and extraversion (Chapter 2) were more likely to engage in networking behaviours. They also found that engaging in professional activities and increasing internal visibility were most associated with career success (i.e., compensation, promotions, and perceived success).[44] However, this applied only to men, despite the fact that men and women engaged in networking equally, except for socializing, where men perhaps had the edge. Forret and Dougherty make the important point that networking has increased in importance as people become more self-reliant and less reliant on organizations to plot their career futures. This is why many MBA and executive MBA programs foster social media such as LinkedIn, Facebook, and Twitter to maintain trusted networks among their alumni.

Being central in a large network provides power because you have access to considerable resources, such as knowledge. This is especially true if the network is diverse (the people you know do not know each other) and consists of those who themselves hold power.[45] One study in a leading bank revealed that those who were promoted most quickly to senior vice-president had very different networks from regular vice-presidents. Their networks bridged the bank, cutting across different divisions and regions and including people of diverse tenure and functional expertise. In turn, these networks were used to make up for the limitations of formal organizational structure.[46]

Networking is an effective way to develop informal social contacts.

Machiavellianism—The Harder Side of Politics

Have you ever known people who had the following characteristics?

- act very much in their own self-interest, even at the expense of others
- cool and calculating, especially when others get emotional
- high self-esteem and self-confidence
- form alliances with powerful people to achieve their goals

These are some of the characteristics of individuals who are high on a personality dimension known as Machiavellianism. **Machiavellianism** is a set of cynical beliefs about human nature, morality, and the permissibility of using various tactics to achieve one's ends. The term derives from the 16th-century writings of the Italian civil servant Niccolo Machiavelli, who was concerned with how people achieve social influence and the ability to manipulate others. Machiavellianism is a stable personality trait (Chapter 2).

Compared with "low Machs," "high Machs" are more likely to advocate the use of lying and deceit to achieve desired goals and to argue that morality can be compromised to fit the situation in question. In addition, high Machs assume that many people are excessively gullible and do not know what is best for themselves. Thus, in interpersonal situations, the high Mach acts in an exceedingly practical manner, assuming that the ends justify the means. Not surprisingly, high Machs tend to be convincing liars and good at "psyching out" competitors by creating diversions. Furthermore, they are quite willing to form coalitions with others to outmanoeuvre or defeat people who get in their way.[47] In summary, high Machs are likely to be enthusiastic organizational politicians.

Do high Machs feel guilty about the social tactics they utilize? The answer would appear to be no. Since they are cool and calculating rather than emotional, high Machs seem to be able to insulate themselves from the negative social consequences of their tactics. You might wonder how successful high Machs are at manipulating others and why others would tolerate such manipulation. After all, the characteristics we detail above are hardly likely to win a popularity contest, and you might assume that targets of a high Mach's tactics would vigorously resist manipulation by such a person. Again, the high Mach's rationality seems to provide an answer. Put simply, it appears that high Machs are able to accurately identify

Machiavellianism. A set of cynical beliefs about human nature, morality, and the permissibility of using various tactics to achieve one's ends.

situations in which their favoured tactics will work. Such situations have the following characteristics:

- the high Mach can deal face to face with those he or she is trying to influence;
- the interaction occurs under fairly emotional circumstances; and
- the situation is fairly unstructured, with few guidelines for appropriate forms of interaction.[48]

In combination, these characteristics reveal a situation in which the high Mach can use his or her tactics because emotion distracts others. High Machs, by remaining calm and rational, can create a social structure that facilitates their personal goals at the expense of others. Thus, high Machs are especially skilled at getting their way when power vacuums or novel situations confront a group, department, or organization. For example, imagine a small family business whose president dies suddenly without any plans for succession. In this power vacuum, a high Mach vice-president would have an excellent chance of manipulating the choice of a new president. The situation is novel, emotion provoking, and unstructured, since no guidelines for succession exist. In addition, the decision-making body would be small enough for face-to-face influence and coalition formation.

Despite sometimes being able to get their own way, research shows that high Machs are unlikely to be high performers. In fact, they are inclined toward counterproductive behaviours such as sabotage and theft.[49]

Defensiveness—Reactive Politics

So far, our discussion of politics has focused mainly on the proactive pursuit of self-interest. Another form of political behaviour, however, is more reactive in that it concerns the defence or protection of self-interest. The goal here is to reduce threats to one's own power by avoiding actions that do not suit one's own political agenda or avoiding blame for events that might threaten one's political capital. Blake Ashforth and Ray Lee describe some tactics for doing both.[50]

Astute organizational politicians are aware that sometimes the best action to take is no action at all. A number of defensive behaviours can accomplish this mission:

- *Stalling.* Moving slowly when someone asks for your cooperation is the most obvious way of avoiding taking action without actually saying no. With time, the demand for cooperation may disappear. The civil service bureaucracy is infamous for stalling on demands from acting governments.
- *Overconforming.* Sticking to the strict letter of your job description or to organizational regulations is a common way to avoid action. Of course, the overconformer may be happy to circumvent his job description or organizational regulations when it suits his political agenda.
- *Buck passing.* Having someone else take action is an effective way to avoid doing it yourself. Buck passing is especially dysfunctional politics when the politician is best equipped to do the job but worries that it might not turn out successfully ("Let's let the design department get stuck with this turkey.").

Another set of defensive behaviours is oriented around the motto "If you can't avoid action, avoid blame for its consequences." These behaviours include

- *Buffing.* Buffing is the tactic of carefully documenting information showing that an appropriate course of action was followed. Getting "sign offs," authorizations, and so on are examples. Buffing can be sensible behaviour, but it takes on political overtones when doing the documenting becomes more important than making a good decision. It is clearly dysfunctional politics if it takes the form of fabricating documentation.

- *Scapegoating.* Blaming others when things go wrong is classic political behaviour. Scapegoating works best when you have some power behind you. One study found that when organizations performed poorly, more powerful CEOs stayed in office and the scapegoated managers below them were replaced. Less powerful CEOs were dismissed.[51]

The point of discussing these defensive political tactics is not to teach you how to do them. Rather, it is to ensure that you recognize them as political behaviour. Many of the tactics are quite mundane. However, viewing them in context again illustrates the sometimes subtle ways that individuals pursue political self-interest in organizations.

ETHICS IN ORGANIZATIONS

In 2008, Linda Keen, the president of the Canadian Nuclear Safety Commission, was dismissed from her post by the Conservative government, citing her "lack of leadership." The commission headed by Keen had ordered a shutdown of the 50-year-old Chalk River nuclear reactor because of safety concerns. The reactor, which generates 40 to 60 percent of the world's vital medical isotopes used in nuclear medicine, was restarted following an emergency measure in the House of Commons. Prime Minster Stephen Harper had called Keen a partisan because she was appointed by the Liberal government. In the following months, heavy water leaks occurred, which eventually forced the shutdown of the reactor.[52] What are the ethics of this story?

For our purposes, **ethics** can be defined as systematic thinking about the moral consequences of decisions. Moral consequences can be framed in terms of the potential for harm to any stakeholders in the decision. **Stakeholders** are simply people inside or outside the organization who have the potential to be affected by the decision. This could range from the decision makers themselves to "innocent bystanders."[53]

Researchers have conducted a number of surveys to determine managers' views about the ethics of decision making in business.[54] Some striking similarities across studies provide an interesting picture of the popular psychology of business ethics. First, far from being shy about the subject, a large majority agree that unethical practices occur in business. Furthermore, a substantial proportion (between 40 and 90 percent according to the particular study) report that they have been pressured to compromise their own ethical standards when making decisions. Finally, in line with the concept of self-serving attributions, managers invariably tend to see themselves as having higher ethical standards than their peers and sometimes their superiors.[55] The unpleasant picture here is one in which unethical behaviour tempts managers, who sometimes succumb but feel that they still do better than others on moral grounds. This situation is not helped by the fact that top managers tend to see their organizations as being more ethical than do those lower in the hierarchy.[56] This is not a recipe for ethical vigilance.

Among business students, undergraduates have been found to be more ethical than MBA students.[57] In fact, in a large survey, 56 percent of MBA students admitted to cheating during the past year, compared with 47 percent of non-business grad students.[58] Research indicates that women are marginally more ethical than men and that older people are marginally more ethical than the young. However, these associations are very small compared to those for personality (discussed below).[59]

The Nature of Ethical Dilemmas

What are the kinds of ethical dilemmas that most frequently face organizational decision makers? Exhibit 12.6 shows the results of a Conference Board study of corporate codes of business ethics. The figures indicate the extent to which various issues are covered for the firms' own employees, its suppliers, and its joint venture partners. As can be seen, contractual and legally

Watch

HONEST TEA:
ETHICS–COMPANY
MISSION AND
VALUES Go to
MyManagementLab
to watch a video about
ethics.

Simulate

ETHICS Go to
MyManagementLab to
complete a simulation
about ethics.

LO 12.8

Define *ethics* and review
the ethical dilemmas
that managers and
employees face.

Ethics. Systematic
thinking about the
moral consequences of
decisions.

Stakeholders. People
inside or outside of an
organization who have the
potential to be affected by
organizational decisions.

EXHIBIT 12.6
Issues covered in corporate codes of ethics.
Source: Berenbeim, R.E. (1999). *Global corporate ethics practices: A developing consensus* (Report Number: R-1243-99-RR), The Conference Board, Inc. www.conference-board.org.

	Employees	Suppliers/ Vendors	Joint Venture Partners
Bribery proper payments	92%	45%	27%
Conflict of interest	92	37	26
Security of proprietary information	92	30	25
Receiving gifts	90	46	25
Discrimination/equal opportunity	86	25	22
Giving gifts	84	48	26
Environment	78	27	24
Sexual harassment	78	22	17
Antitrust	76	27	23
Workplace safety	71	20	18
Political activities	71	11	13
Community relations	62	8	13
Confidentiality of personal information	52	11	11
Human rights	50	14	17
Employee privacy	48	8	10
Whistle-blowing	46	10	10
Substance abuse	42	12	12
Nepotism	28	5	8
Child labour	15	8	7

mandated issues find the most consensus (e.g., bribery, conflict of interest, and proprietary information). The important but more subjective matters at the bottom of the list are less likely to be addressed.

Ethical issues are often occupationally specific. As an example, let's consider the ethical dilemmas faced by the various subspecialties of marketing.[60] Among market researchers, telling research participants the true sponsor of the research has been an ongoing topic of debate. Among purchasing managers, where to draw the line in accepting favours (e.g., sports tickets) from vendors poses ethical problems. Among product managers, issues of planned obsolescence, unnecessary packaging, and differential pricing (e.g., charging more in the inner city) raise ethical concerns. When it comes to salespeople, how far to go in enticing customers and how to be fair in expense account use have been prominent ethical themes. Finally, in advertising, the range of ethical issues can (and does) fill books. Consider, for example, the decision to use sexual allure to sell a product.

In contrast to these occupationally specific ethical dilemmas, what are the common themes that run through ethical issues that managers face? An in-depth interview study of an occupationally diverse group of managers discovered seven themes that defined their moral standards for decision making.[61] Here are those themes and some typical examples of associated ethical behaviour:

- *Honest communication.* Evaluate subordinates candidly; advertise and label honestly; do not slant proposals to senior management.

- *Fair treatment.* Pay equitably; respect the sealed bid process; do not give preference to suppliers with political connections; do not use lower-level people as scapegoats.

- *Special consideration.* The "fair treatment" standard can be modified for special cases, such as helping out a long-time employee, giving preference to hiring the disabled, or giving business to a loyal but troubled supplier.

- *Fair competition.* Avoid bribes and kickbacks to obtain business; do not fix prices with competitors.

- *Responsibility to organization.* Act for the good of the organization as a whole, not for self-interest; avoid waste and inefficiency.

- *Corporate social responsibility.* Do not pollute; think about the community impact of plant closures; show concern for employee health and safety.

- *Respect for law.* Legally avoid taxes, do not evade them; do not bribe government inspectors; follow the letter and spirit of labour laws.

Before continuing, have a look at the You Be the Manager: *Yahoo's Resume Scandal* feature.

YOU BE THE MANAGER

Yahoo's Resume Scandal

"And computer science" were three words that Yahoo CEO Scott Thompson would come to regret. Thompson, the former president of PayPal, had been at Yahoo for only four months when Third Point, an activist shareholder group seeking representation on the board, claimed that he had misrepresented his academic credentials in the Yahoo annual report filed with the U.S. Securities and Exchange Commission. The report, which CEOs must certify as true, stated that "Mr. Thompson holds a B.S. in accounting and computer science from Stonehill College." In fact, Thompson held an accounting degree, but not one in computer science. The press quickly ascertained that Thompson's degree had in the past also been inaccurately stated on the PayPal website, but that it was accurately described in formal SEC filings by PayPal parent eBay and another firm where Thompson was a board member.

The degree scandal occurred against a backdrop of turmoil at Yahoo, which had been losing ground to web-based companies Google, Facebook, and YouTube. The previous CEO had been fired within a year, and there had been recent staff layoffs. Third Point was the largest shareholder in Yahoo and had launched a proxy war to place its founder Daniel Loeb and other Third Point nominees on the board to assert and protect its interests. Discrediting Scott Thompson was a step in this direction.

Was this scenario a serious ethical violation by Scott Thompson or just a manifestation of power and politics?

Yahoo CEO Scott Thompson was challenged concerning resume irregularities.

Questions

1. How serious of an ethical violation was Scott Thompson's misstatement of academic qualifications in the Yahoo annual report? Who are the relevant stakeholders here? What might have motivated this misrepresentation?

2. What should Thompson have done to resolve this? What should the board of directors have done?

To find out what happened, see The Manager's Notebook at the end of the chapter.

Sources: Pepitone, J. (2012, May 13). Yahoo CEO out after resume scandal—reports. *CNNMoney*, http://money.cnn.com/2012/05/13/technology/yahoo-ceo-out-rumor/index.htm; Saginor, J. (2012, May 13). Yahoo! CEO Scott Thompson resigns amid resume scandal. *Digital Trends*, www.digitaltrends.com/web/yahoo-ceo-scott-thompson-resigns-amid-resume-scandal/; Saginor, J. (2012, April 6). Yahoo versus the hedge fund millionaire: A Silicon Valley soap opera. *Digital Trends*, 2012, www.digital trends.com/web/yahoo-versus-the-hedge-fund-billionaire-a-silicon-valley-soap-opera/.

Causes of Unethical Behaviour

Knowing the causes of unethical behaviour can aid in its prevention. Because the topic is sensitive, you should appreciate that this is not the easiest area to research. The major evidence comes from surveys of executive opinion, case studies of prominent ethical failures, business game simulations, and responses to written scenarios involving ethical dilemmas.

GAIN   Although the point might seem mundane, it is critical to recognize the role of temptation in unethical activity. The anticipation of healthy reinforcement for following an unethical course of action, especially if no punishment is expected, should promote unethical decisions.[62] Consider Dennis Levine, an investment banker who was convicted of insider trading in one of Wall Street's biggest scandals.

> It was just so easy. In seven years I built $39 750 into $11.5 million, and all it took was a 20-second phone call to my offshore bank a couple of times a month—maybe 200 calls total. My account was growing at 125% a year, compounded. Believe me, I felt a rush when I would check the price of one of my stocks on the office Quotron and learn I'd just made several hundred thousand dollars. I was confident that the elaborate veils of secrecy I had created—plus overseas bank-privacy laws—would protect me.[63]

A slightly more subtle example of the role of gain can be seen in compensation systems designed around very high bonuses. Such systems have often been implicated in ethically questionable behaviour, as ethics are sacrificed to boost income. In a related vein, pressure from analysts and investors for better and better financial performance has been implicated in ethical lapses among prominent and successful firms.[64]

ROLE CONFLICT   Many ethical dilemmas are actually forms of role conflict (Chapter 7) that get resolved in an unethical way. For example, consider the ethical theme of corporate social responsibility we listed above. Here, an executive's role as custodian of the environment (do not pollute) might be at odds with his or her role as a community employer (do not close the plant that pollutes).

A very common form of role conflict that provokes unethical behaviour occurs when our "bureaucratic" role as an organizational employee is at odds with our role as the member of a profession.[65] For example, engineers who in their professional role opposed the fatal launch of the space shuttle *Challenger* due to cold weather were pressured to put on their bureaucratic "manager's hats" and agree to the launch. Both the insurance and brokerage businesses have been rocked by similar ethics problems. Agents and brokers report being pressured as employees to push products that are not in the best interests of their clients. Frequently, reward systems (i.e., the commission structure) heighten the conflict, which then becomes a conflict of interest between self and client.

STRONG ORGANIZATIONAL IDENTIFICATION   Some employees identify very strongly with their organizations, seeing their membership as an integral part of their identity. This can sometimes lead them to engage in unethical activities to "help" the organization. Many instances of covering up previous ethical violations have this motivation. Strong identifiers seem most likely to do this when they expect their "loyalty" will be reciprocated with favours.[66]

COMPETITION   Stiff competition for scarce resources can stimulate unethical behaviour. This has been observed in both business game simulations and industry studies of illegal acts, in which trade offences, such as price fixing and monopoly violations, have been shown to increase with industry decline.[67] For example, observers cite a crowded and mature market as one factor prompting price-fixing violations in the folding-carton packaging industry.[68] We should note one exception to the "competition stresses ethics" thesis. In cases in which essentially *no* competition exists, there is also a strong temptation to make unethical decisions. This is because the opportunity to make large gains is not offset by market checks and balances. Prominent examples have occurred in the defence industry, in which monopoly contracts to produce military hardware have been accompanied by some remarkable examples of over-charging taxpayers. The understandable monopolies that police forces such as the RCMP have in law enforcement have sometimes been linked to ethical breaches.

PERSONALITY   Are there certain types of personalities that are more prone to unethical decisions? In fact, the cynical and those with external locus of control (Chapter 2) are less tuned in to ethical matters. Also, people with a high need for personal power (especially Machiavellians) may be prone to make unethical decisions, using this power to further self-interest rather than for the good of the organization as a whole.[69] Finally, people with strong economic values (Chapter 4) are more likely to behave unethically than those with weaker economic values.[70]

More broadly, there are marked individual differences in the degree of sophistication that people use in thinking about moral issues.[71] Some people are morally disengaged, rejecting responsibility for their actions and using euphemistic labelling to obscure moral issues.[72] For example, a broken political promise might be described as a "non-core promise" to deflect censure. Other people are morally attentive, spotting moral issues and thinking about moral matters.[73] Research shows that less disengagement and more attentiveness is associated with more ethical behaviour.[74]

Remember that we have a tendency to exaggerate the role of dispositional factors, such as personality, in explaining the behaviour of others (Chapter 3). Thus, when we see unethical behaviour, we should look at situational factors, such as competition and the organization's culture, as well as the personality of the actor.

ORGANIZATIONAL AND INDUSTRY CULTURE   Bart Victor and John Cullen found that there were considerable differences in ethical values across the organizations they studied.[75] These differences involved factors such as consideration for employees, respect for the law, and respect for organizational rules. In addition, there were differences across groups within these organizations. This indicates that aspects of an organization's culture (and its subcultures) can influence ethics.[76] This corresponds to the repeated finding in executive surveys that the conduct of peers and superiors is viewed as strongly influencing ethical behaviour, for good or for bad. The presence of role models helps to shape the culture (Chapter 8). If these models are actually rewarded for unethical behaviour, rather than punished, the development of an unethical culture is likely. In fact, firms convicted of illegal acts often tend to be repeat offenders.[77] Remember, no one thing creates a "culture of corruption" in organizations. Rather, it is often a combination of factors, such as evaluating managers solely "by the numbers," denying responsibility, denying injury to others, and teaching (low power) newcomers corrupt practices that lead to unethical corporate cultures.[78]

Observers of the folding-carton price-fixing scandal we mentioned above noted how top managers frequently seemed out of touch with the difficulty of selling boxes in a mature, crowded market. They put in place goal setting and reward systems (e.g., commission forming 60 percent of income), systems that are much more appropriate for products on a growth cycle, that almost guaranteed unethical decisions.[79] In fact, research shows that upper-level managers generally tend to be naïve about the extent of ethical lapses in those below them. This can easily contribute to a success-at-any-cost culture.[80]

Finally, a consideration of culture suggests the conditions under which corporate codes of ethics might actually have an impact on decision making. If such codes are specific, tied to the actual business being done, correspond to the reward system, and are rigorously enforced, they should bolster an ethical culture. If vague codes that do not correspond to other cultural elements exist, the negative symbolism might actually damage the ethical culture.

Whistle-Blowing

In spite of the catalogue of causes of unethical behaviour discussed above, individuals occasionally step forward and "blow the whistle" on unethical actions. For instance, former tobacco executive Dr. Jeffrey Wigand (portrayed in the movie *The Insider*) leaked evidence to *60 Minutes* that consumers had been misled about the addictiveness of nicotine for many years. Similarly, Catherine Galliford blew the whistle on sexual harassment at the RCMP.

Whistle-blowing.
Disclosure of illegitimate practices by a current or former organizational member to some person or organization that may be able to take action to correct these practices.

Whistle-blowing occurs when a current or former organizational member discloses illegitimate practices to some person or organization that may be able to take action to correct these practices.[81] Thus, the whistle may be blown either inside or outside of the offending organization, depending on the circumstances. The courage of insiders to call attention to organizational misdoing is especially important in large contemporary organizations, because their very complexity often allows for such misdoing to be disguised from outsiders. Also, given pervasive conflicts of interest, there is no guarantee that external watchdogs (such as accounting firms that perform audits) will do the job.[82] Most organizations seem to rely on vague open-door policies rather than having specific channels and procedures for whistle-blowers to follow (see Exhibit 12.6). This is not the best way to encourage principled dissent.

Not everyone at the failed energy-trading giant Enron stood idly by while massive fraud unfolded around them. Sherron Watkins, a vice-president with a master's degree in accounting, courageously spoke out against fraudulent accounting practices and notified the CEO. Watkins' testimony at the hearings into the scandal also provided crucial information as to the breadth and depth of the problems at Enron. At telecommunications giant WorldCom, Cynthia Cooper, an internal auditor, discovered fraudulent bookkeeping entries. Cooper discussed her findings with the company's controller and with the CFO, but was told not to worry about it and to stop her review. Instead, she immediately went over her boss's head and called the board chair's audit committee. Two weeks later, WorldCom disclosed its misstatements, leading to the largest bankruptcy in American history.[83]

People with power rarely blow the whistle. Michael Woodford, CEO of Olympus, producer of medical equipment and cameras, uncovered accounting fraud that stretched back a decade. Although fired for his efforts, he subsequently received an out-of-court financial settlement.[84]

LO 12.9

Sexual Harassment—When Power and Ethics Collide

Define *sexual harassment* and discuss what organizations can do to prevent it and how they should respond to allegations.

As indicated in Exhibit 12.6, 78 percent of the codes of ethics examined by the Conference Board mentioned sexual harassment. In recent years, a number of high-profile sexual harassment cases have made news headlines and brought increased attention to this problem. In addition to numerous cases reported in the American and Canadian military, many organizations, including Mitsubishi, Astra, Sears, and Del Laboratories, have found themselves involved in costly litigation cases.[85] The failure of these organizations to effectively respond to charges of sexual harassment has cost them millions of dollars in settlements as well as lower productivity, increased absenteeism, and turnover. As well, the effects on employees can include decreased job satisfaction and organizational commitment as well as reduced psychological and physical well-being.[86]

The following is a fairly comprehensive definition of sexual harassment:

The EEOC [Equal Employment Opportunity Commission] regulatory guidelines state that unwelcome sexual advances, requests for sexual favours, and other verbal or physical conduct of a sexual nature constitute sexual harassment when submission to requests for sexual favours is made explicitly or implicitly a term or condition of employment; submission to or rejection of such requests is used as a basis for employment decisions; or such conduct unreasonably interferes with work performance or creates an intimidating, hostile, or offensive work environment. On the basis of these guidelines, current legal frameworks generally support two causes of action that claimants may state: coercion of sexual cooperation by threat of job-related consequences (quid pro quo harassment) and unwanted and offensive sex-related verbal or physical conduct, even absent any job-related threat (hostile work environment).[87]

Sexual harassment is a form of unethical behaviour that stems, in part, from the abuse of power and the perpetuation of a gender power imbalance. Managers who use their position, reward, or coercive power to request sexual favours or demonstrate verbal or physical conduct of a sexual nature as a condition of employment or as a basis for employment decisions toward those in less powerful positions are abusing their power and acting in an unethical manner. While the most severe forms of sexual harassment are committed by supervisors, the most frequent perpetrators are actually co-workers. Although co-workers do not necessarily have the same formal power bases as supervisors, power differences often exist among co-workers and can also play a role in co-worker sexual harassment. Whether the harasser is a supervisor or a co-worker, he or she is likely to be more powerful than the person being harassed,[88] and the most vulnerable victims are those who cannot afford to lose their jobs.[89]

Sexual harassment is also prevalent in hostile work environments that perpetuate the societal power imbalance between men and women. For example, the higher incidences of sexual harassment reported in the military are believed to be partly a function of the rigid hierarchy and power differentials in the organizational structure.[90] Incidents of harassment and organizational inaction to complaints of harassment are also more likely in male-dominated industries and organizations in which men attempt to maintain their dominance relative to women.[91]

Clients and customers can also engage in harassment. Many service jobs are performed by women, who are required to spend virtually their entire workday with customers. Other jobs (e.g., sales rep) require the development of strong client relationships. In a web-based survey of professional women, 86 percent reported having experienced sexist hostility, 40 percent reported unwanted sexual attention, and 8 percent reported sexual coercion. Harassment increased when the proportion of men in the client base increased and when the clients were perceived as holding at lot of power (e.g., were very important to company business). Also, minority women were more likely to be harassed.[92] Jennifer Berdahl found that harassment was more likely to be experienced by women who exhibited traditionally masculine personality traits (such as independence, assertiveness, and dominance). In other words, the motive was punishment for gender role "deviance" rather than sexual desire.[93]

Unfortunately, like the RCMP, many organizations are slow to react to complaints of sexual harassment. This phenomenon has been labelled the "deaf ear syndrome," which refers to the "inaction or complacency of organizations in the face of charges of sexual harassment."[94] A review found three main reasons why organizations fail to respond: inadequate organizational policies and procedures for managing harassment complaints; defensive managerial reactions; and organizational features that contribute to inertial tendencies (e.g., international companies in the United States have problems managing sexual harassment).[95]

Organizations can effectively deal with allegations of sexual harassment and increase their responsiveness by taking a number of important measures. Ellen Peirce, Carol Smolinski, and Benson Rosen offer the following recommendations:

- *Examine the characteristics of deaf ear organizations.* Managers should examine their own organizations to determine if they have any of the characteristics that would make them susceptible to the deaf ear syndrome.

- *Foster management support and education.* Sexual harassment training programs are necessary to educate managers on how to respond to complaints in a sensitive and respectful manner.

- *Stay vigilant.* Managers must monitor the work environment and remove displays of a sexual nature and factors that can contribute to a hostile work environment.

- *Take immediate action.* Failure to act is likely to result in negative consequences for the organization and the victims of sexual harassment. Organizations considered to be the best places for women to work are known for their swift action and severe handling of harassers.

- *Create a state-of-the-art policy.* Sexual harassment policies and procedures need to clearly define what constitutes harassment and the sanctions that will be brought to bear on those found guilty of it.

- *Establish clear reporting procedures.* User-friendly policies need to be designed so that there are clear procedures for filing complaints and mechanisms in place for the impartial investigation of complaints. The privacy of those involved must also be protected.[96]

In general, organizations that are responsive to complaints of sexual harassment have top management commitment, provide comprehensive education programs, continuously monitor the work environment, respond to complaints in a thorough and timely manner, and have clear policies and reporting procedures.[97] An example is DuPont, which has developed a sexual harassment awareness program called A Matter of Respect. It includes interactive training programs, peer-level facilitators who are trained to meet with victims or potential victims, and a 24-hour hotline. As the company has become more international, so has its training on sexual harassment, which is now provided in Japan, China, Mexico, and Puerto Rico.[98]

Employing Ethical Guidelines

A few simple guidelines, regularly used, should help in the ethical screening of decisions. The point is not to paralyze your decision making but to get you to think seriously about the moral implications of your decisions before you make them.[99]

- Identify the stakeholders that will be affected by any decision.

- Identify the costs and benefits of various decision alternatives to these stakeholders.

- Consider the relevant moral expectations that surround a particular decision. These might stem from professional norms, laws, organizational ethics codes, and principles such as honest communication and fair treatment.

- Be familiar with the common ethical dilemmas that decision makers face in your specific organizational role or profession.

- Discuss ethical matters with decision stakeholders and others. Do not think ethics without talking about ethics.

- Convert your ethical judgments into appropriate action.

What this advice does is enable you to recognize ethical issues, make ethical judgments, and then convert these judgments into behaviour.[100]

Training and education in ethics have become very popular in North American organizations. Evidence indicates that formal education in ethics does have a positive impact on ethical attitudes.[101]

THE MANAGER'S NOTEBOOK

Yahoo's Resume Scandal

1. Opinions will vary about the seriousness of Scott Thompson's misstatement of his academic qualifications in the Yahoo annual report. Perhaps it was an honest mistake. Alternatively, some might see it as somewhat of a victimless crime, as it is hard pinpoint exactly whose interests were damaged by the event. On the other hand, consider some stakeholders: Yahoo as a company clearly did not need such bad publicity, especially given its recent turmoil. And the board member who headed the search committee that recruited Thompson felt compelled to announce she would step down. Investors might take unwarranted comfort in seeing that the head of a web-embedded company held a computer science degree. Finally, actions such as this by high-profile business leaders may convince some people that "everybody does it," serving as a negative role model for many future leaders. As news stories reported at the time, this was not the first case of a business leader being derailed by bogus academic qualifications. However, the technology and web sectors may be especially prone to this, as some will feel a need to signal their technical legitimacy in web-related matters.

2. Scott Thompson resigned from Yahoo, citing personal reasons, including a diagnosis of thyroid cancer. There is reason to believe that the move was motivated in part by a subcommittee of outside directors who had been appointed to examine the matter, because Daniel Loeb and two Third Point nominees were immediately appointed to the board. All in all, the three words "and computer science" provided a rational excuse for the board to jettison Thompson and resolve a contentious proxy war with Third Point, Yahoo's biggest shareholder.

MyManagementLab   Visit MyManagementLab at **www.mymanagementlab .com** for access to online tutorials, interactive exercises, videos, and much more.

LEARNING OBJECTIVES CHECKLIST

12.1 *Power* is the capacity to influence others who are in a state of dependence. People have power by virtue of their position in the organization (legitimate power) or by virtue of the resources that they command (reward, coercion, friendship, or expertise).

12.2 People can obtain power by doing the right things and cultivating the right people. Activities that lead to power acquisition need to be extraordinary, visible, and relevant to the needs of the organization. People to cultivate include outsiders, subordinates, peers, and superiors.

12.3 *Empowerment* means giving people the authority, opportunity, and motivation to solve organizational problems. Power is thus located where it is needed to give employees the feeling that they are capable of doing their jobs well.

12.4 *Influence tactics* are interpersonal strategies that convert power into influence. They include assertiveness, ingratiation, rationality, exchange, upward appeal, and coalition formation. Rationality (logic, reason, planning, and compromise) is generally the most efficient tactic.

12.5 Effective managers often have a high need for power. While individuals with high *n* Pow can, in some circumstances, behave in an abusive or dominating fashion, they can also use their power responsibly. Managers with high *n* Pow are effective when they use this power to achieve organizational goals.

12.6 Organizational subunits obtain power by controlling *strategic contingencies*. This means that they are able to affect events that are critical to other subunits. Thus, departments that can obtain resources for the organization will acquire power. Similarly, subunits gain power when they are able to reduce uncertainty, when their function is central to the organizational mission or workflow, and when other subunits or outside contractors cannot perform their tasks.

12.7 *Organizational politics* occur when non-sanctioned ends are pursued or when influence in the form of non-sanctioned means is used. The pursuit of non-sanctioned ends is always dysfunctional, but the organization may benefit when non-sanctioned means are used to achieve approved goals. Several political tactics were discussed: *Networking* is establishing good relations with key people to accomplish goals. It contributes to political skill along with political astuteness, interpersonal influence, and apparent sincerity. *Machiavellianism* is a set of cynical beliefs about human nature, morality, and the permissibility of using various means to achieve one's ends. Situational morality, lying, and "psyching out" others are common tactics.

Defensiveness means avoiding taking actions that do not suit one's political agenda and avoiding blame for negative events.

12.8 *Ethics* is systematic thinking about the moral consequences of decisions. Of particular interest is the impact on stakeholders, people who have the potential to be affected by a decision. Ethical dilemmas that managers face involve honest communication, fair treatment, special consideration, fair competition, responsibility to the organization, social responsibility, and respect for law. Causes of unethical behaviour include the potential for gain, role conflict, strong organizational identification, the extremes of business competition (great or none), organizational and industry culture, and certain personality characteristics.

12.9 *Sexual harassment* is a form of unethical behaviour that stems from the abuse of power and the perpetuation of a gender imbalance in the workplace. Steps that can be taken to prevent and deal with harassment include training and education, clear and formal policies, vigilance, detection of the "deaf ear" syndrome, and rapid response.

DISCUSSION QUESTIONS

1. Contrast the bases of power available to an army sergeant with those available to the president of a voluntary community association. How would these differences in power bases affect their influence tactics?

2. Are the bases of individual power easily substitutable for each other? Are they equally effective? For example, can coercive power substitute for expert power?

3. Suppose that you are an entrepreneur who has started a new chain of consumer electronics stores. Your competitive edge is to offer excellent customer service. What would you do to empower your employees to help achieve this goal?

4. Imagine that you are on a committee at work or in a group working on a project at school that includes a "high Mach" member. What could you do to neutralize the high Mach's attempts to manipulate the group?

5. Discuss the conditions under which the following subunits of an organization might gain or lose power: legal department; research and development unit; public relations department. Use the concepts of scarcity, uncertainty, centrality, and substitutability in your answers.

6. Differentiate between power and politics. Give an example of the use of power that is not political.

7. Is it unethical to occasionally surf the internet at work? Is it unethical to download pornography? Defend your answers.

8. Is sexual harassment more likely to be a problem in some occupations and types of organizations? Describe those occupations and organizational cultures where sexual harassment is most likely to be a problem. What can be done to prevent sexual harassment in these occupations and organizations?

INTEGRATIVE DISCUSSION QUESTIONS

1. Consider the role of politics and ethics in decision making. How can organizational politics be a source of effective or ineffective decision making in organizations? In what way can the causes of unethical behaviour influence decision making?

2. How can an organization create an ethical workplace where ethical behaviour is the norm?

Refer to the organizational learning practices in Chapter 2, attitudes in Chapter 4, ethical leadership in Chapter 9, and the contributors to organizational culture in Chapter 8 to answer this question.

ON-THE-JOB CHALLENGE QUESTION

CBC's Steven Smart

Canadian Broadcasting Corporation (CBC) journalist Stephen Smart didn't anticipate that getting married would get him in hot water with his employer. However, Smart, a reporter in the British Columbia provincial legislature, married Rebecca Scott, the Premier's deputy press secretary. Shortly thereafter, the marriage came to the attention of the CBC ombudsperson, who declared that Smart was in a conflict of interest position, and that it was not possible for him to be fair and impartial in his reporting concerning the Premier, given his wife's close connection to her. Mr. Smart's regional director, noting that no evidence of partiality had been presented, explained that ground rules had been established with him regarding his reporting and that no other action would be taken.

Who are the stakeholders in this ethical scenario? What kinds of role conflicts are operating here? Should Smart continue on the provincial legislature beat, or is this ethically unacceptable?

Source: Woo, A. (2012, January 23). Marriage violates CBC standards: Ombudsman. *National Post*, p. A3.

EXPERIENTIAL EXERCISE

Political Skill Inventory

Early in the chapter we discussed political skill. This exercise will allow you to assess your political skill set.

Instructions: Using the following 7-point scale, place the number on the blank before each item that best describes how much you agree with each statement about yourself.

1–Strongly disagree

2–Disagree

3–Slightly disagree

4–Neutral

5–Slightly agree

6–Agree

7–Strongly agree

1. _____ I spend a lot of time and effort at work networking with others.

2. _____ I am able to make most people feel comfortable and at ease around me.

3. _____ I am able to communicate easily and effectively with others.

4. _____ It is easy for me to develop good rapport with most people.

5. _____ I understand people very well.

6. _____ I am good at building relationships with influential people at work.

7. _____ I am particularly good at sensing the motivations and hidden agendas of others.

8. _____ When communicating with others, I try to be genuine in what I say and do.

9. _____ I have developed a large network of colleagues and associates at work whom I can call on for support when I really need to get things done.

10. _____ At work, I know a lot of important people and am well connected.

11. _____ I spend a lot of time at work developing connections with others.

12. _____ I am good at getting people to like me.

13. _____ It is important that people believe I am sincere in what I say and do.

14. _____ I try to show a genuine interest in other people.

15. _____ I am good at using my connections and network to make things happen at work.

16. _____ I have good intuition or savvy about how to present myself to others.

17. _____ I always seem to instinctively know the right things to say or do to influence others.

18. _____ I pay close attention to people's facial expressions.

Scoring and Interpretation

To compute your overall political skill, add up your scores and divide the total by 18. Scores below 2.3 indicate low political skill and scores over 4.6 signal high political skill. You can also compute your scores for the various dimensions of political skill. To deter-

mine your social astuteness, sum answers 5, 7, 16, 17, and 18 and divide by 5. To determine your interpersonal influence, sum answers 2, 3, 4, and 12 and divide by 4. To assess your networking ability, sum answers 1, 6, 9, 10, 11, and 15 and divide by 6. Finally, to compute your apparent sincerity, sum answers 8, 13, and 14 and divide by 3. It is also useful to see how others rate your political skill. Have someone who knows you well use the scale to rate you and compare his or her rating with yours.

Source: Ferris, G.R., Treadway, D.C., Kolodinsky, R.W., Hochwarter, W.A., Kacmar, C.J., Douglas, C., & Frink, D.D. (2005). Development and validation of the Political Skill Inventory. *Journal of Management, 31*, 126–152.

CASE INCIDENT

Doubling Up

The business school at Canadian Anonymous University prided itself on its international programs, which spanned Eastern Europe, North Africa, and South America. Many of the faculty enjoyed teaching in these programs, as it offered them a chance for free travel and the opportunity to sometimes avoid the harsh extremes of the Canadian climate. In addition, the teaching was well paid, offering a more reliable source of additional income than consulting. The university's auditor recently determined that several faculty members had been teaching in the international programs at the same time that they were scheduled to be teaching undergraduate classes at CAU. This was possibly due to the loose connection between the international programs office and the academic departments. After some investigation,

it was determined that these faculty members had been subcontracting their CAU teaching to graduate students (at rather low rates) to enable themselves to teach internationally. One faculty member defended the practice as "gaining global exposure." Another claimed that developing countries "deserved experienced professors." A third claimed to be underpaid without the international teaching.

1. What kind of organizational politics are at work here?

2. What influence tactics might the profs have used to get the grad students to fill in for them?

3. Discuss the ethics of the professors "doubling up" on their teaching.

CASE STUDY

OrangeWerks: A Question of Ethics

Introduction

David Samarin, network administrator for Orange-Werks, laced his shoes as he prepared to head out for his exercise break in Ottawa. It was February 7, 2011, and Samarin needed to decide what to do with the information he had uncovered while performing a routine file-clean of his company's servers.

Located in Ottawa's trendy Glebe neighbourhood, software developer OrangeWerks was prepar-

ing to present to venture capital firms for its first major round of funding. It was also fielding media interview requests the following week from the *Ottawa Citizen* and *The National Post*, both interested in writing news stories about OrangeWerks' phenomenal increase in software licenses for its OrangeWerks App Creator, a mobile application software development platform.

OrangeWerks

OrangeWerks was founded in March 2010 by two successful entrepreneurs to create software applications for the Apple platform. The founders had noticed the growing popularity of Apple devices and wanted to capitalize on the recent launch of the Apple iPad. Furthermore, independent research by firms such as Forrester Research and Gartner suggested that the consumer market would continue to demand these and other products designed to access content on the Internet.

Fuelling the popularity of Apple OS-based devices was Apple's unique combination of appealing design, intuitive user interfaces, and the proliferation of downloadable—and inexpensive—applications (or "apps") for entertainment, business, and other uses.

OrangeWerks had developed an application development platform—OrangeWerks App Creator (OAC)—that allowed novice users to create their own Apple app without any software training. They began to popularize their product by allowing consumers to download a limited version of their software free of charge.

To attract media attention, OrangeWerks had been targeting business customers for OAC, reporting on December 15, 2010, that the number of business software licences awarded for both its rough and beta versions had jumped from 1500 to 20 000 in the last two months.

Staffing OrangeWerks

The founders had assembled their team largely from personal connections, and Samarin was employee number two and their first engineer hired. Although hired as chief product developer, Samarin was initially tasked with everything from setting up desktop computers for the public relations consultants and marketing personnel to fixing broken light bulbs. His projects also included configuring OrangeWerks' hardware and software to run its Web site and internal operations.

Samarin's First Projects

Starting with personal funds of less than Cdn$20 000, the two founders had intended to seek angel funding immediately. To do that, they needed to show that they were on track to building a viable business. First, they needed a Web site, and a staff of developers to create a working model of their software program.

For OrangeWerks' software platform, the company asked Samarin to create a functioning database on top of a UNIX-based operating system. Samarin realized that the 15-year-old server and packet switching hardware that they had recently purchased to run the software was outdated and inadequate. He convinced the founders that they would have to acquire newer equipment to achieve the desired functionality. Reluctantly, Samarin's request was met after a week of indecision.

When the new hardware arrived in April 2010, Samarin offered to telephone the major software companies to purchase the requisite software licenses. Thus, Samarin was surprised when the founders decided to take the discussion out of the office by inviting him to a lunch meeting. OrangeWerks had been in operation for four weeks at this point, and had only five employees.

The Request

Over lunch at the "Market" (as the ByWard Market is known in Ottawa), Samarin was informed that no more funds existed for the purchase of software. Samarin was told that it was his responsibility to load software onto the machines.

Samarin had several other projects that were awaiting his attention, but he did not want to disappoint his friends and new employers. Relying on several industry contacts, Samarin acquired new, cracked[1] version of software required to run OrangeWerks' operations.

Known in the software industry as "warez,"[2] these were fully functional software programs made available to the public by software engineers who had cracked the software's security and validation codes.

Legitimate users typically purchased a software license from the supplier, who included a code to validate to software, making it available for use. Samarin knew that it was not legal to condone the use of warez. He explained:

Of course I know it's an ethical dilemma. But which side of the line do I stand on? The white line, the black line, or do I thread the fine line in the middle?

---

1 "Cracked" refers to the fact that the security code has been cracked, enabling use of the program without purchase.

2 Pronounced "wares."

The Angel Round of Funding

One month later, in May 2010, OrangeWerks secured Cdn$3 million in funding from various angel investors in Canada and the United States. The founders were extremely proud of having secured the amount, in spite of the fact that the continued downturn in the economy was affecting investor confidence. Euphoric, they embarked on an office expansion, hired another 45 people, and prepared a fall marketing campaign.

Samarin was rewarded with a bonus of Cdn$5000, payable upon completion of a year's work, but was reassigned as a network administrator.

Samarin did not notice any attempt by the founders to acquire software licence agreements.

Rapid Growth at OrangeWerks

With the infusion, a newly hired team of 8 engineers began coding the first beta release of OAC. The team of marketers were given the latest Apple iPhones and a travel budget to fly to seminars and conferences to promote OAC at key industry conferences including Apple's WWDC (Worldwide Developers Conference) in San Francisco. The Canadian media, hungry for stories in the slow August to September period, pounced on the chance to tout OrangeWerks as the most promising start-up in the app development market, generating thousands of media impressions in the process.

Progress is Slowed

But the internal climate at OrangeWerks was different. The team of 8 engineers had split into two factions, bickering over creative control of the project. In the process, engineering work for OAC stalled, and key engineers tendered their resignations in frustration. By November 2010, OrangeWerks had only a rough working model of OAC. However, plans were still in place to approach venture capitalists in December for Cdn$15 million, and interested parties were still being promised a December beta release.

The Founders Take Action

The two founders began taking control of the situation in late November, firing 4 of the software engineers and giving the remaining team new goals to meet. Within two weeks, the situation stabilized and a climate of productivity returned. It seemed that a sense of urgency at OrangeWerks had re-emerged, and

on the 12th of December, the founders announced to employees that the beta version was ready.

A press release was issued on the 15th of December, announcing that a limited version of OrangeWerks' OAC was being rapidly adopted by consumers, reaching 20 000 licences awarded. The licences for the limited versions had been awarded at no cost in order to rapidly gain market share.[3] OrangeWerks, paraphrasing a company press release, explained that it intended to charge developers for its 1.0 release.

The Discovery

As part of his monthly duties, Samarin performed a file-clean-up of OrangeWerks' internal file folders. One of the founders had purchased a new laptop and had asked Samarin to load new software and transfer old files for him. While manually transferring the files on the morning of December 28, Samarin recovered a deleted e-mail. In the e-mail fragment, the founder outlined that 15 000 fake accounts had been created by him to download the OAC program. The e-mail had apparently been written to the other founder in order to inform him of this occurrence.

Scrolling further, he chanced upon a more recent e-mail fragment from the Ontario Workplace Safety and Insurance Board (WSIB):

> . . . You have not filled out the necessary forms to register your company with the WSIB . . . the employees of the OrangeWerks are not covered and cannot claim benefits if they are involved in a workplace accident . . . you are in direct violation of workplace safety standards.

Perplexed, Samarin shut down the computers and headed out for his break.

Samarin's Dilemma

Finishing his run, Samarin decided to take an extended lunch to stroll around Ottawa's Parliament buildings. Even though it was unusually warm for a February in Ottawa, Samarin had other things on his mind.

> Has OrangeWerks paid for the software we use to create OAC? What do these e-mail fragments mean?

---

3 It was common practice in the software industry to award free licences to developers willing to test a new software tool. At the company's discretion, a fee could be charged for subsequent software upgrades.

We're not covered under the WSIB. If I had fallen and broken my neck while changing light bulbs or electrocuted myself while wiring computers, I would have been finished.

Calming himself, Samarin headed back to his desk at OrangeWerks. He had a lot to think about.

Ken Mark prepared this case under the supervision of Professor Christina Cavanagh solely to provide material for class discussion. The authors do not intend to illustrate either effective or ineffective handling of a managerial situation. The authors may have disguised certain names and other identifying information to protect confidentiality.

QUESTIONS

1. Discuss the power dynamics at OrangeWerks. What bases of power do the founders hold over David Samarin? What bases of power does he hold over them?

2. What are some likely causes of unethical behaviour in contemporary high-tech start-ups such as OrangeWerks?

3. There are clearly ethical issues at play in the case. Who are the various stakeholders in this ethical drama?

4. Which action is most and least unethical—employing pirated software, creating 15 000 fake download accounts, or failing to register with the Workplace Safety and Insurance Board?

5. Did David act ethically in reading the email fragments?

6. Describe the role conflict faced by David.

7. Discuss how David might employ *influence tactics* and *political skill* to help resolve his ethical dilemma.

8. What should David do now?

CONFLICT AND STRESS

LEARNING OBJECTIVES

After reading Chapter 13, you should be able to:

13.1 Define *interpersonal conflict* and review its causes in organizations.

13.2 Explain the *types of conflict* and the process by which conflict occurs.

13.3 Discuss the various *modes of managing conflict*.

13.4 Review a range of *negotiation techniques*.

13.5 Discuss the merits of *stimulating conflict*.

13.6 Distinguish among *stressors*, *stress*, and *stress reactions*.

13.7 Discuss the role that personality plays in stress.

13.8 Review the sources of stress encountered by various organizational role occupants.

13.9 Describe *behavioural*, *psychological*, and *physiological reactions* to stress, and discuss techniques for managing stress.

THE TORONTO HAIR WAR: GLO VERSUS GLISS

A dispute between two of Yorkville's ritziest hair salons has degenerated into a sniping war involving seized garbage, surprise searches, and a $6.4 million lawsuit. The fight centres on Glo Salon & Spa, a high-end beauty purveyor on [Toronto's] Avenue Road that caters to some of the city's wealthiest women. A Glo cut and colour starts at about $200 and goes up quickly from there.

"(Hairstyling) is a dirty little business, laughed Luis Pacheco, co-owner of nearby Hair on the Avenue, who is watching this scrap from the sidelines. "It's like a cesspool."

Three years ago, hairstylist Perry Neglia and a partner sold Glo to Mary Louise Abrahamse, who was new to the salon business. As part of the $450 000 sale, Neglia agreed to continue working at Glo for a year and not to open a competing business for three years. It's not clear who did what to whom over the next three years, but it's plain that relations between Abrahamse and some of her new staff became strained. On April 1, the day after his non-compete clause expired, Neglia opened a rival salon 100 metres up the street, calling it Gliss. Over the next several weeks, a steady stream of Glo hairstylists and colour technicians followed Neglia the short walk up Avenue Road. More importantly, "a high percentage" of their clients came with them, according to Neglia. He and his new staffers contacted long-time customers to let them know about the switch. "It would be rude not to tell them," Neglia said in an interview. "It would look like we didn't want to take them. They'd feel jilted."

"She thinks she bought the clients," Jarmil Kulik, Neglia's new partner and a former Glo stylist, said of Abrahamse. "And nobody does that," said Neglia. As a result, Glo was left with a denuded staff without well-developed client rosters, according to Abrahamse's lawsuit. One of her lawyers, Bob Klotz, said in an interview that his client's business has been "destroyed." Abrahamse declined comment.

For several weeks, things settled to a low boil. But while Neglia and his staff were building their new business, Abrahamse was working behind the scenes to unsettle them. She hired private investigators to go through Gliss's trash. They sent dummy clients into Gliss to look around. The object of the search was to determine what, if anything, Gliss staff had removed from Glo. Key to that investigation were the so-called "colour cards" that are used to chart the chemical formula for colouring hair. The cards often contain a client's contact info. Abrahamse's legal team asserts that the cards are her property. Neglia counters that cards were the property of individual staffers when he owned Glo, and that the rule was not changed after he sold the business. He claims that his staff copied the information on the cards and left the originals at Glo. "That way (the customers) have a choice about which

Former Glo staff, now at Gliss, embroiled in a $6.4 million suit.

salon they want to go to," said Neglia in an interview. The practice of taking cards and luring away clients often causes ugly breakups in the hairstyling business but is so pervasive that most salon owners grudgingly accept it. "Clients have free will, too. There's no ownership," said Hair on the Avenue owner Pacheco. "Is it fair to take [the cards]? I would say so."

The investigators found enough to persuade a judge to issue an Anton Piller order, an extraordinary legal device that allows a private search without notice so that evidence cannot be destroyed. On the morning of June 4, a team of lawyers and forensic technicians, including a videographer, arrived to search Gliss. "It was like something out of *Law & Order,*" said stylist Stephen Jackson, one of those who left Glo to join Neglia. At the same time, another half-dozen people turned up at Neglia's home. Both groups brought police officers to act as peacekeepers. Staffers at Gliss were told to hand over cellphones, the contents of which were then copied. A total of six computers at the business and at Neglia's home were confiscated and cloned. About a thousand colour cards and binders with client information were also taken and have yet to be returned. All of that property is now being held by an independent auditor. Neglia, Kulik, Jackson and five other former Glo staff members then learned they were being sued for a total of $6.4 million. "It's mind-boggling," said Brian Menzies, a colourist and co-defendant.

The fight has caused a flutter around Yorkville, where dozens of high-end salons have clustered in the years since Vidal Sassoon opened his landmark shop in the late '60s. "I think everyone thinks Mary Louise is out of her mind, that she's crazy," said Marianne Marshall, the city's top beauty trade headhunter. She said both Abrahamse and Neglia are her clients. It's also raising questions among hair professionals and their clients about who owns what in the prim world of beauty salons. "What is she (Abrahamse) suing for?" said Marlene Hore, an advertising exec who moved up the street to Gliss to continue getting her hair done by Jackson. "Don't I have a right to go wherever I want to have my hair cut?"

On Monday, Justice Colin Campbell thought better of the Anton Piller order. He intends to set it aside, dealing a blow to Abrahamse's suit. However, Klotz said that his client intends to continue. "Sure, Mary Louise is mad," said headhunter Marshall. "But suing Perry (Neglia) is not going to accomplish anything. This way, everyone gets dragged through the mud. And, in the end, I don't think she's going to win."[1]

GORDON LAW GROUP: CONFLICT AND NEGOTIATION Go to MyManagementLab to watch a video about conflict and negotiation.

Define *interpersonal conflict* and review its causes in organizations.

Interpersonal conflict. The process that occurs when one person, group, or organizational subunit frustrates the goal attainment of another.

In this chapter, we will define *interpersonal conflict*, discuss its causes, and examine various ways of handling conflict, including negotiation. Then we will explore *work stress*, noting its causes and the consequences that it can have for both individuals and organizations. Various strategies for managing stress will be considered.

WHAT IS CONFLICT?

Interpersonal conflict is a process that occurs when one person, group, or organizational subunit frustrates the goal attainment of another. Thus, the curator of a museum might be in conflict with the director over the purchase of a particular work of art. Likewise, the entire curatorial staff might be in conflict with the financial staff over cutbacks in acquisition funds.

In its classic form, conflict often involves antagonistic attitudes and behaviours, as seen in the drama concerning the Toronto hair salons. As for attitudes, the conflicting parties might develop a dislike for each other, see each other as unreasonable, and develop negative stereotypes of their opposites ("Those scientists should get out of the laboratory once in a while"). Antagonistic behaviours might include name calling, sabotage, or even physical aggression. In some organizations, the conflict process is managed in a collaborative way that keeps antagonism at a minimum. In others, conflict is hidden or suppressed and not nearly so obvious (e.g., some gender conflict).[2]

CAUSES OF ORGANIZATIONAL CONFLICT

It is possible to isolate a number of factors that contribute to organizational conflict.[3]

Group Identification and Intergroup Bias

An especially fascinating line of research has shown how identification with a particular group or class of people can set the stage for organizational conflict. In this work, researchers have typically assigned people to groups randomly or on the basis of some trivial characteristic, such as eye colour. Even without interaction or cohesion, people have a tendency to develop a more positive view of their own "in-group" and a less positive view of the "out-group," of which they are not a member.[4] The ease with which this unwarranted intergroup bias develops is disturbing.

Why does intergroup bias occur? Self-esteem is probably a critical factor. Identifying with the successes of one's own group and disassociating oneself from out-group failures boosts self-esteem and provides comforting feelings of social solidarity. Research by one of your authors, for example, found that people felt that their work group's attendance record was superior to that of their occupation in general (and, by extension, other work groups).[5] Attributing positive behaviour to your own work group should contribute to your self-esteem.

In organizations, there are a number of groups or classes with which people might identify. These might be based on personal characteristics (e.g., race or gender), job function (e.g., sales or production), or job level (e.g., manager or non-manager). Furthermore, far from being random or trivial, differences between groups might be accentuated by real differences in power, opportunity, clients serviced, and so on. For instance, the merger between Air Canada and Canadian Airlines made firm identities very salient for employees, and these identities persisted even after the companies merged into a single entity. The best prognosis is that people who identify with some groups will tend to be leery of out-group members. The likelihood of conflict increases as the factors we cover below enter into the relationship between groups.

The increased emphasis on teams in organizations generally places a high premium on getting employees to identify strongly with their team. The prevalence of intergroup bias suggests that organizations will have to pay special attention to managing relationships *between* these teams.

Interdependence

When individuals or subunits are mutually dependent on each other to accomplish *their own* goals, the potential for conflict exists. For example, the sales staff is dependent on the production department for the timely delivery of high-quality products. This is the only way sales can maintain the goodwill of its customers. On the other hand, production depends on the sales staff to provide routine orders with adequate lead times. Custom-tailored emergency orders will wreak havoc with production schedules and make the production department look bad. In contrast, the sales staff and the office maintenance staff are not highly interdependent. Salespeople are on the road a lot and should not make great demands on maintenance. Conversely, a dirty office probably will not lose a sale.

Interdependence can set the stage for conflict for two reasons. First, it necessitates interaction between the parties so that they can coordinate their interests. Conflict will not develop if the parties can "go it alone." Second, as we noted in the previous chapter, interdependence implies that each party has some *power* over the other. It is relatively easy for one side or the other to abuse its power and create antagonism.

Interdependence does not *always* lead to conflict. In fact, it often provides a good basis for collaboration through mutual assistance. Whether interdependence prompts conflict depends on the presence of other conditions, which we will now consider.

Differences in Power, Status, and Culture

Conflict can erupt when parties differ significantly in power, status, or culture.

POWER If dependence is not mutual but one-way, the potential for conflict increases. If party A needs the collaboration of party B to accomplish its goals but B does not need A's assistance, antagonism may develop. B has power over A, and A has nothing with which to bargain. A good example is the quality control system in many factories. Production workers might be highly dependent on inspectors to approve their work, but this dependence is not reciprocated. The inspectors might have a separate boss, their own office, and their own circle of friends (other inspectors). In this case, production workers might begin to treat inspectors with hostility, one of the symptoms of conflict.

STATUS Status differences provide little impetus for conflict when people of lower status are dependent on those of higher status. This is the way organizations often work, and most members are socialized to expect it. However, because of the design of the work, there are occasions when employees who technically have lower status find themselves giving orders to, or controlling the tasks of, higher-status people. The restaurant business provides a good example. In many restaurants, lower-status servers give orders and initiate queries to higher-status chefs. The latter might come to resent this reversal of usual lines of influence.[6] In some organizations, junior staff are more adept with information technology than senior staff. Some executives are defensive about this reversal of roles.

CULTURE When two or more very different cultures develop in an organization, the clash in beliefs and values can result in overt conflict. Hospital administrators who develop a strong culture centred on efficiency and cost-effectiveness might find themselves in conflict with physicians who share a strong culture based on providing excellent patient care at any cost. A telling case of cultural conflict occurred when Apple Computer expanded and hired professionals away from several companies with their own strong cultures.

> *During the first couple of years Apple recruited heavily from Hewlett-Packard, National Semiconductor, and Intel, and the habits and differences in style among these companies were reflected in Cupertino. There was a general friction between the rough and tough ways of the semiconductor men (there were few women) and the people who made computers,*

> *calculators, and instruments at Hewlett-Packard.... Some of the Hewlett-Packard men began to see themselves as civilizing influences and were horrified at the uncouth rough-and-tumble practices of the brutes from the semiconductor industry.... Many of the men from National Semiconductor and other stern backgrounds harboured a similar contempt for the Hewlett-Packard recruits. They came to look on them as prissy fusspots.[7]*

Ambiguity

Ambiguous goals, jurisdictions, or performance criteria can lead to conflict. Under such ambiguity, the formal and informal rules that govern interaction break down. In addition, it might be difficult to accurately assign praise for good outcomes or blame for bad outcomes when it is hard to see who was responsible for what. For example, if sales drop following the introduction of a "new and improved" product, the design group might blame the marketing department for a poor advertising campaign. In response, the marketers might claim that the "improved" product is actually inferior to the old product.

Ambiguous performance criteria are a frequent cause of conflict between managers and employees. The basic scientist who is charged by a chemical company to "discover new knowledge" might react negatively when her boss informs her that her work is inadequate. This rather open-ended assignment is susceptible to a variety of interpretations. Conflict is not uncommon in the film and entertainment industry, in part because a great deal of ambiguity surrounds just what is needed to produce a hit movie or show. In the up-market atmosphere of Yorkville's hair salons, there is apparent ambiguity about who "owns" client information such as colour cards.

Scarce Resources

In the previous chapter we pointed out that differences in power are magnified when resources become scarce. This does not occur without a battle, however, and conflict often surfaces in the process of power jockeying. Limited budget money, secretarial support, or lab space can contribute to conflict. Scarcity has a way of turning latent or disguised conflict into overt conflict. Two scientists who do not get along very well may be able to put up a peaceful front until a reduction in lab space provokes each to protect his or her domain. In the chapter-opening vignette, the battle between Glo and Gliss was most decidedly provoked by scarce resources—wealthy customers willing to pay $200 for a haircut and colour.

LO 13.2

Explain the *types of conflict* and the process by which conflict occurs.

Relationship conflict. Interpersonal tensions among individuals that have to do with their relationship per se, not the task at hand.

Task conflict. Disagreements about the nature of the work to be done.

Process conflict. Disagreements about how work should be organized and accomplished.

TYPES OF CONFLICT

Is all conflict the same? The answer is no. It is useful to distinguish among relationship, task, and process conflict.[8] **Relationship conflict** concerns interpersonal tensions among individuals that have to do with their relationship per se, not the task at hand. So-called personality clashes are examples of relationship conflicts. **Task conflict** concerns disagreements about the nature of the work to be done. Differences of opinion about goals or technical matters are examples of task conflict. Finally, **process conflict** involves disagreements about how work should be organized and accomplished. Disagreements about responsibility, authority, resource allocation, and who should do what all constitute process conflict.

In the context of work groups and teams, relationship and process conflict tend to be detrimental to member satisfaction and team performance. In essence, such conflict prevents the development of cohesiveness (Chapter 7). Occasionally, some degree of task conflict is actually beneficial for team performance, especially when the task is non-routine and requires a variety of perspectives to be considered and when it does not degenerate into relationship conflict.[9] Thus, not all conflict is detrimental, and we shall return to some potential benefits of conflict later in the chapter.

CONFLICT DYNAMICS

A number of events occur when one or more of the causes of conflict we noted above take effect. We will assume here that the conflict in question occurs between groups, such as organizational departments. However, much of this is also relevant to conflict within teams or between individuals. Specifically, when conflict begins, we often see the following events transpire:

- "Winning" the conflict becomes more important than developing a good solution to the problem at hand.

- The parties begin to conceal information from each other or to pass on distorted information.

- Each side becomes more cohesive. Deviants who speak of conciliation are punished, and strict conformity is expected.

- Contact with the opposite party is discouraged except under formalized, restricted conditions.

- While the opposite party is negatively stereotyped, the image of one's own position is boosted.

- On each side, more aggressive people who are skilled at engaging in conflict may emerge as leaders.[10]

You can certainly see the difficulty here. What begins as a problem of identity, interdependence, ambiguity, or scarcity quickly escalates to the point that the conflict process *itself* becomes an additional problem. The elements of this process then work against the achievement of a peaceful solution. The conflict continues to cycle "on its own steam," as illustrated in the "Hair War" vignette.

MODES OF MANAGING CONFLICT

How do you tend to react to conflict situations? Are you aggressive? Do you tend to hide your head in the sand? As conflict expert Kenneth Thomas notes, there are several basic reactions that can be thought of as styles, strategies, or intentions for dealing with conflict. As shown in Exhibit 13.1, these approaches to managing conflict are a function of both how *assertive* you are in trying to satisfy your own or your group's concerns and how *cooperative* you are in trying to satisfy those of the other party or group.[11] It should be emphasized that none of the five

LO 13.3

Discuss the various *modes of managing conflict.*

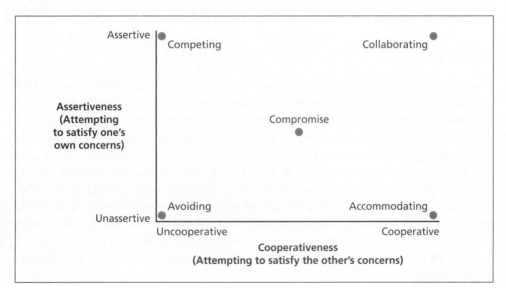

EXHIBIT 13.1
Approaches to managing organizational conflict.
Source: Thomas, K.W. (1992). Conflict and negotiations in organizations" in M.D. Dunnette, & L.M. Hough, (Eds.) *Handbook of industrial and organizational psychology* (2nd Ed., Vol. 3). Palo Alto, CA: Consulting Psychologists Press. Used by permission of the publisher.

✳ Explore

Go to MyManagementLab to see an annotated version of this figure.

styles for dealing with conflict in Exhibit 13.1 is inherently superior. As we will see, each style might have its place given the situation in which the conflict episode occurs. To diagnose how you manage conflict, try the Experiential Exercise at the end of the chapter.

Avoiding

Avoiding. A conflict management style characterized by low assertiveness of one's own interests and low cooperation with the other party.

The **avoiding** style is characterized by low assertiveness of one's own interests and low cooperation with the other party. This is the "hiding one's head in the sand" response. Although avoidance can provide some short-term stress reduction from the rigours of conflict, it does not really change the situation. Thus, its effectiveness is often limited.

Of course, avoidance does have its place. If the issue is trivial, information is lacking, people need to cool down, or the opponent is very powerful and very hostile, avoidance might be a sensible response.

Accommodating

Accommodating. A conflict management style in which one cooperates with the other party while not asserting one's own interests.

Cooperating with the other party's wishes while not asserting one's own interests is the hallmark of **accommodating**. If people see accommodation as a sign of weakness, it does not bode well for future interactions. However, it can be an effective reaction when you are wrong, the issue is more important to the other party, or you want to build good will.

Competing

Competing. A conflict management style that maximizes assertiveness and minimizes cooperation.

A **competing** style tends to maximize assertiveness for your own position and minimize cooperative responses. In competing, you tend to frame the conflict in strict win–lose terms. Full priority is given to your own goals, facts, or procedures. Bill Gates, the billionaire czar of Microsoft, tends to pursue the competing style:

> Gates is famously confrontational. If he strongly disagrees with what you're saying, he is in the habit of blurting out, "That's the stupidest…thing I've ever heard!" People tell stories of Gates spraying saliva into the face of some hapless employee as he yells, "This stuff isn't hard! I could do this stuff in a weekend!" What you're supposed to do in a situation like this, as in encounters with grizzly bears, is stand your ground: if you flee, the bear will think you're game and will pursue you, and you can't outrun a bear.[12]

The competing style holds promise when you have a lot of power, you are sure of your facts, the situation is truly win–lose, or you will not have to interact with the other party in the future. This style is illustrated in the chapter-opening vignette.

Compromise

Compromise. A conflict management style that combines intermediate levels of assertiveness and cooperation.

Compromise combines intermediate levels of assertiveness and cooperation. Thus, it is itself a compromise between pure competition and pure accommodation. In a sense, you attempt to satisfice (Chapter 11) rather than maximize your outcomes and hope that the same occurs for the other party. In the law, a plea bargain is an example of a compromise between the defending lawyer and the prosecutor.

Compromise places a premium on determining rules of exchange between the two parties. As such, it always contains the seeds for procedural conflict in addition to whatever else is being negotiated. Also, compromise does not always result in the most creative response to conflict. Compromise is not so useful for resolving conflicts that stem from power asymmetry, because the weaker party may have little to offer the stronger party. However, it is a sensible reaction to conflict stemming from scarce resources. Also, it is a good fallback position if other strategies fail.

Collaborating

In the **collaborating** mode, both assertiveness and cooperation are maximized in the hope that an integrative agreement occurs that fully satisfies the interests of both parties. Emphasis is put on a win–win resolution, in which there is no assumption that someone must lose something. Rather, it is assumed that the solution to the conflict can leave both parties in a better condition. Ideally, collaboration occurs as a problem-solving exercise (Chapter 11). It probably works best when the conflict is not intense and when each party has information that is useful to the other. Although effective collaboration can take time and practice to develop, it frequently enhances productivity and achievement.[13]

Some of the most remarkable examples of collaboration in contemporary organizations are those between companies and their suppliers. Traditionally, adversarial competition in which buyers try to squeeze the very lowest price out of suppliers, who are frequently played off against each other, has dominated these relationships. This obviously does not provide much incentive for the perpetually insecure suppliers to invest in improvements dedicated toward a particular buyer. Gradually, things have changed, and now it is common for organizations to supply extensive engineering support and technical advice to their suppliers. In a related example, after the 2011 Japanese earthquake and tsunami the country's car manufacturers, usually fierce competitors, collaborated to get the nation's parts suppliers back on line.[14]

Collaboration also helps to manage conflict inside organizations. Our discussion of cross-functional teams in Chapter 7 is a good example. Also, research shows that collaboration between organizational departments is particularly important for providing good customer service.[15]

MANAGING CONFLICT WITH NEGOTIATION

The stereotype we have of negotiation is that it is a formal process of bargaining between labour and management or buyer and seller. However, job applicants negotiate for starting salaries, employees negotiate for better job assignments, and people with sick kids negotiate to leave work early. To encompass all these situations, we might define **negotiation** as "a

Collaborating. A conflict management style that maximizes both assertiveness and cooperation.

LO 13.4

Review a range of *negotiation techniques.*

Negotiation. A decision-making process among interdependent parties who do not share identical preferences.

Collaboration can provide unions and management with win–win solutions.

decision-making process among interdependent parties who do not share identical prefer-ences."[16] Negotiation constitutes conflict management, in that it is an attempt to either pre-vent conflict or resolve existing conflict.

Negotiation is an attempt to reach a satisfactory exchange among or between the parties. Sometimes, negotiation is very explicit, as in the case of the labour negotiation or the buyer–seller interaction. However, negotiation can also proceed in a very implicit or tacit way.[17] For instance, when an employee is trying to get a more interesting job assignment or to take off from work early, the terms of the exchange are not likely to be spelled out very clearly. Still, this is negotiation.

It has become common to distinguish between distributive and integrative negotiation tactics.[18] **Distributive negotiation** assumes a zero-sum, win–lose situation in which a fixed pie is divided up between the parties. If you re-examine Exhibit 13.1, you can imagine that distributive negotiation occurs on the axis between competition and accommodation. In theory, the parties will more or less tend toward some compromise. On the other hand, **inte-grative negotiation** assumes that mutual problem solving can result in a win–win situation in which the pie is actually enlarged before distribution. Integrative negotiation occurs on the axis between avoiding and collaborating, ideally tending toward the latter.

Distributive and integrative negotiations can take place simultaneously. We will discuss them separately for pedagogical purposes.

Distributive Negotiation Tactics

Distributive negotiation is essentially single-issue negotiation. Many potential conflict situ-ations fit this scenario. For example, suppose you find a used car that you really like. Now, things boil down to price. You want to buy the car for the minimum reasonable price, while the seller wants to get the maximum reasonable price.

The essence of the problem is shown in Exhibit 13.2. Party is a consulting firm who would like to win a contract to do an attitude survey in Other's firm. Party would like to make $90 000 for the job (Party's target) but would settle for $70 000, a figure that provides

Distributive negotiation. Win–lose negotiation in which a fixed amount of assets is divided between parties.

Integrative negotiation. Win–win negotiation that assumes that mutual problem solving can enlarge the assets to be divided between parties.

EXHIBIT 13.2
A model of distributive negotiation.
Source: Thomas, K.W. (1992). Conflict and negotiations in organizations" in M.D. Dun-nette, & L.M. Hough (Eds.) *Handbook of industrial and organizational psychology* (2nd Ed., Vol. 3). Palo Alto, CA: Consulting Psychologists Press. Used by permission of the publisher.

 Explore

Go to MyManagementLab to see an annotated version of this figure.

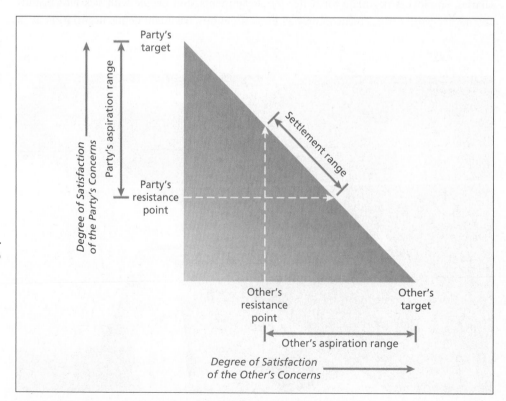

for minimal acceptable profit (Party's resistance point). Other thinks that the survey could be done for as little as $60 000 (Other's target) but would be willing to spend up to $80 000 for a good job (Other's resistance point). Theoretically, an offer in the settlement range between $70 000 and $80 000 should clinch the deal, if the negotiators can get into this range. Notice that every dollar that Party earns is a dollar's worth of cost for Other. How will they reach a settlement?[19]

THREATS AND PROMISES *Threat* consists of implying that you will punish the other party if he or she does not concede to your position. For example, the Other firm might imply that it will terminate its other business with the consulting company if Party does not lower its price on the attitude survey job. *Promises* are pledges that concessions will lead to rewards in the future. For example, Other might promise future consulting contracts if Party agrees to do the survey at a lower price. Of course, the difference between a threat and a promise can be subtle, as when the promise implies a threat should no concession be made.

Threat has some merit as a bargaining tactic if one party has power over the other that corresponds to the nature of the threat, especially if no future negotiations are expected or if the threat can be posed in a civil and subtle way.[20] If power is more balanced and the threat is crude, a counter threat could scuttle the negotiations, despite the fact that both parties could be satisfied in the settlement range. Promises have merit when your side lacks power and anticipates future negotiations with the other side. Both threats and promises work best when they send interpretable signals to the other side about your true position, what really matters to you. Careful timing is critical.

FIRMNESS VERSUS CONCESSIONS How about intransigence—sticking to your target position, offering few concessions, and waiting for the other party to give in? Research shows that such a tactic yields superior economic results, especially in face-to-face negotiations.[21] When some concessions are thought to be appropriate, good negotiators often use face-saving techniques to explain them. For example, the consulting firm might claim that it could reduce the cost of the survey by making it web-based rather than based on paper questionnaires.

PERSUASION Verbal persuasion or debate is common in negotiations. Often, it takes a two-pronged attack. One prong asserts the technical merits of the party's position. For example, the consulting firm might justify its target price by saying "We have the most qualified staff. We do the most reliable surveys." The other prong asserts the fairness of the target position. Here, the negotiator might make a speech about the expenses the company would incur in doing the survey.

Verbal persuasion is an attempt to change the attitudes of the other party toward your target position. Persuaders are most effective when they are perceived as expert, likable, and unbiased. The obvious problem in distributive negotiations is bias—each party knows the other is self-interested. One way to deal with this is to introduce some unbiased parties. For example, the consulting firm might produce testimony from satisfied survey clients. Also, disputants often bring third parties into negotiations on the assumption that they will process argumentation in an unbiased manner.

Salary negotiation is a traditional example of distributive bargaining. A review of studies on gender differences in negotiation outcomes found that although men negotiated significantly better outcomes than women, the overall difference between men and women was small. However, even small differences in salary negotiations would be perpetuated through subsequent salary increases based on percentage of pay. Thus, training programs that enable women to negotiate better starting salaries comparable with men can have short- and long-term benefits.[22] Negotiation is worth doing, as a recent study showed that new hires who negotiated received a $5000 salary premium. Collaborating and competing strategies were superior to compromising and accommodating.[23]

Integrative Negotiation Tactics

As we noted earlier, integrative negotiation rejects a fixed-pie assumption and strives for col-laborative problem solving that advances the interests of both parties. At the outset, it is useful but sobering to realize that people have a decided bias for fixed-pie thinking. A good example is seen in the North American manufacturing sector, where such thinking by both unions and management badly damaged the global competitiveness of manufacturing firms.[24]

Why the bias for fixed-pie thinking? First, integrative negotiation requires a degree of creativity. Most people are not especially creative, and the stress of typical negotiation does not provide the best climate for creativity in any event. This means that many of the role models that negotiators have (e.g., following labour negotiations on TV) are more likely to use distributive than integrative tactics. To complicate matters, if you are negotiating for constitu-ents, they are also more likely to be exposed to distributive tactics and likely to pressure you to use them. Nevertheless, attempts at integrative negotiation can be well worth the effort.[25]

COPIOUS INFORMATION EXCHANGE   Most of the information exchanged in distributive bargaining is concerned with attacking the other party's position and trying to persuade them of the correctness of yours. Otherwise, mum's the word. A freer flow of information is critical to finding an integrative settlement. The problem, of course, is that we all tend to be a bit para-noid about information being used against us in bargaining situations. This means that trust must be built slowly. One way to proceed is to give away some non-critical information to the other party to get the ball rolling. As we noted earlier, much negotiation behaviour tends to be reciprocated. Also, ask the other party a lot of questions, and *listen* to their responses. This is at odds with the tell-and-sell approach used in most distributive negotiations. If all goes well, both parties will begin to reveal their true interests, not just their current positions.

FRAMING DIFFERENCES AS OPPORTUNITIES   Parties in a negotiation often differ in their preferences, for everything from the timing of a deal to the degree of risk that each party wants to assume. Traditionally, such differences are framed as barriers to negotiations. However, such differences can often serve as a basis for integrative agreements because, again, they contain information that can telegraph each party's real interests. For instance, imag-ine that two co-workers are negotiating for the finishing date of a project that they have to complete by a certain deadline. Due to competing demands, one wants to finish it early, and the other wants to just make the deadline. In the course of the discussion, they realize that they can divide the labour such that one begins the project while the other finishes it, satisfying both parties fully (notice that this is not a compromise).

CUTTING COSTS   If you can somehow cut the costs that the other party associates with an agreement, the chance of an integrative settlement increases. For example, suppose that you are negotiating with your boss for a new, more interesting job assignment, but she does not like the idea because she relies on your excellent skills on your current assignment. By asking good questions (see above), you find out that she is ultimately worried about the job being done properly, not about your leaving it. You take the opportunity to inform her that you have groomed a subordinate to do your current job. This reduces the costs of her letting you assume the new assignment.

Integrative solutions are especially attractive when they reduce costs for *all* parties in a dispute. For example, firms in the computer and acoustics industries have joined together to support basic research on technology of interest to all firms. This reduces costly competition to perfect a technology that all parties need anyway.

INCREASING RESOURCES   Increasing available resources is a very literal way of getting around the fixed-pie syndrome. This is not as unlikely as it sounds when you realize that two parties, working together, might have access to twice as many resources as one party. One of your authors once saw two academic departments squabbling to get the approval to recruit one new faculty member for whom there was a budget line. Seeing this as a fixed pie leads to one department winning all or to the impossible compromise of half a recruit for each department. The chairs of the two departments used their *combined* political clout to get the dean to promise that they could also have exclusive access to one budget line the following year. The chairs then flipped a coin to see who would recruit immediately and who would wait a year. This minor compromise on time was less critical than the firm guarantee of a budget line.

INTRODUCING SUPERORDINATE GOALS As discussed in Chapter 7, **superordinate goals** are attractive outcomes that can be achieved only by collaboration.[26] Neither party can attain the goal on its own. Superordinate goals probably represent the best example of creativity in integrative negotiation because they change the entire landscape of the negotiation episode. Many observers have noted how the terrorist attacks on September 11, 2001, created a superordinate goal that prompted collaboration among nations that otherwise might have been mired in conflict over more trivial matters.

Superordinate goals.
Attractive outcomes that can be achieved only by collaboration.

Third Party Involvement

Sometimes, third parties come into play to intervene between negotiating parties.[27] Often, this happens when the parties reach an impasse. For example, a manager might have to step in to a conflict between two employees or even between two departments. In other cases, third party involvement exists right from the start of the negotiation. For example, real estate agents serve as an interface between home sellers and buyers.

MEDIATION The process of mediation occurs when a neutral third party helps to facilitate a negotiated agreement. Formal mediation has a long history in labour disputes, international relations, and marital counselling. However, by definition, almost any manager might occasionally be required to play an informal mediating role.

What do mediators do?[28] First, almost anything that aids the *process* or *atmosphere* of negotiation can be helpful. Of course, this depends on the exact situation at hand. If there is tension, the mediator might serve as a lightning rod for anger or try to introduce humour. The mediator might try to help the parties clarify their underlying interests, both to themselves and to each other. Occasionally, imposing a deadline or helping the parties deal with their own constituents might be useful. Introducing a problem-solving orientation to move toward more integrative bargaining might also be appropriate.

The mediator might also intervene in the *content* of the negotiation, highlighting points of agreement, pointing out new options, or encouraging concessions.

Research shows that mediation has a fairly successful track record in dispute resolution. However, mediators cannot turn water into wine, and the process seems to work best when the conflict is not too intense and the parties are resolved to use negotiation to deal with their conflict. If the mediator is not seen as neutral or if there is dissension in the ranks of each negotiating party, mediation does not work so well.[29]

ARBITRATION The process of arbitration occurs when a third party is given the authority to dictate the terms of settlement of a conflict (there is also non-binding arbitration, which we will not consider here). Although disputing parties sometimes agree to arbitration, it can also be mandated formally by law or informally by upper management or parents. The key point is that negotiation has broken down, and the arbitrator has to make a final distributive allocation. This is not the way to integrative solutions.

In *conventional arbitration*, the arbitrator can choose any outcome, such as splitting the difference between the two parties. In *final offer arbitration*, each party makes a final offer, and the arbitrator chooses one of them. This latter invention was devised to motivate the two parties to make sensible offers that have a chance of being upheld. Also, fear of the all-or-nothing aspect of final arbitration seems to motivate more negotiated agreement.[30]

One of the most commonly arbitrated disputes between employers and employees is dismissal for excessive absenteeism. One study found that the arbitrators sided with the company in over half of such cases, especially when the company could show evidence of a fair and consistently applied absentee policy.[31]

LO 13.5

Discuss the merits of *stimulating conflict.*

IS ALL CONFLICT BAD?

In everyday life, there has traditionally been an emphasis on the negative, dysfunctional aspects of conflict. This is not difficult to understand. Discord between parents and children, severe labour strife, and international disputes are unpleasant experiences. To some degree, this emphasis on the negative aspects of conflict is also characteristic of thinking in organizational behaviour. However, there is growing awareness of some potential *benefits* of organizational conflict.[32] In fact, we suggested this in our previous distinction among task, process, and relationship conflict.

The argument that conflict can be functional rests mainly on the idea that it promotes necessary organizational change:

$$CONFLICT \rightarrow CHANGE \rightarrow ADAPTATION \rightarrow SURVIVAL[33]$$

In other words, for organizations to survive, they must adapt to their environments. This requires changes in strategy that may be stimulated through conflict. For example, consider the museum that relies heavily on government funding and consistently mounts exhibits that are appreciated only by "true connoisseurs" of art. Under a severe funding cutback, the museum can survive only if it begins to mount exhibits with more popular appeal. Such a change might occur only after much conflict within the board of directors.

Just how does conflict promote change? For one thing, it might bring into consideration new ideas that would not be offered without conflict. In trying to "one up" the opponent, one of the parties might develop a unique idea that the other cannot fail to appreciate. In a related way, conflict might promote change because each party begins to monitor the other's performance more carefully. This search for weaknesses means that it is more difficult to hide errors and problems from the rest of the organization. Such errors and problems (e.g., a failure to make deliveries on time) might be a signal that changes are necessary. Finally, conflict may promote useful change by signalling that a redistribution of power is necessary. Consider the human resources department that must battle with managers to get diversity programs implemented. This conflict might be a clue that some change is due in power priorities.

Conflict stimulation.
A strategy of increasing conflict to motivate change.

All this suggests that there are times when managers might use a strategy of **conflict stimulation** to cause change. But how does a manager know when some conflict might be a good thing? One signal is the existence of a "friendly rut," in which peaceful relationships take precedence over organizational goals. Another signal is seen when parties that should be interacting closely have chosen to withdraw from each other to avoid overt conflict. A third signal occurs when conflict is suppressed or downplayed by denying differences, ignoring controversy, and exaggerating points of agreement.[34]

The causes of conflict, discussed earlier, such as scarcity and ambiguity, can be manipulated by managers to achieve change.[35] For example, when he was appointed vice-chairman of product development at General Motors, Robert Lutz sent out a memo entitled "Strongly Held Beliefs." In it, the product czar said that GM undervalued exciting design, and he panned corporate sacred cows such as the extensive use of consumer focus groups and product planning committees. Lutz stimulated conflict by signalling a shift of resources from marketing to design.[36]

Conflict in organizations, warranted or not, often causes considerable stress. Let's now turn to this topic.

A MODEL OF STRESS IN ORGANIZATIONS

During the last two decades, stress has become a serious concern for individuals and organizations. A U.S. National Institute for Occupational Safety and Health survey found that 40 percent of workers found their jobs extremely or very stressful, and the U.S. Bureau of Labor Statistics determined that stress is a leading cause of worker disability.[37] In fact, in an American Psychological Association survey, work was reported to be a potent source of stress, edging out health and relationships.[38] Stress has been estimated to cost U.S. businesses $300 billion annually and Canadian businesses $16 billion.[39] The model of a stress episode in Exhibit 13.3 can guide our introduction to this topic.[40]

Stressors

Stressors are environmental events or conditions that have the potential to induce stress. There are some conditions that would prove stressful for just about everyone. These include such things as extreme heat, extreme cold, isolation, or hostile people. More interesting is the fact that the individual personality often determines the extent to which a potential stressor becomes a real stressor and actually induces stress.

Stress

Stress is a psychological reaction to the demands inherent in a stressor that has the potential to make a person feel tense or anxious because the person does not feel capable of coping with these demands.[41] Stress is not intrinsically bad. All people require a certain level of stimulation from their environment, and moderate levels of stress can serve this function. In fact, one would wonder about the perceptual accuracy of a person who *never* experienced tension. On the other hand, stress does become a problem when it leads to especially high levels of anxiety and tension. Obviously, the "Hair War" described in the chapter-opening vignette has provoked much stress.

Stress Reactions

Stress reactions are the behavioural, psychological, and physiological consequences of stress. Some of these reactions are essentially passive responses over which the individual has little direct control, such as elevated blood pressure or a reduced immune function. Other reactions are active attempts to *cope* with some previous aspect of the stress episode. Exhibit 13.3 indicates that stress reactions that involve coping attempts might be directed toward dealing directly with the stressor or simply reducing the anxiety generated by stress. In general, the former strategy has more potential for effectiveness than the latter because the chances of the stress episode being *terminated* are increased.[42]

LO **13.6**

Distinguish among *stressors, stress,* and *stress reactions.*

 Watch

EAST HAVEN FIRE DEPARTMENT: MANAGING STRESS Go to MyManagementLab to watch a video about managing stress.

Stressors. Environmental events or conditions that have the potential to induce stress.

Stress. A psychological reaction to the demands inherent in a stressor that has the potential to make a person feel tense or anxious.

Stress reactions. The behavioural, psychological, and physiological consequences of stress.

EXHIBIT 13.3 Model of a stress episode.

Go to MyManagementLab to see an annotated version of this figure.

Often, reactions that are useful for the individual in dealing with a stress episode may be very costly to the organization. The individual who is conveniently absent from work on the day of a difficult inventory check might prevent personal stress but leave the organization short-handed (provoking stress in others). Thus, organizations should be concerned about the stress that individual employees experience.

Throughout the book, we have been careful to note cross-cultural differences in OB. However, the stress model presented here appears to generalize across cultures. That is, similar factors provoke stress and lead to similar stress reactions around the globe.[43]

Personality and Stress

LO 13.7

Discuss the role that personality plays in stress.

Personality (Chapter 2) can have an important influence on the stress experience. As shown in Exhibit 13.3, it can affect both the extent to which potential stressors are perceived as stressful and the types of stress reactions that occur. Let's look at three key personality traits.

Locus of control. A set of beliefs about whether one's behaviour is controlled mainly by internal or external forces.

LOCUS OF CONTROL

You will recall from Chapter 2 that **locus of control** concerns people's beliefs about the factors that control their behaviour. Internals believe that they control their own behaviour, while externals believe that their behaviour is controlled by luck, fate, or powerful people. Compared with internals, externals are more likely to feel anxious in the face of potential stressors.[44] Most people like to feel in control of what happens to them, and externals feel less in control. Internals are more likely to confront stressors directly because they assume that this response will make a difference. Externals, on the other hand, are anxious but do not feel that they are masters of their own fate. Thus, they are more prone to simple anxiety-reduction strategies that only work in the short run.

Type A behaviour pattern. A personality pattern that includes aggressiveness, ambitiousness, competitiveness, hostility, impatience, and a sense of time urgency.

TYPE A BEHAVIOUR PATTERN

Interest in the **Type A behaviour pattern** began when physicians noticed that many sufferers of coronary heart disease, especially those who developed the disease relatively young, exhibited a distinctive pattern of behaviours and emotions.[45] Individuals who exhibit the Type A behaviour pattern tend to be aggressive and ambitious. Their hostility is easily aroused, and they feel a great sense of time urgency. They are impatient, competitive, and preoccupied with their work. The Type A individual can be contrasted with the Type B, who does not exhibit these extreme characteristics. Compared with Type B individuals, Type A people report heavier workloads, longer work hours, and more conflicting work demands.[46] We will see later that such factors turn out to be potent stressors. Thus, either Type A people encounter more stressful situations than Type B people do, or they perceive themselves as doing so. In turn, Type A individuals are likely to exhibit adverse physiological reactions in response to stress. These include elevated blood pressure, elevated heart rate, and modified blood chemistry. Frustrating, difficult, or competitive events are especially likely to prompt these adverse reactions. Type A individuals seem to have a strong need to control their work environment. This is doubtless a full-time task that stimulates their feelings of time urgency and leads them to overextend themselves physically.[47]

Research has made it increasingly clear that the major component of Type A behaviour that contributes to adverse physiological reactions is hostility and repressed anger. This may also be accompanied by exaggerated cynicism and distrust of others. When these factors are prominent in a Type A individual's personality, stress is most likely to take its toll.[48]

Negative affectivity. Propensity to view the world, including oneself and other people, in a negative light.

NEGATIVE AFFECTIVITY

Negative affectivity is the propensity to view the world, including oneself and other people, in a negative light. It is a stable personality trait that is a major component of the Big Five personality dimension neuroticism (Chapter 2). People high in negative affectivity tend to be pessimistic and downbeat. As a consequence, they tend to report more stressors in the work environment and to feel more subjective stress. They are particularly likely to feel stressed in response to the demands of a heavy workload.[49]

Several factors might be responsible for the susceptibility to stress of those who are high in negative affectivity. These include (a) a predisposition to *perceive* stressors in the workplace, (b) hypersensitivity to existing stressors, (c) a tendency to gravitate to stressful jobs, (d) a tendency to *provoke* stress through their negativity, or (e) the use of passive, indirect coping styles that avoid the real sources of stress.[50]

STRESSORS IN ORGANIZATIONAL LIFE

A study found that among a sample of employed Canadians, the most common source of stress is *workplace* stressors.[51] In this section, we will examine potential stressors in detail. Some stressors can affect almost everyone in any organization, while others are likely to affect people who perform particular roles.

Executive and Managerial Stressors

Executives and managers make key organizational decisions and direct the work of others. In these capacities, they experience some special forms of stress.

ROLE OVERLOAD **Role overload** occurs when one must perform too many tasks in too short a time period, and it is a common stressor for managers, especially in today's downsized organizations.[52] The open-ended nature of the managerial job is partly responsible for this heavy and protracted workload.[53] Management is an ongoing *process*, and there are few signposts to signify that a task is complete and that rest and relaxation are permitted. Especially when coupled with frequent moves or excessive travel, a heavy workload often provokes conflict between the manager's role as an organizational member and his or her role as a spouse or parent. Thus, role overload may provoke stress, at the same time preventing the manager from enjoying the pleasures of life that can reduce stress.

HEAVY RESPONSIBILITY Not only is the workload of the executive heavy, but it can have extremely important consequences for the organization and its members. A vice-president of

LO 13.8

Review the sources of stress encountered by various organizational role occupants.

Role overload. The requirement for too many tasks to be performed in too short a time period.

"You've been working awfully hard lately.
If you need a little fresh air and sunshine,
you can go to www.fresh-air-and-sunshine.com"

labour relations might be in charge of a negotiation strategy that could result in either labour peace or a protracted and bitter strike. To complicate matters, the personal consequences of an incorrect decision can be staggering. For example, the courts have fined and even jailed executives who have engaged in illegal activities on behalf of their organizations. Finally, executives are responsible for people as well as things, and this influence over the future of others has the potential to induce stress. The executive who must terminate the operation of an unprofitable division, putting many out of work, or the manager who must lay off an employee, putting one out of work, may experience guilt and tension.[54]

Operative-Level Stressors

Operatives are individuals who occupy non-professional and non-managerial positions in organizations. In a manufacturing organization, operatives perform the work on the shop floor and range from skilled craftspeople to unskilled labourers. As is the case with other organizational roles, the occupants of operative positions are sometimes exposed to a special set of stressors.

POOR PHYSICAL WORKING CONDITIONS Operative-level employees are more likely than managers and professionals to be exposed to physically unpleasant and even dangerous working conditions. Although social sensibility and union activity have improved working conditions over the years, many employees must still face excessive heat, cold, noise, pollution, and the chance of accidents.

POOR JOB DESIGN Although bad job design can provoke stress at any organizational level (executive role overload is an example), the designs of lower-level blue- and white-collar jobs are particular culprits. It might seem paradoxical that jobs that are too simple or not challenging enough can act as stressors. However, monotony and boredom can prove extremely frustrating to people who feel capable of handling more complex tasks. Thus, research has found that job scope can be a stressor at levels that are either too low or too high.[55]

Boundary Role Stressors, Burnout, and Emotional Labour

Boundary roles. Positions in which organizational members are required to interact with members of other organizations or with the public.

Boundary roles are positions in which organizational members are required to interact with members of other organizations or with the public. For example, a vice-president of public relations is responsible for representing his or her company to the public. At other levels, receptionists, sale reps, and installers often interact with customers or suppliers.

People are especially likely to experience stress as they straddle the imaginary boundary between the organization and its environment. This is yet another form of role conflict in which one's role as an organizational member might be incompatible with the demands made by the public or other organizations. A classic case of boundary role stress involves sales reps. In extreme cases, customers desire fast delivery of a custom-tailored product, such as a new software application. The sales rep might be tempted to "offer the moon" but at the same time is aware that such an order could place a severe strain on his or her organization's software development team. Thus, the sales rep is faced with the dilemma of doing his or her primary job (selling), while protecting another function (software development) from unreasonable demands that could result in a broken delivery contract.

Burnout. A syndrome of emotional exhaustion, cynicism, and reduced self-efficacy.

A particular form of stress (and accompanying stress reactions) experienced by some boundary role occupants is burnout. **Burnout**, as Christina Maslach, Michael Leiter, and Wilmar Schaufeli define it, is a syndrome made up of emotional exhaustion, cynicism, and low self-efficacy (Chapter 2).[56] Burnout was originally studied among those working in some capacity with people. Frequently, these people are organizational clients who

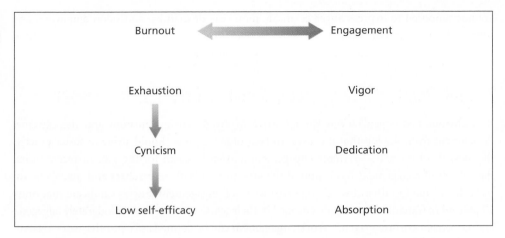

EXHIBIT 13.4
**The burnout–
engagement continuum.**

Explore
_____

Go to MyManagementLab
to see an annotated
version of this figure.

require special attention or who are experiencing severe problems. Thus, teachers, nurses, paramedics, social workers, and police are especially likely candidates for burnout. However, it has now been established that burnout can occur even among non-boundary spanners.

Burnout follows a process that begins with emotional exhaustion (left side of Exhibit 13.4). The person feels fatigued in the morning, drained by the work, and frustrated by the day's events. One way to deal with this extreme exhaustion is to become cynical and distance oneself from one's clients, the "cause" of the exhaustion. In the extreme, this might involve depersonalizing them, treating them like objects, and lacking concern for what happens to them. The clients might also be seen as blaming the employee for their problems. Finally, the burned-out individual develops feelings of low self-efficacy and low personal accomplishment—"I can't deal with these people, I'm not helping them, I don't understand them." In fact, because of the exhaustion and depersonalization, there might be more than a grain of truth to these feelings. Although the exact details of this progression are open to some question, these three symptoms paint a reliable picture of burnout.[57]

Burnout seems to be most common among people who entered their jobs with especially high ideals. Their expectations of being able to "change the world" are badly frustrated when they encounter the reality shock of troubled clients (who are often perceived as unappreciative) and the inability of the organization to help them. Teachers get fed up with being disciplinarians, nurses get upset when patients die, and police officers get depressed when they must constantly deal with the "losers" of society. Gender and personality are also related to burnout. Women are more likely to report emotional exhaustion and men are more likely to report depersonalization. In general, those with high self-esteem, high conscientiousness, and internal control report less burnout.[58]

What are the consequences of burnout? Some individuals bravely pursue a new occupation, often experiencing guilt about not having been able to cope in the old one. Others stay in the same occupation but seek a new job. For instance, the burned-out nurse may go into nursing education to avoid contact with sick patients. Some people pursue administrative careers in their profession, attempting to "climb above" the source of their difficulties. These people often set cynical examples for idealistic subordinates. Finally, some people stay in their jobs and become part of the legion of "deadwood," collecting their paycheques but doing little to contribute to the mission of the organization. Many "good bureaucrats" choose this route.[59]

Much boundary role stress stems from the frequent need for such employees to engage in "emotional labour." You will recall from Chapter 4 that emotional labour involves regulating oneself to suppress negative emotions or to exaggerate positive ones. Thus, police officers are not supposed to express anger at unsafe motorists or drunks, and salon employees are supposed to act friendly and sympathetic to boorish clients. Such suppression and acting takes a toll on cognitive and emotional resources over time.[60]

The Job Demands–Resources Model and Work Engagement

It is obvious that organizations should strive to avoid causing burnout and the extreme detachment from the job that it causes. In fact, organizations should strive to foster exactly the *opposite* of burnout—extreme engagement and enthusiasm for the job. In recent years the subject of engagement has captured the attention of both researchers and managers. In part, this is due to rather low self-reported levels of engagement. Surveys indicate that only 17 percent of Canadians are highly engaged in their work, 66 percent are moderately engaged, and 17 percent are disengaged.[61] **Work engagement** can be defined as "a positive work-related state of mind that is characterized by vigor, dedication, and absorption."[62] (See the right side of Exhibit 13.4.) Vigour involves high levels of energy and mental resilience at work; dedication means being strongly involved in your work and experiencing a sense of significance, enthusiasm, and challenge; absorption refers to being fully concentrated on and engrossed in your work. In particular, the first two dimensions—vigour and dedication—position engagement as the opposite of burnout.[63]

What determines whether employees tend toward engagement versus burnout? According to the **job demands–resources model** the work environment can be described in terms of demands and resources.[64] Job demands are physical, psychological, social, or organizational features of a job that require sustained physical or psychological effort that in turn can result in physiological or psychological costs. Common demands include work overload, time pressure, role ambiguity, and role conflict. Job resources refer to features of a job that are functional in that they help achieve work goals, reduce job demands, and stimulate personal growth, learning, and development. Job resources can come from the organization (e.g., pay, career opportunities, and job security), interpersonal and social relations (e.g., supervisor and co-worker support, team climate), the organization of work (e.g., role clarity, participation in decision making), and the task itself (e.g., task significance, autonomy, and performance feedback). A central assumption of the model is that high job resources foster work engagement, while high job demands exhaust employees physically and mentally and lead to burnout. Indeed, research has found that job demands are related to burnout, disengagement, and health problems, while job resources lead to work engagement, organizational citizenship behaviour, and organizational commitment. Also, it shows that resources can buffer the negative impact of job demands on well-being.[65]

Exhibit 13.5 shows the results of a survey of 11 000 U.K. workers in 26 occupations. The occupations are ranked in terms of several outcomes of stress. The low-ranked jobs are "worse," and those in italics are worse than average. These are the jobs that make high demands while supplying limited resources. Later in the chapter we will suggest some ways to reduce stress or improve the ability to cope that involve reducing demands and/or increasing resources.

Some General Stressors

To conclude our discussion of stressors that people encounter in organizational life, we will consider some that are probably experienced equally by occupants of all roles.

INTERPERSONAL CONFLICT   Interpersonal conflict can be a potent stressor, especially for those with strong avoidance tendencies. The entire range of conflict, from personality clashes to intergroup strife, is especially likely to cause stress when it leads to real or perceived attacks

---

Work engagement.
A positive work-related state of mind that is characterized by vigour, dedication, and absorption.

Job demands–resources model. A model that specifies how job demands cause burnout and job resources cause engagement.

Rank	Physical Health	Psychological Well–being	Job Satisfaction
1	*Ambulance*	*Social services providing care*	*Prison officer*
2	*Teachers*	*Teachers*	*Ambulance*
3	*Social services providing care*	*Fire brigade*	*Police*
4	*Customer services–call centre*	*Ambulace*	*Customer services–call centre*
5	*Bar staff*	*Vets*	*Social services providing care*
6	*Prison officer*	*Lecturers*	*Teachers*
7	*Mgmt (private sector)*	*Clerical and admin*	*Nursing*
8	*Clerical and admin*	*Mgmt (private sector)*	*Medical/dental*
9	*Police*	*Prison officer*	*Allied health professionals*
10	Teaching assistant	*Research–academic*	Bar staff
11	Head teachers	Police	Mgmt (private sector)
12	Secretarial/business support	*Customer services–call centre*	Fire brigade
13	Research–academic	Director (public sector)	Vets
14	Lecturers	Allied health professionals	Clerical and admin
15	Senior police	Bar staff	Mgmt (public sector)
16	Nursing	Nursing	Lecturers
17	Mgmt (public sector)	Medical/dental	Head teachers
18	Allied health professionals	Senior police	Teaching assistant
19	Medical/dental	Secretaria/business support	Secretarial/business support
20	Accountant	Head teachers	Director (public sector)
21	Fire brigade	Mgmt (public sector)	Research–academic
22	Vets	Accountant	Senior police
23	Director (public sector)	Teaching assistant	School lunchtime supervisors
24	Analyst	Analyst	Accountant
25	School lunchtime supervisors	School lunchtime supervisors	Analyst
26	Director/MD (private sector)	Director/MD (private sector)	Director/MD (private sector)

EXHIBIT 13.5
Occupations ranked on physical health, psychological well-being, and job satisfaction.
Source: Johnson S. (2009). Organizational screening: The ASSET model. In S. Cartwright & C.L. Cooper (Eds.), *The Oxford handbook of organizational well-being.* Oxford: Oxford University Press, p. 145.
Note: The most stressful jobs have the lowest ranks. Jobs worse than average are indicated in italics.

on our self-esteem or integrity. Although conflict can lead to stress in many settings outside of work, we often have the option of terminating the relationship, of "choosing our friends," as it were. This option is often not available at work.

A particular manifestation of interpersonal conflict that has received increased attention is workplace bullying. **Bullying** is repeated negative behaviour directed toward one or more individuals of lower power or status that creates a hostile work environment.[66] Research has clearly demonstrated that it is a potent source of stress and negative well-being.[67]

A number of factors distinguish bullying as a stress-inducing form of conflict.[68] Although bullying can involve physical aggression, it is most commonly a more subtle form of psychological aggression and intimidation. This can take many forms, such as incessant teasing, demeaning criticism, social isolation, or sabotaging others' tools and equipment. An essential feature of bullying is its persistence, and a single harsh incident would not constitute such behaviour. Rather, it is the *repeated* teasing, criticism, or undermining that signals bullying. Another key feature of the bullying process is some degree of power or status imbalance between the bully and the victim. Thus, managers have often been identified as bullies by subordinates, and research has even shown that the behaviour can "trickle down" from managers to supervisors to workers.[69] However, power imbalance can be subtle, and in some

Bullying. Repeated negative behaviour directed toward one or more individuals of lower power or status that creates a hostile work environment.

settings even work peers might lack power due to their gender, race, physical stature, low job security, or educational credentials. Also, there is power in numbers, in that subordinates might team up to harass their boss. This is an example of a phenomenon closely associated to bullying called *mobbing*. Mobbing occurs when a number of individuals, usually direct co-workers, "gang up" on a particular employee.[70] Mobbing can be especially intimidating and stressful because it restricts the availability of social support that might be present when there is only a single bully.

The essential point is that victims of bullying and mobbing experience stress because they feel powerless to deal with the perpetrator(s). Most observers note that a combination of factors work together to stimulate this dysfunctional behaviour.

Norway, Sweden, France, and the Canadian provinces of Quebec, Saskatchewan, and Ontario have enacted laws that pertain to bullying in the workplace. Various organizations have also done their part. The U.S. Department of Veterans Affairs and IBM both have active anti-bullying programs. IBM fired several factory workers who mobbed their new supervisor to drive home its seriousness about its policy.[71]

Before continuing, consider You Be the Manager: *Bullying at Veterans Affairs.*

WORK–FAMILY CONFLICT   Work–family conflict occurs when either work duties interfere with family life or family life interferes with work responsibilities.[72] A study found that it is costing Canadian companies $6 billion to $10 billion a year in absenteeism, and the Canadian health care system $425 million in increased visits to the doctor.[73]

Two facts of life in contemporary society have increased the stress stemming from the inter-role conflict between being a member of one's family and the member of an organization. First, the increase in the number of households in which both parents work and the increase in the number of single-parent families has led to a number of stressors centred around child care. Finding adequate daycare and disputes between partners about sharing child care responsibilities can prove to be serious stressors. Second, increased life spans have meant that many people in the prime of their careers find themselves providing support for elderly parents, some of whom may be seriously ill. This inherently stressful elder care situation is often compounded by feelings of guilt about the need to tend to matters at work.[74]

Women are particularly victimized by stress due to work–family conflict, although it is a rapidly growing problem for men as well. Much anecdotal evidence suggests that women who take time off work to deal with pressing family matters are more likely than men to be labelled disloyal or undedicated to their work. Also, many managers seem to be insensitive to the demands that these basic demographic shifts are making on their employees, again compounding the potential for stress.[75]

Occupations that require a high degree of teamwork or responsibilities for others tend to provoke the most work–family conflict (e.g., police detectives, firefighters, and family doctors). At the other extreme, tellers, insurance adjusters, and taxi drivers report much lower levels.[76] Also, people who are highly engaged in their work have been shown to have elevated work to family conflict, but more conscientious employees seem to handle this tension between work and family better.[77]

JOB INSECURITY AND CHANGE   Secure employment is an important goal for almost everyone, and stress may be encountered when it is threatened. During the last decade, organizations have undergone substantial changes that have left many workers unemployed and threatened the security of those who have been fortunate enough to remain in their jobs. The trend toward mergers and acquisitions, along with reengineering, restructuring, and downsizing, has led to increasingly high levels of stress among employees who either have lost their jobs or must live with the threat of more layoffs, the loss of friends and co-workers,

YOU BE THE MANAGER

Bullying at Veterans Affairs

Jobs in the social service sector regularly entail emotional labour, with workers confronted on a daily basis with high demands from clients concerning social, emotional, and medical problems. While such client–service provider interactions can be emotionally draining, such a work environment can also be a breeding ground for workplace aggression and bullying.

With this in mind, the United States Department of Veterans Affairs (VA), in collaboration with university researchers, launched the Workplace Stress and Aggression Project. The VA provides patient care and federal benefits to veterans and their dependents through central offices, benefits offices, and medical facilities. In the post–September 11 era, the VA had seen an increase in activity with the conflicts in Afghanistan and Iraq. The goal of the project was to assess the prevalence of workplace aggression and bullying within the VA, to understand their impact on employee satisfaction, VA performance, and veteran satisfaction, and to develop intervention strategies.

The research team used archival data, questionnaires, interviews, and discussion groups. Results of the initial surveys clearly indicated that workplace aggression and bullying were issues within the VA. Overall, 36 percent of employees surveyed reported being bullied at work. Bullying was defined as persistent patterns of aggression that workers experienced at least once a week. Of the 36 percent, 29 percent indicated they experienced aggression in the workplace one to five times a week, while 7 percent reported experiencing six or more aggression episodes a week. Another 58 percent of employees reported that they experienced workplace aggression, albeit not on a weekly basis, while only 6 percent of employees indicated that they suffered no workplace aggression. Aggression could be physical or verbal, active (e.g., in a confrontation) or passive (e.g., through exclusion), or direct (e.g., personally targeted) or indirect (e.g., defacing property or spreading rumours). Most incidents were of the verbal, passive, and indirect variety.

Employees indicated that 44 percent of the aggression they experienced emanated from co-workers, 35 percent came from supervisors, and 12 percent came from veterans. In terms of impact on personal well-being, they suffered more stress and lower job satisfaction when a supervisor was the source of the aggression than when co-workers or clients were the

High levels of bullying at various Veterans Affairs facilities worried executives.

source. The research team also found that bullying was linked to lower employee and organizational performance and increases in stress, absenteeism, lateness, turnover, and worker compensation claims. With these data in hand, the project team's focus turned to understanding why aggression occurred and what could be done to reduce it.

Questions

1. What do you think some of the primary causes of workplace aggression and bullying within the VA might be? Do you think the causes would be different across the various VA facilities?

2. Suggest an intervention strategy to reduce the incidence of aggression and bullying in the VA workplace. Who should be involved?

To find out how the VA responded, see The Manager's Notebook at the end of the chapter.

Sources: Scaringi, J., et al. (n.d.). *The VA workplace stress and aggression project—Final report*; Neuman, J.H., and Keashly, L. (2005, August). Reducing aggression and bullying: An intervention project in the U.S. Department of Veterans Affairs. In J. Raver (Chair), *Workplace bullying: International perspectives on moving from research to practice*. Symposium presented at the annual meeting of the Academy of Management, Honolulu, HI; Neuman, J.H. (2004). Injustice, stress, and aggression in organizations. In R.W. Griffin and A.M. O'Leary-Kelly (Eds.), *The dark side of organizational behavior*. San Francisco, CA: Jossey-Bass.

and an increased workload.[78] The fear of job loss has become a way of life for employees at all organizational levels.[79]

At the operative level, unionization has provided a degree of employment security for some, but the vagaries of the economy and the threat of technology and other organizational changes hang heavily over many workers. Among professionals, the very specialization that enables them to obtain satisfactory jobs becomes a millstone whenever social or economic forces change. For example, aerospace scientists and engineers have long been prey to the boom-and-bust nature of their industry. When layoffs occur, these people are often perceived as overqualified or too specialized to easily obtain jobs in related industries. Finally, the executive suite does not escape job insecurity. Recent pressures for corporate performance have made cost-cutting a top priority, and one of the surest ways to cut costs in the short run is to reduce executive positions and thus reduce the total management payroll. Many corporations have greatly thinned their executive ranks in recent years.

ROLE AMBIGUITY We have already noted how role conflict—having to deal with incompatible role expectations—can provoke stress. There is also substantial evidence that role ambiguity can provoke stress.[80] From Chapter 7, you will recall that role ambiguity exists when the goals of one's job or the methods of performing the job are unclear. Such a lack of direction can prove stressful, especially for people who are low in their tolerance for such ambiguity. For example, the president of a firm might be instructed by the board of directors to increase profits and cut costs. While this goal seems clear enough, the means by which it can be achieved might be unclear. This ambiguity can be devastating, especially when the organization is doing poorly and no strategy seems to improve things.

SEXUAL HARASSMENT In Chapter 12, we discussed sexual harassment in terms of the abuse of power and a form of unethical behaviour. Sexual harassment is a major workplace stressor, with serious consequences for employees and organizations that are similar to or more negative than those of other types of job stressors.[81] Sexual harassment in the workplace is now considered to be widespread in both the public and private sectors, and most harassment victims are subjected to ongoing harassment and stress.[82] The negative effects of sexual harassment include decreased morale, job satisfaction, organizational commitment, and job performance and increased absenteeism, turnover, and job loss. Sexual harassment has also been found to have serious effects on

EXHIBIT 13.6
Sources of stress at various points in the organization.

Explore

Go to MyManagementLab to see an annotated version of this figure.

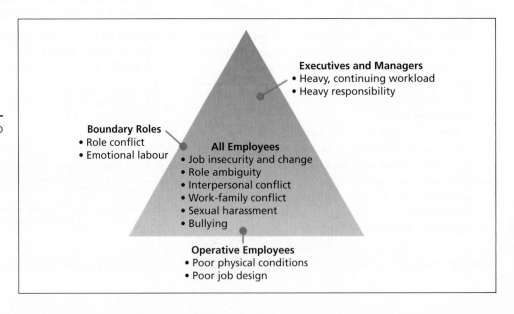

the psychological and physical well-being of harassment victims.[83] Victims of sexual harassment experience depression, frustration, nervousness, fatigue, nausea, hypertension, and symptoms of post-traumatic stress disorder.[84] Organizations in which sexual harassment is most likely to be a problem are those that have a climate that is tolerant of sexual harassment and where women are working in traditionally male-dominated jobs and in a male-dominated workplace.[85]

Exhibit 13.6 summarizes the sources of stress at various points in the organization.

REACTIONS TO ORGANIZATIONAL STRESS

In this section, we examine the reactions that people who experience organizational stress might exhibit. These reactions can be divided into behavioural, psychological, and physiological responses. In general, reactions that result in an addition to one's resources can be seen as good coping with stress. Reactions that increase demands constitute bad coping. Exhibit 13.7 shows how a sample of more than 31 000 Canadian employees reported coping with stress.

Behavioural Reactions to Stress

Behavioural reactions to stress are overt activities that the stressed individual uses in an attempt to cope with the stress. They include problem solving, seeking social support, modified performance, withdrawal, and the use of addictive substances.

PROBLEM SOLVING In general, problem solving is directed toward terminating the stressor or reducing its potency, not toward simply making the person feel better in the short run. Problem solving is reality-oriented, and while it is not always effective in combating the stressor, it reveals flexibility and realistic use of feedback. Most examples of a problem-solving response to stress are undramatic because problem solving is generally the routine, sensible, obvious approach that an objective observer might suggest. Consider the following examples of problem solving.

- *Delegation.* A busy executive reduces her stress-provoking workload by delegating some of her many tasks to a capable assistant.

Coping Strategies	% of Sample Who Use		
	Rarely	Weekly	Daily
Prioritize	9%	21%	69%
Schedule, organize, and plan my time more carefully	22%	32%	47%
Talk with family or friends	26%	29%	45%
Just work harder (I try to do it all)	31%	26%	43%
Find some other activity to take my mind off it	36%	32%	32%
Talk with colleagues at work	40%	27%	32%
Delegate work to others	49%	24%	27%
Search for help from family or friends	51%	25%	23%
Just try and forget about it	60%	20%	19%
Search for help from colleagues at work	65%	19%	16%
Have an alcoholic drink	65%	23%	12%
Use prescription, over-the-counter, or other drugs	86%	4%	11%
Reduce the quality of the things I do	72%	18%	10%

LO 13.9

Describe *behavioural, psychological,* and *physiological reactions* to stress and discuss techniques for managing stress.

EXHIBIT 13.7
How Canadian employees cope with stress.
Source: Higgins, C., Duxbury, L., & Lyons, S. (2006). *Reducing work-life conflict: What works? What doesn't?* Ottawa: Health Canada, p. 131. Reproduced with the permission of the Minister of Public Works and Government Services Canada, 2009.

Explore

Go to MyManagementLab to see an annotated version of this figure.

- *Time management.* A manager who finds the day too short writes a daily schedule, requires his subordinates to make formal appointments to see him, and instructs his secretary to screen phone calls more selectively.

- *Talking it out.* An engineer who is experiencing stress because of poor communication with her non-engineer superior resolves to sit down with the boss and hammer out an agreement concerning the priorities on a project.

- *Asking for help.* A salesperson who is anxious about his company's ability to fill a difficult order asks the production manager to provide a realistic estimate of the probable delivery date.

- *Searching for alternatives.* A machine operator who finds her monotonous job stress-provoking applies for a transfer to a more interesting position for which the pay is identical.

SEEKING SOCIAL SUPPORT Speaking generally, social support simply refers to having close ties with other people. In turn, these close ties can affect stress by bolstering self-esteem, providing useful information, offering comfort and humour, or even providing material resources (such as a loan). Research evidence shows that the benefits of social support are double-barrelled. First, people with stronger social networks exhibit better psychological and physical well-being. Second, when people encounter stressful events, those with good social networks are likely to cope more positively. Thus, the social network acts as a buffer against stress.[86]

Off the job, individuals might find social support in a spouse, family, or friends. On the job, social support might be available from one's superior or co-workers. Research evidence suggests that the buffering aspects of social support are most potent when they are directly connected to the source of stress. This means that co-workers and superiors may be the best sources of support for dealing with work-related stress. But most managers need better training to recognize employee stress symptoms, clarify role requirements, and so on. Unfortunately, some organizational cultures, especially those that are very competitive, do not encourage members to seek support in a direct fashion. In this kind of setting, relationships that people develop in professional associations can sometimes serve as an informed source of social support.

PERFORMANCE CHANGES Stress or stressors frequently cause reduced job performance.[87] However, this statement needs to be qualified slightly. Some stressors are "hindrance" stressors in that they directly damage goal attainment. These include things like role ambiguity and interpersonal conflict. Such stressors damage performance. On the other hand, some stressors are challenging. These include factors such as heavy workload and responsibility. Such stressors can damage performance, but they sometimes stimulate it via added motivation.[88] Because they are discretionary, organizational citizenship behaviours (Chapter 4) are especially likely to decrease under stressful conditions.[89]

WITHDRAWAL Withdrawal from the stressor is one of the most basic reactions to stress. In organizations, this withdrawal takes the form of absence and turnover. Compared with problem-solving reactions to stress, absenteeism fails to attack the stressor directly. Rather, the absent individual is simply attempting short-term reduction of the anxiety prompted by the stressor. When the person returns to the job, the stress is still there. From this point of view, absence is a dysfunctional reaction to stress for both the individual and the organization. The same can be said about turnover if a person resigns from a stressful job on the spur of the moment merely to escape stress. However, a good case can be made for a well-planned resignation in which the intent is to assume another job that should be less stressful. This is actually a problem-solving reaction that should benefit both the individual and the organization in

■ RESEARCH FOCUS

PRESENTEEISM IN THE WORKPLACE

Presenteeism refers to going to work when one is ill. Although both managers and work researchers have been interested in absenteeism for years, it is only recently that presenteeism has become a subject of concerted interest. Some of this interest is stimulated by the finding that the aggregate productivity loss that occurs due to working while ill is much greater than that attributed to absence. Presentees are at work, but they are often not working at full capacity. What would cause people to go to work even though they are suffering from asthma, allergies, migraines, or respiratory problems? Many factors appear to be stress-related. This is ironic because it means that some stressors can cause both absenteeism and presenteeism.

High job demands and time pressure have been associated with presenteeism; people feel under pressure to get work done and sense the work piling up if they are absent. This is especially likely if there is a lack of backup, an increasing possibility in today's downsized organizations. Job insecurity may also prompt people to go to work when they are ill. Thus, non-permanent employees exhibit less absenteeism than their permanent counterparts, and this might signal presenteeism on their part. Strict policies against absence and team-oriented work designs have also been implicated in presenteeism. In team settings, people might feel they are letting the team down if they book off sick.

Depression, which is frequently associated with stress, is one of the most common health problems connected to presenteeism. This may be because people do not view it as a legitimate reason to be absent or fear disclosing it as the reason for their absence.

Source: Johns, G. (2010). Presenteeism in the workplace: A review and research agenda. *Journal of Organizational Behavior, 31,* 519–532.

the long run. Absence, turnover, and turnover intentions have often been linked with stress and its causes.[90] For an ironic counter-example, see the Research Focus: *Presenteeism in the Workplace.*

USE OF ADDICTIVE SUBSTANCES Smoking, drinking, and drug use represent the least satisfactory behavioural responses to stress for both the individual and the organization. These activities fail to terminate stress episodes, and they leave employees less physically and mentally prepared to perform their jobs. We have all heard of hard-drinking newspaper reporters and advertising executives, and it is tempting to infer that the stress of their boundary role positions is responsible for their drinking. Indeed, cigarette and alcohol use are associated with work-related stress.[91]

Psychological Reactions to Stress

Psychological reactions to stress primarily involve emotions and thought processes rather than overt behaviour, although these reactions are frequently revealed in the individual's speech and actions. The most common psychological reaction to stress is the use of defence mechanisms.[92]

Defence mechanisms are psychological attempts to reduce the anxiety associated with stress. Notice that, by definition, defence mechanisms concentrate on *anxiety reduction* rather than on actually confronting or dealing with the stressor. Some common defence mechanisms include the following:

Defence mechanisms. Psychological attempts to reduce the anxiety associated with stress.

- *Rationalization* is attributing socially acceptable reasons or motives to one's actions so that they will appear reasonable and sensible, at least to oneself. For example, a male nurse who becomes very angry and abusive when learning that he will not be promoted to supervisor might justify his anger by claiming that the female head nurse discriminates against men.

- *Projection* is attributing one's own undesirable ideas and motives to others so that they seem less negative. For example, a sales executive who is undergoing conflict about offering a bribe to an official of a foreign government might reason that the official is corrupt.

- *Displacement* is directing feelings of anger at a "safe" target rather than expressing them where they may be punished. For example, a construction worker who is severely criticized by the boss for sloppy workmanship might take out his frustrations in an evening hockey league.

- *Reaction formation* is expressing oneself in a manner that is directly opposite to the way one truly feels, rather than risking negative reactions to one's true position. For example, a low-status member of a committee might vote with the majority on a crucial issue rather than stating his true position and opening himself up to attack.

- *Compensation* is applying one's skills in a particular area to make up for failure in another area. For example, a professor who is unable to get his or her research published might resolve to become a superb teacher.

Is the use of defence mechanisms a good or bad reaction to stress? Used occasionally to temporarily reduce anxiety, they appear to be a useful reaction. For example, the construction worker who displaces aggression in an evening hockey league rather than attacking a frustrating boss might calm down, return to work the next day, and "talk it out" with the boss. Thus, the occasional use of defence mechanisms as short-term anxiety reducers probably benefits both the individual and the organization. In fact, people with "weak defences" can be incapacitated by anxiety and resort to dysfunctional withdrawal or addiction.

When the use of defence mechanisms becomes a chronic reaction to stress, however, the picture changes radically. The problem stems from the very character of defence mechanisms—they simply do not change the objective character of the stressor, and the basic conflict or frustration remains in operation. After some short-term relief from anxiety, the basic problem remains unresolved. In fact, the stress might *increase* with the knowledge that the defence has been essentially ineffective.

Physiological Reactions to Stress

Can work-related stress kill you? This is clearly an important question for organizations, and it is even more important for individuals who experience excessive stress at work. Many studies of physiological reactions to stress have concentrated on the cardiovascular system, specifically on the various risk factors that might prompt heart attacks. For example, work stress is associated with electrocardiogram irregularities and elevated levels of blood pressure, cholesterol, and pulse.[93] Stress has also been associated with the onset of diseases such as respiratory and bacterial infections due to its ill effects on the immune system.[94] The accumulation of stress into burnout has been particularly implicated in cardiovascular problems.[95]

ORGANIZATIONAL STRATEGIES FOR MANAGING STRESS

This chapter would be incomplete without a discussion of personal and organizational strategies to manage stress. In general, these strategies either reduce demands on employees or enhance their resources.

Police officers must deal with a unique type of on-the-job stress: workplace violence. There has been an upswing in psychological counselling for officers experiencing stress reactions.

Job Redesign

Organizations can redesign jobs to reduce their stressful characteristics. In theory, it is possible to redesign jobs anywhere in the organization to this end. Thus, an overloaded executive might be given an assistant to reduce the number of tasks he or she must perform. In practice, most formal job redesign efforts have involved enriching operative-level jobs to make them more stimulating and challenging.

Especially for service jobs, there is growing evidence that providing more autonomy in how service is delivered can alleviate stress and burnout.[96] Call centre workers, fast-food employees, some salespeople, and some hospitality workers are highly "scripted" by employers, with the idea that uniformity will be appreciated by customers. This idea is debatable, but what is not debatable is that this lack of personal control goes against the research-supported prescriptions of job enrichment (Chapter 6) and empowerment (Chapter 12), and the job demands–resources model of stress (this chapter). Boundary role service jobs require a high degree of emotional regulation in any event, and some degree of autonomy allows employees to cope with emotional labour by adjusting their responses to the needs of the moment in line with their own personalities. Guidelines about desired service outcomes can replace rigid scripts, especially for routine (non-emergency) encounters. Also, excessive electronic monitoring should be avoided in call centres.[97]

A special word should be said about the stressful job designs that often emerge from heavy-handed downsizings, restructurings, and mergers. Common symptoms of such jobs are extreme role overload, increased responsibility without corresponding authority to act, and the assignment of tasks for which no training is provided. Executives overseeing such change efforts should obtain professional assistance to ensure proper job designs.

"Family-Friendly" Human Resource Policies

To reduce stress associated with dual careers, child care, and elder care, many organizations are beginning to institute "family-friendly" human resource policies.[98] These policies generally include some combination of formalized social support, material support, and increased flexibility to adapt to employee needs. In the domain of social support, some firms distribute newsletters, such as *Work & Family Life,* that deal with work–family issues. Others have developed company support groups for employees dealing with elder care problems. Some companies have contracted specialized consultants to provide seminars on elder care issues.

A welcome form of material support consists of corporate daycare centres. Flexibility (which provides more *control* over family issues) is also important, and includes flex-time, telecommuting, and job sharing (Chapter 6), as well as family leave policies that allow time off for caring for infants, sick children, and aged dependents. Although many firms boast of having such flexible policies, a common problem is encouraging managers to *use* them in an era of downsizing and lean staffing. According to a Mediacorp study, some of Canada's most family-friendly employers include Pfizer, Manitoba Hydro, Statistics Canada, and Desjardins.[99] There is growing evidence that such policies contribute to improved health, lower turnover, and higher organizational performance.[100] In general, research shows that perceptions of flexibility, a reasonable workload, supportive supervision, and a supportive culture are associated with less work–family conflict and higher job satisfaction and organizational commitment.[101] For an example of a family-friendly government initiative, see the Applied Focus: *Quebec Certifies Work–Life Balance.*

■ APPLIED FOCUS ■

QUEBEC CERTIFIES WORK–LIFE BALANCE

The benefits of work–life balance have been well-touted through surveys, studies, and employee testimonials. But Quebec has decided to take that sentiment a step further in launching a certification standard around work–family balance. Employers of all sizes can now apply to have their work places evaluated by the Bureau de normalisation du Québec (BNQ), with four levels of certification available. The certification requires, at a minimum, employers have a commitment from management around work–family balance (WFB). This should include an internal management policy, demonstrated commitment to WFB, WFB measures for men and women, employee communications, and a designated person responsible for the program. Employers are also required to have a WFB committee that consults with employees; proposes WFB measures and practices; implements, promotes, and evaluates those measures; and presents the results to management and employees every two years.

Frima Studio is a Quebec City-based employer that...[became] the first in the province to attain the standard, according to Stephen Couture, Frima's president. The company started looking at work–life balance in 2008, offering its 275 employees initiatives such as public transportation passes, flexible schedules, longer holidays, fresh fruit, and on-site massages. Frima's program has evolved to include more innovative approaches such as Frima Points. This gives employees points based on their performance, which they can exchange online for different services such as babysitters, plumbers, or gardeners.

"This program was to have our employees spend more time with their families, so (they can) avoid doing extra work when they're home," said Couture. "It's a kind of program for our employees to have a better life outside the hours they spend at work."

As a result, fewer people leave Frima and more people are inclined to stay, he said. And with a competitive video game industry in Quebec and larger companies installing new facilities in the region, there's a lot of pressure on HR and recruitment.

"This kind of program helps to become competitive," he said. "There's a lot of people in the province who have deep pockets for their employees, to attract employees, so we needed to be creative."

Adopting a work–family program is more than just an expense, it's an investment, said Couture.

Source: Excerpted from Dobson, S. (2011, May 23). Quebec certifies work-life balance. *Canadian HR Reporter,* 1,19; see also Dobson, S. (2012, May 7). Quebec certification hits 1-year mark. *Canadian HR Reporter,* 7, 10.

Companies are striving to be much more "family friendly" than in the past. Some organizations offer daycare for children of employees.

Stress Management Programs

Some organizations have experimented with programs designed to help employees "manage" work-related stress. Such programs are also available from independent off-work sources. Some of these programs help physically and mentally healthy employees prevent problems due to stress. Others are therapeutic in nature, aimed at individuals who are already experiencing stress problems. Although the exact content of the programs varies, most involve one or more of the following techniques: meditation, training in muscle-relaxation exercises, biofeedback training to control physiological processes, training in time management, and training to think more positively and realistically about sources of job stress.[102] Evidence suggests that these applications are useful in reducing physiological arousal, sleep disturbances, and self-reported tension and anxiety.[103]

Work–Life Balance, Fitness, and Wellness Programs

Many people have argued that a balanced lifestyle that includes a variety of leisure activities combined with a healthy diet and physical exercise can reduce stress and counteract some of the adverse physiological effects of stress. For some organizations, work–life balance programs and quality-of-life benefits have become a strategic retention tool. Employees are increasingly demanding work–life balance benefits, and employers are realizing that by providing them they can increase commitment and reduce turnover.

At Husky Injection Molding Systems, the cafeteria serves only healthy food. The company's head office in Bolton, Ontario, has a naturopath, a chiropractor, a medical doctor, a nurse, and a massage therapist on staff, and employees are encouraged to use the company's large fitness centre.[104] The DundeeWealth investment firm features weight-loss contests, fitness classes, and consultation on home training programs.[105]

Studies show that fitness training is associated with improved mood, a better self-concept, reduced absenteeism, enhanced job satisfaction, and reports of better performance.[106] Work–life programs are also believed to result in lower health care costs. Some of these improvements probably stem from stress reduction.

■ THE MANAGER'S NOTEBOOK

Bullying at Veterans Affairs

1. Many of the well-known sources of conflict in the workplace can lead to aggression and bullying. Power and status differences between individuals, rivalries between groups, uncertainty and competition, and a noxious organizational culture can all facilitate bullying and aggression. The VA project team found many of these conditions at the various sites. However, they generally found a distinctive pattern of causes of bullying at each facility. At some sites, a lack of cooperation, respect, and fairness were drivers of aggression and bullying. At other sites, diversity management was the primary issue. Sites that had recently made significant new hires often had clashes between newcomers and old-timers. Sites with poor leadership and a lack of goal alignment were also problems. The results were often communication breakdowns, misinformation, and the growth of rumours. Overall, the project team identified issues in the work climate, although they varied in content from site to site, as the key factor in workplace aggression and bullying.

2. The VA project team realized that, unlike many organizational development prescriptions advocating the establishment of best practices to resolve problems, interventions to quell workplace aggression and bullying would need to be customized at each site to deal with each specific work climate. However, the general process they developed to do this was common to all. In the 11 sites that participated in the more comprehensive version of the project, the research team created action teams of organizational members to guide the project and develop needed interventions. The exercise of bringing people together to learn and discuss issues surrounding bullying and aggression in itself transformed the work climate in a positive way. Interventions often focused on some form of what are known as High Involvement Work Systems, involving information sharing and empowerment. In a follow-up two years after the original data gathering exercise, the research team found that, compared with the 15 sites that did not participate in the intervention, the 11 focal sites reported fewer incidents of aggressive behaviour and fewer injury stress–related behaviours. Work attitudes and performance indicators also improved at the 11 intervention sites compared with the 15 other sites.

MyManagementLab   Visit MyManagementLab at **www.mymanagementlab .com** for access to online tutorials, interactive exercises, videos, and much more.

LEARNING OBJECTIVES CHECKLIST

13.1 *Interpersonal conflict* is a process that occurs when one person, group, or organizational unit frustrates the goal attainment of another. Such conflict can revolve around facts, procedures, or the goals themselves. Causes of conflict include intergroup bias, high interdependence, ambiguous jurisdictions, and scarce resources. Differences in power, status, and culture are also a factor.

13.2 *Types of conflict* include *relationship*, *task*, and *process* conflict. Conflict dynamics include the need to win the dispute, withholding information, increased cohesiveness, negative stereotyping of the other party, reduced contact, and emergence of aggressive leaders.

13.3 Modes of managing conflict include *avoiding*, *accommodating*, *competing*, *compromise*, and *collaborating*.

13.4 *Negotiation* is a decision-making process among parties that do not have the same preferences. *Distributive negotiation* attempts to divide up a fixed amount of outcomes. Frequent tactics include threats, promises, firmness, concession making, and persuasion. *Integrative negotiation* attempts to enlarge the amount of outcomes available via collaboration or problem solving. Tactics include exchanging copious information, framing differences as opportunities, cutting costs, increasing resources, and introducing *superordinate goals*.

13.5 When managers perceive that employees are in a rut or avoiding disagreements at the cost of not dealing with important issues, they may want to *stimulate* conflict to reinvigorate the workplace. Although conflict is often considered a negative occurrence, conflict can also be necessary for and beneficial to organizational change initiatives. In the context of change, conflict can generate new ideas, lead to more careful monitoring of the actions of others, and lead to a redistribution of power within the organization.

13.6 *Stressors* are environmental conditions that have the potential to induce stress. *Stress* is a psychological reaction that can prompt tension or anxiety because an individual feels incapable of coping with the demands made by a stressor. *Stress reactions* are the behavioural, psychological, and physiological consequences of stress.

13.7 Personality characteristics can cause some individuals to perceive more stressors than others, experience more stress, and react more negatively to this stress. In particular, people with *external locus of control*, high *negative affectivity*, and *Type A behaviour pattern* are prone to such reactions.

13.8 At the managerial or executive level, common stressors include *role overload* and high responsibility. At the *operative level*, poor physical working conditions and underutilization of potential owing to poor job design are common stressors. *Boundary role occupants* often experience stress in the form of conflict between demands from inside the employing organization and demands from outside. Emotional labour may also provoke stress. *Burnout* may occur when a job produces emotional exhaustion, cynicism, and low self-efficacy. Job insecurity and change, role ambiguity, sexual harassment, interpersonal conflict, and work–family conflicts have the potential to induce stress in all organizational members.

Work engagement is a positive state of mind about work involving dedication, absorption, and vigour. The job demands–resources model explains how demands lead to burnout and resources lead to engagement.

13.9 *Behavioural reactions* to stress include problem solving, modified performance, withdrawal, and the use of addictive substances. *Problem solving* is the most effective reaction because it confronts the stressor directly and thus has the potential to terminate the stress episode. The most common psychological reaction to stress is the use of *defence mechanisms* to temporarily reduce anxiety. The majority of studies on physiological reactions to stress implicate cardiovascular risk factors. Strategies that can reduce organizational stress include job redesign, family-friendly human resource policies, stress management programs, and work–life balance programs.

DISCUSSION QUESTIONS

1. The manager of a fast-food restaurant sees that conflict among the staff is damaging service. How might she implement a superordinate goal to reduce this conflict?

2. A company hires two finance majors right out of college. Being in a new and unfamiliar environment, they begin their relationship cooperatively. However, over time, they develop a case of deep interpersonal conflict. What factors could account for this?

3. What are some of the factors that make it a real challenge for conflicting parties to develop a collaborative relationship and engage in integrative negotiation?

4. Two social workers just out of college join the same county welfare agency. Both find their case loads very heavy and their roles very ambiguous. One exhibits negative stress reactions, including absence and elevated alcohol use. The other seems to cope very well. Use the stress episode model to explain why this might occur.

5. Imagine that a person who greatly dislikes bureaucracy assumes her first job as an investigator in a very bureaucratic government tax office. Describe the stressors that she might encounter in this situation. Give an example of a problem-solving reaction to this stress. Give an example of a defensive reaction to it.

6. What factors might explain why bullying persists? How do workplace bullies get away with it?

7. Compare and contrast the stressors that might be experienced by an assembly line worker and the president of a company.

8. Discuss the advantages and disadvantages of hiring employees with Type A personality characteristics.

INTEGRATIVE DISCUSSION QUESTIONS

1. Does personality influence the way individuals manage conflict? Consider the relationship among each of the following personality characteristics and the five approaches to managing conflict described in this chapter: the Big Five dimensions of personality, locus of control, self-monitoring, self-esteem, need for power, and Machiavellianism.

2. Can leadership be a source of stress in organizations? Refer to the leadership theories described in Chapter 9 (e.g., leadership traits, behaviours, situational theories, participative leadership, strategic leadership, and LMX theory) and explain how leadership can be a source of stress. According to each theory, what can leaders do to reduce stress and help employees cope with it?

ON-THE-JOB CHALLENGE QUESTION

Why Don't People Take Their Vacations?

A Harris/Decima poll determined that almost 25 percent of Canadians fail to use all the vacation days they are entitled to during the year. The unused days ranged from 1.39 in the province of Quebec to 2.81 in Alberta. Although these numbers seem small, they project nationally to 34 million unused days a year. Despite this, 42 percent of those polled reported being tired, stressed, and in need of a vacation. A similar Harris Interactive U.S. poll found that 57 percent of Americans reported unused vacation days.

What do you think explains the reluctance of so many people to forego deserved vacation time? If you were or are a manager, how would you react to staff who don't use all their vacation days? What are the long-term implications of this behaviour?

Sources: Covert, K. (2009, July 9). Vacation phobia spreads. *National Post*, FP11; Censky, A. (2012, May 18). Vacation? No thanks, boss. *CNNMoney*.

EXPERIENTIAL EXERCISE

Strategies for Managing Conflict

Indicate how often you use each of the following by writing the appropriate number in the blank. Choose a number from a scale of 1 to 5, with 1 being "rarely," 3 being "sometimes," and 5 being "always." After you have completed the survey, use the scoring key to tabulate your results.

____ 1. I argue my position tenaciously.

____ 2. I put the needs of others above my own.

____ 3. I arrive at a compromise both parties can accept.

____ 4. I don't get involved in conflicts.

____ 5. I investigate issues thoroughly and jointly.

____ 6. I find fault in other persons' positions.

____ 7. I foster harmony.

____ 8. I negotiate to get a portion of what I propose.

____ 9. I avoid open discussions of controversial subjects.

____ 10. I openly share information with others in resolving disagreements.

____ 11. I enjoy winning an argument.

____ 12. I go along with the suggestions of others.

____ 13. I look for a middle ground to resolve disagreements.

____ 14. I keep my true feelings to myself to avoid hard feelings.

____ 15. I encourage the open sharing of concerns and issues.

____ 16. I am reluctant to admit I am wrong.

____ 17. I try to help others avoid "losing face" in a disagreement.

____ 18. I stress the advantages of "give and take."

____ 19. I encourage others to take the lead in resolving controversy.

____ 20. I state my position as only one point of view.

Scoring Key

Managing Strategy

Total your responses to these questions

Competing 1, 6, 11, 16 _____

Accommodating 2, 7, 12, 17 _____

Compromising 3, 8, 13, 18 _____

Avoiding 4, 9, 14, 19 _____

Collaborating 5, 10, 15, 20 _____

Primary conflict management strategy (highest score): _____

Secondary conflict management strategy (next-highest score): _____

Source: Whetten, D.A., & Cameron, K.S. *Developing management skills* (7th ed.) © 2008. Reproduced by Pearson Education, Inc., Upper Saddle River, NJ. Electronically reproduced by permission of Pearson Education, Inc., Upper Saddle River, NJ.

CASE INCIDENT

Bringing Baby to Work

Ted Swanson liked to think of himself as a progressive, family-friendly kind of guy. Consequently, he couldn't quite believe the words coming out of his mouth, directed at Bryan Papis, his boss and owner of the creative media company ZeusAd. "Bryan, that baby is driving me crazy! The cooing, laughing, and crying are one thing, but some of the creative team and support staff make such a fuss over him that it drives me to distraction. I had a client in here yesterday who didn't know what to make of the whole thing. This just isn't professional."

The four-month-old baby to which Ted was alluding belonged to Glenda Fox, one of the more clever creative types in the company. Although she was eligible for extended maternity leave, she had chosen not to take it. She said she didn't want to "get out of the loop" or let her current project team down. These motives, and Glenda's espoused beliefs in "attachment parenting" had led her to bring her new baby to work on a fairly regular basis, except when her husband could occasionally provide care.

Bryan Papis also prided himself on being a family-friendly employer, but he wondered if ZeusAd needed a formal policy concerning babies at work.

Source: Inspired in part by Boesveld, S. (2012, March 8). When every day is take your kids to work day. *National Post*, A1, A2.

1. A number of news stories have appeared suggesting that babies in the workplace are a source of considerable interpersonal conflict. What are some likely reasons for this?

2. Is bringing a baby to work the ultimate example of work–family integration? Or does it go too far in blurring the distinction between work and family?

3. What considerations should underpin a formal policy concerning babies at work?

CASE STUDY

Tough Guy

A mere half-block away from the office on a pleasing fall day—the kind that caught the attention of most New Yorkers—Jeremy Frazer, an associate at the investment bank Hudson Smith Gordon ("Hudson") thought about Chip Mazey, one of the vice presidents he was working with on a negotiation. Frazer and three other members working on the deal, Jean Fenster, Rich Patten, and Payton Edwards, had finally confided in each other about what it was like to work for the VP.

They found themselves in a difficult situation, one that most of them thought they had no power to change. After all, doing something about Mazey's behavior was tricky business. First was the fear of confronting Mazey. Another concern was the likelihood that Mazey would probably deny his behavior or wouldn't think that a problem existed. Then there was the unease about escalating the discussion to include a conversation with Mazey's boss. Going upstairs might cause a tense situation to become even worse. Not really knowing what to do irked Frazer, though he couldn't exactly say why. He thought about the stories his co-workers had shared.

Bulge, Middle, or Boutique?

The lure of high risk and high reward made investment banking an attractive career for many in the world of finance. Organizations employed investment banks to help work out financial problems. Offering a mix of business activities, investment banks issued securities, helped investors to purchase securities, managed financials assets, traded securities, and provided financial advice. Investment banks came in several sizes. The largest were called "bulge bracket" firms; the "middle market" companies tended to be regionally based; and "boutique" banks were smaller and more specialized. As a "middle market" firm, Hudson was oriented toward financial analysis and program trading.

To support their security sales and trading activities, investment banks hired and maintained large staffs of research analysts. As Frazer described:

> In investment banking, you make deals for companies to raise capital—debt or equity. Research supports that effort. By becoming expert in a particular field, you generate more business. My firm is considered the leading expert on wireless carriers. This reputation translates into wireless communication companies' wanting Hudson to do research on them.

Making the Deal with a Fast-Tracker

Chip Mazey had been with Hudson 10 years and followed the "kiss up, kick down" mantra. His verbal lashings were sharp, unrelenting, and unprovoked. He had developed a nasty reputation among analysts and associates, which was passed to the firm's top management only through their 360° review system. Mazey was very careful not to show his true colors when senior management was within earshot, but as result of the negative comments from below, his initial promotion to vice president was postponed. The decision came as a shock to him, because he believed he had always been submissive to upper management. Despite his poor people skills, Mazey was a solid banker, and he received the promotion as scheduled one year later.

As a vice president, Mazey's swagger and bravado increased exponentially. Mazey always had trouble interacting with his peers, but after his promotion, he was more ruthless to his subordinates than his peers. He often referred to subordinates as "you" or "analyst" and he reminded others of his new title by telling them, "I am superior to you." It was common for him to yell at a subordinate in a rage, only to discover that he had made an error and there was no problem. In such a situation, Mazey would abruptly hang up the phone when he realized his error without a goodbye or apology. The targets of his verbal abuse disliked working with him and tried to spend time working on projects with other bankers.

The first time Frazer worked with Mazey was on a project Mazey was heading up. "I was assigned to this kick-ass multibillion dollar deal," Frazer said. "Even better than that was the fact that the deal team included the vice president, so I was extremely excited about the opportunity." The vice president was in charge of leading the deal and had a reputation of being "dynamic" and on the "fast track." Frazer's enthusiasm faded somewhat when he stepped into Mazey's office. During their initial meeting, Mazey ordered Frazer to stand "right here" and pointed to a spot on the floor in front of his desk. The associate felt uneasy about being spoken to in this manner, but because it was the first time he had worked with Mazey, he decided not to mention anything—it was best to let things go. After all, investment banks had a reputation for being infested with Type A personalities. Some "I-bankers" had told Frazer that the biggest challenge in an investment banking career was to manage upward.

Over the next several weeks, Frazer witnessed Mazey's insulting and derogatory behavior toward other associates and analysts. Tension was part of being around him. "Fortunately, I worked on multiple assignments, reporting to various other managers at the same time," Frazer said. "The dynamics on other assignment were in stark contrast to this particular one. So I realized how much I like the job and how well I fit in—despite being so heavily reprimanded on a continual basis with that VP."

On a Need-to-Know Basis

That Mazey was difficult to deal with was hardly news to most at Hudson. What was worthy of a headline was that Frazer seemed more willing than most to talk about his supervisor's questionable behavior. Others who had been in the organization much longer than Frazer just learned to work around Mazey's behavior—he was a control freak who made a lot of money for the company and that translated into wielding a lot of power. "I became more comfortable with some of my peers and started confiding in a few of them," Frazer said. "I realized my situation was hardly unique since everyone who had at one time worked with that VP had the same story." Things became so ugly, Frazer learned, that some full-time associates within the group bluntly refused to work with him. Jean Fenster, an analyst who also worked with Mazey on a few deals, described her experience:

> When I first started, Chip asked me to complete an assignment which would typically take a novice at least three days to finish. I was handed the assignment at 8 p.m. and instructed to have it finished and on his desk to look at first thing the following morning. I sat through the night cracking on the assignment and finally completed what I thought was a pretty comprehensive product. To my good fortune, there were a few experienced staff members at the office during the night who offered to vet my product. They

> seemed pretty happy with my work. Slightly before dawn, I laid the finalized assignment on Chip's desk. I thought it would be a great idea to go home, catch up on a couple hours of sleep, and clean up. I arrived back at the office at least 15 minutes before Chip—ready to answer any questions.

As expected Fenster was called over to Mazey's desk the next morning. What followed, however, was unexpected. He questioned every assumption she had made, countered every explanation she offered in a derogatory manner, and nitpicked her work for an entire hour. He then asked her to redo the work based on information he forwarded via e-mail. When Fenster sat down at her desk to rework the material, she was shocked to learn that the VP was privy to that additional information *before he handed her the assignment*, information that would have made it easier to complete the work. She just couldn't fathom why this information was not forwarded to her earlier. Even more discouraging was that although she was asked to complete the work within 24 hours, the e-mail indicated they had two weeks before it was even due. That assignment was a nightmare, and every effort Fenster made toward working on it contributed to the bad dream. "Each session I had with Chip included a series of derogatory and demeaning remarks directed toward me," she said. "From my communication skills, my accent, to the way I dressed, this VP was critical."

Fenster's story sounded eerily familiar to Rich Patten, who described a couple of his experiences with the vice president. During a conference call with a client, Patten was unable to answer a question the client posted. Mazey became enraged and began screaming at both him and the other analyst in the room. Patten said he could have helped Mazey answer the client's questions but Mazey's ranting prevented him from even speaking. "The outburst resembled that of a 2-year-old, and both of us were speechless," Patten said. "Then, still in a rage, Chip grabbed a calculator from his desktop and shattered it against the wall, just above my head!"

Later that day, Mazey apologized for his outburst, and Patter believed his apology was sincere. "I had considered going to speak with the vice president who hired me about the incident," Patten said. "But after the apology I changed my mind," Mazey asked the associate to focus on the task at hand. It was 7 p.m. and there were still at least nine hours of work that had to be completed by an 8 a.m. conference call the next morning, Mazey instructed Patten to come in to work an hour early to prepare for the call.

"I spent the entire night working, arrived home at 4:30 a.m., slept for an hour and a half, and then returned to the office at 7 a.m.," Pattern recalled. "Gulping down my coffee, I went to Chip's office only to find it empty." The 8 a.m. showtime came and went without any word from Mazey, who eventually rolled into the office at 10 a.m. without a word. Patten asked him about the meeting, and Mazey simply said that the meeting was changed. Patten asked another associate who was staffed on the deal about the meeting, and found out that no such meeting was ever planned!

Get to Work—Everyone!

Payton Edwards had another Mazey characteristic to share. "He's very bright and certainly very capable, but he demands complete perfection and treats subordinates as if they were subservient to him and only him," Edwards said. "Occasionally, this man would compliment me for a 'job well done.'" Yet within five minutes, Mazey would come back with some reason why it wasn't "quite right" and force him to redo his work. He was also known for forcing people to do useless, menial tasks. For example, he frequently had his administrative assistant, as well as two analysts, complete the *exact* same task. Mazey said he just want to make absolutely sure that when all was said and done, the task was completed perfectly. Eventually, the analysts and administrative assistant found out that they were all assigned the same task and they were peeved. They felt like he didn't trust them—and he didn't. Edwards said,

> *Even when it was apparent that Chip had made a mistake, he never openly acknowledged it. One time, he denied that that there were multiple buyers on a particular deal and created a hostile deal environment for many of the concerned parties. He also did not like initiative-taking, much less even consider rewarding it. When I went to him with ideas on topics to research relevant ongoing deals, he shot down my ideas and told me to work on what he wanted me to get done. When it turned out later that my ideas were good, he never gave me credit and pretended that he*

had thought of them himself. In fact, he went out of his way to discredit me. For example, when I was still a very novice drinker, Chip would get a kick out of having me order the wine at closing dinners. He wanted to embarrass me in public because of my lack of knowledge about wine.

Chip also made fun of the secretary who came from a poorer part of the city and where everyone seemed to have the same last name. At Christmas parties, the support staff was not allowed to bring spouses while analysts and associates were invited to bring their spouses. Chip told me that he did not feel that it was necessary to "pay to feed the secretary's husband."

Any More Questions?

Life for support staff working for Mazey was a challenge as well. He had an incessant need to know what every person was working on at all times. This was even more pronounced the lower an employee was within the organizational hierarchy. His administrative assistant, Gabriela Salaberrios, found it surprising that the VP needed to know what a secretary was typing at a given moment. Yet Mazey had to know where all employees were at all times. He provided Salaberrios with a cell phone so that he could contact her in the middle of the night to work on last-minute deal items. He was never polite, and refused to take no for an answer. More than a few times, Mazey called in the middle of the night and demanded her presence at the office. Many times he had already sent a car to get Salaberrios before she had said yes. One time, she was vacationing in Tunisia, and he called to demand her immediate return—it seemed that his idea on how a deal should go from beginning to end was to be followed by all.

So What?

Proud of his accomplishment in his career so far, Frazer had sashayed into New York with a youthful certainty that attitude would carry him. He held a job he had thought about for some time in a firm he was convinced would offer even more opportunities. Not once had he expected to get sidetracked over some middle-aged, disgruntled vice president.

Yet that same VP possessed many of the characteristics Frazer had expected and indeed admired on Wall Street. Gathering all this information on Mazey had been almost cathartic. Now what, if anything, should he do with it?

QUESTIONS

1. Earlier in the chapter *conflict* was defined as a process that occurs when one person, group, or organizational subunit frustrates the goal attainment of another. Speculate about how Chip Mazey has frustrated the goal attainment of personnel at Hudson Smith Gordon.

2. Is the conflict observed in the case relationship, task, or process conflict? Please explain your reasoning.

3. The chapter outlined a number of causes of conflict. Which seem to be prevalent in this case? Feel free to cite some other contributors as well.

4. The chapter discusses five modes of managing conflict: avoiding, accommodating, competing, compromise, and collaborating. What mode does Chip Mazey employ? What mode does his staff employ?

5. Chip Mazey's subordinates seem to be suffering from stress, but what is its exact causes? That is, how does his behaviour translate into stress for others?

6. Is Chip a bully? Defend your answer.

7. Despite his obvious reputation, how has Chip managed to retain a position of power?

8. What should Jeremy Fraser do now? What should his goals be?

INTEGRATIVE CASE

Deloitte & Touche: Integrating Arthur Andersen

At the end of Part Two of the text, on Individual Behaviour, you answered a number of questions about the Deloitte & Touche Integrative Case that dealt with issues related to learning, perceptions, fairness and job attitudes, motivation, and pay plans. Now that you have completed Part Three of the text and the chapters on Social Behaviour and Organizational Processes, you can return to the Integrative Case and enhance your understanding of some of the main issues associated with social behaviour and organizational processes by answering the following questions that deal with groups, socialization and culture, leadership, communication, conflict, and stress.

QUESTIONS

1. Given that employees from the two firms will be working together in groups, what are the implications for group development and group cohesiveness? What advice would you give the integration team for designing effective work teams?

2. Is organizational socialization relevant for the integration of Arthur Andersen employees? What would you tell the integration team about organizational socialization and how it can be helpful for the integration process?

3. What methods of organizational socialization can be used to integrate the Arthur Andersen employees? Be sure to explain how you would use each of the methods described in Chapter 8 and indicate what you think would be most effective for the successful integration of Arthur Andersen employees.

4. Review the results of the cultural assessment of the two firms and then compare and contrast

their cultures. How are they similar and different and what are the implications for the successful integration of the two firms?

5. What should the integration team do about the cultural differences between the two firms? Should they integrate the Arthur Andersen employees into the existing Deloitte & Touche culture or should they create a new culture? What do you think the integration team should do and how should they proceed?

6. How important is leadership for the successful integration of the two firms? Consider the implications of the different leadership theories described in Chapter 9 (situational theories, leader–member exchange theory, transformational and transactional leadership, ethical and authentic leadership, and strategic leadership)

for the successful integration of the two firms. What type of leadership do you think is most important and likely to be effective, and why?

7. Identify some challenges or barriers to effective communication in the case. How did Deloitte try to counteract these barriers?

8. Although there is no evidence of open conflict in the case, there is plenty of potential for it. What are some factors that might cause conflict between the Deloitte and Andersen contingents?

9. Consider the potential for stress among the employees of both firms. What stressors are employees most likely to experience and why? What can the integration team do to minimize these stressors and help employees cope with stress?

PART

4

THE TOTAL ORGANIZATION

14 Organizational Structure

15 Environment, Strategy, and Technology

16 Organizational Change, Development, and Innovation

ORGANIZATIONAL STRUCTURE

LEARNING OBJECTIVES

After reading Chapter 14, you should be able to:

14.1 Define *organizational structure* and explain how it corresponds to division of labour.

14.2 Discuss the relative merits of various forms of *departmentation*.

14.3 Review the more basic and more elaborate means of achieving organizational *coordination*.

14.4 Discuss the nature and consequences of *traditional structural characteristics*.

14.5 Explain the distinction between *organic* and *mechanistic* structures.

14.6 Discuss the emergence of *ambidextrous*, *network*, *virtual*, *modular*, and *boundaryless* organizations.

14.7 Review important considerations concerning *downsizing*.

14.8 Identify symptoms of structural problems in organizations.

FLIGHT CENTRE: FAMILY, VILLAGE, TRIBE

Flight Centre is an Australian-based firm that grew from a modest two-person bus touring company in 1982 to one of today's largest global travel agencies. It currently runs more than 2000 travel outlets and related businesses in 11 countries and employs more than 13 000 people. Through licensing and reseller agreements, the company also maintains a presence in 60 additional countries.

Flight Centre opened its first Canadian outlet in Vancouver in 1995, which is now the headquarters of Flight Centre Canada. With approximately 200 shops and businesses and 1400 employees, Flight Centre Canada has achieved resounding success; it has been recognized for 10 consecutive years as one of Canada's best companies to work for. The North American subsidiary is not alone. All of Flight Centre's operations have been repeatedly recognized as great places to work.

Flight Centre's high pace of corporate growth is impressive, not only for what it has achieved but also because such growth can often be debilitating, especially if not managed appropriately. So how did Flight Centre manage to grow so effectively? Graham "Sckroo" Turner, Flight Centre's gregarious founder, attributes much of the company's recent success to a concept introduced by Nigel Nicholson, an organizational behaviour professor who contended that people are best motivated if they are organized into hunter–gatherer groups. Nicholson's arguments are based on the idea that human beings have retained many of the survival attributes that were prevalent in the Stone Age, such as fight-or-flight, use of emotion versus reason, and seeking of status, and that people will perform better when they are assembled into smaller groups. Nicholson suggested that corporations should organize around the way people prefer to work, rather than forcing people to work in idiosyncratic organizational cultures.

Turner realized that Flight Centre had been successful due to his own subconscious implementation of Nicholson's ideas. Turner always believed that he and his employees should be responsible for their own work, with limited delegation of tasks: "I feel that if a job needs doing, I should either do it myself or slice off a part of the job and give that whole part of the job to someone else in senior management rather than to a PA or secretary.... This helps to ensure that you make things easier for yourself and develop the people around you." Past corporate performance supported Turner's realization that work needed to be managed holistically by individuals and small teams. Upon analysis, he found that Flight Centre shops that were restricted to six or seven people performed significantly better than larger shops of 10 or more people. The same applied to performance within the company's regions and back-office functions. As soon as team size exceeded groups of seven or so, decision making suffered and performance dropped off.

At Flight Centre, outstanding performance is celebrated at the family, village, and tribe level.

In 1995, when Turner read about Nicholson's evolution-based management ideas, Flight Centre was in the process of becoming a public company, making Turner much more aware of the risks it now faced. He worried that as Flight Centre grew it would lose much of its hunter–gatherer culture, which had been so fundamental to its success. In an effort to prevent employee alienation that can come from centralized decision making, Turner and his executive team incorporated ideas from both Nicholson and another professor, Robin Dunbar, to establish a team-based structure of families, villages, and tribes. This structure reflected Turner's desire to provide every employee with autonomy and responsibility in a supportive environment. In the structure, families represented the customer-facing shops and were limited to teams of three to seven people. Villages were geographically based and included three to five families that would support each other. Tribes replaced the larger regional organizations, consisting of no more than 25 families (approximately 150 people). The tribes were given a single identity and came together for celebrations and interactions. Through this "family, village, tribe" approach, Flight Centre was able to provide employees with a single tribal identity that reinforced their sense of family but equally encouraged competition.

The "family, village, tribe" team design allowed Flight Centre to retain its flat corporate structure and employees' sense of belonging by establishing a set of small businesses within the larger corporation. Flight Centre acknowledges that the team-based structure is somewhat expensive, as more leaders are required than in a traditional corporate hierarchy, but Turner believes that the benefits far outweigh the expense: "We need to ensure that we have the right people in the front line with the right systems and culture so that our people feel that they're a central part of the enterprise."

The "family, village, tribe" team-based approach not only encourages a loyal family atmosphere, it also brings financial reward. As a means to promote ownership, responsibility, and accountability, employee compensation and bonuses are based solely on individual and team performance in key business areas such as profit, turnover, promotions, and net income. Team compensation serves to quell any unproductive competition between stores. As Turner explains, "We used to have a shop [in one town] and another [in a nearby town]. They used to kill each other for bloody business. Even to the extent of maybe phoning the other shop [as a way of occupying their time with phantom business], which was pretty stupid." The "family, village, tribe" approach eliminated this type of competition by encouraging shops within the same "village" to support each other. Compensation programs encourage employees to work together and exceed corporate business objectives.[1]

Why are Flight Centre and other firms organized and structured the way they are? And how does organizational structure affect employees and the overall effectiveness of organizations? These are the kinds of questions that we shall attempt to answer in this chapter and the next.

First we will define organizational structure and discuss the methods for dividing labour and forming departments. Then we will consider some methods for coordinating labour as well as traditional structural characteristics and the relationship between size and structure. Finally, we will review some signals of structural problems.

WHAT IS ORGANIZATIONAL STRUCTURE?

LO

Define *organizational structure* and explain how it corresponds to division of labour.

ORGANIZATIONAL STRUCTURE Go to MyManagementLab to complete a simulation about organizational structure.

In previous chapters, we were concerned primarily with the bits and pieces that make up organizations. First, we analyzed organizational behaviour from the standpoint of the individual member—how his or her learning, personality, perception, attitudes, and motivation affect behaviour. Then we shifted our analysis to groups and to some of the processes that occur in organizations, including communication, leadership, and decision making. In this chapter we adopt yet another level of analysis by looking at the organization as a whole. Our primary interest is the causes and consequences of organizational structure.

Shortly, we will discuss organizational structure in detail. For now, it is enough to know that it broadly refers to how an organization's individuals and groups are *put together* or *organized* to accomplish work. This is an important issue. An organization could have well-motivated individual members and properly led groups but still fail to fulfill its potential because of the way their efforts are divided and coordinated.

In Chapter 1, we defined organizations as social inventions for accomplishing common goals through group effort. In this chapter and the next, we shall see that organizational structure intervenes between goals and organizational accomplishments, and thus influences organizational effectiveness. Among other things, structure affects how effectively and efficiently group effort is coordinated.

To achieve its goals, an organization has to do two very basic things: *divide* labour among its members and then *coordinate* what has been divided. For example, consider how a university divides its labour: some members teach, some run the graduate programs, some take care of accounts, and some handle registration. It is simply unlikely that anyone could do *all* these things well. Furthermore, within each of these subunits, labour would be further divided. For example, the registrar's office would include a director, secretaries, clerks, and so on. With all this division, some coordination is obviously necessary.

We can conclude that **organizational structure** is the manner in which an organization divides its labour into specific tasks and achieves coordination among these tasks.[2]

Organizational structure. The manner in which an organization divides its labour into specific tasks and achieves coordination among these tasks.

THE DIVISION AND COORDINATION OF LABOUR

Labour must be divided because individuals have physical and intellectual limitations. *Everyone* cannot do *everything*; even if this were possible, tremendous confusion and inefficiency would result. There are two basic dimensions to the division of labour: a vertical dimension and a horizontal dimension. Once labour is divided, it must be coordinated to achieve organizational effectiveness.

Vertical Division of Labour

The vertical division of labour is concerned primarily with apportioning authority for planning and decision making—who gets to tell whom what to do? As we can see in

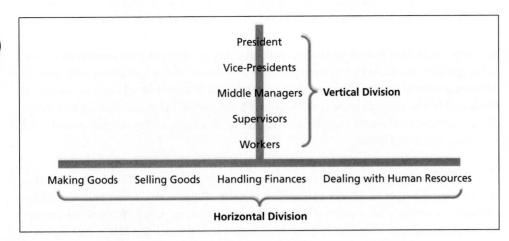

EXHIBIT 14.1
The dimensions of division of labour in a manufacturing firm.

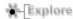 Explore

Go to MyManagementLab to see an annotated version of this figure.

Exhibit 14.1, in a manufacturing firm, the vertical division of labour is usually signified by titles such as president, manager, and supervisor. In a university, it might be denoted by titles such as president, dean, and chairperson. Organizations differ greatly in the extent to which labour is divided vertically. For example, the Canadian Army has 18 levels of command, ranging from full generals to privates. Walmart has five levels between its CEO and its store managers. On the other hand, an automobile dealership might have only two or three levels, and a university would usually fall between the extremes. Separate departments, units, or functions *within* an organization will also often vary in the extent to which they vertically divide labour. A production unit might have several levels of management, ranging from supervisor to general manager. A research unit in the same company might have only two levels of management. A couple of key themes underlie the vertical division of labour.

AUTONOMY AND CONTROL Holding other factors constant, the domain of decision making and authority is reduced as the number of levels in the hierarchy increases. Put another way, managers have less authority over fewer matters. On the other hand, a flatter hierarchy pushes authority lower and involves people further down the hierarchy in more decisions.

COMMUNICATION A second theme underlying the vertical division of labour is communication or coordination between levels. As labour is progressively divided vertically, timely communication and coordination can become harder to achieve. Recall our discussion in Chapter 10 on information filtering as a barrier to communication. As the number of levels in the hierarchy increases, filtering is more likely to occur.

These two themes illustrate that labour must be divided vertically enough to ensure proper control but not so much as to make vertical communication and coordination impossible. The proper degree of such division will vary across organizations and across their functional units.

Horizontal Division of Labour

The horizontal division of labour groups the basic tasks that must be performed into jobs and then into departments so that the organization can achieve its goals. Required workflow is the main basis for this division. The firm schematized in Exhibit 14.1 must produce and sell goods, keep its finances straight, and keep its employees happy. A hospital must admit patients, subject them to lab tests, fix what ails them, and keep them comfortable, all the while staying within its budget. Just as organizations differ in the extent to which they divide labour vertically, they also differ in the extent of horizontal division of labour. In a small business, the owner might be a "jack-of-all-trades," making estimates, delivering the product or service, and keeping the books. As the organization grows, horizontal division of labour is likely, with different groups of employees assigned to perform each of these tasks. Thus, the horizontal division of labour suggests some specialization on the part of the workforce. Up to a point, this increased specialization can promote efficiency. A couple of key themes underlie the horizontal division of labour.

JOB DESIGN   The horizontal division of labour is closely tied to our earlier consideration of job design (Chapter 6). An example will clarify this. Suppose that an organization offers a product or service that consists of A work, B work, and C work (e.g., fabrication, inspection, and packaging). There are at least three basic ways in which it might structure these tasks:

- Form an ABC Department in which all workers do ABC work.
- Form an ABC Department in which workers specialize in A work, B work, or C work.
- Form a separate A Department, B Department, and C Department.

There is nothing inherently superior about any of these three designs. Notice, however, that each has implications for the jobs involved and how these jobs are coordinated. The first design provides for enriched jobs in which each worker can coordinate his or her own A work, B work, and C work. It also reduces the need for supervision and allows for self-managed teams. However, this design might require highly trained workers, and it might be impossible if A work, B work, and C work are complex specialties that require (for example) engineering, accounting, and legal skills. The second design involves increased horizontal division of labour in which employees specialize in tasks and in which the coordination of A work, B work, and C work becomes more critical. However, much of this coordination could be handled by properly designing the head of the department's job. Finally, the third design offers the greatest horizontal division of labour in that A work, B work, and C work are actually performed in separate departments. This design provides for great control and accountability for the separate tasks, but it also suggests that someone above the department heads will have to get involved in coordination. There are several lessons here. First, the horizontal division of labour strongly affects job design. Second, it has profound implications for the degree of coordination necessary. Finally, it also has implications for the vertical division of labour and where control over work processes should logically reside.

DIFFERENTIATION   A second theme occasioned by the horizontal division of labour is related to the first. As organizations engage in increased horizontal division of labour, they usually become more and more differentiated. **Differentiation** is the tendency for managers in separate units, functions, or departments to differ in terms of goals, time spans, and interpersonal styles.[3] In tending to their own domains and problems, managers often develop distinctly different psychological orientations toward the organization and its products or services. Under high differentiation, various organizational units tend to operate more autonomously.

A classic case of differentiation is that which often occurs between marketing managers and those in research and development. The goals of the marketing managers might be external to the organization and oriented toward servicing the marketplace. Those of R&D managers might be oriented more toward excellence in design and state-of-the-art use of materials. While marketing managers want products to sell *now*, R&D managers might feel that "good designs take time." Finally, marketing managers might believe that they can handle dispute resolution with R&D through interpersonal tactics learned when they were

Differentiation. The tendency for managers in separate units, functions, or departments to differ in terms of goals, time spans, and interpersonal styles.

on the sales force ("Let's discuss this over lunch"). R&D managers might feel that "the design speaks for itself" when a conflict occurs. The essential problem here is that the marketing department and the R&D department *need* each other to do their jobs properly![4] Shortly, we will review some tactics to help achieve necessary coordination.

Differentiation is a natural and necessary consequence of the horizontal division of labour, but it again points to the need for coordination, a topic that we will consider in more detail below. For now, let's examine more closely how organizations can allocate work to departments.

Departmentation

As we suggested above, once basic tasks have been combined into jobs, a question still remains as to how to group these jobs so that they can be managed effectively. The assignment of jobs to departments is called departmentation, and it represents one of the core aspects of the horizontal division of labour. It should be recognized that "department" is a generic term; some organizations use an alternative term, such as unit, group, or section. There are several methods of departmentation, each of which has its strengths and weaknesses.

FUNCTIONAL DEPARTMENTATION This form of organization is basic and familiar. Under **functional departmentation**, employees with closely related skills and responsibilities (functions) are located in the same department (Exhibit 14.2). Thus, those with skills in sales and advertising are assigned to the marketing department, and those with skills in accounting and credit are assigned to the finance department. Under this kind of design, employees are grouped according to the kind of resources they contribute to achieving the overall goals of the organization.[5]

What are the advantages of functional departmentation? The most cited advantage is that of efficiency. When all the engineers are located in an engineering department, rather than scattered throughout the organization, it is easier to be sure that they are neither overloaded nor underloaded with work. Also, support factors, such as reference books, specialized software, and laboratory space can be allocated more efficiently with less duplication. Some other advantages of functional departmentation include the following:

- Communication within departments should be enhanced, since everyone "speaks the same language."
- Career ladders and training opportunities within the function are enhanced because all parties will share the same view of career progression.
- The performance of functional specialists should be easier to measure and evaluate when they are all located in the same department.

LO 14.2

Discuss the relative merits of various forms of *departmentation*.

Functional departmentation. Employees with closely related skills and responsibilities are assigned to the same department.

Go to MyManagementLab to see an annotated version of this figure.

EXHIBIT 14.2 Functional departmentation.

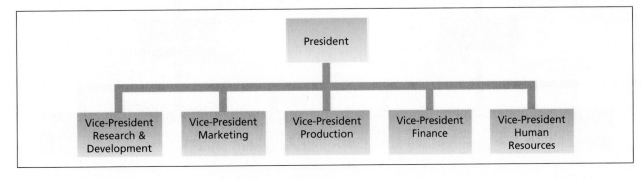

What are the disadvantages of functional departmentation? Most of them stem from the specialization within departments that occurs in the functional arrangement. As a result, a high degree of differentiation can occur between functional departments. At best, this can lead to poor coordination and slow response to organizational problems. At worst, it can lead to open conflict between departments, in which the needs of clients and customers are ignored. Departmental empires might be built at the expense of pursuing organizational goals. There is consensus that functional departmentation works best in small to medium-sized firms that offer relatively few product lines or services. It can also be an effective means of organizing the smaller divisions of large corporations. When the scale gets bigger and the output of the organization gets more complex, most firms gravitate toward product departmentation or its variations.

PRODUCT DEPARTMENTATION   Under **product departmentation**, departments are formed on the basis of a particular product, product line, or service. Each of these departments can operate fairly autonomously because it has its own set of functional specialists dedicated to the output of that department. For example, a personal care firm might have a shampoo division and a cosmetics division, each with its own staff of production people, marketers, and research and development personnel (Exhibit 14.3).

What are the advantages of product departmentation? One key advantage is better coordination among the functional specialists who work on a particular product line. Since their attentions are focused on one product and they have fewer functional peers, fewer barriers to communication should develop. Other advantages include flexibility, since product lines can be added or deleted without great implications for the rest of the organization. Also, product-focused departments can be evaluated as profit centres, since they have independent control over costs and revenues. This is not feasible for most functional departments (e.g., the research and development department does not have revenues). Finally, product departmentation often serves the customer or client better, since the client can see more easily who produced the product (the software group, not Ajax Consulting). All in all, product structures have more potential than functional structures for responding to customers in a timely way.

Are there any disadvantages to product departmentation? Professional development might suffer without a critical mass of professionals working in the same place at the same time. Also, economies of scale might be threatened and inefficiency might occur if relatively

Product departmentation.
Departments are formed on the basis of a particular product, product line, or service.

Explore

Go to MyManagementLab to see an annotated version of this figure.

EXHIBIT 14.3
Product departmentation.

EXHIBIT 14.4
Matrix departmentation.

 Explore

Go to MyManagementLab
to see an annotated
version of this figure.

autonomous product-oriented departments are not coordinated. R&D personnel in an industrial products division and a consumer products division might work on a similar problem for months without being aware of each other's efforts. Worse, product-oriented departments might actually work at cross purposes.

Recently, Canadian Tire moved from a product-oriented structure (e.g., automotive, housewares, and hardware) to a more functional one. This redesign, meant to reduce "silo" thinking and cut costs, centralized such functions as human resources, finance, and information technology.[6]

MATRIX DEPARTMENTATION The system of **matrix departmentation** is an attempt to capitalize simultaneously on the strengths of both functional and product departmentation.[7] In its most literal form, employees remain tied to a functional department such as marketing or production, but they also report to a product manager who draws on their services (Exhibit 14.4). For example, in a firm in the chemical industry, a marketing expert might matrix with the household cleaning products group. Familiar firms that have matrix designs include Procter & Gamble, IBM, Boeing, and BMW.

There are many variations on matrix design. Most of them boil down to what exactly gets crossed with functional areas to form the matrix and the degree of stability of the matrix relationships. For example, besides products, a matrix could be based on geographical regions or projects. For instance, a mechanical engineer in a global engineering company could report to both the mechanical engineering department at world headquarters and the regional manager for Middle East operations. This would probably be a fairly stable arrangement. Recently, Cisco Technical Services, which supplies equipment and 24/7 help desk support worldwide, converted from a regular functional design to a matrix based on geographic regions in order to better provide integrated services.[8] In fact, integrating business in multiple geographic regions is a common stimulus for the matrix design.[9]

Matrix departmentation.
Employees remain
members of a functional
department while also
reporting to a product or
project manager.

On the other hand, a matrix could be based on shorter-term projects. NASA uses this system, as do many consulting firms and research labs. The cross-functional teams that design cars (Chapter 7) draw members from various functions (e.g., styling, marketing, and engineering). When the design is completed, members go on to other assignments.

The matrix system is quite elegant when it works well. Ideally, it provides a degree of *balance* between the abstract demands of the product or project and the people who actually do the work, resulting in a better outcome. Also, it is very flexible. People can be moved around as project flow dictates, and projects, products, or new regions can be added without total restructuring. Being focused on a particular product or project can also lead to better communication among the representatives from the various functional areas (precisely why cross-functional teams are used to design cars).

Two interrelated problems threaten the matrix structure. First, there is no guarantee that product or project managers will see eye-to-eye with various functional managers. This can create conflict that reduces the advantages of the matrix. Also, employees assigned to a product or project team in essence report to two managers, their functional manager and their product or project manager. This violation of a classical management principle (every employee should have only one boss) can result in role conflict and stress, especially at performance review time. The upshot of this is that managers need to be well trained under matrix structures. In your authors' opinion, some of the bad press that matrix designs have received in the past stems from their early application in technical environments where neither functional managers nor project managers had well-developed people-management skills. Also, there may be some cultural limitations to this design. At least one consultant asserts that it is challenging to implement matrix in China due to discomfort with the vague reporting relationships.[10]

OTHER FORMS OF DEPARTMENTATION

Several other forms of departmentation also exist.[11] Two of these are simply variations on product departmentation. One is geographic departmentation. Under **geographic departmentation**, relatively self-contained units deliver the organization's products or services in specific geographic territories (Exhibit 14.5). This form of departmentation shortens communication channels, allows the organization to cater to regional tastes, and gives some appearance of local control to clients and customers. National retailers, insurance companies, and oil companies generally exhibit geographic departmentation.

Geographic departmentation.
Relatively self-contained units deliver an organization's products or services in a specific geographic territory.

Explore

Go to MyManagementLab to see an annotated version of this figure.

EXHIBIT 14.5
Geographic departmentation.

EXHIBIT 14.6
Customer
departmentation.

Go to MyManagementLab to see an annotated version of this figure.

Another form of departmentation closely related to product departmentation is **customer departmentation**. Under customer departmentation, relatively self-contained units deliver the organization's products or services to specific customer groups (Exhibit 14.6). The obvious goal is to provide better service to each customer group through specialization. For example, many banks have commercial lending divisions that are separate from the consumer loan operations. Universities might have separate graduate and undergraduate divisions. An engineering firm might have separate divisions to cater to civilian and military customers. In general, the advantages and disadvantages of geographic and customer departmentation parallel those for product departmentation.

Customer departmentation. Relatively self-contained units deliver an organization's products or services to specific customer groups.

Finally, we should recognize that few organizations represent "pure" examples of functional, product, geographic, or customer departmentation. It is not unusual to see **hybrid departmentation**, which involves some combination of these structures. For example, a manufacturing firm might retain human resources, finance, and legal services in a functional form at headquarters but use product departmentation to organize separate production and sales staffs for each product. Similarly, McDonald's and Walmart centralize many activities at their respective headquarters but also have geographic divisions that cater to regional tastes and promote efficient distribution. The hybrids attempt to capitalize on the strengths of various structures, while avoiding the weaknesses of others.

Hybrid departmentation. A structure based on some mixture of functional, product, geographic, or customer departmentation.

LO 14.3

Basic Methods of Coordinating Divided Labour

When the tasks that will help the organization achieve its goals have been divided among individuals and departments, they must be coordinated so that goal accomplishment is actually realized. We can identify five basic methods of **coordination**, which is a process of facilitating timing, communication, and feedback.[12]

Review the more basic and more elaborate means of achieving organizational *coordination*.

DIRECT SUPERVISION This is a very traditional form of coordination. Working through the chain of command, designated supervisors or managers coordinate the work of their subordinates. For instance, a production supervisor coordinates the work of his or her subordinates. In turn, the production superintendent coordinates the activities of all the supervisors. This method of coordination is closely associated with our discussion of leadership in Chapter 9.

Coordination. A process of facilitating timing, communication, and feedback among work tasks.

STANDARDIZATION OF WORK PROCESSES Some jobs are so routine that the technology itself provides a means of coordination. Little direct supervision is necessary for these jobs to be coordinated. The automobile assembly line provides a good example. When a car comes by, worker X bolts on the left A-frame assembly, and worker Y bolts on the right assembly. These workers do not have to interact, and they require minimal supervision. Work processes can also be standardized by rules and regulations. McDonald's stringent routine for constructing a burger is an example of such standardization.

STANDARDIZATION OF OUTPUTS

Even when direct supervision is minimal and work processes are not standardized, coordination can be achieved through the standardization of work outputs. Concern shifts from how the work is done to ensuring that the work meets certain physical or economic standards. For instance, employees in a machine shop might be required to construct complex valves that require a mixture of drilling, lathe work, and finishing. The physical specifications of the valves will dictate how this work is to be coordinated. Standardization of outputs is often used to coordinate the work of separate product or geographic divisions. Frequently, top management assigns each division a profit target. These standards ensure that each division "pulls its weight" in contributing to the overall profit goals. Thus, budgets are a form of standardizing outputs.

STANDARDIZATION OF SKILLS

Even when work processes and output cannot be standardized and direct supervision is unfeasible, coordination can be achieved through standardization of skills. This is seen very commonly in the case of technicians and professionals. For example, a large surgery team can often coordinate its work with minimal verbal communication because of its high degree of interlocked training—surgeons, anaesthesiologists, and nurses all know what to expect from each other because of their standard training. MBA programs provide some standardized skills (e.g., the ability to read a balance sheet) to people with different functional specialties.

MUTUAL ADJUSTMENT

Mutual adjustment relies on informal communication to coordinate tasks. Paradoxically, it is useful for coordinating the most simple and the most complicated divisions of labour. For example, imagine a small florist shop that consists of the owner–operator, a shop assistant, and a delivery person. It is very likely that these individuals will coordinate their work through informal processes, mutually adjusting to each other's needs. At the other extreme, consider the top executive team of virtually any corporation. Such teams are generally composed of people with a variety of skills and backgrounds (e.g., finance, marketing) and tend to be preoccupied with very non-routine problems. Again, mutual adjustment would be necessary to coordinate their efforts because standardization would be impossible.

As we see in Exhibit 14.7, the coordination methods can be crudely ordered in terms of the degree of *discretion* they permit in terms of task performance. Applied strictly, direct supervision permits little discretion. Standardization of processes and outputs permits successively more discretion. (However, clever employees can "beat" these forms of standardization.) Finally, standardization of skills and mutual adjustment put even more control into the hands of those who are actually doing the work. Obviously, Flight Centre leans toward the right of the continuum.

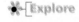
Explore

Go to MyManagementLab to see an annotated version of this figure.

EXHIBIT 14.7
Methods of coordination as a continuum of worker discretion.
Source: Mintzberg, H. (1979). *Structuring of organizations: A synthesis of the research*, 1st ed. Reproduced by Pearson Education, Inc., Upper Saddle River, NJ. Electronically reproduced by permission of Pearson Education, Inc., Upper Saddle River, NJ.

Notice that just as division of labour affects the design of jobs, so does the method of coordination employed. As we move from the left side to the right side of the continuum of coordination, there is greater potential for jobs to be designed in an enriched manner. By the same token, an improper coordination strategy can destroy the intrinsic motivation of a job. Traditionally, much work performed by professionals (e.g., scientists and engineers) is coordinated by their own skill standardization. If the manager of a research lab decides to coordinate work with a high degree of direct supervision, the motivating potential of the scientists' jobs might be damaged. The *manager* is doing the work that *they* should be doing.

The use of the various methods of coordination tends to vary across different parts of the organization. These differences in coordination stem from the way labour has been divided. As we noted, upper management relies heavily on mutual adjustment for coordination. Where tasks are more routine, such as in the lower part of the production subunit, we tend to see coordination via direct supervision or standardization of work processes or outputs.[13] Advisory subunits staffed by professionals, such as a legal department or a marketing research group, often rely on a combination of skill standardization and mutual adjustment.

Finally, methods of coordination may change as task demands change. Under peacetime conditions or routine wartime conditions, the army relies heavily on direct supervision through a strict chain of command. However, this method of coordination can prove ineffective for fighting units under heavy fire. Here, we might see a sergeant with a radio instructing a captain where to direct artillery fire. This reversal of the chain of command is indicative of mutual adjustment. Similarly, the trend toward self-managed work teams (Chapter 7) downplays direct supervision and focuses on mutual adjustment among team members.

Other Methods of Coordination

The forms of coordination we discussed above are very basic, in that almost every organization uses them. After all, when do we see an organization that *does not* exhibit some supervision, some standardization, and some talking things out? Sometimes, however, coordination problems are such that more customized, elaborate mechanisms are necessary to achieve coordination. This is especially true when we are speaking of lateral coordination across highly differentiated departments. Recall that the managers of such departments might vary greatly in goals, time spans, and interpersonal orientation. Figuratively at least, they often "speak different languages." The process of attaining coordination across differentiated departments usually goes by the special name of **integration**.[14] Good integration achieves coordination without reducing the differences that enable each department to do its own job well.[15] For example, in a high-technology firm, we do not *want* production and engineering to be so cozy that innovative tension is lost.[16] Ideally, integration specifies who is accountable for what, enables one department to predict the activities of another, and creates a shared understanding of overarching goals.[17]

Integration. The process of attaining coordination across differentiated departments.

In ascending order of elaboration, three methods of achieving integration include the use of liaison roles, task forces, and full-time integrators.[18]

LIAISON ROLES A **liaison role** is occupied by a person in one department who is assigned, as part of his or her job, to achieve coordination with another department. In other words, one person serves as a part-time link between two departments. Sometimes the second department might reciprocate by nominating its own liaison person. For example, in a university library, reference librarians might be required to serve as liaison people for certain academic departments or schools. In turn, an academic department might assign a faculty member to "touch base" with its liaison in the library. Sometimes, liaison people might actually be located physically in the corresponding department.

Liaison role. A person who is assigned to help achieve coordination between his or her department and another department.

TASK FORCES AND TEAMS

When coordination problems arise that involve several departments simultaneously, liaison roles are not very effective. **Task forces** are temporary groups set up to solve coordination problems across several departments. Representatives from each department are included on a full-time or part-time basis, but when adequate integration is achieved, the task force is disbanded.

Self-managed and cross-functional teams (Chapter 7) are also an effective means of achieving coordination. Such teams require interaction among employees who might otherwise operate in an independent vacuum. Cross-functional teams are especially useful in achieving coordination for new-product development and introduction. At Flight Centre, basing the structure on small teams facilitates coordination.

INTEGRATORS

Integrators are organizational members who are permanently installed between two departments that are in clear need of coordination. In a sense, they are full-time problem solvers. Integrators are especially useful for dealing with conflict between departments that (1) are highly interdependent, (2) have very diverse goals and orientations, and (3) operate in a very ambiguous environment. Such a situation occurs in many high-tech companies.[19] For example, a bio-tech firm might introduce new products almost every month. This is a real strain on the production department, which might need the assistance of the lab to implement a production run. The lab scientists, on the other hand, rely on production to implement last-minute changes because of the rapidly changing technology. This situation badly requires coordination.

Integrators usually report directly to the executive to whom the heads of the two departments report. Ideally, they are rewarded according to the success of both units. A special kind of person is required for this job, since he or she has great responsibility but no direct authority in either department. The integrator must be unbiased, "speak the language" of both departments, and rely heavily on expert power.[20] He or she should also identify strongly with the overall organization and its goals.[21] An engineer with excellent interpersonal skills might be an effective integrator for the electronics firm. A typical job title might be project coordinator.

TRADITIONAL STRUCTURAL CHARACTERISTICS

Every organization is unique in the exact way that it divides and coordinates labour. Few business firms, hospitals, or schools have perfectly identical structures. What is needed, then, is some efficient way to summarize the effects of the vertical and horizontal division of labour and its coordination on the structure of the organization. Over the years, management scholars and practising managers have agreed on a number of characteristics that summarize the structure of organizations.[22]

Span of Control

The **span of control** is the number of subordinates supervised by a manager. There is one essential fact about span of control: The larger the span, the less *potential* there is for coordination by direct supervision. As the span increases, the attention that a supervisor can devote to each subordinate decreases. When work tasks are routine, coordination of labour through standardization of work processes or output often substitutes for direct supervision. Thus, at lower levels in production units, it is not unusual to see spans of control ranging to more than 20. In the managerial ranks, tasks are less routine and adequate time is necessary for informal mutual adjustment. As a result, spans at the upper levels tend to be smaller. Also, at lower organizational levels, workers with only one or a few specialties report to a supervisor. For instance, an office supervisor might supervise only

EXHIBIT 14.8
The relationship between span of control and organizational flatness and tallness.

Go to MyManagementLab to see an annotated version of this figure.

clerks. As we climb the hierarchy, workers with radically different specialties might report to the boss. For example, the president might have to deal with vice-presidents of human resources, finance, production, and marketing. Again, the complexity of this task might dictate smaller spans.[23]

Flat versus Tall

Holding size constant, a **flat organization** has relatively few levels in its hierarchy of authority, while a **tall organization** has many levels. Thus, flatness versus tallness is an index of the vertical division of labour. Again, holding size constant, it should be obvious that flatness and tallness are associated with the average span of control. This is shown in Exhibit 14.8. Both schematized organizations have 31 members. However, the taller one has five hierarchical levels and an average span of two, while the flatter one has three levels and an average span of five. Flatter structures tend to push decision-making powers downward in the organization because a given number of decisions are apportioned among fewer levels. Also, flatter structures generally enhance vertical communication and coordination. The Danish toy company Lego flattened its manufacturing division from four levels of management to three levels composed of teams. In the process, the number of managers was reduced by 40 percent.[24] In general, there has been a North American trend toward flatter organizations, especially with downsizing, a topic we will cover later.

Formalization

Formalization is the extent to which work roles are highly defined by the organization.[25] A very formalized organization tolerates little variability in the way members perform their tasks. Some formalization stems from the nature of the job itself; the work requirements of

Flat organization. An organization with relatively few levels in its hierarchy of authority.

Tall organization. An organization with relatively many levels in its hierarchy of authority.

Formalization. The extent to which work roles are highly defined by an organization.

the assembly line provide a good example of this. More interesting, however, is formalization that stems from rules, regulations, and procedures that the firm or institution chooses to implement. Detailed, written job descriptions, thick procedure manuals, and the requirement to "put everything in writing" are evidence of such formalization. At McDonald's, strict standards dictate how customers are greeted, how burgers are cooked, and how employees are dressed and groomed.

Very complex tasks dictate high formalization. In designing its 777 aircraft, Boeing used information technology to manage the development and modification of thousands of drawings and documents, thus coordinating the work of 5000 individuals at more than 20 locations.[26]

Sometimes, formalization seems excessive. Perhaps this is why so many fast-food employees ignore the hairnet rule. A U.S. Department of Energy document detailing how to change a light bulb in a radioactive area is 317 pages long and specifies duties for 43 people.[27]

Centralization

Centralization. The extent to which decision-making power is localized in a particular part of an organization.

Centralization is the extent to which decision-making power is localized in a particular part of the organization. In the most centralized organization, the power for all key decisions would rest in a single individual, such as the president. In a more decentralized organization, decision-making power would be dispersed down through the hierarchy and across departments. One observer suggests that limitations to individual brainpower often prompt decentralization:

At Food Lion, buying is centralized, but local managers have autonomy to stay close to customers.

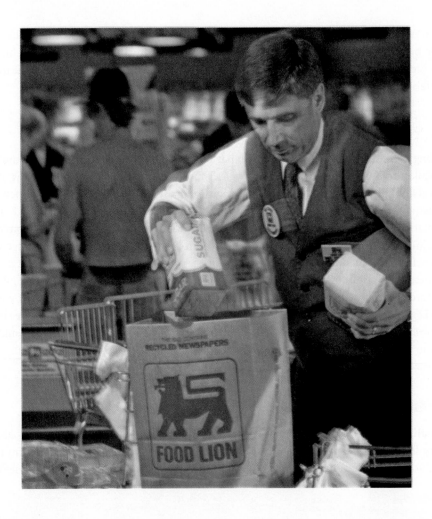

How can the Baghdad salesperson explain the nature of his clients to the Birmingham manager? Sometimes the information can be transmitted to one centre, but a lack of cognitive capacity (brainpower) precludes it from being comprehended there. How can the president of the conglomerate corporation possibly learn about, say, 100 different product lines? Even if a report could be written on each, he would lack the time to study them all.[28]

Of course, the information-processing capacity of executives is not the only factor that dictates the degree of centralization. Some organizations consciously pursue a more participative climate through decentralization. Sckroo Turner explicitly thought about decentralization at Flight Centre. In other organizations, top management might wish to maintain greater control and opt for stronger centralization. One of founder Ray Kroc's innovations was not to permit *regional* franchises that could grow powerful and challenge the basic business principles of McDonald's.[29] The successful North Carolina–based supermarket chain

APPLIED FOCUS

Did BP's Organizational Structure Contribute to the Gulf Oil Spill?

An organization that decentralized with some apparent success was the energy giant British Petroleum (BP). Over the years, the firm became so tall and bureaucratic that both its exploration and production functions suffered from slow, ponderous decision making and a lack of the kind of entrepreneurial spirit that the smaller energy companies had. BP was thus redesigned to allocate these functions into about 20 "assets," smaller business units such as a single oil field. The managers of these assets were accorded much freedom as long as they met performance targets. Since some centralized forces for information sharing and integration were removed with this design, these managers formed small peer groups to share ideas and help each other solve problems.

Although decentralization can facilitate speed and flexibility, it can also damage coordination and remove important oversight. And this can contribute to disaster. In 2010, an explosion on the BP oil rig Deepwater Horizon killed 11 workers and led to the largest oil spill in history. For three months, unprecedented volumes of crude oil gushed into the waters of the Gulf of Mexico, devastating sea life and severely damaging the fishing and tourism industries. Jeffrey Stamps and Jessica Lipnack argued that this ecological disaster occurred in part due to a flat, decentralized organizational structure that was inappropriate for managing the complexity of safely finding and extracting oil from the depths of the seabed. They pointed to conflict and confusion about staunching the oil blowout, getting the cleanup underway, and facilitating claims for damages

as evidence of a lack of coordinated oversight. In similar fashion, a U.S. Department of the Interior report concluded that local business units were responsible for implementing their own operating systems and that this led to localized, idiosyncratic, and inadequate risk management procedures.

Did BP's decentralized design contribute to the Gulf oil disaster?

Sources: Fairtlough, G., & Beckham, R. (2009). Organizational design. In S.R. Clegg & C.L. Cooper (Eds.), *The Sage handbook of organizational behavior* (Vol. 2). London: Sage; Roberts, J. (2004). *The modern firm: Organizational design for growth and performance.* Oxford: Oxford University Press; Stamps, J., & Lipnack, J. (2010, June 23). Why BP crashed and killed the Gulf. *HBR Blog Network*, http://blogs.hbr.org/cs/2010/06/why_bp_crashed_and_killed_the. html; U.S. Department of the Interior. (2011, September 14). *Report regarding the causes of the April 20, 2010 Macondo well blowout.*

Food Lion has generally decentralized with growth, giving local managers more autonomy to stay close to customers and cater to regional differences. However, the buying function and store design and construction have remained centralized to maintain efficiency and contain costs. Also, the lighting in all of its more than 1200 stores spanning 11 states is centralized via a computer system.[30]

Walmart and its French retail competitor Carrefour have pursued different degrees of centralization in their efforts to penetrate the Chinese market. Walmart has mostly replicated its extremely centralized U.S. structure. On the other hand, Carrefour has not centralized logistics and distribution, and it has granted much more autonomy to local store managers. The latter structure seems more appropriate for dealing with China's geographically fragmented and rapidly changing consumer demands.[31]

The proper degree of centralization should put decision-making power where the best *knowledge* is located. Often, this means decentralizing functions with direct customer contact, while centralizing functions that have a more internal orientation (e.g., information technology group). For an example of the pros and cons of centralization, see the Applied Focus: *Did BP's Organizational Structure Contribute to the Gulf Oil Spill?*

Complexity

Complexity. The extent to which an organization divides labour vertically, horizontally, and geographically.

Complexity is the extent to which organizations divide labour vertically, horizontally, and geographically.[32] A fairly simple organization will have few management levels (vertical division) and not many separate job titles (horizontal division). In addition, jobs will be grouped into a small number of departments, and work will be performed in only one physical location (geographic division). At the other extreme, a very complex organization will be tall, will have a large number of job titles and departments, and might be spread around the world. The essential characteristic of complexity is *variety*—as the organization becomes more complex, it has more kinds of people performing more kinds of tasks in more places, whether these places are departments or geographic territories.

LO 14.5

Explain the distinction between *organic* and *mechanistic* structures.

SUMMARIZING STRUCTURE—ORGANIC VERSUS MECHANISTIC

Do the various structural characteristics that we have been reviewing have any natural relationship to one another? Is there any way to summarize how they tend to go together?

If you think back to the very first chapter of the book, you will recall how early prescriptions about management tended to stress employee specialization along with a very high degree of control and coordination. These themes were common to the classical management theorists, Taylor's scientific management, and Weber's bureaucracy. On the other hand, you will also recall how the human relations movement detected some of the problems that specialization and control can lead to—boredom, resentment, and low motivation. Consequently, these human relations advocates favoured more flexible management systems, open communication, employee participation, and so on.

Mechanistic structures. Organizational structures characterized by tallness, specialization, centralization, and formalization.

In general, the classical theorists tended to favour **mechanistic structures**.[33] As Exhibit 14.9 demonstrates, these structures tend toward tallness, narrow spans of control, specialization, high centralization, and high formalization. The other structural and human resources aspects in the exhibit complement these basic structural prescriptions. By analogy, the organization is structured as a mechanical device, each part serving a separate function, each part closely coordinated with the others. Speaking generally, functional structures tend to be rather mechanistic.

Organic structures. Organizational structures characterized by flatness, low specialization, low formalization, and decentralization.

We can contrast mechanistic structures with organic structures. As shown in Exhibit 14.9, **organic structures** tend to favour wider spans of control, fewer authority

Organizational Characteristics	Types of Organization Structure	
Index	**Organic**	**Mechanistic**
Span of control	Wide	Narrow
Number of levels of authority	Few	Many
Ratio of administrative to production personnel	High	Low
Range of time span over which an employee can commit resources	Long	Short
Degree of centralization in decision making	Low	High
Proportion of persons in one unit having opportunity to interact with persons in other units	High	Low
Quantity of formal rules	Low	High
Specificity of job goals	Low	High
Specificity of required activities	Low	High
Content of communications	Advice and information	Instructions and decisions
Range of compensation	Narrow	Wide
Range of skill levels	Narrow	Wide
Knowledge-based authority	High	Low
Position-based authority	Low	High

EXHIBIT 14.9
Mechanistic and organic structures.
Source: From Seiler, J.A. (1967). *Systems analysis in organizational behavior.* Homewood, IL: Irvin, p. 168. This exhibit is an adaptation of one prepared by Paul T. Lawrence and Jay W. Lorsch in an unpublished "Working Paper on Scientific Transfer and Organizational Structure," 1963. The latter, in turn, draws heavily on criteria suggested by Evans, W. (1963). "Indices of hierarchical structure of industrial organizations." *Management Science, 9,* 468–477, Burns and Stalker, op cit., and Woodward, op cit., as well as those suggested by Hall, R.H. (1962). "Intraorganizational structure variables." *Administrative Science Quarterly, 9,* 295–308.

Go to MyManagementLab to see an annotated version of this figure.

levels, less specialization, less formalization, and decentralization. Flexibility and informal communication are favoured over rigidity and the strict chain of command. Thus, organic structures are more in line with the dictates of the human relations movement. Speaking generally, the matrix form is organic.

The labels *mechanistic* and *organic* represent theoretical extremes, and structures can and do fall between these extremes. But is one of these structures superior to the other? To answer this, pause for a moment and consider the structures of a fast-food restaurant chain like McDonald's and the structure of W.L. Gore & Associates, Inc. At the restaurant level, McDonald's is structured very mechanistically. This structure makes perfect sense for the rather routine task of delivering basic convenience food to thousands of people every day and doing it with uniform quality and speed. Of course, McDonald's headquarters, which deals with less routine tasks (e.g., product development, strategic planning), would be more organically structured. W.L. Gore & Associates, Inc. develops and manufactures products that are highly dependent on fast-changing high technology. Although its GORE-TEX brand breathable waterproof fabric is likely most familiar to you, it also produces a wide range of medical and environmental products. Using a philosophy somewhat similar to Flight Centre, Gore limits its plants to 200 people and retains a very flat structure to stimulate communication and innovation. New ideas spin off new business units. Its founder also despised bureaucracy.[34] An organic structure suits Gore perfectly.

There is no "one best way" to organize. In general, more mechanistic structures are called for when an organization's external environment is more stable and its technology is more routine. Organic structures work better when the environment is uncertain, the technology is less routine, and innovation is important. It has to be emphasized that many organizations do not have only a single structure and that structure can and should change over time. Innovation (which we will study in detail in Chapter 16) is one factor that often dictates multiple structures, as we will see in the following section.

ZIP CAR: ORGANIZATIONAL STRUCTURE Go to MyManagementLab to watch a video about organizational structure.

Discuss the emergence of *ambidextrous, network, virtual, modular,* and *boundaryless* organizations.

CONTEMPORARY ORGANIC STRUCTURES

Recent years have seen the advent of new, more organic organizational structures. Global competition and deregulation, as well as advances in technology and communications, have motivated the creation of these structures. Typically, the removal of unnecessary bureaucracy and the decentralization of decision making result in a more adaptable organization. Let's examine some contemporary organic organizational structures.

The Ambidextrous Organization

An **ambidextrous organization** is one that can simultaneously exploit current competencies and explore emerging opportunities.[35] The word "*ambidextrous*" means equally capable of using both hands, and the ideal ambidextrous organization is *partly* organic in form. On the other hand, it also exhibits more mechanistic characteristics. The need for ambidexterity stems from an age-old dilemma—how to pursue the core business while engaging in radical innovation. There is an essential tension between getting the most out of existing technology and the bread-and-butter products or services being offered (the firm's current competencies) and at the same time searching for new opportunities and innovating. This distinction is sometimes described as *exploiting* versus *exploring*. The tension between these two strategies stems from the fact that both require organizational resources, most of which are being generated by exploitation. It also stems from the fact that exploiting is a more certain activity but with diminishing returns, while exploring is a highly uncertain activity but has the potential to unlock fabulous opportunities for renewal. The question then becomes how to manage this essential tension, and it is generally conceded that proper structuring is part of the solution. This solution is important, because ambidexterity is hard to accomplish and thus rare and difficult to imitate, providing a distinct source of competitive advantage.[36] Indeed, ambidexterity has been associated with superior innovation, better financial performance, and longer survival because it provides a dynamic capability for change.[37] It should be noted that any merger of more and less entrepreneurial firms (such as Suncor with Petro-Canada) raises the need to consider ambidexterity.

There is general agreement among experts that exploration and its quest for innovation require a more organic structure, while exploitation—extracting value from existing competencies—requires a more mechanistic approach. This means that ambidexterity provides great pressure for differentiation, clearly separating the creation of new ideas from the fine-tuning of established ideas. We have seen that differentiation in turn requires special attention to integration. This is particularly true in the case of ambidexterity because of the need to have *synergy* between exploitation and exploration while protecting the exploratory unit from creeping bureaucracy. Thus, considerable recent attention has been paid to the most effective integration mechanisms and degree of integration for optimizing ambidexterity.

Charles O'Reilly and Michael Tushman studied how well-established organizations were structured to support radical innovation, the ultimate test of ambidexterity.[38] Some firms tried to innovate using regular functional structures. Others set up completely separate innovation units, the ultimate in differentiation. Some used cross-functional teams within an existing structure. However, the most successful structure for achieving ambidexterity was one in which an innovative unit maintained its own culture, structure, and processes but was integrated with the core of the firm by existing senior management. This structure provided resources and protection for the innovative unit and allowed established units to perfect their own business. This suggests that, with proper structure, exploitation and exploration are complementary rather than contradictory.[39]

O'Reilly and Tushman cite *USA Today* as an example of an organization that made a successful transition to ambidexterity, integrating traditional printed news with the burgeoning but uncertain internet news business. A false start positioned USAToday.com as a completely independent operation from the print unit, so isolated that it could not capitalize on the newspaper's resources. Then the publisher reframed *USA Today* as a news *network* that would span paper, web, and TV coverage. This meant that a valuable resource, news content, would be shared, not hoarded (providing integration), but that each part of the news empire could use the content in its own way (maintaining differentiation).

As the *USA Today* story illustrates, innovations often require difficult decisions about existing structures and how to incorporate the innovation. A particular dilemma is the following: innovations entail a good deal of uncertainty, and more organic structures are best for dealing with uncertainty because of their capacity for adjustment. However, existing organizations are often structured more mechanistically to capitalize on the efficiencies of such a structure. George Westerman, F. Warren McFarlan, and Marco Iansiti studied how existing firms responded to an important innovation—the advent of electronic commerce.[40] The drug chain CVS opted for a highly differentiated structure in that its e-commerce unit was largely autonomous and located at the opposite end of the country from the CVS headquarters. This more organic structure enabled CVS to get an early jump on its competitors. On the other hand, Walgreens pursued a much more integrated structure, fitting the e-commerce operation into its existing offline business, using senior executives as integrators to ensure that the offliners helped the online personnel. There were teething problems, but the integrated approach gradually paid off in efficiency as e-commerce became a more routine business model. Indeed, competitor CVS restructured to a more integrated, less autonomous design as the merits of that approach became apparent. The lesson to be learned here, according to Westerman and colleagues, is that innovations have life cycles and that organizational structures have to correspond to these cycles. Autonomy and differentiation are helpful for introducing innovations, but more integration leads to efficiency as the innovation becomes familiar.

In theory, it makes sense for established firms to pursue ambidexterity by acquiring more innovative exploratory firms. However, research suggests that acquisitions are often assimilated for exploitation unless they are technologically unique and thus incompatible with the existing order.[41]

Network and Virtual Organizations

In a **network organization**, various functions are coordinated as much by market mechanisms as by managers and formal lines of authority.[42] That is, emphasis is placed on who can do what most effectively and economically rather than on fixed ties dictated by an organizational chart. All the assets necessary to produce a finished product or service are present in the network as a whole, not held in-house by one firm. Ideally, the network members cooperate, share information, and customize their services to meet the needs of the network. Indeed, the diffusion of information and innovation are two important outcomes of network forms, especially when the partner firms are technologically diverse.[43] However, via resource synergies, networks can also facilitate exploitation of established assets.[44]

In stable networks, core firms that are departmentalized by function, product, or some other factor contract out some functions to favoured partners so that they can concentrate on the things that they do best (see the left side of Exhibit 14.10). Chrysler, for instance, has its car seats supplied by an upstream firm that also does all the research associated with seating.

Particularly interesting networks are dynamic or virtual organizations, such as that illustrated on the right side of Exhibit 14.10. In a **virtual organization**, an alliance of independent companies shares skills, costs, and access to one another's markets. Thus, they consist of a network of continually evolving independent companies.[45] A "broker" firm with a good idea invents a network in which a large amount of the work is done by other network partners who might change over time or projects. Each partner in a virtual organization contributes only in its area of core competencies. Contemporary book publishers are good examples. These firms do not employ authors, print books, or

Network organization.
Liaisons between specialist organizations that rely strongly on market mechanisms for coordination.

Virtual organization.
A network of continually evolving independent organizations that share skills, costs, and access to one another's markets.

distribute books. Rather, they specialize in contracting authors for a particular project, providing developmental assistance, and marketing the final product. Printing, distribution, and some editorial and design work are handled by others in the network. Such networks are not new, as they have been used for years in the fashion and film industries. However, more firms in other industries, such as computers and biotechnology, now adopt network forms.

A familiar organization that is essentially virtual is Visa, which is at the centre of a network of thousands of financial institutions and many more retailers. Another organization with virtual properties is Google, which licenses its Android operating system at no charge to mobile phone companies and gives applications developers free access to related software. In turn, Google takes a cut of the revenues generated by thousands of applications.[46]

As indicated, a key advantage of the network form is its flexibility and adaptability. A virtual organization is even more flexible than a matrix. Networks also allow organizations to specialize in what they do best. In its network, Chrysler has intentionally positioned itself as a car manufacturer, not a car seat manufacturer. In turn, its supplier has a strong incentive to specialize in its product because Chrysler is a good customer.

The joint operation of specialization and flexibility can be seen in the video game industry.[47] Although there are some exceptions, the development of video games (e.g., *Madden NFL 13*) and the design and sale of video game consoles (e.g., Xbox, PlayStation, and Wii) are done by separate, specialist organizations. In fact, there are hundreds of game developers (e.g., Ubisoft) and just a few console producers. Game developers can and do make choices about which consoles their games can run on, thus establishing a network tie. Factors such as the age and market dominance of the console affect this choice. On their part, console designers such as Sony and Nintendo have to think about the nature and timing of new products so as to cater to the needs of game designers and thus maintain and enlarge their networks. Wireless gaming has led to even more complex networks, involving game developers, wireless carriers (e.g., Bell), handset makers (e.g., Samsung), platform providers (e.g., Oracle), and game publishers (e.g., Sega).[48]

Networking often breeds networking. Ubisoft, a French company, has a large and well-established game development studio in Montreal. Many of its veterans have started their

The video game industry uses networks extensively to develop and design games and gaming consoles.

own ventures which then do business with Ubisoft. Such concentrations of talent, often supported by local universities and government subsidies, foster the advent of network organizations.[49]

Network and virtual organizations face some special problems.[50] Stable networks can deteriorate when the companies dealing with the core firm devote so much of their effort to this firm that they are isolated from normal market demands. This can make them "lazy," resulting in a loss of their technological edge. Virtual organizations lose their organic advantage when they become legalistic, secretive, and too binding of the other partners. On the other side of the coin, virtual partners sometimes exploit their loose structure to profit at the expense of the core firm. The computer industry has experienced both problems with its network arrangements. For instance, the main beneficiaries of the advent of the PC were Microsoft (the operating system supplier) and Intel (the microprocessor supplier), not IBM.[51] Finally, and ironically, despite their capacity for flexibility, network firms sometimes suffer from "structural inertia." That is, network ties are maintained even when they are not economical. This may occur especially among older, larger organizations with large networks.[52]

The Modular Organization

In today's highly uncertain and fast-changing environment, many organizations are realizing that there are advantages to not becoming a large and vertically integrated bureaucracy. Instead, they focus on a few core activities that they do best, such as designing and marketing computers, and let other companies perform all the other activities. A **modular organization** is a network organization that performs a few core functions and outsources other activities to specialists and suppliers. These core functions tend to focus on intellectual property such as patents, brands, advertising, and distribution channels.[53] Services that are often outsourced include the manufacturing of parts, trucking, catering, data processing, and accounting. Thus, modular organizations are like hubs that are surrounded by networks of suppliers that can be added or removed as needed. And unlike a virtual organization, in which the participating firms give up part of their control and are interdependent, the modular organization maintains complete strategic control.[54]

Modular organization. A network organization that performs a few core functions and outsources other activities to specialists and suppliers.

By outsourcing non-core activities, modular organizations are able to keep unit costs low and develop new products more rapidly. It also allows them to use their capital in areas where they have a competitive advantage, such as design and marketing. This has enabled companies such as Dell Computer and Nike to experience large and rapid growth in a relatively short period of time, as they have not had to invest heavily in fixed assets. Nike and Reebok concentrate on designing and marketing high-tech fashionable sports and fitness footwear. Both organizations contract out production to suppliers in countries with low-cost labour.[55]

Modular organizations in the electronics industry buy their products already built, or they buy the parts from suppliers and then assemble them. Dell Computer, for example, assembles computers from outsourced parts, and this allows it to focus on marketing and service. Given this leanness, Dell can afford to invest in areas such as training salespeople and service technicians, although even most of its technicians are outsourced.[56] The automotive industry in North America is heavily involved in outsourcing and is thus increasingly modular. An increasing number of auto makers are now outsourcing major parts of their vehicles (e.g., seats, doors) to parts suppliers like Magna in an effort to improve efficiency and quality. The practice is also apparent in Europe and Japan. For example, Toyota has achieved great success by relying on a network of suppliers.[57] Outsourcing is also taking place among auto parts suppliers, as manufacturers of smaller parts are providing the supplies for those who make the larger parts.[58]

One familiar firm with modular network properties is Sweden's IKEA, the biggest furniture retailer in the world. IKEA restricts its own activities to inventing, distributing, and

Go to MyManagementLab
to see an annotated
version of this figure.

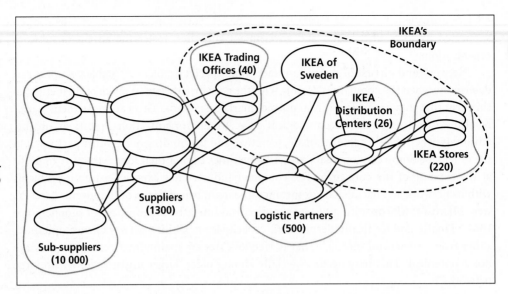

retailing its products. However, as shown in Exhibit 14.11, the company has 1300 suppliers who manufacture these products, 10 000 sub-suppliers (e.g., wood, coatings), and 500 logistical transportation partners. A key strength of IKEA is its skill in working with its suppliers to *develop* its products and to sustain efficiency in its operations.[59]

Although there are many advantages to the modular organization, there are also some disadvantages. Modular organizations work best when they focus on the right speciality and have good suppliers. Because they are dependent on so many outsiders, it is critical that they find suppliers who are reliable and loyal and can be trusted with trade secrets. Modular organizations also must be careful not to outsource critical technologies, which could diminish future competitive advantages. Another disadvantage of the modular organization is that it decreases operational control due to its dependence on outsiders.[60]

In summary, the modular organization is a lean and streamlined organizational structure with great flexibility, making it particularly well suited to organizations in rapidly changing environments. Many modular organizations have become extremely profitable and competitive. And although modular organizational structures have been most popular in the trendy, fast-paced apparel and electronics industries, other industries, such as automotive, steel, chemicals, and photographic equipment, are also becoming more modular.[61] For a sophisticated example of modularity, see the Applied Focus: *Network-Centric Innovation: Boeing's 787 Dreamliner.*

The Boundaryless Organization

**Boundaryless
organization.** An
organization that removes
vertical, horizontal, and
external barriers so that
employees, managers,
customers, and suppliers
can work together, share
ideas, and identify the best
ideas for the organization.

Traditional organizational structures consist of boundaries or barriers that divide people at different hierarchical levels and separate those in different departments. This can be problematic to the extent that the different levels and departments are interdependent, because such interdependence often results in open conflict. For example, in organizations with a tall vertical hierarchy, there can be conflict between employees at the lower levels and management in the upper ranks. In organizations with a functional structure, the various departments often do not coordinate their efforts, even though their tasks are interdependent. Thus, the barriers that exist in traditional organizational structures can stifle productivity and innovation.[62]

Former General Electric CEO Jack Welch developed the idea of the boundaryless organization. In a **boundaryless organization**, the boundaries that divide employees, such

APPLIED FOCUS

NETWORK-CENTRIC INNOVATION: BOEING'S 787 DREAMLINER

Traditionally, firms have directed internal resources toward innovation, but more recently, some organizations have embraced network-centric innovation. This means that a hub firm at the centre of a network commissions modular innovations from its suppliers, who invest in the overall project, and ensures that they are appropriately rewarded for these innovations. The fuel-efficient, carbon composite Boeing 787 Dreamliner was designed in this way, in concert with 14 main global partners (in the U.S., Korea, Japan, India, France, Italy, Sweden) and a host of second-tier suppliers who provided modules that were integrated by Boeing. Satish Nambisan and Mohanbir Sawhney explain the details of this network-centric innovation:

Boeing assembled a set of global partners whom it could trust with the process of creating entire sections of the plane, from concept to production. Boeing made a critical shift from making its partners "build to print" to making them "design and build to performance." The design and development tasks were not just outsourced to these partners; instead, partners made financial investments in those tasks—specifically, partners were required to invest in the project by paying the upfront cost related to design and development (this came to approximately $4 billion of the original $10 billion estimate for the 787 project). Although each global partner had considerable autonomy with regard to the design of the individual components, Boeing remained the central decision maker in the network. Boeing's role as integrator thus required it to envision and clarify the innovation architecture, facilitate and coordinate the innovation activities of the network partners, and integrate the components and bring the finished product to the market (thereby enabling its partners to appropriate value from their innovative contribution). As a platform leader, a hub firm defines and offers the basic innovation architecture, which then becomes the platform or the foundation for other network members to build on through their complementary innovations.

The authors assert that careful "orchestration" of such a complicated project is essential. This includes providing technologies and tools to ensure quality and easy module integration, maintaining the coherence of the various innovations, and ensuring the fair distribution of rewards and intellectual rights stemming from the network partners' investments. The success of Boeing's orchestration was mixed. Early prototypes were too heavy, and a number of reworks and delays were suffered, leading to late deliveries. Organizations are just starting to understand network-centric innovation, and the design of an airliner is surely one of the most complicated projects on which to practice the art.

Source: Excerpt from Nambisan, S., & Sawhney, M. (2011, August). Orchestration processes in network-centric innovation: Evidence from the field. *Academy of Management Perspectives*, 40–57, p. 41.

---

as hierarchy, job function, and geography, as well as those that distance companies from suppliers and customers are broken down.[63] Thus a boundaryless organization removes vertical, horizontal, and external barriers so that employees, managers, customers, and suppliers can work together, share ideas, and identify the best ideas for the organization.

Instead of being organized around functions with many hierarchical levels, the boundaryless organization is made up of self-managing and cross-functional teams that are organized around core business processes that are critical for satisfying customers, such as new-product development or materials handling. The teams comprise individuals from different functional areas within the organization, as well as customers and suppliers. Each business process has an owner who is in charge of the process and process performance. Thus the traditional vertical hierarchy is flattened and replaced by layers of teams, making the organization look more horizontal than vertical.[64] Information and knowledge can be quickly distributed throughout the organization and directly to where it is needed without first being filtered by a tall vertical hierarchy.[65] Boundaryless organizations are able to achieve greater integration and coordination within the organization and with external stakeholders.

While boundaryless organizations have a number of advantages, including the ability to adapt to environmental changes, they have a number of disadvantages. For example, it can be difficult to overcome political and authority boundaries, and it can be time-consuming to manage the democratic processes required to coordinate the efforts of many stakeholders.[66]

In summary, many of the traditional organizational structures are being replaced by more flexible structures that break down external and internal boundaries. For many organizations, traditional structures are no longer effective, so they must find new ways to structure and coordinate their efforts to adapt to environmental changes and remain competitive.

LO 14.7

Review important considerations concerning *downsizing*.

THE IMPACT OF SIZE

It perhaps seems trivial to observe that the giant Walmart is structured differently from a small travel agency. But exactly how does organizational size (measured by number of employees) affect the structure of organizations?[67]

Size and Structure

In general, large organizations are more complex than small organizations.[68] For example, a small organization is unlikely to have its own legal department or market research group, and these tasks will probably be contracted out. Economies of scale enable large organizations to perform these functions themselves, but with a consequent increase in the number of departments and job titles. In turn, this horizontal specialization often stimulates the need for additional complexity in the form of appointing integrators or creating planning departments. As horizontal specialization increases, management levels must be added (making the organization taller) so that spans of control do not get out of hand.[69] To repeat, size is associated with increased complexity.

Complexity means coordination problems, in spite of integrators, planning departments, and the like. This is where other structural characteristics come into play. In general, bigger organizations are less centralized than smaller organizations.[70] In a small company, the president might be involved in all but the least critical decisions. In a large company, the president would be overloaded with such decisions, and they could not be made in a timely manner. In addition, since the large organization will also be taller, top management is often too far removed from the action to make many operating decisions. How is control retained with decentralization? The answer is formalization—large organizations tend to be more formal than small organizations. Rules, regulations, and standard procedures help to ensure that decentralized decisions fall within accepted boundaries.

One exception to the general rule that growth leads to decentralization occurs when the growth comes from acquisitions of other firms. The forest product company Weyerhaeuser found that such growth led to too much decentralization, in that a home builder often had to place orders with multiple divisions. The structure was consequently centralized so that a single salesperson could handle all requests from a builder.[71] In general, acquisitions require restructuring to optimize firm performance.[72]

You will recall that product departmentation is often preferable to functional departmentation as the organization increases in size. Logically, then, organizations with product departmentation should exhibit more complexity and more decentralization than those with functional departmentation. A careful comparison of Exhibits 14.2 and 14.3 will confirm this logic. In the firm structured by product, research, production, and marketing are duplicated, increasing complexity. In addition, since each product line is essentially self-contained, decisions can be made at a lower organizational level.

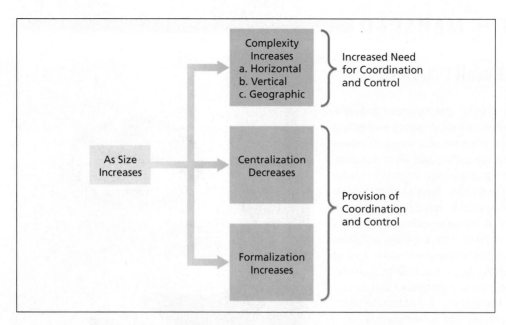

EXHIBIT 14.12
The relationship between size and structure.

Go to MyManagementLab to see an annotated version of this figure.

Finally, we should recognize that size is only one determinant of organizational structure. Even at a given size, organizations might require different structures to be maximally effective. In the next chapter, we will examine other determinants of structure, principally environmental pressures and technology.

Exhibit 14.12 summarizes the relationship between size and structural variables. Before continuing, see You Be the Manager: *The Toyota Recall Problem*.

Downsizing

A reduction in workforce size, popularly called *downsizing*, has been an organizational trend in recent years. Millions of jobs have disappeared as organizations seek to bolster efficiency and cut costs in an era of global competition, government deregulation, mergers, changing consumer preferences, and advancing technologies.[73] Downsizing has a number of implications for organizational structure.

DOWNSIZING AND STRUCTURE **Downsizing** is the intentional reduction in workforce size with the goal of improving organizational efficiency or effectiveness.[74] Notice that this definition does not imply that the organization's fortunes are necessarily in decline, although a shrinking market could motivate downsizing. In fact, firms sometimes downsize during a year of good revenues in anticipation of the need to be more competitive in the future.[75]

Downsizing. The intentional reduction in workforce size with the goal of improving organizational efficiency or effectiveness.

How should downsizing affect organizational structure? It is tempting to "work backwards" through Exhibit 14.12 and simply say that as size *decreases* the firm should reduce its complexity, centralize, and become less formalized. In the case of a very simple downsizing, this logic might work. However, notice its limitations. First, some of the conditions listed above that often prompt downsizing are *new* conditions, not simply the opposite of the factors that led to organizational growth in the past. For example, deregulation has led to a completely new cast of competitors in the banking and telecommunications industries. Second, the logic of simply working backwards through Exhibit 14.12 would assume that downsizing occurs proportionally in all parts of an organization. As you may know, this is not the case. White-collar managerial and staff jobs have been disproportionately reduced in the most recent downsizings, for reasons varying from high salaries to improvements in information technology. The upshot of all this is that a new, downsized structure should not necessarily look like a mini version of the old structure.

YOU BE THE MANAGER

The Toyota Recall Problem

Beginning in the fall of 2009, the Japanese auto producer Toyota announced a series of safety recalls that would eventually result in the recall of about 20 million cars. This was an unbelievable saga for a company that had served as the gold standard for product manufacturing quality for many years. Toyota had quite literally written the book on product quality, serving as an open model for other car manufacturers and firms in a diverse range of other fields. The problems pertained to sudden or unintended acceleration which was at first attributed to ill-fitting floor mats, then to sticky accelerator pedals, and then to mysterious faults in Toyota's electronic throttle system. In addition, in some markets, problems with anti-lock brakes were noted.

Given its culture of obsession with quality, headquarters management in Japan responded slowly and methodically to what it saw as a quality control problem. However local executives in Canada, the United States, and Australia saw an urgent safety problem, and a media circus ensued in which a number of deaths from accidents were attributed to the safety issues. An exhaustive U.S. Department of Transportation probe (aided by NASA) found no evidence for electronic gremlins, and experts have attributed many of the cases of unintended acceleration to driver error. However, Toyota's slow response to feared safety problems did incalculable damage to the company's hard-won reputation for quality. In the U.S., Toyota faced congressional hearings, and was required to pay fines totalling over $48 million for failing to report apparent defects and issue recalls in a timely manner. Hundreds of individual lawsuits concerning unintended acceleration are still pending.

Although Toyota had traditionally been a very conservative company, it embarked on an aggressive growth strategy in 2005. In fact, the strategy seemed to put growth before quality at a time when cars were becoming more and more complex in terms of engineering. To foster growth and cut design lead times, the company chose to contract out engineering work and take on new suppliers, dealing with people who had not been exposed to the Toyota cult of quality. All the while, the company continued with a highly centralized structure in which top management in Tokyo made all key decisions about quality, safety recalls, and the like, even though they were culturally and geographically removed from the key markets where the sudden acceleration and brake problems had surfaced.

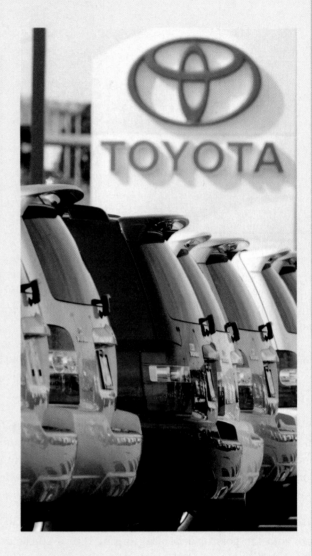

Questions

1. What lessons does the Toyota saga teach us about the connection between size and centralization?

2. What structural changes should Toyota make?

For commentary on these questions, see The Manager's Notebook at the end of the chapter.

Sources: Cole, R.E. (2011, Summer). What really happened at Toyota? *Sloan Management Review*, 29–35; Valdes-Dapena, P. (2011, February 8). Toyota acceleration probe finds no electronic flaws. *CNNMoney.com*; Blackburn, R. (2010, February 13–14). Oh, how they're reeling. *The Sydney Morning Herald*, p. NR7; Taylor, A., III. (2010, February 1). Where Toyota went wrong. *CNNMoney.com*.

Downsizing can be accomplished in a variety of ways. Although layoffs have been common, some organizations have relied on hiring freezes and natural attrition. In practice, downsizing is often accompanied by reducing horizontal or vertical complexity. Vertically, management levels have been removed to make organizations flatter. This has sometimes made sense when information technology enables the remaining managers to more effectively monitor the performance of their subordinates. Also, self-managed teams (Chapter 7) can act as substitutes for a level of management. Horizontally, functions can be combined (e.g., inspection and quality) or removed altogether by contracting them out.

PROBLEMS WITH DOWNSIZING Many organizations have not done a good job of anticipating and managing the structural and human consequences of downsizing. For instance, when faced with serious decline, organizations have a decided tendency to become more mechanistic, particularly more formalized and centralized.[76] Rules are closely enforced, and higher levels of management take part in more day-to-day decisions. This can be useful to get the organization back on track, but it can also reduce flexibility just when it is needed. A good rule to follow is to avoid unnecessary formalization or centralization of matters that might have a negative impact on customers or clients. In other words, do not allow internal tightening up to damage external relationships.

One downsizing tactic has been to greatly reduce or even to eliminate whole departments of headquarters advisory staff. For instance, a human resources department might be downsized or the legal department eliminated. Many such staff units become bloated over the years, and they have been known to isolate top management from divisional concerns and to bureaucratize decision making. Thus, downsizing can provoke decentralization, giving line managers more power and speeding up decisions. On the other hand, some firms have eliminated such positions and then turned around and hired consultants to do the same work. Contracting work out can be a viable strategy, but it is clear that some consulting arrangements have proven more expensive than the original in-house unit.[77] A good rule to follow is to think very carefully about the *work* that needs to be done and *who* should do it before downsizing. Research has shown that downsizing has particularly damaged the performance of firms that are R&D–intensive and knowledge-sensitive (e.g., biotechnology, pharmaceuticals, and advanced electronics).[78] This shows that human-capital considerations cannot take a back seat to short-term financial considerations.

A common downsizing structural error has been to flatten organizations by removing management levels without considering the implications for job design and workload. A glance at Exhibit 14.8 illustrates the crux of the problem: If only the management ranks are thinned, managers have larger spans below them and less support above them. This works well if decentralization is called for and if the people in the lower ranks are ready to assume greater decision-making responsibility. It does not work well if managers are overloaded with work or are incapable of delegating to subordinates. Advanced information technology and training can sometimes assist managers in coping with increased spans of control.

The increased spans that accompany flatter structures have also been implicated in some cases of ethical violation and corporate fraud. Less direct supervision coupled with unclear responsibilities mean that traditional guards against unethical activities may be lacking.

Thinking in advance about the structural aspects of downsizing is not a substitute for involving employees in downsizing plans. Surprising people with workforce cuts is very likely to result in low morale, reduced personal productivity, and continuing distrust of management. Some survivors of downsizing have even reported feeling guilty because they retained their jobs.[79]

In summary, downsizing has the potential to improve organizational effectiveness in certain circumstances, but its impact on structure and morale must be anticipated and managed. A fair amount of evidence shows that downsizing often leads to reduced satisfaction and commitment, increased absenteeism, and damaged health.[80] Perhaps because of this, research has shown that, contrary to expectations, downsizing tends to have a negative effect on stock prices and mixed effects on profitability.[81] The negative outcomes of downsizing, however, are primarily due to poor implementation, such as a lack of supporting activities. When carefully and properly implemented, downsizing can have positive consequences. For example, when discount broker Charles Schwab experienced business losses, it first cut back on management perks and cut executive pay. When the layoffs occurred, employees were given stock options, outplacement services, and $20 000 tuition vouchers.[82]

A FOOTNOTE: SYMPTOMS OF STRUCTURAL PROBLEMS

LO 14.8

Identify symptoms of structural problems in organizations.

Let's conclude the chapter by considering some symptoms of structural problems in organizations.

- *Bad job design.* As we noted at several points, there is a reciprocal relationship between job design and organizational structure. Frequently, improper structural arrangements turn good jobs on paper into poor jobs in practice. A tall structure and narrow span of control in a research and development unit can reduce autonomy and turn exciting jobs into drudgery. An extremely large span of control can overload the most dedicated manager.

- *The right hand does not know what the left is doing.* If repeated examples of duplication of effort occur, or if parts of the organization work at cross purposes, structure is suspect. One author gives the example of one division of a large organization laying off workers while another division was busy recruiting from the same labour pool![83] The general problem here is one of coordination and integration.

- *Persistent conflict between departments.* Managers are often inclined to attribute such conflicts to personality clashes between key personnel in the warring departments. Just as often, a failure of integration is the problem. One clue here is whether the conflict persists even when personnel changes occur.

- *Slow response times.* Ideally, labour is divided and coordinated to do business quickly. Delayed responses might be due to improper structure. Centralization might speed responses when a few decisions about a few products are required (dictating functional departmentation). Decentralization might speed responses when many decisions about many products are required (dictating product departmentation).

- *Decisions made with incomplete information.* In Chapter 11, we noted that managers generally acquire more than enough information to make decisions. If we find that decisions have been made with incomplete information and the information existed somewhere in the organization, structure could be at fault. Structural deficiencies were, in part, responsible for keeping top NASA administrators unaware of the mechanical problems that contributed to the explosion of the space shuttle *Challenger.*[84] This information was known to NASA personnel, but it did not move up the hierarchy properly.

- *A proliferation of committees.* Committees exist in all organizations, and they often serve as one of the more routine kinds of integrating mechanisms. However, when committee is piled on committee, or when task forces are being formed with great regularity, it is often a sign that the basic structure of the organization is being "patched up" because it does not work well.[85] A structural review might be in order if too many people are spending too much time in committee meetings.

THE MANAGER'S NOTEBOOK

The Toyota Recall Problem

1. As discussed in the chapter, there is a tendency for firms to decentralize as they get bigger. In general, this is a good thing. As firms grow, they become more complex, and this leads to information processing and coordination challenges. If they remain centralized, decision making becomes slow, as all important matters have to wind their way up the hierarchy, and decisions are made by those too far removed from localized markets. Observers agreed that the aggressive growth successfully pursued by Toyota was not accompanied by appropriate structural changes, and that the company was structured the same as it was during its entry into the North American market many years ago. When the safety concerns emerged, management in Japan framed them as an engineering issue and reacted too slowly. Not enough information was passed up and down the chain of command. A media circus ensued, and this only magnified the actual recall problem.

2. Toyota should, and did, decentralize a number of functions to put more decision-making power closer to where local knowledge is located, in the various regional markets (e.g., North America, Australia). Top management is certainly responsible for setting overall strategy and maintaining a cultural imperative for safety, quality, and reliability. However, regional management is best placed both geographically and culturally to understand local laws, local media, and data coming in from local dealers. It can thus act more quickly and aggressively to deal with initial quality management and recalls. Of course, major and permanent fixes require a more centralized approach. Toyota also reportedly slowed down its model development process and brought more engineering work in-house where it can be better controlled.

MyManagementLab   Visit MyManagementLab at **www.mymanagementlab .com** for access to online tutorials, interactive exercises, videos, and much more.

LEARNING OBJECTIVES CHECKLIST

14.1 *Organizational structure* is the manner in which an organization divides its labour into specific tasks and achieves coordination among these tasks. Labour is divided vertically and horizontally. *Vertical division of labour* concerns the apportioning of authority. *Horizontal division of labour* involves designing jobs and grouping them into departments.

14.2 While *functional departmentation* locates employees with similar skills in the same department, other forms of departmentation locate employees in accordance with *product, geography,* or *customer requirements*.

14.3 Basic methods of coordinating divided labour include direct supervision, standardization of work processes, standardization of outputs, standardization of skills, and mutual adjustment. Workers are permitted more discretion as coordination moves from direct supervision through mutual adjustment. More elaborate methods of coordination are aimed specifically at achieving integration across departments.

These include liaison roles, task forces, teams, and integrators.

14.4 *Traditional structural characteristics* include span of control, flatness versus tallness, formalization, centralization, and complexity. Larger organizations tend to be more complex, more formal, and less centralized than smaller organizations.

14.5 The classical organizational theorists tended to favour *mechanistic organizational structures* (small spans, tall, formalized, and fairly centralized). The human relations theorists, having noted the flaws of bureaucracy, tended to favour *organic structures* (larger spans, flat, less formalized, and less centralized). However, there is no one best way to organize, and both mechanistic and organic structures have their places.

14.6 Many of the traditional organizational structures are being replaced with more flexible structures that break down external and internal boundaries and facilitate innovation. *Ambi-dextrous organizations* foster both exploitation and exploration. *Network* or *virtual organizations* and *modular organizations* break down or modify external barriers, and *boundaryless organizations* remove both internal and external barriers. As organizations grow in size they tend to become more complex (vertically, horizontally, and geographically), more formalized, and less centralized.

14.7 *Downsizing* is the intentional reduction in workforce size with the goal of improving organizational efficiency or effectiveness. Sensible downsizing avoids mechanistic tendencies, retains necessary personnel, and respects the principles of good job design.

14.8 Symptoms of structural problems include poor job design, extreme duplication of effort, conflict between departments, slow responses, too many committees, and decisions made with incomplete information.

DISCUSSION QUESTIONS

1. Discuss the division of labour in a restaurant. What methods are used to coordinate this divided labour? Do differences exist between fast-food versus more formal restaurants?

2. Is the departmentation in a small college essentially functional or product-oriented? Defend your answer. (*Hint:* In what department will the historians find themselves? In what department will the groundskeepers find themselves?)

3. Which basic method(s) of coordination is (are) most likely to be found in a pure research laboratory? On a football team? In a supermarket?

4. What are the relative merits of mechanistic versus organic structures?

5. Discuss the logic behind the following statement: "We don't want to remove the differentiation that exists between sales and production. What we want to do is achieve integration."

6. As Spinelli Construction Company grew in size, its founder and president, Joe Spinelli, found that he was overloaded with decisions. What two basic structural changes should Spinelli make to rectify this situation without losing control of the company?

7. Describe a situation in which a narrow span of control might be appropriate and contrast it with a situation in which a broad span might be appropriate.

8. Make up a list of criteria that defines a good downsizing effort.

INTEGRATIVE DISCUSSION QUESTIONS

1. How do the structural characteristics of organizations influence leadership, communication, decision making, and power in organizations? Discuss the implications of each of the structural characteristics (i.e., span of control, organization levels, formalization, centralization, and complexity) for leadership behaviour, communication and decision-making processes, and the distribution and use of power in organizations.

2. How do the new forms of organizational structure, such as virtual, modular, and boundaryless

organizations, influence the culture of an organization? In other words, what is the relationship between these types of structures and an organization's culture? What is the relationship between these structures and the use and effectiveness of teams?

ON-THE-JOB CHALLENGE QUESTION

Span of Control at Google

Google, the internet innovator par excellence, relies less on top-down strategies and more on grassroots ideas for new products and services. These ideas are often developed in small project teams that have little supervision. In a typical organization, the span of control of a manager might range between 5 and 30 subordinates. However, according to consultant Gary Hamel, a single manager at Google professed to have 160 employees reporting to him!

What does this structural feature tell you about how work is organized at Google? How does a large span of control promote grassroots innovation?

Source: Hamel, G. (2006, February). The why, what, and how of management innovation. *Harvard Business Review*, 72–84.

EXPERIENTIAL EXERCISE

Organizational Structure Preference Scale

In most organizations, there are differences of opinion and preferences as to how the organization should be structured and how people should conduct themselves. Following are a number of statements concerning these matters. The purpose of this survey is for you to learn about your own preferences regarding the structure of organizations. Please use the response scale below to indicate the extent to which you agree with each statement.

1–Disagree strongly

2–Disagree

3–Neither agree nor disagree

4–Agree

5–Agree strongly

_____ 1. I get most of my motivation to work from the job itself rather than from the rewards the company gives me for doing it.

_____ 2. I respect my supervisors for what they know rather than for the fact that the company has put them in charge.

_____ 3. I work best when things are exciting and filled with energy. I can feel the adrenalin rushing through me and I like it.

_____ 4. I like it best if we can play things by ear. Going by the book means you do not have any imagination.

_____ 5. People who seek security at work are boring. I don't go to work to plan my retirement.

_____ 6. I believe that planning should focus on the short term. Long-term planning is unrealistic. I want to see the results of my plan.

_____ 7. Don't give me a detailed job description. Just point me in the general direction and I will figure out what needs to be done.

_____ 8. I don't expect to be introduced to new people. If I like their looks, I'll introduce myself.

_____ 9. Goals should be set by everyone in the organization. I prefer to achieve my own goals rather than those of someone else.

_____ 10. One of the things I prefer most about a job is that it be full of surprises.

_____ 11. I like a job that is full of challenges.

_____ 12. Organization charts are only needed by people who are already lost.

_____ 13. Technology is constantly changing.

_____ 14. Supervision and control should be face to face.

_____ 15. If organizations focus on problem solving, the bottom line will take care of itself.

_____ 16. I would never take a job that involved repetitive activities.

_____ 17. Organizations are constantly in a state of change. I don't worry about how the players line up.

_____ 18. Every decision I make is a new one. I don't look for precedents.

_____ 19. When people talk about efficiency, I think they really don't want to do a good job.

_____ 20. The people who know the most about the work should be put in charge.

Scoring and Interpretation

To calculate your organizational structure preference score, simply add up your responses to each of the 20 questions. Scores can range from 20 to 100. Your score on this survey indicates your preference for a mechanistic or organic organizational structure. A score of less than 50 indicates a preference for a mechanistic or formal organizational structure. Mechanistic structures tend to favour tallness, narrow spans of control, specialization, centralization, and formalization. Scores above 50 indicate a preference for a more organic or informal organizational structure. Organic structures tend to favour wider spans of control, fewer authority levels, less specialization, less formalization, and decentralization. Flexibility and informal communication are favoured over rigidity and the strict chain of command.

Source: Hoffman, R., & Ruemper, F. (1997). "Exercise 20: Mechanistic or Organic Organizational Design. In" *Organizational behaviour: Canadian cases and exercises*, 3rd ed. Toronto: Captus Press Inc.), 298–299. Reprinted with permission of Captus Press Inc. www.captus.com.

CASE INCIDENT

Conway Manufacturing

Conway Manufacturing is a large organization that manufactures machine tools that are used by workers in various industries. In recent years, sales of the company's products have begun to fall as a result of increasing competition. Customers have also begun to complain about the quality of Conway's products. In response, Conway decided to design some new, high-quality products.

The research and development department was asked to develop some new designs for several of Conway's best-selling products. When the engineering department looked at the designs, they rejected them outright, saying that they were not very good. Engineering then revised the designs and sent them to the production department. However, the production department responded by sending them back to the engineering department, insisting that they would be impossible to produce. In the meantime, the marketing department had begun a campaign based on the material they had received from the research and development department. One year later, Conway was still no closer to producing new products. In the meantime, more customers were complaining and threatening to find new suppliers, and the competition continued to take more and more of Conway's business.

1. Describe the structure of Conway Manufacturing. What are some of the problems that Conway is having? Is organizational structure a factor?

2. What would be the most effective structure to design new, high-quality products in a short period of time? What are some methods for improving coordination?

CASE STUDY

Trojan Technologies Inc.

In March 1998, a group of Trojan Technologies Inc. (Trojan) employees grappled with the issue of how to structure the business to effectively interact with their customers and to manage the company's dramatic growth. The London, Ontario, manufacturer of ultraviolet (UV) water disinfection systems believed that strong customer service was key to its recent and projected growth and had come to the realization that changes would have to be made to continue to achieve both simultaneously. The group hoped to develop a structure to address these issues. Marvin DeVries, executive vice-president, was to lead the development and implementation of the new structure. The transition to the new structure was to begin as of September 1998 to coincide with the new fiscal year.

The Business

Technology

Since 1977, the company had specialized in UV light applications for disinfecting water and wastewater. In essence, Trojan's products killed micro-organisms using high-intensity UV lamps. Water was channelled past the lamps at various speeds, based on the clarity of the water and the strength of the lamps, to achieve the required "kill" rate.

Trojan's UV technology had proved to be an environmentally safe and cost effective alternative to chlorination and was gaining wider recognition and acceptance. Even so, a significant market remained to be tapped, as the company estimated ". . . that only 5 percent to 10 percent of municipal wastewater sites in North America use UV-based technology . . . [and] of the approximate 62 000 wastewater treatment facilities operating worldwide, only 2500 currently utilize UV disinfection systems."[1]

Trojan Technologies Inc.[2]

Trojan was established in 1977 with a staff of three with the goal of developing a viable UV wastewater disinfection technology. Following several years of work, the first UV disinfection system (System UV2000™) was installed in Tillsonburg, Ontario, in 1981. It took another two years, however, before the regulatory approvals were in place to market the technology for municipal wastewater treatment in Canada and the United States. During this time, the company generated revenues through the sale of small residential and industrial cleanwater UV systems.

By 1991, the company had sales in excess of $10 million and had introduced its second-generation technology in the System UV3000™ wastewater disinfection system. As the company's growth continued, a staff of 50 was in place by 1992. The following year, due to capital requirements created by the company's strong growth, an initial public offering on the Toronto Stock Exchange was completed. Also in 1993, a branch office was established in The Hague, Netherlands, expanding Trojan's reach across the Atlantic.

The following year, 1994, saw the launch of the System UV4000™, the construction of a new head office, and sales exceeding $20 million. In 1995, a branch office was opened in California to service the enormous market for wastewater treatment in that state. Two years later, an expansion doubled head office capacity to house 190 staff and meet the demand for sales of more than $50 million.

Well into 1998, the expectation was that sales would reach $70 million by year end and continue to grow by more than 30 percent each year over the next five years, reaching $300 million by 2003. The company was in the process of planning additional capacity expansion in the form of building and property purchases adjacent to head office and expected to quadruple its headcount by 2003 to more than 1000 employees.

Products

In 1997, 93 percent of Trojan's sales were of wastewater products (System UV4000™ and System UV3000™). These systems were designed for use at small to very large wastewater treatment plants and more complex wastewater treatment applications with varying degrees of effluent treatment. The remaining 7 percent of sales were cleanwater products (primarily the System UV8000™ and Aqua UV™) for municipal and residential drinking water and industrial process applications. Growth in the coming year would be driven by increased sales of the wastewater disinfection products in both current and new geographic markets. In the longer term, new products such as the A•I•R•2000™, which was to use UV light with an advanced photocatalytic technology to destroy volatile organic compounds in the air, were expected to further Trojan's sales growth.

Products were typically assembled from component parts at Trojan's head office. The complexity of the product design, manufacture, and service arose from the integration of skills in electronics, biology, controls programming, and mechanical engineering. The company owned patents on its products and was prepared to defend them to preserve its intellectual capital.

Customers

Trojan sold its wastewater treatment products to contractors working on projects for municipalities or directly to municipalities. Typically, the process involved bidding on a project based on the Trojan products required to meet the municipality's specifications, and, therefore, engineering expertise was required as part of the selling process. Project sales typically fell in a $100 000 to $500 000 range, and given the large value of each sale, the sales and marketing function was critical to the company's success. However, for marketing to be effective, this new technology had to be well supported. Municipalities purchasing the wastewater disinfection systems required rapid response to any problems, and expected superior service given the consequences of breakdowns for the quality of water being discharged from their facility. Municipalities also had the ability to discuss Trojan and their UV products with other municipalities before deciding to make their purchase, further underlining the importance of warranty and aftermarket service to customers to ensure positive word-of-mouth advertising.

Trojan's smaller product line, the cleanwater segment, focused on a different customer base from wastewater, and it was difficult to generalize about the nature of this segment's customers. These customers ranged from municipalities to industrial companies to individuals.

Interaction with Customers

The Process

The main points of customer interaction in the wastewater product line included:

1. Quote/bid process
2. Configuration of the project structure
3. Project shipment and system installation
4. Technical support and warranty claims
5. Parts order processing

Each of these is described briefly below:

The quote/bid process was a major function of the marketing department with support from the project engineering department. Although the marketing department took the lead role in assembling the appropriate bid and pricing, the customer would on occasion wish to speak directly to the project engineering department on specific technical questions related to the function of the UV unit within the particular wastewater setting.

After winning a bid, the configuration of project structure involved working with the customer on the detailed specifications for the project and applying the appropriate Trojan systems in a configuration that would meet the customer's needs. The project engineering department took the lead role in this work and either worked through the marketing representative in transmitting technical information to and from the customer or communicated directly with the customer's technical personnel.

Once the project had been configured, it was scheduled for manufacture by the operations department. On completion, and when the customer was ready to integrate the UV system into their wastewater facility, the service department completed the installation and start-up of the unit. The service department would also be involved in demonstrating the proper use of the system to the customer.

After the system was in use by the customer, further interaction came in the form of technical support. The service department would deal with phone calls, site visits, and warranty claims and was the primary contact point for the customer. By its nature, most service work at this stage of the process was completed on an "as-needed" basis by the first available service representative. As a result, it was difficult or impossible to have the same service representative available to respond to a particular customer on every occasion. The service department, therefore, kept a detailed file on each UV installation and all customer contact to ensure the most informed response on each service call.

The final stage of customer interaction was the ordering of replacement parts by the customer after the warranty period was complete. This was handled by a call centre at the Trojan head office in London that was separate from the other departments that had dealt with the customer. The call centre was staffed to receive orders for Trojan replacement parts, but not to provide technical support as with the service department, and would generally not access customer service files in taking the order.

In summary, customers would deal with as many as four different departments during their interaction with Trojan. During the early days of Trojan's growth, the "close-knit" nature of Trojan's workforce allowed a seamless transition between "departments." However, as described below, the company's continued growth began to complicate the transition between departments.

Customer Support in the Early Days

In the 1980s and early 1990s, when Trojan had less than 50 employees and worked on a limited number of wastewater bids and projects during the course of the year, customer support was a collective effort across the entire company. In fact, it was not unusual that virtually everyone in Trojan knew the details of all the major projects in process at any given time. There was a common knowledge base of customer names and issues, which resulted, in DeVries' words, in an "immediate connectivity" to the job at hand. At times during those early days, there were as few as two employees in a "department." Under these conditions, every project received immediate and constant attention from start to finish, ensuring the customer was satisfied and potential issues were addressed in a proactive manner.

Challenges Created by Growth

As the company grew, departments grew. Very quickly, the number of projects multiplied and it became impossible for everyone to know all the customers and active projects, or even all the people in the organization. As departments grew from two to five to ten people, communications became focused internally within the departments. This made it progressively more difficult to ensure timely and effective communication on project status between departments, and the "immediate connectivity" described by DeVries began to break down. The situation was described by many as one where "things began to slip between the cracks" in terms of customer service excellence, because it was no longer possible for employees to shepherd a project though the company from start to finish as had been done in the early days. Once a particular department had finished their component of a project, they immediately had to turn their attention to the other projects they had ongoing, creating the potential for a lag before the next department picked up the customer file.

Project Engineering

Project engineering was one example of a department that had begun to experience problems maintaining service levels to the end-customer as a result of growth. By 1997, there were seven engineers in the department handling the regular support to the marketing department and acting as "specialists" for the various technical components of the products. When engineers were hired into this group, there was no formal training or apprenticeship program in place. The new hire would simply follow along as best he or she could and attempt to learn the complex product line though observation and assistance from others in the department. This type of training was strained by the demand for project engineering services brought on by Trojan's growth.

A "specialist" role, in addition to their support of the marketing department's project bids, had evolved within the project engineering group. To handle specific technical requests, this informal addition to the project engineer's role had occurred somewhat spontaneously within the department. For example, if one of the project engineers had developed a detailed understanding of the electronics included in the System UV4000™ products, that employee acted as the reference point for most detailed queries on this subject and was considered the "electronics specialist." There was no specific training or support to develop these specialists for their roles in place in 1997, nor was hiring particularly targeted at filling the specialist roles described above, as it was a secondary role for the department. As a result of the dual roles and the company's rapid growth, project engineers could not take responsibility to guide a project from bid through customer queries to production and commissioning of the project. The demand for assistance on many bids, coupled with the need to respond to queries in their "specialist" area on active projects, prevented project engineers from acting as a steward on specific projects as they passed through the company. Instead, the department operated more as a pooled resource that was accessed as needed by the marketing department to support bids and by the service group to assist with product support.

Service

The growth of the company and the establishment of new product lines had caused an amplified growth in the service group, because for each new project installed there was a long-term source of potential queries and service needs. The service group covered a broad spectrum of needs, from the initial set up of UV systems to emergency responses to equipment problems or queries (which frequently required site visits). A formal training program had been instituted during early 1998 when the new service manager recognized the need to quickly develop new employees to ensure they could contribute a strong technical background and familiarity with the product. An existing service group member typically instructed new employees for approximately one week, and new employees learned the balance "on the job" through observation and discussion of issues with other service employees. Again, company growth had caused some difficulty in ensuring that new employees received adequate training before they were needed to actively service customer inquiries.

There was a fundamental structuring conflict within the service area on how to best serve the customer. On one hand, customers appreciated the ability to contact one person whenever they had a concern or question. Also, customers frequently needed quick response times to their site for in-person assessments and action by the service employees. This appeared to suggest a need to place service employees physically as close to the end-customer as possible, especially given the company's expanded geographic marketing area. However, the timing of service work was very uncertain. Whereas the project engineering department had some ability to prioritize and schedule their workload, the service department typically had to respond to customer calls immediately, and the geographic distribution of calls was not predictable. Therefore, if Trojan received significant service requests in California, the company could be forced to respond by sending all available service employees there. The uncertainty of the timing and geographic distribution of service calls lent itself more to the centralized pooling of resources that Trojan currently used.

As Trojan had a significant geographic distribution of sales, service work involved substantial travel. In fact, the constant travel presented an additional risk of "burnout" that was unique to the department. To address this, and to ensure a reliable response to calls for assistance from customers, a head office call centre was created in 1998. The call centre was staffed by service technicians who could respond to many customer situations over the phone and by using sophisticated remote monitoring of the UV instalments in some cases. The call centre also provided a place where experienced service personnel who were at risk of "burnout" from constant travel could use their expertise. Also, the call centre provided another opportunity to train new employees before dispatching them directly to customer locations.

Related Issues

Career Ladders

In a small company, career progression and satisfaction typically comes with successes achieved that significantly affect the organization. There was generally not the expectation or the possibility of significant promotion or role development, but this was offset by the potential for involvement of everyone in several major components of company activity. This was certainly the case at Trojan in the early days. As the company grew, however, a need to distinguish between and recognize the various levels of experience developed. The current department structure did not provide for much differentiation of job requirements within the departments, and, therefore, did not recognize the significant difference in experience levels between new and veteran employees.

Training Issues

As Trojan's sales continued to grow, the need to increase staffing was accelerating. In the early days, the addition of a person to the company was informal and supportive. The new employee would be introduced to everyone and would easily be able to approach the appropriate person to ask questions and learn their role within the company. Given the rapid expansion of the company, this informal introduction to the company and its processes was rapidly becoming insufficient to allow new employees to become effective in their new position. Training, therefore, needed to be addressed in many areas.

Decisions

Given the issues developing as Trojan grew, the structuring issue was becoming steadily more important. The structuring team under DeVries envisioned a regional, team-based approach to customer interaction that would replicate the structure used by the company in the early days. One of the difficulties in implementing such a structure, however, would be ensuring that the groups still operated as though they were one company, sharing knowledge and resources as appropriate. Another would be determining what level of centralized support would be appropriate, bearing in mind the need to avoid duplicating activities at head office that should be handled by the regional teams. Employees were now aware that there would be a change in the company structure, and there was a need to come to some conclusions on the new structure quickly to reduce anxiety about the change within the organization.

Notes

1. From the Trojan 1998 annual report.
2. The information in this section was primarily gathered from the Trojan 1997 annual report.

QUESTIONS

1. Discuss how Trojan Technologies coordinated labour in its early days.
2. Discuss the kind of departmentation and the related structure used by Trojan at the time the change is being contemplated. Critique it from the standpoint of differentiation and integration.
3. Discuss the tensions between centralization and decentralization that Trojan faces. What are the merits and demerits of more or less centralization as they apply to Trojan?
4. The Trojan call centre actually uses technology to supplement organizational structure. Explain this.
5. Given the material in the chapter, reflect on how the change in size due to business growth has affected Trojan.
6. What kind of departmentation and structure is being contemplated at the end of the case?
7. Compare the current and contemplated structures in terms of responsiveness to customers.

CHAPTER 15

ENVIRONMENT, STRATEGY, AND TECHNOLOGY

LEARNING OBJECTIVES

After reading Chapter 15, you should be able to:

15.1 Discuss the *open systems* concept of an organization and the components of an organization's *external environment*.

15.2 Explain how *environmental uncertainty* and *resource dependence* affect what happens in organizations.

15.3 Define *strategy* and describe how organizational structure can serve as a strategic response to environmental demands.

15.4 Explain how *vertical integration, mergers, acquisitions, strategic alliances, interlocking directorates,* and the establishment of *legitimacy* reflect strategic responses.

15.5 Describe the basic dimensions of organizational *technology*.

15.6 Explain how organizations must match organizational structure to technology.

15.7 Discuss the impact of *advanced information technology* on job design and organizational structure.

FORD MOTOR COMPANY

Ford Motor Company's Michigan Assembly Plant (formerly known as the Michigan Truck Plant) opened in 1957 when it became the industry's first plant that was constructed exclusively to build station wagons. In 1964, the first truck was made at the plant. For decades the plant made large trucks and SUVs like the Ford Bronco, Ford Expedition, and Lincoln Navigator.

However, today the plant has been transformed into what is called a "flexible" assembly plant that will focus on small and fuel-efficient vehicles. The plant has undergone a $550 million renovation that will allow it to make a variety of models and to equip them with different kinds of powertrains—conventional or electric. The plant has an environmentally friendly workplace with flexible manufacturing capability and a specially trained workforce that will build a new fuel-efficient car.

The flexibility means that multiple models can be built on one or more platforms in the same facility, which makes it easier to respond to changes in customer preferences and needs. For example, if gas prices go up and more consumers demand electric versions of Ford's new generation Focus compact, the plant can shift to making them instead of piston-powered cars. If growing families

reject sedans in favour of the roomier, van-like C-Max "multi-activity vehicle," the plant can easily make the change. The plant will also be able to build subcompacts, such as the Fiesta, which is on a different chassis than the Focus.

Flexibility also reduces the likelihood of plant shutdowns if sales of one type or size of vehicle stall, which can cost millions of dollars and idle workers for months. The flexibility means that the factory can add production of popular models while cutting production of models that are not selling.

Flexible production has implications for the workforce in terms of new processes and a new level of involvement. The Michigan Assembly Plant has 2000 employees in the main assembly plant, and 1300 more in the stamping plant. Managers say all are encouraged to fix issues as they arise. According to plant manager Rob Webber, "We're asking them to be problem solvers." There are feedback boxes throughout the shop floor. Break areas have video setups so that Webber can pass messages to all shifts in the entire factory. He holds meetings with small groups of workers to see how it's going. "We're trying to get people to focus on quality," he says.

The transformation of Ford's Michigan Assembly Plant into a flexible plant means that it can make a variety of models on the same production line.

Production employees also have to be more flexible and learn more skills. Parts and techniques are different. Instead of workers grabbing parts from bins to install, each vehicle has pre-organized kits of items to be installed, a feature of flexible plants. Workers need to know how to install them all under the new system.

The plant is also designed to be environmentally friendly and as green as possible. Vehicles are painted using a three-wet paint application that will save about $3 million in natural gas and electricity during production. The three-wet paint process also produces fewer carbon dioxide (CO_2) emissions per year. The plant itself will operate on a blend of renewable and conventional electricity thanks to one of the largest solar power generation systems in the state, and will offer several electric vehicle charging stations. The cardboard that is used to ship parts to the plant is collected, sorted, and recycled.

The Michigan Assembly Plant is Ford's most flexible and modern manufacturing facility and the first facility in the world that is capable of building a full array of vehicles including gas-powered, battery electric, hybrid, and plug-in hybrid—all on the same production line. In 2011 the plant began production of the new Ford Focus and the Focus Electric, a zero-emissions battery electric vehicle that is the automaker's first commercially available all-electric passenger car.[1]

The story of the Ford Motor Company's new flexible assembly plant illustrates some of the major questions that we will consider in this chapter. How does the external environment influence organizations? How can an organization develop a strategy to cope with the environment? What forms of strategic response do organizations employ to cope with environmental uncertainty? What are the implications of technology for organizational behaviour? In the previous chapter, we concluded that there is no one best way to design an organization. In this chapter, we will see that the appropriate organizational structure is contingent on environmental, strategic, and technological factors.

THE EXTERNAL ENVIRONMENT OF ORGANIZATIONS

External environment. Events and conditions surrounding an organization that influence its activities.

In previous chapters, we have been concerned primarily with the internal environments of organizations—those events and conditions inside the organization—that affect the attitudes and behaviours of members. In this section, we turn our interest to the impact of the **external environment**—those events and conditions surrounding the organization that influence its activities.

There is ample evidence in everyday life that the external environment has tremendous influence on organizations. The OPEC oil embargo of 1973 and subsequent oil price increases shook North American automobile manufacturers to their foundations. Faced with gasoline shortages, increasing gasoline prices, and rising interest rates, consumers postponed automobile purchases or shifted to more economical foreign vehicles. As a consequence, workers were laid off, plants were closed, and dealerships failed, while the manufacturers scrambled to develop more fuel-efficient smaller cars. The emphasis of advertising strategies changed from styling and comfort to economy and value. Significant portions of the manufacturers' environment (Middle East oil suppliers, American consumers, and Japanese competitors) prompted this radical regrouping.

Environmental conditions changed, and by the mid-1980s an international oil surplus pushed gasoline prices down. Consumers responded with increased interest in size, styling, and performance. Auto industry analysts noted that some manufacturers responded to this shift faster than others. Chrysler, trimmed of bureaucracy by its near-demise several years earlier, responded quickly and scored a number of marketing coups.

At the start of the new millennium, the auto industry faced an increasingly fragmented market as well as accelerated global competition, especially to supply the burgeoning middle class in developing countries. The implementation of flexible manufacturing systems as well as joint ventures and mergers between companies have become common. Ford's new flexible manufacturing plant is a good example of this.

Another example of the influence of the external environment is the SARS (Severe Acute Respiratory Syndrome) outbreak of 2003. When SARS hit Toronto, bus, hotel, restaurant, theatre, and travel companies were deluged with cancellations and experienced a sharp decline in business. SARS forced Toronto-based Cullingford Coaches to idle many of its 17 coaches and face the prospect of having part of its fleet repossessed.[2] It has been estimated that the overall effect of SARS on the economy from lost tourism and airport revenues was about $570 million in Toronto and another $380 million in the rest of Canada. The losses were even greater in some Asian countries, which experienced SARS outbreaks that were much worse than what Canada experienced.[3] But many companies noticed that they could operate just as well with less business travel than they had undertaken before SARS. Some realized large savings in time and money by using technology like videoconferencing.[4]

A more recent example of the influence of the external environment is the recent economic crisis and global recession, in which manufacturing production plunged and thousands of employees lost their jobs. Particularly hard hit was the global auto industry. Companies such as GM and Chrysler had to shut down their North American operations and close plants and dealerships in the face of major declines in sales. The rise in gasoline prices triggered the collapse

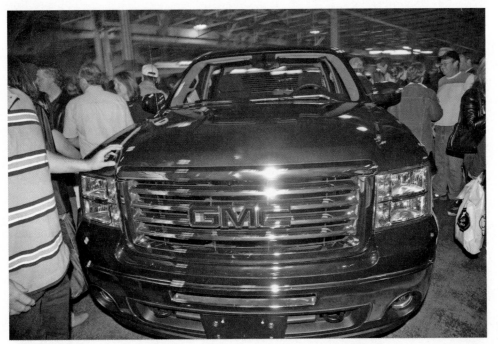

The final truck rolls off the assembly line, marking the close of GM's award-winning truck assembly plant in Oshawa, Ontario.

LO 15.1

Discuss the *open systems* concept of an organization and the components of an organization's *external environment*.

Open systems. Systems that take inputs from the external environment, transform some of them, and send them back into the environment as outputs.

Explore

Go to MyManagementLab to see an annotated version of this figure.

of the market for trucks and SUVs and resulted in the closure of GM's award-winning truck assembly plant in Oshawa, Ontario, after 44 years of operation. As a result, for the first time since 1918, GM stopped manufacturing trucks in Oshawa. GM filed for bankruptcy protection and had to scale back its business by selling off its Hummer and Saab brands and discontinuing the manufacture of Pontiacs. GM and Chrysler made major reductions in their workforce and negotiated new contracts with the Canadian Auto Workers and United Auto Workers unions to cut costs and change work rules. They also received $40 billion in government loans from the U.S. and Canadian governments to restructure. When the federal and Ontario governments announced a combined $10.6 billion in loans to help GM restructure, the headline on the front page of the *Toronto Star* read "Government Motors." The restructuring plan was expected to result in leaner, greener companies that manufacture smaller and more fuel-efficient vehicles.[5] As always, the external environment profoundly shapes organizational behaviour.

Organizations as Open Systems

Organizations can be described as open systems. **Open systems** are systems that take inputs from the external environment, transform some of these inputs, and send them back into the external environment as outputs (Exhibit 15.1).[6] Inputs include capital, energy, materials, information, technology, and people; outputs include various products and services. Some inputs are transformed (e.g., raw materials), while other inputs (e.g., skilled craftspeople) assist in the transformation process. Transformation processes may be physical (e.g., manufacturing or surgery), intellectual (e.g., teaching or programming), or even emotional (e.g., psychotherapy). For example, an insurance company imports actuarial experts, information about accidents and mortality, and capital in the form of insurance premiums. Through the application of financial knowledge, it transforms the capital into insurance coverage and investments in areas like real estate. Universities and colleges import seasoned scholars and aspiring students from the environment. Through the teaching process, they return educated individuals to the community as outputs.

The value of the open systems concept is that it sensitizes us to the need for organizations to cope with the demands of the environment on both the input side and the output side. As we will see, some of this coping involves adaptation to environmental demands. On the other hand, some coping may be oriented toward changing the environment.

First, let's examine the external environment in greater detail.

EXHIBIT 15.1
The organization as an open system.

Components of the External Environment

The external environment of any given organization is obviously a "big" concept. Technically, it involves any person, group, event, or condition outside the direct domain of the organization. For this reason, it is useful to divide the environment into a manageable number of components.[7]

THE GENERAL ECONOMY   Organizations that survive through selling products or services often suffer from an economic downturn and profit from an upturn. When a downturn occurs, competition for remaining customers increases, and organizations might postpone needed capital improvements. Of course, some organizations thrive under a poor economy, including welfare offices and law firms that deal heavily in bankruptcies. In addition, if a poor economy is accompanied by high unemployment, some organizations might find it opportune to upgrade the quality of their staff, since they will have an ample selection of candidates. This is exactly what Research In Motion (RIM) and other tech firms did during the recent recession. RIM hired thousands of employees, including tech gurus laid off by other firms, in hopes of gaining an edge on its competitors. Of course, when RIM faced slumping sales of its BlackBerry smartphones a few years later, it too had to lay off thousands of workers.[8]

We see a clear example of the impact of the general economy in the most recent recession. Faced with falling orders (reduced inputs), thousands of organizations engaged in radical downsizing as a means of cutting costs. As indicated earlier, this was especially felt in the automobile industry.

CUSTOMERS   All organizations have potential customers for their products and services. Piano makers have musicians, and consumer activist associations have disgruntled consumers. The customers of universities include not only their students but also the firms that employ their graduates and seek their research assistance. Organizations must be sensitive to changes in customer demands. For example, the small liberal arts college that resists developing a business school might be faced with declining enrolment.

Successful firms are generally highly sensitive to customer reactions. L'Oréal, the world's largest producer of cosmetics, announced that it would no longer test its products on animals in response to customer demand. More recently, companies like Kraft Foods have begun to remove trans fat from their products, and restaurants like KFC now use trans fat–free cooking oil. Automobile manufacturers are now making smaller and more energy-efficient vehicles as well as hybrids that use less gas; fully electric cars are expected in the next few years. The new flexible Michigan Assembly Plant was a response to the increasing customer demand for fuel-efficient and green vehicles and the new Ford Focus and the Focus Electric are good examples of this.

SUPPLIERS   Organizations are dependent on the environment for supplies, which include labour, raw materials, equipment, and component parts. Shortages can cause severe difficulties. For instance, the lack of a local technical school might prove troublesome for an electronics firm that requires skilled labour. Similarly, a strike by a company that supplies component parts might cause the purchaser to shut down its assembly line.

As alluded to earlier in the text, many contemporary firms have changed their strategy for dealing with suppliers. It used to be standard practice to have many suppliers and to keep them in stiff competition for one's business, mainly by extracting the lowest price. For example, auto manufacturers tend to pressure their suppliers to lower costs, and perhaps not surprisingly, suppliers report poor working relationships with most auto manufacturers.[9] However, more exclusive relationships with suppliers, on the basis of quality and reliable delivery, are becoming more common. Dell Computer reduced its suppliers from 140 to 80 and its freight carriers from 21 to 3.

COMPETITORS   Environmental competitors vie for resources that include both customers and suppliers.[10] Thus, private schools compete for students, and consulting firms compete for clients. Similarly, utility companies compete for coal, and professional baseball teams compete for free-agent ballplayers. Successful organizations devote considerable energy to monitoring the activities of competitors.

The computer software industry provides an instructive lesson in how competition can change over time. In the early days of software development (not very long ago!), there were a large number of players in the field, and small companies could find a profitable niche. There was plenty of room for many competitors in what was essentially a technology-driven business. However, the growing domination of Microsoft, which slashed prices and consolidated multiple functions in its programs, prompted a great number of mergers, acquisitions, and failures among firms dealing in basic consumer software such as word processing and spreadsheets.[11]

For many organizations today the competition has become so aggressive that their environments have been described as hypercompetitive. Organizations that find themselves in hypercompetitive environments must become extremely flexible to respond quickly to changes and cope with hypercompetition.[12]

SOCIAL/POLITICAL FACTORS Organizations cannot ignore the social and political events that occur around them. Changes in public attitudes toward ethnic diversity, the proper age for retirement, the environment, corporate social responsibility, or the proper role of big business will soon affect them. Frequently, these attitudes find expression in law through the political process. Thus, organizations must cope with a series of legal regulations that prescribe fair employment practices, proper competitive activities, product safety, clients' rights, and environmental protectionism.

One example of the impact of social trends on organizations is Walmart's move to ban handgun sales in its stores. Another is the increasing public interest in environmentalism. Many firms have been fairly proactive in their responses. For example, Pacific Gas and Electric works closely with environmental groups and has a dedicated environmentalist on its board. McDonald's has become a visible proponent of recycling and an active educator of the public on environmental issues. Fairmont Hotels and Resorts pioneered the Green Partnership program, which is a commitment to minimize its impact on the environment. Their Green Partnership Guide is distributed to hotel management schools and other hotel chains.[13] Recall how the new Michigan Assembly Plant has been designed not only to be flexible but also to be environmentally friendly.

TECHNOLOGY The environment contains a variety of technologies that are useful for achieving organizational goals. As we shall see, technology refers to ways of doing things, not simply to some form of machinery. The ability to adopt the proper technology should enhance an organization's effectiveness. For a business firm, this might involve the choice of an appropriate computer system or production technique. For a mental health clinic, it might involve implementing a particular form of psychotherapy that is effective for the kinds of clients serviced. For an automotive firm, it might involve flexible manufacturing and smart robots. Ford's newly transformed Michigan Assembly Plant is a good example of this.

An example of the impact of technology on organizational life is the advent of computer-aided design (CAD). With CAD, designers, engineers, and draftspeople can produce quick, accurate drawings via computer. They can store databases and run simulations that produce visual records of the reaction of objects to stress, vibration, and design changes. Some firms have found that CAD reduces design lead times and increases productivity

Now that we have outlined the basic components of organizational environments, a few more detailed comments are in order. First, this brief list does not provide a perfect picture of the large number of actual interest groups that can exist in an organization's environment. **Interest groups** are parties or organizations other than direct competitors that have some vested interest in how an organization is managed. For example, Exhibit 15.2 shows the interest groups that surround a university. As you can see, our list of six environmental components actually involves quite an array of individuals and agencies with which the university must contend. To

Interest groups. Parties or organizations other than direct competitors that have some vested interest in how an organization is managed.

EXHIBIT 15.2

Interest groups in the external environment of a university.

Source: Based on Brown, W.B., & Moberg, D.J. (1980). *Organization theory and management,* p. 45. Copyright © 1980 by John Wiley & Sons, Inc. Reprinted by permission of John Wiley & Sons, Inc.

Explore

Go to MyManagementLab to see an annotated version of this figure.

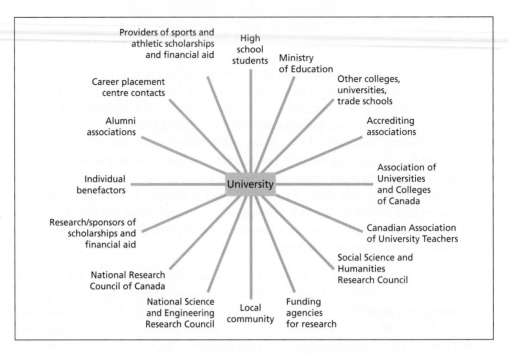

complicate matters, some of these individuals and agencies might make competing or conflicting demands on the university. For instance, sponsors of athletic and sports scholarships might press the university to allocate more funds to field a winning hockey team, while research scholarship sponsors might insist that the university match their donations for academic purposes. Such competition for attention from different segments of the environment is not unusual. Obviously, different interest groups evaluate organizational effectiveness according to different criteria.[14]

Different parts of the organization are often concerned with different environmental components. For instance, we can expect a marketing department to be tuned in to customer demands and a legal department to be interested in regulations stemming from the social/political component. As we indicated in the previous chapter, coordination of this natural division of interests is a crucial concern for all organizations. Also, as environmental demands change, it is important that power shifts occur to allow the appropriate functional units to cope with these demands.

Finally, events in various components of the environment provide both constraints and opportunities for organizations. Although environments with many constraints (e.g., high interest rates, strong competition, and so on) appear pretty hostile, an opportunity in one environmental sector might offset a constraint in another. For example, the firm that is faced with a dwindling customer base might find its salvation by exploiting new technologies that give it an edge in costs or new product development.

 LO 15.2

Explain how *environmental uncertainty* and *resource dependence* affect what happens in organizations.

Environmental uncertainty. A condition that exists when the external environment is vague, difficult to diagnose, and unpredictable.

Environmental Uncertainty

In our earlier discussion of environmental components we implied that environments have considerable potential for causing confusion among managers. Customers may come and go, suppliers may turn from good to bad, and competitors may make surprising decisions. The resulting uncertainty can be both challenging and frustrating. **Environmental uncertainty** exists when an environment is vague, difficult to diagnose, and unpredictable. We all know that some environments are less certain than others. Your hometown provides you with a fairly certain environment. There, you are familiar with the transportation system, the language, and necessary social conventions. Thrust into the midst of a foreign culture, you encounter a much less certain environment. How to greet a stranger, order a meal, and get around town become significant issues. There is nothing intrinsically bad about this uncertainty. It simply requires you to marshal a particular set of skills to be an effective visitor.

Like individuals, organizations can find themselves in more or less certain environments. But just exactly what makes an organizational environment uncertain? Put simply, uncertainty depends on the environment's *complexity* (simple versus complex) and its *rate of change* (static versus dynamic).[15]

- *Simple environment.* A simple environment involves relatively few factors, and these factors are fairly similar to each other. For example, consider the pottery manufacturer that obtains its raw materials from two small firms and sells its entire output to three small pottery outlets.

- *Complex environment.* A complex environment contains a large number of dissimilar factors that affect the organization. For example, the university in Exhibit 15.2 has a more complex environment than the pottery manufacturer. In turn, Ford has a more complex environment than the university.

- *Static environment.* The components of this environment remain fairly stable over time. The small-town radio station that plays the same music format, relies on the same advertisers, and works under the same CRTC (Canadian Radio-television and Telecommunications Commission) regulations year after year has a stable environment. (Of course, no environment is *completely* static; we are speaking in relative terms here.)

- *Dynamic environment.* The components of a highly dynamic environment are in a constant state of change, which is unpredictable and irregular, not cyclical. For example, consider the firm that designs and manufactures microchips for electronics applications. New scientific and technological advances occur rapidly and unpredictably in this field. In addition, customer demands are highly dynamic as firms devise new uses for microchips. A similar dynamic environment faces auto manufacturers, in part owing to the vagaries of the energy situation and cost of fuel and in part owing to the fact that marketing automobiles has become an international rather than a national business. For example, fluctuations in the relative value of international currencies can radically alter the cost of competing imported cars quite independently of anything management does.

As we see in Exhibit 15.3, it is possible to arrange rate of change and complexity in a matrix. A simple/static environment (Cell 1) should provoke the least uncertainty, while a dynamic/complex environment (Cell 4) should provoke the most. Some research suggests that change has more influence than complexity on uncertainty.[16] Thus, we might expect a static/complex environment (Cell 2) to be somewhat more certain than a dynamic/simple environment (Cell 3).

Earlier, we stated that different parts of the organization are often interested in different components of the environment. And we have just shown that some aspects of the environment are less certain than others. Thus, some subunits might be faced with more uncertainty than others. For example, the research and development department of a microchip company would seem to face a more uncertain environment than the human resources department.

Increasing uncertainty has several predictable effects on organizations and their decision makers.[17] For one thing, as uncertainty increases, cause-and-effect relationships become less clear. If we are certain that a key competitor will not match our increased advertising budget, we may be confident that our escalated ad campaign will increase our market share. Uncertainty about the competitor's response reduces confidence in this causal inference. Second, environmental uncertainty tends to make priorities harder to agree on, and it often stimulates a fair degree of political jockeying within the organization. To continue the example, if the consequences of increased advertising are unclear, other functional units might see the increased budget allocation as being "up for grabs." Finally, as environmental uncertainty increases, more information must be processed by the organization to make adequate decisions. Environmental scanning, boundary spanning, planning, and formal management information systems will become more prominent.[18] This illustrates that organizations will act to cope with or reduce uncertainty because uncertainty increases the difficulty of decision making and thus threatens organizational effectiveness. Shortly, we will examine

EXHIBIT 15.3

Environmental uncertainty as a function of complexity and rate of change.

Source: Duncan, R.B. (1972). Characteristics of organizational environments and perceived environment Uncertainty. *Administrative Science Quarterly, 17*(3), 313–327, p. 320. Used by permission of Cornell University Johnson School.

 Explore

Go to MyManagementLab to see an annotated version of this figure.

	Complexity	
	Simple	Complex
Static	**Cell 1** *Low perceived uncertainty* 1. Small number of factors and components in the environment 2. Factors and components are somewhat similar to one another 3. Factors and components remain basically the same and are not changing	**Cell 2** *Moderately low perceived uncertainty* 1. Large number of factors and components in the environment 2. Factors and components are not similar to one another 3. Factors and components remain basically the same
Dynamic	**Cell 3** *Moderately high perceived uncertainty* 1. Small number of factors and components in the environment 2. Factors and components are somewhat similar to one another 3. Factors and components of the environment are in continual process of change	**Cell 4** *High perceived uncertainty* 1. Large number of factors and components in the environment 2. Factors and components are not similar to one another 3. Factors and components of environment are in a continual process of change

Rate of Change

in greater detail the means of managing uncertainty. First, we explore resource dependence, another aspect of the impact of the environment on organizations.

Resource Dependence

Earlier we noted that organizations are open systems that receive inputs from the external environment and transfer outputs into this environment. Many inputs from various components of the environment are valuable resources that are necessary for organizational survival. These include such things as capital, raw materials, and human resources. By the same token, other components of the environment (such as customers) represent valuable resources on the output end of the equation. All this suggests that organizations are in a state of **resource dependence** with regard to their environments.[19] Carefully managing and coping with this resource dependence is a key to survival and success.

Although all organizations are dependent on their environments for resources, some organizations are more dependent than others. This is because some environments have a larger amount of readily accessible resources.[20] A classic case of a highly resource-dependent organization is a newly formed small business. Cautious bank managers, credit-wary suppliers, and a dearth of customers all teach the aspiring owner the meaning of dependence. Also, many organizations in traditional manufacturing industries encounter a much less munificent environment. Investors are wary, customers are disappearing, and skilled human resources are attracted to situations with better career prospects. Historically, the computer and software industries were located in munificent environments. Capital was readily available, human resources were trained in relevant fields, and new uses for computers were continually being developed. Although this is still the case to some extent, we have already alluded to the shakeout in the market for basic software. The days are gone when business amateurs can develop a new word-processing package and become multimillionaires, like the founders of WordPerfect. The big firms have consolidated the market.

Resource dependence. The dependency of organizations on environmental inputs, such as capital, raw materials, and human resources as well as outputs such as customers.

Resource dependence can be fairly independent of environmental uncertainty, and dealing with one issue will not necessarily have an effect on the other. For example, although the computer industry generally faces a fairly munificent environment, this environment is uncertain, especially with regard to rate of change. On the other hand, many mature small businesses exist in a fairly certain environment but remain highly resource-dependent.

Competitors, regulatory agencies, and various interest groups can have a considerable stake in how an organization obtains and transforms its resources.[21] In effect, the organization might be indirectly resource-dependent on these bodies and thus susceptible to a fair degree of social control.

The concept of resource dependence does not mean that organizations are totally at the mercy of their environments. Rather, it means that they must develop strategies for managing both resource dependence and environmental uncertainty.[22]

STRATEGIC RESPONSES TO UNCERTAINTY AND RESOURCE DEPENDENCE

Organizations devote considerable effort to developing and implementing strategies to cope with environmental uncertainty and resource dependence. **Strategy** can be defined as the process by which top executives seek to cope with the constraints and opportunities posed by an organization's environment.

Exhibit 15.4 outlines the nature of the relationship between environment and strategy. At the top, the objective organizational environment is portrayed in terms of uncertainty and available resources, as we discussed above. However, much of the impact that the

LO **15.3**

Define *strategy* and describe how organizational structure can serve as a strategic response to environmental demands.

Strategy. The process by which top executives seek to cope with the constraints and opportunities that an organization's environment poses.

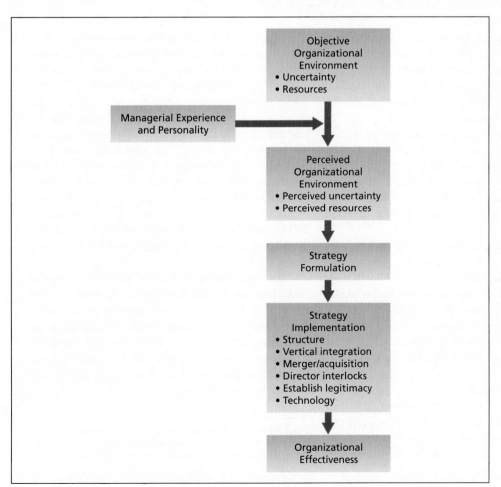

EXHIBIT 15.4
Environment, strategy, and organizational effectiveness.

✳ Explore

Go to MyManagementLab to see an annotated version of this figure.

environment has on organizations is indirect rather than direct, filtered through the perceptual system of managers and other organizational members.[23] By means of the perceptual process we discussed in Chapter 3, personality characteristics and experience may colour managers' perceptions of the environment. For example, the environment might seem much more complex and unstable for a manager who is new to his job than for one who has years of experience. Similarly, the optimistic manager might perceive more resources than the pessimistic manager.[24] It is the perceived environment that comprises the basis for strategy formulation. For a good example of this, see the Research Focus: *CEO Narcissism and Firm Strategy.*

Strategy formulation itself involves determining the mission, goals, and objectives of the organization. At the most basic level, for a business firm, this would even involve consideration of just what business the organization should pursue. Then the organization's orientation toward the perceived environment must be determined. This might range from being defensive and protective of current interests (such as holding market share) to prospecting vigorously for new interests to exploit (such as developing totally new products).[25] There is no single correct strategy along this continuum. Rather, the chosen strategy must correspond to the constraints and opportunities of the environment. Finally, the strategy must be implemented by selecting appropriate managers for the task and employing appropriate techniques, as shown in Exhibit 15.4.

RESEARCH FOCUS

CEO NARCISSISM AND FIRM STRATEGY

Research has found that top executives inject a great deal of themselves into their decisions and that the characteristics of top management teams affect strategic behaviour and performance. However, little attention has been given to one of the most vivid qualities of some CEOs: high levels of narcissism.

Narcissism is a recognized personality dimension that is defined as the degree to which an individual has an inflated sense of self and is preoccupied with having that self-view continually reinforced. The main manifestations of narcissism include feelings of superiority, entitlement, and a constant need for attention and admiration.

Highly narcissistic CEOs are defined as those who have very inflated self-views and who are preoccupied with having those self-views continuously reinforced. Narcissists seek out and pursue actions that are bold, distinctive, risky, and dramatic. As a result, they engage in behaviours and make decisions that have major consequences not only for individuals who interact directly with them but also for broader sets of stakeholders.

But can CEO narcissism influence an organization's strategy? To find out, Arijit Chatterjee and Donald C. Hambrick conducted a study of 111 CEOs in 105 firms in the computer software and hardware industries in the period 1992–2004. They argued that narcissism may impel CEOs to take actions that defy convention as a way to garner attention and applause and that these actions will affect their companies' strategy and performance. They hypothesized that narcissistic CEOs will favour strategic dynamism (the degree of change in an organization's strategy) and grandiosity rather than incrementalism and stability, which will result in extreme performance (big wins or big losses) and wide fluctuations in firm performance. They also predicted that narcissistic CEOs would be involved in more and larger acquisitions because they are among the most visible initiatives a CEO can take. To measure CEO narcissism, the researchers used unobtrusive indicators such as the prominence of the CEO's photograph in the company's annual report.

The results indicated that CEO narcissism is significantly positively related to strategic dynamism, number and size of acquisitions made, extreme performance, and fluctuating performance. Narcissistic CEOs change their organization's strategy more often and engage in bold actions that attract attention (e.g., acquisitions) and result in big wins or big losses and extreme and irregular firm performance.

Organizational Structure as a Strategic Response

How should organizations be structured to cope with environmental uncertainty? Paul Lawrence and Jay Lorsch of Harvard University have studied this problem.[26]

Lawrence and Lorsch chose for their research more and less successful organizations in three industries—plastics, packaged food products, and paper containers. These industries were chosen intentionally because it was assumed that they faced environments that differed in perceived uncertainty. This was subsequently confirmed by questionnaires and interviews. The environment of the plastics firms was perceived as very uncertain because of rapidly changing scientific knowledge, technology, and customer demands. Decisions had to be made even though feedback about their accuracy often involved considerable delay. At the opposite extreme, the container firms faced an environment that was perceived as much more certain. No major changes in technology had occurred in 20 years, and the name of the game was simply to produce high-quality standardized containers and get them to the customer quickly. The consequences of decisions could be learned in a short period of time. The perceived uncertainty faced by the producers of packaged foods fell between that experienced by the plastics producers and that faced by container firms.

Going a step further, Lawrence and Lorsch also examined the sectors of the environment that were faced by three departments in each company: sales (market environment), production (technical environment), and research (scientific environment). Their findings are shown in Exhibit 15.5. The crucial factor here is the *range* of uncertainty across the sub-environments faced by the various departments. In the container companies, producing, selling, and research (mostly quality control) were all fairly certain activities. In contrast, the range of uncertainty encountered by the plastics firms was quite broad. Research worked in a scientific environment that was extremely uncertain. On the other hand, production faced a technical environment that was more routine.

When Lawrence and Lorsch examined the attitudes of organizational managers, the impact of perceived environmental uncertainty became apparent. First of all, because the departments of the plastics firms had to cope with sectors of the environment that differed in certainty, the plastics firms tended to be highly differentiated (Chapter 14). Thus, their managers tended to differ rather greatly in terms of goals, interpersonal relationships, and time spans. For example, production managers were interested in immediate, short-term problems, while managers in the research department were concerned with longer-range scientific development. Conversely, the container firms were not highly differentiated because the environmental sectors with which they dealt were more similar in perceived certainty. The food packaging firms were more differentiated than the container firms but less differentiated than the plastic companies.

Because they faced a relatively certain environment and were fairly undifferentiated, the container firms had adopted mechanistic structures. The most successful was organized along strict functional lines and was highly centralized. Coordination was achieved

✳ Explore

Go to MyManagementLab to see an annotated version of this figure.

EXHIBIT 15.5
Relative perceived uncertainty of environmental sectors in the Lawrence and Lorsch study.
Source: Based on Paul R. Lawrence and Jay W. Lorsch, Organization and Environment: Managing Differentiation and Integration. Boston: Division of Research, Harvard Business School 1967, p. 91. Copyright © 1976 by the President and Fellows of Harvard College. All rights reserved.

through direct supervision and formalized written schedules. All in all, this container firm conformed closely to the classical prescriptions for structure. At the other extreme, the most successful plastics company had adopted an organic structure. This was the most sensible way to deal with an uncertain environment and high differentiation. Decision-making power was decentralized to locate it where the appropriate knowledge existed. Coordination was achieved through informal mutual adjustment, ad hoc teams that cut across departments, and special integrators who coordinated between departments (Chapter 14). In addition, the departments themselves were structured somewhat differently, research being the most organic and production the least organic.

The Lawrence and Lorsch study is important because it demonstrates close connections among environment, structure, and effectiveness. However, follow-up research has not been entirely supportive of their findings, and several contradictory studies exist.[27] For example, a study of new ventures in the internet sector, where the environment is dynamic, turbulent, and uncertain, found that new ventures with a more mechanistic structure (i.e., greater founding team formalization, functional specialization, and administrative intensity) outperformed those with more organic structures. Further, the effect of formalization, specialization, and administrative intensity was greater for larger new ventures. Thus, while mature organizations typically need to become more organic and flexible to adapt to dynamic environments, the opposite seems to be true for new ventures, which tend to be flexible and attuned to their environment but lack the benefits of structure.[28]

The argument presented so far suggests that strategy always determines structure, rather than the other way around. This is a reasonable conclusion when one considers an organization undergoing great change or the formation of a new organization. However, for ongoing organizations, structure sometimes dictates strategy formulation. For instance, highly complex, decentralized structures might dictate strategies that are the product of political bargaining between functional units. More centralized, simple structures might produce strategies that appear more rational and less political (although not necessarily superior in effectiveness).[29]

Let's now turn to a consideration of other ways that organizations can respond to and cope with environmental uncertainty and resource dependence.

LO 15.4

Explain how *vertical integration*, *mergers*, *acquisitions*, *strategic alliances*, *interlocking directorates*, and the establishment of *legitimacy* reflect strategic responses.

Other Forms of Strategic Response

Variations on organizational structure are not the only strategic response that organizations can make. Structural variations often accompany other responses that are oriented toward coping with environmental uncertainty or resource dependence. Some forms of strategy implementation appear extremely routine, yet they might have a strong effect on the performance of the organization. For example, economic forecasting might be used to predict the demand for goods and services. In turn, formal planning might be employed to synchronize the organization's actions with the forecasts. All this is done to reduce uncertainty and to predict trends in resource availability. Lobbying and public relations are also common strategic responses. Simple negotiating and contracting are other forms of implementing strategy.

Some more elaborate forms of strategic response are worth a more detailed look and are discussed below. Notice how many of these concern relationships *between* organizations. The global automotive crisis resulted in dramatic changes and a restructuring of the industry, with a number of examples of strategic responses that involve relationships between organizations such as mergers, acquisitions, and joint ventures.

VERTICAL INTEGRATION Many managers live in fear of disruption on the input or output end of their organizations. A lack of raw materials to process or a snag in marketing products or services can threaten the very existence of the organization. One basic way to buffer the organization against such uncertainty over resource control is to use an inventory policy of stockpiling both inputs and outputs. For example, an automaker might stockpile needed parts in advance of an anticipated strike at a supplier. At the same time, it might have a 30-day supply of new cars in its distribution system at all times. Both inventories serve as environmental "shock absorbers." A natural extension of this logic is **vertical integration**, the strategy of formally taking control of sources of supply and distribution.[30] Major oil companies, for instance, are highly vertically integrated, handling their own exploration, drilling, transport, refining, retail sales, and credit. Starbucks, the Seattle-based chain of espresso bars, imports, roasts, and packages its own coffee and refuses to franchise its bars in order to maintain high quality.

Vertical integration can reduce risk for an organization in many cases. However, when the environment becomes very turbulent, it can reduce flexibility and actually increase risk.[31] Managerial inefficiencies can also develop as a result of control and coordination difficulties, and various bureaucratic costs can also result. However, the results of one study indicate that the benefits of vertical integration outweigh the costs.[32]

MERGERS AND ACQUISITIONS In the last decade, there have been a number of very high-profile mergers and acquisitions. Topping the list was the very bitter and highly contested merger between Hewlett-Packard and Compaq Computer, in which Hewlett-Packard's former CEO Carly Fiorina had to contend with a shareholder revolt against her plan for the merger. Shareholders eventually approved the $19 billion merger, making it the largest technology merger ever.[33] As well, a number of very big Canadian mergers and acquisitions have taken place, such as the merger between Suncor and Petro-Canada.

Mergers of two firms and the **acquisition** of one firm by another have become increasingly common strategic responses in recent years. Some mergers and acquisitions are stimulated simply by economies of scale. For example, a motel chain with 100 motels might have the same advertising costs as one with 50 motels. Other mergers and acquisitions are pursued for purposes of vertical integration. For instance, a paper manufacturer might purchase a timber company. Similarly, Oracle Corp., the world's largest business software company,

Vertical integration.
The strategy of formally taking control of sources of organizational supply and distribution.

Merger. The joining together of two organizations.

Acquisition. The purchase of one organization by another.

acquired Sun Microsystems Inc., which sells high-end servers and key software technologies. The acquisition allows Oracle to offer one-stop shopping for all the hardware and software required for complex corporate networks, thereby joining the ranks of IBM, Hewlett-Packard, Dell, and Cisco.[34]

When mergers and acquisitions occur within the *same* industry, they are being effected partly to reduce the uncertainty prompted by competition. When they occur across *different* industries (a diversification strategy), the goal is often to reduce resource dependence on a particular segment of the environment. A portfolio is created so that if resources become threatened in one part of the environment, the organization can still prosper.[35] This was one motive for Philip Morris to take over food companies such as Kraft; anti-smoking sentiments and legislation have provided much uncertainty for the firm's core cigarette business. However, the benefits and success of mergers and acquisitions are often disappointing. Before continuing, consider You Be the Manager: *Loblaw Companies Limited Buys T&T Supermarket.*

STRATEGIC ALLIANCES We have all heard about bad blood following a merger or acquisition, especially after a hostile takeover. This failure of cultures to integrate smoothly (Chapter 8) is only one reason that mergers that look good from a financial point of view often end up as operational disasters. Is there any way to have the benefits of matrimony without the attendant risks? Increasingly, the answer seems to be **strategic alliances**— that is, actively cooperative relationships between legally separate organizations. The organizations in question retain their own cultures, but true cooperation replaces distrust, competition, or conflict for the project at hand. Properly designed, such alliances reduce risk and uncertainty for all parties and recognize resource *interdependence*. The network organization we discussed in the previous chapter is one form of strategic alliance.

Organizations can engage in strategic alliances with competitors, suppliers, customers, and unions.[36] Among competitors, one common alliance is a research and development consortium in which companies band together to support basic research that is relevant for their products. For example, several Canadian producers of audio speakers formed a consortium under the National Research Council to perfect the technology for "smart speakers" that adjust automatically to room configuration. Another common alliance between competitors is the joint venture, in which organizations combine complementary advantages for economic gain or new experience. In a **joint venture**, two or more organizations form an alliance in the creation of a new organizational entity. Organizations form joint ventures to create new products and services and, in the case of an international joint venture (IJV), to enter new and foreign markets.

In some cases, competitors might form strategic alliances to tackle economic and social concerns. For example, several years ago, America Online, Microsoft, and Yahoo! formed an alliance to address the email spam problem. Spam accounts for an estimated 40 percent of all email traffic and costs businesses $8 billion to $10 billion a year. The companies said that they intend to share complaint data and build evidence files that can be used by state and federal prosecutors.[37]

Strategic alliances with suppliers and customers have a similar theme of reducing friction and building trust and cooperation. At Union Pacific Railroad, for example, customers can place orders and track the progress of their shipments by accessing UP's own mainframe. Magna International formed a strategic alliance with Ford Motor Co. to manufacture an all-electric car.

There are many risks associated with strategic alliances, and almost half of them fail. According to one study, strategic alliances are most successful when there is a vice-president or director of strategic alliances with his or her own staff and resources. Organizations with such a dedicated alliance function achieve a 25 percent higher long-term success rate with their alliances than those without such a function, and they generate almost four times the market wealth whenever they announced the formation of a new alliance. Strategic alliances are also more likely to be successful and stable when the senior managers of the firms

Strategic alliances. Actively cooperative relationships between legally separate organizations.

Joint venture. Two or more organizations form an alliance in the creation of a new organizational entity.

■ YOU BE THE MANAGER ■

Loblaw Companies Limited Buys T&T Supermarket

T&T Supermarket is a Canadian grocery chain that was built by Cindy Lee, a Taiwanese immigrant who found it difficult to find Asian products in Vancouver, which were available only at small stores in Chinatown.

The first T&T stores were opened in British Columbia in 1993, and the company moved into Alberta in 1999. By 2009, T&T had 17 stores and was Canada's largest Asian supermarket chain, with annual sales of $514 million and more than 4000 employees.

T&T caters to Asian consumers, one of the country's fastest-growing consumer segments. It has been dubbed the Asian Loblaw because of its large, clean, well-lit stores and westernized approach to merchandizing.

The chain grew as more new immigrants—especially from greater China—moved to Metro Vancouver. After opening more than 10 stores in British Columbia and Alberta, T&T expanded to Ontario, where it opened its first store in Thornhill in 2002.

By comparison, Loblaw Companies Limited is Canada's largest supermarket chain and food distributor, with more than 1000 stores across the country. With more than 135 000 full-time and part-time employees, it is one of the largest private sector employers in Canada.

However, over the past couple of years Loblaw has tumbled from crisis to crisis and has been struggling to turn around a flawed expansion strategy that left it with problems keeping products in stock and made it difficult to cut prices.

In 2008, amidst a change in senior management, its stock dropped 6 percent, which raised questions about the company's efforts to restore itself to its former glory. At the same time, the company was in the midst of a protracted turnaround to prepare to take on Walmart Canada, which had been building supercentres with fully stocked grocery aisles. One article on Loblaw asked, "Can Loblaw be a great grocery chain again?"

On July 24, 2009, Loblaw announced that it had struck a deal with the shareholders of T&T

Loblaw purchased T&T Supermarket in 2009 for $225 million.

Supermarket to buy the 17-store chain for $225 million. Some industry analysts believed it was a great deal, while others questioned whether it was a wise strategy. What do you think? You be the manager.

Questions

1. What kind of strategic response has Loblaw employed? What are some common reasons for this kind of strategic response?

2. Why do you think Loblaw purchased T&T Supermarket? Will it be an effective strategic response?

To find out more, consult The Manager's Notebook at the end of the chapter.

Sources: Strauss, M. (2008, April 22). Shakeup at Loblaw. *Globe and Mail*, B1, B8; Wells, J. (2008, April 22). It's a sign, Mr. Leighton: Be sure to take stock. *Globe and Mail*, B1, B8; Pitts, G. (2008, April 22). The Weston versus Sobey approach. *Globe and Mail*, B8; Flavelle, D. (2009, August 4). Does big ruin little? *Toronto Star*, B1, B2; Shaw, H. (2009, July 25). Loblaw's buys Asian store chain. *Financial Post*, FP1; Flavelle, D. (2009, July 25). 17-store chain a tasty morsel with huge potential for gain: "Ethnic market is vast... Our objective is to be No. 1 player." *Toronto Star*, B1; Lee-Young, J. (2009, July 25). T&T Supermarkets sold to Loblaws Inc. for $225 million: Founder Cindy Lee promises brand will remain the same. *Vancouver Sun*, E3; Strauss, M. (2009, July 25). Beyond memories of Kashmir. *Globe and Mail*, B3.

meet frequently and when the firms behave "transparently" toward one another, exchanging information quickly and accurately. A prior history of cooperation and a feeling that the partner is not taking unfair advantage of the alliance are also important.[38]

Strategic alliances between global partners are increasingly common. Examples include the Ford–Mazda connection, the European Airbus consortium, and a Canon–Olivetti joint venture in copiers. These global alliances can be especially difficult to manage due to cross-cultural differences in expectations. For example, North Americans favour shorter time horizons and a rather direct approach to conflicts. East Asian cultures favour longer time horizons and "talking around" overt conflict.[39]

INTERLOCKING DIRECTORATES

If we added up all the positions on boards of directors in the country and then added up all the people who serve as directors, the second number would be considerably smaller than the first. This is because of **interlocking directorates**, the condition that is said to exist when one person serves as a director on two or more boards. Such interlocking is legally prohibited when the firms are direct competitors; but as you can imagine, a fine line may exist as to the definition of a direct competitor. Many have recognized that interlocking directorates provide a subtle but effective means of coping with environmental uncertainty and resource dependence. The director's expertise and experience with one organization can provide valuable information for another. Sometimes the value of the interlock is more direct. This is especially true when it is a "vertical interlock," in which one firm provides inputs to or receives outputs from the other (for instance, a director might serve on the board of a steel company and that of an auto producer):

> *In addition to reducing uncertainty concerning inputs or outputs, a vertical interlock may also create a more efficient method of dealing with the environment. The outside director might be able not only to obtain the critical input but also to procure favourable treatment, such as a better price, better payment terms, or better delivery schedules. In addition, the search costs or the complexity involved in dealing with the environment may be reduced.[40]*

Interlocks can also serve as a means of influencing public opinion about the wealth, status, or social conscience of a particular organization. Highly placed university officials, clergy, and union leaders are effectively board members in their own organizations, and they may be sought as board members by business firms to convey an impression of social responsibility to the wider public.[41] Resources are easier to obtain from a friendly environment than from a hostile environment!

ESTABLISHING LEGITIMACY

It is something of a paradox that environmental uncertainty seems to increase the need to make correct organizational responses, but at the same time makes it harder to know which response is correct! One strategic response to this dilemma is to do things that make the organization appear *legitimate* to various constituents.[42] **Establishing legitimacy** involves taking actions that conform to prevailing norms and expectations. This will often be strategically correct, but equally important, it will have the *appearance* of being strategically correct. In turn, management will appear to be rational, and providers of resources will feel comfortable with the organization's actions.

How can legitimacy be achieved? One way is by associating with higher-status individuals or organizations. For example, an organization without much established status might put a high-status outsider on its board or form a strategic alliance with a more prestigious partner. Consider how WestJet first established its legitimacy:

> *In its formative year, the Calgary-based company had no direct experience in running an airline and it expected to be treated with skepticism by potential investors. To pre-empt this, it approached David Neeleman, former president of Morris Air, which had just been acquired by Dallas-based Southwest Airlines. Mr. Neeleman became one of WestJet's initial investors and joined its board of directors. In this way, WestJet was able to demonstrate that it had not just a business plan that copied Southwest's successful style but also an experienced entrepreneur on side, committed to the idea. WestJet took off. WestJet*

Interlocking directorates. A condition existing when one person serves on two or more boards of directors.

Establishing legitimacy. Taking actions that conform to prevailing norms and expectations.

continues to pay attention to public legitimacy, or what its (former) CEO, Clive Beddoe, describes as "winning the hearts and minds of customers and employees."[43]

Another way to achieve legitimacy is to be seen as doing good deeds in the community. Thus, many companies engage in corporate philanthropy and various charity activities. A third way is to make very visible responses to social trends and legal legislation; many firms have appointed task forces and directors of workforce diversity or established official units to deal with employment equity guidelines. For example, the Bank of Montreal has an executive committee that oversees equity and diversity issues. Although such highly visible responses are not the only way to proceed with these matters, they do send obvious signals to external constituents that the organization is meeting social expectations. Probably the most common way of achieving legitimacy is to imitate management practices that other firms have institutionalized.

Attempts to achieve legitimacy can backfire. This is especially evident when management practices from other firms are copied without careful thought. Many firms that "got on the bandwagon" of total quality management (a program aimed at improving the quality of an organization's goods or services, discussed in Chapter 16,) or that downsized without clear rationale have had unsuccessful experiences, despite the appearance of following recognized business trends.

The preceding are just a few examples of the kinds of strategic responses that organizations can implement to cope with the environment. Now, let's examine in greater detail another such response—technological choice.

THE TECHNOLOGIES OF ORGANIZATIONS

LO **15.5**

Describe the basic dimensions of organizational *technology*.

Technology. The activities, equipment, and knowledge necessary to turn organizational inputs into desired outputs.

The term *technology* brings to mind physical devices, such as turret lathes, handsaws, computers, and electron microscopes. However, as we pointed out earlier, this is an overly narrow view of the concept. To broaden this view, we might define **technology** as the activities, equipment, and knowledge necessary to turn organizational inputs into desired outputs. In a hospital, relevant inputs might include sick patients and naïve interns, while desired outputs include healthy people and experienced doctors. In a steel mill, crucial inputs include scrap metal and energy, while desired outputs consist of finished steel. What technologies should the hospital and the steel mill use to facilitate this transformation? More important for our purposes, do different technologies require different organizational structures to be effective?

The concepts of *technology* and *environment* are closely related.[44] The inputs that are transformed by the technology come from various segments of the organization's environment. In turn, the outputs that the technology creates are returned to the environment. In addition, the activities, equipment, and knowledge that constitute the technology itself seldom spring to life within the organization. Rather, they are imported from the technological segment of the environment to meet the organization's needs.

Organizations choose their technologies.[45] In general, this choice is predicated on a desired strategy. For example, the directors of a university mental health centre might decide that they wish to deal only with students suffering from transitory anxiety or mild neuroses. Given these inputs, certain short-term psychotherapies would constitute a sensible technology. More disturbed students would be referred to clinics that have different strategies and different technologies.

Different parts of the organization rely on different technologies, just as they respond to different aspects of the environment as a whole. For example, the human resources department uses a different technology from the finance department. However, research has often skirted this problem, concentrating on the "core" technology used by the key operating function (e.g., the production department in manufacturing firms).

Basic Dimensions of Technology

Organizational technology has been defined, conceptualized, and measured in literally dozens of different ways.[46] Some analysts have concentrated on the degree of automation; others have focused on the degree of discretion granted to workers. Here we will consider other classifications of technologies, specifically those of Charles Perrow, James D. Thompson, and Joan Woodward. These classification schemes are advantageous because we can apply them to both manufacturing firms and service organizations, such as banks and schools.

PERROW'S ROUTINENESS

According to Perrow, the key factor that differentiates various technologies is the routineness of the transformation task that confronts the department or organization.[47] **Technological routineness** is a function of two factors:

Technological routineness. The extent to which exceptions and problems affect the task of converting inputs into outputs.

- *Exceptions.* Is the organization taking in standardized inputs and turning out standardized outputs (few exceptions)? Or is the organization encountering varied inputs or turning out varied outputs (many exceptions)? The technology becomes less routine as exceptions increase.

- *Problems.* When exceptions occur, are the problems easy to analyze or difficult to analyze? That is, can programmed decision making occur, or must workers resort to non-programmed decision making? The technology becomes less routine as problems become more difficult to analyze.

As Exhibit 15.6 demonstrates, the exceptions and problems dimensions can be arranged to produce a matrix of technologies. This matrix includes the following technologies:

- *Craft technologies* typically deal with fairly standard inputs and outputs. Cabinet makers use wood to make cabinets, and public schools attempt to educate "typical" students. However, when exceptions are encountered (a special order or a slow learner), analysis of the correct action might be difficult.

- *Routine technologies*, such as assembly line operations and technical schools, also deal with standardized inputs and outputs. However, when exceptions do occur (a new product line or a new subject to teach), the correct response is fairly obvious.

- *Nonroutine technologies* must deal frequently with exceptional inputs or outputs, and the analysis of these exceptions is often difficult. By definition, research units are set up to deal with difficult, exceptional problems. Similarly, psychiatric hospitals encounter patients with a wide variety of mental health issues. Deciding on a proper course of therapy can be problematic.

- *Engineering technologies* encounter many exceptions of input or required output, but these exceptions can be dealt with by using standardized responses. For example, individuals with a wide variety of physical conditions visit health spas, and each has a particular goal (e.g., weight loss and muscle development). Despite this variety, the recommendation of a training regimen for each individual is a fairly easy decision.

Explore

Go to MyManagementLab to see an annotated version of this figure.

EXHIBIT 15.6
Perrow's matrix of technologies.
Source: From Perrow, C. (1967, April). Framework for the comparative analysis of organizations. *American Sociological Review, 32*(2), Figures 1 and 2, pp. 196, 198. Copyright © by the American Sociological Association. Reprinted by permission.

| | | Exceptions | |
		Few	Many
Problems	Difficult Analysis	**Craft Technology** cabinet making public school	**Nonroutine Technology** research unit psychiatric hospital
	Easy Analysis	**Routine Technology** assembly line vocational training	**Engineering Technology** heavy machinery construction health spa

From most routine to least routine, we can order Perrow's four technological classifications in the following manner: routine, engineering, craft, nonroutine. Shortly, we will consider which structures are appropriate for these technologies. First, though, let's examine Thompson's technological classification and Woodward's production processes.

THOMPSON'S INTERDEPENDENCE

In contrast to Perrow, James D. Thompson was interested in the way in which work activities are sequenced or "put together" during the transformation process.[48] A key factor here is **technological interdependence**, the extent to which organizational subunits depend on each other for resources, such as raw materials or information. In order of increasing interdependence, Thompson proposed three classifications of technology (Exhibit 15.7). These classifications are as follows:

- *Mediating technologies* operate under **pooled interdependence**. This means that each unit is to some extent dependent on the pooled resources generated by the other units but is otherwise fairly independent of those units. Thompson gives rather abstract examples, such as banks, which mediate between depositors and borrowers, and post offices, which mediate between the senders and receivers of letters. However, the same argument can be applied more clearly to the branches of banks or post offices. The health of a bank as a whole might depend on the existence of several branches, but these branches operate almost independently of each other. Each has its own borrowers and depositors. Similarly, post office branches are dependent on other branches to forward and receive mail, but this is the limit of their required interaction. A taxi company is another good example of pooled interdependence.

- *Long-linked technologies* operate under **sequential interdependence**. This means that each unit in the technology is dependent on the activity of the unit that preceded it in a sequence. The transformed product of each unit becomes a resource or raw material for the next unit. Mass production assembly lines are the classic example of long-linked technology. However, many "paper-processing" technologies, such as the claims department of an insurance company, are also sequentially interdependent (claims must be verified before they are adjusted and must be adjusted before they are settled).

Technological interdependence. The extent to which organizational subunits depend on each other for resources, raw materials, or information.

Pooled interdependence. A condition in which organizational subunits are dependent on the pooled resources generated by other subunits but are otherwise fairly independent.

Sequential interdependence. A condition in which organizational subunits are dependent on the resources generated by units that precede them in a sequence of work.

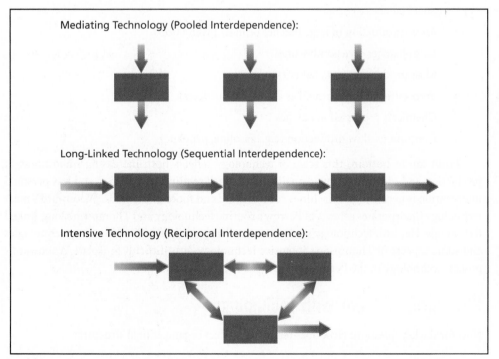

EXHIBIT 15.7
Thompson's technology classification.

✳ Explore

Go to MyManagementLab to see an annotated version of this figure.

Mediating Technology (Pooled Interdependence):

Long-Linked Technology (Sequential Interdependence):

Intensive Technology (Reciprocal Interdependence):

**Reciprocal interde-
pendence.** A condition
in which organizational
subunits must engage
in considerable interplay
and mutual feedback to
accomplish a task.

- *Intensive technologies* operate under **reciprocal interdependence**. This means that considerable interplay and mutual feedback must occur between the units performing the task to accomplish it properly. This is necessary because each task is unique, and the intensive technology is thus a customized technology. One example might be the technology employed by a multidisciplinary research team. Thompson cites a general hospital as a prime example of intensive technology:

> *At any moment, an emergency admission may require some combination of dietary, x-ray, laboratory, and housekeeping or hotel services, together with the various medical specialities, pharmaceutical services, occupational therapies, social work services, and spiritual or religious services. Which of these is needed, and when, can be determined only from evidence about the state of the patient.*[49]

As technologies become increasingly interdependent, problems of coordination, communication, and decision making increase. To perform effectively, each technology requires a tailored structure to facilitate these tasks.

WOODWARD'S PRODUCTION PROCESSES   The most famous study of the relationship between technology and structure is that of Joan Woodward. Woodward examined the technology, structure, and organizational effectiveness of 100 firms in southern Essex, England.[50] This study is especially interesting because it began as an attempt to test the argument that mechanistic structures will prove most effective in all cases. In brief, this test failed—there was no simple, consistent relationship between organizational structure and effectiveness—and many of the successful firms exhibited organic structures. Woodward then analyzed and classified the technologies of the 80 firms in her sample that had clear-cut, stable production processes. She used the classifications *unit*, *mass*, and *process production*. Some examples of these classifications include the following:

- *Unit* (production of single units or small batches)

  Custom-tailored units

  Prototype production

  Fabrication of large equipment in stages (e.g., locomotives)

  Small batches to order

- *Mass* (production of large batches or mass production)

  Large batches on assembly lines

  Mass production (e.g., bakeries)

- *Process* (input transformed as an ongoing process)

  Chemicals processed in batches

  Continuous-flow production (e.g., gasoline, propane)

From top to bottom, this scale of technology reflects both increasing smoothness of production and increasing impersonalization of task requirements.[51] Less and less personal intervention is necessary as machines control more and more of the work. Woodward's mass technology incorporates aspects of Perrow's routine technology and Thompson's long-linked technology. Her unit technology seems to cover Perrow's craft and engineering technologies and some aspects of Thompson's intensive technology. It is difficult to isolate Woodward's process technology in the Perrow or Thompson classifications.

LO **15.6**

Explain how organizations must match organizational structure to technology.

Structuring to Cope with Technology

Now for the key question: How does technology affect organizational structure?

PERROW According to Perrow, routine technologies should function best under mechanistic structures, while nonroutine technologies call for more organic structures. In the former case, few exceptions to the normal course of events and easily analyzable problems suggest high formalization and centralization. In the latter case, many exceptions and difficult problems suggest that decision-making power should be located "where the action is." The craft and engineering technologies fall between these prescriptions. Research has generally supported his notion that more routine technologies adopt more mechanistic structures.[52]

THOMPSON According to Thompson, increasing technological interdependence must be accompanied by increased coordination or integration mechanisms. There is research evidence to support this proposition.[53] Furthermore, the *methods* used to achieve coordination should be reflected in structural differences across the technologies. Mediating technologies, operating only under pooled interdependence, should be able to achieve coordination via standardization of rules, regulations, and procedures. This formalization is indicative of a mechanistic structure (consider banks and the post office). Long-linked technologies must also be structured mechanistically, but the increased demands for coordination prompted by sequential interdependence must be met by planning, scheduling, and meetings. Finally, intensive technologies require intensive coordination, and this is best achieved by mutual adjustment and an organic structure that permits the free and ready flow of information among units.[54]

WOODWARD According to Woodward, structures should vary with technology and this variance should be related to organizational effectiveness. The research evidence supports this. Each of the three technologies tended to have distinctive structures, and the most successful firms had structures that closely approximated the average of their technological groups. For instance, Woodward found that as the production process became smoother, more continuous, and more impersonal, the management of the system took on increasing importance. That is, moving from unit to mass to process, there were more managers relative to workers, more hierarchical levels, and lower labour costs. This is not difficult to understand. Unit production involves custom-tailored craftwork in which the workers can essentially manage their own work activity; however, it is very labour intensive. On the other hand, sophisticated continuous-process systems (such as those used to refine gasoline) take a great amount of management skill and technical attention to start up; once they are rolling, however, a handful of workers can monitor and maintain the system.

Successful firms with unit and process technologies relied on organic structures, while successful firms that engaged in mass production relied on mechanistic structures. For example, the latter firms had more specialization of labour, more controls, and greater formalization (a reliance on written rather than verbal communication). At first glance, it might strike you as unusual that the firms at the extremes of the technology scale (unit and process) both tended to rely on organic structures. However, close consideration of the actual tasks performed under each technology resolves this apparent contradiction. Unit production generally involves custom-building complete units to customer specifications. As such, it relies on skilled labour, teamwork, and coordination by mutual adjustment and standardized skills. The work itself is not machine paced and is far from mechanistic. At the other extreme, process production is almost totally automated. The workers are essentially skilled technicians who monitor and maintain the system, and they again tend to work in teams. While the machinery itself operates according to a rigid schedule, workers can monitor and maintain it at their own pace. Informal relationships with supervisors replace close control.

Woodward's research is a landmark in demonstrating the general proposition that structure must be tailored to the technology the organization adopts to achieve its strategic goals. Her findings have been replicated and extended by others.[55] However, there have been disconfirming studies, and a constant debate has gone on about the relative importance of organizational size versus technology in determining structure.[56]

Discuss the impact of *advanced information technology* on job design and organizational structure.

Advanced information technology. The generation, aggregation, storage, modification, and speedy transmission of information made possible by the advent of computers and related devices.

IMPLICATIONS OF ADVANCED INFORMATION TECHNOLOGY

In concluding the chapter, let's consider some of the implications that ongoing advances in information technology are having for organizational behaviour. Speaking broadly, **advanced information technology** refers to the generation, aggregation, storage, modification, and speedy transmission of information made possible by the advent of computers and related devices. Information technology is equally applicable in the factory or the office. In the factory, examples include robots, computer-controlled machine tools, and automated inventory management. In the office, IT covers everything from word processing to email to automated filing to expert systems. Between the office and the factory, it includes computer-aided design and engineering. However, it is worth noting that there is an important distinction between the adoption and the use of new technology. To learn more, see the Research Focus: *The Adoption and Use of Technology: What's the Difference?*

RESEARCH FOCUS

THE ADOPTION AND USE OF TECHNOLOGY: WHAT'S THE DIFFERENCE?

Although many organizations adopt new technologies (i.e., the purchase of a technology), they are often used very little or not at all. In other words, technology use does not always follow technology adoption. This happens so often with software that the business press refers to it as "shelfware" because the software is purchased and then put on a shelf and never used. Thus, technology adoption and technology use are two distinct phenomena.

This is a serious problem for organizations because the adoption of a new technology will not improve an organization's competitiveness unless it ends up being used. Even worse, if a large investment is made in the adoption of a technology that does not result in technology use, this can have a very negative effect on an organization and can even result in a company going bankrupt. Thus, technology use has important implications for firm performance. The question, then, is why doesn't technology use follow technology adoption?

One reason is that different members of an organization are involved in the decision to adopt the technology and the decision to use and implement the technology. Senior managers make the decision to adopt a new technology. However, those who are responsible for replacing the existing technology and processes with new technology, processes, and routines are responsible for the use of technology and they tend to be more careful and cautious when it comes to making a decision to use a new technology. So when does technology use follow technology adoption?

To study the factors that contribute to technology use, Gianvito Lanzolla and Fernando Suarez studied the adoption of e-procurement, which is an information technology that enables the use of electronic marketplaces in different stages of the purchasing process, from identification of requirements to payment and contract management. They looked at 3158 firms that adopted a prepackaged standard e-procurement software product used to facilitate an organization's interaction with electronic marketplaces.

Their results indicate that technology use is more likely to occur when there are many users of a new technology at the time of adoption, something they refer to as *contiguous user bandwagon*. In other words, the time from technology adoption to technology use is shorter when there are a greater number of users.

The results of this study indicate that contiguous user bandwagon is a key factor of time to technology use. This is an important finding because it suggests that the factors that contribute to technology use are not the same as those that contribute to technology adoption.

One way for organizations to increase user bandwagons is to facilitate communication between prospective users within the organization with actual users of a technology in other organizations. Increasing user awareness and programs to ease the transition from the old to the new technology are also important.

In summary, organizations that want to ensure that technology adoption results in technology use should increase user bandwagons, which are essential to the long-term success of new technologies.

Source: Based on Lanzolla, G., & Suarez, F.F. (2012). Closing the technology-adoption-use divide: The role of contiguous user bandwagon. *Journal of Management, 38,* 836–859.

The Two Faces of Advanced Technology

It is important to recognize that there has been much inaccurate hoopla about advanced information technology. This began even before the first mainframe computers were perfected, and it continues today. To exaggerate only slightly, doomsayers have painted a dark picture of job loss and de-skilling, with technology running wild and stifling the human spirit. Opponents of this view (often vendors of hardware and software) have painted a rosy picture of improved productivity, superior decision making, and upgraded, happy employees. It probably does not surprise you that research fails to support either of these extremes as a general state of affairs. In the early days of mainframe batch data processing, de-skilling, job pacing, and loss of routine clerical jobs did occur. However, as we shall see, the consequences of current advanced information technology are much less deterministic.

This discussion of extremes alerts us to a more realistic issue that we might call the "two faces" of technology.[57] This means that a given form of advanced information technology can have exactly *opposite* effects, depending on how it is employed. For example, the system that is designed to monitor and control employees (say, by counting keystrokes) can also provide feedback and reduce supervision. Additionally, the technology that can de-skill jobs can also build skills *into* jobs. How can these opposite effects occur? They are possible because information technology is so *flexible*. In fact, we are discussing information technology separately from the core technologies discussed earlier because it is so flexible that it can be applied in conjunction with any of them.

The flexibility of information technology means that it is not deterministic of a particular organization structure or job design. Rather, it gives organizations *choices* about how to organize work. The company that wishes to decentralize can use information technology to provide lower-level employees with data to make decisions. The company that wishes to centralize can use the other face of the same technology to gather information from below to retain control. Such choices are a function of organizational culture and management values rather than inherent in the hardware. They should match the strategy the organization is pursuing, as our discussion of advanced manufacturing will show.

For purposes of discussion, we will distinguish between advanced manufacturing technology and advanced office technology. However, as we shall see, this distinction is artificial, since advanced technology has the capability to link the office more closely to the factory or to clients, customers, and suppliers in the outside environment.

Advanced Manufacturing Technology

Three major trends underlie advanced manufacturing technology.[58] The first is an obvious capitalization on computer intelligence and memory. The second is flexibility, in that the technology can accomplish a changing variety of tasks. This is usually the product of an organizational strategy that favours adaptiveness, small batch production, and fast response. In turn, this strategy follows from attempting to find and exploit short-term "niches" in the marketplace rather than hoping to produce large volumes of the same product year after year—precisely why automobile manufacturers like Ford have implemented flexible manufacturing. Consider this textile firm:

> Milliken has reduced its average production run from 20 000 to 4000 yards and can dye lots as small as 1000 yards. Apparel makers, textile and fibre firms, and retailers have recently joined to launch the so-called Quick Response program, designed to improve the flow of information among the various groups and speed order times. The program's goal is to cut the 66-week cycle from fibre to retail in the United States to 21 weeks.[59]

The same thing is happening in the auto industry where there is a trend toward more efficient, flexible manufacturing systems. As described at the beginning of the chapter, with flexible manufacturing, a plant can manufacture a number of different vehicles in the same plant rather than just one vehicle, and it can also quickly and more easily switch model production. With flexible manufacturing, the plant can switch production between different types of cars depending on customer demand simply by reprogramming the robots in the body shop. Flexible manufacturing also makes it possible to serve smaller niches, something that would not be profitable in a traditional plant that is designed to manufacture large numbers of a single vehicle.[60]

In a third trend, advanced manufacturing technologies are increasingly being designed to be integrated with *other* advanced technologies that organizations use. For example, the computer-aided design system that is used to design and modify a product can also be used to design, operate, and modify its production process via computer-aided manufacturing programs (the result being a so-called CAD/CAM system). Ultimately, using most of the technologies mentioned here, computer-integrated manufacturing systems (CIM) that integrate and automate all aspects of design, manufacturing, assembly, and inspection can be put in place. In turn, computerized information systems can link these tasks to supply and sales networks. Exhibit 15.8 compares highly flexible manufacturing systems with traditional mass production.[61]

What are the general implications of advanced manufacturing technology for organizational behaviour? Such technology tends to automate the more routine information-processing and decision-making tasks. Depending on job design, what might remain for operators are the more complex, nonroutine tasks—those dealing with system problems and exceptions. In addition, task interdependence tends to increase under advanced technologies. For example, design, manufacturing, and marketing become more reciprocally than sequentially interdependent in a flexible manufacturing system. Finally, let's remember that such advanced technologies are adopted, in part, to cope with a less certain environment. Thus, many advanced technological systems result in nonroutine, highly interdependent tasks that are embedded in an uncertain environment.[62]

ORGANIZATIONAL STRUCTURE What are the implications of this shift in technology? As Exhibit 15.8 shows, one effect is a movement toward flatter, more organic structures to capitalize on the technology's flexibility.[63] This corresponds to Woodward's finding that unit technologies require more organic designs than mass technologies; the adoption of more flexible, short-term production batches is an example of unit technology. The expectation of flatter structures stems from the fact that more highly automated systems will handle information processing and diagnoses that were formerly performed by middle managers.

EXHIBIT 15.8
Flexible manufacturing compared with traditional mass production.

 Explore

Go to MyManagementLab to see an annotated version of this figure.

Organizational Characteristic	Flexible Manufacturing	Mass Production
Strategy	• Adapt to environment • Produce small batches • Small inventory, fast turnover • Respond fast	• Buffer against environment • Produce large batches • Large inventory, slow turnover • Respond predictably
Product	• Many variations, variable life cycles	• Few variations, long life cycles
Marketing	• Exploit niche markets	• Cater to mass market
Structure	• Organic, integrated	• Mechanistic, differentiated
Suppliers	• Few, chosen for reliability and responsiveness	• Many, chosen on basis of cost
Jobs	• Flexible jobs; teamwork	• Rigid, specialized jobs; little teamwork

Implications of advanced technology for centralization are interesting. On the one hand, matters such as ordering raw materials and scheduling production should become more highly centralized. This is both required by the flexibility of the system and permitted by its enhanced information-processing capability. On the other hand, when problems or exceptions occur or when new designs are conceived, decentralization might be called for to locate decision making in the hands of lower-level specialists. However, the whole thrust of advanced technology dictates greater integration among specialities, such as design, engineering, production, and marketing. This might require a retreat from the rigid functional structures (Chapter 14) that are common in manufacturing firms. Minimally, it suggests the increased use of integrators, task forces, planning committees, and other mechanisms that stimulate coordination. One study of 185 firms that adopted advanced manufacturing technology found a general trend toward decentralization with more formalized rules and procedures to ensure coordination and effective exploitation of the technology.[64] However, another study found that it reduced the number of levels in the hierarchy and centralized operational authority and influence.[65]

JOB DESIGN Advanced manufacturing technology can be expected to affect the design of jobs, and this is where the issue of choice we alluded to earlier clearly comes into play. There is evidence that such technology can reduce worker control over shop floor jobs and water down existing skills.[66] An example is having skilled machinists operate lathes that have been programmed by a remote technician. However, other choices are possible, including teaching the machinists to program the lathe or at least to edit existing programs for local conditions. The latter approaches have been shown to gain cooperation and commitment to the new technology and to enhance performance.[67] Following this logic, since advanced technology tends to automate routine tasks, operative workers must usually acquire advanced skills (e.g., computer skills). Also, since advanced technology tends to be flexible as well as expensive to operate, workers themselves must be flexible and fast to respond to problems. Extreme division of labour can be counterproductive in advanced technology. For example, operators simply might not be able to wait for someone else to perform routine maintenance and thus might have to have the flexibility to do this themselves. Similarly, traditional distinctions between roles (electrical maintenance versus mechanical maintenance or drafting versus design) begin to blur when the needs for coordination that advanced technology imposes are recognized. Recall that the production employees at the Michigan Assembly Plant had to learn more skills and they have to be more flexible.

All this points to the design of jobs for advanced manufacturing technology according to the principles of job enrichment, which we discussed in Chapter 6. The results of a study of 80 manufacturing companies found that integrated manufacturing was positively associated with job enrichment and employee skills development rather than impoverished, low-skill work.[68] As described in Chapter 6, when jobs are enriched, proper training is critical and pay levels should be revised to fit the additional skills and responsibilities prompted by the technology.

Many observers have recommended that self-managed teams (Chapter 7) be made responsible for setting up, running, and maintaining the system.[69] Such teams permit cross-transfer of skills and provide the cross-task integration that is necessary to keep things working smoothly. The team concept is also applicable to other forms of advanced technology. For example, one company organized its CAD/CAM users into teams composed of two designers, a draftsperson, and a toolmaker.[70]

Advanced Office Technology

As we noted above, the label *advanced office technology* can be applied sensibly to everything from word processing to exotic expert decision systems. Advanced office technology illustrates the coming together of some combination of three previously separate technologies—computers, office machines, and telecommunications (for example, a word processor combines a computer and a typewriter). The most common basic functions of the technology are the following:[71]

- text processing;
- communication (e.g., email, fax);
- information storage and retrieval;
- analysis and manipulation of information; and
- administrative support (e.g., electronic calendars).

As with advanced manufacturing technology, we can point to some environmental and strategic concerns that have stimulated the adoption of advanced office technology, although these concerns are more general. One is the potential for *labour saving*. Consider, for example, word processing (revisions are easy), videoconferencing (a trip to the coast is unnecessary), or spreadsheet analysis (many "What if?" scenarios can be probed by one manager). Another major concern stimulating the adoption of advanced technology is *responsiveness*, both within the organization and to customers and suppliers. Speed and personalization of response are common goals. Finally, *improved decision making* is a goal of various decision support systems, expert systems, and the like.

The implications of advanced office technology are far-reaching. What follows is an illustrative sample, again focusing on organizational structure and job design.

ORGANIZATIONAL STRUCTURE At least as it pertains to management jobs, the link between office technology and organizational structure has been dominated by two related issues—the impact of information technology on tallness/flatness and on centralization. Regarding tallness and flatness, advanced technology has enabled a reduction in the number of supervisory and middle-management personnel.[72] Fewer supervisors are needed because electronic monitoring and feedback often replace routine supervision, and existing supervisors can handle larger spans of control. With fewer supervisors, fewer middle managers are required. Also, some advanced technology, such as decision support and expert systems, can make up for analyses performed by middle managers. For its size (over 250 000 employees), FedEx is a flat organization, having only five levels. This is due, in part, to advanced electronic communication systems.

Actual research evidence on all this is rather scanty and mainly targeted at the middle-management issue. Although there are reports of staff reductions, it is difficult to know how much of this is a direct result of office technology as opposed to the imposition of flatness to make organizations more responsive to the external environment. Some research points to increased demands on middle-management jobs as larger spans require them to be in charge of more diverse areas and as their performance is more monitorable by top management due to the technology.[73]

The impact of advanced office technology on centralization of decision making is variable, precisely as it should be.[74] Again, the key is the extreme flexibility of information technology. The same systems that allow senior managers to meddle in lower-level operations might enable junior staffers to assemble data and make decisions. Notice, though, that advanced technology does imply a freer, more democratic flow of information and general communication. This suggests that advanced technology enables a wider range of people at more levels to be involved in organizational decision making.[75] Exactly how this capacity gets played out in decision-making practice is most likely a function of strategy and the prevailing culture of an organization.

JOB DESIGN The impact of advanced office technology on job design and related quality of working life differs considerably with job status. Among clerical and secretarial employees, when jobs have not been lost altogether there is the potential for de-skilling and reduced motivating potential.[76] A good case in point is what occurred in many organizations when word processing was introduced. Because the equipment was then expensive, administrative support was often shifted into word processing pools to make efficient use of the hardware.[77] This frequently resulted in task specialization and a reduction in task identity. However, most observers agree that such technology can actually upgrade skills if it is used to optimal capacity and the work is not highly fragmented.[78] In fact, one study found that the extent to which computers have a positive or negative effect on job characteristics depends on several factors, such as the amount of time spent on computing and non-computing components of a job, the nature of the work done on the computer, and the nature of the work that is done apart from the computer.[79]

Turning to quality of working life, word processing and related video display work have been known to provoke eyestrain, muscular strain, and stress symptoms; proper work station design and work pacing can help employees cope with these problems. Computer monitoring (such as counting keystrokes or timing the length of phone calls by service workers) has also been linked to stress reactions. However, there are studies that show that such monitoring may be viewed favourably by employees when it is used for job feedback rather than as a basis for punishment.[80] Some forms of monitoring such as *awareness monitoring systems* that are meant to improve communications between workers in different geographic locations, can have a number of negative consequences due to concerns over privacy and fairness.[81]

There are many examples of organizations that have had poor success in introducing advanced technology because they ignored the human dimension. This raises the issue of implementing change in organizations, a concern of the next chapter.

THE MANAGER'S NOTEBOOK

Loblaw Companies Limited Buys T&T Supermarket

1. Loblaw's purchase of T&T Supermarket is an example of an acquisition of one firm, usually a larger one, of another, smaller one. Acquisitions are often stimulated by simple economies of scale or vertical integration. When an acquisition occurs within the same industry, as is the case with the Loblaw purchase of T&T, it is usually to reduce the uncertainty that stems from competition. When acquisitions occur across different industries, it is an attempt to reduce resource dependence on the environment.

2. As a strategic response, an acquisition can provide the acquiring organization with a new brand image or enable it to enter a new market segment. Loblaw's goal in purchasing T&T is to reach out to the fast-growing Asian–Canadian population, where T&T has a stronger relationship with consumers and suppliers. According to a Loblaw spokesperson, "The reasons we acquired T&T was to tap into that large, growing market where T&T far surpasses what we offer in our own stores." Former Loblaw president Allan Leighton told analysts, "The ethnic market opportunity in Canada is vast. Today we have a relatively small share. Our objective is to be the No. 1 player. T&T gives us the platform to build to this objective... There is a huge amount of learning we can get from [T&T] in terms of [product] ranges and sourcing, and it should help our core stores, too." According to T&T President and CEO Cindy Lee, "They approached us because they want to break further into Asian groceries. They don't want to change us. We are both thinking the same thing."

T&T provides Loblaw the opportunity to expand into one of the fastest-growing food markets in Canada. It will now control about 70 percent of all Chinese-Canadian grocery spending in Vancouver and 60 percent in Toronto, the two biggest markets.

Since becoming part of Loblaw, T&T has continued to expand. In 2012 it opened its 19th store in Canada and the 8th in Ontario.

MyManagementLab   Visit MyManagementLab at **www.mymanagementlab** **.com** for access to online tutorials, interactive exercises, videos, and much more.

LEARNING OBJECTIVES CHECKLIST

15.1 Organizations are *open systems* that take inputs from the external environment, transform some of these inputs, and send them back into the environment as outputs. The *external environment* includes all the events and conditions surrounding the organization that influence this process. Major components of the environment include the economy, customers, suppliers, competitors, social/political factors, and existing technologies.

15.2 One key aspect of the external environment is its uncertainty. More uncertain environments are vague, difficult to diagnose, and unpredictable. Uncertainty is a function of complexity and rate of change. The most uncertain environments are complex and dynamic—they involve a large number of dissimilar components that are changing unpredictably. More certain environments are simple and stable—they involve a few similar components that exhibit little change. As *environmental uncertainty* increases, cause-and-effect relationships become harder to diagnose, and agreeing on priorities becomes more difficult because more information must be processed. Another key aspect of the external environment is the amount of resources it contains. Some environments are richer or more munificent than others, and all organizations are dependent on their environments for resources. *Resource dependence* refers to the dependency of organizations on environmental inputs, such as capital, raw materials, and human resources and outputs such as customers. Organizations must develop strategies for managing environmental uncertainty and resource dependence for their survival and success.

15.3 *Strategy* is the process that executives use to cope with the constraints and opportunities posed by the organization's environment, including uncertainty and scarce resources. One critical strategic response involves tailoring the organization's structure to suit the environment. In general, as the Lawrence and Lorsch study demonstrates, mechanistic structures are most suitable for more certain environments, and organic structures are better suited to uncertain environments.

15.4 Some of the more elaborate strategic responses include vertical integration, mergers and acquisitions, strategic alliances, interlocking directorates, and establishing legitimacy. Many of these involve relationships between organizations. *Vertical integration* involves taking control of sources of organizational supply and distribution; *mergers* and *acquisitions* involve two firms joining together or one taking over another; *strategic alliances* involve cooperative relationships between legally separate organizations; *interlocking directorates* exist when one person serves on two or more boards of directors; and *establishing legitimacy* involves taking actions that conform to prevailing norms and expectations.

15.5 *Technology* includes the activities, equipment, and knowledge necessary to turn organizational inputs into desired outputs. One key aspect of technology is the extent of its routineness. A routine technology involves few exceptions to usual inputs or outputs and readily analyzable problems. A nonroutine technology involves many exceptions that are difficult to analyze. Another key aspect of technology is the degree of interdependence that exists between organizational units. This may range from simple pooling of resources, to sequential activities, to complex reciprocal interdependence. Woodward classified technologies as unit, mass, or process production, which reflects both increasing smoothness of production and increasing impersonalization of task requirements.

15.6 According to Perrow, routine technologies should function best under mechanistic structures, while nonroutine technologies call for more organic structures. According to

Thompson, mediating technologies require formalization that calls for a mechanistic structure; long-linked technologies must also be structured mechanistically; and intensive technologies require intensive coordination, which is best achieved with an organic structure. The most famous study of the relationship between technology and structure was Joan Woodward's. She determined that unit and process technologies performed best under organic structures, while mass production functioned best under a mechanistic structure. In general, less routine technologies and more interdependent technologies call for more organic structures.

15.7 *Advanced information technology* generates, aggregates, stores, modifies, and speedily transmits information. In the factory, it permits flexible manufacturing that calls for organic structures, enriched jobs, and increased teamwork. In the office and the organization as a whole, the flexibility of advanced information technology means that its effects are highly dependent on management values and culture.

DISCUSSION QUESTIONS

1. Construct a diagram of the various interest groups in the external environment of CBC Television. Discuss how some of these interest groups might make competing or contradictory demands on the CBC. Now do the same for your organization or the most recent organization you worked in.

2. Give an example of vertical integration. Use the concept of resource dependence to explain why an organization might choose a strategic response of vertical integration.

3. Discuss how interlocking directorates can reduce environmental uncertainty and help manage resource dependence.

4. Explain why organizations operating in more uncertain environments require more organic structures.

5. Distinguish among pooled interdependence, sequential interdependence, and reciprocal interdependence in terms of the key problem each poses for organizational effectiveness.

6. Give an example of unit technology, mass technology, and process technology. For which type of technology are the prescriptions of the classical organizational theorists best suited?

7. Imagine that a company is converting from conventional mass technology to a highly flexible, computerized, integrated production system. List structural and behavioural problems that the company might have to anticipate in making this conversion.

8. Discuss this statement: The effects of advanced information technology on job design and organizational structure are highly predictable.

9. What is the meaning of the expression "the two faces of advanced technology" and what are the implications of advanced technology for organizational structure and job design?

10. Why are mergers and acquisitions a common and popular form of strategic response? What are the advantages and disadvantages of each?

INTEGRATIVE DISCUSSION QUESTIONS

1. Consider the effect of environmental uncertainty and resource dependence on power and politics in organizations. To what extent is subunit power and organizational politics a function of environmental uncertainty and resource dependence? Does environmental uncertainty and resource dependence predict and explain the distribution and use of power and politics in organizations?

2. How does technology influence job design? Discuss the effect of technology according to Perrow, Thompson, and Woodward on the following approaches to job design described in Chapter 6: traditional views of job design, the Job Characteristics Model, job enrichment, and relational job design.

3. Discuss the implications of mergers and acquisitions for organizational culture. In particular, consider mergers and acquisitions in light of the assets and liabilities of strong cultures. How will culture influence the success or failure of mergers and acquisitions, and what can organizations do to increase the chances of success?

ON-THE-JOB CHALLENGE QUESTION

The Learjet 60XRs

A few years ago, manufacturers of business jets were soaring thanks to new-found wealth in emerging markets such as Russia. However, in August 2009, Montreal-based Bombardier Inc. announced that it had terminated an order for 110 business jets, valued at about $1.5 billion.

The Learjet 60XRs were for a European private jet service called Jet Republic, which had grounded its operations. The Jet Republic deal was one of Bombardier's largest orders ever for corporate jets and could force it to scale back Learjet output and cut staff. "This is an unfortunate business decision and it's especially unfortunate for the Learjet team; however, we're working closely with them to re-energize sales and move forward," spokesperson Danielle Boudreau said in an interview.

There is also concern that more cancellations could be on the way. Bombardier, like all aircraft manufacturers, is feeling the effects of a slowdown in orders caused by the recession and the global financial crisis. In addition to companies slashing travel budgets, the industry has also had to cope with corporate jets becoming a symbol of the financial excess that brought down Wall Street. A glut of used business jets on the market is also slowing orders for new aircraft and dragging down prices. According to one aerospace analyst, Bombardier faces a long road to recovery in the business jet market.

What environmental factors contributed to the termination of Bombardier's business jet order? Comment on the role of environmental uncertainty and resource dependence. What can Bombardier do to reduce environmental uncertainty and resource dependence? What strategic responses should they consider and why?

Sources: Sorensen, C. (2009, August 21). Bumpy landing for aviation industry. *Toronto Star*, B7; Jang, B. (2009, August 21). Bombardier takes hit on private jets. *Globe and Mail*, B1, B2; Lam, E. (2009, August 19). No rush to buy Bombardier, analyst says. *National Post*, FP7; Anonymous. (2009, August 21). Bombardier cancels US$1.5B Learjet order: Manufacturers Company loses one of the largest business jet orders in its history. *Telegraph-Journal* (Saint John), B3; Anonymous. (2009, August 19). Bombardier facing long road to recovery. *Telegraph-Journal* (Saint John), B3.

EXPERIENTIAL EXERCISE

Diagnosing an Organization

The purpose of this exercise is to choose an organization and to diagnose it in terms of the concepts we covered in the chapter. Doing such a diagnosis should enable you to see better how the degree of "fit" among organizational structure, environment, strategy, and technology influences the effectiveness of the organization.

This exercise is suitable for an individual, a group project completed outside the class, or a class discussion guided by the instructor. In the case of the group project, each group might choose and contact a local organization for information. Alternatively, library resources might be consulted to diagnose a prominent national or international organization. Your instructor might suggest one or more organizations for diagnosis.

1. Discuss in detail the external environment of the chosen organization.

    a. How has the general economy affected this organization recently? Is the organization especially sensitive to swings in the economy?

    b. Who are the organization's key customers? What demands do they make on the organization?

    c. Who are the organization's key suppliers? What impact do they have on the organization?

    d. Who are the organization's important competitors? What threats or opportunities do they pose for the organization?

    e. What general social and political factors (e.g., the law, social trends, and environmental concerns) affect the organization in critical ways?

2. Drawing on your answers to question 1, discuss both the degree of environmental uncertainty and the nature of resource dependence the organization faces. Be sure to locate the firm or institution in the appropriate cell of Exhibit 15.3 and defend your answer.

3. What broad strategies (excluding structure) has the organization chosen to cope with its environment?

4. Describe in as much detail as possible the structure of the organization, and explain how this structure represents a strategic response to the demands of the environment. Is this the proper structure for the environment and the broad strategies that you described in response to the earlier questions?

    a. How big is the organization?

    b. What form of departmentation is used?

    c. How big are the spans of control?

    d. How tall is the organization?

    e. How much formalization is apparent?

f. To what extent is the organization centralized?

g. How complex is the organization?

h. Where does the organization fall on a continuum from mechanistic to organic?

5. Describe the organization's core technology in terms of routineness (Exhibit 15.6) and interdependence (Exhibit 15.7). Is its structure appropriate for its technology?

6. What impact has advanced information technology had on the organization?

EXPERIENTIAL EXERCISE

Effects of Advanced Information Technology

The purpose of this exercise is to learn about an organization that has implemented advanced information technology and the effect it has had on organizational structure and job design.

This exercise is suitable for an individual, a group project completed outside the class, or a class discussion guided by the instructor. In the case of the group project, each group might choose and contact a local organization for information. Your instructor might suggest one or more organizations for this exercise. Alternatively, you can also focus on your own organization if you are currently employed or an organization you have previously worked for. The main requirement is that you choose an organization that has recently implemented some form of advanced information technology.

1. Discuss in detail the advanced information technology implemented by the organization.

a. Describe the advanced information technology that has been implemented in the organization. What is it called and what is it used for?

b. Is this an example of advanced manufacturing technology or advanced office technology?

c. What were the main reasons for implementing the technology in the organization? What are the expected advantages and benefits?

d. Who is expected to use the technology (which job(s)) and what will they be doing with it?

2. Refer to the section in the text on "The Two Faces of Advanced Technology," and then describe the technology implemented by the organization along those lines. In other words, what are the potential "two faces" of the technology that the organization has implemented?

3. What effect has the technology had on the organizational structure? What are some other potential implications of the technology for the organization's structure? Refer to the following from Chapter 14 when answering this question:

a. structural characteristics (i.e., span of control, flat versus tall, formalization, centralization, and complexity);

b. basic methods of coordinating divided labour (i.e., direct supervision, standardization of work processes, standardization of outputs, standardization of skills, and mutual adjustment);

c. other methods of coordination (i.e., liaison roles, task forces and teams, and integrators); and

d. organic versus mechanistic structures.

4. What effect has the technology had on job design? What are some other potential implications of the technology for job design? Refer to the following from Chapter 6 when answering this question:

a. traditional views of job design;

b. job characteristics model;

c. job enrichment; and

d. work design characteristics.

5. What other effects has the technology had on employees and the organization? For example, what has been the effect on the quality of working life? What have been the main outcomes of the technology for the organization and employees? Have there been any problems or disadvantages? Did most employees use the technology, or have there been problems in getting employees to use it?

6. What advice can you give the organization about its implementation and use of technology?

CASE INCIDENT

Technology at the Toronto District School Board

Many organizations are using technology to track employees for things such as start-end times and employee location. Tracking devices such as global positioning systems (GPS) can be attached to company vehicles so employers know exactly where workers are in real time.

The Toronto District School Board (TDSB) recently decided to install GPS tracking devices on all maintenance and construction vehicles following reports of high costs for routine maintenance work, such as replacing an electrical outlet, which cost almost $3000, and installing a pencil sharpener, which cost $143.

The cost of the GPS tracking devices is reported to be $300 000 a year. It is believed that they will reduce fuel consumption and optimize scheduling. It is also believed that they will help to increase the productivity of workers

According to school board chair Chris Bolton, "It is important to know where the vehicles are at any time. What it really allows for is better oversight."

1. Do you think the use of GPS tracking devices is a good use of technology? Explain your answer in terms of the two faces of advanced technology.

2. What effect do you think the GPS tracking devices will have on employees? What effect will it have on the organization?

Sources: Welsh, M., & Donovan, K. (2012, July 11). TDSB spending: Board tracks construction, maintenance workers using GPS. *Toronto Star,* www.thestar.com/printarticle/1224644; Baluja, T., & Hammer, K. (2012, July 11). TDSB: 'Too early' to cut ties with union despite alleged overpricing, *Globe and Mail,* www.theglobeandmail.com; Harder, D. (2012, June 18). Employee monitoring technology increasingly used to prevent time theft. *Canadian HR Reporter, 25*(12), 11, 13.

CASE STUDY

The Rise and Fall of Saturn

Written by Alan M. Saks and Gary Johns.

In February 1984, a radical new experiment began with the establishment of the Group of 99, which consisted of 99 individuals representing a broad cross-section of members of the United Auto Workers (UAW), General Motors (GM) managers, and staff from 55 plants and 14 UAW regions. The group's mission was to study GM divisions as well as other organizations and to create a new approach to building automobiles. The group travelled some two million miles and concluded that employees perform best when they feel part of the decision-making process, which meant that to overcome the traditional difficulties of automobile manufacturing, auto plants would have to operate under a different philosophy.

On January 8, 1985, then-GM Chairman and CEO Roger B. Smith held a press conference in Detroit to make a "historic announcement": the unveiling of Saturn, GM's first new brand in 70 years. Saturn was conceived as a totally new corporation, a wholly owned General Motors subsidiary that delivered its first cars in the fall of 1990. The autonomous division, headquartered in Spring Hill, Tennessee, had its own sales and service operations.

Why did GM decide to separate Saturn so decisively from the existing corporate structure, rather than just add yet another product line to its Chevrolet, Oldsmobile, Pontiac, Buick, and Cadillac lines?

General Motors insiders and auto industry analysts cited two primary reasons. First, GM badly needed to find ways to cut costs to compete in the small-car market, in which estimates suggested that Japanese manufacturers enjoyed a great cost advantage. According to Smith, Saturn's mission was "to develop and produce an American-made small car that will be fully competitive with the best of the imports...[and] affirm that American ingenuity, American technology, and American productivity can once again be the model and the inspiration for the rest of the world."

Second, top GM executives hoped to use the Saturn venture as a testing ground for innovations that could be applied throughout the rest of the organization, especially ones that could get new models to the market more quickly. According to Smith, the techniques GM learned from Saturn would spread throughout the company, "improving the efficiency and competitiveness of every plant we operate... Saturn is the key to GM's long-term competitiveness, survival and success as a domestic producer." To accomplish both these goals, the freedom of a completely "fresh start" and the protection autonomy offered seemed to be essential.

With the exception of the use of plastic for vertical body parts, Saturn cars did not represent a radical technical departure for GM. Rather, it was the way in which the cars were built and marketed that was innovative. A primary goal was to create a culture in which employees had a sense of ownership over the functions they performed and a better understanding and bigger picture of the business. Tasks traditionally performed by management were performed by assembly workers. Extensively trained self-managed work teams assembled the cars, maintained their own equipment, ordered supplies, set work schedules, and even selected new team members. In addition, a consensus-based decision-making process involved employees in decisions that affected them. Each team had to feel 70 percent comfortable with a decision.

To control quality and reduce transport costs, much subassembly was done by suppliers located close to the plant or even within the plant itself, thus fostering a close cooperative arrangement. Parts that did come in from the outside were delivered precisely when they were needed and directly to the location where they were used in assembly. In the marketing domain, dealers were given more exclusive territories than is typical of North American auto manufacturers. As long as they met stiff requirements in several key areas, they were given substantial autonomy to tailor their operations to local needs.

These changes in manufacturing and marketing were supported by a number of departures from conventional structure, management style, and labour relations practices. Saturn had a flatter management structure than the traditional GM divisions. A computerized, "paperless" operation comprising email and a single, highly integrated database sped decisions and countered bureaucracy. Finally, GM agreed to a truly groundbreaking labour contract with the United Auto Workers. The "Memorandum of Understanding," as it was called, meant that Saturn would not be bound by the union's cumbersome contract, which included 200 job classifications at some GM factories and rules prohibiting members of one group performing the work of another group. Rather, Saturn would have only a handful of job classifications. There were no time clocks, and workers were on salaries, although these salaries averaged less than industry hourly wages (80 percent). In addition, restrictive work rules were eliminated to support the team assembly concept. In exchange for these concessions, GM devoted a percentage of the industry hourly wage to performance incentives tied to quality and productivity and a profit-sharing plan for Saturn workers. Also, 80 percent of the workforce was granted what amounted to lifetime employment security. GM agreed that it would not lay off more than 20 percent of the workforce under any circumstances. Union representatives sat on planning and organizing committees. Saturn advertisements used the tagline "A Different Kind of Company. A Different Kind of Car."

Did Saturn fulfill the promise of its multibillion-dollar investment? Early cars suffered from quality glitches that the company attended to quickly, even replacing some faulty cars for free. As a result of such tactics and extremely cooperative dealers (many of whom organized customer picnics and car clinics), intense customer loyalty resulted in Saturn turning a profit three years after the first car rolled off the assembly line.

However, the company operated in the red most years and had not recouped the initial investment. Many observers noted the failure of other parts of GM to embrace the Saturn innovations. The United Auto Workers consistently resisted Saturn-type labour agreements at any other manufacturing sites. Saturn was slow to develop new models, and competitors were outpacing the company in terms of technical refinement and safety, even while copying some of its "buyer-friendly" sales techniques. Although Saturn buyers had good demographics in terms of income and education, the company was slow to develop larger sedans, minivans, and sport utility vehicles to offer them. Gaining investment funds for such projects from GM had been difficult because the parent firm was busy recentralizing much vehicle development and engineering. When Saturn executives sought funds to develop a Saturn SUV, the response from GM was that customers should buy Chevy SUVs.

Four years after its start-up, Saturn became part of the GM Small Car Group. This required Saturn leadership to work even harder to ensure the spirit of the Saturn partnership remained strong. In 1996, a decision was made to build a new mid-size Saturn model at an existing GM plant in Delaware. Even though organizational and market changes challenged Saturn's unique culture, the original memorandum of agreement between Saturn and its workers was renewed in late 1999.

Meanwhile, Saturn had been rebuilding its aging product line. In 1999, the new L-series went on sale, making it the first new Saturn product in nearly a decade. In a long-awaited move, it finally introduced a sport utility vehicle, marking the first expansion in the division's history beyond its coupes, sedans, and station wagons, and sending a signal that Saturn was now in the truck business.

In December 2001, the new Vue sport utility vehicle was unveiled, followed by a complete restyling of its mid-sized L-Series. In 2002, Saturn unveiled the Ion to replace the S-Series, the car that first launched Saturn, and in 2003 it unveiled the Relay minivan. However, these vehicles were, for the most part, similar to models sold by other GM divisions.

In 2004, GM absorbed Saturn into its companywide Global Manufacturing System. Saturn workers voted to return to the GM-UAW master contract giving them the same contract as the rest of GM's workforce. The Saturn plant was renamed GM Spring Hill Manufacturing.

In November 2005, General Motors announced that it would be eliminating 5000 jobs in addition to 25 000 previously announced cuts and would be closing all or part of a dozen plants. This time, however, even Saturn was not to be spared. What had once been the company's centrepiece of workplace innovation was now slated to lose one of its two production lines and as many as 1500 jobs. Production of the Ion compact was shifted to another GM plant, and the Saturn plant would make some non-Saturn vehicles. Why Saturn? According to a GM spokesperson, "We really consider it to be another GM facility, just like any other."

In 2009, GM CEO Rick Wagoner was ousted by the U.S. government as part of a bailout effort to save the company in the midst of the global automobile crisis. GM was given 60 days by the government to submit a new restructuring plan. GM subsequently filed for bankruptcy protection and as part of its restructuring plan decided to sell off several of its brands, including Saturn. GM had initially planned to discontinue and shut down Saturn if a buyer could not be found.

During the global auto crisis, Saturn's sales plunged, leaving dealers with an inventory of 32 647 vehicles. Customer loyalty to the Saturn brand was also faltering, and the Astra, a new model, flopped and was discontinued.

In June 2009, GM made a deal to sell the Saturn brand and the service, parts, and distribution operations to auto-racing magnate Roger Penske and his company, Penske Automotive Group, who planned to find another manufacturer to build Saturn vehicles. In a statement, Penske, who operated more than 300 franchised automobile dealerships, said, "For nearly 20 years Saturn has focused on treating the customer right. We share that philosophy, and we want to build on those strengths."

However, a few months later the deal fell apart because Penske was unable to find an auto maker to manufacture Saturn vehicles.

Roger Smith, who had publicly staked GM's future on Saturn's success, passed away in 2007. While he had hoped to remake GM using Saturn as the model, it now seems that the opposite happened. The experiment to create a "different kind of company" had come to an end. GM stopped producing Saturn vehicles shortly after the Penske deal fell through.

Sources: Austen, I. (1999, March 26). Problem child. *Canadian Business*, 22–31; Bennet, J. (1994, March 29). Saturn, GM's big hope, is taking its first lumps. *New York Times*, A1, A12; Fisher, A.B. (1985, November 11). Behind the hype at GM's Saturn. *Fortune*, 34–49; Garsten, E. (2002, March 28). Saturn jazzes up small-car offerings. *Toronto Star*, C6; Keenan, G. (2002, February 6). GM driven to improve. *Globe and Mail*, C1; Staff. (1994, October 17). Will it work this time? *Autoweek*, 4–5; Taylor, A., III. (1988, August 1). Back to the future at Saturn. *Fortune*, 63–69; Treece, J.B. (1990, April 9). Here comes GM's Saturn. *Business Week*, 56–62; Vaughn, M. (1999, July 5). Smiling happy people. *Autoweek*, 20–21; Woodruff, J. (1992, August 17). Saturn. *Business Week*, 86–91; Kiger, P.J. (2005, December 12). Saturn plant's innovations live on at GM despite cutbacks. *Workforce Management*, 84(14), 3–4; Solomon, C.M. (1991, June). Behind the wheel at Saturn. *Personnel Journal*, 70(6), 72–74; Ingrassia, P. (2009, April 4). Saturn was supposed to save GM. *Newsweek*, 153(15), 20–24; Marr, K. (2009, June 6). Racing magnate Penske to buy Saturn from GM. *The Washington Post* (online), www.washingtonpost.com; Terlep, S., & Stoll, J.D. (2009, June 6). Penske will buy, remake Saturn—Racing legend/auto magnate will add auto brand and dealers to empire. *Wall Street Journal*, B1; Stoll, J.D. (2009, June 29). At Saturn, a split relying on the Penske name. *Wall Street Journal*, B1; Keenan, G. and Krashinsky, S. (2009, October 1). End of the road for Saturn as Penske walks. *Globe and Mail*, B1.

QUESTIONS

1. Discuss the role that environmental constraints and opportunities may have played in the creation and fall of Saturn. What contributed to its inception and its end?

2. Apply the concepts of environmental uncertainty, resource dependence, and strategy to the Saturn case. To what extent does the strategy correspond to the constraints and opportunities of the environment?

3. Consider the relationship between the strategy and structure of the Saturn plant. What came first and how and why is the structure different from the rest of GM?

4. What strategic responses were used by Saturn to try to cope with environmental uncertainty? What other strategic responses might have been considered?

5. Describe the technology of Saturn in terms of Perrow's routineness, Thompson's interdependence, and Woodward's production processes. Does the structure fit the technology? Explain your answer.

6. Describe the nature of advanced manufacturing technology at Saturn. What effect did the technology have on organizational structure and job design?

7. What does the story of Saturn teach us about the linkages between environment, strategy, and technology? What lessons can be learned from the Saturn experiment?

CHAPTER 16

ORGANIZATIONAL CHANGE, DEVELOPMENT, AND INNOVATION

LEARNING OBJECTIVES

After reading Chapter 16, you should be able to:

16.1 Explain the environmental forces that motivate organizational change and describe the factors that organizations can change.

16.2 Explain how organizations learn and what makes an organization a *learning organization*.

16.3 Describe the basic *change process* and the issues that require attention at various stages of change.

16.4 Explain how organizations can deal with *resistance to change*.

16.5 Define *organizational development* and discuss its general philosophy.

16.6 Discuss *team building*, *survey feedback*, *total quality management*, and *reengineering* as organizational development efforts.

16.7 Discuss the problems involved in evaluating organizational development efforts.

16.8 Define *innovation* and discuss the factors that contribute to successful organizational innovation.

16.9 Understand the factors that help and hurt the diffusion of innovations.

BEST BUY

Best Buy operates stores throughout the world and has more than 180 000 employees. Over four decades it became the leading retailer of consumer electronics. Best Buy, however, rose from humble beginnings. Dick Schulze, founder and now chair of the board, opened his first audio components Sound of Music store in 1966. For 15 years, the company grew steadily, with several stores in the Minneapolis–St. Paul region. In 1981, a tornado blew the roof off the company's most profitable store, causing Schulze to hold a massive inventory sale in an adjacent parking lot. Through that experience he learned the importance of turning inventory over unit margins and the need to make discount shopping enjoyable for the consumer.

Schulze subsequently put in place a continual renewal strategy that included a series of progressive concepts that would eventually bring the company as close to the customer as possible. In 1983, he adopted the name Best Buy and focused on a niche market (Concept I), that of the adult male shopper. Toward the end of the decade, he aimed to become the cost leader within the industry

(Concept II), successfully reducing expenses from more than 20 percent of sales to just 11.2 percent. Concept III, launched in the mid-1990s, sought to increase profitability by combining both low- and high-end products within the same store. Concept IV followed at the end of 1990s, with a focus on tailoring products to consumer needs and launching www.bestbuy.com. In 2001, Schulze moved toward selling solutions from selling individual items (Concept V). Sales teams were encouraged to predict customer wants, not just satisfy them. Best Buy also began to expand internationally and experienced an increase in growth margins from 13.5 percent in 1997 to 25 percent in 2003.

In 2002, Brad Anderson took over from Schulze as CEO but, instead of coming in with an entirely new strategy, as many CEOs are inclined to do, Anderson picked up where Schulze left off, albeit with a more aggressive approach. Anderson decided to symbolically skip Concept VI, moving directly to Concept VII—getting closer to the customer—which aimed to control the "last 10 feet to the customer." To achieve Concept VII, Best Buy quantified

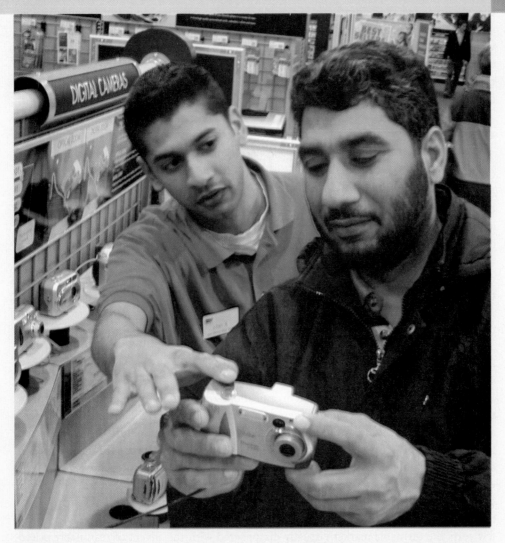

Best Buy has recognized the constant need for change posed by the volatile consumer electronics market.

the profitability of each customer segment and characterized each segment in terms of its needs. From there, Best Buy established value positions for each segment and empowered local management teams to meet the needs of these segments. This customer-centric approach generated a 22 percent growth in earnings by 2006. During this era, the firm also instituted various human resources innovations.

By 2009, however, Best Buy was hit by the same economic recession that led to the demise of a key competitor, Circuit City. Sales, profits, and stock price were all down, as nervous consumers passed on the pricey electronic devices that were at the core of the company's success. If anything, though, the effects of the recession simply obscured the sea change that was occurring in the domain of big-box retailing. This change is highlighted by repeated reports of the practice of "showrooming," in which consumers visit a large retail store to see and try products of interest first hand and then proceed to shop online (sometimes while in the store!) for the best possible price. The big-box chains invested in giant stores and large inventories while internet purveyors such as Amazon.com, which did neither, reaped the benefits. In March of 2012 Best Buy posted a $1.7 billion quarterly loss and announced plans to close 50 stores.

At about this same time Dick Schulze, who had served as chairman of the board for many years, resigned his position on an unrelated matter, along with CEO Brian Dunn. Schulze and the three CEOs who had followed him had all come up through the ranks at Best Buy and were considered "retail guys." Analysts wondered whether more "digital guys" were the solution to Best Buy's problems. Some observers felt that the resignations might ease the strategic transition that was facing Best Buy. The firm that continuously renewed itself was again facing the need for renewal.[1]

This story reflects some key themes of our chapter. Best Buy implemented periodic changes in strategy and culture to foster growth and innovation, but more change is now required. In this chapter we will discuss the concept of organizational change, including the whys and whats of change. Then we will consider the process by which change occurs and examine problems involved in managing change. Following this we will define organizational development and explore several development strategies as well as innovation, a special class of organizational change.

THE CONCEPT OF ORGANIZATIONAL CHANGE

Common experience indicates that organizations are far from static. Our favourite small restaurant experiences s and expands. We return for a visit to our alma mater and observe a variety of new programs and new buildings. Toyota starts building trucks in Texas. As consumers, we are aware that such changes may have a profound impact on our satisfaction with the product or service offered. By extension, we can also imagine that these changes have a strong impact on the people who work at the organizations in question. In and of themselves, such changes are neither good nor bad. Rather, it is the way in which the changes are *implemented* and *managed* that is crucial to both customers and members. This is the focus of the present chapter.

Why Organizations Must Change

All organizations face two basic sources of pressure to change—external sources and internal sources.

In Chapter 15, we pointed out that organizations are open systems that take inputs from the environment, transform some of these inputs, and send them back into the environment as outputs. Organizations work hard to stabilize their inputs and outputs. For example, a manufacturing firm might use a variety of suppliers to avoid a shortage of raw materials and attempt to turn out quality products to ensure demand. However, there are limits on the extent to which such control over the environment can occur. In this case, environmental changes must be matched by organizational changes if the organization is to remain effective. For example, consider the successful producer of record turntables in 1970. In only a few years the turntable market virtually disappeared with the advent of reasonably priced cassette and CD players. Now, downloaded music is commonplace. Best Buy has changed to keep up with these trends.

Probably the best recent example of the impact of the external environment in stimulating organizational change is the increased competitiveness of business. Brought on, in part, by a more global economy, deregulation, and advanced technology, this competitiveness has forced businesses to become, as the cliché goes, leaner and meaner. Many firms laid off thousands of employees and did away with layers of middle managers, developing flatter structures that are more responsive to competitive demands. Mergers, acquisitions, and joint ventures with foreign firms have become commonplace, as have less adversarial relationships with unions and suppliers.

Change can also be provoked by forces in the internal environment of the organization. Low productivity, conflict, strikes, sabotage, and high absenteeism and turnover are some of the factors that signal that change is necessary. Employee opinion can also be a force for change. For example, a number of Microsoft employees publish online blogs, some of which are critical of the firm's business strategy.[2] Very often, internal forces for change occur in response to organizational changes that are designed to deal with the external environment. Thus, many mergers and acquisitions that were to bolster the competitiveness of an organization have been followed by cultural conflict between the merged parties.

A word should be said about the perception of threat and change. Sometimes, when threat is perceived, organizations "unfreeze" (see below), scan the environment for solutions, and

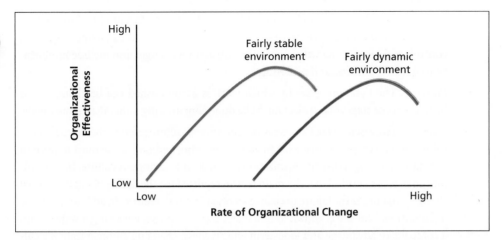

EXHIBIT 16.1
**Relationships among
environmental change,
organizational change,
and organizational
effectiveness.**

✱─Explore

Go to MyManagementLab
to see an annotated
version of this figure.

use the threat as a motivator for change. Other times, though, organizations seem paralyzed by threat, behave rigidly, and exhibit extreme inertia. Change almost always entails some investment of resources, be it money or management time. Also, it almost always requires some modification of routines and processes.[3] If either of these prerequisites is missing, inertia will occur. For example, one of the authors observed a university program threatened by low enrolment. The involved faculty spent many hours ostensibly revising the curriculum. However, the revised curriculum looked much like the old curriculum. Here, resources were invested, but the routines of teaching were not modified to counter the threat.

In spite of trends toward change, the internal and external environments of various organizations will be more or less dynamic. In responding to this, organizations should differ in the amount of change they display. Exhibit 16.1 shows that organizations in a dynamic environment must generally show more change to be effective than those operating in a more stable environment. Also, change in and of itself is not a good thing, and organizations can exhibit too much change as well as too little. The company that is in constant flux fails to establish the regular patterns of organizational behaviour that are necessary for effectiveness, and employees become cynical.

Despite the importance of change, an IBM study, *Making Change Work*, found that most CEOs saw their organizations as being poor at executing change. Project leaders responsible for changes reported only a 41 percent success rate. The majority reported budget, quality, or time problems, and 15 percent of projects were complete failures.[4]

What Organizations Can Change

Since *change* is a broad concept, it is useful to identify several specific domains in which modifications can occur. Of course, the choice of what to change depends on a well-informed analysis of the internal and external forces signalling that change is necessary.[5] Factors that can be changed include

- *Goals and strategies.* Organizations frequently change their goals and the strategies they use to reach these goals. Expansion, the introduction of new products, and the pursuit of new markets represent such changes. Electronics giant Samsung changed its strategy from producing low cost, imitative products to pursuing quality, collaboration, and innovation. Over the years, Best Buy's strategy was reinvented several times to cope with changes in its external environment.

- *Technology.* Technological changes can vary from minor to major. The introduction of online portal access for employees is a fairly minor change. Moving from a rigid assembly line to flexible manufacturing is a major change.

- *Job design.* Companies can redesign individual groups of jobs to offer more or less variety, autonomy, identity, significance, and feedback, as we discussed in Chapter 6.

- *Structure.* Organizations can be modified from a functional to a product form or vice versa. Formalization and centralization can be manipulated, as can tallness, spans of control, and networking with other firms. Structural changes also include modifications in rules, policies, and procedures.

- *Processes.* The basic processes by which work is accomplished can be changed. For instance, some stages of a project might be done concurrently rather than sequentially.

- *Culture.* As we discussed in Chapter 8, organizational culture refers to the shared beliefs, values, and assumptions that exist in an organization, and one of the most important and difficult changes that an organization can make is to change its culture. In fact, culture change is so critical that the main reason reported for the failure of organizational change programs is the failure to change an organization's culture. In addition, because organizational culture is known to be a major factor in providing an organization with a competitive advantage and long-term effectiveness, changing an organization's culture is considered to be a fundamental aspect of organizational change.[6]

- *People.* The membership of an organization can be changed in two senses. First, the actual *content* of the membership can be changed through a revised hiring process. This is often done to introduce "new blood" or to take advantage of the opportunities that a more diverse labour pool offers. At Best Buy, some observers felt that the departure of the CEO and Dick Schulze's departure from the chair's position offered hope for corporate renewal. Second, the existing membership can be changed in terms of skills and attitudes by various training and development methods.

Two important points should be made about the various areas in which organizations can introduce change. First, a change in one area very often calls for changes in others. Failure to recognize this systemic nature of change can lead to severe problems. For example, consider the functionally organized east-coast chemical firm that decides to expand its operations to the west coast. To be effective, this goal and strategy change might require some major structural changes, including a more geographic form and decentralization of decision-making power.

Second, changes in goals, strategies, technology, structure, process, job design, and culture almost always require that organizations give serious attention to people changes. As much as possible, necessary skills and favourable attitudes should be fostered *before* these changes are introduced. For example, although providing bank employees with a revised IT system is a fairly minor technological change, it might provoke anxiety on the part of those whose jobs are affected. Adequate technical training and clear, open communication about the change can do much to alleviate this anxiety.

The Change Process

By definition, change involves a sequence of events or a psychological process that occurs over time. The distinguished psychologist Kurt Lewin suggested that this sequence or process involves three basic stages—unfreezing, changing, and refreezing.[7]

Unfreezing. The recognition that some current state of affairs is unsatisfactory.

UNFREEZING **Unfreezing** occurs when it is recognized that some current state of affairs is unsatisfactory. This might involve the realization that the present structure, task design, or technology is ineffective, or that member skills or attitudes are inappropriate. Crises are especially likely to stimulate unfreezing. A dramatic drop in sales, a big lawsuit, or an unexpected strike are examples of such crises. A visit to Honda's American motorcycle plant by Harley-Davidson executives shocked them. The plant's great efficiency was obtained without extensive information technology and with very few support staff. Samsung's former chairperson, dismayed by product quality, burned 150 000 phones and fax machines in a giant bonfire, a dramatic unfreezing ploy meant to signal crisis. Of course, unfreezing can also occur without crisis. Employee attitude surveys, customer surveys, and accounting data are often used to anticipate problems and to initiate change before crises are reached.

CHANGE **Change** occurs when some program or plan is implemented to move the organization or its members to a more satisfactory state. Change efforts can range from minor to major. A simple skills training program and a revised hiring procedure constitute fairly minor changes, in which few organizational members are involved. Conversely, major changes that involve many members might include extensive job enrichment, radical restructuring, or serious attempts at empowering the workforce. An interesting study found that employees who identified more strongly with the organization showed particular interest in the details of the change process. Those who identified less strongly were more concerned with the outcomes of the change.[8]

REFREEZING When changes occur, the newly developed behaviours, attitudes, or structures must be subjected to **refreezing**—that is, they must become an enduring part of the organization. At this point, the effectiveness of the change can be examined, and the desirability of extending the change further can be considered. It should be emphasized that refreezing is a relative and temporary state of affairs, as can be seen in the Best Buy saga.

In recent years there has been much debate about whether Lewin's simple model of change, especially the refreezing component, applies to firms in so called hyper-turbulent environments, where constant, unpredictable, non-linear change is the norm.[9] Although this turbulence clearly applies to the software, nanotechnology, and biotechnology industries, it can also be seen in a less extreme form in retail, as the Best Buy saga illustrates. While the model probably applies, there is little doubt that organizations in hyper-turbulent environments face special challenges that require them be constantly acquiring, assimilating, and disseminating information so that they are ready for rapid change. Ideally, this permits something that looks like seamless "morphing" rather than the step-like process described by Lewin.[10] To achieve this seamless change, they have to have the qualities of a learning organization, a subject we will now explore.

The Learning Organization

Organizational learning refers to the process through which organizations acquire, develop, and transfer knowledge throughout the organization. There are two primary methods of organizational learning. First, organizations learn through *knowledge acquisition*. This involves the acquisition, distribution, and interpretation of knowledge that already exists but which is external to the organization. Second, organizations also learn through *knowledge development*. This involves the development of new knowledge that occurs in an organization primarily

Change. The implementation of a program or plan to move the organization or its members to a more satisfactory state.

Refreezing. The condition that exists when newly developed behaviours, attitudes, or structures become an enduring part of the organization.

LO 16.2

Explain how organizations learn and what makes an organization a *learning organization*.

Organizational learning. The process through which an organization acquires, develops, and transfers knowledge throughout the organization.

through dialogue and experience. Organizational learning occurs when organizational members interact and share experiences and knowledge, and through the distribution of new knowledge and information throughout the organization.[11] Nokia and Samsung are prominent learning organizations.

Some organizations are better at learning than others because they have processes and systems in place to facilitate learning and the transfer of knowledge throughout the organization. These kinds of organizations are known as learning organizations. A **learning organization** is an organization that has systems and processes for creating, acquiring, and transferring knowledge to modify and change its behaviour to reflect new knowledge and insights.[12] As a result, organizational change is much more likely to occur in a learning organization. In fact, it has even been suggested that a learning organization is "an organization that is adaptive in its capacity for change."[13]

There are four key dimensions that are critical for a learning organization:[14]

- *Vision/support.* Leaders must communicate a clear vision of the organization's strategy and goals, in which learning is a critical part and key to organizational success.

- *Culture.* A learning organization has a culture that supports learning. Knowledge and information sharing, risk taking, and experimentation are supported, and continuous learning is considered to be a regular part of organizational life and the responsibility of everybody in the organization.

- *Learning systems/dynamics.* Employees are challenged to think, solve problems, make decisions, and act according to a systems approach by considering patterns of interdependencies and by "learning by doing." Managers must be active in coaching, mentoring, and facilitating learning.

- *Knowledge management/infrastructure.* Learning organizations have established systems and structures to acquire, code, store, and distribute important information and knowledge so that it is available to those who need it, when they need it. This requires the integration of people, processes, and technology.

Learning organization.
An organization that has systems and processes for creating, acquiring, and transferring knowledge to modify and change its behaviour to reflect new knowledge and insights.

BMO Financial Group's Institute for Learning serves as the organization's strategic learning base and is a tangible symbol of the company's commitment to lifelong learning.

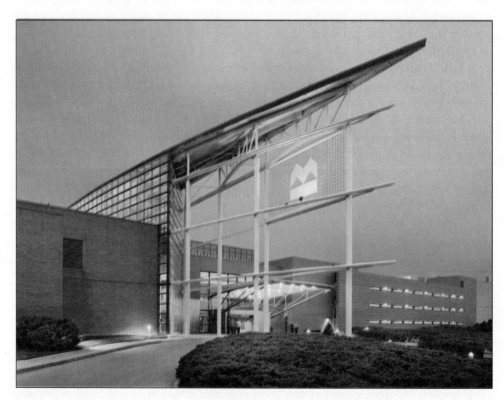

Conference Board of Canada research has shown that learning organizations are almost 50 percent more likely to have higher overall levels of profitability than those organizations not rated as learning organizations, and they are also better able to retain essential employees.[15] Another study also found a positive relationship between learning organization practices and a firm's financial performance.[16]

Some companies, like BMO Financial Group (also known as Bank of Montreal), have realized the strategic importance of learning and the link between learning and achieving business objectives. Thus, the bank invested in the construction of the Institute for Learning, which serves as the organization's strategic learning base and a tangible symbol of BMO's commitment to lifelong learning. The institute serves as an agent of strategic and cultural alignment by providing individuals and teams with opportunities to acquire corporate knowledge and perspective through the learning process, both in a centralized classroom and through distributed learning at or near the employee's work site, thereby increasing access to relevant learning.[17]

One organization that excels at learning is Singapore Airlines. The company has created a culture that values extracting copious information from customers and using the information in a systematic way to improve customer service. In addition to using formal surveys and analyses of complaints, the airline has a system in place to note and codify verbal complaints and suggestions made to aircrew personnel. The level of detail achieved has led to many very specific innovations in customer service, such as in-flight email.[18]

Learning organizations are better able to change and transform themselves because of their greater capacity for acquiring and transferring knowledge. Thus, learning is an important prerequisite for organizational change and transformation. Next, we consider some issues in the change process. But first, consider the Research Focus: *Do Organizations Learn More from Success or Failure?*

■ RESEARCH FOCUS

DO ORGANIZATIONS LEARN MORE FROM SUCCESS OR FAILURE?

As long as organizations survive, they typically improve their performance with increasing experience, and this is generally attributed to organizational learning. But experience includes both successes and failures. Thus, is the experience effect mostly due to the fact that organizations learn from failures, learn from successes, or learn from a combination of the two outcomes? Peter Madsen and Vinit Desai studied the global orbital launch vehicle industry to find out. More precisely, they examined 4220 successful orbital rocket launches and 443 failed launches, beginning with Sputnik's success in 1957. Essentially, they were interested in the impact of launch success versus failure on future launch success, which would be indicative of organizational learning. The authors hypothesized that failure would lead to more learning than success because failure stimulates far greater information search and acquisition. They confirmed their hypothesis that failure is a more potent determinant of organizational learning than success. Although there was some evidence that organizations learned from the failure of other launch organizations, direct experience with failure was a more impactful experience in terms of learning. Also, although major failures (e.g., rocket blew up) contributed to learning, lesser failures (e.g., improper orbit) did not. This is unfortunate because it precludes learning from "near misses." The authors note the paradox that while organizations learn the most from failure, failure is frequently stigmatized, and thus ignored, hidden, or redefined as success. Thus, taking a less punitive, more supportive stance toward failures might garner great benefits. Madsen and Desai discuss evidence that less exotic failures, such as airplane and railroad accidents and automotive safety recalls, may also be stimuli for organizational learning and improved organizational performance.

Source: Madsen, P.M., & Desai, V. (2010). Failing to learn? The effects of failure and success on organizational learning in the global orbital launch vehicle industry. *Academy of Management Journal, 53*, 451–476.

LO 16.3

Describe the basic *change process* and the issues that require attention at various stages of change.

Diagnosis. The systematic collection of information relevant to impending organizational change.

Change agents. Experts in the application of behavioural science knowledge to organizational diagnosis and change.

ISSUES IN THE CHANGE PROCESS

The simple sketch of the change process presented earlier neglects several important issues that organizations must confront during the process. These issues represent problems that must be overcome if the process is to be effective. Exhibit 16.2 illustrates the relationship between the stages of change and these problems, which include diagnosis, resistance, evaluation, and institutionalization.

Diagnosis

Diagnosis is the systematic collection of information relevant to impending organizational change. Initial diagnosis can provide information that contributes to unfreezing by showing that a problem exists. Once unfreezing occurs, further diagnosis can clarify the problem and suggest just what changes should be implemented. It is one thing to feel that "hospital morale has fallen drastically," but quite another to be sure that this is true and to decide what to do about it.

Relatively routine diagnosis might be handled through existing channels. For example, suppose the director of a hospital laboratory believes that many of his lab technicians do not possess adequate technical skills. In conjunction with the hospital human resources manager, the director might arrange for a formal test of these skills. The hospital could devise a training program to correct inadequacies and establish a more stringent selection program to hire better personnel.

For more complex, non-routine problems, there is considerable merit in seeking out the diagnostic skills of a change agent. **Change agents** are experts in the application of behavioural science knowledge to organizational diagnosis and change. Some large firms have in-house change agents who are available for consultation. In other companies, outside consultants might be brought in. In any event, the change agent brings an independent, objective perspective to the diagnosis while working with the people who are about to undergo change.

It is possible to obtain diagnostic information through a combination of observations, interviews, questionnaires, and the scrutiny of records. Attention to the views of customers or clients is critical. As the next section will show, there is usually considerable merit in using surveys to involve the intended targets of change in the diagnostic process.

The importance of careful diagnosis cannot be overemphasized. Proper diagnosis clarifies the problem and suggests what should be changed and the appropriate *strategy* for implementing change without resistance.[19] Unfortunately, many firms imitate the change programs of their competitors or other visible firms without doing a careful diagnosis of their own specific needs. A symptom of this is buying some pre-packaged intervention from a consulting firm. Similarly, managers sometimes confuse symptoms with underlying problems. This usually leads to trouble.

EXHIBIT 16.2 The change process and change problems.

 Explore

Go to MyManagementLab to see an annotated version of this figure.

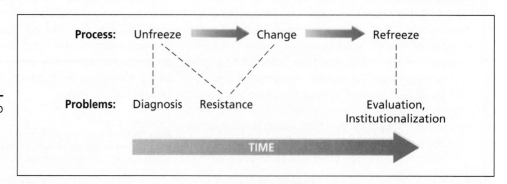

Resistance

As the saying goes, people are creatures of habit, and change is frequently resisted by those at whom it is targeted.[20] More precisely, people may resist both unfreezing and change. At the unfreezing stage, defence mechanisms (Chapter 13) might be activated to deny or rationalize the signals that change is needed.[21] Even if there is agreement that change is necessary, any specific plan for change might be resisted.

When Carly Fiorina became CEO of Hewlett-Packard, there was a great deal of resistance to her plans for change. Although managers and employees did not openly attack her ideas, if they did not like what they heard they would simply ignore it. The resistance was subtle and pervasive.[22] However, when she announced plans to merge with Compaq Computer, she was met with fierce resistance from the founders' families, shareholders, and employees. Many employees were concerned that the changes she was making would destroy the company's cherished culture.

CAUSES OF RESISTANCE
Resistance to change occurs when people either overtly or covertly fail to support the change effort. Why does such failure of support occur, leading to a lack of readiness for change? Several common reasons include the following:[23]

Resistance. Overt or covert failure by organizational members to support a change effort.

- *Politics and self-interest.* People might feel that they personally will lose status, power, or even their jobs with the advent of the change. For example, individual departments will lose power and autonomy when a flat and decentralized structure is centralized and made more hierarchical.

- *Low individual tolerance for change.* Predispositions in personality make some people uncomfortable with changes in established routines. People who seek routine, are cognitively rigid, and have a short-term focus are inclined to resist change.[24] Those who feel self-efficacy to change tend to be committed to proposed changes.[25]

- *Lack of trust.* People might clearly understand the arguments being made for change but not trust the motives of those proposing the change.

- *Different assessments of the situation.* The targets of change might sincerely feel that the situation does not warrant the proposed change and that the advocates of change have misread the situation. For example, at UPS, managers saw the introduction of scanning bar-coded packages as a way to help customers trace goods. Employees saw it as a way to track them and spy on them.[26]

- *Strong emotions.* Change has the capacity to induce strong emotions in people trying to make sense of the change, emotions that often make people feel helpless and resistant.[27]

- *A resistant organizational culture.* Some organizational cultures have especially stressed and rewarded stability and tradition. Advocates of change in such cultures are viewed as misguided deviants or aberrant outsiders. At the time of its bankruptcy, many observers noted that the culture of General Motors was especially resistant to change.[28]

Underlying these various reasons for resistance are two major themes: (1) change is unnecessary because there is only a small gap between the organization's current identity and its ideal identity; and (2) change is unobtainable (and threatening) because the gap between the current and ideal identities is too large. Exhibit 16.3 shows that a moderate identity gap is probably most conducive to increased acceptance of change because it unfreezes people while not provoking maximum resistance.[29]

Exhibit 16.4 highlights the challenges to change reported by IBM's Making Change Work survey respondents. Notice that "soft," OB-type factors top the list rather than harder, technical factors.

EXHIBIT 16.3
**Probability of
acceptance of change.**
Source: Reger, R.K.,
Gustafson, L.T., DeMarie,
S.M., & Mullane, J.V. (1994).
Reframing the organization:
Why implementing total quality
is easier said than done.
*Academy of Management
Review, 19, 565–584.*

Explore

Go to MyManagementLab
to see an annotated
version of this figure.

LO **16.4**

Explain how organiza-
tions can deal with
resistance to change.

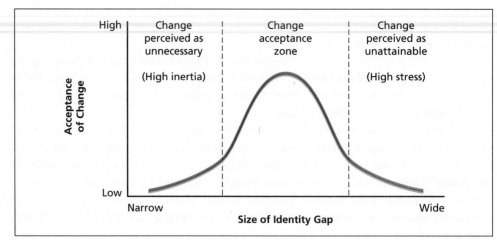

DEALING WITH RESISTANCE Low tolerance for change is mainly an individual matter, and it can often be overcome with supportive, patient supervision.

If politics and self-interest are at the root of resistance, it might be possible to co-opt the reluctant by giving them a special, desirable role in the change process or by negotiating special incentives for change. For example, consider office computing. Initially, many IT directors resisted the proliferation of personal computers, feeling that this change would reduce their power as departments moved away from dependence on the mainframe. Most organizations countered this resistance by giving IT control over the purchase, maintenance, and networking of personal computers, providing an incentive for change.

If misunderstanding, lack of trust, or different assessments are provoking resistance, good communication can pay off. Contemporary organizations are learning that obsessive secrecy about strategy and competition can have more internal costs than external bene-fits. It is particularly critical that lower-level managers understand the diagnosis underly-ing intended change and the details of the change so that they can convey this information to employees accurately. Springing "secret" changes on employees, especially when these changes involve matters such as workforce reduction, is sure to provoke resistance. Manag-ers who are generally perceived as fair have a real advantage here because this can lead to the anticipation that change efforts will unfold fairly.[30]

Involving the people who are the targets of change in the change process often reduces their resistance.[31] This is especially appropriate when there is adequate time for participation,

EXHIBIT 16.4
**Major change
challenges.**
Source: IBM. (2008). *Making
change work.* Somers, NY: IBM
Corporation. Reprinted with
the permission of IBM Global
Services.

Explore

Go to MyManagementLab
to see an annotated
version of this figure.

The most significant challenges when implementing change projects are people-oriented – topping the list are *changing mindsets* and *corporate culture*.

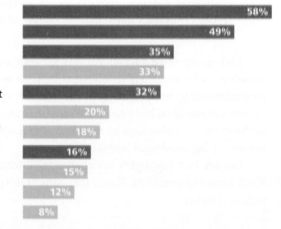

when true commitment ("ownership") to the change is critical, and when the people who will be affected by the change have unique knowledge to offer.

Finally, transformational leaders (Chapter 9) are particularly adept at overcoming resistance to change. One way they accomplish this is by "striking while the iron is hot"— that is, by being especially sensitive to when followers are ready for change. The other way is to unfreeze current thinking by installing practices that constantly examine and question the status quo. One research study of CEOs who were transformational leaders noted the following unfreezing practices:[32]

- An atmosphere is established in which dissent is not only tolerated but encouraged. Proposals and ideas are given tough objective reviews, and disagreement is not viewed as disloyalty.

- The environment is scanned for objective information about the organization's true performance. This might involve putting lots of outsiders on the board of directors or sending technical types out to meet customers.

- Organizational members are sent to other organizations and even other countries to see how things are done elsewhere.

- The organization compares itself along a wide range of criteria *against the competition*, rather than simply comparing its performance against last year's. This avoids complacency.

Transformational leaders are skilled at using the new ideas that stem from these practices to create a revised vision for followers about what the organization can do or be. Often, a radically reshaped culture is the result. In the process, as we suggested in Chapter 9, transformational leaders are good at inspiring trust and encouraging followers to subordinate their individual self-interests for the good of the organization. They are also adept at countering employee cynicism so that the proposed change is not seen as the new "flavour of the month."[33] This combination of tactics keeps followers within the zone of acceptance shown in Exhibit 16.3. By the way, that "flavour of the month" feeling is a bad thing because it suggests poor planning, and perceptions of poor planning provide stressful uncertainty.[34]

Evaluation and Institutionalization

It seems only reasonable to evaluate changes to determine whether they accomplished what they were supposed to and whether that accomplishment is now considered adequate. Obviously, objective goals, such as return on investment or market share, might be easiest and most likely to be evaluated. Of course, organizational politics can intrude to cloud even the most objective evaluation.

Organizations are notorious for doing a weak job of evaluating "soft" change programs that involve skills, attitudes, and values. However, it is possible to do a thorough evaluation by considering a range of variables:

- Reactions—did participants like the change program?
- Learning—what knowledge was acquired in the program?
- Behaviour—what changes in job behaviour occurred?
- Outcomes—what changes in productivity, absence, and so on occurred?[35]

To some extent, reactions measure resistance, learning reflects change, and behaviour reflects successful refreezing. Outcomes indicate whether refreezing is useful for the organization. Unfortunately, many evaluations of change efforts never go beyond the measurement of reactions. Again, part of the reason for this may be political. The people who propose the change effort fear reprisal if failure occurs.

If the outcome of change is evaluated favourably, the organization will wish to institutionalize that change. This means that the change becomes a permanent part of the organizational system, a social fact that persists over time, despite possible turnover by the members who originally experienced the change.[36]

Logic suggests that it should be fairly easy to institutionalize a change that has been deemed successful. However, we noted that many change efforts go unevaluated or are only weakly evaluated, and without hard proof of success it is very easy for institutionalization to be rejected by disaffected parties. This is a special problem for extensive, broad-based change programs that call for a large amount of commitment from a variety of parties (e.g., extensive participation, job enrichment, or work restructuring). It is one thing to institutionalize a simple training program, but quite another to do the same for complex interventions that can be judged from a variety of perspectives.

Studies of more complex change efforts indicate that a number of factors can inhibit institutionalization. For example, promised extrinsic rewards (such as pay bonuses) might not be developed to accompany changes. Similarly, initial changes might provide intrinsic rewards that create higher expectations that cannot be fulfilled. Institutionalization might also be damaged if new hires are not carefully socialized to understand the unique environment of the changed organization. As turnover occurs naturally, the change effort might backslide. In a similar vein, key management supporters of the change effort might resign or be transferred. Finally, environmental pressures, such as decreased sales or profits, can cause management to regress to more familiar behaviours and abandon change efforts.[37]

It stands to reason that many of the problems of evaluation and institutionalization can be overcome by careful planning and goal setting during the diagnostic stage. Let's now examine organizational development, a means of effecting planned change. But first, please consult You Be the Manager: *Changing the Face of the Victoria Police Force*.

ORGANIZATIONAL DEVELOPMENT: PLANNED ORGANIZATIONAL CHANGE

LO

Define *organizational development* and discuss its general philosophy.

Organizational development (OD).
A planned, ongoing effort to change organizations to be more effective and more human.

Organizational development (OD) is a planned, ongoing effort to change organizations to be more effective and more human. It uses the knowledge of behavioural science to foster a culture of organizational self-examination and readiness for change. A strong emphasis is placed on interpersonal and group processes.[38]

The fact that OD is *planned* distinguishes it from the haphazard, accidental, or routine changes that occur in all organizations. OD efforts tend to be *ongoing* in at least two senses. First, many OD programs extend over a long period of time, involving several distinct phases of activities. Second, if OD becomes institutionalized, continual re-examination and readiness for further change become permanent parts of the culture. In trying to make organizations more *effective* and more *human*, OD gives recognition to the critical link between personal processes, such as leadership, decision making, and communication, and organizational outcomes, such as productivity and efficiency. The fact that OD uses *behavioural science knowledge* distinguishes it from other change strategies that rely solely on principles of accounting, finance, or engineering. However, an OD intervention may also incorporate these principles. OD seeks to modify *cultural norms and roles* so that the organization remains self-conscious and prepared for adaptation. Finally, a focus on *interpersonal* and *group* processes recognizes that all organizational change affects members and that their cooperation is necessary to implement change.

Traditionally, the values and assumptions of OD change agents were decidedly humanistic and democratic. Thus, self-actualization, trust, cooperation, and the open expression of feelings among all organizational members have been viewed as desirable.[39] In recent years, OD practitioners have shown a more active concern with organizational effectiveness and with using development practices to further the strategy of the organization. This joint concern with both people and performance has thus become the credo of many contemporary OD change agents. The focus has shifted from humanistic advocacy to generating data or alternatives that allow organizational members to make informed choices.[40]

E MANAGER

: Face of the Victoria Police Force

...ia's Victoria Police Force (VPF), which employs
13 600 people and serves five million citizens, is more
than 150 years old. Established in 1853, the organization reflected many of the norms and values of the
people it served. In the late 20th century, however, as
women began entering what were typically male-dominated professions, the VPF resisted the integration of wom-
en into the police ranks, sidelining them into administrative roles. By 1999, the VPF had the lowest percentage
of women police in Australia, and problems of sexual
harassment, inflexible work arrangements, and negative attitudes were to blame. Visible minorities and homosexuals suffered the same fate. The VPF culture had
come to be known as sexist, racist, and homophobic.

The VPF situation had not gone unnoticed. As
much of society was pushing for change in the area
of diversity and equal opportunity, the VPF made
efforts to integrate women and minorities. In 2000,
the force launched million-dollar recruitment campaigns and leadership programs, but to no avail.
A two-point increase in female membership (to 16.4
percent) was countervailed by high attrition rates. In
parallel, downsizing efforts were taking place, with
many officers taking early retirement. Those who
were left had to take on greater workloads and operate with less support. Effective and sustainable
change was clearly needed.

In 2001, the VPF made a bold move by hiring an
outsider, Christine Nixon, as the first ever female chief
commissioner. Not only was she foreign to the VPF, she
had never actually worked as a police officer. In fact,
Nixon was an academic with organizational change
experience gained while working as director of human
resources in the state of New South Wales. This experience was evident from the start of her tenure as chief,
when she committed to three key objectives: workforce
diversity, inclusivity, and community involvement. Nixon
embodied these commitments immediately after her
appointment by visiting all of the VPF branches and the
communities in which they resided. During these visits
she communicated her vision and encouraged dialogue
with employees and citizens to understand the various issues that were preventing change. In less than
six months she had collected 550 issues, otherwise
known as the "The Force Issues," which fell into the
broad categories of work arrangements, staffing and
development, and promotions. Based on these issues,
Nixon created 30 project teams that were tasked to
further define the problems and propose resolutions.
From 2001 to 2006, these teams (which grew in size
and scope) developed programs and policies that would

Christine Nixon, a transformational
leader, led an effective and sustainable
change effort at the Victoria Police Force.

ultimately reflect the objectives of diversity, inclusivity,
and community involvement.

At the start of her tenure, Nixon also made a series of
immediate changes to tackle the discrimination problems
that plagued the force. Recruitment campaigns targeted
women and non–Australian-born candidates, and practices that disadvantaged these groups were removed. For
example, the obstacle course requirements were modified and non–Australian-background applicants were
provided with a course that closed the knowledge gap
with their Australian counterparts. Additionally, Nixon
boldly led uniformed officers in the 2001 gay and lesbian
parade, requested that she be addressed as "Christine"
in lieu of "Ma'am," redesigned the police uniforms
(relaxing many of the appearance standards), renamed
the top management group from "Executive Command"
to "Corporate Management Group," decentralized many
of the powers of this group, and gave prominence to
human resources management and ethics.

Questions

1. Why did the Victoria Police Force feel the need to
   hire a woman police chief who had no operational
   experience?

2. Describe Nixon's organizational change strategy.
   Do you think it was effective and sustainable? Why
   or why not?

To see what the VPF did, check The Manager's Notebook at the end of the chapter.

Sources: Adapted from Metz, I., & Kulik, C.T. (2008, Summer). Making public
organizations more inclusive: A case study of the Victoria Police Force. *Human
Resource Management, 47*, 369–387; Victoria Police Annual Report
2007–08, www.police.vic.gov.au.

LO 16.6

Discuss *team building*, *survey feedback*, *total quality management*, and *reengineering* as organizational development efforts.

SOME SPECIFIC ORGANIZATIONAL DEVELOPMENT STRATEGIES

The organization that seeks to "develop itself" has recourse to a wide variety of specific techniques. We discussed some of these techniques earlier in the book. For example, job enrichment and management by objectives (Chapter 6) are usually classed as OD efforts, as are diversity training (Chapter 3), self-managed and cross-functional teams (Chapter 7), and empowerment (Chapter 12). In this section, we will discuss four additional OD strategies that illustrate the diversity of the practice. Team building and survey feedback are limited in scope and are often a part of other change efforts. Total quality management and reengineering are broader in scope and lead to more sweeping organizational change.

Team Building

Team building. An effort to increase the effectiveness of work teams by improving interpersonal processes, goal clarification, and role clarification.

Team building attempts to increase the effectiveness of work teams by improving interpersonal processes, goal clarification, and role clarification.[41] (What is our team trying to accomplish, and who is responsible for what?) As such, it can facilitate communication and coordination. The term *team* can refer to intact work groups, special task forces, new work units, or people from various parts of an organization who must work together to achieve a common goal.

Team building usually begins with a diagnostic session, often held away from the workplace, in which the team explores its current level of functioning. The team might use several sources of data to accomplish its diagnosis. Some data might be generated through sensitivity training, outdoor "survival" exercises, or open-ended discussion sessions. In addition, "hard" data, such as attitude survey results and production figures, might be used. The goal at this stage is to paint a picture of the current strengths and weaknesses of the team. The ideal outcome of the diagnostic session is a list of needed changes to improve team functioning. Subsequent team-building sessions usually have a decidedly task-oriented slant—how can we actually implement the changes indicated by the diagnosis? Problem solving by subgroups might be used at this stage. Between the diagnostic and follow-up sessions, the change agent might hold confidential interviews with team members to anticipate implementation problems. Throughout, the change agent acts as a catalyst and resource person.

Outdoor training programs are a popular method of team building in which team members participate in structured outdoor activities to improve their communication and coordination skills and learn how to work together as a team.

is used to develop new work teams, the preliminary diagnostic
mpts to clarify expected role relationships and additional training
n members. In subsequent sessions, the expected task environment
...n role-playing exercises.

...pany used this integrated approach to develop the management team of a new
... In the simulation portion of the development, typical problems encountered in opening a new plant were presented to team members via hypothetical in-basket memos and telephone calls. In role-playing the solutions to these problems, they reached agreement about
how they would have to work together on the job and gained a clear understanding of each
other's competencies. Plant start-ups were always problem-laden, but this was the smoothest
in the history of the company.

Ideally, team building is a continuing process that involves regular diagnostic sessions
and further development exercises as needed. This permits the team to anticipate new problems and to avoid regression to less effective, predevelopment habits.

Survey Feedback

In bare-bones form, **survey feedback** involves collecting data from organizational members
and feeding these data back to them in a series of meetings in which members explore and
discuss the data.[43] The purpose of the meetings is to suggest or formulate changes that emerge
from the data.

As its name implies, survey feedback's basic data generally consist of questionnaires
completed by organizational members. Before data are collected, a number of critical
decisions must be made by the change agent and organizational management. First, who
should participate in the survey? Sometimes, especially in large organizations, the survey
could be restricted to particular departments, jobs, or organizational levels where problems
exist. However, most survey feedback efforts attempt to cover the entire organization. This
approach recognizes the systemic nature of organizations and permits a comparison of survey results across various subunits. It is generally conceded that all members of a target group
should be surveyed. This procedure builds trust and confidence in survey results.

What questions should the survey ask? Two approaches are available. Some change
agents use pre-packaged, standardized surveys, such as the University of Michigan Survey
of Organizations.[44] This questionnaire covers areas such as communication and decision-
making practices and employee satisfaction. Such questionnaires are usually carefully constructed and permit comparisons with other organizations in which the survey has been
conducted. However, there is some danger that pre-packaged surveys might neglect critical
areas for specific consideration and so many change agents choose to devise their own custom-tailored surveys or seek help from consulting firms. Some firms, such as the Hay Group,
have large databases that enable organizations to compare their employees' responses with
those of other organizations on core questions.

Feedback seems to be most effective when it is presented to natural working units in
face-to-face meetings. This method rules out presenting only written feedback or feedback
that covers only the organization as a whole. In a software firm, a natural working unit might
consist of a department, such as development or marketing. In a school district, such units
might consist of individual schools. Many change agents prefer that the manager of the working unit conduct the feedback meeting. This demonstrates management commitment and
acceptance of the data. The change agent attends such meetings and helps facilitate discussion of the data and plans for change.

It bears emphasis that surveys have the most beneficial effects when the results are
indeed reviewed with employees and when action is taken in response to the survey.
Exhibit 16.5 shows the percentage of favourable survey responses in a multinational consumer products company. The survey is delivered in 40 languages in 200 nations. As you

Survey feedback. The
collection of data from
organizational members
and the provision of feedback about the results.

EXHIBIT 16.5

Percentage of favourable responses to a survey in terms of perceptions that results were reviewed with employees and action was taken.

Source: Church, A.H., Golay, L.M., Rotolo, C.T., Tuller, M.D., Shull, A.C., & Desrosiers, E.I. (2012). Without effort there can be no change: Reexamining the impact of survey feedback and action planning on employee attitudes. In A.B. Shani, W.A. Pasmore, & R.W. Woodman (Eds.), *Research in organizational change and development* Vol. 20, 223–264. Emerald Group Publishing.

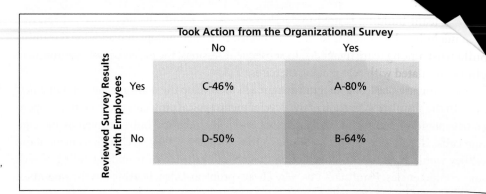

can see, the most favourable responses (80%) occur in quadrant A, where survey results were shared and action occurred as a result of the survey. Sharing results but not acting (C), or doing neither (D), were both associated with much less favourable responses. The motto is clear: Share and act.

IBM was one of the pioneers in employee surveys, beginning back in 1957. Given its business sector, it was also one of the first firms to use computerized surveying with integrated data collection and data processing, allowing for fast feedback. The company currently uses quarterly surveys of random samples of employees in 70 countries using 13 languages.[45] There are 25 core questions and 5 more tailored to local concerns. The company has validated the links from employee job satisfaction to client satisfaction to business performance.

Ford Motor Company also has a comprehensive, yearly, worldwide employee attitude survey called Ford Pulse.[46] Fifty-five core questions that are linked to strategic issues are always completed by salaried employees. Supplemental questions are custom-developed to cover local issues. On average, around 80 000 employees in 50 countries respond online in 23 languages. Ford validated the importance of the Pulse results at 147 Ford Credit branches in Canada and the United States.[47] The results showed that branches with higher Pulse scores had higher customer satisfaction, market share, and business volume and lower loan delinquency and employee turnover. The top part of Exhibit 16.6 shows the association between several Pulse dimensions and customer satisfaction with the branch. The lower part shows the association between Pulse scores and market share. These kinds of bottom-line results go a long way toward enhancing the credibility of the survey to managers and underlining the importance of accountability for "people issues."

Ford is a member of a consortium of over 40 large premier companies known as the Mayflower Group. Other participants include Nike, Microsoft, Best Buy, Boeing, 3M, and Target. Participating firms agree to include a number of core items in their employee surveys and share the responses with the consortium at least once every two years. This has provided a normative benchmarking database of over 3 million employees that enables member companies to compare where they stand on matters such as employee job satisfaction, work engagement, and diversity.[48]

Total Quality Management

Total quality management (TQM). A systematic attempt to achieve continuous improvement in the quality of an organization's products or services.

Total quality management (TQM) is a systematic attempt to achieve continuous improvement in the quality of an organization's products or services. Typical characteristics of TQM programs include an obsession with customer satisfaction; a concern for good relations with suppliers; continuous improvement of work processes; the prevention of quality errors; frequent measurement and assessment; extensive training; and high employee involvement and teamwork.[49]

Prominent names associated with the quality movement include W. Edwards Deming, Joseph Juran, and Philip Crosby.[50] Although each of these "quality gurus" advocates somewhat different paths to quality, all three are concerned with using teamwork to achieve

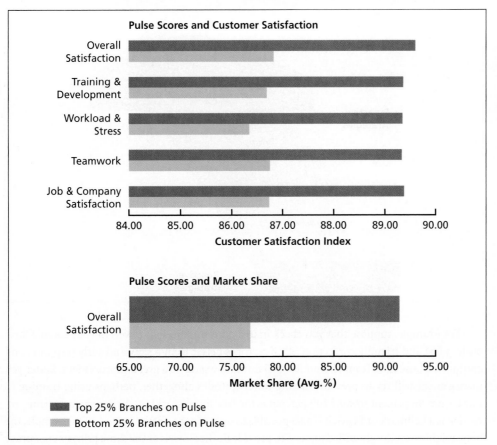

EXHIBIT 16.6
Relationship between Ford Pulse survey scores and customer satisfaction and market share at Ford Credit branches.
Source: Johnson, R.H., Ryan, A.M., & Schmit, M. (1994). Employee Attitudes and Branch Performance at Ford Motor Credit. Presentation at the annual conference of the Society for Industrial and Organizational Psychology, Nashville, Tennessee. © 1994 Raymond Johnson. Used by permission of Dr. R. Johnson on behalf of the authors.

�֍ Explore

Go to MyManagementLab to see an annotated version of this figure.

continuous improvement to please customers. Exhibit 16.7 highlights the key principles underlying customer focus, continuous improvement, and teamwork. In turn, each of these principles is associated with certain practices and specific techniques that typify TQM.

The concept of continuous improvement sometimes confuses students of TQM—how can something be more than 100 percent good? To clarify this, it is helpful to view improvement as a continuum ranging from responding to product or service problems (a reactive strategy) to creating new products or services that please customers (a proactive strategy). Exhibit 16.8 illustrates this continuum.[51]

EXHIBIT 16.7
Principles, practices, and techniques of total quality management.
Source: Dean, J.W., Jr., & Bowen, D.E. (1994). Management theory and total quality: Improving research and practice through theory development. *Academy of Management Review, 19,* 392–418.

	Customer Focus	**Continuous Improvement**	**Teamwork**
Principles	Paramount importance of providing products and services that fulfill customer needs; requires organizationwide focus on customers	Consistent customer satisfaction can be attained only through relentless improvement of processes that create products and services	Customer focus and continuous improvement are best achieved by collaboration throughout an organization as well as with customers and suppliers
Practices	Direct customer contact Collecting information about customer needs Using information to design and deliver products and services	Process analysis Reengineering Problem solving Plan/do/check/act	Search for arrangements that benefit all units involved in a process Formation of various types of teams Group skills training
Techniques	Customer surveys and focus groups Quality function deployment (translates customer information into product specifications)	Flowcharts Pareto analysis Statistical process control Fishbone diagrams	Organizational development methods such as the nominal group technique Team-building methods (e.g., role clarification and group feedback)

EXHIBIT 16.8
A continuum of continuous improvement.
Source: Adapted from Kinlaw, D.C. (1992). *Continuous improvement and measurement for total quality: A team based approach.* San Diego: Pfeiffer. © 1992 John Wiley & Sons Inc. Used by permission of John Wiley & Sons, Inc.

Go to MyManagementLab to see an annotated version of this figure.

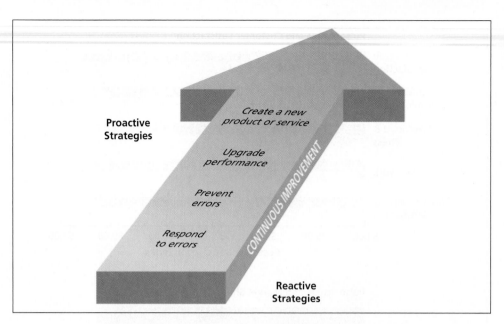

For example, suppose that you check in to a hotel and find no towels in your room. Obviously, a fast and friendly correction of this error is better than a slow and surly response, and cutting response time from 15 minutes to 5 minutes would be a great improvement. Better yet, management will try to prevent missing-towel episodes altogether, perhaps using training to move from 96 percent toward 100 percent error-free towel stocking. Although such error *prevention* is a hallmark of TQM, it is also possible to upgrade the service episode. For example, the hotel might work closely with suppliers to provide fluffier towels at the same price or encourage guests to not use too many towels, thus reducing laundry and room costs. Finally, a new service opportunity might be identified and acted on. For example, the Chicago Marriott hotel discovered (after 15 years of operation) that 66 percent of all guests' calls to the housekeeping department were requests for irons or ironing boards. The manager took funds earmarked to replace black-and-white bathroom TVs with colour sets and instead equipped each room with an iron and ironing board. No one had ever complained about black-and-white TVs in the bathroom.[52]

This series of hotel examples illustrates several features of the continuous improvement concept and TQM in general.[53] First, continuous improvement can come from small gains over time (e.g., gradually approaching 100 percent error-free room servicing) or from more radical innovation (e.g., offering a new service). In both cases, the goal is long-term improvement, not a short-term "fix." Next, improvement requires knowing where we are in the first place. Thus, TQM is very concerned with measurement and data collection—in our examples, we alluded to speed of service, percent of error-free performance, and frequency of customer requests as examples. Next, TQM stresses teamwork among employees and (in the examples given here) with suppliers and customers. Finally, TQM relies heavily on training to achieve continuous improvement.

Although simple job training can contribute to continuous improvement (as in the towel-stocking example), TQM is particularly known for using specialized training in tools that empower employees to diagnose and solve quality problems on an ongoing basis. Some tools, noted in the bottom row of Exhibit 16.7, include:

- *Flowcharts of work processes.* Flowcharts illustrate graphically the operations and steps in accomplishing some task, noting who does what, and when. For instance, what happens when hotel housekeeping receives a guest request for towels?

- *Pareto analysis.* Pareto analysis collects frequency data on the causes of errors and problems, showing where attention should be directed for maximum improvement. For instance, the Marriott data on reasons for calls to housekeeping corresponds to Pareto data.

- *Fishbone diagrams.* Fishbone (cause-and-effect) diagrams illustrate graphically the factors that could contribute to a particular quality problem. Very specific causes ("small bones") are divided into logical classes or groups ("large bones"). In the hotel example, classes of causes might include people, equipment, methods, and materials.

- *Statistical process control.* Statistical process control gives employees hard data about the quality of their own output that enables them to correct any deviations from standard. TQM places particular emphasis on reducing variation in performance over time.

These tools to improve the diagnosis and correction of quality problems will not have the desired impact if they fail to improve quality in the eyes of the customer. An essential problem here is that quality has many different and potentially incompatible definitions. For example, *ultimate excellence, value for the money, conformance to specifications,* or *meeting or exceeding customer expectations* are all potential definitions of quality.[54] Although this last definition would seem to be closest to the TQM principle of customer focus, it is not without its weaknesses. For example, customers might have contradictory expectations. Also, they are more likely to have clear expectations about familiar products and services than about new or creative products or services. Nevertheless, organizations with a real commitment to TQM make heavy use of customer surveys, focus groups, mystery shoppers, and customer clinics to stay close to their customers. Harley-Davidson holds customer clinics and sponsors bike rallies to learn from its customers. Also, survey feedback programs allow organizations to obtain information about internal customers (such as how the adjacent department views your department's performance).

TQM programs reveal a large number of successes in firms such as L.L. Bean, Motorola, and Ritz-Carlton Hotels. However, they have also had their share of problems, all of which ultimately get expressed as resistance. Despite allowing for radical innovation, TQM is mainly about achieving small gains over a long period of time. This long-term focus can be hard to maintain, especially if managers or employees expect extreme improvements in the short term. Despite these problems, the quality movement continues to be one of the most popular of the more elaborate OD efforts.

Reengineering

Of all the forms of change discussed in this chapter, reengineering is the most fundamental and radical. **Reengineering** is the radical redesign of organizational processes to achieve major improvements in such factors as time, cost, quality, or service.[55]

Reengineering does not fine-tune existing jobs, structures, technology, or human resources policies. Rather, it uses a "clean slate" approach that asks basic questions, such as "What business are we really in?" and "If we were creating this organization today, what would it look like?" Then, jobs, structure, technology, and policy are redesigned around the answers to these questions.

A key word in our definition of reengineering is "processes." **Organizational processes** are *activities* or *work* that the organization must accomplish to create outputs that customers (internal or external) value.[56] For example, designing a new product is a process that might involve people holding a variety of jobs in several different departments (R&D, marketing, production, and finance). In theory, the gains from reengineering will be greatest when the process is complex and cuts across a number of jobs and departments. We can contrast reengineering with TQM, in that TQM usually seeks incremental improvements in existing processes rather than radical revisions of processes. However, a TQM effort could certainly be part of a reengineering project.

What factors prompt interest in reengineering? One factor is "creeping bureaucracy," which is especially common in large, established firms. With growth, rather than rethinking basic work processes, many firms have simply tacked on more bureaucratic controls to maintain order. This leads to overcomplicated processes and an internal focus on satisfying bureaucratic procedures rather than tending to the customer. Many corporate downsizings have been unsuccessful because they failed to confront bureaucratic controls and basic work processes.

Reengineering. The radical redesign of organizational processes to achieve major improvements in such factors as time, cost, quality, or service.

Organizational processes. Activities or work that have to be accomplished to create outputs that internal or external customers value.

New information technology has also stimulated reengineering. Many firms were disappointed that initial investments in information technology did not result in anticipated reductions in costs or improved productivity. This is because existing processes were simply automated rather than reengineered to correspond to the capabilities of the new technology. Now, it is commonly recognized that advanced technology allows organizations to radically modify (and usually radically simplify) important organizational processes. In other words, work is modified to fit technological capabilities rather than simply fitting the technology to existing jobs. At Ford Motor Company, for example, a look at the entire process for procuring supplies revealed great inefficiencies.[57] Ford employed a large accounts payable staff to issue payments to suppliers when it received invoices. Now, employees at the receiving dock can approve payment when the *goods* are received. Information technology enables them to tap a database to verify that the goods were ordered and issue a payment to the supplier.

How does reengineering actually proceed? In essence, much reengineering is oriented toward one or both of the following goals:[58]

- The number of mediating steps in a process is reduced, making the process more efficient.
- Collaboration among the people involved in the process is enhanced.

Removing the number of mediating steps in a process, if done properly, reduces labour requirements, removes redundancies, decreases chances for errors, and speeds up the production of the final output. All of this happened with Ford's revision of its procurement process. Enhanced collaboration often permits simultaneous, rather than sequential, work on a process and reduces the chances for misunderstanding and conflict.

Some of the nitty-gritty aspects of reengineering include the following practices. You will notice that we have covered many of them in other contexts earlier in the book.[59]

- *Jobs are redesigned and usually enriched.* Frequently, several jobs are combined into one to reduce mediating steps and provide greater employee control.
- *A strong emphasis is placed on teamwork.* Teamwork (especially cross-functional) is a potent method of enhancing collaboration.
- *Work is performed by the most logical people.* Some firms train customers to do minor maintenance and repairs themselves or turn over the management of some inventory to their suppliers.
- *Unnecessary checks and balances are removed.* When processes are simplified and employees are more collaborative, expensive and redundant controls can sometimes be removed.
- *Advanced technology is exploited.* Computerized technology not only permits combining of jobs, it also enhances collaboration via email, groupware, and so on.

It is easiest to get a feel for the success of reengineering by considering some of the reductions in mediating steps and improvements in speed that have resulted. Using software that allows clients to file electronic claims, Blue Cross of Washington and Alaska handled 17 percent more volume with a 12 percent smaller workforce and halved the time to handle a claim. Using cross-functional teams and advanced technology, Chrysler cut the design time of its successful Jeep Cherokee by 40 percent.[60] Such "concurrent engineering" is now the norm. At popular clothing stores, fashions move from design to store in two months rather than the former two *seasons*. Thus, a firm is much more responsive to fickle swings in trends and taste.

Reengineering is most extensive in industries where (1) much creeping bureaucracy has set in, (2) large gains were available with advanced technology, and (3) deregulation increased the heat of competition. These include the insurance, banking, brokerage, and telecommunications industries.

Because reengineering has the goal of radical change, it requires strong CEO support and transformational leadership qualities. Also, before reengineering begins, it is essential that the organization clarify its overall strategy. What business should we really be in? (Do we want to produce hardware, software, or both?) Given this, who are our customers, and what core processes create value for them? If such strategic clarification is lacking, processes that do not matter to the customer will be reengineered. Strong CEO support and a clear strategy are important for overcoming resistance that simply dismisses people who advocate reengineering as "more efficiency experts." Resistance due to self-interest and organizational politics is likely when radical change may lead to layoffs or major changes in work responsibilities.

Reengineering must be both broad and deep to have long-lasting, bottom-line results—that is, it should span a large number of activities that cut costs or add customer value, and it should affect a number of elements, including skills, values, roles, incentives, structure, and technology.[61] Half-hearted attempts do not pay off.

DOES ORGANIZATIONAL DEVELOPMENT WORK?

Does it work? That is, do the benefits of OD outweigh the heavy investment of time, effort, and money? At the outset, we should reemphasize that most OD efforts are *not* carefully evaluated. Political factors and budget limitations might be prime culprits, but the situation is not helped by some OD practitioners who argue that certain OD goals (e.g., making the organization more human) are incompatible with impersonal, scientifically rigorous evaluation. Two large-scale reviews of a wide variety of OD techniques (including some we discussed in this chapter as well as job redesign, MBO, and goal setting from Chapters 5 and 6) reached the following conclusions:[62]

- Most OD techniques have a positive impact on productivity, job satisfaction, or other work attitudes.

- OD seems to work better for supervisors or managers than for blue-collar workers.

- Changes that use more than one technique seem to have more impact.

- There are great differences across sites in the success of OD interventions.

Exhibit 16.9 summarizes the results of a large number of research studies on the impact of OD efforts on changes in a variety of outcomes such as performance and turnover. Organizational arrangements included changes in formal structure and some quality

LO **16.7**

Discuss the problems involved in evaluating organizational development efforts.

Go to MyManagementLab to see an annotated version of this figure.

EXHIBIT 16.9
Organizational change due to organizational development efforts.
Source: Modified and reproduced by special permission of the Publisher, Davies-Black Publishing, an imprint of CCP Inc., Palo Alto, CA 94303 from Dunnette, M.D., & Hough, L.M. (Eds.). (1992). *Handbook of industrial and organizational psychology*, 2nd ed., vol. 3. Copyright by Davies-Black Publishing, an imprint of CPP, Inc. All rights reserved. Further reproduction is prohibited without the Publisher's written consent.

interventions. Social factors included the use of team building and survey feedback. Technology changes mainly involved job redesign. Finally, physical-setting interventions (which were rare) included things such as changes to open-plan offices.

As you can see, a healthy percentage of studies reported positive changes following an OD effort. However, many studies also reported no change. This underlines the difficulty of introducing change, and it also suggests that variations in how organizations actually implement change may greatly determine its success. The relative lack of negative change is encouraging, but it is also possible that there is a bias against reporting bad outcomes.[63]

Weak methodology has sometimes plagued research evaluations of the success of OD interventions, although the quality of research seems to be improving over time.[64] Some specific problems include the following:[65]

- OD efforts involve a complex series of changes. There is little evidence of exactly which of these changes produce changes in processes or outcomes.

- Novelty effects or the fact that participants receive special treatment might produce short-term gains that really do not persist over time.

- Self-reports of changes after OD might involve unconscious attempts to please the change agent.

- Organizations may be reluctant to publicize failures.

Let's hope that promise will overcome problems as organizations try to respond effectively to their increasingly complex and dynamic environments. Speaking of such responses, let's turn now to innovation.

THE INNOVATION PROCESS

Do you recognize the name Arthur Fry? Probably not. But Arthur Fry is famous in his own way as the inventor of the ubiquitous, sticky-backed Post-it notes, a top seller among paper office supplies. Fry, a researcher at the innovative 3M Company, developed the product that became Post-its in response to a personal problem—how to keep his place marker from falling out of his church choir hymnal.

What accounts for the ability of individuals like Arthur Fry and organizations like 3M to think up and exploit such innovative ideas? This is the focus of this section of the chapter.[66]

What Is Innovation?

Innovation is the process of developing and implementing new ideas in an organization. The term *developing* is intentionally broad. It covers everything from the genuine invention of a new idea to recognizing an idea in the environment, importing it to the organization, and giving it a unique application.[67] The essential point is a degree of creativity. Arthur Fry did not invent glue, and he did not invent paper, but he did develop a creative way to use them together. Then 3M was creative enough to figure out how to market what might have appeared to less probing minds to be a pretty mundane product.

We can roughly classify innovations as product (including service) innovations, process innovations, or managerial innovations.[68] *Product innovations* have a direct impact on the cost, quality, style, or availability of a product or service. Thus, they should be very obvious to clients or customers. It is easiest to identify with innovations that result in tangible products, especially everyday consumer products. Thus, we can surely recognize that the BlackBerry, the iPhone, the iPod, and Post-it notes have been innovative products. Perhaps coming less readily to mind are service innovations, such as purchasing via eBay, researching via Google, and downloading music via Kazaa.

JOBY: INDIVIDUAL BEHAVIOUR Go to MyManagementLab to watch a video about individual behaviour.

ENTREPRENEURSHIP, CREATIVITY AND INNOVATION Go to MyManagementLab to complete a simulation about entrepreneurship, creativity and innovation.

Define *innovation* and discuss the factors that contribute to successful organizational innovation.

Innovation. The process of developing and implementing new ideas in an organization.

Process innovations are new ways of designing products, making products, or delivering services. In many cases, process changes are invisible to customers or clients, although they help the organization to perform more effectively or efficiently. Thus, new technology is a process innovation, whether it be new manufacturing technology or a new management information system.

Managerial innovations are new forms of strategy, structure, human resource systems, and managerial practices that facilitate organizational change and adaptation. Examples might include job enrichment, participation, reengineering, and quality programs.[69] Visa, GE, DuPont, and Procter & Gamble are particularly noted for managerial innovations.[70]

Innovation is often conceived of as a stage-like process that begins with idea generation and proceeds to idea implementation. For some kinds of innovations, it is also hoped that the implemented innovation will diffuse to other sites or locations. This applies especially to process innovations that have begun as pilot or demonstration projects:

IDEA GENERATION → IDEA IMPLEMENTATION → IDEA DIFFUSION

In advance of discussing these stages, let us note several interesting themes that underlie the process of innovation. First, much idea generation is due to serendipity. Thus, IKEA's signature flat-packed "take it home yourself" furniture actually stemmed from a temporary labour shortage, not some grand plan to lower costs and save warehouse space.[71] Second, the beginning of innovation can be pretty haphazard and chaotic, and the conditions necessary to create new ideas might be very different from the conditions necessary to get these ideas implemented. In a related vein, although organizations have to innovate to survive, such innovation might be resisted just like any other organizational change. The result of these tensions is that innovation is frequently a highly political process (Chapter 12).[72] This important point is sometimes overlooked because innovation often involves science and technology, domains that have a connotation of rationality about them. However, both the champions of innovation and the resisters might behave politically to secure or hold onto critical organizational resources. Finally, the generation of good ideas is no guarantee that they will be implemented and diffused. For an example see the Applied Focus: *Why Aren't High-Quality Health Care Innovations Implemented?*

Generating and Implementing Innovative Ideas

Innovation requires creative ideas, someone to fight for these ideas, good communication, and the proper application of resources and rewards.

INDIVIDUAL CREATIVITY Creative thinking by individuals or small groups is at the core of the innovation process. **Creativity** is usually defined as the production of novel but potentially useful ideas. Thus, creativity is a key aspect of the "developing new ideas" part of our earlier definition of innovation. However, innovation is a broader concept, in that it also involves an attempt to implement new ideas. Not every creative idea gets implemented.

Creativity. The production of novel but potentially useful ideas.

When we see a company like Corning, which is known for its innovations, or we see an innovative project completed successfully, we sometimes forget about the role that individual creativity plays in such innovations. However, organizations that have a consistent reputation for innovation have a talent for selecting, cultivating, and motivating creative individuals. Such creativity can come into play at many "locations" during the process of innovation. Thus, the salesperson who discovers a new market for a product might be just as creative as the scientist who developed the product.

What makes a person creative?[73] For one thing, you can pretty much discount the romantic notion of the naïve creative genius. Research shows that creative people tend to have an excellent technical understanding of their domain—that is, they understand its basic practices, procedures, and techniques. Thus, creative chemists will emerge from those who are well trained and up-to-date in their field. Similarly, creative money managers will be

APPLIED FOCUS

WHY AREN'T HIGH-QUALITY HEALTH CARE INNOVATIONS IMPLEMENTED?

North America produces some of the most effective health care innovations on the planet, most of which have been subjected to rigorous standards of testing. Despite this, quality improvements in health care lag behind those of many industries, and preventable deaths, medication mistakes, and hospital-induced infections are all too familiar, as is the associated skyrocketing cost of health care. What accounts for this paradox, the failure of proven innovations to diffuse across the health care system?

Ingrid Nembhard, Jeffrey Alexander, Timothy Hoff, and Rangaraj Ramanujam studied this diffusion problem, which they termed "innovation implementation failure." This means that an innovation is ostensibly adopted but not really implemented as intended. As an example, they cite the failure of the prestigious Cedars-Sinai Medical Center in Los Angeles to successfully implement computerized physician order entry for medical prescriptions, a system meant to replace error-inducing handwritten prescriptions. The multimillion-dollar system was scrapped after its use was boycotted by hospital staff.

What accounts for the failure to implement medical innovations? Nembhard and colleagues claim that physicians are extremely risk-averse and schooled in the Hippocratic dictum to "do no harm" to patients, to the point that they often refuse to engage in proven, evidence-based clinical practices. The tradition of clinical discretion in dealing with patients means that they can do this because they have much more power than hospital managers. Also, many health care innovations require interdisciplinary teamwork, but physicians themselves are highly specialized and status-conscious concerning the roles of the various health professions. This is not a recipe for good teamwork. Finally, physicians' tendency to identify with their profession rather than their hospital means that innovations, which are usually focused on improving the overall performance of a hospital, may not receive dedicated support.

To counter implementation failure, the authors suggest risk-free pilot projects and dry runs and more involvement of physicians and other staff in planning stages. They also suggest framing the innovation as a learning challenge rather than a performance challenge, promoting more identification with the health care organization, and fostering transformational leadership.

Source: Nembhard, I.M., Alexander, J.A., Hoff, T.J., & Ramanujam, R. (2009, February). Why does the quality of healthcare continue to lag? Insights from management research. *Academy of Management Perspectives, 12,* 24–42.

---

among those who have a truly excellent grasp of finance and economics. Notice, however, that the fact that creative people have good skills in their area of specialty does not mean that they are extraordinarily intelligent. Once we get beyond subnormal intelligence, there is no correlation between level of intelligence and creativity.

Most people with good basic skills in their area are still not creative. What sets the creative people apart are additional *creativity-relevant* skills. These include the ability to tolerate ambiguity, withhold early judgment, see things in new ways, and be open to new and diverse experiences. Some of these skills reflect certain personality characteristics, such as curiosity and persistence. Interestingly, creative people tend to be socially skilled but lower than average in need for social approval. They can often interact well with others to learn and discuss new ideas, but they do not see the need to conform just to get others to like them.

Many creativity-related skills can actually be improved by training people to think in divergent ways and to withhold early evaluation of ideas.[74] Some of the methods we discussed in Chapter 11 (electronic brainstorming, nominal groups, and Delphi techniques) can be used to hone creative skills. Frito-Lay and DuPont are two companies that engage in extensive creativity training.

Finally, people can be experts in their field and have creativity skills, but still not be creative if they lack intrinsic motivation for generating new ideas. Such motivation is most likely to occur when there is genuine interest in and fascination with the task at hand. This is not to say that extrinsic motivation is not important in innovation, as we shall see shortly. Rather, it means that creativity itself is not very susceptible to extrinsic rewards.

Having a lot of potentially creative individuals is no guarantee in itself that an organization will innovate. Let's now turn to some other factors that influence innovation.

IDEA CHAMPIONS Again and again, case studies of successful innovations reveal the presence of one or more **idea champions**, people who see the kernel of an innovative idea and help guide it through to implementation.[75] This role of idea champion is often an informal emergent role, and "guiding" the idea might involve talking it up to peers, selling it to management, garnering resources for its development, or protecting it from political attack by guardians of the status quo. Champions often have a real sense of mission about the innovation. Idea champions have frequently been given other labels, some of which depend on the exact context or content of the innovation. For example, in larger organizations, such champions might be labelled *intrapreneurs* or *corporate entrepreneurs*. In R&D settings, one often hears the term *project champion*; *product champion* is another familiar moniker. The exact label is less important than the function, which is one of sponsorship and support.

> **Idea champions.**
> People who recognize an innovative idea and guide it through to implementation.

For a modest innovation whose merits are extremely clear, it is possible for the creative person who thinks up the idea to serve as its sole champion and to push the idea into practice. In the case of more complex and radical innovations, especially those that demand heavy resource commitment, it is common to see more than one idea champion emerge during the innovation process. For example, a laser scientist might invent a new twist to laser technology and champion the technical idea within her R&D lab. In turn, a product division line manager might hear of the technical innovation and offer to provide sponsorship to develop it into an actual commercial product. This joint emergence of a technical champion and a management champion is typical. Additional idea champions might also emerge. For example, a sales manager in the medical division might lobby to import the innovation from the optics division.

What kind of people are idea champions, and what are their tactics? An interesting program of research headed by Jane Howell examined champions who spearheaded the introduction of technology or product innovations in their firms (e.g., new management information systems).[76] This research compared "project champions" with non-champions who had also worked on the same project. The champions had very broad interests and saw their roles as being broad. They were very active in scouting for new ideas, using a wide variety of media for stimulation. They were skilled at presenting the innovation in question as an opportunity rather than framing it as countering a threat (e.g., "This will give us a whole new line of business" versus "This will keep us from getting sued"). Also, they exhibited clear signs of transformational leadership (Chapter 9), using charisma, inspiration, and intellectual stimulation to get people to see the potential of the innovation. They used a wide variety of influence tactics to gain support for the new system. In short, the champions made people truly want the innovation despite its disruption of the status quo.

Some idea champions feel compelled to engage in **creative deviance**, which means they defy orders by management to stop work on a creative idea. This sometimes involves "bootlegging" funds from other (approved) projects or camouflaging one's creative work from management scrutiny. Creative successes as diverse as the production of *The Godfather* to the advent of LED lighting have been attributed to creative deviance.[77]

> **Creative deviance.**
> Defying orders by management to stop working on a creative idea.

EXTERNAL COMMUNICATION Effective communication with the external environment and effective communication within the organization are vital for successful innovation.

The most innovative firms seem to be those that are best at recognizing the relevance of new, external information, importing and assimilating this information, and then applying it.[78] You might recall from earlier in the chapter that such processes are consistent with organizational learning. Experience shows that recognition and assimilation are a lot more chaotic and informal than one might imagine. Rather than relying on a formal network of journal articles, technical reports, and internal memoranda, technical personnel are more likely to be exposed to new ideas via informal oral communication networks. In these networks, key

Gatekeepers. People who span organizational boundaries to import new information, translate it for local use, and disseminate it.

personnel function as **gatekeepers** who span the boundary between the organization and the environment, importing new information, translating it for local use, and disseminating it to project members. These people tend to have well-developed communication networks with other professionals outside the organization and with the professionals on their own team or project. Thus, they are in key positions to both receive and transmit new technical or scientific information.[79] "Well developed" does not necessarily mean large. Strong ties with a sparse but diverse network seem to be key.[80] Also, they are perceived as highly competent and as a good source of new ideas. Furthermore, they have an innovative orientation, they read extensively, and they can tolerate ambiguity.[81] It is important to note that gatekeeping is essentially an informal, emergent role, since many gatekeepers are not in supervisory positions.

Organizations can do several things to enhance the external contact of actual or potential gatekeepers. Generous allowances for subscriptions, telephone use, and database access might be helpful. The same applies to travel allowances for seminars, short courses, and professional meetings.

Technical gatekeepers are not the only means of extracting information from the environment. Many successful innovative firms excel at going directly to users, clients, or customers to obtain ideas for product or service innovation. This works against the development of technically sound ideas that nobody wants, and it also provides some real focus for getting ideas implemented quickly. For example, Nike uses internet-based engagement platforms designed around global customer experiences, such as enthusiasm for soccer or running. These "communities" of customers possess creativity that can find its way into new Nike designs.[82] Willie G. Davidson, recently retired chief styling officer and grandson of one of the founders of Harley-Davidson, got ideas from customers at Harley-Davidson bike rallies, where he often walked around with a notebook in hand and had one-on-one sessions with customers.[83] Notice that we are speaking here about truly getting "close to the customer," not simply doing abstract market research on large samples of people. Such market research does not have a great track record in prompting innovation; talking directly to users does.

Information can also be extracted from the environment by hiring employees with multicultural experience or providing opportunities for such experience, which has been shown to enhance creativity.[84] Also, research shows that firms that put their R&D activities in several geographic locations exhibit higher levels of imitative innovation, because they can access a broader set of knowledge.[85] For instance, appliance giant Whirlpool has design centres in Shanghai; Milan; New Delhi; São Paulo; Monterrey, Mexico; and Benton Harbor, Michigan.[86]

INTERNAL COMMUNICATION Now that we have covered the importation of information into the organization, let's focus on the requirements of *internal* communication for innovation. At least during the idea-generation and early design phase, the more the better. Thus, it is generally true that organic structures (Chapter 14) facilitate innovation more easily than mechanistic structures.[87] Decentralization, informality, and a lack of bureaucracy all foster the exchange of information that innovation requires. To this mixture, add small project teams or business units and a diversity of member backgrounds to stimulate cross-fertilization of ideas. One study of more than 211 000 patents found that the exchange of knowledge between the divisions of diversified firms resulted in the most cited patents.[88] Inter-division communication is a driver of innovation.

In general, internal communication can be stimulated with in-house training, cross-functional transfers, and varied job assignments.[89] One study even found that the actual physical location of gatekeepers was important to their ability to convey new information to co-workers.[90] This suggests the clustering of offices and the use of common lounge areas as a means of facilitating communication. Organizations could give equal thought to the design of electronic communication media.

One especially interesting line of research suggests just how important communication is to the performance of research and development project groups.[91] This research found that

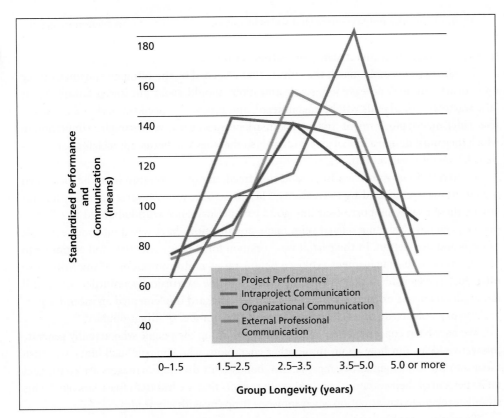

EXHIBIT 16.10
Group longevity, communication, and performance of research and development groups.
Source: From Katz, R. (1992). The effects of group longevity on project communication and performance, Figure 3: Standardized Performance and Communication Means as a Function of Group Longevity. *Administrative Science Quarterly, 27(1),* p. 96. By permission of © Johnson Graduate School of Management, Cornell University.

Explore

Go to MyManagementLab to see an annotated version of this figure.

groups with members who had worked together a short time or a long time engaged in less communication (within the group, within the organization, and externally) than groups that had medium longevity. In turn, performance mirrored communication, the high-communicating, medium-longevity groups being the best performers (Exhibit 16.10). Evidently, when groups are new, it takes time for members to decide what information they require and to forge the appropriate communication networks. When groups get "old," they sometimes get comfortable and isolate themselves from critical sources of feedback. Understand that the age of the group is at issue here, not the age of the employees or their tenure in the organization.

Although organic structures seem best in the idea-generation and design phases of innovation, more mechanistic structures are often better for actually implementing innovations.[92] Thinking up new computer programs is an organic task. Marketing them and distributing them online requires more bureaucratic procedures. This transition is important. Although audio and video recording innovations were pioneered in the United States, it was the Japanese who successfully implemented recording products in the marketplace. In part, this stemmed from a recognition of the different organizational requirements for idea generation versus idea implementation.

RESOURCES AND REWARDS Despite the romance surrounding the development of innovations on a shoestring using unauthorized, "bootlegged" funds, abundant resources greatly enhance the chances of successful innovation. Not only do these resources provide funds in the obvious sense, they also serve as a strong cultural symbol that the organization truly supports innovation.[93]

Funds for innovation are seen as an *investment*, not a *cost*. Several observers have noted that such a culture is most likely when the availability of funding is anarchic and multisourced—that is, because innovative ideas often encounter resistance from the status quo under the best of circumstances, innovators should have the opportunity to seek support from more than one source. At 3M, for instance, intrapreneurs can seek support from their own division, from another division, from corporate R&D, or from a new ventures group.[94] (Notice how other idea champions might be cultivated during this process.)

Money is not the only resource that spurs innovation. *Time* can be an even more crucial factor for some innovations. At Google, employees can devote up to 20 percent of work time to any personal project that will help advertisers or users.[95]

Reward systems must match the culture that is seeded by the resource system. Coming up with new ideas is no easy job, so organizations should avoid punishing failure. Many false starts with dead ends will be encountered, and innovators need support and constructive criticism, not punishment. In fact, Hallmark puts its executives through a simulation in which they must design a line of greeting cards so that they can better appreciate the frustrations felt by the creative staff.

A survey of research scientists found that freedom and autonomy were the *most* cited organizational factors leading to creativity.[96] Since intrinsic motivation is necessary for creativity, these results support rewarding good past performance with enhanced freedom to pursue personal ideas. In a related vein, many organizations have wised up about extrinsic rewards and innovation. In the past, it was common for creative scientists and engineers to have to move into management ranks to obtain raises and promotions. Many firms now offer dual career ladders that enable these people to be extrinsically rewarded while still doing actual science or engineering. When Hewlett-Packard implemented an incentive program to pay researchers for each patent they filed, the number of filings doubled.[97]

We have been concerned here mainly with rewarding the people who actually generate innovative ideas. But how about those other champions who sponsor such ideas and push them into the implementation stage? At 3M, bonuses for division managers are contingent on 25 percent of their revenues coming from products that are less than five years old.[98] This stimulates them to pay attention when someone drops by with a new idea.

To summarize this section, we can conclude that innovation depends on individual factors (creativity), social factors (a dedicated champion and good communication), and organizational factors (resources and rewards).

Diffusing Innovative Ideas

LO **16.9**

Understand the factors that help and hurt the diffusion of innovations.

Diffusion. The process by which innovations move through an organization.

Many innovations, especially process innovations, begin as limited experiments in one section or division of an organization. This is a cautious and reasonable approach. For example, a company might introduce new automated technology for evaluation in one plant of its multi-plant organization. Similarly, an insurance company might begin a limited exploration of job enrichment by concentrating only on clerical jobs at the head office. If such efforts are judged successful, it seems logical to extend them to other parts of the organization. **Diffusion** is the process by which innovations move through an organization. However, this is not always as easy as it might seem!

Richard Walton of Harvard University studied the diffusion of eight major process innovations in firms such as Volvo, Alcan, General Foods, Corning, and Shell UK. Each effort was rigorous and broad-based, generally including changes in job design, compensation, and supervision.[99] All the pilot projects that Walton studied were initially judged successful, and each received substantial publicity, a factor that often contributes to increased commitment to further change. Despite this, substantial diffusion occurred in only one of the observed firms—Volvo. What accounted for this poor record of diffusion?

- Lack of support and commitment from top management.
- Significant differences between the technology or setting of the pilot project and those of other units in the organization, raising arguments that "it won't work here."
- Attempts to diffuse particular *techniques* rather than *goals* that could be tailored to other situations.
- Management reward systems that concentrate on traditional performance measures while ignoring success at implementing innovation.

- Union resistance to extending the negotiated "exceptions" in the pilot project.

- Fears that pilot projects begun in non-unionized locations could not be implemented in unionized portions of the firm.

- Conflict between the pilot project and the bureaucratic structures in the rest of the firm (e.g., pay policies and staffing requirements).

Because of these problems, Walton raises the depressing spectre of a "diffuse or die" principle. That is, if diffusion does not occur, the pilot project and its leaders become more and more isolated from the mainstream of the organization and less and less able to proceed alone. As we noted earlier, innovation can be a highly politicized process. Several of the barriers to diffusion that Walton cites were implicated in limiting the influence that the innovative Saturn project had on General Motors, including top management changes, union resistance, and competition for resources from old-line GM divisions.

Some research suggests that innovations are especially difficult to diffuse in organizations dominated by professionals, who tend to focus on their own "silos." Thus, in hospitals, doctors, nurses, and physiotherapists can have trouble working as multi-disciplinary teams to introduce new practices.[100]

One classic review suggests that the following factors are critical determinants of the rate of diffusion of a wide variety of innovations:[101]

- *Relative advantage.* Diffusion is more likely when the new idea is perceived as truly better than the one it replaces.

- *Compatibility.* Diffusion is easier when the innovation is compatible with the values, beliefs, needs, and current practices of potential new adopters.

- *Complexity.* Complex innovations that are fairly difficult to comprehend and use are less likely to diffuse.

- *Trialability.* If an innovation can be given a limited trial run, its chances of diffusion will be improved.

- *Observability.* When the consequences of an innovation are more visible, diffusion will be more likely to occur.

To this list we might add *adaptability*, since innovations often have to be custom-tailored to diffuse effectively.[102] In combination, these determinants suggest that there is considerable advantage to thinking about how innovations are "packaged" and "sold" so as to increase their chances of more widespread adoption. Also, they suggest the value of finding strong champions to sponsor the innovation at the new site.

A FOOTNOTE: THE KNOWING–DOING GAP

Despite the need for organizations to change, develop, and innovate, they often exhibit considerable inertia. This is particularly ironic in that managers are better educated than ever, and there are well-developed bodies of research (many documented in your text) showing that some management practices are better than others. In addition, short courses, consulting firms, and popular books by management gurus frequently describe in detail the "best practices" of successful firms in various industries. Thus, it seems that many managers know what to do, but have considerable trouble *implementing* this knowledge in the form of action. In a very insightful book, Jeffrey Pfeffer and Robert Sutton describe this situation as the *knowing–doing gap*.[103] To take just one of their examples, they note that the much admired and highly efficient Toyota Production System (TPS) has been featured in many books and articles. Toyota readily gives plant tours to illustrate its features. Despite this, firms have had considerable trouble in trying to imitate Toyota.

Why does the knowing–doing gap happen? Pfeffer and Sutton cite a number of reasons. One is the tendency for some organizational cultures to reward short-term talk rather than longer-term action. Meetings, presentations, documentation, and mission statements thus take precedence over action and experimentation. This is only reinforced when mistrust permeates a firm and employees fear reprisals for mistakes. Also, many changes require cooperation between organizational units, but many organizations foster internal competition that is not conducive to such cooperation. Finally, Pfeffer and Sutton note that when managers do manage to make changes, these changes sometimes fail because techniques are adopted without an understanding of their underlying philosophy. For instance, the TPS is based in part on TQM principles described earlier in this chapter, but some observers just see visible manifestations such as the cords that workers can pull to stop the assembly line. Similarly, one of the authors once heard a consultant say that one of his clients was all in favour of teamwork but did not want to actually implement any teams!

We hope that our book has provided you with the knowing. Now it's your turn to do the doing!

THE MANAGER'S NOTEBOOK

Changing the Face of the Victoria Police Force

1. Although the Victoria Police Force had tried to change its culture in the 1980s and 1990s, the changes were short-lived and not very successful. The culture was so entrenched that change seemed impossible. In 2000, although expensive programs were put in place, the downsizing of the force compounded employee resistance to change because many officers were overworked and in fear of losing their jobs. Opening up the force to women and visible minorities added to this fear. Additionally, understanding the business case for change can be challenging in public service organizations because many of the benefits of diversity are measured in non-financial ways. The leadership at the time was unable to see past the risks of change and appreciate the rewards of inclusivity. By hiring Christine Nixon, the VPF sent a clear message to both the force itself and the community at large. The hiring emphasized the VPF's commitment to enhancing the presence of women in the force and the need for sustainable human resource change. Although gaining immediate respect from the officers in the force was clearly going to be a challenge, Nixon was able to take advantage of her outsider status by changing the rules of the game. Without the burden of previous relationships, Nixon was free to design and implement an organizational change effort on her own terms.

2. As a transformational leader, Nixon took a long-term view of the VPF's organizational change. First, she defined a set of priorities (diversity, inclusivity, and community involvement) that were clear and achievable. Second, she embodied these priorities by establishing a two-way dialogue with the VPF employees and the community at large. Through ongoing and broad communication initiatives, she consistently emphasized the importance of the change initiative and the benefits it would bring. By identifying "The Force Issues" and handing over resolution to the project teams, she was able to encourage a diverse set of solutions to many of the problems. To initiate the unfreezing process, she made immediate changes that signalled to the employees and the community that past behaviours would no longer be tolerated. Simple changes such as changing the way she was addressed (i.e., "Christine" in lieu of "Ma'am") and leading officers in the gay and lesbian parade symbolically represented the dramatic changes that were underway. Two years into her tenure, Nixon established six key values: integrity, leadership, flexibility, respect, support, and professionalism. These values reinforced the behavioural changes needed to move through the change phase into the refreezing phase. To this day, these values represent the VPF's new culture and are the foundation for the force's strategic plan, which seems to be working: the 2007–2008 VPF annual report indicated that women police officers and recruits accounted for over 23 percent of the force, up from 16.5 percent in 2001. As the strategic change agent, Nixon never faltered in her objectives.

LEARNING OBJECTIVES CHECKLIST

16.1 All organizations must change because of forces in the external and internal environments. Although more environmental change usually requires more organizational change, organizations can exhibit too much change as well as too little. Organizations can change goals and strategies, technology, job design, structure, processes, culture, and people. People changes should almost always accompany changes in other factors.

16.2 Organizations learn through the acquisition, distribution, and interpretation of knowledge that already exists but is external to the organization, and through the development of new knowledge that occurs in an organization primarily through dialogue and experience. *Learning organizations* have systems and processes for creating, acquiring, and transferring knowledge throughout the organization to modify and change behaviour.

16.3 The general *change process* involves unfreezing current attitudes and behaviours, changing them, and then refreezing the newly acquired attitudes and behaviours. Several key issues or problems must be dealt with during the general change process. One is accurate diagnosis of the current situation. Another is the resistance that might be provoked by unfreezing and change. A third issue is performing an adequate evaluation of the success of the change effort. Many such evaluations are weak or non-existent.

16.4 Organizations can deal with *resistance to change* by being supportive, providing clear and up-front communication about the details of the intended change, involving those who are targets of the change in the change process, and by co-opting reluctant individuals by giving them a special or desirable role in the change process or by negotiating special incentives for change. Transformational leaders are particularly adept at overcoming resistance to change.

16.5 *Organizational development (OD)* is a planned, ongoing effort to change organizations to be more effective and more human. It uses the knowledge of behavioural science to foster a culture of organizational self-examination and readiness for change. A strong emphasis is placed on interpersonal and group processes.

16.6 Four popular OD techniques are team building, survey feedback, total quality management, and reengineering. *Team building* attempts to increase the effectiveness of work teams by concentrating on interpersonal processes, goal clarification, and role clarification. *Survey feedback* requires organizational members to generate data that are fed back to them as a basis for inducing change. *Total quality management (TQM)* is an attempt to achieve continuous improvement in the quality of products or services. *Reengineering* is the radical redesign of organizational processes to achieve major improvements in time, cost, quality, or service.

16.7 The careful evaluation of OD programs poses special challenges to researchers. OD efforts involve a complex series of changes, so it is difficult to know exactly what changes produce changes in processes or outcomes. Novelty effects or the fact that participants receive special treatment might produce short-term gains that really do not persist over time. Self-reports of changes after OD might involve unconscious attempts to please the change agent, and organizations might be reluctant to publicize failures.

16.8 *Innovation* is the process of developing and implementing new ideas in an organization. It can include new products, new processes, and new management practices. Innovation requires individual creativity and adequate resources and rewards to stimulate and channel that creativity. Also, *idea champions* who recognize and sponsor creative ideas are critical. Finally, internal and external communication is important for innovation. The role of gatekeepers who import and disseminate technical information is especially noteworthy.

16.9 Innovations will diffuse most easily when they are not too complex, can be given a trial run, are compatible with existing practices, and offer a visible advantage over current practices. Factors that can hurt diffusion include a lack of support and commitment from top management, reward systems that focus on traditional performance and ignore success at implementing innovation, union resistance, and conflict between pilot projects and the bureaucratic structures in the rest of the organization.

DISCUSSION QUESTIONS

1. Describe an example of resistance to change that you have observed. Why did it occur?

2. You have been charged with staffing and organizing an R&D group in a new high-tech firm. What will you do to ensure that the group is innovative?

3. What qualities would the ideal gatekeeper possess to facilitate the communication of technical information in his or her firm?

4. Suppose a job enrichment effort in one plant of a manufacturing firm is judged to be very successful. You are the corporate change agent responsible for the project, and you wish to diffuse it to other plants that have a similar technology. How would you sell the project to other plant managers? What kinds of resistance might you encounter?

5. What personal qualities and skills would be useful for an OD change agent to possess? Describe the relative merits of using an internal staff change agent versus an external consultant.

6. Discuss: The best organizational structure to generate innovative ideas might not be the best structure to implement those ideas.

7. Discuss some of the things that an organization can do to improve organizational learning and to become a learning organization. What should organizations know about the linkages between organizational learning and change and innovation?

8. Debate: Survey feedback can be a problematic OD technique because it permits people who are affected by organizational policies to generate data that speak against those policies.

INTEGRATIVE DISCUSSION QUESTIONS

1. Do leadership, organizational culture, and communication influence the effectiveness of organizational change programs? Discuss the effect that leadership behaviour, strong cultures, and personal and organizational approaches to communication have on the change process and change problems. What should organizations do in terms of leadership, culture, and communication to overcome problems and ensure that the change process is effective?

2. How can organizational learning practices, pay, and socialization influence organizational learning and innovation in organizations? Design a program to improve an organization's ability to learn or generate and implement innovative ideas that combines organizational learning practices (Chapter 2), pay systems (Chapter 6), and socialization methods (Chapter 8). What effect does organizational culture have on an organization's ability to learn and innovate?

3. Review the chapter-opening vignette on Best Buy and identify some of the most relevant issues that have been covered in previous chapters. In particular, consider the vignette in terms of some of the following topics: Learning (Chapter 2), Perceptions (Chapter 3), Groups and teamwork (Chapter 7), Culture (Chapter 8), Leadership (Chapter 9), Communication (Chapter 10), Organizational structure (Chapter 14), and Strategy (Chapter 15).

ON-THE-JOB CHALLENGE QUESTION

The Hacker Way at Facebook

Facebook's campus in Menlo Park, California, includes a large sign reading *The Hacker Company* and a giant HACK configured into the surface of one of its many pedestrian plazas. Founder Mark Zuckerberg is fond of extolling the virtues of the Hacker Way, an obsessive-compulsive need to change, fix, and improve systems, rejecting the status quo even in the face of outright resistance or claims that some innovation is impossible to accomplish. The company often sponsors Hackathons in which teams of employees work together to design a new concept in a short spurt of creativity. In fact, the Facebook Timeline service was conceived in a Hackathon.

Given that Facebook itself is the frequent target of malicious hacking, Zuckerberg's use of the term and glorification of the spirit of hacking is ironic. Why does he extol the Hacker Way? How is it connected to the concept of organizational learning? What does it signal to organizational insiders and outsiders about change and innovation?

Source: Hartley, M. (2012, March 19). Facebook makes room for everyone. *National Post*, FP3.

EXPERIENTIAL EXERCISE

Measuring Tolerance for Ambiguity

Please read each of the following statements carefully. Then use the following scale to rate each of them in terms of the extent to which you either agree or disagree with the statement.

Completely disagree		Neither agree nor disagree			Completely agree	
1	2	3	4	5	6	7

Place the number that best describes your degree of agreement or disagreement in the blank to the left of each statement.

____ 1. An expert who does not come up with a definite answer probably does not know too much.

____ 2. I would like to live in a foreign country for a while.

____ 3. The sooner we all acquire similar values and ideals, the better.

____ 4. A good teacher is one who makes you wonder about your way of looking at things.

____ 5. I like parties where I know most of the people more than ones where all or most of the people are complete strangers.

____ 6. Teachers or supervisors who hand out vague assignments give a chance for one to show initiative and originality.

____ 7. A person who leads an even, regular life in which few surprises or unexpected happenings arise really has a lot to be grateful for.

____ 8. Many of our most important decisions are based on insufficient information.

____ 9. There is really no such thing as a problem that cannot be solved.

____ 10. People who fit their lives to a schedule probably miss most of the joy of living.

____ 11. A good job is one in which what is to be done and how it is to be done are always clear.

____ 12. It is more fun to tackle a complicated problem than to solve a simple one.

____ 13. In the long run, it is possible to get more done by tackling small, simple problems than large and complicated ones.

____ 14. Often the most interesting and stimulating people are those who do not mind being different and original.

____ 15. What we are used to is always preferable to what is unfamiliar.

____ 16. People who insist on a yes or no answer just do not know how complicated things really are.

Scoring and Interpretation

You have just completed the Tolerance for Ambiguity Scale. It was adapted by Paul Nutt from original work by S. Budner. The survey asks about personal and work-oriented situations that involve various degrees of ambiguity. To score your own survey, add 8 to each of your responses to the odd numbered items. Then, add up the renumbered *odd* items. From this total, subtract your score from the sum of the *even* numbered items. Your score should fall between 16 and 112. People with lower scores are tolerant of and even enjoy ambiguous situations. People with high scores are intolerant of ambiguity and prefer more structured situations. In Paul Nutt's research, people typically scored between 20 and 80, with a mean around 45. People with a high tolerance for ambiguity respond better to change.

They also tend to be more creative and innovative than those with low tolerance for ambiguity.

Source: From Nutt, P. (1989). *Making tough* decisions. John Wiley & Sons. Reprinted with permission of John Wiley & Sons, Inc.

CASE INCIDENT

Dandy Toys

Company president George Reed had built a successful toy company called Dandy Toys, which specialized in manufacturing inexpensive imitations of more expensive products. However, with increasing domestic and global competition, he became concerned that his cheap imitations would not be enough to maintain the company's current success. George decided to call a meeting with all the company's managers to express his concerns. He told them that Dandy Toys must change and become more innovative in its products. He told the managers that rather than just knock off other companies' toys, they must come up with creative and innovative ideas for new and more upscale toys. "By the end of this year," George told the managers, "Dandy Toys must begin making its own in-house designed quality toys." When the managers left the meeting, they were surprised, and some were even shocked, about this new direction for Dandy Toys.

Although a few of the managers suggested some ideas for new toys during the next couple of months,

nobody really seemed interested. In fact, business pretty much continued as always at Dandy Toys, and by the end of the year not a single new in-house toy had been made.

1. Comment on the change process at Dandy Toys. What advice would you give the president about how to improve the change process? What are some of the things that might be changed at Dandy Toys as part of the change process?

2. Why wasn't the innovation process more successful at Dandy Toys, and what can be done to improve it?

3. Consider the relevance of organizational learning for change and innovation at Dandy Toys. What should the company do to improve learning and will this help to create change and improve innovation?

CASE STUDY

First Canadian Club

Sally Newton was the only purchasing officer of First Canadian Club, a fitness club with 20 centres scattered around Canada. In February 1988, she was thinking of how to handle the resistance coming from some centre managers, especially the "alliance" of three Toronto centres, to the newly introduced centralized purchasing system designed by her one month earlier.

First Canadian Club

First Canadian Club was founded in 1979 and owned by Mr. Jim Stewart, a business administration graduate from the University of Western Ontario. At the age of 25, he opened his first fitness centre in Toronto, Ontario. Over the past 10 years, the club had been growing gradually, and in 1988, it had 20 centres scattered around Canada. The head office, however, remained in Waterloo.

Locations of the 20 Fitness Centres of the First Canadian Club

Location	Number of Centres
Kingston, Ontario	1
Jonquière, Quebec	1
Laval, Quebec	2
London, Ontario	2
North Bay, Ontario	1
Ottawa, Ontario	1
Peterborough, Ontario	2
Sarnia, Ontario	1
Sault Ste. Marie, Ontario	1
Sudbury, Ontario	1
Toronto, Ontario	3
Waterloo, Ontario	1 (including head office)
Windsor, Ontario	2
Winnipeg, Manitoba	1
Total	20

Sally Newton

Sally Newton was 24. Right after earning a diploma in psychology from Fanshawe College, London, Ontario, she joined First Canadian Club in January 1988 as the purchasing officer of the club. Her job responsibilities included the administration of purchasing and inventory control. Before her college studies, she had a number of years of work experience in various areas but none of them specifically related to purchasing or inventory control. As she said herself, "This is my first job in this area."

The Purchase System in First Canadian Club Before Sally Newton

"If there was really a purchasing system in the First Canadian Club before Sally came, I could only say it was a very, very loose one," one staff member commented.

First Canadian Club needed many different kinds of items to keep its centres running. They ranged from parts for machines and equipment like bike parts and suntan bulbs to stationery supplies and toiletries. Before Sally joined the club, each centre was responsible for its own purchasing. Most centres did not keep any inventory and purchased items on an ad hoc basis (i.e., buy when needed at a nearby store). In the head office, there was a part-time employee also doing the purchasing and inventory control job but only for the head office. She did not purchase items for the other 19 centres, but kept records for them.

Sally Newton's New Centralized Purchasing System

During her first week in the First Canadian Club, Sally examined the two binders that were left by the part-time employee. She was surprised to find that the club was using the centre-based ad hoc basis purchasing system and thought that a centralized one might work in this situation. She talked to her boss about this idea, and her boss encouraged her to investigate further.

She then went to do some research work on it and found that a centralized purchasing system could really save a considerable amount of money for the club. For example, she found a supplier that would reduce the cost of toiletry purchases by nearly 50 percent if the club bought in bulk through it. Therefore, along with searching for more suppliers for different items, she spent time on developing the details of the centralized purchasing system.

Basically, the new system that Sally had designed centralized all purchases in the head office. Instead of each centre buying its own supplies, the centre manager was asked to fill in an order form and fax it to the head office. The deadline was 5 o'clock on Monday every week, and the items requested would be sent to the requesting centre on the following Monday. Sally had the authority to disapprove or reduce the amount requested if she thought it was not justified. However, each centre was allowed to have petty cash of one hundred dollars for making any urgent purchases.

By the end of January, she finished the plan, which was approved by her boss immediately. She notified all 20 centres with a memo that explained the reasons for the new purchasing system and the procedures for making the change.

Resistance Received from Centre Managers

After about one month of implementation, Sally was a bit frustrated by the resistance from some of the centre managers. Some managers did not use the order form but just called in right away when they needed some items. The most difficult problem was that the three fitness centres in Toronto "joined" together and resisted changing to the new system.

Sally was thinking of how to handle this situation, especially how to tackle the problem of the "alliance" of the three Toronto centres.

Source: Case prepared by Professor Patrick Yam Keung Chau, University of Hong Kong. Used with permission.

QUESTIONS

1. Was Sally Newton's decision to centralize purchasing technically sound? That is, is this the kind of task that lends itself to centralization? Please explain your answers.
2. Did Sally do a good job of introducing the change to the local fitness centre managers? Could she have used other tactics?
3. Explain the motives for resistance. Why are the local centres against this change?
4. The new purchasing system is an innovation for First Canadian Club. In that context, explain why this innovation is not diffusing throughout the business.
5. Could team building be helpful in dealing with the resistance to this innovation? If so, how and why?
6. Sally is especially concerned about the "Toronto alliance." Could she use it to her advantage?
7. What should Sally do now?

INTEGRATIVE CASE

Deloitte & Touche: Integrating Arthur Andersen

At the end of Part Three of the textbook, on Social Behaviour and Organizational Processes, you answered a number of questions about the Deloitte & Touche Integrative Case that dealt with issues related to groups, socialization and culture, leadership, communication, conflict, and stress. Now that you have completed Part Four and the chapters on The Total Organization, you can return to the Integrative Case and enhance your understanding of some of the main issues associated with the total organization by answering the following questions that deal with organizational structure, the external environment and strategy, and organizational change.

QUESTIONS

1. How would you classify the organizational structures of Deloitte and Andersen? Why is Deloitte structured the way it is?

2. Discuss the role that the external environment played in the integration of the two firms. What constraints and opportunities led to the integration? Do you think that the integration of the two firms was an effective strategic response for each firm? Explain your answer and in doing so consider other forms of strategic responses.
3. There seems to be some resistance to change coming from Deloitte staff. What might account for this?
4. Deloitte has been using Pulse Surveys during the change, and at the end of the case Noble muses about taking employees "to an offsite location" to deal with cultural differences. This latter strategy suggests the possibility of team building. Discuss the merits of surveys and team building to enhance integration. What would you recommend and why?

APPENDIX

RESEARCH IN ORGANIZATIONAL BEHAVIOUR

LEARNING OBJECTIVES

After reading the Appendix, you should be able to:

A.1 Explain what *a hypothesis* is and define the meaning of a *variable*.

A.2 Distinguish between *independent* and *dependent variables* and *moderating* and *mediating variables*.

A.3 Differentiate *reliability* from *validity* and *convergent validity* from *discriminant validity*.

A.4 Understand *observational research* and distinguish between *participant* and *direct observation*.

A.5 Describe *correlational research* and explain why causation cannot be inferred from correlation.

A.6 Explain *experimental research* and the meaning of *internal validity*, and discuss threats to internal validity.

A.7 Discuss the relative advantages and disadvantages of different research techniques.

A.8 Describe *random sampling, random assignment,* and *external validity* and the role they play in the research process.

A.9 Explain *quasi-experimental design* and how it differs from experimental research.

A.10 Explain the *Hawthorne effect* and how it can occur.

A.11 Discuss the basic ethical concerns to which researchers must attend.

Research is a way of finding out about the world through objective and systematic information gathering. The key words here are *objective* and *systematic*, and it is these characteristics that separate the outcomes of the careful study of organizational behaviour from opinion and common sense.

Understanding how researchers conduct their research is important to the study of organizational behaviour for several reasons. First of all, you should be aware of how the information presented in this book was collected. This should increase your confidence in the advantages of systematic study over common sense. Second, you will likely encounter reports, in management periodicals and the popular press, of interventions to improve organizational behaviour, such as job redesign or employee development programs. A critical perspective is necessary to differentiate those interventions that are carefully designed and evaluated from useless or even damaging ones. Those backed by good research deserve the greatest confidence. Occasionally, a manager may have to evaluate a research proposal or consultant's intervention to be carried out in his or her own organization. A brief introduction to research methodology should enable you to ask some intelligent questions about such plans

Trained behavioural scientists who have backgrounds in management, applied psychology, or applied sociology carry out research in organizational behaviour. While this introduction will not make you a trained behavioural scientist, it should provide an appreciation of the work that goes into generating accurate knowledge about organizational behaviour.

Explain what a *hypothesis* is and define the meaning of a *variable*.

Hypothesis. A formal statement of the expected relationship between two variables.

Variables. Measures that can take on two or more values.

Distinguish between *independent* and *dependent variables* and *moderating* and *mediating variables*.

Independent variable. The variable that predicts or is the cause of variation in a dependent variable.

Dependent variable. The variable that is expected to vary as a result of changes to the independent variable.

Moderating variable. A variable that affects the nature of the relationship between an independent and a dependent variable such that the relationship depends on the level of the moderating variable.

Mediating variable. A variable that intervenes or explains the relationship between an independent and a dependent variable.

THE BASICS OF ORGANIZATIONAL BEHAVIOUR RESEARCH

All research in organizational behaviour begins with a question about work or organizations. Sometimes this question might stem from a formal theory in the field. For example, a motivation theory called equity theory (see Chapter 5) is concerned with people's reactions to fairness or lack of it. Equity theory suggests the following research question: What do people do when they perceive their pay to be too low in comparison to other people's pay? Other times, a research question might stem from an immediate organizational problem. For example, a human resources manager might ask herself: How can we reduce absenteeism among our customer service employees?

Often, research questions are expressed as hypotheses. A **hypothesis** is a formal statement of the expected relationship between two variables. **Variables** are simply measures that can take on two or more values. Temperature is a variable, but so are pay, fairness, and absenteeism. A formal hypothesis stemming from equity theory might be this: The less fair people perceive their pay to be, the more likely they will be to resign their jobs. Here, a variable that can take on many values, perceived fairness, is linked to a variable made up of two values, staying or leaving. The human resources manager might develop this hypothesis: The introduction of a small attendance bonus will reduce absenteeism. Here, a variable with two values, bonus versus no bonus, is related to one that can take on many values, days of absenteeism.

Types of Variables

In most research, we are concerned with two kinds of variables: the independent variable and the dependent variable. The **independent variable** is a predictor or cause of variation in a dependent variable. The **dependent variable** is a variable that will vary as a result of changes in the independent variable. So in the first example, pay fairness perceptions is the independent variable and resigning is the dependent variable. In the second example, the attendance bonus is the independent variable and absenteeism is the dependent variable. In both cases, scores on the dependent variable are expected to vary as a function of scores on the independent variable.

Two other kinds of variables that we are sometimes interested in are mediating variables and moderating variables. A **moderating variable** is a variable that affects the nature of the relationship between an independent and a dependent variable such that the relationship depends on the level of the moderating variable. Moderating variables are like contingency variables in that they indicate when an independent variable is most likely to be related to a dependent variable. In the example above about the attendance bonus, a moderating variable might be pay satisfaction. If the attendance bonus only reduces the absenteeism of employees who are *not* satisfied with their pay and has no effect on the absenteeism of employees who *are* satisfied with their pay, then we would conclude that pay satisfaction moderates the effect of the bonus on absenteeism.

Sometimes we want to know why an independent variable predicts or causes a dependent variable. In such cases, we are interested in a mediating variable. A **mediating variable** is a variable that intervenes or explains the relationship between an independent and a dependent variable. To return to the attendance bonus example, we might want to know why the bonus reduces absenteeism. One possibility might be that the bonus increases people's *perceived fairness*. Thus, fairness perceptions intervene or mediate the relationship between the attendance bonus and absenteeism.

Measurement of Variables

Good researchers carefully measure the variables they choose. For one thing, a measure should exhibit high reliability. **Reliability** is an index of the consistency of a research subject's responses. For example, if we ask someone several questions about how fair his or her pay is, the person should respond roughly the same way to each question. Similarly, the person should respond roughly the same way to the same questions next week or next month if there has been no change in pay.

Measures should also exhibit high validity. **Validity** is an index of the extent to which a measure truly reflects what it is supposed to measure. For instance, a good measure of perceived pay fairness should not be influenced by employees' feelings of fairness about other workplace factors, such as supervision. Also, a researcher would expect people who are objectively underpaid to report high pay unfairness and for them to report increased fairness if their pay were increased. Researchers are often able to choose measures with a known history of reliability and validity.

Good measures should also be strongly related to other measures of the same variable and should not be related to measures of different variables. For example, a measure of job satisfaction should be highly correlated to other measures of job satisfaction. This is known as **convergent validity**, and it exists when there is a strong relationship between different measures of the same variable. In addition, good measures should not be related to measures of different variables. For example, a measure of job satisfaction should not be strongly related to measures of job performance. This is known as **discriminant validity**, and it exists when there is a weak relationship between measures of different variables. Good measures should have both convergent and discriminant validity. Thus, a measure of job satisfaction should be more strongly related to other measures of job satisfaction than to measures of job performance.

There are three basic kinds of research techniques: observation, correlation, and experimentation. As you will see, each begins with a research question or questions. Correlation and experimentation are most likely to test specific hypotheses and devote explicit attention to measurement quality.

OBSERVATIONAL TECHNIQUES

Observational research techniques are the most straightforward ways of finding out about behaviour in organizations and thus come closest to the ways in which we develop common-sense views about such behaviour. In this case, *observation* means just what it implies—the researcher proceeds to examine the natural activities of people in an organizational setting by listening to what they say and watching what they do. The difference between our everyday observations and the formal observations of the trained behavioural scientist is expressed by those key words *systematic* and *objective*.

First, the researcher approaches the organizational setting with extensive training concerning the nature of human behaviour and a particular set of questions that the observation is designed to answer. These factors provide a systematic framework for the business of observing. Second, the behavioural scientist attempts to keep a careful ongoing record of the events that he or she observes, either as they occur or as soon as possible afterwards. Thus, excessive reliance on memory, which may lead to inaccuracies, is unnecessary. Finally, the behavioural scientist is well informed of the dangers of influencing the behaviour of those under observation and is trained to draw reasonable conclusions from his or her observations. These factors help ensure objectivity.

LO

Differentiate *reliability* from *validity* and *convergent validity* from *discriminant validity*.

Reliability. An index of the consistency of a research subject's responses.

Validity. An index of the extent to which a measure truly reflects what it is supposed to measure.

Convergent validity. When there is a strong relationship between different measures of the same variable.

Discriminant validity. When there is a weak relationship between measures of different variables.

LO

Understand *observational research* and distinguish between *participant* and *direct observation*.

Observational research. Research that examines the natural activities of people in an organizational setting by listening to what they say and watching what they do.

The outcomes of observational research are summarized in a narrative form, sometimes called a *case study*. This narrative specifies the nature of the organization, people, and events studied; the particular role of and techniques used by the observer; the research questions; and the events observed. In some cases, an observer actively participates in the behaviour under observation, while in other cases he or she does not participate. Let's now consider each of these approaches.

Participant Observation

Participant observation. Observational research in which the researcher becomes a functioning member of the organizational unit being studied.

One obvious way for a researcher to find out about organizational behaviour is to actively participate in this behaviour. In **participant observation** the researcher becomes a functioning member of the organizational unit he or she is studying to conduct the research. At this point you may wonder, "Wait a minute. What about objectivity? What about influencing the behaviour of those being studied?" These are clearly legitimate questions, and they might be answered in the following way: In adopting participant observation, the researcher is making a conscious bet that the advantages of participation outweigh these problems. It is doubtless true in some cases that "there is no substitute for experience." For example, researcher Robert Sutton wanted to find out how employees cope with jobs that require them to express negative emotions.[1] To do this, he trained and then worked as a bill collector. This is obviously a more personal experience than simply interviewing bill collectors.

Another advantage to participant observation is its potential for secrecy—the participants need not know that they are being observed. This potential for secrecy does raise some ethical issues, however. Sociologist Tom Lupton served as an industrial worker in two plants in England to study the factors that influenced productivity.[2] Although he could have acted in secrecy, he was required to inform management and union officials of his presence to secure records and documents, and he thus felt it unfair not to inform his workmates of his purpose. It should be stressed that his goals were academic and that he was *not* working for the managements of the companies involved. Sometimes, however, secrecy seems necessary to accomplish a research goal, as the following study of "illegal" industrial behaviour shows.

Joseph Bensman and Israel Gerver investigated an important organizational problem: What happens when the activities that appear to be required to get a job done conflict with official organizational policy?[3] Examples of such conflicts include the punch press operator who must remove the safety guard from his machine to meet productivity standards, the executive who must deliver corporate money to a political slush fund, or the police officer who cannot find time to complete an eight-page report to justify having drawn her revolver on a night patrol.

The behaviour of interest to Bensman and Gerver was the unauthorized use of taps by aircraft plant workers. A tap is a hard steel hand tool used to cut threads into metal. The possession of this device by aircraft assemblers was strictly forbidden because the workers could use it to correct sloppy or difficult work like the misalignment of bolt holes in two pieces of aircraft skin or stripped lock nuts; both of these problems could lead to potential structural weaknesses or maintenance problems.

Possession of a tap was a strict violation of company policy, and a worker could be fired on the spot for it. On the other hand, since supervisors were under extreme pressure to maintain a high quota of completed work, the occasional use of a tap to correct a problem could save hours of disassembly and realignment time. How was this conflict resolved? The answer was provided by one of the authors, who served as a participant observer while functioning as an assembler. Put simply, the supervisors and inspectors worked together to encourage the cautious and appropriate use of taps. New workers were gradually introduced to the mysteries of tapping by experienced workers, and the supervisors provided refinement of skills and signals as to when a tap might be used. Taps were not to be used in front of inspectors or to correct chronic sloppy work. If "caught," tappers were expected to act truly penitent in response to a chewing out by the supervisors, even if the supervisors themselves had suggested the use of the tap. In short, a *social ritual* was developed to teach and control the use of the tap to facilitate getting the work out without endangering the continued presence of the crucial tool. Clearly, this is the kind of information about organizational behaviour that would be extremely difficult to obtain except by participant observation.

Direct Observation

In **direct observation** the researcher observes organizational behaviour without participation in the activity being observed. There are a number of reasons why one might choose direct observation over participant observation. First, there are many situations in which the introduction of a new person into an existing work setting would severely disrupt and change the nature of the activities in that setting. These are cases in which the "influence" criticism of participant observation is especially true. Second, there are many job tasks that a trained behavioural scientist could not be expected to learn for research purposes. For example, it seems unreasonable to expect a researcher to spend years acquiring the skills of a pilot or banker to be able to investigate what happens in the cockpit of an airliner or in a boardroom. Finally, participant observation places rather severe limitations on the observers' opportunity to record information. Existence of these conditions suggests the use of direct observation. In theory, the researcher could carry out such observation covertly, but there are few studies of organizational behaviour in which the presence of the direct observer was not known and explained to those being observed.

Direct observation. Observational research in which the researcher observes organizational behaviour without taking part in the studied activity.

Henry Mintzberg's study of the work performed by chief executives of two manufacturing companies, a hospital, a school system, and a consulting firm provides an excellent example of the use of direct observation.[4] At first glance, this might appear to be an inane thing to investigate. After all, everybody knows that managers plan, organize, lead, and control, or some similar combination of words. In fact, Mintzberg argues that we actually know very little about the routine, everyday behaviour managers use to achieve these vague goals. Furthermore, if we ask managers what they do (in an interview or questionnaire), they usually respond with a variation of the plan-organize-lead-control theme.

Mintzberg spent a week with each of his five executives, watching them at their desks, attending meetings with them, listening to their phone calls, and inspecting their mail. He kept detailed records of these activities and gradually developed a classification scheme to make sense of them. What Mintzberg found counters the common-sense view that some hold of managers—sitting behind a large desk, reflecting on their organization's performance, and affixing their signatures to impressive documents all day. In fact, Mintzberg found that his managers actually performed a terrific amount of work and had little time for reflection. On an average day, they examined 36 pieces of mail, engaged in five telephone conversations, attended eight meetings, and made one tour of their facilities. Work-related reading encroached on home lives. These activities were varied, unpatterned, and of short duration. Half the activities lasted less than nine minutes, and 90 percent less than one hour. Furthermore, these activities tended to be directed toward current, specific issues rather than past, general issues. Finally, the managers revealed a clear preference for verbal communications by either telephone or unscheduled face-to-face meetings; in fact, two-thirds of their contacts were of this nature. In contrast, they generated an average of only one piece of mail a day.

In summary, both participant and direct observation capture the depth, breadth, richness, spontaneity, and realism of organizational behaviour. However, they also share some weaknesses. One of these weaknesses is a lack of control over the environment in which the study is being conducted. Thus, Mintzberg could not ensure that unusual events would not affect the executives' behaviour. Also, the small number of observers and situations in the typical observational study is problematic. With only one observer, there is a strong potential for selective perceptions and interpretations of observed events. Since only a few situations are analyzed, the extent to which the observed behaviours can be generalized to other settings is limited. (Do most executives behave like the five that Mintzberg studied?) It is probably safe to say that observational techniques are best used to make an initial examination of some organizational event on which little information is available and to generate ideas for further investigation with more refined techniques. Let's now take a closer look at some of these more refined techniques.

Correlational Techniques

Correlational research attempts to measure variables precisely and examine relationships among these variables without introducing change into the research setting. Correlational research sacrifices some of the breadth and richness of the observational techniques for more precision of measurement and greater control. It necessarily involves some abstraction of the real event that is the focus of observation to accomplish this precision and control. More specifically, correlational approaches differ from observational approaches in terms of the nature of the data researchers collect and the issues they investigate.

The data of observational studies are most frequently observer notes. We hope that these data exhibit reliability and validity. Unfortunately, because observations are generally the products of a single individual viewing a unique event, we have very little basis on which to judge their reliability and validity.

The data of correlational studies involve surveys and interviews as well as existing data. **Surveys** involve the use of questionnaires to gather data from participants, who answer questions on the relevant variables. The **interview** is a technique in which the researcher asks respondents a series of questions to gather data on the variables of interest. Interview data can be quantitative and similar to that obtained from a survey or it can be more qualitative and descriptive. The type of data obtained will depend on the purpose of the interview and the nature of the questions asked. **Existing data** come from organizational records and include productivity, absence, and demographic information (e.g., age, gender, and tenure). Variables often measured by surveys and interviews include

- employees' perceptions of how their managers behave on the job;
- the extent to which employees are satisfied with their jobs; and
- employees' reports about how much autonomy they have on their jobs.

It is possible to determine in advance of doing research the extent to which such measures are reliable and valid. Thus, when constructing a questionnaire to measure job satisfaction, the researcher can check its reliability by repeatedly administering it to a group of workers over a period of time. If individual responses remain fairly stable, there is evidence of reliability. Evidence of the validity of a questionnaire might come from its ability to predict which employees would quit the organization for work elsewhere. It seems reasonable that dissatisfied employees would be more likely to quit, and such an effect is partial evidence of the validity of a satisfaction measure.

In addition to differing in the nature of the data collected, correlational studies differ from observational studies in terms of the kinds of events they investigate. Although the questions investigated by observational research appear fairly specific (What maintains an "illegal" behaviour such as tapping? What do executives do?), virtually any event relevant

LO A.5

Describe *correlational research* and explain why causation cannot be inferred from correlation.

Correlational research. Research that attempts to measure variables precisely and examine relationships among these variables without introducing change into the research setting.

Surveys. The use of questionnaires to gather data from participants, who answer questions on the relevant variables.

Interview. A technique in which the researcher asks respondents a series of questions to gather data on the variables of interest.

Existing data. Data that are obtained from organizational records, such as productivity, absence, and demographic information.

to the question is fair game for observation. Thus, such studies are extremely broad-based. Correlational research sacrifices this broadness to investigate the relationship (correlation) between specific, well-defined variables. The relationship between the variables of interest is usually stated as a hypothesis of the relationship between an independent and a dependent variable. Using the variables mentioned above, we can construct three sample hypotheses and describe how they would be tested.

- Employees who are satisfied with their jobs will tend to be more productive than those who are less satisfied. To test this, a researcher might administer a reliable, valid questionnaire to measure job satisfaction and obtain production data from company records.

- Employees who perceive their supervisor as friendly and considerate will be more satisfied with their jobs than those who do not. To test this, a researcher might use reliable, valid questionnaires or interview measures of both variables.

- Older employees will be absent less than younger employees. To test this, a researcher might obtain data concerning the age of employees and their absenteeism from organizational records.

In each case, the researcher is interested in a very specific set of variables, and he or she devotes effort to measuring them precisely.

A good example of a correlational study is that of Belle Rose Ragins and John Cotton, who studied employees' willingness to serve as mentors to newer organizational members.[5] Mentorship was defined as helping a junior person with career support and upward mobility. The major focus of the study was the relationship between gender (the independent variable) and willingness to mentor (the dependent variable). The authors reviewed literature that hypothesized that women may face more barriers to becoming mentors than men because they are in a minority in many employment settings. The authors were also interested in the relationships between age, organizational rank, length of employment, and prior mentorship experience and willingness to mentor.

These variables were measured with questionnaires completed by more than 500 employees in three research and development organizations. The researchers found that men and women were equally willing to serve as mentors, although the women perceived more barriers (e.g., lack of qualifications and time) to being a mentor. They also found that higher rank and prior experience as a mentor or a protègè were associated with greater willingness to mentor. Notice that a study such as this could also incorporate existing data from records. For example, we might hypothesize that those with better performance evaluations would be more confident about serving as mentors.

Correlation and Causation

A final important point should be made about correlational studies. Consider a hypothesis that friendly, considerate supervisors will have more productive employees than unfriendly, inconsiderate supervisors. In this case, a researcher might have some employees describe the friendliness of their supervisors on a reliable, valid questionnaire designed to measure this variable and obtain employees' productivity levels from company records. The results of this hypothetical study are plotted in Exhibit A.1, where each dot represents an employee's response to the questionnaire in conjunction with his or her productivity. In general, it would appear that the hypothesis is confirmed—that is, employees who describe their supervisor as friendly tend to be more productive than those who describe him or her as unfriendly. As a result of this study, should an organization attempt to select friendly supervisors or even train existing supervisors to be more friendly to obtain higher productivity? The answer is no. The training and selection proposal assumes that friendly supervisors *cause* their employees to be productive, and this may not be the case. Put simply, supervisors might be friendly *if their*

EXHIBIT A.1
Hypothetical data from
a correlational study of
the relationship between
supervisory friendliness
and employee
productivity.

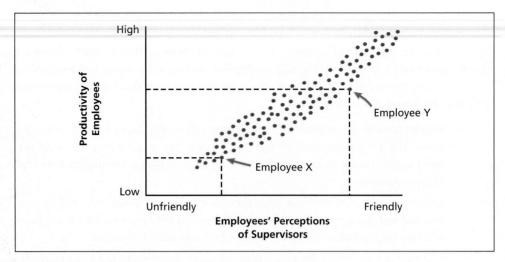

employees are productive. This is a possible interpretation of the data, and it does not suggest that selection or training to make supervisors friendly will achieve higher productivity. This line of argument should not be unfamiliar to you. Heavy smokers and cigarette company lobbyists like to claim that smoking is related to the incidence of lung cancer because cancer proneness prompts smoking, rather than vice versa. The point here is that *correlation does not imply causation*. How can we find out which factors cause certain organizational behaviours? The answer is to perform an experiment. Let's now take a closer look at experimental research techniques.

EXPERIMENTAL TECHNIQUES

LO **A.6**

Explain *experimental
research* and the mean-
ing of *internal validity*,
and discuss threats to
internal validity.

Experimental research.
Research that changes
or manipulates a variable
under controlled condi-
tions and examines the
consequences of this ma-
nipulation for some other
variable.

If observational research involves observing nature, and correlational research involves measuring nature, **experimental research** involves manipulating nature. In an experiment, a variable is manipulated or changed under controlled conditions, and the consequence of this manipulation for some other variable is measured. If all other conditions are truly controlled, and a change in the second variable follows the change that was introduced in the first variable, we can infer that the first change has caused the second change.

In experimental language, the variable that the researcher manipulates or changes is the independent variable. The variable that the independent variable is expected to affect is the dependent variable. Consider the following hypothesis: The introduction of recorded music into the work setting will lead to increased productivity. In this hypothesis, the independent variable is music, which is expected to affect productivity, the dependent variable. Consider another hypothesis: Stimulating, challenging jobs will increase the satisfaction of the workforce. Here, the design of the job is the independent variable and satisfaction is the dependent variable.

Let's return to our hypothesis that friendly, considerate supervisors will tend to have more productive employees. If we wish to determine whether friendly supervision contributes to employee productivity, the style of supervision becomes the independent variable, and productivity becomes the dependent variable. This means that the researcher must manipulate or change the friendliness of some supervisors and observe what happens to the productivity of their employees. In practice, this would probably be accomplished by exposing the bosses to some form of human relations training designed to teach them to be more considerate and personable toward their workers.

Exhibit A.2 shows the results of this hypothetical experiment. The line on the graph represents the average productivity of a number of employees whose supervisors have received our training. We see that this productivity increased and remained higher following the

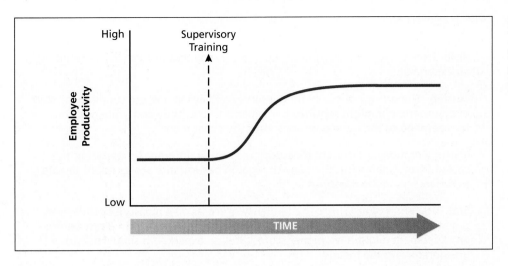

EXHIBIT A.2
Hypothetical data from an experiment concerning human relations training.

introduction of the training. Does this mean that friendliness indeed increases productivity and that we should proceed to train all of our supervisors in this manner? The answer is again no. We cannot be sure that *something else* did not occur at the time of the training to influence productivity, such as a change in equipment or job insecurity prompted by rumoured layoffs. To control this possibility, we need a control group of supervisors who are not exposed to the training, and we need productivity data for their employees. A **control group** is a group of research participants who have not been exposed to the experimental treatment, in this case not exposed to the training. Ideally, these supervisors should be as similar as possible in experience and background to those who receive the training, and their employees should be performing at the same level. The results of our improved experiment are shown in Exhibit A.3. Here, we see that the productivity of the employees whose supervisors were trained increases following training, while that of the control supervisors remains constant. We can, thus, infer that the human relations training affected employee productivity.

The extent to which a researcher can be confident that changes in a dependent variable are due to the independent variable is known as **internal validity**. Note that this is different from the validity of a measure, which was discussed earlier. Internal validity has to do with the validity of an experimental design. To return to the example above, if a control group was not included in the design then the internal validity would be low because other factors

Control group. A group of research participants who have not been exposed to the experimental treatment.

Internal validity. The extent to which a researcher has confidence that changes in a dependent variable are due to the independent variable.

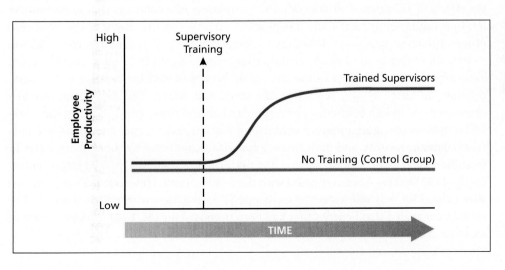

EXHIBIT A.3
Hypothetical data from an improved experiment concerning human relations training.

EXHIBIT A.4
Threats to internal
validity.

Selection of participants. When participants selected for the experimental group differ from those in the control group in some way that influences the results of an experiment.

Testing. The process of completing a survey and answering questions at the start of an experiment might sensitize participants to the study and influence how they respond to the same questions after the experiment.

Instrumentation. If different measures are used at different times during the course of an experiment, then any changes in participants' scores might be due to differences in the measures used.

Statistical regression. This is the tendency of scores on a measure to shift over time toward the mean score. Participants who perform poorly on a test before an experiment might have higher scores after an experiment simply due to regression toward the mean.

History. Events or factors that occur during the course of an experiment and can explain changes in the dependent variable.

Maturation. Natural changes in participants that are due to the passage of time (e.g., job experience) and can result in changes in the dependent variable.

Mortality. When certain types of participants drop out of an experiment before it has ended and those who remain and complete the dependent measures differ in some way from those who dropped out.

might explain the improvement in productivity. What are some of these other factors? Perhaps something happened at the same time that the supervisors were trained, such as a pay increase or bonus, or perhaps new equipment or technology was implemented. Factors that are alternative explanations for the results of an experiment are called *threats to internal validity* (see Exhibit A.4). Without a control group, there are many threats to internal validity that might be responsible for a change in productivity. However, with a control group, one can have much more confidence that the improvement in productivity was due to the training program. Thus, internal validity increases the confidence that one has in concluding that the training program was the cause of the improvement in productivity and not something else.

John Ivancevich and Herbert Lyon conducted an interesting experiment that examined the effects of a shortened workweek on the employees of a company that manufactures food-packaging equipment.[6] The independent variable was the length of the workweek (4 days, 40 hours versus 5 days, 40 hours). Two of the company's divisions were converted to a 4–40 week from a 5–40 week. A third division, remaining on the 5–40 schedule, served as a control group. Workers in the control division were similar to those in the other divisions in terms of age, seniority, education, and salary. The dependent variables (measured one month before the conversion and several times after) included the workers' responses to a questionnaire concerning job satisfaction and stress, absence data from company records, and performance appraisals conducted by supervisors. After 12 months, several aspects of satisfaction and performance showed a marked improvement for the 4–40 workers when compared with the 5–40 workers. However, at 25 months this edge existed for only one aspect of satisfaction—satisfaction with personal worth. The authors concluded that benefits that had been proposed for the 4–40 workweek were of short-term duration.

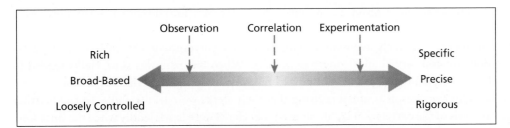

A CONTINUUM OF RESEARCH TECHNIQUES

LO **A.7**

Discuss the relative
advantages and disad-
vantages of different
research techniques.

You might reasonably wonder which of the research techniques just discussed is most effective. As shown in Exhibit A.5, these methods can be placed on a continuum ranging from
rich, broad-based, and loosely controlled (observation) to specific, precise, and rigorous
(experimentation). The method that researchers use to investigate organizational behaviour is dictated by the nature of the problem that interests them. In the writing of this section of the chapter, special pains were taken to choose examples of problems that were well
suited to the research techniques employed to investigate them. Bensman and Gerver were
interested in variables that were not well defined. The variables were thus not easy to isolate and measure precisely, and observation was the appropriate technique. Furthermore,
"tapping" was a controversial issue, and the researchers would have had to develop considerable trust to investigate it with questionnaires or formal interviews. Similarly, Mintzberg
insists that questionnaires and interviews have failed to tell us what executives actually do.
Ragins and Cotton, who studied mentoring, were interested in specific variables that were
relatively easily measured. On the other hand, they were not in a position to manipulate the
causes of intention to mentor. Ivancevich and Lyon were also interested in a specific set of
variables, and they conducted their research on the short workweek in a situation where it
was both possible and ethical to manipulate the workweek. In all these cases, the research
technique the researchers chose was substantially better than dependence on common sense
or opinion.

Although we have described each of these techniques as independent approaches for
studying organizational behaviour, very often they are combined and used to complement
each other. Let's consider how this might be done.

COMBINING RESEARCH TECHNIQUES

Robert Sutton and Anat Rafaeli tested what might seem to be an obvious hypothesis—that
friendly, pleasant behaviour on the part of sales clerks would be positively associated with
store sales.[7] As obvious as this might seem, it would be a good idea to confirm it before
spending thousands of dollars on human relations training for clerks. The study combined
correlational and observational methods. In the quantitative correlational part of the study,
teams of researchers entered a large North American chain's 576 convenience stores and,
posing as shoppers, evaluated the friendliness of the sales clerks on rating scales. They also
recorded other factors, such as the length of the line at the register. Existing data from company records provided the total annual sales each store recorded. When the researchers
analyzed the data, the results were surprising—the "unfriendly" stores tended to chalk up
higher sales!

To understand this unexpected result, the authors resorted to qualitative, observational research techniques. Specifically, each author spent extensive time in many of
the convenience stores directly observing transactions between customers and clerks. In
addition, each spent time as a participant observer, actually doing the sales clerk's job.

This observation resolved the mystery. The researchers found that when the stores were busy, the sales clerks tended to stop the small talk, concentrate on their work, and process customers as quickly as possible. This behaviour corresponded to customers' expectations for fast service in a convenience store. When business was slow, clerks tended to be friendly and engage in small talk to relieve boredom. Since the busier stores generated higher sales, it is not surprising that their clerks were less friendly. In fact, further analysis of the correlational data showed that clerks were less friendly when the lines were longer.

This study illustrates how two research techniques can complement each other. It also shows that correlation does not imply causation. Although sales were negatively correlated with friendliness, volume of sales affected the expression of friendliness, not the other way around. Of course, these results would probably not generalize to sales settings in which customers expect more personal attention.

ISSUES AND CONCERNS IN ORGANIZATIONAL BEHAVIOUR RESEARCH

As in every field of study, particular issues confront researchers in organizational behaviour. Three of these issues include sampling, Hawthorne effects, and ethical concerns.

Sampling

Researchers are usually interested in generalizing the results of their research beyond their study. The extent to which the results of a study generalize to other samples and settings is known as **external validity**. External validity will be greater when the results of a study are based on large, random samples. Large samples ensure that the results they obtain are truly representative of the individuals, groups, or organizations being studied and not merely the product of an extreme case or two.

Random sampling means that the research participants have been randomly chosen from the population of interest. Random samples ensure that all relevant individuals, groups, or organizations have an equal probability of being studied and give confidence in the generalizability of the findings. As was noted earlier, observational studies usually involve small samples, and they are seldom randomized. Thus, generalizing from such studies is a problem. However, a well-designed observational study that answers important questions is surely superior to a large-sample, randomized correlational study that enables one to generalize about a trivial hypothesis.

In experimental research, randomization means **randomly assigning** participants to experimental and control conditions. To illustrate the importance of this, we can reconsider the hypothetical study on human relations training. Suppose that instead of randomly assigning supervisors to the experimental and control groups, managers nominate supervisors for training. Suppose further that to "reward" them for their long service, more-experienced supervisors are nominated for the training. This results in an experimental group containing more-experienced supervisors and a control group containing less-experienced supervisors. If supervisory experience promotes employee productivity, we might erroneously conclude that it was the *human relations training* that led to any improved results and that our hypothesis is confirmed. Poor sampling due to a lack of randomization has biased the results in favour of our hypothesis. To achieve randomization, it would be a good idea to ascertain that the employees of the experimental and control supervisors were equally productive *before* the training began. Random assignment to conditions is another way to lower the threats to internal validity. In this example, the threat to internal validity was due to the fact that the supervisors in the experimental condition had more experience than those in the control group (as shown in Exhibit A.4, this threat to internal validity is called *selection of participants*), and this might explain the results of the experiment. Thus, it is important that when conducting an experiment the participants are randomly assigned to the experimental and control groups. This helps to ensure that the participants in both conditions do not differ on important variables such as experience and increases the internal validity of the experiment.

Sometimes it is not possible to randomly assign participants to the experimental and control conditions such as when the participants work on different shifts or in different plants. When the participants are not randomly assigned to the experimental and control conditions we refer to the study technique as a **quasi-experimental design**. In quasi-experimental designs we cannot be sure that the participants in each condition are similar so it is important that we measure variables that they might differ on (e.g., age, organization tenure, and gender) and then compare them on these variables to determine if there are any differences. If differences are found then we would try to control for them when we analyze the data because such differences might explain any differences between the experimental and control conditions on the dependent variable(s).

Quasi-experimental design. A research technique in which the participants are not randomly assigned to the experimental and control conditions.

Hawthorne Effect

LO

Explain the *Hawthorne effect* and how it can occur.

The Hawthorne effect was discovered as a result of a series of studies conducted at the Hawthorne plant of the Western Electric Company near Chicago many years ago. As explained in Chapter 1, these studies examined the effects of independent variables, such as rest pauses, lighting intensity, and pay incentives, on the productivity of assemblers of electrical components.[8]

In a couple of these loosely controlled experiments, unusual results occurred. In the illumination study, both experimental and control workers improved their productivity. In another study, productivity increased and remained high despite the introduction and withdrawal of factors such as rest pauses, shortened workdays, and so on. These results gave rise to the term **Hawthorne effect**, which refers to a favourable response of participants in an organizational experiment to a factor other than the independent variable that is formally being manipulated. Researchers have concluded that this "other factor" is psychological in nature, although it is not well understood.[9] Likely candidates include participants' reactions to special attention, including feelings of prestige, heightened morale, and so on. The point is that researchers might misinterpret the true reason for any observed change in behaviour because research participants can have unmeasured feelings about their role in the research.

Hawthorne effect. A favourable response by participants in an organizational experiment that is the result of a factor other than the independent variable that is formally being manipulated.

To return to the human relations training experiment, a Hawthorne effect might occur if the experimental participants are grateful to management for selecting them for this special training and resolve to work harder back on the job. The supervisors might put in longer hours thinking up ways to improve productivity that have nothing to do with the training they received. However, the researcher could easily conclude that the human relations training improved productivity.

It is very difficult to prevent Hawthorne effects. However, it is possible, if expensive, to see whether they have occurred. To do so, investigators establish a second experimental group that receives special treatment and attention but is not exposed to the key independent variable. In the human relations experiment, this could involve training that is not expected to increase productivity. If the productivity of the supervisors' employees in both experimental groups increases equally, the Hawthorne effect is probably present. If productivity increases only in the human relations training condition, it is unlikely to be due to the Hawthorne effect.

LO

Ethics

Discuss the basic ethical concerns to which researchers must attend.

Researchers in organizational behaviour, no matter who employs them, have an ethical obligation to do rigorous research and to report that research accurately.[10] In all cases, the psychological and physical well-being of the research participants is of prime importance. In general, ethical researchers avoid unnecessary deception, inform participants about the general purpose of their research, and protect the anonymity of research participants. For example, in a correlational study involving the use of questionnaires, investigators should explain the general reason for the research and afford potential participants the opportunity to decline participation. If names or company identification numbers are required to match responses with data in employee files (e.g., absenteeism or subsequent turnover), investigators must guarantee that they will not make individual responses public. In some observation studies and experiments participants may be unaware that their behaviour is under formal study. In these cases, researchers have special obligations to prevent negative consequences for participants. Ethical research has a practical side as well as a moral side. Good cooperation from research participants is necessary to do good research. Such cooperation is easier to obtain when people are confident that ethical procedures are the rule, not the exception.

MyManagementLab

Visit MyManagementLab at **www.mymanagementlab .com** for access to online tutorials, interactive exercises, videos, and much more.

LEARNING OBJECTIVES CHECKLIST

A.1 All research in organizational behaviour begins with a basic question about work or organizations. Frequently, researchers express the question as a *hypothesis*, a formal statement of the expected relationship between two variables. *Variables* are simply measures that can take on two or more values.

A.2 In most research, we are concerned with two kinds of variables. The *independent variable* is a predictor or cause of variation in a dependent variable. The *dependent variable* is a variable that will vary as a result of changes in the independent variable. Two other kinds of variables that we are sometimes interested in are mediating variables and moderating variables. A *moderating variable* is a variable that affects the nature of the relationship between an independent and dependent variable such that the relationship depends on the level of the moderating variable. A *mediating variable* is a variable that intervenes or explains the relationship between an independent and dependent variable.

A.3 Careful measurement of variables is important in research. *Reliability* is an index of the consistency of a research subject's responses. *Validity* is an index of the extent to which a measure truly reflects what it is supposed to measure. *Convergent validity* exists when there is a strong relationship between different measures of the same variable. *Discriminant validity* exists when there is a weak relationship between measures of different variables.

A.4 In *observational research*, one or a few observers assess one or a few instances of organizational behaviour in its natural setting. In *participant observation*, the observer actually takes part in the activity being observed. In *direct observation*, the assessment occurs without the active participation of the researcher.

A.5 Compared with observation, *correlational research* techniques attempt to measure the variables in question more precisely by using questionnaires, interviews, and existing data. No change is introduced into the research setting. One problem with correlational research is its inability to imply causation. Researchers use experiments to overcome this problem.

A.6 In *experimental research*, the investigator actually changes or manipulates some factor in the organizational setting and measures the effect that this manipulation has on behaviour. In experimental language, the variable that the researcher manipulates or changes is the independent variable and the variable that the independent variable is expected to affect is the dependent variable. Causation can be inferred from a carefully designed experiment that has high internal validity. *Internal validity* refers to the confidence that the researcher has in concluding that changes in the dependent variable are due to the independent variable. Threats to internal validity are alternative explanations for the results of an experiment. The use of a control group and random assignment to experimental and control conditions increases internal validity and lowers threats to internal validity.

A.7 The method that researchers use to investigate organizational behaviour is dictated by the nature of the problem under investigation. When variables are not well defined and not easy to isolate and measure precisely, *observation* is an appropriate technique. Some of the weaknesses of observational research include a lack of control over the environment in which the study is being conducted and the small number of observers and situations in the typical observational study. Observational techniques are best used to make an initial examination of some organizational event on which little information

is available and to generate ideas for further investigation with more refined techniques. When the researcher is interested in specific variables that are well defined and relatively easy to measure but cannot be manipulated, *correlational research* is an appropriate technique. Correlational research provides more precision and greater control than observational techniques; however, it cannot be used to study causation. When the researcher is interested in causation and the effect of an independent variable on a dependent variable and it is both possible and ethical to manipulate the independent variable, *experimental research* is an appropriate technique. Experimental research provides the greatest amount of rigour but sacrifices the breadth and richness of less rigorous techniques like observational research.

A.8 *External validity* refers to the extent to which the results of a study generalize to other samples and settings. External validity will be greater when the results of a study are based on large, random samples. A *random sample* means that the research participants have been randomly chosen from the population of interest. This ensures that all relevant individuals, groups, or organizations have an equal probability of being studied and give confidence in the generalizability of the findings. *Random assignment* means randomly assigning participants to the experimental and control conditions of an experiment.

A.9 In a *quasi-experimental design* the participants are not randomly assigned to the experimental and control conditions. As a result, we cannot be sure that the participants in each condition are similar which is assumed in an experiment where participants are randomly assigned to conditions.

A.10 The *Hawthorne effect* refers to a favourable response of participants in an organizational experiment to a factor other than the independent variable that is formally being manipulated. Researchers have concluded that this "other factor" is psychological in nature, although it is not well understood. Likely candidates include participants' reactions to special attention, including feelings of prestige, heightened morale, and so on. The point is that researchers might misinterpret the true reason for any observed change in behaviour because research participants can have unmeasured feelings about their role in the research.

A.11 Researchers in organizational behaviour have an ethical obligation to do rigorous research and to report that research accurately. In all cases, the psychological and physical well-being of the research participants is of prime importance. In general, ethical researchers avoid unnecessary deception, inform participants about the general purpose of their research, and protect the anonymity of research participants.

Chapter 1

1. Dobson, S. (2011, December 19). CSR program helps boost engagement. *Canadian HR Reporter, 24*(22), 13, 14; www.sodexo.ca (The better tomorrow plan; About us; About Sodexo Canada; Sodexo Canada named one of Canada's Greenest Employers; Sodexo named one of World's Most Admired Companies' by FORTUNE magazine); Chosen as one of Canada's Greenest Employers for 2012 (Sodexo Canada Ltd.), www.eluta.ca/green-at-sodexo; Sodexo-Making every day count: Driving business success through the employee experience (2012 Catalyst Award Winner), www.catalyst.org; 2011 Diversity and Inclusion Annual Report, Sodexo.

2. Pfeffer, J. (2010). Business and the spirity: Management practices that sustain values. In R. A., Giacalone & C. L. Jurkiewicz (Eds.), *Handbook of workplace spirituality and organizational performance* (27–43). Armonk, NY: M. E. Sharpe.

3. Katz, D. (1964). The motivational basis of organizational behavior. *Behavioral Science, 9,* 131–146.

4. Peters, T. (1990, Fall). Get innovative or get dead. *California Management Review,* 9–26.

5. Pfeffer, J. (1994). *Competitive advantage through people: Unleashing the power of the work force.* Harvard Business School Press: Boston.

6. Crook, T. R., Todd, S. Y., Combs, J. G., Woehr, D. J., & Ketchen, D. J. Jr. (2011). Does human capital matter? A meta-analysis of the relationship between human capital and firm performance. *Journal of Applied Psychology, 96,* 443-456.

7. Wren, D. (1987). *The evolution of management thought* (3rd ed.). New York: Wiley.

8. Rousseau, D.M. (2006). Is there such a thing as "evidence-based management"? *Academy of Management Review, 31,* 256–269; Pfeffer, J., & Sutton, R.I. (2006). Evidence-based management. *Harvard Business Review,* 62–74.

9. For a summary of their work and relevant references, see Wren, 1987.

10. Taylor, F.W. (1967). *The principles of scientific management.* New York: Norton.

11. Weber, M. (1974). *The theory of social and economic organization* (A.M. Henderson & T. Parsons, Trans.). New York: Free Press.

12. See Wren, 1987.

13. Roethlisberger, F. J., & Dickson, W. J. (1939). *Management and the worker.* Cambridge, MA: Harvard University Press; Wrege, C. D., & Greenwood, R. G. (1986). The Hawthorne studies. In D. A. Wren & J. A. Pearce II (Eds.) (1986), *Papers dedicated to the development of modern management.* Academy of Management.

14. Argyris, C. (1957). *Personality and organization.* New York: Harper.

15. Likert, R. (1961). *New patterns of management.* New York: McGraw-Hill.

16. Gouldner, A.W. (1954). *Patterns of industrial bureaucracy.* New York: Free Press.

17. Selznick, P. (1949). *TVA and the grass roots: A study in the sociology of formal organizations.* Berkeley: University of California Press.

18. Abrahamson, E. (1991). Managerial fads and fashions: The diffusion and rejection of innovations. *Academy of Management Review, 16,* 586–612; Johns, G. (1993). Constraints on the adoption of psychology-based personnel practices: Lessons from organizational innovation. *Personnel Psychology, 46,* 569–592.

19. Mintzberg, H. (1973). *The nature of managerial work.* New York: Harper & Row. See also Mintzberg, H. (1994, Fall). Rounding out the manager's job. *Sloan Management Review,* 11–26.

20. Gibbs, B. (1994). The effects of environment and technology on managerial roles. *Journal of Management, 20,* 581–604; Kraut, A. I., Pedigo, P. R., McKenna, D. D., & Dunnette, M. D. (1989, November). The role of the manager: What's really important in different management jobs. *Academy of Management Executive,* 286–293.

21. Luthans, F., Hodgetts, R. M., & Rosenkrantz, S. A. (1988). *Real managers.* Cambridge, MA: Ballinger.

22. Kotter, J. P. (1982). *The general managers.* New York: Free Press.

23. Simon, H. A. (1987, February). Making management decisions: The role of intuition and emotion. *Academy of Management Executive,* 57–64; Isenberg, D. J. (1984, November–December). How senior managers think. *Harvard Business Review,* 80–90. See also Sims, H. P., Jr., & Gioia, D. A. (Eds.) (1986). *The thinking organization: Dynamics of organizational social cognition.* San Francisco: Jossey-Bass.

24. Hofstede, G. (1993, February). Cultural constraints in management theories. *Academy of Management Executive,* 81–94.

25. Crawford, M. (1993, May). The new office etiquette. *Canadian Business,* 22–31.

26. Kanungo, R. N. (1998). Leadership in organizations: Looking ahead to the 21st century. *Canadian Psychology, 39*(1–2), 71–82.

27. Mahoney, J. (2005, March 23). Visible majority by 2017. *Globe and Mail,* A1, A7.

28. Mingail, H. (2004, September 29). Wise ways for retraining older workers. *Globe and Mail,* C8.

29. Galt, V. (2006, March 15). 65 means freedom to start a whole new career. *Globe and Mail,* C1, C2.

30. Galt, V. (2005, September 20). Few firms adopt plans to retain aging staff. *Globe and Mail,* B7.

31. Javidan, M., Dorfman, P. W., de Luque, M. S., & House, R. J. (2006). In the eye of the beholder: Cross cultural lessons in leadership from Project GLOBE. *Academy of Management Perspectives, 20,* 67–90.

32. Attersley, J. (2005, November 7). Absence makes the bottom line wander. *Canadian HR Reporter,* R2; May 29; Galt, V. (2003, June 4). Workers rack up increased sick time. *Globe and Mail,* C1, C3.

33. Duxbury, L., & Higgins, C. (2003). *Work–life conflict in Canada in the new millennium: A status report.* Ottawa: Health Canada.

34. Saks, A. M. (2011). Workplace Spirituality and Employee Engagement. *Journal of Management, Spirituality & Religion, 8,* 317–340.

35. Myers, J. (2009, November 13). Nurturing spirituality in the workplace. *Globe and Mail (Breaking News), GMBN.*

36. Avey, J. B., Reichard, R. J., Luthans, F., & Mhatre, K. H. (2011). Meta-analysis of the impact of positive psychological capital on employee attitudes, behaviors, and performance. *Human Resource Development Quarterly, 22,* 127–152.

37. Avey, J. B., Luthans, F., & Youssef, C. M. (2010). The additive value of positive psychological capital in predicting

work attitudes and behaviors. *Journal of Management, 36,* 430–452.

38. Avey et al., 2010, 2011; Culbertson, S. S., Fullagar, C. J., & Mills, M. J. (2010). Feeling good and doing great: The relationship between psychological capital and well-being. *Journal of Occupational Health Psychology, 15,* 421–433; Avey, J. B., Luthans, F., Smith, R. M., & Palmer, N. F. (2010). Impact of positive psychological capital on employee well-being over time. *Journal of Occupational Health Psychology, 15,* 17–28; Peterson, S. J., Luthans, F., Avolio, B. J., Walumbwa, F. O., & Zhang, Z. (2011). Psychological capital and employee performance: A latent growth modeling approach. *Personnel Psychology, 64,* 427–450.

39. Luthans, F., Avey, J. B., Avolio, B. J., & Peterson, S. J. (2010). The development and resulting performance impact of positive psychological capital. *Human Resource Development Quarterly, 21,* 41–67.

40. Ray, R. L. (2011, October). CEO challenge reflections: Talent matters. *The Conference Board.*

41. Lockwood, N. R. (2006). Talent management: Driver for organizational success. *2006 SHRM Research Quarterly.* Alexandria, VA: Society for Human Resource Management.

42. McLaren, C. (2002, February 8). Ways to win top talent. *Globe and Mail,* C1.

43. Bakker, A. B., & Demerouti, E. (2008). Towards a model of work engagement. *Career Development International, 13,* 209–223.

44. Ray, 2011; Saks, A. M. (2006). Antecedents and consequences of employee engagement. *Journal of Managerial Psychology, 21,* 600–619; Christian, M. S., Garza, A. S., & Slaughter, J. E. (2011). Work engagement: A quantitative review and test of its relations with task and contextual performance. *Personnel Psychology, 64,* 89–136; Rich, B. L., Lepine, J. A., & Crawford, E. R. (2010). Job engagement: antecedents and effects of job performance. *Academy of Management Journal, 53,* 617–635; Macey, W. H., & Schneider, B., Barbera, K. M., & Young, S. A. (2009). *Employee engagement: Tools for analysis, practice, and competitive advantage.* Malden, WA: Wiley-Blackwell.

45. Lawler, E. E. (2008). *Talent: Making people your competitive advantage.* San Francisco, CA: John Wiley & Sons.

46. McKay, S. (2001, February). The 35 best companies to work for in Canada. *Report on Business Magazine,* 53–62; Toda, B.H. (2000, February). The rewards: Being a good employer draws talent and unlocks success. *Report on Business Magazine,* 33.

47. Bansal, P., Maurer, C., & Slawinski, N. (2008, January/February). Beyond good intentions: Strategies for managing your CSR performance. *Ivey Business Journal, 72*(1), 1–8.

48. Bansal, P., Maurer, C., & Slawinski, N. (2008, January/February).

49. Birenbaum, R., Lang, H., Linley, D., MacMahon, Mann, B., Sabour, A., Sosa, I., Stein, G., & White, A. (2009, June 22). 50 most socially responsible corporations. *Maclean's, 122*(23), 42–49.

50. About Sodexo Canada, www.sodexo.ca.

51. McLaren, D. (2008, December 10). Doing their part—with goals in mind. *Globe and Mail,* B7.

52. Johne, M. (2007, October 10). Show us the green, workers say. *Globe and Mail,* C1, C6.

53. Aguinis, H., & Glavas, A. (2012). What we know and don't know about corporate social responsibility: A review and research agenda. *Journal of Management, 38,* 932–968.

54. Johne, M. (2007, October 10).

Chapter 2

1. Hubbard, J. (2011, January 31). From awareness to action: Employee wellness. *Canadian HR Reporter, 24*(2), 32; Smith, B. (2011, April 18). TEIG shares wellness program success. *Benefits Canada,* www .benefitscanada.com; Freifeld, L. (2011, January/February). TEIG locks in on leadership. *Training, 48*(1), 34-39.

2. Dobson, S. (2012, February 13). Revving up interest. *Canadian HR Reporter, 25*(3), 13, 18.

3. George, J. M. (1992). The role of personality in organizational life: Issues and evidence. *Journal of Management, 18,* 185–213; Mount, M. K., & Barrick, M. R. (1995). The big five personality dimensions: Implications for research and practice in human resources management. In K. M. Rowland & G. Ferris (Eds.), *Research in personnel and human resources management* (Vol. 13, 153–200). Greenwich, CT: JAI Press.

4. George, 1992; Weiss, H. M., & Adler, S. (1984). Personality and organizational behavior. In B. M. Staw & L. L. Cummings (Eds.), *Research in organizational behavior* (Vol. 6, 1–50). Greenwich, CT: JAI Press.

5. Adler, S., & Weiss, H. M. (1988). Recent developments in the study of personality and organizational behavior. In C. L. Cooper & I. Robertson (Eds.), *International review of industrial and organizational psychology.* New York: Wiley.

6. Tett, R. P., & Burnett, D. D. (2003). A personality trait-based interactionist model of job performance. *Journal of Applied Psychology, 88,* 500–517.

7. Moses, S. (1991, November). Personality tests come back in I/O. *APA Monitor,* 9.

8. Mount & Barrick, 1995.

9. Digman, J. M. (1990). Personality structure: Emergence of the five-factor model. *Annual Review of Psychology, 41,* 417–440; Hogan, R. T. (1991). Personality and personality measurement. In M. D. Dunette & L. M. Hough (Eds.), *Handbook of industrial and organizational psychology* (2nd ed., Vol. 2). Palo Alto, CA: Consulting Psychologists Press; Barrick, M. R., & Mount, M. K. (1991). The big five personality dimensions and job performance: A meta-analysis. *Personnel Psychology, 44,* 1–26; Barrick, M. R., Mount, M. K., & Judge, T. A. (2001). Personality and performance at the beginning of the new millennium: What do we know and where do we go next? *International Journal of Selection and Assessment, 9,* 9–30; Barrick, M. R., Mount, M. K., & Gupta, R. (2003). Meta-analysis of the relationship between the five-factor model of personality and Holland's occupational types. *Personnel Psychology, 56,* 45–74; Ng, T. W. H., Eby, L. T., Sorensen, K. L., & Feldman, D. C. (2005). Predictors of objective and subjective career success: A meta-analysis. *Personnel Psychology, 58,* 367–408.

10. Judge, T. A., Higgins, C. A., Thorensen, C. J., & Barrick, M. R. (1999). The Big Five personality traits, general mental ability, and career success across the life span. *Personnel Psychology, 52,* 621–652.

11. Chiaburu, D. S., Oh, I., Berry, C. M., Li, N., & Gardner, R. G. (2011). The five-factor model of personality traits and organizational citizenship behaviors: A meta-analysis. *Journal of Applied Psychology, 96,* 1140–1166; Hough, L. M., Eaton, N. K., Dunnette, M. D., Kamp, J. D., & McCloy, R. A. (1990). Criterion-related validities of personality constructs and the effect of response distortion on those validities. *Journal of Applied Psychology, 75,* 581–595; Tett, R. P., Jackson, D. N., & Rothstein, M. (1991). Personality measures as predictors of job performance: A meta-analytic review. *Personnel Psychology, 44,* 703–742.

12. Barrick & Mount, 1991; Ones, D. S., Dilchert, S., Viswesvaran, C., & Judge, T. A. (2007). In support of personality assessment in organizational settings. *Personnel Psychology, 60,* 995–1027; Barrick, M. R., Mount, M. K., & Judge, T. A. (2001).

13. Ones, D. S., Viswesvaran, C., & Schmidt, F. L. (1993). Comprehensive meta-analysis of integrity test validities: Findings and implications for personnel selection and theories of job performance. *Journal of Applied Psychology, 78,* 679–703.

14. Judge, Higgins, Thorensen, & Barrick, 1999.

15. Judge, T. A., & Ilies, R. (2002). Relationship of personality to performance motivation: A meta-analytic review. *Journal of Applied Psychology, 87,* 797–807.

16. Judge, T. A., Heller, D., & Mount, M. K. (2002). Five-factor model of personality and job satisfaction: A meta-analysis. *Journal of Applied Psychology, 87,* 530–541; Morgeson, F. P., Reider, M. H., & Campion, M. A. (2005). Selecting individuals in team settings: The importance of social skills, personality characteristics, and team work knowledge. *Personnel Psychology, 58,* 583–611.

17. Kanfer, R., Wanberg, C. R., & Kantrowitz, T. M. (2001). Job search and employment: A personality-motivational analysis and meta-analytic review. *Journal of Applied Psychology, 86,* 837–855.

18. Judge, Higgins, Thorensen, & Barrick, 1999.

19. Rotter, J. B. (1966). Generalized expectancies for internal versus external controls of reinforcement. *Psychological Monographs, 80* (Whole no. 609).

20. Szilagyi, A. D., & Sims, H. P., Jr. (1975). Locus of control and expectancies across multiple organizational levels. *Journal of Applied Psychology, 60,* 638–640.

21. Szilagyi, A. D., Sims, H. P., Jr., & Keller, R. T. (1976). Role dynamics, locus of control, and employee attitudes and behavior. *Academy of Management Journal, 19,* 259–276.

22. Andrisani, P. J., & Nestel, G. (1976). Internal-external control as contributor to and outcome of work experience. *Journal of Applied Psychology, 61,* 156–165.

23. Wang, Q., Bowling, N. A., & Eschleman, K. J. (2010). A meta-analytic examination of work and general locus of control. *Journal of Applied Psychology, 95,* 761–768. For evidence on stress and locus of control, see Anderson, C. R. (1977). Locus of control, coping behaviors, and performance in a stress setting: A longitudinal study. *Journal of Applied Psychology, 62,* 446–451. For evidence on career planning, see Thornton, G. C., III. (1978). Differential effects of career planning on internals and externals. *Personnel Psychology, 31,* 471–476.

24. Snyder, M. (1987). *Public appearances/private realities: The psychology of self-monitoring.* New York: W. H. Freeman; Gangestad, S. W., & Snyder, M. (2000). Self-monitoring: Appraisal and reappraisal. *Psychological Bulletin, 126*(4), 530–555.

25. Snyder, 1987; Gangestad & Snyder, 2000.

26. Day, D. V., Schleicher, D. J., Unckless, A. L., & Hiller, N. J. (2002). Self-monitoring personality at work: A meta-analytic investigation of construct validity. *Journal of Applied Psychology, 87,* 390–401.

27. Kilduff, M., & Day, D. V. (1994). Do chameleons get ahead? The effects of self-monitoring and managerial careers. *Academy of Management Journal, 37*(4), 1047–1060.

28. Brockner, J. (1988). *Self-esteem at work: Research, theory, and practice.* Lexington, MA: Lexington.

29. Brockner, 1988.

30. Brockner, 1988.

31. Pierce, J. L., Gardner, D. G., Cummings, L. L., & Dunham, R. B. (1989). Organization-based self-esteem: Construct definition, measurement, and validation. *Academy of Management Journal, 32,* 622–648; Tharenou, P. (1979). Employee self-esteem: A review of the literature. *Journal of Vocational Behavior, 15,* 1–29.

32. Pierce, J. L., Gardner, D. G., Dunham, R. B., & Cummings, L. L. (1993). Moderation by organization-based self-esteem of role condition–employee response relationships. *Academy of Management Journal, 36,* 271–288.

33. George, J. M. (1996). Trait and state affect. In K. R. Murphy (Ed.), *Individual differences and behavior in organizations.* San Francisco, CA: Jossey-Bass.

34. Johnson, R. E., Tolentino, A. L., Rodopman, O. B., & Cho, E. (2010). We (sometimes) know not how we feel: Predicting job performance with an implicit measure of trait affectivity. *Personnel Psychology, 63,* 197–219.

35. Johnson et al., 2010; George, 1996; Thoresen, C. J., Kaplan, S.A., Barsky, A. P., Warren, C. R., & de Chermont, K. (2003). The affective underpinnings of job perceptions and attitudes: A meta-analytic review and integration. *Psychological Bulletin, 129,* 914–945; Lyubomirsky, S., King, L., & Diener, E. (2005). The benefits of frequent positive affect: Does happiness lead to success? *Psychological Bulletin, 131,* 803–855; Kaplan, S., Bradley, J. C., Luchman, J. N., & Haynes, D. (2009). On the role of positive and negative affectivity in job performance: A meta-analytic investigation. *Journal of Applied Psychology, 94,* 162–176.

36. Crant, M. J. (2000). Proactive behaviour in organizations. *Journal of Management, 26,* 435–462; Seibert, S. E., Kraimer, M. L., & Crant, J. M. (2001). What do proactive people do? A longitudinal model linking proactive personality and career success. *Personnel Psychology, 54,* 845–874.

37. Bateman, T. S., & Crant, J. M. (1993). The proactive component of organizational behavior: A measure and correlates. *Journal of Organizational Behavior, 14,* 103–118.

38. Li, N., Liang, J., & Crant, J. M. (2010). The role of proactive personality in job satisfaction and organizational citizenship behavior: A relational perspective. *Journal of Applied Psychology, 95,* 395–404; Seibert, Kraimer, & Crant, 2001; Thompson, J. A. (2005). Proactive personality and job performance: A social capital perspective. *Journal of Applied Psychology, 90,* 1011–1017; Brown, D. J., Cober, R. T., Kane, K., Levy, P. E., & Shalhoop, J. (2006). Proactive personality and the successful job search: A field investigation with college graduates. *Journal of Applied Psychology, 91,* 717–726.

39. Chen, G., Gully, S. M., & Eden, D. (2001). Validation of a new general self-efficacy scale. *Organizational Research Methods, 4,* 62–83.

40. Chen, Gully, & Eden, 2001.

41. Judge, T. A., Erez, A., Bono, J. E., & Thoresen, C. J. (2003). The core self-evaluation scale: Development of a measure. *Personnel Psychology, 56,* 303–331.

42. Chang, C., Ferris, D. L., Johnson, R. E., Rosen, C. C., & Tan, J. A. (2012). Core self-evaluations: A review and evaluation of the literature. *Journal of Management, 38,* 81–128; Judge, T. A., & Bono, J. E. (2001). Relationship of core self-evaluations traits—self-esteem, generalized self-efficacy, locus of control, and emotional stability—with job satisfaction and job performance: A meta-analysis. *Journal of Applied Psychology, 86,* 80–92; Judge, T. A., Bono, J. E., & Locke, E. A. (2000). Personality and job satisfaction: The mediating role of job characteristics. *Journal of Applied Psychology, 85,* 237–249; Judge, Erez, Bono, & Thoresen, 2003; Judge, T. A., Locke, E. A., & Durham, C. C. (1997). The dispositional causes of job satisfaction: A core evaluations approach. In B. M. Staw & L. L. Cummings (Eds.), *Research in organizational behavior* (Vol. 19, 151–188). Greenwich, CT: JAI Press; Judge, T. A., Bono, J. E., Erez, A., & Locke, E. A. (2005). Core self-evaluations and job and life satisfaction: The role of self-concordance and goal attainment. *Journal of Applied Psychology, 90,* 257–268; Kammeyer-Mueller, J. D., Judge, T. A., & Scott, B. A. (2009). The role of core self-evaluations in the coping process. *Journal of Applied Psychology, 94,* 177–195; Judge, T. A. (2009). Core self-evaluations and work success. *Current Directions in Psychological Science, 18,* 58–62; Johnson, R. E., Rosen, C. C., & Levy, P. E. (2008). Getting to the

core of core self-evaluation: A review and recommendations. *Journal of Organizational Behavior, 29,* 391–413.

43. Day, N. (1998, June). Informal learning gets results. *Workforce,* 31–35.

44. Pfeffer, J. (1994). *Competitive advantage through people: Unleashing the power of the work force.* Boston, MA: Harvard Business School Press.

45. Immen, W. (2012, June 20). Companies boosting incentive programs. *Globe and Mail,* B17.

46. Peterson, S. J., & Luthans, F. (2006). The impact of financial and nonfinancial incentives on business-unit outcomes over time. *Journal of Applied Psychology, 91,* 156–165.

47. Peterson & Luthans, 2006.

48. Luthans, F., & Kreitner, R. (1975). *Organizational behavior modification.* Glenview, IL: Scott, Foresman.

49. However, more research is necessary to establish the extent of this in organizations. See Arvey, R. D., & Ivancevich, J. M. (1980). Punishment in organizations: A review, propositions, and research suggestions. *Academy of Management Review, 5,* 123–132.

50. Punishment in front of others can be effective under restricted conditions. See Trevino, L. K. (1992). The social effects of punishment in organizations: A justice perspective. *Academy of Management Review, 17,* 647–676.

51. Orsgan, D. W., & Hamner, W. C. (1982). *Organizational behavior: An applied psychological approach* (Revised ed.). Plano, TX: Business Publications.

52. See Parmerlee, M. A., Near, J. P., & Jensen, T. C. (1982). Correlates of whistle-blowers' perceptions of organizational retaliation. *Administrative Science Quarterly, 27,* 17–34.

53. Bandura, A. (1991). Social cognitive theory of self-regulation. *Organizational Behavior and Human Decision Processes, 50,* 248–287.

54. Bandura, A. (1989). Human agency in social cognitive theory. *American Psychologists, 44,* 1175–1184. For a presentation of operant learning theory, see Honig, W. K., & Staddon, J. E. R. (Eds.). (1977). *Handbook of operant behavior.* Englewood Cliffs, NJ: Prentice-Hall. For a presentation of social learning theory, see Bandura, A. (1986). *Social foundations of thought and action.* Englewood Cliffs, NJ: Prentice-Hall.

55. Bandura, 1986.

56. Luthans, F., & Kreitner, R. (1985). *Organizational behavior modification and beyond: An operant and social learning approach.* Glenview, IL: Scott, Foresman; Manz, C. C., & Sims, H. P., Jr. (1981). Vicarious learning: The influence of modeling on organizational behavior. *Academy of Management Review, 6,* 105–113.

57. Bandura, 1986; Goldstein, A. P., & Sorcher, M. (1974). *Changing supervisor behavior.* New York: Pergamon.

58. Robinson, S. L., & O'Leary-Kelly, A. M. (1998). Monkey see, monkey do: The influence of work groups on the anti-social behavior of employees. *Academy of Management Journal, 41,* 658–672; Goulet, L. R. (1997). Modelling aggression in the workplace: The role of role models. *Academy of Management Executive, 11,* 84–85.

59. Bandura, A. (1997). *Self-efficacy: The exercise of control.* New York, NY: W. H. Freeman.

60. Bandura, 1997; Stajkovic, A. D., & Luthans, F. (1998). Self-efficacy and work-related performance: A meta-analysis. *Psychological Bulletin, 124,* 240–261.

61. Bandura, 1991; Manz, C. C., & Sims, H. P., Jr. (1980). Self-management as a substitute for leadership: A social learning theory perspective. *Academy of Management Review, 5,* 361–367; Hackman, J. R. (1986). The psychology of self-management in organizations. In M. S. Pollack & R. Perloff (Eds.), *Psychology and work.* Washington, DC: American Psychological Association.

62. Bandura, 1986, 1989, 1991; Kanfer, F. H. (1980). Self-management methods. In F. H. Kanfer & A. P. Goldstein (Eds.), *Helping people change: A textbook of methods* (2nd ed.). New York: Pergamon.

63. Luthans & Kreitner, 1985; Manz & Sims, 1980.

64. Frayne, C., & Latham, G. (1987). Application of social learning theory to employee self-management of attendance. *Journal of Applied Psychology, 72,* 387–392.

65. Frayne, C. A., & Geringer, J. M. (2000). Self-management training for improving job performance: A field experiment involving salespeople. *Journal of Applied Psychology, 85,* 361–372.

66. Gist, M. E., Stevens, C. K., & Bavetta, A. G. (1991). Effects of self-efficacy and post-training intervention on the acquisition and maintenance of complex interpersonal skills. *Personnel Psychology, 44,* 837–861; Stevens, C. K., Bavetta, A. G., & Gist, M. E. (1993). Gender differences in the acquisition of salary negotiation skills: The role of goals, self-efficacy, and perceived control. *Journal of Applied Psychology, 78,* 723–735.

67. Komaki, J., Barwick, K. D., & Scott, L. R. (1978). A behavioral approach to occupational safety: Pinpointing and reinforcing safe performance in a food manufacturing plant. *Journal of Applied Psychology, 63,* 434–445. For a similar study, see Haynes, R. S., Pine, R. C., & Fitch, H. G. (1982). Reducing accident rates with organizational behavior modification. *Academy of Management Journal, 25,* 407–416.

68. Stajkovic, A. D., & Lutans, F. (1997). A meta-analysis of the effects of organizational behavior modification on task performance, 1975–95. *Academy of Management Journal, 40,* 1122–1149; Stajkovic, A. D., & Luthans, F. (2003). Behavioral management and task performance in organizations: Conceptual background, meta-analysis, and test of alternative models. *Personnel Psychology, 56,* 155–194; Stajkovic, A. D., & Luthans, F. (2001). Differential effects of incentive motivators on work performance. *Academy of Management Journal, 44,* 580–590.

69. Markham, S. E., Scott, K. D., & McKee, G. H. (2002). Recognizing good attendance: A longitudinal, quasi-experimental field study. *Personnel Psychology, 55,* 639–660.

70. Anonymous. (2008, April 28). The power of peer recognition. A special report for the Great Place to Work® Institute Canada. *Globe and Mail,* GPTW5; Marron, K. (2006, February 15). High praise from colleagues counts. *Globe and Mail,* C1, C6.

71. Markham, Scott, & McKee, 2002; Well-structured employee reward/recognition programs yield positive results. (1999, November). *HRFocus, 1,* 14, 15.

72. Markham, Scott, & McKee, 2002.

73. Klie, S. (2006, August 14). Recognition equals profits. *Canadian HR Reporter, 19*(14), 18.

74. Saks, A. M., & Haccoun, R. R. (2010). *Managing performance through training and development* (5th ed.). Toronto: Nelson.

75. Taylor, P. J., Russ-Eft, D. F., & Chan, D. W. L. (2005). A meta-analytic review of behavior modeling training. *Journal of Applied Psychology, 90,* 692–709.

76. Taylor, Russ-Eft, & Chan, 2005.

77. Saks, A. M. (1997). Transfer of training and self-efficacy: What is the dilemma? *Applied Psychology: An International Review, 46,* 365–370.

78. DeSimone, R. L., Werner, J. M., & Harris, D. M. (2002). *Human resource development.* Orlando, FL: Harcourt College.

79. Harding, K. (2003, February 5). Firms offer a hand up the ladder. *Globe and Mail,* C3.

80. Brown, D. (2005, June 20). TD gives employees tool to chart career paths. *Canadian HR Reporter, 18*(12), 11, 13.

Chapter 3

1. Klie, S. (2010, April 19). IS Awards honour diversity. *Canadian HR Reporter, 23*(8), 1, 18; Bach, M. (2011, October 24). A little recognition goes a long way. *Canadian HR Reporter, 24*(18), 23; Dobson, S. (2011, November 7). Catalyst honours champions of women in business. *Canadian HR Reporter, 24*(19), 1, 17; Aulakh, R. (2010, March 25). He created a job out of diversity. *Toronto Star,* www.thestar.com; One of Canada's Best Diversity Employers for 2012, www.eluta.ca/diversity-at-kpmg; One of Canada's Top 100 Employers and Greater Toronto's Top Employers for 2012, www.eluta.ca/top-employer-kpmg; www.kpmg.com/ca/en (Catalytst Canada Honors KPMG's very own Michael Bach; Who we are; KPMG named one of Canada's Best Diversity Employers).

2. Cox, T., Jr. (1993). *Cultural diversity in organizations: Theory, research, & practice.* San Francisco: Berrett-Koehler.

3. Ashforth, B. E. (2001). *Role transitions in organizational life: An identity-based persepctive.* Mahwah, NJ: Lawrence Erlbaum Associates, Inc.; Ashforth, B. E., & Mael, F. (1989). Social identity theory and the organization. *Academy of Management Review, 14,* 20–39.

4. Ashforth, 2001; Ashforth & Mael, 1989.

5. Bruner, J. S. (1957). On perceptual readiness. *Psychological Review, 64,* 123–152.

6. Eagly, A. H., Ashmore, R. D., Makhijani, M. G., & Longo, L. C. (1991). What is beautiful is good, but…: A meta-analytic review of research on the physical attractiveness stereotype. *Psychological Bulletin, 110,* 109–128; Hosoda, M., Stone-Romero, E. F., & Coats, G. (2003). The effects of physical attractiveness on job-related outcomes: A meta-analysis of experimental studies. *Personnel Psychology, 56,* 431–462.

7. Stone, E. F., Stone, D. L., & Dipboye, R. L. (1992). Stigmas in organizations: Race, handicaps, and physical unattractiveness. In K. Kelley (Ed.), *Issues, theory and research in industrial/organizational psychology.* New York: Elsevier; Hosoda, Stone-Romero, & Coats, 2003.

8. Judge, T. A., & Cable, D. M. (2004). The effect of physical height on workplace success and income: Preliminary test of a theoretical model. *Journal of Applied Psychology, 89,* 428–441.

9. See Krzystofiak, F., Cardy, R., & Newman, J. E. (1988). Implicit personality and performance appraisal: The influence of trait inferences on evaluations of behavior. *Journal of Applied Psychology, 73,* 515–521.

10. Fiske, S. T. (1993). Social cognition and social perception. *Annual Review of Psychology, 44,* 155–194.

11. Secord, P. F., Backman, C. W., & Slavitt, D. R. (1976). *Understanding social life: An introduction to social psychology.* New York: McGraw-Hill. For elaboration, see Wilder, D. A. (1986). Social categorization: Implications for creation and reduction of intergroup bias. *Advances in Experimental Social Psychology, 19,* 291–349.

12. Dion, K. L., & Schuller, R. A. (1991). The Ms. stereotype: Its generality and its relation to managerial and marital status stereotypes. *Canadian Journal of Behavioural Science, 23,* 25–40.

13. For a more complete treatment see Falkenberg, L. (1990). Improving the accuracy of stereotypes within the workplace. *Journal of Management, 16,* 107–118.

14. Kelley, H. H. (1972). Attribution in social interaction. In E. E. Jones, D. E. Kanhouse, H. H. Kelley, R. E. Nisbett, S. Valins, & B. Weiner (Eds.), *Attribution: Perceiving the causes of behavior.* Morristown, NJ: General Learning Press. For an integrative attribution model, see Medcof, J. W. (1990). PEAT: An integrative model of attribution processes. *Advances in Experimental Social Psychology, 23,* 111–209.

15. This discussion of attribution biases draws upon Fiske, S. T., & Taylor, S. E. (1984). *Social cognition.* Reading, MA: Addison-Wesley.

16. Jones, E. E. (1979). The rocky road from acts to dispositions. *American Psychologist, 34,* 107–117; Ross, L. (1977). The intuitive psychologist and his shortcomings: Distortions in the attribution process. *Advances in Experimental Social Psychology, 10,* 173–220.

17. Mitchell, T. R., & Kalb, L. S. (1982). Effects of job experience on supervisor attributions for a subordinate's poor performance. *Journal of Applied Psychology, 67,* 181–188.

18. Watson, D. (1982). The actor and the observer: How are their perceptions of causality divergent? *Psychological Bulletin, 92,* 682–700.

19. Sonnenfeld, J. (1981). Executive apologies for price fixing: Role biased perceptions of causality. *Academy of Management Journal, 24,* 192–198; Waters, J. A. (1978, Spring). Catch 20.5. Corporate morality as an organizational phenomenon. *Organizational Dynamics,* 2–19.

20. Malle, B. F. (2006). The actor-observer asymmetry in attribution: A (surprising) meta-analysis. *Psychological Bullentin, 132,* 895–919.

21. Greenwald, A. G. (1980). The totalitarian ego: Fabrication and revision of personal history. *American Psychologist, 35,* 603–618; Tetlock, P. E. (1985). Accountability: The neglected social context of judgment and choice. *Research in Organizational Behavior, 7,* 297–332.

22. Pyszczynski, T., & Greenberg, J. (1987). Toward an integration of cognitive and motivational perspectives on social inference: A biased hypothesis-testing model. *Advances in Experimental Social Psychology, 20,* 197–340.

23. This section relies on Jackson, S. E., & Alvarez, E. B. (1992). Working through diversity as a strategic imperative. In S. E. Jackson (Ed.), *Diversity in the workplace: Human resources initiatives.* New York: Guilford Press; Mahoney, J. (2005, March 23). Visible majority by 2017. *Globe and Mail,* A1, A7.

24. Mahoney, 2005, March 23.

25. Mingail, H. (2004, September 29). Wise ways for retraining older workers. *Globe and Mail,* C8; Dobson, S. (2010, April 5). HR by the numbers. *Canadian HR Reporter, 23*(7), 4.

26. Crawford, T. (2006, April 1). A better mix. *Toronto Star,* L1, L2; Galt, V. (2005, March 2). Diversity efforts paying off: Shell CFO. *Globe and Mail,* B1, B20; Vu, U. (2004, November 8). FedEx holds managers accountable for diversity. *Canadian HR Reporter, 17*(19), 3; Shaw, A. (2006, May 22). Hiring immigrants makes good business sense. *Canadian HR Reporter, 19*(10), 21; Keung, N. (2006, March 18). Wanted: Minorities. *Toronto Star,* B1, B3.

27. Cox, 1993; Cox, T., Jr. (1991, May). The multicultural organization. *Academy of Management Executive, 5,* 34–47.

28. Crone, G. (1999, February 18). Companies embracing workplace diversity. *Financial Post,* C11; Galt, V. (2004, January 27). Firms excel with women in senior ranks: Study. *Globe and Mail,* B5; McKay, P. F., Avery D. R., & Morris, M. A. (2009). A tale of two climates: Diversity climate from subordinates' and managers' perspectives and their role in store unit sales performance. *Personnel Psychology, 62,* 767–791.

29. Nguyen, H.-H. D., & Ryan, A. M. (2008). Does stereotype threat affect test performance of minorities and women? A meta-analysis of experimental evidence. *Journal of Applied Psychology, 93,* 1314–1334.

30. Hartley, E. L. (1946). *Problems in prejudice.* New York: King's Crown Press.

31. Alderfer, C. P., & Thomas, D. A. (1988). The significance of race and ethnicity for organizational behavior. In C. L. Cooper & I. Robertson (Eds.), *International*

review of industrial and organizational psychology. New York: Wiley; Cox, T., Jr., & Nkomo, S. M. (1990). Invisible men and women: A status report on race as a variable in organization behavior research. *Journal of Organizational Behavior, 11*, 419–431.

32. Sharpe, R. (1993, September 14). Losing ground. *Wall Street Journal*, A1, 12, 13.

33. King, E. B., & Ahmad, A. S. (2010). An experimental field study of interpersonal discrimination toward Muslim job applicants. *Personnel Psychology, 63*, 881–906.

34. Immen, W. (2007, June 29). Minorities still see barriers in way to the top. *Globe and Mail*, C1.

35. (2007, June 29). Discrimination reported as a continuing issue in U.S. *Globe and Mail*, C1.

36. Greenhaus, J. H., & Parasuraman, S. (1993). Job performance attributions and career advancement prospects: An examination of gender and race effects. *Organizational Behavior and Human Decision Processes, 55*, 273–297.

37. Powell, G. N. (1992). The good manager: Business students' stereotypes of Japanese managers versus stereotypes of American managers. *Group & Organizational Management, 17*, 44–56.

38. Brief, A. P., Umphress, E. E., Dietz, J., Burrows, J. W., Butz, R. M., Scholten, L. (2005). Community matters: Realistic group conflict theory and the impact of diversity. *Academy of Management Journal, 48*, 830–844.

39. Galt, V. (2005, May 4). Glass ceiling still tough to crack. *Globe and Mail*, C1, C2; Flavelle, D. (2005, April 28). Women advance up ranks slowly. *Toronto Star*, D1, D12; Perry, A. (2009, March 6). Women climbing corporate ranks: Study. *Toronto Star*, B3.

40. Brenner, O. C., Tomkiewicz, J., & Schein, V. E. (1989). The relationship between sex role stereotypes and requisite management characteristics revisited. *Academy of Management Journal, 32*, 662–669; Heilman, M. E., Block, C. J., Martell, R. F., & Simon, M. C. (1989). Has anything changed? Current characterizations of men, women, and managers. *Journal of Applied Psychology, 74*, 935–942; Schein, V. E. (1975). Relationships between sex role stereotypes and requisite management characteristics among female managers. *Journal of Applied Psychology, 60*, 340–344.

41. Brenner et al., 1989; Powell, G. N., Butterfield, D. A., & Parent, J. D. (2002). Gender and managerial stereotypes: Have the times changed? *Journal of Management, 28*(2), 177–193; Koenig, A. M., Eagly, A. H., Mitchell, A. A., & Ristikari, T. (2011). Are leader stereotypes masculine? A meta-analysis of three research paradigms. *Psychological Bulletin, 137*, 616–642.

42. Rosen, B., & Jerdee, T. H. (1974). Influence of sex role stereotypes on personnel decisions. *Journal of Applied Psychology, 59*, 9–14.

43. Cohen, S. L., & Bunker, K. A. (1975). Subtle effects of sex role stereotypes on recruiters' hiring decisions. *Journal of Applied Psychology, 60*, 566–572. See also Rose, G. L., & Andiappan, P. (1978). Sex effects on managerial hiring decisions. *Academy of Management Journal, 21*, 104–112.

44. Heilman, M. E., Wallen, A. S., Fuchs, D., & Tamkins, M. M. (2004). Penalties for success: Reactions to women who succeed at male gender-typed tasks. *Journal of Applied Psychology, 89*, 416–427.

45. Parasuraman, S., & Greenhaus, J. H. (1993). Personal portrait: The lifestyle of the woman manager. In E. A. Fagenson (Ed.), *Women in management: Trends, issues, and challenges in managerial diversity*. Newbury Park, CA: Sage; Cleveland, J. N., Vescio, T. K., & Barnes-Farrell, J. L. (2005). Gender discrimination in organizations. In R. L. Dipboye & A. Colella (Eds.), *Discrimination at work: The psychological and organizational bases*. Mahwah, NJ: Lawrence Erlbaum Associates.

46. Tosi, H. L., & Einbender, S. W. (1985). The effects of the type and amount of information in sex discrimination research: A meta-analysis. *Academy of Management Journal, 28*, 712–723.

47. For a review, see Latham, G. P., Skarlicki, D., Irvine, D., & Siegel, J. P. (1993). The increasing importance of performance appraisals to employee effectiveness in organizational settings in North America. In C. L. Cooper & I. Robertson (Eds.), *International review of industrial and organizational psychology*. New York: Wiley. For a representative study, see Pulakos, E. D., White, L. A., Oppler, S. A., & Borman, W. C. (1989). Examination of race and sex effects on performance ratings. *Journal of Applied Psychology, 74*, 770–780; Cleveland, Vescio, & Barnes-Farrell, 2005.

48. Roth, P. L., Purvis, K. L., & Bobko, P. (2012). A meta-analysis of gender group differences for measures of job performance in field studies. *Journal of Management, 38*, 719–739.

49. Galt, 2005, March 2.

50. Galt, 2005, May 4.

51. Rosen, B., & Jerdee, T. H. (1976). The nature of job-related age stereotypes. *Journal of Applied Psychology, 61*, 180–183. See also Gibson, K. J., Zerbe, W. J., & Franken, R. E. (1992). Job search strategies for older job hunters: Addressing employers' perceptions. *Canadian Journal of Counselling, 26*, 166–176.

52. Gibson et al., 1992.

53. Ng, T. W. H., & Feldman, D. C. (2008). The relationship of age to ten dimensions of job performance. *Journal of Applied Psychology, 93*, 392–423; McEvoy, G. M., & Cascio, W. F. (1989). Cumulative evidence of the relationship between employee age and job performance. *Journal of Applied Psychology, 74*, 11–17. For a broader review on age, see Rhodes, S. R. (1983). Age related differences in work attitudes and behavior. *Psychological Bulletin, 93*, 328–367.

54. Rosen, B., & Jerdee, T. H. (1976). The influence of age stereotypes on managerial decisions. *Journal of Applied Psychology, 61*, 428–432. Also see Dietrick, E. J., & Dobbins, G. J. (1991). The influence of subordinate age on managerial actions: An attributional analysis. *Journal of Organizational Behavior, 12*, 367–377.

55. Galt, V. (2002, October 16). What am I, chopped liver? *Globe and Mail*, C1, C6.

56. Galt, 2002, October 16.

57. Dobson, S. (2011, March 14). 50-plus awards celebrate older workers. *Canadian HR Reporter, 24*(5), 1, 6.

58. Falkenberg, 1990; Fiske, S. T., Beroff, D. N., Borgida, E., Deaux, K., & Heilman, M. E. (1991). Use of sex stereotyping research in Price Waterhouse v. Hopkins. *American Psychologist, 46*, 1049–1060.

59. Dobson, S. (2010, May 3). HR by the numbers. *Canadian HR Reporter, 23*(9), 4.

60. Shaw, A. (2008, May 5). Boeing puts diversity to work—silently. *Canadian HR Reporter, 21*(9), 18; Caballero, R., & Yerema, R. (2009, February 19). Employer Review: Boeing Canada Operations Limited: Chosen as one of Canada's Best Diversity Employers for 2009. www.eluta.ca/diversity-at-boeing-canada; Chosen as one of Canada's Best Diversity Employers for 2012. www.eluta.ca/diversity-at-boeing-canada.

61. Caudron, S. (1993, April). Training can damage diversity efforts. *Personnel Journal*, 51–62.

62. Scott, K. A., Heathcote, J. M., & Gruman, J. A. (2011). The diverse organization: Finding gold at the end of the rainbow. *Human Resource Management, 50*, 735–755.

63. Mayer, R. C., & Davis, J. H. (1999). The effect of the performance appraisal system on trust for management: A field quasi-experiment. *Journal of Applied Psychology, 84*, 123–136.

64. Lee, C. (1997, January). Trust. *Training, 34*(1), 28–37.

65. Mayer & Davis, 1999; Davis, J. H., Mayer, R. C., & Schoorman, F. D. (1995, October). The trusted general manager and firm performance: Empirical evidence of a strategic advantage. Paper presented at the 15th annual meeting of the Strategic Management Society, Mexico City, Mexico. Cited in Mayer & Davis, 1999.

66. Davis, Mayer, & Schoorman, 1995; Mayer, R. C., Davis, J. H., & Schoorman, F. D. (1995). An integrative model of organizational trust. *Academy of Management Review, 20*, 709–734; Rousseau, D. M., Sitkin, S. B., Burt, R. S., & Camerer, C. (1998). Not so different after all: A cross-discipline view of trust. *Academy of Management Review, 23*, 393–404.

67. Mayer, Davis, & Schoorman, 1995.

68. Mayer & Davis, 1999; Mayer, Davis, & Schoorman, 1995.

69. Colquitt, J. A., & Rodell, J. B. (2011). Justice, trust, and trustworthiness: A longitudinal analysis integrating three theoretical perspectives. *Academy of Management Journal, 54*, 1183–1206.

70. Dirks, K. T., & Ferrin, D. L. (2002). Trust in leadership: Meta-analytic findings and implications for research and practice. *Journal of Applied Psychology, 87*, 611–628.

71. Neto, J. T. (2009, April 6). About this survey. *A special national report for the Great Place to Work Institute Canada. Globe and Mail*, GPTW2.

72. Colquitt, J. A., Lepine, J. A., Zapata, C. P., & Wild, R. E. (2011). Trust in typical and high-reliability contexts: Building and reacting to trust among firefighters. *Academy of Management Journal, 54*, 999–1015.

73. Rhoades, L., & Eisenberger, R. (2002). Perceived organizational support: A review of the literature. *Journal of Applied Psychology, 87*, 698–714.

74. Rhoades & Eisenberger, 2002.

75. Shanock, L. R., & Eisenberger, R. (2006). When supervisors feel supported: Relationships with subordinates' perceived supervisor support, perceived organizational support, and performance. *Journal of Applied Psychology, 91*, 689–695.

76. Allen, D. G., Shore, L. M., & Griffeth, R. W. (2003). The role of perceived organizational support and supportive human resource practices in the turnover process. *Journal of Management, 29*(1), 99–118.

77. Rynes, S. L., Bretz, R., & Gerhart, B. (1991). The importance of recruitment in job choice: A different way of looking. *Personnel Psychology, 44*, 487–521.

78. Hausknecht, J. P., Day, D. V., & Thomas, S. C. (2004). Applicant reactions to selection procedures: An updated model and meta-analysis. *Personnel Psychology, 57*, 639–683.

79. Campion, M. A., Palmer, D. K., and Campion, J. E. (1997). A review of structure in the selection interview. *Personnel Psychology, 50*, 655–702; McDaniel, M. A., Whetzel, D. L., Schmidt, F. L., & Maurer, S. D. (1994). The validity of employment interviews: A comprehensive review and meta-analysis. *Journal of Applied Psychology, 79*, 599–616; Wiesner, W. H., & Cronshaw, S. F. (1988). A meta-analytic investigation of the impact of interview format and degree of structure on the validity of the employment interview. *Journal of Occupational Psychology, 61*, 275–290.

80. Hakel, M.D. (1982). Employment interviewing. In K. M. Rowland & G. R. Ferris (Eds.), *Personnel management*. Boston: Allyn and Bacon.

81. Hakel, 1982; Dipboye, R. L. (1989). Threats to the incremental validity of interviewer judgments. In R. W. Eder & G. R. Ferris (Eds.), *The employment interview: Theory, research, and practice*. Newbury Park, CA: Sage.

82. Hollmann, T. D. (1972). Employment interviewers' errors in processing positive and negative information. *Journal of Applied Psychology, 56*, 130–134.

83. Rowe, P. M. (1989). Unfavorable information in interview decisions. In R. W. Eder & G. R. Ferris (Eds.), *The employment interview: Theory, research, and practice*. Newbury Park, CA: Sage.

84. Maurer, T. J., & Alexander, R. A. (1991). Contrast effects in behavioral measurement: An investigation of alternative process explanations. *Journal of Applied Psychology, 76*, 3–10; Maurer, T. J., Palmer, J. K., & Ashe, D. K. (1993). Diaries, checklists, evaluations, and contrast effects in measurement of behavior. *Journal of Applied Psychology, 78*, 226–231; Schmitt, N. (1976). Social and situational determinants of interview decisions: Implications for the employment interview. *Personnel Psychology, 29*, 70–101.

85. One of Canada's Best Diversity Employers for 2012, www.eluta.ca/diversity-at-kpmg.

86. Chapman, D. S., & Zweig, D. I. (2005). Developing a nomological network for interview structure: Antecedents and consequences of the structured selection interview. *Personnel Psychology, 58*, 673–702.

87. For other reasons and a review of the interview literature, see Harris, M. M. (1989). Reconsidering the employment interview: A review of recent literature and suggestions for future research. *Personnel Psychology, 42*, 691–726.

88. Balzer, W. K., & Sulsky, L. M. (1992). Halo and performance appraisal research: A critical examination. *Journal of Applied Psychology, 77*, 975–985; Cooper, W. H. (1981). Ubiquitous halo. *Psychological Bulletin, 90*, 218–244; Murphy, K. R., Jako, R. A., & Anhalt, R. L. (1993). Nature and consequences of halo error: A critical analysis. *Journal of Applied Psychology, 78*, 218–225.

89. Kingstrom, P. D., & Bass, A. R. (1981). A critical analysis of studies comparing behaviorally anchored rating scales (BARS) and other rating formats. *Personnel Psychology, 34*, 263–289; Landy, F. J., & Farr, J. L. (1983). *The measurement of work performance*. New York: Academic Press.

90. Roch, S. G., Woehr, D. J., Mishra, V., & Kieszczynska, U. (2012). Rater training revisited: An updated meta-analytic review of frame-of-reference training. *Journal of Occupational and Organizational Psychology, 85*, 370–395.

Chapter 4

1. Excerpted from Nebenzahl, D. (2009, February 28). Managing the generation gap. *The Gazette* (Montreal), G1–G2. Reprinted by the express permission of Montreal Gazette Group Inc., a CanWest Partnership.

2. Hofstede, G. (1980). *Culture's consequences: International differences in work-related values*. Beverly Hills, CA: Sage, 19; see also Rokeach, M. (1973). *The nature of human values*. New York: Free Press.

3. Meglino, B. M., & Ravlin, E. C. (1998). Individual values in organizations: Concepts, controversies, and research. *Journal of Management, 24*, 351–389.

4. Schwartz, S. H. (1992). Universals in the content and structure of values: Theoretical advances and empirical tests in 20 countries. *Advances in Experimental Social Psychology, 25*, 1–65.

5. See for example Hammill, G. (2005, Winter/Spring). Mixing and managing four generations of employees. *FDU Magazine* (online), http://view.fdu.edu/default.aspx?id=1144.

6. Cennamo, L., & Gardner, D. (2008). Generational differences in work values, outcomes and person–organisation fit. *Journal of Managerial Psychology, 23*, 891–906; Hess, N., & Jepsen, D. M. (2009). Career stage and generational differences in psychological contracts. *Career Development International, 14*, 261–283; Wong, M., Gardiner, E., Lang, W., & Coulon, L. (2008). General differences in personality and motivation: Do they exist and what are the implications for the workplace? *Journal of Managerial*

Psychology, 23, 878–890; Deal, J. J. (2007). *Retiring the generation gap: How employees young and old can find common ground.* San Francisco: Jossey-Bass.

7. Westerman, J. W., & Yamamura, J. H. (2007). Generational preferences for work environment fit: Effects on employee outcomes. *Career Development International, 12*, 150–161; Cennamo & Gardner, 2008; Wong et al., 2008.

8. Twenge, J. M. (2010). A review of the empirical evidence on generational differences in work attitudes. *Journal of Business and Psychology, 25*, 201–210.

9. Twenge, 2010; Twenge, J. M., Campbell, S. M., Hoffman, B. J., & Lance, C. E. (2010). Generational differences in work values: Leisure and extrinsic values increasing, social and intrinsic values decreasing. *Journal of Management, 36*, 1117–1142.

10. Deal, 2007.

11. Meglino & Ravlin, 1998; Kristof, A. L. (1996). Person-organization fit: An integrative review of its conceptualizations, measurement, and implications. *Personnel Psychology, 49*, 1–49.

12. Black, J. S., & Mendenhall, M. (1990). Cross-cultural training effectiveness: A review and theoretical framework for future research. *Academy of Management Review, 15*, 113–136.

13. MOW International Research Team. (1987). *The meaning of working.* London: Academic Press.

14. Hofstede, G., Hofstede, G. J., Minkov, M. (2010). *Cultures and organizations: Software of the mind* (3rd ed.). New York: McGraw-Hill.

15. Hofstede, G. (1991). *Cultures and organizations: Software of the mind.* London: McGraw-Hill; Hofstede, G., & Bond, M. H. (1988). The Confucius connection: From cultural roots to economic growth. *Organizational Dynamics, 16*(4), 4–21.

16. House, R. J., Hanges, P. J., Javidan, M., Dorfman, P. W., & Gupta, V. (Eds.) (2004). *Culture, leadership, and organizations: The GLOBE study of 62 societies.* Thousand Oaks, CA: Sage.

17. For a meta-analysis of the correlates of Hofstede's cultural dimensions see Taras, V., Kirkman, B. L., & Steel, P. (2010). Examining the impact of *Culture's Consequences*: A three-decade, multilevel, meta-analytic review of Hofstede's cultural value dimensions. *Journal of Applied Psychology, 95*, 405–439.

18. Hofstede, G. (1984). The cultural relativity of the quality of life concept. *Academy of Management Review, 9*, 389–398; Hofstede, G. (1993, February). Cultural constraints in management theories. *Academy of Management Executive*, 81–94.

19. Young, S. M. (1992). A framework for successful adoption and performance of Japanese manufacturing practices in the United States. *Academy of Management Review, 17*, 677–700; Basadur, M. (1992, May). Managing creativity: A Japanese model. *Academy of Management Executive*, 29–42.

20. Glasman, L. R., & Albarracín, D. (2006). Forming attitudes that predict future behavior: A meta-analysis of the attitude-behavior relation. *Psychological Bulletin, 132*, 778–821.

21. The following syllogistic construction of attitudes can be found in Jones, E. E., & Gerard, H. B. (1967). *Foundations of social psychology.* New York: Wiley.

22. Harrison, D. A., Newman, D. A., & Roth, P. L. (2006). How important are job attitudes? Meta-analytic comparisons of integrative behavioral outcomes and time sequences. *Academy of Management Journal, 49*, 305–325.

23. Locke, E. A. (1976). The nature and causes of job satisfaction. In M. D. Dunnette (Ed.), *Handbook of industrial and organizational psychology.* Chicago: Rand McNally. See also Rice, R. W., Gentile, D. A., & McFarlin, D. B. (1991). Facet importance and job satisfaction. *Journal of Applied Psychology, 76*, 31–39.

24. Smith, P. C. (1992). In pursuit of happiness: Why study general job satisfaction? In C. J. Cranny, P. C. Smith, & E. F. Stone (Eds.), *Job satisfaction.* New York: Lexington.

25. Smith, P. C., Kendall, L. M., & Hulin, C. L. (1969). *The measurement of satisfaction in work and retirement.* Chicago: Rand McNally; Bowling Green State University (2009). *The job descriptive index.* Bowling Green, OH: Department of Psychology, Bowling Green State University.

26. Weiss, D. J., Dawis, R. V., England, G. W., & Lofquist, L. H. (1967). *Manual for the Minnesota satisfaction questionnaire: Minnesota studies in vocational rehabilitation.* Minneapolis: Vocational Psychology Research, University of Minnesota.

27. Locke, E. A. (1969). What is job satisfaction? *Organizational Behavior and Human Performance, 4*, 309–336; Rice, R. W., McFarlin, D. B., & Bennett, D. E. (1989). Standards of comparison and job satisfaction. *Journal of Applied Psychology, 74*, 591–598.

28. Williams, M. L., McDaniel, M. A., & Nguyen, N. T. (2006). A meta-analysis of the antecedents and consequences of pay level satisfaction. *Journal of Applied Psychology, 91*, 392–413.

29. For a good overview of fairness research, see Greenberg, J., & Colquitt, J. A. (2005). *Handbook of organizational justice.* Mahwah, NJ: Lawrence Erlbaum Associates. For empirical reviews of the literature, see Colquitt, J. A., Conlon, D. E., Wesson, M. J., Porter, C. O. L. H., & Ng, K. Y. (2001). Justice at the millennium: A meta-analytic review of 25 years of organizational justice research. *Journal of Applied Psychology, 86*, 425–445; Cohen-Charash, Y., & Spector, P. E. (2001). The role of justice in organizations: A meta-analysis. *Organizational Behavior and Human Decision Processes, 86*, 278–321.

30. Adams, J. S. (1963). Toward an understanding of inequity. *Journal of Abnormal and Social Psychology, 67*, 422–436.

31. See Kulik, C. T., & Ambrose, M. L. (1992). Personal and situational determinants of referent choice. *Academy of Management Review, 17*, 212–237.

32. Sharp, I. (2009, April 15). A few bumps in the road. *Globe and Mail*, B3.

33. Greenberg, J. (1987). A taxonomy of organizational justice theories. *Academy of Management Review, 12*, 9–22.

34. Brockner, J., & Wisenfeld, B. M. (1996). An integrative framework for explaining reactions to decisions: Interactive effects of outcomes and procedures. *Psychological Bulletin, 120*, 189–208; Brockner, J., & Wiesenfeld, B. (2005). How, when, and why does outcome favorability interact with procedural fairness? In Greenberg & Colquitt, 2005.

35. Cropanzano, R., & Folger, R. (1989). Referent cognitions and task decision autonomy: Beyond equity theory. *Journal of Applied Psychology, 74*, 293. See also Folger, R. (1987). Reformulating the preconditions of resentment: A referent cognitions model. In J. C. Masters & W. P. Smith (Eds.), *Social comparison, justice, and relative deprivation: Theoretical, empirical, and policy perspectives.* Hillsdale, NJ: Erlbaum.

36. Colquitt, J. A., Greenberg, J., & Zapata-Phelan, C. P. (2005). What is organizational justice? A historical overview. In Greenberg & Colquitt, 2005; Bies, R. J. (2005). Are procedural justice and interactional justice conceptually distinct? In Greenberg & Colquitt, 2005.

37. Greenberg, J. (2006). Losing sleep over organizational injustice: Attenuating insomniac reactions to underpayment inequity with supervisory training in interactional justice. *Journal of Applied Psychology, 91*, 58–69.

38. Judge, T. A. (1992). The dispositional perspective in human resources research. *Research in Personnel and Human Resources Management, 10*, 31–72. See also Staw, B. M., & Cohen-Charash, Y. (2005). The dispositional approach to job satisfaction: More than

a mirage, but not yet an oasis. *Journal of Organizational Behavior, 26*, 59–78; Bowling, N. A., Beehr, T. A., Wagner, S. H., & Libkuman, T. M. (2005). Adaptation-level theory, opponent process theory, and dispositions: An integrated approach to the stability of job satisfaction. *Journal of Applied Psychology, 90*, 1044–1053.

39. Song, Z., Li, W., & Arvey, R. D. (2011). Associations between dopamine and serotonin genes and job satisfaction: Preliminary evidence from the Add Health Study. *Journal of Applied Psychology, 96*, 1223–1233.

40. Judge, T. A., Heller, D., & Mount, M. K. (2002). Five-factor model of personality and job satisfaction: A meta-analysis. *Journal of Applied Psychology, 87*, 530–541.

41. Judge, T. A., Bono, J. E., & Locke, E. A. (2000). Personality and job satisfaction: The mediating role of job characteristics. *Journal of Applied Psychology, 85*, 237–249.

42. Weiss, H. M., & Cropanzano, R. (1996). Affective events theory: A theoretical discussion of the structure, causes and consequences of affective experiences at work. *Research in Organizational Behavior, 18*, 1–74.

43. Barsky, A., Kaplan, S. A., & Beal, D. J. (2011). Just feelings? The role of affect in the formation of organizational fairness judgments. *Journal of Management, 37*, 248–279.

44. Barsade, S. G. (2002). The ripple effect: Emotional contagion and its influence on group behavior. *Administrative Science Quarterly, 47*, 644–675; see also Vijayalakshmi, V., & Bhattacharyya, S. (2012). Emotional contagion and its relevance to individual behavior and organizational processes: A position paper. *Journal of Business and Psychology*, 1–12.

45. Grandey, A. A., Dickter, D. N., & Sin, H. P. (2004). The customer is *not* always right: Customer aggression and emotion regulation of service employees. *Journal of Organizational Behavior, 25*, 397–418.

46. Hülsheger, U. R., & Schewe, A. F. (2011). On the costs and benefits of emotional labor: A meta-analysis of three decades of research. *Journal of Occupational Health Psychology, 16*, 361–389.

47. Côté, S., & Morgan, L. M. (2002). A longitudinal analysis of the association between emotion regulation, job satisfaction, and intentions to quit. *Journal of Organizational Behavior, 23*, 947–962.

48. Glomb, T. M., Kammeyer-Mueller, J. D., & Rotundo, M. (2004). Emotional labor demands and compensating wage differentials. *Journal of Applied Psychology, 89*, 700–714.

49. This material draws upon Locke, 1976.

50. Hackett, R. D. (1989). Work attitudes and employee absenteeism: A synthesis of the literature. *Journal of Occupational Psychology, 62*, 235–248; Hackett, R. D., & Guion, R. M. (1985). A reevaluation of the absenteeism-job satisfaction relationship. *Organizational Behavior and Human Decision Processes, 35*, 340–381.

51. Johns, G. (2008). Absenteeism and presenteeism: Not at work or not working well. In C. L. Cooper & J. Barling (Eds.), *The Sage handbook of organizational behavior* (Vol. 1). London: Sage; Nicholson, N., & Johns, G. (1985). The absence culture and the psychological contract—Who's in control of absence? *Academy of Management Review, 10*, 397–407.

52. Farris, G. F. (1971). A predictive study of turnover. *Personnel Psychology, 24*, 311–328. However, the more general relationship between performance and voluntary turnover is negative, as shown by Bycio, P., Hackett, R. D., & Alvares, K. M. (1990). Job performance and turnover: A review and meta-analysis. *Applied Psychology: An International Review, 39*, 47–76; Williams, C. R., & Livingstone, L. P. (1994). Another look at the relationship between performance and voluntary turnover. *Academy of Management Journal, 37*, 269–298.

53. Hom, P. W., & Griffeth, R. W. (1995). *Employee turnover*. Cincinnati, OH: South-Western.

54. This model is based on Hom & Griffeth, 1995; Lee, T. W., & Mitchell, T. R. (1994). An alternative approach: The unfolding model of voluntary employee turnover. *Academy of Management Review, 19*, 51–89; Mitchell, T. R., Holtom, B. C., Lee, T. W., Sablynski, C. J., & Erez, M. (2001). Why people stay: Using job embeddedness to predict voluntary turnover. *Academy of Management Journal, 44*, 1102–1121.

55. Hom & Griffeth, 1995.

56. Carsten, J. M., & Spector, P. E. (1987). Unemployment, job satisfaction, and employee turnover: A meta-analytic test of the Muchinsky model. *Journal of Applied Psychology, 72*, 374–381.

57. Boswell, W. R., Boudreau, J. W., & Tichy, J. (2005). The relationship between employee job change and job satisfaction: The honeymoon-hangover effect. *Journal of Applied Psychology, 90*, 882–892; see also Boswell, W. R., Shipp, A. J., Payne, S. C., & Culbertson, S. S. (2009). Changes in newcomer satisfaction over time: Examining the pattern of honeymoons and hangovers. *Journal of Applied Psychology, 94*, 844–858.

58. Judge, T. A., Thoresen, C. J., Bono, J. E., & Patton, G. K. (2001). The job

satisfaction-job performance relationship: A qualitative and quantitative review. *Psychological Bulletin, 127*, 376–407.

59. Iaffaldano, M. T., & Muchinsky, P. M. (1985). Job satisfaction and job performance: A meta-analysis. *Psychological Bulletin, 97*, 251–273.

60. Lawler, E. E., III (1973). *Motivation in organizations*. Monterey, CA: Brooks/ Cole.

61. Riketta, M. (2008). The causal relationship between job attitudes and performance: A meta-analysis of panel studies. *Journal of Applied Psychology, 93*, 472–481.

62. Organ, D. W. (1988). *Organizational citizenship behavior: The good soldier syndrome*. Lexington, MA: Lexington; Podsakoff, P. M., MacKenzie, S. B., Paine, J. B., & Bachrach, D. G. (2000). Organizational citizenship behaviors: A critical review of the theoretical and empirical literature and suggestions for future research. *Journal of Management, 26*, 513–563.

63. Lepine, J. A., Erez, A., & Johnson, D.E. (2002). The nature and dimensionality of organizational citizenship behavior: A critical review and meta-analysis. *Journal of Applied Psychology, 87*, 52–65; Organ, D. W., & Ryan, K. (1995). A meta-analytic review of attitudinal and dispositional predictors of organizational citizenship behavior. *Personnel Psychology, 48*, 775–802; Hoffman, B. J., Blair, C. A., Meriac, J. P., & Woehr, D. J. (2007). Expanding the criterion domain? A quantitative review of the OCB literature. *Journal of Applied Psychology, 92*, 555–566.

64. Organ, 1988.

65. Lepine et al., 2002; Fassina, N. E., Jones, D. A., & Uggerslev, K. L. (2008). Meta-analytic tests of relationships between organizational justice and citizenship behavior: Testing agent-system and shared-variance models. *Journal of Organizational Behavior, 29*, 805–828.

66. George, J. M. (1991). State or trait: Effects of positive mood on prosocial behaviors at work. *Journal of Applied Psychology, 76*, 299–307.

67. Podsakoff, N. P., Whiting, S. W., Podsakoff, P. M., & Blume, B. D. (2009). Individual- and organizational-level consequences of organizational citizenship behaviors: A meta-analysis. *Journal of Applied Psychology, 94*, 122–141.

68. Leavy, B. (2005). Innovation at Xilinx: A senior operating manager's view. *Strategy & Leadership, 33*(4), 33–37.

69. Berry, C.M., Lelchook, A.M., & Clark, M.A. (2011). A meta-analysis of the interrelationships between employee lateness, absenteeism, and turnover:

Implications for models of withdrawal behavior. *Journal of Organizational Behavior, 33*(5), 678–699; Harrison et al., 2006.

70. Harter, J.K, Schmidt, F.L., & Hayes, T.L. (2002). Business-unit level relationship between employee satisfaction, employee engagement, and business outcomes: A meta-analysis. *Journal of Applied Psychology, 87,* 268–279.

71. Laabs, J. (1999, March). The HR side of Sears' comeback. *Workforce,* 24–29.

72. Meyer, J.P., & Allen, N.J. (1997). *Commitment in the workplace.* Thousand Oaks, CA: Sage; for a recent critique and revised conception of commitment see Klein, H.J., Molloy, J.C., & Brinsfield, C.T. (2012). Reconceptualizing workplace commitment to redress a stretched construct: Revisiting assumptions and removing confounds. *Academy of Management Review, 37,* 130–151.

73. Meyer, J.P., Allen, N.J., & Topolnytsky, L. (1998). Commitment in a changing world of work. *Canadian Psychology, 39,* 83–93; see also Meyer, J.P., Jackson, T.A., & Maltin, E.R. (2008). Commitment in the workplace: Past, present, and future. In J. Barling & C.L. Cooper (Eds.), *The Sage handbook of organizational behavior* (Vol. 1). London: Sage.

74. Meyer, J.P, Stanley, D.J., Herscovitch, L., & Topolnytsky, L. (2002). Affective, continuance, and normative commitment to the organization: A meta-analysis of antecedents, correlates, and consequences. *Journal of Vocational Behavior, 61,* 20–52.

75. Meyer et al., 2002.

76. Meyer et al., 2002; for a careful study, see Jaros, S.J., Jermier, J.M., Koehler, J.W., & Sincich, T. (1993). Effects of continuance, affective, and moral commitment on the withdrawal process: An evaluation of eight structural equation models. *Academy of Management Journal, 36,* 951–995.

77. Meyer, J.P., Becker, T.E., & Vandenberghe, C. (2004). Employee commitment and motivation: A conceptual analysis and integrative model. *Journal of Applied Psychology, 89,* 991–1007.

78. Meyer, J.P., Paunonen, S.V., Gellatly, I.R., Goffin, R.D., & Jackson, D.N. (1989). Organizational commitment and job performance: It's the nature of the commitment that counts. *Journal of Applied Psychology, 74,* 152–156.

79. Randall, D.M. (1987). Commitment and the organization: The organization man revisited. *Academy of Management Review, 12,* 460–471.

80. Meyer, Allen, & Topolnytsky, 1998.

81. Cascio, W.F. (1993, February). Downsizing: What do we know? What have we learned? *Academy of Management Executive,* 95–104.

82. Meyer, Allen, & Topolnytsky, 1998; see also Meyer et al., 2008.

Chapter 5

1. Brooks, Y. (2006, December). Handle with care. *BC Business* (online), bcbusinessonline.ca; Colman, R. (2007, March). Packing the perfect HR punch: Great Little Box Company president and CEO Robert Meggy, CMA, FCMA, knows that people make a business. His unique approach to employee engagement proves it. *Entrepreneur* (online), www.entrepreneur.com; Great Little Box Company: A team approach to success. *Managing for Business Success.* Industry Canada, www.ic.gc.ca; Atkinson, C. (2008, July 2). The total package: Anatomy of a great place to work, *Globe and Mail,* B6; Brent, P. (2005, October). Packaging loyalty: A Vancouver maker thrives by finding employees who fit. *National Post,* WK2; Yerema, R. (2009, January 12). Employer Review: The Great Little Box Company Ltd.: Chosen as one of Canada's Top 100 employers and BC's top employers for 2009. www .eluta.ca; Great Little Box Company, www.greatlittlebox.com/about/history; Chosen as one of Canada's Top 100 employers, *Financial Post*'s Ten Best Companies to Work For and BC's Top Employers for 2012, www.eluta.ca/top-employer-great-little-box company.

2. Great Little Box Company: A team approach to success. *Managing for Business Success.* Industry Canada, www .ic.gc.ca.

3. Campbell, J.P., Dunnette, M.D., Lawler, E.E., III, & Weick, K.E., Jr. (1970). *Managerial behavior, performance, and effectiveness.* New York: McGraw-Hill. Also see Blau, G. (1993). Operationalizing direction and level of effort and testing their relationship to job performance. *Organizational Behavior and Human Decision Processes, 55,* 152–170.

4. Dyer, L., & Parker, D.F. (1975). Classifying outcomes in work motivation research: An examination of the intrinsic-extrinsic dichotomy. *Journal of Applied Psychology, 60,* 455–458; Kanungo, R.N., & Hartwick, J. (1987). An alternative to the intrinsic-extrinsic dichotomy of work rewards. *Journal of Management, 13,* 751–766. Also see Brief, A.P., & Aldag, R.J. (1977). The intrinsic-extrinsic dichotomy: Toward conceptual clarity. *Academy of Management Review, 2,* 496–500.

5. Vallerand, R.J. (1997). Toward a hierarchical model of intrinsic and extrinsic motivation. *Advances in Experimental Social Psychology, 29,* 271–360.

6. Deci, E.L., & Ryan, R.M. (1985). *Intrinsic motivation and self-determination in human behavior.* New York: Plenum.

7. Deci & Ryan, 1985.

8. Eisenberger, R., & Cameron, J. (1996). Detrimental effects of reward: Reality or myth? *American Psychologist, 51,* 1153–1166.

9. Guzzo, R.A. (1979). Types of rewards, cognitions, and work motivation. *Academy of Management Review, 4,* 75–86; Wiersma, U.J. (1992). The effects of extrinsic rewards in intrinsic motivation: A meta-analysis. *Journal of Occupational and Organizational Psychology, 65,* 101–114.

10. Gagné, M., & Deci, E.L. (2005). Self-determination theory and work motivation. *Journal of Organizational Behavior, 26,* 331–362.

11. Based on Campbell, J.P., & Pritchard, R.D. (1976). Motivation theory in industrial and organizational psychology. In M.D. Dunnette (Ed.), *Handbook of industrial and organizational psychology.* Chicago: Rand McNally.

12. O'Reilly, C.A. III, & Chatman, J.A. (1994). Working smarter and harder: A longitudinal study of managerial success. *Administrative Science Quarterly, 39,* 603–627.

13. Lang, J.W.B., Kersting, M., Hulsheger, U.R., & Lang, J. (2010). General mental ability, narrower cognitive abilities, and job performance: The perspective of the nested-factors model of cognitive abilities. *Personnel Psychology, 63,* 595–640; Hunter, J.E. (1986). Cognitive ability, cognitive aptitudes, job knowledge, and job performance. *Journal of Vocational Behavior, 29,* 340–362; Schmidt, F.L., & Hunter, J.E. (1998). The validity and utility of selection methods in personnel psychology: Practical and theoretical implications of 85 years of research findings. *Psychological Bulletin, 124,* 262–274; Judge, T.A., Klinger, R.L., & Simon, L.S. (2010). Time is on my side: Time, general mental ability, human capital, and extrinsic career success. *Journal of Applied Psychology, 95,* 92–107.

14. Mayer, J.D., Caruso, D.R., & Salovey, P. (2000). Emotional intelligence meets traditional standards for an intelligence. *Intelligence, 27,* 267–298; Salovey, P., & Mayer, J.D. (1990). Emotional intelligence. *Imagination, Cognition and Personality, 9,*185–211.

15. Mayer, Caruso, & Salovey, 2000.

16. George, J.M. (2000). Emotions and leadership: The role of emotional intelligence. *Human Relations, 53,* 1027–1055.

17. George, 2000.

18. George, 2000.

19. Van Rooy, D.L., & Viswesvaran, C. (2004). Emotional intelligence: A meta-analytic investigation of predictive validity and nomological net. *Journal of Vocational Behavior, 65,* 71–95.

20. O'Boyle, E.H., Jr., Humphrey, R.H., Pollack, J.M., Hawver, T.H., & Story, P.A. (2011). The relation between emotional intelligence and job performance: A meta-analysis. *Journal of Organizational Behavior, 32,* 788–818.

21. Schutte, N.S., Malouff, J.M., Hall, L.E., Haggerty, D.J., Cooper, J.T., Golden, C.J., & Dornheim, L. (1998). Development and validation of a measure of emotional intelligence. *Personality and Individual Differences, 25,* 167–177; Wong, C., & Law, K.S. (2002). The effects of leader and follower emotional intelligence on performance and attitude: An exploratory study. *The Leadership Quarterly, 13,* 243–274; Daus, C.S., & Ashkanasy, N.M. (2005). The case for the ability-based model of emotional intelligence in organizational behaviour. *Journal of Organizational Behavior, 26,*453–466; Joseph, D.L., & Newman, D.A. (2010). Emotional intelligence: An integrative meta-analysis and cascading model. *Journal of Applied Psychology, 95,* 54–78.

22. Côté, S., & Miners, C.T.H. (2006). Emotional intelligence, cognitive intelligence, and job performance. *Administrative Science Quarterly, 51,* 1–28.

23. See Henkoff, R. (1993, March 22). Companies that train best. *Fortune,* 62–75.

24. The distinction between need (content) and process theories was first made by Campbell et al., 1970.

25. Maslow, A.H. (1970). *Motivation and personality* (2nd ed.). New York: Harper & Row.

26. Alderfer, C.P. (1969). An empirical test of a new theory of human needs. *Organizational Behavior and Human Performance, 4,* 142–175. Also see Alderfer, C.P. (1972). *Existence, relatedness, and growth: Human needs in organizational settings.* New York: The Free Press.

27. McClelland, D.C. (1985). *Human motivation.* Glenview, IL: Scott, Foresman.

28. McClelland, D.C., & Winter, D.G. (1969). *Motivating economic achievement.* New York: The Free Press, 50–52.

29. McClelland, D.C., & Boyatzis, R.E. (1982). Leadership motive pattern and long-term success in management. *Journal of Applied Psychology, 67,* 737–743; McClelland, D.C., & Burnham, D. (1976, March–April). Power is the great motivator. *Harvard Business Review,* 159–166. However, need for power might not be the best motive pattern for managers of technical and professional people. See Cornelius, E.T., III, & Lane, F.B. (1984). The power motive and managerial success in a professionally oriented service industry organization. *Journal of Applied Psychology, 69,* 32–39.

30. Wahba, M.A., & Bridwell, L.G. (1976). Maslow reconsidered: A review of research on the need hierarchy theory. *Organizational Behavior and Human Performance, 15,* 212–240.

31. Schneider, B., & Alderfer, C.P. (1973). Three studies of measures of need satisfaction in organizations. *Administrative Science Quarterly, 18,* 498–505. Also see Alderfer, C.P., Kaplan, R.E., & Smith, K.K. (1974). The effect of relatedness need satisfaction on relatedness desires. *Administrative Science Quarterly, 19,* 507–532. For a disconfirming test, see Rauschenberger, J., Schmitt, N., & Hunter, J.E. (1980). A test of the need hierarchy concept by a Markov model of change in need strength. *Administrative Science Quarterly, 25,* 654–670.

32. McClelland, 1985; Spangler, W.D. (1992). Validity of questionnaire and TAT measures of need for achievement: Two meta-analyses. *Psychological Bulletin, 112,* 140–154.

33. Great Little Box Company: A team approach to success. *Managing for Business Success.* Industry Canada, www.ic.gc.ca.

34. Herzberg, F. (1966). *Work and the nature of man.* Cleveland: World Publishing.

35. Lawler, E.E., III. (1973). *Motivation in work organizations.* Monterey, CA: Brooks/Cole.

36. Vroom, V.H. (1964). *Work and motivation.* New York: Wiley.

37. Mitchell, T.R. (1974). Expectancy models of job satisfaction, occupational preference, and effort: A theoretical, methodological, and empirical appraisal. *Psychological Bulletin, 81,* 1053–1077. Also see Pinder, C.C. (1984). *Work motivation: Theory, issues, and applications.* Glenview, IL: Scott, Foresman; Kanfer, R. (1990). Motivation theory in industrial and organizational psychology. In M.D. Dunnette & L.M. Hough (Eds.), *Handbook of industrial and organizational psychology* (2nd ed., Vol. 1). Palo Alto, CA: Consulting Psychologists Press.

38. A good discussion of how managers can strengthen expectancy and instrumentality relationships is presented by Strauss, G. (1977). Managerial practices. In J.R. Hackman & J.L. Suttle (Eds.), *Improving life at work: Behavioral science approaches to organizational change.* Glenview, IL: Scott, Foresman.

39. Adams, J.S. (1965). Injustice in social exchange. *Advances in Experimental Social Psychology, 2,* 267–299.

40. Kulik, C.T., & Ambrose, M.L. (1992). Personal and situational determinants of referent choice. *Academy of Management Review, 17,* 212–237.

41. Carrell, M.R., & Dittrich, J.E. (1978). Equity theory: The recent literature, methodological considerations, and new directions. *Academy of Management Review, 3,* 202–210; Mowday, R.T. (1991). Equity theory predictions of behavior in organizations. In R.M. Steers & L.W. Porter (Eds.), *Motivation and work behavior,* 111–131. New York: McGraw-Hill.

42. Mowday, 1991; Carrell & Dittrich, 1978.

43. See Kulik & Ambrose, 1992.

44. Colman, R. (2007, March).

45. Locke, E.A., & Latham, G.P. (2002). Building a practically useful theory of goal setting and task motivation. *American Psychologist, 57,* 705–717.

46. The best-developed theoretical position is that of Locke, E.A., & Latham, G.P. (1990). *A theory of goal setting and task performance.* Englewood Cliffs, NJ: Prentice-Hall.

47. Locke & Latham, 2002.

48. Locke & Latham, 2002.

49. Locke, E.A., Latham, G.P., & Erez, M. (1988). The determinants of goal commitment. *Academy of Management Review, 13,* 23–39.

50. See Erez, M., Earley, P.C., & Hulin, C.L. (1985). The impact of participation on goal acceptance and performance: A two-step model. *Academy of Management Journal, 28,* 50–66.

51. Latham, G.P., Erez, M., & Locke, E.A. (1988). Resolving scientific disputes by the joint design of crucial experiments by the antagonists: Application to the Erez-Latham dispute regarding participation in goal setting. *Journal of Applied Psychology, 73,* 753–772.

52. Latham, G.P., Mitchell, T.R., & Dosset, D.L. (1978). The importance of participative goal setting and anticipated rewards on goal difficulty and job performance. *Journal of Applied Psychology, 63,* 163–171; Saari, L.M., & Latham, G.P. (1979). The effects of holding goal difficulty constant on assigned and participatively set goals. *Academy of Management Journal, 22,* 163–168.

53. For a discussion of this issue, see Saari & Latham, 1979.

54. Payne, S.C., Youngcourt, S.S., & Beaubien, J.M. (2007). A meta-analytic examination of the goal orientation nomological net. *Journal of Applied Psychology, 92,*128–150; Zweig, D., &

Webster, J. (2004). Validation of a multidimensional measure of goal orientation. *Canadian Journal of Behavioural Science, 36*(3), 232–243.

55. Seijts, G.H., Latham, G.P., Tasa, K., & Latham, B.W. (2004). Goal setting and goal orientation: An integration of two different yet related literatures. *Academy of Management Journal, 47,* 227–239; Button, S.B., Mathieu, J.E., & Zajac, D.M. (1996). Goal orientation in organizational research: A conceptual and empirical foundation. *Organizational Behavior and Human Decision Processes, 67,* 26–48; VandeWalle, D., Brown, S.P., Cron, W.L., & Slocum, J.W., Jr. (1999). The influence of goal orientation and self-regulation tactics on sales performance: A longitudinal field test. *Journal of Applied Psychology, 84,* 249–259; VandeWalle, D., Cron, W.L., & Slocum, J.W., Jr. (2001). The role of goal orientation following performance feedback. *Journal of Applied Psychology, 86,* 629–640; Kozlowski, S.W.J., Gully, S.M., Brown, K.G., Salas, E., Smith, E.M., & Nason, E.R. (2001). Effects of training goals and goal orientation traits on multidimensional training outcomes and performance adaptability. *Organizational Behavior and Human Decision Processes, 85,* 1–31.

56. Latham, G.P., & Seijts, G.H. (1999). The effects of proximal and distal goals on performance on a moderately complex task. *Journal of Organizational Behavior, 20,* 421–429; Seijts, G.H., & Latham, G.P. (2001). The effect of distal learning, outcome, and proximal goals on a moderately complex task. *Journal of Organizational Behavior, 22,* 291–307.

57. O'Leary-Kelly, A.M., Martocchio, J.J., & Frink, D.D. (1994). A review of the influence of group goals on group performance. *Academy of Management Journal, 37,* 1285–1301; Kleingeld, A., van Mierlo, H., & Arends, L. (2011). The effect of goal setting on group performance: A meta-analysis. *Journal of Applied Psychology, 96,* 1289–1304.

58. Locke, E.A., & Latham, G.P. (1984). *Goal setting—A motivational technique that works.* Englewood Cliffs, NJ: Prentice-Hall.

59. Latham, G.P., & Baldes, J.J. (1975). The "practical significance" of Locke's theory of goal setting. *Journal of Applied Psychology, 60,* 122–124; Latham, G.P., & Locke, E. (1979, Autumn). Goal setting—a motivational technique that works. *Organizational Dynamics, 8*(2), 68–80.

60. Payne et al., 2007; Seijts, Latham, Tasa, & Latham, 2004; Seijts, G., & Latham, G.P. (2005). Learning versus performance goals: When should each be used?

Academy of Management Executive, 19, 124–131.

61. Latham & Seijts, 1999; Seijts & Latham, 2001.

62. Seijts, Latham, Tasa, & Latham, 2004; Seijts & Latham, 2005; Latham & Seijts, 1999; Seijts & Latham, 2001.

63. Kagitcibasi, C., & Berry, J.W. (1989). Cross-cultural psychology: Current research and trends. *Annual Review of Psychology, 40,* 493–531.

64. Hofstede, G. (1980). *Culture's consequences: International differences in work-related values.* Beverly Hills, CA: Sage.

65. For a review, see Kagitcibasi & Berry, 1989.

66. Adler, N.J. (1992). *International dimensions of organizational behavior* (2nd ed.). Belmont, CA: Wadsworth.

67. Locke & Latham, 2002.

68. Kirkman, B.L., & Shapiro, D.L. (1997). The impact of cultural values on employee resistance to teams: Toward a model of globalized self-managing work team effectiveness. *Academy of Management Review, 22,* 730–757.

69. Adler, 1992, 159.

Chapter 6

1. Gerstel, J. (2011, November 24). Best GTA employers: Building on a solid foundation, *The Toronto Star,* X4, X5; Chosen as one of Canada's Top 100 Employers, Top Employers for Canadians Over 40 and Greater Toronto's Top Employers for 2012, www.eluta.ca/top-employer-ellisdon; Brent, P. (2008, April 29). Who's on top?: EllisDon, www.workopolis.com; www.ellisdon.com/careers/culture.

2. Rynes, S.L., Gerhart, B., & Minette, K.A. (2004). The importance of pay in employee motivation: Discrepancies between what people say and what they do. *Human Resource Management, 43,* 381–394.

3. Immen, W. (2012, June 20). Companies boosting incentive programs. *Globe and Mail,* B17; Jenkins, G.D., Jr., Mitra, A., Gupta, N., & Shaw, J.D. (1998). Are financial incentives related to performance? A meta-analytic review of empirical research. *Journal of Applied Psychology, 83,* 777–787; Sturman, M.C., Trevor, C.O., Boudreau, J.W., & Gerhart, B. (2003). Is it worth it to win the talent war? Evaluating the utility of performance-based pay. *Personnel Psychology, 56,* 997–1035; Rynes, Gerhart, & Minette, 2004.

4. For reviews, see Chung, K.H. (1977). *Motivational theories and practices.* Columbus, OH: Grid; Lawler, E.E., III. (1971). *Pay and organizational effectiveness: A psychological view.* New York:

McGraw-Hill. For a careful study, see Wagner, J.A., III, Rubin, P.A., & Callahan, T.J. (1988). Incentive payment and nonmanagerial productivity: An interrupted time series analysis of magnitude and trend. *Organizational Behavior and Human Decision Processes, 42,* 47–74.

5. Locke, E.A., Feren, D.B., McCaleb, V.M., Shaw, K.N., & Denny, A.T. (1980). The relative effectiveness of four methods of motivating employee performance. In K.D. Duncan, M.M. Gruneberg, & D. Wallis (Eds.), *Changes in working life.* London: Wiley.

6. Fein, M. (1973, September). Work measurement and wage incentives. *Industrial Engineering,* 49–51.

7. Inspire your team. *Success,* 12; Perry, N.J. (1988, December 19). Here come richer, riskier pay plans. *Fortune,* 50–58; Sharplin, A.D. (1990). Lincoln Electric Company, 1989. In A.A. Thompson, Jr., & A.J. Strickland, III. (Eds.), *Strategic management: Concepts and cases.* Homewood, IL: BPI/Irwin.

8. For a general treatment of why firms fail to adopt state-of-the-art personnel practices, see Johns, G. (1993). Constraints on the adoption of psychology-based personnel practices: Lessons from organizational innovation. *Personnel Psychology, 46,* 569–592.

9. Posner, B.G. (1989, May). If at first you don't succeed. *Inc.,* 132–134.

10. Lawler, 1971.

11. Lawler, 1971; Nash, A., & Carrol, S. (1975). *The management of compensation.* Monterey, CA: Brooks/Cole.

12. Bertin, O. (2003, January 31). Is there any merit in giving merit pay? *Globe and Mail,* C1, C7.

13. Sethi, C. (2006, September 5). Calgary wages rising at record pace. *Globe and Mail,* B1, B2.

14. Young, G.J., Beckman, H., & Baker, E. (2012). Financial incentives, professional values and performance: A study of pay-for-performance in a professional organization. *Journal of Organizational Behavior,* doi: 10.1002/job.1770.

15. Chu, K. (2004, June 15). Firms report lacklustre results from pay-for-performance plans. *Wall Street Journal,* D2.

16. Heneman, R.L. (1990). Merit pay research. *Research in Personnel and Human Resources Management, 8,* 203–263; Tosi, H.L., & Gomez-Mejia, L.R. (1989). The decoupling of CEO pay and performance: An agency theory perspective. *Administrative Science Quarterly, 34,* 169–189; Ungson, G.R., & Steers, R.M. (1984). Motivation and politics in executive compensation. *Academy of Management Review, 9,* 313–323.

17. Haire, M., Ghiselli, E.E., & Gordon, M.E. (1967). A psychological study of pay. *Journal of Applied Psychology Monograph, 51,* (Whole No. 636).

18. Meyer, H.H. (1991, February). A solution to the performance appraisal feedback enigma. *Academy of Management Executive,* 68–76.

19. See Zenga, T.R. (1992). Why do employers only reward extreme performance? Examining the relationships among pay, performance, and turnover. *Administrative Science Quarterly, 37,* 198–219.

20. Benzie, R. (2011, June 25). OLG reports record $6.7B revenues, $11.6M in bonuses. *Toronto Star,* B1, B2.

21. Lawler, E.E., III. (1972). Secrecy and the need to know. In H.L. Tosi, R.J. House, & M.D. Dunnette (Eds.), *Managerial motivation and compensation.* East Lansing, MI: Michigan State University Press.

22. Futrell, C.M., & Jenkins, O.C. (1978). Pay secrecy versus pay disclosure for salesmen: A longitudinal study. *Journal of Marketing Research, 15,* 214–219, 215.

23. For a study of the prevalence of these plans, see Lawler, E.E. III, Mohrman, S.A., & Ledford, G.E. (1992). *Employee involvement and total quality management: Practices and results in Fortune 1000 companies.* San Francisco: Jossey-Bass.

24. Vermond, K. (2008, October 11). Bonus planning in a bear market. *Globe and Mail,* B16; Gooderham, M. (2007, November 20). A piece of the pie as motivational tool. *Globe and Mail,* B8.

25. (2003, October). The goals of stock option programs. www.workforce.com.

26. Gordon, A. (February 2000). 35 best companies to work for. *Report on Business Magazine,* 24–32.

27. Brearton, S., & Daly, J. (2003, January). The 50 Best Companies to Work for in Canada. *Report on Business,* 53–65.

28. Hays, S. (February 1990). "Ownership cultures" create unity. *Workforce, 78*(2), 60–64.

29. Vermond, K. (2008, March 29). Worker as shareholder: Is it worth it? *Globe and Mail,* B21.

30. Graham-Moore, B., & Ross, T.L. (1990). *Gainsharing: Plans for improving performance.* Washington, DC: Bureau of National Affairs; Markham, S.E., Scott, K.D., & Little, B.L. (1992, January–February). National gainsharing study: The importance of industry differences. *Compensation & Benefits Review,* 34–45; Miller, C.S., & Shuster, M.H. (1987, Summer). Gainsharing plans: A comparative analysis. *Organizational Dynamics,* 44–67.

31. Davis, V. (1989, April). Eyes on the prize. *Canadian Business,* 93–106.

32. Graham-Moore & Ross, 1990; Moore, B.E, & Ross, T.L. (1978). *The Scanlon way to improved productivity: A practical guide.* New York: Wiley.

33. Perry, N.J. (1988, December 19). Here come richer, riskier pay plans. *Fortune,* 50–58; Lawler, E.E. (1984). Whatever happened to incentive pay? *New Management, 1*(4), 37–41.

34. Arthur, J.B., & Huntley, C.L. (2005). Ramping up the organizational learning curve: Assessing the impact of deliberate learning on organizational performance under gainsharing. *Academy of Management Journal, 48,* 1159–1170.

35. Hammer, T.H. (1988). New developments in profit sharing, gainsharing, and employee ownership. In J.P. Campbell & R.J. Campbell (Eds.), *Productivity in organizations.* San Francisco: Jossey-Bass.

36. Cooper, C.L., Dyck, B., & Frohlich, N. (1992). Improving the effectiveness of gainsharing: The role of fairness and participation. *Administrative Science Quarterly, 37,* 471–490.

37. Lawler, E.E., III, & Jenkins, G.D., Jr. (1992). Strategic reward systems. In M.D. Dunette & L.M. Hough (Eds.), *Handbook of industrial and organizational psychology* (2nd ed., Vol. 3). Palo Alto, CA: Consulting Psychologists Press.

38. Murray, B., & Gerhart, B. (1998). An empirical analysis of a skill–based pay program and plant performance outcomes. *Academy of Management Journal, 41,* 68–78.

39. Peterson, S., & Luthans, F. (2006). The impact of financial and nonfinancial incentives on business-unit outcomes over time. *Journal of Applied Psychology, 91,* 156–165.

40. Erez, M. (2010). Culture and job design. *Journal of Organizational Behavior, 31,* 389–400.

41. Immen, W. (2009, February 27). Meaning means more than money at work: Poll. *Globe and Mail,* B14; Immen, W. (2008, January 23). Forget pay: Challenging work counts for top talent. *Globe and Mail,* C2.

42. Taylor, F.W. (1967). *The principles of scientific management.* New York: Norton.

43. This discussion draws upon Gibson, J.L., Ivancevich, J.M., & Donnelly, J.H., Jr. (1991). *Organizations* (7th ed.). Homewood, IL: Irwin.

44. Ray, R. (2006, April 19). New assignments a stretch but not a yawn. *Globe and Mail,* C1, C6.

45. Immen, W. (2007, October 17). Starting rotation adds bench strength. *Globe and Mail,* C1, C2.

46. Hackman, J.R., & Oldham, G.R. (1980). *Work redesign.* Reading, MA: Addison-Wesley.

47. Oldham, G.R., Hackman, J.R., & Stepina, L.P. (1979). Norms for the job diagnostic survey. *JSAS Catalog of Selected Documents in Psychology, 9,* 14. (Ms. No. 1819).

48. See, for example, Johns, G., Xie, J.L., & Fang, Y. (1992). Mediating and moderating effects in job design. *Journal of Management, 18,* 657–676.

49. Humphrey, S.E., Nanhrgang, J.D., & Morgeson, F.P. (2007). Integrating motivational, social, and contextual work design features: A meta-analytic summary and theoretical extension of the work design literature. *Journal of Applied Psychology, 92,* 1332–1356.

50. Johns et al., 1992; Tiegs, R.B., Tetrick, L.E., & Fried, Y. (1992). Growth need strength and context satisfactions as moderators of the relations of the Job Characteristics Model. *Journal of Management, 18,* 575–593.

51. Brown, S.P. (1996). A meta-analysis and review of organizational research on job involvement. *Psychological Bulletin, 120,* 235–255.

52. This section draws in part on Hackman & Oldham, 1980.

53. Dumaine, B. (1989, November 6). P&G rewrites the marketing rules. *Fortune,* 34–48, 46.

54. Campion, M.A., Mumford, T.V., Morgeson, F.P., & Nahrgang, J.D. (2005). Work redesign: Eight obstacles and opportunities. *Human Resource Management, 44,* 367–390.

55. Stonewalling plant democracy (1977, March 28). *Business Week.*

56. Morgeson, F.P., & Humphrey, S.E. (2006). The work design questionnaire (WDQ): Developing and validating a comprehensive measure for assessing job design and the nature of work. *Journal of Applied Psychology, 91,* 1321–1339; Humphrey et al., 2007.

57. Grant, A.M. (2008). Does intrinsic motivation fuel the prosocial fire? Motivational synergy in predicting persistence, performance, and productivity. *Journal of Applied Psychology, 93,* 48–58.

58. Grant, A.M. (2007). Relational job design and the motivation to make a prosocial difference. *Academy of Management Review, 32,* 393–417.

59. Grant, 2008; Grant, A.M. (2008). The significance of task significance: Job performance effects, relational mechanisms, and boundary conditions. *Journal of Applied Psychology, 93,* 108–124; Grant, A.M., Campbell, E.M., Chen, G., Cottone, K., Lapedis, D., & Lee, K. (2007). Impact and the art of motivation maintenance: The effects of contact with beneficiaries on persistence behavior. *Organizational Behavior and Human Decision Processes, 103,* 53–67; Grant,

A.M., & Parker, S.K. (2009). Redesigning work design theories. *The Academy of Management Annals, 3,* 317–375.

60. Good descriptions of MBO programs can be found in Mali, P. (1986). *MBO updated: A handbook of practices and techniques for managing by objectives.* New York: Wiley; Odiorne, G.S. (1965). *Management by objectives.* New York: Pitman; Raia, A.P. (1974). *Managing by objectives.* Glenview, IL: Scott, Foresman.

61. Beer, M., & Cannon, D. (2004). Promise and peril in implementing pay-for-performance. *Human Resource Management, 43,* 3–48.

62. Brearton, S., & Daly, J. (2003, January). The 50 best companies to work for in Canada. *Report on Business,* 53–66.

63. Brearton & Daly, 2003; Rodgers, R., & Hunter, J.E. (1991). Impact of management by objectives on organization productivity. *Journal of Applied Psychology, 76,* 322–336.

64. Rodgers & Hunter, 1991.

65. See Rodgers, R., Hunter, J.E., & Rogers, D.L. (1993). Influence of top management commitment on management program success. *Journal of Applied Psychology, 78,* 151–155.

66. For discussions of these and other problems with MBO, see Levinson, H. (1979, July–August). Management by whose objectives. *Harvard Business Review,* 125–134; McConkey, D.D. (1972, October). 20 ways to kill management by objectives. *Management Review,* 4–13; Pringle, C.D., & Longenecker, J.G. (1982). The ethics of MBO. *Academy of Management Review, 7,* 305–312.

67. Myers, J. (2010, June 26). The flex factor. *Globe and Mail,* B15.

68. See Nollen, S.D. (1982). *New work schedules in practice: Managing time in a changing society.* New York: Van Nostrand Reinhold; Ronen, S. (1981). *Flexible working hours: An innovation in the quality of work life.* New York: McGraw-Hill; Ronen, S. (1984). *Alternative work schedules: Selecting, implementing, and evaluating.* Homewood, IL: Dow Jones-Irwin.

69. For a good study showing absence reduction, see Dalton, D.R., & Mesch, D.J. (1990). The impact of flexible scheduling on employee attendance and turnover. *Administrative Science Quarterly, 35,* 370–387.

70. Baltes, B., Briggs, T.E., Huff, J.W., Wright, J.A., & Neuman, G.A. (1999). Flexible and compressed workweek schedules: A meta-analysis of their effects on work-related criteria. *Journal of Applied Psychology, 84,* 496–513.

71. Golembiewski, R.T., & Proehl, C.W. (1978). A survey of the empirical literature on flexible workhours: Character

and consequences of a major innovation. *Academy of Management Review, 3,* 837–853; Pierce, J.L., Newstrom, J.W., Dunham, R.B., & Barber, A.E. (1989). *Alternative work schedules.* Boston: Allyn and Bacon; Ronen, 1981 and 1984.

72. Baltes et al., 1999.

73. Ronen, 1984; Nollen, 1982.

74. Pierce et al., 1989; Ronen, 1984; Ronen, S., & Primps, S.B. (1981). The compressed workweek as organizational change: Behavioral and attitudinal outcomes. *Academy of Management Review, 6,* 61–74.

75. Pierce et al., 1989; Ivancevich, J.M., & Lyon, H.L. (1977). The shortened workweek: A field experiment. *Journal of Applied Psychology, 62,* 34–37.

76. Johns, G. (1987). Understanding and managing absence from work. In S.L. Dolan & R.S. Schuler (Eds.), *Canadian readings in personnel and human resource management.* St. Paul, MN: West.

77. Ivancevich & Lyon, 1977; Calvasina, E.J., & Boxx, W.R. (1975). Efficiency of workers on the four-day workweek. *Academy of Management Journal, 18,* 604–610; Goodale, J.G., & Aagaard, A.K. (1975). Factors relating to varying reactions to the 4-day workweek. *Journal of Applied Psychology, 60,* 33–38.

78. Baltes et al., 1999.

79. This section relies on Pierce et al., 1989.

80. MacGregor, A. (2001, December 29). Sharing jobs gets trendy. *The Gazette,* Montreal, C1.

81. Popplewell, B. (2009, March 10). Staying at home so others don't have to. *Toronto Star,* B1, B4; Grant, T. (2009, June 23). Buying jobs and buying time. *Globe and Mail,* B4.

82. DeFrank, R.S., & Ivancevich, J. M. (1998). Stress on the job: An executive update. *Academy of Management Executive, 12,* 55–66.

83. Grensing-Pophal, L. (1997, March). Employing the best people—from afar. *Workforce, 76*(3), 30–38; Piskurich, G.M. (1998). *An organizational guide to telecommuting: Setting up and running a successful telecommuter program.* Alexandria, VA: American Society for Training and Development.

84. Grensing-Pophal, 1997.

85. DeFrank & Ivancevich, 1998; Goldsborough, R. (1999, May 14). Make telecommuting work for you. *Computer Dealer News,* 19–20; Fortier, B. (2005, June 6). Ergonomics for teleworkers often overlooked. *Canadian HR Reporter, 18*(11), 18, 21.

86. Galt, V. (2003, September 24). Drive is on for telework. *Globe and Mail,* C7; Vu, U. (2006, August 14). A variety of options gives boost to remote work. *Canadian HR Reporter, 19*(14), 15, 21;

Myers, R.C. (2008, March 8). The back and forth of working from home. *Globe and Mail,* B16.

87. DeFrank & Ivancevich, 1998; Grensing-Pophal, 1997.

88. Gajendran, R.S., & Harrison, D.A. (2007). The good, the bad, and the unknown about telecommuting: Meta-analysis of psychological mediators and individual consequences. *Journal of Applied Psychology, 92,* 1524–1541.

89. Bailey, D.S., & Foley, J. (1990, August). Pacific Bell works long distance. *HRMagazine,* 50–52.

90. Myers, 2008.

91. Klie, S. (2008, June 2). Mistrust "number one barrier" to telework. *Canadian HR Reporter, 21*(11), 13, 19; Grensing-Pophal, 1997.

92. Rynes et al., 2004.

Chapter 7

1. www.fastcompany.com/mic/2010/profile/ideo; www.ideo.com/images/uploads/home/IDEO_Fact_Sheet.pdf; Brown, T. (2009). *Change by design: How design thinking transforms organizations and inspires innovation.* New York: HarperCollins; www.businessweek.com/careers/content/jan2001/ca20010111_923.htm (Strong quote); http://pages.towson.edu/aclardy/Working%20Papers/IDEO.pdf; www.ideo.com/work/the-tube/; http://charleslawportfolio.com/charleslaw_assets/charleslaw_creativeessay.pdf; www.ideo.com/images/uploads/hcd_toolkit/IDEO_HCD_ToolKit.pdf.

2. Tuckman, B.W. (1965). Developmental sequence in small groups. *Psychological Bulletin, 63,* 384–399; Tuckman, B.W., & Jensen, M.A.C. (1977). Stages of small-group development revisited. *Group & Organization Studies, 2,* 419–427.

3. Harris, S.G., & Sutton, R.I. (1986). Functions of parting ceremonies in dying organizations. *Academy of Management Journal, 29,* 5–30.

4. Seger, J.A. (1983). No innate phases in group problem solving. *Academy of Management Review, 8,* 683–689. For a study comparing phases with punctuated equilibrium, see Chang, A., Bordia, P., & Duck, J. (2003). Punctuated equilibrium and linear progression: Toward a new understanding of group development. *Academy of Management Journal, 46,* 106–117.

5. Ginnett, R.C. (1990). Airline cockpit crew. In J.R. Hackman (Ed.), *Groups that work (and those that don't).* San Francisco: Jossey-Bass.

6. Gersick, C.J.G. (1989). Marking time: Predictable transitions in task groups. *Academy of Management Journal, 32,*

274–309; Gersick, C.J.G. (1988). Time and transition in work teams: Toward a new model of group development. *Academy of Management Journal, 31,* 9–41.

7. Gersick, 1989, 1988; Hackman, J.R., & Wageman, R. (2005). A theory of team coaching. *Academy of Management Review, 30,* 269–287.

8. Hare, A.P. (1976). *A handbook of small group research.* New York: The Free Press; Shaw, M.E. (1981). *Group dynamics: The psychology of small group behavior* (3rd ed.). New York: McGraw-Hill; Jones, E.E., & Gerard, H.B. (1967). *Foundations of social psychology.* New York: Wiley.

9. Hare, 1976; Shaw, 1981.

10. The following discussion relies upon Steiner, I.D. (1972). *Group process and productivity.* New York: Academic Press.

11. Steiner, 1972; Hill, G.W. (1982). Group versus individual performance: Are n+1 heads better than one? *Psychological Bulletin, 91,* 517–539.

12. Williams, K.Y., & O'Reilly, C.A. III. (1998). Demography and diversity in organizations: A review of 40 years of research. *Research in Organizational Behavior, 20,* 77–140; Jackson, S.E., Stone, V.K., & Alvarez, E.B. (1993). Socialization amidst diversity: The impact of demographics on work team oldtimers and newcomers. *Research in Organizational Behavior, 15,* 45–109.

13. Watson, W.E., Kumar, K., & Michaelson, L.K. (1993). Cultural diversity's impact on interaction process and performance: Comparing homogeneous and diverse task groups. *Academy of Management Journal, 36,* 590–602.

14. Webber, S.S., & Donahue, L.M. (2001). Impact of highly and less job-related diversity on work group cohesion and performance: A meta-analysis. *Journal of Management, 27,* 141–162.

15. Bell, S.T., Villado, A.J., Lukasik, M.A., Belau, L., & Briggs, A.L. (2011). Getting specific about demographic diversity variable and team performance relationships: A meta-analysis. *Journal of Management, 37,* 709–743; see also Joshi, A., & Roh, H. (2009). The role of context in work team diversity research: A meta-analytic review. *Academy of Management Journal, 52,* 599–627.

16. Bell et al., 2011; Joshi & Roh, 2009.

17. Harrison, D.A., Price, K.H., & Bell, M.P. (1998). Beyond relational demography: Time and effects of surface- and deep-level diversity on work group cohesion. *Academy of Management Journal, 41,* 96–107; see also Bell, S.T. (2007). Deep-level composition variables as predictors of team performance: A meta-analysis.

18. For an example of the social process by which this sharing may be negotiated in a new group, see Bettenhausen, K., & Murnighan, J.K. (1991). The development of an intragroup norm and the effects of interpersonal and structural challenges. *Administrative Science Quarterly, 36,* 20–35.

19. Kanter, R.M. (1977). *Men and women of the corporation.* New York: Basic Books, 37.

20. Leventhal, G.S. (1976). The distribution of rewards and resources in groups and organizations. In L. Berkowitz & E. Walster (Eds.), *Advances in experimental social psychology* (Vol. 9). New York: Academic Press.

21. See Mitchell, T.R., Rothman, M., & Liden, R.C. (1985). Effects of normative information on task performance. *Journal of Applied Psychology, 70,* 48–55.

22. Kleingeld, A., van Mierlo, H., & Arends, L. (2011). The effect of goal setting on group performance: A meta-analysis. *Journal of Applied Psychology, 96,* 1289–1304.

23. Jackson, S.E., & Schuler, R.S. (1985). A meta-analysis and conceptual critique of research on role ambiguity and role conflict in work settings. *Organizational Behavior and Human Decision Processes, 36,* 16–78. For a methodological critique of this domain, see King, L.A., & King, D.W. (1990). Role conflict and role ambiguity: A critical assessment of construct validity. *Psychological Bulletin, 107,* 48–64.

24. Jackson & Schuler, 1985; Tubre, T.C., & Collins, J.M. (2000). Jackson and Shuler (1985) revisited: A meta-analysis of the relationship between role ambiguity, role conflict, and job performance. *Journal of Management, 26,* 155–169.

25. O'Driscoll, M.P., Ilgen, D.R., & Hildreth, K. (1992). Time devoted to job and off-job activities, interrole conflict, and affective experiences. *Journal of Applied Psychology, 77,* 272–279.

26. See Latack, J.C. (1981). Person/role conflict: Holland's model extended to role-stress research, stress management, and career development. *Academy of Management Review, 6,* 89–103.

27. Jackson & Schuler, 1985.

28. Shaw, 1981.

29. Fiske, S.T. (2010). Interpersonal stratification: Status, power, and subordination. In S.T. Fiske, D.T. Gilbert, & G. Lindzey (Eds.), *Handbook of social psychology* (5th ed., Vol. 2). Hoboken, NJ: Wiley.

30. Kiesler, S., & Sproull, L. (1992). Group decision making and communication technology. *Organizational Behavior and Human Decision Processes, 52,* 96–123; Fiske, 2010.

31. Strodbeck, F.L., James, R.M., & Hawkins, C. (1957). Social status in jury deliberations. *American Sociological Review, 22,* 713–719.

32. Kiesler & Sproull, 1992.

33. For other definitions and a discussion of their differences, see Mudrack, P.E. (1989). Defining group cohesiveness: A legacy of confusion? *Small Group Behavior, 20,* 37–49.

34. Stein, A. (1976). Conflict and cohesion: A review of the literature. *Journal of Conflict Resolution, 20,* 143–172. For an interesting example, see Haslam, S.A., & Reicher, S. (2006). Stressing the group: Social identity and the unfolding dynamics of responses to stress. *Journal of Applied Psychology, 91,* 1037–1052.

35. Cartwright, D. (1968). The nature of group cohesiveness. In D. Cartwright & A. Zander (Eds.), *Group dynamics: Research and theory* (3rd ed., pp. 91–109). New York: Harper & Row.

36. Lott, A., & Lott, B. (1965). Group cohesiveness as interpersonal attraction: A review of relationships with antecedent and consequent variables. *Psychological Bulletin, 64,* 259–309.

37. Anderson, A.B. (1975). Combined effects of interpersonal attraction and goal-path clarity on the cohesiveness of task-oriented groups. *Journal of Personality and Social Psychology, 31,* 68–75; see also Cartwright, 1968.

38. Aronson, E., & Mills, J. (1959). The effects of severity of initiation on liking for a group. *Journal of Abnormal and Social Psychology, 59,* 177–181.

39. Cartwright, 1968; Shaw, 1981.

40. Schacter, S. (1951). Deviation, rejection, and communication. *Journal of Abnormal and Social Psychology, 46,* 190–207; see also Barker, J.R. (1993). Tightening the iron cage: Concertive control in self-managing teams. *Administrative Science Quarterly, 38,* 408–437.

41. Beal, D.J., Cohen, R.R., Burke, M.J., & McLendon, C.L. (2003). Cohesion and performance in groups: A meta-analytic clarification of construct relations. *Journal of Applied Psychology, 88,* 989–1004; Mullen, B., & Copper, C. (1994). The relation between group cohesiveness and performance: An integration. *Psychological Bulletin, 115,* 210–227.

42. Podsakoff, P.M., MacKenzie, S.B., & Ahearne, M. (1997). Moderating effects of goal acceptance on the relationship between group cohesiveness and productivity. *Journal of Applied Psychology, 82,* 974–983.

43. Seashore, S. (1954). *Group cohesiveness in the industrial workgroup.* Ann

Arbor, MI: Institute for Social Research; see also Stogdill, R.M. (1972). Group productivity, drive, and cohesiveness. *Organizational Behavior and Human Performance, 8,* 26–43. For a critique, see Mudrack, P.E. (1989). Group cohesiveness and productivity: A closer look. *Human Relations, 42,* 771–785.

44. Gulley, S.M., Devine, D.J., & Whitney, D.J. (1995). A meta-analysis of cohesion and performance: Effects of level of analysis and task interdependence. *Small Group Research, 26,* 497–520.

45. Shepperd, J.A. (1993). Productivity loss in small groups: A motivation analysis. *Psychological Bulletin, 113,* 67–81; Kidwell, R.E., III, & Bennett, N. (1993). Employee propensity to withhold effort: A conceptual model to intersect three avenues of research. *Academy of Management Review, 18,* 429–456.

46. Shepperd, 1993; Kidwell & Bennett, 1993; George, J.M. (1992). Extrinsic and intrinsic origins of perceived social loafing in organizations. *Academy of Management Journal, 35,* 191–202.

47. Barnes, C.M., Hollenbeck, J.R., Jundt, D.K., DeRue, D.S., & Harmon, S.J. (2011). Mixing individual incentives and group incentives: Best of both worlds or social dilemma? *Journal of Management, 37,* 1611–1635.

48. Guzzo, R.A., & Dickson, M.W. (1996). Teams in organizations: Recent research on performance and effectiveness. *Annual Review of Psychology, 47,* 307–338.

49. Kirkman, B.L., & Shapiro, D.L. (1997). The impact of cultural values on employee resistance to teams: Toward a model of globalized self–managing work team effectiveness. *Academy of Management Review, 22,* 730–757.

50. Guzzo & Dickson, 1996; Kirkman & Shapiro, 1997; Banker, R.D., Field, J.M., Schroeder, R.G., & Sinha, K.K. (1996). Impact of work teams on manufacturing performance: A longitudinal field study. *Academy of Management Journal, 39,* 867–890.

51. Tasa, K., Taggar, S., & Seijts, G.H. (2007). The development of collective efficacy in teams: A multi-level and longitudinal perspective. *Journal of Applied Psychology, 92,* 17–27; Gibson, C.B., & Earley, P.C. (2007). Collective cognition in action: Accumulation, interaction, examination, and accommodation in the development and operation of efficacy beliefs in the workplace. *Academy of Management Review, 32,* 438–458; Tasa, K., Sears, G.J., & Schat, A.C.H. (2011). Personality and teamwork behavior in context: The cross-level moderating role of collective efficacy. *Journal of Organizational Behavior, 32,* 65–85;

Stajkovic, A.D., Lee, D., & Nyberg, A.J. (2009). Collective efficacy, group potency, and group performance: Meta-analyses of their relationships, and test of a mediation model. *Journal of Applied Psychology, 94,* 814–828.

52. Hackman, J.R. (1987). The design of work teams. In J.W. Lorsch (Ed.), *Handbook of organizational behavior.* Englewood Cliffs, NJ: Prentice-Hall; see also Hackman, J.R. (2002). *Leading teams: Setting the stage for great performances.* Boston: Harvard Business School Press.

53. Campion, M.A., Medsker, G.J., & Higgs, A.C. (1993). Relations between work group characteristics and effectiveness: Implications for designing effective work groups. *Personnel Psychology, 46,* 823–850.

54. Wall, T.D., Kemp, N.J., Jackson, P.R., & Clegg, C.W. (1986). Outcomes of autonomous workgroups: A field experiment. *Academy of Management Journal, 29,* 280–304.

55. Parts of this section rely on Hackman, 1987.

56. See Ashforth, B.E., & Mael, F. (1989). Social identity theory and the organization. *Academy of Management Review, 14,* 20–39.

57. Wall et al., 1986; Cordery, J.L., Mueller, W.S., & Smith, L.M. (1991). Attitudinal and behavioral effects of autonomous group working: A longitudinal field study. *Academy of Management Journal, 34,* 264–276.

58. van der Vegt, G.S., Bunderson, S., & Kuipers, B. (2010). Why turnover matters in self-managing work teams: Learning, social integration, and task flexibility. *Journal of Management, 36,* 1168–1191.

59. Bainbridge, J. (2009). Inspire and innovate: Personal services. www.guardian.co.uk.

60. Hayward, D. (2003, May 20). Management through measurement. *Financial Post,* BE5.

61. Manz, C.C., & Sims, H.P., Jr. (1987). Leading workers to lead themselves: The external leadership of self-managing work teams. *Administrative Science Quarterly, 32,* 106–128.

62. For reviews of research on self-managed teams, see Chapter 3 of Cummings, T.G., & Molloy, E.S. (1977). *Improving productivity and the quality of working life.* New York: Praeger; Goodman, P.S., Devadas, R., & Hughes, T.L.G. (1988). Groups and productivity: Analyzing the effectiveness of self-managing teams. In J.P. Campbell & R.J. Campbell (Eds.), *Productivity in organizations.* San Francisco: Jossey-Bass; Pearce, J.A., III, & Ravlin, E.C. (1987). The design

and activation of self-regulating work groups. *Human Relations, 40,* 751–782.

63. Campion, M.A., Papper, E.M., & Medsker, G.J. (1996). Relations between work team characteristics and effectiveness: A replication and extension. *Personnel Psychology, 49,* 429–452; Campion, Medsker, & Higgs, 1993.

64. Kirkman & Shapiro, 1997; Banker et al., 1996.

65. Farnham, A. (1994, February 7). America's most admired company. *Fortune,* 50–54; Dumaine, B. (1993, December 13). Payoff from the new management. *Fortune,* 103–110.

66. Waterman, R.H., Jr. (1987). *The renewal factor.* New York: Bantam Books; McElroy, J. (1985, April). Ford's new way to build cars. *Road & Track,* 156–158.

67. Pinto, M.B., Pinto, J.K., & Prescott, J.E. (1993). Antecedents and consequences of project team cross-functional cooperation. *Management Science, 39,* 1281–1297; Henke, J.W., Krachenberg, A.R., & Lyons, T.F. (1993). Cross-functional teams: Good concept, poor implementation! *Journal of Product Innovation Management, 10,* 216–229. Mustang examples from White, J.B., & Suris, O. (1993, September 21). How a "skunk works" kept the Mustang alive—on a tight budget. *Wall Street Journal,* A1, A12.

68. Mathieu, J., Maynard, M.T., Rapp, T., & Gilson, L. (2008). Team effectiveness 1997–2007: A review of recent advancements and a glimpse into the future. *Journal of Management, 34,* 410–476; Mesmer-Magnus, J.R., & DeChurch, L.A. (2009). Information sharing and team performance. *Journal of Applied Psychology, 94,* 535–546; Mohammed, S., Ferzandi, L., & Hamilton, K. (2010). Metaphor no more: A 15-year review of the team mental model construct. *Journal of Management, 36,* 876–910; DeChurch, L.A., & Mesmer-Magnus, J.R. (2010). The cognitive underpinnings of effective teamwork: A meta-analysis. *Journal of Applied Psychology, 95,* 32–53.

69. Cronin, M.A., & Weingart, L.R. (2007). Representational gaps, information processing, and conflict in functionally diverse teams. *Academy of Management Review, 32,* 761–773, p. 761.

70. Lipnack, J., & Stamps, J. (2000). *Virtual teams: People working across boundaries with technology.* (2nd ed.). New York: Wiley; Axtell, C.M., Fleck, S.J., & Turner, N. (2004). Virtual Teams: Collaborating across distance. *International Review of Industrial and Organizational Psychology, 19,* 205–248; Staff. (2010, First Quarter). Successfully transitioning to a virtual organization:

Challenges, impact and technology. *SHRM Research Quarterly*. Alexandria, VA: Society for Human Resource Management.

71. Willmore, J. (2000, February). Managing virtual teams. *Training Journal*, 18–21.

72. Joinson, C. (2002, June). Managing virtual teams. *HR Magazine*, 68–73.

73. Cascio, W.F. (2000, August). Managing a virtual workplace. *Academy of Management Executive*, 81–90; see also Malhotra, A., Majchrzak, A., & Rosen, B. (2007). Leading virtual teams. *Academy of Management Perspectives*, 60–70; and Gibson, C.B., & Gibbs, J.L. (2006). Unpacking the concept of virtuality: The effects of geographic dispersion, electronic dependence, dynamic structure, and national diversity on team innovation. *Administrative Science Quarterly*, *51*, 451–495.

74. Willmore, 2000.

75. Mesmer-Magnus, J.R., DeChurch, L.A., Jimenez-Rodriguez, M., Wildman, J., & Shuffler, M. (2011). A meta-analytic investigation of virtuality and information sharing in teams. *Organizational Behavior and Human Decision Processes*, *115*, 214–225.

76. Cascio, 2000; Joinson, 2002; Kirkman, B.L., Rosen, B., Gibson, C.B., Tesluk, P.E., & McPherson, S.O. (2002, August). Five challenges to virtual team success: Lessons from Sabre, Inc. *Academy of Management Executive*, *16*, 67–79.

77. Allen, N.J., & Hecht, T.D. (2004). The "romance of teams": Toward an understanding of its psychological underpinnings and implications. *Journal of Occupational and Organizational Psychology*, *77*, 439–461.

78. Vallas, S.P. (2003). Why teamwork fails: Obstacles to workplace change in four manufacturing plants. *American Sociological Review*, *68*, 223–250; Tudor, T.R., Trumble, R.R., & Diaz, J.J. (1996, Autumn). Work-teams: Why do they often fail? *S.A.M. Advanced Management Journal*, 31–39.

Chapter 8

1. Anonymous (2012, April 19). Canada's best workplaces: Google Canada tops list of large employers. *A Special National Report for the Great Place to Work Institute, Globe and Mail*, GPTW1, GPTW6; Anonymous (2009, April 6). Canada's best workplaces: Google Canada, World's top search engine also ranked Canada's best place to work. *A Special National Report for the Great Place to Work Institute, Globe and Mail*, GPTW1, GPTW3; Abel, K. (2008, November 24). Google Canada's new eco-friendly home enjoys playful

work philosophy: Part One and Part Two [Web log message]. www.krisable. ctv.ca/blog; Mills, E. (2007, April 27). Newsmaker: Meet Google's culture czar. *CNET News*, www.news.cnet.com; Google Corporate Information, The Google Culture, www.google.ca.

2. See Morrison, E.W. (1993). Newcomer information seeking: Exploring types, modes, sources, and outcomes. *Academy of Management Journal*, *36*, 557–589.

3. The terms information dependence and effect dependence are used by Jones, E.E., & Gerard, H.B. (1967). *Foundations of social psychology*. New York: Wiley.

4. Salancik, G. R., & Pfeffer, J. (1978). A social information processing approach to job attitudes and task design. *Administrative Science Quarterly*, *23*, 224–253.

5. Festinger, L. (1954). A theory of social comparison processes. *Human Relations*, *7*, 117–140; Thomas, J., & Griffin, R. (1983). The social information processing model of task design: A review of the literature. *Academy of Management Review*, *8*, 672–682.

6. Kelman, H.C. (1961). Processes of opinion change. *Public Opinion Quarterly*, *25*, 57–78.

7. Bauer, T.N., Morrison, E.W., & Callister, R.R. (1998). Organizational socialization: A review and directions for future research. In G.R. Ferris & K.M. Rowland (Eds.), *Research in Personnel and Human Resources Management*, (Vol. 16, pp. 149–214). Greenwich, CT: JAI Press; Saks, A.M., & Ashforth, B.E. (1997a). Organizational socialization: Making sense of the past and present as a prologue for the future. *Journal of Vocational Behavior*, *51*, 234–279.

8. Saks, A.M., & Ashforth, B.E. (1997b). A longitudinal investigation of the relationships between job information sources, applicant perceptions of fit, and work outcomes. *Personnel Psychology*, *50*, 395–426.

9. Kristof-Brown, A.L., Zimmerman, R.D., & Johnson, E.C. (2005). Consequences of individuals' fit at work: A meta-analysis of person-job, person-organization, person-group, and person-supervisor fit. *Personnel Psychology*, *58*, 281–342; Kristof, A.L. (1996). Person-organization fit: An integrative review of its conceptualizations, measurement, and implications. *Personnel Psychology*, *49*, 1–49; Saks & Ashforth, 1997b; Saks, A.M., & Ashforth, B.E. (2002). Is job search related to employment quality? It all depends on the fit. *Journal of Applied Psychology*, *87*, 646–654.

10. Ashforth & Saks, 1996; Riketta, M. (2005). Organizational identification: A meta-analysis. *Journal of Vocational Behavior*, *66*, 358–384.

11. Van Maanen, J., & Schein, E.H. (1979). Toward a theory of organizational socialization. *Research in Organizational Behavior*, *1*, 209–264.

12. Feldman, D.C. (1976). A contingency theory of socialization. *Administrative Science Quarterly*, *21*, 433–452.

13. Wanous, J.P. (1992). *Organizational entry: Recruitment, selection, orientation, and socialization of newcomers*. (2nd ed.). Reading, MA: Addison-Wesley.

14. Wanous, J.P. (1976). Organizational entry: From naive expectations to realistic beliefs. *Journal of Applied Psychology*, *61*, 22–29; Wanous, J.P., Poland, T.D., Premack, S.L., & Davis, K.S. (1992). The effects of met expectations on newcomer attitudes and behaviors: A review and meta-analysis. *Journal of Applied Psychology*, *77*, 288–297.

15. See Breaugh, J.A. (1992). *Recruitment: Science and practice*. Boston: PWS-Kent.

16. Morrison, E.W., & Robinson, S.L. (1997). When employees feel betrayed: A model of how psychological contract violation develops. *Academy of Management Review*, *22*, 226–256.

17. Robinson, S.L., & Rousseau, D.M. (1994). Violating the psychological contract: Not the exception but the norm. *Journal of Organizational Behavior*, *15*, 245–259.

18. Zhao, H., Wayne, S.J., Glibkowski, B.C., & Bravo, J. (2007). The impact of psychological contract breach on work-related outcomes: A meta-analysis. *Personnel Psychology*, *60*, 647–680.

19. Bordia, P., Restubog, S.L.D., Bordia, S., & Tang, R.L. (2010). Breach begets breach: Trickle-down effects of psychological contract breach on customer service. *Journal of Management*, *36*, 1578–1607; Ng, T.W.H., Feldman, D.C., & Lam, S.S.K. (2010). Psychological contract breaches, organizational commitment, and innovation-related behaviors: A latent growth modeling approach. *Journal of Applied Psychology*, *95*, 744–751.

20. Morrison & Robinson, 1997.

21. Morrison & Robinson, 1997.

22. Montes, S.D., & Zweig, D. (2009). Do promises matter? An exploration of the role of promises in psychological contract breach. *Journal of Applied Psychology*, *94*, 1243–1260.

23. Wanous, 1992; Breaugh, 1992.

24. Wanous, 1992; Breaugh, 1992.

25. Galt, V. (2005, March 9). Kid-glove approach woos new grads. *Globe and Mail*, C1, C3.

26. Harding, K. (2003, July 16). Police aim to hire officers. *Globe and Mail*, C1.

27. Phillips, J.M. (1998). Effects of realistic job previews on multiple organizational outcomes: A meta-analysis. *Academy of Management Journal*, *41*, 673–690.

28. Premack, S.L., & Wanous, J.P. (1985). A meta-analysis of realistic job preview experiments. *Journal of Applied Psychology, 70,* 706–719. See also Wanous, J.P., Poland, T.D., Premack, S.L., & Davis, K.S. (1992). The effects of met expectations on newcomer attitudes and behaviors: A review and meta-analysis. *Journal of Applied Psychology, 77,* 288–297.

29. Earnest, D.R., Allen, D.G., & Landix, R.S. (2011). Mechanisms linking realistic job previews with turnover: A meta-analytic path analysis. *Personnel Psychology, 64,* 865–897.

30. Premack & Wanous, 1985; McEvoy, G.M., & Cascio, W.F. (1985). Strategies for reducing employee turnover: A meta-analysis. *Journal of Applied Psychology, 70,* 342–353.

31. Morrison & Robinson, 1997.

32. Wanous, J.P., & Reichers, A.E. (2000). New employee orientation programs. *Human Resource Management Review, 10,* 435–451.

33. Mitchell, B. (2012, January 30). Power to the people. *Canadian HR Reporter, 25*(2), 23, 25.

34. Klein, H.J., & Weaver, N.A. (2000). The effectiveness of an organizational-level orientation training program in the socialization of new hires. *Personnel Psychology, 53,* 47–66.

35. Schettler, J. (2002, August). Welcome to ACME Inc. *Training, 39*(8), 36–43.

36. Van Maanen, J., & Schein, E.H. (1979). Toward a theory of organizational socialization. In B.M. Staw (Ed.), *Research in organizational behavior,* Vol. 1. Greenwich, CT: JAI Press, 209–264.

37. Ashforth, B.E., & Saks, A.M. (1996). Socialization tactics: Longitudinal effects on newcomer adjustment. *Academy of Management Journal, 39,* 149–178; Jones, G.R. (1986). Socialization tactics, self-efficacy, and newcomers' adjustments to organizations. *Academy of Management Journal, 29,* 262–279.

38. Ashforth & Saks, 1996; Jones, 1986; Cable, D.M., & Parsons, C.K. (2001). Socialization tactics and person-organization fit. *Personnel Psychology, 54,* 1–23; Rollag, K., Parise, S., & Cross, R. (2005). Getting new hires up to speed quickly. *MIT Sloan Management Review,* 35–41.

39. Haggard, D.L., Dougherty, T.W., Turban, D.B., & Wilbanks, J.E. (2011). Who is a mentor? A review of evolving definitions and implications for research. *Journal of Management, 37,* 280–304.

40. Kram, K. (1985). *Mentoring.* Glenview, IL: Scott, Foresman.

41. Weinberg, F.J., & Lankau, M.J. (2011). Formal mentoring programs: A mentor-centric and longitudinal analysis. *Journal of Management, 37,* 1527–1557; Allen,

T.D., Eby, L.T., & Lentz, E. (2006a). Mentorship behaviours and mentorship quality associated with formal mentoring programs: Closing the gap between research and practice. *Journal of Applied Psychology, 91,* 567–578; Murray, M. (1991). *Beyond the myths and magic of mentoring: How to facilitate an effective mentoring program.* San Francisco, CA: Jossey-Bass; Lawrie, J. (1987). How to establish a mentoring program. *Training & Development Journal, 41*(3), 25–27.

42. Harding, K. (2003, March 12). Your new best friend. *Globe and Mail,* C1, C10.

43. Cox, T., Jr. (1993). *Cultural diversity in organizations: Theory, research, & practice.* San Francisco: Berrett-Koehler; Noe, R.A. (1988). Women and mentoring: A review and research agenda. *Academy of Management Review, 13,* 65–78; Ragins, B.R. (1989). Barriers to mentoring: The female manager's dilemma. *Human Relations, 42,* 1–22.

44. Dreyfus, J., Lee, M.J., & Totta, J.M. (1995, December). Mentoring at the Bank of Montreal: A case study of an intervention that exceeded expectations. *Human Resource Planning, 18*(4), 45–49.

45. O'Brien, K.E., Biga, A., Kessler, S.R., & Allen, T.D. (2010). A meta-analytic investigation of gender differences in mentoring. *Journal of Management, 36,* 537–554.

46. Ragins, B., & McFarlin, D. (1990). Perceptions of mentor roles in cross-gender mentoring relationships. *Journal of Vocational Behavior, 37,* 321–339.

47. O'Brien et al., 2010.

48. Weinberg & Lankau, 2011.

49. Burke, R., & McKeen, C. (1990). Mentoring in organizations: Implications for women. *Journal of Business Ethics, 9,* 317–322; Dennett, D. (1985, November). Risks, mentoring helps women to the top. *APA Monitor, 26*; Morrison, A., White, R., & Van Velsor, E. (1987). *Breaking the glass ceiling: Can women reach the top of America's largest corporations?* Reading, MA: Addison-Wesley.

50. Purden, C. (2001, June). Rising to the challenge. *Report on Business Magazine, 17*(12), 31.

51. Ramaswami, A., Dreher, G. F., Bretz, R., & Wiethoff, C. (2010). Gender, mentoring, and career success: The importance of organizational context. *Personnel Psychology, 63,* 385–405.

52. Purden, 2001.

53. Church, E. (2001, March 8). Mentors guide women through career roadblocks. *Globe and Mail,* B12.

54. Cox, 1993; Ibarra, H. (1993). Personal networks of women and minorities in management. *Academy of Management Review, 18,* 56–87.

55. Nkomo, S., & Cox, T. (1989). Gender differences in the upward mobility of black managers: Double whammy or double advantage? *Sex Roles, 21,* 825–839.

56. Thomas, D. (1989). Mentoring and irrationality: The role of racial taboos. *Human Resource Management, 28,* 279–290; Thomas, D. (1990). The impact of race on managers' experiences of developmental relationships: An intraorganizational study. *Journal of Organizational Behavior, 11,* 479–492.

57. Papmehl, A. (2002, October 7). Diversity in workforce paying off, IBM finds. *Toronto Star.* www.thestar.com.

58. Dalton, G.W., Thompson, P.H., & Price, R. (1977, Summer). The four stages of professional careers—A new look at performance by professionals. *Organizational Dynamics,* 19–42; Fagenson, E. (1988). The power of a mentor: Protégés and nonprotégés' perceptions of their own power in organizations. *Group and Organization Studies, 13,* 182–192; Fagenson, E. (1989). The mentor advantage: Perceived career/job experiences of protégés versus non-protégés. *Journal of Organizational Behavior, 10,* 309–320; Scandura, T. (1992). Mentorship and career mobility: An empirical investigation. *Journal of Organizational Behavior, 13,* 169–174; Dreher, G., & Ash, R. (1990). A comparative study of mentoring among men and women in managerial, professional and technical positions. *Journal of Applied Psychology, 75,* 539–546; Whitely, W., Dougherty, T., & Dreher, G. (1991). Relationship of career mentoring and socioeconomic origin to managers' and professionals' early career progress. *Academy of Management Journal, 34,* 331–351.

59. Allen, T.D., Eby, L.T., Poteet, M.L., Lentz, E., & Lima, L. (2004). Career benefits associated with mentoring for protégés: A meta-analysis. *Journal of Applied Psychology, 89,* 127–136.

60. Chao, G., Walz, P., & Gardner, P. (1992). Formal and informal mentorships: A comparison on mentoring functions and contrast with nonmentored counterparts. *Personnel Psychology, 45,* 619–636; Noe, R. (1988). An investigation of the determinants of successful assigned mentoring relationships. *Personnel Psychology, 41,* 457–479; Allen, Eby, & Lentz, 2006a; Allen, T.D., Eby, L.T., & Lentz, E. (2006b). The relationship between formal mentoring program characteristics and perceived program effectiveness. *Personnel Psychology, 59,* 125–153.

61. Dobrow, S.R., Chandler, D.E., Murphy, W.M., & Kram, K.E. (2012). A review of

developmental networks: Incorporating a mutuality perspective. *Journal of Management, 38,* 210–242.

62. Ostroff, C., & Kozlowski, S.W.J. (1992). Organizational socialization as a learning process: The role of information acquisition. *Personnel Psychology, 45,* 849–874; Saks, A.M., & Ashforth, B.E. (1996). Proactive socialization and behavioral self-management. *Journal of Vocational Behavior, 48,* 301–323.

63. Morrison, E.W. (1993). Newcomer information seeking: Exploring types, modes, sources, and outcomes. *Academy of Management Journal, 36,* 557–589; Morrison, E.W. (1993). Longitudinal study of the effects of information seeking on newcomer socialization. *Journal of Applied Psychology, 78,* 173–183.

64. Ashford, S.J., & Black, J.S. (1996). Proactivity during organizational entry: The role of desire for control. *Journal of Applied Psychology, 81,* 199–214; Griffin, A.E.C., Colella, A., & Goparaju, S. (2000). Newcomer and organizational socialization tactics: An interactionist perspective. *Human Resource Management Review, 10,* 453–474; Wanberg, C.R., & Kammeyer-Mueller, J.D. (2000). Predictors and outcomes of proactivity in the socialization process. *Journal of Applied Psychology, 85,* 373–385; Whitely, W.T., Peiró, J.M., Feij, J.A., & Taris, T.W. (1995). Conceptual, epistemological, methodological, and outcome issues in work-role development: A reply. *Journal of Vocational Behavior, 46,* 283–291.

65. Ostroff & Kozlowski, 1992; Ashforth, B.E., Sluss, D.M., & Saks, A.M. (2007). Socialization tactics, proactive behavior, and newcomer learning: Integrating socialization models. *Journal of Vocational Behavior, 70,* 447–462; Saks, A.M., Gruman, J. A., & Cooper-Thomas, H. (2011). The neglected role of proactive behavior and outcomes in newcomer socialization. *Journal of Vocational Behavior, 79,* 36–46.

66. Deveau, D. (2012, February 3). Canada's 10 most admired corporate cultures ('People here really believe in our purpose'). *National Post,* JV6.

67. For a more complete discussion of various definitions, theories, and concepts of culture, see Allaire, Y., & Firsirotu, M.E. (1984). Theories of organizational culture. *Organization Studies, 5,* 193–226; Hatch, M.J. (1993). The dynamics of organizational culture. *Academy of Management Review, 18,* 657–693; Schein, E.H. (1992). *Organizational culture and leadership,* 2nd ed. San Francisco: Jossey-Bass; Smircich, L. (1983). Concepts of culture and

organizational analysis. *Administrative Science Quarterly, 28,* 339–358.

68. Sackmann, S.A. (1992). Culture and subculture: An analysis of organizational knowledge. *Administrative Science Quarterly, 37,* 140–161.

69. Gregory, K.L. (1983). Native-view paradigms: Multiple cultures and culture conflicts in organizations. *Administrative Science Quarterly, 28,* 359–376.

70. Deal, T.E., & Kennedy, A.A. (1982). *Corporate cultures: The rites and rituals of corporate life.* Reading, MA: Addison-Wesley; Kilmann, R., Saxton, M.J., & Serpa, R. (1986, Winter). Issues in understanding and changing culture. *California Management Review,* 87–94. For a critique, see Saffold, G.S., III. (1988). Culture traits, strength, and organizational performance: Moving beyond "strong" culture. *Academy of Management Review, 13,* 546–558.

71. Holloway, A. (2006, April 10–23). Hilti (Canada) Corp. *Canadian Business, 79*(8), 78.

72. Quinn, P. (2008, January 30). WestJet locks in top spot on corporate culture honour poll. *Financial Post* (online), www.financialpost.com; (2009). *Canada's 10 Most Admired Corporate Cultures 2008.* Toronto: Waterstone Human Capital; (2008). *Canada's 10 Most Admired Corporate Cultures 2007.* Toronto: Waterstone Human Capital.

73. Verburg, P. (2000, December 25). Prepare for takeoff. *Canadian Business, 73*(24), 94–99; (2008). *Canada's 10 Most Admired Corporate Cultures 2007.* Toronto: Waterstone Human Capital.

74. Gordon, G.G., & Di Tomaso, N. (1992). Predicting corporate performance from organizational culture. *Journal of Management Studies, 29,* 783–798. For a critique of such work, see Siehl, C., & Martin, J. (1990). Organizational culture: A key to financial performance. In B. Schneider (Ed.), *Organizational climate and culture.* San Francisco: Jossey-Bass.

75. Sheridan, J.E. (1992). Organizational culture and employee retention. *Academy of Management Journal, 35,* 1036–1056.

76. Lorsch, J.W. (1986, Winter). Managing culture: The invisible barrier to strategic change. *California Management Review,* 95–109.

77. Verburg, P. (2000, December 25).

78. (2009). *Canada's 10 Most Admired Corporate Cultures 2008.* Toronto: Waterstone Human Capital.

79. Mount, I. (2002, August). Out of control. *Business 2.0, 3*(8), 38–44.

80. Cartwright, S., & Cooper, C.L. (1993, May). The role of culture compatibility

in successful organizational marriage. *Academy of Management Executive,* 57–70.

81. Fordahl, M. (2002, March 28). Hp, Compaq face ghosts of mega-mergers past. *Globe and Mail,* B17.

82. Kets de Vries, M.F.R., & Miller, D. (1984). *The neurotic organization: Diagnosing and changing counterproductive styles of management.* San Francisco: Jossey-Bass.

83. Lardner, J. (2002, March). Why should anyone believe you? *Business 2.0, 3*(3), 40–48; Waldie, P., & Howlett, K. (2003, June 11). Reports reveal tight grip of Ebbers on WorldCom. *Globe and Mail,* B1, B7; Wells, J. (2009, August 6). Now playing: Garth Drabinsky stars in the 7-year stretch. *Toronto Star,* A1, A12; Blackwell, R., & MacMillan, J. (2009, August 6). They built a theatre empire that crumbled, bilking investors and cleaning out creditors. Now Garth Drabinsky and his partner are going to jail for their "deception" and "dishonest dealing." *Globe and Mail,* A1, A7.

84. McKenna, B. (2003, August 27). Shuttle probe blasts NASA's dysfunctional atmosphere. *Globe and Mail,* A9; Schwartz, J., & Wald, M.L. (2003, August 27). Shuttle probe faults NASA. *Toronto Star* (online), www.thestar.ca (orig. pub. *New York Times*).

85. Maccharles, T. (2011, November 17). Sexual harassment tops RCMP agenda. *Toronto Star,* A4; Keller, J. (2012, May 10). RCMP corporal files sexual harassment suit. *The Canadian Press,* www .metronews.ca/news.

86. See Schein, 1992.

87. Papmehl, 2002.

88. Uttal, B. (1985, August 5). Behind the fall of Steve Jobs. *Fortune,* 20–24.

89. Pascale, R. (1985, Winter). The paradox of "corporate culture": Reconciling ourselves to socialization. *California Management Review,* 26–41. For some research support, see Caldwell, D.F., Chatman, J.A., & O'Reilly, C.A. (1990). Building organizational commitment: A multifirm study. *Journal of Occupational Psychology, 63,* 245–261.

90. Deveau, D. (2012, February 3). Canada's 10 most admired corporate cultures (Culture aids recruiting process). *National Post,* JV1.

91. Deveau, D. (2012, February 3). Canada's 10 most admired corporate cultures (No cultural divides for Agrium employees). *National Post,* JV4.

92. Gordon, A. (2000, February). 35 best companies to work for. *Report on Business Magazine,* 24–32.

93. Hatch, 1993; Ornstein, S. (1986). Organizational symbols: A study of their meanings and influences on perceived

organizational climate. *Organizational Behavior and Human Decision Processes, 38*, 207–229.

94. Nulty, P. (1989, February 27). America's toughest bosses. *Fortune,* 40–54.

95. Trice, H.M., and Beyer, J.M. (1984). Studying organizational cultures through rites and ceremonials. *Academy of Management Review, 9*, 653–669.

96. Deveau, D. (2012, February 3). Canada's 10 most admired corporate cultures ('People here really believe in our purpose'). *National Post,* JV6.

97. Martin, J., Feldman, M.S., Hatch, M.J., & Sitkin, S.B. (1983). The uniqueness paradox in organizational stories. *Administrative Science Quarterly, 28*, 438–453.

98. Peters, T., & Austin, N. (1985). *A passion for excellence: The leadership difference.* New York: Random House.

Chapter 9

1. O'Grady, M. (2012, February 16). The Bay's Bonnie Brooks leads Lord & Taylor. *Canadian Business,* www.canadianbusiness.com/article/71119; Shaw, H. (2012, January 23). Bonnie Brooks adds top job at Lord & Taylor. *Financial Post,* www.business.financialpost.com/2012/01/23/bonnie-brooks; Flavelle, D. (2012, January 23). Brooks to oversee the Bay and Lord & Taylor. *Toronto Star,* www.thestar.com/printarticle/1120081; Hudson's Bay Company Press Releases (Hudson's Bay Company Acquires Lord & Taylor; Leadership: Bonnie Brooks), www2.hbc.caom; Long, C.D. (2011, Autumn). Room for change (Bonnie Brooks and The Bay). *Montecristo Magazine,* www.montecristomagazine.com; Lawrence, C. (2011, October 6). Retail arbiter. *Women of Influence,* www.womenofinfluence.ca/retail-arbiter/; Kingston, A. (2009, March 16). Bonnie of the Bay. *Maclean's, 122*(9), 34–36; Stren, O. (2008, December). Shop girl. *Toronto Life,* www.torontolife.com/features/shop-girl; Strauss, M. (2009, April 23). The pragmatic fashionista. *Globe and Mail,* B1, B7.

2. Daly, J. (2003, February). The toughest SOBs in business. *Report on Business Magazine, 19*(8), 34–42; Various contributors (2005, November). The power 25. *Report on Business Magazine, 22*(4), 49–82.

3. Hiller, N.J., DeChurch, L.A., Murase, T., & Doty, D. (2011). Searching for outcomes of leadership: A 25-year review. *Journal of Management, 37*, 1137–1177.

4. Ireland, R.D., & Hitt, M.A. (1999). Achieving and maintaining strategic competitiveness in the 21st century: The role of strategic leadership. *Academy of Management Executive, 13*, 43–57.

5. Judge, T.A., Bono, J.E., Ilies, R., & Gerhardt, M.W. (2002). Personality and leadership: A qualitative and quantitative review. *Journal of Applied Psychology, 87*, 765–780.

6. Bass, B.M. (1990). *Bass & Stogdill's handbook of leadership: A survey of research* (3rd ed.). New York: Free Press.

7. Derue, D.S., Nahrgang, J.D., Wellman, N., & Humphrey, S.E. (2011). Trait and behavioral theories of leadership: An integration and meta-analytic test of their relative validity. *Personnel Psychology, 64*, 7–52.

8. This list is derived from Bass, 1990; House, R.J., & Baetz, M.L. (1979). Leadership: Some empirical generalizations and new research directions. *Research in Organizational Behavior, 1*, 341–423; Locke, E.A. & Associates (1992). *The essence of leadership: The four keys to leading effectively.* New York: Free Press; Lord, R.G., DeVader, C.L., & Alliger, G.M. (1986). A meta-analysis of the relationship between personality traits and leadership perceptions: An application of validity generalization procedures. *Journal of Applied Psychology, 71*, 402–410.

9. Derue et al., 2011; Judge et al., 2002; Grant, A.M., Gino, F., & Hofmann, D.A. (2011). Reversing the extraverted leadership advantage: The role of employee proactivity. *Academy of Management Journal, 54*, 528–550; Van Iddekinge, C.H., Ferris, G.R., & Heffner, T.S. (2009). Test of a multistage model of distal and proximal antecedents of leader performance. *Personnel Psychology, 62*, 463–495.

10. Judge, T.A., & Bono, J.E. (2000). Five-factor model of personality and transformational leadership. *Journal of Applied Psychology, 85*, 751–765; Judge, T.A., Colbert, A.E., & Ilies, R. (2004). Intelligence and leadership: A quantitative review and test of theoretical propositions. *Journal of Applied Psychology, 89*, 542–552.

11. Derue et al., 2011.

12. Kirkpatrick, S.A., & Locke, E.A. (1991). Leadership: Do traits matter? *Academy of Management Executive, 5*, 48–60.

13. Derue et al., 2011.

14. Hannon, G. (2004, January). The great transformation. *Report on Business Magazine, 20*(7), 43–46.

15. Judge, T.A., Piccolo, R.F., & Ilies, R. (2004). The forgotten ones? The validity of consideration and initiating structure in leadership research. *Journal of Applied Psychology, 89*, 36–51.

16. Kerr, S., Schriesheim, C.A., Murphy, C.J., & Stogdill, R.M. (1974). Toward a contingency theory of leadership based upon the consideration and initiating structure literature. *Organizational Behavior and Human Performance, 12*, 62–82.

17. Podsakoff, P.M., Bommer, W.H., Podsakoff, N.P., & MacKenzie, S.B. (2006). Relationships between leader reward and punishment behaviour and subordinate attitudes, perceptions, and behaviors: A meta-analytic review of existing and new research. *Organizational Behavior and Human Decision Processes, 99*, 113–142.

18. Verburg, P. (2000, December 25). Prepare for takeoff. *Canadian Business, 73*(24), 94–99.

19. Fiedler, F.E. (1967). *A theory of leadership effectiveness.* New York: McGraw-Hill; Fiedler, F.E. (1978). The contingency model and the dynamics of the leadership process. In L. Berkowitz (Ed.), *Advances in experimental social psychology* (Vol. 11). New York: Academic Press; Fiedler, F.E., & Chemers, M.M. (1974). *Leadership and effective management.* Glenview, IL: Scott, Foresman.

20. Fiedler, F.E. (1989). The effective utilization of intellectual abilities and job-relevant knowledge in group performance: Cognitive resource theory and an agenda for the future. *Applied Psychology: An International Review, 38*, 289–304. Fiedler, F.E. (1995). Cognitive resources and leadership performance. *Applied Psychology: An International Review, 44*, 5–28.

21. For a summary, see Fiedler, 1978.

22. See Ashour, A.S. (1973). The contingency model of leader effectiveness: An evaluation. *Organizational Behavior and Human Performance, 9*, 339–355; Graen, G.B., Alvares, D., Orris, J.B., & Martella, J.A. (1970). The contingency model of leadership effectiveness: Antecedent and evidential results. *Psychological Bulletin, 74*, 285–296.

23. Peters, L.H., Hartke, D.D., & Pohlmann, J.T. (1985). Fiedler's contingency theory of leadership: An application of the meta-analysis procedures of Schmidt and Hunter. *Psychological Bulletin, 97*, 274–285; Schriesheim, C.A., Tepper, B.J., & Tetreault, L.A. (1994). Least preferred co-worker score, situational control, and leadership effectiveness: A meta-analysis of contingency and performance predictions. *Journal of Applied Psychology, 79*, 561–573; Strube, M.J., & Garcia, J.E. (1981). A meta-analytic investigation of Fiedler's contingency model of leadership effectiveness. *Psychological Bulletin, 90*, 307–321.

24. Fiedler, 1995; Fiedler, F.E., Murphy, S.E., & Gibson, F.W. (1992). Inaccurate reporting and inappropriate variables: A reply to Vecchio's (1990) examination

of cognitive resource theory. *Journal of Applied Psychology, 77,* 372–374.

25. Fiedler, Murphy, & Gibson, 1992; Vecchio, R.P. (1990). Theoretical and empirical examination of cognitive resource theory. *Journal of Applied Psychology, 75,* 141–147.

26. House, R.J., & Dessler, G. (1974). The path-goal theory of leadership: Some post hoc and a priori tests. In J.G. Hunt & L.L. Larson (Eds.), *Contingency approaches to leadership.* Carbondale, IL: Southern Illinois University Press; House, R.J., & Mitchell, T.R. (1974, Autumn). Path-goal theory of leadership. *Journal of Contemporary Business,* 81–97. See also Evans, M.G. (1970). The effects of supervisory behavior on the path-goal relationship. *Organizational Behavior and Human Performance, 5,* 277–298.

27. Filley, A.C., House, R.J., & Kerr, S. (1976). *Managerial process and organizational behavior* (2nd ed.). Glenview, IL: Scott, Foresman; House & Dessler, 1974; House & Mitchell, 1974; Wofford, J.C., & Liska, L.Z. (1993). Path-goal theories of leadership: A meta-analysis. *Journal of Management, 19,* 857–876.

28. See, for example, Greene, C.N. (1979). Questions of causation in the path-goal theory of leadership. *Academy of Management Journal, 22,* 22–41; Griffin, R.W. (1980). Relationships among individual, task design, and leader behavior variables. *Academy of Management Journal, 23,* 665–683.

29. Mitchell, T.R. (1973). Motivation and participation: An integration. *Academy of Management Journal, 16,* 160–179.

30. Maier, N.R.F. (1970). *Problem solving and creativity in individuals and groups.* Belmont, CA: Brooks/Cole; Maier, N.R.F. (1973). *Psychology in industrial organizations* (4th ed.). Boston: Houghton Mifflin.

31. Maier, 1970, 1973.

32. Vroom, V.H., & Jago, A.G. (1988). *The new leadership: Managing participation in organizations.* Englewood Cliffs, NJ: Prentice-Hall; Vroom, V.H., & Yetton, P.W. (1973). *Leadership and decision-making.* Pittsburgh: University of Pittsburgh Press.

33. Vroom & Yetton, 1973, 13.

34. See Vroom & Jago, 1988, for a review. See also Field, R.H.G., Wedley, W.C., & Hayward, M.W.J. (1989). Criteria used in selecting Vroom-Yetton decision styles. *Canadian Journal of Administrative Sciences, 6*(2), 18–24.

35. Reviews on participation reveal a complicated pattern of results. See Miller, K.I., & Monge, P.R. (1986). Participation, satisfaction, and productivity: A meta-analytic review. *Academy*

of *Management Journal, 29,* 727–753; Wagner, J.A., III, & Gooding, R.Z. (1987a). Shared influence and organizational behavior: A meta-analysis of situational variables expected to moderate participation–outcome relationships. *Academy of Management Journal, 30,* 524–541; Wagner, J.A., III, & Gooding, R.Z. (1987b). Effects of societal trends on participation research. *Administrative Science Quarterly, 32,* 241–262; Huang, X., Iun, J., Liu, A., & Gong, Y. (2010). Does participative leadership enhance work performance by inducing empowerment or trust? The differential effects on managerial and non-managerial subordinates. *Journal of Organizational Behavior, 31,* 122–143.

36. Graen, G.B., & Uhl-Bien, M. (1995). Relationship-based approach to leadership: Development of leader–member exchange (LMX) theory of leadership over 25 years: Applying a multi-level, multi-domain perspective. *Leadership Quarterly, 6*(2), 219–247.

37. Walumbwa, F.O., Mayer, D.M., Wang, P., Wang, H., Workman K., & Christensen, A.L. (2011). Linking ethical leadership to employee performance: The roles of leader-member exchange, self-efficacy, and organizational identification. *Organizational Behavior and Human Decision Processes, 115,* 204–213; Walumbwa, F.O., Cropanzano, R., & Goldman, B.M. (2011). How leader–member exchange influences effective work behaviors: Social exchange and internal-external efficacy perspectives. *Personnel Psychology, 64,* 739–770.

38. Gerstner, C.R., & Day, D.V. (1997). Meta-analytic review of leader-member exchange theory: Correlates and construct issues. *Journal of Applied Psychology, 82,* 827–844; Graen, & Uhl-Bien, 1995; Schriesheim, C.A., Castro, S.L., & Cogliser, C.C. (1999). Leader–member exchange (LMX) research: A comprehensive review of theory, measurement, and data-analytic practices. *Leadership Quarterly, 10*(1), 63–113; House, R.J., & Aditya, R.N. (1997). The social scientific study of leadership: Quo vadis? *Journal of Management, 23,* 409–473; Tierney, P., Farmer, S.M., & Graen, G.B. (1999). An examination of leadership and employee creativity: The relevance of traits and relationships. *Personnel Psychology, 52,* 591–620.

39. Gerstner, & Day, 1997; Graen, & Uhl-Bien, 1995; Ilies, R., Nahrgang, J.D., & Morgeson, F.P. (2007). Leader-member exchange and citizenship behaviors: A meta-analysis. *Journal of Applied Psychology, 92,* 269–277; Liao, H., Liu, D., & Loi, R. (2010). Looking at both sides of the social exchange coin: A

social cognitive perspective on the joint effects of relationship quality and differentiation on creativity. *Academy of Management Journal, 53,* 1090–1109.

40. Judge, T.A., & Piccolo, R.F. (2004). Transformational and transactional leadership: A meta-analytic test of their relative validity. *Journal of Applied Psychology, 89,* 755–768.

41. The transformational/transactional distinction is credited to Burns, J.M. (1978). *Leadership.* New York: Harper & Row.

42. Bass, B.M. (1985). *Leadership and performance beyond expectations.* New York: Free Press; Bass, B.M. (1990, Winter). From transactional to transformational leadership: Learning to share the vision. *Organizational Dynamics, 19,* 31.

43. Judge & Piccolo, 2004.

44. Judge & Piccolo, 2004; Bono, J.E., & Judge, T.A. (2004). Personality and transformational and transactional leadership: A meta-analysis. *Journal of Applied Psychology, 89,* 901–910.

45. House, R.J. (1977). A 1976 theory of charismatic leadership. In J.G. Hunt & L.L. Larson (Eds.), *Leadership: The cutting edge.* Carbondale, IL: Southern Illinois University Press.

46. DeGroot, T., Kilker, D.S., & Cross, T.C. (2000). A meta-analysis to review organizational outcomes related to charismatic leadership. *Canadian Journal of Administrative Sciences, 17,* 356–371; Fuller, J.B., Patterson, C.E.P., Hester, K., & Stringer, D.Y. (1996). A quantitative review of research on charismatic leadership. *Psychological Reports, 78,* 271–287.

47. Agle, B.R., Nagarajan, N.J., Sonnenfeld, J.A., & Srinivasan, D. (2006). Does CEO charisma matter? An empirical analysis of the relationships among organizational performance, environmental uncertainty, and top management team perceptions of CEO charisma. *Academy of Management Journal, 49,* 161–174; Waldman, D.A., Ramirez, G.G., House, R.J., & Puranam, P. (2001). Does leadership matter? CEO leadership attributes and profitability under conditions of perceived environmental uncertainty. *Academy of Management Journal, 44,* 134–143.

48. Judge & Piccolo, 2004.

49. Derue et al., 2011.

50. Colbert, A.E., Kristof-Brown, A.L., Bradley, B.H., & Barrick, M.R. (2008). CEO transformational leadership: The role of goal importance congruence in top management teams. *Academy of Management Journal, 51,* 81–96; Ling, Y., Simsek, Z., Lubatkin, M.H., & Veiga, J.F. (2008). The impact of transformational CEOs on the performance of small- to medium-sized firms: Does organizational

context matter? *Journal of Applied Psychology, 93,* 923–934.

51. Seo, M., Taylor, M.S., Hill, N.S., Zhang, X., Tesluk, P.E., & Lorinkova, N.M. (2012). The role of affect and leadership during organizational change. *Personnel Psychology, 65,* 121–165; Oreg, S., & Berson, Y. (2011). Leadership and employees' reactions to change: The role of leaders' personal attributes and transformational leadership style. *Personnel Psychology, 64,* 627–659; Herold, D.M., Fedor, D.B., Caldwell, S., & Liu, Y. (2008). The effects of transformational and change leadership on employees' commitment to a change: A multilevel study. *Journal of Applied Psychology, 93,* 346–357.

52. Hoffman, B.J., Bynum, B.H., Piccolo, R.F., & Sutton, A.W. (2011). Person-organization value congruence: How transformational leaders influence work group effectiveness. *Academy of Management Journal, 54,* 779–796; Wang, H., Law, K.S., Hackett, R.D., Wang, D., & Chen, Z.X. (2005). Leader–member exchange as a mediator of the relationship between transformational leadership and followers' performance and organizational citizenship behaviour. *Academy of Management Journal, 48,* 420–432; Piccolo, R.F., & Colquitt, J.A. (2006). Transformational leadership and job behaviours: The mediating role of core job characteristics. *Academy of Management Journal, 49,* 327–340; Walumbwa, F.O., Avolio, B.J., & Zhu, W. (2008). How transformational leadership weaves its influence on individual job performance: The role of identification and efficacy beliefs. *Personnel Psychology, 61,* 793–825

53. Gregersen, H.B., Morrison, A.J., & Black, J.S. (1998, Fall). Developing leaders for the global frontier. *Sloan Management Review,* 21–32.

54. Javidan, M., Dorfman, P.W., de Luque, M.S., & House, R.J. (2006). In the eye of the beholder: Cross-cultural lessons in leadership from Project GLOBE. *Academy of Management Perspectives, 20,* 67–90.

55. Gregersen, Morrison, & Black, 1998.

56. Gregersen, Morrison, & Black, 1998; Javidan et al., 2006.

57. Javidan et al., 2006.

58. Gregersen, Morrison, & Black, 1998; Church, E. (1999, January 7). Born to be a global business leader. *Globe and Mail,* B8.

59. Moore, K. (2002, August 21). Multicultural Canada breeds managers with global outlook. *Globe and Mail,* B9.

60. Avolio, B.J., Walumbwa, F.O., & Weber, T.J. (2009). Leadership: Current theories, research, and future directions. *Annual Review of Psychology, 60,* 421–449.

61. Zhang, X., & Bartol, K.M. (2010). Linking empowering leadership and employee creativity: The influence of psychological empowerment, intrinsic motivation, and creative process engagement. *Academy of Management Journal, 53,* 107–128.

62. Ahearne, M., Mathieu, J., & Rapp, A. (2005). To empower or not to empower your sales force? An empirical examination of the influence of leadership empowerment behavior on customer satisfaction and performance. *Journal of Applied Psychology, 90,* 945–955.

63. Zhang & Bartol, 2010.

64. Brown, M.E., Trevino, L.K., & Harrison, D.A. (2005). Ethical leadership: A social learning perspective for construct development and testing. *Organizational Behavior and Human Decision Processes, 97,* 117–134; Brown, M. E., & Trevino, L.K. (2006). Ethical leadership: A review and future directions. *The Leadership Quarterly, 17,* 595–616.

65. Thomas, T., Schermerhorn, J.R., & Dienhart, J.W. (2004). Strategic leadership of ethical behavior in business. *Academy of Management Executive, 18,* 56–66.

66. Carpenter, D. (2006, July 3). Boeing CEO sitting pretty one year in. *Globe and Mail,* B5.

67. Mayer, D.M., Aquino, K., Greenbaum, R.L., & Kuenzi, M. (2012). Who displays ethical leadership, and why does it matter? An examination of antecedents and consequences of ethical leadership. *Academy of Management Journal, 55,* 151–171; Kacmar, K.M., Bachrach, D.G., & Harris, K.J. (2011). Fostering good citizenship through ethical leadership: Exploring the moderating role of gender and organizational politics. *Journal of Applied Psychology, 96,* 633–642; Schminke, M., Ambrose, M.L., & Neubaum, D.O. (2005). The effects of leader moral development on ethical climate and employee attitudes. *Organizational Behavior and Human Decision Processes, 97,* 135–151.

68. Walumbwa et al., 2011; Piccolo, R.F., Greenbaum, R., Hartog, D.N.D., & Folger, R. (2010). The relationship between ethical leadership and core job characteristics. *Journal of Organizational Behavior, 31,* 259–278.

69. Brown, Trevino, & Harrison, 2005; Mayer, D.M., Kuenzi, M., Greenbaum, R., Bardes, M., & Salvador, R. (2009). How low does ethical leadership flow? Test of a trickle-down model. *Organizational Behavior and Human Decision Processes, 108,* 1–13.

70. Hannah, S.T., Avolio, B.J., & Walumbwa, F.O. (2011). Relationships between authentic leadership, moral courage, and ethical and pro-social behaviors. *Business Ethics Quarterly, 21,* 555–578; Gardner, W.L., Avolio, B.J., Luthans, F., May, D.R., & Walumbwa, F. (2005). "Can you see the real me?" A self-based model of authentic leader and follower development. *The Leadership Quarterly, 16,* 343–372; Ilies, R., Morgenson, F.P., & Nahrgang, J.D. (2005). Authentic leadership and eudaemonic well-being: Understanding leader-follower outcomes. *The Leadership Quarterly, 16,* 373–394.

71. Pitts, G. (2008, December). The testing of Michael McCain. *Report on Business,* 60–66; Pitts, G. (2008, August 30). Man under fire. *Globe and Mail,* B1, B6.

72. Walumbwa, F.O., Avolio, B.J., Gardner, W.L., Wernsing, T.S., & Peterson, S.J. (2008). Authentic leadership: Development and validation of a theory-based measure. *Journal of Management, 34,* 89–126.

73. Walumbwa et al., 2008; Hannah et al., 2011; Walumbwa, F.O., Wang, P., Wang, H., Schaubroeck, J., & Avolio, B.J. (2010). Psychological processes linking authentic leadership to follower behaviors. *The Leadership Quarterly, 21,* 901–914.

74. Walumbwa, F.O., Luthans, F., Avey, J.B., & Oke, A. (2011). Authentically leading groups: The mediating role of collective psychological capital and trust. *Journal of Organizational Behavior, 32,* 4–24.

75. Hannah, S.T., Walumbwa, F.O., & Fry, L.W. (2011). Leadership in action teams: Team leader and members' authenticity, authenticity strength, and team outcomes. *Personnel Psychology, 64,* 771–802.

76. Van Dierendonck, D. (2011). Servant leadership: A review and synthesis. *Journal of Management, 37,* 1228–1261.

77. Van Dierendonck, 2011.

78. Van Dierendonck, 2011; Mayer, D.M., Bardes, M., & Piccolo, R.F. (2008). Do servant-leaders help satisfy follower needs? An organizational justice perspective. *European Journal of Work and Organizational Psychology, 17,* 180–197; Neubert, M.J., Kacmar, K.M., Carlson, D.S., Chonko, L.B., & Roberts, J.A. (2008). Regulatory focus as a mediator of the influence of initiating structure and servant leadership on employee behavior. *Journal of Applied Psychology, 93,* 1220–1233.

79. Walumbwa, F.O., Hartnell, C.A., & Oke, A. (2010). Servant leadership, procedural justice climate, service climate, employee attitudes, and organizational citizenship behavior: A cross-level investigation. *Journal of Applied Psychology, 95,* 517–529; Ehrhart, M.G. (2004).

Leadership and procedural justice climate as antecedents of unit-level organizational citizenship behavior. *Personnel Psychology, 57,* 61–94.

80. Javidan et al., 2006.

81. Javidan et al., 2006.

82. Javidan et al., 2006.

83. Eagley, A.H., & Johnson, B.T. (1990). Gender and leadership style: A meta-analysis. *Psychological Bulletin, 108,* 233–256.

84. Kass, S. (September 1999). Employees perceive women as better managers than men, finds five-year study. *ADA Monitor, 30*(8), 6.

85. Derue et al., 2011.

86. Eagly, A.H., Johannesen-Schmidt, M.C., & van Engen, M.L. (2003). Transformational, transactional, and laissez-faire leadership styles: A meta-analysis comparing women and men. *Psychological Bulletin, 120,* 569–591.

87. Financial Post Staff (2011, December 11). Canada's most powerful women: Top 100, *Financial Post,* www.financialpost.com; www.ge.com.ca/en/company/leadership,bios/elyse_allan.html

88. Wohlbold, E., & Chenier, L. (2011). Women in senior management: Where are they? *The Conference Board of Canada.* Ottawa; Kopun, F. (2011, August 31). Women's workplace mobility 'flatlined.' *Toronto Star,* B4; McFarland, J., & McNish, J. (2010, October 15). Firms creating diversity programs to break down systemic barriers. *Globe and Mail,* A14; Klie, S. (2009, April 6). Women make small gains. *Canadian HR Reporter, 22*(7), 1, 2; Morra, M. (2008, June–July). The broad perspective. *HR Professional,* 22–28.

89. Eagly, A.H., & Carli, L.L. (2007, September). Women and the labyrinth of leadership. *Harvard Business Review, 85,* 63–71.

90. Eagly & Carli, 2007.

91. Koenig, A.M., Eagly, A.H., Mitchell, A.A., & Ristikari, T. (2011). Are leader stereotypes masculine? A meta-analysis of three research paradigms. *Psychological Bulletin, 137,* 616–642.

Chapter 10

1. Excerpted from Tamburri, R. (2009, May). Communicating in bad times. *University Affairs,* 18–20.

2. LePine, J.A., & Van Dyne, L. (2001). Voice and cooperative behavior as contrasting forms of contextual performance: Evidence of differential relationships with Big Five personality characteristics and cognitive ability. *Journal of Applied Psychology, 86,* 326–336; for a review of voice and silence, see Morrison, E.W. (2011). Employee voice behavior: Integration and directions for future research. *Academy of Management Annals, 5,* 373–412.

3. Morrison, E.W., Wheeler-Smith, S.L., & Kamdar, D. (2011). Speaking up in groups: A cross-level study of group voice climate and voice. *Journal of Applied Psychology, 96,* 183–191; Ng, T.W.H., & Feldman, D.C. (2012). Employee voice behavior: A meta-analytic test of the conservation of resources framework. *Journal of Organizational Behavior, 33,* 216–234; LePine & Van Dyne, 2001.

4. Detert, J.R., & Treviño, L.K. (2010). Speaking up to higher-ups: How supervisors and skip-level leaders influence employee voice. *Organization Science, 21,* 249–270.

5. Edmondson, A. (1999). Psychological safety and learning behavior in work teams. *Administrative Science Quarterly, 44,* 350–383.

6. Ng & Feldman, 2012.

7. Detert, J.R., & Edmondson, A.C. (2011). Implicit voice theories: Taken-for-granted rules of self-censorship at work. *Academy of Management Journal, 54,* 461–488.

8. Tesser, A., & Rosen, S. (1975). The reluctance to transmit bad news. In L. Berkowitz (Ed.), *Advances in experimental social psychology* (Vol. 8). New York: Academic Press.

9. Read, W. (1962). Upward communication in industrial hierarchies. *Human Relations, 15,* 3–16; for related studies, see Jablin, F.M. (1979). Superior–subordinate communication: The state of the art. *Psychological Bulletin, 86,* 1201–1222.

10. Evidence that subordinates suppress communicating negative news to the boss can be found in O'Reilly, C.A., & Roberts, K.H. (1974). Information filtration in organizations: Three experiments. *Organizational Behavior and Human Performance, 11,* 253–265. For evidence that this is probably self-presentational, see Bond, C.F., Jr., & Anderson, E.L. (1987). The reluctance to transmit bad news: Private discomfort or public display? *Journal of Experimental Social Psychology, 23,* 176–187.

11. Ashford, S.J. (1989). Self-assessments in organizations: A literature review and integrated model. *Research in Organizational Behavior, 11,* 133–174; Heidemeier, H., & Moser, K. (2009). Self-other agreement in job performance ratings: A meta-analytic test and a process model. *Journal of Applied Psychology, 94,* 353–370.

12. Noon, M., & Delbridge, R. (1993). News from behind my hand: Gossip in organizations. *Organization Studies, 14,* 23–36.

13. Davis, K. (1977). *Human behavior at work* (5th ed.). New York: McGraw-Hill.

14. Bartlett, C.A., & Ghosal, S. (1995, May–June). Changing the role of top management: Beyond systems to people. *Harvard Business Review,* 132–142; for more on gossip, see the June 2004 special issue of the *Review of General Psychology.*

15. Van Hoye, G., & Lievens, F. (2009). Tapping the grapevine: A closer look at word-of-mouth as a recruitment source. *Journal of Applied Psychology, 94,* 341–352.

16. Rosnow, R.L. (1980). Psychology of rumor reconsidered. *Psychological Bulletin, 87,* 578–591.

17. Rosnow, R.L. (1991). Inside rumor: A personal journey. *American Psychologist, 46,* 484–496; see also DiFronzo, N. & Bordia, P. (2007). *Rumor psychology: Social and organizational approaches.* Washington, DC: American Psychological Association.

18. Kanter, R.M. (1977). *Men and women of the corporation.* New York: Basic Books.

19. For reviews, see Heslin, R., & Patterson, M.L. (1982). *Nonverbal behavior and social psychology.* New York: Plenum; Harper, R.G., Wiens, A.N., & Matarazzo, J.D. (1978). *Nonverbal communication: The state of the art.* New York: Wiley; for a popular treatment, see Goman, C.K. (2008). *The nonverbal advantage: Secrets and science of body language at work.* San Francisco: Berrett-Koehler.

20. Mehrabian, A. (1972). *Nonverbal communication.* Chicago: Aldine-Atherton.

21. Mehrabian, 1972; see also Hall, J.A., Coats, E.J., & Smith LeBeau, L. (2005). Nonverbal behavior and the vertical dimension of social relations: A meta-analysis. *Psychological Bulletin, 131,* 898–924.

22. DePaulo, B.M. (1992). Nonverbal behavior and self-presentation. *Psychological Bulletin, 111,* 203–243.

23. Edinger, J.A., & Patterson, M.L. (1983). Nonverbal involvement and social control. *Psychological Bulletin, 93,* 30–56.

24. Rasmussen, K.G., Jr. (1984). Nonverbal behavior, verbal behavior, resume credentials, and selection interview outcomes. *Journal of Applied Psychology, 69,* 551–556.

25. Campbell, D.E. (1979). Interior office design and visitor response. *Journal of Applied Psychology, 64,* 648–653. For a replication, see Morrow, P.C., & McElroy, J.C. (1981). Interior office design and visitor response: A constructive replication. *Journal of Applied Psychology, 66,* 646–650.

26. Gosling, S.D., Ko, S.J., Mannarelli, T., & Morris, M.E. (2002). A room with a cue: Personality judgments based on offices

and bedrooms. *Journal of Personality and Social Psychology, 82,* 379–398.

27. Elsbach, K.D. (2004). Interpreting workplace identities: The role of office decor. *Journal of Organizational Behavior, 25,* 99–128.

28. Molloy, J.T. (1993). *John T. Molloy's new dress for success.* New York: Warner; Molloy, J.T. (1987). *The woman's dress for success book.* New York: Warner.

29. Rafaeli, A., & Pratt, M.G. (1993). Tailored meanings: On the meaning and impact of organizational dress. *Academy of Management Review, 18,* 32–55; Solomon, M.R. (Ed.). (1985). *The psychology of fashion.* New York: Lexington; Solomon, M.R. (1986, April). Dress for effect. *Psychology Today,* 20–28.

30. Forsythe, S., Drake, M.F., & Cox, C.E. (1985). Influence of applicant's dress on interviewer's selection decisions. *Journal of Applied Psychology, 70,* 374–378.

31. Dress for Success Worldwide, www.dressforsuccess.org.

32. Solomon, 1986.

33. Tannen, D. (1994). *Talking from 9 to 5.* New York: William Morrow.

34. Koonce, R. (1997, September). Language, sex, and power: Women and men in the workplace. *Training & Development,* 34–39.

35. Tannen, D. (1995, September–October). The power of talk: Who gets heard and why. *Harvard Business Review,* 138–148.

36. Koonce, 1997.

37. Tannen, 1994.

38. Koonce, 1997; Tannen, 1995.

39. Adler, N.J. (1992). *International dimensions of organizational behavior* (2nd ed.). Belmont, CA: Wadsworth, 66.

40. Ramsey, S., & Birk, J. (1983). Preparation of North Americans for interaction with Japanese: Considerations of language and communication style. In D. Landis & R.W. Brislin (Eds.), *Handbook of intercultural training* (Vol. 3). New York: Pergamon.

41. Ekman, P., & Rosenberg, E. (1997). *What the face reveals.* New York: Oxford University Press.

42. Furnham, A., & Bochner, S. (1986). *Culture shock: Psychological reactions to unfamiliar environments.* London: Methuen, 207–208; for a more general perspective on how gestures relate to verbal communication, see Hostetter, A.B. (2011). When do gestures communicate? A meta-analysis. *Psychological Bulletin, 137,* 297–315.

43. Examples on gaze and touch draw on Argyle, M. (1982). Inter-cultural communication. In S. Bochner (Ed.), *Cultures in contact: Studies in cross-cultural interaction.* Oxford: Pergamon; Furnham & Bochner, 1986.

44. Collett, P. (1971). Training Englishmen in the non-verbal behaviour of Arabs: An experiment on intercultural communication. *International Journal of Psychology, 6,* 209–215.

45. Furnham & Bochner, 1986; Argyle, 1982.

46. Ramsey & Birk, 1983.

47. Furnham & Bochner, 1986; Argyle, 1982.

48. Tannen, 1995.

49. Levine, R., West, L.J., & Reis, H.T. (1980). Perceptions of time and punctuality in the United States and Brazil. *Journal of Personality and Social Psychology, 38,* 541–550.

50. Hall, E.T., & Hall, M.R. (1990). *Understanding cultural differences.* Yarmouth, ME: Intercultural Press.

51. Dulek, R.E., Fielden, J.S., & Hill, J.S. (1991, January–February). International communication: An executive primer. *Business Horizons,* 20–25.

52. Daft, R.L., & Lengel, R.H. (1984). Information richness: A new approach to managerial behavior and organizational design. *Research in Organizational Behavior, 6,* 191–233.

53. Dennis, A.R., & Wixom, B.H. (2001). Investigating the moderators of the group support systems use with meta-analysis. *Journal of Management Information Systems, 18,* 235–257.

54. McGuire, T., Kiesler, S., & Siegel, J. (1987). Group and computer-mediated discussion effects in risk decision making. *Journal of Personality and Social Psychology, 52,* 917–930.

55. Baltes, B.B., Dickson, M.W., Sherman, M.P., Bauer, C.C., & LaGanke, J.S. (2002). Computer-mediated communication and group decision making: A meta-analysis. *Organizational Behavior and Human Decision Processes, 87,* 156–179.

56. Wilson, J.M., Straus, S.G., & McEvily, B. (2006). All in due time: The development of trust in computer-mediated and face-to-face teams. *Organizational Behavior and Human Decision Processes, 99,* 16–33.

57. Kasper-Fuehrer, E.C., & Ashkanasy, N.M. (2001). Communicating trustworthiness and building trust in interorganizational virtual organizations. *Journal of Management, 27,* 235–254.

58. O'Mahony, S., & Barley, S.R. (1999). Do digital telecommunications affect work organization? The state of our knowledge. *Research in Organizational Behavior, 21,* 125–161; Thomson, R., & Murachver, T. (2001). Predicting gender from electronic discourse. *British Journal of Social Psychology, 40,* 193–208.

59. Kruger, J., Epley, N., Parker, J., & Ng, Z.W. (2005). Egocentrism over e-mail: Can we communicate as well as we think? *Journal of Personality and Social Psychology, 89,* 925–936; see also Byron, K. (2008). Carrying too heavy a load? The communication and miscommunication of emotion by email. *Academy of Management Review, 33,* 309–327.

60. Byron, 2008.

61. Vignovic, J.A., & Thompson, L.F. (2010). Computer-mediated cross-cultural collaboration: Attributing communication errors to the person versus the situation. *Journal of Applied Psychology, 95,* 265–276.

62. Gajendran, R.S., & Harrison, D.A. (2007). The good, the bad, and the unknown about telecommuting: Meta-analysis of the psychological mediators and individual consequences. *Journal of Applied Psychology, 92,* 1524–1541.

63. Golden, T.D., Veiga, J.F., & Dino, R.N. (2008). The impact of professional isolation on teleworker job performance turnover intentions: Does time spent teleworking, interacting face-to-face, or having access to communication-enhancing technology matter? *Journal of Applied Psychology, 93,* 1412–1421.

64. Lengel, R.H., & Daft, R.L. (1988, August). The selection of communication media as an executive skill. *Academy of Management Executive,* 225–232.

65. The following relies in part on Athos, A.G., & Gabarro, J.J. (1978). *Interpersonal behavior.* Englewood Cliffs, NJ: Prentice-Hall; DeVito, J.A. (1992). *The interpersonal communication book* (6th ed.). New York: HarperCollins; Whetten, D.A., & Cameron, K.S. (2007). *Developing management skills* (7th ed.). Upper Saddle River, NJ: Prentice Hall.

66. Chamberlin, J. (2000, January). Cops trust cops, even one with a PhD. *Monitor on Psychology,* 74–76.

67. Dulek et al., 1991.

68. Bobocel, D.R., & Zdaniuk, A. (2005). How can explanations be used to foster organizational justice? In J. Greenberg & J.A. Colquitt (Eds.), *Handbook of organizational justice* (pp. 469–498). Mahwah, NJ: Lawrence Erlbaum; Greenberg, J., & Lind, E.A. (2000). The pursuit of organizational justice: From conceptualization to implication to application. In C.L. Cooper & E.A. Locke (Eds.), *Industrial and organizational psychology: Linking theory with practice.* Oxford: Blackwell, 72–105.

69. Shaw, J.C., Wild, E., & Colquitt, J.A. (2003). To justify or excuse? A meta-analytic review of the effects of explanations. *Journal of Applied Psychology, 88,* 444–458.

70. Smither, J.W., London, M., & Reilly, R.R. (2005). Does performance improve following multisource feedback? A theoretical model, meta-analysis, and review of empirical findings. *Personnel Psychology, 58,* 33–66.

71. For a good description of how to develop and use organizational surveys, see Kraut, A.I. (Ed.). (1996) *Organizational surveys*. San Francisco: Jossey-Bass; Edwards, J.E., Thomas, M.D., Rosenfeld, P., & Booth-Kewley, S. (1996). *How to conduct organizational surveys: A step-by-step guide*. Thousand Oaks, CA: Sage.

72. Wintrob, S. (2003, May 20). Awards can bring rewards. *Financial Post*, BE1, BE6.

73. Taft, W.F. (1985). Bulletin boards, exhibits, hotlines. In C. Reuss & D. Silvis (Eds.), *Inside organizational communication* (2nd ed.). New York: Longman.

74. Tamburri, R. (2011, January). Making it safe to report wrongdoing. *University Affairs*, 12–16.

75. Chamine, S. (1998, December). Making your intranet an effective HR tool. *HR Focus*, 11–12.

76. Burnaska, R. (1976). The effects of behavior modeling training upon managers' behaviors and employees' perceptions. *Personnel Psychology, 29*, 329–335.

77. Capella, J.N. (1981). Mutual influence in expressive behavior: Adult–adult and infant–adult dyadic interaction. *Psychological Bulletin, 89*, 101–132.

Chapter 11

1. Excerpted from Silver-Greenberg, J., & Schwartz, N.D. (2012, May 15). Warnings said to go unheeded by Chase bosses. *New York Times*, A1, B5.

2. Mintzberg, H. (1979). *The structuring of organizations*. Englewood Cliffs, NJ: Prentice-Hall.

3. MacCrimmon, K.R., & Taylor, R.N. (1976). Decision making and problem solving. In M.D. Dunnette (Ed.), *Handbook of industrial and organizational psychology*. Chicago: Rand McNally.

4. Anonymous. (2008, November). No left turn. *Road & Track*, 40.

5. Nebraska lawmakers vote to limit safe-haven law. (2008, November 21). www.cnn.com.

6. Simon, H.A. (1957). *Administrative behavior* (2nd ed.). New York: Free Press. See also: Kahneman, D. (2003). A perspective in judgment and choice: Mapping bounded rationality. *American Psychologist, 56*, 697–720.

7. Bazerman, M. (2006). *Judgment in managerial decision making* (6th ed.). Hoboken, NJ: Wiley; Kahneman, 2003.

8. Russo, J.E., & Schoemaker, P.J.H. (1989). *Decision traps*. New York: Doubleday; Whyte, G. (1991, August). Decision failures: Why they occur and how to prevent them. *Academy of Management Executive*, 23–31.

9. The latter two difficulties are discussed by Huber, G.P. (1980). *Managerial decision making*. Glenview, IL: Scott, Foresman. For further discussion of problem identification, see Cowan, D.A. (1986). Developing a process model of problem recognition. *Academy of Management Review, 11*, 763–776; Kiesler, S., & Sproull, L. (1982). Managerial response to changing environments: Perspectives on problem sensing from social cognition. *Administrative Science Quarterly, 27*, 548–570.

10. Whyte, 1991; Russo & Schoemaker, 1989.

11. Tversky, A., & Kahneman, D. (1973). Availability: A heuristic for judging frequency and probability. *Cognitive Psychology, 5*, 207–232. Also see Taylor, S.E., & Fiske, S.T. (1978). Salience, attention, and attribution: Top of the head phenomena. In L. Berkowitz (Ed.), *Advances in experimental social psychology* (Vol. 11). New York: Academic Press.

12. Lichtenstein, S., Fischhoff, B., & Phillips, L.D. (1982). Calibration of probabilities: The state of the art in 1980. In D. Kahneman, P. Slovic, & A. Tversky (Eds.), *Judgment under uncertainty: Heuristics and biases*. Cambridge: Cambridge University Press.

13. Tingling, P. (2009, April 21). Fact or fantasy. *National Post*, FP12.

14. Miller, J.G. (1960). Information input, overload, and psychopathology. *American Journal of Psychiatry, 116*, 695–704.

15. Manis, M., Fichman, M., & Platt, M. (1978). Cognitive integration and referential communication: Effects of information quality and quantity in message decoding. *Organizational Behavior and Human Performance, 22*, 417–430; Troutman, C.M., & Shanteau, J. (1977). Inferences based on nondiagnostic information. *Organizational Behavior and Human Performance, 19*, 43–55; Wiltermuth, S.S., & Neale, M.A. (2011). Too much information: The perils of nondiagnostic information in negotiation. *Journal of Applied Psychology, 96*, 192–201.

16. Tsai, C.I., Klayman, J., & Hastie, R. (2008). Effects of amount of information on judgment accuracy and confidence. *Organizational Behavior and Human Decision Processes, 107*, 97–105.

17. Feldman, M.S., & March, J.G. (1981). Information in organizations as signal and symbol. *Administrative Science Quarterly, 26*, 171–186.

18. Gino, F. (2008). Do we listen to advice just because we paid for it? The impact of advice cost on its use. *Organizational Behavior and Human Decision Processes, 107*, 234–245. For a review of advice taking, see Bonaccio, S., & Dalal, R.S. (2006). Advice taking and decision-making: An integrative literature review and implications for the organizational sciences. *Organizational Behavior and Human Decision Processes, 101*, 127–151.

19. Kahneman et al., 1982; Tversky, A., & Kahneman, D. (1976). Judgment under uncertainty: Heuristics and biases. *Science, 185*, 1124–1131.

20. Northcraft, G.B., & Neale, M.A. (1987). Experts, amateurs, and real estate: An anchoring-and-adjustment perspective on property pricing decisions. *Organizational Behavior and Human Decision Processes, 39*, 84–97.

21. Johns, G. (1999). A multi-level theory of self-serving behavior in and by organizations. *Research in Organizational Behavior, 21*, 1–38; Tetlock, P.E. (1999). Accountability theory: Mixing properties of human agents with properties of social systems. In L.L. Thompson, J.M. Levine, & D.M. Messick (Eds.), *Shared cognition in organizations: The management of knowledge*. Mahwah, N.J.: Lawrence Erlbaum.

22. Simon, H.A. (1957). *Models of man*. New York: Wiley; Cyert, R.M., & March, J.G. (1963). *A behavioral theory of the firm*. Englewood Cliffs, NJ: Prentice-Hall. For an example, see Bower, J., & Zi-Lei, Q. (1992). Satisficing when buying information. *Organizational Behavior and Human Decision Processes, 51*, 471–481.

23. Nutt, P.C. (2004, November). Expanding the search for alternatives during strategic decision-making. *Academy of Management Executive,* 13–28.

24. Posavac, S.S., Kardes, F.R., & Brakus, J.J. (2010). Focus induced tunnel vision in managerial judgment and decision making: The peril and the antidote. *Organizational Behavior and Human Decision Processes, 113*, 102–111.

25. Dalal, R.S., & Bonaccio, S. (2010). What types of advice do decision-makers prefer? *Organizational Behavior and Human Decision Processes, 112*, 11–23.

26. Bazerman, M. (1990). *Judgment in managerial decision making* (2nd ed.). New York: Wiley.

27. Kahneman, D., & Tversky, A. (1979). Prospect theory: An analysis of decision under risk. *Econometrica, 47*, 263–291; see also Holmes, M.R. Jr., Bromiley, P., Devers, C.E., Holcomb, T.R., & McGuire, J.B. (2011). Management theory applications of prospect theory: Accomplishments, challenges, and opportunities. *Journal of Management, 37*, 1069–1107.

28. Sitkin, S.B., & Pablo, A.L. (1992). Conceptualizing the determinants of

risk behavior. *Academy of Management Review, 17,* 9–38.

29. For a detailed treatment and other perspectives, see Northcraft, G.B., & Wolf, G. (1984). Dollars, sense, and sunk costs: A life cycle model of resource allocation decisions. *Academy of Management Review, 9,* 225–234.

30. Brockner, J. (1992). The escalation of commitment to a failing course of action: Toward theoretical progress. *Academy of Management Review, 17,* 39–61; Staw, B.M. (1997). Escalation of commitment: An update and appraisal. In Z. Shapira (Ed.), *Organizational decision making.* Cambridge: Cambridge University Press; for a recent meta-analysis, see Sleesman, D.J., Conlon, D.E., McNamara, G., & Miles, J.E. (2012). Cleaning up the big muddy: A meta-analytic review of the determinants of escalation of commitment. *Academy of Management Journal, 55,* 541–562.

31. Staw, B.M. (1981). The escalation of commitment to a course of action. *Academy of Management Review, 6,* 577–587. For the limitations on this view, see Knight, P.A. (1984). Heroism versus competence: Competing explanations for the effects of experimenting and consistent management. *Organizational Behavior and Human Performance, 33,* 307–322.

32. Arkes, H.R., & Blumer, C. (1985). The psychology of sunk cost. *Organizational Behavior and Human Decision Processes, 35,* 124–140.

33. Whyte, G. (1986). Escalating commitment to a course of action: A reinterpretation. *Academy of Management Review, 11,* 311–321.

34. Wong, K.F.E., Yik, M., & Kwong, J.Y.Y. (2006). Understanding the emotional aspects of escalation of commitment: The role of negative affect. *Journal of Applied Psychology, 91,* 282–297.

35. Ku, G., Malhotra, D., & Murnighan, J.K. (2005). Towards a competitive arousal model of decision-making: A study of auction fever in live and internet auctions. *Organizational Behavior and Human Decision Processes, 96,* 89–103.

36. Simonson, I., & Nye, P. (1992). The effect of accountability on susceptibility to decision errors. *Organizational Behavior and Human Decision Processes, 51,* 416–446; Simonson, I., & Staw, B.M. (1992). Deescalation strategies: A comparison of techniques for reducing commitment to losing courses of action. *Journal of Applied Psychology, 77,* 419–426; Whyte, 1991.

37. Whyte, G. (1993). Escalating commitment in individual and group decision making: A prospect theory approach.

Organizational Behavior and Human Decision Processes, 54, 430–455.

38. Hawkins, S.A., & Hastie, R. (1990). Hindsight: Biased judgments of past events after outcomes are known. *Psychological Bulletin, 107,* 311–327; for a recent refinement, see Fessel, F., Epstude, K., & Roese, N.J. (2009). Hindsight bias redefined: It's about time. *Organizational Behavior and Human Decision Processes, 110,* 56–64.

39. Greenwald, A.G. (1980). The totalitarian ego: Fabrication and revision of personal history. *American Psychologist, 35,* 603–618.

40. Forgas, J.P., & George, J.M. (2001). Affective influences on judgments and behavior in organizations: An information processing perspective. *Organizational Behavior and Human Decision Processes, 86,* 3–34.

41. Hayward, M.L.A., & Hambrick, D.C. (1997). Explaining the premiums paid for large acquisitions: Evidence of CEO hubris. *Administrative Science Quarterly, 42,* 103–127.

42. Forgas & George, 2001; Weiss, H.M. (2002). Conceptual and empirical foundations for the study of affect at work. In R.G. Lord, R.J. Klimoski, & R. Kanfer (Eds.), *Emotions in the workplace: Understanding the structure and role of emotions in organizational behavior.* San Francisco: Jossey-Bass; Davis, M.A. (2009). Understanding the relationship between mood and creativity: A meta-analysis. *Organizational Behavior and Human Decision Processes, 108,* 25–38; Baas, M., De Dreu, C.K.W., & Nijstad, B.A. (2008). A meta-analysis of 25 years of mood-creativity research: Hedonic tone, activation, or regulatory focus? *Psychological Bulletin, 134,* 779–806.

43. Au, K., Chan, F., Wang, D., & Vertinsky, I. (2003). Mood in foreign exchange trading: Cognitive processes and performance. *Organizational Behavior and Human Decision Processes, 91,* 322–338; see also Fenton-O'Creevy, M., Soane, E., Nicholson, N., & Willman, P. (2011). Thinking, feeling and deciding: The influence of emotions on the decision making and performance of traders. *Journal of Organizational Behavior, 32,* 1044–1061.

44. Mitchell, T.R., & Beach, L.R. (1977). Expectancy theory, decision theory, and occupational preference and choice. In M.F. Kaplan & S. Schwartz (Eds.), *Human judgment and decision processes in applied settings.* New York: Academic Press.

45. Pinfield, L.T. (1986). A field evaluation of perspectives on organizational decision making. *Administrative Science Quarterly, 31,* 365–388.

46. Nutt, P.C. (1989). *Making tough decisions.* San Francisco: Jossey-Bass.

47. Nutt, P.C. (1999, November). Surprising but true: Half the decisions in organizations fail. *Academy of Management Executive,* 75–90.

48. Salas, E., Rosen, M.A., & DiazGranados, D. (2010). Expertise-based intuition and decision making in organizations. *Journal of Management, 36,* 941–973; Kahneman, D., & Klein, G. (2009). Conditions for intuitive expertise: A failure to disagree. *American Psychologist, 64,* 515–526; Gigerenzer, G., & Gaissmaier, W. (2011). Heuristic decision making. *Annual Review of Psychology, 62,* 451–482.

49. Shaw, M.E. (1981). *Group dynamics* (3rd ed.). New York: McGraw-Hill, 78.

50. Hill, G.W. (1982). Group versus individual performance: Are n+1 heads better than one? *Psychological Bulletin, 91,* 517–539.

51. Shaw, 1981; Davis, J.H. (1969). *Group performance.* Reading, MA: Addison-Wesley; Libby, R., Trotman, K.T., & Zimmer, I. (1987). Member variation, recognition of expertise, and group performance. *Journal of Applied Psychology, 72,* 81–87.

52. Van Ginkel, W.P., & van Knippenberg, D. (2009). Knowledge about the distribution of information and group decision making: When and why does it work? *Organizational Behavior and Human Decision Processes, 108,* 218–229; Brodbeck, F.C., Kerschreiter, R., Mojzisch, A., & Schulz-Hardt, S. (2007). Group decision making under conditions of distributed knowledge: The information asymmetries model. *Academy of Management Review, 32,* 459–479.

53. Park, G., & DeShon, R.P. (2010). A multilevel model of minority opinion expression and team decision-making effectiveness. *Journal of Applied Psychology, 95,* 824–833.

54. Janis, I.L. (1972). *Victims of groupthink.* Boston: Houghton Mifflin.

55. Esser, J.K. (1998). Alive and well after 25 years: A review of groupthink research. *Organizational Behavior and Human Decision Processes, 73,* 116–141.

56. Aldag, R.J., & Fuller, S.R. (1993) Beyond fiasco: A reappraisal of the groupthink phenomenon and a new model of group decision processes. *Psychological Bulletin, 113,* 533–552; McCauley, C. (1989). The nature of social influence in groupthink: Compliance and internalization. *Journal of Personality and Social Psychology, 57,* 250–260; Baron, R.S. (2005). So right it's wrong: Groupthink and the ubiquitous nature of polarized group decision making. *Advances in Experimental Social Psychology, 37,* 219–253.

57. Janis, 1972.

58. This is our analysis. The data cited are from Capers, R.S., & Lipton, E. (1993, November). Hubble error: Time, money, and millionths of an inch. *Academy of Management Executive*, 41–57 (originally published in *Hartford Courant*).

59. Hart, P. (1998). Preventing groupthink revisited: Evaluating and reforming groups in government. *Organizational Behavior and Human Decision Processes, 73*, 306–326.

60. Stoner, J.A.F. (1961). *A comparison of individual and group decisions involving risk.* Unpublished Master's thesis. School of Industrial Management, Massachusetts Institute of Technology.

61. Lamm, H., & Myers, D.G. (1978). Group-induced polarization of attitudes and behavior. In L. Berkowitz (Ed.), *Advances in experimental social psychology* (Vol. 11, pp. 145–195). New York: Academic Press.

62. Isenberg, D.J. (1986). Group polarization: A critical review and meta-analysis. *Journal of Personality and Social Psychology, 50*, 1141–1151.

63. Kiesler, S., & Sproull, L. (1992). Group decision making and communication technology. *Organizational Behavior and Human Decision Processes, 52*, 96–123; Sia, C.L., Tan, B.C.Y., & Wei, K.K. (1999). Can a GSS stimulate group polarization? An empirical study. *IEEE Transactions on Systems, Man, and Cybernetics Part C—Applications and Reviews, 29*, 227–237.

64. Nutt, 1999.

65. Maier, N.R.F. (1973). *Psychology in industrial organizations* (4th ed.). Boston: Houghton Mifflin; Maier, N.R.F. (1970). *Problem solving and creativity in individuals and groups.* Belmont, CA: Brooks/Cole.

66. Tjosvold, D. (2000). *Learning to manage conflict: Getting people to work together productively.* Lanhan, MD: Lexington; Tjosvold, D. (1985). Implications of controversy research for management. *Journal of Management, 11*, 21–37.

67. Schwenk, C.R. (1984). Devil's advocacy in managerial decision-making. *Journal of Management Studies, 21*, 153–168; for a study, see Schwenk, C., & Valacich, J.S. (1994). Effects of devil's advocacy and dialectical inquiry on individuals versus groups. *Organizational Behavior and Human Decision Processes, 59*, 210–222.

68. Osborn, A.F. (1957). *Applied imagination.* New York: Scribners.

69. See for example Madsen, D.B., & Finger, J.R., Jr. (1978). Comparison of a written feedback procedure, group brainstorming, and individual brainstorming. *Journal of Applied Psychology, 63*, 120–123.

70. Sutton, R.I., & Hargadon, A. (1996). Brainstorming groups in context: Effectiveness in a product design firm. *Administrative Science Quarterly, 41*, 685–718.

71. Gallupe, R.B., Dennis, A.R., Cooper, W.H., Valacich, J.S., Bastianutti, L.M., & Nunamaker, J.F., Jr. (1992). Electronic brainstorming and group size. *Academy of Management Journal, 35*, 350–369; see also Dennis, A.R., & Valacich, J.S. (1993). Computer brainstorms: More heads are better than one. *Journal of Applied Psychology, 78*, 531–537.

72. Delbecq, A.L., Van de Ven, A.H., & Gustafson, D.H. (1975). *Group techniques for program planning: A guide to nominal group and Delphi processes.* Glenview, IL: Scott, Foresman, and Co.

73. Delbecq et al., 1975.

Chapter 12

1. Root out sexual harassment from the RCMP. (2011, Nov 16). Retrieved from *Globe and Mail*, www.theglobeandmail.com/news/opinions/editorials/root-out-sexual-harassment-from-the-rcmp/article2238700/; Expand RCMP sexual harassment hearings, Liberals urge. (2012, Apr 23). Retrieved from CBCnews, www.cbc.ca/news/canada/story/2012/04/23/rcmp-sexual-harassment-hearings-paulson.html; Bailey, I. (2011, Dec 20). Lawyers preparing possible class-action suit against RCMP. Retrieved from *Globe and Mail*, www.theglobeandmail.com/news/politics/lawyers-preparing-possible-class-action-suit-against-rcmp/article2278817/; Burgmann, T. (2012, Apr 16). RCMP to train B.C. officers to investigate sex harassment within force. Retrieved from *Globe and Mail*, www.theglobeandmail.com/news/national/rcmp-to-train-bc-officers-to-investigate-sex-harassment-within-force/article2403389/; Clancy, N. (2011, Nov 07). B.C. Mountie alleges years of sexual harassment. Retrieved from CBCnews British Columbia: www.cbc.ca/news/canada/british-columbia/story/2011/11/07/bc-rcmp-harassment-galiford.html; Gillis, C., & MacQueen, K. (2011, Nov 28). The RCMP: a Royal Canadian disgrace Retrieved from Macleans.ca, http://www2.macleans.ca/2011/11/18/a-royal-canadian-disgrace/; Keller, J. (2012, Jan 06). Another sexual harassment suit filed against RCMP. Retrieved from *Globe and Mail*, www.theglobeandmail.com/news/national/british-columbia/another-sexual-harassment-suit-filed-against-rcmp/article2294125/; Mason, G. (2011, Dec. 03). Former Mountie paints picture of near daily harassment.

Retrieved from *Globe and Mail*, www.theglobeandmail.com/news/national/former-mountie-paints-picture-of-near-daily-harassment/article2259072/; Mason, G. (2011, Dec 12). Inaction in RCMP harassment scandal should bother us all. Retrieved from *Globe and Mail*, www.theglobeandmail.com/news/national/british-columbia/gary_mason/inaction-in-rcmp-harassment-scandal-should-bother-us-all/article2268808/; Mason, G. (2011, Dec 05). RCMP took two years to respond to officer's sexual harassment complaint. Retrieved from *Globe and Mail*, www.theglobeandmail.com/news/national/british-columbia/gary_mason/rcmp-took-two-years-to-respond-to-officers-sexual-harassment-complaint/article2261049/; Theodore, T. (2012, Mar 27). Ex-Mountie's lawsuit accuses RCMP of bullying, sexual discrimination. Retrieved from *Globe and Mail*, www.theglobeandmail.com/news/national/british-columbia/ex-mounties-lawsuit-accuses-rcmp-of-bullying-sexual-discrimination/article2383538/.

2. Brass, D.J., & Burkhardt, M.E. (1993). Potential power and power use: An investigation of structure and behavior. *Academy of Management Journal, 36*, 441–470; see also Kim, P.H., Pinkley, R.L., & Fragale, A.R. (2005). Power dynamics in negotiation. *Academy of Management Review, 30*, 799–822.

3. These descriptions of bases of power were developed by French, J.R.P., Jr., & Raven, B. (1959). In D. Cartwright (Ed.), *Studies in social power.* Ann Arbor, MI: Institute for Social Research.

4. Rahim, M.A. (1989). Relationships of leader power to compliance and satisfaction with supervision: Evidence from a national sample of managers. *Journal of Management, 15*, 545–556; Tannenbaum, A.S. (1974). *Hierarchy in organizations.* San Francisco: Jossey-Bass.

5. Podsakoff, P.M., & Schriesheim, C.A. (1985). Field studies of French and Raven's bases of power: Critique, reanalysis, and suggestions for future research. *Psychological Bulletin, 97*, 387–411.

6. Heider, F. (1958). *The psychology of interpersonal relations.* New York: Wiley.

7. Podsakoff & Schriesheim, 1985.

8. Ragins, B.R., & Sundstrom, E. (1990). Gender and perceived power in manager-subordinate dyads. *Journal of Occupational Psychology, 63*, 273–287.

9. The following is based upon Kanter, R.M. (1977). *Men and women of the corporation.* New York: Basic Books. For additional treatment see Pfeffer, J. (1992). *Managing with power: Politics and influence in organizations.* Boston: Harvard Business School Press.

10. Goldstein, N.J., & Hays, N.A. (2011). Illusory power transference: The vicarious experience of power. *Administrative Science Quarterly, 56*, 593–621.

11. See Thomas, K.W., & Velthouse, B.A. (1990). Cognitive elements of empowerment: An "interpretative" model of intrinsic task motivation. *Academy of Management Review, 15*, 668–681; Conger, J.A., & Kanungo, R.N. (1988). The empowerment process: Integrating theory and practice. *Academy of Management Review, 13*, 471–482. For a good review of this area, see Spreitzer, G. (2008). Taking stock: A review of more than twenty years of research on empowerment at work. In J. Barling and C.L. Cooper (Eds.), *The Sage handbook of organizational behavior* (Vol. 1). London: Sage.

12. Chen, G., Kirkman, B.L., Kanter, R., Allen, D., & Rosen, B. (2007). A multilevel study of leadership, empowerment, and performance in teams. *Journal of Applied Psychology, 92*, 331–346; Srivastava, A., Bartol, K.M., & Locke, E.A. (2006). Empowering leadership in management teams: Effects on knowledge sharing, efficacy, and performance. *Academy of Management Journal, 49*, 1239–1251.

13. Tichy, N.M., & Sherman, S. (1993, June). Walking the talk at GE. *Training and Development*, 26–35.

14. Lowe, E. (2005, October). Responseability and the Power to Please: Delta Hotels. *Social Innovations*, 7–8; Vanier Institute of the Family. www.vifamily.ca/library/social/delta.html.

15. Seibert, S.E., Wang, G., & Courtright, S.H. (2011). Antecedents and consequences of psychological and team empowerment in organizations: A meta-analytic review. *Journal of Applied Psychology, 96*, 981–1003; Maynard, M.T., Gilson, L.L., & Mathieu, J.E. (2012). Empowerment–fad or fab? A multilevel review of the past two decades of research. *Journal of Management, 38*, 1231-1281; Wall, T.D., Wood, S.J., & Leach, D.J. (2004). Empowerment and performance. *International Review of Industrial and Organizational Psychology, 19*, 1–46.

16. Bowen, D.E., & Lawler, E.E., III. (1992, Spring). The empowerment of service workers: What, why, how, and when. *Sloan Management Review*, 31–39.

17. Kipnis, D., Schmidt, S.M., & Wilkinson, I. (1980). Intra-organizational influence tactics: Explorations in getting one's way. *Journal of Applied Psychology, 65*, 440–452; Kipnis, D., & Schmidt, S.M. (1988). Upward-influence styles: Relationship with performance evaluation, salary, and stress. *Administrative Science Quarterly, 33*, 528–542; Bolino, M.C., Kacmar, K.M., Turnley, W.H., & Gilstrap, J.B. (2008). A multi-level review of impression management motives and behaviors. *Journal of Management, 34*, 1080–1109.

18. See Brass & Burkhardt, 1993.

19. Kipnis et al., 1980. See also Keys, B., & Case, T. (1990, November). How to become an influential manager. *Academy of Management Executive*, 38–51.

20. Kipnis & Schmidt, 1988.

21. Westphal, J.D., & Stern, I. (2006). The other pathway to the boardroom: Interpersonal influencing behavior as a substitute for elite credentials and majority status in obtaining board appointments. *Administrative Science Quarterly, 51*, 169–204.

22. Kipnis, D. (1976). *The powerholders*. Chicago: University of Chicago Press.

23. McClelland, D.C. (1975). *Power: The inner experience*. New York: Irvington.

24. Winter, D.G. (1988). The power motive in women—and men. *Journal of Personality and Social Psychology, 54*, 510–519.

25. McClelland, D.C., & Burnham, D.H. (1976, March–April). Power is the great motivator. *Harvard Business Review*, 100–110.

26. Tang, J., Crossan, M., & Glenn Rowe, W. (2011). Dominant CEO, deviant strategy, and extreme performance: The moderating role of a powerful board. *Journal of Management Studies, 48*, 1479–1503.

27. Salancik, G.R., & Pfeffer, J. (1977, Winter). Who gets power—and how they hold on to it: A strategic contingency model of power. *Organizational Dynamics*, 3–21.

28. Salancik, G.R., & Pfeffer, J. (1974). The bases and use of power in organizational decision making: The case of a university. *Administrative Science Quarterly, 19*, 453–473. Also see Pfeffer, J., & Moore, W.L. (1980). Power in university budgeting: A replication and extension. *Administrative Science Quarterly, 25*, 637–653. For conditions under which the power thesis breaks down, see Schick, A.G., Birch, J.B., & Tripp, R.E. (1986). Authority and power in university decision making: The case of a university personnel budget. *Canadian Journal of Administrative Sciences, 3*, 41–64.

29. Hickson, D.J., Hinings, C.R., Lee, C.A., Schneck, R.E., & Pennings, J.M. (1971). A strategic contingency theory of intra-organizational power. *Administrative Science Quarterly, 16*, 216–229; for support of this theory, see Hinings, C.R., Hickson, D.J., Pennings, J.M., & Schneck, R.E. (1974). Structural conditions of intraorganizational power. *Administrative Science Quarterly, 19*, 22–44; Saunders, C.S., & Scamell, R. (1982). Intraorganizational distributions of power: Replication research. *Academy of Management Journal, 25*, 192–200; Hambrick, D.C. (1981). Environment, strategy, and power within top management teams. *Administrative Science Quarterly, 26*, 253–276.

30. Kanter, 1977, 170–171.

31. Hickson et al., 1971; Hinings et al., 1974.

32. Hickson et al., 1971; Hinings et al., 1974; Saunders & Scamell, 1982.

33. Nulty, P. (1989, July 31). The hot demand for new scientists. *Fortune*, 155–163.

34. Nord, W.R., & Tucker, S. (1987). *Implementing routine and radical innovations*. Lexington, MA: Lexington Books.

35. Mayes, B.T., & Allen, R.W. (1977). Toward a definition of organizational politics. *Academy of Management Review, 2*, 672–678.

36. Porter, L.W., Allen, R.W., & Angle, H.L. (1981). The politics of upward influence in organizations. *Research in Organizational Behavior, 3*, 109–149.

37. Porter et al., 1981; Madison, D.L., Allen, R.W., Porter, L.W., Renwick, P.A., & Mayes, B.T. (1980). Organizational politics: An exploration of managers' perceptions. *Human Relations, 33*, 79–100.

38. Chang, C.-H., Rosen, C.C., & Levy, P.E. (2009). The relationship between perceptions of organizational politics and employee attitudes, strain, and behavior: A meta-analytic examination. *Academy of Management Journal, 52*, 779–801.

39. Treadway, D.C., Ferris, G.R., Hochwarter, W., Perrewé, P., Witt, L.A., & Goodman, J.M. (2005). The role of age in the perceptions of politics-job performance relationship: A three-study constructive replication. *Journal of Applied Psychology, 90*, 872–881.

40. Ferris, G.D., Davidson, S.L., & Perrewé, P.L. (2005). *Political skill at work: Impact on effectiveness*. Mountain View, CA: Davies-Black, 7; see also Ferris, G.R., Treadway, D.C., Kolodinsky, R.W., Hochwarter, W.A., Kacmar, C.J., Douglas, C., & Frink, D.D. (2005). Development and validation of the Political Skill Inventory. *Journal of Management, 31*, 126–152.

41. Perrewé, P.L., Zellars, K.L., Ferris, G.R., Rossi, A.M., Kacmar, C.J., & Ralston, D.A. (2004). Neutralizing job stressors: Political skill as an antidote to the dysfunctional consequences of role conflict. *Academy of Management Journal, 47*, 141–152; Harvey, P., Harris, R.B., Harris, K.J., & Wheeler, A.R. (2007). Attenuating the effects of social stress: The impact of political skill. *Journal*

of Occupational Health Psychology, 12, 105–115.

42. Kotter, J.P. (1982). *The general managers.* New York: Free Press.

43. Forret, M.L., & Dougherty, T.W. (2004). Networking behaviors and career outcomes: Differences for men and women. *Journal of Organizational Behavior, 25,* 419–437; Forret, M.L., & Dougherty, T.W. (2001). Correlates of networking behavior for managerial and professional employees. *Group & Organization Management, 26,* 283–311.

44. See also Wolff, H-G., & Maser, K. (2009). Effects of networking on career success: A longitudinal study. *Journal of Applied Psychology, 94,* 196–206.

45. Brass, D.J., Galaskiewicz, J., Greve, H.R., & Tsai, W. (2004). Taking stock of networks and organizations: A multilevel perspective. *Academy of Management Journal, 47,* 795–817.

46. Cross, R., Cowen, A., Vertucci, L., & Thomas, R.J. (2009). How effective leaders drive results through networks. *Organizational Dynamics, 38,* 93–105.

47. Geis, F., & Christie, R. (1970). Overview of experimental research. In R. Christie & F. Geis (Eds.), *Studies in Machiavellianism.* New York: Academic Press; Wilson, D.S., Near, D., & Miller, R.W. (1996). Machiavellianism: A synthesis of the evolutionary and psychological literatures. *Psychological Bulletin, 119,* 285–299.

48. Geis & Christie, 1970; Wilson et al., 1996.

49. O'Boyle, E.H., Jr., Forsyth, D.R., Banks, G.C., & McDaniel, M.A. (2012). A meta-analysis of the Dark Triad and work behavior: A social exchange perspective. *Journal of Applied Psychology, 97,* 557–579.

50. What follows relies on Ashforth, B.E., & Lee, R.T. (1990). Defensive behavior in organizations: A preliminary model. *Human Relations, 43,* 621–648.

51. Boeker, W. (1992). Power and managerial dismissal: Scapegoating at the top. *Administrative Science Quarterly, 37,* 400–421.

52. Galloway, G. (2009, May 21). Watchdog predicted reactor's demise. *Globe and Mail,* A5; (2008, January 16). Nuclear safety watchdog head fired for "lack of leadership": Minister. www.cbc.ca/news.

53. This draws loosely on Glenn, J.R., Jr. (1986). *Ethics in decision making.* New York: Wiley.

54. For reviews, see Treviño, L.K. (1986). Ethical decision making in organizations: A person-situation interactionist model. *Academy of Management Review, 11,* 601–617; Tsalikis, J., & Fritzsche, D.J. (1989). Business ethics: A literature review with a focus on marketing ethics. *Journal of Business Ethics, 8,* 695–743.

55. Tyson, T. (1992). Does believing that everyone else is less ethical have an impact on work behavior? *Journal of Business Ethics, 11,* 707–717.

56. Treviño, L.K., Weaver, G.R., & Brown, M.E. (2008). It's lovely at the top: Hierarchical levels, identities, and perceptions of organizational ethics. *Business Ethics Quarterly, 18,* 233–252.

57. Kaynama, S.A., King, A., & Smith, L.W. (1996). The impact of a shift in organizational role on ethical perceptions: A comparative study. *Journal of Business Ethics, 15,* 581–590.

58. McCabe, D.L., Butterfield, K.D., & Treviño, L.K. (2006). Academic dishonesty in graduate business programs: Prevalence, causes, and proposed action. *Academy of Management Learning & Education, 5,* 294–305.

59. Kish-Gephart, J.J., Harrison, D.A., & Treviño, L.K. (2010). Bad apples, bad cases, and bad barrels: Meta-analytic evidence about sources of unethical decisions at work. *Journal of Applied Psychology, 95,* 1–31; see also Pan, Y., & Sparks, J.R. (2012). Predictors, consequence, and measurement of ethical judgments: Review and meta-analysis. *Journal of Business Research, 65,* 84–91.

60. Tsalikis & Fritzsche, 1989.

61. Bird, F., & Waters, J.A. (1987). The nature of managerial moral standards. *Journal of Business Ethics, 6,* 1–13.

62. Hegarty, W.H., & Sims, H.P., Jr. (1978). Some determinants of unethical behavior: An experiment. *Journal of Applied Psychology, 63,* 451–457; Treviño, L.K., Sutton, C.D., & Woodman, R.W. (1985). *Effects of reinforcement contingencies and cognitive moral development on ethical decision-making behavior: An experiment.* Paper presented at the annual meeting of the Academy of Management, San Diego.

63. Levine, D.B. (1990, May 21). The inside story of an inside trader. *Fortune,* 80–89, 82.

64. Mishina, Y., Dykes, B.J., Block, E.S., & Pollock, T.G. (2010). Why "good" firms do bad things: The effects of high aspirations, high expectations, and prominence on the incidence of corporate illegality. *Academy Management Journal, 53,* 701–722.

65. Grover, S.L. (1993). Why professionals lie: The impact of professional role conflict on reporting accuracy. *Organizational Behavior and Human Decision Processes, 55,* 251–272.

66. Umphress, E.E., & Bingham, J.B. (2011). When employees do bad things for good reasons: Examining unethical pro-organizational behaviors. *Organization Science, 22,* 621–640; Umphress, E.E., Bingham, J.B., & Mitchell, M.S. (2010). Unethical behavior in the name of the company: The moderating effect of organizational identification and positive reciprocity beliefs on unethical pro-organizational behavior. *Journal of Applied Psychology, 95,* 769–780.

67. Staw, B.M., & Szwajkowski, E.W. (1975). The scarcity-munificence component of organizational environments and the commission of illegal acts. *Administrative Science Quarterly, 20,* 345–354.

68. Sonnenfeld, J., & Lawrence, P.R. (1989). Why do companies succumb to price fixing? In K.R. Andrew (Ed.), *Ethics in practice: Managing the moral corporation.* Boston: Harvard Business School Press.

69. Hegarty & Sims, 1978; Hegarty, W.H., & Sims, H.P., Jr. (1979). Organizational philosophy, policies, and objectives related to unethical decision behavior: A laboratory experiment. *Journal of Applied Psychology, 64,* 331–338.

70. Kish-Gephart et al., 2010; Detert, J.R., Treviño, L.K., & Sweitzer, V.L. (2008). Moral disengagement in ethical decision making: A study of antecedents and outcomes. *Journal of Applied Psychology, 93,* 374–391.

71. Colby, A., & Kohlberg, L. (1987). *The measurement of moral judgment. Volume 1: Theoretical foundations and research validation.* Cambridge: Cambridge University Press; see also Treviño, 1986; Grover, 1993.

72. Detert et al., 2008.

73. Reynolds, S.J., (2008). Moral attentiveness: Who pays attention to the moral aspects of life? *Journal of Applied Psychology, 93,* 1027–1041.

74. Kish-Gephart et al., 2010.

75. Victor, B., & Cullen, J.B. (1988). The organizational bases of ethical work climates. *Administrative Science Quarterly, 33,* 101–125.

76. Kish-Gephart et al., 2010; Tenbrunsel, A.E., & Smith-Crowe, K. (2008). Ethical decision making: Where we've been and where we're going. *Academy of Management Annals, 2,* 545–607.

77. Baucus, M.S., & Near, J.P. (1991). Can illegal corporate behavior be predicted? An event history analysis. *Academy of Management Journal, 34,* 9–16.

78. Anand, V., Ashforth, B.E., & Joshi, M. (2004, May). Business as usual: The acceptance and perpetuation of corruption in organizations. *Academy of Management Executive,* 39–53.

79. Sonnenfeld & Lawrence, 1989; see also Hosmer, L.T. (1987). The institutionalization of unethical behavior. *Journal of Business Ethics, 6,* 439–447.

80. Morgan, R.B. (1993). Self- and co-worker perceptions of ethics and their relationships to leadership and salary. *Academy of Management Journal, 36,* 200–214.

81. This definition and other material in this paragraph are from Miceli, M.P., & Near, J.P. (2005). Standing up or standing by: What predicts blowing the whistle on organizational wrongdoing? *Research in Personnel and Human Resources Management, 24,* 95–136.

82. Moore, D.A, Tetlock, P.H., Tanlu, L., & Bazerman, M.H. (2006). Conflicts of interest and the case of auditor independence: Moral seduction and strategic issue cycling. *Academy of Management Review, 31,* 10–29.

83. Ripley, A. (2002, December 30/2003, January 6). The night detective. *Time,* 45; Morse, J., & Bower, A. (2002, December 30/2003, January 6). The party crasher. *Time,* 53.

84. Kageyama, Y. (2012, May 31). Olympus settles with whistleblower. *The Gazette* (Montreal), B8.

85. Peirce, E., Smolinski, C.A., & Rosen, B. (1998, August). Why sexual harassment complaints fall on deaf ears. *Academy of Management Executive,* 41–54.

86. O'Leary-Kelly, A.M., Bowes-Sperry, L., Bates, C.A., & Lean, E.R. (2009). Sexual harassment at work: A decade (plus) of progress. *Journal of Management, 35,* 503–536; Willness, C.R., Steel, P., & Lee, K. (2007). A meta-analysis of the antecedents and consequences of workplace sexual harassment. *Personnel Psychology, 60,* 127–162.

87. Schneider, K.T., Swan, S., & Fitzgerald, L.F. (1997). Job-related and psychological effects of sexual harassment in the workplace: Empirical evidence from two organizations. *Journal of Applied Psychology, 82,* 401–415.

88. O'Leary-Kelly et al., 2008.

89. Seppa, N. (1997, May). Sexual harassment in the military lingers on. *APA Monitor,* 40–41.

90. Seppa, 1997.

91. Peirce et al., 1998; Seppa, 1997.

92. Gettman, H.J., & Gelfand, M.J. (2007). When the customer shouldn't be king: Antecedents and consequences of sexual harassment by clients and customers. *Journal of Applied Psychology, 92,* 757–770.

93. Berdahl, J.L. (2007). The sexual harassment of uppity women. *Journal of Applied Psychology, 92,* 425–437.

94. Peirce et al., 1998.

95. Peirce et al., 1998.

96. Peirce et al., 1998.

97. Flynn, G. (1997, February). Respect is key to stopping harassment. *Workforce,* 56.

98. Peirce et al., 1998.

99. This draws on Waters, J.A., & Bird, F. (1988). *A note on what a well-educated manager should be able to do with respect to moral issues in management.* Unpublished manuscript.

100. See Jones, T.M. (1991). Ethical decision making by individuals in organizations: An issue-contingent model. *Academy of Management Journal, 16,* 366–395.

101. Weber, J. (1990). Measuring the impact of teaching ethics to future managers: A review, assessment, and recommendations. *Journal of Business Ethics, 9,* 183–190.

Chapter 13

1. Excerpted from Kelly, C. (2009, June 17). Rival Yorkville hair salons in ugly battle. www.thestar.com. Reprinted with permission of TorStar Syndication Services.

2. Kolb, D.M., & Bartunek, J.M. (Eds.) (1992). *Hidden conflict in organizations: Uncovering behind-the-scenes disputes.* Newbury Park, CA: Sage.

3. This section relies partly on Walton, R.E., & Dutton, J.M. (1969). The management of interdepartmental conflict: A model and review. *Administrative Science Quarterly, 14,* 73–84; see also De Dreu, C.K.W., & Gelfand, M.J. (2008). Conflict in the workplace: Sources, functions, and dynamics across multiple levels of analysis. In C.K.W. De Dreu & M.J. Gelfand (Eds.), *The psychology of conflict and conflict management in organizations.* New York: Lawrence Erlbaum.

4. Ashforth, B.E., & Mael, F. (1989). Social identity theory and the organization. *Academy of Management Review, 14,* 20–39; Kramer, R.M. (1991). Intergroup relations and organizational dilemmas: The role of categorization processes. *Research in Organizational Behavior, 13,* 191–228; Messick, D.M., & Mackie, D.M. (1989). Intergroup relations. *Annual Review of Psychology, 40,* 45–81.

5. Johns, G. (1994). Absenteeism estimates by employees and managers: Divergent perspectives and self-serving perceptions. *Journal of Applied Psychology, 79,* 229–239.

6. See Whyte, W.F. (1948). *Human relations in the restaurant industry.* New York: McGraw-Hill.

7. Moritz, M. (1984). *The little kingdom: The private story of Apple Computer.* New York: Morrow, 246–247.

8. Jehn, K.A., & Mannix, E.A. (2001). The dynamic nature of conflict: A longitudinal study of intragroup conflict and group performance. *Academy of Management Journal, 44,* 238–251.

9. De Dreu, C.K.W., & Weingart, L.R. (2003). Task versus relationship conflict, team performance, and team member satisfaction: A meta-analysis. *Journal of Applied Psychology, 88,* 741–749; de Wit, F.R.C., Greer, L.L., & Jehn, K.A. (2012). The paradox of intragroup conflict: A meta-analysis. *Journal of Applied Psychology, 97,* 360–390.

10. See Blake, R.R., Shepard, M.A., & Mouton, J.S. (1964). *Managing intergroup conflict in industry.* Houston: Gulf; Sherif, M. (1966). *In common predicament: Social psychology of intergroup conflict and cooperation.* Boston: Houghton Mifflin; Wilder, D.A. (1986). Social categorization: Implications for creation and reduction of intergroup bias. *Advances in Experimental Social Psychology, 19,* 291–349; Pruitt, D.G. (2008). Conflict escalation in organizations. In De Dreu & Gelfand, 2008.

11. Thomas, K.W. (1992). Conflict and negotiation in organizations. In M.D. Dunnette & L.M. Hough (Eds.), *Handbook of industrial and organizational psychology* (2nd ed., Vol. 3). Palo Alto, CA: Consulting Psychologists Press.

12. Seabrook, J. (1994, January 10). E-mail from Bill. *The New Yorker,* 48–61, 52.

13. Johnson, D.W., Maruyama, G., Johnson, R., Nelson, D., & Skon, L. (1981). Effects of cooperative and individualistic goal structures on achievement: A meta-analysis. *Psychological Bulletin, 89,* 47–62; see also Tjosvold, D. (1991). *The conflict-positive organization.* Reading, MA: Addison-Wesley.

14. Keenan, G. (2011, December 28). Earthquake. Tsunami. Floods. How Japan's car makers are rebuilding after a year of disasters. *Globe and Mail,* B1, B4, B5.

15. Tjosvold, D., Dann, V., & Wong, C. (1992). Managing conflict between departments to serve customers. *Human Relations, 45,* 1035–1054.

16. Neale, M.A., & Bazerman, M.H. (1992, August). Negotiating rationally: The power and impact of the negotiator's frame. *Academy of Management Executive,* 42–51, p. 42; for a recent review, see Thompson, L.L., Wang, J., & Gunia, B.C. (2010). Negotiation. *Annual Review of Psychology, 61,* 491–515.

17. Wall, J.A., Jr. (1985). *Negotiation: Theory and practice.* Glenview, IL: Scott, Foresman.

18. Walton, R.E., & McKerzie, R.B. (1991). *A behavioral theory of labor negotiations* (2nd ed.). Ithaca, NY: ILR Press.

19. What follows draws on Pruitt, D.G. (1981). *Negotiation behavior.* New York: Academic Press.

20. Wall, J.A., Jr., & Blum, M. (1991). Negotiations. *Journal of Management, 17,* 273–303.

21. Hüffmeier, J., Freund, P.A., Zerres, A., Backhaus, K., & Hertel, G. (2011). Being tough or being nice? A meta-analysis on the impact of hard- and softline strategies in distributive negotiations. *Journal of Management*, 0149206311423788.

22. Stuhlmacher, A.F., and Walters, A.E. (1999). Gender differences in negotiation outcome: A meta-analysis. *Personnel Psychology, 52*, 653–677; see also Kulik, C.T., & Olekalns, M. (2012). Negotiating the gender divide: Lessons from the negotiation and organizational behavior literatures. *Journal of Management, 38*, 1387–1415.

23. Marks, M., & Harold, C. (2011). Who asks and who receives in salary negotiation. *Journal of Organizational Behavior, 32*, 371–394.

24. Bazerman, M.H. (1990). *Judgment in managerial decision making* (2nd ed.). New York: Wiley.

25. The following draws on Bazerman, M.H., & Neale, M.A. (1992). *Negotiating rationally*. New York: The Free Press; see also Bazerman, M.H. (2006). *Judgment in managerial decision making* (6th ed.). Hoboken, NJ: Wiley.

26. Sherif, 1966; Hunger, J.D., & Stern, L.W. (1976). An assessment of the functionality of the superordinate goal in reducing conflict. *Academy of Management Journal, 19*, 591–605.

27. Goldman, B.M., Cropanzano, R., Stein, J., & Benson, L. III. (2008). The role of third parties/mediation in managing conflict in organizations. In De Dreu & Gelfand, 2008.

28. Pruitt, 1981; Kressel, K., & Pruitt, D.G. (1989). *Mediation research*. San Francisco: Jossey-Bass.

29. Kressel & Pruitt, 1989.

30. Pruitt, 1981; Wall & Blum, 1991.

31. Moore, M.L., Nichol, V.W., & McHugh, P.P. (1992). Review of no-fault absenteeism cases taken to arbitration, 1980–1989: A rights and responsibilities analysis. *Employee Rights and Responsibilities Journal, 5*, 29–48; Scott, K.D., & Taylor, G.S. (1983, September). An analysis of absenteeism cases taken to arbitration: 1975–1981. *The Arbitration Journal, 61–70.*

32. For a spirited debate on this, see De Dreu, C.K.W. (2008). The virtue and vice of workplace conflict: Food for (pessimistic) thought. *Journal of Organizational Behavior, 29*, 5–18, and Tjosvold, D. (2008). The conflict-positive organization: It depends on us. *Journal of Organizational Behavior, 29*, 19–28.

33. Robbins, S.P. (1974). *Managing organizational conflict: A nontraditional approach*. Englewood, Cliffs, NJ: Prentice-Hall, 20.

34. Brown, L.D. (1983). *Managing conflict at organizational interfaces*. Reading, MA: Addison-Wesley.

35. Robbins, 1974; see also Brown, 1983.

36. Raynal, W., & Wilson, K.A. (2001, October 15). What about Bob? *Autoweek*, 5.

37. Keita, G.P. (2006, June). The national push for workplace health. *Monitor on Psychology, 32.*

38. American Psychological Association (2012). *Stress in America: Our health at risk*. Washington, DC: APA.

39. Tangri, R. (2007, September). Putting a price on stress. *Canadian Healthcare Manager, 14*, 24–25.

40. This model has much in common with many contemporary models of work stress. For a comprehensive summary, see Kahn, R.L., & Byosiere, P. (1992). Stress in organizations. In M.D. Dunnette & L.M. Hough (Eds.), *Handbook of industrial and organizational psychology* (2nd ed., Vol. 3). Palo Alto, CA: Consulting Psychologists Press.

41. McGrath, J.E. (1970). A conceptual formulation for research on stress. In J.E. McGrath (Ed.), *Social and psychological factors in stress*. New York: Holt, Rinehart, Winston.

42. Roth, S., & Cohen, L.J. (1986). Approach, avoidance, and coping with stress. *American Psychologist, 41*, 813–819.

43. Glazer, S., & Beehr, T.A. (2005). Consistency of implications of three role stressors across four countries. *Journal of Organizational Behavior, 26*, 467–487.

44. Ng, T.W.H., Sorensen, K.L., & Eby, L.T. (2006). Locus of control at work: A meta-analysis. *Journal of Organizational Behavior, 27*, 1057–1087.

45. Friedman, M., & Rosenman, R. (1974). *Type A behavior and your heart*. New York: Knopf.

46. Chesney, M.A., & Rosenman, R. (1980). Type A behavior in the work setting. In C.L. Cooper and R. Payne (Eds.), *Current concerns in occupational stress*. Chichester, England: Wiley. For a typical study, see Jamal, M., & Baba, V.V. (1991). Type A behavior, its prevalence and consequences among women nurses: An empirical examination. *Human Relations, 44*, 1213–1228.

47. Fine, S., & Stinson, M. (2000, February 3). Stress is overwhelming people, study shows. *Globe and Mail*, A1, A7; Matthews, K.A. (1982). Psychological perspectives on the Type A behavior pattern. *Psychological Bulletin, 91*, 293–323.

48. Booth-Kewley, S., & Friedman, H.S. (1987). Psychological predictors of heart disease: A quantitative review. *Psychological Bulletin, 101*, 343–362;

Smith, D. (2003, March). Angry thoughts, at-risk hearts. *Monitor on Psychology, 46–48*; Ganster, D.C., Schaubroeck, J., Sime, W.E., & Mayes, B.T. (1991). The nomological validity of the Type A personality among employed adults. *Journal of Applied Psychology, 76*, 143–168.

49. Houkes, I., Janssen, P.P.M., de Jonge, J., & Bakker, A.B. (2003). Personality, work characteristics, and employee well-being: A longitudinal analysis of additive and moderating effects. *Journal of Occupational Health Psychology, 8*, 20–38; Grant, S., & Langan-Fox, J. (2007). Personality and the stressor-strain relationship: The role of the Big Five. *Journal of Occupational Health Psychology, 12*, 20–33; Kammeyer-Mueller, J.D., Judge, T.A., & Scott, B.A. (2009). The role of core self-evaluations in the coping process. *Journal of Applied Psychology, 94*, 177–195.

50. Spector, P.E., Zapf, D., Chen, P.Y., & Frese, M. (2000). Why negative affectivity should not be controlled in stress research: Don't throw out the baby with the bath water. *Journal of Organizational Behavior, 21*, 79–95. For a relevant study, see Barsky, A., Thoresen, C.J., Warren, C.R., & Kaplan, S.A. (2004). Modeling negative affectivity and job stress: A contingency-based approach. *Journal of Organizational Behavior, 25*, 915–936.

51. Fine, S., & Stinson, M. (2000, February 3). Stress is overwhelming people, study shows. *Globe and Mail*, A1, A7.

52. Parasuraman, S., & Alutto, J.A. (1981). An examination of the organizational antecedents of stressors at work. *Academy of Management Journal, 24*, 48–67.

53. Mintzberg, H. (1973). *The nature of managerial work*. New York: Harper & Row.

54. An excellent review of managerial stressors can be found in Marshall, J., & Cooper, C.L. (1979). *Executives under pressure*. New York: Praeger.

55. Xie, J.L., & Johns, G. (1995). Job scope and stress: Can job scope be too high? *Academy of Management Journal, 38*, 1288–1309.

56. Maslach, C., Leiter, M.P., & Schaufeli, W. (2009). Measuring burnout. In S. Cartwright & C.L. Cooper (Eds.), *The Oxford handbook of organizational well-being*. Oxford: Oxford University Press; Maslach, C., & Leiter, M.P. (2008). Early predictors of burnout and engagement. *Journal of Applied Psychology, 93*, 498–512; Maslach, C., & Jackson, S.E. (1984). Burnout in organizational settings. In S. Oskamp (Ed.), *Applied social psychology annual* (Vol. 5). Beverly Hills, CA: Sage.

57. Maslach, C., Schaufeli, W.B., & Leiter, M.P. (2001). Job burnout. *Annual*

Review of Psychology, 52, 397–422; Cordes, C.L., & Dougherty, T.W. (1993). A review and integration of research on job burnout. *Academy of Management Review, 18,* 621–656. For a comprehensive study, see Lee, R.T., & Ashforth, B.E. (1993). A longitudinal study of burnout among supervisors and managers: Comparisons of the Leiter and Maslach (1988) and Golembiewski et al. (1986) models. *Organizational Behavior and Human Decision Processes, 54,* 369–398.

58. Purvanova, R.K., & Muros, J.P. (2010). Gender differences in burnout: A meta-analysis. *Journal of Vocational Behavior, 77,* 168–185; Alarcon, G., Eschleman, K.J., & Bowling, N.A. (2009). Relationships between personality variables and burnout: A meta-analysis. *Work & Stress, 23,* 244–263.

59. See Pines, A.M., & Aronson, E. (1981). *Burnout: From tedium to personal growth.* New York: The Free Press.

60. Hülsheger, U.R., & Schewe, A.F. (2011). On the costs and benefits of emotional labor: A meta-analysis of three decades of research. *Journal of Occupational Health Psychology, 16,* 361–389; see also Mesmer-Magnus, J.R., DeChurch, L.A., & Wax, A. (2012). Moving emotional labor beyond surface and deep acting: A discordance–congruence perspective. *Organizational Psychology Review, 2,* 6–53.

61. Galt, V. (2005, November 15). Fewer workers willing to put in 110%. *Globe and Mail,* B8; Carniol, N. (2005, November 15). Fewer workers willing to give 100 percent. *Toronto Star,* D1, D11; Galt, V. (2005, January 26). This just in: Half your employees ready to jump ship. *Globe and Mail,* B1, B9.

62. Schaufeli, W.B., Bakker, A.B., & Van Rhenen, W. (2009). How changes in job demands and resources predict burnout, work engagement, and sickness absenteeism. *Journal of Organizational Behavior, 30,* 893–917; see also Bakker, A.B., & Demerouti, E. (2008). Towards a model of work engagement. *Career Development International, 13,* 209–223.

63. Cole, M.S., Walter, F., Bedeian, A.G., & O'Boyle, E.H. (2012). Job burnout and employee engagement: A meta-analytic examination of construct proliferation. *Journal of Management, 38,* 1550–1581.

64. Bakker, A.B., & Demerouti, E. (2007). The job-demands-resources model: State of the art. *Journal of Managerial Psychology, 22,* 309–328.

65. Bakker & Demerouti, 2007; Schaufeli et al., 2009.

66. Salin, D. (2003). Ways of explaining workplace bullying: A review of enabling, motivating and precipitating structures in the work environment. *Human Relations, 56,* 1213–1232.

67. Bowling, N.A., & Beehr, T.A. (2006). Workplace harassment from the victim's perspective: A theoretical model and meta-analysis. *Journal of Applied Psychology, 91,* 998–1012.

68. Salin, 2003; Rayner, C., & Keashly, L. (2005). Bullying at work: A perspective from Britain and North America. In S. Fox & P.E. Spector (Eds.), *Counterproductive work behavior: Investigations of actors and targets.* Washington, DC: American Psychological Association.

69. Mawritz, M.B., Mayer, D.M., Hoobler, J.M., Wayne, S.J., & Marinova, S.V. (2012). A trickle-down model of abusive supervision. *Personnel Psychology, 65,* 325–357.

70. This is one interpretation of the distinction between bullying and mobbing. See Zapf, D., & Einarsen, S. (2005). Mobbing at work: Escalated conflicts in organizations. In Fox & Spector, 2005.

71. Dingfelder, S.F. (2006, July–August). Banishing bullying. *Monitor on Psychology,* 76–78.

72. See Ford, M.T., Heinen, B.A., & Langkamer, K.L. (2008). Work and family satisfaction and conflict: A meta-analysis of cross-domain relations. *Journal of Applied Psychology, 92,* 57–80.

73. Duxbury, L., & Higgins, C. (2003). *Work–life conflict in Canada in the new millennium: A status report.* Ottawa: Health Canada.

74. For a review of the antecedents of work–family conflict, see Michel, J.S., Kotrba, L.M., Mitchelson, J.K., Clark, M.A., & Baltes, B.B. (2011). Antecedents of work-family conflict: A meta-analytic review. *Journal of Organizational Behavior, 32,* 689–725.

75. Bellavia, G.M., & Frone, M.R. (2005). Work–family conflict. In J. Barling, E.K. Kelloway, & M.R. Frone (Eds.), *Handbook of work stress.* Thousand Oaks, CA: Sage.

76. Dierdorff, E.C., & Ellington, J.K. (2008). It's the nature of the work: Examining behavior-based sources of work–family conflict across occupations. *Journal of Applied Psychology, 93,* 883–892.

77. Halbesleben, J.R.B., Harvey, J., & Bolino, M.C. (2009). Too engaged? A conservation of resources view of the relationship between work engagement and work interference with family. *Journal of Applied Psychology, 94,* 1452–1465.

78. For job loss in particular, see McKee-Ryan, F.M., Song, Z., Wanberg, C.R., & Kinicki, A.J. (2005). Psychological and physical well-being during unemployment: A meta-analytic study. *Journal of Applied Psychology, 90,*

53–76; for mergers and acquisitions, see Cartwright, S. (2005). Mergers and acquisitions: An update and appraisal. *International Review of Industrial and Organizational Psychology, 20,* 1–38.

79. DeFrank, R.S., & Ivancevich, J.M. (1998, August). Stress on the job: An executive update. *Academy of Management Executive,* 55–66.

80. Jackson, S.E., & Schuler, R.S. (1985). Meta-analysis and conceptual critique of research on role ambiguity and conflict in work settings. *Organizational Behavior and Human Decision Processes, 36,* 16–78. For a critique of some of this research, see Fineman, S., & Payne, R. (1981). Role stress—A methodological trap? *Journal of Occupational Behaviour, 2,* 51–64.

81. Fitzgerald, L.F., Drasgow, F., Hulin, C.L., Gelfand, M.J., & Magley, V.J. (1997). Antecedents and consequences of sexual harassment in organizations: A test of an integrated model. *Journal of Applied Psychology, 82,* 578–589; Schneider, K.T., Swan, S., & Fitzgerald, L.F. (1997). Job-related and psychological effects of sexual harassment in the workplace: Empirical evidence from two organizations. *Journal of Applied Psychology, 82,* 401–415.

82. Fitzgerald et al., 1997; Schneider et al., 1997.

83. O'Leary-Kelly, A.M., Bowes-Sperry, L., Bates, C.A., & Lean, E.R. (2009). Sexual harassment at work: A decade (plus) of progress. *Journal of Management, 35,* 503–536; Willness, C.R., Steel, P., & Lee, K. (2007). A meta-analysis of the antecedents and consequences of workplace sexual harassment. *Personnel Psychology, 60,* 127–162.

84. Peirce, E., Smolinski, C.A., & Rosen, B. (1998, August). Why sexual harassment complaints fall on deaf ears. *Academy of Management Executive,* 41–54; Schneider et al., 1997.

85. Fitzgerald et al., 1997; Glomb, T.M., Munson, L.J., Hulin, C.L., Bergman, M.E., & Drasgow, F. (1999). Structural equation models of sexual harassment: Longitudinal explorations and cross-sectional generalizations. *Journal of Applied Psychology, 84,* 14–28.

86. Cohen, S., & Wills, T.A. (1985). Stress, social support, and the buffering hypothesis. *Psychological Bulletin, 98,* 310–357; Kahn & Byosiere, 1992. For recent treatments of social support and relational views of work, see Grant, A.M., & Parker, S.K. (2009). Redesigning work design theories: The rise of relational and proactive perspectives. *Academy of Management Annals, 3,* 317–375, and Baran, B.E., Shanock, L.R., & Miller, L.R. (2012).

Advancing organizational support theory into the twenty-first century world of work. *Journal of Business and Psychology, 27*, 123–147.

87. Gilboa, S., Shirom, A., Fried, Y., & Cooper, C. (2008). A meta-analysis of work demand stressors and job performance: Examining main and moderating effects. *Personnel Psychology, 61*, 227–271. For a classic study, see Jamal, M. (1984). Job stress and job performance controversy: An empirical assessment. *Organizational Behavior and Human Performance, 33*, 1–21.

88. LePine, J.A., Podsakoff, N.P., & LePine, M.A. (2005). A meta-analytic test of the challenge stressor-hindrance stressor framework: An explanation for inconsistent relationships among stressors and performance. *Academy of Management Journal, 48*, 764–775.

89. Eatough, E.M., Chang, C.-H., Miloslavic, S.A., & Johnson, R.E. (2011). Relationships of role stressors with organizational citizenship behavior: A meta-analysis. *Journal of Applied Pscyhology, 96*, 619–632.

90. Johns, G. (1997). Contemporary research on absence from work: Correlates, causes and consequences. *International Review of Industrial and Organizational Psychology, 12*, 115–173; Darr, W., & Johns, G. (2008). Work strain, health, and absenteeism from work: A meta-analysis. *Journal of Occupational Health Psychology, 13*, 293–318; Podsakoff, N.P., LePine, J.A., & LePine, M.A. (2007). Differential challenge stressor-hindrance stressor relationships with job attitudes, turnover intentions, turnover, and withdrawal behavior: A meta-analysis. *Journal of Applied Psychology, 92*, 438–454.

91. Beehr, T.A., & Newman, J.E. (1978). Job stress, employee health, and organizational effectiveness: A facet analysis, model, and literature review. *Personnel Psychology, 32*, 665–699; Kahn & Byosiere, 1992; Frone, M.R. (2008). Employee alcohol and illicit drug use: Scope, causes, and organizational consequences. In J. Barling & C.L. Cooper (Eds.), *Sage handbook of organizational behavior* (Vol 1). London: Sage.

92. For reviews, see Cramer, P. (2000). Defense mechanisms in psychology today: Further processes for adaptation. *American Psychologist, 55*, 637–646; Baumeister, R.F., Dale, K., & Sommer, K.L. (1998). Freudian defense mechanisms and empirical findings in modern social psychology: Reaction formation, projection, displacement, undoing, isolation, sublimation, and denial. *Journal of Personality, 66*, 1081–1124.

93. Beehr & Newman, 1978. For a later review and a strong critique of this work, see Fried, Y., Rowland, K.M., & Ferris, G.R. (1984). The physiological measurement of work stress: A critique. *Personnel Psychology, 37*, 583–615. See also Fried, Y. (1989). The future of physiological assessments in work situations. In C.L. Cooper & R. Payne (Eds.), *Causes, coping, and consequences of stress at work*. Chichester, England: Wiley & Sons.

94. Cohen, S., & Herbert, T.B. (1996). Health psychology: Psychological and physical disease from the perspective of human psychoneuroimmunology. *Annual Review of Psychology, 47*, 113–142; Cohen, S., & Williamson, G.M. (1991). Stress and infectious disease in humans. *Psychological Bulletin, 109*, 5–24.

95. Melamed, S., Shirom, A., Toker, S., Berliner, S., & Shapira, I. (2006). Burnout and risk of cardiovascular disease: Evidence, possible causal paths, and promising research directions. *Psychological Bulletin, 132*, 327–353; Kivimaki, M., Virtanen, M., Elovainio, M., Kouvonen, A., Vaananen, A., & Vahtera, J. (2006). Work stress in the etiology of coronary heart disease: A meta-analysis. *Scandinavian Journal of Work, Environment and Health, 32*, 431–442; see also the special issue Stress and the Heart, *Stress and Health*, August 2008.

96. Grandey, A.A., Fisk, G.M., & Steiner, D.D. (2005). Must "service with a smile" be stressful? The moderating role of personal control for American and French employees. *Journal of Applied Psychology, 90*, 893–904; Grandey, A.A., Dickter, D.N., & Sin, H.P. (2004). The customer is not always right: Customer aggression and emotion regulation of service employees. *Journal of Organizational Behavior, 25*, 397–418.

97. See Spriggs, C.A., & Jackson, P.R. (2006). Call centers as lean service environments: Job related strain and the mediating role of work design. *Journal of Occupational Health Psychology, 11*, 197–212.

98. This section relies on a *Wall Street Journal* special section on Work & Family (1993, June 21) and Shellenbarger, S. (1993, June 29). Work & family. *Wall Street Journal*, B1.

99. Canadastop100.com/family/, retrieved May 25, 2012.

100. Ngo, H.-Y., Foley, S., & Loi, R. (2009). Family friendly work practices, organizational climate, and firm performance: A study of multinational corporations in Hong Kong. *Journal of Organizational Behavior, 30*, 665–680; Van Steenbergen, E.F., & Ellemers, N. (2009). Is managing the work–family interface worthwhile? Benefits for employee health and performance. *Journal of Organizational Behavior, 30*, 617–642.

101. Kelly, E.L., Kossek, E.E., Hammer, L.B., Durhman, M., Bray, J., Chermack, K., Murphy, L.A., & Kaskubar, D. (2008). Getting there from here: Research on the effects of work-family initiatives on work-family conflict and business outcomes. *Academy of Management Annals, 2*, 305–309.

102. Richardson, K.M., & Rothstein, H.R. (2008). Effects of occupational stress management intervention programs: A meta-analysis. *Journal of Occupational Health Psychology, 13*, 69–93; Ivancevich, J.M., Matteson, M.T., Freedman, S.M., & Phillips, J.S. (1990). Worksite stress management interventions. *American Psychologist, 45*, 252–261; Cartwright, S., & Cooper, C. (2005). Individually targeted interventions. In Barling et al., 2005.

103. Richardson & Rothstein, 2008; Ivancevich et al., 1990.

104. Lush, T. (1998, October 3). Company with a conscience. *The Gazette* (Montreal), C3.

105. Immen, W., & Brown-Bowers, A. (2008, April 16). Employers get the fitness bug. *Globe and Mail*, C1, C2.

106. Parks, K.M., & Steelman, L.A. (2008). Organizational wellness programs: A meta-analysis. *Journal of Occupational Health Psychology, 13*, 58–63; DeGroot, T., & Kiker, D.S. (2003). A meta-analysis of the non-monetary effects of employee health management programs. *Human Resource Management, 42*, 53–69; Jex, S.M. (1991). The psychological benefits of exercise in work settings: A review, critique, and dispositional model. *Work & Stress, 5*, 133–147.

Chapter 14

1. Kirby, A., & Jones, K. (2004). Family fortunes at Flight Centre. *Human Resource Management International Digest, 12*(6), 33–34; www.flightcentre.ca; www.flightcentre.com.au; Johnson, M. (2005). *Family village tribe: The story of Flight Centre Limited*. Sydney: Random House; First and second Turner quotes are from Turner, G., & Teare, R. (2006). Reflections on leadership. *International Journal of Contemporary Hospitality Management, 18*(6), 519; Last Turner quote is from Palmer, I., & Dunford, R. (2002). Managing discursive tension: The co-existence of individualist and collaborative discourses in Flight Centre. *Journal of Management Studies, 39*, 1045–1069; updates: personal

communication from Flight Centre's Haydn Long and Allison Wallace, June 26, 2012.

2. Mintzberg, H. (1979). *The structuring of organizations*. Englewood Cliffs, NJ: Prentice-Hall. For a more recent review of some of the issues involved in structuring organizations, see Dunbar, R.L., & Starbuck, W.H. (2006). Learning to design organizations and learning from designing them. *Organization Science, 17*, 171–178.

3. Lawrence, P.R., & Lorsch, J.W. (1969). *Organization and environment: Managing differentiation and integration*. Homewood, IL: Irwin.

4. For an extended treatment of the role of interdependence between departments, see McCann, J., & Galbraith, J.R. (1981). Interdepartmental relations. In P.C. Nystrom & W.H. Starbuck (Eds.), *Handbook of organizational design* (Vol. 2). Oxford: Oxford University Press.

5. For a comparison of functional and product departmentation, see McCann & Galbraith, 1981; Walker, A.H., & Lorsch, J.W. (1968, November–December). Organizational choice: Product vs. function. *Harvard Business Review*, 129–138.

6. Flynn, A., & Freeman, S. (2010, September 16). Canadian Tire tweaks managers' roles. *Globe and Mail*, B10.

7. Galbraith, J.R. (2009). *Designing matrix organizations that actually work*. San Francisco: Jossey-Bass; see also Davis, S.M., & Lawrence, P.M. (1977). *Matrix*. Reading, MA: Addison-Wesley.

8. Novak, B. (2008, July–August). Cisco connects the dots: Aligning leaders with a new organizational structure. *Global Business and Organizational Excellence*, 22–32.

9. Qiu, J.X.J., & Donaldson, L. (2011). Stopford and Wells were right! MNC matrix structures do fit a "high-high" strategy. *Management International Review*, 1–19.

10. Karlsson, P.J. (2008, June 23). Matrix organization—possible in China? *China Daily* (Hong Kong edition, *China Business Weekly* section), 4.

11. Treatment of these forms of departmentation can be found in Daft, R.L. (2009). *Organization theory and design* (10th ed.). Mason, OH: Thompson South-Western; Robey, D. (1991). *Designing organizations* (3rd ed.). Homewood, IL: Irwin.

12. Mintzberg, 1979.

13. See Hall, R.H. (1962). Intraorganizational structural variation: Application of the bureaucratic model. *Administrative Science Quarterly, 7*, 295–308.

14. Lawrence & Lorsch, 1969.

15. Galbraith, J.R. (1977). *Organization design*. Reading, MA: Addison-Wesley.

16. See Birnbaum, P.H. (1981). Integration and specialization in academic research. *Academy of Management Journal, 24*, 487–503.

17. Okhuysen, G.A., & Bechky, B.A. (2009). Coordination in organizations: An integrative perspective. *Academy of Management Annals, 3*, 463–502.

18. This discussion relies on Galbraith, 1977.

19. Lawrence & Lorsch, 1969.

20. Galbraith, 1977.

21. Richter, A.W., West, M.A., Van Dick, R., & Dawson, J.F. (2006). Boundary spanners' identification, intergroup contact, and effective intergroup relations. *Academy of Management Journal, 49*, 1252–1269.

22. These definitions of structural variables are common. However, there is considerable disagreement about how some should be measured. See Walton, E.J. (1981). The comparison of measures of organizational structure. *Academy of Management Review, 6*, 155–160.

23. Research on these hypotheses is sparse and not always in agreement. See Dewar, R.D., & Simet, D.P. (1981). A level specific prediction of spans of control examining effects of size, technology, and specialization. *Academy of Management Journal, 24*, 5–24; Van Fleet, D.D. (1983). Span of management research and issues. *Academy of Management Journal, 26*, 546–552.

24. Lüscher, L.S., & Lewis, M.W. (2008). Organizational change and managerial sensemaking: Working through paradox. *Academy of Management Journal, 51*, 221–240.

25. For a study, see Hetherington, R.W. (1991). The effects of formalization on departments of a multi-hospital system. *Journal of Management Studies, 28*, 103–141.

26. Groth, L. (1999). *Future organizational design: The scope for the IT-based enterprise*. Chichester, England: Wiley.

27. *60 Minutes*, October 17, 1993.

28. Mintzberg, 1979, 182.

29. Ritzer, G., (1993). *The McDonaldization of society*. Thousand Oaks, CA: Pine Forge Press.

30. Personal communication from Food Lion's Jeff Lowrance, August 7, 2006.

31. Chuang, M.-L., Donegan, J.J., Ganon, M.W., & Wei, K. (2011). Walmart and Carrefour experiences in China: Resolving the structural paradox. *Cross Cultural Management, 18*, 443–463.

32. Daft, 2009.

33. The terms *mechanistic* and *organic* (to follow) were first used by Burns, T., & Stalker, G.M. (1961). *The management of innovation*. London: Tavistock Publications. For a relevant study, see

Courtright, J.A., Fairhurst, G.T., & Rogers, L.E. (1989). Interaction patterns in organic and mechanistic systems. *Academy of Management Journal, 32*, 773–802.

34. Anfuso, D. (1999, March). Core values shape W. L. Gore's innovative culture. *Workforce*, 48–53; Deutschman, A. (2004, December). The fabric of creativity. *Fast Company*, 54–62; Weinreb, M. (2003, April). Power to the people. *Sales and Marketing Management*, 30–35.

35. Raisch, S., Birkinshaw, J., Probst, G., & Tushman, M.L. (2009). Organizational ambidexterity: Balancing exploitation and exploration for sustained performance. *Organization Science, 20*, 685–695; Simsek, Z., Heavey, C., Viega, J.F., & Souder, D. (2009). A typology for aligning ambidexterity's conceptualizations, antecedents, and outcomes. *Journal of Management Studies, 46*, 864–894.

36. Jansen, J.J.P., Tempelaar, M.P., van den Bosch, F.A.J., & Volberda, H.W. (2009). Structural differentiation and ambidexterity: The mediating role of integration mechanisms. *Organization Science, 20*, 797–811.

37. O'Reilly, C.A. III, & Tushman, M.L. (2008). Ambidexterity as a dynamic capability: Resolving the innovator's dilemma. *Research in Organizational Behavior, 28*, 185–206.

38. O'Reilly, C.A. III, & Tushman, M.L. (2004, April). The ambidextrous organization. *Harvard Business Review*, 74–82; see also Jansen et al., 2009, and O'Reilly, C.A. III, Tushman, M.L. (2011, Summer). Organizational ambidexterity in action: How managers explore and exploit. *California Management Review, 53*, 5–22.

39. Farjoun, M. (2010). Beyond dualism: Stability and change as a duality. *Academy of Management Review, 35*, 202–225.

40. Westerman, G., McFarlan, F.W., & Iansiti, M. (2006). Organization design and effectiveness over the innovation life cycle. *Organization Science, 17*, 230–238; see also Puranam, P., Singh, H., & Zollo, M. (2006). Organizing for innovation: Managing the coordination-autonomy dilemma in technology acquisitions. *Academy of Management Journal, 49*, 263–280.

41. Phene, A., Tallman, S., & Almeida, P. (2012). When do acquisitions facilitate technological exploration and exploitation? *Journal of Management, 38*, 753–783.

42. Miles, R.E., & Snow, C.C. (1992, Summer). Causes of failure in network organizations. *California Management Review*, 53–72; Snow, C.C., Miles, R.F.,

& Coleman, H.J., Jr. (1992, Winter). Managing 21st century network organizations. *Organizational Dynamics, 20,* 5–20.

43. Brass, D.J., Galaskiewicz, J., Greve, H.R., & Tsai, W. (2004). Taking stock of networks and organizations: A multilevel perspective. *Academy of Management Journal, 47,* 795–817; Phelps, C.C. (2010). A longitudinal study of the influence of alliance network structure and composition on firm exploratory innovation. *Academy of Management Journal, 53,* 890–913.

44. Parmigiani, A., & Rivera-Santos, M. (2011). Clearing a path through the forest: A meta-review of interorganizational relationships. *Journal of Management, 37,* 1108–1136.

45. Dess, G.G., Rasheed, A.M.A., McLaughlin, K.J., & Priem, R.L. (1995, August). The new corporate architecture. *Academy of Management Executive, 9,* 7–20.

46. Magder, J. (2011, February 12). Risky business of Google. *The Gazette* (Montreal). B1, B4.

47. This example is from Venkatraman, N., & Lee, C.H. (2004). Preferential linkage and network evolution: A conceptual model and empirical test in the U.S. video game sector. *Academy of Management Journal, 47,* 876–892.

48. Ozcan, P., & Eisenhardt, K.M. (2009). Origin of alliance portfolios: Entrepreneurs, network strategies, and firm performance. *Academy of Management Journal, 52,* 246–279.

49. Hartley, M. (2012, May). Doubling down. *Financial Post Magazine,* 24–28.

50. Miles & Snow, 1992.

51. Chesbrough, H.W., & Teece, D.J. (2002, August). Organizing for innovation: When is virtual virtuous? *The Innovative Enterprise,* 127–134.

52. Kim, T.Y., Oh, H., & Swaminathan, A. (2006). Framing interorganizational network change: A network inertia perspective. *Academy of Management Review, 31,* 704–720.

53. Davis, G.F. (2009, August). The rise and fall of finance and the end of the society of organizations. *Academy of Management Perspectives,* 27–44.

54. Dess et al., 1995; Tully, S. (1993, February 8). The modular corporation. *Fortune,* 106–114.

55. Tully, 1993; Dess et al., 1995.

56. Magretta, J. (1998, March–April). The power of virtual integration: An interview with Dell Computer's Michael Dell. *Harvard Business Review,* 72–84; Tully, 1993.

57. Dess et al., 1995.

58. Berman, D. (1996, September). Car and striver. *Canadian Business,* 92–99.

59. Baraldi, E. (2008, Summer). Strategy in industrial networks: Experiences from IKEA. *California Management Review,* 99–126.

60. Dess et al., 1995; Tully, 1993.

61. Tully, 1993.

62. Dess et al., 1995.

63. Tichy, N.M., & Sherman, S. (1993, January 25). Jack Welch's lessons for success. *Fortune,* 86–93. Excerpt from *Control your destiny or someone else will* (1993), Toronto: Doubleday.

64. Jacob, R. (1992, May 18). The search for the organization of tomorrow. *Fortune,* 92–98; Rao, R.M. (1995, April 3). The struggle to create an organization for the 21st century. *Fortune,* 90–99.

65. Jacob, 1992.

66. Dess et al., 1995.

67. For a good general review of size research, see Bluedorn, A.C. (1993). Pilgrim's progress: Trends and convergence in research on organizational size and environments. *Journal of Management, 19,* 163–191.

68. Much of this research was stimulated by Blau, P.M. (1970). A theory of differentiation in organizations. *American Sociological Review, 35,* 201–218. For a review and test, see Cullen, J.B., Anderson, K.S., & Baker, D.D. (1986). Blau's theory of structural differentiation revisited: A theory of structural change or scale? *Academy of Management Journal, 29,* 203–229.

69. Dewar, R., & Hage, J. (1978). Size, technology, complexity, and structural differentiation: Toward a theoretical synthesis. *Administrative Science Quarterly, 23,* 111–136; Marsh, R.M., & Mannari, H. (1981). Technology and size as determinants of the organizational structure of Japanese factories. *Administrative Science Quarterly, 26,* 33–57.

70. Hage, J., & Aiken, M. (1967). Relationship of centralization to other structural properties. *Administrative Science Quarterly, 12,* 79–91; Mansfield, R. (1973). Bureaucracy and centralization: An examination of organizational structure. *Administrative Science Quarterly, 18,* 77–88.

71. Carleton, J. (2006, April 20). Forestry company Weyerhaeuser tries to become more nimble. *Globe and Mail,* B16.

72. Barkema, H.G., & Schijven, M. (2008). Toward unlocking the full potential of acquisitions: The role of organizational restructuring. *Academy of Management Journal, 51,* 695–722.

73. DeWitt, R.L. (1993). The structural consequences of downsizing. *Organization Science, 4,* 30–40.

74. Freeman, S.J., & Cameron, K.S. (1993). Organizational downsizing: A convergence

and reorientation framework. *Organization Science, 4,* 10–29.

75. See Datta, D.K., Guthrie, J.P., Basuil, D., & Pandey, A. (2010). Causes and effects of employee downsizing: A review and synthesis. *Journal of Management, 36,* 281–348.

76. DeWitt, 1993; Sutton, R.L., & D'Aunno, T. (1989). Decreasing organizational size: Untangling the effects of money and people. *Academy of Management Review, 14,* 194–212.

77. Cascio, W.F. (1993, February). Downsizing: what do we know? What have we learned? *Academy of Management Executive,* 95–104.

78. Guthrie, J.P., & Datta, D.K. (2008). Dumb and dumber: The impact of downsizing on firm performance as moderated by industry conditions. *Organization Science, 19,* 108–123.

79. Brockner, J. (1988). The effects of work layoffs on survivors: Research, theory, and practice. *Research in Organizational Behavior, 10,* 213–255.

80. Datta et al., 2010; Kammeyer-Mueller, J., Liao, H., & Arvey, R.D. (2001). Downsizing and organizational performance: A review of the literature from a stakeholder perspective. *Research in Personnel and Human Resources Management, 20,* 269–329; Johns, G. (2010). Presenteeism in the workplace: A review and research agenda. *Journal of Organizational Behavior, 31,* 519–542.

81. Datta et al., 2010.

82. Cascio, W.F. (2002, August). Strategies for responsible restructuring. *Academy of Management Executive,* 80–91; see also Burke, W.W. (1997, Summer). The new agenda for organization development. *Organizational Dynamics,* 7–18.

83. Child, J. (1984). *Organization: A guide to problems and practice.* London: Harper & Row.

84. Presidential Commission. (1986). *The report on the space shuttle Challenger accident.* Washington, DC: U.S. Government Printing Office.

85. Pugh, D.S. (1979, Winter). Effective coordination in organizations. *Advanced Management Journal, 44,* 28–35.

Chapter 15

1. Woodyard, C. (2011, February 28). Ford focuses on flexibility at its factories, *USA Today,* www.usatoday.com; Anonymous (2011, March 17). Ford opens flexible, green Michigan Assembly Plant with production of all-new Ford Focus. www.media.ford.com; Anonymous. Case study: Michigan Assembly Plant: A symbol of Ford's transformation. *Sustainability Report, 2010/11,* www.corporate.ford.com; Michigan Assembly

Plant transformed to produce fuel-efficient cars of the highest quality, www.ford.com.

2. McNish, J. (2003, June 11). Skittish travelers shifting bus tour firm into reverse. *Globe and Mail,* B1, B4.

3. Little, B. (2003, June 11). Second SARS outbreak barely noticed. *Globe and Mail,* B4.

4. Neuman, S. (2003, June 4). SARS travel slump could last. *Globe and Mail,* B6.

5. Scoffield, H. (2009, May 16). Manufacturing production sinks 2.7%. *Globe and Mail,* B6; Ferguson, R., & Van Alphen, T. (2009, June 2). Government Motors. *Toronto Star,* A1, A12; Keenan, G., Howlett, K., & McCarthy, S. (2009, June 2). High stakes, high costs and high hopes. *Globe and Mail,* A1, A14; Van Alphen, T. (2009, May 15). Truck stop. *Toronto Star,* B1, B4; Van Alphen, T. (2009, May 15). Oshawa reels as truck plant closes. *Toronto Star,* B4.

6. Katz, D., & Kahn, R.L. (1978). *The social psychology of organizations* (2nd ed.). New York: Wiley.

7. This list relies on Duncan, R. (1972). Characteristics of organization environments and perceived environmental uncertainty. *Administrative Science Quarterly, 17,* 313–327.

8. Friend, D. (2009, March 13). RIM stays ahead of the curve with hiring frenzy. *Globe and Mail,* B14; Rubin, J. (2012, May 26). RIM expected to announce major layoffs this week. *Toronto Star,* www.thestar.com/printarticle/1197035.

9. Durbin, D. (2005, May 31). Parts firms' trust in big three drops. *Globe and Mail,* B12.

10. See Khandwalla, P. (1981). Properties of competing organizations. In P.C. Nystrom & W.H. Starbuck (Eds.), *Handbook of organization design* (Vol. 1). Oxford: Oxford University Press.

11. Zachary, G.P. (1994). Consolidation sweeps the software industry; small firms imperiled. *Wall Street Journal,* A1, A6.

12. Volberda, H.W. (1996). Toward the flexible form: How to remain vital in hypercompetitive environments. *Organization Scene, 7,* 359–374.

13. Kirkpatrick, D. (1990, February 12). Environmentalism: The new crusade. *Fortune,* 44–55; Dobson, S. (2007, March 26). Fairmont finds it's easy being green. *Canadian HR Reporter, 20(6),* 14.

14. Connolly, T., Conlon, E.J., & Deutsch, S.J. (1980). Organizational effectiveness: A multiple-constituency approach. *Academy of Management Review, 5,* 211–217.

15. Duncan, 1972. Just how to measure uncertainty has provoked controversy; see Downey, H.K., & Ireland, R.D. (1979). Quantitative versus qualitative:

Environmental assessment in organizational studies. *Administrative Science Quarterly, 24,* 630–637; Milliken, F.J. (1987). Three types of perceived uncertainty about the environment: State, effect, and response uncertainty. *Academy of Management Review, 12,* 133–143.

16. Duncan, 1972; Tung, R.L. (1979). Dimensions of organizational environments: An exploratory study of their impact on organization structure. *Academy of Management Journal, 22,* 672–693. For contrary evidence, see Downey, H., Hellriegel, D., & Slocum, J. (1975). Environmental uncertainty: The construct and its application. *Administrative Science Quarterly, 20,* 613–629.

17. See Leblebici, H., & Salancik, G.R. (1981). Effects of environmental uncertainty on information and decision processes in banks. *Administrative Science Quarterly, 26,* 578–596.

18. See At-Twaijri, M.I.A., & Montanari, J.R. (1987). The impact of context and choice on the boundary-spanning process: An empirical extension. *Human Relations, 40,* 783–798.

19. Pfeffer, J., & Salancik, G.R. (1978). *The external control of organizations: A resource dependence perspective.* New York: Harper & Row; Yasai-Ardekani, M. (1989). Effects of environmental scarcity and munificence on the relationship of context to organizational structure. *Academy of Management Journal, 32,* 131–156.

20. Castrogiovanni, G.J., (1991). Environmental munificence: A theoretical assessment. *Academy of Management Review, 16,* 542–565.

21. Pfeffer & Salancik, 1978.

22. Hillman, A.J., Withers, M.C., & Collins, B.J. (2009). Resource dependence theory: A review. *Journal of Management, 35,* 1404–1427.

23. Boyd, B.K., Dess, G.G., & Rasheed, A.M.A. (1993). Divergence between archival and perceptual measures of the environment: Causes and consequences. *Academy of Management Review, 18,* 204–226.

24. For an analogue, see Miller, D., Dröge, C., & Toulouse, J.M. (1988). Strategic process and content as mediators between organizational context and structure. *Academy of Management Journal, 31,* 544–569.

25. Miles, R.C., & Snow, C.C. (1978). *Organizational strategy, structure, and process.* New York: McGraw-Hill.

26. Lawrence, P.R., & Lorsch, J.W. (1967). *Organization and environment: Managing differentiation and integration.* Homewood, IL: Irwin. For a follow-up

study, see Lorsch, J.W., & Morse, J.J. (1974). *Organizations and their members: A contingency approach.* New York: Harper & Row.

27. For a review, see Miner, J.B. (1982). *Theories of organizational structure and process.* Chicago: Dryden.

28. Sine, W.D., Mitsuhashi, H., & Kirsch, D.A. (2006). Revisiting Burns and Stalker: Formal structure and new venture performance in emerging economic sectors. *Academy of Management Journal, 49,* 121–132.

29. Frederickson, J.W. (1986). The strategic decision process and organizational structure. *Academy of Management Review, 11,* 280–297.

30. Romme, A.G.L. (1990). Vertical integration as organizational strategy formation. *Organization Studies, 11,* 239–260.

31. Chatterjee, S., Lubatkin, M., & Schoenecker, T. (1992). Vertical strategies and market structure: A systematic risk analysis. *Organization Science, 3,* 138–156; D'Aveni, R.A., & Ilinitch, A.Y. (1992). Complex patterns of vertical integration in the forest products industry: Systematic and bankruptcy risks. *Academy of Management Journal, 35,* 596–625.

32. D'aveni, R.A., & Ravenscraft, D.J. (1994). Economies of integration versus bureaucracy costs: Does vertical integration improve performance? *Academy of Management Journal, 37(5),* 1167–1206.

33. Anders, G. (2003, February). The Carly Chronicles. *Fast Company,* 66–73; Wong, T. (2006, January 31). Fairmont fetches $3.9 billion U.S.: Saudi prince, allies purchase chain Royal York among hotels, resorts sold. *Toronto Star,* D1; Perkins, T. (2006, August 18). Executive suite vacated at mining firm's headquarters. *Toronto Star,* F1, F8; Perkins, T. (2006, August 24). Domtar creates fine-paper giant in deal with U.S. firm. *Toronto Star,* C1, C8.

34. Hartley, M. (2009, April 21). Oracle deal for Sun creates one-stop shop. *Globe and Mail,* B13.

35. Lubatkin, M., & O'Neill, H.M. (1987). Merger strategies and capital market risk. *Academy of Management Journal, 30,* 665–684; Pfeffer & Salancik, 1978; Hill, C.W.L., & Hoskisson, R.E. (1987). Strategy and structure in the multiproduct firm. *Academy of Management Review, 12,* 331–341.

36. Kanter, R.M. (1989, August). Becoming PALS: Pooling, allying, and linking across companies. *Academy of Management Executive,* 183–193.

37. Krim, J. (2003, April 28). 3 E-mail providers join spam fight: AOl, Microsoft, Yahoo seek ways to curtail unwanted solicitations. *The Washington Post,* A2.

38. Dyer, J.H., Kale, P., & Singh, H. (2001). How to make strategic alliances work. *MIT Sloan Management Review, 42*(4), 37–43; Parkhe, A. (1993). Strategic alliance structuring: A game theoretic and transaction cost examination of interfirm cooperation. *Academy of Management Journal, 36*, 794–829. See also Ring, P.S., & Van de Ven, A.H. (1994). Developmental processes of cooperative interorganizational relationships. *Academy of Management review, 19*, 90–118.

39. Parkhe, A. (1993). Partner nationality and the structure-performance relationship in strategic alliances. *Organizational Science, 4*, 301–324.

40. Schoorman, F.D., Bazerman, M.H., & Atkin, R.S. (1981). Interlocking directorates: A strategy for reducing environmental uncertainty. *Academy of Management Review, 6*, 243–251, 244. For a more recent study, see Haunschild, P.R., (1993). Interorganizational imitation: The impact of interlocks on corporate acquisition activity. *Administrative Science Quarterly, 38*, 564–592.

41. Schoorman et al., 1981.

42. See Davis, G.F., & Powell, W.W. (1992). Organization-environment relations. In M.D. Dunnette & L.M. Hough (Eds.), *Handbook of industrial and organizational psychology* (2nd ed., Vol. 3). Palo Alto, CA: Consulting Psychologists Press; Oliver, C. (1991). Strategic responses to institutional processes. *Academy of Management Review, 16*, 145–179.

43. Greenwood, R., & Deephouse, D. (2001, December 26). Legitimacy seen as key. *Globe and Mail,* B7.

44. Rousseau, D.M. (1979). Assessment of technology in organizations: Closed versus open systems approaches. *Academy of Management Review, 4*, 531–542.

45. Child, J. (1972). Organizational structure, environment and performance: The role of strategic choice. *Sociology, 6*, 2–22.

46. Gillsepie, D.F., & Mileti, D.S. (1977). Technology and the study of organizations: An overview and appraisal. *Academy of Management Review, 2*, 7–16; Rousseau, 1979.

47. Perrow, C.A. (1967). A framework for the comparative analysis of organizations. *American Sociological Review, 32*, 194–208.

48. Thompson, J.D. (1967). *Organizations in action.* New York: McGraw-Hill.

49. Thompson, 1967, 17.

50. Woodward, J. (1965). *Industrial organization: Theory and practice.* London: Oxford University Press.

51. Mintzberg, H. (1979). *The structuring of organizations.* Englewood Cliffs, NJ: Prentice-Hall.

52. Miller, C.C., Glick, W.H., Wang, Y.D., & Huber, G.P. (1991). Understanding technology-structure relationships: Theory development and meta-analytic theory testing. *Academy of Management Journal, 34*, 370–399. For information on measurement, see Withey, M., Daft, R.L., & Cooper, W.H. (1983). Measures of Perrow's work unit technology: An empirical assessment and a new scale. *Academy of Management Journal, 26*, 45–63.

53. Cheng, J.L.C. (1983). Interdependence and coordination in organizations: A role-system analysis. *Academy of Management Journal, 26*, 156–162.

54. Van de Ven, A.H., Delbecq, A.L., & Koenig, R., Jr. (1976). Determinants of coordination modes within organizations. *American Sociological Review, 41*, 322–338.

55. Keller, R.T., Slocum, J.W., Jr., & Susman, G.J. (1974). Uncertainty and type of management in continuous process organizations. *Academy of Management Journal, 17*, 56–68; Marsh, R.M., & Mannari, H. (1981). Technology and size as determinants of the organizational structure of Japanese factories. *Administrative Science Quarterly, 26*, 33–57; Zwerman, W.L. (1970). *New perspectives on organizational theory.* Westport, CT: Greenwood.

56. Singh, J.V. (1986). Technology, size, and organizational structure: A reexamination of the Okayma study data. *Academy of Management Journal, 29*, 800–812.

57. Walton, R.E. (1989). *Up and running: Integrating information technology and the organization.* Boston: Harvard Business School Press.

58. Child, J. (1987). Organizational design for advanced manufacturing technology. In T.D. Wall, C.W. Clegg, & N.J. Kemp (Eds.), *The human side of advanced manufacturing technology.* Sussex, England: Wiley.

59. From the Massachusetts Institute of Technology report *Made in America,* as excerpted in *Fortune,* May 22, 1989, 94.

60. Keenan, G. (2003, May 24). Chrysler future lies in flexibility. *Globe and Mail,* B3.

61. This table draws in part on Jelinek, M., & Goldhar, J.D. (1986). Maximizing strategic opportunities in implementing advanced manufacturing systems. In D.D. Davis (Ed.), *Managing technological innovation.* San Francisco: Jossey-Bass; Main, J. (1990, May 21). Manufacturing the right way. *Fortune,* 54–64; Nemetz, P.L., & Fry, L.W. (1988). Flexible manufacturing organizations: Implications for

strategy formulation and organization design. *Academy of Management Review, 13*, 627–638.

62. Cummings, T.G., & Blumberg, M. (1987). Advanced manufacturing technology and work design. In T.D. Wall, C.W. Clegg, & N.J. Kemp (Eds.), *The human side of advanced manufacturing technology.* Sussex, England: Wiley.

63. The following draws upon Child, 1987; Nemetz & Fry, 1988; Zammuto, R.F., & O'Connor, E.J. (1992). Gaining advanced manufacturing technologies' benefits: The roles of organizational design and culture. *Academy of Management Review, 17*, 701–728.

64. Dean, J.W., Jr., Yook, S.J., & Susman, G.I. (1992). Advanced manufacturing technology and organizational structure: Empowerment or subordination? *Organization Science, 3*, 203–229.

65. Collins, P.D., Ryan, L.V., & Matusik, S.F. (1999). Programmable automation and the locus of decision-making power. *Journal of Management, 25*, 29–53.

66. Wall, T.D., & Davids, K. (1992). Shopfloor work organization and advanced manufacturing technology. *International Review of Industrial and Organizational Psychology, 7*, 363–398.

67. Wall, T.D., Corbett, J.M., Martin, R., Clegg, C.W., & Jackson, P.R. (1990). Advanced manufacturing technology, work design, and performance: A change study. *Journal of Applied Psychology, 75*, 691–697; Wall, T.D., Jackson, P.R., & Davids, K. (1992). Operator work design and robotics systems performance: A serendipitous field study. *Journal of Applied Psychology, 77*, 353–362.

68. Patterson, M.G., West, M.A., & Wall, T.D. (2004). Integrated manufacturing, empowerment, and company performance. *Journal of Organizational Behavior, 25*, 641–665.

69. Cummings & Blumberg, 1987; Blumberg, M., & Gerwin, D. (1984). Coping with advanced manufacturing technology. *Journal of Occupational Behaviour, 5*, 113–130.

70. From an unpublished paper by C.A. Voss, cited in Child, 1987.

71. Long, R.J. (1987). *New office information technology: Human and managerial implications.* London: Croom Helm.

72. Long, 1987.

73. Dopson, S., & Stewart, R. (1990). What is happening to middle management? *British Journal of Management, 1*, 3–16.

74. See Bloomfield, B.P., & Coombs, R. (1992). Information technology, control and power: The centralization and decentralization debate revisited. *Journal of Management Studies, 29*, 459–484; Dewett, T., & Jones, G.R. (2001). The role of information technology in the

organization: A review, model and assessment. *Journal of Management, 27,* 313–346.

75. Huber, G.P. (1990). A theory of the effects of advanced information technologies on organizational design, intelligence, and decision making. *Academy of Management Review, 15,* 47–71.

76. Long, 1987; Hughes, K.D. (1989). Office automation: A review of the literature. *Relations Industrielles, 44,* 654–679.

77. Long, 1987.

78. Medcof, J.W. (1989). The effect and extent of use of information technology and job of the user upon task characteristics. *Human Relations, 42,* 23–41.

79. Medcof, J.W. (1996). The job characteristics of computing and non-computing work activities. *Journal of Occupational and Organizational Psychology, 69,* 199–212.

80. Long, 1987.

81. Zweig, D., & Webster, J. (2002). Where is the line between benign and invasive? An examination of psychological barriers to the acceptance of awareness monitoring systems. *Journal of Organizational Behavior, 23,* 605–633.

Chapter 16

1. Coverage through 2006 from Chakravarthy, B., & Lorange, P. (2007). *Strategy & Leadership, 35*(6), 4–11; subsequent coverage from Best Buy CEO Brad Anderson to retire. (2009, January 12): *MPRnews.* http://minnesota.publicradio.org/display/web/2009/01/21/best_buy/; Bustillo, M. (2012, April 12). Best Buy chief executive quits. *The Wall Street Journal,* 18.

2. Kirby, J. (2006, June 19). Awakening Microsoft. *National Post,* FP1, FP4.

3. Gilbert, C.G. (2005). Unbundling the structure of inertia: Resource versus routine rigidity. *Academy of Management Journal, 48,* 741–763; see also Vincente-Lorente, J.D., & Zúñiga-Vicente, J.A. (2006). Testing the time-variancy of explanatory factors of strategic change. *British Journal of Management, 17,* 93–114.

4. Jørgensen, H.H., Owen, L., & Neus, L. (2009). Stop improvising change management! *Strategy & Leadership, 37,* 38–44.

5. This list relies mostly on Leavitt, H. (1965). Applied organizational changes in industry: Structural, technological, and humanistic approaches. In J.G. March (Ed.), *Handbook of organizations.* Chicago: Rand McNally.

6. Cameron, K.S., & Quinn, R.E. (1999). *Diagnosing and changing organizational culture.* Reading: MA. Addison-Wesley.

7. Lewin, K. (1951). *Field theory in social science.* New York: Harper & Row; see also Burnes, B. (2004). Kurt Lewin and the planned approach to change: A re-appraisal. *Journal of Management Studies, 41,* 977–1002.

8. Van Knippenberg, B., Martin, L., & Tyler, T. (2006). Process-orientation versus outcome-orientation during organizational change: The role of organizational identification. *Journal of Organizational Behavior, 27,* 685–704.

9. Rafferty, A.E., & Griffin, M.A. (2008). Organizational change. In J. Barling & C.L. Cooper (Eds.), *The Sage handbook of organizational behavior* (Vol. 1). London: Sage.

10. Marshak, R.J. (2004). Morphing: The leading edge of organizational change in the twenty-first century. *Organization Development Journal, 22,* 8–21.

11. Tetrick, L.E., & Da Silva, N. (2003). Assessing the culture and climate for organizational learning. In S.E. Jackson, M.A. Hitt, and A.S. Denisi (Eds.), *Managing knowledge for sustained competitive advantage.* San Francisco, CA: Jossey-Bass.

12. Garvin, D.A. (1993, July–August). Building a learning organization. *Harvard Business Review,* 78–91.

13. Corley, K.G., & Gioia, D.A. (2003). Semantic learning as change enabler: Relating organizational identity and organizational learning. In M. Easterby-Smith and M.A. Lyles (Eds.), *Handbook of organizational learning and knowledge management.* Oxford: Blackwell.

14. Harris-Lalonde, S. (2001). *Training and development outlook 2001.* Ottawa: The Conference Board of Canada.

15. Harris-Lalonde, 2001.

16. Ellinger, A.D., Ellinger, A.E., Baiyin, Y., & Howton, S.W. (2002). The relationship between the learning organization concept and firms' financial performance: An empirical assessment. *Human Resource Development Quarterly, 13,* 5–21.

17. Flynn, G. (1997, December). Bank of Montreal invests in its workers. *Workforce,* 30–38.

18. Wirtz, J., Heracleous, L., & Menkhoff, T. (2007). Value creation through strategic knowledge management: The case of Singapore Airlines. *Journal of Asian Business, 23,* 249–263.

19. See Levinson, H. (2002). *Organizational assessment: A step-by-step guide to effective consulting.* Washington, DC: American Psychological Association; Howard, A. (Ed.) (1994). *Diagnosis for organizational change: Methods and models.* New York: Guilford.

20. Ford, J.D., & Ford, L.W. (2009). Resistance to change: A reexamination and extension. *Research in Organizational Change and Development, 17,* 211–239.

21. Sonenshein, S. (2010). We're changing—or are we? Untangling the role of progressive, regressive, and stability narratives during strategic change implementation. *Academy of Management Journal, 53,* 477–512.

22. Anders, G. (2003, February). The Carly chronicles. *Fast Company,* 66–73.

23. The first five reasons are from Kotter, J.P., & Schlesinger, L.A. (1979, March–April). Choosing strategies for change. *Harvard Business Review,* 106–114.

24. Oreg, S., Bayazit, M., Vakola, M., Arciniega, L., Armenakis, A., Barkauskiene, R., Bozionelos, N., et al. (2008). Dispositional resistance to change: Measurement equivalence and the link to personal values across 17 nations. *Journal of Applied Psychology, 93,* 935–944.

25. Herold, D.M., Fedor, D.B., & Caldwell, S.D. (2007). Beyond change management: A multilevel investigation of contextual and personal influences on employees' commitment to change. *Journal of Applied Psychology, 92,* 942–951.

26. Frank, R. (1994, May 23). As UPS tries to deliver more to its customers, labor problems grow. *Wall Street Journal,* A1, A8.

27. George, J.M., & Jones, G.R. (2001). Towards a process model of individual change in organizations. *Human Relations, 54,* 419–444. Unfortunately, research has often ignored the emotional component of change; see Rafferty, A.E., Jimmieson, N.L., & Armenakis, A.A. (2012). Change readiness: A multilevel review. *Journal of Management.*

28. Brooks, D. (2009, June 9). The quagmire ahead. *National Post,* A10.

29. The following relies partly on Kotter & Schlesinger, 1979.

30. Rodell, J.B., & Colquitt, J.A. (2009). Looking ahead in times of uncertainty: The role of anticipatory justice in an organizational change context. *Journal of Applied Psychology, 94,* 989–1002.

31. For reviews, see Macy, B.A., Peterson, M.F., & Norton, L.W. (1989). A test of participation theory in a work redesign field setting: Degree of participation and comparison site contrasts. *Human Relations, 42,* 1095–1165; Filley, A.C., House, R.J., & Kerr, S. (1976). *Managerial process and organizational behavior* (2nd ed.). Glenview, IL: Scott, Foresman.

32. Tichy, N.M., & Devanna, M.A. (1986). *The transformational leader.* New York: Wiley.

33. Bommer, W.H., Rich, G.A., & Rubin, R.S. (2005). Changing attitudes about change: Longitudinal effects of transformational leader behavior on employee cynicism about organizational change. *Journal of Organizational Behavior, 26*, 733–753; Herold, D.M., Fedor, D.B., Caldwell, S., & Liu, Y. (2008). The effects of transformational and change leadership on employees' commitment to change: A multilevel study. *Journal of Applied Psychology, 93*, 346–357.

34. Rafferty, A.E., & Griffin, M.A. (2006). Perceptions of organizational change: A stress and coping perspective. *Journal of Applied Psychology, 91*, 1154–1162.

35. Catalanello, R.F., & Kirkpatrick, D.L. (1968). Evaluating training programs— The state of the art. *Training and Development Journal, 22*, 2–9.

36. Goodman, P.S., Bazerman, M., & Conlon, E. (1980). Institutionalization of planned organizational change. *Research in Organizational Behavior, 2*, 215–246.

37. Goodman et al., 1980.

38. For a review of various definitions, see Porras, J.I., & Robertson, P.J. (1992). Organizational development: Theory, practice, and research. In M.D. Dunnette & L.M. Hough (Eds.), *Handbook of industrial and organizational psychology,* (2nd ed., Vol. 3). Palo Alto, CA: Consulting Psychologists Press.

39. French, W.L., & Bell, C.H., Jr. (1973). *Organization development.* Englewood Cliffs, NJ: Prentice-Hall.

40. Beer, M. (1980). *Organization change and development: A systems view.* Glenview, IL: Scott, Foresman; Beer, M., & Walton, E. (1990). Developing the competitive organization: Interventions and strategies. *American Psychologist, 45*, 154–161.

41. Beer, M. (1976). The technology of organizational development. In M.D. Dunnette (Ed.) *Handbook of industrial and organizational psychology.* Chicago: Rand McNally. See also Dyer, W. (1987). *Team building: Issues and alternatives* (2nd ed.). Reading, MA: Addison-Wesley.

42. Wakeley, J.H., & Shaw, M.E. (1965). Management training: An integrated approach. *Training Directors Journal, 19*, 2–13.

43. This description relies upon Beer, 1980; Huse, E.F., & Cummings, T.G. (1985). Organization development and change (3rd ed.). St. Paul, MN: West; Nadler, D.A. (1977). *Feedback and organization development: Using data-based methods.* Reading, MA: Addison-Wesley.

44. Taylor, J., & Bowers, D. (1972). *Survey of organizations: A machine-scored standardized questionnaire instrument.* Ann Arbor, MI: Center for Research on Utilization of Scientific Knowledge, Institute for Social Research, University of Michigan.

45. Weiner, S.P. (2006). *Driving change with IBM's bimonthly global pulse survey.* Paper presented at the annual conference of the Society for Industrial and Organizational Psychology, Dallas, Texas.

46. Smith, R.L., Rauschenberger, J.M., Bastos, M.W., Jayne, M.A.E., Mills, N.E., & Tripp, R.E. (2006). *Ford Motor Company Pulse trend analysis—Making and breaking trends.* Paper presented at the annual conference of the Society for Industrial and Organizational Psychology, Dallas, Texas; see also Pulse Survey Offers Employee a Voice, Measures Satisfaction. (2011, August 26) www.at.ford.com/news/cn/Pages/Pulse%20Survey%20Offers%20Employee%20a%20Voice%20Measures%20Satisfaction.aspx.

47. Johnson, R.H., Ryan, A.M., & Schmit, M. (1994). Employee attitudes and branch performance at Ford Motor Credit. Presentation at the annual conference of the Society for Industrial and Organizational Psychology, Nashville, Tennessee.

48. Mayflower Group, www.mayflower-group.org.

49. For an eclectic view of TQM concerns, see the Total Quality Special Issue of the July 1994 *Academy of Management Review.*

50. Crosby, P.B. (1979). *Quality is free.* New York: McGraw-Hill; Deming, W.E. (1986). *Out of the crisis.* Cambridge, MA: Massachusetts Institute of Technology Center for Advanced Engineering Study; Juran J.M. (1992). *Juran on quality by design.* New York: Free Press.

51. Kinlaw, D.C. (1992). *Continuous improvement and measurement for total quality: A team-based approach.* San Diego: Pfeiffer.

52. Berry, L.L., Parasuraman, A., & Zeithaml, V.A. (1994, May). Improving service quality in America: Lessons learned. *Academy of Management Executive, 8*, 32–45.

53. Kinlaw, 1992; Bounds, G., Yorks, L., Adams, M., & Ranney, G. (1994). *Beyond total quality management: Toward the emerging paradigm.* New York: McGraw-Hill.

54. Reeves, C.A., & Bednar, D.A. (1994). Defining quality: Alternatives and implications. *Academy of Management Review, 19*, 419–445.

55. Greengard, S. (1993, December). Reengineering: Out of the rubble. *Personnel Journal,* 48B–48O; Hammer, M., & Champy, J. (1993). *Reengineering the corporation: A manifesto for business revolution.* New York: HarperBusiness; Stewart, T.A. (1993, August 23). Reengineering: The hot new management tool. *Fortune,* 41–48.

56. Hammer & Champy, 1993.

57. Hammer & Champy, 1993.

58. Teng, J.T.C., Grover, V., & Fiedler, K.D. (1994, Spring). Business process reengineering: Charting a strategic path for the information age. *California Management Review, 36*, 9–31.

59. Hammer & Champy, 1993; Teng et al., 1994.

60. Examples from Greengard, 1993; Teng et al., 1994.

61. Hall, G., Rosenthal, J., & Wade, J. (1993, November–December). How to make reengineering really work. *Harvard Business Review,* 119–131.

62. Guzzo, R.A., Jette, R.D., & Katzell, R.A. (1985). The effects of psychologically based intervention programs on worker productivity: A meta-analysis. *Personnel Psychology, 38*, 275–291; Neuman, G.A., Edwards, J.E., & Raju, N.S. (1989). Organizational development interventions: A meta-analysis of their effects on satisfaction and other attitudes. *Personnel Psychology, 42*, 461–489.

63. For a meta-analytic summary, see Robertson, P.J., Roberts, D.R., & Porras, J.I. (1993). Dynamics of planned organizational change: Assessing support for a theoretical model. *Academy of Management Journal, 36*, 619–634. See also Macy, B.A., & Izumi, H. (1993). Organizational change, design, and work innovation: A meta-analysis of 131 North American field studies—1961–1991. *Research in Organizational Change and Development, 7*, 235–313.

64. Porras, & Robertson, 1992; Nicholas, J.M., & Katz, M. (1985). Research methods and reporting practices in organization development: A review and some guidelines. *Academy of Management Review, 10*, 737–749.

65. White, S.E., & Mitchell, T.R. (1976). Organization development: A review of research content and research design. *Academy of Management Review, 1*, 57–73.

66. For reviews of creativity and innovation research, see George, J.M. (2007). Creativity in organizations. *Academy of Management Annals, 1*, 439–477; Shalley, C.E., & Gibson, L.L. (2004). What

leaders need to know: A review of social and contextual factors that can foster or hinder creativity. *Leadership Quarterly, 15*, 33–53; Anderson, N., De Dreu, C.K.W., & Nijstad, B.A. (2004). The routinization of innovation research: A constructively critical review of the state-of-the-science. *Journal of Organizational Behavior, 25*, 147–173; Hennessey, B.A., & Amabile, T.M. (2010). Creativity. *Annual Review of Psychology, 61*, 569–598.

67. For an attempt to provide some order to this subject, see Wolfe, R.A. (1994). Organizational innovation: Review, critique and suggested research directions. *Journal of Management Studies, 31*, 405–431.

68. Tushman, M., & Nadler, D. (1986, Spring). Organizing for innovation. *California Management Review, 28*, 74–92; Damanpour, F., & Aravind, D. (2012). Managerial innovation: Conceptions, processes, and antecedents. *Management and Organization Review, 8*, 423–454.

69. Damanpour & Aravind, 2012.

70. Hamel, G. (2006, February). The why, what, and how of management innovation. *Harvard Business Review*, 72–84.

71. Birkinshaw, J., Hamel, G., & Mol, M.J. (2008). Management innovation. *Academy of Management Review, 33*, 825–845.

72. Frost, P.J., & Egri, C.P. (1991). The political process of innovation. *Research in Organizational Behavior, 13*, 229–295.

73. This three-part view of creativity is from Amabile, T.M. (1988). A model of creativity and innovation in organizations. *Research in Organizational Behavior, 10*, 123–167; see also Woodman, R.W., Sawyer, J.E., & Griffin, R.W. (1993). Toward a theory of organizational creativity. *Academy of Management Review, 18*, 293–321.

74. Basadur, M. (1994). Managing the creative process in organizations. In M.A. Runco (Ed.), *Problem finding, problem solving, and creativity*. Norwood, NJ: Ablex; Kabanoff, B., & Rossiter, J.R. (1994). Recent developments in applied creativity. *International Review of Industrial and Organizational Psychology, 9*, 283–324.

75. Galbraith, J.R. (1982, Winter). Designing the innovating organization. *Organizational Dynamics*, 4–25.

76. Howell, J.M. (2005, May). The right stuff: Identifying and developing effective champions of innovation. *Academy of Management Executive*, 108–119; Howell, J.M., & Higgins, C.A. (1990). Champions of technological innovation.

77. Definition and examples from Mainemelis, C. (2010). Stealing fire: Creative deviance in the evolution of new ideas. *Academy of Management Review, 35*, 558–578.

78. Cohen, W.M., & Levinthal, D.A. (1990). Absorptive capacity: A new perspective on learning and innovation. *Administrative Science Quarterly, 35*, 128–152.

79. Tushman, M.L., & Scanlan, T.J. (1981a). Characteristics and external orientations of boundary spanning individuals. *Academy of Management Journal, 24*, 83–98; Tushman, M.L., & Scanlan, T.J. (1981b). Boundary spanning individuals: Their role in information transfer and their antecedents. *Academy of Management Journal, 24*, 289–305.

80. McFadyen, A.M., Semadeni, M., & Cannella, A.A., Jr. (2009). Value of strong ties to disconnected others: Examining knowledge creation in biomedicine. *Organizational Science, 20*, 552–564.

81. Keller, R.T., & Holland, W.E. (1983). Communicators and innovators in research and development organizations. *Academy of Management Journal, 26*, 742–749.

82. Ramaswamy, V. (2008). Co-creating value through customers' experiences: The Nike case. *Strategy & Leadership, 36*, 9–14.

83. Bertin, O. (2003, July 14). Harley-Davidson's great ride to the top. *Globe and Mail*, B1, B4.

84. Leung, A.K.-Y., Maddux, W.W., Galinsky, A.D., & Chiu, C.-Y. (2008). Multicultural experience enhances creativity: The when and how. *American Psychologist, 63*, 169–181.

85. Leiponen, A., & Helfat, C.E. (2011). Location, decentralization, and knowledge sources for innovation. *Organization Science, 22*, 641–658.

86. Wilson, K.A. (2011, February 7). From the inside, out. *Autoweek*, 22–23.

87. Kanter, R.M. (1988). When a thousand flowers bloom: Structural, collective, and social conditions for innovation in organization. *Research in Organizational Behavior, 10*, 169–211; Nord, W.R., & Tucker, S. (1987). *Implementing routine and radical innovations*. Lexington, MA: Lexington Books; Damanpour, F. (1991). Organizational innovation: A meta-analysis of effects of determinants and moderators. *Academy of Management Journal, 34*, 555–590.

88. Miller, D.J., Fern, M.J., & Cardinal, L.B. (2007). The use of knowledge for technological innovation within diverse

firms. *Academy of Management Journal, 50*, 308–326.

89. Tushman & Scanlan, 1981b.

90. Keller & Holland, 1983.

91. Katz, R. (1982). The effects of group longevity on project communication and performance. *Administrative Science Quarterly, 27*, 81–104.

92. For a review, see Nord & Tucker, 1987. However, this prescription is controversial. For other views, see Kanter, 1988; Marcus A.A. (1988). Implementing externally induced innovations: A comparison of rule-bound and autonomous approaches. *Academy of Management Journal, 31*, 235–256.

93. Damanpour, 1991; Kanter, 1988.

94. Galbraith, 1982.

95. Hamel, 2006.

96. Amabile, 1988.

97. Damsell, K. (2003, October 29). CEO Fiorina touts HP's ability to adapt. *Globe and Mail*, B3.

98. Galbraith, 1982.

99. Walton, R.E. (1975, Winter). The diffusion of new work structures: Explaining why success didn't take. *Organizational Dynamics, 3*, 3–22.

100. Ferlie, E., Fitzgerald, L., Wood, M., & Hawkins, C. (2005). The nonspread of innovations: The mediating role of professionals. *Academy of Management Journal, 48*, 117–134.

101. Rogers, E.M. (2003). *Diffusion of innovations* (5th ed.). New York: Free Press.

102. Ansari, S.M., Fiss, P.C., & Zajac, E.J. (2010). Made to fit: How practices vary as they diffuse. *Academy of Management Review, 35*, 67–92.

103. Pfeffer, J., & Sutton, R.I. (2000). *The knowing-doing gap: How smart companies turn knowledge into action*. Boston: Harvard Business School Press; see also Johns, G. (1993). Constraints on the adoption of psychology-based personnel practices: Lessons from organization innovation. *Personnel Psychology, 46*, 569–592.

Appendix

1. Sutton, R.I. (1991). Maintaining norms about expressed emotions: The case of bill collectors. *Administrative Science Quarterly, 36*, 245–268.

2. Lupton, T. (1963). *On the shop floor.* Oxford: Pergamon.

3. Bensman, J., & Gerver, I. (1963). Crime and punishment in the factory: The function of deviancy in maintaining the social system. *American Sociological Review, 28*, 588–598.

4. Mintzberg, H. (1973). *The nature of managerial work.* New York: Harper & Row.

5. Ragins, B.R., & Cotton, J.L. (1993). Gender and willingness to mentor in organizations. *Journal of Management, 19,* 97–111.

6. Ivancevich, J.M., & Lyon, H.L. (1977). The shortened workweek: A field experiment. *Journal of Applied Psychology, 62,* 34–37.

7. Sutton, R.I., & Rafaeli, A. (1988). Untangling the relationship between displayed emotions and organizational sales: The case of convenience stores. *Academy of Management Journal, 31,* 461–487.

8. Greenwood, R.G., & Wrege, C.D. (1986). The Hawthorne studies. In D.A. Wren & J.A. Pearce II (Eds.), *Papers dedicated to the development of modern management.* The Academy of Management; Roethlisberger, F.J., & Dickson, W.J. (1939). *Management and the worker.* Cambridge, MA: Harvard University Press.

9. Adair, J.G. (1984). The Hawthorne effect: A reconsideration of the methodological artifact. *Journal of Applied Psychology, 69,* 334–345.

10. See Academy of Management. (2011). Academy of Management code of ethics. *Academy of Management Journal, 54,* 1299–1306. *Academy of Management Journal, 51,* 1246–1253; Lowman, R.L. (Ed.). (1998). *The ethical practice of psychology in organizations.* Washington, DC: American Psychological Association.

INDEX

A

abdication of leadership, 317
ability, 101
Aboriginal people
  Centre for Aboriginal Human Resource
    Development, 99
  as workforce demographic, 19
Abrahamse, Mary Louise, 452–453
absence cultures, 237
absence schedules, 237
absenteeism
  and extraversion, 47
  and group norms, 237
  and job satisfaction, 136–137
  and self-regulation, 64
  and work environment, 20–21
acceptance, 318–319
accommodating approach to conflict, 458
achievement needs, 162
achievement-oriented behaviour, 316
acquisitions, 543–544, 557
active listening, 374
actor–observer effect, 90
Adams, J. Stacey, 168
adaptability, 595
addictive substances, 476
additive tasks, 233
adjourning, 231
Adler, Nancy, 178
advanced information technology
  defined, 552
  manufacturing technology, 553–555
  office technology, 555–557
  opposite effects of, 553
  and reengineering, 586
  two faces of, 553
advanced manufacturing technology
  and flexibility, 554f
  and job design, 555
  and organizational structure, 554–555
  trends in, 553–554
advanced office technology
  functions of, 556
  and job design, 556–557
  and organizational structure, 556
Advancement of Women Initiative, 336
affective commitment, 141, 142
affiliation needs, 162
affiliative managers, 428
age
  four generations in the workplace, 121f
  and perception, 112–113
  stereotyping, 96–98
  and values, 120–121
  as workforce demographic, 20
agenda implementation, 17
agendas, managerial, 17

agenda setting, 17
agentic leadership, 335, 335f
agreeableness, 47
Alderfer, Clayton, 161
Alderfer's ERG theory, 160f, 163, 202
Alexander, Jeffrey, 590
Allan, Elyse, 334
Allen, Natalie, 141, 143
Allfirst Bank, 396
Alliance for Equality of Blind Canadians, 113
alternatives, searching for, 475
alternative working schedules
  compressed workweek, 213–214
  flex-time, 212–213, 212f
  job sharing, 214–215
  telecommuting, 215–216
  work sharing, 214–215
ambidextrous organization, 509–510
ambiguity, 456
American Express Canada, 100, 108
American Psychological Association, 465
America Online, 544
anchoring effect, 392
Andersen Worldwide SC, 35
Anderson, Brad, 566
anticipatory socialization, 267
Anton Piller order, 453
Antozyk, John, 301
anxiety reduction, 476
Apex Public Relations, 198
apologies, 364, 375
apparent sincerity, 433
Apple Computer, 286, 322, 323, 455–456
Applied Focus
  Boeing, 514
  Bureau de normalisation du Québec, 480
  Cedars-Sinai Medical Center, 590
  decision making, 404
  Delta Chelsea Hotel, 24
  empowerment, 426
  Frima Studio, 480
  green management, 24
  innovation implementation failure, 590
  network organization, 514
  organizational culture and customer service, 283
  organizational structure, 507
  Print Audit, 283
  RIM, 404
  Scotiabank, 336
  Tim Hortons, 426
  virtual teams, 251
  women in leadership, 336
  work-life balance, 480
arbitration, 463–464
Argyris, Chris, 13
Armstrong, Anne, 297
Arthur Andersen, 34–40, 225–226, 488–489

Ash, Mary Kay, 285
Ashforth, Blake, 436
asking for help, 475
assertiveness, 331*f*, 427
assigned roles, 236
Association for Canadian Studies, 126
Association for the Fifty-Plus, 97, 98
astuteness, 433
attitudes
    and behaviour, 126–127
    defined, 126
    job satisfaction. *see* job satisfaction
    organizational citizenship behaviour, 139–140
    organizational commitment, 141–144
attractiveness, 85
attribution
    in action, 89
    actor–observer effect, 90
    biases in, 89–91
    consensus cues, 88
    consistency cues, 88
    cue combinations, 89*f*
    defined, 87
    dispositional attributions, 87
    distinctiveness cues, 88–89
    fundamental attribution error, 90
    self-serving bias, 90–91
    situational attributions, 87
Australia
    bonus initiative, 111
    and values, 123
Austria, 123
authentic leadership, 328–330
autonomous leadership, 332
autonomous motivation, 156
autonomy, 203, 204*f*, 209*f*, 495
avoiding, as approach to conflict, 458

B

baby boomers
    background of, 120
    and skills gap, 22
    stereotyping, 120
    values of, 118
Bach, Michael, 78–79
Baker, Richard, 306
Baker, Ross, 399
balanced processing, 329
Balsillie, Jim, 404
Bandura, Albert, 61
Bank of Montreal, 547, 572, 573
Bardswick, Kathy, 310, 311
Bartz, Carol, 380
Bass, Bernard, 322–323
Bazerman, Max, 393
Beddoe, Clive, 284, 547
behaviour *see* individual behaviour; organizational behaviour
behaviour modelling training, 68
behaviourally anchored rating scale, 107, 107*f*
behavioural plasticity theory, 50
behavioural science knowledge, 578
Belgium, 121
Bell Canada, 215, 276
Bell Helicopter Textron, 199, 200
belongingness needs, 160

benevolence, 101
Bennett, Sarah, 147–151
Benotto, Mary Lou, 285
Bensman, Joseph, 606, 612
Berdahl, Jennifer, 443
Best Buy, 566–567, 570
best companies to work for
    Co-operators, 311
    EllisDon Corporation, 188
    employee recognition, 66
    Enron, 35
    Flight Centre, 492
    Four Seasons, 370
    Google Canada, 263
    Great Little Box Company Ltd., 152
    KPMG, 79
    management practices of, 8, 23
    Modern Appliances, 298
    motivational practices, 216
    and profitability, 9
    Scotiabank, 188
    stock options, 198
    turnover rate, 23
    for women, 96*f*
Best Diversity Employers, 79, 108
Best Employer Awards for 50-plus Canadians, 97, 98
Best Employers for New Canadians, 79
biases
    actor–observer effect, 90
    in attribution, 89–91
    fundamental attribution error, 90
    implicit personality theories, 85
    intergroup bias, 454–456
    in person perception, 84–87
    primacy effect, 84
    projection, 85
    recency effect, 84
    reliance on central traits, 85
    self-serving bias, 90–91
    stereotyping, 86–87
    weight-based bias, 86, 111
Big Five. *see also* Five-Factor Model
    and job satisfaction, 131
    self-esteem, 50–51
biometric screening clinics, 42
Black, Stewart, 325
Black, Susan, 3
blogs, 251, 359
Blue Cross, 586
boasting, 363
body language, 360–361, 374
Boeing, 99, 248, 328, 505, 514
Bolton, Chris, 562
Bombardier Inc., 560
Bond, Michael, 123
Bono, Joyce, 74
book publishers, 511
Booth, Alan, 36
bootlegged funds, 593
boss-relationship building, 279*f*
Bostock, Roy, 380
Boston Pizza, 281
boundaryless organization, 514–515
boundary roles, 468
bounded rationality, 388, 392, 400*f*
Bradshaw, James, 295–298, 301

brainstorming, 407–408
Branson, Richard, 324
breadth, 201
Brin, Sergey, 262
Britain, 122
British Petroleum, 507
broad tendency, 120
broker firms, 511
Brooks, Bonnie, 304–306, 334
Brown, David, 111
Brown, Tim, 228
Bruner, Jerome, 83–84
buck passing, 436
buffing, 436
Buhler Industries Inc., 214
bullying, 470–472, 473, 481
Bulos, Anastasia, 382
bureaucracy
    creeping bureaucracy, 585
    critique of, 13–14
    defined, 13
    qualities of, 13
Bureau de normalisation du Québec, 480
burnout, 468–469, 469f
Business Development Bank of Canada,
    311, 337
Butler, Mark, 111

C
CAD, 535, 554
Cadsby, C. Bram, 196
Cajun Sensation, 414
Calgary Airport Authority, 68
Cameo Corp., 24
Campbell, Colin, 453
Campion, Michael, 247
Canada
    best workplaces for women, 96f
    cultural intelligence, 126
    diversity in, 91
    and gender roles, 123
    immigrant unemployment rate, 94
    and values, 123
    visible minorities, 19–20, 91
    women in corporate officer positions, 94
Canada's Best Diversity Employers, 99
Canada's Greenest Employers, 2
Canadian Auto Workers, 220, 533
Canadian Broadcasting Corporation, 447
Canadian HR Reporter, 79, 108
Canadian National Institute for the Blind, 113
Canadian Nuclear Safety Commission, 437
Canadian Tire, 499
Capital One, 136, 144
Capital Power, 272
Cardinal, Jean, 119
Career Advisor, 69
career development
    discussed, 69
    and gender, 276–277
    and job satisfaction, 134
career success, and personality, 48
Carli, Linda, 334, 337f
CARP, 111
Carrefour, 508
Carrier, 199

case incidents
    Cajun Sensation, 414
    Canadian Anonymous University, 448
    Canadian National Institute for the Blind, 113
    communication, 382
    compensation and job satisfaction, 147
    Conway Manufacturing, 524
    Courier Cats, 75
    Dandy Toys, 600
    decision making, 414
    Fran-Tech, 344
    group assignment, 258–259
    job characteristics, 222–223
    Mayfield Department Stores, 184
    Monkland Pharmaceuticals, 382
    organizational behaviour, 29–30
    organizational change, 600
    organizational politics, 448
    organizational structure, 523
    reality shock, 295
    technology, 561–562
    Toronto District School Board, 561–562
    work-family balance, 484–485
    ZeusAd, 485
case studies, 524–528
    Chang Koh Metal Ptd. Ltd., 223–225
    communication and hiring, 382–384
    conflict, 485–488
    creative development committee, 259–261
    CTV Newsnet, 114–117
    Datatronic, 184–187
    decision making, 414–416
    employee engagement, 295–302
    ethics, 448–451
    external environment, 562–565
    Facebook, 382–384
    First Canadian Club, 600–602
    General Motors, 562–565
    Gen Y in the Workforce, 147–151
    Howe 2 Ski Stores, 75–77
    Hudson Smith Gordon, 485–488
    ICRISAT, 345–351
    Modern Appliances, 295–302
    motivation, 184–187, 223–225
    OrangeWerks, 448–451
    organizational change, 600–602
    organizational structure, 524–528
    Saturn, 562–565
    A Zero Wage Increase Again?, 30–34
Catalyst Award, 3, 336
categories, social, 82
categorization theory, 310
causation, 609
cause-and-effect diagrams, 585
Cedars-Sinai Medical Center, 590
Center for Creative Leadership, 121, 378
centrality
    and power, 430
    of work, 121–122
centralization, 14, 505–506, 515, 517, 519
central tendency, 106, 106f
central traits, 85
Centre for Aboriginal Human Resource
    Development, 99
CEO narcissism, 540
Ceridian Canada Ltd., 66

chain of command, 355–356
challenge, 171, 178
change. *see also* organizational change
 defined, 571
 rate of, 537, 538*f*
 resistance to, 284
 and stress, 472
change agents, 574
Chang Koh Metal Ptd. Ltd., 223–225
Chaparral Steel Company, 287
Chapman, Derek, 104
character, 325
charisma, 323–324
charismatic/value-based leadership, 332
Charles Schwab, 520
Chastain, Charles, 414–416
chat systems, 372
Chatterjee, Arijit, 540
Chau, Patrick Yam Keung, 601
cheating culture, 285
China
 an empowering leadership, 327
 and values, 123
Christie, Hugh, 426
Chrysler, 511, 533, 586
Circuit City, 567
Cisco Technical Services, 499
Citizens Medical Centre, 111
classical viewpoint, 11–13
clichés, 375
client relationships, 206
clothing, 362–363
CN Rail, 292–293
coalition formation, 427
Coast Capital Savings Credit Union, 280, 288
codes of ethics, 438*f*
coercive power, 421
cognitive ability, 156–157
cognitive biases, 388, 390, 391, 392, 400*f*
cognitive demands, 132–133, 133*f*
cognitive resource theory, 315
cohesiveness, 240–243, 241*f*, 243*f*
collaborating, 459
collective efficacy, 244
collective socialization tactics, 273*f*
collectivism, 123, 176–177
Colombia, 123
combining tasks, 206
commitment
 affective commitment, 141, 142
 continuance commitment, 141, 142
 and goals, 171, 171–172
 normative commitment, 141, 142
 organizational commitment, 141–144
 and participation, 172
 and rewards, 172
 and supportiveness, 172
committees, 230, 520
common manager, 355
common vocabulary, 360
communal leadership, 335, 335*f*
communication
 basics of, 355–356
 blogs, 251, 359
 chain of command, 355
 computer-mediated communication, 371–373, 379

cross-cultural communication. *see* cross-cultural
 communication
 and cue availability, 371*f*
 defined, 354
 and division of labour, 495
 downward communication, 355
 and ethics, 438
 explanations, 375–376
 filtering, 355
 gatekeepers, 592
 gender differences in, 363–364
 grapevine, 357–358
 horizontal communication, 355
 informal communication, 355
 and innovation, 591–593, 593*f*
 intranets, 377
 management training, 377–378
 mum effect, 356–357
 non-verbal language of work, 360–363
 office decor, 361–362, 362*f*
 organizational approaches to, 375–378
 personal approaches to, 373–375
 podcasts, 377
 principles of, 373–374
 process of, 354*f*
 props, artifacts, and costumes, 361–363
 psychological safety, 356
 query systems, 377
 routine communication, 16
 self-presentation bias, 367
 suggestion systems, 376–377
 surveys, 376
 synchronization, 371*f*
 telephone hotlines, 377
 360-degree feedback, 376
 clothing and communication, 362–363
 upward communication, 355
 verbal language of work, 359–360
 voice, 356
 webcasts, 377
 and workforce diversity, 98*f*
Compaq Computer, 284–285, 322, 543, 575
compatibility, 595
compensation. *see also* pay
 as defence mechanism, 477
 employee stock ownership plans, 198, 200*f*
 gainsharing, 198–199, 200*f*
 and job satisfaction, 134
 merit pay plans, 193–197
 and motivation theories, 190
 pay for knowledge, 199–200
 and performance on production jobs, 190–193
 and performance on white-collar jobs, 193–197
 piece-rate, 190
 profit sharing, 198, 200*f*
 skill-based pay, 199–200, 200*f*
 teamwork pay plans, 197–200, 200*f*
 wage incentive plans, 190–193
competing approach to conflict, 458
competition, 240, 241*f*, 440–441
competitive advantage
 and employee learning, 53
 and employee relations, 9
 and employee satisfaction, 136
 and organizational behaviour, 7
 and workforce diversity, 92*f*

Competitive Advantage Through People, 7
competitors, 534–535
complex environment, 537, 538*f*
complexity
    and division of labour, 507
    and downsizing, 516, 518
    and environmental uncertainty, 537, 538*f*
    and innovation, 595
    job complexity, 209*f*
    and organizational behaviour, 16
    and organizational structure, 515, 516*f*
    and self-managed teams, 245–246
compliance, 265
compliments, 364
compressed workweek, 213–214
compromise, 458
computer-aided design, 535, 554
computer-mediated communication,
    371–373, 377
COMVOC, 360
concessions, 461
Conference Board of Canada, 437, 442, 573
confidence, 363
confirmation bias, 390
conflict
    accommodating approach, 458
    and ambiguity, 456
    arbitration, 463–464
    avoiding approach, 458
    benefits of, 464
    causes of, 454–456
    collaborating approach, 459
    competing approach, 458
    compromise approach, 458
    conflict simulation, 464
    and culture, 455–456
    defined, 454
    dynamics of, 457
    group identification, 454–456
    interdependence, 455
    intergroup bias, 454–456
    interpersonal conflict, 454
    management strategies, 484
    managing, 457–459, 457*f*
    mediation, 463
    and negotiation, 459–464
    and organizational change, 464
    organizational conflict, 454–456
    and power, 455
    process conflict, 456
    relationship conflict, 456
    and scarce resources, 456
    and status, 455
    and structural problems, 519
    task conflict, 456
    third party involvement, 463–464
    types of, 456
    work-family conflict, 472
conflict resolution, 282
conflict simulation, 464
conformity, 242, 265, 403, 436
congruence, 374
conjunctive tasks, 234
Connelly, Catherine, 432
conscientiousness, 47, 139
consensus cues, 88

conservative shifts, 405–406, 405*f*
consideration, 310–311, 312, 323
consistency, 84, 105, 287
consistency cues, 88
constancy, 84
contemporary contingency approach, 14–15
context
    and job satisfaction, 135
    and socialization, 273
contextual characteristics, 208, 209*f*
contiguous user bandwagon, 552
contingencies, strategic, 429–431
contingency approach, 14–15
contingency theory, 313–315, 314*f*
contingent reward behaviour, 322
continuance commitment, 141, 142
continuous improvement,
    583–584, 583*f*, 584*f*
contrast effects, 104, 105*f*
control group, 610
controlled motivation, 156
controversy, 407
conventional arbitration, 463
convergent validity, 605
Cooper, Cynthia, 442
cooperation, reduced, 192
Co-operators, 310
coordination, 282, 501–504
coordination of labour
    direct supervision, 501
    integration, 503
    integrators, 503–504
    liaison roles, 503
    methods of, 501–504, 502*f*
    mutual adjustment, 502–503
    standardization of outputs, 501–502
    standardization of skills, 502
    standardization of work processes, 501
    and structural problems, 519
    task forces, 503
    teams, 503
core job characteristics, 203–205, 203*f*, 204*f*
core self-evaluations, 52–53, 74
Corning Inc., 272, 589
corporate culture *see* organizational culture
corporate entrepreneurs, 591
corporate social responsibility, 23–25, 439.
    see also organizational citizenship
    behaviour
Corporate Social Responsibility Report, 25
correlational research, 608–609, 610*f*
cost cutting, 462
Cotton, John, 609, 613
counselling, 276
courtesy and cooperation, 140
Couture, Stephen, 480
co-workers, and job satisfaction, 134–135
craft technologies, 548, 548*f*, 551
Crawford, Neil, 188
creative development committee, 259–261
creative deviance, 591
creativity, 589–591
creativity-relevant skills, 590
credit, 363
creeping bureaucracy, 585
critical psychological states, 203*f*, 205

Cropanzano, Russell, 131, 132
Crosby, Philip, 582
cross-cultural communication
    cultural context, 368–371, 369f
    differences, 375
    etiquette and politeness, 366–367
    language differences, 365
    non-verbal communication, 365–366
    and pace of life, 368f
    social conventions, 367–368
cross-functional teams, 248–250, 503
CTV Inc., 114–117
Cubbon, Paul, 426
cue combinations, 89f
Cullen, John, 441
Cullingford Coaches, 532
cultural assessment, 38f, 39f
cultural awareness, 53
cultural context, 368–371, 369f
cultural intelligence, 126
culturally contingent, 332
culturally endorsed implicit leadership theory, 332
cultural maps, 123, 125f
culture
    and absenteeism, 237
    appreciation of global customers, 125
    and communication. see cross-cultural
        communication
    and conflict, 455–456
    and gender roles, 123
    and leadership, 331–332, 333f
    and management style, 19
    and motivation, 175–178
    and organizational behaviour theories, 124
    and organizational change, 570
    organizational culture. see organizational culture
    and organizational learning, 572
    and power distance, 123
    and uncertainty avoidance, 123
    vacation policy, 122f
    and value differences, 121–126, 124f
culture clash, 284–285
customer departmentation, 500, 501f
customer focus, 583f
customers, 534
customer satisfaction, 140–141
cutting costs, 462
CVS, 511

D
Dana, 199
Dandy Toys, 600
Dar, William, 345–351
Darroch, Monica, 188–189
Davidson, Willie G., 592
deaf ear syndrome, 443
debasement, 287
decentralization, 515
Dechief, Diane, 94
decisional roles, 16
decision-based evidence making, 390
decision making
    and advanced technology, 556
    brainstorming, 407–408
    cognitive biases in, 388, 390, 391,
        392, 400f

and controversy, 407
    defined, 386
    Delphi technique, 409
    employee participation in, 318f
    framing, 388, 389–390
    group decision making. see group decision making
    ill-structured problems, 387
    improving, 406–409
    nominal group technique, 408
    and participative leadership, 320f
    rational decision-making model. see rational
        decision making
    Toronto General Hospital, 399
    training for, 406
    well-structured problems, 386–387
Deepwater Horizon, 507
defence mechanisms, 476–478
defensiveness, 436–437
delegation, 475
Dell, Michael, 18
Dell Computer, 513, 534
Deloitte & Touche, 34–40, 225–226,
    277–278, 488–489
Deloitte Touche Tohmatsu, 34
Delphi technique, 409
Delta Hotels, 24, 425
Deming, W. Edwards, 582
demographics, 19–20
Denmark, 123
departmentation
    customer departmentation, 500, 501f
    functional departmentation, 497–498, 497f
    geographic departmentation, 500, 500f
    hybrid departmentation, 500–501
    matrix departmentation, 499–500, 499f
    product departmentation, 498, 498f
dependent variables, 604
depression, 477
depth, 201
Desai, Vinit, 573
developmental networks, 278
development, and workforce diversity, 98f
devil's advocate, 407
DeVries, Marvin, 524
diagnosis
    of job design problems, 207
    in organizational change, 574
Dickson, William J., 13
Dienhart, John, 327
differential opportunity, 191–192
differentiation, 496–497
diffusion, 594–595
diffusion of responsibility, 401
Digital Equipment Corp., 285
Dimon, Jamie, 384–385
direction, 155
directive behaviour, 316
direct supervision, 501
disabilities, persons with
    Canadian National Institute for
        the Blind, 113
    Society for Manitobans with Disabilities, 99
    as workforce demographic, 19
discrepancy production, 64
discrepancy reduction, 64
discrepancy theory, 128

discretion, 502
discriminant validity, 605
discrimination. *see also* stereotyping
    age, 97
    in merit pay plans, 195
    name discrimination, 94
    religious, 93
    in United States, 93
    weight-based, 86
disjunctive socialization tactics, 273*f*
disjunctive tasks, 234
Disney, 122, 125, 285, 287, 289, 322
Disney, Walt, 285
displacement, 477
disposition, 131
dispositional approach, 45
dispositional attribution, 87
disseminator roles, 16
distal goals, 173, 174
distant staffing, 215
distinctiveness cues, 88–89
distributed work programs, 215
distributive fairness, 128–130, 140
distributive justice, 128–130
distributive negotiation, 460–461, 460*f*
disturbance handler roles, 16
diversification strategy, 544
diversity. *see also* workforce diversity
    diversity training programs, 99
    of groups, 233*f*, 241–242
    as management concern, 19–20
    and motivation, 163
    and perception, 91–101
    and reinforcement, 56
    of teams, 246
diversity programs, 98*f*
divestiture socialization tactics, 273*f*
division of labour
    coordination of, 501–504
    departmentation, 497–501
    horizontal division of labour,
        495–497, 495*f*
    and structural problems, 519
    vertical division of labour,
        494–495, 495*f*
domination, 403
dot.com meltdown, 398
Dougherty, Thomas, 433–434
Douglas, Rachel, 426
Down, Steven, 359
downsizing, 516–519
downward communication, 355
Drabinsky, Garth, 285
Dress for Success, 363
dress norms, 236
Drew, Ina, 384
Drucker, Peter, 211
duality, 325
Dun & Bradstreet Canada, 69
Dunbar, Robin, 493
DundeeWealth, 481
Dunn, Brian, 567
DuPont, 444
Durham, Cathy, 52
dynamic environment, 537, 538*f*
dynamics of conflict, 457

E

Eagly, Alice, 334, 337*f*
Eckel, Peter, 353
Economical Insurance, 42–43
economy, 534
education, and performance, 157
Edwards, Payton, 486
effect dependence, 264
effective communication, 354, 355
effort, 154
Eggers, John, 524
Eisner, Michael, 322
electronic brainstorming, 408
Elliott, William, 341, 419
EllisDon Corporation, 188–189
Ellison, Larry, 284
Elsbach, Kimberly, 361
emergent roles, 237
emoticons, 372
emotion
    and decision making, 396–397
    defined, 132
    and job satisfaction, 132–133
    and perception, 81
    and resistance to change, 575
emotional contagion, 132
emotional intelligence, 157–158, 158*f*, 178
emotional labour, 132–133, 133*f*, 469
emotional regulation, 132
emotional stability, 46
empathy, 374
employee engagement, 23
employee orientation programs, 271–272
employee recognition programs, 66–67, 66*f*
employee selection, 286
employee stock ownership plans, 198, 200*f*
employee surveys, 376
employee time theft, 182–183
employee turnover, 20–21
employee well-being, 20–22
Employment Equity Act, 20
employment interviews, 104–105
Employment Standards Act, 176
empowering leadership, 326–327, 330
empowerment, 424–427
encounter, 267
Eng, Susan, 111
engineering technologies, 548, 548*f*, 551
Enron, 35–36, 285, 442
entrepreneur roles, 16
environment *see* external environment
environmental change, 569*f*
environmental uncertainty
    and acquisitions, 543–544
    and establishing legitimacy, 546–547
    factors affecting, 536–538, 541*f*
    as function of complexity and rate of change, 538*f*
    and interlocking directorates, 546
    and mergers, 543–544
    and organizational structure, 541–542
    and strategic alliances, 544–546
    and strategy, 539–547, 539*f*
    and vertical integration, 542–543
equality of outcomes, 130
equilibrium, 232
equipment use, 209*f*

equity theory
  and cultural differences, 177
  defined, 129, 168
  and gender, 169
  integrated with other theories, 178f, 180
  and job satisfaction, 129
  managerial implications of, 170
  and motivation, 168–170
  research question, 604
  research support for, 169
Erez, Amir, 74
ergonomics, 209f
ERG theory
  explained, 161
  and job scope, 202
  research evidence, 163
Ernst & Young, 36
error prevention, 399, 409, 584
escalation of commitment, 394–395
establishing legitimacy, 546–547
esteem needs, 160
Ethical Focus
  blogs, 359
  escalation of commitment, 396
  incentive compensation, 196
  knowledge hiding, 432
  name discrimination, 94
  socialization tactics, 275
ethical leadership, 327–328
ethical leadership scale, 341–342
ethics
  causes of unethical behaviour, 440–441
  codes of ethics, 438f
  comparisons, 437
  defined, 437
  ethical behaviours, 438–439
  guidelines for, 444
  in leadership, 327–328
  nature of ethical dilemmas, 437–439
  in organizations, 437–444
  in research, 615
  sexual harassment, 318–319, 442–444
  whistle-blowing, 442
ethnicity, and mentoring, 278
ethnic stereotyping, 93–94
etiquette, 366–367
evaluations, 126
evaluation standardization, 105
Evans, Martin, 315
evasive hiding, 432
evidence-based decision making, 390
evidence-based management, 11
exceptions, 548, 548f
exchange, 427
existence needs, 161
existing data, 608
expectancy, 165
expectancy theory
  boosting expectancies, 167–168
  and cultural differences, 177
  defined, 164
  and diversity, 168
  expectancy, 165
  force, 165
  instrumentality, 164
  integrated with other theories, 178, 178f

  and job scope, 202
  managerial implications of, 167–168
  models of, 165f, 166f
  outcomes, 164, 165f
  research support for, 167
  and reward contingencies, 168
  valence, 164
expectations, 268
experimental research, 610–612
expertise, 246
expert power, 422
explaining organizational behaviour, 10
explanations, 375–376
exploiting versus exploring, 509
external environment
  competitors, 534–535
  complex environment, 537, 538f
  components of, 534–536
  customers, 534
  defined, 532
  dynamic environment, 537, 538f
  general economy, 534
  impact of, 532–533
  interest groups, 535–536, 536f
  open systems, 533, 533f
  resource dependence, 538–539
  simple environment, 537, 538f
  social/political factors, 535
  static environment, 537, 538f
  and strategy, 539f
  suppliers, 534
  and technology, 535–536, 547
  uncertainty. see environmental uncertainty
external partnership, 98f
external validity, 614
extinction, 58, 59f
extraordinary activities, 423
extraversion, 46, 47
extrinsic motivation, 155–156

F
Facebook, 382–383, 599
face saving, 177
facet satisfaction, 127
facial expressions, 365–366
fair competition, 439
Fairmont Hotels and Resorts, 24, 535
fairness
  and cultural differences, 131
  as ethical behaviour, 438
  and job satisfaction, 128–130
  and organizational citizenship behaviour, 140
  perceived fairness, 604
family, village, tribe team design, 492–493
family-friendly HR policies, 479
family life, 336
Fan, Jinyan, 271
fast-trackers, 287
Fayol, Henri, 11
Fecan, Ivan, 114, 115
feedback
  in communication, 364, 374
  as core job characteristic, 204, 204f
  direct, 207
  and gender, 364
  and goals, 171, 178

feedback *(continued)*
  from job, 209*f*
  multisource feedback, 376
  and organizational development, 581
  from others, 209*f*
  and performance, 56
  survey feedback, 376
  360-degree feedback, 376
feedback seeking, 279*f*
Feldman, Daniel C., 157
Fenster, Jean, 485
Ferris, Gerald, 433
Fiedler, Fred, 313–315
figurehead roles, 15
filtering, 355–356
final offer arbitration, 463
financial success, 283–284
Fiorina, Carly, 322, 543, 575
Fire Force Five, 148–151
firmness, 461
First Canadian Club, 600–602
fishbone diagrams, 585
fit, 46, 266
fitness programs, 481
Fit-Rite Jeans, 241
Five-Factor Model
  dimensions of, 46–47, 46*f*
  locus of control, 48–49, 48*f*
  research evidence, 47–48
  self-monitoring, 49–50
fixed-pie thinking, 460, 462
fixed socialization tactics, 273*f*
flaming, 372
flat organization, 504, 505*f*
flexibility
  and advanced technology, 553–554, 554*f*
  benefits of, 14
  at Ford Motor Company, 530–531
  strategic flexibility, 49
flex-time, 212–213, 212*f*
Flight Centre, 289, 492–493
flowcharts, 584
folklore, 287, 289
Follett, Mary Parker, 13
Food Lion, 506
force, 165
Ford, Tracy, 24
Ford Motor Company, 141, 530–531, 544, 582, 586
Ford Pulse, 582, 583*f*
formal authority, 14
formal mentoring programs, 276
formal socialization tactics, 273*f*
formal work group, 230
forming a group, 231
Forret, Monica, 433–434
Fortune magazine
  100 Best Companies to Word For, 9, 35, 136, 370
  Most Admired Companies, 2, 263
  top companies for leaders, 337
founder's role, 285–286
Four Seasons, 129–130, 287, 370, 378
Fox, Glenda, 485
Fox, Maggie, 27
frame-of-reference training, 108
framing, 388, 389–390, 462

France, 126
Fran-Tech, 344
Fraser Papers, 199
Frazer, Jeremy, 485–488
free rider effect, 244
French, John, 420
friendliness, 613
friendly rut, 464
Frima Studio, 480
Fry, Arthur, 588
Fulmer, Ingrid, 9
functional departmentation, 497–498, 497*f*
functional foremanship, 13
functional specialty, 389
fundamental attribution error, 90
future orientation, 331*f*

G
gainsharing, 198–199, 200*f*
Galliford, Catherine, 418, 419, 442
gatekeepers, 592
Gates, Bill, 61, 285, 458
Gawande, Atul, 410
gaze, 366
gender
  and career development, 276–277
  and communication, 363–364
  culture and, 123
  and equity theory, 169
  and feedback, 364
  and leadership, 332–336, 335*f*, 337*f*
  and perception, 81*f*
  and questions, 364
  stereotyping, 94–96
  and values, 123
gender egalitarianism, 331*f*
gender roles
  in Canada, 123
  in United States, 123
general cognitive ability, 156–157, 178
general economy, 534
General Electric, 142, 199, 296, 334, 378, 424–425, 514
General Foods, 207
General Motors, 249, 464, 533, 562, 575, 595
general self-efficacy, 52, 73
general socializing, 279*f*
generations, 120–121, 121*f*
Generation Shock, 118
Generation X
  background of, 120
  stereotyping, 120
  values of, 118–119
Generation Y, 147–151
  background of, 120
  stereotyping, 120
  values of, 118–119
geographic departmentation, 500, 500*f*
Gerhart, Barry, 9
Germany, 19
Gerstner, Louis, Jr., 286
Gerver, Israel, 606, 612
gestures, 366
Giambrone, Adam, 12

Glass, Marjorie, 415–416
glass ceiling, 334
Gliss, 452–453
Global Focus
    cross-functional teams, 249
    cultural intelligence, 126
    cultural socialization, 271
    fairness, 131
    job design, 210
    ROPES, 271
    self-presentation bias, 367
globalization
    and cultural differences, 125
    developing global employees, 126
    and diversity, 20
    and stereotyping, 93
global leadership, 325–326
Global Leadership and Organizational Behaviour
    Effectiveness,
    331–332, 331f, 333f
GLOBE project, 123
Glomb, Theresa, 132
Glo Salon & Spa, 452–453
goal orientation, 173
goals
    accomplishment of, 5
    challenge of, 171, 178
    and commitment, 171, 171–172
    defined, 170
    and feedback, 171
    and group cohesiveness, 240–241, 242–243
    group goals, 173
    limitations of, 174
    and management by objectives, 211
    and motivation, 155, 170–174
    and organizational change, 569
    and organizational politics, 431
    for self-regulation, 64
    self-test, 183–184
    specificity, 171, 178
    subconscious goals, 175
    superordinate goals, 249, 463
goal setting theory
    and challenge, 171, 178
    and commitment, 171, 171–172
    defined, 170
    enhancing goal commitment, 171–172
    factors affecting, 173–174
    and feedback, 171
    goal orientation, 173
    integrated with other theories, 178, 178f
    kinds of goals, 170–171
    managerial implications of, 174
    mechanisms of, 171f
    and participation, 172
    and proximity, 173
    research support for, 173–174
    and rewards, 172
    specificity, 171, 178
    subconscious goals, 175
    and supportiveness, 172
good sports, 139
Google, 135, 262–263, 282, 286, 511, 522, 594
Gordon, Joe, 359
Gottlieb, Myron, 285

Gouldner, Alvin, 13
Government of Canada, 214
Grant, Adam, 208
grapevine, 357–358
Graves, Carol, 382
Great Britain
    cultural intelligence, 126
    and values, 121, 123
Great Little Box Company Ltd., 152–153
Great Place to Work Institute Canada, 101
Greece, 123
green initiatives
    as corporate social responsibility, 24
    Delta Chelsea Hotel, 24
    Fairmont Hotels and Resorts, 535
    Ford Motor Company, 530, 534
    Google Canada, 262
    Sodexo Canada, 2
Greenleaf, Robert, 330
Green Partnership Guide, 535
Gregersen, Hal, 325
group cohesiveness, 240–243, 241f, 243f
group decision making
    disadvantages of, 402–405
    quality of decisions, 402
    reasons for using groups, 401
    and risk, 405–406
group development, 231–233, 231f
group effort, 5
Group of 99, 562
groups
    and authentic leadership, 330
    cohesiveness of, 240–243, 241f
    and conflict, 454–456
    defined, 230
    effectiveness of, 248f
    and innovation, 592–593, 593f
    punctuated equilibrium model, 232–233, 232f
    and social loafing, 243–244
    structure of. see group structure
    teams. see teams
    types of, 230
group structure
    consequences of, 233–240
    defined, 233
    diversity, 235, 241–242
    group size, 233–235, 233f, 241–242
    norms, 235
    roles, 236–239
    and status, 239–240
    tasks, 233–234
groupthink, 403
growth needs, 161
growth need strength, 205

H

Hackman, J. Richard, 203–205, 210, 245
Haines, Avery, 114, 116–117
Hair on the Avenue, 452, 453
Hallmark, 594
halo effect, 106
Hambrick, Donald C., 540
hard factors, 576f
Hargadon, Andrew, 407
Harley-Davidson, 199, 570, 585, 592

Harper, Stephen, 437
harshness, 106, 106*f*
Hawthorne effect, 615
Hawthorne studies, 13
hazing, 287
helping behaviour, 139
Herrmann, Pol, 49
Hewlett-Packard, 211, 284–285, 322, 543, 575, 594
high-context cultures, 369*f*
Hilti (Canada) Corp., 281
hindrance stressors, 476
hindsight, 395–396
history, 612*f*
Hobbs, Leona, 27
Hodgetts, Richard, 16
Hoff, Timothy, 590
Hofstede, Geert, 19, 122–124
Holyday, Doug, 217
Honda, 570
honeymoon-hangover effect, 139*f*
Hong Kong, 123
hope, 22
Hore, Marlene, 453
horizontal communication, 355
horizontal division of labour, 495–497, 495*f*
hotlines, 377
House, Robert, 123, 315–317
Howe, Maria, 75–77
Howe 2 Ski Stores, 75–77
Howell, Jane, 591
Howell, Peggy, 111
Hudson's Bay Company, 25, 198, 304–306
humane orientation, 331*f*, 332
human relations movement, 13–14
human relations training, 610, 611*f*, 613, 614, 615
human resources
    employment interviews, 104–105
    and perception, 103–108
    performance appraisal, 105–108
    recruitment and selection, 103–104
human resources management, 6, 16
humility, 330
Humphrey, Stephen, 208
Husky Injection Molding Systems Ltd., 25, 198, 481
hybrid departmentation, 500–501
hypothesis, 604

I

Iansiti, Marco, 511
IBM, 27, 278, 284, 285, 286, 287, 582
ICRISAT, 345–351
idea champions, 591
idealized influence, 323–324
identification, 265, 440
identity, 82–83
IDEO, 228–229, 407
IKEA, 513, 514*f*, 589
Iksil, Bruno, 384
ill-structured problems, 387
illusion of invulnerability, 403
illusion of morality, 403
illusion of unanimity, 403
immigrants, 19–20, 91
Immigrant Success Awards, 108
implicit leadership theory, 331–332
implicit personality theories, 85

incentive compensation, 196. *see also* motivation
increasing resources, 462–463
independent variables, 604
indirectness, 364
individual behaviour
    and attitudes, 126–127
    extinction, 58
    increasing probability of, 54–56
    of leaders, 310–313
    negative reinforcement, 55
    persistent behaviour, 57
    positive reinforcement, 54–55
    and punishment, 58–60
    reducing probability of, 58–60
    reinforcement, 54–56
    reinforcement strategies, 57–58, 58*f*
    self-efficacy beliefs, 62–63, 63*f*
    self-regulation, 63–64
individualism, 123, 125*f*, 176–177
individualized consideration, 323
individualized socialization, 272–274, 272*f*
individual socialization tactics, 273*f*
Industrial Revolution, 201
industry culture, 441
influence, 433
influence tactics, 427–428
informal communication, 355
informal group, 230
informal socialization tactics, 273*f*
informational roles, 16
information dependence, 264
information exchange, 462
information overload, 390–391
information processing, 209*f*
information richness, 371
information search, 390–391
information seeking, 279*f*
information technology *see* advanced
    information technology
infrastructure, 98*f*
ingratiation, 427
in-group collectivism, 331*f*
initiating structure, 312
initiation, 242
innovation
    creative deviance, 591
    creativity, 589–591
    defined, 588
    and diffusion, 594–595
    and external communication, 591–592
    factors affecting, 594
    group longevity, communication
        and performance of R&D, 593*f*
    idea champions, 591
    idea generation, 589–594
    and internal communication, 592–593
    managerial innovations, 589
    process innovations, 589
    product innovations, 588
    and resources, 593–594
    and rewards, 594
innovation implementation failure, 590
Innovations in Diversity Award, 3
inputs, 129
inquisitiveness, 325
inspirational motivation, 323

institutional collectivism, 331*f*
institutionalization, 577–578
institutionalized socialization, 272–274, 272*f*
institutional managers, 428
instrumentality, 164, 178
instrumentation, 612*f*
integration, 503
integrative case, 34–40, 225–226, 488–489, 602
integrative negotiation, 460, 462–463
integrators, 503–504
integrity, 101
intellectual stimulation, 323
intelligence
    emotional intelligence, 157–158, 158*f*
    general cognitive ability, 156–157
    and performance, 156–159
intensive technologies, 549*f*, 550, 551
interactional fairness, 130, 140
interactional justice, 130
interactionism, 45
interactionist approach, 45, 50
interaction outside the organization, 209*f*
interdependence, 209*f*, 455, 544
interest groups, 535–536, 536*f*
interlocking directorates, 546
internalization, 265
internalized moral perspective, 329
internal validity, 611, 612*f*
International Crops Research Institute for the
    Semi-Arid Tropics, 345–351
international managers, 18–19
interpersonal acceptance, 330
interpersonal conflict, 454, 470–472. *see also* conflict
interpersonal influence, 433
interpersonal roles, 15
interpersonal skills, 53
interpretation, 80
interrole conflict, 238
intersender role conflict, 238
interviews
    for employment, 104–105
    as research, 608
intranets, 377
intrapersonal skills, 53
intrapreneurs, 591
intrasender role conflict, 238
intrinsic motivation, 155–156, 163
intuition, 18
investiture socialization tactics, 273*f*
ISE Communications, 257
Isenberg, Daniel, 18
Israel, 123
Ivancevich, John, 612, 613

J

J.C. Penney Company, 107
Jackson, Stephen, 453
Jago, Arthur, 319–321
Jameson, Al, 113
Janis, Irving, 403
Janssen-Ortho Inc., 211
Japan
    and absenteeism, 237
    job design, 210
    management style, 19
    and values, 121, 122, 123, 124

jargon, 359–360, 375
Javelin Technologies Inc., 202
Jedwab, Jack, 126
Jen, Mark, 359
Jet Republic, 560
job change negotiation, 279*f*
job characteristics model
    core job characteristics, 203–205
    critical psychological states, 205
    diagrammed, 203*f*
    introduced, 203
    moderators, 205
    and national culture, 210
    outcomes, 205
    research evidence, 205
job complexity, 209*f*
job demands-resources model, 470
Job Descriptive Index, 127
job design
    and advanced technology, 555, 556–557
    breadth, 201
    core job characteristics, 203–205, 203*f*, 204*f*
    defined, 200
    depth, 201
    and diagnosis, 207
    and division of labour, 496
    job characteristics model, 203–206, 203*f*
    job enlargement, 207
    job enrichment, 206–208
    job involvement, 206
    job rotation, 203
    job scope, 201–203, 201*f*
    and motivation, 201–203
    and national culture, 210
    new developments in, 208–210
    relational architecture of jobs, 209
    relational job design, 208–210
    rewards, demand for, 207
    socio-technical systems, 210
    as stressor, 468
    and structural problems, 519
    supervisory resistance, 208
    traditional views of, 201
    union resistance, 207
    and wage incentive plans, 192
    work design, 208, 209*f*
Job Diagnostic Survey, 204
job engorgement, 207
job enlargement, 207
job enrichment, 206–208
job feedback, 204, 204*f*
job insecurity, 472
job involvement, 206
job previews, 269–271, 270*f*
job redesign, 478
job rotation, 203
Jobs, Steve, 197, 323
job satisfaction
    and absenteeism, 136–137
    aspects of, 127
    and career opportunities, 134
    and cognitive demands, 132–133, 133*f*, 134
    consequences of, 136–141
    contributors to, 134–135
    and cultural differences, 131

job satisfaction *(continued)*
  and customer satisfaction, 140–141
  defined, 127
  determinants of, 128–133, 134*f*
  discrepancy theory, 128
  and disposition, 131
  and distributive fairness, 128–130, 140
  and emotion, 132–133, 133*f*
  equity theory, 129
  and fairness, 128, 140
  honeymoon-hangover effect, 139*f*
  and inputs, 129
  and interactional fairness, 130, 140
  and mentally challenging work, 134
  and mood, 132–133
  and organizational citizenship behaviour, 139–140
  and organizational commitment, 142
  and outcomes, 129
  and pay, 133, 134
  and people, 134–135
  and perception, 128
  and performance, 138–139
  and personality, 47, 53
  and procedural fairness, 130, 140
  and profit, 140–141
  progression of withdrawal, 140*f*
  ranking of occupations, 471*f*
  surveys, 127–128
  and turnover, 137–138
  and values, 128
  "very important" aspects of, 135*f*
job scope, 201–203, 201*f*
job search, 48
job sharing, 214–215
Johns, Gary, 237
joint venture, 544
Jones, Micah, 249
JPMorgan Chase, 384–385
Judge, Timothy, 52, 74
Juran, Joseph, 582
justification, 394–395

K

Kahneman, Daniel, 393
Kaljuste, Kadi, 426
Kammeyer-Mueller, John, 132
Kammeyer-Mueller, John D., 275
Kanter, Rosabeth Moss, 360, 423
Kapitonov, Vlad, 249
Keen, Linda, 437
Kelleher, Herb, 322
Kerviel, Jérôme, 396
KFC, 534
Kim, Steve, 249
Kirmac Collision Services, 42
Klotz, Bob, 452, 453
knowing-doing gap, 595–596
knowledge acquisition, 571
knowledge characteristics, 208, 209*f*
knowledge development, 571
knowledge hiding, 432
knowledge infrastructure, 572
knowledge management, 572
knowledge of results, 205
König, Cornelius, 367
Kotter, John, 17

Kowalski, Henry, 114, 116–117
KPMG, 36, 78–79
Kraft Foods, 534
Kroc, Ray, 285, 289, 506
Kruger, Jason, 373
Kulik, Jarmil, 452–453

L

L&H Marketing Research, 415–417
L'Oréal, 118–119, 534
labour
  coordination of, 501–504
  departmentation, 497–501
  division of, 494–501, 495*f*
  horizontal division of, 495–497, 495*f*
  vertical division of, 494–495, 495*f*
labour saving, 556
labour shortage, 22–23
labyrinth, 334
laissez-faire leadership, 333
Lanzolla, Gianvito, 552
Larsen & Shaw Ltd., 198
latchkey kids, 120
Latham, Gary, 175
law, respect for, 439
Lawrence, Paul, 541
Lazaridis, Mike, 404
leader behaviour, 316
leader-member exchange theory, 321–322
leader punishment behaviour, 312–313
leader reward behaviour, 312–313
leadership
  agentic leadership, 335, 335*f*
  authentic leadership, 328–330
  behaviour of leaders, 310–313, 316
  cognitive resource theory, 315
  communal leadership, 335, 335*f*
  consideration, 310–311, 312
  contingency theory, 313–315, 314*f*
  culturally endorsed implicit leadership
    theory, 332
  and culture, 331–332, 333*f*
  defined, 306
  development of, 311
  empowering leadership, 326–327
  ethical leadership, 327–328
  ethical leadership scale, 341–342
  and gender, 332–336, 335*f*, 337*f*
  global leadership, 325–326
  implicit leadership theory, 331–332
  initiating structure, 312
  laissez-faire leadership, 333
  leader categorization theory, 310
  leader-member exchange theory, 321–322
  management by exception, 322
  new and emerging theories of, 326–330
  participative leadership, 317–321, 332
  path-goal theory, 315–317, 316*f*
  punishment behaviour, 312–313
  and racial bias, 310
  reward behaviour, 312–313
  servant leadership, 330
  situational factors, 316–317
  situational theories of, 313–3107
  social exchange theory, 321–322
  strategic leadership, 306–307

traits of, 308–309, 308f
trait theory of leadership, 307–309
transactional leadership, 322
transformational leadership, 322–325, 577
Leadership Action Plan, 69
leadership roles, 15
Learjet, 560
learning
  cultural awareness, 53
  defined, 53
  employee learning, 53
  interpersonal skills, 53
  intrapersonal skills, 53
  learning effects, 59f
  observational learning, 61–62
  operant learning theory. see operant learning theory
  organizational learning practices, 65–69
  personal skills, 53
  practical skills, 53
  self-efficacy beliefs, 62–63, 63f
  self-regulation, 63–64
  social cognitive theory. see social cognitive theory
learning dynamics, 572
learning goal orientation, 173
learning organization, 572
learning systems, 572
least-preferred co-worker, 313
Le Calvez, Didier, 370
Lee, Cindy, 545
Lee, Ray, 436
Lee, SangYup, 249
Leeson, Nick, 396
legitimacy, 546–547
legitimate power, 420–421
Lego, 504
Leiter, Michael, 468
leniency, 106, 106f
Leonardelli, Geoffrey, 310
Levine, Dennis, 440
Lewenza, Ken, 220
Lewin, Kurt, 570, 571
Lewis, Josh, 147–151
Li, Andrew, 131
liaison roles, 15, 503
life satisfaction, 47
Likert, Rensis, 13
Lilliman, Nicole, 426
Lincoln Electric Company, 191, 287
Lipnack, Jessica, 507
listening, 374
Livent Inc., 285
lobbying, 542
Loblaw Companies Limited, 545, 557
Locke, Edwin, 52
locus of control, 48–49, 48f, 466
long-linked technologies, 549, 549f, 551
long-term orientation, 123
Lord & Taylor, 306
Lorsch, Jay, 541
Los Angeles Metropolitan Transportation
  Authority, 146
low-context cultures, 369f
loyalty, 123
lubricant expressions, 367
lump sum bonus, 195
Lupton, Tom, 606

Luthans, Fred, 16
Lutz, Robert, 464
Lyon, Herbert, 612, 613

M

Machiavellianism, 435–436
MacInnes, John, 283
Maclean's, 24
Macris, Achilles, 384
Madsen, Peter, 573
Magna International, 285, 513, 544
management. see also managers; organizational
    behaviour
  behavioural requirements, 19
  and bureaucracy, 11–13
  case incident, 29–30
  classical view, 11–13
  contemporary concerns, 19–25
  contemporary contingency approach, 14–15
  and corporate social responsibility, 23–25
  and culture, 19
  defined, 11
  diversity, 19–20
  early prescriptions for, 11–14
  and employee engagement, 23
  and employee well-being, 20–22
  evidence-based management, 11
  and globalization, 20
  human relations movement, 13–14
  scientific management, 13
  talent management, 22–23
  of teams, 247
  traditional management, 16
  trickle-down effects of abusive
      management, 62
  and work engagement, 23
  and work environment, 20–22
  of workforce diversity, 98–101
management by exception, 322
management by objectives, 210–212
management practices, 7, 8f
management training, 377–378
managerial activities, 16–17, 17f
managerial innovations, 589
managerial minds, 18
managerial roles, 15–16, 15f
managers
  activities of, 16–17, 17f
  agenda implementation, 17
  agenda setting, 17
  agendas of, 17
  international managers, 18–19
  managerial minds, 18
  networking, 17
  and power, 428, 429f
  roles of, 15–16, 15f
managing organizational behaviour, 11
Mancuso, Maureen, 352–353
manufacturing technology, 553–555
Maple Leafs Foods, 328, 329
Marriott, 584
Marshall, Marianne, 453
Martin, Rolin, 184–187
Mary Kay Cosmetics, 285, 289
Maslach, Christina, 468
Maslow, Abraham, 159

Maslow's hierarchy of needs, 159–160, 160*f*, 161, 163, 202
mass technologies, 550, 551
matrix departmentation, 499–500, 499*f*
maturation, 612*f*
Mawritz, Mary Bardes, 62
maximization, 392, 393
Mayer, John, 158
Mayflower Group, 582
Mayo, Elton, 13
Mazey, Chip, 485–488
McCain, Michael, 328, 329
McClelland, David, 162–163, 428
McClelland's theory of needs, 162–163
McDonald's, 285, 289, 505, 506, 508–509, 535
McFarlan, F. Warren, 510
McNerney, Jim, 328
meaningfulness, 205
mechanistic structure, 508–509, 508*f*
mediating technologies, 549, 549*f*, 551
mediating variables, 604
mediation, 463
Meggy, Robert, 153, 154
Mehta, Sunita, 345
mentoring
    career functions of, 276
    explained, 275–276
    formal programs, 276
    psychosocial functions of, 276
    and race/ethnicity, 278
    research evidence, 278, 609
    and women, 276–278
mentors, 275, 424
Menzies, Brian, 453
Meredith, Jeff, 301
mergers, 543–544
merit pay plans
    defined, 193
    discrimination, 195
    ineffectiveness of, 195
    pay secrecy, 196–197, 197*f*
    problems with, 195–197
    small increases, 195
Merlo, Kamet, 419
Mesmer-Magnus, Jessica, 253
Mexico, 123
Meyer, John, 141, 143
Michaels, Barry, 414–416
Microsoft, 135, 285, 535, 544, 568
midpoint transition, 232
Milczyn, Peter, 194, 217
Milliken, 553
Mills, Dennis, 115
mindguards, 403
Minnesota Satisfaction Questionnaire, 127
Mintzberg, Henry, 15, 326, 607, 613
mobbing, 471
models
    of expectancy theory, 165*f*, 166*f*
    Five-Factor Model, 46–51, 46*f*
    integrative model of motivation theories, 178*f*
    job characteristics model, 205
    job demands-resources model, 469–470
    of job design, 203–206, 203*f*
    model of stress episode, 465*f*

of participative leadership, 319–321, 320*f*
punctuated equilibrium model, 232–233, 232*f*
of rational decision making, 388*f. see* rational decision making
for self-regulation, 64
of turnover, 138*f*
Vroom and Jago's model, 319–321, 320*f*
moderating variables, 604
moderators, 205
Modern Appliances, 295–302
modular organization, 512–513, 513*f*
Molloy, John T., 362
monitor roles, 16
mood
    and decision making, 397–398
    defined, 132
    and job satisfaction, 132–133
Mooney, James D., 11
Moore, Karl, 326
Morgeson, Frederick, 208
Morrison, Allen, 325
mortality, 612*f*
motivation
    autonomous motivation, 156
    characteristics of, 154–155
    and compensation. *see* compensation
    controlled motivation, 156
    and culture, 175–178
    defined, 154
    and direction, 155
    and diversity, 163
    and effort, 154
    and goals, 155
    inspirational motivation, 323
    intrinsic motivation, 155–156, 163
    money as motivator. *see* compensation
    motivation-performance relationship, 159
    and participative leadership, 318
    and performance, 156–159
    and persistence, 154
    and personality, 47, 52
    prosocial motivation, 209
    reasons to study, 154
    and self-determination theory, 156
motivation practices
    alternative working schedules, 212–216
    compensation, 190–200
    employee stock ownership plans, 198
    gainsharing, 198–199
    job design, 200–210
    management by objectives, 210–212
    merit pay plans, 193–197
    in perspective, 216–217
    profit sharing, 198
    skill-based pay, 199–200
    teamwork pay plans, 197–200, 200*f*
    wage incentive plans, 190–193
motivation theories
    and compensation, 190
    equity theory, 168–170
    expectancy theory, 164–168
    extrinsic motivation, 155–156
    goal setting theory, 170–174
    integrating theories of, 178–180
    integrative model of motivation theories, 178*f*
    and job scope, 202

need theories of work motivation.
    see need theories of work motivation
process theories of work motivation.
    see process theories of work motivation
theories of. see motivation theories
Motorola, 199
multisource feedback, 376
mum effect, 356–357
mutual adjustment, 502–503

N

Nadkarni, Sucheta, 49
Nambisan, Satish, 514
name discrimination, 94
narcissism, 540
NASA, 257–258, 285, 397, 403, 500, 518, 520
National Association to Advance Fat
    Acceptance, 111
National Institute for Occupational Safety and
    Health, 465
National Research Council, 544
Nebenzahl, Donna, 118
need, and distributive fairness, 130
need for achievement, 162
need for affiliation, 162
need for power, 162–163, 428
needs
    Alderfer's ERG theory, 161, 163
    Maslow's hierarchy of, 159–160, 163
    Maslow's versus Alderfer's, 160f, 161
    McClelland's theory of, 162–163
need theories of work motivation
    Alderfer's ERG theory, 161
    defined, 159
    and diversity, 163
    integrated with other theories, 178f, 180
    and intrinsic motivation, 163–164
    managerial implications of, 163–164
    Maslow's hierarchy of needs, 159–160
    Maslow's versus Alderfer's, 160f, 161
    McClelland's theory of needs, 162–163
    research support for, 163
Neeleman, David, 546–547
negative affectivity, 51, 466–467
negative reinforcement, 55, 59f
Neglia, Perry, 452–453
negotiation
    arbitration, 463–464
    defined, 459
    distributive negotiation, 460–461, 460f
    integrative negotiation, 460, 462–463
    mediation, 463
    third party involvement, 463–464
negotiator roles, 16
Nembhard, Ingrid, 590
nepotism, 368
Netflix, 27
Netherlands, 19
networking
    as managerial activity, 16, 17
    as political skill, 433–434, 434f
    as proactive socialization behaviour, 279f
network organization, 510–512, 511f, 514
neuroticism, 46
Newton, Sally, 600–602
New Zealand, 123

NeXT Computers, 197
Ng, Thomas W.H., 157
Nicholson, Nigel, 492–493
Nigeria, 123
Nike, 512, 592
Nixon, Christine, 579, 596
Noble, Terry, 34–40
Nolin, Rosalie, 119
nominal group technique, 408
nonroutine technologies, 548, 548f, 551
non-sanctioned means, 431f, 432
non-verbal communication, 360–363,
    365–366, 371, 373
Nordstrom, 425
NORDX/CDT, 214
normative commitment, 141, 142
norming, 231
norms
    in action, 237
    conformity to, 265
    defined, 235
    development of, 235–236
    types of, 236
North America
    demographics, 19–20
    management style, 19
not-sanctioned ends, 431f, 432
n Pow, 162–163, 428
Nucor, 191
Nutt, Paul, 393

O

O'Reilly, Charles, 510
O'Sullivan, Sonia, 175
objective measures, 105–106
observability, 595
observational learning, 61–62
observational research
    and causation, 609
    correlational research, 608–609, 610f
    defined, 605
    direct observation, 607–608
    ethical issues, 606
    participant observation, 606–607
occupation ranking, 471f
office decor, 361–362, 362f
office technology, 555–557
Oldham, Greg, 203, 210
Olympus, 442
one up, one down, 363, 364
Ontario Human Rights Commission,
    97, 98
Ontario Lottery and Gaming
    Corporation, 195
openness to experience, 47
open systems, 533, 533f
operant learning theory
    defined, 54
    and diversity, 56
    increasing probability of behaviour, 54–56
    negative reinforcement, 55
    organizational errors, 55–56
    positive reinforcement, 54–55
    reducing probability of behaviour, 58–60
    reinforcement strategies, 57–58
    rewards versus reinforcers, 55, 69

optimism, 22
Oracle Corp., 543–544
Oracle Corporation, 284
Orange, 252, 254
Oreopoulos, Philip, 94
organic structure, 508–509, 508*f*
organizational behaviour. *see also* management
　areas of study, 5
　best companies, 8, 9
　and bureaucracy, 11–13
　case incident, 29–30
　classical view, 11–13
　contemporary contingency approach, 14–15
　cultural implications, 124
　defined, 5
　and diversity, 19–20
　early prescriptions for, 11–14
　and employee engagement, 23
　and employee well-being, 20–22
　explaining, 10
　goals of, 10–11
　and green initiatives, 24
　and group effort, 5
　human relations movement, 13–14
　human resources management. *see*
　　human resources management
　importance of, 7
　interactionist approach, 45, 50
　interesting nature of, 7
　issues in, 6
　knowledge of, 8–10
　and management style, 19
　managing, 11
　negative affectivity, 51
　new developments in, 50–53
　in the news, 29
　and personality, 45–51
　positive affectivity, 51
　practices of effective companies, 7, 8*f*
　predicting, 10
　reasons to study, 6–8
　research into. *see* organizational
　　behaviour research
　scientific management, 13
　and self-monitoring, 49–50
　situational approach, 45
　for survival and adaptation, 5
　and talent management, 22–23
　and teamwork, 5
　trait activation theory, 46
　on TV, 28–29
　and work environment, 20–22
organizational behaviour modification,
　65–66, 65*f*
organizational behaviour research
　combining techniques, 613
　continuum of techniques, 612–613, 613*f*
　and ethics, 615
　experimental techniques, 610–612
　Hawthorne effect, 615
　hypothetical data, 611*f*
　issues in, 614–615
　measurement of variables, 605
　observational research techniques, 605–610
　sampling, 614
　variables, 604–605

organizational change. *see also* organizational
　development
　challenges in, 576*f*
　change agents, 574
　and culture, 570
　diagnosis, 574
　and environmental change and organizational
　　effectiveness, 569*f*
　and evaluation, 577
　factors that can be changed, 569–570
　goals and strategies, 569
　innovation process, 588–595
　institutionalization of, 577–578
　issues in, 574–578
　and job design, 569
　knowing-doing gap, 595–596
　and organizational development. *see*
　　organizational development
　and organizational learning, 571–574
　and people, 570
　planned change, 578
　probability of acceptance, 576*f*
　problems with, 574*f*
　and processes, 570
　process of, 570–571, 574*f*
　reasons for, 568–569
　refreezing, 571
　resistance to, 575–577
　and structure, 570
　and technology, 569
　unfreezing, 570
organizational citizenship behaviour, 139–140.
　see also corporate social responsibility
organizational commitment
　consequences of, 142
　contributors to, 142
　defined, 141
　types of, 141
　and workplace changes, 143
organizational culture
　Canada's 10 most admired, 282*f*
　contributors to, 285–287
　core culture, 287
　defined, 280
　diagnosing, 287–289
　and ethics, 441
　founder's role, 285–286
　and resistance to change, 575
　and socialization, 286–287
　strong culture, 281–285
　Victoria Police Force, 579
organizational development. *see also*
　organizational change
　effectiveness of, 587–588, 587*f*
　and organizational change, 578
　organizational processes, 585
　problems with, 588
　reengineering, 585–587
　strategies for, 580–587
　survey feedback, 581–582, 582*f*
　team building, 580–581
　total quality management,
　　582–585, 583*f*
organizational folklore, 287
organizational identification, 266, 440
organizational justice theory, 103–104

organizational learning
  behaviour modelling training, 68
  career development, 69
  dimensions of, 572
  employee recognition, 66–67, 66f
  importance of, 573
  methods of, 571
  organizational behaviour modification, 65–66
  peer recognition, 66–67, 69
  training and development, 67–68
organizational politics
  basics of, 431–433
  defensiveness, 436–437
  defined, 431
  dimensions of, 431f
  Machiavellianism, 435–436
  political skill, 433–434
organizational processes, 585
organizational socialization
  employee orientation programs,
    271–272
  explained, 265
  job previews, 269–271, 270f
  mentoring, 275–279
  methods of, 269–279
  proactive socialization, 279, 279f
  process of, 266f
  research evidence, 274
  stages of, 266–267, 267f
  steps in, 286f
  and strong culture, 286–287
  tactics of, 272–274, 272f, 273f, 275
organizational structure
  and advanced technology, 554–555, 556
  ambidextrous organization, 509–510
  boundaryless organization, 514–515
  centralization, 505–506
  complexity, 507, 515
  contemporary structures, 509–515
  coordination of labour, 501–504
  defined, 494
  division of labour, 494–501, 495f
  downsizing, 516–519
  and environmental uncertainty,
    541–542
  flat organization, 504, 505f
  formalization, 505
  mechanistic structure, 508–509, 508f
  modular organization, 512–513, 513f
  network organization, 510–512, 511f, 514
  organic structure, 508–509, 508f
  and organizational change, 570
  and size, 515–519, 516f
  span of control, 504, 505f
  symptoms of structural problems,
    519–520
  tall organization, 504, 505f
  and technology, 550–551
  traditional characteristics of, 504–508
  virtual organization, 511–512, 511f
organizational support theory, 102
organizations
  characteristics of, 4–5
  defined, 4
  and expectations, 267–269
  and goal accomplishment, 5

  and group effort, 5
  social influence in, 264–265
  as social inventions, 4–5
orientation, 271–272
Orkin/PCO Services Corp., 20
outcomes
  defined, 129
  and expectancy theory, 164, 165f
  in job characteristics model, 203f, 205
outsiders, 423
overall satisfaction, 127
overconforming, 436
overpayment, 169

P

pace of life, 368f
Pacheco, Luis, 452, 453
Pacific Gas and Electric, 535
Page, Larry, 262
Pakistan, 123, 125f, 176
Pandry, George, 184–187
Papis, Bryan, 484–485
para-verbal cues, 371
pareto analysis, 584
Parsons, Rick, 382–384
participant observation, 606–607
participant selection, 612f, 614
participation, 172
participative leadership
  advantages of, 318–319
  defined, 316, 317, 332
  problems of, 319
  range of participation, 318f
  Vroom and Jago's model, 319–321, 320f
Pascale, Richard, 286
path-goal theory, 315–317, 316f
Patten, Rich, 485
Paulson, Bob, 340–341
pauses, 374
pay. see also compensation
  and job satisfaction, 133, 134
  overpayment, 169
  underpayment, 169
pay for knowledge, 199–200
pay secrecy, 196–197, 197f
PCL Constructors, 198
Pearsons, Lee, 188
peer recognition, 69
peer recognition programs, 66–67
peers, 424
Peirce, Ellen, 443
people
  and job satisfaction, 134–135
  and organizational change, 570
perceived organizational support,
  101–103, 103f
perceiver, 81
perception
  and attribution, 87–91
  basic biases in person perception,
    84–87
  components of, 80–82
  defined, 80
  and diversity, 91–101
  in employment interview, 104–105
  factors that influence, 81f

perception *(continued)*
    in human resources, 103–108
    implicit personality theories, 85
    and job satisfaction, 128
    perceptual process, 83–84, 83*f*
    and performance appraisal, 105–108
    primacy effect, 84
    projection, 85
    and race and gender, 81*f*
    recency effect, 84
    in recruitment and selection, 103–104
    reliance on central traits, 85
    signalling theory, 103
    and social identity theory, 82–83
    stereotyping, 86–87
    of trust, 101–103
    weight-based bias, 86
perceptual defence, 81, 389
perceptual process, 83–84, 83*f*
perfect rationality, 387–388, 400*f*
performance. *see also* motivation
    changes in, 476
    defined, 156
    and education, 157
    and emotional intelligence, 158
    factors contributing to, 156*f*
    and group structure, 233–235, 233*f*
    and intelligence, 156–159
    and job satisfaction, 138–139
    and motivation, 156–159
    motivation-performance relationship,
        159
    and organizational commitment, 142
    and pay on production jobs, 190–193
    and pay on white-collar jobs, 193–197
    and personality, 156
    and power, 427*f*
    and subconscious goals, 175
performance appraisals
    behaviourally anchored rating scale,
        107, 107*f*
    central tendency, 106, 106*f*
    frame-of-reference training, 108
    halo effect, 106
    harshness, 106, 106*f*
    leniency, 106, 106*f*
    objective measures, 105–106
    and perception, 105–108
    rater errors, 106–108
    similar-to-me effect, 106–107
    subjective measures, 106–108
performance-avoid goal orientation,
    173
performance feedback, 56, 162
performance goals, 170
performance norms, 236
performance orientation, 331*f*
performance-prove goal orientation,
    173
performing, 231
Perrow, Charles, 548, 551
persistence, 154
persistent behaviour, 57
person–situation debate, 45
personal character, 325
personal identity, 82

personality
    agreeableness, 47
    behavioural plasticity theory, 50
    Big Five, 46–51, 46*f*, 131
    and career success, 48
    of CEO, and firm performance, 49
    conscientiousness, 47
    core self-evaluations, 52–53
    defined, 44
    dispositional approach, 45
    emotional stability, 46
    and ethics, 441
    extraversion, 46
    Five-Factor Model, 46–51, 46*f*
    general self-efficacy, 52, 73
    interactionist approach, 45, 50
    and job satisfaction, 47, 131
    and job search, 48
    locus of control, 48–49, 48*f*
    and motivation, 47
    negative affectivity, 51
    neuroticism, 46
    new developments in, 50–53
    openness to experience, 47
    and organizational behaviour, 45–51
    and performance, 156
    plasticity, 50
    positive affectivity, 51
    proactive behaviour, 52
    proactive personality, 52, 73
    research on, 47–48
    self-efficacy, 22
    self-efficacy beliefs, 62–63, 63*f*
    self-esteem, 50–51
    self-monitoring, 49–50
    situational approach, 45
    and stress, 466–467
    trait activation theory, 46
personal power managers, 428
personal skills, 53
person-job fit, 266
person-organization fit, 266
person perception *see* perception
persons with disabilities
    Canadian National Institute for
        the Blind, 113
    Society for Manitobans with
        Disabilities, 99
    as workforce demographic, 19
persuasion, 461
Peters, Tom, 5, 249
Pfeffer, Jeffrey, 7, 595–596
Philip Morris, 544
Philippines, 123
Phillips, Katherine, 310
Photon Control Inc., 214
physical appearance, 85, 86
physical demands, 209*f*
physical health, 471*f*
physiological needs, 159
piece-rate, 190
Pitney Bowes Canada, 203
Pixar, 135
plasticity, 50
playing dumb, 432
playing hooky, 72

podcasts, 377
politeness, 366–367
political skill, 433–434
politics
  as external factor, 535
  organizational politics. *see*
    organizational politics
  and power, 431–437
  and resistance to change, 575
pooled interdependence, 549, 549*f*
poppies, 411–412
Portugal, 123
positive affectivity, 51
positive reinforcement, 54–55, 59*f*
Post-it notes, 588
power
  bases of, 420–422, 427
  and centrality, 430
  coercive power, 421
  and conflict, 455
  defined, 420
  employee response to, 422*f*
  empowerment, 424–427
  expert power, 422
  influence tactics, 427–428
  legitimate power, 420–421
  need for power, 162–163, 428
  obtaining, 423–424, 429–431
  and performance, 427*f*
  and politics, 431–437
  power seekers, 428–429
  referent power, 421
  reward power, 421
  and scarcity, 429–430
  and strategic contingencies, 429–431
  and uncertainty, 430
power and substitutability, 430–431
power distance, 123, 125*f*, 177, 331*f*
power needs, 162
practical skills, 53
predicting organizational behaviour, 10
preference, 120
presenteeism, 237, 477
Pret A Manger, 247
primacy effect, 84, 104
proactive behaviour, 52
proactive personality, 52, 73
proactive socialization, 279, 279*f*
problems, 386–387, 389–390, 548, 548*f*
problem solving, 209*f*, 475
procedural fairness, 130, 140
procedural justice, 130
process, and organizational change, 570
process conflict, 456
process innovations, 589
process losses, 234
process technologies, 550, 551
process theories of work motivation
  defined, 164
  equity theory, 168–170
  expectancy theory, 164–168
  goal setting theory, 170–174
product champion, 591
product departmentation, 498, 498*f*
product innovations, 588
production jobs, 190–193

productivity
  and absenteeism, 21
  and group cohesiveness, 243*f*
  and psychological and social processes, 13
  restriction of, 192–193
  and wage incentive plans, 192–193, 193*f*
Profiles in Diversity Journal, 3
profit, and job satisfaction, 140–141
profit sharing, 198, 200*f*
programs, 386
project champion, 591
project groups, 592–593
projection, 85, 477
project team, 230
promises, 461
promotion, 287
prosocial motivation, 209
prototypes, 82
proximal goals, 173, 174
Prue, Michael, 176
psychological capital, 22
psychological contract, 268–269
psychological contract breach, 268–269
psychological safety, 356
psychological states, 205
psychological well-being, 471*f*
public relations, 542
Pulse Survey, 34, 37, 37*f*, 39
punctuality, 368
punctuated equilibrium model,
  232–233, 232*f*
punishment
  defined, 58
  effective use of, 59–60
  learning effects, 59*f*
punishment behaviour, 312–313

Q

quality
  definitions of, 585
  and participative leadership, 318
  and wage incentive plans, 191
quality control circles, 210
quasi-experimental design, 615
query systems, 377
question consistency, 105
questions
  and gender, 364
  and good communication, 374
question sophistication, 105

R

race
  and leadership, 310
  and mentoring, 278
racial stereotyping, 93–94
Rae, John, 113
Rafaeli, Anat, 613
Rafferty, John M., 113
Ragins, Belle Rose, 609, 613
Ramanujam, Rangaraj, 590
random assignment, 614
random sampling, 614
random socialization tactics, 273*f*
rapport building, 105, 373
rater errors, 106–108

rational decision making
  alternative development, 391–393
  bounded rationality, 388, 392, 400*f*
  cognitive biases, 388
  and emotions, 396–397
  framing, 388, 389–390
  information search, 390–391
  justification, 394–395
  model of, 388*f*
  and mood, 397–398
  perfect rationality, 387–388, 400*f*
  problem identification, 389–390
  risk, 393–394
  solution evaluation, 394–395
  solution implementation, 394
rationality, 427
rationalization, 403, 477
rationalized hiding, 432
Raven, Bertram, 420
RCMP, 285, 340–341, 418–419
reaction formation, 477
realistic job previews, 269–271, 270*f*
Realistic Orientation Program for Entry Stress,
  271–272
reality shock, 268, 269
recency effect, 84
reciprocal interdependence, 549*f*, 550
recognition programs, 66–67, 66*f*, 69
recruitment
  and perception, 103–104
  signalling theory, 103
  for virtual teams, 253
  and workforce diversity, 98*f*
Redies, Tracy, 280
Red River College, 99
reduced cooperation, 192
Reebok, 512
Reed, George, 600
reengineering, 585–587
referent power, 421–422
refreezing, 571
rehearsing, for self-regulation, 64
Reichardt, Carl, 288
reinforcement
  defined, 54
  and diversity, 56
  extinction, 58
  negative reinforcement, 55
  and organizational behaviour
    modification, 65–66, 65*f*
  organizational errors, 55–56
  performance feedback, 56
  positive reinforcement, 54–55
  and punishment, 58–60
  rewards versus reinforcers, 55
  for self-regulation, 64
  social recognition, 56
  sources of, 56
  strategies for, 57–58, 58*f*
relatedness needs, 161
relational architecture of jobs, 209
relational job design, 208–210
relational transparency, 329
relationship building, 279*f*
relationship conflict, 456
relationship orientation, 313–315

relative advantage, 595
relevant activities, 423
reliability, 605
reliance on others, 206
religious stereotyping, 93–94
research *see* organizational behaviour research
Research Focus
  best companies, 9
  CEO narcissism and firm strategy, 540
  CEO personality and firm performance, 49
  education and job performance, 157
  leadership and racial bias, 310
  norms in action, 237
  organizational learning, 573
  presenteeism, 477
  subconscious goals and motivation, 175
  technology, 552
  trickle-down effects of abusive management, 62
  weight-based bias, 86
Research in Motion, 135, 404, 534
resilience, 22
resistance, 284, 575–577
resource allocation roles, 16
resource dependence, 538–539
responsibility, 205, 467
restriction of productivity, 192–193
retention, 98*f*
reward allocation norms, 236
reward behaviour, 312–313
reward power, 421
rewards. *see also* compensation
  and commitment, 172
  demand for, 207
  and innovation, 594
  versus reinforcers, 55, 69
  and socialization, 287
  suggestion systems, 376–377
  and teams, 247
Rich, Bruce L., 275
Riddiford, David, 305
RIM, 135, 404, 534
Rising Entertainment, 147–151
risk, 393–394, 405–406, 405*f*
risky shifts, 405–406, 405*f*
ritual opposition, 364
rituals, 288–289
Ritz-Carlton, 411–412
Roberts, Chris, 2
Robertson, Russ, 36
Roddick, Anita, 358
Roethlisberger, Fritz, 13
Rogers Communications, 214
role ambiguity, 237–238, 474
role assumption process, 237*f*
role conflict, 238–239, 440, 468
role management, 267
role models, 276, 287
role overload, 467
role-playing, 412–413
roles
  conflict in, 238–239
  in groups, 236–239
Rompré, Marjolaine, 118
ROPES, 271–272
Rosen, Benson, 443
Rosenkrantz, Stuart, 16

Rosette, Ashleigh, 310
Rotundo, Maria, 132
Rousseau Muskoka, 176
routine communication, 16
routineness, 548–549, 548*f*
routines, 386
routine technologies, 548, 548*f*, 551
Royal Bank of Canada, 198
Royal Canadian Mounted Police, 285, 340–341,
    418–419
Rudolph, Cort, 86
rules, 14, 386
rules of thumb, 386
Rumour Mill, 352–353
rumours, 358
Rusnak, John, 396
Russia, 123

S

safe haven law, 387
safety needs, 159–160
Salomn, Mika, 186–187
Salovey, Peter, 158
Samarin, David, 448–451
sampling, 614
Samsung, 125, 569, 570
sanctioned ends, 431, 431*f*
sanctioned means, 431, 431*f*, 432
SARS, 532
satisficing, 392–393
Saturn, 595
Savaria, Dominic, 119
saving face, 177
savvy, 325
Sawhney, Mohanbir, 515
Scanlon, Joe, 199
Scanlon Plan, 199
scapegoating, 437
scarcity, 429–430, 456
Schaufeli, Wilmar, 468
Schein, Edgar, 272
Schermerhorn, John, 327
Schulze, Dick, 566, 567, 570
Schwarzkopf, "Stormin'" Norman, 323
scientific management, 13
Scotiabank, 336
Scott, Kimberly, 9
Scott, Rebecca, 447
Sears, 141
security, 118
selection, and perception, 103–104
selection of participants, 612*f*, 614
selectivity, 84
self-actualization needs, 160, 176
self-awareness, 329
self-censorship, 403
self-determination theory, 156
self-efficacy, 22
self-efficacy beliefs, 62–63, 63*f*
self-esteem, 50–51, 454
self-interest, 575
self-managed teams, 245–247, 503
self-monitoring, 49–50
self-observation data, 64
self-presentation bias, 367
self-protective leadership, 332

self-regulation, 63–64
self-selection, 270
self-serving bias, 90–91
sense of ownership, 198
sequential interdependence, 549, 549*f*
sequential socialization tactics, 273*f*
serial socialization tactics, 273*f*
servant leadership, 330
sexual harassment, 418–419, 442–444, 474
Shantz, Amanda, 175
shared mental models, 250
Sharma, Surya Kant, 345
Shaw, Miranda, 382–384
shelfware, 552
Shell Canada Ltd., 96
shock absorbers, 543
shocks, 137–138
short-term orientation, 123
showrooming, 567
Sicard, John, 288
sick leave, 64
signalling theory, 103
silos, 595
Silva, Fernanda, 100
similar-to-me effect, 106–107
Simon, Herbert, 18
Simon, Lauren S., 275
simple environment, 537, 538*f*
sincerity, 433
Singapore
    management style, 19
    and values, 123
Singapore Airlines, 573
situation, as component of perception, 82
situational approach, 45
situational attribution, 87
situational factors, 316–317
situational theories of leadership, 313–3107
size, 515–519, 516*f*
skill-based pay, 199–200, 200*f*
skills
    communication skills, 377–378
    and intelligence, 590
    interpersonal skills, 53
    intrapersonal skills, 53
    practical skills, 53
skill variety, 203, 204*f*, 208, 209*f*
Skinner, B.F., 54
slang, 375
Slovakia, 123
Smart, Steven, 447
Smith, Bob, 414–416
Smith, Roger B., 562
Smolinski, Carol, 443
social astuteness, 433
social categories, 82
social characteristics, 208, 209*f*
social cognitive theory
    explained, 60–61
    observational learning, 61–62
    self-efficacy beliefs, 62–63, 63*f*
    self-regulation, 63–64
social conformity, 265
social conventions, 367–368
social exchange theory, 321–322
social identity theory, 82–83

social influence, 264–265
social information processing theory, 264
social inventions, 4–5
socialization, 265. *see also*
  organizational socialization
socialization tactics, 272–274, 272f, 273f, 275
social loafing, 243–244
Social Media Group, 27
social/political factors, 535
social recognition, 56
social responsibility, 23–25
social ritual, 607
social support, 209f, 475–476
Société Générale, 396
Society for Human Resource Management, 135
Society for Manitobans with Disabilities, 99
socio-technical systems, 210
Sodexo Canada, 2–3, 23–24
soft factors, 576f
Solar Press, 192
solution evaluation, 394–395
solution implementation, 394
solutions, 389
Song, Fei, 196
South Korea, 123
Southwest Airlines, 322
span of control, 504, 505f, 522
speaking up, 356
specialization, 14, 209f
specificity, 171, 178
spiritual workplace, 21
spokesperson roles, 16
sponsors, 424
Sputnik, 573
stability, 246
staffing and infrastructure, 98f
stakeholders, 437
stalling, 436
Stamps, Jeffrey, 507
Standard Grooming Products, 414–416
standardization of outputs, 501–502
standardization of skills, 502
standardization of work processes, 501
standard operating procedures, 386
Starbucks, 543
static environment, 537, 538f
statistical process control, 585
statistical regression, 612f
status
  and conflict, 455
  defined, 239
  in groups, 239–240
Staw, Barry, 394
Steelcase, 191
Steele, Nancy, 100, 108
stereotype threat, 93
stereotyping
  age, 96–98
  defined, 86
  in employment interview, 104
  ethnic, 93–94
  explained, 86–87
  gender, 94–96
  of generations, 120
  of outsiders, 403
  racial, 93–94

religious, 93–94
  stereotype threat, 93
  and workforce diversity, 92–98
stewardship, 330
Stewart, Jim, 600
stockpiling, 542
Stoner, J.A.F., 405
stories, 287, 289
storming, 231
straight talk, 369
strategic alliances, 544–546
strategic contingencies, 429–431
strategic flexibility, 49
strategic leadership, 306–307
strategy
  acquisitions, 543–544, 557
  and CEO narcissism, 540
  defined, 539
  and environmental uncertainty,
    539–547, 539f
  establishing legitimacy, 546–547
  interlocking directorates, 546
  mergers, 543–544
  and organizational change, 574
  organizational structure as, 541–542
  strategic alliances, 544–546
  vertical integration, 542–543
stress. *see also* stressors
  behavioural reactions to, 475–476
  consequences of, 465–466
  coping strategies, 475f
  defined, 465
  family-friendly HR policies, 479
  job demands-resources model, 469–470
  and job redesign, 478
  management strategies, 478–481
  model of stress episode, 465f
  and personality, 466–467
  physiological reactions to, 478
  psychological reactions to, 476–478
  reactions to, 474–478
  stress-management programs, 479–481
  work-life balance programs, 481
stress episode, 465f
stressors. *see also* stress
  boundary role stressors, 468, 474f
  bullying, 470–472
  burnout, 468, 469f
  change, 472
  defined, 465
  emotional labour, 470
  executive and managerial stressors,
    467–468, 474f
  hindrance stressors, 476
  interpersonal conflict, 470–472
  job insecurity, 472
  operative-level stressors, 468, 474f
  role ambiguity, 474
  sexual harassment, 474
  types of, 467–474
  work-family conflict, 472
stress reactions, 465–466
stretch assignments, 202
Stronach, Frank, 285
strong culture
  assets of, 282–284

defined, 281
    liabilities of, 284–285
    pathology of, 285
structural inertia, 512
Suarez, Fernando, 552
subconscious goals, 175
subcultures, 281
subjective measures, 106–108
subordinates, 423–424
substance abuse, 476
substitutability, 430–431
success
    financial success, 283–284
    and group cohesiveness, 240–241,
        241f, 242
    and group diversity, 242
sucker effect, 244
suggestion systems, 376–377
Summerlee, Alastair, 352–353
sunk costs, 394
Sun Microsystems Inc., 544
superiors, 424
superordinate goals, 249, 463
supervision, 206
supervisory resistance, 208
suppliers, 534
supportive behaviour, 316
supportiveness, 172
survey feedback, 581–582, 582f, 583f
surveys, 376, 581–582, 608
Sutton, Robert, 407, 595–596, 606, 613
Swanson, Ted, 484–485
Sweden, 123
Switzerland, 237
symbols, 287–288
symptoms, 389
synchronous communication, 371, 371f
Szczepanowski, Janine, 188

T

T&T Supermarket, 545, 557
Taiwan
    management style, 19
    and values, 123
talent management, 22–23
talking it out, 476
tall organization, 505, 505f
Tannen, Deborah, 363–364
Tapon, Francis, 196
target
    of attitudes, 126
    as component of perception, 81–82
task characteristics, 208, 209f, 220–221
task conflict, 456
task forces, 230, 503
task identity, 204, 204f, 209f
task orientation, 313–315
task significance, 204, 204f, 209f
task variety, 208, 209f
Taylor, Bryce, 399, 409
Taylor, Frederick, 13, 201, 210
TD Bank Financial Group, 69
team building, 580–581
team-oriented leadership, 332
teams
    composition of, 246–247

and coordination of labour, 503
    cross-functional teams, 248–250, 503
    defined, 244, 580
    designing, 245–253
    effectiveness of, 248f, 249–250
    as panacea, 254
    self-managed teams, 245–247, 503
    supporting, 247
    tasks for, 245–246
    virtual teams, 250–253
teamwork
    and motivational pay, 197–200, 200f
    and organizational behaviour, 5
    and total quality management, 582, 583f, 584
technological interdependence, 549–550, 549f, 551
technological routineness, 548–549, 548f
technology
    adoption and use of, 552
    advanced information technology, 552–557
    craft technologies, 548, 548f, 551
    defined, 547
    dimensions of, 548–550
    engineering technologies, 548, 548f, 551
    and environment, 547
    as external factor, 535–536
    intensive technologies, 549f, 550, 551
    long-linked technologies, 549, 549f, 551
    mass technologies, 551
    mediating technologies, 549, 549f, 551
    nonroutine technologies, 548, 548f, 551
    and organizational change, 569
    and organizational structure, 550–551
    Perrow's routineness, 548–549, 548f, 551
    pooled interdependence, 549, 549f
    process technologies, 551
    reciprocal interdependence, 549f, 550
    routineness, 548–549, 548f
    routine technologies, 548, 548f, 551
    sequential interdependence, 549, 549f
    technological interdependence, 549–550, 549f, 551
    Thompson's interdependence, 549–550, 549f, 551
    unit technologies, 551
    Woodward's production processes, 550, 551
telecommuting, 215–216
telephone hotlines, 377
TELUS, 21–22
Telvent Canada Ltd., 276
Teo, Andrew, 223–225
Teo, Kai San, 223–225
testing, 612f
The Bay, 25, 198, 304–306
The Hacker Company, 599
The Manager's Notebook
    American Express Canada, 108
    bullying, 481
    Business Development Bank of Canada, 337
    Calgary Airport Authority, 69
    Capital One, 144
    centralization, 420
    cross-cultural communication, 378
    employee recognition, 69
    error prevention, 409
    ethics, 445
    Four Seasons, 378
    immigrant strategy, 69
    job satisfaction, 144

The Manager's Notebook *(continued)*
   Kinaxis, 290
   leadership practices, 337
   Loblaw Companies Limited, 557
   merit pay plans, 217
   motivation, 179
   Orange, 254
   organizational behaviour, 25
   organizational change, 596
   organizational culture, 290, 596
   Rousseau Muskoka, 179
   T&T Supermarket, 557
   Toronto City Hall, 217
   Toronto General Hospital, 409
   Toronto Transit Commission, 25
   Toyota, 520
   Veterans Affairs, 481
   Victoria Police Force, 596
   virtual teams, 254
   Yahoo!, 445
Thomas, Kenneth, 457
Thomas, Terry, 327
Thompson, James D., 548, 551
Thompson, Scott, 439, 445
Thompson's interdependence,
   549–550, 549*f*
Thoresen, Carl, 74
threat, 240
threats, 461
threats to internal validity, 611, 612*f*
3M Company, 588, 593, 594
360-degree feedback, 376
time, and innovation, 594
time management, 475
time theft, 182–183
Tim Hortons, 426
tips, 176
Toews, Vic, 341
top employers, 189
Topolnytsky, Laryssa, 143
Toronto City Hall, 194, 217
Toronto District School Board, 72, 561–562
Toronto General Hospital, 399, 409
Toronto Region Immigrant Employment
   Council, 108
Toronto Transit Commission, 12, 25
total quality management, 582–585, 583*f*
touch, 366
Touché, Christophe, 414
Toyota, 517, 595
Traditionalists
   background of, 120
   stereotyping, 120
   values of, 118
traditional management, 16
training
   and decision making, 406
   and development, 67–68
   diversity training programs, 99
   management training, 377–378
   and socialization, 287
   and teams, 247
   and total quality management, 584–585
   types of, 247
   for virtual teams, 253
   and workforce diversity, 98*f*

trait activation theory, 46
traits, 308–309, 308*f*
trait theory of leadership, 308–309
transactional leadership, 322
transformational leadership, 322–325, 577
Tremblay, Cynthia, 68
triadic reciprocal causation, 61
trialability, 595
Trougakos, John, 432
trust
   defined, 101
   and perceived organizational support,
      101–103, 103*f*
   perceptions of, 101–103
   and resistance to change, 575
Trust Index, 101, 102*f*
Turner, Graham "Sckroo", 492–493, 506
turnover
   factors in, 137–138
   and job satisfaction, 137–138
   model of, 138*f*
   and organizational behaviour, 10
   and organizational commitment, 142
Turtle Island Recycling, 24
Tushman, Michael, 510
Tversky, Amos, 393
Type A behaviour pattern, 466

U

U.S. Department of Energy, 506
Ubisoft, 512, 513
unbridled inquisitiveness, 325
uncertainty, 430. *see also* environmental uncertainty
uncertainty avoidance, 123, 331*f*
underinvestment in social capital, 336
underpayment, 169
unethical behaviour, 440–441
unfreezing, 568, 570
Unilever Canada, 24
Union Pacific Railroad, 544
unions
   Canadian Auto Workers, 220
   and job enrichment, 207
   United Auto Workers, 533, 562
United Auto Workers, 533, 562
United States
   and gender roles, 123
   and values, 121, 123
unit technologies, 550, 551
University of Guelph, 352–353
University of Michigan Survey of Organizations, 581
unlimited vacation policy, 27
unrealistic expectations, 268
UPS, 386–387
Upton, Greg, 524
upward appeal, 427
upward communication, 355
Urwick, Lyndall, 11
USA Today, 510

V

vacation, unused, 484
vacation policy, 27, 122*f*
valence, 164–165
validity, 605

values
    appreciation of global customers, 125
    and attitudes, 127
    collectivism, 123
    cross-cultural comparisons, 124f
    cultural differences, 121–126
    defined, 120
    generational differences, 120–121
    global employees, 126
    Hofstede's study, 122
    individualism, 123, 125f
    and job satisfaction, 128
    long-term orientation, 123
    loyalty, 123
    power distance, 123, 125f
    short-term orientation, 123
    uncertainty avoidance, 123
    work centrality, 121–122
Van Maanen, John, 272
variables, 604–605
variable socialization tactics, 273f
Venezuela, 123
verbal language of work, 359–360
vertical division of labour, 494–495, 495f
vertical integration, 542–543
vertical interlock, 546
Veterans Affairs, 473, 481
Victor, Bart, 441
Victoria Police Force, 579, 596
video games, 512
vignettes
    The Bay, 304–306
    Best Buy, 566–567
    Economical Insurance, 42–43
    EllisDon Corporation, 188–189
    Flight Centre, 492–493
    Ford Motor Company, 530–531
    Gliss, 452–453
    Glo Salon & Spa, 452–453
    Google Canada, 262–263
    Great Little Box Company Ltd., 152–153
    IDEO, 228–229
    JPMorgan Chase, 384–385
    KPMG, 78–79
    L'Oréal Canada, 118–119
    RCMP, 418–419
    Rumour Mill, 352–353
    Sodexo Canada, 2–3
    University of Guelph, 352–353
virtual organization, 511–512, 511f
virtual teams, 250–253
Visa, 511
visible activities, 423
visible minorities, 19–20, 91
vision, 572
voice, 356
Volvo, 594
Vroom, Victor, 164, 319–321

W

W.L. Gore & Associates, Inc. At, 508–509
wage incentive plans
    defined, 190
    differential opportunity, 191–192
    piece-rate, 190
        problems with, 191–193
        and productivity, 191
        and quality, 191, 191–193
        reduced cooperation, 192
        restriction of productivity, 192–193
wage increases, 30–33
Waldmeir, Rebecca, 249
Walgreens, 511
Walmart, 97, 98, 285, 506, 535
Walton, Richard, 594, 595
Walton, Sam, 285
Wanous, John P., 271
Waterstone's, 359
Watkins, Sherron, 442
Watson, Thomas, 286
Webber, Rob, 530
webcasts, 377
Weber, Max, 13
Webster, Gary, 12
Webster, Jane, 432
Wei, Jian, 223–225
weight-based bias, 86, 111
Weiss, Howard, 132
Welburn, Ed, 249
Welch, Jack, 61, 296, 514
wellness programs, 42–43, 481
Wells Fargo, 288
well-structured problems, 386
Westerman, George, 510
Western Electric Company, 13, 615
WestJet Airlines, 198, 281–282, 284, 313, 546–547
Weyerhaeuser Company, 173, 174, 515
Whirlpool, 592
whistle-blowing, 238, 442
white-collar jobs, 193–200
Wigand, Jeffrey, 442
withdrawal, 476
women
    best workplaces in Canada, 96f
    in corporate Canada, 94
    and gender stereotyping, 94–96
    and leadership, 332–336
    and mentoring, 276–278
    qualities of successful women executives, 335f
    and sexual harassment, 442–444
    as workforce demographic, 19
Woodford, Michael, 442
Woodward, Joan, 548, 551
Woodward's production processes, 550
work centrality, 121–122
work conditions, 209f
work context characteristics, 208, 209f
work design, 208. see also job design
work design characteristics, 208, 209f
Work Design Questionnaire, 208
work engagement, 23, 470
work environment, 20–22
work-family conflict, 472
workforce diversity. see also diversity
    and the changing workplace, 91
    and competitive advantage, 92f
    defined, 91
    diversity programs, 98f
    managing, 98–101
    and stereotypes, 92–98
    valuing, 91–92

working conditions, 468
working schedules
    alternative. *see* alternative working
        schedules
    traditional, 212
work-life balance, 480, 481
work-life conflict, 21, 21*f*
work motivation *see* motivation
workplace
    changes in, 91
    and organizational commitment, 143
workplace spirituality, 21
work sharing, 214–215
work teams, 206
WorldCom, 285, 442
World Wildlife Fund, 3

X

Xilinx, 140

Y

Yahoo!, 380, 439, 445, 544
Yetton, Philip, 319, 321
You Be the Manager
    American Express Canada, 100
    bullying, 473
    Business Development Bank of Canada, 311
    Calgary Airport Authority, 68
    Capital One, 136
    centralization, 518
    cultural context, 370

customer service, 12
employee recognition, 68
error prevention, 399
ethics, 439
Four Seasons, 370
job satisfaction, 136
Kinaxis, 288
leadership development, 311
Loblaw Companies Limited, 545
merit pay plans, 194
motivation and performance, 176
Orange, 252
organizational change, 579
organizational culture, 288
Rousseau Muskoka, 176
strategic response, 545
T&T Supermarket, 545
Toronto City Hall, 194
Toronto General Hospital, 399
Toronto Transit Commission, 12
Toyota, 518
Veterans Affairs, 473
Victoria Police Force, 579
virtual teams, 252
workplace diversity, 100
Yahoo!, 439

Z

zero wage increase, 30–33
Zimbabwe, 123
Zuckerberg, Mark, 599
Zweig, David, 105, 184, 432

PHOTO CREDITS

Preface

Page xxviii: (top) photo by David Ward; (bottom) Ken Jones.

Part Openers

Piano: Digital Vision/Getty Images; Trumpet: Digital Vision/Getty Images; Saxophone: Digital Vision/Getty Images; Xylophone: Studio Blond/Getty Images.

Chapter 1

Page 3: Sodexo Canada; The Canadian Press/Chris Young; page 12: The Canadian Press/Fred Lum/The Globe and Mail; page 18: The Canadian Press/AP Photo/Jacquelyn Martin; page 19: Rehan Qureshi/Shutterstock.com.

Chapter 2

Page 44: Waterloo Region Record Staff; page 45: Courtesy of Kirmac Collision Services; page 58: David Anderson; page 68: David Anderson; page 69: The Canadian Press/Richard Buchan.

Chapter 3

Page 79: The Canadian Press/Kevin Van Paassen/The Globe and Mail; page 80: P.C. Vey; page 97 (top) © Queen's Printer for Ontario, 2003. Reproduced with permission; (bottom) ZUMA Press/Newscom; page 100: Aaron Harris; page 104: © Masterfile.

Chapter 4

Page 119: Phil Carpenter, The (Montreal) Gazette; page 122: Kyodo /Landov; page 136: AP Photo/Mark Lennihan; page 141: A.G.E. Foto Stock/First Light.

Chapter 5

Page 153: Courtesy of Great Little Box Company; page 172: Randy Glasbergen; page 174: Weyerhauser; page 176: Sergej Khackimullin/Fotolia; page 177: The Canadian Press/Bebeto Matthews.

Chapter 6

Page 189: Colin Mcconnell/GetStock.com; page 191: David Anderson; page 192: Mikhallshin Iqor/ITAR-TASS/Landov; page 194: Christopher Drost/ZUMA Press/Newscom; page 199: Jean B. Heguy Photo/First Light; page 202: PHOTOFEST; page 213: David W. Harbaugh; page 215: David Anderson.

Chapter 7

Page 229: Courtesy of IDEO; page 241: © Ashley Cooper/CORBIS; page 249: Norman Mayersohn/The New York Times/Redux; page 252: Eyecandy Images/GetStock.com.

Chapter 8

Page 263: Courtesy of Kris Abel; page 274: © Leif Skoogfors/Corbis; page 277: © Dennis MacDonald/Alamy; page 285: The Canadian Press/Adrian Wyld; page 288: Courtesy of Kinaxis Inc.; page 289: Daniel Alan/Stone/Getty.

Chapter 9

Page 305: The Canadian Press/Deborah Baic/The Globe and Mail; page 307: Roy Delgado; page 310: Philip Lengden Photography; page 311: Photo courtesy of Business Development Bank of Canada; page 314: The Canadian Press/Kevin Frayer; page 324: The Canadian Press/Aaron Harris; page 329: The Canadian Press/Ryan Remiorz; page 334: The Canadian Press/Frank Gunn.

Chapter 10

Page 353: Photo courtesy of University of Guelph; page 358: www.CartoonStock.com; page 362: Terry Vine/Stone/Getty Images; page 370: © Hemis/Alamy; page 372: © Dennis MacDonald/Alamy.

Chapter 11

Page 385: REUTERS/Brendan McDermid; page 389: ScienceCartoonsPlus.com; page 391: © allOver photography/Alamy; page 397: © Ariel Skelley/Corbis; page 399: Brasiliao/Shutterstock.

Chapter 12

Page 419: The Canadian Press/Darryl Dyck; page 425: The Canadian Press/Steve White; page 426: © Philip Bird/Alamy; page 435: © Mark Leibowitz/Masterfile; page 439: Noah Berger/Polaris/Newscom.

Chapter 13

Page 453: Carlos Osorio/GetStock.com; page 459: Michael Stuparyk/GetStock.com; page 467: Randy Glasbergen; page 473: Chip Somodevilla/Getty Images; page 479: The Canadian Press/Fred Chartrand; page 480: Dick Hemingway.

Chapter 14

Page 493: Courtesy of Flight Centre Canada; page 506: Will Mcintyre/Time & Life Pictures/Getty Images; page 507: © US Coast Guard Photo/Alamy; page 511: The Canadian Press/AP Photo/John Froschauer; page 517: The Canadian Press/AP Photo/David Zalubowski.

Chapter 15

Page 531: The Canadian Press/AP Photo/Paul Sancya; page 533: Joe Sarnovsky, CAW Local 222; page 543: David Anderson; page 545: Richard Lautens/GetStock.com.

Chapter 16

Page 567: Brian Dexter/GetStock.com; page 571: Bradford Veley; page 572: BMO Financial Group/Richard Johnson Photography Inc.; page 579: AAP via AP Images/Julian Smith; page 580: © Royalty Free/CORBIS.